INVESTIGACIONES CONTEMPORÁNEAS SOBRE HISTORIA DE MÉXICO

Published in the United States
for the Institute of Latin American Studies
by the University of Texas Press,
Austin & London

INVESTIGACIONES CONTEMPORÁNEAS SOBRE HISTORIA DE MÉXICO

MEMORIAS DE LA TERCERA REUNIÓN
DE HISTORIADORES MEXICANOS
Y NORTEAMERICANOS

OAXTEPEC, MORELOS, 4 - 7 de noviembre de 1969

UNIVERSIDAD NACIONAL AUTÓNOMA DE MÉXICO

EL COLEGIO DE MÉXICO

THE UNIVERSITY OF TEXAS AT AUSTIN

México, 1971

PALABRAS PRELIMINARES
DE DANIEL COSÍO VILLEGAS,
PRESIDENTE DE LA REUNIÓN

El lector podrá ver una nota de mi viejo y querido amigo Lewis U. Hanke, en que hace una breve reseña de las circunstancias en que se celebraron las dos reuniones anteriores. [1] Así, por una vez, se alivia a un historiador de la tarea de hacer historia. Pero no de señalar que, según Hanke, mi conversión ha sido de ciento ochenta grados, pues de escéptico del trabajo colectivo como aparezco pintado por él en la Primera Reunión, he pasado a presidir la tercera, y de allí a redactar estas palabras preliminares.

Por celebrarse en el Monterrey mexicano y en el Austin texano, los trabajos de las dos primeras reuniones quedaron confinados al salón donde se presentaron, de modo que no tuvieron propiamente repercusión pública. Fue distinto el caso de la tercera, pues aun cuando se celebró fuera de la ciudad de México, en el sedante poblado de Oaxtepec, la prensa periódica, la radio y aun la televisión informaron de los preparativos y de las principales vicisitudes de ella. Así, los miembros de los Comités Organizadores, norteamericano y mexicano, y aun algunos participantes, nos vimos ante la necesidad de explicar al público por qué los mexicanos invitábamos y acogíamos a un grupo de extranjeros para conversar sobre la historia de México. No debió faltar quien sintiera que se trataba de una nueva invasión, y en el sagrado recinto de la historia patria, al que sólo pueden entrar los nacionales, y eso dejando en las afueras los pesados y ruidosos zapatos que calzan, para orar en el templo dentro del más concentrado recogimiento.

Es de esperarse que un fruto menor, pero no de escasa importancia, de este volumen, sea mostrar al lector cómo, en efecto, es, puede y debe ser internacional el interés por la historia de México.

La primera preocupación de los comités organizadores fue, por supuesto, el tema o los temas de la Tercera Reunión. En las dos anteriores primero se determinó la lista de los invitados, y después, de sus respectivas especialidades, aun de sus gustos personales, nacieron los temas a tratar. Es de suponerse que los organizadores de esas dos primeras reuniones le hallaron a ese proceder señaladas ventajas: haciéndose la selección de los participantes por su excelencia académica, la reunión alcanzaría un brillo estelar; además, tendría un grado superlativo

---

[1] Lewis Hanke, "Hail!", en el folleto III *Reunión de historiadores mexicanos y norteamericanos*, México, 1969.

*de espontaneidad, ya que los invitados se moverían en su propio me-
dio, y, por añadidura, en un medio elegido por ellos.*

*Sin desconocer los méritos y los atractivos probados ya de este pro-
cedimiento, los comités organizadores de la Tercera Reunión decidieron
adoptar el contrario, o sea fijar primero los temas y después seleccionar los historiadores que los expusieran. Vino en seguida la duda de
si habría un tema único o si tres o cuatro, importantes en sí mismos,
pero sin relación directa entre ellos. Los comités resolvieron adoptar
un gran tema único y eligieron el de la historiografía pensando que
ningún otro podría superarlo en importancia, ya que la historiografía
nutre toda enseñanza y cualquier investigación. La última decisión fue
dividir ese tema mayor en un buen número de subtemas, sea usando
el criterio de las épocas históricas, sea el de las ramas de la historia, digamos la política, la económica, la social, etcétera.*

*No se ocultó a los comités organizadores que estas decisiones iban
a introducir en los trabajos de la reunión la rigidez o la disciplina
que trae consigo toda norma. Sin embargo, las mantuvieron confiados
en que el fruto final resultaría más rico justamente por haber sido
cultivado con sistema.*

*Valdrá la pena destacar otras dos ideas principales adoptadas por los
comités organizadores. La primera, componer los grupos que se ocuparían de cada subtema de modo que hubiera una representación nacional muy finamente equilibrada: si el ponente, digamos, era norteamericano o europeo, la réplica la haría un mexicano, y a la inversa en
el siguiente caso. Por esta misma razón se hizo un esfuerzo especial
para asegurar el concurso de sabios europeos interesados también en la
historia de México.*

*Más importante fue la idea de darle en esta reunión un papel pre-
ponderante a los historiadores jóvenes. De hecho, se llevó hasta el punto
de asignarles las ponencias para darles ocasión de apreciar críticamente
la obra de sus mayores. Y a éstos se les puso, como si dijéramos, en una
posición defensiva al pedirles la réplica a esas ponencias.*

*A pesar de que los comités organizadores se sintieron satisfechos de
las ideas que presidieron la organización de esta Tercera Reunión y
de los resultados prácticos obtenidos en su aplicación real, resolvieron
que, en principio, no debiera intentarse otra vez un programa de una
magnitud tan grande como ésta, sino que los temas de las subsecuentes
reuniones fueran más restringidos.*

*Del resultado final de todos estos esfuerzos y esperanzas juzgará el
lector de este volumen. Encontrará en él las ponencias y sus réplicas,
así como algunas intervenciones de los participantes. En cambio, no
hallará el texto de las discusiones orales que suscitaron los textos escritos de las ponencias y sus réplicas, pues aun cuando se acarició la idea*

de registrarlas en cinta magnetofónica, no se logró sistematizar el trabajo para ofrecerlas al público en este volumen.

No vacilo en calificar de rotundo el éxito alcanzado en esta Tercera Reunión. Tampoco en atribuirlo al fácil y continuo buen entendimiento que reinó entre los comités organizadores norteamericano y mexicano, y a la actividad que cada uno desplegó en cumplir sus respectivos cometidos. Por lo que toca al comité mexicano, el peso mayor recayó en tres historiadores distinguidos y jóvenes: Luis González, Alejandra Moreno y Romeo Flores. También debe reconocerse la ayuda valiosísima de don Agustín Yáñez, Secretario de Educación; de don Víctor L. Urquidi, presidente del Colegio de México; y de los dirigentes de la empresa Condumex.

Por sobre todas las cosas, sin embargo, el buen éxito se debió al espíritu de genuina camaradería de todos y cada uno de los participantes en esta Tercera Reunión de Historiadores Mexicanos y Norteamericanos.

INTRODUCCIÓN

El análisis de las principales aportaciones contemporáneas, en el campo de la historiografía mexicana, fue el tema de la Tercera Reunión de Historiadores Mexicanos y Norteamericanos, celebrada en Oaxtepec, Morelos, del 4 al 7 de noviembre de 1969. Aproximadamente desde un año antes dos comités de historiadores, uno mexicano y otro norteamericano, estuvieron trabajando para organizar esta reunión. El creciente interés por los estudios sobre los distintos periodos del pasado de México justificaba plenamente tanto el tema escogido como la celebración de este congreso, designado con el nombre más sencillo de reunión.

Entre otras cosas pareció oportuno continuar así la confrontación de pareceres y la valoración de aportaciones que, dos veces, habían tenido ya lugar. En 1949 se celebró la primera de estas reuniones en la ciudad de Monterrey, Nuevo León, promovida principalmente por los doctores Silvio Zavala y Lewis Hanke. En 1958, en Austin, Texas, tuvo lugar la segunda con un enfoque muy definido y que fue el de la "frontera mexicano-norteamericana".

Al comenzar a organizarse desde 1968 la Tercera Reunión, cuyas Memorias aquí se publican, se decidió abrir las posibilidades de participación a investigadores de otras varias nacionalidades. Tan buen acuerdo tuvo por consecuencia que en la Reunión de Oaxtepec estuvieran presentes estudiosos de la historia de México procedentes de Francia, España, República Federal Alemana, República Democrática Alemana, Checoslovaquia, Suecia e Inglaterra.

En tres formas distintas pudieron participar los historiadores que concurrieron a Oaxtepec. Primeramente ha de mencionarse la de quienes presentaron ponencias en las que se analizan y valoran las investigaciones recientes sobre un periodo o aspecto determinado de la historia de México. Otra forma de participación consistió en preparar comentarios escritos en relación con las ponencias que, con bastante anticipación, se hicieron circular. Finalmente los demás historiadores que asistieron a esta reunión tuvieron asimismo ocasión de intervenir haciendo uso de la palabra en las distintas sesiones de trabajo.

Esta Tercera Reunión distribuyó sus actividades en once grupos de trabajo y en tres mesas redondas. Los temas tratados en los grupos de trabajo fueron los siguientes: historiografía prehispánica, historiografía novohispana de los siglos xvi y xvii, historiografía del siglo xviii y de la revolución de independencia, síntesis de la historia de México,

*historias de tema regional y parroquial, biografía, historiografía de la
vida económica, historiografía de la vida social, historiografía de la vida
política, problemas comunes de la investigación histórica e historiografía
de las relaciones internacionales.*

*Las tres mesas redondas, que se celebraron con la asistencia de la
mayor parte de los concurrentes a esta reunión, versaron sobre los
siguientes temas: nuevas direcciones y métodos de la investigación histórica, problemas sobre historia de las ideas y el contenido social de la
literatura y las artes.*

*En conjunto se presentaron por escrito treinta y dos ponencias y
veinticuatro comentarios, que son precisamente los que integran las
presentes Memorias. Debe consignarse, como dato de particular interés,
que las ponencias fueron elaboradas, en su mayoría, por jóvenes de
las más recientes promociones de historiadores. Los correspondientes
comentarios fueron preparados por especialistas en los distintos campos
sobre los que versaron las ponencias. Además de contarse en cada grupo
de trabajo con la participación de otros distinguidos historiadores, asistieron a la reunión, especialmente invitados, estudiantes de la carrera
de historia de la Facultad de Filosofía y Letras de la Universidad Nacional, de El Colegio de México y del Instituto Nacional de Antropología e Historia. Correspondió a varios de ellos colaborar como relatores
en las varias sesiones. Los trabajos de relatoría se publican asimismo en
las Memorias.*

*Al reunir y dar a conocer aquí los logros alcanzados en la Tercera
Reunión de Historiadores Mexicanos y Norteamericanos, expresamente
se hace constar que en la publicación de estas Memorias han participado conjuntamente la Universidad Nacional Autónoma de México,
a través de su Instituto de Investigaciones Históricas, El Colegio de
México y la Universidad de Texas. Como es obvio, el éxito de la reunión
se debió al espíritu de colaboración de todos los participantes. Los
comités organizadores, mexicano y norteamericano, estuvieron integra-
dos por Daniel Cosío Villegas, que fue elegido Presidente de la Reunión,
Edmundo O'Gorman, Luis González, Miguel León-Portilla, Romeo
Flores Caballero, Alejandra Moreno, Howard F. Cline, Stanley F. Ross,
Charles Gibson, Stanley J. Stein y James Wilkie. Como patrocinadores
de la reunión deben mencionarse: la Secretaría de Educación Pública
de México, la Universidad Nacional Autónoma de México, El Colegio de México, el Instituto de Estudios Latinoamericanos de la Universidad de Texas, la Conferencia de Historia Latinoamericana, la Fundación Hispánica de la Biblioteca del Congreso de Washington,
Fundación Cultural de Condumex, la Henry L. and Grace Doherty
Foundation, el Joint Comitte on Latin American Studies of the American Council of Learned Societies y el Social Science Research Council,
los señores Carlos Prieto y Juan Sánchez Navarro, y muy especialmente*

al Instituto Mexicano del Seguro Social, que proporcionó su Centro Vacacional de Oaxtepec para la celebración de esta Reunión.

Se deja igualmente constancia de la colaboración especial de las siguientes personas: Mercedes Carrera, Françoise Carner, Jorge Jufresa, Victoria Lerner, Elsa Malvido, Miguel Marín Bosch, Álvaro Matute, José María Muriá, Julia Tuñón de Muriá, Alicia Orive y María de los Ángeles Yáñez, que actuaron como relatores en la reunión. Igualmente participaron en la preparación de estas Memorias para la imprenta los historiadores Luis González, Andrés Lira, Jorge A. Manrique, Miguel León-Portilla, Alfredo López Austin, Luis Muro, Josefina Vázquez de Knauth y Josefina García Quintana.

Los comités organizadores

I. HISTORIOGRAFÍA PREHISPÁNICA

4 de noviembre de 1969

Presidente: Wigberto Jiménez Moreno, director del Departamento de Investigaciones Históricas del Instituto Nacional de Antropología e Historia.

Ponentes: Alfredo López Austin, investigador y secretario del Instituto de Investigaciones Históricas, UNAM; Henry B. Nicholson, profesor de antropología, Universidad de California, Los Ángeles.

Comentaristas: Miguel León-Portilla, director del Instituto de Investigaciones Históricas, UNAM; Donald Robertson, profesor asociado de arte, Universidad de Tulane.

Participantes: Fernando Anaya Monroy, investigador del Instituto de Historia, UNAM; Ignacio Bernal, director del Instituto Nacional de Antropología e Historia; Pedro Carrasco, profesor asociado de antropología, Universidad de California, Los Ángeles; Barbro Dahlgren Jordán, subdirectora del Departamento de Investigaciones Históricas, INAH; Charles E. Dibble, profesor catedrático de antropología, Universidad de Utah; Doris Heyden, investigadora de la Sección de Antropología, UNAM; Fernando Horcasitas, Investigador de la Sección de Antropología, UNAM; Carlos Martínez Marín, subdirector en funciones de director de la Escuela Nacional de Antropología; John F. Scott, Metropolitan Museum of Art., USA; Elizabeth Mary Smith, profesora asistente de historia del arte, Universidad de Nuevo México, Alburquerque; Ronald Marvin Spores, profesor asistente de antropología, Universidad de Massachussets.

Participante europeo: Günter Zimmerman, Director del Instituto de Antropología y Etnografía, Hamburgo.

Relator: José María Muriá Rouret, profesor de la Universidad de Guadalajara.

LOS TEXTOS EN IDIOMA NÁHUATL
Y LOS HISTORIADORES CONTEMPORÁNEOS

Alfredo López Austin

INTRODUCCIÓN

Las últimas décadas de la investigación acerca del México antiguo se han caracterizado por una marcada tendencia a buscar en el pasado indígena una imagen integral del hombre. Estos estudios, que a juicio de uno de sus seguidores se encuentran apenas en una fase inicial, aunque vigorosa, [1] han recibido sus principales impulsos de los importantísimos descubrimientos arqueológicos, del desciframiento progresivo de los códices pictográficos y de un nuevo tratamiento dado a los textos indígenas en idioma náhuatl.

He elegido el estudio de los textos nahuas como base para este trabajo por razones de crítica histórica y hasta cierto punto también apologéticas. Creo que ignorar la existencia de los textos es renunciar a la posibilidad de obtener una visión más completa, justa y adecuada del México antiguo. Pude haber escogido, en igual forma, el estudio acerca de los logros obtenidos a través de la arqueología o de la lectura de los códices pictográficos, ya que, como antes dije, también han contribuido en gran parte a que se obtenga esta nueva visión de nuestra historia prehispánica. Motivos muy personales —mayor conocimiento de los textos que de la arqueología y de los códices pictográficos, a más del gusto por los primeros— son los que dan origen a mi elección.

La influencia del nuevo tratamiento dado a los textos indígenas sobre la actual visión del hombre prehispánico no ha sido unilateral; también el sentido de los estudios de los textos y la aplicación de los métodos lingüísticos y filológicos obedecen a la búsqueda de dicha imagen integral. Lo cierto es que la concepción del hombre náhuatl ha variado en una forma tan radical que hay la impresión de un absoluto desconocimiento anterior y de una potencialidad inmensa de nuevos descubrimientos.

En mis prerrogativas de autor baso la elección de nueve historiadores contemporáneos. Son todos ellos de los más distinguidos, aunque otros hay que no incluyo, a partir de figuras que tan honda huella dejaron

[1] Justino Fernández, "Estudios humanistas sobre la cultura náhuatl", *Homenaje a Rafael García Granados*, México, Instituto Nacional de Antropología e Historia, 1960, 364 pp., pp. 185-193, esta nota en p. 185.

como Francisco del Paso y Troncoso, Eduard Seler o Walter Lehmann. Fijándome aquí en investigadores contemporáneos he tratado de tipificar actitudes más que de hablar de personas. Bajo este ángulo debe entenderse mi comentario sobre cada uno. No deberá extrañar, por tanto, que nada tenga que ver el orden de exposición con el cronológico de sus obras, ni aparecerán los cambios accidentales que en tendencias, predilecciones de temas o en métodos hayan podido tener. No podrá achacárseme haber omitido injustificadamente, por ejemplo, la importantísima labor en materia de arqueología al referirme a Alfonso Caso, o no haber tocado el punto de su interpretación de los códices pictográficos. Hablo también de Garibay sin mencionar sus traducciones de los clásicos del Viejo Mundo. Es que el Caso y el Garibay que por el momento me interesan son únicamente los que me pueden dar una visión, por cierto aún superficial, de su actitud frente a los textos nahuas. Y así del resto de los historiadores.

I. LOS PASOS INICIALES

a) *Wigberto Jiménez Moreno*. Apenas unas líneas arriba he dicho que de ninguna manera pretendo hablar de los historiadores tomando como base un orden cronológico de sus obras. El nombre de este apartado se deriva del enfoque que eligen los dos investigadores en él mencionados.

Jiménez Moreno, en primer término, afirma que la historia es por un lado registro de sucesos importantes, y por otro la explicación del pasado.[2] Si atendemos a este doble carácter, el proceso lógico indudable es la iniciación del trabajo de investigación histórica en la apreciación, ordenamiento y concordancia de los informes registrados, para concluir en la explicación. Jiménez Moreno, ante el cúmulo de noticias de las fuentes que en ocasiones dan la impresión de un tremendo caos, se echa a cuestas la labor de limpiar, purificar y ordenar la trama que servirá de fundamento indispensable para ir colocando después otro tipo de elementos de juicio, los que darán base a la explicación o serán explicación de la vida del hombre en el pasado prehispánico.

El material registrado tiene bajo su mano una tajante división: los informes acerca de un hombre que se confunde en el mito, de un ser del que en ocasiones no se sabe si es humano o divino, y los referentes al que surge en el momento en que una fecha y un topónimo hacen que se inicie la historia documentada, la historia en sentido es-

---

[2] Wigberto Jiménez Moreno, José Miranda y María Teresa Fernández, *Historia de México*, 3ª ed. México, Editorial E.C.L.A.L.S.A., 1967, 576 pp., ils. y mapas. Aunque la obra está escrita por tres autores, se afirma en nota de la p. xxii que el autor del prólogo es Jiménez Moreno.

tricto. [3] Es este hombre —y en particular sus fechas, sus migraciones, los nombres de sus gobernantes y pueblos— el que interesa a Jiménez Moreno. Si estima que el grado de desarrollo cultural de los pueblos del México antiguo los hace depender en gran parte de las condiciones ambientales, principalmente las orohidrográficas, [4] no es raro que el historiador busque en un primer paso la identificación de los sitios habitados y las rutas de sus constantes viajes. La fijación de las fechas dará a conocer los contactos étnicos producto de las migraciones. Una vez establecido el esquema espacio-temporal, con auxilio de los datos arqueológicos, podrán investigarse sobre terreno más sólido las relaciones entre la naturaleza y el hombre y entre el hombre y el hombre. Mientras tanto el aspecto cultural que sobre todo merece una atención detallada es el de los sistemas calendáricos, en tanto es auxiliar de la fijación de la cronología. Hay afirmación expresa en el sentido de que México es uno de los mejores laboratorios para el estudio de las ciencias del hombre; [5] pero es necesario tener la trama completa antes de hacer uso de la rica información que este país puede proporcionar al mundo.

Esta posición influye notablemente en la actitud de Jiménez Moreno frente a los textos en lengua náhuatl: reconoce que el material de los informantes indígenas de Sahagún es más extenso y completo que la *Historia general de las cosas de Nueva España* [6] y que los textos en náhuatl recogidos por el franciscano permiten penetrar en la mentalidad del indígena; [7] pero estudios que sin duda estima más urgentes lo hacen esperar el momento propicio para la edición en castellano de tan importantes documentos.

Su conocimiento del idioma náhuatl le es auxiliar en su labor de fijación de esquema. Precisa con ayuda de la traducción la existencia de personajes, [8] la paternidad de las fuentes, la vida de sus autores, el orden que guardaron en un principio los capítulos de una obra. [9] Sus versiones sobrepasan la obtención del dato escueto cuando Jiménez Mo-

[3] Wigberto Jiménez Moreno, "Historia precolonial del Valle de México", *Revista Mexicana de Estudios Antropológicos*, t. xiv, primera parte, 1954-55, pp. 219-236, pp. 219-220.
[4] Wigberto Jiménez Moreno y Alfonso García Ruiz, *Historia de México. Una síntesis*, México, Instituto Nacional de Antropología e Historia, 1962, 136 pp., ils., (Serie Historia, VII), pp. 9-10.
[5] *Ibid*, p. 11.
[6] Jiménez Moreno, Wigberto, "Fray Bernardino de Sahagún y su obra", en fray Bernardino de Sahagún, *Historia general de las cosas de Nueva España*, edición de Joaquín Ramírez Cabañas, nota preliminar de Wigberto Jiménez Moreno, estudios de Nicolás León e Ignacio Alcocer, 5 vols., México, Editorial Pedro Robredo, 1938, ils., vol. i, pp. xiii-lxxxiv, y dos desplegados, pp. liii y liv.
[7] *Ibid.*, xxxviii.
[8] Jiménez Moreno, "Historia precolonial . . .", p. 222.
[9] Por ejemplo en Jiménez Moreno, "Fray Bernardino de Sahagún . . .", xxviii-xxix; lvi-lvii, n. 14; lix n. 27; lxv, n. 46; lxix, n. 65; lxix-lxx, n. 67.

reno es el colaborador de historiadores que investigan la cultura náhuatl; pero para su propia obra ha concedido por ahora a la presentación de los textos un secundario papel.

b) *Paul Kirchhoff.* En su trabajo sobre la *Historia tolteca-chichimeca*, señala Kirchhoff su actividad como la elaboración de una guía de estudio para quien, como primer paso en la comprensión de lo más profundo del pensamiento y las tradiciones nahuas, desee conocer las complejidades de la historia y la historiografía indígenas. [10] Es consciente, según se desprende de esta afirmación, de la gran importancia de los textos indígenas en su lengua original; pero parece elegir también el camino de preparación del esquema espacio-temporal que servirá de base a estudios posteriores de otro tipo.

Estima que la fuente es demasiado oscura. Su papel es dedicarse al análisis y comparación de los datos con los que otras fuentes aportan. Aparentemente parece consistir "sólo de nombres y más nombres, tanto de personajes como de lugares". [11] Esto es precisamente lo que ha de aclararse, y no sólo por lo que se refiere a la *Historia tolteca-chichimeca*, sino a toda la historia del México antiguo. Lo importante —cuando menos de inmediato— es la ubicación del mayor número posible de lugares por donde pasaron o donde se establecieron los grupos en migración, los componentes étnicos de una ciudad, los títulos de sus gobernantes y sus lugares de asiento, la extensión geográfica de los imperios, el número de pueblos y ciudades sujetos a ellos, el sistema de gobierno que los unía en una sola entidad política, la fecha de fundación de una ciudad o de un imperio y la de su ruina, la lista de reyes. [12]

La búsqueda de este tipo de material ocupa gran parte de su labor como investigador. Temas culturales de fundamental importancia han sido ofrecidos sólo en bocetos, que algunas veces contienen una útil

[10] Paul Kirchhoff, "La Historia Tolteca-Chichimeca. Un estudio histórico-sociológico", en *Historia Tolteca-Chichimeca. Anales de Quauhtinchan*, versión preparada y anotada por Heinrich Berlin en colaboración con Silvia Rendón, prólogo de Paul Kirchhoff, México, Antigua Librería Robredo de José Porrúa e hijos, 1947, 147 pp., xxv láms. y un mapa (Fuentes para la Historia de México, colección publicada bajo la dirección de Salvador Toscano, 1), pp. xvii-lxiv, p. xix.

[11] *Ibid.*

[12] Así se desprende de las cuestiones que plantea en "La ruta de los tolteca-chichimeca entre Tula y Cholula", *Miscellanea Paul Rivet. Octogenario Dicata*, 2 vols., México, XXXI Congreso Internacional de Americanistas y Universidad Nacional Autónoma de México, 1958, pp. 485-494, cuadros y mapas, p. 485; en "Composición étnica y organización política de Chalco según las Relaciones de Chimalpahin", *Revista Mexicana de Estudios Antropológicos*, vol. xiv, primera parte, 1954-955, pp. 297-298, y en "Quetzalcóatl, Huémac y el fin de Tula", *Cuadernos Americanos*, año xiv, vol. lxxxiv, núm. 6, noviembre-diciembre 1955, pp. 163-196, 163-164.

recomendación de método para quien desee profundizar en su estudio. [13] Asuntos de organización política y de calendarios están tratados al servicio de la precisión del esquema. [14] Indudablemente desea esperar, como Jiménez Moreno, un punto de precisión mayor, una final concordancia de los informes más objetivos de las fuentes, para penetrar en los problemas de la cultura.

Su enfoque hace que las obras en lengua náhuatl le sean fuentes de rica información, y las utiliza a menudo. Sin embargo, deben ser tratadas a su juicio con el cuidado que es necesario por su particular origen: aunque provienen de un pueblo de desarrollado sentido histórico y con profundo interés en el registro de fechas, [15] el uso de sistemas distintos en el cómputo del tiempo hace indispensable la cautela. Es necesaria la investigación acerca de la existencia de pluralidad de fuentes pictográficas de tradición distinta, como origen de la crónica estudiada, cuando los informes presenten contradicción en materia de fechas, ya sea la contradicción interna o frente a otros documentos. [16] Es más, el método adecuado obliga a suponer derivados de una tradición, y por tanto realmente compatibles, sólo los informes que en la fuente conocida se encuentran inmediatos e inmersos en una redacción que indica procedencia de fuente única. [17]

Aun tratadas con estas precauciones, las fuentes en idioma náhuatl no serán nunca suficientemente precisas y claras. [18] En todo caso sus informes tendrán suficiente valor al ser ratificados por los descubrimientos arqueológicos. [19]

Por lo demás el contenido de la información que de los documentos en lengua náhuatl puede obtenerse no varía del de otras fuentes: nombres, fechas, títulos, rutas, que no hacen indispensable una traducción directa. Para él parece ser absolutamente válida la versión de versión, [20]

[13] Baste citar como ejemplos Mesoamérica. Sus límites geográficos, composición étnica y caracteres culturales, 2ª ed., México, Escuela Nacional de Antropología e Historia, Sociedad de Alumnos, 1960, (iv)-18 pp., un cuadro (Suplemento de la revista Tlatoani, 3); "Dos tipos de relaciones entre pueblos en el México Antiguo", A Pedro Bosch-Gimpera en el septuagésimo aniversario de su nacimiento, México, Instituto Nacional de Antropología e Historia y Universidad Nacional Autónoma de México, 1963, LXIV-448 pp., pp. 255-259, y "Land tenure in Ancient Mexico. A preliminary sketch", Revista Mexicana de Estudios Antropológicos, vol. XIV, primera parte, México, 1954-1955, pp. 351-361.
[14] Kirchhoff, "La Historia Tolteca-Chichimeca . . .", pp. XXXIV y XXXV, y "Calendarios tenochca, tlatelolca y otros", Revista Mexicana de Estudios Antropológicos, vol. XIV, primera parte, 1954-1955, pp. 257-267.
[15] Kirchhoff, "Quetzalcóatl, Huémac . . .", p. 171.
[16] Kirchhoff, "La Historia Tolteca-Chichimeca . . .", pp. XXIII-XXIV.
[17] Kirchhoff ,"Calendarios . . .", pp. 259-260.
[18] Kirchhoff, "La Historia Tolteca-Chichimeca . . .", p. XIX.
[19] Kirchhoff, "Dos tipos de relaciones . . .", p. 255; "¿Se puede localizar Aztlán?", Anuario de Historia, año I, 1961, pp. 59-67, un mapa y un desplegado, p. 67.
[20] Por ejemplo en "Calendarios . . ." p. 260; "¿Se puede localizar? . . .", passim.

puesto que no modifica el dato que interesa una traducción indirecta. Apenas es útil el conocimiento del idioma cuando hay que hablar del significado de una palabra equivocada [21] o, ya en un plan más elevado, para encontrar por similitud o diferencia de estilos la paternidad de un documento. Pero, en este caso, se puede remitir a la autorizada opinión de un nahuatlato. [22]

c) *Comentarios.* He de tomar como absolutamente válidas las posiciones que ante la elaboración de la historia ocupan los distintos investigadores. Por ahora mis comentarios se reducen a la forma en que hacen uso de las fuentes en lengua náhuatl, problema de tipo predominantemente metodológico que ha de subordinarse al concepto que tienen de la historia y de su propio papel.

Siendo así, estimo que los textos nahuas, en la forma en que Jiménez Moreno y Kirchhoff los utilizan, aportan información en cantidad y calidad muy considerables, más si son analizados con una previa crítica de fuentes que sirva de pauta para darles un acertado valor en cada uno de los casos. Pero esa misma crítica que Jiménez Moreno y Kirchhoff realizan en torno de fechas, penetrando en el problema de los diversos sistemas de cómputo calendárico, hacen pensar si no es útil adoptar un semejante rigor con otras instituciones culturales, directamente relacionadas con el valor de los datos puramente objetivos. Para exponerlo en una pregunta-ejemplo: ¿No es útil alguna previa penetración en las instituciones económicas y políticas de los antiguos nahuas para valorar el informe que aporta datos sobre migraciones y dirigentes?

II. LA CULTURA Y LA LENGUA NÁHUATL

a) *Pedro Carrasco.* En el extenso campo de estudio del mundo cultural elige cada autor, con libertad amplia, los sectores que responden plenamente a su particular interés. La organización social indígena es el tema que con preferencia aborda Pedro Carrasco en sus investigaciones, y demuestra una especial inclinación a la búsqueda de fuentes en los archivos. Sigue en esto una pauta de trabajo aconsejada por Kirchhoff, el análisis de documentos que se refieren a casos concretos de fenómenos jurídicos, argumentando que

El régimen de la tierra entre los indios del siglo XVI tanto en la época prehispánica como en la colonial ha sido discutido por lo general tomando como base la obra de Alonso de Zurita. Si bien ésta merece toda la

21 Kirchhoff, "Calendarios . . .", p. 266.
22 Paul Kirchhoff, "El autor de la segunda parte de la Crónica Mexicáyotl", *Homenaje al Doctor Alfonso Caso*, México, Imprenta Nuevo Mundo, S. A., 1951, 460 pp., pp. 225-227 y un desplegado, pp. 225-227.

atención que le ha sido prestada y aun más todavía, es preciso notar que Zurita presentó sus propias interpretaciones y generalizaciones y no incluyó en su obra el material concreto en que se basó y al que sólo alude en su conocida *Relación*. Cosa parecida puede decirse de autores como Torquemada, Ixtlilxóchitl y otros cuyos datos sobre la tenencia de la tierra son de suma importancia, pero que rara vez presentan casos concretos acerca de lugares, fechas, personas o terrenos identificables. Como lo ha hecho notar Paul Kirchhoff, es necesario complementar las descripciones generales de las fuentes con el análisis de casos concretos en documentos cuya búsqueda y recopilación apenas se ha iniciado. [23]

En principio, estima Carrasco que todo documento que aporte informes de utilidad para estudios sociológicos y jurídicos debe ser publicado, sea o no tema que él pueda aprovechar de inmediato en sus particulares investigaciones. Así saca a la luz documentos que se encuentran en español en los archivos [24] y versiones al castellano de otros cuyos originales están escritos en lenguas indígenas. [25] Pero es indudable que lo que tiene para él mayor interés es el aprovechamiento de las fuentes en sus propios estudios sociológicos.

El conocimiento de la lengua náhuatl le permite una aproximación mayor, sobre todo por la comprensión de la etimología, al concepto que los indios tenían de los diversos cargos, dignidades e instituciones jurídicas y sociales. [26] Por otra parte puede descubrir entre los documentos que duermen en los archivos los que verdaderamente podrán ofrecer un caudal apreciable de información acerca de la organización social, política o fiscal. Un libro de matrimonios escrito en lengua náhuatl, por ejemplo, le permite determinar de qué modo la filiación de barrio era parte de la regulación del matrimonio en San Andrés Chiauhtla a fines del siglo XVI y principios del XVII. [27] Documentos de este tipo, trabajados con modernos métodos sociológicos, [28] sin duda alguna aportan una información que servirá para complementar en gran

[23] Pedro Carrasco, "Las tierras de dos indios nobles de Tepeaca en el siglo XVI", *Tlalocan*, vol. IV, núm. 2, 1963, pp. 97-119, p. 97.

[24] Por ejemplo, Pedro Carrasco, "Más documentos sobre Tepeaca", *Tlalocan*, vol. VI, núm. 1, 1969, pp. 1-37.

[25] Pedro Carrasco, "La exogamia según un documento cakchiquel", *Tlalocan*, vol. IV, núm. 3, 1963, pp. 193-196.

[26] Ver, por ejemplo, Pedro Carrasco, "The civil-religious hierarchy in Mesoamerican communities; pre-Spanish background and Colonial development", *American Anthropologist*, vol. 63, núm. 3, June, 1961, pp. 483-497.

[27] Pedro Carrasco, "El barrio y la regulación del matrimonio en un pueblo del Valle de México en el siglo XVI", *Revista Mexicana de Estudios Antropológicos*, t. XVII, 1961, pp. 7-26.

[28] Véase el método utilizado, por ejemplo, en "Tres libros de tributos del Museo Nacional de México y su importancia para los estudios demográficos", XXXV *Congreso Internacional de Americanistas. México, 1962*, 3 vols., México, Comité Organizador, 1964, pp. 373-378.

parte las muchas veces oscuras relaciones de autores que en las primeras décadas del virreinato trataron de comprender tipos de organización social muy alejados de los entonces vigentes en Europa. La investigación con bases en documentos escritos en lengua náhuatl no termina, sin embargo, con el trato que puede darse a la información proporcionada como si fuese, una vez traducida, un material de la misma categoría que el que proporcionan las fuentes en español. Muy importante es la labor de Carrasco en lo que se ha mencionado; pero tiene obra en la que la naturaleza de la fuente es aún más aprovechada. La lengua es uno de los mejores reflejos de la cultura, y en el estudio filológico puede apoyarse gran parte de la investigación acerca de la organización social. En particular Carrasco se dedica al estudio de los grados de parentesco en idioma náhuatl del siglo xvi, y a través de sus análisis aclara gran parte de las relaciones familiares prehispánicas y las variaciones que sufrieron los términos para adaptarse a las que entraron en vigor por la introducción del derecho canónico. [29] La investigación de la fuente en lengua náhuatl va adquiriendo así peculiaridades que la colocan por encima de la fuente escrita en español.

b) *Alfonso Caso.* La investigación dirigida a los puntos claves de la cultura es preocupación constante del segundo de los historiadores mencionados en este apartado. Aun en los casos en que parece enfocar su atención en problemas de ubicación geográfica simple, hay el impulso de esclarecer para proporcionar información que sea auxiliar inmediato en el estudio de las instituciones:

> Una de las cuestiones que ha preocupado siempre a los investigadores de la organización social, económica y política de los aztecas, es cuál era la distribución de los barrios y su localización en las dos ciudades gemelas de Tenochtitlan y Tlatelolco.
> Se conocían los datos de Vetancourt en su *Teatro mexicano*, sobre las parroquias con los nombres de los santos patronos y de los barrios indígenas y, en algunos casos, podían localizarse cuando las parroquias se habían conservado, pero no podían marcarse los límites de los barrios que en tiempos precortesianos eran, además de divisiones territoriales, los lugares de residencia de los antiguos clanes, que tan importante papel jugaban en la vida social y política de los aztecas. [30]

Este afán por el conocimiento de la cultura descansa en la concepción misma que Alfonso Caso tiene del hombre. Para él todo ser humano

[29] Pedro Carrasco, "Sobre algunos términos de parentesco en el náhuatl clásico", *Estudios de Cultura Náhuatl*, vol. vi, 1966, pp. 149-166.
[30] Alfonso Caso, "Los barrios antiguos de Tenochtitlan y Tlatelolco", *Memorias de la Academia Mexicana de la Historia*, t. xv, núm. 1, enero-marzo de 1956, pp. 7-63, tres planos en desplegado y una ilustración, pp. 7-8.

es partícipe de una identidad en lo fundamental, ya presente en la conciencia puramente racional, "la mente abstracta", [31] ya en una necesidad de carácter universal que desemboca en la plasmación concreta de una idea capaz de subsistir por encima de las particularidades de las culturas y las contingencias de la historia. [32] Esta identidad produce en las culturas una similitud de evolución; marca un proceso peculiar de perfeccionamiento que se inicia en la concepción mágica para ir pasando por el politeísmo, el dualismo, el monoteísmo y va a terminar en el pensamiento científico. Pero esto no ha de entenderse como curso único e invariable ni como desarrollo fatal. [33] Simplemente el hombre, en lo que tiene de semejante, puede ser estudiado en diversas latitudes y épocas tomando como base ese fundamento que lo hace obrar igual en circunstancias iguales. En México los pueblos no son diferentes a los del resto del mundo cuando otorgan a sus dioses un origen de concepción milagrosa, cuando caen en aberraciones por el fanatismo religioso o cuando una misión divina les sirve como pretexto para dominar y explotar a sus semejantes. [34]

El estudio del hombre, sin embargo, no debe detenerse cuando las similitudes desaparecen. Si el paso de la mente abstracta al pensamiento concreto hace surgir la incomprensión de las culturas, el científico tiene la obligación de sobreponerse y tratar de "entender a otros espíritus, prescindiendo, hasta cierto punto, del propio espíritu". [35] Debe pasarse entonces del dominio de la lógica pura al de la psicología y la etnografía. [36] No es extraño, bajo este ángulo, que para este autor sí tenga una importancia fundamental el mito. [37]

Caso maneja en forma constante las fuentes escritas en náhuatl. La recolección de informes de que hace uso en el estudio de los calendarios debe buena parte de su calidad a textos en idioma indígena. [38] En ocasiones reconoce que el valor de un documento es único en el estudio de un problema determinado. [39] Pero, ya considerados los textos

[31] Alfonso Caso, Los calendarios prehispánicos, México, Universidad Nacional Autónoma de México, Instituto de Investigaciones Históricas, 1967, x-268 pp., ils. y cuadros, (Serie de Cultura Náhuatl, Monografías, 6), p. 41.
[32] Alfonso Caso, "El águila y el nopal", Memorias de la Academia Mexicana de la Historia, t. v. núm. 2, abril-junio de 1946, pp. 93-104, ils., p. 95.
[33] Alfonso Caso, El pueblo del Sol, figuras de Miguel Cobarrubias, México, Fondo de Cultura Económica, 1953, 136 pp., xvi láms., pp. 11-16 y 123-124.
[34] Ibid., pp. 69, 95-96 y 121-122.
[35] Caso, Los calendarios ..., p. 41.
[36] Ibid.
[37] Véase Caso, "El águila ..."
[38] Véanse, por ejemplo, Alfonso Caso, "La fecha de la conquista de Tlatelolco por Tenochtitlan", Tlatelolco a través de los tiempos, vol. v, 1945, pp. 30-31, p. 30; Caso, Los calendarios ..., pp. 4-5, 40, 50, 53, 72 y 86-90.
[39] Por ejemplo el de la obra en náhualtl de Cristóbal del Castillo para el tema de los "señores de la noche", en Caso, Los calendarios ..., pp. 114-115.

en el conjunto de las fuentes, su posición no se encuentra en el primer término:

Consideramos que las piedras con inscripciones son la más genuina fuente de conocimientos sobre el modo de pensar de los antiguos indios. De igual valor son las pinturas, muy escasas por cierto, que se han descubierto en los monumentos. En ambos casos tenemos datos absolutamente auténticos sobre el pensamiento indígena, y sólo puede incurrirse en error por una mala lectura de la inscripción o porque el escriba se haya equivocado al hacerla, lo que es muy poco probable.

Casi del mismo valor son los códices precortesianos, aunque no se puede estar tan seguro de su origen como del de las piedras con inscripciones o los frescos. Aquí la dificultad estriba en la escasez del material, pues los códices que indudablemente fueron pintados antes de la conquista son muy raros, mientras que los códices posthispánicos son bastante numerosos.

El tercer lugar corresponde precisamente a estos códices posthispánicos; de preferencia los que fueron pintados en el siglo xvi, y aquellos que tienen leyendas en español o en alguna de las lenguas indígenas. Del mismo valor son las noticias que nos proporcionan los cronistas, indios o españoles, sobre todo los que escribieron pocos años después de la conquista y, entre los autores indígenas, los que ya eran personas mayores en 1521.

De menos valor son las noticias proprocionadas por los escritores de los siglos xvii y xviii y las opiniones de eruditos y viajeros de estos siglos, que casi nunca hicieron una investigación propia, sino que se conformaron con las noticias que les proporcionaba otro escritor, al que por falta de comparación consideraron indiscutible.

Por último, sin valor como fuentes, pero con gran valor como estudios, están los escritos de los sabios del siglo pasado y del presente, que se han ocupado de la cuestión. [40]

Tal vez debamos considerar esta posición expresa de Caso referida en forma muy particular al problema del estudio de los calendarios y, aun dentro de este contexto, en relación a los datos de carácter más objetivo. Otro tipo de estudios, en los que se tratan ideales de conquista o pensamiento religioso y mágico, hace que el historiador busque esa liga en la que su propio espíritu trata de diluirse para captar la débil imagen de pensamiento de un hombre distinto que quedó grabada en forma objetiva. Esa comunicación de tipo psicológico debe encontrarla en fuente que da una comunicación más directa: la palabra. Aun en este caso la especificación es mayor: son indispensables aquellos textos en que, en honor a la belleza, el hombre deja escapar mucho de su naturaleza interna. Discurso y poesía pasan algunas veces a las

[40] *Ibid.*, pp. 41-42.

obras de Alfonso Caso como medios únicos para aproximarse realmente al pensamiento prehispánico. [41]

c) *Comentarios*. Estimo que en los trabajos de estos dos autores hay un alto grado de concordancia entre la petición que se hace a la fuente y el valor de la respuesta que de ella se obtiene. Sólo quiero detenerme brevemente en esa opinión transcrita en relación al grado de valor de las fuentes, jerarquización que, llevada a la práctica por mentes menos ágiles y críticas, podría ser peligrosa. Haciendo a muy grueso modo un ordenamiento que tomara como base la capacidad de comunicación, el cuadro quedaría totalmente invertido, y una gráfica que sacara el promedio de ambos valores, tal vez diera como resultado una elevación considerable de esa porción central que ocupan los documentos en lengua náhuatl. Pero no creo que en esta materia los cuadros y las gráficas sean aconsejables. Todos los tipos de fuentes tienen valores muy especiales, establecidos por los objetos particulares de estudio, por los enfoques de la investigación y aun por la capacidad de manejo de los distintos historiadores. Volviendo al tema de las migraciones, sería estimable poder contar con relaciones indígenas de carácter netamente histórico que dieran información sobre la ruta, los descubrimientos arqueológicos que indicaran los sitios de asentamiento, los textos que en forma directa o indirecta permitieran deducir la información de carácter económico, social, político y cultural del grupo emigrante, modernos estudios ecológicos referentes a las zonas recorridas, y muchísimos otros más.

El cuadro de jerarquías tal vez deba entenderse referido, como anteriormente opiné, sólo a la valoración del material más objetivo en relación con los problemas calendáricos. Un mal entendimiento podría ser deformante.

III. EL VALOR DEL DOCUMENTO

a) *Robert H. Barlow*. Es discutible el valor que puede concederse en el campo de la crítica histórica a expresiones vagas, a términos que tal vez de manera inconsciente quedaron registrados. Muy diferente método es el nuestro al del psicólogo, y mucho más lo es el tipo de conocimientos. Pese a ello, creo deber transcribir dos párrafos de Robert H. Barlow, de los que me he tomado la libertad de subrayar sendas palabras:

Desde hace varios meses saltaban a la vista las posibilidades que ofrece Tlatelolco para hacer exploraciones cuyos resultados vengan a *sumarse*

[41] Caso, "El águila . . .", pp. 97-98, y Caso, *El Pueblo . . .*, pp. 44, 99-100, 123, etc.

a los datos de carácter pictórico y literario que ya existen sobre ese lugar. [42]

De los templos y señores de aquel lejano Tula se han ocupado otros investigadores, sobre todo el señor Jiménez Moreno, y solamente pretendemos difundir un documento que viene a *completar* la historia de Tula después de su ruina. [43]

Desde un punto de vista muy personal estimo que el decir de una fuente, al ser descubierta, se *suma* a las ya existentes, y que un documento —o inclusive un estudio— sirve para *completar* la historia de un pueblo, señala una particular visión de lo que es la historia, así como señalaría otra el afirmar que un documento que acaba de descubrirse puede dar pie, interpretado y utilizado en una forma dada, para presentar una particular visión de un fenómeno histórico. No es mi intención —y debo aclararlo— conceder a una de estas o de otras posiciones mayor o menor valor, puesto que por el momento no es ese el objeto de mi estudio. Pero sí será de utilidad hacer notar esta particularidad para entender por qué Barlow obró en forma determinada frente a los textos nahuas.

George T. Smisor relata que Barlow y él, al iniciar su contacto con el México prehispánico, quedaron sobrecogidos frente a los restos arqueológicos, pero encontraron que estaban aquellos objetos lejos de comunicarles una verdadera significación. Su iniciación en el estudio de la lengua náhuatl les dio a conocer la inmensa cantidad de documentos existentes, y la respuesta que daría su traducción a las preguntas que no habían podido contestar aquellos objetos de piedra y cerámica. [44]

Tlalocan fue el vehículo para dar a conocer una gran cantidad de documentos en lenguas indígenas que ayudarían a los investigadores a abandonar la viciosa costumbre de hacer la historia antigua de México a través de las citas de Clavijero; [45] pero, a pesar de proporcionar valiosas fuentes para la investigación, no sería una revista dedicada a publicar el fruto de dichos estudios. [46] *Tlalocan* —y Barlow y Smisor— se unieron a una opinión de García Icazbalceta: "Cada día echa mayores raíces en mi ánimo la convicción de que más se sirve a nuestra

[42] R. H. Barlow, "Pozos estratigráficos de Tlaltelolco núms. I y II", *Tlaltelolco a través de los tiempos*, vol. ı, 1944, pp. 72-74, p. 72.
[43] R. H. Barlow, "Anales de Tula, Hidalgo, 1361-1521", *Tlalocan*, vol. ııı, núm. 1, 1949, pp. 2-13, ils., p. 2.
[44] George T. Smisor, "R. H. Barlow and 'Tlalocan'", *Tlalocan*, vol. ııı, núm. 2, 1952, pp. 97-102, pp. 98-99.
[45] R. H. Barlow y George T. Smisor, "Introducing Tlalocan" (Re-Introducing Tlalocan), *Tlalocan*, vol. ıv, núm. 1, 1962, pp. 1-2, p. 1.
[46] *Ibid.*, p. 2.

historia ... con publicar documentos inéditos o muy raros, que con escribir obras originales, casi nunca exentas de deficiencias y errores." [47]

Esta posición hizo que Barlow, acompañado muchas veces de Byron McAfee, realizara una importantísima labor de traducción y publicación de documentos valiosos para el conocimiento del México antiguo. [48] No fue de menos utilidad el estudio que hizo acerca de fuentes, ya indígenas, ya de éstas derivadas, muy especialmente la que lo llevó a establecer las relaciones que guardaban algunas de las obras antiguas más conocidas con la llamada *Crónica X*. [49]

La dedicación a estas fuentes hizo nacer en Barlow un gran cariño por el idioma náhuatl, y entre sus actividades, algo apartadas éstas de la historia, se cuentan la recolección de cuentos populares y la edición de un periódico en la lengua indígena. [50] Esto pudiera hacer suponer que Barlow deseaba abordar temas etnohistóricos. Hay, sin embargo, características muy notables en su obra que es necesario hacer destacar: los documentos históricos traducidos son en su gran mayoría de los que aportan casi exclusivamente datos tan objetivos como fechas, nombres de persona, topónimos, registros de hechos es-

---

[47] *Ibid.*

[48] Basten como ejemplos, en versión de él, "Tlatelolco en el periodo tepaneca", *Tlatelolco a través de los tiempos*, vol. I, 1944, pp. 23-42; y "La construcción del templo actual de Santiago Tlatelolco. Fragmentos de los 'Anales de Tlatelolco y México núm. 1', (1519-1633) de la Colección de Anales de México y sus contornos", *Tlatelolco a través de los tiempos*, vol. VI, pp. 62-64. Y con versión de él y de Byron McAfee, "La guerra entre Tlatelolco y Tenochtitlan según el Códice Cozcatzin", *Tlatelolco a través de los tiempos*, vol. VII, 1946, pp. 45-54; "La segunda parte del Códice Aubin", *Tlatelolco a través de los tiempos*, vol. IX, 1947, pp. 35-61, ils.; "Anales de la conquista de Tlatelolco en 1473 y en 1521", *Tlatelolco a través de los tiempos*, vol. V, 1945, pp. 32-45, ils. y "The titles of Tezcotzinco (Santa María Nativitas)", *Tlalocan*, vol. II, núm. 2, 1946, pp. 110-127, ils.

[49] R. H. Barlow, "La Crónica X. Versiones coloniales de la historia de los mexica tenochca", *Revista Mexicana de Estudios Antropológicos*, t. VII, 1945, pp. 65-88, ils. y un cuadro. También para este trabajo se sirvió de sus conocimientos de la lengua náhuatl, precisando por el análisis del contenido que fue indígena el autor de la versión original. Son también importantes, aunque breves, las críticas que hizo a un pequeño documento, "Anales de la conquista de Tlatelolco ...", arriba citado y en su "Resumen analítico de 'Unos anales históricos de la Nación Mexicana'", en *Anales de Tlatelolco. Unos anales históricos de la Nación Mexicana y Códice de Tlatelolco*, versión preparada y anotada por Heinrich Berlin, con un resumen de los anales y una interpretación del códice por Robert H. Barlow, México, Antigua Librería Robredo de José Porrúa e Hijos, 1948, XXIV-135 pp., 5 láms. y 2 desplegados (Fuentes para la Historia de México, colección publicada bajo la dirección de Salvador Toscano, 2), pp. IX-XXIII, p. IX.

[50] Véanse R. H. Barlow, "Un cuento sobre el día de los muertos", *Estudios de Cultura Náhuatl*, vol. II, 1960, pp. 77-82, y R. H. Barlow y Valentín Ramírez, "Tonatiw iwan meetstli. El Sol y la Luna", *Tlalocan*, vol. IV, núm. 1, 1962, pp. 55-61. En realidad los dos cuentos fueron preparados por Barlow, pero publicados por sus amigos después de su muerte.

cuetos, listas de reyes, etcétera; en sus estudios usó las fuentes escritas
en lengua náhuatl para apoyar sólo detalles históricos de este mismo
tipo;[51] usó indistintamente la traducción directa y la versión de versión, o aún la cita de documentos nahuas en francés;[52] y, por último,
fue consciente de la necesidad de abordar los temas de carácter político y tributario, pero no lo hizo.[53]

Tal vez su concepto de la historia, el que se refleja en sumar y
completar, hizo innecesario que tocara los temas de la cultura; tal
vez también él creía indispensable completar primero el esquema espacio-temporal, y tomó como obligación propia la de aportar documentos
que proporcionaran datos, sin tener la de traducir al español o al
inglés los ya conocidos en idiomas modernos. O tal vez, aunque parezca
paradójico, no creía en la capacidad comprensión-expresión del traductor:

> ...las traducciones son, cuando mucho, juguetes sin valor. Ninguna
> dimensión de ingeniosa paráfrasis permite suplantar los documentos
> originales...[54]

b) *Arthur J. O. Anderson y Charles E. Dibble*. Merece cada uno
de los autores aquí citados un lugar especial por la importancia de
sus investigaciones. Sin embargo el enfoque de este trabajo hace que
sean considerados principalmente por una magna empresa que ambos
firman: la versión al inglés del *Códice florentino*, cuya publicación
fue iniciada hace diecinueve años y está, según parece, por concluir
con la aparición del sexto de los doce libros de los informantes de
fray Bernardino de Sahagún y el volumen introductorio.[55]

Es indudable que la elección de un trabajo como es enfrentarse a
la versión de la que ha sido considerada enciclopedia de la cultura
náhuatl presupone la coincidencia de fuertes inclinaciones que, aun-

---

[51] Véanse, por ejemplo, sus artículos "Tlatelolco en el periodo...", pp. 28-32,
en notas 8, 10, 14, 19, 19A, 20 y 22; "Tlatelolco como tributario de la Triple
Alianza", *Tlatelolco a través de los tiempos*, vol. IV, 1945, pp. 30-35, p. 28, nota
11, y "Los 'cónsules' de Tlatelolco", *Tlatelolco a través de los tiempos*, vol. VIII,
1946, pp. 23-26, *passim*.

[52] "Anales de Tula...", p. 3; R. H. Barlow, "El Códice de Tlatelolco", en
Anales de Tlatelolco..., *op. cit.*, p. 110.

[53] R. H. Barlow, *The extent of the empire of the Culhua Mexica*, Berkeley and
Los Angeles, University of California Press, 1949, VIII, 144 pp., un mapa (Ibero-
Americana, 28).

[54] "...traslations are at best worthless toys. No amount of ingenious paraphrase
can possibly supplant the original documents...", *Ibid.*, p. v.

[55] *Florentine Codex. General History of the things of New Spain*, translated
from the Aztec into English, with notes and illustrations, by Arthur J. O. Anderson
and Charles E. Dibble, 11v., Santa Fe, New Mexico, The School of American
Research and The University of Utah, 1950-1963.

que no necesariamente iguales, dieron en el proyecto como común denominador.

Anderson se interesa por el problema netamente cultural. Prefiere temas acerca del saber indígena —mucho de las ciencias naturales y la medicina— y parece considerar necesarios dos grupos de cuestiones: el primero comprendería las preguntas relacionadas con el grado de conocimientos que tenían los nahuas antes de la llegada de los españoles; el segundo, las relativas al método utilizado por Sahagún, principalmente para descubrir si las respuestas corresponden a la realidad de la antigua cultura náhuatl o son producto ya de la aculturación española.[56] Este segundo grupo de preguntas está en función del primero.

Dibble prefiere el aspecto historiográfico. Sus temas elegidos son los que se relacionan con el origen y la historia de las fuentes. Entre ellos son de importancia los que buscan la influencia europea en la escritura de los códices indígenas poshispánicos.[57] Encuentra también interesante la forma en que el orgullo de un pueblo, el chichimeca, afecta la veracidad de una crónica.[58] Busca en las fuentes la similitud que indique una derivación.[59] En ocasiones penetra a la minucia y dedica todo un artículo al estudio de un vocablo oscuro.[60]

Unidos el afán por la cultura antigua, el interés por las fuentes y el amplio conocimiento del idioma náhuatl, pudieron Dibble y Anderson proyectar y ya casi concluir la versión completa al inglés del *Códice florentino*. Sin duda fueron guiados por una idea de interrelación de los elementos de la cultura. Y si a esto se agrega el valor verdaderamente enciclopédico de la obra de Sahagún, habrá que reconocer que algo de razón tienen los que abogan por el mérito de la simple

[56] Véanse sus artículos "Medical practices of the Aztecs", *El Palacio*, v. 68/2, Summer, 1961, pp. 113-118; "Sahagún's Nahuatl texts as Indigenist documents", *Estudios de Cultura Náhuatl*, vol. II, 1960, pp. 31-42; "Materiales colorantes prehispánicos", *Estudios de Cultura Náhuatl*, vol. IV, 1963, pp. 73-84, y en colaboración con Spencer L. Rogers, "El inventario anatómico sahaguntino", *Estudios de Cultura Náhuatl*, vol. V, 1965, pp. 115-122.

[57] Véanse sus artículos "Spanish influence of the Aztec writing system", *Homenaje a Rafael García Granados*, México, Instituto Nacional de Antropología e Historia, 1960, 364 pp., pp. 171-177, y "Glifos fonéticos del Códice Florentino", *Estudios de Cultura Náhuatl*, vol. IV, 1963, pp. 55-60, ils.

[58] Véanse sus obras *Códice Xólotl*, palabras preliminares de Rafael García Granados, México, Universidades de Utah y México, Instituto de Historia de la Universidad Nacional Autónoma de México, 1951, 168 pp., lams., mapas y cuadros, y "Los chichimecas de Xólotl", *Revista Mexicana de Estudios Antropológicos*, vol. XIV, primera parte, 1954-1955, pp. 285-288, *passim*.

[59] Dibble, *Códice Xólotl*, *passim*. y Dibble, "Apuntes sobre la plancha X del Códice Xólotl", *Estudios de Cultura Náhuatl*, vol. V, 1965, pp. 103-106, ils.

[60] Charles E. Dibble, "Náhuatl names for body parts", *Estudios de Cultura Náhuatl*, vol. I, 1959, pp. 27-29.

publicación de documentos. Siempre, claro está, que los documentos sean de esta magnitud.

c) *Comentarios.* Unidos los autores que se mencionan en este apartado por el alto valor que conceden a la fuente en sí, hay una total divergencia en cuanto al objeto particular de su estimación: por un lado la fuente que proporciona el preciso dato histórico; por el otro, la de la información acerca de la cultura. Del primero poco puede decirse, puesto que entregó buenas versiones de utilísimos textos dentro de los límites que él consideró apropiados: dar a conocer todo documento que, a más de haber pasado inadvertido proporciona valioso informe que no puede utilizarse por no estar escrito en lengua de comprensión asequible. De los segundos hay que tomar en consideración que aún no publican el volumen introductorio al *Códice florentino,* en el que indudablemente se referirán a los objetivos de su traducción. Algunos puntos pudieran adelantarse; pero es justo esperar que los autores mismos den razón de su proceder.

Una rápida alusión a la forma de dar a conocer los textos nahuas es, sin embargo, indispensable. Se proporciona al lector, por regla general, un recto sentido que elude las dificultades de versión conservadora de matices y de comprensión laboriosa para un público vasto. Doy como ejemplo un párrafo en el que esta forma de traducción es notable. El caso, debo reconocerlo, es extremo y nada frecuente en su gravedad. Lo he elegido porque ilustra; pero sería injusto no dar a conocer que son pocos los que en tan grande obra simplifican así el contenido. El original dice, refiriéndose a quienes nacen en el día Uno Ciervo:

> In aquin ipan tlacati pilli, in tetzon, in teizti, in tetzicueuhca, in tetzicuehuallo, in tetlapanca, in tetechpa quiz, yol, in tehuitztzo, in teahuayo, in tetentzon, in teixcuamol, in teezzo, in tetlapallo, tlatocayotia, hualmotenyotiaya. [61]

La versión de Anderson y Dibble es la siguiente:

> El que entonces nacía siendo noble, era de noble linaje, se convertía en gobernante y obtenía fama. [62]

Una traducción más apegada al original sería:

> El que nacía entonces, [si era] noble —cabellera, uña de la gente, salpicadura, lo que de la gente rebota, pedazo de la gente, que de la gente provino y vivió por la gente, la púa, la espínula de la gente, la barba,

---

[61] Transcribo con ortografía moderna.
[62] "He who was then born a nobleman, who was of noble lineage, became a ruler and gained fame", *Florentine Codex,* vol. iv-v, p. 9. En nota 1 remite a Olmos, Sahagún y Siméon, diciendo que en ellos podrá verse que los términos no traducidos son sinónimos de parientes.

la ceja de la gente, la sangre, el color de la gente— gobernaba, venía a afamarse.

Esta versión no quedaría completa todavía sin una detallada anotación que diera a conocer las particularidades filológicas que, sin duda, ayudan a comprender mejor su sentido —el concepto a que pudiera referirse el pronombre personal indefinido, el uso de la terminación de abstracto en los posesivos, la traducción etimológica de *tzicuehua*, etcétera—, no meros complementos eruditos que pudieran juzgarse estériles, sino elementos que servirían para entender el concepto que los nahuas tenían de los *pipiltin* o nobles.

IV. LOS TEXTOS NAHUAS COMO FUENTE INDISPENSABLE

a) *Ángel Ma. Garibay K.* La vida humana en el Nuevo Continente, lejos de todo influjo, asombrará al mundo cuando serena y amorosamente acabe de hacerse la investigación sobre sus orígenes y contenido. Así lo estimaba Garibay en los momentos en que descubría un nuevo rostro del México antiguo y encontraba, junto a elementos netamente originales de la historia humana, una asombrosa identidad que le hacía maravillarse ante la bella experiencia en la que el hombre había demostrado ser siempre Hombre.[63] Ésta fue para él la mayor razón del estudio de la cultura náhuatl: el mérito de entrar en la corriente universal del pensamiento con hombres que poseyeron plenamente las emociones que en todo tiempo y lugar norman la percepción estética humana.[64] La idea de la igualdad del hombre estuvo muy lejos de sujetarlo a un supuesto humanismo que desconoce el valor de las particularidades de las culturas y trata de ajustar todo comportamiento a los patrones establecidos por un pueblo guía. Ese pueblo no existe.[65] Toda actitud que se niegue a comprender al hombre en su cultura, o que quiera entender ésta fuera de su campo y ambiente propio, es lo más opuesto al verdadero humanismo.[66] Para quien quiera encerrarse en moldes occidentales o vivir las nostalgias de lo helénico, serán incomprendidos "un Tláloc enigmático, una Coatlicue espantosa, un

[63] Ángel Ma. Garibay K., *Historia de la Literatura Náhuatl*, 2 vols., México, Editorial Porrúa, S. A., 1953-1954 (Biblioteca Porrúa, 1 y 5), vol. ii, p. 9.
[64] *Ibid.*, vol. i, p. 171.
[65] *Ibid.*, i, 151-332; Ángel María Garibay K., *Poesía Náhuatl*, 3 vols., paleografía, versión, introducción, notas y apéndices de —————, México, Universidad Nacional Autónoma de México, Instituto de Investigaciones Históricas, 1964-1968, (Serie de Cultura Náhuatl, Fuentes, 4, 5 y 6), vol. ii, p. xv, y Prólogo a la obra de Miguel León-Portilla, *La Filosofía Náhuatl estudiada en sus fuentes*, 3ª ed., México, Universidad Nacional Autónoma de México, Instituto de Investigaciones Históricas, 1966, xxiv-414 pp., ils., (Serie de Cultura Náhuatl, Monografías, 10), p. xxii.
[66] Garibay, *Historia de la Literatura*..., vol. i, pp. 206-207.

Xochipilli en su ademán de quietud en la alegría, una Coyolxauhqui bañada por el hondo misterio de la muerte, pero guardando aún sus misterios de la vida". [67] Sigue diciendo que "si la vida del México antiguo es una obsesión religiosa, es también un vaho de sangre que horripila a los neuróticos de la cultura, que no cierran los ojos ante los nefastos crímenes internacionales de la vida moderna". [68]

El hombre lo es con los mismos atributos en todo lugar y tiempo. Sin embargo llega a mayores o menores alturas que se estiman por la realización de su humanidad. Aunque el entendimiento es su rasgo distintivo, "lo que no viste la imaginación no lo atesora el entendimiento". [69] Lo mejor del hombre "no es por cierto la inteligencia pura, ya angélica, sino la emoción, la pasión, el anhelo, el dolor y la entusiasta exaltación... es decir, la poesía"; [70] y ésta es "la más completa y perfecta de todas las artes, es la expresión musical del pensamiento". [71] Sobre todo es ella el vehículo de la religión, [72] la posibilidad de comunicación con la divinidad.

La poesía es directriz en la obra de Garibay. Es el hombre universal, el Hombre, el que importa. La palabra del hombre es la poesía, eslabón que lo une con el hombre y con Dios. Pero la obra de Garibay —cuando menos la principal y la que aquí interesa— no es la poesía sino su estudio, la apreciación de un fenómeno con el mayor deseo de objetividad, [73] sostenido por una larga preparación [74] y un profundo conocimiento de la lengua. Así, es al mismo tiempo su historia la que se hace desde un plano de absoluta seriedad profesional, y la emotiva, la que intenta "revivir un mundo", [75] no la de los "zurcidores de textos sin alma". [76]

Si la poesía es lo más humano —y por tanto el más común de los denominadores— lógico fue que encontrara constantemente similitud entre la obra de los nahuas y el resto del mundo. [77] Pero pudo apreciar también, y en buen grado, todas aquellas peculiaridades de belleza expresiva de los nahuas. La lengua le fue altamente estimada, [78] por

[67] *Ibid.*, vol. I, p. 149.
[68] *Ibid.*, vol. I, p. 108.
[69] *Ibid.*, vol. I, p. 387.
[70] *Ibid.*, vol. I, p. 109.
[71] *Ibid.*, vol. I, p. 60.
[72] *Ibid.*, vol. I, p. 109.
[73] *Ibid.*, vol. I, pp. 48, 331 y 421. Garibay, Prólogo a la obra de León-Portilla, *La Filosofía Náhuatl...*, p. XXI.
[74] Garibay, *Historia de la Literatura...*, vol. I, pp. 49-50.
[75] *Ibid.*, vol. II, p. 298.
[76] *Ibid.*, vol. II, p. 243.
[77] *Ibid.*, vol. I, pp. 59, 145, 171, 200, 296; Garibay, *Poesía Náhuatl*, vol. I, p. XXVI, vol. II, p. XVII, etcétera.
[78] Garibay, *Historia de la Literatura...*, vol. I, pp. 17-18 y 20; Garibay, *Poesía Náhuatl*, vol. II, p. XXVI.

sus méritos tanto de expresión estética como filosófica. Algunas de sus características permitían el paso a lenguas modernas con feliz éxito; otras, en cambio, reservaban buena parte del valor estético sólo a quienes iban a la fuente original. El carácter interno de la contextura no podía ser destruido en las versiones, por ser más bien modalidad de pensamiento que de lenguaje;[79] pero la volatilidad y la musicalidad de los ritmos verbales, por ejemplo, no eran transladables al castellano.[80] Difícil problema para quien se daba el papel no sólo de informar al mundo de la existencia de aquella poesía, sino el de servir de intermediario en la comunicación bella de los hombres.

Ofreció sus traducciones buscando un punto medio entre la fidelidad y el uso correcto y bello del castellano, entre la versión inteligible y la simplicidad sospechosa de traición al texto, entre la conservación del matiz original y la extorsión irrecatada de la lengua receptora. En un constante empeño de equilibrio, deja varias versiones distintas de una misma poesía.

La penetración en el mundo literario de los pueblos nahuas dio a Garibay profundísimos conocimientos de la cultura toda en el México antiguo. En sus obras históricas, apartado del método y de los intereses de los por él llamados "zurcidores de textos sin alma", los documentos en lengua náhuatl alcanzaron un valor inapreciable. La palabra náhuatl es necesaria, según él, para llegar a comprender la mentalidad de aquellos hombres;[81] da conocimientos que permiten restaurar cuadros enteros de la vieja cultura;[82] acerca al descubrimiento del mundo conceptual;[83] proporciona muchas veces materiales que no pueden obtenerse de otra fuente;[84] sirven en particular los textos de los informantes de Sahagún, en resumen, porque aportan datos netamente objetivos acerca de lugares, personas, hechos, cosas; de usos y costumbres; dan información literaria; proporcionan medios para conocer la mentalidad antigua; dan a conocer las particularidades de la estilística y son un tesoro en el campo de la lexicografía.[85] Por estas

[79] Garibay, *Historia de la Literatura* . . . , vol. I, p. 65.
[80] *Ibid.*, vol. I, pp. 120, 189 y 191.
[81] Ángel Ma. Garibay K., *Veinte himnos sacros de los nahuas*, versión, introducción, notas de comentario y apéndices por —————————, México, Universidad Nacional Autónoma de México, Instituto de Investigaciones Históricas, 1958, 280 pp., (Fuentes Indígenas de la Cultura Náhuatl, Informantes de Sahagún, 2), p. 9.
[82] Ángel Ma. Garibay K., *Vida económica de Tenochtitlan. 1. Pochtecáyotl* (*Arte de Traficar*), paleografía, versión, introducción y apéndices por —————, México, Universidad Nacional Autónoma de México, Instituto de Historia, 1961, 190 pp., (Fuentes Indígenas de la Cultura Náhuatl, Informantes de Sahagún, 3), p. 23.
[83] Garibay, *Poesía Náhuatl*, I, p. XXIII.
[84] Garibay, *Historia de la Literatura* . . . , vol. II, p. 85.
[85] Garibay, *Vida económica* . . . , pp. 15-16.

razones su historia, la que intenta "revivir un mundo", nada tiene que ver, en el uso de las fuentes, con las versiones de versiones. [86]

b) *Miguel León-Portilla*. Varias décadas de investigación arqueológica y un siglo escaso de acercamiento de tipo moderno a códices y textos han hecho, según León-Portilla, que al fin la historia de los pueblos del México prehispánico llegue a ocupar su posición adecuada en el ámbito de la historia universal. [87] Muchos aspectos de la cultura náhuatl pueden ser comparados actualmente con los conocidos en el Viejo Mundo sin temor de ocupar un sitio inferior. El pensamiento filosófico, por ejemplo, tomando en cuenta todas sus peculiaridades y diferencias, es equiparable a las ideas de algunos sabios griegos e indostánicos. [88]

La ubicación de la historia antigua de México en el contexto universal y la comparación de logros culturales carecerían en absoluto de importancia si no hubiera en el mundo, aparte de los contactos entre los pueblos —que entre los nahuas y el Viejo Continente no los hubo—, otro tipo de relación objetiva. Según León-Portilla deben buscarse en la historia, con un criterio objetivo, las posibles significaciones de los hechos que se estudian. [89] Si dice, por otra parte, que la labor del historiador puede estar encaminada a una *recreación*, siempre que no se entienda ingenuamente como tal la búsqueda de una imagen "exacta" del pasado, y si usa como método válido el "dejar hablar" a los hombres a través de sus propios textos, [90] es lógico considerar que acepta una vasta posibilidad de comunicación entre los hombres, independientemente de su ubicación en el tiempo y en el espacio. Es más, esta comunicación tiene un alto grado significativo, objetivo, que presupone la idea no sólo de existencia de situaciones humanas muy semejantes, sino de posibilidad, en algunas épocas y lugares, de aprovechar la palabra y la experiencia de los hombres del pasado. [91] La historia adquiere con esto una fuerte razón de ser.

[86] Véanse *Veinte himnos* . . . , p. 24 y la *Historia de la Literatura* . . . , vol. ii, p. 247.

[87] Miguel León-Portilla, *Trece poetas del mundo azteca*, México, Instituto de Investigaciones Históricas, 1967, 260 p., ils., (Serie de Cultura Náhuatl, Monografías, 11), p. 15.

[88] *Ibid.*, pp. 39 y 49.

[89] Josefina Vázquez de Knauth, Luis González, Miguel León-Portilla, Juan A. Ortega y Medina, "¿Qué piensan de la Historia los maestros que la escriben y la enseñan?", *La cultura en México*, núm. 382, 4 de junio de 1969, pp. vii-x, p. ix.

[90] Miguel León-Portilla, *Los antiguos mexicanos a través de sus crónicas y cantares*, dibujos de Alberto Beltrán, México, Fondo de Cultura Económica, 1961, 200 pp., p. 11.

[91] Véase, por ejemplo, el problema de la aculturación en Miguel León-Portilla,

La posibilidad de comunicación hace suponer la existencia de un conjunto de interrogaciones universales. No es extraño que los pueblos, al apartarse del mito y responder las cuestiones planteadas, lleguen a similares contestaciones. León-Portilla encuentra en el México prehispánico respuestas que a veces son similares a las surgidas en filosofías de otros puntos del globo. [92] Pero no son las semejanzas, sino las muy particulares contestaciones que da el hombre náhuatl, las que son importantes para el mundo. El conjunto de cuestiones filosóficas a las que los pueblos han de enfrentarse no llega jamás a ser respondido de manera definitiva. La posibilidad de comunicación por medio de la historia otorga un sentido a la ubicación adecuada del hombre náhuatl. Se convierte en un colaborador del hombre contemporáneo, un legatario cultural:

> Examinando las fuentes indígenas, lo más elevado de la cultura del México antiguo, las manifestaciones de su sentido espiritualista, podrá ensayarse la presentación de lo que pudiera llamarse su legado cultural: los diversos valores que aún hoy día pueden encontrar resonancia en el pensamiento de todo ser humano interesado en los problemas del hombre. [93]

> ... conocer el alma del artista y el sentido del arte en el mundo náhuatl no es algo estático y muerto. Puede constituir una verdadera lección de sorprendente novedad dentro del pensamiento estético contemporáneo. En la concepción náhuatl del arte hay atisbos e ideas de una profundidad apenas sospechada. Recuérdese solamente que para los sabios nahuas la única manera de decir palabras verdaderas en la tierra era encontrando la "flor y el canto de las cosas", o sea el simbolismo que se expresa por el arte. [94]

El legado surge de todo un mundo de cultura. Es visión particular de un pueblo que se encuentra distante de la tradición a la que hoy se entrega. Su lenguaje, lejano, no tiene la nitidez que en una simple traducción lo vuelva cristalino; tiene, en cambio, por su propia naturaleza, la posibilidad de descubrir sus tesoros conceptuales a través del esfuerzo filológico. Glosa y etimología son indispensables por estas razones. Con ambas, [95] y con la preparación filosófica que al historiador exige, [96] León-Portilla hace entrega del legado.

"Los chichimecas de Xólotl", *Estudios de Cultura Náhuatl*, vol. VII, 1967, pp. 59-86, ils., p. 61.

[92] Véanse ejemplos en *La Filosofía Náhuatl...*, pp. 68-69, 170 nota 75 y 215.

[93] León-Portilla, *Los antiguos mexicanos*, p. 12.

[94] León-Portilla, *La Filosofía Náhuatl...*, pp. 270-271.

[95] Véase el método de trabajo en Miguel León-Portilla, *La Filosofía Náhuatl...*, *passim*.

[96] Josefina Vázquez de Knauth, Miguel León-Portilla *et al.*, "¿Qué piensan...?", p. IX.

Aprecia también el resto de las fuentes: reconoce que se podrá penetrar en el pensamiento estético sólo relacionando hallazgos arqueológicos, códices, textos y cronistas;[97] que para dar una descripción de la ciudad azteca es preferible la fuente que proviene de la mirada azorada del forastero y no la del indio acostumbrado a ella;[98] y que los textos de los informantes indígenas de Sahagún y la *Historia general de las cosas de Nueva España* son fuentes que se complementan mutuamente.[99] Pero los títulos de sus obras principales dan a conocer que su afán más grande es descubrir a través de las palabras de los nahuas sus conceptos filosóficos, su mente, su literatura. La glosa detallada, el estudio filológico, la aportación de textos, dan a sus obras características inconfundibles.

c) *Comentarios*. Muy distintos son los enfoques de Garibay y León-Portilla. El primero buscó en el hombre universal el valor más alto, la poesía. Fue ésta el eje de sus investigaciones —tal vez de su vida—, y el hombre náhuatl vino a ser para él otro productor de obra; sólo que en adversas condiciones, en un continente apartado, viviendo la recurrencia de bellas pero eternas fórmulas.[100]

León-Portilla, por el contrario, ve en la separación del mundo prehispánico una de las razones por las que la cultura de sus hombres ha de ser estimada en más alto grado. Es que para él importa el hombre, en particular éste, el del México antiguo en toda su orinalidad, y cree posible mostrar que fue capaz de alcanzar notables cumbres.

Pero el deseo de Garibay por conocer la obra y el de León- Portilla por conocer al hombre los condujeron a intereses comunes. Garibay, con el tesón de afirmarse plenamente en realidades, eligió para su estudio las formas literarias de los pueblos cuya cultura se propuso conocer a fondo. El pueblo náhuatl fue uno de los elegidos. León-Portilla comprendió que todo intento de demostrar el valor del hombre náhuatl sería vano si el conocimiento fuera superfluo, y hubo de penetrar también profundametne en su cultura. Ambos tuvieron necesidad de fundamentar su investigación básicamente en los textos nahuas. Otro método de trabajo sería inútil: no podía estudiarse la

[97] León-Portilla, *La Filosofía Náhuatl* . . . , pp. 269-270.
[98] León-Portilla, *Los antiguos mexicanos* . . . , p. 107.
[99] Miguel León-Portilla, *Ritos, sacerdotes y atavíos de los dioses*, introducción, paleografía y notas de —————————, presentación de Henrique González Casanova, México, Universidad Nacional Autónoma de México, Instituto de Historia, 1958, 176 pp., ils., (Fuentes Indígenas de la Cultura Náhuatl, Textos de los informantes indígenas de Sahagún, 1), p. 164.
[100] Véase lo relativo a su opiniones sobre la separación del hombre náhuatl en *Poesía Náhuatl*, vol. II, p. xv, y en *Historia de la Literatura* . . . , vol. I, pp. 171, 230, 262, etcétera, y vol. II, p. 233.

literatura en versiones o la filosofía a través de la interpretación de otro pueblo. Y los textos respondieron con una riqueza que tal vez no fué inicialmente sospechada. Para ambos el camino fue el mismo, y al recorrerlo han dado a conocer a un hombre de rostro muy diferente al que se le había supuesto.

CONCLUSIÓN

Ha sido este trabajo exposición crítica más que defensa. Inicialmente afirmé que tenía sentido apologético, y lo tiene, en cuanto la intención es encaminar al joven historiador hacia el conocimiento de las lenguas indígenas. La razón es tan obvia que, si sólo se afirma, corre el riesgo de quedar inadvertida. Creí que era preferible mostrar un poco de la aventura de descubrir a un hombre en el México prehispánico.

He querido dar a conocer diversas actitudes frente a los textos en lengua náhuatl, no para que se tome partido, no para que por fuerza se encuentre el ejemplo. Son diversas formas de utilizar los textos para buscar al hombre. Son más las que ha habido. Muchas más las posibles. El texto es material noble.

PRE-HISPANIC CENTRAL MEXICAN HISTORIOGRAPHY

H. B. NICHOLSON

> Los indígenas no sólo de México, sino
> de toda Mesoamérica, poseían una ver-
> dadera vocación histórica y relataban y
> *escribían* historia ... No me parece justo,
> después de quemarles a los indios sus
> historias, declarar que no las escribían.
>
> ALFONSO CASO

INTRODUCTION

One of the leading diagnostics of the Mesoamerican Area Co-Tradition
was the detailed recording of past events over relatively long time spans.
This "chronicle conciousness", as I have elsewhere (Nicholson 1955b)
referred to it, was much more fully developed here than in any other
aboriginal New World region. Even many Old World cultures assigned
to a substantially higher rung on the ladder of cultural complexity cannot
offer historical records nearly as rich or extending over such long
periods. Students interested in the historical aspect of Mesoamerican
studies have always intensively utilized these native chronicles, but
less attention has been directed to the native *concepts* of history and
to *transmission media and techniques*. In a preliminary paper, delivered orally 9 years ago an published only in brief abstract form (Nicholson 1963), I briefly discussed the former aspect. Mesoamerican
concepts of history —which would include consideration of why such
a strong interest in history fluorished in this area— deserve much
more analysis than they have yet received. [1] However, this paper
will not be concerned with concepts but rather will focus on the
methods employed to transmit knowledge of the past and the kinds
of events recorded —its historiography, if you will— in one Mesoamerican sub-area, Central Mexico. [2]

[1] Citing only recent students, Radin (1920), Garibay (1953-1954, I: 275-329,
449-478; 1963: 71-90, 117-138), and Leon-Portilla (1956 [1959, 1966]: 258-264
[1963: 154-166]; 1961: 48-75), among others, have concerned themselves with
this topic to some extent.
[2] Typical previous discussions of significance would include: León y Gama 1832,
Pt. 2: 29-45; Aubin 1849 (1885); Brasseur de Bourbourg 1857-1859; Bancroft 1874-1875, v: 133-149; Orozco y Berra 1960 (1880, I: 231-340); Chavero 1887: Introducción; Simeon 1889: iii-xii; Lehmann 1909: 10-30; Radin

Central Mexico is of key importance in relation to this topic because it offers by far the largest number and variety of surviving Mesoamerican historical records and also because the cultures which generated them can be most fully reconstructed. As with so many other aspects of Mesoamerican culture, this extensively documented area serves as a useful touchstone for the less well documented regions. Although Central Mexican historiographical techniques cannot be mechanically projected into the rest of Mesoamerica, the area co-tradition crearly possessed sufficient overall similarity in fundamental culture patterns that many, if not most, of the devices employed to transmit knowledge of past events in this area undoubtedly were utilized —to a greater or lesser degree and with various regional modifications— in other parts of Mesoamerica, above all in the other "nuclear" or "climax" zones. [3]

Some professional historians might be disposed to question the legitimacy of the term "historiography" in this context on the ground that it normally connotes a tradition of *written* history —and Meso-america lacked a fully developed phonetic system of writing. However, the essentially picto-ideographic system—with limited use of the homophonic or rebus principle—of late pre-Hispanic Central Mexico can certainly qualify within abroad definition of "writing", and I submit that only an over-literal definition of "historiography" would exclude the methods of historical transmission (including oral) of pre-Hispanic Central Mexico.

Our knowledge of this subject is largely derived from 3 major categories of sources, which represent the 3 major types of history transmission techniques in the area: 1) "archaeological"; 2) "written" records; 3) orally transmitted historical information. Each will be discussed in turn.

ARCHAEOLOGICAL RECORDS

The first category excludes the artifactual and architectural data, the "witnesses in spite of themselves", as Bloch termed them, which constitute the "normal" evidence sought and utilized by the New World field archaeologist to reconstruct the past. Here our only concern is with surviving records which were consciously intended to commemorate actual events in some fashion for posterity and which

1920; Garibay 1945 (1964), 1953-1954, i: caps. v, ix, 1963: 71-90, 117-138; León Portilla 1956 (1959, 1966): 258-264 (1963: 154-166), 1961: 48-75, 1964: 129-146 (1969: 116-131); Robertson 1959: *passim*.
    [3] Caso (1960) has contributed a very useful general discussion of pre-Hispanic pictorial historiography in the Mixteca.

thus constitute, in a broad definition, a kind of very abbreviated "written" history.

This category is, unfortunately, not a large one. It is most prominently represented by various carvings and paintings featuring dates in the native calendar which appear to have historical rather than ritual referents —and sometimes associated scenes and/or symbols. These may go back to at least as early as the Early Classic (Caso 1967: 143-163; 1968), during the height of Teotihuacan civilization. However, even if some of the tiny handful of dates painted and carved on Teotihuacan objects and structures have historical referents, the significant historical information they convey is about nil. In the Late Classic and during the transition to the Postclassic more materials become available, which would include, possibly, the Tenango del Valle stela (Romero Quiroz 1963: 101-132; Caso 1967: 161-162; possibly Early Classic) and cliff carvings (Romero Quiroz 1963: 75-100; Nicholson 1966: Fig. 7), the Xico stela (Peñafiel 1890, Plates, vol. II: Lam. 293), the Maltrata boulder carvings (Medellín Zenil 1962), and, above all, the extensive carvings on the Pyramid of the Feathered Serpent, Xochicalco, plus a few other isolated carvings from that site.

The Xochicalco Pyramid of the Feathered Serpent reliefs, with many dates (Peñafiel 1890, Plates, vol. II: Lams. 170-211; Seler 1902-1923, II: 128-167), probably represent the best pre-Aztec representational historical record. A plausible interpretation is that they commemorate an important event, a meeting or "congress" of priests (and rulers?) from different communities —with calendric problems or "reform" perhaps an important item on the agenda. [4] A number of the sacerdotal figures represented on the various friezes are identified by what are almost certainly place and/or name glyphs (one of which [Cook de Leonard 1959: 132, Fig. 9] may well designate a town which still exists: Orizaba [Ahuilizapan]). Although some of the dates are certainly year dates, none can be correlated with the Christian calendar because of the familiar 52 year cycle repetition problem. Most important among the lesser carved Xochicalco monuments which may contain some historical referents are the "Piedra Seler" (Peñafiel 1890, Plates, vol II: Lam. 204), the "Piedra del Palacio" (Caso 1967: 166), and, possibly, the 3 recently discovered stela (Sáenz 1961; Caso 1967: 166-186). The "Piedra del Palacio" is particularly important for it resembles a page from a pictorial manuscript and thus may, in fact, provide some notion of the appearance of a Xochicalco historical record on paper and/or skin.

[4] For recent expressions of this view see Cook de Leonard 1959: 132; Jiménez Moreno 1959 (1966): 1072.

Although some of the most important structures in the ceremonial heart of the site have been excavated, substantially fewer carvings with possible historical referents of the kind just discussed have so far been discovered at Tula, the Toltec capital and the type site for the archaeology of the Central Mexican Early Postclassic. Dates (Acosta 1956-1957: Fig. 22) [5] are particularly scarce and none are certainly of years rather than days or of certain historical rather than ritual reference. Perhaps the best candidates for Tula carvings with some genuine historical reference are the warrior figures, with name-glyphs (and/or titles), carved on the sectioned square pillars of Structure B (Acosta 1956-1957: Fig. 24), which probably represent historical personages in power at the time of the dedication of this important structure. Similar pillar figures are common at Chichén Itzá, northern Yucatán, where Toltecs from Tula apparently set them-selves up as a ruling elite over the native Maya, and where various wall paintings, relief carvings, and embossed sheet gold pectorals almost certainly depict actual historical events, either in an essentially rea-listic or symbolic way (Tozzer 1952, Text: 98, and *passim*).

The largest number of monuments bearing representations with possible, probable, or virtually certain historical referents belong to the Late Postclassic or Aztec period. Most of them display dates. Lehmann (1909: 14-17) reviewed some of these, and a few years ago I prepared a preliminary list, with concise discussion of each, of all known Aztec period objects bearing dates with possible historical reference (Nicholson 1955a) —and I have since located many ad-ditional examples. Many of the monuments consist solely of dates; some of these, if not the majority, were probably commemorative stones associated with structures. Even if certain of these dates can be tentatively correlated with those in the Christian calendar, sep-arated now from the structures they once dated, they convey no signific-ant historical information.

A few monuments, however, in addition to their dates, feature representational scenes and/or symbolic motifs and thus constitute an historically somewhat more informative category. To illustrate, one of the most important of these is the Dedication Stone of the Great Temple of Tenochtitlan (e.g., Caso 1967: 60) [6] which displays one very large date in a square cartouche and above it a much smaller date, without a cartouche, associated with a stylized scene of 2 figures

---

[5] 3-5, 3 dates from the Cerro de la Malinche cliff reliefs, however, must be eliminated as Toltec period dates for they are clearly post-Toltec in age (see Nicholson 1955a: 17-19).

[6] This important monument was first published (drawing) and interpreted (with essential correctness) by Ramírez (1845). Unfortunately, he provided no data on the precise circumstances, time, and place of its discovery.

in priestly attire standing on either side of a *zacatapayolli* (grass ball for the insertion of blood smeared maguey spines) and drawing blood from their ear lobes. They are identified as the 7th and 8th rulers of Tenochtitlan, Tizoc (1481-1486) and Ahuitzotl (1486-1502), by their name-glyphs. Although there is no direct reference to the Templo Mayor, the large date, 8 Acatl, must be 1487, the well documented date for the dedication of this structure. The referent for the small date, 7 Acatl, is ambiguous, but it can perhaps be most congently interpreted as that of a day within the 8 Acatl year, 1487 (in the Caso correlation the 20th day of Panquetzaliztli, perhaps the most appropriate day for the dedication of the principal temple to Huitzilopochtli; see Nicholson 1955a: 3-4; Caso 1967: 64-67). Thus, although this famous stone canot be fully interpreted without the aid of the Tenochtitlan histories, it provides an indisputable confirmation —and may add the precise day— of what may have been the bloodiest dedication of a sacred structure in the history of the world.

Interestingly, the Aztec carving which provides the greatest amount of significant historical information, the *cuauhxicalli* of Tizoc, bears no date. However, since one of the 15 triumphant figures of Huitzilopochtli, patron deity of Tenochtitlan, bears the name glyph of Tizoc (i.e., represents him in the guise of the god), who enjoyed the shortest reign of all the Tenochca rulers, it can undoubtedly be dated to the period 1481-1486 or very shortly thereafter (in case it might have been posthumously commemorative). The great historical value of this monument lies in the fact that it constitutes the only record of a series of Tenochca conquests outside the pictorial and textual histories —apart from its considerable value to the student of the writing system in providing the largets group of place-glyphs of indubitable pre-Hispanic date. [7]

After the Tizoc stone, perhaps the Chapultepec cliff sculpture of Motecuhzoma II (Nicholson 1961a) provides the most historical information; probably: the year of Motecuhzoma's birth (1 Acatl, 1947), the day of his coronation (1 Cipactli, in the year, apparently undesignated, 10 Tochtli, 1502), the year of the last pre-Conquest New Fire ceremony (2 Acatl, 1507), and, possibly, the place-glyph of one of Motecuhzoma's conquests or a commemoration of the remarkable temporary alliance with an old hereditary enemy, Huexotzinco, which occurred late in his reign. Again, these interpretations are largely dependent on the recordation of these events in the pictorial and textual Tenochtitlan histories, but this monument, in turn,

[7] No really satisfactory thorough study of this famous monument has ever been published, nor has it ever been adequately illustrated. The classic studies are: León Gama 1832, Pt. 2: 46-73; Orozco y Berra 1877; Chavero 1887: 774-779; Seler 1902-1923, II: 801-810; Peñafiel 1910: 27-33; Saville 1928: 44-50.

confirms them and further reveals what events in the native view were considered to be most significant in the life of their supreme ruler —thus constituting a significant historical record in its own right.

Most of the other Aztec period archaeological pieces which may have been intended to commemorate actual past events convey only a bare minimum of historical information.[8] On the other hand, future discoveries, such as the recovery of the "piedra pintada" (apparently a twin to the Tizoc *cuauhxicalli*) in the Zócalo (Caso 1969), might well substantially increase the historical data provided by items assigned to this archaeological category.

"WRITTEN" RECORDS

This second category is much more important. Before proceeding, however, some very brief clarification of the "writing" system involved is in order. From at least Late Classic times —and probably considerably before, perhaps from the beginnings of Teotihuacan or even earlier— historical records in Central Mexico were apparently "written" in the form of pictorial narrations on screenfolds of bark paper or animal skin or, often superimposed on cartographic layouts, on large sheets of cotton cloth, bark paper, or skin (singlyor as a collection of sequent "pages").[9] Apparently no indubitably pre-Hispanic specimens of these pictorial histories have survived, although thousands must have been in existence at the advent of Cortés. However, a few pre-Hispanic pieces were copied in early post-Conquest times and others were composed on the pre-Hispanic model, so a fair number are available for study —and most of the major examples have been published and studied to a greater or lesser extent.

This corpus has provided the essential basis for modern understanding of the principles of the writing system (e.g., Dibble 1940, 1966; Barlow and McAfee 1949; Nowotny 1959). The system is basically pictographic but symbolic or ideographic elements are also of

[8]Typical examples are the "Chimalli Stone of Cuernavaca" (e.g., Seler 1902-1923, ii: 165), which may commemorate the accession of Axayacatl in 3 Calli, 1469, and/or a military campaign early in his reign, and the stone "year bundle stones", or *xiuhmolpilli*, which commemorate the 2 Acatl "New Fire" years at the end of one 52 year cycle and the commencement of another — some of which at least were "interred" in ritual "tombs" (Caso 1967: 129-140). See discussion in Nicholson 1955a: 4-5, 7-10.

[9] Jiménez Moreno (1966 [1959]: 44) has suggested that ". . .a true historiography arose only with the conditions of anguish and chaos that seem to have prevailed in Central Mexico from the end of the great Teotihuacan epoch in about A.D. 650, i.e. only when the Classic world was beginning to disintegrate".

great importance, and in some of the place and name-glyphs (which
are naturally especially common in the historical records) a phonetic
principle is operative utilizing homophones ("rebus principle"). By
"pictographic" is meant that most of the historical information is
conveyed by small stylized pictorial representations of events and
persons and objects in a fashion generally somewhat similar to the
techniques of some modern cartoons or "comic strips". In spite of
the obvious limitations of such a system, by the exercise of considerable imagination and ingenuity a surprisingly detailed narration
of events could at times be achieved. On the other hand, the majority of the surviving pictorial histories are, in fact, quite limited and
stylized in the kinds of historical information they convey. The development of this system of picto-ideographic writing provided the essential mechanism which permitted record keeping of a decidedly
more permanet and tangible kind than would have been possible on
the basis of purely oral transmission.

No annalistic system can be very effective without some method
of reasonably accurate chronologic control, and the other basic tool
which made possible the compilation of detailed historical records
in our area was a typical version of the advanced Mesoamerican
calendric system. In spite of some problems which require further
clarification, the fundamental principles of this system are well understood and well-known (e.g., Caso 1967). A cycle of 20 day signs was
combined with a cycle of 13 numbers ("numerical coefficients") to form
a permutating cycle of 260 days, the *tonalpohualli*. This very ancient
cycle was employed largely for divinatory purposes, but the *tonalpohualli* days were also used for secular record keeping ends. The
365 days vague year, which regulated the agricultural cycle and
the major public rituals, for structural mathematical reasons could
only begin or end (i.e., the 360th day; the last 5 days were in theory
supernumerary) on 4 of the 20 *tonalpohualli* days, which, at least
since Xochicalco times in Central Mexico, were Calli, Tochtli, Acatl,
and Tecpatl. These *tonalpohualli* days, with their "numerical coefficients" 1-13 (succeeding each other in the order: 1 Tochtli, 2 Acatl,
3 Tecpatl, 4 Calli, 5 Tochtli, etc.), served as designations for the
years, forming a re-entering cycle of 52 years. Most of the surviving
annals are content to specify the year of the occurrence of an event,
but occasionally the day (and sometimes the veintena) is indicated
as well (rarely, the day without the year). Apparently no "long
count" system (counting consecutively from a fixed "zero point")
was used, as far as is known, and this 52 year repetition problem can
be a serious one for the modern student. Another serious problem
—concerning which more below— is that different year counts appear
to have been in use at different times and in different places, although

for at least the last century or so before the Conquest the calendars
of most Central Mexican communities seem to have been standardized
(1 Acatl = 1519 [January 26, 1519-January 24, 1520, in the Caso
correlation]).

The presence, then, in pre-Hispanic Central Mexican culture of
2 key devices, a relatively sophisticated type of picto-ideographic writing and an unusually advanced calendric system, greatly facilitated
accurate historical record keeping. We now turn to the records themselves.

A number of distinct types of pictorial histories were employed.
Probably most are represented in the surviving corpus. Various Nahuatl
terms were applied to them. No one, to my knowledge, has attempted
to work out a thorough typology of extant Central Mexican native
pictorial histories or compile a reasonably complete list of the relevant
Nahuatl terminology. [10] A somewhat simplified, preliminary breakdown might appear something like this (with citation of typical
specimens and the apparent most appropriate Nahuatl designations,
derived largely from Molina (1944) and the various Nahuatl histories
themselves):

1) *Continuous year count annals* ([ce]*xiuhamatl*, "year-paper or
book"; [ce]*xiuhtlapohualamatl*, "year count-paper or book"; [ce]*xiuh-
tlacuilolli*, "year-paintings"; [ce]*xiuhtlapohualtlacuilolli*, "year count-
paintings"; *xiuhtonalamatl*, "year sign-book"). This important type is
distinguished by the recordation of a continuously sequent record of
years with picto-ideographic notations of events usually assigned to
particular years.

The best known (citing only those with a substantial pre-Hispanic
portion) are members of a famous group from Mexico Tenochtitlan
or communities in its direct orbit: *Códices Boturini* (probably 1116-
1303 [unfinished]), *Aubin* (probably 1116-1608, with 1 cycle omitted),
Mendoza (1324-1521), *Telleriano-Remensis/Vaticanus* A (1195-1562),
Mexicanus (1168-1590), *Azcatitlan* (ostensibly 1168-1382, probably
1116-1330), "*Histoire Mexicaine depuis 1221 jusqu'en 1591*" (Aubin-
Goupil # 40) (probably 1116-1573, with gaps), and "*Fragment de
l'Histoire des Anciens Mexicains*" (Aubin-Goupil # 85) (1196-1405).
The Acolhuaque area yields only 2: *Tira (Mapa) de Tepechpan* (1298-
1596) and *Códice en Cruz* (1402-1559). Two hail from communities
north of the Basin of Mexico: *Códice de Huichapan* (1403-1528,

10 Although Aubin (1885 [1849]: 50) drew up a small list, Simeon (1889:
Introduction) was the first to compile a fairly extended vocabulary of the commonest
Nahuatl terms relating to history and historians, with French translations of their
meanings, which Radin (1920: 7) summarized, with English translations of Simeon's
French versions. Garibay (1953-1954, I: *passim*) also mentioned most of the com-
monest terms.

with gaps) and *Anales de Tula* (1402-1521), and one from just south of it, *Códices de Tlaquiltenango* (precise years uncertain). Only one derives from the Basin of Puebla, *Historia Tolteca-Chichimeca* (1116-1544). One is of uncertain —but certainly Central Mexican— provenience, *"Codex Saville"* (1407-1535). Although from a Guerrero coastal community technically located outside the Central Mexican area, the *Códices de Azoyu 1* (1299-1565?) and 2 (obverse: 1428-1564?; reverse-*Humboldt Fragment 1*: 1487-1522, with gap?) deserve mention here because stylistically and iconographically they are so similar (in spite of a variant calendric notation) to the Central Mexican examples. [11]

It is perhaps worth noting that, with the one exception noted, all surviving Mesoamerican continuous year count pictorial anals stem from Central Mexico. All seem to be post-Conquest; most, however, are at least in part copies or versions of pre-Hispanic specimens. Only 5 (*Aubin*, Aubin-Goupil # 40 and # 85, *Huichapan, and Tula*) were annotated with fairly extensive explanatory texts in native languages (all Náhuatl but *Huichapan*, wich is Otomí) —the pictorial parts of *Historia Tolteca-Chichimeca* are more in the nature of illustrations to the very extensive Nahuatl text. Some of the others bear very brief Nahuatl annotations. *Telleriano-Remensis* and *Mendoza* are fairly extensively annotated in Spanish. None of them, if the most probable correlations of their year sequences with the Christian calendar be accepted, goes back earlier than 1116, or a little over 4 centuries before Cortés. All of those which begin their year counts this early or from some other point in the 12th century, however, commence with migratory sequences which, at best, are obviously highly

[11] I do not include the inadequately studied *"Códice Moctezuma"* in this list (which is not intended to be exhaustive), attributed to Morelos, and which has a sequence of year dates the beginning of which is difficult to discern but which, in its later portion, runs at least from 1493 to 1523. This piece is a tira, annotated in Nahuatl, with the stream of year signs running up the left hand margin and the picto-ideographic historical data occupying the remainder of the strip, in large compartments. There are some apparent anomalous stylistic features in this piece, which deserves further analysis (an unpublished study, incomplete, by R. Barlow and S. Mateos Higuera, is in the library of the University of the Americas). To avoid tedious over-citation, it will suffice to indicate here that all of the primary native historical sources mentioned from this point on, generally under their most commonly accepted titles, can be located by consulting, particularly: Boban 1891, Lejeal 1902, Kubler and Gibson 1951, García Granados 1952-1953, León-Portilla and Mateos Higuera 1957, Alcina Franch 1955-1956, Robertson 1959, Bernal 1962, Carrera Stampa 1962-1963, Glass 1964, and, above all, the comprehensive "censuses" of both textual and pictorial native sources in the forthcoming vol. 13 of the *Handbook of Middle American Indians* (preliminary versions, with limited distribution: Gibson 1964-1967; Glass 1966-1967; Nicholson 1960, 1961b; for Tlaxcalan and Pueblan native tradition pictorials see also Nicholson 1967, 1968).

patterned and stereotyped; the more genuinely historical sections do not usually begin until well into the 14th century. [12]

Various formats were employed, although this is complicated by obvious rearrangement and modification in some of the post-Conquest copies and versions (e.g., Robertson 1959: 109-110). The simplest (represented by the *Códices Mexicanus* and *Huichapan*, the *Tira de Tepechpan*, and the *Anales de Tula*) was a continuous stream of sequent year dates, with one exception (*Tepechpan*: round) in square cartouches, painted on long strips ("tira") or on individual pages, with the picto-ideographic notations of the historical events drawn adjacent to the years when they occurred —and often connected to them by lines. A special peculiarity of *Tepechpan* is that it is a bi-community history, Tepechpan above the row of year signs, Tenochtitlan below (probably reflecting the part-Tenochca origin of the ruling dynasty of this community otherwise in the Acolhuaque political sphere).

An interesting "abbreviation" of this format is provided by the "*Codex Saville*", where the notation of the years is reduced to a continuous stream of blue circles (= turquoise disks, *xihuitl* = year), each standing for a year (with some of the years also indicated by the normal picto-ideogram with its "numerical coefficient"). Some of the *Tlaquiltenango* (Morelos) fragments display what appear to be similar records, in this case with the blue circles filled with the standard cross-hatching (to indicate mosaic).

What amount to variations on this format are the meander arrangements of the year cartouches of *Boturini* (and one section of *Vaticanus A*), the "page frame" arrangements of the year rows of *Mendoza*, *Telleriano-Remensis/Vaticanus A*, and *Azoyu 1* and *2*, where the rows edge the sides of the pages (in the first 2 mentioned perhaps an adaptation to the European page format by the copyist), and the "block" formats of *Aubin*, *Azcatitlan*, and Aubin-Goupil # 40 and # 85, where the rows of cartouches are often grouped into (frequently irregular) blocks. The most unique format is the "cross" layout of the *Códice en Cruz* —each year assigned a long narrow strip with year sign at one end and picto-ideographic information in the remainder of the compartment. Some of these pictorial histories utilize different formats in different sections; again, at least in some cases this may be the result of their post-Conquest copy status rather than reflecting

---

[12] Continuous year count pictorial histories with much longer temporal coverages almost certainly existed, as evidenced, among other things, by some Spanish accounts directly derived from lost native pictorials, to be described below. If Torquemada (1943, II: 310) can be believed ("...se podía tener noticia de sus cosas, y referir con puntualidad lo sucedido de mil Años atrás, como lo hazen"), some of them extended back to ca. A. D. 500 — cf. Motolinia 1903: 349, who speaks of continuous year count annals commencing A.D. 694.

authentic pre-Hispanic practice, although the latter is certainly not unlikely.

These continuous year count histories obviously constitute the most systematic annalistic Central Mexican treatments of history. Although the historical information they convey is often rather sketchy, their precise dating and strictly sequential ordering lend them special value to the modern student.

Some of the most important textual histories, both Spanish and Nahuatl, obviously derive more or less directly from these continuous year pictorial annals. A particularly clear example is the *Historia de los mexicanos por sus pinturas* (1891), 'compiled by an anonymous (Fray Andrés de Olmos?) Franciscan in Spanish, which amounts to an invaluable Mexica "world history" from the creation of the universe (which can be calculated at about A.D. 986) to ca. 1532-33. The important *Juan Cano Relaciones*, [13] also compiled at about the same date (1532) by another anonymous Franciscan and, according to explicit statements in them, based on detailed Mexica and Colhuaque pictorial histories, present continuous sequences, mostly in reign lengths, from ca. 770 to 1532 —but no native years are explicitly named. The "migrational portion" of Muñoz Camargo's history of Tlaxcala (1948: chaps. 1-4) seems to have derived from a continuous year count record, as did at least some of Torquemada's material on Mexica history (1943, I: book II). Certainly Alva Ixtlilxochitl (1952) must have had some access to this type of chronicle, although, if so, his utilization of them was obviously not very systematic.

Turning to the Nahuatl sources, much of that extraordinarily meaty compilation of many independent histories, the *Anales de Cuauhtitlan*, is obviously ultimately derived from various continuous year pictorial histories from different communities, [14] as is much of Chimalpahin's *Relaciones* (see discussion of his sources in Zimmermann 1960). In the case of both these sources many independent chronicles were fitted —obviously often quite artificially— into single continuous master year count schemes which ostensibly cover the longest periods of any native

[13] I employ this name for convenience instead of their cumbersome and somewhat misleading separate titles: *Relación de la genealogía y linaje de los Señores que han señoriado esta tierra de la Nueva España, después que se acuerdan haber gentes en estas partes* ... and *Origen de los Mexicanos*. Although García Icazbalceta, who first published them (1886-1892, III: 263-308), practically implied that the latter was a copy of the former, it is obvious that both must derive, with significant variations, from a lost common prototype.

[14] Barlow (1947) published a fairly detailed outline of this complex composite source. His breakdown, however, suffers from lack of an attempt at specification of the many histories from different communities. Garibay (1953-1954, I: 36-38, 69-70, 454-456) discussed these in a general, preliminary fashion. A thorough analysis of this key source and breakdown into its constituent parts is still very much a high priority desideratum in Mesoamerican studies.

Central Mexican histories (*Cuauhtitlan*: 635-1519; Chimalpahin, total coverage of all *Relaciones*: 670-1612). [15]

The most important continuous year count chronicle from a single community is *Anales de Tlatelolco*, doc. v (1155-1522). Also deserving of mention in this regard are Zapata's *Historia Cronología de la N. C. de Tlaxcala en Mexicano* (begins 1168?; truly continuous 1477-1692), the early portions of the *Anales de Tecamachalco* (1398-1590), *Anales de Tlaxcala # 1* (1453-1603), *Anales Mexicanos # 2* (1168-1546), and "*Fragment d'une Histoire de Mexique en Langue Nahuatl*" (Aubin-Goupil #217) (1398-1595) —the last 2 quite closely related to the *Codex Aubin*.

2) *Sporadically dated, or undated, annals* (Nahuatl terminology uncertain, perhaps *nemilizamatl, nemiliztlacuilolli*, "life-paper or book", "life-paintings"). How important this category was in pre-Hispanic times is difficult to estimate. A typical example seems to be the second section of the *Códice Azcatitlan*, which chronicles in order, but without dates, the reigns of the rulers of Tenochtitlan, their conquests, and other major events, including the Conquest. Another lost pictorial Tenochca "world history", of which the unfortunately truncated "*Leyenda de los Soles*" is a Nahuatl commentary of 1558, might also have been of this "sporadically" dated type. At least the crude sketch (p. 78) of one scene would suggest this, as well as the scattered dates provided by the text itself. The pictorial aspect of the hypothetical "*Crónica X*" (Barlow 1945) might also have qualified for this category —as well as some of the original pictorials on which the colonial "composite histories" were ultimately based. Various items in the next category might be considered to belong here as well, but they will be treated separately below.

3) *Cartographic layouts combined with historical, dynastic, and/or genealogical depictions* (Nahuatl terminology uncertain; *altepetlacuilolli?*, "community-paintings"). This is one of the most original and interesting categories of Mesoamerican pictorial histories, one which is by no means confined to Central Mexico (it is perhaps even more characteristic of Oaxaca and the Gulf Coast). It constitutes an unusual kind of history in which there is more focus upon the spatial co-ordinates of the events depicted than the temporal co-ordinates. Outstanding in this category are 3 well-known Acolhuaque pictorial histories: *Códice Xolotl*, and *Mapas Quinatzin* and *Tlotzin*. The first named is especially important; it consists of a series of 9 maps —surprisingly accurate in general layout— of the Basin of Mexico and immediately surrounding

---

[15] On the chronologic artificiality of one of Chimalpahin's *Relaciones* ("*Memorial Breve acerca de la Ciudad de Culhuacán*"), see Kirchhoff 1961a (1964).

territory with detailed depictions of historical events and genealogies of ruling dynasties of major communities superimposed on this cartographic layout. Each map belongs to a different period, in sequence, but specific dates are scarce and —because they are not part of a continuous series— sometimes of uncertain correlation with the Christian calendar (see discussions in Dibble 1951; Nicholson in press).

Another well-known group is Pueblan, the *Mapas de Cuauhtinchan 1-4*, plus some similar layouts in the *Historia Tolteca-Chichimeca*; again, with the partial exception of the *Mapa de Cuauhtinchan 2*, dates are very scarce or absent. Only one example appears to be almost certainly from Tenochtitlan itself or its immediate orbit, the famous *Mapa de Sigüenza*, whose cartographic aspect is the most highly schematized of all known examples of this class and which is temporally confined to the migratory period up to the founding of Tenochtitlan-Tlatelolco. Dates are lacking; only groups of little circles to indicate the number of years spent by the migrators at the various stops and an unusual version of the *xiuhmolpilli*, "tying of the years" symbol, are employed. Other significant and typical examples of this category are: *Mapa de Popotla* and *"pièce d'un Procès"* (Aubin-Goupil # 392), from the Basin of Mexico; *Lienzo of the Heye Foundation*, of uncertain provenience but undoubtedly Central Mexico; *Lienzo de Tetlama, Mapa de Coatlan del Rio*, and *"Plan Topographique de Hueyapan"*, from Morelos; *Lienzo de Cuauhquechollan, Circular Map of Cuauhquechollan, Mapa de Ehecatepec y Huitziltepec, Codice de la Cueva* and *Map and Dynasty of Tecamachalco (Lienzo Vischer 1)*, from central Puebla; and *Map of Metlaltoyuca* and *Lienzo de Oyametepec y Huitzilatl*, from northern Puebla. Typically, few contain more than a handful of dates; the emphasis is on events and their geographical loci rather than temporal aspects. The categories of historical information most commonly depicted on these maps are migrations and conquests and, especially, genealogical layouts and dynastic sequences.

To what extent some of the textual chronicles might have in part derived from these "cartographized histories" is difficult to judge. Alva Ixtlilxochitl's close dependence on the *Códice Xolotl* for a major part of his history is undoubtedly the clearest example. Whenever community and/or provincial mojoneras are listed in detail some cartographic pictorial was probably the ultimate source, as in the known case of the *Historia Tolteca-Chichimeca*. However, oral traditions might also have occasionally included fairly extensive lists of this type.

4) *Genealogies* (*tlacamecayoamatl*, "genealogy-paper or book", *huehuetlatocatlacamecayotlacuilolli*, "ancient rulers-genealogy-paintings"). This category comprises those pictorials which are virtually exclusively

devoted to conveying genealogical information; many, of course, include genealogical along with other historical data. These were certainly common in pre-Hispanic times; it is likely that every important noble family possessed them. Many have survived, some introduced as exhibits in post-Conquest litigations. Although all those extant appear to be colonial in date, most probably reproduce authentic native formats. Interestingly, these genealogies are very rarely dated. The most common additional information they contain is related to land ownership; the relevant properties are often depicted adjacent to the genealogical layout itself.

A fair number of Central Mexican genealogies are extant, particularly from Tlaxcala and neighboring provinces. [16] Space limitations preclude their detailed itemization, but some typical examples are: *Circular Genealogy of the Descendants of Nezahualcoyotl, Genealogía de los Príncipes Mexicanos* (Aubin-Goupil # 72), *Colhuacan: Proceso de Marta Petronila y Augustín de la Luna contra Juan Francisco, María y Juana* (Aubin-Goupil # 110), and *Xochimilco: Juliana Tlaco contra Petronila Francisca*, from the Basin of Mexico; *Tlacotepec: Piece du Proces de Pablo Ocelotl et Ses Fils contre Alonzo Gonzales* (Aubin-Goupil # 32), from the Basin of Toluca; *Genealogía de Tetlamaca y Tlametzin*, of unknown provenience but undoubtedly from Central Mexico; *Lienzo Chalchihuitzin Vázquez, Genealogía de una Familia de Tepeticpac, Genealogy and Properties of Descendants of Ocelotzin*, "*Genealogie von 33 Personen*", *Lienzo de Don Juan Chichimecatecuhtli, Genealogía de Zolin*, and *Genealogía des Tlatzcantzin*, from Tlaxcala; *Genealogía de Cuauhquechollan-Macuilxochitepec*, from central Puebla; and "*Papers of Itzcuintepec*", from northern Puebla.

The most common format is the depiction of the founding ancestor at the top of the layout, sometimes in a house (especially common in Tlaxcalan genealogies; see Nicholson 1967), with his descendants linked to him with lines or cords; marital partners are sometimes linked with dotted lines. Usually, but not invariably, the name-glyph of each person depicted is included. The detail and complexity of these genealogies is often remarkable; some represent well over 50 individuals.

Various textual histories, both in Náhuatl and Spanish, obviously contain significant information derived from pictorial genealogies. Good examples are the detailed genealogies contained in the Náhuatl *Crónica Mexicayotl*, plus many briefer ones in the *Historia Tolteca-Chichimeca, Anales de Cuauhtitlan*, Chimalpahin's *Relaciones*, etc., and, in Spanish, in the histories of Muñoz Camargo and Alva Ixtlilxochitl. A major textual genealogical source is the Latin letter of Pablo Nazareo, 16th century cacique of the province of Xaltocan and husband of Motecuh-

---

[16] The lists in Nicholson 1967 and 1968 include over 25 genealogies.

zoma II's niece (Paso y Troncoso 1940, x: 89-129); his data must have derived ultimately from pictorial genealogies (see chart in Jiménez Moreno 1950).

5) *Dynastic lists* (Nahuatl terminology uncertain; e.g., *tecuhamatl?*, "lords-paper or book"). A category closely related to that justa discussed consists of pictorial dynastic sequences —without the specification of geneaological connections. These dynastic lists usually involve just the depiction of each ruler in sequence (top to bottom or left to right are the most common formats), with his name-glyph, commonly seated on a throne. Often, but not invariably, their reigns are dated or at least the total number of years they ruled is recorded. Good examples of these "straight" pictorial dynastic lists are: one section of the *Codex Cozcatzin*; *Codex Aubin*, second section; and Sahagún's *"Primeros Memoriales"* (Tetzcoco, Tenochtitlan, and Huexotlan dynasties) and *"Florentine Codex"* (Tlatelolco dynasty).

Textual lists which consist just of the enumeration of rulers by name and the eyars and/or lengths of their reigns, and which might thus be derived from pictorial dynastic lists of this type, are rare. A few examples, however, can be cited, e.g.: the one page *"Relación de los Señores que Fueron de Méjico"* (Tudela de la Orden 1954: 388); Torquemada's (1943, I: book III, chap. VI) Azcapotzalco ruler list, and Alva Ixtlilxochitl's Xochimilco dynastic sequence in his *"Relación del Origen de los Xuchimilcas"* (1952, I: 455-456).

Probably the great majority of surviving Central Mexican native histories can be assigned to one or more of the categories just discussed. However, the existence of other types, not clearly represented by any extant items, can be deduced from the available Nahuatl terminology (mostly from Molina 1944). A remarkably detailed type of history apparently existed: *cecemilhuitlacuilolli, cecemilhuiamoxtli*, "ystoria de dia en dia", unless these terms were concocted after the Conquest for the European type of diary. Closely related must have been the "ystoria de lo presente", *quinaxcannemilizamatl*. A form of biography seems to be indicated by the verb *nemilizpoa*, "narrar o relatar historia, o vida de otro", and the substantive *nemiliztlacuilolli*, "chronica, historia, o leyenda" (cf. *nemiliztlacuiloani*, "cronista o historiador") probably included biographical narrations —but probably also connoted a broader type of historical recounting as well. For the generic term "ystoria" Molina gives as one term *nemilizamatl*, "life-paper or book".

ORALLY TRANSMITTED HISTORY

The final major category, orally transmitted historical information, was tremendously important. It is, however, the most difficult to analyze and to understand. At the outset, a basic division can probably be made: the "attached" oral narrations which served as direct annotatory accompaniments to the pictorial histories, on the one hand, and, on the other, the oral narrations which had an "independent" existence —although certainly no very sharp line can be drawn between them and there must have been much overlap. The former will be first considered since it relates so closely to the major category just discussed.

The surviving native language texts which directly annotate the pictorial histories (see above, p. 46), or are obviously directly derived from those which did, evidence a considerable formularization of these oral accompaniments. It is possible that a standardized "explanatory" verbal narration, memorized virtually word-perfect, accompanied every pictorial history. However, the precise nature of the relationship between them and their oral accompaniments is not very clear, and the relevant statements of the primary choniclers are too general to be of much aid. The extant texts range from the most laconic, minimal conveyances of the picto-ideographic information to very long narrations, some seemingly in verse, for which the pictorial data obviously only served as a kind of mnemonic stimulus. As Garibay (especially, 1953-1954, I: 319) has particularly discerned, these "over the minimum" verbal passages appear to include, inter alia, whole or portions of poetic "epics", long "prose" historical and biographical narratives, essentially "novelistic romances" (even if based on actual historical figures and events), and poetic songs or chants (apparently sometimes prosified).

Whether these longer narrations were normally "inserted" at key points as the pictorial was "read" is difficult to judge. It seems likely, but it must be recognized that the surviving textual histories were compiled in post-Hispanic times for somewhat different ends and their organization and contents may not reflect altogether faithfully the manner in which the pre-Hispanic "reader" orally conveyed the contents of a pictorial history. I suspect, however, that, in general, they do, at least the ones which most clearly annotate a single pictorial history (e.g., *Leyenda de los Soles*, and sections of the *Anales de Tlatelolco*, *Anales de Cuauhtitlan*, and Chimalpahin's *Relaciones*). In addition to these more formal, carefully memorized oral accompaniments, it does not seem unlikely that more informal, extemporaneous verbal explanations of the pictorial scenes must also have been made to interested parties in pre-Hispanic times —almost certainly, if nowhere else, in a pedagogical context— by the composers and custodians of these histories.

The phrasing and style of those which only have textual explanations in Spanish are much more informal than their Náhuatl-Otomí counterparts, but in these cases probably no real attempt was made literally to "translate" the standarized native language accompaniments. These Spanish annotations, rather, probably resulted from repeated questioning of supposedly knowledgeable informants concerning the meaning of the picto-ideographic scenes. [17]

We are dealing, then, with a kind of "dual media history", or "bigraphic", as Simeon (1889: IX) suggested it be called, involving 2 simultaneous and complementary methods of transmission, picto-ideographic and oral. The former provided a "stability factor" and a useful mnemonic function, the latter added richness of color and detail as well as psychological nuances which could be conveyed in no other way. In some cases the surviving specimens provide us with both halves of this equation, in other cases, either one or the other. But no history of this type can be considered truly complete unless both the picto-ideographic and oral segments are extant.

Turning to the "independent" oral category, it is now clear, particularly after the devoted studies over the past few decades of, above all, Garibay and his followers and fellow students, that an oral literature of considerable richness and sophistication was an outstanding feature of late pre-Hispanic Central Mexican culture. [18] This extensive corpus can be classified into a number of different genres, and there have been various attempts to do so. The leading modern student (Garibay 1953-1954; 1963) suggested this scheme, on the broadest level: 1) poetry: lyric, epic, and dramatic; 2) prose: historical, didactic, and imaginative. In all of these categories, except perhaps didactic prose, historical information could be, and was, conveyed.

The most important was "historical prose", oral narratives —by definition, for the purposes of the present category, not directly tied to pictorial histories— which were intended to convey information concerning human past events which were believed to have actually occurred.

[17] Judging from the frequency of obvious errors in these accounts (especially serious in the case of the *Telleriano-Remensis*), the informants were seemingly not always so knowledgeable or perhaps at times deliberately misled their Spanish interrogators; on the other hand, simple failures of communication resulting from the language barrier and possibly other factors might have been responsible.

[18] Garibay's contributions were voluminous and scattered, but his most fundamental study was his *Historia de la Literatura Nahuatl* (1953-1954); see also Garibay 1937, 1940a (1952, 1962), 1940b, 1942, 1945 (1964), 1958, 1963, 1964a, 1964b, 1965, 1968. León-Portilla (e.g. 1961, 1964 [1969], 1967) has been his most important disciple; see also Irene Nicholson 1959a, 1959b, and Taggart 1957. Citations and brief appraisals of most of the works of his predecessors were included in his magnum opus by Garibay. There has been, in the writer's opinion, a tendency on the part of his followers to accept some of Garibay's hypotheses too uncritically — and a thorough appraisal and critique of his landmark contribution is an obvious need. Significant recent independent studies and publications of the Nahuatl literary corpus, especially the poetry, would include: Nowotny 1956, Van Zantwijk 1957, Kutscher 1958, Mendoza 1958, 1959, Lambert 1958, 1961, Horcasitas 1959, Simmons 1960, and, especially, Schultze Jena 1957.

Garibay (1953-1954, I: 478) estimated that this category composed one-half to two-thirds of the oral literature with historical content. Some of these appear to contain traces of metered versification or at least regularly patterned rhythms —which would have greatly facilitated their memorization. However, it is precisely the lack of clear-cut versification that most obviously justifies categorizing these narrations as "prose" (Garibay 1963: 112).

It is possible that every important community had individuals who had committed to memory most or all of its oral historical corpus and who might have been called upon to recite appropriate segments of it on appropriate occasions. This corpus also probably constituted an "official", virtually canonized oral version of each community's history, which was progressively added to, probably frequently modified in response to local political-dynastic vicissitudes, and carefully transmitted to younger successors to these community "oral historians". It is likely that these latter probably also utilized the pictorial annals in close conjunction with the verbal narratives.

These historical oral prose accounts obviously provide much of the information, over and above the standardized explanatory oral accompaniments to the pictorials, contained in the more important textual histories. Most of the primary Nahuatl histories (*Anales de Tlatelolco, Anales de Cuauhtitlan, Historia Tolteca-Chichimeca, Leyenda de los Soles, Codex Aubin, Crónica Mexicayotl*, Chimalpahin's *Relaciones*, Cristóbal del Castillo, Zapata, Aubin-Goupil # 40, etc.) appear to contain many examples of authentic pre-Hispanic historical prose narrations recorded virtually verbatim in the Roman alphabet. [19] It is also likely that much of the content of the native histories in Spanish is derived, directly or indirectly, from these Nahuatl prose narratives; some of them may be fairly close translations of these originals. Perhaps the prime example would be the Tezozomoc and Durán histories of Tenochtitlan probably derived from cognate (but not identical) versions of a lost Nahuatl chronicle which Barlow (1945) dubbed the "*Crónica X*". Many sections in the histories of Alva Ixtlilxochitl, Muñoz Camargo, Torquemada and other Spanish language native histories undoubtedly ultimately stem from these Nahuatl prose oral historical narrations, as do some portions of the *Histoire du Mexique* (1905), preserved only in a 16th century French translation from a lost Spanish original.

The "epic poems" or "sagas" as Garibay (1940a; 1945; 1953-1954, I: chap. v; 1963; chap. 3) and others have defined them, represent much more consciously esthetic productions, with more formal rhythms and

---

[19] Garibay (1953-1954, I: caps. v and ix) identified and translated many of the most striking examples.

metered versifications. They range, in Garibay's definition, from the completely mythological to those closely based on genuine historical persons and events. Although technically belonging more to the realm of art than of history, if handled with critical caution these "epics" can provide a wealth of priceless historical data, even those with an obvious heavy infusion of legendary, romantic, and folkloristic elements. Particularly well-known examples are the Topiltzin Quetzalcoatl of Tollan Tale (Nicholson 1957), another cycle including the rather enigmatic "Copil Tale", revolving around the foundation of Tenoch-titlan, and a cycle concerned with the Mexica "Babylonian captivity" in Colhuacan. Garibay (especially 1945, 1953-1954, I: chap. v) believed that most of the preserved native histories were studded with these metered epic poems, usually in fragmentary form —and he identified and translated quite a number of them. He recognized, however, the difficulty of clearly separating them from the prose accounts and the novelistic romances and, in fact, often assigned them to more than one category. This genre may have had the great importance which he suggested (cf. Horcasitas 1959: 200-203); in any case, further study and analysis is certainly indicated.

What might be called "hero tales" could be assigned to either this category, when essentially versified, or to the prose narration category, discussed above. A good example is the tragi-romantic story of the champion Otomi warrior from Tlaxcala, Tlalhuicole, unfortunately known only in 2 late Spanish versions (Muñoz Camargo 1948: 138-140; Durán 1967, II: 455-457; Tezozomoc 1944: 475-477 —the last 2 cognate versions ultimately from a single original). Some of the recountings of Nezahualcoyotl's adventures fall into this category, particularly as chronicled by Alva Ixtlilxochitl and one section of the *Anales de Cuauhtitlan*, as does the "*Crónica X*" story of the Tenochca prince, the Ezhuahuacatl Tlacahuepan, and his heroic selfsacrifice while in the power of the Chalcans (Durán 1967, II: 145-147; Tezozomoc 1944: 88-90). Even the exploits of Tlacaellel, half brother of Motecuhzoma I, so obviously over—glorified in the "*Crónica X*" and other sources derived from it, might be included here. In spite of their folkloristic and even novelistic overtones, these heroic narratives undoubtedly contain a certain core of genuine historicity. Their appeal as romantic stories would, as in all times and places, favor their indefinite preservation in the oral literary corpus and, as a consequence, whatever actual historical data they contain.

Garibay's "dramatic poems" or "poemas mímicos" (1953-1954, I: cap. VI; 1963: 90-107; 1968) are also essentially esthetic productions, but often their themes were taken directly from significant historical events. Consequently, they, too, if handled critically, can provide some useful historical data. The best known of these is the first "*teponaz-*

cuicatl" of the *Cantares Mexicanos* (fols. 26v-27v), the "Toltec Elegy" of Lehmann (1922 [1941]; cf. Garibay 1968. No. 1), which laments the flight from Tollan of Topiltzin Quetzalcoatl and which provides, inter alia, priceless historical allusions to personages and places prominent durin the Toltec period. The *Cantares Mexicanos* contains a few other specimens of this genre which also provide some significant historical allusions; e.g., the *"Tlapapal cuextecayotl"*, *"Matlatzinca-yotl"*, and *"Huehuecuicatl"* (respectively, fols. 36r-v, 53v, and 73v-74v; Garibay 1968, Nos. 12, 19, and 21).

The "lyric poems" (Garibay 1937; 1940b (1952, 1962); 1953-1954, I: cap. III; 1964b; 1965), as would be expected because of their nature, in general contain fewer significant historical allusions than the categories just discussed. However, Garibay recognized various subclasses within this broad grouping, and poems within one, which might be labeled "the exaltation of war and in praise of military heroes" (*cuauh-cuicatl, yaocuicatl, tecuhcuicatl*), and within another, the elegiac poems (*icnocuicatl*), often contain allusions to battles, persons, and places of considerable historical value. One prime example is "The Usurpation of Tezozomoc" (*Cantares Mexicanos*, fol. 7v-9r; Garibay 1965: 90-93; cxv-cxvII), which Radin even included (in Brinton's inaccurate translation) among his selections of primary historical sources. Some of these might have been composed as funeral dirges, "cantatas funerales", as Garibay (1953-1954, I: 203) called them. Because of the importance of the deceased or the particular beauty of the song, they might have been preserved for many generations; if so, they would, in effect, have constituted a kind of "contemporary" record, however poeticized, of actual events in the life of an historically prominent individual.

Even the "pure" lyric poems (*xochicuicatl, xopancuicatl*) occasionally contain historical tidbits of value. One *Cantares Mexicanos* poem (fol. 60v-r), in fact, labeled a *xopancuicatl*, is entirely devoted to a remembrance of the "Chapultepec Defeat", when the Mexica were conquered and dispersed by a coalition of neighboring communities, and contains many valuable historical references (Garibay 1942 (1940): 47-48; 1953-1954, I: 92-93, 474-475). Like the so-called epic and dramatic poems, lyric poems or fragments of them were apparently often inserted into the historical chronicles; certainly many of the post-Conquest histories appear to contain them. The most famous of these is the "Song of the Chapultepec Defeat", which is found, whole or in part, in different sources (*Anales de Tlatelolco*, doc. 5; *Anales de Cuauhtitlan*, *"Cédula de Cuauhtémoc"*; Garibay 1953-1954, I: 93-94, 221-222, 475-476). The "Moquihuix Cuetlaxtlan Victory Song" of the *Anales de Tlatelolco*, doc. 5 (Barlow 1948: 133, 144; Garibay 1953-1954, I: 225-226, 476), is another well-known example. Even the religious poetic songs or chants, represented particularly by the 20 examples collected by Sahagún in Tepepulco (Brinton 1887; Seler 1902-1923, II: 959-1107; Garibay 1953-1954, I: cap. II, 1958; Sahagún 1950-1963, Pt. III: 207-214), contain a few allusions, especially to places, that conceivably have some historical value.

Statements are occasionally found in some primary sources (e.g., Sahagún 1950-1963, Pt. IV: 55; Tovar in García Icazbalceta 1947, IV: 92) that songs, both religious and secular, and the "parlamentos que hacían los oradores" were "written" in books ("los figuraban con sus caracteres"). Nothing like these, to my knowledge, have survived, and I share Garibay's (1953-1954, I: 289; 1968: XXXVIII) perplexity as to just how such "written" versions of the songs and oral narrations would have appeared. It is true that imaginative utilization of series of pictograms and ideograms could well have served a very useful mnemonic function for the oral productions, and "songbooks" of this type might have been employed. If so, this would provide another significant link between the pictorial and oral techniques of transmission.

A considerable Nahuatl terminology appears to have developed for the different types of oral transmissions with historical content. Concentrating just on the substantives, the most generic terms were those like *tlatolli*, "palabra, plática o habla ... cuento", *huehue tlatolli* and *huecauh tlatolli*, "ystoria de los tiempos antiguos", *quinaxcantlatolli*, "ystoria de lo presente", *tlatollotl*, "historia", *nemiliztlatollotl*, "chronica, historia, o leyenda", *nemilizcotl*, "ystoria", *tenonotztli* (*tenonotzaliztli*), "historia que se cuenta o relación que se haze de alguna cosa", *nenonotzalli* (*huehuenenotzal*), "(ancient) tradition", *itoloca*, "that which is said of someone" (see León-Portilla 1956: 261), and *icacoca*, which Garibay (1953-1954, I: 55) suggests might be best translated as "historieta". Many of these terms contain stems of the verbs *itoa*, *tlatoa*, *notza*, *nonotza*, *nonetza*, to speak, to tell, to relate, emphasizing the spoken word aspect (cf. English tale, German saga, Spanish cuento, etc.). The well-known generic for the poem-songs is *cuicatl*.

Space limitations prevent a truly adequate analysis and discussion of this rich, complex oral literature with historical content. In spite of the extremely valuable landmark contributions of Garibay and his followers, more critical studies by other scholars equipped with a thorough mastery of Classical Nahuatl are certainly indicated. Garibay, although interested in the historical aspect, consciously concentrated more or less exclusively on the strictly literary aspect. The student interested in this extensive corpus primarily for its possible historical value is faced with some formidable problems of analysis and evaluation before he can utilize with any confidence these data for his historical reconstructions. The poetic compositions, particuarly, so inextricably combine history, legend, folklore, romance, and myth that the task of culling out of them the genuine historical nuggets is a task not to be undertaken lightly —but often the effort pays off.

THE HISTORIANS

The different types of history transmission techniques in pre-Hispanic Central México have been concisely reviewed. Some consideration of the transmitters themselves, the compilers and composers of these histories, is now in order. The basic question, of course, is *who*? Who were the historians in the pre-Hispanic Central Mexican communities? Were there specialists, trained by older specialists, who played this role, or was historical record keeping essentially a "sideline", a task performed by individuals who were more concerned with other matters in their societies? I do not believe that simple, definitive answers to these questions can be advanced at this time. Certainly some rather generalized statements in various primary and secondary sources appear to indicate that there were more or less professional annalists and genealogists. [20] Molina provides some terms for "coronista": *altepetlacuilo* ("community-painter"), *xiuhtlacuilo* ("year-painter"), and *tenemilizicuiloani* ("painter of someone's life"), which certainly refer to the composers of the picto-ideographic histories. The "painter" in general, as is well-known, was called *tlacuilo*; he was the specialist in the picto-ideographic writing system who produced the screenfold books and other "written" records needed in his society. His was clearly a recognized full-time profession. However, the typical *tlacuilo* seems to have been essentially a scribe, working under the supervision of others (priests, government officials, etc.). Perhaps the implication of Molina's definitions is that there were professional annalists, "coronistas", who also could do the "writing" as well as the composing of history. This seems entirely possible, but the point is not very clear. Certainly there are positive statements relating to some Mesoamerican areas that professional priests also painted sacred books (e.g., Las Casas 1958, II: 422: Totonacapan; Landa 1941: 27: Yucatán). If some at least of the priests could be trained as *tlacuiloque*, there would seem to be no good reason for not training historical record keepers in the same skill. Certainly, from the standpoint of practical economy of labor this would have been the most efficient system.

Molina also defines what may have been another type of historian, the "contador de historia", *tenemilizpoa*, *tenemilizpoani*; these cate-

[20] Among the best descriptions in the primary sources of the kinds of historians and the kinds of records they kept are: Motolinia 1903: 3, 8-9, 150, 349; Durán 1967, I: 222-223, 226; Pomar 1964: 175, 186, 190; Tovar (letter of 1587 to Acosta; e.g., García Icazbalceta 1947, IV: 91-93; English translation: Kubler and Gibson 1951: 77-78); Torquemada 1943, II: 301, 544; Alva Ixtlilxochitl 1952, II: 17-18.

gories may have referred to those who concentrated particularly on memorizing the oral narrations. He also includes the "relator", *tenonetzani, tlanonotzani*. For "ystoriador" Molina gives *tlatolicuiloani* and *nemiliztlatolicuiloani* (these terms, however, possibly reflect some Spanish influence, as Molina gives the meaning of the first as "historiador, o cronista, o el que escriue las palabras que otros dizen").

Some native historians appear to have been officials supported by the state (Torquemada 1943, ii: 544), although this pattern was probably confined to the largest and most important cabeceras such as Mexico Tenochtitlan and Tetzcoco. As indicated above, it seems likely that every community, even the smaller ones, had at least one "official local historian". They must have stemmed largely from the ranks of the nobility; in any case, the histories they compiled, pictorial and/or oral, certainly strongly reflected the attitudes and interests of the upper class. They may have assisted in the formal educational institutions, the *calmecac* and the *telpochcalli*. They surely trained others to succeed them in their duties and responsibilities as compilers and transmitters of the community's history.

Some historians are even named in different sources. Durán (1967, ii: 216), for example, speaks of a "historiador real ... viejo de muchos años", Cuauhcoatl, who flourished during the reign of Motecuhzoma II. Alva Ixtlilxochitl, (1952, ii: 21), commencing his *Historia Chichimeca*, cites: "Los más graves autores y históricos que hubo en la antigüedad de estos naturales, se halla haber sido Quetzalcoatl el primero; y de los modernos Nezahualcoyotzin rey de Tetzcuco, y los dos infantes de Mexico, Itzcoatzin y Xiuhcozcatzin, hijos del rey Huitzilihuitzin, sin otros muchos que hubo ..." He also attributes the *Códice Xolotl* to 2 individuals whom he names (1952, ii: 144) "Cemilhuitzin y el otro Quauhquechol" —but this, as Dibble (1965) has shown, is based on a misinterpretation of certain scenes in the lower right hand corner of Sheet 10. The clear existence of professionalism in historical record keeping is fully congruent with the overall level of cultural complexity of these societies. It also assures that the historical data available for these societies are bound to be much more numerous and sophisticated than one usually encounters in so-called "primitive" societies, to which category some earlier students unjustifiably assigned the cultures of late pre-Hispanic Central Mexico.

The fact must be faced that our knowledge of the activities of these ancient Central Mexican compilers of history is quite inadequate. Concentrating on the pictorial historians, various key questions can be posed, to which answers are not easily forthcoming. How, for example, did the native chroniclers actually go about gathering historical information for and composing their annals? What were their sources? What exactly were in those mysterious "archives"? How were the individual histories stored and "catalogued"? How old were the oldest extant at Contact? Just how were "new editions" prepared? What was the precise nature of the relationship between the *altepetlacuilo* and the local rulers and priests who obviously were very much interested in protecting and perpetuating a "correct" image of their community's past? Were new histories subjected to some kind of scrutiny —"censorship", if you will— and, if so, by whom? How did the chronicler, if he were utilizing data contained in different older records reconcile discrepancies, which he must frequently have encountered? What was the rate of loss of pictorial histories? The Tlaxcalteca, according to Alva Ixtlilxochitl (1952, I: 414; II: 362), apparently deliberately burned the great Tetzcoco archive; was this standard practice in the wake of successful military assaults on leading communities? [21] Certainly the chief temple was burned, as a symbolic gesture of triumph over the community's patron deity and to rub in the humiliation of defeat; was it also normal practice to include the local archives? What occurred in Tollan at its fall ... and Azcapotzalco? Is this one reason for the rather skimpy and generalized —and often contradictory— available histories of these centers? [22] Or did their successors in power simply choose to downplay the histories of their predecessors and to focus essentially on the histories of their own communities and provinces?

This interrogation could be greatly extended. Hopefully, some of these questions might receive at least partial answers as our knowledge increases and new discoveries are made. In any case, usually before questions can be satisfactorily answered they have to be asked, and keeping queries such as these constantly in mind might help us eventually to ascertain some of the answers.

TYPES OF HISTORICAL INFORMATION CONVEYED

We turn now to the fundamental question of what kinds of historical information were conveyed by the different techniques and media discussed above. Or, to put it another way, what types of events were considered worthy of permanent recordation?

In the archaeological category, the information transmitted was obviously quite limited. It consists mainly of dates, usually dedicatory,

[21] Alva Ixtlilxochitl (1952, I: 362), apropos of the destruction of the Tetzcoco "archivos reales", labeled the Tlaxcalteca "los primeros destruidores de las historias de esta tierra" — but this seems to be stated in the context of the later post-Conquest destructions of native records under Spanish missionary auspices.

[22] However, the "*Anonimo Mexicano*" (Barlow 1948: xxii-xxiii), which provides an important ruler list for Azcapotzalco, attributes the lack of more detailed historical information for this center to the loss of the records at the time of the Spanish Conquest.

"portraits" of historical individuals, and, in the case of one monument (Tizoc *cuauhxicalli*), a few conquests. More detailed and explicit historical information, e.g., representational scenes involving major events such as battles and construction projects, of the ancient Egyptian and Mesopotamian type, have not yet been discovered in pre-Hispanic Central Mexico —although their occasional presence in Toltec Chichén Itzá suggests that some may eventually turn up, particularly at Tula.

In the pictorials, various classes of information received major attention: dynastic succession (births, accessions, and deaths of rulers, etc.); conquests and battles; migrational sequences; erections and dedications of structures (principally temples but occasionally other construction projects [aqueducts, canals, etc.]); genealogies; various natural phenomena (solar eclipses, earthquakes, locust plagues, storms, floods, comets and unusual celestial occurrences, etc.); important religious ceremonies, particularly sacrifices; foundings of communities and community subdivisions and establishments of boundaries (especially important from the standpoint of the "legal charter" use of these histories); and a large miscellaneous category much too numerous for detailed itemization.

Included in this last category would be one of the most interesting types, which might be called "anecdotal" or "personal pictorial narrative", in which sequences of actions of an individual or a group are portrayed in a series of quite graphic pictographic scenes. Here obviously the ingenuity and imagination of the *tlacuilo* or his "supervisor" must have played a considerable role, although traditional, stereotyped formats probably were followed as much as possible. The best examples are found in the *Códice Xolotl*, particularly its sequences (Sheets 9-10) depicting the adventures of Nezahualcoyotl; no other Central Mexican pictorial, in fact, provides nearly as much material of this type. Also unique to the *Códice Xolotl* is what might be called the "ideogram stream", a series of compact ideographic representations in a line issuing, like a kind of elaborate speech scroll, from the mouth of an individual and denoting the key ideas in an oral report or command (see Dibble 1940: 110-112). Whether this interesting technique is truly pre-Conquest, however, is questionable.

Clearly, political, dynastic, and genealogical information dominated native Central Mexican pictorial historiography, as it has tended to dominate the historiography of nearly all early civilizations. It is remarkable, however, that so much additional information was recorded, some of it of considerable value to the modern culture historian.

That part of the oral history category which consists of the standardized verbal accompaniments to the pictorial records more or less directly reflects, of course, the types of information conveyed by the latter. The "independent" oral narratives, on the other hand, conveyed about all that the pictorial records could convey and much more —and therein, as indicated above, lies their great importance. Above all, they provide much more of what has been called the "fill" of history, the innumerable details of incident and color which were quite beyond the transmitting power of the most skilled and imaginative *tlacuilo*. They also frequently "explain" the events, providing motives and rationales, in a way not possible or extremely difficult utilizing only the picto-ideographic writing system. Although there are perhaps no major categories of historical information exclusively confined to the oral division, in every case they can and usually do provide much more context and detail than the same categories in the pictorial records.

Another positive advantage of the oral narratives —one which has probably not received sufficient stress— is that they provide a more explicit and unambiguous account of events. Although the composers and interpreters of the pictorial records probably were quite skilled in "reading" those produced by others, particularly as time passed the problems of correct interpretation must have greatly increased. If any original Toltec period pictorial histories were extant at Contact, for example, would all of the expert historians of, say, Tenochtitlan, Tetzcoco, Cholollan, and/or Tlaxcallan have agreed in their "readings" of these records painted centuries before their time? We know that the same place and name-glyphs were occasionally interpreted differently by native informants in the colonial period, [23] and it seems likely that this must also have occurred in the pre-Hispanic period, particularly when very old records were involved. Copyists' mistakes and misunderstandings (as older, delapidated pictorial histories were copied to create "new editions" and updated) also must have contributed sometimes to errors and inadvertent changes of meaning. The oral narratives, on the other hand, might be memorized incorrectly and/or portions might be lost through time, but at least most of what was extant was explicit and unambiguous. The personal and place-names included, for example, were not the result of interpretations of picto-ideograms but were transmitted verbatim.

In spite of the obvious capacity of the oral narratives to provide much more detailed historical information than the pictorials, they were not completely open-ended and flexible in their conveyance of information but rather display definite format stereotypings which limit and channel their data in recognizable ways. This is particularly obvious, of course, in the case of the versified poetic compositions which by their very nature exert a strongly selective influence on the historical information they can transmit —entirely apart from the necessary re-

[23] The occasional variants in the place names of the "official" lists of Tenochca conquests can most readily be explained in this way (Barlow 1946, 1949).

shaping and simplifying of the infinite complexity of actual events inherent in all historiography. In the case of the prose historical narrations, this process of patterning and stereotyping also strongly determined the final from of the conveyance of the historical data. A kind of "pattern history" emerged, then, particularly for the earlier periods when cosmological and cosmogonical preconceptions obviously exerted a profound influence. Even for the recording of the very recent past certain stylistic characteristics of these oral narratives exerted great influence on the manner in which historical events were conceived to have occurred. The "strings of concrete images" technique of conveying ideas and events, the frequent repetitions and parallelisms, the rich use of metaphor and poetic imagery, the stereotyped speeches and conversations, the strong influence of sacred numbers, and the many other stylistic and phraseological peculiarities of all Nahuatl prose combined to produce a very characteristic and unmistakable type of historical narrative. [24]

VALUE AND RELIABILITY OF PRE-HISPANIC CENTRAL MEXICAN HISTORIES

Finally, we come to the basic question of the reliability of the surviving records, archaeological, pictorial, and oral, of past events in pre-Hispanic Central Mexico. While the central focus of this paper is on the *manner* in which history was preserved and conveyed in this area, some examination of the *value* of the available historical information so transmitted also seems appropriate. Many difficult problems face the investigator here. Broad generalizations serve little purpose. Each source, each body of historical data, must be thoroughly analyzed on its own merits, and these analyses must be informed with as complete a knowledge as possible of the culture(s) which generated the putatively historical information under scrutiny. [25]

First of all, it is obvious that some data in these records are so clearly mythological, legendary, novelistic, romantic, and/or folkloristic that their acceptance as accurate accounts of past events, "wie es eigentlich gewesen", in pre-Hispanic Central Mexico would be extremely nave. The mythological type of material, especially, can be rather readily discerned. A more or less accepted canon of about 10 major cosmogonical episodes, in sequence, can be reconstructed for Tenochtitlan-Tlatelolco and its orbit, from original genesis to 2 final episodes I (Nicholson 1964: 7-8) have labeled "9) The Institution of Terrestrial

[24] Garibay, in his various publications on Nahuatl literature previously cited, has devoted the most attention to the stylistic aspect (see, especially, Garibay 1953-1954, I: caps. I and VII).

[25] Vansina 1965 has presented the most comprehensive general discussion of the historical value of oral tradition; McCall 1969, although devoted to Africa, is also of considerable general applicability in this regard.

War and Human Sacrifice to Feed the Gods and Sustain the Universe; 10) The Quasi-Historical Legends of the Chichimecs and the Toltecs". Obviously, it is during these episodes —and possibly during a slightly earlier "Tamoanchan era"— that out and out myth begins to fade to be gradually replaced by traditions which have some claim to at least partial historicity. And here, in this penumbra zone between the realm of obvious myth and the "documented" age of more or less continuous chronicle, that very difficult evaluation problems begin to confront us.

That a certain amount of historicity attaches to even the "Mixcoatl-Mimixcoa cycle" and almost certainly to the Topiltzin Quetzalcoatl of Tollan cycle has been widely accepted. However, the whole question of the accurate reconstruction of Toltec history —concerning which our knowledge is almost entirely confined to oral narrations, although some of these must be directly derived from (post-Toltec) pictorial histories— is an extremely difficult and embroiled one. This is hardly the place to discuss the "Toltec question", but the problems here well illustrate the methodological issues which must be faced by the would-be reconstructor interested in distinguishing any reasonably reliable traditions from the welter of legendary, novelistic, and folkloristic tales that surround this epoch. The primary accounts often differ considerably, even those ostensibly from the same community, and those from different communities (a.g., Colhuacan vs. Tenochtitlan vs. Tetzcoco) often are at major variance with one another. The widely differing reconstructions of highly respected authorities (e.g., Kirchhoff 1955b, 1961a [1964] vs. Jiménez Moreno 1945, 1954-1955, 1966, n.d.) reflect these great divergencies.

One obvious problem is the lack of adequate cross-cheks on the oral traditions that purport to provide historical accounts of the Toltec period. This should be most clearly provided by "dirt" archaeological evidence, which is now abundant from Tula itself. However, the methodological problems inherent in the attempt to correlate artifactual-architectural sequences with native historical traditions, previously discussed by the writer (Nicholson 1955b, 1959), continue to inhibit very successful correlations of these very dissimilar sets of data. Some very generalized ones can perhaps be suggested, but so far the available archaeological data has not appreciably helped to establish the "correct" Toltec dynastic sequence, much less to confirm or deny the details of Toltec history (most apparently near its end) contained in the different basic accounts.

As we move forward from the Toltec era, the amount of "hard" history in our sources obviously increases but seemingly only rather slowly at firts. The politically disruptive conditions of the "chichimec interregnum" which followed Tollan's downfall would, by their very nature, hardly be conducive to detailed, accurate record keeping —apart

from the supposed cultural backwardness of many of the newcomer
groups who were surging to power in Central Mexico. A number of
detailed migration accounts apparently refer to this period or just before
or not long after. By far the best documented, both pictorially and
orally, is that of the ancestors of the founders of Tenochtitlan-Tlatelolco, the Azteca-Mexitin or Mexica. The problems and controversies
surrounding the "Aztec migration problem" also well illustrate the
difficulties inherent in attenmpting to cull out authentic history from
these types of sources. Again, the 2 leading students (Kirchhoff 1961b
vs. Jiménez Moreno 1966, unpublished lectures given in 1968) differ
widely in their reconstructions. My own attitude is somewhat more
skeptical of the historicity of these migration accounts. The concept
of "pattern history" seems particularly applicable to these migration
"histories". Religious and cosmological influences were obviously
strongly at work here, while legendary, novelistic, and folkloristic
clements are clearly legion. While the fundamental fact of migration
of at least some of the ancestors of the later inhabitants of Tenochtitlan-Tlatelolco from an area north-west of the Basin of Mexico near
the end of, at, or not long after the break-up of the Toltec imperium
can probably be accepted, the details of itinerary, sojourn durations,
and chronology provided by the many primary accounts —which differ
widely among themselves— can hardly be accepted as reliable history
except in very broad outline. [26]

A new era obviously dawns about the middle of the 14th century,
at least for the Basin of Mexico and immediately surrounding territory.
With the rise of Tezozomoc of Azcapotzalco to paramount power in
this region and the steady build-up of the Tepanec Empire during the
final decades of that century, there appears to be little doubt that
the major events can be reconstructed with considerable accuracy from
the many extant pictorial and oral-textual sources. And the amount
of usable history steadily increases until, in the third and fourth decades
of the following century, a quantum leap occurs at about the time of
the fall of Azcapotzalco and the creation of the "Triple Alliance" of Te-
nochtitlan-Tetzcoco-Tlacopan —which established the essential political
order which flourished from this time until the Conquest. For this
last period of pre-Hispanic Central Mexican history of little less than
a century's duration we possess a truly extraordinary amount of historical data, the bulk of which, after thorough critical evaluation, can
certainly be generally accepted.

Although there are many puzzling discrepancies even for very late
events, careful analysis of all relevant sources can usually establish

[26] No through study of the "Aztec migration problem" has been published.
Acosta Saignes 1946, however brief and incomplete, is useful and has been much
cited.

the most likely overall sequence of events with some confidence. Local "propagandistic bias" is ubiquitous (merely expressing the intense political localism which was one of the leading cultural diagnostics of Mesoamerica), but it often is so obvious that it can be rather readily recognized.[27] Even the chronologic discrepancies, such a challenging problem for the earlier epochs, now considerably lessen and events can sometimes be dated accurately to the very day. Novelistic and folkloristic accounts still abound, but, with the "control" now available of the mass of obviously reliable history, their detection is much easier than for the earlier periods.

The spatial coverage is somewhat uneven. For some communities (above all, Tenochtitlan-Tlatelolco; "core Acolhuacan" [especially Tepetlaoztoc, Tepechpan, Chiauhtlan, Tetzcoco, Huexotlan, Coatlinchan, Coatepec, and Chimalhuacan]; Tepanecapan [Azcapotzalco, Tlacopan, Tenanyocan, Coyoacan, etc.]; the "Nauhtecuhtli" [Colhuacan, Huitzilopochco, Mexicaltzinco, Itztapalapan]; Cuauhtitlan; Xaltocan; Xochimilco; Cuitlahuac; Chalco [Chalco Atenco, Tlalmanalco, Amaquemecan, Tenanco, Chimalhuacan Chalco, etc.]; "Tochimilco"; Cuauhnahuac; Cuauhquechollan; Totomihuacan; Cuauhtinchan; Tecamachalco-Quecholac; Tepeyacac; Zacatlan; Tlaxcallan; Tollan; Huichapan) abundant or sizable data are available —fairly full dynastic. records, if nothing else. For others, even leading communities, it is quite scanty: the whole Toluca Basin; most of the Otomi-Nahuatl region north of the Basin of Mexico; most of the Sierra de Puebla communities (except as they relate to the history of Acolhuacan); parts of the Basin of Puebla (including, surprisingly, the great centers of Huexotzinco and Cholollan, except as they relate to the histories of their neighbors); and Morelos and northern Guerrero (apart from Cuauhnahuac and its immediate sphere —which is not too well covered). By far the most details are available, of course, for the great twin city, Tenochtitlan-Tlatelolco, and the history of this community will always be the touchstone for all pre-Hispanic Central Mexican history. Tetzcoco is not too far behind, while in the *Relaciones of* Chimalpahin much detail is recorded for the Chalco province cabeceras and the *Anales de Cuauhtitlan* provides a particularly rich coverage of the history of the important community which gives its name to this composite source.

Most of the extant native histories, both pictorial and oral, are local histories, or at least concentrate largely on one major community and/or province. The histories of other communities are usually inclu-

[27] An excellent example is the famous post-Tepanec War "guerra fingida" or "pretended conquest of Tetzcoco" ("*Cronica X*" through Tezozomoc 1944: caps. XIX-XX and Duran 1967, II: cap. XV) vs. "the symbolic conquest of Tenochtitlan (Alva Ixtlilxochitl 1952, II: cap. XXXIV).

ded only wen they impinge directly on that of the local community. Prominent partial exceptions are the *Tira de Tepechpan*, with its dual history of Tepechpan and Tenochtitlan, and, particularly, the *Códice Yolotl*, which is unusually panoramic in its coverage of at least the dynastic histories of the major communities of the Basin of Mexico and immediately surrounding territory —although the viewpoint is always clearlfy that of "core Acolhuacan".

The highly composite history, incorporating and trying to fit into a single overall chronologic scheme many independent histories, such as, in Nahuatl, the *Anales de Cuauhtitlan* and the *Relaciones* of Chimalpahin, and, to some extent, the histories, in Spanish, of Alva Ixtlilxóchitl, Torquemada, and Muñoz Camargo were probably unknown in pre-Hispanic times. However, some systematic compilation of the histories of other communities and provinces, particularly those with whom the home communities possessed dynastic and/or politic-military alliances —and even some attempt to meld them into a fairly consistent overall pattern— might well have been undertaken, particularly in the imperial seats. Certainly the *Codice Xolotl* goes a long step in this direction, and many other pictorial and verbal chronicles note, to some extent, dynastic successions and other events in other communities —particularly in Tenochtitlan because of its preeminent military-political position during the last few decades before the Conquest.

As it did for the early colonial compilers, the strongly localistic orientation of most of these native histories creates serious problems for the modern student attempting to reconstruct a more panoramic, integrated history for the area. Attempts to reconcile divergent accounts have often been extremely forced. The problem of deciding which of 2 accounts is correct when they are diametrically opposed on some specific point is admittedly a challenging one. In modern syntheses, the criteria of choice are often not made sufficiently explicit. On the other hand, a positive advantage of this multiplicity of local histories is that we are often provided with accounts of major events seen from different, localistically-conditioned angles —and this can actually result in a more objective perspective concerning these events on the part of the student. For example, one can easily imagine the distortion in our understanding of Triple Alliance politics and impeperialism if we only possessed either the Tenochca or the Tetzcocan account but not the other. In fact, we have probably gained a very distorted view of the events surrounding the Tepanec War because the victors, as always, wrote the histories (poor Richard III!).

The problem of the "objectivity" of these Central Mexican native histories can only be dealt with briefly. Certainly, these histories to some extent served as a kind of propaganda vehicle for the community, particularly its ruling lineage of the moment, in addition to other related functions, such as that of a "community charter", a vindication of its rights and privileges and integrity as an independent entity (even if politically subservient at any given period to another community or federation of communities). Bias in recounting its past there certainly was; its triumphs are typically extolled and recorded in detail, its defeats often omitted or glossed over. Certainly rewriting was going on all the time, especially whenever basic dynastic and/or political changes occurred. That there was even some deliberate "book-burning" we know from the celebrated incident attributed by Sahagun's Tlatelolco informants (Sahagún 1950-1963, Pt. XI: 191) to Itzcoatl of Tenochtitlan (1428-1440). However, the real motivation of this cursorily reported act is still quite obscure despite the usual assumption of his desire to "erase" the lowly past political position of the Mexica. Careful scrutiny, on the other hand, reveals that defeats were not by any means always concealed. The semi-legendary "Chapultepec Defeat" was even commemorated in a famous song, and the greatest of all Triple Alliance military defeats, against the Tarascans on their one great expedition of conquest into eastern Michoacan during the reign of Axayacatl (1469-1481), was recounted in detail in the "Crónica X" (Tezozomoc, 1944: caps. LII-LIII; Durán 1967, II: caps. XXXVII-XXXVIII), a chronicle otherwise devoted to exalting Tenochca glory and power. Also, in the recording of basic facts, such as successions of rulers, major military and political events, and the occurrences of various natural phenomena, the pre-Hispanic Central Mexican annalists seem to have exhibited an unusual degree of objectivity —and the basic reliability of these narrations must, I think, be assumed.

A special word, however brief, is in order concerning a particular problem in using the data of these native Central Mexican histories. Technically it is strictly a chronologic one, but it has broader implications. This is the problem of correlating years in the native calendar with those in the Christian calendar. First of all, there is the familiar 52 year cycle repetition problem. For events close to the Conquest this is no particular problem; for more remote events it can be quite serious. Much more serious, however, is the possibility that different year counts were used in Central Mexico, at least in pre-Tepanec Empire times, and that the native annalists often recorded events as if they were in the standard 1 Acatl = 1519 count when they were in fact in other counts, which in some cases would make considerable difference in years. Particularly for the period between the fall of Tollan and the rise of Azcapotzalco, the "Chichimec interregnum", the existence of different year counts could pose quite a problem in correlating and integrating historical information from different centers.

At Contact a different years count (13 Acatl = 1519) was centainly
employed in western Oaxaca and southern Puebla by the Mixtec and
Popoloca-speaking communities of this region (Jiménez Moreno
1940). A different year count (3 In thihui [Acatl] = 1519) also seems
to have been in use among at least some of the Matlatzinca-speaking
communities of the Toluca Basin (Caso 1967: 226-240). However,
whether the different Nahua-speaking communities of the Basin of
Mexico and surrounding territory had differing year counts, up to a
possible "unification" in the 14th or early 15th century, is a much
murkier question. Kirchhoff (1950, 1955a) believes he is able to identify quite a number (including different *tonalpohualli* counts), Jiménez Moreno (1961, n.d.) nearly as many. However, they have yet to
present their evidence in full. Although there is undoubtedly some
evidence in favor of their views, so many obscurities still surround
this complex topic that the prudent course would seem to be that of
analyzing each chronologic problem on its own merits, hypothesizing
different year counts only when this is the most satisfactory and eco-
nomical explanation of all the facts.

Whatever the reliability of these pre-Hispanic Central Mexican
records from the standpoint of the genuine historicity of the events
recounted, one great value is undeniable: the information they provide
on cultural values, preoccupations, themes, patterns, etc. In other
words, entirely apart from the question of their value as histories, their
ethnographic value is immense. Anthropologists, particularly, should
appreciate this —and, more importantly, should take fuller advantage
of it than they have so far done. As Tylor (1958 [1871]: 416) long ago
pointed out, with reference to "poetic legend":

> ... unconsciously, and as it were in spite of themselves, the shapers
> and transmitters of poetic legend have preserved for us masses of sound
> historical evidence. They moulded into mythic lives of gods and heroes
> their own ancestral heirlooms of thought and word, they displayed in
> the structure of their legends the operations of their own minds, they
> placed on record the arts and manners, the philosophy and religion of
> their own times, times of which formal history has often lost the very
> memory.

The records we have have been discussing certainly are far more than
"poetic legends", but Tylor's remarks would still seem quite pertinent,
particularly for those which hark back to "Chichimec interregnum"
and Toltec times.

CONLUDING REMARKS

There are many other aspects of pre-Hispanic Central Mexican historiography, particularly various important sociocultural correlates, which very much deserve discussion. These aspects, however, must be reserved for another occasion —along with further examination of native concepts of history. If nothing else, it is hoped that this brief summary of a complex topic has pointed up the wealth of material available to the Mesoamericanist interested in historical reconstruction in the Central Mexican area. There is obvious need for more critical and through analyses of the extant sources, archaeological, pictorial, and oral, to clarify their interrelationships, to distinguish what is reliable history in them, and then, with this indispensable evaluatory task completed, to go on to create new historical syntheses. In spite of the existence of an extensive and often quite valuable literature in this area, I am convinced that the greatest achievements lie ahead. If this little paper helps point the way toward improved knowledge and understanding of an extremely important aspect of pre-Hispanic Central Mexican civilization, it will have more than served its purpose.

REFERENCES CITED

Acosta, J.
1956-57 "Interpretación de algunos de los datos obtenidos en Tula relativos a la época Tolteca." *Revista Mexicana de Estudios Antropológicos* 14 (2nd. Pt.): 75-110.

Acosta Saignes, M.
1946 Migraciones de los Mexicas." *Memorias de la Academia Mexicana de la Historia* 5, 2: 177-187 (Tlatelolco a través de los tiempos, 7: IV).

Alcina Franch, J.
1955-56 "Fuentes indígenas de Méjico. Ensayo de sistematización bibliográfica." *Revista de Indias* 15, 61-62: 421-521. Also (1956) issued as separate, with added index.

Alva Ixtlilxóchitl, F. de
1952 *Obras históricas de Don Fernando de Alva Ixtlilxóchitl.* Publicadas y anotadas por Alfredo Chavero. 2 vols. 2nd ed. México, Editorial Nacional.

Aubin, J. M. A.
1849 "Memoire sur la peinture didactique et l'ecriture figurative des anciens Mexicains." Paris, Paul Dupont. Republished, with introduction by E. T. Hamy in: *Mission scientifique au Mexique et dans l'Amérique Centrale,* ouvrage publié par ordre du Ministre de l'Instruction Publique, vol. 3, recherches historiques et archéologiques, publiées sous la direction de M. E. T. Hamy, conservateur du Musée d'Ethnographie, première partie, histoire. Paris, Imprimerie Nationale, 1885.

BANCROFT, H. H.

1874-75 The native races of the Pacific states. 5 vols. San Francisco, A. L. Bancroft and Company, Publishers.

BARLOW, R.

1945 "La Crónica X: versiones coloniales de la historia de los Mexica Tenoch-ca." *Revista Mexicana de Estudios Antropológicos* 7, 1-3: 65-87.

1946 "Materiales para una cronología del imperio de los Mexica." *Revista Mexicana de Estudios Antropológicos* 8, 1-3: 207-215.

1947 Review of P. F. Velázquez edition of the *Anales de Cuauhtitlan* and the *Leyenda de los Soles* (Mexico, 1945). *Hispanic American Historical Review* 27: 520-526.

1948 Resumen analítico de "Unos annales históricos de la nación Mexicana." *In Anales de Tlatelolco: Unos annales históricos de la nación Mexicana* y *Códice de Tlatelolco*. Fuentes para la Historia de México; Colección Publicada bajo la Dirección de Salvador Toscano, 2. H. Berlin, ed. México, Antigua Librería Robredo, de José Porrúa e Hijos.

1949 "Las conquistas de Moteczuma Xocoyotzin." *Memorias de la Academia Mexicana de la Historia* 8, 2: 159-172.

BARLOW, R. and B. MCAFEE

1949 *Diccionario de elementos fonéticos en escritura jeroglífica (Códice Mendocino)*. Universidad Nacional Autónoma de México, Publicaciones del Instituto de Historia, Primera Serie, 9.

BERNAL, I.

1962 "Bibliografía de arqueología y etnografía: Mesoamérica y norte de México, 1514-1960." México, Instituto Nacional de Antropología e Historia, *Memorias* 7.

BOBAN, E.

1891 *Documents pour servir à l'histoire du Mexique*. Catalogue raisonné de la collection de M. E. Eugene Goupil (ancienne collection J. M. A. Aubin). 2 vols. and atlas. Paris, Ernest Leroux.

BRASSEUR DE BOURBOURG, C. E.

1857-59 *Histoire des nations civilisées du Mexique et de l'Amérique Centrale, durant les siècles antérieurs a Christophe Colomb, écrite sur des documents originaux et entièrement inédits, puisés aux anciennes archives des indigènes*. 4 vols. Paris, Arthus Bertrand.

BRINTON, D.

1887 *Ancient Nahuatl poetry, containing the Nahuatl text of XXVII ancient Mexican poems*, with a translation, introduction, notes and vocabulary. Brinton's Library of Aboriginal American Literature 7. Philadelphia, D. G. Brinton.

Carrera Stampa, M.

1962-63   "Fuentes para el estudio del mundo indígena." *Memorias de la Academia Mexicana de la Historia* 21, 3: 261-312; 21, 4: 375-413; 22, 1: 31-110; 22, 2: 152-212; 22, 3: 261-326; 22, 4: 361-420.

Caso, A.

1960   "Valor histórico de los códices Mixtecos." *Cuadernos Americanos*, año 19, 109, 2: 139-147.

1967   *Los calendarios prehispánicos.* Universidad Nacional Autónoma de México, Instituto de Investigaciones históricas, Serie de Cultura Náhuatl, Monografías 6.

1968   *Dioses y signos Teotihuacanos.* Sociedad Mexicana de Antropología: Teotihuacan, Onceava Mesa Redonda: 249-279.

1969   Y mientras el mundo exista, no cesará la gloria de México-Tenochtitlan: La legendaria "Piedra Pintada", regio monumento prehispánico puede ser rescatado ahora, al abrirse la ruta del "metro". *Nuestra Gente; Revista al Servicio de la Seguridad Social* 33: 30-37 (republication of article first published in the Sunday supplement of El Nacional, May 28, 1939).

Chavero, A.

1887   "Historia antigua y de la conquista." *México a través de los siglos,* V. Riva Palacio, ed., vol. 1. Mexico and Barcelona, Espasa.

Cook de Leonard, C.

1959   "La escultura." In *Esplendor del México antiguo.* C. Cook de Leonard, ed. México, Centro de Investigaciones Antropológicas de México.

Dibble, C.

1940   "El antiguo sistema de escritura en México." *Revista Mexicana de Estudios Antropológicos* 4, 1-2: 105-128.

1951   *Códice Xolotl.* Universidad Nacional Autónoma de México, Publicaciones del Instituto de Historia, Primera Serie 22.

1965   "Apuntes sobre la Plancha X del Códice Xolotl." *Estudios de Cultura Náhuatl* 5: 103-106.

1966   "The Aztec writing system." In *Readings in anthropology.* J. D. Jennings and E. A. Hoebel, eds. New York, McGraw Hill.

Durán, F. D.

1967   *Historia de las Indias de Nueva España y Isla de la Tierra Firme.* A. M. Garibay K., ed. 2 vols. México, Editorial Porrúa.

García Granados, R.

1952-53   *Diccionario biográfico de historia antigua de Méjico.* 3 vols. Universidad Nacional Autónoma de México, Publicaciones del Instituto de Historia, Primera Serie, 23.

García Icazbalceta, J.

1886-92 *Nueva colección de documentos para la historia de México.* 5 vols. México, Andrade y Morales and F. Díaz de León.

1927 *Don Fray Juan de Zumárraga, primer Obispo y Arzobispo de México.* Edición de R. Aguayo y A. Castro Leal. 4 vols. Colección de Escritores Mexicanos, 41-44. México, Editorial Porrúa.

Garibay K., A. M.

1937 *La poesía lírica Azteca: esbozo de síntesis crítica.* México.

1940a "La épica Azteca." *Ábside* 4, 1: 48-74; 4, 3: 18-25; 4, 5: 26-37.

1940b *Poesía indígena de la altiplanicie.* Divulgación literaria. Universidad Nacional Autónoma de México, Biblioteca del Estudiante Universitario, 11. 2nd ed., 1952. 3rd ed., 1962.

1942 "Poesía indígena precortesiana." *Ábside* 6, 2: 119-141.

1945 *Épica Náhuatl.* Divulgación literaria. Universidad Nacional Autónoma de México, Biblioteca del Estudiante Univeritario, 51. 2nd ed., 1964.

1953-54 *Historia de la literatura Náhuatl.* 2 vols. Biblioteca Porrúa 1, 5. México, Editorial Porrúa.

1958 *Veinte himnos sacros de los Nahuas.* Universidad Nacional Autónoma de México, Instituto de Historia: Seminario de Cultura Náhuatl, Fuentes Indígenas de la Cultura Náhuatl, Informantes de Sahagún 2.

1963 *Panorama literaria de los pueblos Nahuas.* Colección "Sepan cuantos . . ." 22. México, Editorial Porrúa.

1964a *La literatura de los Aztecas.* México, Editorial Joaquín Mortiz.

1964b *Poesía Náhuatl,* I, Romances de los Señores de la Nueva España, manuscrito de Juan Bautista de Pomar, Tezcoco, 1582. Universidad Nacional Autónoma de México, Instituto de Historia: Seminario de Cultura Náhuatl, Fuentes Indígenas de la Cultura Náhuatl 4.

1965 *Poesía Náhuatl,* II, Cantares Mexicanos, manuscritos de la Biblioteca Nacional de México, primera parte. Universidad Nacional Autónoma de México, Instituto de Investigaciones Históricas, Fuentes Indígenas de la Cultura Náhuatl 5.

1968 *Poesía Náhuatl,* III, Cantares Mexicanos, manuscrito de la Biblioteca Nacional de México, segunda parte. Universidad Nacional Autónoma de México, Instituto de Investigaciones Históricas, Fuentes Indígenas de la Cultura Náhuatl 6.

Gibson, C.

1964-67 *Native prose sources. II. Census of Meso-American prose documents in the native historical tradition; Guide to EHS essays, Essay 21, Prose sources in the native tradition. Handbook of Middle American Indians, Guide to Ethnohistorical Sources, Working Papers* 38, 64. Limited reference circulation (multilithed). Washington, Library of Congress, Reference Department, Hispanic Foundation.

GLASS, J.

1964 *Catálogo de la colección de códices.* México, Museo Nacional de Antropología.

1966-67 *A survey and census of native Middle American pictorial Manuscripts. Handbook of Middle American Indians, Guide to Ethnohistorical Sources, Working Papers* 53, 54, 60, 61. Limited reference circulation (multilithed). Washington, Library of Congress, Reference Department, Hispanic Foundation.

HISTORIA DE LOS MEXICANOS POR SUS PINTURAS

1891 *In* García Icazbalceta 1886-1892, III: 228-262.

HISTOYRE DU MECHIQUE

1905 *Journal de la Société des Americanistes de Paris,* n.s., 2: 1-41. E. de Jonghe, ed.

HORCASITAS, E.

1959 "La prosa Náhuatl." In *Esplendor del México antiguo.* C. Cook de Leonard, ed. México, Centro de Investigaciones Antropológicas de México.

JIMÉNEZ MORENO, W.

1940 *Signos cronográficos del códice y calendario Mixteco. Códice de Yanhuitlan;* edición en facsimile y con un estudio preliminar por Wigberto Jiménez Moreno y Salvador Mateos Higuera: 69-76. México, Secretaría de Educación Pública, Instituto Nacional de Antropología e Historia, Museo Nacional.

1945 Introducción, *Guía arqueológica de Tula* (A. Ruz Lhuillier). México, Ateneo Nacional de Ciencias y Artes de México.

1950 "The importance of Xaltocan in the ancient history of Mexico." *Mesoamerican Notes* 2: 133-138.

1954-55 "Síntesis de la historia precolonial del Valle de México." *Revista Mexicana de Estudios Antropológicos* 14 (Pt. 1): 219-236.

1959 "Síntesis de la historia pretolteca de Mesoamérica." In *Esplendor del México antiguo.* C. Cook de Leonard, ed. México, Centro de Investigaciones Antropológicas de México. English translation, slinghtly modified, in *Ancient Oaxaca: discoveries in Mexican archeology and history.* J. Paddock, ed. Stanford, California, 1966.

1961 "Diferente principio del año entre diversos pueblos y sus consecuencias para la cronología prehispánica." *El México Antiguo* 9: 137-152.

1966 "Unidad VI: Horizonte Postclásico." In *Compendio de historia de México.* W. Jiménez Moreno, J. Miranda, and M. T. Fernández. México, Editorial E.C.L.A.L.S.A.

n.d.   *Historia antigua de México* (duplicated from class lecture notes).

Kirchhoff, P.

1950   *The Mexican calendar and the founding of Tenochtitlan-Tlatelolco.* Trans-
        actions of the New York Academy of Sciences, Series II, 12, 4: 126-132.

1955a   *Las fechas indígenas mencionadas para ciertos acontecimientos en las
        fuentes, y su importancia como índice de varios calendarios* (ms. presented
        to Mesa Redonda on calendric problems of ancient Central Mexico, Cha-
        pultepec, December 5-12, 1955, sponsored by the Sociedad Mexicana de
        Antropología).

1955b   "Quetzalcóatl, Huémac y el fin de Tula." *Cuadernos Americanos,*
        año 14, 84, 6: 163-196.

1961a   "Der Beitrag Chimalpahins zur Geschichte der Tolteken." In *Beiträge zur
        Völkerforschung: Hans Damm zum 65. Geburstag.* Berlin, Akademie-
        Verlag. Spanish translation in *Anales de Antropología* 4: 77-90, México,
        1964.

1961b   "¿Se puede localizar Aztlán?" *Anales de Antropología* 1: 59-67.

Kubler, G. and C. Gibson

1951   "The Tovar Calendar: an illustrated Mexican manuscript of ca. 1585.
        Reproduced with a commentary and handlist of sources on the Mexican
        365-day year." *Memoirs of the Connecticut Academy of Arts and Scien-
        ces* 11.

Kutscher, G.

1958   The translation of the "Cantares Mexicanos" by Leonhard Schultze Jena.
        Proceedings of the Thirty Second International Congress of Americanists,
        Copenhagen, 8-14 August, 1956: 253-258. Copenhagen, Munksgaard.

Lambert, J. C.

1958   *Chants lyriques des Azteques.* Paris, Seghers.

1961   *Les poesies mexicaines.* Paris.

Landa, F. D.

1941   *Landa's Relación de las cosas de Yucatán:* a translation. Edited with
        notes by A. M. Tozzer. Papers of the Peabody Museum of American
        Archaeology and Ethnology, Harvard University 18.

Las Casas, F. B. de

1958   *Apologética historia.* Biblioteca de Autores Españoles desde la Formación
        del Lenguaje hasta Nuestros Días, 105-106: Obras Escogidas de Fray
        Bartolomé de Las Casas, iii-iv. Estudio Crítico Preliminar y Edición por
        J. Pérez Tudela Bueso. 2 vols. Madrid, Sucs. J. Sánchez de Ocaña.

Lehmann, W.

1909   *Methods and results in Mexican research.* Translated from the German . . .
        by S. de Ricci. Published at the expense of the Duke of Loubat. Paris.

1922 "Ein Toltekenklagegesang." In *Festschrift Eduard Seler. Stuttgart, Strecker und Schroeder*. Spanish translation by P. R. Hendrichs, with introductions and annotations by W. Jiménez Moreno: *Una elegía Tolteca*, Publicaciones de la Sociedad "México-Alemana, Alejandro de Humboldt", folleto núm. 2, México, 1941.

LEJEAL, L.

1902 *Les antiquités mexicaines (Mexique, Yucatan, Amérique-Centrale)*. Bibliothèque de Bibliographies Critiques Publiée par la Société des Etudes Historiques. Paris, Alphonse Picard et Fils.

LEÓN Y GAMA, A.

1832 *Descripción histórica y cronológica de las dos piedras, que con ocasión del nuevo empedrado que se está formando en la plaza principal de México, se hallaron en ella el año de 1790*. 2nd ed., augmented, C. M. de Bustamante, ed. México, Imprenta del Ciudadano Alejandro Valdés.

LEÓN-PORTILLA, M.

1956 *La filosofía Náhuatl; estudiada en sus fuentes*. Ediciones especiales del Instituto Indigenista Interamericano. México. 2nd. edition, enlarged, 1959. 3rd edition, 1966. English translation, *Aztec thought and culture: a study of the ancient Nahuatl mind*, Norman, Oklahoma, 1963.

1961 *Los antiguos Mexicanos a través de sus crónicas y cantares*. México, Fondo de Cultura Económica. 2nd edition, 1968.

1964 *Las literaturas precolombinas de México*. Colección Pormaca 5. México, Editorial Pormaca. English translation, modified, Pre-Columbian literatures of Mexico, Norman, Oklahoma, 1969.

1967 *Trece poetas del mundo Azteca*. Universidad Nacional Autónoma de México, Instituto de Investigaciones Históricas, Serie de Cultura Náhuatl, Monografía 11.

LEÓN-PORTILLA, M. and S. MATEOS HIGUERA

1957 *Catálogo de los códices indígenas del México antiguo*. Suplemento del Boletín Bibliográfico de la Secretaría de Hacienda, año 3, 111.

McCALL, D.

1969 "Africa in time-perspective: a discussion of historical reconstruction from unwritten sources." New York, *Oxford University Press*.

MEDELLÍN ZENIL, A.

1962 "El monolito de Maltrata, Veracruz." *La Palabra y El Hombre* 24: 555-562.

MENDOZA, V. T.

1958 "El ritmo de los cantares mexicanos recolectados por Sahagún." In *Miscellanea Paul Rivet: octogenaria dicata*. México, Universidad Nacional Autónoma de México.

1959   "La música y la danza." In *Esplendor del México antiguo*. C. Cook de
        Leonard, ed. México, Centro de Investigaciones Antropológicas de México.

MOLINA, F. A. DE

1944   *Vocabulario en lengua Castellana y Mexicana de Fray Alonso de Molina
        impreso en Méjico, 1571*. Colección de Incunables Americanos, Siglo XVI,
        4, Madrid, Ediciones Cultura Hispánica.

MOTOLINIA (FRAY TORIBIO DE BENAVENTE)

1903   *Memoriales de Fray Toribio de Motolinia*. Documentos Históricos de Mé-
        jico, 1. L. García Pimentel, ed. México, en Casa del Editor; París, en Casa
        de A. Donnamette; Madrid, Librería de Gabriel Sánchez.

MUÑOZ CAMARGO, D.

1948   *Historia de Tlaxcala*. A. Chavero, ed. Republication, with additions, of
        edition of 1892. México, Talleres Gráficos Laguna de Apolonia B. Arzate
        e Hijos.

NICHOLSON, H. B.

1955a   *Aztec style calendric inscriptions of possible historical significance a
        survey* (photoduplicated; presented at Mesa Redonda on calendric pro-
        blems of ancient Central Mexico, Chapultepec, December 5-12, 1955,
        sponsored by the Sociedad Mexicana de Antropología).

1955b   "Native historical traditions of Nuclear America and the problem of
        their archaeological correlation." *American Anthropologist* 57, 3: 594-613.

1957   "Topiltzin Quetzalcoatl of Tollan: a problem in Mesoamerican ethno-
        history." Ph. D. dissertation, Harvard University.

1959   *The synchronization of culture historical sequences derived from archaeo-
        logical excavation with native Mesoamerican historical traditions*. Paper
        presented at 58th Annual Meeting of the American Anthropological
        Association, Mexico City, December, 1959.

1960   *Preliminary Checklist of Mesoamerican Pictorial Documents in the Na-
        tive Tradition ("Codices")*. Multilithed, Washington, Library of Congress,
        Reference Department, Hispanic Foundation.

1961a   "The Chapultepec cliff sculpture of Motecuhzoma Xocoyotzin." *El
        Mexico Antiguo* 9: 379-444.

1961b   *Preliminary checklist of Mesoamerican pictorial manuscripts in the na-
        tive tradition ("Codices")*. Greatly augmented, revised version of Nicholson
        1960. Duplicated.

1963   *The concept of history in pre-Hispanic Mesoamerica*. Abstract. VI Con-
        grès International des Sciences Anthropologiques et Ethnologiques, Paris,
        30 Juillet-6 Aout, 1960, Tome 2, Ethnologie (Premier Volume): 445.
        Paris.

1964   *Pre-Hispanic Central Mexico: religión*. Mimeographed. Paper submitted for publication in the Handbook of Middle American Indians; distributed by permissión of the Editor.

1966 "The significance of the 'looped cord' year symbol in pre-Hispanic Mexico: an hypothesis." *Estudios de Cultura Náhuatl* 6: 135-148.

1967 "A 'royal headband' of the Tlaxcalteca." *Revista Mexicana de Estudios Antropológicos* 21: 71-106.

1968 *Native tradition pictorials from the state of Puebla, México:a preliminary classification and analysis.* Duplicated. Distributed to those attending the oral presentation at the 38th International Congress of Americanists, Stuttgart, August 13, 1968.

In press *The problem of the historical identity of the Cerro Portezuelo/ San Antonio archaeological site: an hypothesis.* Symposium volume of papers presented at the eleventh Mesa Redonda of the Sociedad Mexicana de Antropología. "El Valle de Teotihuacan y su contorno", Mexico City, August 8-13, 1966.

NICHOLSON, Irene

1959a *Firefly in the night: a study of ancient Mexican poetry and symbolism.* London, Faber and Faber.

1959b "La poesía Náhuatl." *In Esplendor del México antiguo.* C. Cook de Leonard, ed. México, Centro de Investigaciones Antropológicas de México.

NOWOTNY, K. A.

1956 *Die Notation des "Tono" in den Aztekischen Cantares.* Baessler Archiv, n.f., 4 (29 Band): 185-190.

1959 "Die Hieroglyphen des Codex Mendoza: der Bau einer mittelamerikanischen Wortschrift." In *Amerikanistische Miszellen.* Mitteilungen aus dem Museum für Völkerkunde in Hamburg, XXV; Festband Franz Termer. Hamburg, Kommissionsverlag Ludwig Appel.

OROZCO Y BERRA, M.

1960 *Historia antigua y de la conquista de México.* 4 vols. Biblioteca Porrúa 17-20. México, Editorial Porrúa. Republication of original edition of 1880, with added materials by A. M. Garibay K. and M. León-Portilla.

1877 "El cuauhxicalli de Tizoc." *Anales del Museo Nacional de México* 1: 3-36.

PASO Y TRONCOSO, F. DEL

1940 *Epistolario de Nueva España*: 1505-1818. 16 vols. Biblioteca Histórica Mexicana de Obras Inéditas, Segunda Serie, 1-16. México, Antigua Librería Robredo, de José Porrúa e Hijos.

PEÑAFIEL, A.

1890 *Monumentos del arte mexicano antiguo.* 1 vol. text, 2 vols. plates. Berlin, Asher.

1910 *Destrucción del Templo Mayor de México antiguo.* México, Imprenta y Fototipia de la Secretaría de Fomento.

Pomar, J. Bautista
1964   *Relación de Tezcuco.* In Garibay 1964: 152-219. Republication of original
        edition *in* García Icazbalceta, 1886-1892, iii: 1-69.

Radin, P.
1920   *The sources and authenticity of the history of the ancient Mexicans.*
        University of California Publications in American Archaeology and Eth-
        nology 17, 1.

Ramírez, J. F.
1845   "Descripción de cuatro lápidas monumentales conservadas en el Museo
        Nacional de México, seguida de un ensayo sobre su interpretación."
        William Prescott, *Histo·ia de la Conquista de México,* i. Cumplido,
        ed., ii: 106-124. México.

Robertson, D.
1959   "Mexican manuscript painting of the early colonial period: the metro-
        politan schools." *Yale Historical Publications, History of Art* 12. New
        Haven, Yale University Press.

Romero Quiroz, J.
1963   *Teotenanco y Matlatzinco (Calixtlahuaca).* Toluca, Ediciones del Gobierno
        del Estado de México.

Sáenz, C.
1961   "Tres estelas en Xochicalco." *Revista Mexicana de Estudios Antropoló-
        gicos* 17: 39-65.

Sahagún, F. B. de
1950-63 *Florentine Codex. General history of the things of New Spain.* Fray
        Bernardino de Sahagún. Translated from the Aztec into English with
        notes and illustrations, by C. E. Dibble and A.J.O. Anderson. Monographs
        of The School of American Research, Santa Fe, New Mexico (Published
        by The School of American Research and The University of Utah)
        Number 14, Parts II-VI, VIII-XIII. Santa Fe and Salt Lake City.

Saville, M.
1928   *Tizoc, great lord of the Aztecs, 1481-1486.* Contributions from the
        Museum of the American Indian, Heye Foundation 7, 4.

Seler, E.
1902-23 *Gesammelte Abhandlungen zur Amerikanischen Sprach-und Alterthums-
        kunde.* 5 vols. Berlin, Asher and Behrend.

Simeón, R.
1889   *Annales de Domingo Francisco de San Anton Muñon Chimalpahin
        Quauhtlehuanitzin; sixième et septième relations* (1258-1612). Biblio-
        thèque Lingüistique Américaine 12. Paris, Maisonneuve et Ch. Leclerc,
        Editeurs.

Simmons, M. L.
1960 "Pre-Conquest narrative songs in Spanish America." *Journal of American Folklore* 73, 288: 103-111.

Schultze Jena, L.
1957 *Alt-Aztekische Gesänge, nach Einer in der Biblioteca Nacional von Mexiko aufbewahrten Handschrift.* Nach seinem Tode herausgegeben von G. Kutscher. Quellenwerke zur alten Geschichte *Amerikas aufgezeichnet in den Sprachen der Eingebornen, Herausgegeben von der Ibero-Amerikanischen Bibliothek,* Berlin (Schriftleitung: Kutscher) 6. Stuttgart, W. Kohlhammer Verlag.

Taggart, B.
1957 *Flores de Anáhuac: literatura náhuatl prehispánica.* México.

Tezozómoc, H. Alvarado
1944 *Crónica Mexicana.* México, Editorial Leyenda.

Torquemada, F. J. de
1943 *Monarquía Indiana,* vols. I-II. Facsimile of Madrid edition of 1723. México, Editorial Chávez Hayhoe.

Tozzer, A. M.
1957 "Chichen Itza and its cenote of sacrifice: a comparative study of contemporaneous Maya and Toltec." *Memoirs of the Peabody Museum of Archaeology and Ethnology,* Harvard University 11, 12.

Tudela de la Orden, J.
1954 *Los manuscritos de América en las bibliotecas de España.* Madrid, Ediciones Cultura Hispánica.

Tylor, E.
1958 *The origins of culture (Primitive culture).* Harper Torchbooks 33. New York, Harper and Brothers Publishers. Republication of Chaps. I-X of original edition, London, 1871.

Vansina, J.
1965 *The oral tradition: a study in historical methodology.* Chicago, Aldine Publishing Co.

Van Zantwijk, R.
1957 "Aztec hymns as the expresión of the Mexican philosophy of life." *International Archives of Ethnography* 48, Pt. 1: 67-118.

Zimmermann, G.
1960 "Das Geschichtswerk des Domingo de Muñon Chimalpahin Quauhtlehuanitzin (Quellenkritische Studien zur frühindianischen Geschichte Mexikos)." *Beiträge zur mittelamerikanischen Völkerkunde herausgegeben vom Hamburgischen Museum für Völkerunde und Vogeschichte 5*

COMENTARIO

Es un hecho que, durante las últimas décadas, se ha incrementado muy considerablemente el estudio de las diversas formas de testimonios históricos prehispánicos del área mesoamericana. Al destacar esto pienso no solamente en los numerosos trabajos monográficos en los que se han utilizado muchos de esos testimonios sino también, y de modo particular, en los estudios y publicaciones de las fuentes mismas, bien sea de códices o de textos transcritos ya con el alfabeto latino en idioma indígena, y asimismo en las investigaciones dirigidas a mostrar la significación histórica de determinados hallazgos arqueológicos.

Por lo que toca a los códices picto-ideográficos de contenido histórico son un ejemplo las ediciones y estudios que, acerca de varios de origen mixteco, ha publicado Alfonso Caso (1952, 1960a, 1960b, 1964 y 1966) o los de W. Jiménez Moreno sobre el *Códice de Yanhuitlán* (1940), de R. H. Barlow acerca del *Azcatitlan* (1949), de Ernst Mengin sobre el *Mexicanus* (1952) y los de Charles E. Dibble en relación con el *Códice Xólotl* (1951), el *En Cruz* (1953) y el *Aubin* (1958).

En el campo de los testimonios en lengua indígena, escritos durante el siglo XVI con el alfabeto latino, deben mencionarse las ediciones que de algunos de ellos han preparado: Konrad R. Preuss y Ernst Mengin (1937-1938), Ernst Mengin (1939-1940), Walter Lehmann (1938, 1949), Primo F. Velázquez (1945), Ralph L. Roys (1933, 1946, 1965), Robert H. Barlow (1946), Adrián León (1949), Charles E. Dibble y Arthur J. O. Anderson (1950-1962), Gerdt Kutscher (1958), Alfredo Barrera Vásquez (1948, 1949, 1965), Ángel Ma. Garibay K. (1958, 1961, 1964, 1965, 1968), Miguel León-Portilla (1958 y 1968), Alfredo López Austin (1967, 1969) y Günter Zimermann (1963, 1965). Finalmente el propio H. B. Nicholson, entre otros, se ha ocupado de manera directa de algunos monumentos arqueológicos en los que se consignan acontecimientos y fechas de particular significación histórica (1955a, 1955b, 1961a).

Por otra parte, corroborando el mismo moderno interés por las fuentes históricas mesoamericanas, deben mencionarse las listas o catálogos que de las mismas se han dado a conocer durante los últimos años. Son de mencionarse al menos los trabajos preparados por Alcina Franch (1955-56), Mateos Higuera y León-Portilla (1956), Robertson (1959), Nowotny (1961), Glass (1964), así como las muy importantes recopilaciones en proceso de elaboración de Charles E. Gibson, "Catálogo de documentos mesoamericanos en prosa dentro de la tradición histórica nativa", y de John B. Glass, "Examen y catálogo de los manuscritos pictóricos mesoamericanos".

Y a todo lo anterior deben sumarse las investigaciones en torno a los sistemas calendáricos mesoamericanos e igualmente sobre las diversas formas de escritura en los distintos grupos de esta gran área cultural. En este contexto deben citarse al menos los nombres de quienes han hecho aportaciones sumamente valiosas como J. Eric S. Thompson, T. H. Barthel, L. Satterwaite, C. Lizardi Ramos, H. Berlin y Günter Zimermann, por lo que toca al área maya, y de Alfonso Caso, Wigberto Jiménez Moreno y Paul Kirchhoff por lo que se refiere a otras áreas mesoamericanas.

La breve recordación de estos estudios, aparecidos durante las últimas décadas, muestra a las claras que ha sido un acierto de H. B. Nicholson, en el trabajo que aquí presenta, atender al tema de la historiografía prehispánica. En su estudio, deliberadamente circunscrito a la historiografía indígena de la región central de México, hace una lúcida descripción de las categorías en que pueden distribuirse estas formas de producción histórica e igualmente se ocupa de puntos tan importantes como son los enunciados por las siguientes preguntas: ¿Quiénes eran los historiadores nativos? ¿Qué tipo de información proporciona la historia indígena? ¿Cuál es el valor y la confianza que pueden inspirar las crónicas e historias de origen prehispánico?

En este comentario, en vez de detenerme en un examen de cada una de las secciones que integran el trabajo de Nicholson, prefiero atender a algunos de los problemas que él mismo se plantea y a otros que parecen derivarse de lo que él expone.

Comenzaré por decir algo respecto de la distribución y descripción que hace Nicholson de los diversos tipos de fuentes y testimonios. Siguiendo un criterio, enunciado ya por otros investigadores, distribuye Nicholson los testimonios históricos en las siguientes categorías:

1. Los que provienen de la investigación arqueológica: inscripciones en monumentos;

2. Los designados generalmente como códices picto-ideográficos;

3. Los que se sitúan en la categoría de "historia trasmitida oralmente".

Esta última la subdivide a su vez Nicholson, destacando primeramente los textos que de un modo o de otro se muestran ligados al contenido de los códices picto-ideográficos y a continuación los que aparecen como más autónomos o sea como más puro resultado de diversas formas de tradición oral.

El primer punto que deseo comentar se refiere a los testimonios derivados de los hallazgos estrictamente arqueológicos. Señala Nicholson (p. 39) que "aquí nuestro único interés se refiere a los testimonios sobrevivientes en los que aparece una intención consciente de conmemorar de algún modo acontecimientos que sucedieron, para el recuerdo de la posteridad, y que constituyen, en una amplia definición, una especie de muy abreviada historia 'escrita' ".

Al destacar esta afirmación de Nicholson me parece pertinente confrontarla con lo que ha escrito algunas líneas antes: "La primera categoría (o sea la de estos testimonios arqueológicos), excluye los datos de la arquitectura y de otras producciones o artefactos, testigos a pesar de sí mismos, como los ha nombrado Bloch, que constituyen la evidencia 'normal' buscada y utilizada por los arqueólogos de campo en el Nuevo Mundo, para reconstruir el pasado" (p. 39).

Quiere trazar así Nicholson una línea divisoria entre los testimonios arqueológicos que son portadores de esa especie de "historia escrita abreviada", o sea las inscripciones que registran fechas y acontecimientos, y el gran cúmulo de los otros hallazgos arqueológicos que innegablemente —y aunque a veces "a pesar de sí mismos"— son también fuente importantísima para la historia cultural y desde luego imprescindibles para establecer los distintos horizontes, épocas y periodos en la secuencia histórica de un grupo determinado.

A mi parecer, y reconociendo el sentido que da Nicholson a lo que aquí expone, quiero plantear una cuestión. El hecho de que, en determinados monumentos, se incluyan glifos calendáricos o representativos de nombres de persona o de lugar u otras formas de inscripción, ofrece muchas veces base para considerar a algunos de estos testimonios como de una naturaleza esencialmente igual, aunque con una expresión más sucinta, a la de las noticias que, con una grafía semejante, proporcionan los códices picto-ideográficos. O sea que esas inscripciones pueden ser resultado del mismo propósito de consignar para la posteridad el recuerdo de algo y por consiguiente entran de lleno en el campo de lo que se ha llamado conciencia indígena de la historia. Existe sin embargo un problema que no debe pasarse por alto y que precisamente muestra la necesidad de estudiar la historiografía prehispánica, no como una institución aislada, sino en el contexto integral de la cultura de la que formó parte. Hay en diversos monumentos, esculturas, pinturas, etcétera, anotaciones calendáricas que no hacen necesariamente referencia a lo que podría llamarse un hecho histórico. Daré un ejemplo quizá demasiado evidente. En la conocida pequeña escultura de Xólotl que se conserva en el Museo de Stuttgart se encuentran varios glifos calendáricos tanto en el tocado de la deidad como en sus brazaletes y en su máxtlatl. El análisis de esos glifos, tal como lo hizo Eduard Seler, muestra que, lejos de referirse a un hecho histórico, se trata de una forma distinta de connotación. Por medio de esos glifos se señalan las relaciones del dios Xólotl con determinadas deidades evocadas éstas a través de sus nombres calendáricos. (Seler, 1960, ii, 392-409.)

Aunque el ejemplo aducido, como ya dije, se presta a un análisis bastante obvio, puede haber otros muchos casos de monumentos con inscripciones de contenido a primera vista histórico, y respecto de las cuales solamente un examen más minucioso podrá revelar su verdadera significación.

Atender, por consiguiente, a la categoría de las inscripciones con probable contenido histórico supone en todos los casos particular cautela. Por otra parte, no estará de más reiterar, para no perder de vista la correlación que estos estudios deben tener con la arqueología, que el fijarse aquí en estas inscripciones en modo alguno implica que, para el moderno historiador, dejen de ser asimismo testimonios de gran valor todas las otras formas de monumentos y hallazgos arqueológicos. Nunca estará de más insistir en la necesidad que tiene el investigador de correlacionar hasta donde sea posible la historiografía nativa con el gran cúmulo de evidencias derivadas de los descubrimientos arqueológicos. Sólo así podrá reconstruirse algo de la historia cultural, más allá de los escuetos elencos de fechas y nombres.

Pasando a otro punto, me parece de sumo interés la insistencia de Nicholson en buscar, a propósito de las diversas formas de producción histórica, los términos y conceptos indígenas con que éstas fueron designadas y concebidas. De hecho el análisis lingüístico y filológico de esos vocablos puede ayudar grandemente a lograr una comprensión más honda de lo que significó para el hombre prehispánico la historia. Dado que ésta no existía como algo aislado, sino esencialmente integrada en la totalidad de su cultura, es necesario inquirir cuáles fueron sus diversas formas de interrelación con el pensamiento religioso y mitológico, con el sentido astrológico de los cómputos del tiempo, con la visión del mundo y los propios sistemas de valores. Por mi parte me he planteado diversos problemas relacionados con lo anterior al estudiar el pensamiento maya acerca del tiempo y del espacio (León-Portilla, 1968). Si las medidas del tiempo, con todas sus cargas y connotaciones, fueron elemento inevitablemente presente en la conciencia indígena acerca del pasado, parece claro que debieron influir en sus diversas formas de preservar para la posteridad el conocimiento del mismo.

Justamente esto hace difícil trazar una línea de tajante división entre los recuerdos míticos y la memoria de los acontecimientos que parecen históricos. Por ello es necesario buscar muchas veces el sentido más hondo de algunos relatos en función de la antigua visión del mundo o de las connotaciones de determinados signos calendáricos. Ofreceré un ejemplo de esto tomado de un trabajo de Alfonso Caso, en el que se ocupa de la fundación de Tenochtitlan. (Caso, 1946, 96-97). "La tribu azteca —escribe Caso—, que había emprendido larga peregrinación, salió de Aztlan el año Ce-técpatl (1116 d.C.), según el más fehaciente documento que conservamos, la llamada *Tira de la peregrinación* o *Códice Boturini*, y duró en sus andanzas 208 años o sea, exactamente cuatro siglos indígenas de 52 años."

"Habiendo salido de Aztlan en Ce-técpatl, 1-pedernal (1116) —continúa Alfonso Caso—, tenía forzosamente que iniciar su nueva vida en un año del mismo nombre. Por eso la fundación de Tenochtitlan se hace también en un año 1-*técpatl*, 1324, según el intérprete del *Códice Mendocino*, aunque la pintura que ya los representa asentados en Tenochtitlan, está enmarcada por una serie de años que principia por Ome-calli, 2-casa, 1325, o sea precisamente el año siguiente ... Otro hecho muy importante para los aztecas, consignan sus anales, acaecidos en Ce-técpatl: es el nombramiento de su primer rey Acamapichtli, que sucede precisamente cuando habían transcurrido 52 años de la fundación de la ciudad, es decir en 1376 ..."

La coincidencia, en modo alguno fortuita, de la misma fecha calendárica Ce-técpatl, 1-pedernal, a propósito de estos tres acontecimientos tan significativos para los antiguos mexicanos, hizo que el propio Alfonso Caso se planteara formalmente la siguiente pregunta: "¿qué razón tuvieron los aztecas para elegir precisamente los años Ce-*técpatl* para estos acontecimientos tan importantes?" La respuesta nos la ofrece el mismo investigador. Si los aztecas estaban al servicio de un ideal religioso y llegaron a ser conocedores acuciosos del *tonalpohualli*, tuvieron plena conciencia de que "el día Ce-*técpatl*, está dedicado al dios Huitzilopochtli, por ser el día de su nacimiento, y por esta razón Huitzilopochtli, el dios tribal de los aztecas, se llama por su nombre calendárico Ce-*técpatl*; así como el gran dios de los toltecas, Quetzalcóatl, se llamaba Ce-*ácatl*, 1-caña. El año que se llamaba como su dios, debe haber sido considerado por los sacerdotes y adivinos como particularmente dichoso y propicio para intentar aquellas cosas que

iban a tener una importancia fundamental en la vida de la tribu; el inicio
de la peregrinación, la fundación de la ciudad, la creación de la monarquía".

El análisis de Caso muestra claramente en este ejemplo la necesidad de
atender a las connotaciones míticas de lo calendárico para poder alcanzar
una significación más honda de esos tres hechos del pasado de los mexicas.
Puede afirmarse por consiguiente que, en este caso, esa historia en parte
legendaria estaba implícitamente estructurada en el sistema de connotaciones propias de los cómputos del tiempo.

Complemento indispensable del tipo de información que presenta Nicholson en su trabajo parece ser por consiguiente el requerido estudio de
lo que significó la historia indígena en el más amplio contexto de la cultura intelectual del mundo mesoamericano.

Atendiendo ahora más directamente a lo que Nicholson con razón considera rica producción historiográfica prehispánica, me parece necesario señalar, como en alguna ocasión lo hace él mismo, cuáles pueden ser los varios
desiderata, de innegable prioridad en nuestros estudios sobre la historiografía indígena. Es cierto que actualmente son relativamente numerosas las
publicaciones en las que se dan a conocer estos testimonios. Principalmente
en México, los Estados Unidos de Norte América y Alemania hay investigadores que, como ya lo dijimos al principio, se han dedicado durante las
últimas décadas a preparar ediciones de diversos manuscritos de contenido
histórico en lengua indígena y también de algunos códices. Sin querer juzgar ahora el valor de esos estudios en lo que toca a la fidelidad de las traducciones, o de la lectura e interpretación de los glifos, a la metodología
crítica, etcétera, mencionaré al menos aspectos determinados que requieren
particular atención.

Primeramente está el problema, no siempre debidamente atendido de
determinar cuáles son la naturaleza y el origen de los testimonios que se
estudian. ¿Se trata de un testimonio en el que se trasmiten conocimientos
total o sólo parcialmente de origen prehispánico? Pienso ahora, dentro de
este contexto, en la amplia recopilación de textos, de suma importancia
para la historia cultural del mundo náhuatl, llevada al cabo por fray Bernardino de Sahagún. A no dudarlo en esos centenares de folios hay textos
de origen esencialmente prehispánico como son, por ejemplo, los himnos
a los dioses, buena parte de los *huehuetlatolli* y quizás también otras porciones como aquellas en las que se incluyen los mitos acerca de Huitzilopochtli y Quetzalcóatl. Otra parte de los textos recogidos por Sahagún contienen en cambio las respuestas dadas por los informantes indígenas a los
cuestionarios que el franciscano previamente había elaborado, siguiendo un
esquema adoptado por él mismo. Hay finalmente otros testimonios, sobre
todo en los *Memoriales*, que parecen ser transcripción de lo que más espontáneamente manifestaron los mismos informantes respecto de determinados puntos. Desde luego el valor que críticamente pueda concederse a testimonios como éstos, tan distintos entre sí, dependerá del conocimiento que
se tenga de su origen y de la forma como fueron obtenidos.

El segundo problema, sumamente arduo, pero que urge atender, es el de
la génesis e interrelación de los testimonios que integran el cuerpo de la
historiografía indígena. Robert H. Barlow, mostró por ejemplo, la manifiesta
interrelación, y por tanto el origen en común, de fuentes como el *Códice*

Ramírez, la *Historia mexicana* de Tezozómoc y una parte de la *Historia* de Durán, derivados todos de una cierta "Crónica X".

Una elemental familiaridad con textos como los de las *Relaciones de Chimalpain*, la *Crónica Mexicáyotl*, el *Códice Aubin*, la *Historia* de Cristóbal del Castillo, el manuscrito número 40 de la Colección de MS. Mexicanos de la Biblioteca Nacional de París, muestra que hay en ellos no pocas porciones enteramente iguales o por lo menos muy semejantes. La pregunta surge necesariamente: ¿cuál fue la génesis o proceso de elaboración de estos testimonios? Desde otro punto de vista, la heterogénea información que incluyen, por ejemplo, los *Anales de Cuauhtitlan*, lleva asimismo a preguntarse en qué forma se llevó al cabo la recopilación de testimonios de tan distintas procedencias para integrar con ellos una especie de relación *syncronológica* (correlacionada temporalmente), de lo que sucedió en diversos lugares del Valle de México.

Y esta cuestión, de tanta importancia para valorar críticamente la información de las distintas fuentes, debe hacerse extensiva a muchos de los testimonios incluidos en las obras de cronistas e historiadores tanto españoles, como indígenas y mestizos del siglo xvi y principios del xvii. Mientras estemos desprovistos de estudios dirigidos a investigar con sentido crítico la génesis y posibles interrelaciones de nuestras fuentes, será en extremo difícil poder aprovecharlas debidamente.

Una última proposición es la de considerar la conveniencia de que quienes nos dedicamos al estudio de los testimonios historiográficos mesoamericanos, pensemos en formular un elenco de prioridades por lo que toca a la preparación de ediciones de los mismos. Algunos de ellos fueron publicados hace ya bastante tiempo y desde luego hacen falta nuevas versiones preparadas con un criterio de revisión y eminentemente crítico.

El trabajo sistemático de H. B. Nicholson, al igual que la elaboración de los elencos de las fuentes que hasta hoy conocemos, muestran a las claras que es éste un campo mucho más rico de lo que pudiera pensarse. Paralelamente a las investigaciones arqueológicas, el estudio, debidamente llevado al cabo, de la historiografía prehispánica nos dará la clave para el acercamiento a lo que fue la trayectoria cultural de la civilización en Mesoamérica.

REFERENCIAS BIBLIOGRÁFICAS

Alcina Franch, José, "Fuentes Indígenas de México", *Revista de Indias*, v. vi,
1955-56   núms. 61-62: 425-521.

Barrera Vázquez, Alfredo, *El libro de los libros de Chilam Balam*. Fondo de
1948   Cultura Económica, México.

————, *The Maya Chronicles*. Publication 585 of the Carnegie Institution of
1949   Washington, Washington, D. C.

————, *El libro de los cantares de Dzitbalché*. Instituto Nacional de Antropología e Historia, México.
1965

BARLOW, Robert H., "Códice Azcatitlan", *Journal de la Société des Americanistes*
1946b   de Paris, v. 38: 101-135, París.

CASO, Alfonso, "El águila y el nopal", *Memorias de la Academia Mexicana de la*
1946   *Historia*, v. v, 93-104, México.

———, "Explicaciones del Reverso del Códice Vindobonensis", *Memorias del*
1952   *Colegio Nacional*, v. v, 9-46, México.

———, "Valor Histórico de los códices mixtecos", *Cuadernos Americanos*, año
1960a   19, 109, 2: 139-147, México.

———, *Códice Bodley*, Interpretación del Códice Bodley 2858. Sociedad Mexicana
1960b   de Antropología, México.

———, *Códice Selden*, Interpretación del Códice Selden 3135 (A.2). Sociedad
1964   Mexicana de Antropología, México.

———, *Códice Colombino*, Interpretación del Códice Colombino. Sociedad
1966   Mexicana de Antropología, México.

DIBBLE, Charles E., *Códice en Cruz*. México.
1942

———, *Códice Xólotl*, Introducción de Rafael García Granados. Universidades
1951   de México y de Utah, 168 láminas, cuadros y mapas, México.

———, *Códice de 1576 o Códice Aubin*, edición, introducción, notas, índices,
1963   versión paleográfica y traducción directa del náhuatl. Colección Chimalis-
tac, Madrid.

——— y ANDERSON, Arthur J. O., *Florentine Codex*, libros I, II, III, IV-V, VII,
1950-63   VIII, IX, X, XI, XII, Translated from the Aztec into English, with notes
and illustrations, Published by the School of American Research and the
University of Utah. Santa Fe, New Mexico.

GARIBAY K., Ángel María, *Veinte himnos sacros de los nahuas*. UNAM, Instituto
1958   de Investigaciones Históricas, México.

———, *Vida económica de Tenochtitlan*, Fuentes Indígenas de Cultura Náhuatl 3.
1961   UNAM, Instituto de Investigaciones Históricas, México.

———, *Poesía náhuatl I*, (Romances de los señores de la Nueva España manus-
1964   crito de Juan Bautista de Pomar, Texcoco, 1582), paleografía, versión,
introducción, notas y apéndices. UNAM, Instituto de Investigaciones
Históricas, México.

———, *Poesía náhuatl II*, (Cantares Mexicanos, manuscrito de la Biblioteca Nacio-
1965   nal de México, primera parte), paleografía, versión, introducción y notas
explicativas. UNAM, Instituto de Investigaciones Históricas, México.

———, *Poesía náhuatl III*, Cantares Mexicanos. UNAM, Instituto de Investiga-
1968   ciones Históricas, México.

GLASS, John B., *Catálogo de la colección de códices del Museo Nacional de Antro-
1964   pología*. México.

JIMÉNEZ MORENO, Wigberto y MATEOS HIGUERA, Salvador, *Códice de Yanhuitlán.*
1940 Museo Nacional, México.

LEHMANN, Walter, *Die Geschichte der Königreiche von Colhuacan und Mexiko,*
1938 en Quellenwerke sur alten Geschichte Amerikas Bd. I, Text mit Uberse-
tzung. Stuttgart.

————, *Sterbende Götter und Christliche Heilsbotschat,* Wechselreden Indianischer
1949 vornehmer und Spanischer Glaubenapostel in Mexiko, 1524, Spanischer
und Mexicanischer text. Stuttgart.

LEÓN-PORTILLA, Miguel, *Ritos, sacerdotes y atavíos de los dioses,* introducción,
1958 paleografía, versión y notas. UNAM, Instituto de Investigaciones Históricas, México.

————, *Trece poetas del mundo azteca.* UNAM, Instituto de Investigaciones His-
1967 tóricas, México.

———— y Salvador Mateos Higuera, *Catálogo de los códices indígenas del México
1957 antiguo,* Suplemento del Boletín Bibliográfico de la Secretaría de Hacienda, año 3, núm. 111, junio de 1957.

LÓPEZ AUSTIN, Alfredo, *Juegos rituales aztecas.* UNAM, Instituto de Investigaciones
1967 Históricas, México.

————, *Augurios y abusiones,* Introducción versión y notas. UNAM, Instituto de
1969 Investigaciones Históricas, México.

MENGIN, Ernst, *Anales de Tlatelolco,* Traducción del náhuatl al alemán por Ernst
1948 Mengin, publicado en *Baessler Archiv,* t. XXII, cuadernos 2 y 3 (traducido
del alemán al castellano por Berlín Enrique en *Fuentes para la historia
de México.* Antigua Librería Robredo, México).

————, *Codex Mexicanus* (23-24), Bibliothèque Nationale de Paris. *Société des
1952 Americanistes* XLI, 387-498, París.

———— y Preuss Konrad, *Historia tolteco-chichimeca,* Die mexikanischen Belder-
1937- handschreft, Historia tolteca-chichimeca, übersetz und erläutert von . . .
38 *Baessler Archiv,* Teil 1-2. Berlin.

NICHOLSON, H. B., "Aztec style Calendaric inscriptions of possible historical
1955a significance" (Mesa Redonda on Calendar problems of ancient Central
Mexico), Chapultepec, 5 al 12 de diciembre, *Sociedad Mexicana de
Antropología,* México.

————, "Native Historical traditions of nuclear America and the problem of
1955b their Archaeological correlation", *American Anthropologist,* 57, 3, 594-
613.

————, "The Chapultepec cliff aculpture of Motecuhzoma Xocoyotzin", *El
1961a México Antiguo* 9, 379-444, México.

NOWOTNY, Karl Anton, *Tlacuilolli,* Die mexikanischen Bilderhandschriften, Stil
1961a und Inhalt mit einem Katalog den . . . (Ibero-Americanische Bibliothek,
Monuments American III). Berlin.

ROBERTSON, D., *Mexican manuscript painting in the early colonial period*, The
1959   Metropolitan Schools, Yale Historical publications, History of Art 12.
     New Haven.

ROYS, Ralph L., *The Book of Chilam Balam of Chumayel*. Publication 438 of
1967   the Carnegie Institution, University of Oklahoma Press.

SELER, Eduard, "Des Grünsteinidol des Stuttgarter Museums", *Verhandlungen des*
1960   *XIV. Internationalem Amerikaniste Kongresses Stuttgart 1904*. En: *Ges-*
     ammelte Abhandlungen zur Amerikanischen Sprach und Altertumskunde,
     III, 392-409. Graz, Austria.

TEZOZÓMOC, Fernando Alvarado, *Crónica Mexicayótl*. Traducción del náhuatl por
1949   Adrián León. UNAM, Instituto de Investigaciones Históricas, México.

VALÁZQUEZ, Primo Feliciano, *Códice Chimalpopoca, Anales de Cuauhtitlan y*
1945   *Leyenda de los Soles*, traducción directa del náhuatl. UNAM, Instituto
     de Investigaciones Históricas, México.

ZIMMERMAN, Günter, *Das Geschichtswerk des Domingo de Muñon Chimalpahin*
1960   *Quauhtlehuanitzin* (Quellenkritische Studien zur frühindianischen Ges-
     chichte Mexikos). Beitrage zur mittelamerikanischen Völkerkunde heraus-
     gegeben von Hamburgischen Museum für Völkerkunde unl Vorgeschichte
     5.

————, Domingo Chimalpahin Cuauhtlehuanitzin, *Die Relationen Chimalpahin's*
1963-65 *zur Geschichte Mexico's*, Universität Hamburg, Abhandlungen aus dem
     Gebiet der Auslandskund, v. 38 y 39. Hamburg.

COMMENTARY

DONALD ROBERTSON

The papers of Professors López Austin and Nicholson both give us valuable and related introductions to the materials they cover. López Austin writes on scholarship on the Nahuatl texts and limits the area of his discussion to major authorities, presenting his material in compact and manegeable form. Nicholson's paper is on how they came into being and their value.

Nicholson has given us more than he promised, since in his initial statement he says that he will limit himself to the *"transmission media and techniques"* of the historical aspect of Mesoamerican studies at the expense of "native concepts" of history. However, he does give us some insights into native concepts of history and a large bibliographic guide to the material. His summary of the "writing" and calendars is most useful and handy. His advice that we should analyze each chronological problem on its own merits and then later attempt a synthesis is useful. He also observes that the records of the native past are valuable for the data they preserve to us in terms of traditional history. I was disappointed that he did not emphasize more that they also contain information, as he put it, "on cultural values, preoccupations, themes patterns, etc.".

From the data presented in this paper we emerge with a picture of history as essentially a "chronological" series of dated objects related to people and to events taking place at specific places and in specific moments of time. But history is also the analysis of such persons, places and events so that from them changes or evolutions in the style of a people's art, a people's religion and even the evolution of a state can be derived. This "synthesizing" aspect of history seems to be of less interest in the paper than the more easily handled "chronological" aspect.

The sources for Pre-Columbian history which Nicholson discusses are classified into a number of categories. I would take issue with the name he gives his first category, "archaeological records", and point out that archaeology is essentially method and technique; thus the "archaeological records", as he calls them, are examples of sculpture (he excludes architecture and "artifacts"). As sculpture they are really works of art, of varying quality to be sure, but still products of the sculptor's art; they are only made available to us by the archaeologist. This is more important than it might seem, because as works of art they can potentially give us more information on the milieu than merely the dates they carry. This aspect of their value only touched upon in the paper is capable of greater expansion.

Within Nicholson's classification of the types of written and pictorial documents which have come down to us from the early colonial period I would also question the validity of his category "sporadically dated or undated annals". To me this is merely a sub-category whose members come from compressed colonial documents, but is would have made little or no sense to the native scribe. I also feel that the category of "dynastic lists" is not really as valid in contrast with the "genealogies" as he would have it; one is essentially a sub-category of the other. One might mention in passing that the tribute documents are an important part and source of pre-Hispanic history that should have received a greater emphasis.

The assumption that "the typical *tlacuilo* seems to have been essentially a scribe, working under others ..." is also questionable. I would submit that the distinction between writing and composing history is again Nicholson's. In contradiction, he himself later cites passages in Las Casas and Landa which strongly indicate that this division of labor was not a native idea.

The role of the "written" manuscripts as mnemonic devices and their relation to oral versions of the "texts" is not really resolved for us. If, however, the burden of this paper is to be "transmission media and techniques", one can fairly ask that positive statements on the relationship between these two aspects of pre-Hispanic history be made.

For instance, the burning of archives, the re-writing of history and the preservation of historical traditions over a long period of time, whether through oral *or* written sources or a combination of both, raise many questions. If a person or a group of persons among themselves had committed to memory all the history encompassed in the "written" documents, using them only as mnemonic devices, then the burning of archives would not be an irretrievable loss; the human "memory banks" could be called upon to record again in written (*i.e.*, painted) form the mnemonic clues for future memorizers. The whole archive could be reconstituted with only those lacunae due to the faulty memory of individual "memorizing historians". If the "written" texts were not merely mnemonic devices but, as I believe, actually documents which were "read", then the loss of an archive is closer to a total loss and of much graeter moment in the historical culture of the society.

To answer this key question is to throw light on several aspects of pre-Hispanic society, including, among others, the problem of transmission media and techniques. One can note here in passing that data in some written texts of the Relaciones Geográficas of 1579-1586, hitherto unused in this context, does give evidence of the use of painted manuscripts, oral traditions, and the use of oral explanations accompanying pictorial manuscripts. Sahagun also states that his informants used pictorial manuscripts supplemented by oral comments. In some pages of his early work the oral explanations have been put down in writing and associated with the appropriate items to explain the pictorial representations.

Nicholson's paper, in agreement with most students of sixteenth century Mexican sources, points out the need for critical evaluation of the sources but does not give us a clear-cut method for doing this. Instead he advises us to deal with the specific rather than the general and thus, because he has too many specific sources to deal with, avoids performing this service. After reading a list of eighteen unanswered questions in an unbroken sequence and others throughout the copy at my disposal before this meeting, it occurred to me that some of these questions have been answered by Dibble in his Sahagun paper read before the International Congress of

Americanists in Argentina (1966) and that my own work on Mexican manuscript painting published ten years ago both phrased such questions and, if only tentatively, answered a significant number of them.

Perhaps a study in detail of one or more specific instances would have enabled useful deductions to be made from which methods for solving some of the problems might emerge. For what we really need are just such carefully thought out methods presented in a theoretical framework which can be applied and tested against a limited number of sources, refined, and then be used to test other sources.

To illustrate, let me pose the question of evaluating the relative native and European components in a small part of Sahagun's work, an important monument in pre-Hispanic history.

Father Garibay stated, in his introduction to Book Ten of Sahagun's *Historia*, that he thought this book gave us a picture of Indian life and society before Cortes. Following a suggestion of Nicholson's in footnote 18 that Garibay's theories deserve more criticism than they receive from his followers, I would like to demonstrate why I agree with Nicholson, why I cannot agree with Garibay's statement as it stands unqualified, how it can be tested, and in the process of testing suggest a method for wider application in the study of sixteenth century sources in general.

Book Ten is concerned in the early chapters with the men and women of native Mexico. In Chapter Eight the craftsmen, especially the carpenter, stone mason, and the painter, are discussed. The Spanish Text (Garibay) and the Nahuatl text in English translation (Dibble and Anderson) and especially the illustrations reprinted in Dibble and Anderson, describe carpentry in such a way as to suggest a considerable degree of acculturation. The English translation where it says the carpenter drives nails is quite clearly not native. The illustrations accompanying this section of the text show the use of a European plane, saw, and carpenter's square. Work is being done on a masonry building with gable ends and a European Renaissance base moulding. A column is being carved on a Renaissance pedestal base. The next section, dealing with "the stone cutter the stone breaker" the *"cantero"*, describes the making of "curved stones" in the English translation, perhaps voussoirs; this is more explicitly stated in the Spanish text where the *cantero* can make "arches", certainly not known in the pre-Cortesian period. Again the illustrations show Renaissance pedestals and the European carpenter's square. The plumb line is a marginal case (did it appear in the repertory of native tools?). The description of the scribe (*tlacuilo*) says that the good scribe makes shadows (English translation); the Spanish text says that he can make shadows, paint space and folliage. None of these are part of the repertory of pre-Columbian artists from south central Mexico and appear in the manuscript paintings of the early colonial period with time in increasing degree only as other elements of artistic style also become more European.

In Chapter Ten of Book Ten the description of the good tailor has him making tailored clothes, not unfitted pre-Cortesian garments. In the accompanying illustration he is wearing tailored trousers and using European scissors. The spinner in the next section in the English translation spins on a spindle whorl (see also Chapter Fourteen where she spins in her lap), but the illustration shows the use of the European spinning wheel. In the description of weaving the weaver pushes the headle bar down with her foot but is shown in the illustration using the native back-strap loom. In these last two examples we see the mixture of Mexico and Europe. In the first the description is of an Indian technique, the illustration of a European machine. In the second, the technique is European, but the illustration is Indian.

From studying these examples chosen because their European elements were so obvious we can deduce that the selected passages in Book Ten demonstrate acculturation. This method can be applied to other historical material: Deduct all elements which upon critical examination are surely European in inspiration with the thought that what is left will be native. The method can be applied as we have done it in terms of text and illustrations considered as parts of a single whole. Where only text or only illustrations are present the task is more demanding but still applicable. However, the task is not simple, for in the demonstration just made I made no statement on the use of the plum line —is it native or European? Nor did I deal with technical questions of carpentry, tailoring, and masonry techniques as described in the passages under discussion. In other words, the analysis must go forther than this did before one can say all European elements have been abstracted and what is left is native.

We should now amend Father Garibay's statement in the introduction to Book Ten that its contents offer a picture of Indian life *"before Cortés"* by adding *"and also after Cortés"* and reiterate his warning (also voiced by Barlow in slightly more picturesque fashion in the first issue of *Tlalocan*) that we do not reconstruct a world with intuitions.

Using a similar approach to written source materials I arrived at the conclusion that Tlacaelel shows such strong evidence of influence from European romances of chivalry and rests upon such a limited historical base that he too can serve as an evidence of European influence upon the history and literature of the Aztecs. Perhaps much of the oral tradition which gives so much difficulty may turn out to be less native than one tends to think.

The role of the oral tradition and the use of earlier written (painted) sources is more difficult to define when studying another important group of native sources which are not part of the traditional bibliography and thus were not mentioned by either Professors López Austin or Nicholson in their papers: I refer to the Techialoyan códices. López Austin uses an outline which in a way precludes discussing his materials out of the context of the main individual editors and translators. The Techialoyans are perhaps better discussed as a series of texts with illustrations rather than in the context of the several scholars who have transcribed and translated them (Rosales, Chimalpopoca, Barlow, McAfee, and Jiménez Moreno). Nicholson, noting the almost complete absence of sources for the Otomí-Nahuatl region north of the Basin of Mexico an the Toluca Basin area, does not have this somewhat mechanical reason for omitting them. However, they do cast light upon a stage of scholarship in the study of Náhuatl and *are* the remaining sources in the native tradition otherwise lacking in this large and important arc north and west of the capital.

The pertinence of these códices to our discussion today can be pointed out quite succinctly: they are late seventeenth or early eighteenth century texts of significant length written in Nahuatl. Their content includes sections dealing with pre-Hispanic history, and these sections stand pretty much alone, in splendid isolation, as historical sources for an important area of pre-Hispanic Mexico. Following a simple outline, the Techialoyan códices give histories of the pueblos they come from —the first native conquerors, genealogy of the rulers, and the Spanish entrada with references to the *statu quo* at the point when the Spaniards arrive on the scene. The historical content follows a stereotyped format, as do other classes of native history. On the basis of other areas of content in the group, such as the description of the lands belonging to the pueblo in question which testing indicates to be reliable, their pre-Spanish history must not be disregarded but rather analyzed critically and then used to fill an important gap in our knowledge.

My studies of the Techialoyan group began from the point of view of the historian of Mexican art; thus, I was mainly interested in their pictorial content. With time my interest in the written Nahuatl texts increased. I found no theoretical study which would help me to unravel the relationships linking them with either a surviving oral transmission technique or pictorial manuscripts now lost but probably still existing when the Techialoyan manuscripts were written and painted (*i.e.*, edited). Possibly both kinds of sources played a part in the creation of the Techialoyans, but in any event this older material was edited to a standard pattern when being written down in Nahuatl. Because of the distance in time from the pre-Hispanic period, anachronisms occur which must be, as always, critically analyzed by the historian. These I have explained and pointed out elsewhere.

Commentators always run the risk, like book reviewers, of discussing the paper they would have written rather than the one presented. Perhaps to be a commentator is to have a more valid right to this privilege of speaking from one's own point of view than the book reviewer has. It is not fair in a way for the book reviewer to complain about omissions if the author states clearly that he has intentionally omitted certain aspects of the problem and is concentrating on others. The commentator, however, seems to have this as on of his built-in duties.

RELATORÍA

JOSÉ MARÍA MURIÁ ROURET

La sesión se inició con un intercambio de ideas en torno a la influencia poscortesiana existente en los documentos escritos por los indígenas en sus propias lenguas, aunque utilizando la grafía latina. Se consideró que era a todas luces evidente la necesidad de filtrar los elementos de influencia al utilizar dichas fuentes, más si se toma en cuenta que muchas de ellas, aunque de indudable autenticidad, falsean la realidad en busca de fines ajenos a la historia. Tal es el caso, por ejemplo, de muchos certificados y títulos de propiedad *fabricados* especialmente para retener u obtener tierras, o escritos más extensos, de índole historiográfica, como los de Fernando de Alva Ixtlilxóchitl, que pretende destacar los méritos de su pueblo y de su familia. Sin embargo se consideró relativa la falsedad de estos documentos, puesto que pueden ser de gran valor para el estudio de la época en que fueron escritos y, tras los estudios críticos necesarios, para la obtención de conocimientos importantes del mundo prehispánico.

Se señaló que, para lograr filtrar estas influencias españolas, podría ser útil el estudio de los métodos de trabajo en la elaboración de la historia, tanto por lo que se refiere al México prehispánico como a la Europa de la época. De gran utilidad sería también estudiar la formación individual de los cronistas e historiadores para estimar debidamente el valor particular de sus obras.

Otro de los temas interesantes considerado en la sesión fue el relacionado con los problemas de connotación plural de algunos términos indígenas, que puede llevar a errores de interpretación. Este problema aumenta en los textos que contienen algunas formas de lenguaje esotérico.

Se señalaron también los problemas inherentes a la interpretación de los textos por la confusión entre lo histórico y lo legendario, y a los errores de escritura en la elaboración de copias por escribanos no diestros en idiomas indígenas.

En relación con los fines de la arqueología y la historia se consideró que, a pesar de la diferencia metodológica, tanto el arqueólogo como el historiador persiguen la obtención del conocimiento de la misma realidad. Se aceptó, por tanto, que no existe ningún motivo para que los especialistas de ambas disciplinas trabajen sin la debida comunicación. A este respecto se mencionó que existen infinidad de monumentos y piezas arqueológicas que poseen inscripciones de evidente significado histórico, que la arqueología pudiera investigar en beneficio de la historia.

Se plantearon problemas derivados de la carencia de fuentes tradicionalmente consideradas como formales o explícitas, principalmente por lo que se refiere a las culturas maya y mixteca. Sin embargo, se advirtió que el historiador podría auxiliarse de materiales de carácter informal o implícito, abundantes en toda Mesoamérica.

Finalmente se planteó la importancia de publicar fuentes que aún permanecen inéditas y de elaborar ediciones críticas de muchos de los textos publicados con anterioridad. Para este fin se consideró de utilidad establecer un elenco de prioridades que determinara las fuentes merecedoras de ser tomadas primero en cuenta para su estudio y publicación.

II. HISTORIOGRAFÍA NOVOHISPANA DE LOS SIGLOS XVI Y XVII

Presidente: Charles Gibson, profesor de historia, Universidad de Michigan.

Ponentes: Jorge A. Manrique, profesor e investigador de El Colegio de México y del Instituto de Investigaciones Estéticas, UNAM; John L. Phelan, profesor de historia, Universidad de Wisconsin.

Comentaristas: Carlos Martínez, subdirector en funciones de director de la Escuela Nacional de Antropología; Charles Gibson.

Participantes: Woodrow Borah, profesor de historia, Universidad de California, Berkeley; Rosa Camelo, investigadora del Instituto de Historia UNAM; Guillermo Céspedes, profesor de historia latinoamericana y española, Universidad de California, La Jolla; Howard F. Cline, director de *The Hispanic Foundation*, Biblioteca del Congreso, Washington D. C.; Lothar Knauth, director del Centro de Estudios Orientales, UNAM; Úrsula Lamb, investigadora asociada de historia, Universidad de Yale; Roberto Moreno, investigador de la Biblioteca Nacional de México; Josefina Muriel, investigadora del Instituto de Historia, UNAM; Edmundo O' Gorman, profesor emérito de la Facultad de Filosofía y Letras, UNAM; John H. Parry, profesor Gardiner de Historia Oceánica, Universidad de Harvard; Guadalupe Pérez San Vicente, investigadora del Instituto de Historia, UNAM.

Participantes Europeos: Jean Pierre Berthe, Subdirector de estudios en la *Ecole Pratique des Hautes Études*, Vía, Sección, París; Manfred Kossok, profesor de historia general; encabeza el *Latin American Research Group* del Departamento de Historia de la Universidad Karl Marx, Leipzig.

Relatoría: Álvaro Matute: Becario del Instituto de Historia, UNAM.

LA ÉPOCA CRÍTICA DE LA NUEVA ESPAÑA
A TRAVÉS DE SUS HISTORIADORES

JORGE ALBERTO MANRIQUE

> Las letras son alas: cada uno mire cómo
> vuela con ellas.
> (A. Dávila Padilla: *Historia de la funda-*
> *ción y discurso* ... 575).

Entre los historiadores mexicanos de los siglos XVI y XVII, han sido muy vistos, muy estudiados, muy manoseados los primeros grandes escritores, desde Cortés hasta Sahagún, pasando por Motolonía, Bernal Díaz, Gómara y toda la pléyade de autores que se refieren ya a las antigüedades de los indios prehispánicos, ya a las circunstanicas, peripecias y aconteceres de la Conquista. Se les conoce bien. No, ciertamente, que no haya todavía mucho que hacer sobre ellos, como muy recientemente nos lo muestra el empeño de algunos estudiosos; [1] a poco que se rasque, se advierte que no están tan bien leídos como se había supuesto, que sobre ellos se han hecho y repetido muchas afirmaciones que no resisten una crítica cuidadosa y que, a fin de cuentas, cada vez se hacen más necesarias ediciones críticas, serias, académicas de esas obras. Pero lo dicho no mengua, ni el prestigio de aquellos historiadores, ni el hecho de que sean mucho más conocidos que los que les siguieron o se ocuparon de otros temas.

Sin duda dos criterios han sido la base para colocar a tales autores en el pedestal que ocupan: el de su *veracidad* y el de su *originalidad*. Se supone que en la gran mayoría de los casos nos dicen la "verdad" de lo que pasó (y para esto no se entra en demasiadas honduras sobre cuáles pueden ser los parámetros que la determinen) y que, además, son los "primeros" que nos la dicen. Por este camino se llega a curiosas conclusiones; valga de ejemplo el hecho de elevar a Bernal Díaz, para lo que se refiere a los acontecimientos de la Conquista, muy por encima de Gómara: se sabe que Bernal, juez y parte, tiene una visión interesada, pero eso no es obstáculo para que *a priori* se le suponga más veraz que el capellán de Cortés, puesto que estuvo presente en los hechos que relata y fue actor de ellos. Y respecto al criterio de origina-

---

[1] Me refiero a, v. gr., el trabajo que desde hace algunos años han realizado con tanto fruto Angel Ma. Garibay (q.e.p.d.), Miguel León-Portilla y Alfredo López Austin sobre la obra de los informantes de Sahagún; o a la nueva visión que de Motolinía está empeñado en darnos Edmundo O'Gorman: o a la que ya nos dio de Las Casas en su edición de la *Apologética*.

lidad, basta hacer referencia al desprecio con que se consideran los autores que "copiaron" de fuentes anteriores; no se les quita el sambenito de plagiarios, incapaces de ningún valor, puesto que repiten lo que ya otros (los primeros, los originales) habían investigado. Su crimen no para ahí: al repetir lo dicho por otros se permiten modificarlo, adobarlo, decirlo "a su manera"; es decir, lo falsean.

Quizá el ejemplo mejor que puede traerse a cuento sobre estos modos de juzgar nuestra historiografía colonial es el interesante libro *Estudios de historiografía de la Nueva España*, publicado hace algo más de veinte años por El Colegio de México, que reúne trabajos de los entonces jóvenes egresados de esa institución. [2] El ejemplo es válido, porque se trata de estudios serios, hechos cuidadosamente y con entusiasmo. Válido también porque, a pesar de algunos atisbos aislados, la tónica de la actual apreciación de aquellos viejos historiadores sigue, creo, siendo la misma. Ahí, en la introducción de Ramón Iglesia, que fue quien dirigió los estudios de referencia y quien los avala, puede leerse que "Muñoz Camargo podría haberse quedado muy a gusto en su oscuro rincón sin que perdiéramos gran cosa", que "casi lo mismo puede decirse de Dorantes de Carranza . . .", y que "los elogios que se les vienen tributando (a otros) . . . proceden tan sólo de que nadie hasta ahora había sometido sus textos a exámenes tan minuciosos". [3] Sus discípulos le siguen: ". . . Aquí el historiador no encontrará nada más que una transcripción . . . desaliñada, interpolada . . . una crónica de valor casi nulo . . .", "más que la verdad de los hechos y la justeza de la narración, le interesaba el provecho que con ellas podía obtener . . ."; "la obra en conjunto nos aleja de la verdad en lugar de acercarnos a ella . . ." y suma y sigue. [4]

Creo, en verdad, que esos criterios de apreciación siguen siendo actuantes en nuestra historiografía. (Y al decir "nuestra historiografía" no me refiero sólo a la mexicana, sino a la de nuestros días.) Así, se puede establecer una gradación de valores, según lo que se concede a cada historiador. En un primerísimo grupo estarían los autores que *vieron* los hechos, a los que se da normalmente la máxima aceptación;

[2] *Estudios de historiografía de la Nueva España*, introducción de Ramón Iglesia, México, El Colegio de México, 1945. Reúne los siguientes trabajos: Hugo Díaz-Thomé, "Francisco Cervantes de Salazar y su *Crónica de la Conquista de la Nueva España*"; Fernando B. Sandoval, "La relación de la conquista de México en la *Historia* de Fray Diego Durán"; Manuel Carrera Stampa, "Algunos aspectos de la *Historia de Tlaxcala* de Diego Muñoz Camargo"; Carlos Bosch García; "La conquista de México de las *Décadas* de Antonio de Herrera y Tordesillas"; Ernesto de la Torre Villar, "Baltazar Dorantes de Carranza y la *Sumaria Relación*"; Enriqueta López Lira, "*La Historia de la Conquista de México* de don Antonio de Solís"; Julio Le Riverand, "*La Historia Antigua de México* del padre Francisco Javier Clavijero".
[3] *Op. cit.*, introducción, pp. 11 y 14.
[4] *Op. cit.*, pp. 42, 211, 283.

se trata del "valor testimonio-verdad"; Hernán Cortés [5] y Bernal Díaz del Castillo [6] ocuparían los primeros lugares, y vendrían seguidos de autores como Tapia [7] y el Conquistador Anónimo [8] —a quienes se concede menos importancia en razón de lo limitado y fragmentario de sus escritos—; bastante más abajo de ellos se colocaría Gómara [9] que no fue testigo, pero que estuvo cerca de testigos, lo que le da una valiosa aura, si bien arruinada por el hecho de obedecer a "mezquinos intereses"; en esa misma línea, pero ya revolcado en el desprestigio, estaría después Cervantes de Salazar, [10] que ni fue testigo, ni estuvo cerca de los actores, que es posterior en tiempo, obedecía también a intereses mezquinos y que, además, fue tan irresponsable de adobar a su modo muchos datos que tomó de otros autores; en fin, ya en las profundidades del averno, está un lugar reservado a Solís [11] a quien muy pocos historiadores actuales se atreven a tomar en serio. [12]

En otro grupo estarían los *primeros* que se ocuparon de la cultura indígena, que recogieron informaciones sobre ella de sus moribundos representantes, y que tuvieron el cuidado de escribirla y la suerte de que se conservara. Muy importante es el que se refieran a tal tema, pero parece incluso más importante el hecho de que fueron los primeros que lo hicieron; se trata aquí del "valor originalidad". Motolinía [13] encabezaría este grupo, porque, con excepción del perdido Olmos, [14]

---

[5] Hernán Cortés: *Cartas de Relación, passim.*

[6] Bernal Díaz del Castillo: *Verdadera historia de la conquista de la Nueva España,* introducción y notas de Joaquín Ramírez Cabañas, México, Robredo, 1939.

[7] Bernardino Vázquez de Tapia, *Relación de méritos y servicios...,* edición de Jorge Gurría Lacroix, México Robredo, 1953.

[8] La relación del llamado "conquistador Anónimo" en *Colección de documentos para la Historia de México,* editada por Joaquín García Icazbalceta, México, 1858-1866.

[9] Francisco López de Gómara, *Historia de la Conquista de México,* introducción y notas de Joaquín Ramírez Cabañas, México, Robredo, 1943.

[10] Francisco Cervantes de Salazar, *Crónica de Nueva España,* vol. I, Madrid, 1914; vols. II y III, México, 1936.

[11] Antonio de Solís y Rivadeneira, *Historia de la conquista de México, población y progreso de la América Septentrional, conocida por el nombre de Nueva España.* Madrid, Imprenta de don Antonio de Sancha, 1783-1784. La primera edición es de 1684.)

[12] Pienso en el prólogo de Edmundo O'Gorman a la más reciente edición de Solís (México, Porrúa, 1968, prólogo de E. O'G., notas de José Valero Silva), como una de las excepciones.

[13] Fray Toribio de Motolinía o de Benavente, *Historia de los indios de la Nueva España,* en *Colección de documentos para la historia de México,* editada por Joaquín García Icazbalceta, México, 1858-1866, I, pp. 3-249.

[14] Sobre la perdida "Relación" de fray Andrés de Olmos puede verse Bartolomé de las Casas, *Apologética historia sumaria...,* cap. 224; y Gerónimo de Mendieta: *Historia eclesiástica indiana,* lib. II, "Prólogo al cristiano lector". Puede, para una discusión moderna, consultarse Las Casas: *Los indios de México y Nueva España. Antología,* edición, prólogo y notas de Edmundo O' Gorman, con la co-

nadie le precede en tiempo y porque dedica no poco espacio a las culturas antiguas; estaría muy de cerca seguido por Sahagún, [15] que bien posterior en tiempo, lo supera en abundancia y en método; [16] no muy lejos de ellos estarían Durán, Ixtlixóchitl y Muñón Chimalpahin, [17] el uno por ser original, los otros porque, aunque sus escritos sean menos estructurados, tienen la ventaja de ser indios, lo que les da un cierto carácter de "testigos". Zurita, [18] por haber copiado tanto a Motolinía, tiene un sitio bastante más bajo, y Mendieta y Torquemada [19] quedan cerca del sótano, pues no resultan ya casi nada originales. Y todavía después de ellos vendrían gente como Muñoz Camargo y Dorantes de Carranza: [20] sobre ser muy tardíos —lo que los convierte en repetidores de otras fuentes— están afectados del vicio de la parcialidad, uno encargado de ensalzar la república tlaxcalteca para conseguir preminencias y fueros, el otro dedicado a escribir con el único fin de conseguir empleos reales.

En fin, un tercer grupo, ya francamente despreciado todo él, es el de los cronistas oficiales de las órdenes religiosas. Con excepción de algún cronista temprano, como Motolinía, que es apreciado justamente por temprano, según el valor "originalidad" que he explicado; y con

laboración de J. A. Manrique, México, Porrúa, 1966, en las notas 104, 182, 206, 230, 242, 260 y especialmente 241.

[15] Fray Bernardino de Sahagún, *Historia general de las cosas de Nueva España*, edición de Angel María Garibay K., México, Porrúa, 1956.

[16] Sobre el método empleado por Sahagún han abundado en sus estudios Miguel León-Portilla y Alfredo López Austin; pueden verse, entre otros, del primero su introducción a *Ritos, sacerdotes y atavíos de los dioses*, México, UNAM, 1958; del segundo la suya a *Augurios y abusiones*, México, UNAM, 1969.

[17] Fray Diego Durán, *Historia de las Indias de Nueva España y islas de Tierra Firme*, edición de José F. Ramírez, Imp. de J. M. Andrade y Escalante, 1867-1880. Fernando de Alva Ixtlixóchitl, *Historia de la nación chichimeca*, edición de Alfredo Chavero, México, 1892. Domingo Francisco de San Antón Muñón Chimalpahin Quauhtlehuanitzin, *Annales. Sixième et septième relations*, edición de Rémi Simeón, París, 1889; y *Relaciones originales de Chalco Amaquemecan*, edición de Silvia Rendón, México, 1965.

[18] Alonso de Zorita o Zurita, *Breve y sumaria relación de los señores y maneras y diferencias que había de ellos en la Nueva España*, en *Nueva colección de documentos para la historia de México*, editada por Joaquín García Icazbalceta, México, Impr. Díaz de León, 1886-1892.

[19] Fray Gerónimo de Mendieta, *Historia eclesiástica indiana*, edición de Joaquín García Icazbalceta, México, Impr. Díaz de León, 1870. Fray Juan de Torquemada, *Primera (segunda y tercera) parte de los veinte y un libros rituales y monarquía indiana* . . . , Sevilla, 1615.

[20] Diego Muñoz Camargo, *Historia de Tlaxcala*, editada por Alfredo Chavero, México, Secretaría de Fomento, 1892. Baltazar Dorantes de Carranza, *Sumaria relación de las cosas de Nueva España, con noticia individual de los descendientes de los conquistadores y primeros pobladores españoles*, la publica por primera vez el Museo Nacional de México, paleografiado del original por el señor don José María de Agreda, prólogo de Luis González Obregón, México, Impr. del Museo Nacional, 1902.

excepción de algunos como Mendieta y Torquemada, ya vistos con más sospecha pero que parecen atendibles por lo mucho de sus escritos que está dedicado a las antiguallas de los indios, los frailes cronistas tardíos no gozan de mayor crédito. Aun en el caso, más bien raro, de que un historiador actual acuda a ellos para obtener tal o cual pequeño dato (que sólo para esto se les utiliza), casi nunca lo hace sin aprovechar darle un coscorrón, tachándolo ya de "farragoso", ya de "ingenuo", ya francamente de "inútil".

Con poco que reflexione uno, advierte que los criterios para juzgar de nuestra historiografía de los siglos XVI y XVII, y para conceder y perdonar vidas según el cuadro esquemático que queda hecho en los párrafos anteriores, son, en realidad, los viejos criterios clásicos de la historia cientificista y positivista: su tan conocida crítica de las fuentes. Los valores "veracidad-testimonio" y "originalidad" son de hecho valores de la historia positivista. [21] Hacerse esta reflexión no deja de tener interés. Tiende uno a pensar que ciertas formas de historiar ya están o caducas o suficientemente desprestigiadas, después de todo lo que en el panorama de la teoría de la historia se ha dado en lo que va de nuestro siglo; pero a poco advierte que en realidad, la historiografía positivista no ha muerto, sino que subsiste, si bien vergonzante, disfrazada con las ropas de historia económica o de estructuralismo, o de lo que se quiera.

Si se acepta, aunque sea sólo en lo general, el esquema de graduación de valores que aquí se ha expuesto, es muy fácil comprender que los historiadores y cronistas mexicanos de finales del siglo XVI y principios del XVII se encuentran, frente al común de los estudiosos actuales, en bastante mala situación. No fueron veraces testigos, ni fueron los primeros en dar cuenta de la cultura prehispánica, y esto ya es suficiente para que se les conceda muy poco crédito.

Para colmo de males estos pobres historiadores tardíos tienen todavía una tacha más: la falta de interés de los temas que tratan. Aunque se encontrará en sus obras alguna referencia al suceso de la Conquista, y aunque siempre haya también algo referente a las antigüedades de los indios, no son siempre la parte más voluminosa de su obra (amén de que siempre resultan de segunda mano). El hecho de que sean religiosos apologistas de sus respectivas órdenes, o mestizos ambiciosos de reconocimiento, o descendientes de conquistadores pedigüeños de empleos acaba con lo poco que pudieran tener de prestigio. El curioso que cada día que, por casualidad, los lee, encuentra que tal

---

[21] Entre la numerosísima literatura sobre la historiografía positivista, cientificista y "crítica", puede consultarse Herry Elmer Barnes, *A History of Historical Writing*, Nueva York, Dover, 1962, cap. X, pp. 239-276; para una crítica a la crítica de fuentes de esa historia, puede consultarse la demoledora de Edmundo O'Gorman, *Crisis y porvenir de la ciencia histórica*, México, UNAM, 1947, especialmente Primera Parte, II, 3 y 4, pp. 54-100.

o cual dato está tomado de otro autor, se soba las manos de contento: queda demostrado una vez más que se trata de un plagiario indigno de crédito.

Y bien, quizá justamente las que han sido tradicionalmente consideradas deficiencias de estos historiadores tardíos puedan, con otra perspectiva, convertirse en sus cualidades.

Esto es, si no se atiende exclusivamente a su cualidad de "no testigos", y no se usa el problemático valor de "veracidad-testimonio" como único parámetro para medirlos.

Si, por otra parte, no se atiende sólo a su no originalidad; es decir, si deja de preocupar el hecho de que hayan copiado y, en cambio, preocupa el hecho, fundamentalísimo, de *cómo* copiaron. Aun en el caso de que pueda decirse que al inspirarse en otras fuentes distorsionaron la verdad, si lo que interesa no es tanto el que la hayan distorsionado, sino la forma en que la distorsionaron. (Y aquí, obviamente, queda implícito el decir que, si torcieron la verdad fue *para* encontrar otra verdad: su verdad.)

En fin, sus "defectos" pueden convertirse quizá en cualidades si se atiende, por lo tanto, a la visión que estos tardíos escritores pueden darnos, no de un pasado ya para ellos remoto, sino de su propio mundo: del mundo que les tocó vivir a fines del siglo xvi y principios del xvii. O si se atiende a la perspectiva con que ellos miraban aquellos hechos pasados, los del mundo prehispánico, los de la Conquista, los de la primera colonización y la primera evangelización, pero no tanto por lo que pueda aportarnos sobre un problemático conocimiento objetivo de ellos, sino por lo que nosotros podemos saber de esos mismos historiadores a través de sus juicios sobre los hechos pasados y presentes. Es decir, los tardíos historiadores novohispanos mendaces y plagiarios para la historiografía científica, fuentes de segunda mano —como con tanto desprecio suele decirse— pueden tal vez resultarnos muy otros si sus escritos nos sirven para concerlos a ellos mismos, para conocer y palpar la realidad que les tocó vivir y, en buena medida, construir: la realidad novohispana del tardío siglo xvi y de los primeros años del xvii. Ninguna obra de ningún historiador puede, quizá, servir para más que eso; lo cual, por cierto, no es poco servir.

Decir que este trabajo pretende sacar del olvido a los historiadores novohispanos del tardío xvi y primer xvii sería una pedantería lastimosa. Los estudiosos aquí reunidos saben muy bien que no son desconocidos. De ellos hay ediciones, algunas incluso de los últimos veinte años (si bien casi siempre muy limitadas) y pocos serán los que, trabajando la historia de la Nueva España, no hayan acudido a ellos en más de una ocasión, ya para buscar un dato, ya para precisar algún nombre o alguna fecha. Lo que aquí se pretende es sólo hacer un esfuerzo por contemplar esa historiografía bajo la nueva luz que se ha propuesto párrafos arriba. Esto es, atendiendo no a sus categorías de veracidad y originalidad según las entiende la historiografía cientificista, sino al derecho que les asistió de contemplar y opinar sobre su pasado y sobre su presente en la época en que lo hicieron. Y así, intentar por ese medio una visión nuestra de la Nueva España que ellos mismos conocieron, vivieron, odiaron y amaron.

"Quien mucho abarca poco aprieta", dice el refrán, y yo, convencido de que vale más hablar de poco todo lo que se pueda que de mucho mal, convencido de que para hacer un análisis, así sea mínimamente cuidadoso, es necesario concentrar la atención en un número limitado de cosas, intentaré llevar adelante lo que me propongo con la pequeña muestra de sólo tres autores Agustín Dávila Padilla, Diego Muñoz Camargo y Baltazar Dorantes de Carranza. La selección es tan arbitraria como pudiera serlo cualquiera otra: para mí tengo que otros tres darían resultados muy similares, puesto que a cualquier cosa puede escapar un hombre, menos a su circunstancia histórica. El único criterio de selección fue el de escoger tres personas diversas entre sí: un cronista religioso y apologético, un cacique mestizo empeñado en recalcar la importancia de sus abuelos tlaxcaltecas, y un laico ansioso de oficios y de fama. Es decir, se trata de autores de muy diversa extracción y condición, y que, por lo tanto, responden a solicitaciones diversas y están movidos por intereses (personales y de grupo) también muy diferentes entre sí. Y, sin embargo, los tres están unidos por el hecho de haber vivido un mismo momento, haber conocido una misma realidad, e incluso haber nacido los tres en la Nueva España.

EL PARAÍSO PERDIDO

La primera actitud, muy notable, que puede advertirse en los hombres novohispanos de la época a que me refiero, es la de una gran nostalgia por un pasado que ellos ya no conocieron, pero cuyos hechos, pasados de boca en boca y de crónica en crónica, adquieren en sus días un aura magnífica. La Conquista, la primera evangelización y aun con todas las reservas debidas, el pasado prehispánico en algunos casos, son momentos que nuestros cronistas hubieran deseado vivir. Dorantes, entregado al arte de embaucar mujeres, casarse y descasarse, y al de abrir antesalas imposibles, no deja de suspirar —y esto se revela en todo el tono de su libro— por la posibilidad de haber empuñado una espada en combates audaces, o de haber realizado hazañas como las que, con tanto sabor y admiración, nos cuenta de Cortés, de Alvarado o de su propio padre. [22] A Dávila se le llena la boca de relatarnos las inauditas obras de los primeros misioneros, verdaderos nuevos apóstoles a sus ojos, de hablarnos sobre sus virtudes magníficas e inalterables; con cuánto gusto habría cambiado su birrete universitario, su teología y su filosofía, y hasta su cargo de cronista de la orden [23] por haber participado en la gran aventura de la cristianización primera:

> ... quien considera lo que aquellos padres benditos hicieron y la estrecha pobreza que guardaron y el desprecio grande que de las riquezas de esta tierra tuvieron, entenderá que tornaban a brotar con grande fecundidad los hechos de los apóstoles, y que retoñecía en esta Nueva España la primera predicación del Santo Evangelio. [24]

Muñoz Camargo, por su parte, cogido en el compromiso de aceptar como buena la Conquista, se dedica a elogiar principalmente la actuación de sus antepasados tlaxcaltecas en esa aventura; sin embargo, también se las arregla para cimentar la gloria de éstos desde antes de la presencia española. Para él también el pasado es heroico, grande, envidiable. Y encuentra el modo de relatarnos con gran entusiasmo la increíble hazaña del Tlahuicole; [25] o de hablarnos asimismo de los tiempos santos de la primera iglesia mexicana; [26] pero quizá donde más sentimos la aguda nostalgia de un mundo magnífico, perdido para siempre, ya no recuperable pero siempre prestigioso y digno de ser recordado es en aquella bella frase que remata una larga evocación de las estupendas fiestas de los tlaxcaltecas anteriores a la Conquista: "no había en el mundo más que ver, lo cual todo se ha vedado por la honestidad de nuestra religión". [27] La frase contiene también otro elemento, fundamental, al que me referiré más tarde: el elemento contradicción; de una vez quiero apuntar que sería ingenuo suponer que Muñoz es falso al alabar a la honesta religión que terminó con

[22] Sobre la vida curiosa de Baltazar Dorantes de Carranza véase el apéndice a su *Sumaria relación* ... (cit. en nota 20); de Fernando Benítez, "Los criollos del xvi en el espejo de su prosa", *Historia Mexicana*, i:2 (oct.-dic. 1951); y del mismo *Los primeros mexicanos. La vida criolla en el siglo XVI.* El Colegio de México, 1953 (segunda edic., México, Era, 1962); y el artículo de Ernesto de la Torre citado en la nota 2.
[23] El capítulo general de México le encomendó la tarea de escribir la historia de la provincia en 1589, el general de los predicadores lo hizo cronista general de la orden en 1597.
[24] Fray Agustín Dávila Padilla, *Historia de la fundación y discurso de la provincia de Santiago de México, de la Orden de Predicadores, por las vidas de sus varones insignes, y casos notables de la Nueva España*, en Madrid, en casa de Pedro Madrigal, 1596, segunda edición en Bruselas, Juan de Meerbeque, 1626; ésta es la que reprodujo en México la Editorial Academia Literaria, 1955, con prólogo de Agustín Millares Carlo, y que aquí cito, p. 24.
[25] Muñoz Camargo, *op. cit.* en nota 20, pp. 125-128.
[26] Muñoz Camargo, pp. 267-269.
[27] Muñoz Camargo, pp. 135.

el esplendor antiguo. Para él era soberbio aquel mundo, pero también era buena y honesta la religión cristiana y positivo el hecho de que hubiera suspendido las viejas prácticas. No hay falsedad, sino contradicción interna en el personaje.

Quizá la cualidad príncipe de aquel mundo sesenta u ochenta años anterior a nuestros autores es su dimensión heroica. Ésa es la que le da colores de epopeya. La dimensión heroica de Tlaxcala asediada por México, siempre incólume, o la de la espada cortesiana, o la heroicidad —de otro tipo pero no de menos quilates— de los primeros misioneros. Con un dejo de sorna nos cuenta Muñoz cómo los primeros tres franciscanos, Tecto, Aora y Gante, fueron vistos como "locos" por los indios que no se entendían por qué andaban vestidos así, ni por qué procedían de modo tan extraño, ni qué pretendían realmente; pero el episodio en el fondo sirve para exaltar más lo que llegaron a hacer y el prestigio y respeto que fueron capaces de adquirir, a partir de tan humildes y extraños inicios. [28]

Aquel mundo heroico, del que nada queda, ha dejado, sin embargo, alguna especie de testimonio. Si Dorantes de Carranza se ocupa en apuntar los mitos de algunos pájaros famosos, el cuitlacochi y el huitzitzil, [29] es porque el mito es la manera en que el pasado heroico se actualiza; más que encarecer una rareza actual, los mitos de los pájaros son el testimonio moderno de una grandeza ida.

Un tiempo y una historia irrecuperables, verdadera "edad de oro". Otros tuvieron la suerte de gozarla o de sufrirla: de vivirla; nuestros autores no tienen ya más que el recuerdo. No deja de ser curioso cómo para ellos es claro que el suyo no es ya el tiempo de las hazañas; y, sin embargo, la posibilidad de acometerlas estaba ahí, en el inmenso norte al que apenas se habían hecho débiles e inconsistentes entradas, en toda la tierra caliente, apenas tocada y en tanta parte virgen a la industria y aun a la planta de otros que no fueran sus antiguos pobladores. Todavía más: en el mar, sea el Atlántico ya infestado de piratas, sea en el Pacífico —su Mar del Sur— tan desconocido todavía, la posibilidad de probar fuerzas estaba a la mano. Y estaba también, en otro orden de cosas, en las numerosísimas poblaciones indias alejadas de los centros importantes. No se trata de que ya no hubiera campo para los hombres valerosos ni de que faltaran las oportunidades para que mostraran la madera de que estaban hechos los nietos de los conquistadores. El mundo de las cosas no había cambiado tanto: los que habían cambiado eran los hombres. Eran ellos los que no tenían ya aquella dimensión heroica, e incapaces de emular a sus antepasados, esperaban sólo salvarse mágicamente, por el brillo prestado que pudie-

28 Muñoz Camargo, pp. 162-165.
29 Dorantes, *op. cit.* en nota 20, pp. 126-127.

ra tocarles en esta nueva aventura, tan de otro tipo, que era historiar el pasado. Salvarse en la aventura de la pluma, substituto de la espada.

EL MILENARISMO

Rememorar un paraíso perdido implica, por lo menos, que puesto que es perdido no existe más. A la alabanza de una edad dorada tiene que oponerse, de necesidad, un juicio menos favorable de nuestra edad actual. La contraparte es obligada y está implícita. Don Quijote, estricto contemporáneo de nuestros tres autores, empezó su discurso de los cabreros: "Dichosa edad y siglos dichosos aquellos a quien los antiguos pusieron nombre de dorados", y a un cierto momento tuvo que decir: "y no como en nuestra edad de hierro..." El solo sentimiento de que hubo una edad dorada es revelador del sentimiento de que los tiempos no son ahora tan buenos. Así, pues, la segunda actitud notable en los hombres que vivían la Nueva España setenta años después de la conquista es la apreciación negativa de ese mundo que les tocó la mala suerte de vivir.

Nuestros autores no se conforman con decir que sus tiempos no son ya tan buenos como fueron los de la Conquista o la primera evangelización. Sino que tienen un prurito especialísimo por mostrarnos lo mala que es su época. No sólo parece pobre en comparación con los pasados tiempos heroicos; más bien son aquéllos los que crecen desmesuradamente en la comparación con la actual pequeñez, con la nueva mediocridad. Pocas épocas habrán tenido deturpadores tamaños.

Diversas son las acusaciones que los criollos hacen a su tiempo. Una es sin duda la opacidad, la carencia de brillo, la falta de lo heroico y aun de lo santo. Es la intención de aquel soneto anónimo de "un práctico y aun theórico" que incluye Dorantes en su *Sumaria Relación*, "niños soldados, mozos capitanes". Las armas son ya sólo de oropel, las glorias pequeñas, los capitanes son mozos, figurines disfrazados (ya no los viejos hombres recios), ya no hay guerra verdadera, sino guerra de juego, en que combaten niños soldados, los caballeros se han acabado y quedan substituidos por mercaderes y villanos:

> ... Seco el hidalgo el labrador florece,
> y en este tiempo de trabajos grandes
> se oye, se mira, se contempla y calla. [30]

O lo que podemos leer en otro soneto recogido por el mismo Dorantes:

[30] Dorantes, pp. 115-116.

> ... caballeros de serlo deseosos,
> con toda presunción bodegoneros ... [31]

Durán, contemporáneo de nuestros autores, es movido por los mismos hilos de resentimiento hacia su época y responde en idéntica forma.

> ... estos infelices y desdichados tiempos ... las calamidades que esta fertilísima, riquísima y opulentísima tierra y la ciudad de México ha pasado y decaído, desde aquellos tiempos a acá, y la caída de su grandeza y excelencia con pérdida de tanta nobleza de que estaba poblada y acompañada y de la miseria y pobreza a que ha venido. [32]

En ese mismo orden de cosas fray Agustín Dávila Padilla se refiere a que el tiempo suyo ya no es el de lo grande, sino el de lo mediocre y pequeño. Frente a los tamaños de los viejos misioneros las órdenes no tienen más que poner sino su pequeña cotidianeidad de vicios y virtudes medianas. Mundo de lo bueno y de lo malo, pero nunca de lo grande, ni para bien ni para mal. Inclusive cuando siente la tentación de equiparar a alguno de sus modernos hermanos de religión con los antiguos dominicos, pronto reconoce que es imposible. Así, nos habla de la santidad de fray Alonso Garcés, de cómo murió por salvar las santas especies en la villa de San Ildefonso, en la tierra mixe (lo cual, por cierto, lo lleva a curiosas discusiones teológicas), y de cómo se apareció después de muerto; pero el caso es bastante doloroso: sentimos los esfuerzos que el escritor hace por convencerse a sí mismo, la lucha que mantiene, pero acaba rindiéndose. No tiene más remedio que terminar confesándose, de alguna manera, derrotado en su intento. La vida, acaba diciéndonos, "no sé que tiene" (la vida nuestra, de hoy, debe entenderse) que no deja parecer la santidad. Es poco estimada la santidad de "los que vimos y conversamos", "los que vivieron en nuestra compañía, parece que fueron como nosotros". Es decir, la mediocridad de nuestra vida, de nuestro tiempo, viene a ser como una infección que contamina todas las cosas, incluso aquéllas que —como la santidad del padre Garcés— parecían estar destinadas a algo grande. [33]

Quizá a solas con su conciencia, Dávila —y la misma actitud reflexiva corresponde también a su tiempo, que es de la reflexión y no ya el de la acción— quizá a solas con su conciencia, digo, recordaría aquello de que nos había hablado antes: que en la historia

> no hay licencia para arbitrar, sino declarando lo que fuere conjetura, para que tenga la propia libertad el que leyere: no he querido atreverme

[31] Dorantes lo cita como "soneto de un curial", p. 114.
[32] Durán, *Historia* ... (cit. en nota 17), II, p. 68.
[33] Dávila Padilla, pp. 549-560 (vida de fray Alonso Garcés), las citas en la p. 558.

a dar más circunstancias a la verdad, de las que la historia refería, contentándome con ser en la ocasión verdadero, que en las circunstancias curioso. [34]

El otro agravio —muy referido éste a su circunstancia concreta— que nuestros historiadores hacen a su tiempo es el de su pobreza. Si ha pasado el tiempo de lo heroico, también ha pasado el de la abundancia. Se entiende fácilmente que hay una estrecha relación entre ambas cosas; no todo lo que relumbra es oro, pero sí mucho de ello. No es nuestro propósito tratar en este trabajo de la contracción económica del tiempo que estudiamos; otros, que saben de eso, lo han hecho ya, y podemos creerles mientras no haya prueba en contrario. [35] Como quiera que sea, es indudable que por lo menos había en la Nueva España de entonces el desconcierto lógico en la transisión de un sistema económico a otros, con la ruina definitiva de la encomienda. Y lo que ciertamente interesa para este tema es la forma en que el novohispano de entonces resentía esa situación, por él interpretada como de terrible decaimiento y pobreza. La cita que hemos hecho del padre Durán podría servir tanto en el lugar que fue utilizada, como aquí; la tierra era "riquísima y opulentísima", y ahora "ha pasado y decaído". [36] Nuestros historiadores están plagados de referencias a ese hecho. Muñoz Camargo nos habla de cómo los ganados han "dañificado" a los indios de paz (respirando seguramente por la herida), [37] de cómo los indios entendieron la moneda de cobre como un fraude por la carencia de oro y, considerándola sin ningún valor, la arrojaron a la laguna. [38]

Dávila, al hablarnos del sedero Miguel de Zamora, nos dice que, después de hacer aquí fortuna y volver a España fingiéndose pobre, regresó a México para tratar de rehacer su dinero (pues el primero lo había dejado a su padre), y "halló la tierra delgada, y las ganancias más cortas", [39] tanto que, arruinado, tomó asco a las cosas de este mundo . . . y decidió hacerse lego predicador.

Ahí se trata sólo de algo incidental, pero en otras ocasiones el problema es tratado con mayor amplitud, incluso en casos que importan para la santidad de la orden. Fray Tomás del Rosario (o de San Juan, como se llamó primero) se oponía a que los conventos dominicanos tuvieran bienes, así fuera en común, por lo que podía introducir de desarreglo, y por un prurito de atenerse a las constituciones originales:

[34] Dávila, p. 103.
[35] Woodrow W., Borah, *New Spain's Century of Depression*, Berkeley y Los Ángeles, 1943 (Iberoamericana, 35).
[36] Durán, cit. en nota 32.
[37] Muñoz Camargo, p. 265.
[38] Muñoz Camargo, p. 266.
[39] Dávila Padilla, p. 473.

> Consuelo es acordarnos de aquellos buenos deseos que tuvo el bendito padre fray Tomás con otros de aquellos padres antiguos: pero si hubieran vivido algunos años más, hubieran experimentado la necesidad de la tierra, y cómo su abundancia primera fue flor de maravilla, que aunque la causó entonces con la sobra, le tenemos ahora todos conocida la falta. Con la muerte de los indios, y con el copioso número de españoles que todos los años vienen en cargazones de España, está la tierra tan delgada que ya que no ha quebrado la devoción... han faltado las limosnas, y obligado a los conventos a que tengan rentas de qué sustentarse... [40]

Esta justificación, un poco reparable, del por qué empezaron a tener rentas los conventos, al mismo tiempo que es una acusación de la pobreza de la tierra, es interesante porque resulta una confesión de parte: el autor reconoce implícitamente que la santidad ya no era de los mismos quilates, porque, al fin y al cabo, si el reino empobrecía ¿qué importaba para los que habían hecho vocación de pobre? Es también, puede verse, una referencia a la edad dorada, y además, interesa porque ahí empieza a asomarse el culpable: los gachupines que todos los años vienen en cargazón de España.

Dorantes de Carranza, siempre tan definitivo y exagerado, no precisa más que de una frase para dejar contundentemente sentada su apreciación sobre la ruina en que ha caído la Nueva España: "ya hay más pobres en las Indias que en Castilla la Vieja, Montañas o Galicia" [41] ¿Se necesita más para explicar hasta dónde han ido a parar las cosas?

La Nueva España no es ya lo que fue, la Nueva España, antes "flor de maravilla" no es ahora más que "tierra flaca", venida a la pobreza y miseria. Pero eso no es todo. La visión negativa que nuestros criollos tenían de su mundo y de su tiempo va más lejos, no sólo las cosas están mal, sino que irán de mal en peor. Todo se acabará, la consumación está cercana.

> Siempre lo bueno ha ido en disminución en todo el mundo, y los principios han sido más fervorosos en todo lo loable. [42]

Nos dice Dávila. Antes "daba Dios tan liberalmente", y ahora parece retirarlo todo. Para el dominico la más clara muestra de este fin próximo es el acabamiento de los indios. Y es indudable que no sólo para él, sino para todos sus contemporáneos, los estragos de las pestes, terribles, que asolaron a México de la segunda mitad del siglo XVI, creaban la idea de un fin ineluctable. La peste de 1545, primero, luego el tabardillo de 1558, y después la más terrible de 1576 y 1577, seguidas

---

[40] Dávila Padilla, p. 368.
[41] Dorantes, p. 260.
[42] Dávila Padilla, p. 148.

de otras parciales como la de 1591 y 1592, la continua disminución de los indios, daban una especie de certeza sobre la destrucción total.

Se recordaron entonces las profecías sobre la destrucción de las Indias: la de fray Bartolomé de las Casas, la de don Vasco de Quiroga, la de fray Domingo de Betanzos. La de este último es la que con más riqueza glosa fray Agustín. Según ella pronto no quedaría ni memoria del color y la figura de los primeros habitantes de la Nueva España; si atendemos a lo que está pasando, "hallaremos con evidencia que se va cumpliendo", y añade, agudo, "con más priesa que quisieran los encomenderos..."[43] El derrotismo lo invade todo, pues tanta desgracia no puede tener causas sobre las cuales haya algún arbitrio posible: por eso se echa por delante la profecía, que implica un futuro ya delineado de antemano.

"Decía también el fundador que cuanto los españoles trazasen para bien de los indios, todo se les había de convertir en mal, y las trazas de su argumento habían de redundar en su disminución."[44] Y trae a cuento el viejo refrán: si la piedra va al cántaro, mal para el cántaro, y si el cántaro va a la piedra, mal para el cántaro. Seguramente algunos de los pasajes más conmovedoramente bellos de las páginas del cronista de los predicadores son aquellos en que relata las desgracias de las epidemias, cuando "todos los accidentes, aunque fuesen entre sí contrarios, concordaban en quitar la vida a los indios", que "hallaban la muerte tan cruel enemiga, que de puro miedo se postraban los vivos, antes que les acometiese". Y nos cuenta, en fin, de qué modo, ante lo inútil de los esfuerzos por aliviarlos, "encendíanse con rabiosa furia, por verse llevar tan atropellados de la muerte, sin que su enfermedad se atreviese con los españoles",[45] y trataban de inficionarlos arrojando los cadáveres a las fuentes y los acueductos.

Todo lo que se hiciese por los indios redundaría en su contra, pues así estaba dicho en la profecía. De esta manera, las congregaciones en pueblos, que se impusieron justamente en el paso entre los dos siglos, aunque pensadas para su beneficio, tendrían un resultado contrario; Dávila, agudo observador, y conocedor cierto del carácter de sus evangelizados, observa que

así como se conserva el pece en el agua y el ciervo en el monte, así el indio en su natural es amicísimo de la soledad de su vivienda... No hay para el venado aflicción de asirle de los pies, como para el indio la de detenerle en poblado fuera de su nacimiento y querencia.[46]

[43] Dávila Padilla, p. 100.
[44] Dávila Padilla, p. 102.
[45] Dávila Padilla, pp. 517-518.
[46] Dávila Padilla, p. 102.

En fin, el teólogo cronista, pronto obispo, indudablemente conmovido de tantas desgracias, que de alguna manera le llegaban muy de cerca y le escocían en carne propia, y también, siempre reflexivo y conocedor de lo que a los indios se debía, nos dice en uno de sus párrafos más conmovedores, que seguramente la profecía de Betanzos era

> para avivar nuestro cuidado en doctrinarlos y regalarlos, pues faltándonos ellos nos ha de faltar la ocasión de agradecerles el bien y riqueza que sus tierras nos han dado: y es bien agradecerles con enseñanzas y buen tratamiento, lo que si se acaba, no podremos. [47]

Baltazar Dorantes de Carranza, seglar atrabancado y envidioso, está lejos de tener en sus reflexiones la conciencia y la madurez y mesura del dominico. Sin embargo —y casi se sorprende uno de encontrarlo— también se conmueve de tantas desdichas de los indios, y también en cierto sentido parece hacerse solidario de ellas, y hace la defensa de "estos miserables indios". [48] Recuerda a Las Casas (cuya *Apologética historia* conoció y aún poseyó en manuscrito) y lo alaba. Sin embargo, su mayor preocupación no llega a ser la del acabamiento de la raza, sino la desgracia de la tierra. Tanto la quiere, como lo demuestra (y más adelante veremos cómo), que en arranques contradictorios lanza sus famosas imprecaciones a las Indias. Éstas son bastante conocidas para citarlas aquí; sin embargo, baste recordar ciertos de sus apelativos que demuestran a saciedad esa furia impotente y ese amor-odio a que también me referiré después: "es llegada la sazón donde luce más el engaño y la mentira", "confusión de tropiezos", "alcahuete de haraganes", "banco donde todos quiebran", "hinchazón de necios", "burdel de buenos, locura de cuerdos, destrucción de la virtud", "anzuelo de flacos, casa de locos, algunas cualidades pegadas con alfileres", "mal francés, dibujo del infierno", "tráfago de behetría, igualdad en el trato, comunidad de todos lados", "¿no veis cómo vuestros bienes, vuestro oro, vuestra plata y vuestras piedras preciosas no se perpetúan en esta tierra?" [49]
Otro tipo de desastres contribuyen a crear en nuestros autores, y en los hombres de su tiempo, la idea del acabamiento próximo: los tres nos relatan con más o menos detalles, pero siempre con dolor y desesperación, los desastres sufridos en el mar frente a los corsarios, o los saqueos de puertos a manos de piratas, o —sobre todo— los desastres de la Florida. [50] El relato que hace Dávila del desastre de 1553 y del triste fin que encontraron los españoles a manos de los indios es de tal

[47] Dávila Padilla, p. 103.
[48] Dorantes, p. 256.
[49] Dorantes, pp. 112-114.
[50] Dávila Padilla, pp. 184 ss.

manera vivo y tiene tal fuerza de evocación, que uno no puede menos
que recordar a Tucídides hablándonos de la derrota siciliana de Atenas. [51]

La idea de un acabamiento próximo y de una pérdida de la antigua
heroicidad y grandeza, surgida en primer lugar de la reflexión sobre
la circunstancia inmediata, también se combina con un orden más amplio de sucesos. Así, en nuestros autores surge la idea de la caída y
disminución ya no sólo de la Nueva España, ni siquiera sólo de las
Indias, sino de todo el imperio español.

Este sentimiento se apodera de Muñoz Camargo en el breve espacio
que dedica a los robos y tropelías cometidas por los corsarios en ambos
océanos ante la impotencia de las armadas españolas. [52] Dorantes recuerda a Las Casas y sus amenazas sobre España, que parecen irse
cumpliendo. [53] Dávila Padilla también encuentra que la profecía del
defensor de los indios se va realizando, cuando habla del saco de Santo
Domingo y del de Cartagena, y, más reflexivo, entiende que

> Pocos años ha que tenía España guerra... y el turco le temía, y Alemania se humillaba y Francia dejaba preso su rey y Flandes pedía paz:
> y ahora una mujercilla hereje, infame y deshonesta trae confusa la Cristiandad y hacen lances sus soldados y navíos tan a nuestra costa como
> hemos visto... [54]

LOS CRIOLLOS DESPOSEÍDOS

Si se tiene una visión tan pesimista del momento que se vive, es
normal que se trate de dar una explicación. La Nueva España va a la
ruina, no es ni sombra de su pasado glorioso ni de su riqueza. ¿Quién
es el culpable? Nuestros autores encuentran dos tipos de razones a esta
situación: unas que pudiéramos llamar inmanentes y otra, trascendente.
Si esta tierra indiana ha decaído hasta su actual estado, eso es debido
al poco producto de las minas, a la disminución de los indios, a los
daños del ganado, pero, sobre todo, a la presencia de los gachupines. El
término, en esa aplicación, data de entonces, y de entonces data también la primera inquina entre criollos y peninsulares. El recién llegado
es la peor peste que tiene que padecer el criollo: viene a desplazarlo,
a aprovecharse de las riquezas del país, a desbancarlo de preeminencias y
de oficios. Los herederos de los conquistadores y de los primeros pobladores, que, como dice Dorantes "ya son casi unos", [55] se consideran los legítimos dueños del reino y se sienten desposeídos abusiva-

---

[51] Dávila Padilla, p. 276.
[52] Muñoz Camargo, p. 276.
[53] Dorantes, p. 255.
[54] Dávila Padilla, p. 341.
[55] Dorantes, p. 12.

mente. Ha surgido ya, además, lo que pudiéramos llamar un estilo de vida criollo, [56] con alguna forma de refinamiento, que resiente la rudeza de los peninsulares.

> Viene de España por la mar salobre
> a nuestro mexicano domicilio
> un hombre tosco, sin ningún auxilio,
> de salud falto y de dinero pobre.

Así, surge un mutuo desprecio entre los nacidos aquí y los venidos de fuera:

> Y desprecia después el lugar donde
> adquirió estimación, gusto y haberes
> ¡Y tiraba la jábega en San Lúcar! [57]

Ya veíamos párrafos arriba cómo el moderado agustino Dávila atribuía parte del enflaquecimiento de la tierra al "copioso número de españoles que todos los años vienen en cargazones de España" (y nótese todo lo peyorativo que la expresión "cargazones" puede tener). Pero sin duda es Dorantes de Carranza quien muestra más a gritos ese resentimiento. Después del triste resultado de la conjura del marqués del Valle, hay un convencimiento de que todo está perdido en ese sentido, y de que la Nueva España ha quedado subyugada definitivamente a los empleados reales; él mismo recomienda al marqués Pedro que, "si es cuerdo", no venga a las Indias, "porque esta tierra no sufre más señor que al que aquí nos gobierna por su majestad". [58] Ante la impotencia, pues, no queda más que el resentimiento que mana en tantas de las páginas de su *Relación*: "...sangre derramada y servicios personales y en hijos del reino, premio merecen sin que advenedizos se le frusten". La Nueva España es a sus ojos "madre de extraños, abrigo de foraxidos y delincuentes", "madrastra de vuestros hijos y destierro de vuestros naturales, azote de propios... risa de los virtuosos..." Y alaba el establecimiento del Santo Oficio porque la tierra está ahora llena "de diferentes y ajenas naciones, muchas gentes de linajes y tierras sospechosas..." E incluye una queja anónima en octavas:

> Madrastra nos has sido rigurosa,
> y dulce madre pía a los estraños;
> con ellos de tus bienes generosa,
> con nosotros repartes de tus daños.
> Ingrata patria, adiós, vive dichosa
> con hijos adoptivos largos años,

[56] Sobre esto véase Fernando Benítez, *Los primeros mexicanos*, cit. en nota 22.
[57] Dorantes, p. 114.
[58] Dorantes, p. 102.

que con tu disfavor fiero, importuno,
consumiendo nos vamos uno a uno. [59]

LA GRAN CULPA

Todas estas razones inmanentes, entre las que sobresale tanto la presencia de los extraños y advenedizos, sin embargo, a pesar de su importancia, no llegan a explicar el cúmulo de males y desgracias: "¿do están los siglos de oro? ¿qué es del pago, / que sólo veo cenizas de Cartago? / ... ¿Qué daño es este que tras ti camina, / que tan trocada estás de lo que fuiste?" [60] Ante la imposibilidad de una explicación suficiente, los hombres novohispanos tienen que acudir a causas trascendentes. Aparece así el sentimiento de que algo, desde los primeros tiempos, estuvo mal, de que en la Conquista misma, tan positiva como se quiera, existió alguna tacha fundamental. Existió un pecado primero, una culpa original, que comprometió para siempre la existencia de la Nueva España. Sólo así puede entenderse que los conquistadores mismos hayan sido desgraciados, y que la maldición se perpetúe en sus hijos y sus nietos.

De paso vale la pena aquí hacer siquiera una referencia al problema que plantea el providencialismo de nuestros autores, de sus contemporáneos, de los que les antecedieron y de los que les sucedieron. Es muy común en los críticos modernos hacer una referencia más o menos burlona al providencialismo de los viejos autores, y con eso condenarlos definitivamente como incapaces de comprender los fenómenos históricos. Sin embargo, al mirar con algún cuidado el asunto, puede uno advertir que toda referencia a un destino dictado desde lo alto no necesariamente puede tener un mismo sentido. De hecho el providencialismo no es más el reconocimiento de un mundo trascendente al hombre, de una realidad superior de la cual él depende; pero las posibilidades de interpretación a esos dictados superiores son infinitas, aun dentro de un mundo cristiano, y aun dentro de un mundo católico. De tal modo que la referencia a una instancia superior de ningún modo implica el negarse a dar una explicación a los fenómenos históricos mismos, por más que esa explicación se entienda como la interpretación de los designios providenciales. Y esa explicación-interpretación nos da, necesariamente, la actitud de quien la hace frente a las situaciones mismas que trata de entender. Baste, en apoyo de lo dicho, considerar la diferencia que hay entre los primeros autores de nuestro siglo XVI, para quienes la providencia había abierto el mundo americano con el fin de que, evangelizado, pudiera ser el espejo más perfecto del

[59] Dorantes, pp. 18-23.
[60] Dorantes, *ib*.

ideal cristiano, con la de un Muñoz Camargo, para quien la providencia tenía "reservados" a los tlaxcaltecas para que contribuyeran a la destrucción del reino del demonio, o con la interpretación a que ahora me refiero sobre el acabamiento de la Nueva España.

En la charnela entre los dos siglos, pues, los criollos, sintiéndose desahuciados, entienden que hubo una culpa original en el hecho mismo que da nacimiento a la Nueva España. La Conquista fue, en sí, un hecho positivo. Esto es innegable: trajo el evangelio a estas tierras, dio la posibilidad de la redención a tantas naciones que estaban engañadas por el demonio. Dios indudablemente dispuso el descubrimiento de las Indias y su conquista para extender la redención a todo el género humano. Pero los hombres que llevaron eso a cabo, como servidores de los designios providenciales, no aceptaron humildemente su papel, sino que venían llenos de ambición y de crueldad. Nuestros historiadores empiezan a advertir que esa bella época heroica por la que tanto suspiran es también una época de violencia, de vicio, de crueldad, de ambición desmedida, de traición. La providencia, que había elegido a sus servidores, los castiga, y con ellos a sus descendientes y a toda la tierra: "...porque [dice Dorantes] predicar el Evangelio con la spada en la mano y derramando sangre, es cosa tan temerosa que parece acá, al juicio humano, que sus descendientes van haciendo penitencia desta soltura". [61] Los fines fueron buenos, pero los modos malos y errados.

Por eso Las Casas, el gran impugnador de los modos como fue llevada adelante la Conquista, cobra en estos fines del siglo XVI una gran importancia: todos lo citan y lo glosan. Dorantes, que poseyó y perdió después un manuscrito de Fray Bartolomé, dice, siempre tan exagerado, que "diera por él no sólo dineros, pero la sangre de mis brazos". [62]

Durán censura en varios pasajes las crueldades de Cortés y de su hueste en Cholula, y lo injusto de la prisión de Moctezuma, [63] y en general la ambición de los conquistadores. [64] Dávila Padilla encuentra que "es afrenta a la nobilísima y cristianísima nación española el que hayan salido de ella tales monstruos inhumanos...". [65] Refiriéndose a la matanza del templo mayor relata que "en sus cantares que dicen en sus mitotes y danzas (que son como romances de los españoles) lamentan el día de hoy esta pérdida y no les faltará de la memoria, ni el sentimiento de los corazones, hasta que del todo se acaben", [66] y

[61] Dorantes, p. 17.
[62] Dorantes, p. 256.
[63] Durán, *Historia*..., II, pp. 30-36.
[64] Durán, *Historia*..., II, pp. 48-49 y 67-68.
[65] Dávila Padilla, p. 178.
[66] Dávila Padilla, p. 318.

agrega que, "nosotros", por el sólo hecho de ser hombres, sentimos la fuerza de esa injusticia.

En Baltazar Dorantes de Carranza aparece muy claro cómo la gran culpa, la culpa trascendente, se va componiendo de culpas individuales, que tienen su castigo individual, y luego un castigo colectivo. Nos relata la vida heroica pero pecaminosa de Alvarado, y el fin que, como consecuencia, tienen él y su estirpe. [67] El desastrado fin que tuvieron los orgullosos, hermosos y riquísimos hermanos Ávila también es explicado por Suárez de Peralta por la falta que cometieron los padres. [68] Dorantes alaba por un lado a Cortés como hombre heroico, pío, honrado, "otros", en cambio deben llamarse más "fures, ladrones, porque hacían lo que hace hoy el inglés, enemigo común", que es robar pueblos, cambiar cuentas por oro y arrear a la gente a trabajar en las minas y en los campos. Y la venganza divina está presente en todo momento: si la perpetuidad de las encomiendas no se consiguió fue "por estos rastros y malos tratamientos que hicieron a los indios". A fin de cuentas el mismo Cortés resulta culpable. No podía ser de otro modo; como capitán, su pecado es mayor, y no sólo, sino que sus traiciones y sus malos procederes se extienden a su generación personal (la desgracia del segundo marqués) y a toda su hueste y la descendencia de ella. Así como el pecado del rey Edipo se extiende a toda la ciudad, del mismo modo la culpa del caudillo es castigada en el reino que fundó: de hecho la idea de la falta se concentra en el capitán, del mismo modo que en él se concentra la idea de la empresa misma de la conquista. Dorantes encuentra que sólo él "hizo mejor su hacienda que los otros conquistadores... Y para mí, Dios me lo perdone si miento, sospecho que en los secretos no les fue tan buen tercero ni padrino..." [69]

La traición de Cortés a Narváez es también muestra de esa podredumbre que iba contaminando a toda la empresa conquistadora. [70] En fin, el criollo acude a la cita poética para dar mayor peso a su idea (y cabe decir, de paso, que la inclusión de tantos trozos poéticos tiene para él, más que el sentido de "agradar" a que se refiere en alguna ocasión, el de dar mayor fuerza a su dicho: la forma poética prestigia lo que se dice, y digamos, es capaz de hacer más verdad a la verdad):

> ...que se atribuye a vos alguna culpa,
> culpa que ya jamás tendrá disculpa

[67] Dorantes, pp. 25 ss.
[68] Juan Suárez de Peralta, *Noticias históricas de la Nueva España (Tratado del descubrimiento de Indias y su conquista... y de los virreyes y gobernadores que las han gobernado...)*, editada por Justo Zaragoza, Madrid, 1878. *La conjuración de Martín Cortés y otros temas*, selección de Agustín Yáñez, México, UNAM, 1945, pp. 49-53.
[69] Dorantes, p. 237.
[70] Dorantes, p. 15.

Eso, en fin, es la verdadera causa de que

> ...sólo a ti, triste México, ha faltado
> lo que a nadie en el mundo le es negado
> ...llorosa Nueva Spaña, que deshecha
> te vas en llanto y duelo consumiendo,
> vente mis tristes ojos tan strecha,
> va el pernicioso daño así cundiendo
> ...de tiempo en tiempo siempre a más tristeza,
> en más miserias, hambres y pobreza.
> ¿...de dolor en dolor a peor estado
> qué te condena ya el precioso hado? [71]

La alabanza de la tierra

En las páginas anteriores se ha ido mostrando la visión tan profundamente negativa que los hombres de esta tierra, vividos en el paso entre los siglos XVI y XVII, tuvieron de su mundo y de su tiempo. Y se han mostrado también las consecuencias y las implicaciones y explicaciones que tal visión traía consigo. Hasta ahí todo aparece, espero, con una cierta coherencia. Pero ¿qué pensar cuando el mismo Dorantes, después de desfogarse en las imprecaciones que hemos transcrito arriba y de entregarse al más profundo pesimismo, encuentra, apenas unas páginas más adelante de su *Relación*, que México es "tan grande y tan de ver como lo mayor que hay en Spaña ni otras provincias del mundo, y en absoluto lo mayor y mejor de las Indias"? [72] Se trata, creo, de esa feroz contradicción en que se debaten nuestros autores, y con ellos —debemos entenderlo así— todo el mundo novohispano coetáneo. Mientras por un lado hay esa consideración pesimista y oscura de su patria, y esa añoranza de la edad dorada, por otro empieza la carrera desenfrenada de la alabanza ditirámbica. Mayores horrores que los que ellos dijeron de México difícilmente podrán encontrarse y, simultáneamente, empieza la apología desenfrenada. La actitud contradictoria se explica porque los hombres de esa época se sentían realmente abandonados, perdidos, insatisfechos de su situación; sin embargo tienen la necesidad de afianzarse a algo, de robustecerse e incluso definirse frente al mundo: de ahí la alabanza, el ditirambo, la apología. De ahí, en una palabra, el orgullo criollo y novohispano.

> ¿...Qué ciudad hay en el mundo que tenga más lindas y graciosas entradas y salidas, ni más llenas de hermosos campos y campiñas odoríferas, llenas de todas estas flores, y claveles, y árboles y frescura...?

---

[71] Dorantes, pp. 18-23.
[72] Dorantes, p. 115.

...Tuviera bien que decir Plinio si resucitara, de las cosas naturales más en novedad e monstruosidad que en todas las provincias del mundo ... [73]

Esto nos dice Dorantes de Carranza, y encuentra que todas las cosas de las Indias son de milagro, y que desde la naturaleza hasta los hombres, nada hay mejor en el mundo que lo de su tierra.

Muñoz Camargo discute sobre si es mejor la carne nuestra que la de los ganados de España, y termina diciendo, con gran desprecio, que aquí la abundancia es tal que ni se fija uno en la calidad, mientras que en la península la escasez hace que cualquier pedazo de res les sepa a gloria. [74]

El reflexivo y mesurado Dávila Padilla también encuentra —no podía no ser— lugar para la apología. Le parece que conforme el grano se siembre en tierra fértil, así suele ser estimada la tierra por sus frutos, que la Nueva España y especialmente la provincia de México gozan de los más piadosos cielos, y del mejor temple que hay en el mundo; de tal modo que no es de extrañar que México comenzara "a dar flores de gallardos ingenios y frutos de obras virtuosas". [75] No tiene empacho en decirnos, después de lamentarse de los perdidos tiempos heroicos y gloriosos de la evangelización, que "después acá se han subido a más primor y perfección" las cosas. Y en fin, en un arranque de entusiasmo poco común en él, venir a decirnos que "quisiera yo que los aires de México volaran por todo el mundo, pudiendo decir lo que han oído". [76]

Para darnos cuenta de que si el paso entre los dos siglos es la época de las visiones negativas, también es la de los elogios, baste recordar que la *Grandeza mexicana* de Bernardo de Balbuena se editó precisamente en el año de 1604. Mayor elogio de México no podía hacerse, y sin embargo, a Dorantes le parece que se queda corto, no sea más que porque no se refiere a las provincias de la Nueva España. [77]

Se trata, pues, de esa contradicción inherente e indescifrable para ellos mismos. Un caso típico de ella es la consideración del indio: se le alaba y se le injuria simultáneamente, y no acaba uno de saber qué es lo que piensan de los habitantes naturales del reino. Ya hemos visto cómo ante el desastre de las pestes se compadecen de ellos y aun se solidarizan con su desgracia. En otras ocasiones se refieren con entusiasmo a sus glorias anteriores a la Conquista, y a sus excelentes cualidades naturales; y todo esto no obsta para que, a renglón seguido, se expresen de los indios con un profundo desprecio.

[73] Dorantes, pp. 125-126 y 116.
[74] Muñoz Camargo, p. 262.
[75] Dávila Padilla, p. 519.
[76] Dávila Padilla, p. 382.
[77] Dorantes, p. 116.

Dávila exalta sus virtudes en muy numerosas ocasiones, los cree capaces de llegar a hacer obras de mucha estimación, y aun en algún caso encuentra que son más virtuosos que los españoles; hace también el elogio de la lengua náhuatl, de sus elegancias y derivaciones y de lo retóricos que son los indios en la significación de sus metáforas.[78] Pero todo eso no obsta que otras muy numerosas ocasiones se exprese de ellos con profundo desprecio, como gente que tiene "corazón de piedra", flacos y de corto ingenio, y con quienes es necesaria una infinita paciencia, ya por su carácter novelero "como de niños", ya porque dadas sus pocas luces necesitan la comida de la doctrina no sólo sazonada, "sino casi en la primera digestión".[79] Muñoz Camargo hace también el gran elogio de la lengua —que desde luego él hablaba corrientemente— como "la más amplia y copiosa que se ha hallado; después de la dignidad es suave y amorosa y en sí muy señoril y de gran presunción, compendiosa y fácil y dócil, que no se le halla fin ni cabo...".[80] Gran parte de su obra está encaminada a exaltar las virtudes y grandezas de los indios, especialmente de sus antepasados tlaxcaltecas. Pero en él también se da la contradicción a la que parece que ninguno de sus contemporáneos podría escapar. Después de tantas alabanzas, encuentra que

El desmentirse unos a otros no lo tenían en nada, ni por punto de honra, ni lo recibían por afrenta. Esta nación es muy vanagloriosa... es gente cobarde a solas, pusilánime y cruel, y acompañada, con los españoles son demonios, atrevidos y osados... carecen de razón y de honra según nuestro modo, tienen los términos de su honra por otro modo muy apartado del nuestro... son grandes mentirosos y tramposos, aunque hay de todo...[81]

Véase, pues, cómo estos hombres, cogidos en una contradicción insuperable, repudian su mundo y tiempo, pero —y quizá por eso mismo— empiezan a exaltarlo fuera de toda mesura. Es una exaltación que de algún modo se acepta como retórica y metáfora (y esto es precisamente lo que tiene de curioso), pero no por eso deja de tener una realidad. Todo el resto del siglo XVII y buena parte del XVIII se desarrollará increíblemente esa forma de hacer. Bástenos aquí indicar que la generación de la que estamos tratando es la que señala, justamente, la transición entre el mundo de la acción del siglo XVI y el de la retórica de la centuria siguiente. Por ese su sentido de transición es una generación crítica: y lo es en dos sentidos, tanto porque inicia una "revisión" de las bases de la Nueva España echadas por sus abuelos (y en este sentido piénsese por un momento en la desconfianza con

---

[78] Dávila Padilla, pp. 64, 112, 131, 256-258.
[79] Dávila Padilla, pp. 423, 479, 505, 547.
[80] Muñoz Camargo, p. 25, también en p. 160.
[81] Muñoz Camargo, p. 143.

que los Mendieta, Torquemada, Grijalva o el mismo Dávila veían los resultados de la evangelización), como por qué está ella misma en crisis. De ahí su desconcierto, su indecisión, su desencanto. Es la generación de los hombres reflexivos; pero su misma reflexión los condenaba a la inactividad, los paralizaba, como, contemporáneamente a ellos, al príncipe danés de la obra de Shakespeare. Tanto piensan sobre su tierra, su naturaleza, sus animales y sus habitantes, que acaban no sabiendo qué pensar. Tanto cavilaron sobre su historia y sus circunstancias que llegaron a actitudes contradictorias acerca de ellas. Tanto se preguntaron, en fin, sobre sí mismos, que terminaron no sabiendo quiénes eran ni a dónde iban. Es una generación sin estímulos, sin seguridad, sin ideas definidas, sin empresas por las que luchar.

Por último, no quisiera terminar sin hacer notar que si bien estos hombres tienen tal actitud y tal comportamiento debido a la especialísima circunstancia en que se encontraban, participan, más allá de la Nueva España, de un tiempo y de una circunstancia no sólo local, sino general, por lo menos, al mundo católico de la Contrarreforma. He hablado aquí de desencanto, de desasosiego, de pesimismo, de incertidumbre, de reflexión, de crítica, de temor, de contradicciones. Éstas son, entre otras, las características de ese curioso mundo europeo de la segunda mitad del siglo XVI, que cada vez con más atención se trata de definir en oposición, por un lado, al Renacimiento, y por otro la época barroca: el mundo del *manierismo*. [82] Y si hay algún término que pueda definir la actitud que he tratado de esbozar en los párrafos que anteceden, es justamente el término de *manieristas*. La Europa de la segunda mitad del siglo XVI se encontraba también falta de seguridad, al garete, desconcertada e indecisa. También para ella había sido un fracaso las grandes empresas intentadas en el Renacimiento. He citado aquí a Cervantes y a Shakespeare, lo mismo podría hacer traído a cuento a Montaigne o a Lope de Vega, todos ellos expresión de la cultura manierista. De nuestros tres historiadores y de sus contemporáneos podríamos decir que participan de una especial forma de manierismo, dependiente de su muy particular situación, de la misma manera que los pintores o arquitectos de su época participan de un especial modo de arte manierista. En todo caso, la Nueva España abandonaba definitivamente los sueños del siglo XVI y sus empresas, pero todavía no tenía una idea clara de quién era ni de cuál sería su suerte, del mismo modo que la Europa de ese tiempo, dejados atrás los ideales del alto Renacimiento, tampoco era todavía capaz de definirse en términos de conciencia.

[82] Entre las diversas caracterizaciones del fenómeno manierista que se han hecho últimamente, yo aceptaría como más válida (y en ella pienso al escribir este párrafo, a pesar de que no coincido en todo con él) la de Arnold Hauser: *Mannerism. The crisis of the Renaissance and the origin of modern art*, Londres, Routledge & K. Paul, 1965.

MANY CONQUESTS: SOME TRENDS AND SOME CHALLENGES IN MEXICAN HISTORIOGRAPHY (1945-69): THE SIXTEENTH AND SEVENTEENTH CENTURIES

JOHN LEDDY PHELAN

The obvious fact of the history and the historiography of this period is the conquest and its long-range cultural consequences. Since 1945 historians have become increasingly aware that the conquest was a process of cultural *mestizaje*. Ideologically speaking, the conquest was a "double conquest". The conquerors and the conquered influenced each other reciprocally. It is this context which has provided the framework for much of the significant history of Hapsburg México published since the end of World War II.

This paper makes no pretense to a complete coverage of the literature in a quantitative sense. Its purpose is the more modest one of focusing attentions on some of the major new trends as reflected in a series of books that I consider to be representative. Some attention is also given to the challenges of the immediate future. Hence the criterian to some extent, at least, is subjective. Some may call it opinionated. Therefore this essay may provoke controversy. Hopefully more light than heat will ensue.

No attention will be paid to the republication of important primary sources unless those editions contain substantive prologues.

THE "DEMOGRAPHIC" CONQUEST

The central fact of early Mexican colonial history is demographic in nature. How many Indians were there in 1519 and what happened to the population curve between 1519 and 1700? The history of Hapsburg México can not be written without attempting to answer these questions. The institutional, the cultural, the religious, the economic and even the artistic developments of these two centuries were molded to a significant degree by the changes in the Indian population and the growth of the European and mestizo communities.

Demographic estimates are sharply divergent. Don Ángel Rosenblat has given us no absolute population figures. His concern has been to delimit the trends and to analyze their causes. His thesis is that the Indian population in the sixteenth century remained essentially static. There was a slow replacement and absortion in mixed bloods rather

than massive destruction. [1] His arguments are founded on a technique
of textual criticism developed by institutional and legal historians in
Spain prior to 1936. This methodology consists of a complex series
of rejections, selections and alternate interpretations of documents.
As Woodrow. W. Borah (admittedly a not disinterested observer) has
pointed out, "Unfortunately, as the technique is used in this essay,
scholars can disagree endlessly about which source is reliable, which
ought to be discarded, which interpretation of the text is correct and
so on." [2]

Señor Rosenblat is the most articulate opponent of the Berkeley
school of Mexican colonial demography. In a remarkable series of
monographs the first one of which was published in 1948 by Lesley
Byrd Simpson and Sherburne Cook, Cook and Borah have presented
us with some startling conclusions. In 1948 the Cook-Simpson estimate
for the Indian population in 1519 was 11,000,000 with a drastic decline
to about 1,500,000 by 1650. A gradual recovery took place in the eighteenth century until in 1793 the Indian population had climbed to
3,700,000. The 1963 Borah-Cook estimate has raised the preconquest
population to an approximate figure of 25,200,000 million. The demographic nadir was reached in 1605 when the Indian population had
declined to about 1,075,000. [3]

The Berkeley method is statistical reconstruction and verification
based on a sophisticated use of the tribute rolls and other quantitative
data which are amazingly plentiful by the middle of the sixteenth
century.

My confidence in the findings of the Berkeley school rests in part
on my own research in the history of ideas. The Franciscan chronicler
Gerónimo de Mendieta, was a practical man who knew how to count and
who likewise held positions of leadership in the Franciscan order. He
was also a Franciscan mystic who was deeply troubled by the drastic
diminution of the Indian population which occurred during his residence in New Spain between 1555 and 1596. His interpretation of the
acute demographic crisis was personal and subjective. He saw it as an
apocalyptical catastrophe. [4] His contemporary, Friar Bernardino de

---

[1] Angel Rosenblat, *La población de América en 1492: Viejos y nuevos cálculos*
(México, El Colegio de México, 1967). An earlier edition was published in
Buenos Aires in 1945.

[2] Woodrow W. Borah's review of Rosenblat in *Hispanic-American Historical
Review*, August, 1968, p. 475.

[3] The first volume of the Berkeley school was published by Cook and Simpson
in 1948 in the Ibero-American series of the University of California Press. In the
same series volumes 43 (1960), 44 (1960), 45 (1963), 50 (1968) Borah and
Cook have published their major demografic findings.

[4] John Leddy Phelan, *The Millennial Kingdom of the Franciscans in the New*

Sahagún, was equally explicit about the drastic decline of the Indian population, but he refused to give an apocalyptical interpretation to that event. [5] Sahagún envisaged the future of New Spain as a community of mestizos rather than Indians. He turned out to be an accurate prophet.

Charles Gibson in his study of the valley of México agrees with the essential soundness of the Cook-Borah thesis. So does José Miranda. [6]

In dealing with colonial demography there is no alternative but to employ a statistical and quantitative approach. We have an abundant amount of data that lends itself to quantification. It could be that some of the Borah-Cook conclusions may be modified, but the Berkeley school must be met on their ground of quantitative methodology. No critic of the Berkeley school has yet met this challenge.

Hence, until modified or refuted, their demographic findings form the firm foundation upon which to reconstruct the whole history of early colonial Mexico.

Perhaps the most imaginative achievement of Cook-Borah and Simpson is to have demonstrated, nearly twenty years ago, how the social sciences can be profitably applied to the history of early colonial Mexico, just as these same methods have long been used to survey contemporary issues. While we can never renounce the humanistic tradition òf historiography, the future of early colonial mexican studies, to some extent at least, lies with those who will apply some social science methodologies with discretion, imagination and sophistication.

THE CONQUEST OF THE "CONQUERORS"

A whole new dimension to the conquest has been opened by Irving A. Leonard in his *Books of the Brave* (1949) and Ida Rodríguez Prampolini in her *Amadises de América: la hazaña de Indias como empresa caballeresca* (1948). Both scholars amply document how the conquistadores were deeply influenced by the novels of knight errantry and that the principal chronicles of the conquest vividly reflect this lifestyle. Thus popular culture clashed with the rationalist spirit of the Renaissance led by moralists and intellectuals molded in the image of Erasmus. Both authors persuasively argue that the ideal of chivalry with

World: *A Study of the Writings of Gerónimo de Mendieta, 1525-1604* (Berkeley and Los Angeles, University of California Press, 1956), pp. 88-92.

[5] See the second, revised edition of the *Millennial Kingdom* scheduled for release in the fall of 1969 by the University of California Press, Ch. X.

[6] Charles Gibson, *The Aztecs Under Spanish Rule: A History of the Valley of Mexico, 1519-1810* (Stanford University Press, 1964), p. 142. José Miranda, "La población indígena de México en el siglo xvii", *Historia mexicana*, xii (1962-63), 182-189.

its reliance on faith and intuition and its scorn for prudence and reason were deeply embedded in the Spanish temperament.

On the occasion of the centenary of the death of William H. Prescott the *Hispanic-American Historical Review* dedicated its February, 1959 issue to the patriarch of North-American hispanists. David Levin in his seminal article in that issue subjected Prescott to a historicist analysis. [7] Prescott articulated the bias of the Romantic age in which he lived. But Prescott was fortunate in that he did not have to impose "romantic formulae" on the sixteenth centuries accounts that he used. Bernal, Cortés, López de Gómara, Herrera were "romantics" three centuries before Romanticism was a literary vogue.

Our knowledge of the conquest has been broadened by several regional case-studies. One is Robert S. Chamberlin's *The Conquest and Colonization of Yucatán, 1517-50* (1948), and Philip Wayne Powell's *Soldiers, Indians and Silver: The Northward Advance of New Spain, 1550-1600* (1952). The Spanish advance into the Chichimeca country, the "second conquest" of México, took forty years to accomplish in contrast to the rapidity of the "first conquest". Employing all the techniques of guerrilla warfare, the nomadic Chichimecas could not be conquered until the Spaniards could make them sedentary. The Spanish recipe for victory was the proverbial carrot and the stick, sixteenth century style. The importance of the "second conquest" can scarcely be exaggerated, for it laid the territorial basis of what was to become the modern Mexican nation.

Another original contribution is C. Harvey Gardiner's *Naval Power in the Conquest of Mexico*, a study with some fresh insights into this heretofore neglected aspect. Maurice G. Holmes' *From New Spain by Sea to the Californias: 1519-1668* (1964) is a well-researched synthesis of the activities of New Spain's most active explorers of the Pacific from Cortés to Ulloa.

The controversial and brilliant personality of Hernán Cortés has been the subject of continuing polemic. Salvador de Madariaga, now a venerable octogenarian and one of the last surviving spokesmen of the Spanish Republican generation, has given us an elegantly written biography that is zestfully Spanish in tone (*Hernán Cortés*, 1941). The late, distinguished Manuel Giménez Fernández in his *Hernán Cortés y su revolución comunera en la Nueva España* (1948) advanced the arresting but not totally convincing thesis that there was a parallel between the revolt of Cortés against Velásquez and the contemporary Comunero revolt in Spain. R. H. Wagner in his *The Rise of Fernando*

---

[7] David Levin, "History as Romantic Art: Structure, Characterization and Style in the *Conquest of Mexico*", February, 1959, pp. 20-45. Also see James D. Cockcroft, "Prescott and His Sources", *Ibid.*, February, 1968, pp. 59-74.

Cortés (1944) has unearthed some new documentation and has offered some new interpretations.

One of the most insightful innovations in the historiography of the conquest are two essays of the late Ramón Iglesias on the endless debate between the partisans of Bernal Díaz and López de Gómara. Lesley Byrd Simpson has commented:

[These essays were] in reality a study of the growth of a historian, himself, in the light of experience. He had written the first essay prior to 1936. Like most of us he had written in his study, workins from documents. Upon the outbreak of the Spanish Civil War he joined the Loyalist army in which he served until the débàcle of 1939. In those heart-breaking years he learned something of history in the raw and a great deal about the virtues of military leadership, and by 1939 he found himself in complete disagreement with the Ramón Iglesia of 1936 with respect to Bernal Díaz's evaluation of Cortés. In this reversal he discovered a new regard for Gómara, and in his second essay he re-established Gómara as our first authority on the conquest of Mexico. [8]

Ramón Iglesias saw history as an art form. He realized more than most of us that to be a historian was also to be a philosopher of history. Another contribution was the volume he supervised in which his students at the *Colegio de México* subjected some of our most respectable primary sources on the history of the conquest of Mexico to a critical and still largely valid analysis. The *Estudios de historiografía de la Nueva España* (1945) is still indispensable reading.

Controversial and partisan though it may be, Eulalia Guzmán's *Relaciones de Hernán Cortés* (1958) cannot be ignored. Doña Eulalia, who began her career in José Vasconcelos' ministry of education, writes with passion and hatred for everything Spanish. Her history is *l'histoire engagé*. She sets out to prove that Cortés was a Machiavellian villain, a confirmed liar and ruthless tyrant. Her examination of Cortés' letters against the other sources, in particular the Indian accounts, is rigorous if not selective and often partisan. Yet no one can now accept the account in Cortés' letters as the simple veracity of specific events of the military conquest. Señorita Guzmán has raised too many questions that can not be brushed under the carpet. Although the *Relaciones de Hernán Cortés* can not be discounted, any new interpretation of Cortés' character and role will scarcely conform to doña Eulalia's one-sided portrait.

The literature of the conquest has been polemical and acrimonious since Francisco Javier Clavijero published his *Historia antigua de México* in 1780-81. The often agonizing process of Mexicans searching for the Mexican has been characterized by a wide polarity. Ideological traditionalists and conservative politicians have identified with *lo Cortés*,

[8] *Ibid.*, May, 1948, p. 163.

and ideological innovators and supportetrs of political liberalism have sought historical justification in *lo Cuauhtémoc*. Eulalia Guzmán may be one of the last representatives of the liberal identification with *lo Cuauhtémoc*.

As Mexicans achieve a more secure and articulate sense of national identity, a reconciliation between the Hispanic and the indigenous traditions seems both desirable and possible. The history of the conquest in recent years is beginning to be written in the spirit of those accurate words inscribed on a plaque in the Plaza de Tres Culturas:

> El 13 de Agosto de 1521
> Heroicamente defendido por Cuauhtémoc
> Cayó Tlatelolco en Poder de Hernán Cortés
> No fue Triunfo ni Derrota
> Fue el Doloroso Nacimiento del Pueblo Mexicano
> Que es el México de Hoy

THE CONQUEST OF THE "VANQUISHED"

Evidence of the gradual rapprochement of the Hispanic and the indigenous traditions is the non-polemical tone with which the conquest of the "vanquished" has been written in recent decades. A most significant innovation is that the conquest is no longer seen only in a Spanish perspective. The Indian response, at long last, has been documented with compassion, sophistication and with some objectivity.

The Aztecs are no longer judged by the standards of Renaissance Europe but are now understood in terms of the historical development of Nahuatl culture and society. This important innovation owes much to the anthropological investigations of Manuel Gamio, Alfonso Caso, Robert H. Barlow, Wigberto Jiménez Moreno, S. G. Morley, G. S. Vaillant, to mention only a few. These contributions, important though they may be, are somewhat beyond the scope of this paper. Attention now needs to be focused on the new historical portrait of Aztec society on the eve of the conquest and the dramatic confrontation of the two cultures at the time of the conquest.

An outstanding contribution is that of the French anthropologist, Jacques Soustelle, *La vie quotidienne des Azteques a la veille de la conquete espagnole* (Paris, 1959). This richly documented study is an outstanding example of social history in the classic tradition of French synthesis. As Ralph L. Beals has commented:

> For him the calpulli was a territorial organization, not a clan or clan-derived, and Mexico-Tenochtitlan is not an overgrown pueblo but a great urban center of civilization, head of an expanding empire. Aztec

society is not an emergent tribalkingship structure but a markedly hierarchical society in vigorous development. While avenues of upward mobility still existed for the freemen, an increasingly powerful nobility was facing the growing wealth and power of the merchant class. [9]

Manuel Moreno has given us new insights and new data in his *La organización política y social de los Aztecas* (1962).

Another new dimension is the emphasis now being placed on intellectual history. Ángel María Garibay has published an important *Historia de la literatura náhuatl* (1953) as well as several other monographs and texts of literary history. Miguel León-Portilla's *La filosofía náhuatl* (1956-59), also translated in English, has taken Werner Jaeger's *Paideia* as a model. León-Portilla has reconstructed with imagination and sensitivity the philosophical world-view of the Aztecs, an indispensable prerequisite to any understanding as to why Montezuma II acted the way he did in his confrontation with Cortés. [10]

There is not a more zestfully written nor a more imaginatively conceived portrait of Montezuma than R. C. Padden's *The Hummingbird and the Hawk, Conquest and Sovereignty in the Valley of Mexico* (1967). The recreation of the world of the priestly monarch of the Aztecs is moving, lively and three-dimenisonal. The Renaissance world of Cortés, on the other hand, is flat and insipid.

Miguel León-Portilla's *Visión de los vencidos, relaciones indígenas de la conquista* (1956), a series of translations from Aztec sources, is a many-sided picture of the responses of the Indians to the apocalyptical event of the Spanish conquest.

A common spirit animates all of these studies. It is the desire to reconstruct the Aztec world in Aztec terms without falling into the trap of the dichotomy between *lo Cortés* and *lo Cuauhtémoc*.

THE "IDEOLOGICAL" CONQUEST

Some exciting history has been written within the framework of the conquest as a clash of ideas and ideals. Nowhere can this new approach to the conquest as an intellectual enterprise be more fully appreciated than in the celebrated polemic between Lewis Hanke and Edmundo O'Gorman. Hanke believed that the great debate concerned the nature of the American Indian. O'Gorman, a spiritual student of Dilthey and Ortega, argued that the issue in the debate was the nature of

[9] *Ibid.*, February, 1956, p. 102.
[10] Also see by Miguel Leon-Portilla *Ritos, sacerdotes y atavios de los dioses* (Mexico City, 1948) and *Siete ensayos sobre la cultura náhuatl* (Mexico City, 1958).

man apropos of the American Indian. Hanke saw Las Casas' ideal as
justice *per se* with Las Casas' opponents as champions of injustice.
O'Gorman preferred to view the great debate as a struggle between
two different conceptions of justice, which were reflections of the
ideological and spiritual crisis of the sixteenth century. While focusing
clearly on the philosophical differences between Las Casas and Sepúlveda, O'Gorman also stressed the *zeitgeist* that the two thinkers
shared in common. [11]

At the Valladolid debate Las Casas and Sepúlveda were mutually
incomprehensible. Las Casas was a Scholastic philosopher working for
the universal interests of the Christian commonwealth and Sepúlveda
a Renaissance Aristotelian serving the political interests of Spanish
nationalism. Both men shared the Aristotelian view that the more
perfect should rule the less perfect. To Las Casas this proposition
meant spiritual assistance to pagan peoples by converting them ra-
tionally and peacefully to Christianity. To Sepúlveda this Aristotelian
principle meant the abrogation of pagan peoples' sovereignty and their
conquest by force. Las Casas expressed the ancient-medieval ideal of
the brotherhood of man linked together by a common supranatural
destiny. Sepúlveda spoke for the more modern ideal of the fraternity
of all men belonging to one nation that was destined to include all
humanity. Only in this context can one understand how Las Casas
might accuse his opponents of being unchristian, and they in turn
denounce him for being unpatriotic.

Scholars will be debating for some time to come the issues raised
in the Hanke-O'Gorman polemic. These questions, of course, will
never be resolved, for each generation will see a new dimension in
these ancient juridical-theologian disputes. But all of us, who have
written about the history of early colonial Mexico, should be deeply
grateful to both Lewis Hanke and Edmundo O'Gorman for having
raised these issues.

One of the major contributions to the ideological aspect of the
conquest has been the important role that the thought of Erasmus and
Thomas More played. Silvio Zavala was the pioneer who first explored
this road. [12] George Kubler, Fintan B. Warren, Marcel Bataillon among
others have also made additional contributions. [13] The late José Mi-

[11] For the bibliography on the Hanke-O'Gorman polemic see Edmundo O'Gorman's edition of Fray Bartolomé de las Casas, *Apologética historia sumaria* (2 vols.,
Universidad Nacional Autónoma de México, 1967), i, cxiii-cxv, cxvii-cxviii.

[12] The most concise statements of Zavala's contribution are *Recuerdo de don
Vasco de Quiroga* (México, 1967) and *Filosofía de la conquista* (México, 1947).

[13] Marcel Bataillon's has a concluding chapter on Erasmian influence in Mexico
in the Spanish edition of *Érasme et l'Espagne* (Paris, 1937). Fintan B. Warren,
Vasco de Quiroga and his Pueblo-Hospitals of Santa Fe (Washington, Academy
of American Franciscan History, 1963).

randa and Richard E. Greenleaf have expressed some reservations and doubts. Miranda in his *Victoria y los intereses de la conquista de América* (1947) pointed out that Archbishop Zumárraga's borrowings from the European humanists were selective and opportunistic. Many of the affinities, he argued, were in fact coincidental. On such major issues as worship of the saints and the adoration of images the first Archbishop of Mexico and the Norther European humanists were poles apart. Richard E. Greenleaf in his *Zumárraga and the Mexican Inquisition: 1536-43* (1962) has provided us with a meticulously documented portrait of the Archbishop as a intolerant burner of heretics. I would argue that being a witchhunter and being an Erasman humanist were not mutually exclusive. Such were the contradictions of the time. Be this as it may, *philosophia Christi* left a recognizable imprint on indeological developments. The critical skepticism of Miranda and Greenleaf refines but actually fortifies this important fact.

Ever since the publication of James Brown Scott's *The Spanish Origin of International Law* in 1934 scholars have recognized the central role of the thought of Thomas Aquinas in the ideological conquest of America. This influence found its most articulate expression in Aquinas's two most significant, sixteenth century disciples —Francisco de Vitoria and Bartolomé de las Casas. All those who have worked on Las Casas have made significant contributions to defining this Tomistic influence. Among them are Marcel Bataillon, Lewis Hanke, Manuel Giménez Fernández and Edmundo O'Gorman. Once again the late José Miranda played the role of skeptic. While not denying the importance of Victoria's theories as an ideological defense of the natural rights of the Indians, Miranda also stressed that these were also theories that defended ecclesiastical authority against the encroachments of temporal power. Hence the Dominicans were not totally disinterested defenders of the Indians.

The publication of Robert Ricard's magisterial study underscored the decisive role of the Franciscans in the missionary enterprise. In his *Millennial Kingdom of the Franciscans in the New World,* John L. Phelan explored with a historicist criterion the "political theology" of the Franciscans of which the missionary enterprise was its practical expression. The heir of a long tradition of Franciscan apocalyptical mysticism which was closely identified with the followers of the prophet Joachim of Fiore, the discovery of the New World foreshadowed the End of the World, according to Mendieta. Before that awesome event could come to pass, the Franciscans and the Indians together could create the millennial kingdom on earth. Mendieta's Franciscan stance differed sharply from Philip II's policies and also from the aims of both the Dominicans and the Jesuits.

Others who have explored the Franciscan ideology are Luis González Cárdenas, the late Ramón Iglesias and José Antonio Maravall. [14] The biographical study of Sahagún published by Luis Nicolau D'Olwer deserves special mention. Howard Cline, Alejandra Moreno Toscano and John L. Phelan have reestablished the importance of Juan de Torquemada's *Monarquía indiana,* which has been unjustly disdained as a work of plagerism ever since Joaquín García Icazbalceta's pioneer study. [15]

The Franciscan view will soon be enriched by two forthcoming studies. Edmundo O'Gorman's seminar is currently preparing a new edition of Motolinía's works, an edition which will also contain one of O'Gorman's lucid prologues. Miguel León-Portilla's seminar is preparing a similar critical edition of Torquemada's *Monarquía indiana.*

THE "PHILOSOPHICAL" CONQUEST

Edmundo O'Gorman has developed a highly original and ecumenical vision of the discovery of the New World which he calls the "philosophical" discovery. Deeply influenced by the "perspectivism" of José Ortega y Gasset, the historicism of Wilhelm Dilthey and the existentialism of Martin Heidegger, O'Gorman asked the ontological question: "What is America"? For O'Gorman America is not merely a geographical entity: it is an idea.

In his *Crisis y porvenir de la ciencia histórica* O'Gorman lucidly explained his historicist philosophy of history. In 1951 he published his *Idea del descubrimiento de América.* Columbus did not "discover" America. America did not yet exist as a "thing in itself" fully predestined and constituted and thus an object ripe for discovery.

In a sequel, *La invención de América: el universalismo de la cultura de Occidente* (1958) O'Gorman argued that America was "invented" rather than discovered. The when and the how of America's appearance in the historical cinsciousness of Europe is the principal focus of America: 1) the "geographical" and 2) the "historical". The focus is this book. O'Gorman concentrated on two aspects of the invention of on a rigorous analysis of the texts of Columbus and Vespucci.

O'Gorman's approach to the philosophical invention is dialectical

[14] Luis Gonzalez Cardenas, "Fray Geronimo de Mendieta, pensador politico e historiador", *Revista de historia de America,* núm. 28 (December, 1949), pp. 331-376. Ramon Iglesia, "Invitacion al estudio de Fr. Jeronimo de Mendieta", *Cuadernos americanos,* iv (July-August, 1945), 156-72. Jose Antonio Maravall, "La utopia politico-religiosa de los franciscanos en Nueva España", *Estudios Americanos,* i (January 1949), 197-227.

[15] See Howard Cline's article on Torquemada's sources in the Spring, 1969, issue of *The Americas.*

and Hegelian. Richard Morse defined the paradox of O'Gorman's analysis when he wrote:

> Western culture is at once Europocentric and universalistic. The "invention" of America is therefore a step toward the historic fulfillment and toward the "ontological disintegration" or "self-liquidation" of Europe. Likewise, America both fulfills and "annihilates" herself as she becomes aware of her ecumenical role.

Morse added:

> One may criticize Professor O'Gorman for his oracular tone, for his tendency to verbalize, for the narrow range of evidence with which he supports sweeping ideas, and for his parochialism that tinges his ecumenical vision. He opens a fruitful approach, however, for studying the Americas as a whole, and he provides moments of intellectual stimulation rarely matched in the often pedestrian historiography of the lands of Amerigo. [16]

THE "SPIRITUAL" CONQUEST

Our knowledge of the missionary enterprise still rests on the firm foundation laid by Robert Ricard in his now classic, La "conquête spirituelle" du Mexique. First published in 1933 it has been translated into both Spanish and English. This study is epocal not only for the high quality of its research but also for the historical moment in which it was published. Mexico in 1933 was then emerging from more than two decades of turmoil and bloodshed out of which was painfully evolving a new definition of nationhood. In that agonizing quest for self-identity Mexicans were often anti-Hispanic, anti-clerical and anti-Catholic. Ricard, a Frenchman, implicitly told the Mexicans: "Know yourself, look back into your past and examine it with compassion and with as much objetivity as possible."

What has been done since 1945 has been to build a superstructure on Ricard's foundation. The Spanish Franciscan, Pedro Borges, in his Métodos misionales en la cristianización de América (1960) has published a readable, learned and objective survey of the whole missionary enterprise in the Indies, of which Mexico was a very important chapter. Dionisio Victoria Moreno has given us an interesting study in failure in his Los Carmelitas descalzos y la conquista espiritual de México: 1585-1612 (1967). This monograph is an analysis as to why the discalced Carmelites did not enter the missionary field. Fidel de Lejarza, another Franciscan, has written on the spiritual conquest of Nuevo Santander

[16] *Hispanic-American Historical Review*, May, 1959, p. 274.

(*La conquista espiritual del Nuevo Santander*, 1947). Still another Franciscan, Francis Borgia steck has published a study on the famous Franciscan college of Santa Cruz de Tlatelolco, some of whose founders initially favored training an Indian clergy (*El primer colegio de América, Santa Cruz de Tlatelolco*, 1944).

Arthur Ennis' *Fray Alonso de la Veracruz, O. S. A., 1507-84: A Study of His Contribution to the Religious and Intellectual Affairs of Early Mexico* (1957) and Amancio Bolaño e Isla have added to our knowledge about the life and times of that important Augustinian friar. Richard E. Greenleaf's study of Archbishop Zumárraga as an inquisitor is sharply focused. A meticulosly documented monograph by Georges Baudot on the struggle of the second archbishop to impose the collection of tithes on the Indians in the face of the bitter opposition of the friars sheds much new light on this old controversy. [17]

Rafael Heliodoro Valle's *Santiago en América* (1946) is an arresting study of social iconography. Santiago and St. Christopher were the two most popular saints in early colonial Mexico. Santiago, the fighting saint with his sword unleashed, was the symbol of men at war. And Saint Christopher, recently banished from the calendar of saint, with his staff and an infant on his back, represents the peaceful traveller and the colonist who seeks good and on which to build his home and to rear his family.

Where do we go from here? A series of regional studies which would test Ricard's hypotheses might be useful. Another promising approach would be to study the missionary enterprise with methods borrowed from the social sciences as case-studies in culture change.

One of the most prominent lacuna is a deeper awareness of the reigiosity of the Baroque world of the seventeenth century. The social functions of cofradias, compadrazgo, particular cults of saints and the popularities of certain santuaries need to be studies systematically. In that plural and multi-racial society religion was the one common bond that could cut across ethnic divisions. Hence a greater understanding of the social aspects of seventeenth century religious sentiment could reveal the historical roots of *mexicanidad*, that life-style that lends to Mexico its unique personality.

THE "BUREAUCRATIC" CONQUEST

The reigns of Charles V and Philip II were dominated in part, at least, by bureaucratic institution-making. During the seventeenth century, on the other hand, as the creoles were developing a self-cons-

[17] Georges Baudot, "L'institution de la dime pour les Indies du Mexique", *Melanges de la casa de Velazquez* (Madrid, 1965).

ciousness and as centralized control from Spain was weakenin, these bureaucratic institutions served new ends. It is surprising how little has been done in the field of institutional history since 1945. There can be no quarrel with its quality, but the quantity is somewhat disappointing.

The foundation of our knowledge is the one provived by Clarence Haring in his classic *The Spanish Empire in America* (1947). Although not confined exclusively to Mexico, no Mexicanista can afford to neglect this still useful synthesis. Haring should be supplemented by John H. Parry's *The Spanish Seaborne Empire* and Charles Gibson's *Spain in America*, both published in 1966. Both books are well-structured syntheses which incorporate the new scholarship of their generation.

John H. Parry, *The Audiencia of New Galicia in the Sixteenth Century: A Study in Spanish Colonial Government* (1948) is a meticulously documented monograph that is a model for institutional history. What is surprising is that it stands alone. What happened to the Audiencia of New Galicia in the seventeenth century when social conditions were quite different? We do not know yet. Someone should enlighten us. There is not to my knowledge well-documented and soundly interpreted study of the Audiencia of Mexico. This is an embarrassing gap. We need several studies on the role of the Audiencia as the intermediary between the central authorities in Spain and the local elites and non-elites. We should look forward to the eventual publication of Woodrow W. Borah's study on the *Juzgado de Indios*, the Audiencia as a tribunal for Indian litigations.

What the study of the bureaucracy probably needs most of all is a powerful injection of new theoretical constructs. The place to begin is S. N. Eisenstadt's *The Political Systems of Empires* (1963). Unreadable though this book may be, it does contain a wealth of hypotheses that could be profitably applied to the Habsburg bureaucracy in New Spain and, for that matter, the whole Spanish Empire.

The year, 1598, is one important watershed in Mexican history. By the end of the reign of Philip II massive demographic changes had taken place. Indian Mexico was giving way to creole and mestizo Mexico. That is the meaning of the seventeenth century. The institution-making of Philip II's time was replaced with institution-consolidation of the later Hapsburgs. 1598 also represents the beginning of the end of the plural society in wich economic, political and social functions were largely determined in terms of ethnic origins and the genesis of the multi-racial society that did not come to dominate Mexico until the twentieth century.

José Miranda in his *España y Nueva España en la época de Felipe II* (1962) has well synthesized the larger meaning of the sixteenth century characterized by the growth of bureaucratic centralism, the subjection of the remaining Indians to the demands of the new silver economy and the emergence of latifundia and stockraising.

The outlines of a synthesis for seventeenth century, which would provide a larger conceptual framework for the writing of institutional and bureaucratic history, have been suggested by Lesley Byrd Simpson, François Chevalier and Irving Leonard.

José Ignacio Rubio Mañé's *Introducción al estudio de los virreyes de la Nueva España 1535-1746* (1959-61) is a solid documentary base for beginning to study the viceregal institution. Much more needs, however, needs to be done. Two types of studies should be on any priority list. Monographs on individual vicerys would be useful. Even more desirab'e would be a series of studies dealing with the origin and the development of certain key functions of viceroys studied over a long time span. Among these topics might be: the viceroy as captain general, the viceroy as president of the Audiencia, the viceroy vis-á-vis the local elites and non-elites.

Above all else, institutional and bureaucratic history should not be written in the old-fashioned legalistic spirit of the past but rather in the new and vital framework of social history. Here again we should not be shy in borrowing from the social sciences. Viceroys, audiencias and alcaldes mayores were men of fresh and blood, seeking to maneuver in the face contradictory pressures in a society undergoing gradual but meaningful social change. They should be portrayed as skilled bureaucratic politicians, practitioners of the art of the possible.

The field of regional institutionalized history is virtually a *tabula rasa*. Studies such as those of Charles Gibson and François Chevalier contain a host of insights on local government but that perspective clearly is not their major focus. What we first need is a broadbased synthesis of the rich primary sources comparable to what Guillermo Lohmann Villena did for the *corregidor de Indios* in Habsburg Peru. But such a survey, useful though it would certainly be, will not suffice. We need a whole series of regional studies with a time focus depth in which the societal, economic and political roles of the alcaldes mayores will be tested by hypotheses borrowed in part, at least, from the social sciences.

The Mexican cabildos have not been well studied. Dominated by the creole elites, the cabildos should not be examined in a narrow, legalistic sense but rather for their vital and dynamic socio-political role. They were the spokesmen of the emerging creole elites. And the Council of the Indies, the viceroys and the Audiencias acted at their own peril if they did not seriously take into account the views of the cabildos.

THE "SOCIETAL" CONQUEST

The acculturation of the Indians to Spanish norms has been the topic of Charles Gibson's two major works. His methodological approach is one that all social historians might well emulate. His focus is regional and multi-disciplinary. The historical geographer, Carl Sauer's *Colima of New Spain in the Sixteenth Century* (1948) is another example of the usefulness of the regional and multi-disciplinary approaches.

In his first major book published in 1952 Gibson examined Tlaxcala in the time span of the sixteenth century. His conclusions stressed the humanitarian concern of Spanish colonial policy for the welfare of the Indian community. Gibson stressed the wide variety of Tlaxcala responses to hispanization from rejection to full acceptance in the course of one generation. The clear implication is that a new kind of Hispano-Indian society was emerging as a consequence of the conquest in which the Indians were playing a creative cultural role.

Quite a different perspective emerges from Gibson's second major work published fifteen years later. Again he concentrates on a particular region, this time the valley of Mexico, but his time span is much longer covering the three hundred years of Spanish colonial rule. Out of his massive documentation comes a somber conclusion:

> The Black Legend provides a gross but essentially accurate interpretation of the relations between the Spaniards and the Indians... The substantive content of the Black Legend asserts that the Indians were exploited by the Spaniards and in empirical fact they were... The hacienda combined its essential control of land with secondary controls over labor and tribute, and the result was the most comprehensive institution yet devised for Spanish mastery and Indian subordination. [18]

The Indian pueblo did survive aided by the cofradia and the fiesta, but the incipient cultural florescence of the early sixteenth century was aborted. Societal demoralization expressed itself in the form of alcoholism.

The definitive study of the encomienda is Lesley Byrd Simpson's *The Encomienda in New Spain: The Beginning of Spanish Mexico* was first published in 1929 but extensively revised in 1950. The only incomplete aspect is that Simpson did not unearth the kind of social data of how particular encomiendas actually functioned as social units. James Lockhart did just this for the same period in Perú. [19]

Silvio Zavala's *La libertad de movimiento de los Indios de Nueva*

[18] Gibson, *The Aztecs*, pp. 403, 407.
[19] James Lockhart, *Spanish Peru, 1532-60, A Colonial Society* (University of Wisconsin Press, 1968), pp. 11 ff.

España (1948) is a model of its kind, which stresses the dynamic interplay between the law and its observance. Deriving from a royal cedula of 1480 the Indians did enjoy substantial freedom of movement, however, with some notable restrictions.

The most promising approach to the study of acculturation of Indian communities is that of ethnohistory, which combines historical techniques with those of the social sciences, in particular, anthropology. Howard F. Cline, Ralp Roys, Charles Gibson, George Kubler, John Rowe, John L. Phelan and Herbert Harvey have all experimented with this method. [20] This approach should serve as a model for subsequent research.

One aspect of the class structure in Indian society, i. e., the survival of the Indian nobility, has been studied from a rather narrow genealogical view by both Delfina López Sarrelangue and the late Guillermo S. Fernández de Recas. [21] Both authors gave ample evidence that *cacicazgos* survived in many areas until the time of independence. What now needs to be done is to formulate a few bold hypotheses about the dynamic role of the caciques as cultural brokers between the conquerors and the conquered, which might best be tested in a series of regional studies.

A solidly documented study of the Negro in Mexico is Gonzalo Aguirre Beltran's *La población negra en México* (1946). Blacks and Afro-mestizos played a vital role in Mexico prior to 1650, far out of proportion to their actual numbers, in pulling New Spain through her "century of depression". Their participation in the urban craft guilds, the obrajes, mining and stockraising increased production in those key sectors of the economy at a time when the Indian labor force was drastically declining. In capitalist industries such as the obrajes, mining and sugar plantations Mexican Black slavery could be as "oppressive" and as "exploitative" as its betterknown Anglo-Saxon version. Such is the well-documented conclusion of a Ph. D. thesis recently written by Colin Palmer at the University of Wisconsin.

Social changes among the Spanish colonists were as significant as they were among the Indians. José Durand's pioneer study, *La transformación social del conquistador* (1953) broke new ground, but much more needs to be done. The comprehensive use of notorial archives will afford a more complete picture of the whole process of the Spaniards' adaptation to the New World scene. James Lockhart's *Spanish Peru*:

[20] See especially Howard Cline, "Problems of Mexican Ethno-History, The Ancient Chinantla", *The Hispanic-American Historical Review* August, 1957, pp. 273-95.

[21] Guillermo S. Fernández de Recas, *Cacicazgo y nobiliario indígena de la Nueva España* (México, 1961) and Delfina López Sarrelangue, *La nobleza indígena de Patzcuaro en la epoca virreinal* (Mexico, 1965).

1532-1560: A Colonial Society (1968) provides a model for the same period in Mexico.

Another useful study in social transformation is Norman F. Martin's *Los vagabundos en la Nueva España, siglo XVI* (1957). C. E. Marshall has written a pioneer article about the origins of the single most important social fact of Mexican history—*mestizaje*. [22] While not concentrating exclusively on Mexico Magnus Mörner has provided us with a broad framework inside of which to study the emergence of the mestizo community. [23]

One of the most exciting challenges facing the social historians of the next generation is to explore the emergence of the non-elites —in particular, the Mestizos— and to probe the complex web of relationships between the elites and the non-elites. The French historians have formulated some stimulating theoretical constructs. Let us apply them by going into the archives.

As has already been mentioned, 1598 is a convenient watershed in early Mexican colonial history. Much needs to be done in the field of social history of the seventeenth century. We have only made a beginning, a few striking monographs.

Lesley Byrd Simpson's short article, "Mexico's Forgotten Century" is seminal in its implications. [24] Simpson cogently argues the case for the historical importance of the seventeenth century, the century in which some of the basic social characteristics of Mexico emerged. A century, which saw the growth of the creole elite and the Mestizo non-elite, the rise of latifundia, the consolidation of neo-Scholasticism in the universities and the flowering of the Baroque style in architecture, needs to be studied far more intensively than it has been.

The pathos, the grandeur and the misery of the exotic Baroque world comes to life in the elegantly written pages of Irving Leonard's *Baroque Times in Old Mexico* (1959). This book is a worthy sequel to the monograph of his youth, *Carlos de Sigüenza y Góngora* (1929) which still remains the standard text of that topic. Leonard has made a promising beginning, but much more remains to be done before all the facets of the Baroque mentality will come to life. Francisco de la Maza's *El guadalupanismo Mexicano* (1953) is an excellent example of the kind of socio-intellectual history of the Baroque period that can and should be done.

<hr/>

[22] C. E. Marshall, "The Birth of the Mestizo in New Spain", reprinted in *Readings in Latin American History*, Lewis Hanke, ed., (2 vols., Thomas Y. Crowell, 1966), I, 139-153.

[23] Magnus Mörner, *Race Mixture in the History of Latin America* (1967).

[24] Lesley Byrd Simpson, "Mexico's Forgotten Century", reprinted in *Latin American History: Essays on Its Study and Teaching, 1898-1965*, Howard Cline, ed. (2 vols., University of Texas Press, 1967), II, 500-506.

E. P. Simmons has made a useful summary of the recent literature of the most spectacular jurisdictional battle of early colonial Mexico, that is, the clash between Bishop Palafox and the Jesuits. [25] In this connection Alberto María Carreño also has a helpful monograph. [26] While the main contours of the ideological struggle have become visible, the societal implications have not yet been sufficiently exploited.

The life-style, the imagery and the folk customs of Baroque times need much study. A systematic exploration of the abundant archives of the Inquisition is one place to begin. The chronicles of the seventeenth century might be examined for their implicit and explicit "world-views". A historicist approach would be desirable in such a quest.

Stimulated by an earlier evocative study by Richard Morse, Lyle N. McAlister has given us a seminal article on social structure and social change in colonial Mexico. [27] His formulation of a neo-medieval corporate society divided into racial "estates" and socio-economic functional corporations has provided us with a stimulating set of questions with which to interrogate the documents of social history. His abstract model should be given some flesh and blood by a host of monographic studies.

The myth of the seventeenth century as a "colonial siesta" has fortunately been laid to rest. It was in fact a period of significant social change. Behind a Baroque façade of apparent immobility, society was seething with unrest. We need to take a careful look at social disturbances in this period. Under what conditions does the conciliatory machinery of the bureaucracy break down, thus creating a vacuum which is filled by armed violence? Revolts on the northern frontier, which fall under the category of primary resistance of superficially hispanized Indians, must be distinguished from social disturbances in the more hispanized central-southern Mexico. Concern should center on those movements where there was considerable interaction among the various racial groups.

The urban riots in Mexico City in 1624 and in 1692, reminiscent of recent urban explosions in the United States, are particularly apropos. A useful over-view of these two celebrated riots is the article of Chester Lyle Guthrie. [28] More attention needs to be focused on the interaction

---

[25] E. P. Simmons, "Palafox and His Critics: Reappraising a Controversy", *Hispanic-American Historical Review*, November, 1966, pp. 394-408.

[26] *Cedulario de los siglos XVI and XVII: El obispo don Juan de Palafox y Mendoza y el conflicto con la compañia de Jesus*, Alberto Maria Carreño, ed. (Mexico, 1947).

[27] Both Richard M. Morse's article "Toward a Theory of Spanish American Government" and L. N. McAlister's "Social Structure and Social Change in New Spain" are reprinted in Cline's *Latin American History*, II, 506-521 and 750-764.

[28] Chester Lyle Guthrie, "Riots ni Seventeenth Century Mexico City", in

of creoles, mestizos, mulatoes, Blacks and Indians. Herbert Klein's article on the Tzeltal revolt is an illuminating example of how a Hispanized Indian community bursts into revolt. [29] David Davidson's article on Negro resistance also deserves special mention. [30]

If we agree that 1598 is a convenient watershed, I would submit that 1700 is a meaningless terminal date. The same social forces operating in the seventeenth century continued during the reigns of Philip V and Ferdinand VI. The decisive change does not come until 1759, when Charles III begins the intensive introduction of some phases of the Enlightenment. Nancy Farriss' illuminating *Crown and Clergy in colonial Mexico, The Crisis of Ecclesiastical Privilege* (1968) underscores the usefulness of considering the period from 1598 to 1759 as a single unity in mexican history.

THE "ECONOMIC" CONQUEST

In the field of economic history three books stand out, not only because of their intrinsic merit but also because they are seminal in the questions they pose and the methodologies they employ. Those authors are François Chevalier, Lesley Byrd Simpson and Woodrow Borah.

In commenting on François Chevalier's *La formation des grands domaines au Mexique* (1952) Simpson remarked: "This work should be a challenge and an inspiration to the rest of us." [31] Chevalier used the methodology that Marc Bloch applied to medieval French agricultural society to the vast amount of then incoherent data about the origins and the rise of latifundia in New Spain. What emerges is an impressive example of Gallic synthesis. Woodrow Borah has asked a pertinent question: "Has M. Chevalier's splendid French training with its emphasis on synthesis led him to detect a pattern not in the data? In the present state of Mexican studies, we cannot answer the question with assurance." [32]

The ultimate justification of a book as good as this one is that it should stimulate other books. Chevalier did not use quantitative data.

Greater America, Essays in Honor of Herbert Eugene Bolton (University of California Press, 1955), pp. 243-58. Also see Rosa Feijoo, "El tumulto de 1624", and "El tumulto de 1692", in *Historia mexicana*, July-September, 1964 and April-June, 1965, pp. 42-70 and 656-679.

[29] Herbert S. Klein, "Peasant Communities in Revolt: The Tzeltal Republic of 1712", *Pacific Historical Review*, August, 1966, pp. 247-263.

[30] David Davidson, "Negro Slave Control and Resistance in Colonial Mexico," *Hispanic-American Historical Review*, August, 1966, pp. 235-53.

[31] *Ibid.*, February, 1953, p. 113.

[32] *Ibid.*, November, 1957, p. 506.

Such a method now is a necessity. Another new approach would be to pay much more attention to the social implications of the emergence of the rise of latifundia than Chevalier did. What was the social impact of the rise of commercial production of sugar and wool? What were the effects of these changes on the people who did the work? Above all else the hypotheses formulated in the Chevalier synthesis for the whole of New Spain should be tested in a series of regional studies in order to learn patterns of divergences. Certainly the latifundia complex operated somewhat differently in areas as diverse as Yucatán, the valley of Mexico, the Bajío or northern Mexico. Chevalier has made a splendid beginning. Now the job should be finished.

Lesley Byrd Simpson's *The Exploitation of Land in Central Mexico in the Sixteenth Century* (1952) is of pioneer importance in that he used a quantitative method to measure the extent of ecological change between 1519 and 1620. The future of the field of economic history in early colonial Mexico lies in the use of quantitative, statistical data. Simpson's study was one of the first to point the way. Simpson estimates that almost 80 per cent of Indian agricultural land came to be vacated and that this land was taken over by other forms of plant and animal life. An outgrowth of his first demographic study with Cook published in 1948, Simpson's conclusion is that livestock to a considerable extent replaced Indians on the Mexican landscape.

The economic history of early colonial Mexico cannot be written without taking into account Woodrow W. Borah's *New Spain's Century of Depression* (1951). Borah shattered the view that New Spain from 1521 onward had enjoyed a steadily expanding economy. This depression, beginning with the great epidemic of 1576-79, was precipitated by the rapid decline of native labor available, the increase of the non-Indian population and the lavish use of native labor especially by the regular and secular clergy for their extensive architectural enterprises. The non-Indian population was determined to maintain its customary standard of living with the result that the pressure on the rapidly diminishing Indians became all but intolerable. Stop-gap measures such as the establishment of public granaries and a crude system of price fixing did not prove effective. What eventually arrested the contracting economy during the second half of the seventeenth century was the end of Indian demographic decline, the *repartimiento* and most important of all the consolidation of latifundia.

The Borah hypothesis undoubtedly needs to be tested in a series of regional studies with the use of statistical data.

No economic historian of this period cannot be grateful to Silvio Zavala and María Castelo for the publication of their many volumed *Fuentes para la historia del trabajo en México* (1946). Lesley Byrd Simpson did ask a question that must vex every editor of a collection of primary sources. The difficulty of answering the question, however, should not discourage an editor of primary source materials. Simpson queried:

> Hence he had to make a violent selection, admittedly based on a "subjective criterion", but he fails to come to grips with the nature of that subjective criterion and he leaves us with the uneasy feeling that another person might have made a selection totally at variance with his. [33]

In the somewhat neglected topic of inter-colonial trade Woodrow Borah and Edwardo Arcila Farías have published useful monographs on Mexico's trade with Peru and Venezuela respectively. [34] In a suggestive monograph Pierre Chaunu has incorporated the Manila galleon trade into his grand design of imperial commerce. Thus he has added a new dimension to William L. Schurz's pioneer study on the Manila Galleon. [35] In the *Archivo de la Nación* in Mexico City there is a large amount of material on the Manila Galleon trade, which no one heretofore has explored.

Our knowledge of early colonial economic institutions has been enriched by several studies. Among them are M. Carrera Stampa on the gremios, Fernando B. Sandoval on sugar, Willim Dusenberry on the mesta and Woodrow Borah on silk raising.

The abundant archives of the *Hospital de Jesús* offers a striking challenge to the economic historian, for the *Marquesado* along with the Jesuit estates were the two most profitable capitalist enterprises of the colonial period. Cortés himself was the first capitalist entrepreneur of New Spain. His heirs and their administrators were indeed successful capitalists. A suggestive monograph by Richard E. Greenleaf points up the possibilities of this rich archival collection now housed in the *AGN*, where statistical data abounds. [36] The operations of the Jesuit estates invites further study. [37] Woodrow Borah's article on the collection of tithes in the Bishopric of Oaxaca suggests possibilities

[33] *Ibid.*, May, 1947, pp. 290-91.

[34] Woodrow W. Borah, *Early Colonial Trade and Navigation Between Mexico and Peru* (University of California Press, Ibero-Americana: 38). Eduardo Arcila Farias, *Comercio entre Venezuela y México en los siglos XVI y XVII* (México, 1950).

[35] Pierre Chaunu, *Les Philippines et le Pacifique des Ibériques (XVIᵉ, XVIIᵉ, XVIIIᵉ Siècles)* (Paris, 1960).

[36] Richard E. Greenleaf, "Viceregal Power and the Obrajes of the Cortés Estate," *Hispanic-American Historical Review*, August, 1968, pp. 365-79. For a juridical analysis of the Cortés Estate see Bernardo García-Martínez, *El marquesado del valle* (El Colegio de Mexico, 1969).

[37] See Francois Chevalier, ed. *Instrucciones a los hermanos jesuitas administradores de haciendas* (Mexico, 1950).

for similar studies for other episcopal sees. [38] In this connection there is valuable data in the *Archivo General de Indias* in Sevilla. A dynamic and vibrant history of the early colonial Mexican economy can be written from a comprehensive exploitation of the abundant data on the tithes.

In short we have only made a beginning in exploring the economic history of this period. The future lies with those who are willing to acquire the tools of economic analysis and quantitative methodology.

THE "ARCHITECTURAL" CONQUEST

In surveying all the many cultural consequences flowing from the conquest one of the most durable and the most universal is in the field of ecclesiastical architecture. A general history of the Baroque style, for example, cannot be written without taking into account the Mexican contribution.

One Mexican art historian stands out as the pioneer in the study of Mexico's rich and varied colonial art. As Elizabeth Wilder Weisman commented on the work of the late Manuel Toussaint: "Everyone working in the field of colonial art in Mexico must think of himself as Toussaint's pupil." [39] Among his major works were his studies of Mudéjar art in America and his monumental study of that noble building, the Cathedral of Mexico. His general synthesis, *Arte colonial de México* (1948) is still a classic. Durable though his own achievements as a scholar were, don Manuel was equally important in stimulating and guiding other students in the field of Mexican art for both the pre-conquest, colonial and modern periods. He played a decisive role in organizing the *Instituto de Investigaciones Estéticas* of the *Universidad Nacional Autónoma de Mexico* and in founding its scholarly journal, *Anales*. Both the journal and the *Instituto*, ably led by Dr. Justino Fernández from 1955 until 1968, have provided institutional vehicles for a wide-ranging series of publications covering the whole field of Mexican art.

The accomplishments and the trends in the historiography of colonial art since 1945 are personified in the works of George Kubler, John McAndrew and Francisco de la Maza.

George Kubler's *Mexican Architecture in the Sixteenth Century* (1948) connects the design of ecclesiastical buildings with the mainstream of sixteenth century life. Therein lies its importance. Kubler relates architecture to the lay-out cities, building methods, recruit-

---

[38] Woodrow W. Borah, "Tithe Collection in the Bishopric of Oaxaca", *Hispanic-American Historical Review*, November, 1941, pp. 498-517.

[39] *Ibid.*, May, 1956, p. 270.

ment of labor, the acculturation of the Indians and the ideological formation of the missionary-architects. The result is that no historian of the sixteenth century, whatever his particular specialty may be, can afford to neglect Kubler's two volumes.

John McAndrew's general thrust was the same as Kubler's —to relate architecture to the larger fabric of society. But in contrast to Kubler, who looked at the whole achievement of architecture in the sixteenth century, McAndrew concentrated on only one aspect in his *The Open Air Churches of Sixteenth Century Mexico* (1965). The Open Air Churches were an art form unique to sixteenth century Mexico. In order to point up their uniqueness McAndrew ranged far beyond the more technical aspects of architectural history. In so doing he throws new light on missionary methods, the role of children as missionaries and preachers and the special efficacy of European music in catechizing the natives. He also pays particular attention to how native craftsmen subtly changed Spanish styles.

One of the most prolific and imaginative disciples of Manuel Toussaint is Francisco de la Maza. One example of his many monographs is *Las piras funerarias en la historia y en el arte de México* (1946). Art history, yes, but it also illuminates social history written by a person with sensitive insights into the subtle, often elusive relationships between art and society.

SOME SUGGESTIONS

The study of Mexico's colonial past is no longer submerged in the anti-Hispanic tradition of the Revolution of 1910. Now it is viewed ad just one of Mexico's many historical experiences that should be understood in its own terms. The study of New Spain is increasingly divorced from the ideological trends of today and tomorrow.

From this discussion five principal trends seem to have emerged since 1945. They are 1) ethno-history, 2) historicism, 3) the broad synthesis, 4) the multi-disciplinary approach, and 5) the statistical-quantitative method.

Ethno-history has been practiced by Mexicans, North-Americans and Frenchmen alike. The result has been the emergence for the first time of a three-dimensional perspective of the history of the Indians both before and after the Spaniards. The conquest has become a "double conquest". This indeed is a major accomplishment.

Partially as a consequence of the appeal of the philosophies of Ortega, Dilthey and Heidegger in Mexico (and there are sound historical reasons for this trend) some Mexican historians have been strongly attracted to historicism. Some North Americans have also tried it.

Among the former are Durand, Iglesia, León-Portilla, Maza and O'Gorman. Among the latter are Levin, Padden and Phelan. Historicism is subjective and relativist to some extent, at least. It puts a high priority on the importance of ideas and the desirability of defining the *Zeitgeist* of a particular period. Historicism has been most often applied to the sixteenth century. It now should be used for the seventeenth century.

The French have excelled in broad synthesis that have created some order out of heretofore incoherent masses of raw data. Although these syntheses represent some of the most evocative scholarship done since 1945, they should be considered not as end but as a beginning to research in these topics. Synthetic hypotheses should be tested by regional case-studies.

The multi-disciplinary approach has enjoyed popularity among the North Americans. Some very exciting history can be written by those who generously but discriminately borrow from the social sciences.

However deeply tied we as historians may be to the humanist tradition, we should not hesitate to use a statistical and quantitative approach to social and to economic history when the data is available. And available it often is.

Our view of history should be pluralistic. None of us can practice all of these methods simultaneously, but each of us can profit from the application of these various methods by others.

Although much remains to be done in writing the history of the "many conquests" of Mexico, I would venture that some of the most exciting opportunities lie in the fields of social and economic history. Historicism and quantification, contrasting though they may be, offer some stimulating challenges.

COMMENTARIES

CHARLES GIBSON

I. COMMENTARY ON "MANY CONQUESTS"

"Conquest" once referred to the historical events described by Prescott, events that were in large part military and confined to the period 1519-21. It is true that Prescott, like others, dipped into the Aztec past at the beginning and sketched the subsequent career of Cortés at the end. But neither Prescott nor others saw this beginning and end as accomplishing more than the sounding out of a narrative. They were necessary in a formal sense for the reader's understanding, but they were the parts about which Prescott himself had the most serious doubts, and they fell outside the self-contained dramatic entity. I agree with what Professor Phelan says concerning the romantic character of the sources, for they are obviously rich in the elements of romanticism, and equally obviously it was essentially these elements that inspired Prescott.

Consider what a change has come over the term "conquest". The change began in the Spanish world in the 16th century, in the area of moral-judicial thought, and its rapid development resulted in an official discreditation while the lesser conquests were still in progress. Prohibition of the term, and the substitution of euphemisms, made up one phase of the 16th century revision, and they suggest the degree to which a sensitive estate sought to interpret itself in the least controversial light. "Pacification", a bland word compared with "conquest", put the emphasis on another aspect, one incidentally that held very little interest for Prescott. To my knowledge the first extension of the conquest concept in a new direction occurred with the phase "spiritual conquest", according to which the military was subordinated to the religious, and the missionaries appeared as metaphorical soldiers engaged in Christian campaigns. Much more could be said about the uses of these terms in the 16th and 17th centuries, for they continued a verbal interplay of religion and militarism that is as old as Christianity itself, and they have relevance both to the "real" character of Spanish imperialism and to the very complex problem of its justification.

Professor Phelan's paper, in its main subdivisions, carries the process of conquest expansion farther than I have seen it carried before, and it is to this feature that my commentary will be partly directed. Variants of conquest make up the successive themes. Demographic conquest, conquest of the conquerors, conquest of the vanquished, ideological conquest, philosophical conquest, spiritual conquest, bureaucratic conquest, "societal" conquest, economic conquest, and architectural conquest are put down here for us to ponder. Old-fashioned military conquest, incidentally, is still present, but it is diffused among other categories, and this fits both with the subjective tone of the paper, to which Professor Phelan refers and which is one of its major strengths, and with the general trend of modern historical writing.

The demographic conquest is important, but to my mind it laks the absolutely central position to which Professor Phelan assigns it. It is a "conquest", I suppose, in the sense that a dominant people deliberately as well as involuntarily became the effective "cause" of a sharp population decline, and in this sense it represents perhaps as legitimate a use of the term "conquest" as does any of the others. A methodological conquest, in the application of quantitative techniques, may also be implied. But it is worth questioning, if only to provoke the discussion that we all value, whether or not in fact the central issue of early Mexican colonial history is demographic. One might suspect so from the intensity of recent controversy. But substantive controversy, in this matter, has been limited to a small number of historians, the majority seemingly being willing to await consensus. With regard to numbers, my sympathies are where Professor Phelan's are, and where he says they are. But an interesting feature of the new demographic conclusions is that they can be accommodated within existing understandings of the history, a large part of which remains whether the population was large or small. Is population more "central" than conquest itself? This is perhaps a question without significance.

"Conquest" changes its meaning when one speaks of both the conquest of que conquerors and the conquest of the vanquished. With respect to our knowledge of the Indian, Professor Phelan is surely right that much recent research lies outside the limits of a paper on the 16th and 17th centuries. But much does not, and my own inclination would be to include the important codical and manuscript interpretations of recent years with reference to post-conquest 16th century life by Carrasco, Dibble, Galarza, Leander, and others. Some impressive gains have been made in this area, and the best scholars are meticulous workers deserving our recognition. They rarely write whole books or present bold comprehensive theories, but I wonder if the bold theories may not be receiving, in this paper, an attention that displaces some less "brilliant" but equally substantial contributions. For the record, as a commentator, I should like to add, in various areas of "conquest", names such as Jiménez Moreno, Romero de Terreros, Muriel, De la Torre, Berthe, Malagón, López de Meneses, Zambrand, Durand-Forest, De la Torre Villar, Millares Carlo, and Burrus. Clearly neither the main paper nor the comment can mention every worker in the vineyard, and it may be expected that the discussion will yield further relevant names. But I mention these as examples of persons whose work I admire and think important.

"Spiritual", "societal", "economic", and "architectural" are terms that fit the traditional sense of conquest better than do "ideological" and "philosophical", because they refer, at least in part, to further extensions of the domination of Spaniards over Indians. Ideological and philosophical conquests bear rather upon the historicits interpretation identified near the end of Professor Phelan's paper. With respect to ideological conquest, the meaning is not that Spaniards conquered Indians ideologically, as they did "spiritually" in the spiritual conquest. It is rather that subject of ideological conquest embraces the clash of Spanish ideas that the real conquest engendered. The equivalent comment concerning "philosophical conquest" cannot however be supported, for "philosophical conquest" relates to problems of discovery, not of conquest, and my impression is that the conquest theme breaks down at this point. With respect to "architectural", the term appears narrow when we consider that other arts were also involved.

Leaving the excellent material of the further sub-headings for discussion, I conclude with an effort to point the discussion in a particular direction. Between the large synthesis and the detailed study, between historicism and quantification, it is of course true that the paper urges further work in all areas, and this is as it should be. But my own feel for the paper's emphasis is that historicism and synthesis receive a certain preference. The impression seems supported by the comments on Iglesia, Soustelle, Chevalier, and others, and by the statement that what our study of the bureaucracy principally needs is "a powerful injection of new theoretical constructs". It is perhaps relevant that one may understand Chevalier's major work not as "Gallic synthesis" but as a far-reaching scholarly inquiry into the subject of Latifundia during a defined period. I do not see so clearly as Professor Phelan does the "stimulating theoretical constructs" provided by French—or any other—historians in these studies. In any case, if this interpretation of the paper's emphasis is correct, I would rejoin with the opposite emphasis. My own sense of progress to date in Mexican history and of expectable progress in the future, is that theory still suffers from want of evidence, and that in improving our present position we should stress and bring to light the neglected data of our abundant archives.

II. COMMENTARY ON "HISTORIOGRAFÍA NOVOHISPANA"

The seminar of Ramón Iglesia, which resulted in the publication *Estudios de historiografía de la Nueva España* in 1945, focussed its attention on post-conquest historians of conquest. Its members, presumably under instructions, were seeking defects in the conquest literature of the mid-sixteenth century and after, and with considerable enthusiasm and self-assurance they found what they sought. These later colonial interpreters of conquest were shown to have been slipshod and biased plagiarists, whose contributions to information on the conquest could be understood as limited at best.

Jorge Manrique's perceptive paper classifies the Iglesia studies as scientific, positivist history, and rightfully so. Partly in their defense I think it worth mentioning that the seminar members deliberately eschewed the perspective that Manrique adopts and develops, that their acknowledged concern was with the writers as historians of conquest, not as interpreters of their own time. Cervantes de Salazar, for example, appears wholly derivative in those portions of his work that deal with conquest, and it was precisely—and I shall add almost exclusively—to these portions that Díaz-Thome, in the interests of the seminar, directed his attention. The students, in some instances, gleefully overstated their case. But within the limits set for them, their conclusions were more accurate than not.

If we locate the principal value of a piece of historical writing in the circumstance that it informs us of the historian's own time, the effect is to bring historical writing into conformity with all other writing, indeed all other expressions, of the period. It is to bring to light attributes of the work that the writer himself may only half-consciously have intended. It is to identify in historical writing the themes, ideas, feelings, and other qualities of the age that the positivist historian seeks to demote but that no writer can prevent himself from reflecting. Sooner or later, historians do seem to be interpreted in this way—as when the writings of Thucydides are connected with the development of Greek objective science, or when over a period the historical attitudes toward Caesar or toward Napoleon are demonstrated to have matched exactly the periods in which they appeared. Manrique's important achievement is to fit the post-conquest Mexican historians in their intellectual age, and he performs his task so skilfully that we are obliged to revise our understanding not only of the historians but of the age as well, seeing its tensions in a new perspective. The age cast light on the historians, and the historians in turn cast light on the age. By rejecting the misapplied positivist criteria, by turning the "defects" into usable qualities (p. 106), this paper raises us to a new level of understanding.

A commentator too is expected to make a contribution, and a commentator's natural reaction, when a subject is moved wholesale from the area of old Wissenschaft to the area of new Geisteswissenschaft, might be that the writer has gone too far, that he has protested too much. The charge would be difficult to sustain in the case of the present paper, distinguished as it is by an unusual equanimity of judgment. It might yet be added that even from a positivist point of view the writers examined in the Iglesia seminar—I think especially of Muñoz Camargo, Cervantes de Salazar, Durán, and Dorantes de Carranza—are informative sources for the post-conquest sixteenth century. In those portions of their works that deal with events from 1525 on, they are less vulnerable to the standard positivist accusations, and if one reads a little between the lines it becomes evident that the students of the Iglesia seminar understood this very well. For this period the historians became eye-witnesses, and they did not copy from one another, or from third parties, at least to the same degree. For this period they meet far more successfully the "classic criteria of scientific and positivist history" (p. 105). To the rehabilitation of their reputation that Manrique bases on non-positivist values might then be added a rehabilitation in old-fashioned scientific terms. To a person like myself, who has sought to collect simple data on the external events, the overt history of happening, in the post-conquest sixteenth century, these writings are informative sources, and they are informative for their explicit content quite apart from their nostalgia, their millenarianism, and the other qualities that this paper so convincingly exposes.

COMENTARIO

CARLOS MARTÍNEZ MARÍN

Este bien logrado trabajo del doctor Phelan se inicia advirtiendo que la historiografía del periodo de la Conquista se ha incrementado notablemente desde 1945 en adelante, es decir, durante el periodo que cubre la revisión de la historiografía de México que aborda el Congreso que ahora se realiza. Que esto se debe a que la época de la Conquista se considera desde entonces como la época de un proceso de mestizaje; es decir, que al considerar a la época colonial se ha producido un cambio ideológico cualitativo en la consideración histórica sobre aquella época y que ahora se concibe como un doble proceso en el cual tanto los conquistadores, como los conquistados, participan de un mismo proceso y sufren influencias recíprocas. Que dentro de este contexto es en el que mucho se ha adelantado en la historia de México en las épocas de gobierno de los Habsburgo españoles.

Efectivamente ese nuevo rumbo de la historiografía colonial mexicana de los siglos XVI y XVII, así como su avance, es evidente y ha abierto otras perspectivas al trabajo de investigación, debido al abandono de lo que podríamos llamar las posiciones unilaterales (la indigenista o la hispanista), para así tomar una ruta bidimensional, que a mi modo de ver debería ser más plural, ya que no sólo hubo indios y españoles en el escenario de la vida novohispana, nueva dimensión que cabe dentro del contexto que plantea Phelan de acciones recíprocas entre conquistadores (los españoles peninsulares) y los conquistados (los indios, más los negros y los grupos derivados). Sin embargo, por lo que respecta a los dos grupos, ahora ya tradicionalmente considerados como los principales de Nueva España (blancos e indios), noto que en el trabajo que se comenta, no se ha incluido uno que precisamente plantea esta interinfluencia cultural, desde el momento en que tiene lugar el contacto de los conquistadores y de los conquistados, hasta que se produce lo que ya en verdad se puede llamar una cultura colonial. Me refiero al trabajo de George M. Foster "Conquista y Cultura. La herencia cultural española en América", en cuyas páginas, aunque muy etnográficas, se nos ofrece un marco teórico de referencia, mediante el cual podemos explicarnos cómo se verificó el o los procesos recíprocos de aculturación y cambio entre los grupos en contacto. Sin embargo, es indudable la bondad de la premisa de que en buena parte se ha abandonado la investigación y hechura de historias excluyentes, en los últimos años.

Continúa el doctor Phelan aclarando que a pesar de lo mucho que se ha publicado desde 1945 hasta la fecha, en su trabajo no hará un examen exhaustivo de todo lo que se ha dado a la letra, sino que exclusivamente se ocupará de aquellos trabajos que le parecen más significativos y que representan un camino y un reto al futuro inmediato de las investigaciones.

Advierte que su criterio no es extensivo y por lo mismo es subjetivo pero que persigue fundamentalmente provocar la controversia. Creo que ha obrado con razón, es preferible en campos tan vastos, adoptar un criterio selectivo, aun cuando se corra el riesgo de olvidar algunos buenos trabajos, sin intención deliberada de hacerlo, a caer en un interminable inventario de todo lo publicado. Creo que el material que presenta el autor puede servir para una amplia discusión, como él lo pretende.

En el texto de su trabajo el doctor Phelan ha hecho una clasificación temática, agrupando los trabajos por él considerados, según los asuntos que tratan y que considera más representativos. Para él esos trabajos deben ser considerados como los que mejor ilustran las "varias conquistas" que se verificaron en el país durante los siglos de la Conquista. Así, nos habla de la Conquista "demográfica", la Conquista de los "conquistadores", la Conquista de los "conquistados", la Conquista "ideológica", la Conquista "filosófica", la Conquista "espiritual", la Conquista "burocrática", la Conquista "de la sociedad", la Conquista "económica" y la Conquista "de la arquitectura".

En los apartados propuestos se incluyen los principales trabajos acerca de esos temas y se consideran sus principales aportaciones, con buenas discusiones acerca de su naturaleza, con las explicaciones, aclaraciones e informaciones pertinentes acerca de los aspectos institucionales, culturales, religiosos, económicos, sociales, artísticos, filosóficos e ideológicos que tocan.

No faltan los juicios del autor acerca de los supuestos, las hipótesis, aportaciones, posiciones filosóficas o históricas de cada trabajo y de cada autor y se presentan también, cuando es necesario, los puntos de vista diferentes y las controversias que existen en el tratamiento de temas similares, lo que enriquece la ponencia. Así, para dar unos pocos ejemplos, de los varios que al respecto toca el autor, en lo que él llama la Conquista "demográfica", señala claramente las diferencias que existen entre los que siguen a Rosenblat y el grupo de Berkeley que ha trabajado sobre el tema, tanto en las cuantificaciones de la población indígena en el momento del contacto, como entre los factores causales de la disminución de la población indígena, haciéndonos ver que las diferencias parten indudablemente de los diversos métodos y de las hipótesis seguidas en la investigación.

En otro aspecto, en el de la Conquista "ideológica" nos presenta en forma destacada la controversia Hanke-O'Gorman, según la cual Hanke se inclinó por considerar dos diferentes concepciones del mundo español acerca de la justicia en la conquista de América, representadas en las dos corrientes sostenidas, una por Sepúlveda y otra por Las Casas, mientras que O'Gorman prefiere considerarlas como dos puntos de vista de una misma justicia. En cuanto a la Conquista "filosófica" nos señala la continuidad en los libros de O'Gorman sobre América, acerca del problema ontológico y existencial del nuevo continente en la conciencia de los europeos que la descubrieron, proceso que tiene lugar independientemente de la realidad geográfica previa americana.

A pesar del abandono de la historiografía unilateral, Phelan no se desentiende de los trabajos que se han producido en el periodo estudiado y que corresponden a las dos corrientes tradicionales, la hispanista y la indigenista, identificándolos con lo que él llama "lo Cortés" y "lo Cuauhtémoc", que para él representa una dicotomía que responde al deseo de reconstruir el mundo de los aztecas. Respecto de estos trabajos hay que aclarar por nuestra parte, que afortunadamente la mayor parte de los que se han producido, tienen efectivamente la intención que señala Phelan, conocer más ese mundo indígena anterior a la Conquista y lo que ésta representó para los conquistados, pero que otros siguen preocupados por alimentar posiciones previas, más que lograr contribuciones científicas.

Y así continúa el ponente comentando, explicando y valorando los mejores trabajos de historia social, historia económica, de historia de la administración pública, de historia de la evangelización y de otras instituciones principalmente indígenas; considerando también a la menos trabajada historiografía del siglo xvii, anotando cuidadosamente cuándo tiene lugar el cambio fundamental de aquella época del diez y siete a la época del xviii o de la ilustración y comenta que a pesar de haberse tenido durante mucho tiempo por una etapa de "fachada barroca aparentemente inmóvil" fue indudablemente un siglo en el que se presentaron problemas importantísimos en el proceso de integración de la Colonia, así como sus consecuencias y contradicciones, tales como las revueltas indígenas del norte del país y las del sureste, así como los motines citadinos.

En fin, podríamos extendernos más hasta tratar aquí cada una de las partes de la ponencia, pero creo que no sería lo adecuado; baste señalar que estoy de acuerdo en lo medular del trabajo y prefiero, de acuerdo con los deseos del autor, dejar para su momento la ampliación o los desacuerdos de esta interesante ponencia.

Sin embargo, sí creo importante dejar sentado mi desacuerdo con el título principal de la ponencia y con los subtítulos que señalan la diferente temática de los trabajos que se incluyeron. Indudablemente que por necesidades metodológicas era necesario elaborar un cuadro de clasificación en el cual agrupar los trabajos según su distinta naturaleza, para lograr un orden comprensible, para poder valorar los trabajos en sí y aun para poder compararlos; pero el término general empleado de "Varias conquistas" no me parece el más apropiado; para mí es confuso y desorienta, pues siempre he pensado que en la realidad hubo una sola conquista, que indudablemente presenta múltiples y variados aspectos: el militar, el material, el religioso, el económico, etcétera, que conforman temas que a lo largo del trabajo historiográfico novohispano, se han elegido por lo general de acuerdo a necesidades impuestas por el trabajo científico pero que presentaron indisoluble unidad en la época en que acontecieron y que la presentan en la apreciación global; resulta además difícil aceptar el significado forzado de algunos términos como los calificativos "demográfica", "burocrática" o de "la arquitectura". Hubiera sido preferible usar el término llano de "tema" o "aspecto" que con mayor sencillez designaría la diferente temática con que se ha trabajado la conquista española de México.

RELATORÍA

ÁLVARO MATUTE

La revisión de la historiografía de tema novohispánico publicada en los últimos veinticinco años, y el análisis de las obras de tres cronistas considerados tradicionalmente de "segunda", ocasionaron interesantes discusiones sobre la necesidad de ubicar cronológicamente la época cubierta y la distinción entre las diversas etapas que cubre la historia de este periodo. Se planteó la dificultad de establecer una periodización uniforme por la existencia de hechos sobresalientes que marcan el inicio y fin de una época, y que pertenecen a la historia del arte, a la historia económica y aun a la historia política. Se aclaró que la periodización es instrumental y no real, que es útil sólo en relación a la interpretación particular que se haga de una época histórica.

El tema que ocupó la mayor parte de la sesión fue el de la distinción entre el criollismo novohispano y los diversos regionalismos que aparecieron de manera coetánea en todo el imperio español. Aunque hubo distintas opiniones se acordó que las diferencias estructurales son específicas, pero que la actitud espiritual es concordante. Todo obedecería, en última instancia, a la relación entre las regiones y el aparato central burocrático del imperio español de la época de Carlos V y Felipe II. Con respecto a este asunto se insistió en que debe procederse a estudiar a la Nueva España en relación con la historia universal y no limitarla a la investigación de lo sucedido en la región central de México.

En relación con los criterios que se pueden utilizar para la lectura e interpretación de los textos de la época, se destacó, por un lado, su lectura con el criterio clásico positivista y, por el otro, verlos como expresión de su época. Igualmente se insistió en la necesidad de proceder al examen de otras crónicas.

III. HISTORIOGRAFÍA DEL SIGLO XVIII Y DE LA REVOLUCIÓN DE INDEPENDENCIA

6 de noviembre de 1969

Presidente: Rafael Moreno, director de la Dirección General de Publicaciones, UNAM.

Ponente: Peggy Korn, lectora de historia colonial latinoamericana, Swarthmore College.

Comentarista: Bernabé Navarro, profesor e investigador de la Facultad de Filosofía y Letras, UNAM.

Participantes: Bernard Bobb, Washington State University; Ernesto de la Torre director de la Biblioteca Nacional de México; presidente de la Sección Nacional de México IPGH; Nancy Farris, lectora de estudios hispanoamericanos, Universidad de West Indies, Jamaica; Virginia Guedea, investigadora del Instituto de Historia, UNAM; Asunción Lavrin, lectora de historia, Rosary College, III; Roberto Moreno, investigador de la Biblioteca Nacional; Clement Motten, profesor de historia; director de Actividades Culturales Internacionales, Universidad de Temple; Stanley J. Stein profesor de Historia en la Universidad de Princeton; Masae Sugawara, investigador del Archivo General de la Nación.

Participantes Europeos: M. S. Al'Perovich. Institut Istorii Latinskoi Ameriki, Moscu; Manfred Kossok, director del *Latin American Research Group* del Departamento de Historia de la Universidad Karl Marx, Leipzig; John Lynch, lector de historia hispánica y lationamericana de la Universidad de Londres.

Relator: Diego Sandoval, estudiante del Centro de Estudios Históricos de El Colegio de México.

TOPICS IN MEXICAN HISTORIOGRAPHY, 1750-1810; THE BOURBON REFORMS, THE ENLIGHTENMENT, AND THE BACKGROUND OF REVOLUTION

PEGGY K. KORN

All historians work backward from today. The more perceptive recognize that they do so. Therefore, rather than attempt an all-inclusive examination of subsequent writing and publishing of the history of Mexico in the eighteenth century, let us limit discussion to the historiography of a set of priorities, to themes of great interest to present-day historians. In so doing, we are after all but acknowledging that often what we now consider shortcomings of past histories are but interpretations predicated upon premises and concerns of ages other than ours.

Can a general statement be made concerning what historians of today most want to know about the eighteenth century? The collective impact of recent work does allow, as we shall see, the formulation of a tentative listing of queries subdivided as follows. We want to know, first of all, what was life in Mexico like in the eighteenth century? And what sort of changes took place in the latter decades of that rather general time span, and in the first decade of the 19th century to distinguish it from the preceding centuries of Spanish domination. Secondly, we seek to discover the extent to which the changes realized do or do not provide a continuum or continuing process culminating in revolution. Finally, we wish to assess the nature and magnitude of external influences on internal conditions and developments in Mexico in this period and especially to evaluate how these impulses from without may have contributed to a climate propitious to revolution, or even to actively fostering independence from Spain.

These, then, are our questions. We can not fault other historians in other times for asking different ones. We trust scholars of the future will smile kindly, and not too condescendingly, upon us and our sense of what is important. Recognizing that questions put to a body of historical material come to serve as boundaries imposed on the answers, we should note some of the more outstanding queries and responses of the past before considering in detail the work of today.

1830 TO 1910: GENERAL HISTORIES

An historian's attitude toward *the* big event in Mexican history between the Conquest and the Revolution of the twentieth Century, the Revolution of 1810, often determined, consciously or unconsciously, how accounts of the eighteenth century were to be written. Indeed, from the immediate post-revolutionary period henceforth it often determined whether or not one should bother to consider the eighteenth century at all.

In general, historians writing in the nineteenth century either put down the unrest from 1810 to 1821 as a struggle between gachupines and creoles, or between Spain and its American dependencies, or between liberty and despotism, or even between Spanish law and order, on one hand, and the Mexican tendency to anarchy and chaos on the other. Whatever was said of the eighteenth century most often either remained lumped with the history of the two preceding centuries or was brought in as a curtain-raiser to revolution. And so it often is still. Such handling was simply more obvious at a time when most accounts of the eighteenth century appeared in general histories of Mexico or, most frequently, of all Spanish America.

Here we should note an apparent exception which turns out to be a case in point: the multi-volumed, indeed magisterial, work of H. H. Bancroft, *Mexico* (6 v. San Francisco, 1883-1888). It was *the* Mexican history written in the United States of America before the 1920s and, if recently neglected, still not superseded. Bancroft's sanguine and enthusiastic spirit permeates a mini-library compiled with the aid of obviously diligent assistants. A vociferous liberal in the great, late tradition of the nineteenth century, Bancroft applauded the end of the Spanish regime in America; he observed that, by 1823, "America and Europe are pretty well separated politically, never again, thank God, to be united".[1]

And how was Spanish dominion brought low?

> Looking well into the causes of the Spanish American revolt, we find there the full catalogue of wrongs and injustice common to political subordinates of this nature and in addition some of the blackest crimes within the power of tyranhy to encompass. What were such matters as duties per cent, free coming and going, sumptuary regulations, or even local laws and legislation beside intellectual slavery, the enforcement of superstition, the subordination of soul, the degradation of both the mental and spiritual in man.[2]

[1] v. 4, p. 7.
[2] *ibid.*, p. 13.

In short, Bancroft assumed that nothing of historical importance went on in the stagnant atmosphere of oppressed Mexico. Accordingly, his volume on the eighteenth century is a narrative account largely of political and institutional developments, and as such it is still of great value to historians today. His sources include diaries of the period and other treasures, many of them, unfortunately, since ignored. [3]

Bancroft provides a stellar example of the nineteenth century vantage point. He could not see any activity in progress in the viceroyalty of New Spain except that set in motion by, or in regard to, Spain.

Independence was the favorite theme of nineteenth century historians. Most of them accepted political liberty as a concomitant of progress. There was a widespread belief in the fashionable assumption that "when the fruit is ripe, it will drop". In conformity with this school of thought, the desire for independence was indicative of a general American maturity. Little or no consideration was given to the ripening process. No need, then, to set down the history of the eighteenth century, a task by implication analagous to recounting the daily adventures of a pear hanging on a bough. [4]

In short, to most European and Anglo-American historians, Mexico in the eighteenth century was beside the point. They concentrated, when they wrote of Mexico, on the independence movement. Hidalgo and Morelos simply *happened*, thrust forward by destiny (shades of Napoleón!). When specific cause for revolution was ascribed, it was laid, as by Bancroft, to the individious policies and ill health, indeed

[3] Among them, in a series published in Mexico in 1854 by Diario Oficial, José Manuel de Castro Santa-Ana, *Diario de sucesos notables* [1752-1758], (3 v., *Documentos para la historia de Méjico*, ser. I. IV-VI). The same series, v. VII, contains José Gómez, *Diario curioso de México* [1776-1798].

[4] Dominque de Pradt, *Des colonies et de la revolution actuelle de L'Amerique* (2 v., Paris, 1817), for example, saw all revolutionary activity in America as a chain reaction proceeding from that announcing United States maturity in 1776. For other aspects of de Pradt's ideas and their influence, see Arthur P. Whitaker, *The United States and the Independence of Latin America* (Johns Hopkins Univ., 1941). Also writing in the glow of the revolutionary period was the British charge d'affaires in Mexico, H. G. Ward, *Mexico in 1827* (2 v., London, 1828). De Pradt defined maturity in terms of population and natural resources. Mexico began as inferior to the metropolis, he stated, but had come to equal and would soon overtake it. Cf. William Davis Robinson, *Memoirs of the Mexican Revolution* (2 v., London, 1821), who wrote that Alexander von Humboldt "has flattered the Spanish government" in regard to the extent of reform in Mexico, that injustice and oppression were the sum total of Mexican history until 1808. Spanish historians in the 1800s, of course, had their own cause for concern with Mexican independence. See Melchor Almagro Fernández, *La emancipación de América y su Reflejo en la Conciencia Española* (Madrid, Instituto de Estudios Políticos, 1944) and Luis Felipe Muro Arias, "La Independencia Americana vista por Historiadores Españoles del siglo XIX", in *Estudios de Historiografía Americana* (colegio de México, 1948), pp. 207-388.

prostration, of mother Spain. In this sense, Mexican independence was described as a reaction *against* Spain rather than as a movement *for* national liberty.

It was when Mexicans looked to their own past that the writing of their eighteenth century history proper can be said to have begun. In the two decades after achieving independence, liberals and conservatives began to think back, if selectively, to a time when their land, politically oppressed or not, was at least more prosperous. So José María Luis Mora, even though avidly anti-clerical, in his *Obras sueltas* (Paris, 1837), included some of the writings of Manuel Abad y Queipo, Archbishop-Elect of Michoacán at the inception of revolution in 1810, for, said Mora, "they contain knowledge fundamental to the understanding of questions relating to the public credit of the Mexican Republic". So Carlos María de Bustamante, declaring history to be the surest guide to legislation, published the annalistic history by Andrés Cavo of, in the main, the *ayuntamiento* of Mexico City, under the inflated title of *Los tres siglos de Méjico* (México, 1836). Bustamante more than doubled its volume and added immeasurable to its scholarly worth by the supplement for the years 1767-1821 he appended. So Lucas Alamán in works published 1844-1849 looked back longingly to the general order and stability maintained by the viceregal system of government. [5] To Alamán, to employ a rather anachronistic and international analogy, New Spain approximated Camelot.

Alamán, generally considered the most informative of Mexican historians writing about the eighteenth century, presented the early Bourbon regime as a triumph of enlightened rule. Spain and New Spain, according to his conservative, flourished until the serpent bearing the apple —that is, France profering the Family Pact— brought war and ruin. A weak and exceedingly ill-advised king, Charles IV, then gave the *coup de grace*. Not decay of Spanish institutions but the effect of external meddling and one weak king lost the empire. He related, as if subsidiary and completely dependent on manipulation from abroad, something of what transpired within Mexico. Changes in economy and administration introduced in the regime of Charles III brought salutary reforms conducive to economic prosperity and, as he mentioned in passing, "aumento de la Ilustración". He attributed to Bourbon reforms not only Enlightenment, but also the growth of Mexican *conciencia de sí* or self-awareness. His interest in his fellow-

---

[5] *Disertaciones sobre la historia de la república megicana desde la época de la conquista* (3 v., Mexico, 1844-1849). Volume three includes a history of Spain in which he praises the constitution of the Habsburgs. *Historia de Méjico desde los primeros movimientos que prepararon su independencia en el año de 1808 hasta la época presente* (5 v., México, 1849). Volume one includes a summary of the outstanding institutions and events of the late eighteenth century.

creoles was subsidiary to his estimation of the importance of the Spaniards who governed; he relegated the role of Mexicans to that of passive subjects of Spain, if harboring a traditional antagonism to gachupines. There was, he implied, some reaction in Mexico to Spanish policies and to other external influences on the country, but he was not terribly concerned with any of it until 1808, when reaction to the overthrow of the viceroy by Spaniards somehow produced a "creole party" who initiated a revolution. Where these men came from, who they were, what they had been doing before 1808, and the content of their discontents were all outside the sphere of his inquiry. Alamán's goal was to present New Spain as a model of institutionalized stability, with change carefully imposed and regulated by government. In this sense, he looks at the Revolution of 1810 much as Edmund Burke surveyed contemporary affairs in France in 1790.

Alamán saw widespread creole disaffection from the old ordes spring full-blown from the Spanish deposition of the viceroy, José de Iturriga-ray, in 1808. Bustamante, his more liberal contemporary, recorded the presence of a good deal of positive activity of all sorts among the Mexicans and indicated something of the social complexities of the late eighteenth century. Unfortunately, he never tells us enough. What he intimates, however, is tantalizing. He mentions, for example, enlightened viceroys and educated creoles sharing many economic and social concerns. To him Spanish involvement in war with England from 1796 on was not, as Alamán implied, simply a presage of greater disaster to come, but an event allowing some Mexicans to bolster the country's internal economy. Is Bustamante's account of the sporadic and arbitrary governmental harrassment he suffered while editing the *Diario de México* indicative of how the Spanish regime hampered and discouraged enterprising Mexicans from engaging in legitimate activity of all sorts? If all too sketchily, Bustamante nevertheless contributes much information on the nature of adverse Mexican reaction to a number of what have been subsequently termed "the Bourbon reforms", from the popular displeasure at the expulsion of the Jesuits in 1767 to the outcry raised against the attempt by the government to alienate the real property of hospitals, poor houses, and other religious institu-tions by the Consolidation Act of 1804. It's a pity that neither Busta-mante nor Alamán left us reminiscences of their formative years.

Two trends predominate in the writing of Mexican history from the next generation born after the revolution, to 1910. First of all, Mexican historians were less interested in solving immediate national problems and more concerned with the eighteenth century as a part of the national heritage. Secondly, this interim span was a period of tug-of-war, and ocassionally synthesis, between historical writing as *belles lettres* and as a science.

Synthesis is most apparent in the work of Joaquín García Icazbalceta. Both meticulous research and what used to be referred to as a felicitious style mark the series of biographical sketches and commentaries on historians born in eighteenth century Mexico which he contributed to the *Diccionario Universal de Historia y Geografía* (10 v. México, 1853-56). He commented pungently on Cavo's annals "anotadas año por año con lamentable prolijidad", on Bustamante's supplement to them, as not very good but the best thing Bustamante wrote, on Alamán, as a writer infinitely superior to Bustamante. Highest praise to all writers about America he reserved for Alexander von Humboldt. He included notes on the Spaniards, Manuel Abad y Queipo and the enlightened viceroy, Revillagigedo the Younger, who "always knew how to reconcile the good of the country [Mexico] with the benefit of the metropolis". [6] García Icazbalceta, a pivotal figure in Mexican historiography, noted the contributions of both creoles and enlightened Spaniards to Mexican culture. Although primarily interested in the first Spanish century in Mexico, his lifelong devotion to recovering colonial documents and primary sources gave impetus to publication and republication of much eighteenth century material, as well as to greater reliance on it by other historians. [7]

[6] Vol. 8-10 were an Apendice edited by Manuel Orozco y Berra. Selections from it reappeared in Joaquín García Icazbalceta, *Opúsculos y biografías*, edited by Julio Jiménez Rueda (Universidad Nacional Autónoma de México, [hereafter UNAM], 1942). Also see Manuel Guillermo Martínez, *Don Joaquín García Icazbalceta; his place in Mexican historiography* (Catholic Univ. of America, 1947). García Icazbalceta's works have been collected in *Obras* (10 v, México, 1896-1899).

[7] García Icazbalceta published in *Renacimiento*, 2 (1894), a letter Humboldt wrote to José de Iturrigaray on March 28, 1803. His collections of sixteenth century documents are well known. He also edited *Opúsculos inéditos latinos y castellanos del P. Francisco Javier Alegre* (México, 1889) and published the *Noticias de México* (México, 1880), a manuscript left by the Mexican bookseller, Francisco Sedano (1742?-1812).

Eighteenth century Mexican documents, manuscripts, and histories were selected for publication in accord with the interests of historians writing at the time. In the first half of the century, even during the revolutionary years, works of "economic" import appeared or reappeared. Notable among them were:

1813: *Colección de los escritos más importantes que en diferentes épocas dirigió al gobierno Don Manuel Abad y Queipo* (México, 1813).

1816-1821: José Mariano Beristáin de Souza, *Biblioteca hispanoamericana septentrional...*, an attempt to complete the *Biblioteca mexicana* begun by Juan Eguiara y Eguren (1755).

1820: Juan Antonio Ahumada, *Representación político-legal a la majestad del Sr. D. Felipe V en favor de los empleos políticos, de guerra y eclasiásticos*, originally published in Madrid in 1725.

1831: José Antonio Alzate y Ramírez, *Gacetas de Literatura de México* (4 v, Puebla).

1831: *Instrucción reservada que el conde de Revilla Gigedo dio a su sucesor en el mando, Marqués de Branciforte*.

Manuel Orozco y Berra, the title of whose *Historia de la dominación española en México* (4 v., México, 1906) indicates he wrote from the point of view of what Spain did, in his volume IV, "El Poder Real,

1831: Hipólito Villarroel, *México por dentro y fuera bajo el gobierno de los vireyes. O sea Enfermedades Políticas que padece la capital de la Nueva España en casi todos los cuerpos de que se compone* (1788).

1845-1853: Fabián de Fonseca y Carlos de Urrutia, *Historia general de la real hacienda* (6 v).

(From the 1850s on, García Icazbalceta's influence is in evidence, culminating around the turn of the century with the publication of a number of outstanding collections of documents, and beginning in 1854 with the publication, mentioned above (note 3) of *Documentos para la historia de Méjico*. From this time on, too, material by or relating to the expelled Mexican Jesuits appeared. It is discussed on p. 35).

1853-1857: Manuel Orozco y Berra, comp., *Documentos para la historia de México* (4 series). See above, note 3.

1856: Matías de la Mota Padilla (1688-1776), *Historia de Nueva Galicia.*

1867-73: *Instrucciones que los virreyes de Nueva España dejaron a sus sucesores* (2 v). Later printings of individual instructions include:

1960: Norman F. Martin, ed., *Instrucciones del Marquez de Croiz que deja a su sucesor, Antonio María Bucareli.*

1960: Ernesto de la Torre, ed., *Instrucción reservada que dio don Miguel José de Azanza a su sucesor don Félix Berenguer de Marqueña* (1800).

1965: Norman F. Martin, ed., *Instrucción reservada del Obispo-virrey Ortega Montañés al Conde de Moctezuma.*

1966: Conde de Revilla Gigedo, *Informe sobre las Misiones* (1793) *e Instrucción Reservada al Marqués de Branciforte* (1794), edited by José Bravo Ugarte.

1867: José de Gálvez (Marqués de Sonora), *Informe general que instruyó y entregó... al Virrey, D. Antonio Bucarely y Ursúa... 31 diciembre, 1771.*

1869: Alexander von Humboldt, "Tablas geográfico-políticas del reino de la Nueva España (en el año de 1803) presentadas al señor virrey del mismo reino en enero de 1804", in *Boletín de la Sociedad Mexicana de Geografía y Estadística*, 2ª época, 1.

1869: Fernando Navarro y Noriega, "Memoria sobre la población del Reino de Nueva España" (1814), *ibid.*, pp. 281-291.

1877-1882: Juan E. Hernández y Dávalos, ed., *Colección de Documentos para la historia de la guerra de independencia de México de 1808-1821* (6 v).

1905-1911: Genaro García and Carlos Pereyra, eds., *Documentos inéditos o muy raros para la historia de México* (36 v), includes vol. 10: *Tumultos y rebeliones acaecidos en México;* vol. 11: *El clero de México y la Guerra de Independencia;* and vol. 15: *El clero de México durante la Dominación Española.*

1910: Genaro García, ed., *Documentos históricos mexicanos* (7 v) vol. 1, 2 and 7 include documents for the years, 1807-1810.

1930: *Boletín del Archivo General de la Nación*, 1, included the text of the *Carta Reservada* of Revillagigedo of August 31, 1793. Subsequent editions contain innumerable documents in eighteenth century history.

1933-1936: Luis Chávez Orozco, ed., *Documentos para la historia económica de México* (11 v).

1939-1942: Francisco del Paso y Troncoso, ed., *Epistolario de Nueva España*, 1505-1818 (16 v), vol. 13 includes eighteenth century materials.

1939-1945: Silvio Zavala and Mario Castelo, eds., *Fuentes para la Historia del Trabajo en Nueva España* (8 v), vol. 8:1575-1805.

1701-1789", acknowledged his reliance on a number of primary materials, as do the contributors to the first full-scale Mexican history, edited by Vicente Riva Palacios, *México a través de los siglos* (5 v. México, 1889[?]). [8] Its authors expressed their indebtedness to the scholarship of García Icazbalceta.

As Edmundo O'Gorman has observed, they achieved the synthesis of the Indian and Spanish pasts in conceiving of their project as properly concerned with the historical evolution of the Mexican people and in assuming that "people" to be a corporate body, an organism formed in the bosom of the viceroyalty and evolving through time and space. Within the weighty compendium born of this broad and lofty vision, however, the pages on the eighteenth century reflect a potpourri of old attitudes. While emphasizing Mexican reaction to European wars and to the American and French revolutions, they were largely devoted to charting material progress (although here Riva Palacio erred in so important a matter as avering that no change occurred in the production of agriculture and mining from the 1600s to 1810). It is a history of events (individuals are unimportant), on one level, and of the Mexican spirit on another. Determinism, in this case sired by positivism, prevails. Mind and body naturally progress toward liberty; there is no need to examine how they interact. At its end, the nineteenth century remained a treasure trove of eighteenth century history yet to be written.

1949: Francisco González de Cossío, ed., *Gacetas de México*.

1953: Xavier Tavera Alfaro, "Documentos para la historia de periodismo mexicano (siglo XVIII)", en homenaje a Silvio Zavala, *Estudios históricos americanos* (Colegio de México), pp. 317-344.

1963: —— *El Nacionalismo en la prensa mexicana del siglo* XVIII.

1960: Juan Vicente de Güemes de Padilla, Conde de Revillagigedo, *El Comercio Exterior y su influjo en la Economía de la Nueva España* (1793), This is vol. 4 in the *Colección de documentos para la historia del comercio exterior de México* edited by Luis Chávez Orozco.

1962: Francisco Eduardo Tresguerras, *Ocios literarios*. Edited by Francisco de la Maza.

Note should be made here of Tadeo Ortiz de Ayala, *México considerado como nación independiente y libre* ... (Burdeos, 1832), by the creole tutor of the sons of Iturrigaray who, in chap. 5, included a bibliography of Mexican authors and artists of the colonial period; of Nicolás León monumental *Bibliografía mexicana del siglo* XVIII (5 v, México, 1902-1908); of the popular biographies in *Hombres Ilustres Mexicanos* (México, 1873-1874), edited by Eduardo Gallo E., and of the most balanced of nineteenth-century works on our period, Carlos Pereyra, *Historia de América Española* (7 v, Madrid, 1876), vol. 3: *México*.

[8] Eighteenth century history is found in vol. 2: *El Virreinato*, by Riva Palacio, and the first decade of the nineteenth century in vol. 3, *La Guerra de Independencia*, by Julio Zárate.

GENERAL HISTORIES SINCE 1920

General histories written in the twentieth century by non-Mexicans, despite information accumulating in specialized studies, have brought too little change, for the most part, in approach to eighteenth century Mexican history. Spanish activity in Mexico is all. Internal events appear only as reactions. Notable exceptions, of course, are works emanating from East Germany and Russia. From the United States, Mexican histories by Ernest Gruening (*Mexico and its Heritage*, New York and London, 1928), Lesley B. Simpson (*Many Mexicos*, Univ. of California, 1952), Henry B. Parkes, (*A History of Mexico*, Boston, 1950), and most recently, Charles C. Cumberland (*Mexico. The Struggle for Modernity*, New York, 1968) illustrate this trend.

The earliest, Gruening, followed in the tradition of Bancroft, discerning no change in the (unenlightened) policies of Spanish government throughout the viceregal period. Simpson confined his discussion of the eighteenth century to a brief mention of "the Bourbon revolution" bringing progress to New Spain. Parkes placed the entire century in a chapter on the growth of liberalism, mentioned some of "the precursors of revolution", by which he meant the scattered and sporadic local uprisings (whose inclusion may well be a contributing factor to why this history was translated into Russian), then went confidently on to the events of 1810. Cumberland, who by 1968 should have known better, lumped the viceregal period, as so often done of yore, and ignored as much as possible (more, in fact), the more recent materials available concerning the history of the eighteenth century.

Here special mention must be made of Lillian Estelle Fisher's *The Background of the Revolution for Mexican Independence* (Boston, 1934). Closest to an attempt at a general history of the late colonial period by a non-Mexican, it is full of information badly assembled, less a goldmine than a grab-bag. For all of that, the book *is* a response to scholarly enquiry.

The approach to the late eighteenth century taken by M. S. Alperovich in *Voina za Nezavisimost Meksiki* (Moscow, 1964) should stimulate other historians to attenmpt syntheses of our period. He beguis by attacking the proclivity of "conservative and reactionary bourgeois historians" to rehabilitate Spanish colonialism, mentioning in particular the writings of Cecil Jane, Salvador de Madariaga, Richard Konetzke, and Pierre Chaunu, all of whom he claims see the independence movement os a conservative reaction of creole aristocrats to the liberal reforms of the Bourbon government. Alperovich, instead, explains the revolution as a bourgeois one in which large groups of colonial society participated. He seeks its origins in the late eighteenth century and finds them, not surprisingly, stemming from economic conditions. [9]

He interprets the policy of Charles III not as one of determined reform but as the result of indecision and inconsequence. The government could neither prevent increase in industry, agriculture, and trade nor could it create the conditions necessary to resolve the attendant economic problems. He finds that Mexicans, long thrust upon their own resources, had developed a revolutionary ideology subsequently stimulated by events in Anglo-America and in France. Alperovich reverses the older cause-and-effect relationship historians such as Simpson posited between the Bourbon reforms and the Mexican independence movement. Citing as evidence the more than 100 risings in the colonial period, he assumes that all of them embodied a desire for political emancipation from Spain. The Bourbon reforms he then interprets as introduced in reaction to this growth of a widespread emancipation movement *before* 1760.

Fault may be found with his conceptual framework, particularly with his assumption that all local disturbances had political content, but is perhaps as well to write history from a relatively inflexible ideological point of view, obvious to all, as from a firm, but mistaken, conviction that one is objective and possesses no preconceptions whatsoever.

POLITICAL AND ECONOMIC HISTORY

Specialists in political history, especially in the United States, have tended to cluster around a study of what although largely instituted in the reign of one Bourbon, Charles III, and in some aspects retrogressive — have come to be known as the Bourbon reforms. [10] In 1913

[9] As *Historia de la Independencia de México* (1810-1824), it was translated by Adolfo Sánchez Vázquez (México, 1967). Also see Manfred Kossok, "Revolution und Bourgoisie in Latinamerika. Zum, Charakter der Lateinamerikanischen unabhängigkeitsbewegung, 1810-1826", *Zeitschrift für Geschichtswissenschaft*, Jahrgang, 9 (1961), Sonderheft, pp. 123-143; M. Kossok and Walter Markov, "Konspekt über das spanische Kolonialsystem", *Wissen Zeit, Gesellschafts*, 5:2 (1955-1956), pp. 121-268; and their "Las indias non [sic] eran colonias? Hintergründe einer Kolonialapologetik", in *Lateinamerika zwischen Emanzipation und Imperialismus, 1810-1960* (Berlin, Academie-Verlag 1961), pp. 1-34. From Spain, Jaime Vicèns Vives, ed., *Historia social y económica de España y América* (5 v, Barcelona, 1957-1959), vol. 4, pt. 1 on Mexico. And now being published in London, Peter Calvert, *México*.

[10] Excellent discussion of Bourbon economic policies in Spanish America and an indication of their effects are supplied by J. H. Parry, in *The Spanish Seaborne Empire* (New York, 1966), and R. A. Humphreys, "Economic Aspects of the Fall of the Spanish American Empire", *Revista de Historia de América*, 30 (1950), pp.

Donald E. Smith, assuming "There was no great change in government in the late eighteenth century", unhesitatingly based his institutional history of *The Viceroy in New Spain* (Univ. of California), largely on a study of viceregal administration there in the time of Charles III. Three years later, Herbert I. Priestley in his study of *José de Gálvez, Visitor-General of New Spain, 1765-1771* (Univ. of California), described economic reforms that were not, he stated, fundamental changes in the operation of fiscal machinery but only an enforcement of the existing system, since of "Paramount interest to Spain" was "the productive wealth of New Spain". Reforms introduced due to the visit of Gálvez centralized administration of revenues, enforced monopoly regulations, effectively warred against smuggling, and fostered Spanish manufacture and commerce. However, Priestley added, they also succeeded in making New Spain take up more of the burden of empire, and made local and general government more pervasive and more pervasively Spanish.

A decade later, Lillian E. Fisher surveyed obvious innovation in her study of the *The Intendant System in America* (Univ. of California, 1929), introduced in New Spain in 1787, to promote and administer the reform program on a regional level. Fisher described what was clearly viewed as change by contemporaries who judged the success of the system in large part in accord with their opinions about whether change itself was good or bad. Together with more recent assessments, her work points to the system achieving some reform in finance, civil administration, military matters, and in indian affairs. At the same time, the system provoked an adverse Mexican reaction, by intervening in municipal government and local life, which in some instances overshadowed what it achieved in its stated purposes of bureaucratic organization and revenue increase. [11] In a recently completed disserta-

450-456. For contemporary awareness of the new spurt of Spanish energy in New Spain, see William Robertson, *History of América* (2 v, London, 1777), book 8. *Historia Mexicana*, 17; 3 (1968), in memory of José Miranda is dedicated to general but informative articles on eighteenth-century economic history.

[11] A summary of Fisher's findings appeared as "The Intendant System in Spanish America", *Hispanic American Historical Review* (hereafter *HAHR*), 8 (1928), pp. 3-13. See also Luis Navarro García, *Intendencias en Indias* (Seville, 1959), and for documents concerning the system, Gisela Marazzani de Pérez Enciso, *La Intendencia en España y América* (Caracas, 1966); Víctor A. Belaúnde, "Factors of the Colonial Period in South America working toward a New Regime", *HAHR*, 9 (1929), pp. 144-153, concluded that older divisive traditions, notably regionalism, "received new strength from the reforms of the Bourbons. These reforms were intended to strengthen and reaffirm the bonds between colonies and mother country, but the results were just the contrary". John Lynch, *Spanish Colonial Administration 1782-1810: The Intendan System in the Viceroyalty of the Río de la Plata* (London, 1958), is the sort of study needed for New Spain. See also the essay on the intendancy system in the forthcoming book by David Brading, *Three Essays on Bourbon México*.

tion, B. R. Hamnett suggests some of the longer-range effects of the Mexican interaction and reaction in "The Intendant System and the Landed Interest in Mexico: the Origins of Independence, 1768-1808" (Cambridge Univ. 1968).

Studies of this system (which put the principles of enlightened despotism to work regionally) were followed by reconsiderations of the nature of the office of viceroy in this period of greatest (Spanish) Bourbon aspiration. Dissertations by James M. Manfredini and Edwin H. Carpenter, both completed in 1949, stress the benign, indeed beneficient aspects of the administration of the viceroy who epitomized the spirit of the program, Juan Francisco de Güemes y Horcasitas, el Conde de Revillagigedo. [12] Manfredini noted Revillagigedo's interest in encouraging agriculture, mining, public health and social welfare in general, primary, technical and professional education, and freer trade. In the capital, Revillagigedo pursued an exceedingly enlightened policy. He cleaned and lit the streets, forbid bathing and other personal functions in public fountains, admonished the populace to clothe itself, waged war on drunkenness, regulated the food supply, and encouraged clean hospitals, roadbuilding, libraries, and schools, including those of architecture and mining, and periodicals disseminating useful knowledge.

It was, as you recall, García Icazbalceta who long ago recognized the fine balance Revillagigedo sought, and momentarily achieved, in the harnessing of Mexican prosperity to the needs of the *real hacienda*, in other words, that the dual nature of the reforms he imposed or attempted —he admitted there were some problems he could not solve— clearly reflected the combination of enlightened principles with autocratic aims and methods. All were designed, ultimately, to increase the national wealth of Spain.

How the Crown, fearing England, especially after the occupation of Havana in 1762, innovated initially in dispatching an army to New Spain is recounted by María del Carmen Velásquez in *El estado de guerra de Nueva España, 1760-1808* (Colegio de México, 1950). She and Lyle N. McAlister, studying *The Fuero Militar in New Spain, 1764-1800* (Univ. of Florida, 1957), relate how a new semi-autonomous corporation, the army, was imposed, buttressed by a Mexican militia,

---

[12] See also J. Ignacio Rubio Mañé, "Síntesis histórica de la vida del II Conde de Revillagigedo, virrey de Nueva España", *Anuario de Estudios Americanos*, 6 (Seville, 1949), pp. 451-496; Lillian E. Fisher, *The Viceregal Administration in the Spanish American Colonies* (Univ. of California, 1926); Gaston Desdevises du Dezert, "Vice-Rois et Captaine Généraux de Indes Espagnoles a la fin du XVIII e siècle", *Revue Historique*, 125 (1917), pp. 225-264; Bernard E. Bobb, *The Viceregency of Antonio María Bucareli in New Spain, 1771-1779* (Univ. of Texas, 1962), and Isidoro Vázquez de Acuña, "El capitán General don Matías de Gálvez", *Revista de Historia Militar* (Madrid), 10 (1966).

and served to stimulate further changes in royal policy and in internal arragements. Dra. Velásquez concentrated on the latter, describing Bourbon reforms within a larger historical context. She approached Mexico as the subject of change rather than as its object, and stressed the non-benign aspects of reform.

In studies of the mining reforms, in particular, scholars first sought to understand how Spanish policies related to economic change and to delineate how measures introduced under royal aegis best illustrated the sometimes happy confluence of the two faces of reform, the beneficial and the acquisitive. Arturo Arnáiz y Freg, Walter Howe, Clement Motten, and Arthur P. Whitaker have written of how the Crown sponsored schools, legislation, and scientific endeavors to promote the output of the Mexican silver mines, in the process benefiting Mexicans, Spaniards, and government, and resulting in increasing Mexican economic prosperity and intellectual stimulation. These studies, pursued in the 1930s for the most part, prepared the way for more intensive and extensive works on the Enlightenment in Mexico. David A. Brading, in a book now being published, *Three Essays on Bourbon Mexico*, a study of the Guanajuato silver mining industry in the main, continues on to a consideration of these measures within a broader, social context. [13]

Most indicative of the autocratic nature of Bourbon reform were its manifestations in pursuit of a policy ground in regalism. They are surveyed in general by Alberto de la Hera and in particular by Magnus Mörner who considers regalism to be a prime factor in the expulsion of the Jesuits in 1767. [14] How the Bourbons transformed traditional

[13] Arturo Arnáiz y Freg, *Andrés Manuel del Río* (México, 1936); his "Don Fausto de Elhuyar y Zubice", *Revista de Historia de América*, 6 (1939), pp. 75-96; and his "Don Andrés del Río, descubridor del Eritronio (Vanadio)", *ibid.*, 25 (1948), pp. 27-68; Arthur P. Whitaker, "The Elhuyar Mining Missions and the Enlightenment", *HAHR*, 31 (1951), pp. 558-585; Walter Howe, *The Mining Guild of New Spain and its Tribunal General, 1770-1821* (Harvard Univ., 1949); Clement G. Motten, *Mexican Silver and the Enlightenment* (Univ. of Pennsylvania, 1950); David A. Brading, "la minería de la plata en el siglo XVIII: el caso Bolaños", *HM*, 18 (1969), pp. 314-33; and Germán Somolinos d'Ardois, "Historia de la ciencia", *HM*, 15 (1966), pp. 275-287 for bibliography.

[14] Alberto de la Hera, *El regalismo borbónico en su proyección indiana* (Madrid, 1963); also Gaston Desdevises du Dezert, "L'Église espagnole des Indes au fin du XVIIIe siècle", *Revue Hispanique*, 39 (1917), pp. 112-292; Vicente Rodríguez Casado, "Notas sobre las relaciones de la Iglesia y el Estado en las Indias en el Reinado de Carlos III", *Revista de Indias*, 11 (1951), pp. 97 ff; Mario Góngora, "Estudios sobre el galicanismo y la Ilustración católica en América española", *Revista Chilena de Historia y Geografía*, 125 (1957), pp. 96-151; Richard Konetzke, "Staat und Gesellschaft in Hispanoamerika am Vorabend der Unabhängigkeit", *Saeculum*, 12 (1961); Magnus Morner, "The Expulsion of the Jesuits from Spain and Spanish America in 1767 in the light of Eighteenth Century Regalism", a paper read at the 79th Annual Meeting of the American Historical Association, Dec. 29, 1964.

policy in imposing direct state control over most aspects of Mexican religious life and institutions is described by N. M. Farriss in *Crown and Clergy in Colonial Mexico, 1579-1821. The Crisis of Ecclesiastical Privilege* (London, 1968). Here regalistic policies are explained as one aspect of the broader program designed to ensure the subservence of all traditionally autonomous and semi-autonomous corporations and organizations to the control of the state.

Meanwhile, Eduardo Arcila Farías, recognizing the essentially economic cast of the reform program, provided a model for interpreting the myriad relationships of governmental policies and practices with internal Mexican change and economic development. In his *El Siglo Ilustrado en América: reformas económicas del siglo XVIII* (Caracas, 1955), he concluded that these governmental policies augmented agriculture and mining production and commerce, modified conditions of work, and even distribution of capital, and abetted economic growth in general. While industry lagged, official mercantilist policy discouraging colonial industry was leniently applied and the making of such goods as cheap cotton cloth, not in competition with Spanish manufacture, boomed. [15]

For what is largely a report of regalistic attitudes of the period, notably of José de Gálvez: Raúl Flores Guerrero, "El imperialismo jesuita en Nueva España", *HM*, 4 (1954), pp. 159-173; and for a related discussion on the Inquisition as a political instrument see the differing views of Lewis A. Tambs, "The Inquisition in Eighteenth Century Mexico", *The Americas*, 22 (1965), pp. 167-181, and Richard E. Greenleaf, "The Mexican Inquisition and the Enlightenment, 1763-1805", *New Mexico Historical Review*, July 1966, pp. 181-196; also see his "North American Protestants and the Mexican Inquisition, 1765-1820", *A Journal of Church and State*, 8 (1966), pp. 186-99.

[15] Cf. Alperovich. A number of books and, especially, articles have appeared on Mexican economic conditions. Among them are the following: the great number of studies published and pursued by Luis Chávez Orozco, from his *Historia económica y social de México* (México, 1938), to his "Orígenes de la política de seguridad social", *HM*, 16 (1966), pp. 155-183; and his collections of documents (see above, note 7); Earl J. Hamilton, "Monetary Problems in Spain and Spanish America, 1751-1800", *Journal of Economic History*, 4 (1944), pp. 21-48; the research of Jesús Silva Herzog, including his edition of *Relaciones estadísticas de Nueva España de principios del siglo XIX* (México, 1944), and the unpublished manuscript by Clark W. Reynolds, "The Per Capita Income of New Spain before Independence and after the Revolution" (1967), and also the issue of *HM* cited above (note 10).

Documents concerning royal regulations of working conditions were collected by Silvio Zavala and Mario Castelo (see above, note 7). Aspects of embryonic industry appear in M. Carrera Stampa, *Los gremios mexicanos. La organización gremial de Nueva España* (México, 1954); his "El Obraje novohispano", in *Memorias de la Academia Mexicana de la Historia*, 20 (1961) pp, 148-171; and Richard Greenleaf, "The Obraje in the late Mexican Colony", *The Americas*, 23 (1967), pp. 227-50. Mining conditions appear in D. A. Brading (see above, p. 17 and note 13) and Luis Chávez Orozco, *Conflicto de trabajo con los mineros de Real del Monte, año de 1766* (México, 1960).

An increasing number of works pertaining to trade and commerce include

Recently, several historians have gone beyond the reforms introduced under Charles III to investigate aspects of the economic policies invoked under his successor, Charles IV. Romeo Flores Caballero in "Las representaciones de 1805", (*Historia mexicana* (hereafter *HM*) 17, (1968), pp. 469-473) and in "La consolidación de vales reales en la economía, la sociedad y la política novohispanas", (*HM*, 18, (1969), pp. 334-378) discussed the issuing of *reales vales* from 1780 on, the royal need for funds to amortize them leading to the *real cédula de consolidación de vales reales* of December 26, 1804, the attempt to enforce the decree in New Spain and the economic, social, and political responses. He concluded that the act affected all sectors of society, was a factor in making Spain appear inept and extortionist; government, previously a unifying force, now assumed the role of a divisive social factor. In this sense, Manuel Abad y Queipo might well blame revolution on the bad government of Charles IV.

Flores Caballero indicated that he had consulted a number of *representaciones* written in response to the *cédula* of 1804 and that they will soon be published in the *Boletín del Archivo General de la Nación* by Masae Sugawara H. Sugawara has studied the impact of the *vales reales*, as among "Los antecedentes coloniales de la deuda pública de

Robert S. Smith's articles, "Shipping in the Port of Veracruz, 1790-1821", HAHR, 23 (1943), pp. 5-20; "The Institution of the Consulado in New Spain", HAHR, 24 (1944), pp. 61-83; "The Puebla Consulado", *Revista de Historia de América*, 21 (1946), pp. 19-28; "*The Wealth of Nations* in Spain and Hispanic America", *Journal of Political Economy*, 65 (1957), pp. 104-125; and with Irving A. Leonard, "A proposed library for the Merchant Guild of Veracruz", *HAHR*, 24 (1944), pp. 84-102; José Flores Ramírez, *El Real Consulado de Guadalajara* (Guadalajara, 1952); Luis Chávez Orozco, ed., vol. 1: *El comercio de España y sus Indias* in *Colección de documentos para la historia del comercio exterior* ... (see above, note 7); Sergio Villalobos R., "El comercio extranjero a fines de la Dominación Española", *Journal of Inter-American Studies*, 4 (1962), pp. 517-542; Stanley J. Stein, "Merchants and Monarchs: Interest Groups in Policy-making in Eighteenth Century Spain and New Spain", a paper read at the 79th Annual Metting of the American Historical Association, Dec. 30, 1964; Jesús Silva Herzog, "El comercio de México durante la época colonial", *Cuadernos Americanos*, 153: 4 (jul-ag. 1967), pp. 127-153; and the collections of documents, Secretaría de Educación Pública, *El Comercio de Nueva España* (México, 1945) and Banco Nacional de Comercio Exterior, *El contrabando y el comercio exterior en la Nueva España* (México, 1967).

One of the most fruitful —and this with no unintended— economic areas studied to date, since it was the principal industry of the period, hasta been agricultura. See Luis Chávez Orozco, *La crisis agrícola novo-hispana de 1784-1785* (México, 1953), and his *Documentos sobre las alhóndigas y pósitos de Nueva España* (11 v, México, 1955-1959); François Chevalier, "Survivances seigneuriales et présages de la Révolution agraire dans le Nord du Mexique fin du xviii e xix siècles", *Revue Historique*, 222 (Jul-Sept. 1959), pp. 1-18; Delfina E. López Sarrelangue, *Una villa mexicana en el siglo xviii* (UNAM, 1969); and the important book by Enrique Florescano, *Precios de maíz y crisis agrícolas en México, 1708-1810* (El Colegio de México, 1969) mentioned below, p. 193.

México".[16] In his introduction to Part i: "España: Los Vales Reales, orígenes y desarrollo de 1780 a 1804", Sugawara contends that *all* Spanish policies represented only an inept reaction to forces pressing upon Spain from without, did not contribute to prosperity in the empire, and were of no help in solving the economic problems of Mexico. He implicitly refutes the thesis of Arcila Farías and seconds that of Alperovich.

Sugawara relates royal measures to wider Western economic history at one end and to Mexican development at the other. Here again a Marxist-Leninist orientation points up the present need for more works of tentative synthesis embracing the Bourbon reforms in New Spain and their relationship to Western history in our period as a whole.

Earlier assessments, seemingly at least half-forgotten now, of the origins of the reform program, too, sought to place the extended visit made by Gálvez within the sphere of European international affairs. Notable among them are the articles concerning French and British interest in Spanish American, and particularly Mexican, trade. Vera Lee Brown, Arthur S. Aiton, and Allan Christelow found French intrigue behind the decision to reform and the ultimate choice of José de Gálvez to implement the policy.[17] It is high time the Gálvez mission

[16] *BAGN*, 8 (1967), pp. 129-402. And see the excellent survey by Brian R. Hamnett, "The Appropriation of Mexican Church Wealth by the Spanish Bourbon Government, the 'Consolidación de Vales Reales', 1805-1809", *Journal of Latin American Studies*, 1 (1969), pp. 85-113.

[17] Vera Lee Brown, "Anglo-Spanish Relations in America in the closing years of the Colonial Era", *HAHR*, 5 (1922), pp. 327-483; Arthur S. Aiton, "Spanish Colonial Reorganization under the Family Compact", *HAHR*, 12 (1932), pp. 269-280; Allan Christelow, "French Interest in the Spanish Empire during the Ministry of the Duc de Choiseul (1759-1771)", *HAHR*, 21 (1941), pp. 515-537, and Dorothy B. Goebel, "British Trade to the Spanish Colonies, 1796-1823", *AHR*, 43 (1938), pp. 288-320. For ongoing foreign influence in Mexico: John Rydjord, *Foreign Interest in the Independence of New Spain* (Duke Univ., 1935); for French influence; Rafael Heliodoro Valle, "Algunos franceses en México", *Filosofía y Letras*, 2 (1943), pp. 153-159; Jacques Houdaille, "Frenchmen and Francophiles in New Spain from 1760 to 1810", *The Americas*, 13 (1956), pp. 1-30; and his "Gaëtan Souchet D'Alvimart, the Alleged Envoy of Napoleón to México, 1807-1809", *ibid.*, 13 (1959), pp. 109-132; Jesús Reyes Heroles, "Rousseau y el liberalismo mexicano", *Cuadernos Americanos*, 21 (1962), pp. 159-185; Jefferson R. Spell, *Rousseau in the Spanish World before 1833* (Univ. of Texas, 1938) and his more specific "Rousseau in Spanish America ", *HAHR*, 15 (1935), pp. 260-267; and, most recent, Richard E. Greenleaf, "The Mexican Inquisition and the Masonic Movement, 1751-1820", *New Mexico Historical Review* (1969), 42, pp. 93-117. For British influence and relations: William Kaufmann, *British Policy and the Independence of Latin America, 1804-1828* (Yale Univ., 1951); the introduction by Sir Charles K. Webster to *Britain and the Independence of Latin America* (Oxford Univ., 1944); and John Lynch, "British Policy and Spanish America, 1783-1808", *Journal of Latin American Studies*, 1 (1969), pp. 1-30. The classic study of French policy is W. S. Robertson, *Franca and Latin American Independence* (Johns Hopkins

be connected to the whys of reform, to the ongoing problems of the borderlands, where, after all, he spent three years, and to the subsequent history of official policies and appointments, notably those of Matías and son, Bernardo, as viceroys, and Teodoro de Croix as Capitain General of the Provincias Internas. Had *afrancesados* or true French agents captured the government of New Spain?

The works of Richard Herr, Jean Sarrailh, and Luis Sánchez Agesta supply the necessary Spanish background to policies carried out in Mexico. [18] They indicate a complexity of purpose lay behind the multi-

Univ., 1939), and of the United States, Arthur P. Whitaker, *The United States and the Independence of Latin America, 1800-1830* (see above, note 4).

Lilian E. Fisher wrote a brief article on "Teodoro de Croix", HAHR, 9 (1929), pp. 488-504; see Alfred B. Thomas, ed. and tr., *Teodoro de Croix and the Northern Frontier of New Spain, 1776-1783* (Univ. of Okla., 1941), and Roberto Moreno y de los Arcos, "Teodoro de Croix. Su actuación en América" (unpblished thesis, UNAM, 1967). For José de Gálvez: Priestley; the 1771 *Informe* (see above, note 7), Luis Navarro García, *Don José de Gálvez y la comandancia general de las provincias internas del norte de Nueva España* (Seville, 1964). For his nephew, Donald E. Worcester, ed., *Bernardo de Gálvez's Instructions for Governing the Interior Provinces of New Spain (1786)* (Berkelev, 1951); Guillermo Porras Muñoz, "Bernardo de Gálvez", in homenaje a D. Antonio Ballesteros Beretta, *Miscelánea Americanista*, III (Madrid, 1952), pp. 575-620. On Bernardo's father-in-law, Ramón Ezquerra, "Un patricio colonial: Gilberto de Saint-Maxent, teniente gobernador de Louisiana", *ibid.*, I (Madrid, 1951), pp. 429-502. Also see J. Ignacio Rubio Mañé, "Política del virrey Flores en la Comandancia General de las Provincias Internas, 1787-1789", BAGN, 24 (1953), pp. 213-257; Bernard E. Bobb, "Bucareli and the Interior Provinces", HAHR, 34 (1954), pp. 20-36; For the classic statement: Herbert E. Bolton, *The Spanish Borderlands* (Yale Univ., 1921). A. P. Nasatir is currently engaged in research concerning the frontiers of Spanish Louisiana and particularly the Anglo-Spanish frontier on the Upper Mississippi, 1796-1804. Also for Lousiana: Jack D. L. Holmes, *Gayoso: the Life of a Spanish Governor in the Mississippi Valley, 1789-1799* (Baton Rouge, 1965); and V. Vital-Hawell, "La actividad del cónsul de España y de los emisarios franceses en Nueva Orleans de 1808 a 1809", *Revista de Indias* (jul-dic. 1963), and John P. Moore, "Antonio de Ulloa. A Profile of the first Spanish Governor of Louisiana", *Louisiana History*, 8: 3 (1967), pp. 189-218; Arthur P. Whitaker, "Antonio de Ulloa", HAHR, 15 (1935), pp. 155-194. Other important works on the frontiers include Isabel Eguiloz de Prado, *Los indios del nordeste de Méjico en el siglo XVIII* (Seville, 1965); Michael E. Thurman, *The Naval Department of San Blas, New Spain's Bastion for Alta California* (Glendale, Calif., 1967); Max L. Moorhead, *The Apache Frontier. Jacobo Ugarte and Spanish-Indian Relations in Northern New Spain, 1769-1791* (Univ. of Oklahoma, 1968); and Mark Simmons, *Spanish Government in New Mexico* (New Mexico, 1968). Also see the older works: Bolton, R. W. Manning, "The Nootka Sound Controversy", *American Historical Association Annual Report* (1904), pp. 279-478; and V. Alessio Robles, "Las condiciones sociales en el norte de la Nueva España", in *Memorias de la Academia Mexicana de la Historia*, 4: 2, (1945).

[18] Luis Sánchez Agesta, *El pensamiento político del despotismo ilustrado* (Madrid, 1953); Jean Sarrailh, *L'Espagne éclairée de la seconde moitié du XVIIIeme siècle* (Paris, 1954); Richard Herr, *The Eighteenth Century Revolution in Spain* (Princeton Univ., 1958). There is also quite a bit of periodical literature, and some books, on specific personages involved in and aspects of royal policy, including

faceted program, that under Charles III the royal policy in New Spain sprang from the desire to swell the *Real Hacienda,* from an increasing fear of England and, finally, as Richard Konetzke has documented, from the deeply-felt need "to make the colonies love the nation". [19] Much light would be shed on reform and its ramifications in Mexico by comparative study with contemporary policy and activity in Spain. A brief survey, "La Reorganización Imperial en Hispanoamérica, 1760-1810", *Iberomanskt,* (Stockholm), 4:1, (1969), pp. 1-36, by Magnus Mörner, is our most recent and most balanced account, short but beautifully organized.

Study to date, then, finds the predominating (Western) view is that Bourbon reforms, enlightened and autocratic, initiated largely under Charles III as an attempt at increased assertion of control, acted as catalysts but not originators of Mexican economic prosperity, as stimulants to social, cultural, and intellectual change, demographic change and increase and, finally, as we shall see, to the development of a new revolutionary state of mind. The reforms belong, in proper historical perspective, among the factors abetting change that would at length prove conducive to movement toward independence. And it must be remembered, as Earl J. Hamilton, R. A. Humphreys, Stanley J. Stein, and Masae Sugawara remind us, that both reform and prosperity were responses to an increasing European demand for products and markets. [20]

Political and economic history, then, largely centered on Spanish activity (or lack of it) under Charles III, has yielded some underst-

Ricardo Krebs Wilckens, *El pensamiento histórico, político y económico del Conde de Campomanes* (Santiago de Chile, 1960); José Loredo Aparicio, ed. and comp., *Jovellanos* (México, 1946); José María Ots Capdequi, "Sobre la política económica y el régimen fiscal del Estado español en América al tiempo de la independencia", in homenaje a don Ramón Carande, (2 v, Madrid, 1963), II, pp. 331-345; John H. R. Polt, "Jovellanos and his English Sources", *Transactions of the American Philosophical Society,* new series, 54 (1964); José Cepada Adán, "La política americana vista por un cortesano de Carlos III", *Anuario de Estudios Americanos,* 21 (1964), pp. 437-487; Marcelo Bitar Letayf, "El conde de Campomanes y el comercio español con Indias", *Cuadernos Hispanoamericanos,* 205 (1967), pp. 91-97; and José Antonio Gómez Marín, "La reforma agraria y la mentalidad ilustrada", *ibid.,* 229 (1969), pp. 151-160.

[19] Richard Konetzke, "La condición legal de los criollos y las causas de independencia", *Estudios Americanos,* 2 (1950), pp. 31-54. He cites the fiscales, Campomanes and Floridablanca, of the royal council (el Consejo Extraordinario) in a session of March 5, 1768 (p. 45).

[20] Earl J. Hamilton, *op. cit.* (note 15); also his "Money and Economic Recovery in Spain under the First Bourbon, 1701-1746", *Journal of Modern History,* 15 (1943), pp. 192-206, and *War and Prices in Spain, 1651-1800* (Harvard Univ., 1947); R. A. Humphreys, *op. cit.* (note 10); Stanley J. Stein, *op. cit.* (note 15) and, with Barbara H. Stein, The Colonial Heritage of Latin America: *Perspectives on Economic Dependence* (Oxford Univ., 1969).

anding of what went on in Mexico in the later eighteenth century. Until recently, however, while infusing the period with shape and motion, such accounts gave little indication of internal vitality. In effect, they continued to leave an impression of material progress, abetted or hampered by Spansh policy, or both, depending on the year, paralleling the emergence of a Mexican spirit. Thus Justo Sierra, for example, in his ebullient essay, *Evolución Política del pueblo mexicano* (México, 1900-1902), still tended to describe Mexico in the eighteenth century as an organism becoming conscious of its personality. With equal, if not greater, zest, José Vasconcelos, in his *Breve historia de México* (México, 1937) stated that New Spain under Spain had been the most cultured and enlightened of colonies *until* the advent of Charles III, who "interrumpe el desarrollo nativo y crea problemas y situaciones nefastos". Vasconcelos returned, nearly full circle, to the outlook of Alamán and, oddly enough, looked forward at the same time to the argument of Alperovich. Such delightfully impressionistic characterizations of the eighteenth century as those of Sierra and Vasconcelos were to be made obsolete in the writing of the history of the 1700s, by the inminent wedding of the material and the spiritual.

CULTURAL AND INTELLECTUAL HISTORY

Since 1940 an increasing number of historians, especially in Mexico itself, have come to consider of primary historical importance not political and general institutional arrangements so much as the predominating suppositions or commonly-held assumptions supporting such institutions in a given time and place. Especially do they seek to ascertain the goals and values common to a society or the more dominant segments of it; they assume politics and institutions in general to compose a superstructure reared upon and supported by them. Political and even economic history are seen as outcroppings jutting from the subsoil of ideology.

According to this view, the intellectual preoccupations of an era, are determinants of culture, responsible for setting social values, concerns, and goals.

Whereas Marx posited an economic determinism derived — to vary a cliche —from upending the Hegelian concept of the dialectic— this school of historians appears closer in philosophy to the original Hegelian idea that non-material (indeed for Hegel, spiritual) forces to a large extent shape present history and direct its future course. To this school, then, political and economic determinism occupy the same causative level. Both, in turn, are more products than producers of history. Instead, it is how a society views itself and its relationship to its environment in time and through time the point of view it maintains as its predominant philosophy —or philosophies —and the alterations these undergo, that are the most important determining factors in the history of a community or social entity. A concomitant notion, then, is that past history influences the making of present individual and collective decisions and thus also affects the future. In effect, this outlook has achieved a predominant position in the writing of Mexican history in the past 20 years and has been translated into an ongoing analysis of what earlier historians were content simply to personify as "the Mexican spirit".

John Phelan, among others, has described how history and philosophy have joined forces in the common endeavor "to discover the national ethos of the Mexican culture". [21] Embracing cultural nationalism as a subdivision of universalism, a group of scholars has adopted a position intrinsically humanistic and, like humanists of the sixteenth —and eighteenth— centuries, they assert, in Phelan's phrase, that "the historians' task is to illustrate how the past conditions and determines the range of alternatives for the future". This idea of man as a decision-maker may well be a subtle variation on an eighteenth-century comment on the great chain of being, Voltaire's observation that "Every effect evidently has its cause... but every cause has not its effect... Everythnig is begotten, but everything does not

[21] P. 309, John L. Phelan, "México y lo Mexicano", *HAHR*, 36 (1956), pp. 309-318. Also see Samuel Ramos, "Las Tendencias Actuales de la Filosofía en México", (also in English) in *Intellectual Trends in Latin America* (Austin, 1945), pp. 44-65; Bernabé Navarro, "La Historización de Nuestra Filosofía", *Filosofía y Letras*, 18 (1949), pp. 263-280; Patrick Romanell, *The Making of the Mexican Mind* (Univ. of Nebraska, 1952); Hugo Díaz-Thome, "El mexicano y su historia", *HM*, 2 (1952), pp. 248-258; Julio Le Riverend, "Problemas de historiografía", *HM*, 3 (1954), pp. 62-68; Luis González y González, "En torno de la integración de la realidad mexicana", in homenaje a Silvio Zavala, *Estudios Históricos Americanos* (México, 1953), pp. 407-424; Luis Villoro, "The Historian's Task: the Mexican Perspective", in Archibald Lewis and Thomas F. McGann, eds., *The New World Looks at its History* (Univ. of Texas, 1963), pp. 173-182; Edmundo O'Gorman, "La Revolución Mexicana y la Historiografía", in *Seis Estudios Históricos de Tema Mexicano* (Univ. Veracruzana, 1960), pp. 203-220; and his "Tres etapas de la historiografía mexicana", *Anuario de Historia* (UNAM), 2, (1962), pp. 11-19; Arturo Arnáiz y Freg, "Mexican Historical Writing", in A. Curtis Wilgus, ed., *The Caribbean: Mexico Today* (Univ. of Florida, 1964), pp. 216-224; the more general essay by Arthur P. Whitaker, "The Enlightenment in Spanish America", *Proceedings of the American Philosophical Society*, 102: 6 (1958), pp. 555-559; and the outstanding collection of bibliographical essays published as *HM*, 15: 2-4 (1966), "Veinticinco años de investigación histórica en México". For philosophers seeking *lo mexicano*: Antonio Caso, *México (Apuntamientos de cultura patria)* (UNAM, 1943); José Gaos, *En torno a la filosofía* (2 v, México, 1952); Silvio Zavala, *Aproximaciones a la historia de México* (México, 1953); and Francisco Larroyo, *La filosofía americana: su razón y sin razón de ser* (UNAM, 1958).

beget". [22] For us it has meant a new interest in the eighteenth century not simply negatively as the time before the revolution but positively as a seedbed and transmission period of values and traditions specifically Mexican. Wigberto Jiménez Moreno distinguished this new tendency as

> La de hincar el análisis sobre las ideas y los sentimientos, que son, junto con las primeras necesidades, los verdaderos motores de los hechos. Esto, unido a un examen más certero de los factores económicos y sociales, desplaza el centro de gravedad de nuestros estudios, trayéndolos de la historia política hacia la historia cultural, y de la mera narración de los sucesos, a la interpretación de lo que significan. [23]

Renewed interest in the non-material aspects of history, in culture and intellectual activity, has brought the eighteenth century into great prominence. Pedro Henríquez-Ureña what seems long ago observed, "El siglo XVIII fue, dentro de los límites impuestos por el régimen político de la Colonia, acaso el siglo de mayor esplendor intelectual autóctono que ha tenido México". [24] More recently, our period has come into favor with a broader range of scholars who, whether concerned with the history of philosophy or the philosophy of history take a Collingwood-like stance and contribute to both fields simultaneously. [25] Precursors of this tendency in historical thought include not only historians of literature such as Henríquez-Ureña, Francisco Pimentel, José María Vigil, Luis G. Urbina, Julio Jiménez Rueda, Carlos González Peña and Alfonso Reyes, but also historians of art and architecture such as Manuel Toussaint, Manuel Romero de Terreros, and Francisco de la Maza, of philosophy such as Emeterio Valverde y Téllez, and of academic culture, notably John Tate Lanning. [26]

[22] From his *Philsophical Doctionary* in *The Works of Voltaire*, translated by T. Smollett (Paris, 1901).
[23] P. 455; Wigberto Jiménez Moreno, "50 Años de Historia Mexicana", *HM*, 1 (1952), pp. 449-455.
[24] Cited by B. Navarro, *op. cit.* (note 22), p. 268.
[25] See R. G. Collingwood, "Human Nature and Human History" (1936), in *The Idea of History* (New York, 1956), pp. 205-230.
[26] See Manuel Toussaint, *Arte colonial en México* (México, 1948); Pal Kelemen, *Baroque and Rococo in Latin America* (New York, 1951); George Kubler and M. Soria, *Art and Architecture in Spain and Portugal and their American Dominions, 1500-1800* (London, 1959); Pedro Henríquez Ureña, "Las traducciones y paráfrasis en la literatura mexicana de la época de independencia (1800-1821)", *Anales del Museo Nacional de Arqueología, Historia y Etnología* (ser. 3), 5 (1913), pp. 51-64, 379-381; *Diccionario de Escritores Mexicanos* (UNAM, 1967); Emeterio Valverde y Téllez, *Bibliografía Filosófica Mexicana* (México, 1907), and his *Crítica Filosófica y Estudio Bibliográfico y Crítico de las Obras de Filosofía* (México, 1904); John Tate Lanning, *Academic Culture in the Spanish Colonies* (New York, 1940),

Bernabé Navarro has traced an upsurge of monographs approaching the Mexican past in this fashion and insinting on the cultural importance of the eighteenth century to 1940 when José Gaos began in a seminar at the Colegio de México to investigate the most important intellectual themes relating to Mexico, when *México y la Cultura,* including chapters by Silvio Zavala and Samuel Ramos appeared, when Antonio Caso published a trendsetting article on Juan Benito Díaz de Gamarra y Dávalos, the eighteenth century educator and eclectic, and when Gabriel Méndez Plancarte began his seminar on Mexican philosophy and history in the Seminario Tridentino. In 1941 Méndez Plancarte published his *Humanistas del siglo XVIII;* the following year *La historia de la filosofía en México* by Samuel Ramos appeared. [27]

In that same year of 1942, a group of scholars in the United States, in a slim volume, *Latin America and the Enlightenment* edited by Arthur P. Whitaker, expressed recognition of the importance for all Spanish America of that great cultural trend of the eighteenth century, the Enlightenment. Seeking to allay for all time the notion that Spain kept Latin America enfolded in obscurantism and oppression, they discussed aspects of the official and unofficial introduction of enlightened ideas, particularly the emphasis on useful knowledge, from various European countries, and presented evidence of their dissemination throughout Latin America.

Monelisa Lina Pérez-Marchand, in *Dos etapas ideológicas del siglo XVIII en México a través de los papeles de la Inquisición* (Colegio de México, 1945) corroborated through a study of Inquisition records that enlightened notions had indeed spread throughout Mexico by the latter part of the eighteenth century. In the previous year, Mariano Picón-Salas beautifully resurveyed and depicted within his work on colonial culture, *De la Conquista a la Independencia* (México, 1944) the fabric of intellectual life in Mexico in the late viceregal period. These two books carried into the writing of history proper the thesis of Ramos that in the late eighteenth century in Mexico as in Europe a new philosophy, indeed ideology, came to challenge the older established one, and that some of the best minds in Mexico forsook the world view dominant since the Conquest to embrace the new truth.

Problems remained of definition, of origins, of when and how the

his earlier "La Real y Pontifical Universidad de México y los preliminares de la Independencia", *Universidad de México,* 2: 9 (1936), pp. 3-4; and, most recent, "Tradition and the Englightenment in the Spanish Colonial Universities", *Journal of World History,* pt. 4 (1967); David Mayagoitia, *Ambiente Filosófico de la Nueva España* (México, 1946).

[27] Navarro, *op. cit.*

Enlightenment was introduced and developed in Mexico, and of how it affected subsequent history, notably the independence movements. Among the earliest of such monographic studies were those by Agustín Millares Carlo who recognized the importance of the writings of the Galician Benedictine monk, Benito Gerónimo Feijóo y Montenegro, and especially of his *Teatro crítico universal* (9 v. Madrid, 1739) in transporting the Enlightenment from France to Spain, in marrying French (and English) rationalism to religious orthodoxy, and so in producing an eclectic blend of Catholocism with the critical spirit.[28] Enlightened notions, wrapped in eclecticism, then travelled from Spain to Mexico, where they remained associated with Feijóo's name and with Catholicism.

A private printing of Victoria Junco's *Gamarra o el eclecticismo en México* (México, 1944) and an edition of a selection of Gamarra's writings, *Tratados* (UNAM, 1947) by José Gaos established that advocate of Feijóo's eclecticism as the principal introducer of modern or enlightened philosophy in Mexico. Bernabé Navarro subsequently summarized the contribution of Gamarra in a critical essay introducing his translation of Gamarra's *Elementos de filosofía moderna*, vol. 1 (UNAM, 1963).

Ramos had mentioned not only Gamarra's work but the contributions of certain young creole Jesuits to Mexican philosophy. Navarro, in *La introducción de la filosofía moderna en México* (Colegio de México, 1948) discussed the modern concepts embedded in some of the *cursus philosophicus* that denoted the content of courses in philosophy, taught in the Jesuit colegios, by individual members of the order. His work spaned the period between Feijóo and Gamarra, putting back enlightenment in México to at least mid-century and finding the "modern" outlook to have been an ongoing one within the country.

Monographs and articles published during the 1950s described numerous individual and social manifestations of enlightened concepts, thus drawing attention to the more popular modes of acceptance of the new currents of thougth. Pablo González Casanova in the first issue of *Historia mexicana* (Colegio de México, 1951) commented on the appearance in the late 1700s of popular satire containing advanced "philosophical" notions, then expanded his findings into a book, *La literatura perseguida en la crisis de la colonia* (Colegio de México,

[28] Agustín Millares Carlo "Feijóo en América", *Cuadernos Americanos*, 3 (1944), pp. 139-160; his *Dos Discursos de Feijóo sobre América* (México, 1945), and his edition of Feijoo's *Teatro Crítico Universal* (Madrid, 1923-1925). Also Gaspard Delpy, *L'Espagne et l'esprit europeen: l'oeuvre de Feijóo* (Paris, 1936), and for other eclectic importations: María del C. Rovira, *Eclécticos portugueses del siglo* XVIII *y algunas de sus influencias en América* (México, 1958).

1958). Henceforward *Historia mexicana* printed a number of outstand
ing contributions to eighteenth century history.

Juan Hernández Luna had earlier edited selections from the writings of *José Antonio Alzate* (México, 1945). Rafael Moreno now
discussed Alzate as a prime propagandist for the new ideas concerning
educational reform and in an article appearing a decade later, for
the importance of the natural and phisical sciences.[29] In the same
period, Xavier Tavera Alfaro edited a number of the writings of this
admirer of Gamarra and Mexican savant of encyclopedic interests.[30]
As intellectual and cultural innovation were discerned, Jesús Reyes
Heroles, in the first volume of *El liberalismo mexicano* (3 v, UNAM,
1957-1961) and Francisco López Cámara, in *La génesis de la conciencia liberal en México* (Colegio de México, 1954) reminded readers of a continuation of liberal ideas predating the Enlightenment
by pointing to the liberalism, also descried by Ramos and Méndez
Plancarte, inherent in the Spanish and Mexican traditions of Christian
humanism.

By the 1960s, in *Estudios de la historia de la filosofía en México*
(UNAM, 1963), Rafael Moreno could contribute an essay summar-
izing much of this research. Bernabé Navarro had accumulated sufficient data to postulate, beyond the emergence of a modern philosophy,
the appearance of a *Cultura mexicana moderna en el siglo XVIII*
(UNAM, 1964). Mexican history had come a long way since the
days when Riva Palacio and Justo Sierra wrote airily of a Mexican
spirit progressing toward liberty.

Yet subsequent thought and study has not proved them wrong.
Leopoldo Zea, in *América como conciencia* (México, 1951) had discerned during the course of the viceregal period the emergence of a
particularly American self-awareness expressed by Mexican creoles.
Earlier, Millares Carlo had noted the influence on creole attitudes
of Feijóo's insistence on considering America as a geographical and
cultural entity distinct from Spain. Millares Carlo also translated from
Latin into Castilian an early manifestation of creole particularism or
criollismo, the 1755 edition of the *Prólogos de la Biblioteca Mexicana*
of Juan José de Eguiara y Eguren (México, 1944 rev.ed., Maracaibo,
1963). Juan Hernández Luna then characterized Eguiara y Eguren
as "El iniciador de la historia de las ideas en México" (*Filosofía*

---

[29] Rafael Moreno, "Alzate, Educador ilustrado", *HM*, 2 (1953), pp. 389; and
his "La concepción de ciencia en Alzate", *HM*, 13 (1964), pp. 346-378; also see his
earlier, "José Antonio Alzate y la fisolofía de la Ilustración", *Memorial y Revista
de la Academia Nacional de Ciencias*, 57 (1952), pp. 55-84. For Bartolache: *Los
exámenes universitarios del doctor José Ignacio Bartolache en 1772* appeared in
print (México, 1948) illustrating reawakened interest in Alzate's enlightened contemporary.

[30] Xavier Tavera Alfaro, *op. cit.* (note 7).

y Letras, 25 [1953], pp. 65-80), while Bernabé Navarro pointed out how the *Biblioteca* came to written to defend "La cultura mexicana frente a Europa", (*HM*, 3 (1954), pp. 547-561). Articulate *criollismo*, they concluded, emerged as a reaction to European slurs and gachupín pretensions and as a growing creole pride in the Mexican *patria*.

Luis González y González (1948) explained how the interaction of this sentiment of *conciencia de sí* with enlightened notions stimulated the growth and hardening among a number of articulate Mexicans of a sense of national identity.[31] The patriotic and anti-gachupín outlook latent in criollismo gained form and direction from the enlightened emphasis on national sovereignty and, above all, from the prime characteristic of the movement, the spirit of optimism. Literate creoles, González y González stated, shared a feeling of nationalistic optimism. In the work of Eguiara y Eguren, Alzate, the creole Jesuits, and other articulate Mexicans he discerned a chain or, better, a net of inter-related concepts and attitudes forming an intellectual continuum from the ideas of enlightened creoles to thoughts of national autonomy. José Miranda, in *Las ideas y las instituciones políticas mexicanas* (México, 1952) described the (largely latent) political content of this continuum.

A central point to González y González was the impetus the visit (sponsored by Charles IV) and writings of Alexander von Humboldt gave to creole optimism. This too was a theme developed by José Miranda in *Humboldt y México* (UNAM, 1962). Miranda succinctly summarized how enlightened trends preceded Humboldt to Mexico, how he served as a catalyst to certain notions; especially did he fan a creole spirit of self-help and aid through inculcating in Mexicans a pride in their national resources and an inflated confidence in the potential of their country.[32]

[31] Luis González y González, "El optimismo nacionalista como factor de la independencia de México", in *Estudios de historiografía americana* (Colegio de México, 1948), pp. 155-215; John L. Phelan, "Neo-Aztecism in the Eighteenth Century and the Genesis of Mexican Nationalism", in Stanley Diamond, ed., *Culture in History. Essays in honor of Paul Radin* (Columbia Univ., 1960). See also F. López Cámara and X. Tavera Alfaro, *op. cit.*; Francisco Larroyo, "El movimiento de independencia. Las influencias educativas", *Excelsior* (Mexico City), May 10, 1953; Rafael Moreno, "La creación de la nacionalidad mexicana", *HM*, 12 (1963), pp. 531-551; and Jorge Alberto Manrique, "El pesimismo como factor de la independencia de México", in *Escritos en homenaje a Edmundo O'Gorman, Conciencia y Autenticidad Históricas* (UNAM, 1968), pp. 177-196.

[32] See also Carlos Pereyra, *Humboldt en América* (Madrid, 1917); Juan A. Ortega y Medina, Humboldt desde México (UNAM, 1960), Marianne O de Bopp, *et al*, *Ensayos sobre Humboldt* (UNAM, 1962); Catalina Sierra, *El nacimiento de México* (UNAM, 1960), analyzes some of the consequences of this over-optimism. Most recent: Manfred Kossok, "Alejandro de Humboldt y el lugar histórico de la revolución de independencia latinoamericana", in *Festschrift fur Alexander von*

Commitment to, indeed outsized faith in, material progress exemplified an increasing secularization of thought. Yet this does not mean that a secular culture evolved, but only a *more* secular mood. Throughout the eighteenth century, too, churchmen remained a dominant factor in cultural and intellectual life. When proponents of modern philosophy confronted supporters of traditional orthodoxy, as Pablo González Casanova has shown in *El misoneísmo y la modernidad cristiana en el siglo* XVIII (Colegio de México, 1948) they most often did so from within the Church.

For the most part, as Farriss and others have pointed out, modernism in religion was espoused by certain membrers of the lower clergy and particularly of the Franciscan, Jesuit and Mercedarian orders.[33] On the other hand, among this sort of churchmen were also to be found what may have been the overwhelming majority of *misoneístas*. Certainly the moderns, what ever their number, proved to be a vociferous minority, as has so often been the case with the Party of the Future. Scholarly fascination with the Jesuits, especially, has shed light on the content of this modern or enlightened movement, on Bourbon regalism, on popular reaction to Bourbon innovation, and on the climate of opinion, both elitist and popular, found in Mexico throughout our period.

Ramos found modernism first apparent among a small group of young creole Jesuits who considered "the teachings of scholasticism not in accord real life". Méndez Plancarte observed a new modern spirit, united with a revitalized humanism, in their desire to

Humboldt (Berlin, 1969), pp. 27-52, wherein Humboldt is discussed as championing the social and political emancipation of colonial peoples.

Also see, for the continuation of Eguiara y Eguren's work, A. Millares Carlo, "Don José Mariano Beristáin de Souza y su *Biblioteca Hispanoamericana Septentrional*", *Inter-American Review of Bibliography*, 16 (1966), pp. 20-57; and Beristáin, *op. cit.* (note 7).

[33] Farriss, *op. cit.* See also Manuel Jiménez Fernández, *El concilio IV Provincial Mejicano* (Seville, 1939); Mariano Cuevas, S. J., *Historia de la Iglesia en México* (5 v, El Paso, Texas, 1928); José Bravo Ugarte, "El clero y la independencia...", *Ábside*, 5 (1941), pp. 612-630; *ibid.*, 7 (1943), pp. 406-409; Félix Alvarez Brun, "La ilustración, la expulsión de los jesuitas, y la independencia de América", *Cuadernos Americanos*, 17 (1958), pp. 148-167; Karl Schmitt, "The Clergy and the Enlightenment in Latin America: an analysis", *The Americas*, 15 (1959), pp. 381-391; and his "The Clergy and the Independence of New Spain", *HAHR*, 34 (1954), pp. 289-312; Elías Martínez, "Los franciscanos y la independencia de México", *Ábside*, 24 (1960), pp. 129-166; and Michael P. Costeloe, *Church Wealth in Mexico* (Cambridge Univ., 1968). For an outstanding exception, an enlightened bishop (elect) critical of many royal policies: Lillian E. Fisher, *Champion of Reform: Manuel Abad y Queipo* (New York, 1955) and Secretaría de Educación Pública, *Estudios de Abad y Queipo* (México, 1947). For one disaffected Franciscan; Ernesto de la Torre Villar, "Fray Vicente de Santa María y su Relación histórica", in *Escritos* en homenaje a Edmundo O'Gorman, *Conciencia y Autenticidad Históricas* (UNAM, 1968), pp. 365-398.

reform education, and instill Mexicans with useful knowledge and thus to promote material and social progress.

Here was discerned an indigenous variety of the Enlightenment apparent before the then commonly-accepted date of its introduction, the 1760s. Enlightenment, then, did not originate in Mexico as a byproduct of the reforming tendencies of the ministers and officials of Charles III. In editing selections concerning the reforming Jesuits written by their contemporaries, Juan Luis Maneiro and Manuel Fabri, Bernabé Navarro in *Vidas de mexicanos ilustres del siglo XVIII* (UNAM, 1956), by extracting concrete examples of their early activities, indicated how Rafael Campoy, Agustín Pablo Castro, Javier Clavijero, Diego José Abad, and Francisco Javier Alegre sought to return to the classics in literature, the writings of the church fathers and great schoolmen in theology, and to replace disputation and scholastic method in philosophy with the tenets of rationalism and critical analysis. All exhibited encyclopedic interests. Members of the group explored languages, the natural and exact sciences, history, and archaeology, Campoy formulated a plan to increase the population of his native region of Sinaloa. They had an enlightened faith in the ability of Mexicans through use of individual reason, if well-educated, to change and better life on earth. Gerard Decorme, in *La Obra de los jesuitas mexicanos durante la época colonial* (2 v, México, 1941) and Delfina Esmeralda López Sarrelangue, in *Los colegios jesuitas de la Nueva España* (México, 1941), noted that Francisco Ceballos, the enlightened Provincial of the Order in Mexico, had planned to institute a reform of method and curriculum in Jesuit colegios on the eve of expulsion.

Scholarly interest in the expulsion itself has established the existence and given some indication of the nature of popular disaffection in 1767. Accounts by Orozco y Berra and Priestley relying on the report of José de Gálvez (1771), documents published by José Toribio Medina, Mariano Cuevas and Beatriz Ramírez Camacho, an article by Richard Konetzke, as well as other sources, describe popular reaction to the royal order as widespread, proceeding from initial shock to subsequent expression ranging from resigned amazement to over rebellion. [34] Mexicans witnessed the rigorous maner of expulsion,

[34] See José Mariano Dávila y Arrillaga, *Continuación de la Historia de la Compañía de Jesús en Nueva España* . . . (2 v, Puebla, 1889). Orozco y Berra, *Dominación* . . . *op. cit.*, and Priestley, *op. cit.* José Toribio Medina, *Noticias Bio-Bibliográficas de los Jesuitas expulsos de América en 1767* (Santiago de Chile, 1914); Mariano Cuevas, S. J., ed., *Tesoros Documentales de México, siglo* XVIII. *Priego Zelis, Clavijero* (México, 1944); Beatriz Ramírez Camacho, "Breve relación sobre la expulsión de los jesuitas de Nueva España", *BAGN*, 7 (1966), pp. 875-890; Alberto Pradeau y Avilés, *La expulsión de los Jesuitas de las provincias de Sonora, Ostimuri*

the secrecy, speed, and severity with which the government shipped out even the old and the infirm. Many Mexicans of all segments of society expressed a sense of loyalty to schoolmasters, local priests, friends, relatives and even, in some regions, to the Jesuits as representatives of royal government. For all these reasons the expulsion became an ongoing symbol of all grievances against the Spanish authorities. In addition, events attendant upon the banishment signified adverse reaction to the Bourbon reform program in general and attested to the basically conservative nature of the Mexican populace.

Certainly from the late eighteenth century to today, publication of works written by Jesuits in exile is indicative of (and contributes to) ongoing interest in the problem of Jesuit influence in Mexico. Bustamante edited and published not only Cavo's history but also an edition of the *Historia de la Compañía de Jesús en Nueva España* of Francisco Javier Alegre (México, 1841-1842). García Icazbalceta translated the life of Alegre by Fabri from Latin into Castilian. In 1871 a list of expelled Jesuits compiled by Rafael de Zelis was printed. José Mariano Dávia y Arrillaga wrote a *Continuación de la Historia de la Compañía de Jesús en Nueva España del P. Francisco Javier Alegre* (2 v, Puebla, 1888-1889). Rafael Landívar's *Rusticatio Mexicana* has been translated into Castilian and had several Mexican editions. Most outstanding, and most widely known and read, is of course the *Storia Antica de Messico* (Cesena, 1780-81) of Clavijero. [35]

These writings demonstrate how earlier tendencies became intensified and channelled in exile into protestations of Mexican patriotism and national identiy. Maneiro and Fabri list the works and interest of this group while in Italy. All appear to have been devotees of the

y Sinaloa en 1767 (México, 1959); Konetzke, *op. cit.* (note 19), and Peggy K. Korn, "Contributions of the Jesuits to Mexican Nationalism", (unpublished ms.).

35 The most scholarly translation of Francisco Javier Alegre is *Historia de la Provincia de la Compañía de Jesús de Nueva España* (4 v, Rome, 1959-1960), edited by Ernest J. Burrus, S. J. and Félix Zubillaga, S. J. García Icazbalceta's translation of Manuel Fabri's life of Alegre from Latin to Castilian appears in his *Obras*, vol. 4, pp. 180-184. Spanish translations of Rafael Landívar's *Rusticatio Mexicana*, one by Federico Escobedo and another by Ignacio Loureda, were first published in Mexico in 1924. Reputedly best is the prose version by Octaviano Valdés, *Por los Campos de México* (Mexico, 1941). Also see Jorge A. Ruedas de la Serna, "Un poema desconocido del P. José Julián Parreño, Jesuita expulso en 1767", *BAGN*, 7 (1966), pp. 863-874; Ignacio Osario R., "Diego José Abad, bibliografía", *Boletín de la Biblioteca Nacional*, 14 (1963), pp. 71-97; Justino Fernández, "Pedro José Márquez en el recuerdo y en la crítica", *Anales del Instituto de Investigaciones Estéticas* (UNAM), 8 (1963), pp. 5-20. For early bibliography of Clavijero see Luis González Obregón, *El Abate Francisco Javier Clavijero. Noticias bio-bibliográficas* (Mexico, 1927); Rubén García, *Bio-Bibliografía del Historiador Francisco Javier Clavijero* (México, 1931).

Mexican Virgen de Guadalupe. Extensive scholarly interest in Clavijero, in particular, corroborates the importance of these Jesuits. Antonelli Gerbi, José Miranda, Julio le Riverend Brusone, and Víctor Rico González present Clavijero as a somewhat enlightened creole intent on defending his Mexican *patria* and its ancient cultures against European detractors. Luis Villoro and Charles E. Ronan, S.J., write of him as a great *indigenista*. John Phelan placed the Jesuit among those authors who extolled the ancient indigenous civilizations as the classical antiquity of the Mexican creoles. Gloria Grajales included excerpts from Clavigero's writings in her study of *Nacionalismo incipiente en los historiadores coloniales* (UNAM, 1961). His work is an example, then, of an aristocratic and enlightened criollismo embracing a sense of Mexican cultural nationalism at odds with the Spanish tradition. [36]

These Jesuit exiles maintained ties with New Spain; their writings had an inmediate impact within the country. Maneiro and Fabri note that creole corporations supported Jesuit literary activities. Cavo wrote his history at the behest of the ayuntamiento of Mexico City. The rector and university claustro underwrote distribution of Clavijero's history to distinguished persons in the capital. Alzate eulogized it, as did the viceroy, Bernardo de Gálvez. Gamarra wrote a Latin prologue to the poem *Musa Americana* by Abad, published anonymously in Madrid in 1769. Clavijero's history and Landivar's poem were said to be in the library of Miguel Hidalgo y Costilla. With good reason Navarro emphasized the role played by these Jesuits in introducing and continuing a revolution in the climate of opinion.

Ramos, Pérez Marchand, and González Casanova are among those who have indicated that, paradoxically enough, the intellectual premises predicated by the moderns received impetus thereafter in part as a result of the removal of their proponents. In teaching and preaching, they note, the Jesuits had long been a moderating force reconciling old and new, if seeking to modify yet intent upon upholding traditional values and insititutions. After them, is the implication, the

---

[36] Antonello Gerbi, *Viejas Polémicas sobre el Nuevo Mundo* (3ª ed., Lima, 1943), and his *Disputas del nuevo mundo* (México, 1949); José Miranda, "Clavijero en la Ilustración mexicana", *Cuadernos Americanos*, 5 (1946), pp. 180-196; Julio Le Riverend Brusone, "*La Historia Antigua de México* del Padre Francisco Javier Clavijero", in *Estudios de Historiografía de la Nueva España* (Colegio de México, 1945), pp. 293-321; Víctor Rico González, *Historiadores Mexicanos del Siglo* XVIII (UNAM, 1949); Luis Villoro, *Los grandes momentos del indigenismo en México* (Mexico 1950); and his "La naturaleza americana en Clavijero", *La Palabra y el Hombre* (Oct.-Dic. 1963), pp. 543-550; Charles Edward Ronan, S. J., "Francisco Javier [Mariano] Clavijero (1731-1787)", in the forthcoming vol. 12 of *The Handbook of Middle American Indians*; Phelan, "Neo-Aztecism", *op. cit.* (note 31); Francisco de la Maza, *El Guadalupanismo mexicano* (Mexico, 1953).

intellectual climate tended to polarize. *Post hoc ergo propter hoc?*
Or was the steady hand gone from the ideological tiller in New Spain?
This corpus of studies gives evidence that *misoneístas* and proponents
of secular education found less and less meeting ground. In education
the Jesuits were committed to maintain the Thomistic balance between
temporal and spiritual; the expulsion left education to less adroit
maestros. Gamarra although avowedly orthodox in his writings was
exceedingly clumsy, or at least insufficiently adept, if such was his
purpose, at propounding a philosophy reconciling temporal progress
with the traditional static worldview perpetuated in scholastic thought.
A secular and anti-authoritarian spirit infused the periodicals edited
by Alzate and the doctor of medicine and mathematician, José Ignacio
Bartolache. Alzate and Bartolache were Jesuit-educated, as were most
of the creoles who attended school. Alzate was a priest. In Mexico
City Revillagigedo, in accord with enlightened economic and social
policies, encouraged periodicals and the teaching of useful knonledge
Intendants and enlightened cleries did the same thing in regional
centers. Alamán wrote of Jesuit colegios now, under government
sponsorship, become secular institutions instilling in creole students
all sorts of "useful" information and little respect for tradition.
Did the government zealously hack away at its own ideological
underpinnings?

Further, was the Bourbon administration in good part responsible
after all for the introduction of enlightened notions? Campoy, Castro,
Alegre and Clavijero read copies of Feijóo, and other eclectics, belonging to their *peninsulare* fathers, all of whom held administrative
positions in the government. We should investigate the *fathers* of
these Jesuit fathers.

The young moderns, then, were forerunners of relatively aristocratic
and extremely (in relation to total population) small groups of creole
devotees of enlightenment, in centers throughout Mexico, who considered it important, and fashionable, to be in the intellectual van-
guard. They found in enlightened ideology an alternative to the
traditional doctrines still dominant in Mexico. Modernism was *not*
so widespread as it was in France, for example, but it was there.
And among the overwhelming majority of those who were enlightened, intellectual revolution preceded hope for economic and social
advancement. Notions of independence from Spain, as opposed to
freedom from Spanish governors, often came late among the moderns
and in many cases probably not at all. Here we need to look further
into the social milieu and political attitudes of such upstanding enlightened creole supporters of the Establishment as Gamboa, León
y Gama, and Velázquez de León, men Humboldt lauded as superior
in scientific acumen to the now much better known Alzate. What

of that acquaintance of Humboldt, the enlightened loyalist, José Mariano Beristáin de Souza? Miguel Ramos Arizpe, too, informs us of how enlightened creoles could as late as 1812 cling to the dream of autonomy within the empire.

A rapid survey, then, finds these few enlightened Jesuits belonging to an intellectual and professional creole elite, in influence out of all proportion to their numbers. It indicates further that to speak of the Enlightenment in Mexico is to mean a limited phenomenon, a gloss overlaying a very different popular culture. The importance of ideas, the degree to which they determine events, however, does not necessarily corrolate proportionately with their common acceptance. Moreover, it is becoming ever clearer that one enlightened principle, the zest for innovation, provides the strongest link between Enlightenment and revolution. Other enlightened concepts succeeded in turning creole thought to active civil responsibility, to common cause with fellow-inhabitants of Mexico, but it was the shattering of the moral tie to Spain by the denial of the value of eternal sameness in the temporal sphere that allowed enlightened creole leaders of the movement for independence to justify their defection and conservatives to rebel in an attempt to restore the old order. Perhaps Sir Lewis Namier was right; that after all, "new ideas are not so potent as broken habits". [37]

And, as Luis Villoro recently said, the history of ideas "sólo puede tener sentido si las ideas se estudian como expresiones e instrumentos utilizados por hombres concretos en determinadas situaciones reales". [38] One of our most important tasks now is to connect ideas with their individual proponents and to scrutinize these individuals in relation to their social milieu. What better individual figure to begin with than Miguel Hidalgo y Costilla, whose formative years span our period, and who so greatly affected the course of Mexican history.

Numerous biographies and genealogical studies tell us Hidalgo was born to a creole family of middling economic and social position, and that he first studied at the Jesuit colegio at Valladolid (now Morelia) for a few months before the expulsion. [39] Was his first formal

[37] Sir Lewis Namier, Vanished Supremacies (New York, 1963), p. 23.

[38] Luis Villoro, "Historia de las Ideas", HM, 15 (1966), p. 166.

[39] José de la Fuente, Arbol genealógico de la familia Hidalgo y Costilla (México, 1910), and his Hidalgo Íntimo (México, 1910); also in that centenary year of the revolution, Genaro García, in Documentos históricos mexicanos, op. cit. (note 7), included documents concerning Hidalgo and related to him; William S. Robertson, "Miguel Hidalgo y Costilla", in the Rise of the Spanish American Republics as told in the lives of their Liberators (New York and London, 1912); Luis Castillo Ledón, Hidalgo (2 v, México, 1948); Jesús Amaya, El padre Hidalgo y los suyos (México, 1952); Jesús Rodríguez Frausto, "Los gentilicios de Hidalgo", Excelsior, May 10, 1953; and his Hidalgo no era guanajuatense (Mexico, 1953); selections from the

education provided in accord with a curriculum reformed by Clavijero? He next attended the Colegio de San Nicolás (now the University of Morelia), a school with a long humanistic tradition dating back to Vasco de Quiroga. [40] Pérez-Marchand noted that in the colegio and the town interest in modern books and ideas was fully evident. Was Valladolid a rather typical provincial center or did it and the surrounding region harbor an unusual number of *afrancesados* and *inquietos?*

There is no evidence that Hidalgo received anything but a traditional education, if perhaps he later thought it less filled with scholastic trivia than that he underwent at the university. [41] Yet he partook of an intellectual atmosphere apparently tending to radicalization. As a teacher of theology (and later as rector), at San Nicolás in the years 1783-1792, his notions of proper education appear part of a general trend toward a more secular-minded approach to *all* branches of knowledge. While the modern-minded Jesuits never tampered with revealed truth, in his "Disertación sobre el Verdadero Método de estudiar la teología escolástica" (1784), Hidalgo did. [42] This document has been noted by among others, José de la Fuente, Luis Castillo Ledón, and Samuel Ramos. It has been analyzed by Gabriel Méndez Plancarte, Juan Hernández Luna, and Rafael Moreno. [43] It

Cuadro Histórico de la Revolución Mexicana of Carlos María de Bustamante, published as *Hidalgo* (Mexico, 1953); Agustín Cué Cánovas, *Hidalgo* (Mexico, 1953); Jesús Romero Flores, *Don Miguel Hidalgo y Costilla* (México, 1953); Hugh M. Hamill, Jr., *The Hidalgo Revolt* (Univ. of Florida, 1966); and two theses: María de los Ángeles Hernández Díaz, "Biografía de Don Miguel Hidalgo y Costilla" (Instituto Federal de Capacitación del Magisterio. Escuela Normal Oral), and Luz María López Licona, "Biografía de don Miguel Hidalgo y Costilla", at the same institution; both are dated 1967. Also see Rafael Heliodoro Valle, "Bibliografía sobre Don Miguel Hidalgo y Costilla", *Boletín de la Biblioteca Nacional*, 10 (1959; and *adenda* by Emilia Romero de Valle, *ibid.*, 11: 1 (1960); the historiographical study, Juan Hernández Luna, *Imágenes Históricas de Hidalgo* (UNAM, 1953), and Peggy K. Korn, "The Beginnings of Mexican Nationalism: the Growth of an Ideology, 1521-1810" (unpublished dissertation, 1965).

[40] Salvador Reyes Hurtado, "Hidalgo en San Nicolás", *Letras Nicolaítas* (Morelia), 4 (1953; Enrique Arreguín Vélez, ed., *Hidalgo en el colegio de San Nicolás. Documentos Inéditos* (Morelia, Univ. Michoacana, 1956); Julián Bonavit, *Historia del colegio de San Nicolás* (Univ. Michoacana, 1958); Pablo G. Macías, *Hidalgo, reformador y maestro* (UNAM, 1959); and the general biographies listed above.

[41] See Nicolás Rangel, "Estudios Universitarios de los principales caudillos de la independencia. Miguel Hidalgo y Costilla, 1753-1811", *BAGN*, 1 (1930).

[42] The *Disertación* was originally written in both Spanish and Latin. The Spanish version only is known and is in the Museo de Morelia. The text, with the original orthography, appeared in *Anales del Museo Michoacano*, 1 (1939), pp. 58-74; and in modern form as an appendix to Bonavit, *op. cit.*, pp. 413-435, as well as in Gabriel Méndez Plancarte, *Hidalgo. Reformador intelectual* (Mexico, 1945). Also see Rafael Heliodoro Valle, *op. cit.*, *BBN*, 10: 2, p. 42.

[43] La Fuente, *op. cit.*; Luis Castillo Ledón, "Una disertación de Hidalgo", *Re-*

reveals Hidalgo to have been a quick-witted young academician who
prided himself on his present mindedness. He belongs among those
who sought independence from the past, first in education, later, as
a parish priest, through economic and social reform and, finally,
abruptly through rebellion. [44]
What were the roots of his disaffection? Was he in debt to a
Spaniard? Why was he sent from San Nicolás to the outlying parish
of Colima? Did he feel advancement in the Church impossible for
a creole? As a landed proprietor to what extent was he affected by
the *Consolidación* decree of 1804? What was the nature of his relationship with Abad y Queipo? Were his workshops at San Felipe
and Dolores a trend of the times, having official impetus and sanct-
ion as did analogous enterprises, according to Herr, in Spain? How
did he react to the events of 1808? When did he begin to plot against
the Spaniards and did he seek independence, autonomy, or only creole
predominance?
At the other end of the spectrum, information is sparse concerning
the people who responded to the *Grito*. And in order to obtain it,
we need to know much more of social conditions and changes than
we do now. All the political and economic studies cited earlier serve
as a beginning. Silvio Zavala, Luis Villoro, Hugh Hamill, and M. S.
Alperovich have written overviews of the immediate background of
revolution. [45] We have documents on social history compiled by Richard Konetzke and Luis Chávez Orozco, demographic studies including a re-edition of the 1814 *Memoria sobre la población del reino de
Nueva España*, edited by Fernando Navarro y Noriega (México, 1954)
and of the Spanish version of Humboldt's *Ensayo...* by Juan A.
Ortega y Medina, as well as comments on them by Victoria Lerner

vista Mexicana de Estudios Históricos, 1 (1927), pp. 180-184; Ramos, *Historia*,
op. cit.; G. Méndez Plancarte, *Hidalgo, op. cit.*; Juan Hernández Luna, "El mundo intelectual de Hidalgo", HM, 3 (1953), pp. 157-177, appeared in the bicentennial
year of Hidalgo's birth; Rafael Moreno, "La teología ilustrada de Hidalgo", HM,
5 (1956), pp. 321-336. For Hidalgo's intellectual proclivities before 1810 also see
Filosofía y Letras, 47-48 (1952) and HM, 3: 2 (1953), issues devoted to Hidalgo;
Jesús Reyes Heroles, "Continuidad del liberalismo mexicano", *Cuadernos Americanos*, 13 (1954), pp. 169-202; Agustín Rivera, *Hidalgo el joven teólogo* (Guadalajara, 1954); Alfonso García Ruiz, *Ideario de Hidalgo* (México, 1955); Edmundo
O'Gorman, "Hidalgo en la Historia", *Memoria de la Academia Mexicana de la
Historia*, 23 (1964), pp. 221-247; and Luis Villoro, *El proceso ideológico de la revolución de independencia* (UNAM, 1967), the revised edition of his *La Revolución de Independencia* (UNAM, 1953).
[44] See the documents relevant to Inquisition records concerning Hidalgo and
those of his *causa* in Hernández y Dávalos, *op. cit.* (note 7), and other documents
concerning those years published in various issues of *BAGN*.
[45] Silvio Zavala, "México. La Revolución. La Independencia", in Ricardo Levene,
ed., *Historia de América* (13 v, Buenos Aires, 1940-1941), vol. 7 and 11; Luis
Villoro, *op. cit.* (note 43) and Hamill, *op. cit.* (note 39).

and related articles by Sherburne F. Cook and Donald B. Cooper. [46] Lyle N. McAlister has posited a model of "Social Structure and Social Change in New Spain", (*HAHR*, 43 (1963), pp. 349-370), and Ángel Palerm Vich assessed the emergence of an embryonic middle class in "Factores históricos de la clase media en México" (in Miguel Othón de Mendizábal, *et al.*, *Las clases sociales de México*, pp. 63-84). Luis González Obregón early depicted the social milieu of the year of revolution in *La vida de México en 1810* (México, 1943). Sergio Morales Rodríguez noted changes in social customs and beliefs under Bourbon rule. Luis Navarro García has described rural society, while some important social sectors have received individual attention from Charles Gibson (Indians), Gonzalo Aguirre Beltrán (Negroes), and Romeo R. Flores Caballero (Spaniards). [47]

Of tremendous value is Eric Wolf's "The Bajio in the Eighteenth Century; an analysis of cultural integration". (*Publications of the Middle American Research Institute of Tulane University*, 17, 1955) and the essay by Eusebio Dávalos Hurtado, "La morfología social de Nueva España, móvil de su independencia" (in *Estudios antropológicos en homenaje al Dr. Manuel Gamio*, México, 1956, pp. 593-603). We historians would do well to emulate the conceptual framework, lucidity, and style of these social anthropologists. We would also learn much by concerning ourselves with more of the more local and regional history of the late colonial period.

Most exciting because they indicate a trend toward synthesis of the more formal subdivisions of history into a conceptual whole, are a number of recent theses and dissertations and some works in progress

[46] Richard Konetzke, *Colección de Documentos para la Historia de la Formación social de Hispanoamérica, 1493-1810* (3 v, Madrid, 1962); Chávez Orozco, *Documentos, op. cit.* (note 15); Victoria Lerner, "Consideraciones sobre la población de la Nueva España (1793-1810) según Humboldt y Navarro y Noriega", *HM*, 17 (1968), pp. 327-348; Sherburne F. Cook, "The Population of Mexico in 1793", *Human Biology*, 14 (1942), pp. 499-515; and his "The Smallpox Epidemic of 1797 in Mexico", *Bulletin of the History of Medicine*, 7 (1939), pp. 937-969; also Donald B. Cooper, *Epidemic Disease in Mexico City, 1761-1813: An administrative, social, and medical study* (Univ. of Texas, 1965).

[47] Sergio Morales Rodríguez, "Costumbres y creencias en la Nueva España", in *Estudios históricos americanos, op. cit.*, pp. 425-476; Luis Navarro García, "La sociedad rural de México en el siglo XVIII", *Anales de Universidad Hispalense*, 1 (1963); also see V. Alessio Robles, "Las condiciones sociales en el norte de la Nueva España", in *Memorias de la Academia Mexicana de la Historia*, 4 (1945); Charles Gibson, "The Transformation of the Indian Community in New Spain, 1500-1810", *Journal of World History*, 2: 3 (1955), and his *The Aztecs under Spanish Rule* (Stanford Univ., 1964); also see Delfina E. López Sarrelangue, "Población indígena de la Nueva España en el siglo XVIII", *HM*, 12 (1963), pp. 516-530; Gonzalo Aguirre Beltrán, *La población negra de México, 1519-1610* (México, 1946); and Romeo Flores Caballero, *Los españoles en la vida política y social de México, 1804-1838*, soon to be published by El Colegio de México.

and in press. Among them are Isabel González Sánchez, "Situación social de los indios y de las castas en las fincas rurales, en vísperas de la Independencia" (tesis, UNAM, 1963), the book by David Brading and the dissertation and article by Brian R. Hamnett, mentioned earlier, the other studies, underway, on the *Consolidación* decree of 1804 by Masae Sugawara and Flores Caballero, current research by Norman F. Martin, S.J., on the unemployed (los vagabundos), the dissertation by Virginia Guedea, "Criollos y peninsulares en 1808" (Universidad Iberoamericana, México, 1964), and the dissertations in progress: "Le Rôle des 'Ilustrados' et des liberaux creoles et espagnols dans le mouvement d'independence au Mexique", (Thèse Lettres, 3º cycle, Univ. de Paris, Institut des Hautes Études de l'Amerique Latine), and Doris Ladd Speck, "The Aristocracy of Mexico at Independence: an Introduction" (Ph. D. dissertation, Stanford Univ.). The social and economic consequences for our period of the study by Enrique Florescano of *Precios del maíz y crisis agrícolas en México (1708-1810)* (Colegio de México, 1969), are enormous. The Mexican revolution of 1810, like the French, of 1789, was preceded by a Great Hunger.

Here then we have the start of the investigation of the complexities of society and social change. We need to know much more. How much of the creole population could in truth claim *limpieza de sangre?* How did the distribution of wealth change throughout the century? Certainly it can no longer be assumed that gachupines held all the wealth, nor that all creoles were anti-Spanish, nor that those who were chose to rebel only because Spain hindered their economic wellbeing and advancement. What sorts of influence on Mexican pocketbooks and premises had England and the United States after 1797? Finally, who were the Mexicans who joined Hidalgo? No longer can we dismiss them as Indian hordes or as "peasants" only, nor can we characterize the rebellion of 1810 as a people's revolt for political independence.

The current state of historiography now allows several possible hypotheses about the eighteenth century which help to answer our initial questions. Overriding is the conviction that Mexican history must be studied as part of a wider Western culture; autonomous developments can not otherwise be understood. We know, thanks especially to intense investigation of cultural history centered on the introduction and development in Mexico of the Enlightenment or *modernismo*, that European currents of thought circulated and kindred attitudes were adapted to a number of varying needs and aspirations. It is also clear that the new Bourbon regime in Spain allowed freer ingress of outside cultural influences in general, just as it authorized, or its functionaries in Mexico overlooked, increasing foreign trade and contraband. Further, in many ways the government abetted such innovation, notably through sending in a new Spanish bureaucracy inculcated with enlightened notions borrowed largely from France, of fomenting material progress through governmental activity. A remaining problem is just when these minions of enlightened despotism began to exert such a leavening influence.

Political innovation converged with rising population and economic prosperity to bring social change, increase to some extent social mobility, and concomitantly to give impetus to questioning of assumptions supporting the tradicional social arrangements. A new breed of creole, or a significant increase in an old sort, educated in a profession, became increasingly aggressive in demands for social and political preeminence in Mexico. At the same time, hacendados and mineowners maintaining a traditional ethos of criollismo enjoyed prosperity, then watched it dribbling away as the government of Charles IV, appearing inept in comparison to that of his predecessor and enmeshed in wars with France and Britain, exerted ever more pressure on Mexican resources. Increasingly, they found more profitable markets for their wares in England and through the United States.

Meanwhile, a populace periodically plagued by famine and subsequent epidemics, taxed ever more efficiently, was increasingly disoriented by political and economic reform. Larger sectors earned money income or simply wandered, broken away from traditional communities, especially in the Bajío. Mexicans rose sporadically in various locales to protest innovation because it was innovation and because it weighed heavily on their daily lives and, perhaps in the case of the expulsion of the Jesuits, also because it put in jeopardy what was more important than life to at least some, their immortal souls.

In the crisis of 1808, elements of enlightened creole professionals, notably members of the ayuntamiento of Mexico City, joined by a few of the creole aristocrats, sought unsuccessfully to achieve their economic and social aspirations through political means. [48] Adherents

[48] See José Miranda, *Las Ideas, op. cit.*; Manuel Giménez Fernández, *Las doctrinas populistas en la independencia de Hispano-América* (Seville, 1947); Villoro, *El proceso* and *La Revolución, op. cit.*, Juan López Cancelada, *Conducta del Excelentísimo Señor Don José Iturrigaray* (Cadiz, 1812); and his *La Verdad Sabida y Buena Fe Guardada* (Cadiz, 1811); the rejoinder by Fray Servando Teresa de Mier (José Guerra), *Historia de la Revolución de la Nueva España* (2 v, London, 1813); Genaro García, *El plan de independencia de la Nueva España en 1808* (México, 1903); William E. Robertson, "The Juntas of 1808 and the Spanish Colonies", *English Historical Review*, 31 (1916), pp. 573-585; A. F. Zimmerman, "Spain and its Colonies, 1808-1820", *HAHR*, 11 (1931), pp. 439-463; Enrique Lafuente Ferrari, *El virrey Iturrigaray y los orígenes de la Independencia de México* (Madrid, 1941); Frances M. Foland, "Pugnas políticas en el México de 1808", *HM*, 5 (1955), pp. 30-41; also, on the mysterious Talamantes: Luis González Obregón, "Fray Melchor de Talamantes", in *Ensayos históricos y biográficos* (México, 1937);

of this group in the next two years mobilized popular discontent to gain numbers to their creole cause. In 1810, brief unity was achieved. Led by an enlightened creole, Miguel Hidalgo, and by more conservative elements of the militia, a throng in hope of redress of present and specific grievances and of opportunity for plunder, joined these creoles in what Hidalgo called for, and what Anastasio Zerecero, among others, has referred to, as "an explosion of national sentiment".

Eighteenth century studies to date have enabled us to form the desired continnum to 1810, and to provide with a vital, and anatomically complex, body the Mexican spirit. By our next meeting may we know much more not simply of the mental processes, but also about the blood and guts of that body, Mexican society, in all its diversity.

Genaro García, *Documentos* (1910) *op. cit.*, vol. 7; and Emila Romero de Valle, "Fray Melchor de Talamantes", *HM*, 11 (1961), pp. 28-56; and her "Bibliografía de Fray Melchor Talamantes", *ibid.*, pp. 443-486. For earlier disaffection, Nicolás Rangel, *Los precursores ideológicos de la Guerra de Independencia, 1789-1794* (México, 1929).

COMENTARIO

BERNABÉ NAVARRO

La exposición general de la señorita Korn así como algunas de sus acertadas observaciones sobre nuestra historia cultural del siglo xviii me han hecho reflexionar de nuevo acerca de lo que todos venimos llamando historia de las ideas. Parece que en algunos casos, al menos, fue concebida ésta como una historia abstracta, como si las ideas o los pensamientos tuvieran una historia interna y propia —con Hartmann diríamos objetiva—, en cierto modo independiente de los hombres y de los hechos, de lo subjetivo. En la tradición parece haber dominado siempre el punto de vista de que sólo lo último es susceptible de tener historia y de ser descrito como determinado por y dentro de la temporalidad. De acuerdo con esto la historia de las ideas propiamente es algo muy nuevo. Ello también puede explicar la tardía aparición de la expresa y consciente historia de la filosofía —siglos xvii y xviii: Stanley, Purchot, Brucker. Antes, y aun entonces, dicha historia y semejantes no tenían otro designio que describir la presencia o aparición sucesiva en el tiempo de estructuras ideales más bien intemporales; o, en otras palabras, informar sobre la manifestación del mundo ideal en el real.

A mi parecer, habría, según lo dicho, dos posiciones inadecuadas —desde el punto de vista de una verdadera historia de las ideas: la de una historia interna o inmanente de éstas, y la que describiera simplemente su presencia o manifestación en un medio heterogéneo. En la primera podría estudiarse una serie de relaciones dinámicas entre las ideas mismas —movimientos, choques, impulsos, derivaciones, influjos, modificaciones, etcétera—, que tendrían una dependencia al menos indirecta de los fenómenos temporales. En la segunda tal vez se hayan señalado o pudieran señalarse algunos efectos en los puntos de contacto con el mundo real, pero localizados sobre todo en campos más cercanos al mundo ideal, como el espiritual y religioso. En ambos casos, la realidad plena o los sectores más fuertes de ella se desarrollarían fuera del alcance o de la acción de las ideas.

Quizá pudiéramos encontrar un paralelo de esta problemática en la famosísima cuestión, tan debatida desde la Edad Media hasta el xviii y tratada especialmente por Descartes, pero que en Platón sobre todo y en Aristóteles tuvo sus premisas: la cuestión sobre las relaciones entre el alma y el cuerpo. La teoría del cuerpo como una nave o máquina y del alma como piloto o principio motor, la doctrina de la animación o del influjo físico y la tesis de la armonía preestablecida nos ofrecen en la explicación de esas relaciones algunos aspectos que claramente coinciden con los descritos antes, en forma tan sumaria, sobre el problema tocado aquí.

El cambio de actitud en ambos casos puede deberse fundamentalmente a la transformación de los conceptos mismos, con tendencia a eliminar la heterogeneidad absoluta: entre alma y cuerpo, espíritu y materia, objetivo y subjetivo, idea y hecho, pensamiento y acción. La posibilidad de interacción entre el alma y el cuerpo aumenta o disminuye según la mayor o menor diferencia entitativa entre ellos, es decir, si se los concibe como *substancias* heterogéneas, o más bien como fuerzas o elementos —*accidentes*— afines, homogenizables. A su vez, la posibilidad de influjo o determinación del pensamiento y las ideas sobre la acción y los hechos —es decir, de la explicación de los segundos por los primeros— crecerá o decrecerá según el mayor o menor acercamiento entre esos polos, esto es, al concebirse las facultades del hombre y sus objetos o contenidos menos radicalmente distintos y separados, como aspectos accidentales de un solo obrar fundamental, tomando en su sentido verdadero y profundo la unidad radical significada por el ζῷον λόγον ἔχον: animal operante por medio de la razón, y el ζῷον πολιτικόν: animal asimismo esencialmente político y social.

Vayan estas disquisiciones —o divagaciones— como preámbulo al comentario mismo sobre el trabajo de la señorita Korn. La crítica que en ellas pueda haber quiero aplicármela fundamentalmente a mí mismo, y se refiere no a la impropiedad de lo que otros estudiosos y yo hemos hecho en el campo de la historia de las ideas, sino más bien a la falta de una conciencia cabal sobre el problema que dicha historia plantea en el fondo. Todos hemos ido descubriendo a través de los documentos mismos la enorme importancia que han tenido las ideas y las corrientes ideológicas en la historia de nuestro siglo XVIII —siguiendo, sin duda, en forma directa o indirecta, planteamientos semejantes de autores europeos— y hemos dispuesto, teóricamente, de razones para fundamentar en principio ese punto de vista. Mas creo que nadie, en lo que conozco, ha tratado expresa y sistemáticamente el problema de la relación entre las ideas y los hechos, es decir, la determinación específica que aquéllas pueden causar sobre éstos, con exclusión, como predominantes, de otras causas, que podrían ser: necesidades, sentimientos, emociones, presiones externas, etcétera, o también, otros hechos.

Tal vez no se ha considerado necesario un planteamiento filosófico tan riguroso, porque el asunto puede abordarse en una forma sencilla, como por ejemplo ésta: si en las mentes bullen las ideas de libertad, justicia, independencia, legitimidad, mejoramiento, renovación —o las contrarias—, entonces, y dado que los hechos y las acciones corresponden a tales ideas, las causas de éstos serían aquéllas. Sin embargo, creo difícil que un filósofo o un historiador profundo aceptara hoy contentarse con una actitud que no deja de ser obvia, pero también ingenua.

No es mi intento abordar aquí este problema en la forma indicada, porque no sería su lugar, aunque sí deseo proponer algunas cuestiones —además, por supuesto, de la fundamental planteada en las páginas anteriores. Sin pretender un orden determinado ni una formulación definitiva, yo propondría éstas: 1ª ¿A qué condiciones está sujeto el influjo efectivo de las ideas? Porque parece evidente que no basta su sola presencia; 2ª ¿Qué tipo de ideas tienen mayor influjo? Porque, también, se ha manifestado que algunas lo tuvieron y otras no; 3ª ¿Cuál sería, frente a otras causas posibles, el criterio para determinar el predominio específico de las ideas?; 4ª ¿Es posible, en general, atribuirles un papel primario, o deben considerarse absolutamente como factores secundarios?; 5ª ¿Qué debe decirse, a propósito de nuestro asunto particular, sobre el problema general de las relaciones causales en la historia?; 6ª ¿Cuáles serían las razones precisas de por qué la historiografía anterior no destacó el papel de las ideas en la transformación del siglo xviii orientada hacia la independencia?

La señorita Korn ha visto y señalado claramente la nueva actitud de muchos de nuestros historiadores que, al investigar las causas de la revolución de Independencia, se fijaron en las ideas expresadas y manejadas por aquellos hombres y, como es natural, buscaron sus antecedentes, próximos o remotos, mexicanos o europeos. Sin embargo, es pertinente advertir que también ha habido un camino inverso, diríamos, de los antecedentes a los resultados: es decir, de la Modernidad e Ilustración a la Independencia. El primero sería de los hechos a las ideas y el segundo de éstas a aquéllos. En general puede decirse que se trató, en un caso, de historiadores que tomaron mayor conciencia del sentido de la explicación histórica o se esforzaron por lograr ésta en forma más completa, y en otro caso, de pensadores o historiadores —a veces improvisados— de la filosofía, quienes advirtieron que las doctrinas de los filósofos o su espíritu e influjo aparecían también después en los hombres de acción. Ambos sectores unieron sus esfuerzos y recíprocamente se ofrecieron luz en sus trabajos, no sin antes haber discutido muchas veces, aun acaloradamente, sobre métodos y resultados, lográndose, empero, a fin de cuentas, muchos aspectos positivos en la tarea común: la historia verdadera e íntegra, en sus antecedentes y consecuentes, en las ideas y los hechos, del movimiento de emancipación espiritual y material, ideológico y político, económico y social, llamado Independencia, que abarca desde la 2ª mitad del siglo xviii hasta por lo menos el 1er. cuarto del siguiente.

El trabajo de la señorita Korn presenta cuatro secciones, que en realidad se reducen a tres: 1ª *Historias generales* entre 1830 y 1910, y desde 1920; 2ª *Historia económica y política*, y 3ª *Historia cultural e intelectual*. A este cuerpo del estudio va antepuesto un preámbulo teórico y añadida una especie de conclusión. Mi comentario pasará por alto las dos primeras partes, en vista de que caen fuera de aquel campo a que he dedicado algunos estudios. Únicamente haría yo una observación acerca de su pleno sentido en un trabajo que parece tener como tema fundamental la historia ideológica sobre el siglo xviii y principios del xix. Su inclusión se explica formalmente por el título de la ponencia y el tema general de la III Sección; objetivamente se justificaría por tratarse de la referencia a unos campos y momentos, que servirían como de punto de partida para entender la actitud actual y de contraste entre dos enfoques de la historia de esa época. Sin embargo, en mi opinión, si el tema fundamental fuera el que digo, bastaría un breve resumen al respecto.

Las precisiones acerca del tema y de su enfoque expuestas en el preámbulo me parecen correctas y necesarias, debido al inmenso material a la disposición, que no obstante, sea dicho de paso, la autora muestra conocer tal vez en su totalidad. Sobre las tres cuestiones fundamentales (o más bien cuatro) que interesan a los historiadores de hoy —formuladas ahí debo decir que me extrañó no ver ninguna mención directa del aspecto idoelógico o cultural, al que, sin embargo, está dedicada la parte más extensa de la exposición posterior.

El desarrollo de la parte correspondiente a la historia cultural e intelectual va precedido también de otro breve preámbulo teórico. En él se reconoce la nueva actitud de "un creciente número" de historiadores sobre el siglo XVIII, en su mayor parte mexicanos, la que es formulada certeramente por la autora mediante los conceptos de "supraestructura" —las "instituciones políticas" y las demás en general— y "subestructura" —la "ideología". Sobre lo asentado aquí (p. 177) acerca de la conexión o antecedentes de tal actitud respecto de la doctrina hegeliana correspondiente, debería a mi juicio precisarse que en muchos autores dichas tesis están ausentes o sólo tienen un influjo indirecto. La referencia de la autora, es cierto, podría tener el carácter de una interpretación o conceptuación propia, y no de la afirmación de un hecho real y general: en este caso no sólo es aceptable, sino cierta y valiosa. Y en cuanto a su propia postura crítica al respecto (p. 178), yo la entendería, y compartiría, en el sentido de que más que andar recurriendo a teorías cuya presencia es incierta o confusa, debe atenderse a lo que la realidad histórica misma contiene y manifiesta, sea en el campo de los hechos sea en el de las ideas. Expresado de otro modo, yo diría que la historia debe hacerse —o empezarse— de abajo arriba, de los hechos y datos a la teoría, y no de ésta a aquéllos —entendiendo aquí no la teoría o concepción de la historia misma en general, como ciencia y método (que sí debe preceder), sino en particular una teoría determinada, sobre todo como filosofía o concepción del mundo, que se pretendiera aplicar forzadamente a la realidad.

Otro problema apuntado ahí (p. 178) es el de lo que podría llamarse la *continuidad histórica*, es decir, de las "influencias" que la historia del pasado tiene sobre el presente y el futuro. ¿En qué términos debe plantearse ese influjo? ¿Qué sentido y alcance tendría el hablar de una *determinación* en la historia, sobre todo frente al problema de la libertad y de las infinitas posibilidades del hombre? ¿Sería lo histórico en cuanto tal lo que significara el influjo o la determinación, o más bien otros factores, digámoslo así, "contenidos" o manifestados en la historia? Queden ahí por ahora estas interrogantes, las cuales pueden mostrar la densidad que encierran algunas formulaciones del trabajo comentado.

Creo que a muchos estudiosos mexicanos —por lo menos lo digo de mí— la señorita Korn ofrece en este estudio valiosos informes sobre lo que sus compatriotas —u otros investigadores— han aportado a nuestra historiografía cultural del siglo XVIII. En este punto me refiero en concreto a la obra de Phelan (comentada en la página 178), que según la reseña de la autora ha precisado tan objetivamente la tarea que, "filósofos" e "historiadores" en conjunto, nos hemos impuesto en general al hacer tal historia. Pero también debe decirse lo mismo acerca de la obra editada por Whitaker (página 180), que se ocupa de la Ilustración no sólo en México sino en toda Latinoamérica; o acerca del trabajo de Farris sobre el papel de las órdenes religiosas en la difusión de las ideas modernas (página 184); así como sobre tantos otros autores, consagrados allende el Bravo al estudio de nuestra historia, citados sea dentro de la exposición misma —por ejemplo en las páginas 191-195— sea en las numerosísimas referencias bibliográficas contenidas en las notas.

En lo que se refiere a la bibliografía mexicana sobre la historia cultural —y política, económica y social— de esa época, considero un deber declarar que es asombroso el conocimiento que muestra la autora de la totalidad de las obras fundamentales o más importantes, faltando sólo uno que otro pequeño artículo o alguna aportación secundaria. No me es conocido ningún trabajo semejante entre nosotros, que tenga tan amplias bases como el de la señorita Korn. Y creo que es también mi deber manifestarle a ella, así como a todos los estudiosos de la nación vecina que tan entusiastamente se consagran a la investigación de nuestra historia, nuestro profundo reconocimiento por la labor desarrollada.

El aspecto de comentario bibliográfico que a veces se destaca sobremanera en la ponencia de la señorita Korn podría causar una impresión falsa sobre su verdadero carácter. En efecto, en repaso ligero de sus páginas resaltan sobre todo los títulos, autores y fechas de las innumerables obras reseñadas, quedando en el trasfondo su estructura, método y sentido. Es necesario ver las cosas con más atención a fin de percibir, diríamos, la subestructura, y advertir cómo los datos bibliográficos son sólo puntos de referencia para presentar una visión y un enfoque propios del tema estudiado. En manera alguna se trata de un acumulamiento de breves reseñas más o menos en orden cronológico, sino que es un estudio, sumario pero substancioso, sobre la historia misma, cultural e ideológica del siglo XVIII mexicano, y sobre su historiografía desde el siglo pasado hasta nuestros días. Otra justificación del aspecto bibliográfico sería, por una parte, la objetividad y concreción metódicas —tan propias del modo de ser práctico y realista de nuestros vecinos, y tan valiosas— y, por otra, la enormidad del material que debería estudiar un trabajo semejante, así como la amplitud de la época considerada. Pienso que, puestas estas premisas, todo estudio breve como el de la señorita Korn, si pretendiera objetividad y resultados concretos, debería ofrecer más o menos las características del presente. Con esto no se niega la posibilidad de otro tipo de estudio, pero habría de tener otras dimensiones o concretarse a desarrollos generales teorizantes.

Acerca del fondo o estructura de la concepción misma, a que me he referido, advierto que el hilo conductor (en la tercera parte —página 177 a 195—, única examinada por mí) es el concepto y fenómeno de la *Ilustración*, que debe reconocerse sin duda como central y fundamental. En relación con éste se exponen los otros conceptos afines o derivados y los contrarios, como Modernidad o Modernismo, secularización, autoconciencia, eclecticismo, renovación, optimismo, afrancesamiento, etcétera, o los antecedentes y generales, como el humanismo. No me parece que falte ninguna de las corrientes ideológicas fundamentales o de los hechos más notables conectados con ellas, como la expulsión de los jesuitas, la visita de Humboldt, las medidas de gobierno de Carlos III, las útiles disposiciones de Revillagigedo, etcétera. Sin embargo, en lo que respecta al orden o secuencia de los temas —y de los autores y obras—, debo confesar que en algunos momentos no pude encontrar la razón de aquéllos: no es un orden cronológico, ni de los hechos o de la manifestación de las ideas, ni de las obras o escritos; tampoco pude encontrar un orden temático justificado. He dicho sólo "en algunos momentos". Porque, en lo general se hace referencia cronológicamente primero a los humanistas como predecesores teóricos, después a todos los autores ilustrados y al fin, como su culminación, a Hidalgo. A veces parece seguirse la sucesión cronológica de las investigaciones, a veces la de los movimientos históricos, pudiendo causar confusión en el lector. En este aspecto falta, a mi juicio, un orden más sistemático.

En las observaciones de la señorita Korn acerca de los efectos de la expulsión de los jesuitas hay un punto digno de destacarse, porque implica, a mi juicio, una visión nueva, al menos para mí. Se trata del estrecho vínculo que la reacción de la mayor parte de los hombres y las clases novohispanas contra el decreto de expulsión significa con respecto a la Independencia misma. He aquí dos asertos capitales: "Muchos mexicanos de todos los sectores de la sociedad manifestaron un sentido de lealtad hacia sus maestros, sacerdotes, amigos, parientes y aun, en algunas regiones, hacia los jesuitas como representantes del gobierno real. Por todas estas razones la expulsión se convirtió en un *creciente símbolo de todas las indisposiciones contra el gobierno español*" (página 186); y luego más claramente: "Estos escritos —los publicados de algunos jesuitas— demuestran cómo ciertas tendencias anteriores llegaron en el exilio a intensificarse y a canalizarse en protestas de patriotismo mexicano e identificación nacional" (página 186). No creo o no recuerdo haber leído este pensamiento en algún autor, ni a mí mismo se me hizo presente, a pesar de haberme ocupado de "los jesuitas y la Independencia", y a pesar de que resulta bastante obvio y verosímil.

Frente a esta valiosa observación encuentro otras, en cambio, que me parecen faltas de base o precisión suficientes. Son juicios expresados en breves fórmulas, muy a tono con el carácter del trabajo. Quizá por esto resultan incorrectas. Mas como se trata de problemas de fondo, precisamente por ello también habría que evitarlas, empleando desarrollos más amplios. Son tres afirmaciones y se localizan todas en la página 188.

La primera dice: "Los *misoneístas* y los proponentes de una educación secular no encontraron campo de reunión". Mi primera pregunta aquí, como sobre las otras afirmaciones, es por la base documental. La segunda es sobre el sentido y alcance de la afirmación. Si se la hace con carácter *total*, yo la rechazo y pueden darse muchos argumentos en contra. Si su sentido es que hubo muchos individuos que se cerraron y encastillaron radicalmente en sus posiciones tradicionales sin dar oportunidad para la plática y el acuerdo, pero que asimismo hubo muchas otras que facilitan el diálogo y la conciliación, entonces la suscribo gustoso y la sostengo. ¿De qué otra manera, si no, se explica el mismo avance de la renovación? ¿Acaso por la dominación total de los modernos ilustrados *puros* sobre los tradicionales *absolutos*? Tal vez se diga que la afirmación tiene un sentido *objetivo*, que se refiere al campo doctrinal, y no al subjetivo de los hombres mismos. Aun así, no creo que pueda demostrarse una radicalidad absoluta en la oposición entre el punto de partida del misoneísmo y el de la modernidad.

La segunda afirmación dice así: "En la educación los jesuitas habían mantenido el equilibrio tomista entre lo temporal y lo espiritual; la expulsión lo destruyó". Me imagino que el término "educación" tiene el más amplio sentido, abarcando todos los niveles de la educación, hasta el de la universidad, en que laboraban los jesuitas; si no, habría que extenderlo. ¿A qué bases documentales podría recurrirse en nuestros jesuitas para acreditar concretamente ese "equilibrio tomista" o se trata más bien de una deducción general? Yo mismo no estaría muy seguro para hacer tal afirmación. Otras preguntas: ¿Sólo los jesuitas mantuvieron ese equilibrio? ¿Qué bases habría para designar tal equilibrio sólo o privativamente como tomista? ¿En qué proporción y cómo lo "destruyó" la "expulsión"? Probablemente haya que responder a esto que "en el ámbito o campo de acción jesuítico", mas entonces habría una exagerada tendencia, por lo menos, a identificar lo jesuítico con lo novohispano en el terreno de la educación. Creo que sobre este punto deban hacerse varias precisiones.

Contra la tercera afirmación siento el mayor rechazo. Dice así: "Gamarra, aunque declaradamente ortodoxo en sus escritos fue excesivamente torpe al proponer una filosofía que reconciliaba el progreso temporal con la estática concepción tradicional del mundo, perpetuada en el pensamiento escolástico". En primer lugar quisiera saber qué acepción da la autora aquí al término inglés "clumsy" (torpe, pesado, rudo, tosco, etcétera), y de acuerdo con tal acepción desearía me explicara en qué consiste para ella la "clumsy" actitud de Gamarra. Basándose su trabajo en la literatura sobre Gamarra, también querría con gran deseo saber en qué escritos se funda; si, por lo contrario, parte de su propia lectura de nuestro filósofo, me urgiría asimismo saber de dónde lo deduce y cómo lo demuestra. ¿Estaría por otra parte, lo "clumsy" propiamente en su actitud misma, o habría que referirla objetivamente a la posición filosófica conciliadora que adoptó? ¿Proviene su juicio de la comparación con otros pensadores mexicanos ilustrados y modernos, como Alzate y Bartolache (a quienes en seguida menciona), o acaso del paralelo con importantes pensadores europeos? Si fuera esto último me inclinaría a aceptarla, pero haciendo las aclaraciones necesarias sobre la diversidad de circunstancias. Otro punto, difícil aquí es la referencia a la "ortodoxia" como opuesta de algún modo a la filosofía que concilia el progreso temporal, aceptándolo naturalmente. Yo he tratado el punto en varios escritos y creo haber mostrado cómo los documentos no permiten afirmaciones globales en tal sentido y que es necesaria ante todo una distinción entre la ortodoxia diríamos de las "doctrinas" mismas (es decir, de la iglesia como dogma y doctrina) y la pretendida por los sujetos particulares sobre todo con jerarquía de superiores dentro de las órdenes religiosas. Finalmente, tampoco entiendo bien el sentido del "aunque" (although), pues, en general, sería precisamente la ortodoxia la que causaría la torpeza o pusiera obstáculos en la tarea de conciliar lo moderno con lo tradicional.

Quizá debiera aclarar más mis dudas y oposición sobre los puntos anteriores, pero el espacio concedido no lo permite. Sin duda lo haremos después en común, la autora y los participantes, en las discusiones de la sesión consagrada al tema. Aquí, para terminar, sólo quiero advertir que las conclusiones del estudio de la señorita Korn son eco fiel de lo desarrollado en su exposición. También ahí se encuentra, a mi juicio, una clara prueba de lo que dije antes acerca del carácter y de la calidad del trabajo: que no se trata simplemente de un mero comentario bibliográfico, sino de un estudio con estructura interna que presenta una visión y un enfoque propios de nuestra historia e historiografía cultural-ideológica del siglo xviii.

COMENTARIO

RAFAEL MORENO

1. Salvo en el aspecto económico, donde alcanza por cierto a trazar líneas importantes, cabe afirmar que la autora proporciona sobre la segunda mitad del siglo XVIII y los años inmediatos a la revolución una síntesis y una visión valiosa, que a los mexicanos nos hacían falta. A los datos añade juicios; de los libros deduce reflexiones que utiliza para caracterizarlos dentro de la historiografía; cada una de las obras cobra un sentido y un lugar en la descripción de ese todo que forman los acontecimientos comprendidos entre 1750 y 1810. Enriquece, por otra parte, la mera cronología de los autores y las obras con la aplicación de un método genético, de manera que la ponencia, con las limitaciones propias de un estudio de esta naturaleza, indica de hecho el origen, el proceso, la evolución historiográfica, o sea, entiende bien las distintas maneras cómo los mexicanos y los no mexicanos —principalmente los que pertenecen a su lengua y cultura— han concebido los tiempos anteriores a las campanas de Dolores.

Otros méritos de la ponencia consisten en realizar un inventario de los problemas que son interrogantes para el historiador y para el estudioso de las ideas: cuestiones que se desprenden de una bibliografía manejada sagazmente desde el extranjero; también en comprender desde dentro la época y en tratar sentimental, amorosamente, uno de los capítulos más significativos de la historia mexicana.

Debe reconocerse desde luego que cumple su propósito, a saber, analizar y, en algunos casos, interpretar el material histórico, entendiendo por esto la bibliografía fundamental y la bibliografía monográfica. Con tales utensilios obtiene elementos para presentar un trabajo que señala certeramente los procesos mentales —acercándose apenas a la "sangre e intestinos de . . . la sociedad mexicana en toda su diversidad". Atisba los cambios económicos y políticos de la unidad histórica estudiada y logra captar tanto los cambios mismos como también las categorías ideológicas que presiden la época. Puede decirse por esto que aprehende al continuo que va de los inicios de la mentalidad nueva a la revolución de Independencia. Señala, además, con precisión las influencias externas y, se decide, tras algunas vacilaciones, por la tesis de que es el propio colonial quien evoluciona y cambia, desde dentro, por sí mismo, en contacto o con las medidas reformadoras del gobierno español o con las ideas y corrientes europeas.

Sorprende a un estudioso mexicano el manejo familiar de las obras o del material histórico, y sorprende más el que la autora haya visto con claridad la relación entre las reformas económicas y políticas de los gobernantes españoles con el progreso de la Nueva España, con el avance intelectual y con la creación de un estado mental revolucionario. No advierte sólo el progreso material, aumentado o frenado, sino que muestra la vitalidad interna y el crecimiento de un espíritu cada vez más mexicano.

2. Natural es que los apremios de la síntesis, la necesidad de encontrar fórmulas simples que sirvan para definir el fenómeno prerrevolucionario, la obligación de señalar lo esencial de una obra, han llevado a la autora a ciertas imprecisiones, las cuales son el resultado de la historiografía que se usó. Esto equivale a aceptar que somos, en primer lugar los mexicanos, los responsables de que todavía no se comprenda cabalmente el siglo XVIII. Existen, sobre todo, en el campo de la historia de las ideas, las monografías indispensables para que se lleve a cabo la obra de conjunto, mas ésta, no está realizada. De ahí que sea conveniente hacer una empresa, como las del XVIII de desengaños, al menos sobre algunos aspectos fundamentales desde el punto de vista de las ideas y su historia.

3. *Primer desengaño*: la mentalidad ilustrada no es uniforme, ni siquiera en el mismo autor. En aquellos tiempos las actitudes, las intenciones y las doctrinas cambiaron y progresaron rápidamente; no sólo los grados de modernidad son distintos, sino que las ideas y las etapas se cruzan entre sí. Pueden, a título de guía, fijarse la atención en las siguientes fechas:

I. De 1748 a 1767 predomina el magisterio de los jesuistas; no expresan la introducción del pensamiento moderno, son la apertura definitiva a todas las corrientes modernas, lo que trae por consecuencia la conciliación de lo antiguo en lo nuevo, pero con una definitiva inclinación por la física experimental.

II. En 1761 Bartolache, que no es discípulo de los jesuitas, enseña en la Universidad sus *lecciones matemáticas*, o lecciones sobre el método matemático concebido como el único verdadero. Bartolache afirma que todo conocimiento puede y debe tratarse con el método que establecieron Descartes, Leibniz, Wolff y los lógicos de Port-Royal. Desde esa temprana edad, enseña que los temas de la sagrada teología pertenecen a otra esfera del conocimiento. Por estas afirmaciones es el autor más ilustrado y más moderno del siglo.

III. 1768, cuando Alzate comienza sus publicaciones periódicas, señala la difusión de la física, de las ciencias, del espíritu y la razón crítica, y a la vez del método experimental.

IV. 1774 es el año clave para precisar la aceptación de los textos modernos en los medios oficiales, pues los *elementos de filosofía moderna* de Gamarra son reconocidos por la Universidad Real y Pontificia.

V. 1779, con la llegada de sabios españoles y la organización del Jardín Botánico y un poco más tarde del Seminario de Minería, muestra el crecimiento de la investigación rigurosa, con apego a los métodos del siglo.

VI. 1784 es el año en que Hidalgo pronuncia la *disertación sobre el verdadero método para estudiar teología escolástica*, estudio que significa el avance de la Modernidad hasta el fundamento mismo de la tradición.

VII. 1790 señala la difusión de las ideas de los filósofos modernos, un decaimiento de la enseñanza académica, y los inicios de las ideas políticas revolucionarias.

4. *Segundo desengaño*: los jesuitas. De acuerdo con la tradición historiográfica mexicana, que fundan Pedro Henríquez Ureña y Gabriel Méndez
Plancarte, la autora concede a los jesuitas una preponderancia que no
tuvieron. Formaron, cierto es, un grupo significativo, pero esto fue posible
porque existía la tendencia modernizante. Ni Alzate, ni Bartolache, ni
Gamarra, ni las tesis de Hidalgo, para no hablar de los sabios León y
Gama, Velázquez de León, se pueden explicar históricamente como una
influencia de la enseñanza jesuita. Lo mismo acontece con los franciscanos,
y los mercedarios, que sostuvieron tesis más modernas que las de los jesuitas.
Por lo tanto no es posible atribuir a los jesuitas una importancia tal, que
a partir de su expulsión se polarice el movimiento ilustrado; ni tampoco se
puede afirmar que a partir de 1767 haya dejado de existir una fuerza
moderadora, de conciliación entre los nuevos valores y los valores tradicionales, y que por faltar los jesuitas, los misoneístas y los modernos no
hayan encontrado un campo de unión.

5. *Tercer desengaño*: ¿Fueron los ilustrados una minoría? Los dos factores anteriores nos hacen comprensible cómo la autora pueda afirmar que
los ilustrados fueron una minoría y que la Ilustración fue cultivada sobre
todo por el bajo clero. Pérez Calama y Abad y Queipo bastarían para
mostrar que la última afirmación no es del todo veraz. Claro que la
Ilustración es cultivada por los criollos y que éstos eran un grupo reducido
en comparación con los habitantes de la Nueva España. Mas no puede
asegurarse que los ilustrados sólo formaran grupos "extremadamente pequeños y relativamente aristocráticos", diseminados por todo el país. Las
mismas fuentes manejadas dan los argumentos para decir que las ideas
modernas invadieron las mentes directoras de la nación y que los amantes
de lo antiguo, los aristotélicos o escolásticos, quedaron reducidos a una
minoría tal, que no determinaba ya la orientación de la inteligencia ni los
fines de la enseñanza.

Lo cual no tuviera importancia si la Ilustración no significara la independencia mental con respecto al pasado, y si las nuevas ideas no hubieran
servido después como base para levantar la ideología de la insurgencia.

6. *Cuarto desengaño*: la Ilustración no implica conflicto interior. Parece
que la autora concibe la Modernidad, o la Ilustración prerrevolucionaria
fundamentalmente como una secularización de la cultura y por eso como
una separación y conciliación a la vez de lo espiritual y de lo temporal.
Éste fue el planteamiento de los misoneístas y de los escolásticos, pero
no el de los modernos. Los modernos inclinaron radicalmente la balanza
hacia lo temporal, mas en ningún momento negaron lo espiritual. En
consecuencia no es lícito afirmar que con la expulsión de los jesuitas se
terminó el balance tomista entre lo espiritual y lo temporal. De la misma
manera no se puede afirmar que Gamarra conciliara al progreso temporal
con la concepción escolástica. Cabe distinguir entre lo logrado por los
modernos y su intención, pues procuraron la reforma completa de la mentalidad. Razón por la cual adoptaron un eclecticismo que Gaos califica
como *sui generis* y como una contribución filosófica a la historia general
de la filosofía.

7. *Quinto desengaño*: no hay Ilustración mexicana. Si por Ilustración, según el modelo francés y alemán, se entiende el abandono y la negación de los valores tradicionales, y particularmente un espíritu deista desligado de la Iglesia, así como el establecimiento de una cosmovisión sólo secular, entonces no existieron en sentido estricto ilustrados mexicanos. Habrá, en consecuencia, que pensar, contra lo que hemos venido escribiendo, más bien en un eclecticismo y en una Modernidad, tal como han sido caracterizados por José Gaos y su escuela.

COMENTARIO *

M. S. ALPEROVICH

1. En tanto que el informante se refiere a mi apreciación de las reformas realizadas por los Borbones durante los años 60-80 del siglo XVIII, quisiera precisar una circunstancia. Yo, de ninguna manera afirmé que estas reformas no tuvieron en absoluto ningún significado para la solución de los problemas económicos de la Nueva España. En verdad, en el texto de la edición mexicana de mi libro *Lucha por la Independencia de México* efectivamente está escrito: "Las reformas de los años 60-80 del siglo XVIII no marcaron progreso alguno en el desarrollo económico de México..." (*Historia de la Independencia de México*. México, 1967, p. 74).[1] Sin embargo la traducción en español correspondiente al original ruso no es preciso ya que en la edición soviética, publicada en Moscú en 1964, claramente se dice: "Las reformas de los años 60-80 *indudablemente propiciaron, en cierta medida, algunos adelantos en el desarrollo económico de México y de otras colonias,* pero de ningún modo eliminaron los principales obstáculos que frenaban este proceso...", etcétera (ver página 94).

2. La idea de que las reformas de Carlos III no condujeron a cambios radicales en el régimen colonial de la Nueva España no es nueva. Fue expresada antes, en parte, por el investigador norteamericano Donald Smith en su trabajo *The Viceroy of New Spain* [2] (publicado en 1913), donde él también señala que estas reformas fueron dictadas no por los intereses de las colonias españolas, sino exclusivamente por los intereses de la misma metrópoli.

3. La política de los Estados Unidos e Inglaterra en relación con la guerra de la Independencia de México es más o menos conocida. Sin embargo, la posición de otras potencias se ha estudiado muy poco. Y en lo que se refiere a la política de Rusia, casi nada se ha investigado.

Mientras tanto, como es sabido, en el año de 1799 fue creada la Compañía Ruso-Americana, y en 1812 en las costas de California Norte se fundó el Fuerte Ross, así que en ese tiempo, en determinado sentido, México y Rusia fueron vecinos. Los trabajos de los científicos soviéticos L. Y. Slezkin *Rusia y la guerra de independencia en la América Española* (Moscú, 1964) y N. N. Bolkhatinov *Establecimiento de relaciones ruso-americanas, 1775-1815* (Moscú, 1966), señalan algunos nuevos intentos de Rusia dados para establecer relaciones comerciales con la Nueva España, específicamente con California Norte.

---

* Traducción de Elva Macías G.
[1] en español en el original.
[2] en inglés en el original. Notas del traductor.

Es necesario continuar el trabajo en este terreno de la investigación, buscar documentos en los archivos de la Unión Soviética, México y Estados Unidos.

RELATORÍA

DIEGO SANDOVAL

La ponencia de la doctora Korn sirvió como base para la iniciación de los debates en general, y propició la formulación de varias sugerencias para la mejor comprensión del tema cubierto.

Algunas de las intervenciones sugirieron la inclusión de investigaciones de tipo económico y social para redondear el periodo. Entre ellas: el estudio de crisis agrícolas, salarios y problemas demográficos. Hubo varias intervenciones tendientes a interesar a los especialistas a que examinaran ideas acerca de la interacción de fuerzas sociales, la influencia de la violencia como factor de cambio, y las causas que originaron el aislamiento de importantes sectores de la población mexicana.

La discusión sobre la historia de las ideas para cubrir este periodo, además de interesante, planteó algunas preguntas a fin de que se reconsideraran algunas generalizaciones comunmente aceptadas, por ejemplo ¿Por qué, si se considera que la Iglesia se encontraba en decadencia, ésta propició la invasión y el cultivo de las tesis modernas especialmente en España e Iberoamérica? Igualmente se hicieron consideraciones acerca de la necesidad de que las ideas, se interpretaban y se aplicaban de acuerdo con los intereses particulares de los grupos y clases en conflicto.

El tema de la actuación de la Compañía de Jesús fue debatido con interés, planteándose la interrogante de considerar ¿En qué medida influían los intereses materiales de la Compañía de Jesús en la distribución que hacían de la mano de obra especialmente de la del indio y la del negro? Otros sugirieron estudiar lo que se ha llamado estructura feudal de la Colonia; y otros más consideraron que era necesario aclarar metodológicamente lo que se entendía como español, criollo, "regalismo", "reformismo" y "liberalismo".

Finalmente algunas intervenciones elogiaron los esfuerzos realizados para la elaboración de la ponencia.

IV. SÍNTESIS DE LA HISTORIA DE MÉXICO

Presidente: Leopoldo Zea, director de la Facultad de Filosofía y Letras, UNAM; profesor en El Colegio de México.

Ponentes: Josefina Vázquez de Knauth, profesora e investigadora de El Colegio de México; Robert A. Potash, profesor de historia, Universidad de Massachussets.

Comentaristas: Edmundo O'Gorman, profesor emérito de la Facultad de Filosofía y Letras, UNAM; Charles C. Cumberland, profesor de historia, Michigan State University.

Participantes: Arturo Arnáiz y Freg, Academia Mexicana de la Historia; Anita Brenner, editora de *Mexico this month*; Alfonso García Ruiz, profesor en la Facultad de Filosofía y Letras; Ernest Gruening, senador al Congreso de los Estados Unidos de América, retirado; José A. Matesanz, profesor de la Facultad de Filosofía y Letras, UNAM; Martín Quirarte, subdirector del Archivo Histórico de la Secretaría de Relaciones Exteriores.

Relator: Elías Trabulse, estudiante del Centro de Estudios Históricos de El Colegio de México.

SÍNTESIS DE LA HISTORIA DE MÉXICO DE HISTORIADORES MEXICANOS

JOSEFINA VÁZQUEZ DE KNAUTH

Repudiada o defendida la historia nunca ha dejado de tener un papel importantísimo en la vida mexicana a través del tiempo. Postulada a raíz de la Independencia, como base imprescindible para la formación del ciudadano, su enseñanza fue defendida como única vía para sustituir la falta de experiencia política del pueblo. Al iniciarse las luchas políticas la historia iba a servir para fundamentar las incipientes ideologías. Los conservadores trataron de demostrar con la historia por qué el país no podía desprenderse de su tradición, mientras que los liberales la usaron para demostrar lo contrario: la necesidad de destruir las huellas del inicuo pasado. Más tarde, triunfante la facción republicana-liberal, se le iba a otorgar a la historia una nueva tarea: la de fortalecer la lealtad del ciudadano a su patria, representada por el gobierno republicano, exigencia que para los años noventas se iba a institucionalizar.

Las síntesis de historia de México han sido casi todas producto de finalidades pragmáticas; sólo unas cuantas han llegado a ser el producto de la meditación final, del estudio concienzudo de la historia del país. Las que no han sido elaboradas como libros de texto no han dejado de tener metas pragmáticas: una conferencia, información sucinta para extranjeros, introducción histórica para un libro sobre México o fundamentación de una posición política.

Tocó a José María Luis Mora, a Wenceslao Barquera y a Lorenzo de Zavala ser los primeros en insistir en la necesidad de formar a los ciudadanos de la nueva República, de hacerlos conscientes mediante la enseñanza de la historia patria. Desde 1821 hasta el momento en que la educación por la que propugnaban comenzó a ser una realidad, a partir de 1861, se iban a repetir constantemente los argumentos, aunque poco o nada se pondría en práctica. En primer lugar hacía falta un sistema de educación pública, inexistente antes de 1867; en segundo lugar, hacían falta síntesis adecuadas para tal objeto. El caos constante en que se mantuvo la República hizo imposible poner en práctica las buenas intenciones que en varias ocasiones, incluso, se plasmaron en ley.

La guerra con los Estados Unidos conmovió hondamente a los mexicanos que hasta entonces no habían logrado darse cuenta, con claridad, de su identidad nacional. El golpe que representó la pérdida de más de la mitad del territorio iba a despertar nuevas actitudes. Dentro de ese nuevo espíritu un joven de 18 años, al sentir que era necesario aumentar la conciencia nacional de los mexicanos, publicó la primera síntesis de historia de México para niños en 1851. Se trataba del *Compendio de la historia de México, desde antes de la conquista hasta los tiempos presentes, estractada de los mejores autores para la instrucción de la juventud*, de Epitacio de los Ríos. [1] Como síntoma del trauma que aun representaba la reciente guerra no había ni siquiera una vaga mención a ésta y se despachaba la historia de la República con una lista de gobernantes, porque "el estudio de la minuciosa historia de esas épocas, no es para los niños".

La primera síntesis de historia iniciaba así una tradición funesta: la de negarse a dar una idea de la época contemporánea, tradición que ha persistido en gran medida hasta nuestros días.

El segundo libro de texto fue el de José María Roa Bárcena, *Catecismo de la historia de México, desde su fundación hasta mediados del siglo XIX, formado con vista de los mejores autores y propio para servir de texto a la enseñanza de instrucción pública*, publicado en 1862. Un conservador elaboraba, así, el primer texto que pretendía servir para cumplir con la ley de instrucción pública de 1861, la cual obligaba la enseñanza de la historia del país en la escuela primaria perfecta. El autor confesaba que le movía a hacerlo el evitar que los ciudadanos entraran con tal ceguedad a la vida política, "cuyo norte más seguro, después de la justicia, es el conocimiento de los antecedentes del país en cuya administración se toma parte". [2] El autor incluía la guerra con los Estados Unidos, pero cerraba su relato en 1848 y evitaba, por tanto, la relación de la guerra de Reforma.

A partir de 1867, con el triunfo de la República, se inició la organización del país y, con ella, la de la educación pública. El gobierno se daba cuenta de que no había más que un medio de vencer verdaderamente a los conservadores que consistía en formar a los nuevos ciudadanos dentro de un nuevo espíritu. La enseñanza de la historia ocupaba un lugar importante en este empeño; por lo que pronto se empezaron a publicar una multitud de pequeños textos, los cuales siguieron el modelo de la tercera síntesis de historia de México, la de Manuel Payno, *Compendio de la historia de México para el uso de los establecimientos de Instrucción Pública de la República Mexicana, publicada en 1870*. Los libros de Roa y Payno, que tuvieron larga vigencia, sir-

[1] De los Ríos, Epitacio, *Compendio de la historia de México.* México, s.p.i., 1852, p. 231.
[2] Roa Bárcenas, J. M., *Catecismo elemental de historia de México.* Andrade y Escalante, México, 1867 (2ª edición), p. 4.

vieron lo mismo para niños que para jóvenes y como todos los libros de su época, estaban escritos a base de preguntas y respuestas.

Fue la década de 1880 la que vio aparecer las dos primeras síntesis formales de historia de México. En 1883 apareció el *Compendio de la historia de México, desde sus primeros tiempos hasta la caída del Segundo Imperio*, de Luis Pérez Verdía y hacia 1886 el libro de Guillermo Prieto, *Lecciones de historia patria, escritas para los alumnos del Colegio Militar*. Tenían el gran mérito de preceder a la publicación total del *México a través de los siglos*, la primera gran historia general de México, publicada entre los años de 1884 y 1889. Tocado del cientificismo histórico de su tiempo, Pérez Verdía se preocupaba sobre todo por la imparcialidad, para lo cual consultó no sólo los libros existentes, sino numerosos documentos y corrigió constantemente las ediciones que se hicieron antes de su muerte. Al segundo, aunque aquí y allá hablaba de imparcialidad, le importaba más transmitir el mensaje de la interpretación liberal y confesaba que:

> exaltar el sentimiento de amor a la patria, enaltecer a sus hombres eminentes por sus virtudes, señalar los escollos en que puede tropezar su marcha y alumbrar el camino que la lleve a la prosperidad y a la gloria, tales han sido los objetos de mi *Compendio*, porque estoy persuadido que la enseñanza debe ser *intencional*, es decir, conducir al educando por el camino del bien, conforme con la libertad y los sistemas del país. [3]

Los dos libros ponían las bases de lo que sería la interpretación oficial de la historia de México, especialmente el de Prieto. En ellos triunfaba la interpretación antihispanista enrraizada en los resentimientos criollos coloniales. Se negaba a Cortés y a Iturbide y se encumbraba como héroes a Hidalgo, Morelos y Juárez.

En la década de los noventas, con su empeño nacionalista de fomentar "la religión de la patria" y de estimular la unión nacional, haciendo converger todas las fuerzas positivas en la idea de un México mestizo, la línea oficial favorecía una visión más conciliadora. La ideología positivista y spenceriana vigente facilitaba la tarea con su visión evolutiva de la historia, en la que cada etapa se consideraba un paso adelante. Las interpretaciones que vieron la luz en las dos primeras décadas del siglo XX estaban teñidas en mayor o menor grado de esta posición. Justo Sierra tal vez sea el que ofrezca la más acabada interpretación positivista en la síntesis histórica que servía como introducción general a los tomos del libro *México, su evolución social* (1900-1902). [4] Pero, aunque con diferencias notables, el libro de Nicolás León,

[3] Prieto, Guillermo, *Lecciones de historia patria*. Secretaría de Fomento, México, 1891, p. 464.
[4] La mayor parte del ensayo apareció con el título de "Historia política", t.

Compendio de historia general de México (1902), el de Carlos Pereyra, *Historia del pueblo mejicano* (1909) y el de Ignacio Loureda, *Elementos de historia de México* (1919), también lograron el objetivo de ver la historia de México evolutivamente. León no dejaba de tener sus toques providencialistas y se extendía con devoción en la historia precortesiana. Loureda, quien escribía después de la Revolución, un poco en plan defensivo, destacaba la obra de España durante la Colonia. A Sierra y a Pereyra les preocupaba más seguir la lenta búsqueda del camino del progreso en la época independiente. Pero todos veían con optimismo su presente.

La Revolución truncó "la evolución" a la vez que cambió muchos de los ideales del país. Se replantearon los problemas que la primacía dada al desarrollo material durante el Porfiriato había dejado al margen. Los revolucionarios, en su empeño de buscar nuevas formas de solución a los viejos problemas, volvían a encontrar como enemigo al grupo tradicionalista. En la posición revolucionaria no dejaban de existir huellas tradicionalistas como reacción a un siglo de intentos por adaptar soluciones extranjeras a problemas mexicanos. Los mexicanos ahora estaban convencidos de que debían de buscar soluciones propias y en este empeño muchas veces volvieron a la tradición colonial como fuente de inspiración. Sin embargo, al aflorar los problemas del campo y del indio, el nativismo, que siempre había estado presente, volvió a provocar la exaltación del pasado indígena. Conforme las medidas revolucionarias contra la Iglesia iban entrando en vigor provocaban una reacción clerical que, a su vez, radicalizaba la posición oficial.

Justamente en 1926, coincidiendo con el inicio del nuevo problema religioso, se publicó el *Compendio de historia de México* de Alfonso Toro que, durante treinta años, fue el texto más popular de enseñanza media. Más que indigenista el punto de vista del autor era antihispanista y anticlerical, y en ese momento convergía con las reacciones oficiales. A pesar del largo silencio que habían guardado los conservadores la radicalización que trajeron los años treinta originó los dos primeros libros de texto conscientemente conservadores, el de Agustín Anfossi, *Apuntes de historia de México,* (fines de 1930) y el de Joaquín Márquez Montiel, *Apuntes de historia genética mejicana* (1934 y 1940) y los de divulgación antioficialistas como el de José Vasconcelos, *Breve historia de México* (1938) y el de Mariano Cuevas, *Historia de la nación mexicana* (1940). Al mismo tiempo, acordes con el ambiente que imperaba, hicieron su aparición las primeras interpretaciones marxistas de la historia de México: Alfonso Teja Zabre, *Historia de México. Una*

---

i, vol. i, *pp.* 33-314, el resto lo constituía el capítulo "La era actual" (t. ii, pp. 415-434) en *México, su evolución social.* Ballesca y Cía., México, 1900-1902. Se publicó junto por primera vez con el título de *Evolución política del pueblo mexicano* en 1940.

moderna interpretación (1935), Rafael Ramos Pedrueza, *La lucha de clases a través de la historia de México* (1936) y Hernán Villalobos Lope, *Interpretación materialista de la historia de México* (1937). Fueron muchos los problemas que provocó el "socialismo" del Plan Sexenal, los cuales, para el momento de la expropiación petrolera, parecían indicar que hacía falta una conciliación interna que terminara con la discordia. El mismo peligro de una guerra mundial y de la acción de facciones internacionales en el país, hacía muy importante buscar fuerzas que terminaran con los partidarismos y que estimularan la unidad nacional. En la polémica indigenismo-hispanismo se había llegado a extremismos, tales como los que mostraban por un lado los libros oficiales de la Secretaría de Educación, los artículos del general Rubén García y el mural de Rivera en la escalera del Palacio Nacional; y, por el otro, los libros de los religiosos Cuevas y Márquez Montiel, que no se quedaban atrás en el extremismo de sus juicios. Todavía durante la década de 1940 se presenciaría la representación teatral sobre los encuentros de los restos de Cortés y de Cuauhtémoc y la aparición de una versión tradicionalista de divulgación, a manera de tira cómica, del padre García Gutiérrez. Pero todo conspiraba ya contra los extremismos, incluso la llegada, al final de la década de 1930, de los refugiados políticos españoles. Por un lado constituían un nuevo tipo de inmigrante español que rompía el estereotipo acuñado y, por el otro, venían, bajo los auspicios del gobierno revolucionario, atacados por los "hispanistas" tradicionalistas mexicanos, lo cual daba una nueva dimensión a la antigua polémica. Además los intelectuales españoles, con su aportación de nuevas ideas, iban a contribuir poderosamente tanto a renovar el ambiente cultural mexicano, como a acelerar la confrontación de la cultura mexicana consigo misma, proceso que se había iniciado con el libro de Samuel Ramos, *El perfil del hombre y la cultura en México* (1934) y que había de conducir a la preocupación de "México y lo mexicano".

Los libros que aparecieron a partir de 1940 mostraban, en general, un ánimo menos polémico y más conciliador en sus juicios. Indigenismo e hispanismo no habían desaparecido, pero habían madurado y reconocían la realidad mestiza de México. Sin embargo la polémica no fue estéril, la pasión de los dos grupos estimuló interés en la etapas prehispánica y colonial y produjo estudios interesantes que conducirían a una apreciación más justa del pasado mexicano.

Las décadas de los cuarentas y de los cincuentas fueron, por tanto, de transición. Los autores se empeñaron conscientemente en ser justos, aunque algunos expresaran su simpatía hacia la hispanidad como José Bravo Ugarte o hacia lo indígena como Luis Chávez Orozco. Bravo Ugarte iba a dedicar diez y ocho años a la publicación de los cuatro volúmenes de su *Historia de México*, preocupado por precisar, mediante el estudio acucioso de las fuentes, el mayor número de hechos sobre el pasado mexicano.

Pero la preocupación fundamental estaba en la importancia y las consecuencias de la transmisión de la interpretación del pasado mexicano, que se complicaba con la preocupación que había de legar el libro de Samuel Ramos sobre el complejo de inferioridad del mexicano. Para muchos el rechazo constante de la raíz española o de la raíz indígena de nuestro ser agravaba el problema. Historiadores y profesores de historia expresaron su preocupación por la enseñanza de la historia de México durante el II Congreso Mexicano de Historia (1943) y lograron reunir una Conferencia de Mesa Redonda para el estudio de los problemas de la enseñanza de la historia de México (1944). Torres Bodet al inaugurarla enfocaba certeramente el problema.

> Bien está ... que se cancelen los odios en la redacción de los libros de historia ... asimismo que se emprenda una campaña depuradora para arrancar a los textos las páginas negativas ... pero como funcionario y también como hombre, habré siempre de preocuparme porque en nuestro empeño de eliminar errores, no terminemos absurdamente por confundir los juicios con los prejuicios. [5]

Las resoluciones constituyeron una serie de peticiones a la Secretaría de Educación sobre las exigencias a que debían sujetarse los libros de texto en nivel primario y secundario. En el primer concurso (1945) salió premiado el libro de Jorge Fernando Iturribarría, *Historia de México*, que no llegaría a ver la luz sino hasta 1951. En el segundo concurso (1950), para libro de texto de segunda enseñanza, se iba a premiar el libro de Efrén Núñez Mata, *México en la historia*. Y aunque todavía aparecieron textos plagados de errores, como el de los profesores González Blackaller y Guevara, las exigencias fijadas por la Conferencia obligaron a los autores a fijarse mayor calidad como meta. Sobresalían por su calidad la parte de la época colonial del libro de Chávez Orozco, *Historia de México* (1946) y la prehispánica del libro de Elvira de Loredo-Jesús Sotelo Inclán (1951).

Pero la preocupación oficial por la interpretación del pasado mexicano iba a provocar la publicación de libros como *México, historia de su evolución constructiva* (1945) y *México y la cultura* (1946). Este último libro parecía ser la culminación de la idea que patrocinó la publicación del primero y pretendía responder a las preguntas: ¿Qué busca México? ¿Hacia dónde va? ¿Qué ha dado en historia, en fuerza, en belleza, en lucidez, el saber de los mexicanos? Lo iniciaba la *Síntesis de la historia del pueblo mexicano* de Silvio Zavala. La frialdad

[5] Ramírez Rafael y otros, *La enseñanza de la historia en México*. I.P.G.H., México, 1948, p. 72.

científica del historiador y sus conocimientos sólidos permitieron que cumpliera con su cometido; relataba la historia del pueblo mexicano sin mutilaciones y sin agravios, simplemente como proceso de constitución de un pueblo a través de vicisitudes muchas veces trágicas, lo que en última instancia había preparado al "espíritu mexicano para enfrentarse a la vida con valor y resistencia" y, "a veces, también con dotes creadoras, que otorgan a este pueblo algún derecho de ser estimado como miembro apto de la gran familia humana".

La preocupación de los años sesenta es, como tenía que ser, más madura. De los libros considerados sólo uno fue llevado a cabo por un extraño a la profesión. Dos son libros de texto: Wigberto Jiménez Moreno, María Teresa Fernández, José Miranda, *Historia de México* (1963) y Martín Quirarte, *Visión panorámica de la historia de México* (1965). *La síntesis histórica de México* de Arturo Arnáiz y Freg (1960), escrita en ocasión de la reunión de la Asociación Internacional de Universidades, es un apretado esquema para información de los visitantes. Las de Wigberto Jiménez Moreno, Alfonso García Ruiz, *Historia de México* (1962), López Gallo, *Economía y política en la historia de México* (1965) y José Valadés, *Historia del pueblo de México* (1967) están destinadas a la divulgación. Por último podemos considerar la síntesis de Edmundo O'Gorman *El triunfo de la República, en el horizonte de la historia* que, aunque escrita para una conmemoración, puede considerarse como la interpretación de una parte de la historia de México, producto de una vida dedicada a la historia.

Si exceptuamos el libro de López Gallo, intento semifracasado de interpretación marxista de la historia de México, que continúa arrastrando juicios liberales del siglo XIX con respecto a España, sin fundamentación, todos los demás han superado la polémica de las raíces nacionales. Aquí y allá se notan huellas de antiguas heridas.

A mí, mestizo mexicano, la historia de la conquista me deja cada vez más tranquilo. La miro como un pleito de familia. Como requisito indispensable para que una mitad de mí mismo, se uniera con la otra mitad. [6]

En el libro de Jiménez Moreno-Fernández-Miranda, el texto mejor logrado en términos generales, se acepta que el "trauma" de la conquista se ha superado, pero creen que "queda, sin embargo, otro trauma por superar, el de la Reforma". Sin duda les asiste la razón, aunque nosotros añadiríamos un nuevo "trauma", el de la Revolución, que ellos no se atreven a enfrentar al terminar su historia en 1910. Pocos son los historiadores que, como Valadés y López Gallo, estudian los acontecimientos hasta el momento de la publicación. El primero hace incluso gala de valor al reprobar las acciones del presidente actual.

[6] Arnáiz y Freg, Arturo, *Síntesis histórica de México*. México, s.p.i., 1960, p. 20.

López Gallo proporciona material muy interesante para las últimas
décadas.

El doctor O'Gorman, como siempre, es caso aparte. No se ocupa
del total de la historia mexicana, pero como en otros ensayos del mismo
tipo [7] se aparta de las explicaciones habituales y cala hondo para en-
tregarnos la significación de los acontecimientos, el porqué y el cómo
sucedieron. O'Gorman interpreta la historia de México, nación independiente, como la historia de un proceso "de forcejeo por encontrar
un fundamento histórico a nuestra individualidad, a fin de poder cobrar
conciencia de lo que somos". En el ensayo mencionado se ocupa de la
historia mexicana de 1821 a 1867, la etapa constitutiva, como la llamó
Bravo Ugarte, que tan poca atención ha merecido en su conjunto. Con
su interpretación dinámica O'Gorman descubre como razón de la
lucha dramática que precedió al triunfo de la República, la existencia
de dos posibilidades en el ser del México que se independizó. Dos Mé-
xicos distintos, el republicano y el monárquico, lucharon para imponerse uno sobre el otro. Al entenderlo así, dice O'Gorman, "ya no
resultará ni sorprendente, ni vergonzoso el triste rosario de asonadas,
cuartelazos, rebeliones, planes políticos y cartas constitutivas que exhi-
ben los anales de cincuenta años de nuestra biografía nacional". [8]

Evaluación: Puede apreciarse, en la rápida revisión de la aparición
de las síntesis históricas de México, cómo éstas han respondido a las
demandas y necesidades de cada etapa. En una historia de la historiografía mexicana —tarea todavía por realizar— las síntesis de la historia
podrían servir como fuente muy expresiva de las ideas y creencias fundamentales del momento histórico que las produjo. Desgraciadamente
el tiempo no nos ha bastado para familiarizarnos con los autores y
situarlos debidamente en sus circunstancias como para hacer un análisis completo de las obras que nos ocupan. Por tanto no nos queda
sino sugerir las ideas que una revisión somera de ellas nos ha provocado.

Para nosotros resulta un agrupamiento de las obras en dos etapas.
La primera se inicia con la urgencia de De los Ríos y Roa Bárcena de
formar ciudadanos más patriotas o más civiles mediante el estudio
de la historia. La intención para ellos es más importante que la materia y, a pesar de representar a un partido de la contienda, evitan la
polémica cortando aquellas partes que la provocan. El triunfo de la República acalla prácticamente en este renglón al partido conservador [9]

[7] Ver sus *Seis estudios históricos de tema mexicano*. Universidad Veracruzana,
Xalapa, 1960.
[8] O'Gorman, Edmundo, "El triunfo de la república en el horizonte de su historia" en *A cien años del triunfo de la república*. Secretaría de Hacienda y Crédito
Público, México, 1967, p. 339.
[9] Hay algunos textos conservadores en la década de 1880, como Tirso Rafael
Córdoba que publicó su *Historia elemental de México* en 1881.

y los historiadores liberales tratan de fundamentar la nacionalidad mexicana "republicana" en el pasado indígena, rechazando en gran medida
el pasado español. Se provoca una polémica ardiente durante los años
ochentas y noventas la que evidentemente trataron de superar los autores de principios de siglo, Sierra, Pereyra, León, con la idea de un
México mestizo.

La Revolución dio fin a esta primera conciliación y provocó las bases
del nuevo rompimiento con sus medidas anticlericales que reavivaron el
fuego semiapagado. El problema religioso, iniciado en 1926, estimuló
la aparición de libros partidaristas, ya fuera de conservadores tradicionalistas, ya de liberales y marxistas. Durante los treinta la contienda
alcanzó sus máximas expresiones violentas, tanto que a partir de 1940
se sintió la necesidad de una historia menos radical y volvió a aplicarse la fórmula ni indio, ni español: mestizo. Para los sesentas nuestros profesionales han producido interpretaciones más maduras de
nuestra historia.

En la primera etapa los historiadores pueden clasificarse en tres
grupos: los conservadores tradicionalistas, los liberales oficialistas y los
conciliadores positivistas. En la segunda, la que más nos interesa, encontramos cuatro grupos: conservadores tradicionalistas, liberales y oficialistas, marxistas y el grupo de los historiadores cuyo interés vital por
el pasado les permite superar, en gran medida, sus simpatías políticas.

A diferencia del pasado el grupo tradicionalista no ha producido historiadores de gran talla. El mejor, Bravo Ugarte, por su gran esfuerzo
por comprender el pasado merece formar parte del último grupo. El
grupo oficialista ha logrado a menudo síntesis valiosas de historia política en su empeño por justificar "la obra de la Revolución", aunque
ha mantenido viva la polémica de la Reforma. El grupo marxista
es el peor representado, puesto que, en una forma u otra, sus componentes son parte del *establishment* y además sus conocimientos de
marxismo son superficiales como para poder aplicarlos con seriedad al
caso mexicano. Algunos de los autores, como Teja Zabre, Chávez Orozco
y García Ruiz, que han estado atraídos por el materialismo histórico,
tenemos que considerarlos como parte del último grupo, puesto que
su conocimiento de la historia se impuso al final sobre cualquier dogmatismo. La única característica que puede unificar a todos los autores
es el nacionalismo. En todos se siente una viva preocupación por México y escriben historia ya para "hacer conciencia patria", [10] ya para
explicarnos en forma dinámica el ser de la patria. [11]

[10] Valadés, José, *Breviario de historia de México*. Editorial Patria, México,
1949, p. 81: "Si algún fin tiene la historia, éste es hacer conciencia patria."
[11] O'Gorman, *op. cit.*, p. 342: "el ser de México ... radica en el modo en que
esos hombres concibieron y en la manera cabal en que cumplieron sus responsa-
bilidades en la esfera de los intereses de la nación. Tal la esencia de toda entidad

La influencia de las ciencias sociales, particularmente de la sociología y de la economía, es también una característica bastante general. Las excepciones (entre el grupo de los historiadores sin calificativo) serían tal vez el padre Bravo Ugarte y Edmundo O'Gorman. Bravo Ugarte hace un intento considerable no sólo por rectificar puntos confusos, sino también por incluir la historia en sus diversas expresiones. Es, desde luego, él el que más esfuerzos hace para caracterizar la vida cultural del país. El doctor O'Gorman nos ofrece una interpretación más que un relato y, en última instancia, es el único totalmente original en pensamiento.

La historiografía mexicanista mexicana tiene, por supuesto, un defecto que es común a todas las historiografías nacionales: el regionalismo. Los autores no dan muestras de poseer conocimientos de otras áreas aparte de la historia hispanoamericana —y ésta sólo colonial. Esto les priva de luces que les permitiría ver con mayor relieve los acontecimientos mexicanos y que, en ocasiones, les lleva a achacar a influencias del exterior lo que es un producto del acontecer mexicano. Valadés y Teja Zabre parecen tener una información más general de historia de las Américas; pero, por ejemplo, Martín Quirarte incluye un apartado, sobre la independencia de los Estados Unidos, que demerita su obra, uno de los mejores ensayos de síntesis de historia política mexicana. El pequeño apartado parece sufrir la influencia de un infortunado libro de Pereyra [12] cuando en la actualidad hay muchos estudios de primer orden sobre el problema. El punto que él subraya, la Constitución Norteamericana, como producto de una plutocracia, debería mencionar por lo menos la tesis de Beard y la de sus oponentes. Estoy segura que un mejor conocimiento de la historia de los Estados Unidos permitiría ver desde una nueva perspectiva muchos de los problemas nacionales. Y, si bien, también estaría de acuerdo con Valadés [13] en la falacia de importar valores extraños, pienso que hay grandes ventajas en adquirir una perspectiva más amplia, puesto que no puede negarse que desde la Conquista, México ha tenido que estar sujeto a la interacción con el exterior.

histórica; tal es pues, la de México; proceso que se despliega en la historia y que descansa y depende de la responsabilidad de sus hijos".

[12] Pereyra, Carlos, *La constitución de los Estados como instrumento de dominación plutocrática.* Editorial América, Madrid, s.f.

[13] Valadés, *op. cit.* p. XII: "no han cesado los empeños en dilatar las judicaturas extranjerizantes, ya literarias, ya económicas, ya políticas, en el curso de la historia de México, con lo cual en vez de alcanzar el conocimiento de nuestras cosas materiales y espirituales, hemos caído en el error de creernos débiles e infortunados, cerreros y perezosos ... el historiador mexicano debe cerrar las ventanas de su conciencia a las erudiciones extranjeristas, para perseguir incansablemente todos los signos de la naturaleza nacional que constituyen en la verdad de la realidad las culturas patrias".

Ya en el ambiente del relato mismo todos aceptan "por razones obvias" la división de la historia de México en tres etapas. Aún los que como Márquez Montiel, afirman:

Dicen bien los que dicen que propiamente la historia de México empieza con la Conquista española y dicen bien porque antes de la llegada de los españoles... no existía lo que hoy es México como nación, ni los indígenas pudieron transmitir, ni menos escribir una verdadera historia. [14]

Y se resignan a relatar la etapa prehispánica, aunque no sea propiamente parte de la historia de México, porque las diversas culturas se desarrollaron "en nuestro territorio y aportaron su elemento humano para la construcción de la nueva sociedad". [15]

Algunos historiadores, como Teja Zabre y otros autores de textos oficiales, consideran una nueva etapa a partir de la Revolución de 1910, pero en realidad sus razones no han conquistado verdaderamente un amplio auditorio.

La etapa prehispánica, que solía ser la peor tratada en las síntesis históricas, ha logrado en los últimos libros, gracias a la intervención de un especialista en dos de las síntesis, un tratamiento adecuado. Wigberto Jiménez Moreno ofrece un ensayo interpretativo muy atractivo en su libro con García Ruiz y una síntesis descriptiva muy completa en el libro con María Teresa Fernández y José Miranda.

El periodo colonial siempre estuvo monopolizado por la narración de la Conquista que en algunos libros, como en el de Toro, alcanzó a ocupar casi el 80% del espacio dedicado a la Nueva España. Con los libros de Bravo Ugarte y Chávez Orozco esto comenzó a remediarse. Se abordó la Conquista de grupos ajenos al imperio azteca y se dio debida atención a las instituciones sociales, políticas y económicas, así como a la vida cultural. José Miranda, conocedor del periodo, ofreció un excelente esquema de éste. En muchos autores el antihispanismo sirvió de importante obstáculo para comprender esa etapa tan importante en la formación de nuestro ser nacional, como ha sucedido a una gran mayoría de historiadores norteamericanos que también se han empeñado en exhibir simplemente la crueldad y la superstición españolas, en vez de tratar de comprender los acontecimientos.

Al enfrentarse a la historia nacional, a partir de la década de los cuarentas, se nota un menor partidarismo y como resultado, quizá, del conocimiento más profundo de las etapas anteriores, un espíritu más comprensivo. Valadés ha tratado de revisar muchos de los juicios su-

[14] Márquez Montiel, Joaquín, *Apuntes de historia genética mexicana.* México, 1940 (2ª edición), p. 9. Vasconcelos en su *Breve historia de México* sostiene la misma opinión.
[15] Bravo Ugarte, José, *Historia de México.* Editorial Jus, México, 1940, vol. I, p. 17.

perficiales de la era santanista, misma a la que O'Gorman ha dedicado dos ensayos. Se notan sin embargo, lagunas en la narración de la separación de Texas y de la guerra con los Estados Unidos, porque en general han ignorado las aportaciones historiográficas norteamericanas al respecto. La Reforma, la Intervención y la era Porfirista se abordan, en general, incorporando gran parte de la información que han proporcionado los voluminosos estudios de los últimos tiempos.

La etapa que se inicia con la Revolución de 1910 sigue sin merecer la atención debida. México, al igual que el resto del mundo, ha sufrido varias transformaciones con la revolución tecnológica del siglo xx, el desarrollo increíble de las comunicaciones, las transformaciones sociales, políticas y económicas en todos los continentes producto de las conflagraciones mundiales y de los factores enumerados. Pero el empeño de ver sólo el aspecto político de la historia y para colmo, la interpretación de todo el lapso que sucede a 1910, como "era revolucionaria", impide penetrar en lo más importante. Cierto que como afirman algunos críticos, muchos de los problemas del país siguen, en el fondo, siendo los mismos. Pero qué duda cabe que México cambió profundamente con la Revolución y que ha seguido cambiando, debido a factores que nada tienen que ver con ella. Toda esa transformación queda fuera de las síntesis, a pesar de que sería el tema que más interesaría al público al que se destinan las obras. Valadés, quien se aventura en su reciente libro hasta los años sesenta, considera terminada la Revolución cuando "la doctrina del pueblo —Democracia, Soberanía, Sufragio, Libertad— de 1910, quedó en escombros en el transcurso de medio siglo, por la fuerza del Estado —Orden, Paz, Continuidad, Autoridad". En el fondo del problema está el viejo dilema de fijar principio y fin a los acontecimientos humanos que, sujetos siempre a una complejidad infinita, constituye una de las tareas más difíciles para el historiador. Seguramente habrá terminado antes de lo que afirma el gobierno que no ha encontrado una justificación más importante que el ser revolucionario. Lo que no es comprensible es que los historiadores se empeñen en aceptar la oficial, como una periodización válida.

Nuevas orientaciones: Cuando repasamos en nuestra mente la impresión que nos han dejado la casi totalidad de las obras revisadas, no podemos sino evocar el mural de Diego Rivera en la escalera del Palacio, miles de retratos y de escenas violentas que se amontonan sin demasiado orden. Hay cambio en los vestidos, pero no sabemos exactamente por qué. Todo parece estar dominado por las caras de soldados, de religiosos y de los múltiples héroes y gobernantes. Por supuesto que algunos autores han superado la simple relación política; como ya dijimos, además de una que otra buena síntesis de historia política, hay obras que, bajo la influencia de las ciencias sociales, se han ocupado con éxito de otros aspectos del pasado. Sin embargo lo que no se ha logrado es dar la idea de los efectos que el paso del tiempo van causando en el pueblo mexicano. Falta pintar la transformación de la vida cotidiana bajo la influencia de las revoluciones, de la importación de las modas o de las ideas. Describir la interacción de las ideas y de los hechos, el paso de unas ansiedades, supersticiones, creencias e ideales, a otras diferentes. Para lograr esto hace falta dejar atrás la relación meramente cronológica, plantear una periodización que permita estudiar unidades temporales, desde todos los ángulos. Algunos historiadores han proporcionado un esquema interpretativo de referencia; otros, como Teja Zabre y Valadés, se han planteado la necesidad de una renovación en la forma de historiar. El primero se daba cuenta de que era tarea para ser emprendida por toda una generación, para que resultara una visión más generosa y humana de nuestra realidad nacional. [16] Valadés se fija en cierta forma una meta cercana a la que nosotros planteamos, si interpretamos debidamente su lenguaje barroco.

La idea, pues, está en el ambiente. No es justificación ya la falta de información para llevarla a cabo, lo que sí hará falta, sin duda, es una buena pluma que sea capaz de hacer lo hecho por Luis González en su *Pueblo en vilo*, verdadera síntesis de la historia de México, desde la perspectiva de una pequeña comunidad rural, que puede servir de ejemplo.

La otra posibilidad sería una mirada general a la historia de México a la manera de Edmundo O'Gorman, que interpretara ésta como una unidad. Sí, filosofía de la historia de México, si así prefieren llamarla, que estimulara nuevos acercamientos a problemas que, por el enfrentamiento simplemente datístico y con el peso de los múltiples clichés que hemos heredado, no han podido llegar a comprenderse.

LISTA DE LAS SÍNTESIS HISTÓRICAS DE MÉXICO
CONSIDERADAS EN LA PONENCIA,
EN ORDEN CRONOLÓGICO

Epitacio de los Ríos, *Compendio de la historia de México desde la conquista hasta los tiempos presentes, extractada de los mejores autores para la instrucción de la juventud*. Publícola Simón Blanquel. Imprenta de la Voz de la Religión, México, 1852.

José María ROA BÁRCENA, *Catecismo de la historia de México, desde su fundación hasta mediados del siglo XIX, formado con vista de las mejores obras y propio para servir de texto a la enseñanza de instrucción pública*. Andrade y Escalante, México, 1862.

[16] Teja Zabre, Alfonso, *Historia de México, Una moderna interpretación*. Editorial Botas, México, 1948 (2ª edición), p. 10.

Manuel Payno, *Compendio de la historia de México para uso de los establecimientos de instrucción pública en la República Mexicana.* Imprenta de Francisco Díaz de León, México, 1870.

Luis Pérez Verdia, *Compendio de la historia de México, desde sus primeros tiempos hasta la caida del Segundo Imperio.* Tipografía del autor, Guadalajara, 1883.

Guillermo Prieto, *Lecciones de historia patria, escritas para los alumnos del Colegio Militar.* Oficina Tipográfica de la Secretaría de Fomento, México, 1890 (2ª edición).

Justo Sierra, "Historia política" en *México, su evolución social.* Ballescá y Cía., México, 1901, t. i, vol. i, pp. 33-314 y "La era actual", en la misma obra, t. ii, pp. 415-434.

Nicolás León, *Compendio de historia general de México, desde los tiempos prehispánicos hasta el año de 1900.* México, 1902.

Carlos Pereyra, *Historia del pueblo mejicano.* J. Ballescá y Cía., México, s.f. [1909].

Ignacio Loureda, *Elementos de historia de Méjico.* Librería Española, México, 1919.

Alfonso Toro, *Compendio de historia de México.* Sociedad de Ediciones y Librería Franco-Americana, S. A., México, 1926.

Joaquín Márquez Montiel, *Apuntes de historia genética mexicana.* Puebla, 1940 (2ª edición).

Agustín Anfossi, *Apuntes de historia de México, ajustados a los programas vigentes de la secundaria y de preparatoria. México independiente y mirada retrospectiva a México Colonial.* Editorial Progreso, México, s.f. [1938].

Alfonso Teja Zabre, *Historia de México. Una moderna interpretación.* Secretaría de Relaciones Exteriores, México, 1935.

Rafael Ramos Pedrueza, *La lucha de clases a través de la historia de México.* Talleres Gráficos de la Nación, México, 1936.

Alfonso Reyes, *México en una nuez.* Buenos Aires, 1937.

Hernán Villalobos Lope, *Intepretación materialsita de la historia de México.* México, 1937.

José Vasconcelos, *Breve historia de México.* Polis, México, 1938.

Mariano Cuevas, *Historia de la nación mexicana.* Talleres Tipográficos Modelo, México, 1940.

José Bravo Ugarte, *Historia de México.* Editorial Jus, México, 1940-1958.

Compendio de historia de México. Editorial Jus, México, 1945.

Félix F. Palavicini, *México: Historia de su evolución constructiva.* Distribuidora Editorial Libro, México, 1945.

Jesús García Gutiérrez, *Historia de México.* Buena Prensa, México, 1946.

Silvio ZAVALA, *Síntesis de la historia del pueblo mexicano*, en México y la cultura. SEP, México, 1946, pp. 3-45.

Luis CHÁVEZ OROZCO, *Historia de México*. Editorial Patria, México, 1946 (*etapas precortesiana y colonial*).

José VALADÉS, *Breviario de historia de México*. Editorial Patria, México, 1949.

Jorge Fernando ITURRIBARRÍA, *Historia de México*. SEP, México, 1951.

Ciro GONZÁLEZ BLACKALLER y Luis GUEVARA RAMÍREZ, *Síntesis de historia de México*. Editora Mexicana El y San, México, 1950.

Manuel B. TRENS, *Síntesis histórica de la nación mexicana*. Archivo General de la Nación, México, 1954.

Efrén NÚÑEZ MATA, *México en la historia*. México, 1951.

Elvira de LOREDO y Jesús SOTELO INCLÁN, *Historia de México* (*etapas precortesianas y colonial*). Editorial Patria, México, 1954 (3ª edición).

Carlos ALVEAR ACEVEDO, *Elementos de historia de México*. Editorial Jus, México, 1958 (3ª edición).

Síntesis de historia mexicana. Editorial Jus, México, 1962.

Ángel MIRANDA BASURTO, *La evolución de México* (*de la independencia a nuestros días*). Editorial Herrero, México, 1958.

Wigberto JIMÉNEZ MORENO y Alfonso GARCÍA RUIZ, *Historia de México: una síntesis*. I.N.A.H., México, 1962.

Arturo ARNÁIZ Y FREG, *Síntesis histórica de México*. Comité Organizador Mexicano. III Conferencia General de la U.I.U. México, 1960.

Wigberto JIMÉNEZ MORENO, María Teresa FERNÁNDEZ y José MIRANDA, *Historia de México*. Editorial Porrúa, México, 1963.

Martín QUIRARTE, *Visión panorámica de la historia de México*. México, 1965.

Manuel LÓPEZ GALLO, *Economía y política en la historia de México*. Editorial Solidaridad, México, 1965.

José C. VALADÉS, *Historia del pueblo de México, desde sus orígenes hasta nuestros días*. Editores Mexicanos Unidos, México, 1967.

Edmundo O'GORMAN, "Epílogo: El triunfo de la república en el horizonte de su historia" en *A cien años del triunfo de la república*. Secretaría de Hacienda y Crédito Público, México, 1967, pp. 333-441.

SYNTHESES OF MEXICAN HISTORY: THE U. S. WRITERS

ROBERT A. POTASH

Any examination of Mexican historical syntheses produced by United States scholars ought properly to begin with an explanation of the term. For a work to qualify under the rubric of a synthesis it must, in my opinion, provide a view, at once systematic and balanced, of Mexico's entire history from pre-conquest times down to the present, or at the very least examine the unfolding of that history from the onset of the independence movement to the time of writing. A work that focuses on the Porfiriato or on the 20th century Revolution no matter how broadly defined does not constitute a synthesis of Mexican history. Moreover, while articles have sometimes presented a birdseye view of that history, the concern of this paper is with the more substantial works, the one-volume or multi-volume studies of Mexican history.

Under this definition it becomes immediately apparent that syntheses of Mexican history are rare if not exactly exotic things. While our colleagues who teach United States, British, or even Russian history have bookcases that groan under the weight of the numerous syntheses that pour from the presses on their respective fields, those of us interested in Mexican history are confronted by a condition of scarcity. Indeed, if all the syntheses published originally in English since 1880 were put together, they would scarcely fill a single bookshelf. Even with the addition of translations —and in this regard the recent appearance of Justo Sierra's *Evolución política del pueblo mexicano* is a cause for rejoicing the situation would not be much better. [1] By any reckoning, there are not more than a dozen titles that fall under our designation, and not all of these merit extended discussion.

The first serious attempt to provide a general view of Mexican history in English dates from the 1880's when the businessman-historian, Hubert H. Bancroft, devoted to that task six of the thirty-nine volumes that comprise his *Works*. [2] To be sure, the northern regions of Mexico were treated in detail in two other volumes, and the Indian cultures in his "Native Races", but it is to his six-volume *History of Mexico* that one must look for systematic coverage of events

---

[1] Justo Sierra, *The political Evolution of the mexican People* (Austin, 1969). Tr. by Charles Ramsdell. This is actually the second English translation, the first having appeared, in mangled prose, in Justo Sierra, ed., *Mexico, Its Social Evolution* (2 vols. in 3, Mexico, 1900-1904).

[2] H. H. Bancroft, *Works* (39 vols., San Francisco, 1882-1890).

from the era of the conquest to the Díaz regime. [3] Bancroft of course did not write these works alone —it was a collective enterprise for which he, improperly, took too much credit, but the net result was a monumental study that still retains value today and probably will continue to be useful a century after publication. [4]

The reasons for this are to be found in the very nature of the work. While Bancroft reflected very much the values of his times —he was a successful businessman, a California pioneer, an admirer of Porfirio Díaz— his aim was not to try to moralize from history or set forth a theory of human development, but rather to provide, as he phrased it, "a clear and concise statement of facts bearing upon the welfare of the human race in regard to men and events, leaving the reader to make his own deductions and form his own opinions". [5] To achieve this aim, Bancroft kept five men employed for ten years just in making references. [6] As a result, this 5000-page *History of Mexico* is a mine of information and the bibliographic references alone guarantee continued consultation by serious scholars. Other attractive features are its balanced treatment of the major periods of Mexican history and the vigorous style in which much of it was written. Its inadequacies are partly those that are the inevitable product of the passage of time, partly those inherent in the work itself. It is strictly a political history despite the mass of data of an economic and social nature offered up to the reader in undigested fashion in the last seven chapters. Moreover, for all of Bancroft's boast that he and his staff consulted 10,000 authorities, this history rests primarily on printed sources, thus permitting future scholars to amend or elaborate on its story through the exploitation of archival materials. [7] But despite all that might be said against it, Hubert H. Bancroft's *History of Mexico* is a unique work. No other U. S. historian, or group of historians, has as yet undertaken to produce a work of comparable scope and one is left to wonder whether the conditions that govern the publishing industry in the United States will ever again permit the appearance of a multi-volume general history of Mexico.

[3] Bancroft planned his *Works* so that each component series would have its own numeration. The volumes of interest here are: *Native Races of the Pacific States* (5 vols., New York, 1874-1875); *History of Mexico* (6 vols., San Francisco, 1883-1888); *History of the North Mexican States and Texas* (2 vols., San Francisco, 1884-1889).

[4] The best assessment of Bancroft is John W. Caughey, *Hubert Howe Bancroft: Historian of the West* (Berkeley and Los Angeles, 1946). See especially pp.253-277. Bancroft's own account of his labors is set forth in his *Literary Industries* (New York, 1891). See especially pp. 134-167, 330-348.

[5] Reproduced in Caughey, opp. p. 385.

[6] Bancroft, *Literary Industries*, p. 321.

[7] *Ibid.*; Caughey, p. 169.

The one-volume format, brief enough neither to exhaust the general reader nor to exceed the patience of the undergraduate student, has been the characteristic feature of the syntheses that have appeared in the U. S. since Bancroft's time. Hardly worth mentioning is Arthur Noll's *A Short History of Mexico* issued in 1890, except to say that he was moved to write it because of his own ignorance of Bancroft's work. "If any comprehensive history of Mexico exists in the English language", he wrote in March 1890, two years after the appearance of the last of Bancroft's six volumes, "its name fails to appear in any of the long lists of books on Mexico which the present writer has diligently searched".[8] Without bibliography or notes, his work nevertheless satisfied a temporary need and can safely be relegated to the obscurity it has since enjoyed. The same may be said of the one-volume *History of Mexico* which Bancroft himself brought out in 1914, a reissue in expanded form of his *Popular History of the Mexican People* originally published in 1887.

The early 1920's saw the appearance of the first synthesis written by a professional historian, Herbert I. Priestley's *The Mexican Nation, A History*.[9] Issued originally in 1923 and reprinted without change as late as 1935, it constituted for almost two decades the standard text in those few colleges which offered courses devoted to Mexico.

Although Priestley wrote it shortly after the First World War and following a decade of revolutionary violence in the neighboring country, it was less these events than his training as a colonial historian that appears to have influenced his format and approach. Practically half the volume was taken up with the colonial experience, but here Priestley avoided the temptation, to which other synthesizers have succombed, of dwelling at length on the exploits of Cortés and his generation.[10] It was with the introduction and development of institutions, political, social, and economic, but especially political that Priestley was mainly concerned, for he saw Mexico's troubled history after independence and even down to his own day as an outgrowth of a rich but defective Spanish inheritance, in which personalism, autocratic rule, and class struggle were baneful influences.[11]

Writing for a U.S. audience, Priestley embraced to a certain extent the Greater American concept made famous later by his California colleague, Bolton. This is seen especially in Priestley's interpretation of the breakdown of the Spanish mercantilist empire and the beginnings of independence. In dealing with the 19th century, he likens Gómez

[8] Arthur H. Noll, *A Short History of Mexico* (Chicago, 1890), p. v.
[9] H. I. Priestley, *The Mexican Nation, A History* (New York, 1923).
[10] Of the 455 pages of text, 205 are devoted to the period before 1810 and of these only 14 are used to discuss the exploration and occupation of the mainland.
[11] Priestley, p. XIII.

Farías to an Andrew Jackson, seeing him as the personification of the rise of a new proup and likens Juárez to Lincoln as defenders of national integrity. Priestley stops short of pushing these analogies, for he his well aware of the distinctive cultural patterns of the two countries. [12]

Writing as he did in the early 1920's Priestley reveals a remarkable indifference to the *indigenista* spirit that had been generated by the Revolution, a spirit that was being reflected in art, archaeology, and other ways even as his book appeared. The Revolution to Priestley, insofar as it had social significance, revolved around the mestizo, not the Indian. [13] Indeed, as he saw it, "The progress of the mestizo type has been the cause and effect of the three great revolutionary movements which have marked the trend of Mexican history during the past century and a quarter". [14]

As stated earlier, Priestley's chief preoccupation was with political development. He himself firmly believed that Mexico needed strong centralized government in which the balance of power lay with the executive rather than the legislature. [15] His book accordingly devoted considerable attention to the various constitutions devised for Mexico, and to an analysis of their strengths and weaknesses. No apologist for autocracy, however, he had only condemnation for militarist adventurers whether in the 19th or 20th centuries. His heroes, as one might expect, are Hidalgo, Morelos and Juárez. He acknowledged Díaz' extraordinary achievement in bringing stability and material progress to Mexico, but condemns him for halting Mexico's political development and for making Mexico an economic colony of the United States. "The ambitions of Díaz for his people", Priestley observed, "were excellent, benevolent and laudable whatever may be said of his egotism, his selfishness, his overwhelming lust for power. Neither he nor his enthusiastic admirers ever caught an inkling of the crime he committed. But his success was transitory because he set personal ambition against the trend of his country's history ever since independence by denying it the political evolution which had barely begun at the fall of Maximilian". [16] With this judgement one may still agree or at least until such time as Daniel Cosío Villegas brings out his long-awaited volume on the Porfirian era.

Priestley's treatment of the Revolution of 1910 is extremely weak,

---

[12] *Ibid.*, pp. xi-xiv.
[13] *Ibid.*, p. 125-126.
[14] *Ibid.*, p. 119.
[15] As he saw it (p. 262); "The Mexican system of government, to be successful, must be strongly centralized until political experience and judgment become more nearly universal than the are today."
[16] Priestley, p. xv.

understandably perhaps since he was writing at a time when its main thrust was difficult to discern amidst the resurgence of militarized politics and political violence. But Priestley also reveals a social conservatism that blinded him to the need for, and significance of, land reform. It is curious to note that this book, published in 1923, has but few references to Zapata as a military leader, and makes no mention whatsoever of the Plan of Ayala.

Priestley's narrowly political approach combined with his failure to update his text despite a third printing in 1935 created a need for a new synthesis that would take the reader beyond Carranza's ouster, one that could provide insight into the Revolution as a continuing phenomenon. The challenge to prepare such a work was taken up by another professional historian, Henry B. Parkes. Before examining in any detail his one-volume synthesis, which appeared in 1938, note should be taken of two works that had appeared in the intervening years, Ernest Gruening's *Mexico and Its Heritage* (New York, 1928) and Frank Tannenbaum's *Peace By Revolution: An Interpretation of Mexico* (New York, 1933).

Neither of these works provides a balanced view of Mexican history, and stricktly speaking neither constitutes a synthesis under the definition used in this paper, but each one has been widely read and each has had considerable influence in shaping the views of many Northamericans toward the Revolution. Neither writer it should be noted was trained as a professional historian. Gruening went to Mexico in 1922 as a journalist for Collier's magazine and, having convinced himself of the inadequacy of existing explanations of the Revolution as well as of a simply political approach, he devoted the next six years to producing the massive tome that has been constantly cited ever since. The work contains an introductory historical summary down to 1910 and a chapter on the Revolution through 1927, but it is the thematic chapters with their wealth of detail on the Obregón-Calles period that have had greatest impact. Gruening's practice of quoting extensively from primary sources and of citing his authorities has given his book a weight transcending that usually assigned to journalistic efforts. Still Gruening never thought of himself as a historian and his sole interest in exploring the past was to indentify that which he felt would enlighten the present. Relevance was his watchword as it is today of a new student generation. [17]

Tannenbaum's *Peace by Revolution*, published a few years after the

[17] Gruening's insistence on relevance is seen in his opening chapter, in his flat dismissal of the years 1825-1850, when he wrote (p. 51): "The history of this period is wholly unimportant except as it reveals the extent of national weaknesses and thereby sheds light on some of the paradoxes of contemporary Mexico."

appearance of his study on the agrarian situation, [18] was devoted primarily to an examination of the Revolution of 1910, particularly to its social aspects. The first third of his volume, however, presented an interpretation of Mexican history from the Spanish conquest onward that should at least be mentioned here. In its original edition, and in the new paperback edition issued in 1966, it has brought its particular version of Mexican history to a wide array of readers. With Tannenbaum sociology invaded history, the sweeping generalization replacing narrative chronological reconstruction. Because of the author's literary flair and also his determination to avoid jargon, the reader emerges with a sense of excitement, as mountains of fact are swept aside magically to reveal fundamental processes presented as enduring truths.

In *Peace by Revolution* Tannenbaum offered his American readership an *indigenista* interpretation of Mexican history. The Revolution was presented as the last stage in a 400-year struggle to destroy the consequences of the Spanish Conquest. The Indian, long suppressed by a white minority, was now emerging triumphant. Biologically the white man was disappearing. "Mexico is returning to the children of the Indian mother", he wrote, "and will be colored largely by her blood and her cultural patterns". [19] In this final stage, the *hacienda*, the last surviving major institution of oppression implanted by the Spaniards, was under attack. Arrayed against it was the Indian village which had resisted all attempts at domination or assimilation. It was to the village that Tannenbaum, in 1933, looked for the strength and moral purpose that could bring about a peaceful reconstruction of the country even as he viewed the Indians as "the rock upon which the future civilization and culture of Mexico has to be built". [20] There was a simplicity and beauty to his prescription for the future, undoubtedly a reflection of his passionate commitment to rural Mexico. Time and the perversity of man, if one can so designate the population explosion, urbanization and industrialization, have frustrated its fulfillment.

The year 1938 saw the appearance of Henry B. Parkes' *A History of Mexico*. Parkes, it might be noted, was not a specialist in this field. An Englishman trained to be an historian of the United States, his venture into Mexico was a temporary diversion from his usual interests.

Parkes' volume, as suggested earlier, supplanted Priestley's as the principal text used in the colleges. A comparison with the earlier work reveals it to be similar in format but written with greater attention to the dramatic and in a far more lively style. In Parkes' work the Conquest occupies much greater space at the expense of colonial political history. The seventeenth century, except for brief reference to aes-

[18] *The Mexican Agrarian Revolution* (New York, 1929).
[19] *Peace By Revolution*, pp. 6, 21-23.
[20] *Ibid.*, pp. 181-182.

thetic achievements, disappears from view. Another difference is Parkes' concern with national characteristics. Here as elsewere he was not afraid to state his views.

What gave his volume a special attraction was his use of the present, that is the Mexico of the 1920's and 30's, to illuminate the past. Sensitive to the changes brought by the Revolution and especially the recongnition given to the Indian and Indian culture, Parkes, whether dealing with the Conquest, or the growth of colonial society, or the liberalism of the nineteenth century, directed his readers' attention to the contemporary scene. The failures of the past were contrasted with achievement of the Revolution in giving Mexico a sence of national purpose and in instilling the rural masses with a new confidence in their future.

The air of immediacy with which Parkes was able to endow the past gave his volume great appeal. But it was the immediacy of the 1930's and with the passage of time the volume inevitably lost its freshness. To be sure, in subsequent editions, the last of which came out in 1960, the author added chapters at the end and tinkered here and there with the text; but it is still essentially a book written a generation ago in the atmosphere of the Cárdenas revolution in Mexico and the New Deal in the U.S., and on the basis of a bibliography long out of date. [21]

From 1938 to 1968, although many volumes were published in the United States on various aspects of Mexican history, there was not a single book that attempted to exploit the rising tide of monographs, biographies and special studies to produce a fresh synthesis. To be sure, many important works appeared, some representing years of labor, but they were all devoted to the parts and not to the whole. One need only mention Cook and Borah's studies of colonial demography, Gibson's work on the Valley of Mexico, or the writings of Cline, Quirk, Cumberland, Ross, and more recently Wilkie, on Mexico after 1910. [22]

---

[21] Except for an addendum of nine titles under the heading "Modern Mexico", the Bibliography contains nothing published after 1948. None of the monographs produced by U.S. scholars in the 1950's to say nothing of the early volumes of the *Historia moderna de México* receive any mention.

[22] Sherburne F. Cook and Woodrow Borah, *The Population of Central Mexico in 1548: An Analysis of the Suma de visitas de pueblos* (Berkeley and Los Angeles, 1960); *The Indian Population of Central Mexico, 9531-1610* (Berkeley and Los Angeles, 1960); *The Aboriginal Population of Central Mexico on the Eve of the Spanish Conquest* (Berkeley and Los Angeles, 1963; Charles Gibson, *The Aztecs under Spanish Rule* (Stanford, 1964); H. F. Cline, *The United States and Mexico* (Cambridge, 1953); also his *Mexico: Revolution to Evolution, 1940-1960* (London, New York and Toronto, 1962); Robert E. Quirk, *The Mexican Revolution 1914-1915* (Bloomington, 1960); Charles C. Cumberland, *The Mexican Revolution: Genesis Under Madero* (Austin, 1952); Stanley R. Ross, *Francisco I. Madero, Apostle of Mexican Democracy* (New York, 1955);

The reader interested in Mexico and hoping to find the results of the latest research synthesized in a single work had no place to go. The closest substitute was a modest-sized volume whose author made no claim for it as a history of Mexico, but rather presented it as a "work of exposition and digestion", one in which he limited himself, as he put it, to a "discussion of such institutions, of such habits of life and thought, and of the lives of such men as, in my opinion have left the deepest impress on the country". [23] With these words Leslie Byrd Simpson launched the first edition of his *Many Mexicos* in 1941. Three more editions have since appeared, the latest in 1966, of what is probably the most widely-read general work on Mexico in the United States. With each edition, Simpson has added to the original text, especially in the third and fourth editions in which he elaborated on his earlier presentation and added occasional notes and a selected reading list of standard works in English.

Simpson's predilection for the Spanish period is clearly revealed in this work. Indeed, as he indicated in the preface to the first edition, he intended this book to serve as a corrective to existing treatments which failed to show sufficient appreciation of the positive features of the Spanish administration. [24] The result is seen in the allocation of space and in the very tone of the work. Almost 65% of the entire text of the 1941 edition was devoted to Mexico before 1810. Even in the expanded 1966 edition, which embodied another quarter century of contemporary experience, the chapters devoted to that earlier period still occupied 55% of the printed pages. It was not only quantitatively that Simpson showed his preferences. His treatment of the colonial era reveals a warmth of understanding, a genuine affection for the subject, like that of a parent who loves his children even when they misbehave. In contrast, he treats Mexico's history after 1810 like the proverbial stepchild. It is as if he regarded it as a distasteful matter about which the less said the better. Indeed, he disposes of the period 1821-1854 as if it were a comic opera not deserving of serious examination. In the 150 years after 1810 he finds few men of stature. Only Morelos and Juárez emerge with a full claim to our respect, where as the colonial era is peopled with a series of distinguished figures from Hernán Cortés to Revillagigedo.

The continuing appeal of *Many Mexicos* is a tribute to its style as well as to its content. Simpson enlivens his prose with extensive quotations from primary sources and by calling on his own experiences as

James W. Wilkie, *The Mexican Revolution: Federal Expenditure and Social Change Since 1910* (Berkeley and Los Angeles, 1967).
    [23] Leslie B. Simpson, *Many Mexicos* 2nd. ed. (New York, 1946), "Preface to First Edition", p. XI.
    [24] *Ibid.*

a visitor in Mexico. The anecdote, the satirical thrust, the apt choice of word ("the General Indian Court... for two hundred and thirty years acted as a shock absorber between the races of New Spain") all assist him in getting his message across. Whatever its weakness in interpretation and coverage, *Many Mexicos* has a special charm that assures it a permanent place in the literature on Mexico.

The year 1968 witnessed the appearance of the first completely new scholarly synthesis, since the first editions of Parkes and Simpson a generation before, in Charles C. Cumberland's *Mexico: The Struggle for Modernity* (New York, 1968). [25] Cumberland, whose earlier research focused on the twentieth century, explains his book as "an attempt to clarify and explain the special and economic issues which gave the Mexican Revolution such a distinctive stamp and to account for the direction and nature of the change". [26] Faithful to his stated purpose, Cumberland has produced a work with teleological overtones. Optimistic about the present and the future, he tends to deprecate the past. His chapter titles clearly reflect his approach. Under the title "Marking Time" he disponses of the entier period from the achievement of independence in 1821 to the rise of Díaz in 1876. The political drama of these years is not allowed to emerge; the Reform and Intervention are disposed of in a single paragraph. It is as if a mantle of gray were dropped over all the men whose conflicts over ideas and interests gave meaning to that period. His final chapter, entitled "At Last", reveals Cumberland's belief that Mexico has now reached the stage where it is able to achieve economic growth and at the same time deal justly with the aspirations of its people. The recent unrest in intellectual circles or the sense of disillusionment with the workings of the political system that is also a part of present day Mexico are not allowed to intrude.

It might be argued that as part of a series devoted to economic and social history, this volume necessarily had to be selective of its subject matter, and that neither political nor intellectual history was its main concern. [27] But such an argument serves only to strengthen the case for a new and broader synthesis than the one under discussion here.

[25] I pass over in silence Bishop Joseph Schlarman's polemical *Mexico: Land of Volcanoes* (Milwaukee, 1950) and Victor Alba's *The Mexicans* (New York, 1967). The latter is presented to the public as an English-language original and not a translation. Whatever its origin, it was apparently put together hastily and cannot be relied on for its factual information.

[26] Cumberland, *Mexico*, p. v.

[27] The dustcover description of the series(Oxford's Latin American Histories) states that the "books are general histories of Latin American countries which concentrate on social, economic, and cultural backgrounds, rather than on political figures and national wars". Cumberland's volume ignores the cultural dimension.

Within the limits set for himself, however, Cumberland has provided an excellent picture of economic and social conditions and their evolution over 450 years. A wealth of data is skilfully presented on topics that earlier synthesizers have tended to slight, topics such as Mexico's fiscal problems, the evolution of transportation, agricultural and industrial development. Even in treating such well-worn topics as the Church, landholding and labor conditions, Cumberland has something fresh to say. His discussion of the mining industry in the colonial economy and its vicissitudes since 1810 is outstanding. Thanks to this writer, the general reader in the U.S. now has access to some of the fruits of recent scholarship embodied in the numerous volumes published on both sides of the border over the past twenty years.

Cumberland's volume, as suggested above, does not foreclose the need for another synthesis. Rather it should serve as a stimulus for the preparation of a study that would be more comprehensive in its treatment, one that might take a comparative approach to the history of Mexico. Such a synthesis might very well be planned for two volumes, for it is apparent that 300-400 pages of text are inadequate to provide sufficiently detailed coverage of the various facets of Mexican history. Moreover, a two-volume approach would permit the collaboration of a colonialist and a modernist, each of whom might be able to convey to the other the empathy he feels for his own period.

It is not my intention to set forth here the prospectus for such a synthesis. As a student of nineteenth century Mexico, however, I would like to suggest that the experiences of the twentieth century and not just of Mexico can help us understand the difficulties that beset that country after independence. Mexico in 1821 was a new state confronted by the problems that other Latin American states had to face and not unlike those that recently emancipated areas in Africa and Asia are facing. As a new state, Mexico had to try to combine economic viability with institucional reform, and to seek political stability in the face of sharp internal differences over the direction and rate of change. That military men emerged as the dominant political force or that periods of anarchy alternated with dictatorship hardly seems surprising judged from the vantage point of the mid-20th century. The achievement of longterm stability on other than dictatorial terms for most states is the exception rather than the rule, and Mexico's 19th century experience should be seen in this light.

There are of course a number of key themes that can serve to provide a sense of unity to Mexican history over and above the more or less common thread found in Tannenbaum, Parkes and Cumberland: the enslavement for the masses by the Spanish, their long subjugation, and their eventual emergence through the violence of the Revolution.

With the passage of time, the significance of the Revolution as a permanent redemptive movement for the downtrodden is being increasingly questioned, and it would be well to cast about for other perspectives from which to examine the past. The future synthesizer might well consider using as a unifying theme the continuing quest for identity, the search for a national ethos. This would have implications not only for racial attitudes and relationships but also for interregional and ultimately international relationships. The conflict between regional and national interests is still another theme that links the uncertain present to the colonial past. Related to both the problem of identity and the issue of balance between center and periphery is the series of efforts to modernize the society. The roles played therein by the governing burocracies constitute a framework within which much of Mexico's history from the Bourbons to the present can be told.

Let me state, in conclusion, that the synthesizer for the U.S. reader should by no means ignore the work of his counterparts in Mexico. However, judging from the observations of my panel colleague on Mexican syntheses and from what we know of European efforts, the classic synthesis of Mexican history has yet to make its appearance in any language.

COMENTARIO

EDMUNDO O'GORMAN

Antes que nada quiero felicitar a la señora Josefina Vázquez de Knauth por el esfuerzo de síntesis que representa su ponencia, y a esa congratulación debo añadir el testimonio de mi gratitud por las bondadosas palabras con que incluyó en su análisis alguno de mis trabajos históricos. Fue un acierto el partido general de dividir el asunto en dos grandes apartados, el primero dedicado a una reseña histórica de las obras de síntesis de la historia de México que han aparecido durante el periodo nacional, y el segundo, a una crítica valorativa de esas obras y del proceso que entrañan.

Por lo que toca a lo primero, estimo adecuado y suficiente el inventario de las obras consideradas en la ponencia, puesto que deben tenerse en cuenta la índole del trabajo, sus propósitos de información general y la limitación de espacio, para excusar omisiones que, en otras circunstancias, parecerían injustificadas. A este respecto, sin embargo, me parece pertinente una observación, y es que, a mi juicio, la ponencia debió haber considerado con algún detenimiento la relevancia de *México a través de los siglos*, la obra cumbre de la historiografía sintética mexicana y en su género, no superada entre nosotros por ninguna otra hasta nuestros días. Unas cuantas líneas dedicadas al prólogo que escribió para aquel libro don Vicente Riva Palacio —el inspirador y alma de la mpresa— habrían destacado en mayor relieve la importancia de su tesis acerca del mestizaje espiritual del pueblo mexicano, de tanta significación en el proceso ideológico subsecuente de nuestra historiografía. Porque, en efecto, esa tesis no sólo es el antecedente teórico del predominio que alcanzó la escuela evolucionista del positivismo preconizado por don Justo Sierra, sino la base de las tendencias conciliadoras que sobrevivieron al naufragio filosófico de aquella escuela y de las que, con razón, hace tanto mérito la ponencia como síntoma de la madurez característica de los años posteriores. Y si, en lo personal, pienso que aquella tesis ofrece la dificultad proveniente de su substancialismo, como he pretendido mostrarlo en otra parte, no por eso desconozco que se sigue postulando, conscientemente o no, como el *apriori* de lo más de la producción historiográfica contemporánea.

Pero lo importante para nuestro presente empeño es que las anteriores observaciones, no sólo no invalidan el panorama general que ofrece la ponencia, sino que lo robustecen, de manera que no constituyen una objeción, sino meramente el señalamiento de una laguna.

El mérito más sobresaliente del primer apartado de la ponencia estriba en haber mostrado el sentido pragmático-político que ha orientado, desde sus orígenes, la tarea de los historiadores cuyo empeño fue y ha sido ofrecer una síntesis de la historia de México. En muchos casos esa orientación se proclama abiertamente, pero lo interesante es que, al parecer, se trata de algo ineludible, porque aun en los historiadores que no adoptan conscientemente esa actitud, el propósito de influir en la vida pública es poco menos que obvio. Todos, más o menos abiertamente, aspiran a que sus obras sirvan de textos para la enseñanza, y aquellos que la ponencia distingue como más maduros y serenos por su interés en el pasado y por sus tendencias conciliadoras, no hacen excepción, pues sólo revelan el sentido neutro y conciliador de sus convicciones políticas. Y el más claro síntoma de que, por lo visto, un pragmatismo político es indisoluble a toda síntesis histórica, consiste en la existencia de eso que se llama "la historia oficial" y a la que, secreta o confesadamente, aspiran a llegar a ser todas las interpretaciones que no han recibido ese espaldarazo.

Tal parece, pues, que por más imparcialidad que se suponga en el historiador, por más pureza que se atribuya a su interés en conocer el pasado, un pragmatismo político, en el mejor sentido del término, es de la esencia de su tarea, a no ser, quizá, que se llegue a concebir a ésta de un modo distinto.

El conjunto de estas observaciones no sólo me parece digno de nuestra atención, sino que me atreveré a decir que es el principal asunto en que debemos ocuparla, porque, en definitiva, involucra, desde el centro, las justas críticas que se hacen valer en la ponencia, y las nuevas orientaciones que en ella se sugieren.

Pero antes de terminar quiero puntualizar una distinción que quizá sea de utilidad para orientar desde un principio nuestras reflexiones. Me parece, en efecto, que debemos diferenciar entre lo que es un "compendio" y lo que, propiamente hablando es una "síntesis histórica". Desde luego no se trata primariamente de una cuestión de tamaño, circunstancia más o menos accidental; es cuestión de índole. Un compendio, extenso o breve, es por su naturaleza un resumen de hechos que se consideran establecidos, y en lo esencial, es un relato en el que domina el puro nexo cronológico. Esto implica, ciertamente, un género de interpretación, pero como mera resultante de un ordenamiento ajeno e independiente de toda visión personal del historiador. La síntesis, en cambio, supone un propósito hermenéutico deliberado que tiene por finalidad poner al descubierto el sentido de los sucesos y el significado de lo acontecido para presentarlo como un proceso unitario e inteligible a base de conexiones internas que respetan, pero trascienden, la mera secuencia temporal.

Si esta distinción es aceptable, me parece que deberíamos atenernos a ella y dirigir nuestra atención a sólo aquello que merezca el nombre de síntesis de acuerdo con las condiciones arriba enunciadas.

COMMENTARY

CHARLES C. CUMBERLAND

Mr. Potash has clearly demonstrated the paucity of material in English which might come under the general rubric of "Synthesis of Mexican History"; and he also poses some interesting questions in that field. I would hold that such a synthesis is impossible within the confines of any one book or two, and that furthermore it is impossible at the present moment in view of the lack of sufficient solid monographic material which could be used to construct such a history. The idea of tying together the multitudinous social, political, economic and intellectual threads, from pre-Hispanic times to the present, to construct a flowing whole is enormously attractive; but I would shudder to think of undertaking that monumental task. Mr. Potash has very kindly included my most recent book in his discussion of syntheses, and has quite correctly indicated that it does not obviate the necessity for other and more comprehensive works. I would take issue with him only on one point: my work is not a synthesis and was not intended to be. It was merely an attempt to follow a few highly selected themes through history in order to explain a relatively modern Mexican phenomenon. A synthesis must be much more than that.

But at the moment we do not have the basic tools with which to work. Until we have, for example, a much more sophisticated view of the actual pressures, movements and conditions during the age of Santa Anna, we can scarcely construct a synthesis of that period. How can we tie together the various aspects of the Mexican society of that age, and relate those to conditions of an earlier age, when to date no one has given an adequate explanation of Santa Anna's power? When we have only a vague notion of economic patterns? When we have an even more vague idea of the actual conditions under which the great majority of the society lives? Until we know with greater precision the interplay of the various factors in the society, until we can see that age much more clearly, we can neither develop a synthesis of that age of synthesize that period with those before and after. The same might be said for many other periods.

In his concluding paragraphs, Mr. Potash suggests an approach which I find much more fruitful than that of attempting to put everything together within the covers of one book. Whether the themes he suggests are the most important may be debated, perhaps, but the thematic perception could lead to some excellent works which would give greater depth of comprehension. Mr. Costeloe's researches and publications, for example, show quite clearly that the general assumptions of the past with regard to the Church may well be questioned. A thorough examination of that institution, clarifying both the actual role of that institution and the perceived role from the beginning of the conquest until the present, would be of inestimable value. This type of "synthesis", in which many aspects of the society become subordinate to the principal theme, is manageable.

Another manageable form of synthesis is that of periodization, in which a significant era is studied in depth in order to determine the interaction of the various forces within the society, to indicate whether the institutions are viable or static, to see whether there is "movement", and if so in what direction. This has been, perhaps, the form most often used in the past, but very few scholars have been able to achieve the goal of true synthesis within the period. A conscious effort to synthesize might well be the most profitable approach.

RELATORÍA

ELÍAS TRABULSE

Las sesiones efectuadas se centraron primordialmente en dos temas: la síntesis de la historia de México y los problemas filosóficos que entraña el conocimiento histórico en general.

I. LA SÍNTESIS DE HISTORIA DE MÉXICO

Inicialmente fueron planteadas las deficiencias que poseen las síntesis más conocidas de la historia de México, las cuales versan, sobre todo, sobre historia política. Esta limitación priva sobre todo en los libros de texto, muchos de ellos concebidos en forma de compendio que no es otra cosa que un resumen carente de la interpretación personal la cual debe ser inherente a una verdadera síntesis.

Se puso en relieve la palpable crisis actual de los estudios históricos, pues las nuevas generaciones carecen de una verdadera formación geográfica e histórica lo que constituirá un peligro futuro dado que la humanidad no poseerá el acervo de experiencia que el estudio del pasado proporciona. Por otra parte fue discutido el carácter eminentemente pragmático de la historia patria cuyo fin era crear una conciencia nacional y aprovechóse este giro de la sesión para discutir sobre el carácter "antihispanista" de las síntesis norteamericanas, carentes del equilibrio que debe poner la historia mexicana la cual debe sopesar en la justa proporción el carácter hispánico de la cultura mexicana.

Volviéndose nuevamente sobre los textos de historia de México se puntualizó sobre la influencia que ejercen las instituciones gubernamentales en la enseñanza de la historia, sobre todo en lo concerniente a la ideología que sustentan los textos gratuitamente distribuidos. En consecuencia fue planteada la distinción entre historiografía oficial de carácter educativo y la historiografía como labor del historiador. Esta última se identifica con el conocimiento ontológico del pasado.

En algunos casos, la carencia de bases científicas impide que muchos temas sean tratados con precisión, sobre todo en las síntesis destinadas a la educación en forma de texto gratuito. Es, pues, recomendable distribuir el texto gratuito sólo a nivel de primaria ya que la secundaria y la preparatoria requieren de una formación histórica más completa. Por otra parte, el libro de texto gratuito no es una obra de difusión sino de formación, pero es en ésta "formación" donde encontramos el principal núcleo de deficiencias propio a la historiografía de tipo institucional u oficial, de manifiesta inclinación nacionalista, lo cual les impide, en muchos casos, juzgar imparcialmente sucesos que atañen a otros países (en el caso mexicano la historiografía de los EE.UU. debería procurar tratar con más justicia los nexos históricos con nuestro país).

Por último, dentro de esta temática, fue mencionada la necesidad de que los historiadores que elaboran síntesis destinadas a la juventud no carezcan de una cierta preparación filosófica, la cual debe complementar a la antes mencionada "imparcialidad de juicio" con respecto a otros países.

II. LA VALIDEZ DEL CONOCIMIENTO HISTÓRICO

Apoyados en la necesidad de que el historiador posea una determinada preparación filosófica, algunos comentaristas de la sesión vespertina dieron un nuevo giro a la temática debatida, la cual pasó del análisis de lo que debería ser la síntesis ideal de la historia de México a la discusión del conocimiento histórico como forma válida de conocimiento. Inicialmente fue reconocida la imposibilidad de que el historiador abarque todos los aspectos del suceso que narra, debiéndose llenar esta deficiencia con la interpretación personal del historiador. Esta interpretación, que no es otra cosa que una visión personal del acaecer histórico, no requiere de todos los matices del suceso que narra, sino únicamente de unos cuantos que le permitan reconstruir el pasado y comprenderlo. Pero inmediatamente surge la cuestión sobre hasta qué punto la interpretación subjetiva es válida, pues "ignorar paladinamente los hechos" conduce a "ensueños" sin contacto con la realidad objetiva, de la cual, por otra parte, no poseemos más que huellas. Por tanto a la historia hemos de situarla en el límite entre la ficción y la realidad, quedando por otra parte diferenciada de la novela, en que ésta es una ficción concebida a priori por el novelista y la historia es una resurrección subjetiva elaborada por el historiador a posteriori del conocimiento objetivo de los hechos. De ahí que el historiador requiera de un cierto "calor imaginativo" cuasi literario que le permita "dotar de ser" (O'Gorman) al pasado.

Pero fueron inmediatamente puestos en relieve los peligros de esta postura puramente subjetivista que impide que el conocimiento que un historiador posee del pasado sea transmitido a otro individuo, ya que éste, a su vez, podrá darle al mismo hecho histórico, un significado diferente. Al final del debate fue reconocido que el adoptar una postura ecléctica o intermedia, es lo más aceptable. Dicha postura que concilia ambas tendencias, postularía que el historiador debe, inicialmente, investigar exhaustivamente un hecho, mismo que posteriormente interpretará. El conocimiento histórico quedaría así apoyado en el hecho en sí (conocimiento objetivo) y en la interpretación del mismo (conocimiento subjetivo).

V. HISTORIA DEL TEMA REGIONAL Y PARROQUIAL

Presidente: Antonio Pompa y Pompa, director de Archivos Históricos y Biblioteca del Instituto Nacional de Antropología e Historia.

Ponente: Luis González, profesor e investigador de El Colegio de México.

Comentaristas: Wigberto Jiménez Moreno, director del Departamento de Investigaciones Históricas del Instituto Nacional de Antropología e Historia; Harry Bernstein, profesor de historia, Brooklyn College.

Participantes: Israel Cavazos Garza, director de Archivo General del Estado de Nuevo León; Peter Gerhard, Investigador de historia de México, época Colonial; Charles Gibson, profesor de historia en la Universidad de Michigan; Ricardo Lancaster-Jones, profesor de genealogía y heráldica y de historia de México en la Universidad Autónoma de Guadalajara; Delfina López Sarrelangue, investigadora del Instituto de Historia de la UNAM.

Participante Europeo: Pierre Goubert, director de Estudios en la Escuela Práctica de Altos Estudios, París.

Relator: Elsa Malvido, investigadora del Departamento de Investigaciones Históricas del INAH.

LA HISTORIOGRAFÍA LOCAL: APORTACIONES MEXICANAS

LUIS GONZÁLEZ

I. PROPÓSITOS Y DISCULPAS

La historiografía local no figura en el balance que hizo El Colegio de México en 1966 con el nombre de *Veinticinco años de investigación histórica en México*.[1] Cuando se proyectaba esa obra alguien recordó la carta escrita diez años antes por don Alfonso Reyes a don Daniel Cosío Villegas.

Allí se lee: "Es tiempo de volver los ojos hacia nuestros cronistas e historiadores locales y recoger, así, la contribución particular de tanto riachuelo y arroyo en la gran corriente de nuestra epopeya nacional... Habría que comenzar por un inventario, por una bibliografía metódica, que usted bien pudiera encargar a los excelentes colaboradores de su revista".[2]

En 1965 nadie aceptó la tarea solicitada por don Alfonso, nadie se prestó a levantar el censo de las historias locales. Los obstáculos eran y siguen siendo múltiples. Para hacer una lista más o menos completa de nuestras crónicas lugareñas es necesario, entre otras cosas, recorrer uno a uno y minuciosamente todos los rincones de la República. La razón es clara: muchas de esas crónicas, no obstante la diligencia de don Wigberto Jiménez Moreno o don Antonio Pompa y Pompa, no se encuentran todavía en los lugares frecuentados por los investigadores, en los anaqueles de las bibliotecas y los archivos públicos. Algunas, en copia a máquina o en manuscrito, están en las casas pueblerinas de sus autores. Otras, que han llegado a la reproducción en mimeógrafo, circulan entre una clientela local. Aquellas de las que una imprenta provinciana hizo cien y hasta quinientos ejemplares, rara vez alcanzaron el honor de ser acogidas por una biblioteca.

Además de buscar por todos los rincones del país el investigador pedido por don Alfonso debe proceder, antes de ponerse en obra, a un deslinde: fijar los límites de la microhistoriografía para no exponerse a sumar peras y manzanas. En este caso, la imprecisión lo envuelve todo. Habrá que convenir qué es comunidad marginal, regional y pa-

---

[1] También se publicó en los núms. 58 a 60 de *Historia Mexicana*.

[2] Alfonso Reyes, *Las burlas veras. Primer ciento*. Tezontle, México, 1957, p. 106.

rroquial y qué es etnohistoria e historia de regiones ciudades y parroquias. Quizá la etnohistoria que se ocupa de tribus y grupos marginados, la historia regional que toma como asunto la gran división administrativa de un Estado, la entretenida en las vicisitudes y pormenores de las ciudades y la historia de aldeas y pueblos no sean la misma cosa, probablemente ni hermanas y ni siquiera primas. No es fácil confundir y agavillar estudios relativos a los huicholes, el municipio de San Miguel el Alto, la ciudad de México, el barrio de la Cohetera, el distrito de Jiquilpan, el Valle del Fuerte, la diócesis de Tulancingo, la arquidiócesis de Morelia, el Estado de Campeche, la Península de Yucatán, el vastísimo norte, las ruinas prehispánicas de Tula, la conquista de la Nueva Galicia, la sociedad de Zacatecas en los albores de la época colonial, los misioneros muertos en el norte de la Nueva España, la Independencia en Xochimilco, la Intervención Francesa en Michoacán, la revuelta de la Noria, Porfirio Díaz en Chapala, Zapata y la Revolución en Morelos, los cristeros del volcán de Colima, Yucatán desde la época más remota hasta nuestros días, las artes gráficas en Puebla, la instrucción pública en San Luis Potosí, la bibliografía de Tlaxcala y el Congreso de Chilpancingo.

Como quiera, la petición de don Alfonso Reyes ya es tiempo de que sea atendida. Y mientras se da con la persona hábil y paciente que junte, discrimine y estudie a crónicas e historias locales, no está por demás aventurar un juicio, decir una primera palabra, puesto que nada se ha dicho del conjunto. Por lo mismo, mi ponencia llega muy temprano, y siempre será penoso el llegar con demasiada anticipación a un quehacer o a una fiesta.

Hace poco que empecé a reunir, en horas robadas a otros quehaceres, la bibliografía. Naturalmente no pude establecer en tan breve plazo y desde México un catálogo como el que hace falta. Por otra parte la Reunión ante quien se presentan estos apuntes señaló que no quería oír ni leer una lista de nombres de autores y títulos de obra. Hubo, pues, que pasar de la bibliografía incipiente al escrutinio de lo poco catalogado, y aquí los logros fueron mínimos. Había que examinar 400 libros, debía leer más de cien mil páginas, pero el tiempo sólo alcanzó para hojear apresuradamente poco más de cinco mil páginas escogidas al azar, o casi.

Lo hecho adrede fue la exclusión en el catálogo y en el examen de los estudios de arqueología y etnohistoria, bibliografías, colecciones documentales y otros trabajos auxiliares de la historia, las semihistorias que sólo miran una de las parcelas de la cultura, las cuantiosas y ricas contribuciones extranjeras (la mayoría norteamericanas) que tocan nuestra vida local. Tampoco admití, por la dificultad de dar con ellos, textos mecanográficos y mimeográficos y estudios aparecidos en publicaciones periódicas. Me quedé con obras impresas separadamente y no con todas. Excluí los opúsculos que no llegaban a las cincuenta páginas. Por último, me limité a la producción del último siglo, de 1870 para acá.

En suma, traigo a cuento algunos libros de asunto regional, en los que se usa región en el sentido de las divisiones territoriales, mayores y administrativas de México: las estudiadas por don Edmundo O'Gorman en una obra clásica, o parroquial, donde se usa parroquia en el sentido de patria minúscula, la que Unamuno llama de campanario, "la patria ya no chica si no menos que chica, la que podemos abarcar de una mirada, como se puede abarcar Bilbao desde muchas alturas".[3] En otros términos, las historias que suelen ser expresión de dos emociones de mala fama: el aldeanismo y el provincialismo. En el caso de México, emociones perturbadoras de algo tan grave y sonoro como son las consolidación de la nacionalidad y el patriotismo.

Y aunque el provincialismo y el aldeanismo corresponden a los "ismos" de larga e intensa vida y son más viejos que el amor a la patria por ser herencia proveniente de los pueblos precortesianos y de España, y aunque la historiografía que los expresa nace antes que México se prescinde de todo lo anterior a 1870. Sería llevar las cosas demasiado lejos si comenzara con Juan Gil de Zamora, el historiador del siglo XIII que inaugura el género en España con *De preconiis civitates Numantine*, o con los códices precortesianos de contenido histórico que rara vez rebasan el estrecho círculo de la ciudad o la aldea. Con la Reforma se produce un corte tan profundo en la vida de México que, a partir de su triunfo, es posible comenzar la historia de muchos aspectos de lo mexicano.

La fecha inicial no se ha escogido por puro capricho. Alrededor de ella y en un quinquenio aparecen las obras de Longinos Banda, Gerónimo del Castillo, Manuel Rivera Cambas, Ignacio Navarrete, Manuel Gil y Sáenz y Alejandro Prieto que en buena medida rompen con la tradición y sirven de modelo al porvenir. Quizá más azarosa que el punto de arranque sea la división de la materia en tres periodos: el porfírico, el revolucionario y el actual. Quizá un estudio a fondo del problema aniquile esa periodización.

II. LA REBELIÓN DE LAS PROVINCIAS

Desde mediados del siglo XIX, "las invasiones extranjeras y la presencia constante de un vecino todopoderoso"[4] habían robustecido, en

---

[3] Miguel de Unamuno cit. por Alfonso de Alba, *La provincia oculta*. Editorial Cultura, México, 1949, p. 26.
[4] Seymour Menton, "El nacionalismo y la novela" en *América Indígena*, vol. XXIX (abril de 1969), p. 407.

la aristocracia y la mesocracia de las ciudades mexicanas, un nacionalismo desconfiado, a la defensiva, triste y proselitista. La doctora Vázquez de Knauth cuenta los ardides de que se valieron aquellos hombres
para contagiar su patriotismo a la gran masa de la población.[5] La
élite patriótica, casi toda ella liberal y positivista, hizo lo indecible por
hacer a todos los vecinos de la República, patriotas, prácticos y libres.
Combatió como antiguallas, amores y filias regionales y aldeanas, y
procuró aniquilar su expresión política: el cacicazgo. Como defensa,
los intereses políticos estatales esgrimieron la doctrina del federalismo
y los municipales, la del ayuntamiento libre. Pero no fueron esas las
únicas armas esgrimidas. La historiografía local entró también a la
pelea.

Algunos gobernadores de los Estados (José Eleuterio González de
Nuevo León, Eustaquio Buelna de Sinaloa, Eligio Ancona de Yucatán,
Joaquín Baranda de Campeche, Manuel Muro de San Luis Potosí y
Ramón Corral de Sonora) en sendos libros de historia, destacaron,
con su puño y letra, la personalidad de sus respectivas entidades políticas. Otros gobernadores únicamente promovieron la factura de esas
historias. Nunca como entonces la historiografía local se vio tan favo-
recida por las autoridades. Nunca tampoco ha vuelto a tener tan buenos operarios esa mies.

Ninguno fue historiador profesional porque no había profesión de
historia, pero casi todos se distinguieron por su vasta y variada cultura,
su inteligencia, su mucho mundo y su entrañable cariño a la patria
chica. Aparte de gobernadores ilustrados, anduvieron metidos en la reconstrucción histórica provinciana el obispo Crescencio Carrillo, el
ministro de la Suprema Corte Eduardo Ruiz, el ingeniero y periodista
Manuel Rivera Cambas, el canónigo Vicente de P. Andrade, los sacerdotes Manuel Gil, Antonio Gay y Lucio Marmolejo, el jefe político
de Ejutla y diputado al Congreso de la Unión Manuel Martínez Gracida, el coronel y poeta Elías Amador y los distinguidos abogados y
educadores Francisco Molina Solís, Luis Pérez Verdía y Francisco Medina de la Torre. Si no se puede decir que estaban a la altura del
conjunto de los historiadores de la vida nacional es porque eran generalmente más altos.

Según nuestra bibliografía se publicaron 71 libros de historia local
en tiempos de don Porfirio; algo así como dos por año. Dentro de un
periodo de cuatro décadas, fueron temporadas fecundas las de 1881-
1886, 1899-1905 y 1909-1910. En este último bienio se produjo la cuarta
parte del total. La celebración del centenario de la Independencia explica la anomalía. Con este motivo se escribió acerca de mil co-

---

[5] Josefina Vázquez de Knauth, *Nacionalismo y educación*. El Colegio de México, México, 1970.

sas pertenecientes a Oaxaca, Puebla y Guanajuato. [6] Se aprovechó también el máximo momento del nacionalismo para expedir obras tan monumentales como el *Bosque histórico de Zacatecas*, en dos volúmenes, de Elías Amador; las *Recordaciones históricas*, en dos volúmenes, y la *Historia civil y eclesiástica de Michoacán*, en tres, de Mariano de Jesús Torres; los *Anales históricos de Campeche*, en dos volúmenes, de Francisco Álvarez; la *Historia de San Luis Potosí*, en tres volúmenes, de Luis Pérez Verdía, y la *Historia de Yucatán durante la dominación española*, también en tres volúmenes, de Juan Francisco Molina Solís. [7]

Entonces la historia de los estados fue más cultivada que la municipal. El 71% de los libros del periodo cubren la vida conjunta de 24 de los 28 estados de la Federación. Los más historiados fueron Jalisco, Michoacán y Yucatán, con ocho obras cada uno. El aspecto predominante en la historiografía estatal es el político pero no faltan los trabajos de índole enciclopédica como los que hicieron Manuel Gil, de Tabasco; Alejandro Prieto, de Tamaulipas; Eustaquio Buelna, de Sinaloa; Serapio Baqueiro, de Yucatán; Ignacio Rodríguez, de Colima, y Francisco Belmar, de Oaxaca. Con todo, donde más predomina la tendencia enciclopédica, donde casi nunca deja de conjugarse el tema histórico con el geográfico y económico, es en la historiografía de corte parroquial, en los volúmenes de Juan de la Torre, sobre Morelia; Ramón Sánchez, sobre Arandas y Jiquilpan; Luis Escandón, sobre Tula, y Francisco Medina de la Torre, sobre San Miguel el Alto. [8]

Muchas de las obras de la época porfiriana no traen aparato erudito; no se ve ni una nota a lo largo de la narración. Los laicos las pueden leer a sus anchas, pero no los profesionales de la historia, siempre tan mal pensados. Lo primero que se ocurre es que aquellos enormes libros son fruto del magín o del plagio y no de la paciente y surtida búsqueda en documentos, tepalcates, periódicos y crónicas. De hecho, abundan los no exentos de fantasía, sobre todo en la parte concerniente a la antigüedad prehispánica, pero aun los más fantásticos, como el

[6] Andrés Portillo, *Oaxaca en el centenario de la independencia. Noticias históricas y estadísticas de la ciudad de Oaxaca y algunas leyendas tradicionales.* Imprenta del Estado, Oaxaca, 1910. 996 pp. más apéndice de 92 pp. Ignacio Herrerías y Mario Vitoria, *Puebla en el Centenario*, Imprenta Lacaud, México, 1910, 116 pp. Fulgencio Vargas, *La insurrección de 1810 en el Estado de Guanajuato*, 153 pp.
[7] Además, Eduardo Gómez Haro, *La ciudad de Puebla y la guerra de independencia*; Francisco R de los Ríos, *Puebla de los Ángeles y la orden dominicana*; Adalberto J. Argüelles, *Reseña del Estado de Tamaulipas*; José María Ponce de León, *Reseñas históricas del Estado de Chihuahua*; Manuel Cambre, *Gobierno y gobernantes de Jalisco*; Rafael Garza Cantú, *Algunos apuntes acerca de Nuevo León*.
[8] Vid. Bibliografía aparte.

de Ignacio Navarrete sobre Jalisco, [9] no carecen de erudición, y algunos ya son tan sobradamente documentados como los que vendrán después. En varios, además de documentos y monumentos, se echa mano de la tradición oral. Entonces comienza, con el beneplácito del positivismo, la historiografía que se autollamó científica.

Los historiadores científicos de ahora encuentran muchas imperfecciones de método en los historiadores de la edad porfírica: dizque no se informaron exhaustivamente, usaron más fuentes impresas que manuscritas, creyeron en cosas increíbles, o dieron alguna vez rienda suelta a la pasión. Como quiera, no fueron perezosos ni ingenuos. Creían, con don Nicolás León, que "el conocimiento de las producciones literarias de los ingenios de aquellos tiempos, y el estudio crítico de ellas son la única base en que debe estribar la apreciación imparcial tocante a la ciencia de nuestros antepasados". [10] Y no tomaron a la ligera las operaciones del análisis histórico porque querían conseguir verdades históricas tan firmes como las de la ciencia natural a fin de que pudieran ser útiles. Pensaban que la historia, al proceder como la anatomía y la fisiología, sería aprovechada por los médicos de la sociedad; por los políticos.

Como no se daba aún en la costumbre de agotar las energías en las tareas del análisis histórico, varios de aquellos historiadores meditaron, compusieron y escribieron con arte y sosegadamente sus obras. En lo que toca a la composición lo común fue adaptar moldes añosos; efemérides, catecismos, centones biográficos, etcétera. Hubo un par de innovaciones, no muy felices, pero sí muy imitadas. A la primera le corresponde como remoto antepasado la relación histórico geográfica, la que dispuso hacer Felipe II, la analizada por Alejandra Moreno Toscano en un reciente y novedoso libro. [11] Para designarla se usaron muchos nombres: noticias geográficas, estadísticas e históricas; historia, geografía y estadística; apuntes históricos, geográficos, estadísticos y descriptivos; noticias históricas y estadísticas, etcétera. *El bosquejo estadístico e histórico del distrito de Jiquilpan* de don Ramón Sánchez, es un buen ejemplo de esa arquitectura. Se abre el libro con un retrato, un prólogo en elogio del retratado y una alabanza de éste al gobernador de Michoacán.

La obra misma se reparte en 50 capítulos de muy desigual tamaño y una brevísima conclusión; el que lleva el nombre de historia cubre 50 páginas; en cambio, la página 48 alberga cuatro capítulos: aguas termales, pozos, pozos artesianos y arcas de agua. El capítulo de la

[9] Véase el análisis de José Bravo Ugarte, *Historia sucinta de Michoacán. Provincia mayor e intendencia.* Editorial Jus, México, 1966.
[10] Nicolás León, *Bibliografía mexicana del siglo xviii,* t. i, p. vii.
[11] Alejandra Moreno Toscano, *Geografía Económica de México. Siglo xvi.* El Colegio de México, México, 1969, 176 pp.

religión consta de tres líneas y el de los hombres célebres y notables del distrito de 20 páginas. Otras divisiones se destinan a la posición astronómica, el clima, los ríos, los reinos de la naturaleza, la población, las enfermedades, las diversiones públicas, cívicas y religiosas, la educación, la justicia, el fisco, la agricultura, el giro mercantil, la industria, los baños públicos y las mejoras materiales. Cierra la obra otro elogio para el autor, esta vez en verso.

Para vaciar las investigaciones enciclopédicas de los estudiosos locales, se usó también la forma del diccionario. Don Gerónimo del Castillo compuso el *Diccionario histórico, biográfico y monumental de Yucatán* publicado en 1866 y el abogado, político y polígrafo don Mariano de Jesús Torres, entre 1905 y 1915, dio a conocer en entregas su vastísimo diccionario histórico, biográfico, geográfico, botánico de Michoacán, con artículos suyos y ajenos, con multitud de datos erróneos y en un estilo muy descuidado.

Los cronistas locales de la época fueron generalmente arquitectos monstruosos, pero buenos prosistas. Varios han sido recibidos en las historias de la literatura mexicana, y otros deberían serlo, como don Primo Feliciano Velázquez.

No se cuenta con suficiente información para medir el éxito alcanzado por los libros de historia de asunto regional o parroquial de la era porfiriana. No hay indicios de que alguno haya sido best-seller. Quizá varios tuvieron una modesta acogida local; otros, ni esto. No pocos, a poco andar se volvieron canteras de datos para eruditos. Los de don Eduardo Ruiz, y quizá alguno más, tuvieron desde su aparición un notable círculo de lectores dentro del gran público. Ninguna de aquellas historias ha llegado a ser clásica nacional, aunque casi todas sean clásicas locales. No sé de ninguna que haya sido traducida a otra lengua. Muy pocas han soportado una segunda edición, pero la mayoría figura en las listas de libros raros y son muy buscadas por bibliófilos y bibliómanos. También deberían de aparecer algunas en las listas de mejores libros mexicanos.

III. LA PROVINCIA ES LA PATRIA

La Revolución Mexicana que estalló en 1910 fue tan nacionalista como la Reforma; se hizo en todo México y para México, pero la hicieron una mayoría de campesinos, y no de hombres de la ciudad como sucedió con la Reforma. Los caudillos de ésta pugnaron contra regionalismos y aldeanismos. El grueso de los revolucionarios defendió la tesis de que se podía ser patriota sin dejar de ser localista y aun la extremó con aquel dicho de Héctor Pérez Martínez en Guadalajara: "Para merecer el título de buen mexicano es condición la de ser buen provinciano." [12] La nueva orden fue ir a la provincia y venir de la provincia. Se convirtió en virtud lo que fuera vicio: "la adhesión calurosa a la tierra nativa".

El afecto revolucionario no iba contra la corriente mundial. Los más universalistas de nuestros intelectuales, nuestros hombres de letras, estaban al tanto del gusto por el colorido local que manifiestan las obras de Francis Jammes, Maurice Barrés, Eça de Queiroz, Ivan Bunin, Charles Wagner, José María de Pereda, Santiago Rusiñol, Vicente Blasco Ibáñez y la generación del 98 que, al estilo de los revolucionarios mexicanos, alentó la conciencia y el sentimiento nacionales a fuerza de exaltar lo trivial y pueblerino. Así Azorín, Unamuno, Baroja y Miró. Y así también sus admiradores de México, empezando por el más universal de todos. Don Alfonso Reyes admitió que la República es un haz de provincias, valioso "por sus espigas más que por la guía que las anuda". [13] Ramón López Velarde empequeñeció a la capital "ojerosa y pintada" y alabó a la "aromosa tierruca", y otro tanto hicieron los jaliscienses Francisco González León, Manuel Martínez Valadez y Mariano Azuela; los michoacanos José Rubén Romero y Alfredo Maillefert, y muchos aguascalenteños, guanajuatenses, yucatecos y poblanos. Entre 1910 y 1940 la literatura de tema local estuvo de moda y los escritores provincialistas fueron mimados, con puestos burocráticos, embajadas, cátedras y premios por el régimen de la Revolución.

Los hombres de letras, no los del gremio de la historia. El provincialismo se expresó sobre todo por boca de vates y novelistas, no de historiadores. Los de más nota entre éstos prefirieron nadar en otras corrientes: el indigenismo, el colonialismo, el hispanoamericanismo. Los más se enrtegaron al "desenterramiento de toda una guardarropía". Don Luis González Obregón, Manuel Romero de Terreros (que se subtituló Marqués de San Francisco), Francisco Pérez Salazar, Federico Gómez de Orozco, Artemio de Valle Arizpe... desenterraron "prelados y monjas, cerámica de China, galeones españoles, oidores y virreyes, palaciegos y truhanes, palanquines, tafetanes, juegos de cañas, quemadores inquisitoriales, hechiceros, cordobanes, escudos de armas, gacetas de 1770, pendones, especiería, sillas de coro, marmajeras, retratos de cera" y la fabla del "habedes". [14]

Pero el máximo promotor y crítico del colonialismo, el redondo don Genaro Estrada, no se contentó con el barrio capitalino y "sus capillas pobres, en donde hay nazarenos sucios de terciopelo y de moscas", y con el corazón de la capital y sus patios, fuentes barrocas, casas de tezontle y portones nobilarios. También se dejó atraer por "el hechizo de la provincia". Había nacido en Mazatlán y fue en aquel puerto, re-

[12] Cf. Alfonso de Alba, *op. cit.*, p. 31.
[13] Alfonso Reyes, *A Lápiz*.
[14] Genaro Estrada, *Pero Galín*, México, Editorial Cultura, 1926.

portero, cronista y redactor de tres periódicos. La Revolución lo trans-
terró a México donde obtuvo altos puestos burocráticos en la Secretaría
de Relaciones, y desde ellos impulsó los estudios históricos de tema regional, y sobre todo los de cimiento, los de carácter bibliográfico. A
partir del 1926 lanza la serie de bibliografías de los Estados. Heredia
hace la de Sinaloa; Alessio Robles, la de Coahuila; Romero Flores,
la de Michoacán; Díez, la de Morelos; Chávez Orozco, la de Zacatecas;
Santamaría, la de Tabasco; Díaz Mercado, la de Veracruz; Teixidor, la
de Yucatán, etcétera. [15]

Varios de esos bibliógrafos estatales fueron los primeros en servirse
de listas de libros acabadas de hacer; se convirtieron o por lo menos
se confirmaron como cronistas de la provincia. Así el maestro de toda
erudición norteña, el ingeniero y militar Vito Alessio. Así también el
profesor Jesús Romero Flores. Ambos, por otra parte, contaron con
alguna protección oficial. Pero lo común fue el no obtener ayuda y
estímulos oficiales. La gran mayoría trabajó por mera afición, en horas
restadas al ejercicio de la abogacía, la ingeniería, la medicina, la chamba
burocrática o la enseñanza. Casi ninguno se preparó especialmente
para investigar las acciones humanas del pasado. En este periodo, no
siempre con justicia, se empezó a desdeñar al microhistoriador.

Según nuestra incompleta bibliografía, y no obstante los feos que
les hacían a los investigadores provincianos, en la etapa destructiva
de la Revolución se publicaron 148 libros de historia local, sin contar
catálogos bibliográficos. Entre 1910 y 1924 aparecieron dos libros
anualmente, y de 1925 a 1940, ocho. No encontré ninguno editado en
1915, y di con doce publicaciones en 1940.

El 57% de esa clase de libros, algunos multivoluminosos, caen en
la categoría de historias regionales; el 43%, muchos casi folletos, tratan asuntos de parroquia. Entre éstos la mayoría se refiere a las ciudades de fuste: Pachuca, Querétaro, León, Guanajuato, San Luis Potosí,
Saltillo, Morelia, Torreón, Puebla, Monterrey, Mérida y Guadalajara.
Los temas políticos mantienen su predominio; las monografías enciclopédicas no ceden tampoco sus posiciones; irrumpen con fuerza dos
nuevos asuntos: el etnográfico, puesto de moda por don Manuel Gamio, y el artístico, cuyo principal impulsor fue don Manuel Toussaint.
Lo común es que las crónicas locales abarquen desde los tiempos más
remotos hasta nuestros días, pero en la etapa revolucionaria se dan
cada vez más las que sólo abordan una época, especialmente la colonial.
Sirvan como botones de muestra algunas obras de Vito Alessio Robles;
la *Conquista* y la *Rebelión de Nueva Galicia* de José López Portillo y

[15] Luis González (*et. al.*), *Fuentes de la Historia contemporánea de México*,
El Colegio de México, México, 1961, t. I pp. LII-LIV.

Weber, numerosas monografías de Dávila Garibi y los *Apuntes para la historia de Nueva Vizcaya* de Atanasio González Saravia. [16]

Por lo que mira a la investigación en archivos, bibliotecas y sitios arqueológicos, los logros de la etapa revolucionaria son más cuantitativos que cualitativos. Se acrece el uso de las fuentes primarias. Se hacen compilaciones de documentos a nivel regional y local. Manuel Mestre Ghigliazza documenta a Tabasco, Ignacio Dávila Garibi a Ocotlán, Guadalajara y otros puntos de Jalisco, y Luis Páez Brotchie ve a *La Nueva Galicia a través de su viejo archivo judicial.* También cunde el uso de crónicas conventuales y memorias de conquistadores y pobladores de la época colonial.

En otros aspectos del análisis histórico no se advierten progresos dignos de nota. La debilidad crítica sigue manifestándose sobre todo en los capítulos concernientes a la época precolombina. Sin embargo, las huellas documentales de los periodos virreinales y republicano son tratadas a veces con gran desconfianza, que no gran finura crítica. También escasean las buenas interpretaciones.

El vasto material recogido por los investigadores de la etapa revolucionaria se vació casi todo en formas viejas y difíciles: efemérides (de León, por Sóstenes Lira; de Guanajuato, por Crispín Espinoza; de Hidalgo, por Teodomiro Manzano; de Colima, por Miguel Galindo); monografías geoestadísticas (de Tulancingo, por Canuto Anaya; de Tehuacán, por Paredes Colín; de Yuririapúndaro y otros lugares, por Fulgencio Vargas; de Tlaxcala, por Higinio Vázquez: de Aguascalientes, por Jesús Bernal); diccionarios (de Chihuahua y Colima, por Francisco R. Almada); colecciones de estampas y episodios (de la región de Jalisco, por Ignacio Dávila Garibi; de San Luis Potosí, por Julio Betancourt; de Morelos, por Miguel Salinas; de Hidalgo, por Miguel A. Hidalgo; de Veracruz, por José de J. Núñez y Domínguez; de Acapulco, por Vito Alessio Robles; de Tuxtepec, por Antonio Acevedo Gutiérrez y de Zapotlán, por Guillermo Jiménez); narraciones cronológicas (de Querétaro, por Valentín F. Frías; de Nuevo León, por David A. Cossío; de Toluca, por Miguel Salinas; de Michoacán, por Jesús Romero Flores; de Jalisco por Luis Páez Brotchie, y de Oaxaca, por Jorge Fernando Iturribarría). Fueron novedades las estructuras que les dieron a sus obras los de la escuela histórico artística (Tasco, de Manuel Toussaint; San Miguel Allende, de Francisco de la Maza y la Valenciana y otros puntos de Antonio Cortés); y los primeros etnohistoriadores: Wigberto Jiménez Moreno y Gonzalo Aguirre Beltrán que debutaron, desde la década de los treinta, con estudios ejemplares. Otra manera, en parte novedosa, fue la de la guía turística. En 1934 se conocieron las asombrosas *Calles de Puebla,* de Hugo Leicht.

---

[16] *Vid.* bibliografía aparte.

Lo cierto es, que salvo pocas e ilustres excepciones, aquella historiografía no se distinguió por la unidad y la secuencia de las obras; lo predominante fue la dispersión y el desorden. Tampoco en la manera de contar hubo pocos aciertos. El estilo va de lo extremadamente ampuloso a lo extremadamente árido y pobre.

No sólo debe atribuirse a sus escasos méritos intrínsecos el que el grueso de la historiografía del periodo revolucionario haya tenido escasa acogida en su época y casi ninguna después. Con todo, algunos librotes gozaron de prestigio en el círculo culto y a sus autores se les premió haciéndolos miembros de la Academia Mexicana de la Historia o de la Sociedad de Geografía y Estadística. Al gran público llegaron pocos y casi nunca los mismos aclamados por las academias y sociedades cultas. A los mejor informados se les tuvo por aburridos y algunos de los menos sabios gozaron fama de amenos e interesantes. De los muertos, ya pocos se acuerdan; de sus obras, casi ninguna se ha reeditado, aunque más de alguna será llamada a la segunda vida por un juez literario o un historiador de la historia o (todo es posible), por el reclamo del público.

IV. LA HISTORIOGRAFÍA NINGUNEADA

El nacionalismo mexicano es otro desde 1940. Se ha vuelto más popular y también más aguado y tibio. Ya no profesa odios vigorosos contra lo extranjero y ve a la provincia con indiferencia. Ya no se dice: "La provincia es la patria." Tampoco se sostiene la tesis opuesta. La política busca el fin de la desigualdades regionales, no la muerte de la personalidad de cada región y parroquia. De hecho, la distancia entre lo provinciano y lo capitalino está en vías de desaparecer. Por su parte, también el provincialismo y el aldeanismo se han entibiado.

Aunque todavía muchos de los dioses mayores de la literatura mexicana (Agustín Yáñez, Juan Rulfo y Juan José Arriola) toman inspiración de la provincia, el grueso de los literatos de las tres últimas generaciones anda por otras rutas. El que disminuya día a día el número de poetas y novelistas nacidos y formados fuera de la capital, es una causa menor del fenómeno.

La historiografía mayor se ha apartado del localismo. Wigberto Jiménez Moreno, Gonzalo Aguirre Beltrán, Ignacio Rubio Mañé, Justino Fernández y Héctor Pérez Martínez que se dieron a conocer como historiadores locales, pronto abandonaron ese género. Los demás grandes nunca se han sentido atraídos por él. La república de la historia tiene su asiento en la ciudad capital. La gran mayoría de los investigadores viven en la gran urbe, y desde ella no es fácil hacer historia provinciana. Aquí disfrutan de toda clase de alicientes económicos y honoríficos;

gozan de regulares sueldos; pueden dedicar la mayor parte de sus jornadas a la investigación; los editores de revistas y libros están siempre bien dispuestos a publicarles los frutos de su actividad. Cuando dan a luz, los críticos bibliográficos se encargan de que los que leen periódicos, los radioescuchas y los televidentes lo sepan; se les invita a participar en reuniones y academias de sabios; ganan fácilmente pan, tiempo y nombradía y están a la última moda. Los cronistas locales andan muy lejos de esa gloria.

Desde 1940 no ha dejado de acentuarse la diferencia entre historiadores capitalinos y provincianos. En tiempos de don Porfirio no era perceptible la desigualdad económica, social y profesional entre unos y otros. En la etapa siguiente, varios de los cronistas locales cayeron en la categoría de hermanos pobres, torpes e ignorantes. En los últimos treinta años un abismo separa al historiador de la capital que ha hecho estudios *ad hoc*, presentando una tesis profesional, visitado universidades de Francia, Inglaterra y Estados Unidos, leído obras en inglés y francés y poseído los seguros y ayudas de nuestros institutos de investigación, del cronista local, solo, informe, sin oportunidades de formarse. Algunos ni siquiera han terminado los estudios de la educación primaria, y aunque no faltan los que ostentan títulos universitarios, éstos son de abogacía o medicina. Son muy pocos los profesionales de la historia, y aún éstos no cuentan con los necesarios auxilios para trabajar. La gran mayoría está en mala situación económica, sin conexiones con el gremio, al margen de las nuevas corrientes historiográficas, a la zaga, muy a la zaga, fuera de onda, completamente *out*, pero no inactiva.

De 1941 a lo que va del año de 1969 han aparecido, según mi lista, 292 historias de tema regional y parroquial; esto es, diez por año, el doble de las publicadas en el periodo de 1911-1940 y el triple de las que produjo el Porfiriato. Han sido años de gran fecundidad los de 42, 56 y 57, con catorce libros cada uno. Probablemente en el último trentenio no ha aumentado la producción de artículos, pero sí, con toda seguridad, la de obras que circulan en copias mecanográficas, y mimeográficas, no mencionadas aquí. En fin, por el volumen, la cosecha no es nada desdeñable.

Si mi bibliografía no engaña, las historias de tema parroquial han aventajado en número a las de asunto regional. Va de salida la moda de hacer historias de los Estados. El 60 por ciento de la producción es local. Todavía más: crece la cifra de libros que toman como asunto ciudades pequeñas y aun pueblos de escaso bulto y renombre. La mayoría de los sitios estudiados pertenecen a la región central y Yucatán. Como quiera, don Leonardo Pasquel ha puesto a Veracruz a la cabeza. Nuevo León y el noroeste vienen poco detrás, pero a gran prisa. En la temática no ha habido revolución alguna. Siguen siendo mayoría los cronistas locales empeñados en hacer listas de personas y hechos políticos y militares. Otros siguen adictos a la manera enciclopédica. El influjo de la escuela etnohistórica ha penetrado poco en la provincia, pero, desde la capital algunos etnohistoriadores del arte, también capitalinos, han ensanchado el campo de sus investigaciones localistas. El reciente ejemplo de Carlos Martínez Marín se expande.

A pesar de su aislamiento, los cronistas locales de la época actual han entrado al club de los adoradores de las fuentes primarias y el aparato erudito. Confeccionan sus crónicas y monografías con noticias extraídas de los papeles del Archivo General de la Nación, de los archivos estatales, los registros de bautismo, matrimonios y defunciones de las parroquias y vicarías y los libros de notarios. También acuden con mayor frecuencia a periódicos y ruinas. Los trabajos sobre *Tlapacoyan* y *Misantla*, de Ramírez Lavoignet; Zamora y Jacona de Rodríguez Zetina; Oaxaca, de Iturribarría; Ameca, de Jesús Amaya Topete y los varios de Gabriel Agraz García de Alba, han sido construidos sobre una vasta plataforma documental. Naturalmente que los hechos por profesionales de la historia, como Israel Cavazos Garza y Delfina López Sarrelangue, aúnan a la labor heurística un fino talento crítico.

En términos generales, los cronistas lugareños han hecho avances notables por lo que mira al manejo de las fuentes históricas a pesar de la falta de oficio en tantos. Por otra parte, sobre la forma como proceden en el análisis varía muchísimo de unos individuos a otros. No se puede decir nada que los abarque a todos. Son pocos los que le saben sacar provecho a sus materiales. Los hay que son auténticos historiadores de tijera y engrudo; los hay que pasan de la más pura fantasía a la erudición más espesa.

Seguramente la gran mayoría de nuestros cronistas locales carecen del vicio moderno del "profesionalismo". Por este lado están en gran desventaja con respecto a los historiadores capitalinos. Por otro, les llevan la delantera. Los estudiosos lugareños ganan en vocación, en experiencia vital y sobre todo en cariño hacia su objeto de estudio. Es difícil escoger entre el profesional que es todo inteligencia y oficio y el aficionado, *dilettante* o amateur que es todo corazón.

A veces lo peor de los historiadores localistas es lo que tienen de profesionales. Muchos comparten con éstos la maladada manera de reconstruir la historia. Se meten en explicaciones farragosas y siempre discutibles. En nombre de la ciencia, construyen con sus materiales castillos vericuetosos que nada tienen que ver con las articulaciones reales de la vida histórica. Al verse rodeado de tantas efemérides, monografías histórico-geográfico-estadísticas, relaciones deshilvanadas, informes etnohistóricos y otras deformidades, se añoran la sencillez y la espontaneidad arquitectónica de Bernal Díaz de Castillo, Toribio de Motolinía, Jerónimo de Mendieta y demás fundadores de la historiografía mexicana. ¿Por qué tanto brinco si el suelo está parejo?

Otro aspecto, que tampoco es privativo de la historiografía local, es el de la dignidad de la prosa histórica, digna a fuerza de ser aburrida, pobre, reverente, *camp*. Pero tampoco aquí se puede generalizar. Entre lo poco que conozco, hay magníficas excepciones: el humorismo de Salvador Novo en la *Breve historia de Coyoacán*, las evocaciones laguenses de Alfonso de Alba, la prosa vivificadora de José Fuentes Mares y quizá muchas que ignoro.

Han sido modestos los logros editoriales alcanzados en el último trentenio por las obras de tema regional y parroquial. Algunas no han dado con editor o se han impreso en ediciones cortas y miserables pagadas por quien las escribió. Otras han salido a luz gracias a la caridad oficial o de los paisanos del escribiente. A veces las editoriales universitarias se dignan imprimirlas, pero las de carácter comercial temen meterse con esa clase de libros, lo que parece indicar que el lectorio y el auditorio de los historiadores provincianos sigue siendo reducido y pobre. En el círculo académico seguramente gozan de escasa estima, los críticos rara vez les conceden un rato de atención y el público general difícilmente se percata de su existencia.

Y sin embargo, volviendo a don Alfonso Reyes, "en muchos de estos historiadores locales están las aguas vivas". Yo puedo decir que he leído con mucho agrado y he aprendido mucho en *Tetela del Volcán*, de Carlos Martínez Marín, en el *Consulado* y en la *Insurgencia en Guadalajara* de José Ramírez Flores, en *Cosas de viejos papeles*, de Leopoldo I. Orendáin, en las Colimas de Daniel Moreno, en las historias michoacanas, de don Jesús Romero Flores, en la monografías nuevoleonesas, de Israel Cavazos Garza, en la *Historia del Valle del Yaqui*, de Claudio Dabdoub y en la del Fuerte, de Mario Gill, en la *Historia sucinta de Michoacán*, de José Bravo Ugarte, en la *Huasteca veracruzana* de Joaquín Meade, en las reconstrucciones chihuahuenses de José Fuentes Mares, en las obras sobre Lagos de Alfonso de Alba, en Héctor Pérez Martínez, Rosendo Taracena, Eduardo Villa, Francisco R. Almada, Santiago Roel, José Corona Núñez, Ricardo Lancaster Jones, José Cornejo Franco, Jesús Amaya Topete, Jesús Sotelo Inclán, Jorge Fernando Iturribarría, Estéban Chávez, el benemérito Leonardo Pasquel, el gran promotor Mario Colín y muchos más.

V. RECOMENDACIONES

A pesar de que hasta ahora la historiografía mexicana moderna de tema local no ha conocido todavía un momento de gran esplendor, hay dignos indicadores de la cercanía de un buen temporal. El género ya está de moda en algunos países ricos como Alemania, Estados Unidos, Francia e Inglaterra. En nuestro medio ya empiezan a oirse las siguientes ideas: "La educación histórica de la niñez debe comenzar con el relato del pequeño mundo donde el niño vive." "La historiografía de áreas cortas es un gimnasio ideal para desenvolver los músculos historiográficos de los estudiantes de historia porque esa disciplina exige, como ninguna otra, la aplicación de todas las técnicas heurísticas, críticas, interpretativas, etiológicas, arquitectónicas y de estilo." "En la vida de un pueblo está la vida de todos y por lo reducido del objeto es posible recrearla en toda su amplitud." "Cada una de las aldeas de una nación reproduce en miniatura la vida nacional en que está inmersa." [17] "En los historiadores locales están las aguas vivas, los gérmenes palpitantes. Muchos casos nacionales se entenderían mejor procediendo a la síntesis de los conflictos y sucesos registrados en cada región." [18] En la microhistoria y en la microsociología "el sociólogo y el historiador tienen en México una riqueza que apenas comienza a explotarse".

No sólo entre los cultos, también en el círculo popular se perciben signos de mayor acercamiento a la microhistoria. Fuera de los clientes seguros que en cada región y parroquia ya tienen sus propios cronistas, los hombres de ciudad miran con buenos ojos los relatos de la vida que muere, quizá porque añoran la vida apacible, quizá porque creen que los lugareños tienen algo que enseñar, que todas las comunidades por pequeñas que sean, incluso las más apartadas del comercio y la cultura, aportan experiencias humanas ejemplares.

En el Congreso Científico Mexicano celebrado en México, D. F., durante el mes de septiembre de 1951, don Wigberto Jiménez Moreno afirmó: "Espero que se dará mayor énfasis a la historia regional, como corresponde a la visión de un México múltiple." [19] Y él, mejor que nadie, hubiera podido decir las medidas adecuadas para conseguir la realización de su esperanza. Él puede hacerlo todavía ahora, salvo que crea que el auge de la historiografía local llegará de cualquier manera.

A reserva de que don Wigberto Jiménez Moreno y don Antonio Pompa y Pompa, como máximos expertos y animadores del género que se discute aquí digan lo conducente sobre el caso, aventuro algunas ocurrencias al parecer practicables. Entre las medidas de orden institucional, anoto las siguientes:

1. Que la Secretaría de Educación Pública y las direcciones educativas de los Estados hagan sitio a la historia regional y parroquial en los niveles de enseñanza primaria y secundaria;

[17] Luis González, *Pueblo en vilo. Microhistoria de San José de Gracia.* El Colegio de México, México, 1968, pp. 12-14.
[18] Alfonso Reyes, *Las burlas veras*, p. 107.
[19] Wigberto Jiménez Moreno, "50 años de historia mexicana" en *Historia Mexicana*, vol. I, núm. 3 (enero-marzo, 1952), p. 454.

2. Que nuestras universidades y centros de alta cultura (en especial los de provincia) abran seminarios y cátedras donde se enseñen y apliquen los principios y métodos de la historia local;

3. Que a los pasantes de historia con vocación por la historiografía local se les conceda beca para investigar y organizar durante un año archivos provincianos y que el informe de sus exploraciones se le tome como tesis para optar a una licenciatura o maestría (la ocurrencia de este servicio histórico social es de Jean Meyer);

4. Que el mecenazgo del gobierno y las fundaciones se extienda a la historiografía de tema regional y parroquial en forma de becas, o sinecuras burocráticas, o premios a la labor hecha, o mediante la edición y distribución de las obras de nuestros cronistas locales;

5. Que se reanuden los congresos de historia que tanto sirvieron, desde 1933, para establecer el contacto entre historiadores de la capital y de la provincia y promover las investigaciones de historia regional;

6. Que se forme una asociación de historiadores locales con sede en México o en la capital de alguno de los Estados.

Por lo que toca a reformas interiores, de puertas adentro, sería conveniente revisar los sujetos, los objetos y los procederes de la historiografía local. Paul Leuilliot asegura que "los principios de la historia local son autónomos y aun opuestos a los de la historia general". Aquella es "cualitativa y no cuantitativa"; requiere "une certaine souplesse, c'est une histoire a mailles Lâches"; "debe ser concreta", lo más próximo posible a la vida cotidiana, y debe ser diferencial, procurar medir la distancia entre la evolución general y la de las localidades. [20] Por su parte el profesor inglés H.P.R. Finberg apunta otros rasgos específicos. [21]

Según el profesor Finberg, el historiador local necesita madurez, lecturas amplias, mucha simpatía y piernas robustas. Por madurez entiende una larga y surtida experiencia entre los hombres, un buen equipaje de vivencias. Como lecturas recomienda, aparte de otras, las de libros de historia nacional e internacional. La simpatía que exige es por aquello de que sólo lo semejante conoce a lo semejante y aquello otro de que sólo se conoce bien lo que se ama. La exigencia de las piernas robustas alude a la necesidad que tiene el historiador pueblerino de recorrer a pie, una y otra vez, la sede de su asunto, y de visitar personalmente el mayor número posible de parroquianos.

[20] Paul Leuilliot, "Defense et illustration de l'histoire locale" en *Annales*, 22 année, núm. 1 (enero-febrero, 1967), pp. 154-177.
[21] H.P.R. Finberg: *Aproaches to history*, London, Routledge & Kegan Paul, 1962, pp. 111-125.

Por lo que parece, "el ejercicio de la historiografía circunscrita a una pequeña zona tiene que echar mano de todos los recursos de la metodología histórica y de varios más. En este tipo de investigación, a cada una de las operaciones historiográficas se oponen numerosos obstáculos... No es fácil partir, como en otros campos de la historia, con un equipo adecuado de esquemas anteriores, de interrogatorios hechos, de hipótesis de trabajo y de modelos". Otro problema reside en la escasez y la dispersión de las fuentes. Incluso se ha dicho que no puede hacerse la historia parroquial por que faltan los documentos esenciales.

"La historiografía local, como la biografía, parece estar más cerca de la literatura que los otros géneros históricos, quizá porque la vida concreta exige un tratamiento literario, quizá porque gran parte de la clientela del historiador local es alérgica a la aridez acostumbrada por los historiadores contemporáneos. El redactor de una historia local debiera ser un hombre de letras." [22] De cualquier historia se puede decir con Simpson que "nacerá muerta a menos que esté escrita en un estilo atractivo", pero nunca con tanta razón como de la microhistoria. A los encargados de formar a los historiadores locales del futuro no se les podrá exigir que hagan poetas, pero sí prosistas legibles.

[22] Luis González, *op. cit.*, p. 22.

COMENTARIO

WIGBERTO JIMÉNEZ MORENO

Quiero, en primer término, rendir homenaje al ponente, uno de los jóvenes historiadores mexicanos más expertos y de perspectivas más amplias, en las que no deja de situarse aunque se ocupe de la "microhistoria". Con su acostumbrada destreza ha abordado el tema, en cuyo rubro preferiría yo sustituir por "local" el calificativo "parroquial".

También llamaría "localistas" a los autores que el denomina "lugareños". Estoy de acuerdo en que "habría que comenzar por un inventario, por una bibliografía metódica", —como sugería don Alfonso Reyes a don Daniel Cosío Villegas— y aunque Luis González ha compilado ya una amplia lista y yo sólo una corta —a pesar de que poseo un buen acervo de geografía e historia regional y local— lo aconsejable sería que, en *Historia Mexicana*, se publicase un repertorio selecto de fichas de tal índole para cada entidad de la República. Como se habrá advertido, amplío la sugerencia de don Alfonso a don Daniel incluyendo estudios geográficos —a los que son afines los estadísticos y demográficos— porque se complementan la geografía y la historia y gran parte de la producción pertinente las abarca a ambas, las que tomo en sentido lato, lo que permite incluir libros, folletos, artículos y documentos sobre la evolución de las artes gráficas y de las artes plásticas, la música y el folklore y la literatura, lo mismo que la instrucción pública y el desarrollo de las denominaciones religiosas.

Coincido, sin embargo, con Luis González en la necesidad de "fijar los límites de la microhistoriografía" y de deslindar "qué es comunidad marginal, regional y parroquial" y "qué es etnohistoria e historia de regiones, ciudades y parroquias". Aunque en la enumeración que él hace de varios tópicos, resalta lo disímbolo de ellos, todos me parecen objeto válido de la microhistoria con tal que se les clasifique dentro de un temario adecuado y bajo las etapas y periodos pertinentes. Hechas las distinciones necesarias, una comunidad marginada como Tetelcingo tiene tan buenos títulos como Tepoztlán —que ya no lo está, o sólo en menor grado— para ser asunto plausible del tipo de investigación cuyas peculiaridades analizamos. Si se trata de la etapa prehispánica, lo relativo a las ruinas arqueológicas es tan admisible como la descripción de los conventos y la narración de sus vicisitudes lo son para la colonial, o como lo referente a los teatros y a los palacios de gobierno o municipales lo es para la nacional.

El ponente se concreta a examinar —con las exclusiones a que alude— "algunos libros de verdadera historia, hechos por mexicanos entre 1870 y 1869, de asunto regional... o parroquial que son expresión de actitudes emotivas de "aldeanismo" y "provincialismo". Como colaborador —y de los mejores— de la *Historia moderna de México* dirigida por Cosío Villegas, cuyo punto de partida es la fecha de la restauración de la República, era de esperarse que cerca de ese año —redondeando a 1870 la cifra 1867—, fijara Luis González su punto de arranque. Que la producción pertinente, de entonces a acá, sea la más madura, en general —aunque con múltiples excepciones— y, por lo tanto, la más propicia a este análisis, es indudable. Dentro de esa centuria señala un periodo —el "porfírico"— de 40 años (1870-1910), seguido de otro de 30: el "revolucionario" (1910-1940) y otro más de 29: el actual (1940-1969).

Reconocemos lo aconsejable de concentrar nuestra atención en el último siglo o, preferiblemente —por razones que aduciremos—, en el lapso de 1821 hasta la fecha, pero, antes de restringir nuestras consideraciones al México independiente, queremos hacer una rápida alusión a las épocas prehispánica y colonial.

Como existe en este congreso una sección de historiografía prehispánica, estimo ocioso insistir aquí en que hubo historia regional y local antes de la conquista española, y que sólo existía la historia "parroquial". Nuestros indígenas carecían del concepto de historia general y en lápidas o en códices consignaban sucesos relativos a su comunidad, rebasando este estrecho marco sólo cuando se trataba de conquistas efectuadas en lugares más o menos distantes, o cuando se aludía a lejanos puntos de partida de donde procedían algunos inmigrantes. La historia precolombina es, pues, casi siempre, "microhistoria".

Por lo que respecta a la época colonial, aunque —como anota Luis González— ya los españoles habían mostrado interés en la historia local por lo menos desde que, en el siglo XIII, Juan Gil de Zamora escribió acerca de Numancia, en nuestro país es sólo hasta el siglo XVIII cuando podemos encontrar obras verdaderamente valiosas de historia regional y local: ejemplo de lo primero es la *Historia de la conquista del reino de la Nueva Galicia* de don Matías López de la Mota Padilla (1742) y de lo segundo son el *Compendio de las cosas más notables contenidas en los libros del cabildo de esta ciudad de Nuestra Señora de los Zacatecas desde el año de su descubrimiento, 1546, hasta 1730* y la *Descripción breve de la muy noble y leal ciudad de Zacatecas*, escritas ambas por don José Rivera Bernárdez (1730 y 1732). El más ambicioso esfuerzo de historia "parroquial" es el de don Mariano Fernández Echeverría y Veytia: *Historia de la fundación de la Ciudad de Puebla de los Ángeles en la Nueva España.* Contra lo que podría esperarse, la ciudad de México no tuvo, hasta el siglo XIX, cronistas equiparables a los que tuvieron Zacatecas y Puebla. Al lado de estas obras de mayor importancia y de ámbito espacial o temporal más amplio, las "relaciones y descripciones geográficas" de los siglos XVI, XVII y XVIII, son ricas vetas de información "microhistórica". Al iniciarse nuestra vida independiente aparecen, antes que nada, noticias geográficas y estadísticas que, por su enfoque, recuerden aquellas antiguas "relaciones" y "descripciones".

Anticipé ya que estimaba preferible abarcar un lapso de cerca de siglo y medio (1821-1969) para centrar en él nuestra atención en vez de circunscribirnos, como prefiere el ponente, al de 1870-1969. La razón que él invoca es que "con la Reforma se produjo un corte tan profundo en la vida de México que, a partir de su triunfo, es posible comenzar la historia de muchos aspectos de lo mexicano", y esto a pesar de que —como él lo reconoce— "el provincialismo y el aldeanismo son aquí más viejos que el amor a la patria, por ser herencia recibida de los pueblos precortesianos y de España".

La fase crucial de la Reforma se inicia con la Revolución de Ayutla en 1854 y culmina con el triunfo de Juárez al final de 1860. Sin embargo, el primer acto de este trascendental proceso se tiene bajo Gómez Farías en 1833-34. Por otra parte, el triunfo de los liberales no se consolida sino hasta que cae el Segundo Imperio en 1867 y hasta que, en noviembre de 1874, las Leyes de Reforma son elevadas al rango de constitucionales. Sin desconocer lo que el pensamiento liberal mexicano debe a sus antiguas fuentes españolas, y a la ideología de la Revolución Francesa, lo que acelera y precipita el proceso de la Reforma es, en primer término, el contacto con los Estados Unidos, por medio de su enviado Poinsett desde 1825, y la guerra con esa nación en 1846-47. De hecho la voluntad inexorable de estructurar un México nuevo, de espaldas al pasado, ha surgido ya sin titubeos casi inmediatamente después de firmarse el Tratado de Guadalupe Hidalgo en 1848. Es, a partir de entonces, cuando se advierte un espíritu nuevo en la historiografía regional y local, sobre todo, desde que, de 1851 a 1858, se publica los *Apuntes históricos de la heroica ciudad de Veracruz,* de don Miguel Lerdo de Tejada.

Es sólo hasta 1850-51 cuando se reorganiza la Sociedad Mexicana de Geografía y Estadística que hasta entonces llevaba vida letárgica y es éste un hecho trascendental ya que esta sociedad es la que desde 1833, en que se fundó, había venido auspiciando el estudio de la geografía e historia regionales y, después de su reestructuración, fomentaría más decididamente ese linaje de investigaciones. A partir de 1851 conviven en la ciudad de México tres grandes historiadores: don Joaquín García Icazbalceta, don José Fernando Ramírez y don Manuel Orozco y Berra. Aún vivía Alamán —primer historiador mexicano de corte moderno— y él no sólo había impulsado los estudios geográficos e históricos, sino que fue también uno de los iniciadores de una magna empresa: la de preparar y editar el monumental *Diccionario universal de historia y geografía* en diez volúmenes publicados de 1853 a 1856, de los cuales los tres últimos constituyen un Apéndice referente a México, en el que colaboraron, entre otros, Ramírez y Orozco y Berra. No menos importante fue la aparición, en 1853, del *Atlas geográfico, estadístico e histórico de la República Mexicana* de don Antonio García Cubas. Mientras no existiera un diccionario como el publicado de 1853 a 1856, mientras no se pudiera disponer de un *Atlas geográfico* como el aparecido en 1853, y mientras no se dispusiera de modelos como la *Historia de México* de Alamán (1849-1852) en cuanto a la historia del país y de las *Noticias históricas y estadísticas de Durango* de don José Fernando Ramírez (1851) para la historia de los Estados y de los *Apuntes históricos* de Miguel Lerdo de Tejada (1851-1858) para la de las ciudades, no se podría abrir un nuevo derrotero, que implicara mayor madurez, a las investigaciones de historia regional y local.

Para alcanzar esta madurez que se advierte a partir de 1851 —y que no todos, aún hoy, logran— mucho habían servido esfuerzos previos como los de Juan José Lejarza (1785-1824), autor de un *Análisis estadístico de la provincia de Michuacán, en* 1822 (publicado en 1824) y los de Benigno Bustamante y Septién (1784-1858) que dio a luz una *Memoria geográfica y estadística del Estado de Guanajuato* en 1839. Se destacan, a continuación, unas *Noticias geográficas y estadísticas del departamento de Jalisco*, aparecidas en 1843 (de autor anónimo que usa las iniciales M. L. C.) y la *Noticia histórica de Soconusco* de Manuel Larráinzar editada en ese mismo año. Vienen luego las *Noticias estadísticas del Estado de Durango* y las *Noticias estadísticas de Sonora y Sinaloa*, ambas dadas a luz en 1849 por José Agustín Escudero, quien ya en 1834 había dado a conocer sus *Noticias estadísticas del estado de Chihuahua*. Aparte de una de las obras de Escudero ya aludida, Sonora contó desde 1835, con la *Rápida ojeada* de Ignacio Zúñiga y, desde 1850, con las *Noticias estadísticas* de José Francisco Velasco. Mencionemos, de paso, que los más antiguos de estos autores, es decir, Lejarza y Bustamante y Septién, fueron miembros de la generación que llamo "pleni-insurgente", que es también la de los primeros reformistas, como Valentín Gómez Farías y El Pensador Mexicano. A la de 1797-1809 —la de Juárez y Gutiérrez Estrada— pertenecieron José Fernández Ramírez, Manuel Larráinzar y Jerónimo del Castillo, autor este último de un *Diccionario histórico, biográfico monumental de Yucatán*, editado sólo hasta el año de su muerte (1866).

A partir de 1851 se publican obras de historia regional y local de autores de la generación que llamo "proto-reformista" —la de Ocampo, Ramírez y Prieto, la de los nacidos entre 1810 y 1823— a la que pertenecen Miguel Lerdo de Tejada, José Guadalupe Romero, José Antonio Septién y Villaseñor, José María Pérez Hernández (oriundo de Cuba, según se afirma) e Hilarión Romero Gil. Las *Noticias para formar la historia y la estadística del obispado de Michoacán* (escritas por 1860-1861 e impresas en 1862-63) significan un adelanto considerable por cuanto implican el desplazamiento de un centro de interés localizado en la geografía y la estadística hacia otro arraigado en la historia. Análogo progreso se constata en la *Memoria estadística del estado de Querétaro, precedida de una noticia histórica que comprende desde la fundación del mismo hasta el año del 1821*, de José Antonio Septién y Villaseñor, lo que puede comprobarse comparando esta obra, publicada a la muerte de su autor, en 1875, con dos anteriores sobre la misma entidad: las *Notas estadísticas del Estado de Querétaro* impresas en 1848 y la *Estadística del estado de Querétaro* formada por el ciudadano Juan María Balbontín en los años de 1854, aparecida en 1867. En los diversos trabajos acerca de la historia de Nuevo León, escritos por un coetáneo de los anteriores —don José Eleuterio González, "Gonzalitos"—, se advierte un mayor aprovechamiento de los fondos documentales de los archivos, actitud que se extrema ulteriormente en los *Apuntes para la historia antigua de Coahuila y Texas* de Esteban L. Portillo (1886).

En la generación que designo como "pleni-reformista" —la de los nacidos entre 1824 y 1837, la de Mariano Escobedo y Porfirio Díaz— milita una nutrida hueste de historiadores regionales y locales: aparece con ellos la historia de los Estados: la de Tabasco por Manuel Gil Sáenz; la de Oaxaca por José Antonio Gay; la de Yucatán por Eligio Ancona y Crescencio Carrillo y Ancona; la de Aguascalientes por Agustín R. González y la de Sinaloa por Eustaquio Buelna. Como síntoma de acentuado localismo surgen, en 1883-84, las *Efemérides guanajuatenses* de Lucio Marmolejo, uno de los más ejemplares esfuerzos pioneros de escribir la historia de una ciudad. La capital de México encuentra al fin su cronista en don José María Marroqui. A esta generación pertenece Antonio García Cubas, a quien tantas aportaciones beneméritas se le deben. A ella también Cayetano Esteva, que a los 80 años publica su *Geografía histórica del Estado de Oaxaca* (1913). Para la historia local son excelentes aportaciones las monografías sobre Jiquilpan y sobre Arandas de Ramón Sánchez, aunque son, ante todo, de carácter estadístico.

A la promoción siguiente —la de los nacidos entre 1838 y 1850, la de Justo Sierra y los "epi-reformistas" y "proto-científicos"— corresponden otros autores de historias de los Estados como Alejandro Prieto para Tamaulipas; Joaquín Baranda y Francisco Álvarez para Campeche; Juan Francisco Molina Solís para Yucatán; Manuel Martínez Gracida para Oaxaca; Eduardo Ruiz para Michoacán (entidad federativa a la que otro coetáneo —Mariano de Jesús Torres— consagró un *Diccionario histórico biográfico, geográfico, estadístico, zoológico, botánico y mineralógico*). Elías Amador escribió sobre historia de Zacatecas; Mariano Bárcena y Manuel Cambre historiaron Jalisco; Cecilio Robelo, Morelos. Flavio Paniagua reunió documentos para Chiapas. Manuel Rivera Cambas siguió las huellas de Marroquí en su *México pintoresco, artístico y monumental*, aparte de elaborar una valiosa historia de Jalapa. La de Orizaba fue realizada por Marcos Arroniz.

Entre los miembros de la generación "pleni-científica" —la de los nacidos 1850 y 1863, la de Limantour, Huerta y Carranza— algunos cultivaron la historia de los Estados: la de Sonora, sucintamente, Ramón Corral; la de Morelos, Francisco Plancarte y Navarrete; tanto la de ese Estado como la del México, Miguel Salinas. Los más ejemplares logros son los de Luis Pérez Verdía para Jalisco y de Primo Feliciano Velázquez para San Luis Potosí. Adviértase, empero, que algunas de estas obras se publicaron antes del estallido de la Revolución Mexicana o cuando ésta ocurría (como en el caso de la *Historia particular del Estado de Jalisco*), mientras otras (como la de Velázquez) se imprimieron en el periodo "actual", posterior a 1940. A un género peculiar corresponden las *Leyendas y tradiciones queretanas* (1896-98 y 1900) y *Las calles de Querétaro* (1910) de Valentín F. Frías. La *Geografía local del Estado de Guanajuato*, de Pedro González, contiene un cierto grado de información histórica.

Los historiadores del siguiente estrato de edades —el de los "epi-científicos" y "proto-revolucionarios", nacidos entre 1864 y 1875 —emplean abundantemente los papeles de archivos. Así lo hace, al reconstruir la vida de la ciudad de México don Luis González Obregón, cuyo coetáneo es don Jesús Galindo y Villa, a quien se debe una de las mejores síntesis de la historia de la dicha capital. Ejemplo de esta actitud son los cuatro tomos de *Documentos y datos para la historia de Tabasco* compilados por Manuel Mestre Ghiliazza (1916-1940) y lo son también los documentos sobre el obispado de Chiapas y sobre el arzobispado de Guadalajara, cuya publicación auspició don Francisco Orozco y Jiménez. Innovación importante representa la obra de Gustavo Martínez Alomia: *Historiadores de Yucatán* (1906), cuyo enfoque sólo sería superado en *Los historiadores de Jalisco* (1918) de don Juan B. Iguíniz, de una generación posterior. A la que

veníamos aludiendo pertenecen también Enrique Santibáñez y Marcos
Becerra que se ocupan de Chiapas, y Carlos R. Menéndez que historia
Yucatán. Una importante contribución a la historia parroquial son los
Apuntes para la historia de San Ángel (1913) de Francisco Fernández
del Castillo.

La promoción que llamo "pleni-revolucionaria" —la de los nacidos entre
1875 y 1889, la de Obregón, Villa y Zapata— dio valiosas aportaciones
a las historias de los Estados, como las de Vito Alesio Robles sobre Coahuila, en primer término; de David Alberto Cossío y Santiago Roel sobre
Nuevo León; de Atanasio Sarabia sobre Durango; de Fulgencio Vargas
sobre Guanajuato; de Jesús Romero Flores sobre Michoacán; de Miguel
Galindo sobre Colima y de Enrique Juan Palacios sobre Puebla. Diversos
aspectos de la historia de Jalisco han estudiado Iguíniz, antes aludido,
J. Ignacio Dávila Garibi y José T. Laris. A Genaro Estrada se le debe el
haber impulsado la preparación de numerosas bibliografías de los Estados,
editadas por él. Aunque con tendencia novelesca, Artemio del Valle Arizpe
sigue los pasos de don Luis González Obregón. Joaquín Ramírez Cabañas
y Francisco Pérez Salazar tocaron incidentalmente algunos temas de historia local. La aportación mayor es, sin duda, la de Alessio Robles.

En manera análoga podríamos aludir a la producción "micro-historiográ-
fica" de las generaciones más recientes: la "epi-revolucionaria" (de los nacidos entre 1890 y 1903), la de 1904-1917, a la que pertenezco, y la de
1917-30, de la que es miembro el ponente. Su extraordinaria obra *Pueblo
en vilo* representa la culminación de la historia parroquial. Esta producción es posterior a la Revolución armada y se inicia en lo que podría
llamarse "la fase sonorense" (1920-1935) pero corresponde, en su mayor
parte, al periodo "actual".

Dentro de nuestra perspectiva generacional, en el México independiente
distinguimos cuatro sucesivos climas o atmósferas socioculturales que abarcan los periodos de 1821 a 1860, 1861 a 1900, 1901 a 1938/40 y, finalmente, el último, que se inició hacia esta última fecha y acabará en la
próxima década, por 1980, siguiendo el ritmo de las etapas precedentes,
si bien esta fase postrera puede ser más corta, dada la aceleración del acontecer histórico en nuestro tiempo.

Señala con acierto Luis González que en el periodo por él llamado
"porfírico" (que incluye también lo que Cosío Villegas denomina "La
República restaurada") "la élite patriótica, casi toda ella liberal y positivista . . . combatió . . . amores y filias regionales y aldeanas . . . Como defensa, . . . la historiografía local entró también a la pelea". Hasta hubo
gobernadores que historiaron las entidades políticas que regían. En ese
periodo —agrega el ponente— "la historia de los Estados fue más cultivada
que la municipal" y "los más historiados fueron Jalisco, Michoacán y
Yucatán". "En la historiografía de corte parroquial" es "donde más predomina" —según él— "la tendencia enciclopédica". Cita como ilustración
el variado contenido de algunos estudios como los que Ramón Sánchez
dedicó a Jiquilpan y a Arandas. En general, tanto los historiadores regionales como los locales, con típica actitud científico-positivista —en el sentir
del ponente— "querían conseguir verdades históricas tan firmes como las
de la ciencia natural, a fin de que pudieran ser útiles" y varios de ellos

"meditaron, compusieron y escribieron con arte y sosegadamente". Luis González ve como innovaciones el tipo de obras ejemplificado en las de Ramón Sánchez, ya aludidas, por una parte, y por otra los diccionarios como el consagrado a Yucatán por Jerónimo Castillo (1866). Por último, anota que los cronistas locales eran "arquitectos monstruosos, pero buenos prosistas" y como representativo de esta cualidad nombra a Primo Feliciano Velázquez.

En contraste con las del periodo "porfírico", las características del "revolucionario" (1910-1940), son otras. "Se convirtió en virtud . . . la adhesión calurosa a la tierra nativa" ya que "el grueso de los revolucionarios defendió la tesis de que se podía ser patriota sin dejar de ser localista". Ello coincidía con el "gusto por el colorido local" que se advierte en obras de grandes literatos europeos de fines del siglo xix y principios del xx. En la literatura mexicana, el caso de Ramón López Velarde —paladín de las virtudes de la provincia ingenua y sin artificio frente a la capital "ojerosa y pintada"— no fue aislado y "el provincialismo se expresó por boca de vates y novelistas, no de historiadores". Éstos, sin embargo, fueron alentados por Genaro Estrada, quien "impulsó los estudios históricos de tema regional, y sobre todo . . . los de carácter bibliográfico". "Varios de estos bibliógrafos estatales . . . se convirtieron, o, por lo menos, se confirmaron, como historiadores de la provincia". Sin embargo, "lo común fue el no obtener la ayuda y estímulos oficiales". Un buen número de libros —muchos de los cuales son casi folletos— se refieren a ciudades importantes. Aparecen dos nuevos enfoques: el etnohistórico y el histórico-artístico. "Se acrece" —asevera la ponencia— "el uso de las fuentes primarias, se hacen compilaciones de documentos a nivel regional y local, . . . cunde el uso de crónicas conventuales y memorias de conquistadores y pobladores de la época colonial". Muchas de esas obras se vaciaron en los viejos moldes y "en la manera de contar hubo pocos aciertos". Tuvieron "escasa acogida en su época y casi ninguna después".

Refiriéndose ahora al periodo "actual" observa Luis "que el nacionalismo es otro desde 1940 . . . y ve a la provincia con indiferencia". "La distancia entre lo provinciano y lo capitalino está en vías de desaparecer". "El provincialismo y el aldeanismo se han entibiado" y "la historiografía mayor se ha apartado de lo local". "La república de la historia tiene su asiento en la ciudad capital". "La gran mayoría (de los historiadores provincianos) está . . . al margen de las nuevas corrientes historiográficas". "Las historias de tema parroquial han aventajado en número a las de asunto regional. Va de salida la moda de hacer historias de los Estados . . . crece la cifra de libros que toman como asunto ciudades pequeñas y aún pueblos de escaso bulto y renombre". Muchos de estos historiadores localistas "han hecho avances notables por lo que mira al manejo de las fuentes históricas" y aunque no son profesionales, sus obras "ganan en vocación, en experiencia vital y, sobre todo, en cariño hacia su objeto de estudio". A pesar de ciertas deficiencias, "en muchos de estos historiadores locales están las aguas vivas".

Estamos de acuerdo, básicamente, con la atinada caracterización que, de los tres periodos —"porfírico", "revolucionario" y "actual"— bosqueja

Luis González y que hemos resumido, con sus propias palabras en los tres anteriores párrafos.

Convencidos de que, *sin buena historia regional y local, no puede haber buena historia nacional,* nos solidarizamos con sus recomendaciones, particularmente la relativa a la reanudación de los congresos de historia, los que, a partir del celebrado en Guanajuato en 1945, habían venido consagrando particular atención a la historia de regiones y Estados.

Además de las seis recomendaciones del ponente, proponemos otras tantas a continuación:

7. Que en cada capital de Estado y en otras poblaciones de importancia, se procure la fundación de juntas de geografía e historia locales, integradas por personas idóneas, conocedoras del ambiente geográfico en que viven y de los antecedentes históricos del lugar;

8. Que se procure la instalación adecuada de ciertos archivos locales importantes, y la catalogación de sus fondos documentales, mediante la colaboración de los gobiernos de los Estados o de las autoridades municipales con el Instituto Nacional de Antropología e Historia;

9. Que se introduzcan libros de lectura especiales para cada Estado, en que los temas sean, con preferencia, la geografía, la flora, la fauna, el folklore, la arqueología, la etnografía y la historia de la región, lo mismo que datos de carácter lingüístico y juicios sobre el valor de los productos artísticos regionales, revinculando por estos y otros medios a los habitantes con la región;

10. Que se promueva la creación de un instituto de Geografía e Historia Regionales, preferentemente dentro de la UNAM, con el apoyo de las universidades estatales y en colaboración con ellas. Tal instituto contaría con mapoteca, biblioteca, hemeroteca y archivo documental de micropelícula;

11. Que se pida a El Colegio de México auspicie la elaboración de una historia de la historiografía mexicana y dentro de ella se consagre atención a la historiografía regional y local;

12. Que se solicite a El Colegio de México encargue a persona, o personas idóneas, la elaboración de una bibliografía de la historia regional de México;

13. Que se recomiende a los gobiernos y universidades de los Estados patrocinen la publicación de bibliotecas de autores regionales, consistentes en series en las que se den a conocer o se reimpriman, obras importantes de historiografía regional.

COMMENTARY

HARRY BERNSTEIN

Many factors and forces of local expression and politics lend meaning and life to Mexican history and historiography. Some of these are of obvious ethnic cultural origin. Others, such as the cabildo, the corregidor, the bishop, and the Intendant are of obvious Hispanic provenience. The last of these Spanish-Mexican political import, the Intendancy, had a regional uniqueness and sectional influence over later political history which survived into the national era, in the rise of federalism, and was located within the states' rights sentiments of Valentín Gómez Farías, and even of Mariano Otero. The contribution of Edmundo O'Gorman to "geographic-territorial history" and the formation of the later Mexican states already discovered one effect of the Intendancy, who was both a local administrator and an imperial official. The territory which the Intendant tried to develop economically had always to be viewed as the spoke of the axle and wheel of Spanish Empire. To paraphrase Pierre Chaunu, the Intendant had always to look over his shoulder and watch the attitudes of Mexico City, Veracruz, Seville and Madrid.

Something ought to be said, briefly, about the educated and intellectual level of these intendants. On the whole, they were a non-noble elite, most of them were intelligent commoners. Perhaps we ought to look for a phrase like the "noblesse de la robe" to describe their values, the *letrados*, officials, aides, office staffs and others who worked for them. Those Intendants who came to colonial Mexico were products of the economic societies of Spain, and the generation of the Bourbon Reforms. In Mexico, as in Brazil, both the Iberian colonial systems entrusted their basic wealth and the administration of their overseas domains, to enlightened men of science, merchants, university graduates, experienced military, and others suitable to that age of "useful" (i.e. relevant) knowledge.

Many intendants and their staffs in Mexico (judging from the applications filled out and filed in the Ramo de Intendencia in Mexico's Archivo General de la Nación) were certainly forerunners of the "civil servant". Just by widening this single factor and comparing it with Brazil, it is surprising how many Intendants and their staffs were part of the literate elite scattered throughout both Ibero-American viceroyalties. What Humboldt said with admiration about the Intendant Amat of New Spain, has been said about the Intendant Camara of Brazil. The scientific-civilian library found in Guanajuato in 1802 can only be matched with that remarkable library of the Conde da Barca in Brazil in 1816. Many of the intendancy staffs brought their rich libraries with them and left them in America when they died. It is not far-fetched at all to suppose that when they got to their posts in the provinces and intendancies they always found a few Mexican creoles eager to talk with them about the new world being born in the Old World. Creole Mexico talked "shop", books, and about ideas and events in Paris and Philadelphia with this Hispanic elite. [1]

No one who has studied and handled the applications and certificates for intendancy jobs, found in the Ramo de Intendencia can any longer believe that everyone coming to Mexico from Spain was a *peruleiro* who made a lot of money, or a *gachupín* who could only put on airs. Although from the Intendant down these officeholders were not part of any large population migration, they nevertheless seeded Mexico's local places, cabildos, and larger regions with a civil service ability and the habit (good and bad) of keeping records and paper. This literacy, although done in excess in cases, also provided the subscribers for Alzate's *Gazeta de México*, as well as Humboldt's favorable opinions.

The movement of Western European men and ideas into Mexico, from the time of Father Kino, survived the expulsion of the Jesuits. The Intendancy officials were literary and conversational, and their enlightenment did something in the localities to replace the teaching void. Unfortunately, there is little or no written record of their advices, conversations, suggestions, and "spiritual" role.

Some Intendants, like Francisco Rendón of Oaxaca, did all they could in their home Intendancies, and even while visiting others, to promote and develop the local industry. They were good and faithful servants of the *Sociedades Económicas de Amigos del País* of Spain. In the little—known manuscript journal of Josiah Smith (father of the well-known Hispanist

---

[1] A little comparative historiography, on the French and Spanish intendant systems, would be worth while here. The latest historical study, which also connects most closely the intendancy with the elite of the French Enlightenment is by Vivian R. Gruder, *The Royal Provincial Intendants. A Governing Elite in Eighteenth Century France*. Cornell University Press, Ithaca, New York, 1968. A marginal remark in this book refers to the Intendants as "little kings" of the ancien regime.

Two articles in the Spanish journal, *Revista de Indias*, are worth attention: Alain Viellard-Baron, "L'Intendant Americain et l'Intendant Français", *Revista de Indias*, año XI, enero-junio, 1951, N° 43-44, pp. 237-250, and Miguel Artola "Campillo y las Reformas de Carlos III", *Revista de Indias*, año XII, oct-dec. 1952, núm. 50, pp. 685-715.

In addition to John Lynch's administrative account of the intendancy of La Plata, and Lillian Fisher's overall Spanish American intendancy, two more useful studies should be cited. For a recente work on the entire intendant system, see Dra. Gisela Morazzini de Pérez Enciso, *La Intendencia en España y en América*. Caracas: 1966, with a lively introduction by E. Arcila Farías.

A model study of the scientis-Intendant, with basic documents and sources, is Marcos Carneiro de Mendoça, *O Intendente Camara. Manuel Fereira de Câmara Bethencourt e Sa, Intendente Geral das Minas e dos Diamantes, 1764-1835*. São Paulo. Companhia Editora Nacional, 1958. [Brasiliana series], volume 301.

Had Old Spain allowed Andres del Río to be an Intendant in New Spain, the comparison of the Hispano-Mexican scientist with the Luso-Brazilian would have been complete. So far as I have read no men of science became political administrators or Intendants in Mexico, or elsewhere in Spanish America. They had legally, administratively, economically or militarily-trained intendants as a rule.

Buckingham Smith), Josiah kept the journal or memorandum of his Journey from Veracruz to the City of Mexico.

Written in 1815-1816, Smith gives an account of the economic life of the Intendancy of Puebla. In addition the Smith notes give a glimpse of one of the Intendants of that day, the rather unique figure of Francisco Rendón. Already known to us from the Diary of Francisco de Miranda, the Venezuelan, and the several monographs on Spain and the American Revolution. Identified by Smith as the Intendant of Oaxaca, Rendon "who speaks English" seems to have been visiting Puebla when Smith arrived. He took him to meet the governor, and around the city. With Rendon, as his guide, Smith saw the development of Puebla's famous local manufactures:

> These of earthenware are carried to far greater perfection than I should suppose with the machinery which they have. It is very well shap'd and the patterns and colours are pretty ... all kinds of articles are made.

But Smith also found the prices "are high compar'd with English ware".

As to the other manufactures which the Intendant kept alive in Puebla, Smith described the woolen manufacture, cotton textiles, hats, saddlery, boots and shoes. What was most astonishing to him was the absence of tools in the many manufactories ("they have very few tools and no machinery"), with Indians providing the working force. The Intendants of New Spain were unable to bring in any Industrial Revolution, and the woolen looms were very clumsy. The Puebla wool prices, notwithstanding the cheap Indian labor, were as much as 250 to 300 percent higher than British machine-produced. He liked the green glass, which he compared in quality to the Dutch.

In this part of Mexico, a few years later, we also have the writings and the lobbying of Esteban Antuñano on the industry of Puebla, and the advance of manufactures there. The special place of Puebla was not only well served by the Intendancy there. The Spanish-Mexican consulados, between Veracruz and Mexico City, maintained the Camino Real. It was not only Josiah Smith who praised the road as "deserving as much praise as any in the whole of Christendom". Soldiers, mule harriers, and convoys of teamsters were part of the throng which took Josiah Smith to Mexico City. This artery, which linked the commerce of the Atlantic seaboard with Mexico City almost guaranteed that the middleman-merchant interest of those intendancies would dominate over the infant and undeveloped manufactures of Puebla, no matter how Antuñano argued later. [2]

If this was the politically and economically important route of Mexican history, from the beginning, other observers preferred to draw attention

[2] Jesús Reyes Heroles, "El Caso Antuñano", *Historia Mexicana*, XI, oct.-dec. 1961, núm. 2, pp. 246-262, as well as his 3 volume work on Mexican liberalism; Pierre Chaunu, "Veracruz en la Segunda Mitad del Siglo XVI y Primera del XVII", *Historia Mexicana*, IX, abril-junio 1960, pp. 521-557. Chaunu streesses the importance of the same highway that held together the commercial capitalism of the 16th century that Josiah Smith travelled in the early 19th century. It must have been very importante, and well kept and guarded.

to the important of the North region of Mexico. The Bishop of Durango in 1765, like Henry Ward later on in 1827, favored the wealth, character, and customs of the *provincias internas* and Durango. As Powell and Dusenberry have indicated in recent historical writing the Iberian influences on mining and ranching were much greater than in commerce or in manufactures. Mesta practices and the *minería* prevailed from Coahuila up to Texas. The Intendants there did little to harm the vast ranching properties of the Aguayos, whose records are in the Sánchez Navarro collection at the University of Texas. [3] It took the generation after independence for the advocates of more industry in those northern regions of Mexico to take up the theme of protective tariffs. As in Puebla, at about the same time, northern voices spoke out for industry and manufactures, in addition to mining and ranching. One of them was the noted Mexican historian and bibliographer, José F. Ramírez, native to the region but a national figure just the same.

Long after the Intendancy had come and gone, the local natural resources like the political powers, had come under both the economic and political controls of Mexico City. [4]

In fact the Intendancy had more direction over local and regional economic and fiscal growth than the later Mexican federal states had. The *Museo Mexicano* of 1843, the later *Museo Nacional*, as well as the *Noticias Estadísticas* of many writers, and even of comisiones de hacienda in the national Congress, reveal the political process and shift in this matter. But 19th century historians were slow to find out, and in the Díaz Era (1892) one individual still protested against the 19th century historians who scorned the regional studies and ignored the important history which the Mexican provinces and states had made. By a coincidence of chronology, almost 100 years before (about 1792) an Intendant had argued right up to the level of the Viceroy for the greater autonomy, local control and local use, of the vast silver riches of Zacatecas. He asserted his own responsibility to the "intendancy in his charge", and in my opinion, was far more courageous politically for local rights than many a state governor during the later federal period. [5]

[3] Gloria Grajales, *Guía de Documentos para la Historia de México existentes en la Public Record Office de Londres* (1827-1830). Comisión de Historia del Instituto Panamericano de Geografía e Historia. Comité Interamericano de Archivos, Publicación núm. 5. México: Editorial Fournier, 1967, citing F. O. 50/42 (1828), item N° 77: ff. 85-86, 302, 306, and "Respecto de la Compra de la Propiedad del Marqués de San Miguel de Aguayo, en el Estado de Texas y Coahuila por la Cía. Baring en 1825", p. 8.

[4] On the matter of the Intendancy and the local cabildo, see the essays in Nettie Lee Benson, ed. *Mexico and the Spanish Cortes, 1810-1822*. Latin American Monographs, núm. 5. University of Texas, Institute of Latin American Studies, Austin, 1966. Of the 8 essays by these graduate students which deal with the intendancy and the decline of the ayuntamientos and cabildos, the most pointed is R. L. Cunnif, "Mexican Municipal Electoral Reform, 1810-1822", pp. 59-86.

[5] The instructions of the Viceroy Garibay (1809) to provide elections of deputies to the Cortes of Cadiz opened up arguments between those who favored election by ayuntamiento and the Viceroy "who called for the elections to be held

The three Mexican monarchies of the 19th century (Spain, Iturbide, Maximilian) were different in the ways in which they tried to balance Mexico's interior parts with the center. The Spanish Intendant seems to me to provide more locally helpful recognition. They had little chance to make use of their military talents. Their expertise lay mainly in administrative, economic and related roles. But they could also talk about Jovellanos, Campomanes, Yriarte, Voltaire, even Franklin. Some of them, as we have seen, and Humboldt noted in Guanajuato, brought *buen gusto* to their regions, probably adding a touch of salon to the intendancy capitals. In sum, they brought with them an enlightened elite and an educated civil force to the capitals, alongside the creole society of the cabildos. Through them, the new Spain of the Bourbons, Basques and Castilian regalism fitted the Mexican New Spain to creole independence of mind, but did not completely fit the parts to the center.

On the other hand the intendancy records show very well how the plural intendancies kept their controls over the civic liberties of the creole cabildos. Their bigger influence upon future history of Mexico was the emergence of the states from the territorial boundaries and the very names of the 12 original intendancies. Of course it is not enough to merely recite the similarity of the names of the intendancies with those of many states. The facts of history, interest, protest and federalism created local counter-pressures which altered political boundaries and names. Localism became freed within former intendancies so that one or more new states were carved from the one intendancy. Moreover, without shrinking the shadow of the intendancy over the states, it is also quite necessary to make room in this explanation for the popular forces, the ethnic elements, and even the individual biography of important Mexicans to bring all the factors into the story. Some of these in fact show contradictions, and indicate that men of many regions and even remote localities were the very ones who sustained political centralism and nationalism. In the biography of Matías Romero, later in the 19th century, and indeed in the lives and politics of the so-called "Oaxaca Dynasty", from Juárez to Díaz or the

in each capital of an intendancy". Nettie Lee Benson, ed. and trans. "A Governor's Report on Texas in 1809", 58, Offprint Series, Institute of Latin American Studies, Austin, 1968, reprinted from Southwestern Historical Quarterly, LXXXI, núm. 4, April, 1968, p. 607.

The political position of the intendants, and the recommendations of the Viceroy of New Spain (acting) opens on to the suggestion that the Intendants, who had centralized the local cabildo, Indian villages, local funds, wage-labor, road-building, and administration under his own power, put these elements under Mexico City, and then under Seville and Madrid. While without the Intendancy there would be no Mexican state, and only incomplete urban and community studies, it is equally worth suggesting that the Intendancy nurtured within the Spanish Empire what might have become a commonwealth or dominion idea, working with creoles who would be political equal to Iberians. Certinly the Intendants, if not enemies of audiencia judges and the Viceroy's, were not as "tory". The Intendancy system seems to have elements which might have forestalled nationalism and Independence, while keeping trade, mining, and politics within the empire.

"Sonora Dynasty" from Corral to Calles, we can see the region blended into, and even lost, within Mexico's nationalism.

Nevertheless, what is meant is that national growth moved as a graduation from the unit to the whole, and not as either a romantic-doctrinaire nationalism, or one held by a core of logic. As Torres Bodet, in his first Ministry of Education, pointed out rather aptly the first cultural experience after the family was the local environment, the town, and the region, then the state, and then the nation. If education were close to history, it would then follow that path and, like history, move to the national and the international. In this process of development both the intendancy at the beginning of nationhood, and *indigenismo* in more recent days have given meaning to Mexican events and aims.

The intendancy, as name and fact, continued into the Iturbide years, even if Iturbide dropped the name, but kept the local divisions under the names of "provinces". Just as the intendant dropped the office of "corregidor", Iturbide ended the *partido*. The political-provincial geagraphy and territorial outline was about the same as the intendancy. The evolution of the states, territories, "Distrito Federal", departements, prefectures, well reflect the political talk and the historical effect of all these local forces [6] But that was only one aspect of the political legacy. There was another. It may be that the intendants brought with them libraries, an awareness of the Age of Enlightenment, and a commitment to some sort of economic and administrative change. But they continued to charge a political price for this. The intendancy system perpetuated local and regional ignorance of the art and practice of politics. Only a few creoles took part in the modernization of the Mexican mind; fewer still took part in the political process.

The ups-and-downs of the localities and regions, especially when the time came for representative government, revealed that an inexperience in politics, compared with Mexico City, was another legacy from the Intendancy. Confusion, vacillation, and ignorance of tactics, undermined the

[6] Two historians, Edmundo O'Gorman today, and Orozco y Berra in the 19th century, have combined history and geography to trace and depict the century of regional political division and subdivision since the creation of the 12 intendancies. See also the essays by Howard Cline and Peter Gerhard in the forthcoming Handbook of Middle American Ethnology, dealing with intendancies, municipios and community plus regional roots.

In his essay on New Spain Humboldt mapped the original intendancies, while their outlines are given by O'Gorman and by Navarro García (1964). Cline (figure 23) has superimposed Humboldt's map of the intendancies upon modern Mexican states to show the derivation and connection.

Compared with the Humboldt map of 1811, the map numbered 1306 and called "Carta General de la Nueva España dividida en intendencias como era en 1810, República Mexicana, 1849", lays down some new outlines. It is in the Orozco y Berra Collection or Mapoteca, in the Dirección de Geografía, Meteorología e Hidrología, at Tacubaya, México. Most outlines of the intendancies would have to start with the map by Dr. Carlos de Urrutia, made for the second Viceroy Conde de Revillagigedo, and approved by Miguel Constansó in 1793, which is numbered 1061 in the mapoteca "Catálogo de los Planes de la Colección de Orozco y Berra".

effectiveness of municipio and states' rights power, even if they did produce great political leaders and many talents. José María Bocanegra tells the story very well in his *Memorias para la Historia de México Independiente, 1822-1846:* [7]

> Preciso es de confesar que los diputados de las provincias fuimos [Bocanegra was elected from Zacatecas as one of the 25 from Aguascalientes] víctimas de nuestra inexperiencia y falta de conocimiento en la táctica de la asamblea [of 1821-2]. Lo cierto es que tampoco los contrarios eran hombres muy versados en la táctica de los cuerpos legislativos; pero tenían dos ventajas sobre los de las provincias: primera, su mayor facilidad para dirigir y lograr las maniobras y trabajos, como que su residencia en México y sus viages a Europa les habían dado y daban práctica, y más conocimiento del mundo; y segunda, la combinación y acuerdos directivos de sus logias.

That the very same politically backward provinces could also produce clear political talent, on a different level however, can be seen from the parallel fact that Valentín Gómez Farías was elected with Bocanegra to the same Congress of 1821. There were provincial political brains, but no grass-roots political life.

Bocanegra was explicit in making clear, in his *Carta de Un Payo a un Mexicano*, that local life, provincialism in customs, and remoteness from the center of things should not lead to a provincialism of spirit because it wanted equality of representation in national government and politics with the sophisticated capital. He felt that a larger number of provincial deputies would protect the region from the influential few, and presumably would insure against the defects of inexperience and political ignorance. It is strange that he never raised the economic question of how much wealth Zacatecas (and other regions) produced for Mexico, and what political equality it should get in return. Bocanegra, who was also an elected member of the Zacatecas *Sociedad de Amigos del País* fought against the politically harmful effects of the lack of unity among the separate provinces (for that matter, so did Iturbide at the end, in 1824), but the province of the state never attained the singleness of direction and administrative direction that the larger entity of region-Intendancy possessed. Feuds, rivalry and internal disunity added to the separateness of the states under the federal system. Mexico City prevailed. Bocanegra blamed the federal system for a great deal. He blamed it for the ruin of Chihuahua. Greed and indolence in the capital prevented help to Chihuahua from the wild Indian tribes; Chihuahuans grew to hate Mexico. Many in the North became angry at the alientation of mineral resources, and especially of lands which were "quickly honey for speculators in land". Guanajuato remained aloof, and he accused its upper classes of being tied to the Spaniards, even after the expulsion laws. "Nowhere in Mexico have peninsular ideas such a hold" (II, 396). Guanajuato's rich governor was not interested in representative government, and saw only a phantom in Federalism.

[7] Edición oficial dirigida por J. M. Vigil, 2 tomos, México: Imprenta del Gobierno Federal, 1892-1897, I, 39.

They already knew that many of the changes and revolutions of the central states had little effect upon the outer departments, wrote Bocanegra. [8] There were others however, who saw matters in the language and self-interest of economics. When Mariano Otero wrote a short biography of F. Gamboa, another native of Jalisco (1717-1794) he added accusations against Mexico's monopoly of the coinage of the silver and the consequent effect on the economy of the regions. He was especially concerned with the producers of Guanajuato, Zacatecas, Chihuahua, Sonora. Prices were high in the interior regions; there were no competitive ports for shipment or for import. Otero used an 18th century life to report the same thing existing in his own day: [9]

> In the interior all articles were very high and circulation of money so scarce that Sr. Gamboa mentions the fact that money to pay salaries of the Guadalajara audiencia had several times to be sent from Mexico. We may calculate what influence this one privilege of the capital exercised upon the population, industry, and wealth of the republic.

Nationalism, when it became secure, changed both the positive and negative side of the intendancy heritage. The creation of the states and of representative government, and the rise of strong political figures provided both force and political power. Although both Juárez and Díaz governed Mexico basically as a single national state, they were not able to go too far or too fast. The era of the restored republic and of Díaz heard many regional voices and negotiated many local problems. There were indeed many Mexicos outside of Mexico City and Veracruz, and they began to be heard through Tampico, Monterrey, Jalisco, Yucatán, Sonora and other local places. [10]

If the basic aim of Jalisco was for railways, or that of Tampico for modern port works, the issue of the tariff marks the economic face of regionalism for other states and regions. There were many other issues to identify the cause and to supply a shape and a name. Some dealth with education, and with the state university. Recent claims point to need for dams, roads, and local agrarian needs. Regionalism has many roots in history, although few in historiography. There are too many social, ethnic and cultural elements in Mexican nationality to see the parts that are too

[8] Political events did not send strong shock waves into the interior. It may be that the contemporary hydrographic and hydroelectric regionalism, with dams, roads, population, and industry may hit deeper local roots, in spite of the government one-party system.

[9] *Museo Mexicano*, t. II (1844), Mariano Otero, "Apuntes para la Biografía de Francisco Xavier Gamboa", pp. 53-64.

[10] Emperor Maximilian could never carry out his full intention of visiting the provinces. Therefore the official government journal of the Department of Jalisco, tomo I, Sept. 1864, reminded him in an editorial:

"Jalisco has always been, as a considerable part of Nueva Galicia, or as a state, or as a Department, one of the most important parts of Mexican territory. The gifts which God has given us, the fertility of our soil, the abundance of all the elements of our prosperity, the physical and geographical location of our lands, have given Jalisco a high importance in the destiny of the whole nation".

far from the center. The exceptions to this enter history when the local leaders became great national figures. Historical biography notices this, and this brief commentary has passingly drawn attention to the Oaxaca an Sonora groups. But the first figures to provide recognizable local interest and accent were the intendants, and the intendancy was the first institution to provide an agency. Although they in turn were loyal servants of Spain-in-Mexico, the intendants gave outline, if not impulse, to what was to become Mexico. Even when viewed so briefly here, the Spanish contribution was not all bad for Mexico's growth.

RELATORÍA

ELSA MALVIDO

Los participantes estuvieron de acuerdo con lo dicho por el ponente; exhibieron las virtudes de la historiografía regional y local, y manifestaron su asombro ante el poco uso que hacen de ella los historiadores ocupados en la historia nacional de México. Coincidieron en la necesidad de poner en marcha los puntos propuestos por el ponente y por el comentarista Wigberto Jiménez Moreno. Se habló de las instituciones que podrían patrocinar la formación de historiadores especializados en historia local, las reuniones periódicas de cronistas lugareños, la confección de una bibliografía, etcétera.

Para concluir, los participantes estuvieron de acuerdo en organizar una agrupación de historiadores y cronistas que cultiven la micro-historia profesionalmente con el fin de procurar ampliar y mejorar el género.

VI. HISTORIOGRAFÍA BIOGRÁFICA

"The Status of Biography in Mexican Historiography".
Hugh M. Mamill Jr.

COMENTARIOS

Arturo Arnáiz y Freg
Frank A. Knapp Jr.

RELATORÍA

Julia Tuñón de Muriá

Presidente: Stanley R. Ross, director del Instituto de Estudios Latinoamericanos, Universidad de Texas.

Ponente: Hugh Hamill, profesor asociado de historia, Universidad de Connecticut.

Comentaristas: Arturo Arnáiz y Freg, Academia Mexicana de la Historia; Frank Knapp, profesor de historia y ciencia política.

Participantes: Lowell Blaisdell, profesor de historia, Texas Technological College; Clementina Díaz y de Ovando, directora del Instituto de Investigaciones Estéticas, UNAM; Tarsicio García Díaz, director del Colegio de Historia, Universidad Iberoamericana; Richard Greenleaf, profesor de Historia, Universidad de Tulane; Rosaura Hernández, investigadora del Instituto de Historia, UNAM; Michael Meyer, profesor asistente de historia, Universidad de Nebraska; Josefina Muriel de González Mariscal, investigadora del Instituto de Historia, UNAM; Jorge Ignacio Rubio Mañé, director del Archivo General de la Nación; Donald Chipman, profesor de Historia, North Texas State University, John Street, miembro del Fitzwilliam College, Cambridge y director del Center of Latin American Studies.

Relator: Julia Tuñón de Muriá, profesora de la Universidad de Guadalajara.

THE STATUS OF BIOGRAPHY
IN MEXICAN HISTORIOGRAPHY

HUGH M. HAMILL JR.

I. INTRODUCTION: WHERE HAVE ALL THE SCHOLARS GONE?

Hundreds upon hundreds of biographies crowd the libraries, book stalls and uncritical bibliographies which specialize in Mexican history yet it is unlikely that a responsible list of the ten most significant contributions to historiography will give published lives of Mexico's historical figures a prominent place. This relative scarcity of distinguished works about individuals is not unique to Mexican historiography. In his germinal study of the genre, John Garraty has commented that "for a literary form with a long history, biography has produced fewer recognized masterpieces than any other type of writing..."[1] Nevertheless, the absence of many first rate biographies of Mexicans is curious in a society where personalist leadership has played such an important role.

The reasons for this phenomenon, especially in recent scholarship, have something to do with the growing vogue of the behavioral sciences on the one hand and the sustained emphasis on the history of impersonal institutions, revolutions and causes on the other. Even works which are touted as biographies are more properly classified in other ways. John Womack's admirable and exhaustive treatise on the agrarian revolt in Morelos might better have been entitled *Zapatismo and the Mexican Revolution,* for Emiliano Zapata himself emerges almost incidental to the movement.[2]

It is the special demands of biographical research and writing which are, however, principally to blame for the shortage of first rate biographies of Mexicans. The first problem has to do with the biographer's critical response to his subject. Truth must be his touchstone but, as in the assessment of anyone with whom we have intimate contact, it is the qualities of personality which are most difficult to describe and assess. The love-hate relationship that frequently develops between scholar and historical figure must be unsnarled through dispassionate self-criticism at the time of writing and editing. Research into impersonal institutions requires special skills, detachment and restraint but the

---

[1] John A. Garraty, *The Nature of Biography* (New York, 1957).
[2] John Womack, Jr., *Zapata and the Mexican Revolution* (New York, 1969).

temptation to fall into the gulf of polemical writing has often fatal
attractions for the biographer. Moreover, good biography requires the
most severe literary discipline of all historiographical writing. Writers
of fiction often preëmpt the place of the professional schalor because
they are more adept at revealing personality. Were Carlos Fuentes
to write *La muerte de Álvaro Obregón* after four years of training in
the canons of historical scholarship the result might well be epic!
Conversely, historians might learn much about how to treat the subtle
contours of personality from novelists before attempting biography.
Nor has any Mexican personage yet received the probing attention of
the historian trained in psychological techniques. Erik H. Erikson's
Young Man Luther: a Study in Psychoanalysis and History suggests
perspectives which should be carefully considered by Mexicanists. [3]

The biographical approach to Mexican historiography is plagued
by one other condition that is not necessarily shared among historians
involved with impersonal studies. This is, of course, the matter of
source materials. It has not been easy, especially for the non-Mexican
scholar, to gain access to family archives and the private papers of
important public figures, nor is there a well founded tradition of donat-
ing private collections of manuscripts to public archives where they
may be freely consulted. There are certainly many exceptions to this
but the condition remains. The result has been that many would-be
biographers have not taken the trouble to search beyond available
public records and published materials, and have relied upon secondary
testimonials and autobiographies for those insights into personality
which can project a three dimensional subject into two dimensional
print. The determination with which Edmundo O'Gorman and his
students in the Centro de Estudios de Historia de México have
approached the preliminary biographical study of Carlos María de Bustamante is one of several indications, however, that the matter of source
availability is being systematically attacked. [4]

For recent history, it should be remarked that there is an important
new development in the oral history techniques developed by James
Wilkie, among others. Taped interviews, if properly handled, can
provide biographers with a wealth of organized personal recollections
of profund importance. [5]

[3] (New York, 1958).
[4] Edmundo O'Gorman, *Guía bibliográfica de Carlos María de Bustamante*
(México, 1967).
[5] James W. Wilkie and Edna Monzón de Wilkie, comps., *México visto en el
siglo XX: entrevistas de historia oral: Ramón Beteta, Marte R. Gómez, Manuel
Gómez Morín, Vicente Lombardo Toledano, Miguel Palomar y Vizcarra, Emilio
Portes Gil, Jesús Silva Herzog* (México, 1969).

II. PURPOSE

Given that biography is a difficult genre and that it has proportionately less appeal for the serious scholar (and a proportionately greater appeal for the polemicist —the hero worshipper and the debunker) the task of assessing the status of Mexican biographical writing remains. Surely the vehicle of biography is a worthy one and it is the purpose of this paper to encourage the publication of new and imaginative lives of notable Mexicans. Such encouragement may result if the bulk of this paper devotes critical attention to recent works, indicates some research already in progress, and reveals tempting lacunae.

A secondary goal is to encourage those who are engaged in bibliographical work to make discrete identification of biographies in separate sections in future publications. My own task in preparing this paper would have been far easier if I had had a critical and well organized bibliography of biographies for the years from 1960 to 1968 to complement the section on biography in Luis González y González, *et al.,* *Fuentes de la historia contemporánea de México: Libros y folletos.* [6] In spite of its many admirable qualities, the new periodical *Bibliografía Histórica Mexicana* has no section on biography. Such an innovation would provide a useful cross-reference tool. [7]

III. LIMITS

Although a concentrated search for biographies preceded the composition of this paper, there is no intent to make exhaustive reference to all published lives of all Mexicans. My focus has been narrowed to those biographies written with scholarly intent and methodology about Mexican figures involved in public affairs and social questions between 1800 and 1940. To achieve the purpose described earlier I have emphasized studies completed and in progress during the 1960's. Where especially significant but older books about prominent individuals stand out and have not been superseded, I have tried to mention them.

This focus has meant the exclusion of some forms which are sometimes loosely gathered under the rubric of "biography". Autobiography and the memoire are not treated on the grounds that they are really primary sources which historical biographers must relate to the rest of a man's record. Collected testimonials in honor of an individual,

[6] (México, 1961-62), I, 184-232.
[7] (México, 1967).

whether during or after his lifetime, may be useful for the students of hagiography but they seldom serve as valid biography. Likewise, polemical lives of the great and the ungrateful have been excluded. Scholarly articles in journals are also not covered in this paper because their scope is most often restricted to a single phase or episode in a man's career. The best of these, anyway, are usually sample chapters from subsequently published full-scale biographies brought out to pad personal bibliographies in the time honored fashion of academic gamesmanship. I have in such cases mentioned only the final book length study. Foreigners whose careers included involvement in Mexican affairs have not been treated on the grounds that their lives belong to the historiography of the country of origin. As the literal minded reader will perceive, however, this rule has not been strictly followed for I will discuss the lives of certain Europeans like Iturrigaray and Maximilian. There is no great consistency in my inclusion of artists, men of letters and scientists although an attempt has been made to discuss biographies of those who were also involved in public affairs. As for collective biographies like that of Villaseñor y Villaseñor and *Los gobernantes de México* by Manuel García Purón, they have no place in this discussion. [8] The urge to beg for a monumental dictionary of Mexican national biography, however, cannot be surpressed. Such an undertaking by a group of scholars would be warmly received by all students of Mexican history.

IV. BIOGRAPHIES ASSESSED: 1800-1940

Attention paid by biographers to historical figures for any given period is roughly comparable in volume to that assigned to other facets of historiography. A statistical study might demonstrate, however, that Independence, the Era of Reform and Intervention, and the Revolution of 1910 have drawn an even higher proportion of biographies. These were times of crisis in which chance and the breakdown of institutions propelled an abundance of military and personalist leaders into prominence. Ambitious and talented men who came to maturity on the eve of these crises had opportunities to win praise, eternal damnation or scholarly attention that was denied men who were born to less critical ages. Stephen Vincent Benet once indulged in a bit of whimsy when he arbitrarily set Napoleon's birthday back some thirty years. The crusty soldier, whose brain teemed with elaborate military campaigns,

[8] Alejandro Villaseñor y Villaseñor, *Biografías de los héroes y caudillos de la independencia*, 2 vol. (México, 1962); Manuel García Purón, *México y sus gobernantes: biografías* (México, 1964).

was too old to capitalize on the coming French Revolution and died a frustrated major of artillery in 1789. [9]

A. Independence

It is not a surprise, then, that the years from 1800 to 1821 continue to attract biographers. The 150th anniversary of the Grito de Dolores in 1960 was a stimulus and one can hope that the final triumph of the Army of the Three Guarantees will be similarly noted in 1971 by new lives of Iturbide and Guerrero. It is also no surprise that recent scholarship has focused on insurgent leaders rather than their enemies. Lives of Hidalgo and Morelos continue to dominate. Castillo Ledón's two volume biography of Hidalgo remains the fullest treatment of the Cura of Dolores despite its uncritical methodology and unabashed hero worship. [10] My own work on the rebellion of 1810 began as a biography but developed into a history of the movement itself. [11] A sensitive full dress treatment of this complicated and misunderstood priest is very much needed but it will require the discovery of a fresh lode of source materials by and about Hidalgo. Morelos has drawn the attention of at least five biographers in the 1960's but only Ernesto Lemoine Villicaña and Wilbert H. Timmons have approached him with scholarly intent. Lemoine bolstered his succinct sketch of Morelos' life with a wealth of documents and Timmons has produced a balanced life in English. [12] Other insurgents who have been studied recently are Allende, López Rayón and Matamoros. [13] Except for a study in progress of Tadeo Ortiz by W. H. Timmons it appears that no new critical biographies of promoters of independence will appear in the immediate future. [14]

What is most reprehensible, however, is not that we are without

[9] "The Curfew Tolls", in S. V. Benet, *Selected Works: Prose* (New York, 1942), pp. 383-98.

[10] Luis Castillo Ledón, *Hidalgo: la vida del héroe*, 2 vol. (México, 1948-49).

[11] Hugh M. Hamill, Jr. *The Hidalgo Revolt: Prelude to Mexican Independence* (Gainesville, 1966).

[12] Ernesto Lemoine Villicaña, *Morelos: Su vida revolucionaria a través de sus escritos y de otros testimonios de la época* (México, 1965); Wilbert H. Timmons, *Morelos of Mexico: Priest, Soldier, Statesman* (El Paso, 1963).

[13] Armando de María y Campos, *Allende: Primer soldado de la nación* (México, 1964); A. María y Campos, *Matamoros: Teniente general insurgente* (México, 1964); Luciano Alexanderson Joublanc, *Ignacio López Rayón: Libertador, unificador y primer legislador de México* (México, 1963). None of these reveals suficiente scholarly objectivity to be considered of major importance.

[14] Wilbert H. Timmons, "Tadeo Ortiz: Mexican Economist and Colonizer", Research in progress. See *Latin American Research Review*, II (1967), hereafter cited as *LARR*. The last number corresponds to research inventory, not to page.

the needed wave of definitive and balanced lives of the *insurgentes*
but that the other side, the royalists and defenders of the Establishment, have been so utterly neglected. Abad y Queipo, the Bishop-elect
of Michoacán who excommunicated his old friend Hidalgo, has been
routinely treated,[15] but only by casting Iturbide up as a "defender
of the status quo" is it possible to find another figure who fought
against the insurgents most of his career and who has been adequately
studied. Even in his case, I am not convinced that William Spence
Robertson has delved as thoroughly as desirable into Iturbide's life
before his victory in September 1821.[16] The sage comment made by
Ernesto de la Torre Villar in his brief assessment of a book about
Miramón, el caudillo conservador applies to Independence as well as
to the Reform era:

> Este libro, hecho con simpatía, con conocimiento, llena una laguna
> dentro de la historia mexicana. Es de desearse que los historiadores se
> atrevan a ocuparse de esos hombres que también han hecho la historia
> mexicana, sin mostrarse vergonzantes, y sin injuriar a sus enemigos.
> Sánchez Navarro [the author] superó estas dificultades y su biografía
> es valiosa por su postura serena y sincera.[17]

There are certainly many figures who "have also made Mexican history"
during the years which ended in political emancipation. The viceroys,
for example, have been avoided by scholars everywhere. To be sure,
Iturrigaray has been thoroughly examined by Enrique Lafuente Ferrari,
but the documentation is limited to non-Mexican archives.[18] Besides,
Iturrigaray's flirtation with criolloism before his ouster in Yermo's coup
is sufficient to cast him on the side of nationalist righteousness. The
others, however, await serious examination. It is too much to expect
that Pedro Garibay and Lizana y Beaumont deserve extensive book
length studies, although the latter, tool that he may have been, is a
figure whose life might reveal much about the clerical hierarchy and
the social and political undercurrents of New Spain in the decade
before the Grito de Dolores.

Francisco Javier de Venegas has been written off in curt phrases
as an irascible lecher, but a study of his term as viceroy (1810-1813)
—if not a full fledged life— would reveal that Venegas was a vigorous
and capable leader who may have done more than any other figure

---

[15] Lillian E. Fisher, *Champion of Reform: Manuel Abad y Queipo* (New York,
1955).

[16] William S. Robertson, *Iturbide of Mexico* (Durham, 1952).

[17] E. de la Torre V. and Arturo Gómez Camacho, "La intervención francesa",
Historia Mexicana, xv (1965-66), 607-08.

[18] E. La fuente Ferrari, *El Virrey Iturrigaray y los orígenes de la independencia de Méjico* (Madrid, 1941).

including Calleja to contain the rebellion. Félix María Calleja himself deserves a dispassionate biography. The scholar who attempts a balanced life of Calleja will be able to explore the career of a peninsular who spent more than a quarter century in New Spain; who developed criollo attitudes, family ties and landed property; who was ambivalent toward independence and who developed an extraordinary capacity to frustrate the insurgent cause. Neither C. M. de Bustamante's *Campañas de Calleja*... nor the life of Calleja's wife by Núñez y Domínguez fulfill this need. [19] Juan Ruiz de Apodaca, who took over as viceroy from Calleja in 1816, served through five years of relative serenity... years which have been little studied by historians. Apodaca's life would provide an appropriate lever to enter Mexican politics and to understand the subtleties of restored Bourbon rule. But no one has assayed this delicate task. Lesser figures, too, deserve more attention than they have received but the lack of work at the viceregal level is sufficient to indicate the dimensions of the problem.

B. *The Early Republic*

If we accept that peak interest in individuals conforms to the major crises in Mexican history (Independence, the Reform, the Revolution of 1910) it is no surprise to discover that the years from 1821-1854, which encompass a most significant generation, have attracted much less attention from biographers. I hold this to be understandable... but not good.

To be sure, there is some indication of research in progress which is heartening. Carlos María de Bustamante should be well served by Edmundo O'Gorman and Valentín Gómez Farías has a new biographer in C. A. Hutchinson. [20] Earlier appraisals of Lucas Alamán and his ideology by Arturo Arnáiz y Freg and Moisés González Navarro may be complemented by Stanley C. Green's current investigation. [21] David Brading and Ward M. Morton have research projects into the life and thought of Fray Servando Teresa de Mier; these woul be in addition to Alfonso Junco's *El increíble Fray Servando*. [22] But beyond research

[19] Carlos María de Bustamante, *Campañas del General D. Félix María Calleja*... (México, 1828); José de Núñez y Domínguez, *La virreina mexicana*: Doña María Francisca de la Gándara de Calleja (México, 1950).

[20] On Bustamante, see p. 3 above; C. A. Hutchinson, "Valentín Gómez Farías: a Biography", Research in Progress, See LARR, II (1966), 346.

[21] A. Arnáiz y Freg, *Lucas Alamán* (México, 1939); M. González Navarro, *El pensamiento político de Lucas Alamán* (México, 1952); S. G. Green, "Lucas Alamán", Ph. D. Disertation, In Progress, Texas Christian University.

[22] D. A. Brading, "The Ideology of Mexican Independence: an essay devoted to the life and thought of Fray Servando Teresa de Mier (1763-1827) ...",

completed on the life of Miguel Ramos Arizpe by the ubiquitous Lillian Estelle Fisher, I find very little more to report by way of fresh studies. [23]

We are left then with a limited number of actual contributions in this decade. Fortunately, in the case of José María Luis Mora, the calibre is high. Charles Hale may argue that his work is a study of liberalism and not properly a traditional biography of Mora. Nevertheless, Mora has been so judiciously treated that the work will stand for a long time. [24] Guillermo Prieto, whose career carried over to the Porfiriato, has been the subject of several recent studies, most notably Malcolm McLean's well-balanced biography and Carlos J. Sierra's combined biography-anthology. [25]

There are, of course, older studies, completed before 1960, which have admirable and enduring qualities. Raymond Estep's life of Lorenzo de Zavala holds up well as does Thomas Cotner's traditional biography of José Joaquín Herrera. [26] Miguel A. Quintana has demonstrated in his two volume study of the entrepreneur Estevan de Antuñano that economic historians can find important subjects for biographical treatment. [27]

Curiously, some figures of greatest political prominence in the early republican history of Mexico have not been adequately examined. Both Vicente Guerrero and Guadalupe Victoria belong to the era of the wars for independence as well as to the 1820's and yet the responsible literature on them is slight. William Sprague's life of Guerrero lacks research in Mexican archives and is too short to be the penetrating study which is needed of a *guerrillero* caught in the broils of an unstable political environment. [28] Mexico's first republican president, Guadalupe Victoria, has also escaped exhaustive critical analysis. Antonio López de Santa Anna, whose name has been so often attached —for better or worse— to the period between independence and the Reforma, has

Research in Progress, See *LARR*, iii (1968), 838; W. M. Morton, "Biography of Fray Servando de Mier", Research in Progress, See *LARR*, ii (1967), 598; A. Junco, *El increíble Fray Servando: Psicología y epistolario* (México, 1959).

[23] L. E. Fisher, "Patriot and Constitution Maker: Miguel Ramos Arizpe", Research in Progress, See *LARR*, iii (1968), 973.

[24] Charles A. Hale, *Mexican Liberalism in the Age of Mora, 1821-1853* (New Haven, 1968).

[25] Malcolm D. McLean, *Vida y obra de Guillermo Prieto* (México, 1960); C. J. Sierra, *Guillermo Prieto* (México, 1962).

[26] R. Estep, *Lorenzo de Zavala: Profeta del liberalismo mexicano* (México, 1952); T. E. Cotner, *The Military and Political Career of José Joaquín de Herrera* (Austin, 1949).

[27] M. A. Quintana, *Estevan de Antuñano: Fundador de la industria textil en Puebla*, 2 vols. (México, 1957).

[28] W. F. Sprague, *Vicente Guerrero, Mexican Liberator: a Study in Patriotism* (Chicago, 1939).

been the subject of several responsible and important studies. Those by Rafael Felipe Muñoz, Carmen Flores Mena and, especially, José Fuentes Mares in Spanish and by Wilfred H. Callcott in English are best known. [29] None of these biographies, however, provide the definitive work on that complex man and his times nor does the recent contribution by Oakan L. Jones, Jr. [30]

Spotting lacunae among the biographies of significant Mexicans from the second quarter of the nineteenth century is a good deal easier than it should be. To give some examples, there is an absence of recent and effective lives of Andrés de Quintana Roo, Manuel Gómez Pedraza, Anastasio Bustamante, Mariano Paredes y Arrillaga, Mariano Otero, Manuel Peña y Peña, Mariano Arista and José María Gutiérrez de Estrada. It may well be that documentary resources are inadequate for one or more of these figures but they are significant actors who deserve serious evaluation. Some of them, in their careers as politicians, jurists, soldiers, ideologues and plotters, overlap earlier or later periods.

C. From Reform to Restoration

The mid-nineteenth-century Mexican Reform generation is a rich one for biographers. Although fascination with the heroes of the Revolution of Ayutla has produced a good harvest, there is still ample room for dedicated scholars. As with the wars for independence, the lacunae are much greater among the conservatives, the opponents of the 1857 Constitution, the monarchists and the francophile interventionists. This is not to say that their liberal opponents are universally revered in the existing biographical literature. The polemical attacks on Juárez are an obvious example. But it is clear that those who "have also made Mexican history" have received short shrift. Biographically inclined scholars can choose from a long list which includes Juan Almonte, José Manuel Hidalgo y Esnaurrízar, Leandro Márquez, Tomás Mejía and Félix Zuloaga among the diplomatic-military-political types and Bishops Pelagio Antonio de Labastida y Dávalos and Clemente de Jesús Munguía among the anti-Reform clergy. To be sure, as de la Torre has reminded us, the Sánchez Navarro biography of Miguel Miramón is a mature and measured study of one foe of the Reform, but it is

[29] R. F. Muñoz, *Santa Anna, el que todo lo ganó y todo lo perdió* (Madrid, 1936); Carmen Flores Mena, *El general don Antonio López de Santa Anna, 1810-1833* (México, 1950); J. Fuentes Mares, *Santa Anna: Aurora y ocaso de un comediante* (México, 1956); W. H. Callcott, *Santa Anna: the Story of an Enigma Who Once Was Mexico* (Norman, 1936). The latter has been reprinted: Hamden, Conn., 1964.

[30] O. L. Jones, Jr., *Santa Anna* (New York, 1968).

dificult to find others. [31] Santiago Vidaurri, the powerful boss of
Nuevo León who left the liberals to support Maximilian and faced a
firing squad for his mistake, is the subject of a study by Edward
Mosley. [32] The moderate Ignacio Comonfort, who sought to temporize
between irreconciliables, is also the subject of current research by Ray
F. Broussard. [33] This will supplement and extend the biographical
sketch of Comonfort in Rosaura Hernández Rodríguez' valuable documentary compilation. [34] Jesús González Ortega, another Reform commander who broke with Juárez over political succession, has been
studied by Eliseo Rangel Gaspar. [35]

Maximilian, the ultimate dupe, has, of course, attracted more
attention than any other exponent of a lost cause in Mexican history.
"Eventful hero" rather than "event maker", in Sidney Hook's terminology, Maximilian's romantic tragedy has stimulated biographers in
abundance. [36] Egon C. Corti's classic study has just been reissued in its
English version and one of the more compelling recent works is *Maximilien et Charlotte* by Suzanne Desternes and Henriette Chandet. [37]

Turning to the beneficiaries of the Ayutla revolution against Santa
Anna, the figure of Benito Juárez has attracted continous attention.
It may be, however, that "the definitive biography" of Juárez will
remain as illusive as the man and that any new biographer will be
drawn into the polemical world of hero worship or character assassination. This is not to say that there have been no good works on
Juárez and his times. There is certainly merit in the scholarly four
volumes which José Fuentes Mares produced in spite of his unconcealed
dislike of Juárez for his failure to support democratic principles. [38] Ralph
Roeder's older study and the more recent examination of Juárez by
Charles A. Smart err on the other side. [39] Roeder's ability to recreate

[31] Carlos Sánchez Navarro y Peón, *Miramón, el caudillo conservador* (México,
1945).

[32] E. H. Mosley, "Biography of Santiago Vidaurri", Research in Progress,
See *LARR*, ii (1967), 3.

[33] Ray F. Broussard, "Biography of Ignacio Comonfort", Research in Progress, See *LARR*, i (1965-66), 131.

[34] R. Hernández Rodríguez, *Ignacio Comonfort: Trayectoria política, Documentos* (México, 1967).

[35] E. Rangel Gaspar, *Jesús González Ortega: Caudillo de la Reforma* (México,
1960).

[36] Sidney Hook, *The Hero in History* (Boston, 1955), Ch. IX.

[37] E. C. Corti, *Maximilian and Charlotte of Mexico*, 2 vol. in 1 (Hamden,
Conn., 1968); S. Desternes and H. Chandet, *Maximilien et Charlotte* (Paris,
1964).

[38] *Juárez y los Estados Unidos* (México, 1964); *Juárez y la intervención* (México, 1962); *Juárez y el imperio* (México, 1963); *Juárez y la República* (México,
1965).

[39] R. Roeder. *Juárez and his Mexico*, 2 vol. (New York, 1947); C. A. Smart,
Viva Juárez! (Philadelphia, 1963).

the political and social *ambiente* of the Reform and the Intervention, however, have made the work durable in both English and Spanish editions. Not so Smart's *Viva Juárez!* which has been sharply and effectively criticized by Walter V. Scholes, among others, as infected by the "occupational disease for biographers: hero worship", an opinion I share. [40] Scholes' own admirable study of politics in the period, though not a biography, suggests that he or some other careful scholar should at least attempt the difficult task of an exhaustive balanced life of the Reform's most famous figure. [41] Will the *real* Benito Juárez please stand up?

Fortunately, some others in the Reform ranks have received adequate attention from biographers. A sensitive and carefully researched life of Melchor Ocampo was produced fifteen years ago by José Valadés. [42] Ocampo's complex and subtle mind, however, deserves more penetrating attention from another scholar. The journalistic and political career of Francisco Zarco has been placed in clear perspective by Óscar Castañeda Batres and Raymond C. Wheat. [43] Guillermo Prieto, another journalist, has already been discussed. Leandro Valle, the martyred poet, has been treated with compassion and scholarly restraint by Alfonso Teja Zabre. [44] The diplomat and treasury minister Matías Romero is among the bastions of the Reform who is only now being given the attention he deserves by Robert R. Miller and Harry Bernstein. [45]

Military men, as in other periods of crisis, have received a major share of attention. Juan Álvarez, the old soldier from the south, is the subject of a detailed but undigested biography, published ten years ago by Daniel Muñoz y Pérez. The documents gathered in the last two-thirds of the volume will be useful as a point of departure for a major life of Álvarez. [46] May 5, 1962, the centenary of the Battle of Puebla, occasioned the publication of at least four biographies of Ig-

[40] Review in *The Hispanic American Historical Review*, xlv (1965), 647-48.

[41] W. V. Scholes, *Mexican Politics During the Juárez Regime, 1855-1872* (Columbia, Mo., 1957). A paperback versión appeared in 1969.

[42] J. C. Valadés, *Don Melchor Ocampo: Refomador de México* (México, 1954).

[43] O. Castañeda Batres, *Francisco Zarco* (México, 1961); Castañeda Batres, *Francisco Zarco ante la intervención francesa y el imperio, 1863-1864* (México, 1958); R. C. Wheat, *Francisco Zarco: El portavoz liberal de la Reforma* (México, 1957).

[44] A. Teja Zabre, *Leandro Valle: Un liberal romántico* (México, 1956).

[45] R. R. Miller, "Matías Romero: Mexican Ambassador to the United States", Research in Progress, See *LARR*, i (1965), 133; H. Bernstein, "Matías Romero", Research in Progress, See *LARR*, ii (1966), 44.

[46] D. Muñoz y Pérez, *El General don Juan Álvarez: ensayo biográfico seguido de una selección de documentos* (México, 1959).

nacio Zaragoza. Those by Luis Ramírez Fentanes and Guillermo Colín
Sánchez are the most scholarly. [47]

Sebastián Lerdo de Tejada moves as a vital figure through the
critical twenty years from the early Reform to the Restored Repubilc.
Happily a fellow member of this session has resurrected the president
squeezed between Juárez and Díaz from the obscurity the mythologists
had designed for him. Frank Knapp's 1951 biography was translated
into Spanish ten years later and remains the only work of major
substance on Sebastián Lerdo and one of the most readable of balanced
biographies of nineteenth-century Mexicans. [48]

On the other hand, Sebastian's older brother, Miguel Lerdo de
Tejada, has been strangely neglected. Although typhus killed him during his effort to win the presidency in 1861, Miguel's dynamic career
in the Reform entitles him to the searching examination of an able
biographer. Another man for whom we have no first rate extensive biography is the orator Ignacio Altamirano. One of Robert Quirk's students
at Indiana, Charles A. Weeks, has, I believe, elected to do an exhaustive biography of Altamirano for his dissertation. Among the soldiers,
Santos Degollado, the successful loser, awaits a skillful hand. So, too,
does the more complicated Jesús González Ortega, who has so far
attracted only polemical or immature treatment. The broad panorama
of personalities at mid-century doubtless reveals others who are neglected
but these notes will serve to suggest where some opportunities lie.

D. The Porfiriato

Recent trends in general Mexican historiography demonstrate a
resurgence of interest in the decades of the Porfiriato *qua* Porfiriato.
In spite of the attraction of the Mexican Revolution and its origins,
the multiple volumes composed under Cosío Villegas' direction have
encouraged scholars to consider the years from 1876 to 1910 as worthy
of study in themselves. [49] No longer are they merely an opportunity to
categorize the *grandes problemas nacionales* which provoked the great
upheaval of 1910-1917. Unhappily this trend has had little discernible
effect upon the art of biography. The Porfiriato is another trough
between ridges of greater interest for biographers.

[47] L. Ramírez Fentanes, *Zaragoza* (México, 1962); G. Colín Sánchez, *Ignacio Zaragoza: Evocación de un héroe* (México, 1963).
[48] Frank A. Knapp, Jr. *The Life of Sebastián Lerdo de Tejada, 1823-1889:
a Study in Influence and Obscurity* (Austin, 1951). Spanish translation: Jalapa,
1961.
[49] Daniel Cosío Villegas, *et al. Historia moderna de México: El Porfiriato*, 4
vol. in 5 (México, 1957-65).

The problem appears even with respect to the dictator himself. Porfirio Díaz has attracted scores of polemicists, sycophants and detractors, but precious few scholarly biographers. Obviously the central figure for a third of a century, it is remarkable that there is as yet no biography which might excite the critics to exclaim "Definitive!" Jorge Fernando Iturribaria has made the most recent effort to assess Don Porfirio with reasonable objectivity. [50] Permitting the chips to fall where they might, Iturribaria neither condemns nor deifies his subject. His research is not as profound as it might be, but the work is commendable and better defined than the interesting but cumbersome two volume memoire of Agustín Aragón. [51] Both José C. Valadés and Daniel Cosío Villegas have produced older works which examine the years of Díaz ascendancy with a healthy mixture of serious scholarship and literary verve. *Porfirio Díaz y la revuelta de la Noria* has the special advantage of explaining Díaz in the years before 1876 when he was learning to make the transition from soldier to politician. Both studies are biographical fragments, however, and have not preëmpted the field from would-be Díaz biographers. [52]

Men whose careers belong primarily to the Porfiriato have been even less well served than Díaz. Where, for example, is a firts class biography for the 1960's and '70's of José Ives Limantour? Granted there is the 1922 life of Díaz' financial wizard by Carlos Díaz Dufoo but is it adequate to discourage a new attempt? [53] Manuel González was something more than a stooge who sat in for Díaz for four years as president. No probing biography exists which might illuminate the years from 1880 to 1884. And Ramón Corral, a heartbeat away from the presidency; where is a serious study of him? The members of Díaz' clique, and especially the *Científicos*, have simply not received the individual attention which would enrich our understanding of those individuals who bolstered the most durable of regimes. Another example is Justo Sierra, that most Olympian of public men in Porfirian Mexico. Sierra has never been approached by a scholar intent upon writing a thorough biography of the historian-educator-jurist. Agustín Yáñez has produced the best work on Sierra but, as Robert Potash wrote at the opening of this decade, it is "less a self-contained study than it is an encouragement to browse through the *Obras completas"*. [54]

[50] J. F. Iturribaria, *Porfirio Díaz ante la historia* (México, 1967).
[51] A. Aragón, *Porfirio Díaz: Estudio histórico-filosófico*, 2 vol. (México, 1962).
[52] D. Cosío Villegas, *Porfirio Díaz y la revuelta de la Noria* (México, 1953); J. C. Valadés. *El Porfirismo: Historia de un régimen: i. El nacimiento, 1876-1884* (México, 1941).
[53] C. Díaz Dufoo, *Limantour* (México, 1922).
[54] A. Yáñez, *Don Justo Sierra: Su vida, sus ideas y su obra* (México, 1950); R. A. Potash, "Historiography of Mexico Since 1821", *HAHR*, xl (1960), 409.

Some figures in the Porfiriato have, to be sure, drawn biographical interest. Francisco Bulnes, whose acid views and debunking tactics often concealed a dedicated and progressive spirit, has been the subject of one of the few serious studies of the period. George Lemus accomplished this in 1965. [55] Richard Stillinger's current research stresses Bulnes' attitudes toward the Díaz regime and may be less biographical than Lemus' when it is completed. [56] At least Bulnes is coming under close scrutiny. Bernardo Reyes has also been the subject of an excellent biography which meets the most rigorous of scholarly demands. This life of Reyes by E.V. Niemeyer, Jr., skillfully weaves the subject's military-political career into the fabric of Porfirian society. [57] In progress is another study of Reyes which the researcher, Anthony T. Bryan, calls "not simply a biography". The focus is upon the years 1900 to 1913 with an effort made to describe "the potential for [a politician's] adaptation in the last years of the Porfiriato and the early revolution". [58]

Although they fall within the Porfiriato time span, it has become customary to dub those who actively opposed the Díaz regime for years and even decades before 1910 as "precursors" of the Revolution. If no revolution had occurred, what would we call them? Dissenters from the Establishment, perhaps? Whatever the terminology, many did stay on to play active roles in the maderista revolution and other phases of the movement. James D. Cockcroft has written an admirable book which serves as a guide to the hard core of journalists, poets and other intellectuals who shifted along the spectrum from tolerable criticism to revolutionary preachment and organization. [59] To mention his work violates a ground rule of this paper but the clarity of exposition and the depth of research into the lives of six principal dissenters, among others, warrants comment here. Four of them were from the state of San Luis Potosí: Camilo Arriaga, Librado Rivera, Juan Sarabia and Antonio Díaz Soto y Gama. Two others were added by Cockcroft: Ricardo Flores Magón and Francisco Madero. In addition to Cockcroft's sensitive treatment of these men as they interacted, most, but not all, of them have been subjects of individual biographies by recent scholars. Díaz Soto y Gama is, surprisingly, neglected by researchers. Cockcroft mentions that the four interviews

[55] G. Lemus, *Francisco Bulnes: Su vida y sus obras* (México, 1965).

[56] R. I. Stillinger, "The Political, Economic and Social Thought of Francisco Bulnes, with Emphasis on his Attitudes Toward the Regime of Porfirio Díaz", Ph. D. Dissertation, In Progress, Columbia University.

[57] E. Víctor Niemeyer, Jr., *El General Bernardo Reyes* (Monterrey, 1966).

[58] A. T. Bryan, "General Bernardo Reyes and Mexican Politics, 1900-1913", Ph. D. Disertation, In Progress, University of Nebraska.

[59] J. D. Cockcroft, *Intellectual Precursors of the Mexican Revolution, 1900-1913* (Austin, 1968).

he had with the octogenarian in 1965-66 were the best source of biographical information about him. One recent study, an unpublished doctoral dissertation by Blanche B. DeVore, is devoted to Díaz Soto y Gama's link to the agrarian revolution and does not seem to be a full biography. [60] Camilo Arriaga, the mining engineer with an elite background, is also inadequately represented and deserves a thorough study. Luis I. Mata's slim but useful biography of Filomeno Mata, published a quarter of a century ago, could well be superseded by a more extensive work. [61] Librado Rivera and Juan Sarabia have been examined in recent biographies by Alicia Pérez Salazar and Eugenio Martínez Núñez respectively. [62] Obviously the two non-Porfirians, Flores Magón and Madero, are in a special category of scholarly attention and may be treated in the context of the Revolution itself.

E. The Revolutionary Generation

The richness of Mexico's character and experience is nowhere more apparent than in the history of her twentieth-century Revolution. In those years of instability and subsequent search for new political, social, economic and cultural directions the position of individuals becomes especially important. As earlier in the rhythm of Mexican history, men of ambition and vision found their talents in great demand. It is also true that the intensity of national response to events and to caudillos, statesmen and champions of cultural innovation has been so great that publications about them have been characterized more by passionate polemics than by sober analysis. Nowhere is this more true than in the realm of biography. Men of the Revolution were either the ultimate heroes or the basest scoundrels. They were invariably bigger than life. The result is that we have many lives and infinite sources but a meager list of dispassionate scholarly biographies. The passage of time and the consequent perspective has meant, however, that the decade of the 1960's has seen important steps taken to provide incisive and responsible biographies of the men of the Revolution. The work has only begun, to be sure, and the present generation of young scholars has ample invitations to contribute a battery of excellent biographies.

[60] B. B. De Vore, "The Influence of Antonio Díaz Soto y Gama on the Agrarian Movement in Mexico", Unpublished Ph. D. Dissertation, University of Southern California, 1963.

[61] L. T. Mata, *Filomeno Mata: Su vida y su labor* (México, 1945).

[62] A. Pérez Salazar, *Librado Rivera: Un soñador en llamas* (México, 1964); E. Martínez Núñez, *Juan Sarabia, apóstol y mártir de la revolución mexicana* (México, 1965).

In order to give the examination some coherence, let us set the limits of the Revolutionary generation as the conventional 1910 to 1940. This is not the place to debate periodization or the degrees of mortality associated with the Revolution by various scholars. Those thirty years, however, will serve to focus an assessment of twentieth century biography and will also provide a suitable time with which to terminate this historiographic overview.

What is the status of the biographer's craft with respect to the period's notables? The diminutive figure of Francisco Madero looms largest at the movement's outset as the "apostle of Mexican democracy". Dozens of portraits have been attempted and more will surely follow. José Valadés' two volumes study and A. Aguirre Benavides' sympathetic portrait and compilation of letters and newspaper accounts have added something to our store of information about Madero, but Stanley Ross' carefully written and richly detailed biography remains fundamental and is also one of the most durable of the genre in Mexican historiography. [63] The admirable Fabela documentary collection, among other materials, will doubtless, however, stimulate new efforts to interpret Madero for the 1970's. [64] The most recent book, an unscholarly study of *Madero y la democracia* by Jorge Fernández de Castro y Finck, however, suggests that greater perspective and the availability of more extensive documentation are not in themselves guarantees of excellence. [65]

At an opposite pole from Madero along the Revolutionary ideological spectrum was the anarchist and true believer, Ricardo Flores Magón. He has been the subject of intense research from a number of writers. James Cockcroft's concern has already been mentioned to which must be added the first of the solid biographies of Flores Magón by Ethel Duffy Turner, an unpublished Ph. D. dissertation by Ward S. Albro, III, on the precursor role his subject played and the excellent exploration of the Baja California revolution and Flores Magón's later career by Lowell L. Blaisdell. [66] José Muñoz Cota's treatment might

---

[63] J. C. Valadés, *Imaginación y realidad de Francisco I. Madero*, 2 vol. (México, 1960); A. Aguirre Benavides, *Madero el inmaculado* (México, 1962); S. R. Ross, *Francisco I. Madero: Apostle of Mexican Democracy* (New York, 1955).

[64] Isidro Fabela, ed., *Documentos históricos de la revolución mexicana*, 10 vol. (México, 1960-1966).

[65] (México, 1966).

[66] E. Duffy Turner, *Ricardo Flores Magón y el Partido Liberal Mexicano* (Morelia, 1960); W. S. Albro, III, "Ricardo Flores Magón and the Liberal Party: an Inquiry into the Origins of the Mexican Revolution of 1910", Unpublished Ph. D. Disertation, University of Arizone, 1967; L. Blaisdell, *The Desert Revolution: Baja California, 1911* (Madison, 1962).

have added understanding of Flores Magón's ideology were it not so one sided in its praise and so unrelated to historical conditions. [67]

The early years of the Revolution were populated by many other figures. Some, like Bernardo Reyes, had national careers in Porfirian days which spurted briefly again after 1910. Others, like Pancho Villa and Pascual Orozco, transcended obscurity and local limits to become national leaders in step with the *maderista* revolt against Díaz. Orozco's break with Madero in 1912 and his subsequent rapprochement with Huerta have tarnished his image within the traditional Revolutionary mythology. Happily Michael Meyer has, in brief compass, carefully examined Orozco's career and the validity of the charges levelled against him. [68] One of Meyer's students, William H. Beezley, has just completed a dissertation on Orozco's Chihuahua colleague Abraham González which should complement the pro-González biography by Francisco Almada. [69]

Villa has, understandably, attracted a multitude of writers of all persuasions. No one has conjured up a sobriquet for Villa as harebrained as "The Crimson Jester", applied to Zapata, but someone will surely try. [70] There is a fair sample of responsible writing about Villa but it can safely be said that the definitive life has not yet been published. Martín Luis Guzmán's *Memoirs of Pancho Villa*, which has gone through at least three Spanish editions since 1951 and is now available in an excellent English translation, remains the most satisfying single volume. [71] Federico Cervantes, an ardent *villista* who served as aide to Felipe Ángeles, wrote a sympathetic but cumbersome tome in 1960 which is more useful as a collection of source materials than as a biography. [72] Clarence Clendenen's study of Villa's relationship with the United States has some biographical implications but eschews involvement in the Mexican milieu. [73] More a compilation than a creative work, Antonio Vilanova Fuentes' *Muerte de Villa* is broader

[67] J. Muñoz Cota, *Ricardo Flores Magón: Un sol clavado en la sombra* (México, 1963).

[68] M. C. Meyer, *Mexican Rebel: Pascual Orozco and the Mexican Revolution, 1910-1915* (Lincoln, 1968).

[69] W. H. Beezley, "Revolutionary Governor: Abraham González and the Mexican Revolution in Chihuahua, 1909-1913", Unpublished Ph. D. Dissertation, University of Nebraska, 1969; F. R. Almada, *Vida, proceso y muerte de Abraham González* (México, 1967).

[70] Reference is to H. H. Dunn, *The Crimson Jester: Zapata of Mexico* (New York, 1934).

[71] (Austin, 1965).

[72] F. Cervantes M., *Francisco Villa y la revolución* (México, 1960).

[73] C. C. Clendenen, *The United States and Pancho Villa: a Study in Unconventional Diplomacy* (Ithaca, 1961).

than the title suggests and explores many of Villa's social, moral and political attitudes. [74]

But if some supporters of the early Madero revolution have attracted scholars, others have not. Francisco Vázquez Gómez and José María Pino Suárez, especially the former, are among the interesting politicians who deserve thorough study. Luis Cabrera is the subject of an earnest but unscholarly appreciation by Armando Porras y López, published in 1968. [75] Cabrera's continuing significance into Carranza's government should attract a vigorous and sensitive biographer.

The agrarian revolution's most prominent hero is, of course, Emiliano Zapata. As indicated earlier in this paper, John Womack's exhaustive treatment of Zapatismo tends to dwarf its progenitor. This may well be an appropriate antidote to the excessive hero worship and focus upon caudillos which characterize so much of Mexican historiography. Morelos was sprinkled in Zapata's time with semi-autonomous caciques like Genovevo de la O. They and the little people from hamlets like Anenecuilco gave Zapatismo its real tonalities. These are among the many revelations of Womack's book. Nevertheless, Emiliano's life is certainly there and eager biographers should spend their talents elsewhere. They need not go far. As already indicated, Díaz Soto y Gama and Vásquez Gómez are fair game and Gildardo Magaña, Zapata's heir, would make an excellent subject for a major biography.

The *decena trágica* created a regime and a situation which recalls the concern expressed earlier for those who "have also made Mexican history". Victoriano Huerta has attracted more verbal brickbats than perhaps any other Mexican president yet the problem of a balanced assessment of his life remains unresolved. Guidelines for such a reappraisal were laid down by William L. Sherman and Richard E. Greenleaf nearly ten years ago in a brief revisionist study which has no pretensions of being definitive. [76] Michael Meyer's current research is focused upon the Huerta regime and we may reasonably expect that the much needed biography of Huerta will be the result. [77]

Felipe Ángeles is another military man who moved through those turbulent years and who has so far escaped adequate biographical attention. Venustiano Carranza has received much more attention than Ángeles but none of it of sufficiently high calibre. Alfonso Taracena and Ignacio Suárez G. have made contributions in the 1960's but the

[74] A. Vilanova Fuentes, *Muerte de Villa* (México, 1966).

[75] A. Porras y López, *Luis Cabrera: Revolucionario e intelectual* (México, 1968).

[76] W. L. Sherman and R. E. Greenleaf, *Victoriano Huerta: a Reappraisal* (México, 1960).

[77] M. C. Meyer, "The Victoriano Huerta Presidency", Research in Progress. See *LARR*, III (1968), 564.

first is a popular biography which fails to come to grips with the First
Chief when he was in power and the second is derivative in its materials and excessively devoted to the details of Carranza's death. [78]
Given the position Carranza had in Mexican history between 1913
and 1920 it is imperative that a major biography be devoted to him.
Carranza's lieutenant, Pablo González, is another of our neglected
"also mades" but the research might be too depressing to be sustained.

Obregón's career as military commander and adroit politician has
attracted substantial scholarly interest. Part of this interest is suggested
by a comment James Wilkie made recently with respect to the realities
of political power in modern Mexico:

> The president of Mexico has great power to use federal funds in almost
> any way he sees fit in order to carry out his programs. [79]

Among the current attempts to understand Obregón as one of Mexico's most powerful presidents who understood his budgets are two
doctoral dissertations in progress. Nelson De Lavan is exploring Obregón's public life and Randall G. Hansis is involved with the relation
of political interest groups to the president. [80] The most substantial
recent work on Álvaro Obregón is not a full scale biography but a
thoughtful study of his political thought by Narciso Bassols Batalla. [81]

It is curious that neither of the two major figures who quarrelled
over the right to succeed Obregón in 1924, Plutarco Elías Calles who
won and Adolfo de la Huerta who lost, have inspired the measured
biographical treatment which they both deserve. Where have all the
scholars gone, indeed!

Lázaro Cárdenas has fared somewhat better and we should soon
know how much better. Albert Michaels, James Wilkie and Lyle Brown
have been conducting an intensive project to study the political philosophy and methodology of Cárdenas throughout his career. [82] This
will surely supersede the warmly appreciative Townsend biography and
Brown's own study, which is not widely available. [83]

[78] A. Taracena, *Venustiano Carranza* (México, 1963); I. Suárez G., *Carranza: Forjador del México actual: su vida, su muerte: relato documentado* (México, 1965).

[79] J. B. Wilkie, *The Mexican Revolution: Federal Expenditure and Social Change Since 1910* (Berkeley, 1967), p. 276.

[80] N. De Lavan, "The Public Life of Álvaro Obregón", Ph. D. Dissertation, In Progress, Texas Technological College. R. G. Hansis, "President Álvaro Obregón and Political Interest Groups", Ph. D. Dissertation, In Progress, University of New Mexico.

[81] N. Bassols Batalla, *El pensamiento político de Álvaro Obregón* (México, 1967).

[82] A. L. Michaels, James B. Wilkie and Lyle C. Brown, "A Study of General Lázaro Cárdenas", Research in Progress, See *LARR*, III (1968), 1186.

[83] William C. Townsend, *Lázaro Cárdenas: Mexican Democrat* (Ann Arbor,

Some other men, prominent in the 1920's and 1930's have been given at least as much serious attention as the presidents. José Vasconcelos is a good example. He has been approached by Bar Lewaw Mulstock in 1965, by Gabriella de Beer in 1966 and by John Haddox in 1967. [84] The work by the philosopher Haddox is an admirable but overly brief exploration of Vasconcelos' complex mind. The life by de Beer is extensive but neatly avoids the philosophical works. A synthesis of these two might result in the definitive biography we need of Vasconcelos.

Other figures have been inadequately represented. Luis Morones is sorely neglected in the field of labor relations, and the efforts to produce a solid biography of Vicente Lombardo Toledano have been unavailing. Robert P. Millon's attempt might have succeeded had he examined his subject critically within the context of the Mexican experience. [85] Tomás Garrido Canabal and Saturnino Cedillo are powerful personalities who have been represented only in pristine white or jet black but never in the grays of reality. A significant figure throughout the whole Revolutionary generation, Francisco Múgica, has also been treated in polemical terms but never in an adequate biography. Múgica, as an architect of the Constitution of 1917 and one of Cárdenas' most influential advisers and potential heirs, is presently being examined in depth by Julia G. Shepard. [86]

Bertram Wolfe's *Fabulous Life of Diego Rivera* is among a few other worthy biographies which should probably be mentioned for their literary verve and scholarship. [87] But any further recitation of leaders, lives and lacunae would be futile. Whoever attempts an appraisal of biographies in Mexican historiography a decade from now will, I trust, encounter new books about many significant figures whose careers have thus far been distorted by friends and enemies or neglected by professional historians.

1952); L. C. Brown, *General Lázaro Cárdenas and Mexican Presidential Politics, 1933-1940: a Study in the Acquisition and Manipulation of Political Power* (Austin, 1964) (Mimeographed).

[84] B. L. Mulstock, *José Vasconcelos: Vida y obra* (México, 1965); G. de Beer, *José Vasconcelos and His World* (New York, 1966); J. H. Haddox, *Vasconcelos of Mexico: Philosopher and Prophet* (Austin, 1967). I was unable to consult the work by Mulstock.

[85] R. P. Millon, *Vicente Lombardo Toledano: Mexican Marxist* (Chapel Hill, 1966).

[86] J. G. Shepard, "Francisco Múgica", Ph. D. Dissertation, In Progress, University of Connecticut.

[87] (New York, 1963).

COMENTARIO

ARTURO ARNÁIZ Y FREG

Considero muy afortunado el hecho de que los organizadores de esta Tercera Reunión de Historiadores Mexicanos y Norteamericanos hayan escogido al joven y brillante historiador norteamericano, profesor Hugh M. Hamill Jr., catedrático de historia latinoamericana de la Universidad de Connecticut, por el amplio conocimiento que tiene sobre el tema y por los méritos intelectuales que se le reconocen, sobre todo después de haber publicado hace tres años su libro sobre *La Revolución de Hidalgo, preludio de la Independencia Mexicana*.

En su comunicación el profesor Hamill observa desde luego la relativa escasez de amplios trabajos en este campo. Señala que el género biográfico ha producido quizás menos obras maestras que cualquier otro tipo de trabajo historiográfico, y no deja de mostrar su asombro de que esto ocurra con relación a una sociedad como la mexicana en donde el impacto personalista y la dirección individual han jugado y juegan un papel tan importante. Considera con razón que una buena biografía requiere la más severa disciplina literaria que en este tipo de trabajos pueda aplicarse.

La extensa lista que de los libros escritos por autores norteamericanos sobre vidas de hombres de México nos ha presentado, es sumamente interesante, muy orientadora y, a pesar de las limitaciones a las que debe ceñirse un trabajo que debe presentarse ante una reunión como ésta, ofrece de hecho una adecuada selección de los libros del género que han sido escritos en los Estados Unidos. Acompaña su enumeración con observaciones que nos dan la medida clara de su agudeza crítica y de su amplio conocimiento de este tema.

El justo elogio que hace del libro *Juárez y su México* de Ralph Roeder, aparece ante nosotros con una significación particular, sobre todo después de la muerte de este eminente escritor, ocurrida en México hace menos de dos semanas. En rápida revista alude al valioso libro de Raymond Estep sobre *Lorenzo de Zavala* y, al llevar su información hasta los días más recientes, destaca los méritos del libro que James D. Cockcroft ha publicado hace unos meses sobre *Los precursores intelectuales de la Revolución Mexicana*, libro al que, con plena justicia, el profesor Hamill llama "admirable".

El profesor Hamill no deja de advertir que las décadas más recientes no parecen haber sido propicias para el género biográfico, en años como éstos en los que pienso, la influencia de escritores como Macaullay, Carlyle y Nietzsche ha llegado a ser menos intensa.

Parece ocurrir ahora que los escritores modernos están un poco menos atentos hacia las vidas de los hombres que han marcado huella profunda y que, en su época, han determinado en buena parte el curso de la historia.

Al observar que algunos novelistas se ven atraídos por la tentación de substituir al historiador profesional para ocuparse de una personalidad sobresaliente, el profesor Hamill llega a plantearse la posibilidad de que un joven escritor mexicano como Carlos Fuentes escribiera la muerte de Álvaro Obregón después de cuatro años de entrenamiento dentro de los cánones de la investigación histórica, y llega a exclamar: "¡El resultado pudiera ser épico!"

Por fortuna la literatura mexicana ofrece ya, entre otros muy notables ejemplos, el caso del gran novelista don Martín Luis Guzmán quien al reconstruir las *Memorias de Pancho Villa* nos ha dejado desde hace varias décadas un testimonio elocuente de las altas calidades que un novelista, un gran escritor, puede alcanzar cuando emplea su pluma en temas como ese, tan cercanos al género biográfico.

El profesor Hamill hace también un interesante escrutinio sobre los libros que los hombres de México han escrito para hacer la biografía de alguno o algunos de sus compatriotas, y se queja de la falta de libros de consulta que permitan orientarse en el manejo de ese material. Muy útil para esto es la consulta de la *Bibliografía biográfica mexicana* de don Juan B. Iguíniz, que ha llegado en este año a su segunda edición. Pronto aparecerá el segundo volumen. El *Diccionario Porrúa*, compilado bajo la dirección real de don Felipe Teixidor, permite al lector actual obtener información de manera muy rápida sobre algunos de los mejores trabajos que dentro del género biográfico se han publicado entre nosotros.

Tiene razón el profesor Hamill cuando advierte que en México se han escrito muy pocas biografías de personas nacidas fuera de la nación, quizás por la consideración, no enteramente acertada, de que sus vidas pertenecen más bien a la historia de su país de origen. Lamenta la ausencia de un número suficiente de biografías de los virreyes que tuvo la Nueva España bajo la dominación española, pero al hablar de esto, considero que el extenso trabajo que don Ignacio Rubio Mañé ha elaborado sobre el segundo Conde de Revilla Gigedo debiera ser objeto de mención especial. Con relación a las biografías que se han escrito sobre fray Servando Teresa de Mier, lamento que omita la mención, que me parece enteramente necesaria, de lo que el doctor Edmundo O'Gorman ha escrito con particular brillantez sobre este tema. El libro de Carlos A. Echánove Trujillo sobre Manuel Crescencio Rejón y los trabajos de Reyes Heroles sobre Mariano Otero deben ser tomados muy en cuenta. Cuando menciona que don Justo Sierra, "el más olímpico de los hombres públicos de México de la época porfiriana" nunca ha sido enfocado a través de un estudio adecuado, parece que justifica plenamente el esfuerzo que a lo largo de años ha desarrollado el distinguido investigador francés, Claude Dumas, profesor de la Universidad de Lille, quien publicará próximamente una obra sobre el autor del *Juárez su obra y su tiempo*, libro en el que ha trabajado a lo largo de casi diez años.

Al repasar las biografías de que se ocupa el valioso trabajo del profesor Hamill, resulta evidente la gran riqueza bibliográfica y documental que han manejado los norteamericanos que han escrito sobre las vidas de algunas figuras notables dentro de la vida histórica de México. Qué envidiable resulta la abundancia de medios con que cuentan los investigadores en ese país de archivos bien catalogados y bibliotecas ricas y bien organizadas.

Y, al hablar sobre este tema, recuerdo ahora una conversación que tuve con la señorita Adina de Zavala, nieta de don Lorenzo de Zavala, —primer vicepresidente de la República de Texas—, a la que interrogué en la ciudad de San Antonio sobre la opinión que ella tenía sobre una excelente biografía, escrita en lengua inglesa por un laborioso e inteligente profesor norteamericano a quien ella había permitido, con generosidad, la más amplia consulta de sus archivos familiares.

Miss Adina de Zavala, se unió a los elogios que yo hacía de este buen libro del género biográfico. Y me dijo con plena convicción: "Sí, en esa biografía están todas las fechas, todos los datos alusivos a los altos puestos públicos que desempeñó mi abuelo, está la lista entera de los libros que escribió, se encuentra ahí la descripción precisa de todos y cada uno de los viajes que hizo, la numeración rigurosa de las leyes y de todos los decretos que redactó pero —agregó, lanzando un prolongado suspiro—, me temo que tendrá que venir después alguna gente de México para que en una biografía de mi abuelo *aparezca cabalmente el espíritu*".

Toda civilización es un sistema de secretos. A la tarea, muchas veces admirable de los historiadores e investigadores norteamericanos, debemos la publicación de libros importantes, particularmente dentro del género biográfico. Me complace reconocerlo así, sobre todo en una reunión como ésta, porque considero que una colaboración más estrecha entre los historiadores de los dos países permitirá obtener, especialmente dentro del género biográfico, resultados cada vez más valiosos y fecundos.

COMMENTARY

FRANK A. KNAPP JR.

It is with a nostalgic remembance of things past and a genuine pleasure that I make these brief remarks on Professor Hugh Hamill's balanced, interpretative, and informative paper dealing with the status of biography in Mexican historiography. This may sound like the most prosaic of all prosaic beginnings but I have both special and general reasons —or motives.

Perhaps I should feel on the defensive in some degree. Those who have read the analysis will immediately draw the conclusion that I am reciprocating with gratitude for Professor Hamill's generous and kindly comments about a biographic monograph I published several years ago *The Life of Sebastián Lerdo de Tejada.* That is partly correct. I am indeed grateful to learn that Lerdo, in his opinion, has managed to wear well with time and weather subsequent historical research. I should also confess to another minor fact related to my study on Don Sebastián. I was twenty years younger and I did not then realize that I would never again be capable of mustering the same dedication, zest, sustaining and all-encompassing interest, and spirit of pioneering which I applied to that research project. And I have undertaken and completed many —mostly anonymously— in subsequent years.

In truth, I am not only in basic agreement with all of the major conclusions in Professor Hamill's paper but they hold a highly personal meaning for me. He demonstrates clearly that there has been little basic change in Mexican biographic history over many years. At one time, I had grandiose plans for literary production in Mexican biographic history, an ambition which led me to conduct my own survey of the gaps and needs. The results of my personal compilation were strikingly similar to those of Professor Hamill, adjusted of course for subsequent production.

Having stated my virtual agreement with the selections and interpretations in this paper, I will add only comments which are primarily *obiter dicta,* not major substantive suggestions or criticisms: With regard to the criteria clearly set forth by the author for selecting titles, I recognize that this is the writer's prerogative, and Professor Hamill has adhered to his own framework of limitations, with a few exceptions. However, there are many biographical essays and essay collections of considerable merit which never see the light of print in the form of a full-dress monograph. Some of these titles deserve a place at least in a more detailed bibliographical compilation of Mexican biography, particularly because there are such wide gaps in this field of literature.

One other minor dissent which I have Professor Hamill's approach is his elimination of foreigners from the Mexican biographic scene. He states: "Foreigners whose careers included involvement in Mexican affairs have not been treated on the grounds that their lives belong to the historiography of the country of origin" (p. 288) Should the dividing line be so sharp on the basis of nationality? A more flexible criterion would be the importance of the individual foreigner's role in Mexican political, economic, cultural, or social affairs.

The introduction to this paper contains the enduring enigma in Mexican historiography, as germaine today as it was to me twenty years ago. Professor Hamill notes: "Nevertheless, the absence of many first rate biographies of Mexicans is curious in a society where personalist leadership has played such an important role" (p. 285). Leaders in different spheres worthy of biographic study are products of their times, which make the framework of their activities and opportunities. Yet it is equally axiomatic that prominent public leaders influence the course of events in perceptible ways. This applies to Mexico where strong executive leadership has been, and is, the tradition. Far more perhaps than in countries where political and governmental power is diffused and boxed in with elaborate institutional structures, bureaucracies, and rooted traditions. Hence, biography should rate in Mexico as an ideal medium for organizing political, economic, or cultural history. Still, Professor Hamill's study and selections demonstrate that biography is neglected in Mexico and indeed relatively more attractive to the *norteño* specialist than the Mexican scholar.

In partial explanation, he points out that the vogue of "behavioral sciences" and institutional studies have crowed biography with its literary pitfalls from the polemical-muckraking approach at one extreme to the saintly eulogy at the other. This may account for the concentrated biographycal production on Benito Juárez, Porfirio Díaz, and a few other national figures and the scholarly indifference to a multitude of other worthy subjects, but not the almost complete absence of truly classical biographies. For example, where is a work comparable to Robert K. Massie's *Nicholas and Alexandra?*

Professor Hamill may have struck the key reason in the practice of retaining private source collections in private hands. When carrying out research in Mexico in 1947, I became fascinated with the idea of writing a biography of Matías Romero and had access to his published works and some of his scattered personal letters in other mss. collections. I obtained an interview with the elderly descendant, who had inherited Romero's personal papers —reputedly voluminous. He was most courteous in his treatment of me and sympathetic toward my proposal; but he also firmly refused me any use of these materials for somewhat esoteric political reasons. I wondered at the time whether this problem of access to original sources might not be a serious obstacle to Mexican historical output, particularly biographic.

Professor Hamill also notes another hurdle to biographic history which is hardly confined to Mexico. This is the seemingly universal reflection of nationalism, accepted national symbols, and national heroes in the writing of national history. As a consequence, the so-called "losers" in the struggles over national ideals, principles, and issues are relegated to the discard heap or perform in history as traitors or villains. This factor may render partly understandable the oversight in biographic studies of the last of the Viceroys, the clerical-conservative leaders of the Reform and Intervention periods, and many of the prominent Porfiristas after the Revolution of 1910. In truth, the cult of national hero worship (or iconoclasm) places biographic history in an intolerant straightjacket and chases scholars to less controversial fields of endeavor. As Germán Arciniegas has stated: "Our heroes, like the Greeks, constantly get farther from being men and approach closer to the gods". And he adds that Latin American historians have led the world to believe that the entire nineteenth century was nothing but "heroes of the Independence and caudillos". (*Este pueblo de América* [México, D. F.: 1945], 119-121.)

Because I once harbored lofty ambitions to produce Mexican biographic history, I cannot resist the temptation to append a few ideas of my own to the gaps in the field which Professor Hamill has adeptly enumerated. I am convinced that one of the most valuable historical projects for the nineteenth century in Mexico would combine historiography with political and cultural biography. Many of the great figures of this era were not only prominent in national politics but also in literary pursuits, especially historical writing and journalism. Their political roles could be closely correlated to their historical "methodology" and interpretations. I have in mind such men as Manuel Payno, Lucas Alamán, José María Luis Mora, Francisco Zarco, Ireneo Paz, Vicente Riva Palacio, Guillermo Prieto, Justo Sierra, Miguel Lerdo de Tejada, José María Iglesias, and others. In addition, the opportunities seem almost unlimited for biographies related to local leaders who attained a measure of prominence on the national scene at some juncture in their careers. Equally unexplored is the sphere of economic biography —the major landholders, the "captains" of industrial development, and even the principal economic planners and financiers of this century.

Professor Hamill's discussion of research in progress suggests the value of compiling a comprehensive guide on unpublished theses and dissertations on Mexican biographic topics. Apart from serving as a convenient guide to research, such a compilation might open a few doors to publishing houses. Certainly a select few of these buried titles, with revision and some additional research, might merit the printed page.

The development of oral biographic history, which Professor Hamill mentions briefly, does appear to offer biographers a new and relatively unique primary source, the importance of which cannot be evaluated accurately at this stage. Obviously, the persons interviewed are fully conscious of recording their thoughts for history and hence their statements must be weighed in much the same manner as a memoir or autobiography. Nevertheless, this technique holds the promise of being of more value to biographers than some of the "methodology" in vogue among behavioralists. The recorded voice and the style of expression give the listener a sense of reality; the "actor" has the opportunity to explain his motivation at critical periods in his career, albeit with the benefit of calm retrospect; and he may be willing to express his opinions on the influence of others with whom he was associated in public and private life. Certainly, a great deal of strictly biographical factual data on a subject, which is often time-consuming to locate, can be concentrated in taped interviews.

In concluding this commentary on Professor Hamill's excellent synthesis,

I can only hope that the audience of distinguished scholars will receive my rather candid criticisms on the status of research in the field with a measure of tolerance. I am guilty in a small way in not carrying out some of these grandiose biographic projects which I had in mind some twenty years ago. I shall duck behind the pages of *Sebastián Lerdo* and take refuge in the kindly remarks of Professor Hamill. And I feel confident that his presentation of biographic problems will be a stimulus to some of the renowned historians at this meeting and possibly in turn to their students.

RELATORÍA

JULIA TUÑÓN DE MURIÁ

El debate general se inició con la exposición de algunas ideas en torno a la necesidad de estudiar al biografiado dentro de su propia circunstancia histórica, para poderlo así entender como producto y participante de ella, y no como un ente ajeno a su realidad. De esta manera, el historiador-biógrafo, para lograr identificarse con el biografiado, deberá hacer participar a éste del espíritu de su tiempo, buscando así aprehender al personaje en su propio medio y, a través de él, al medio mismo. Además, el biógrafo debe, con el fin de entender el tiempo y la situación del personaje objeto de su biografía, y para poder lograr un trabajo más integrado, familiarizarse con la ciencia de carácter social y económico.

Otro punto interesante del debate fue el relacionado con la necesidad de ampliar los trabajos de índole biográfica al estudio de figuras de menor relieve, y no limitarla al estudio de personajes que se han distinguido en la política nacional. Se consideró que, aunque estos personajes son más fáciles de investigar, y quizá revelen con más claridad la realidad histórica en que se desenvuelven, también se debe estudiar a otras personalidades representativas tales como los líderes de la llamada *oposición* a la historia *oficial*, ya que ellos son también representantes y afectantes de su tiempo.

Se señalaron algunas de las dificultades que implica la investigación biográfica, especialmente en el uso de archivos públicos y privados por el mal estado en que se encuentran. Además, se hizo hincapié en la necesidad de manejar los archivos notariales, los privados y los familiares en la investigación, por la utilidad de datos que se pueden obtener.

Finalmente se hicieron notar algunas dificultades que representa la utilización de las fuentes orales en la investigación biográfica, especialmente en relación con la conciencia de ser fuente de conocimiento que puede tener el entrevistado, lo que le impide, actuar con espontaneidad, especialmente cuando se tratan hechos que afectan o han afectado su propia vida. Un problema similar se puede presentar en la utilización de otras fuentes tales como cartas personales, autobiografías, memorias y otros documentos de esta naturaleza. Sin embargo, a pesar de estos inconvenientes, este tipo de fuente es válida si se maneja con precaución. Es decir que para lograr que estas fuentes den el rendimiento adecuado, no se debe pensar en ellas como un recurso técnico válido en sí mismo, sino que su utilidad dependerá de la forma en que sean trabajadas.

Algunos participantes, al manifestar sus experiencias sobre este punto, indicaron que ha mejorado mucho la conservación y acceso a la documentación. Fueron elogiados los esfuerzos de varias instituciones por conseguir y conservar documentos personales de hombres importantes de la historia de México. Entre ellas se mencionaron la Secretaría de Hacienda y Crédito Público, el Banco de México, el Instituto de Investigaciones Históricas de la UNAM, el Departamento de Estudios Históricos del Instituto Nacional de Antropología e Historia y CONDUMEX, S. A. Igualmente se mencionó que ha mejorado el servicio y acceso al Archivo Histórico de la Secretaría de Relaciones y se presentaron algunas opiniones acerca de la dificultad para consultar el riquísimo fondo del Archivo de la Defensa Nacional.

VII. HISTORIOGRAFÍA DE LA VIDA ECONÓMICA

4 de noviembre de 1969

Presidente: François Chevalier, director de la Casa Velázquez, Madrid.

Ponentes: Enrique Florescano, profesor e investigador del El Colegio de México; Clark W. Reynolds, investigador del Food Research Institute, Stanford University.

Comentaristas: Víctor L. Urquidi, presidente de El Colegio de México; y Stanley J. Stein, profesor de historia, Universidad de Princeton.

Participantes: Jan Bazant, investigador de El Colegio de México; Marvin Bernstein, profesor asociado de ciencias sociales, State University of New York, Fredonia; Calvin P. Blair, Fundación Ford; David Brading, profesor asistente de historia, Universidad de California, Berkeley; Luis Cossío Silva, subjefe del departamento de Estudios Económicos del Banco de México, S. A.; Romeo Flores Caballero, profesor e investigador de El Colegio de México; Brian Hamnett, State University of New York, Stony Brook; William P. McGreevey, director del Instituto de Estudios Latinoamericanos, Universidad de California, Berkeley; Laura Randall, Institute of Latin American Studies, Columbia; Robert Schafer, profesor de historia, Syracuse University.

Participante europeo: Ruggiero Romano, director de Estudios en la Escuela Práctica de Altos Estudios Sorbona, VI sección, París.

Relator: Alicia Orive, estudiante del Centro de Estudios Históricos de El Colegio de México.

PERSPECTIVAS DE LA HISTORIA ECONÓMICA EN MÉXICO

ENRIQUE FLORESCANO

I. EL PESO DE UNA TRADICIÓN

Contra la tradición que exige a las nuevas generaciones de historiadores continuar el camino de sus antecesores, cada época demanda a los hombres que reconstruyen el pasado "reescribir la historia", fecundar su oficio con las ideas, los métodos y los problemas de su tiempo. La historia-vida como la historia-ciencia no podrían avanzar sin esta interacción continua entre tradición y cambio.

Para los historiadores mexicanos que hoy comienzan a formarse o a escribir, la tradición es la historia-acontecimiento, visible en su representación más exaltada: la historia política, y manifiesta sobre todo en una determinada manera de concebir y practicar la historia (crónica, historia de "los grandes momentos", servidumbre al documento, historia de tijera y engrudo, historia calendárica, etcétera). Bajo una u otra forma, esta clase de historia domina desde hace tiempo el grueso de la producción mexicana y aspira a perpetuarse. Tiene detrás apoyos nobles que parecen justificar sus pretensiones: en su momento de esplendor produjo algunas obras de primer orden que hacen mayoría en el reducido grupo de "nuestros clásicos". Y no debe olvidarse que fueron sus cultivadores más eminentes quienes asestaron el primer golpe a la crónica —el más tradicional de los relatos— al imponer rigor y método en las investigaciones. Fue esa tradición que entonces era vanguardia la que introdujo la costumbre de criticar y exigir veracidad a los testimonios. Fue ella, en fin, la que en una época que carecía de escuelas e institutos de historia, hizo de esta actividad un ejercicio profesional. Pero estoy hablando de una tradición que nació al comenzar el siglo XIX y alcanzó su punto más alto en la segunda mitad de esa centuria.

Hoy los productos de esa clase de historia han dejado de ser creativos. Sus seguidores, a fuerza de no innovar, han terminado por repetir sus temas y exacerbar sus defectos. La vanguardia se convirtió en tradición cuando por una esclerosis progresiva derivó en la gran corriente que se empeñó en cultivar esa visión esencialmente política que desde el siglo XIX tienen los mexicanos de su historia. Ni siquiera los sujetos de estudio han variado y por eso persiste ese interés excesivo por los "hechos singulares", las figuras notables y las instituciones. En

cuanto a los métodos: se repiten sin modificación los que heredamos
de la crónica y la historia positivista. En fin, del legado más importante de esa tradición se desprende una cronología, una serie de instantá-
neas y hechos políticos sin apoyo en los procesos sociales, económicos
y mentales que han contribuido a modelar la historia del país. De ahí
proviene esa imagen deformada de nuestro pasado que se va amplifican-
do a medida que se desciende de la monografía especializada a las
historias generales. Y, finalmente, como herencia última de esa tradición, queda una mentalidad, una manera de concebir y practicar la
historia que además de sus limitaciones evidentes opone una barrera a todo intento de renovación.

Hace poco comenzaron a minar esa barrera los investigadores que
después de 1930 propusieron nuevos campos de estudio: historia social
y económica, historia de las ideas, historia del arte y de la cultura,
antropología, etnohistoria, etcétera. Pero los treinta años transcurridos
desde que se inició ese movimiento muestran que hace falta algo
más que el deseo de explorar nuevas áreas de estudio para transformar
hábitos tan arraigados.

La tradición es un proceso de sumas, adaptaciones y sincretismos
cuyo objetivo último es evitar el cambio cualitativo, el salto pleno que
rompe con el pasado y abre una nueva época. Adaptarse a los nuevos
aires sin realmente cambiar, tal ha sido hasta el momento la constante
más significativa de nuestra historiografía. Lo prueba la producción
de los historiadores mexicanos de 1940 a la fecha. [1] En ese periodo el
aumento cuantitativo de artículos y libros dedicados a la historia económica, social, de las ideas, del arte y de la cultura puede considerarse
prodigioso en relación a lo que se hacía antes. Sin embargo, si excluimos
algunas obras notables, el cambio cualitativo es insignificante. No puede
hablarse de cambio sustancial cuando lo nuevo en historia económica
es simplemente el tema; no puede haber creación ni impulso renovador
cuando en la historia del arte se describen e interpretan los fenómenos
estéticos de la misma manera que lo hacían los historiadores decimonó-
nicos; no se puede estimular el cambio cuando los investigadores de
los hechos sociales recurren a las recetas estereotipadas de la historia
política. Cierto que al aparecer todas esas obras se fracturó definitivamente el monopolio que antes ejercía la historia política. Y es cierto
también que la mayoría de esos estudios son contribuciones valiosas
por el simple hecho de que aportan datos sobre lo que no se sabía.
Con todo, lo trascendente es que en la mayoría de esas obras siguen
imperando los viejos hábitos, los métodos gastados y la incapacidad

---

[1] Véase el volumen colectivo *Veinticinco años de investigación histórica en
México*. El Colegio de México, México, 1966 (edición especial de la revista
Historia Mexicana, donde originalmente fueron publicados los ensayos bibliográficos
que integran el volumen).

creativa de la historia tradicional. Y es que el aire fresco que comenzaba a respirarse se vició sin remedio cuando el interés que despertaron esas especialidades no se acompañó de un interés correlativo en los nuevos métodos e ideas que en otras partes renovaban desde adentro a la vieja Clío.

La voluntad de permanecer sin transformarse se revela también en la reticencia o aceptación condicional con que se acostumbra recibir a los estudios que de alguna manera se apartan de la corriente tradicional. Si se reconoce "la importancia y el mérito" de una nueva manera de enfocar nuestro pasado, inmediatamente se le aisla en los casilleros de la cuasihistoria, se realzan sus limitaciones y nadie piensa seriamente en probar si las cualidades antes destacadas pueden fecundar su propio campo. Es así como las aportaciones trascendentes que han producido los cultivadores de algunas especialidades se tornan infecundas en el momento mismo de nacer. Para el vecino de enfrente son como frutos exóticos a los que de antemano se les niega capacidad de transplante en la parcela propia. De ahí que, una vez dividido el gran edificio de la historia en numerosos apartamientos, cada quien viva encerrado en el suyo, mirando de reojo al vecino sólo para conocer y difundir después sus defectos.

El extremo a que nos ha llevado esa práctica, que impide que las aportaciones de una especialidad fecunden a las demás, está a la vista en esas obras pequeñas o ambiciosas donde hay de todo, pero dividido en estancos que no se comunican entre sí: aquí historia política, más allá económica, en otro lado social, y así sucesivamente. El procedimiento no es de ninguna manera casual, nace del instinto de conservación. Permitir el contacto directo, el flujo y la influencia recíprocas de los métodos e ideas que animan a las nuevas especialidades, sería tanto como destruir las bases sobre las que reposa la concepción tradicional que se tiene de la historia.

Hay, pues, muchos signos que muestran que la historiografía tradicional ha agotado sus posibilidades internas de renovación. Ha perdido, como se decía en otro tiempo, su "impulso vital". Pero se esfuerza desesperadamente por sobrevivir y, en ese intento, acaba por convertirse en un obstáculo para las corrientes innovadoras, o busca nulificarlas a través de un proceso de cooptación más hábil y provechoso, puesto que simultáneamente evita el enfrentamiento radical y aísla a los focos renovadores. De manera que el cambio sustantivo, si cambio ha de haber, tiene que revolucionar el subsuelo que hasta hoy determina el sentido y la manufactura de las obras históricas.

II. UN CAMBIO NECESARIO: HACIA UNA HISTORIA ABIERTA Y EXPERIMENTAL

No sólo en México, en muchos países la concepción tradicional de la historia está en crisis. Padece desgarramientos internos y sufre el ataque desconsiderado de heterodoxos y francotiradores. El culpable es el gran desarrollo teórico e instrumental de las ciencias vecinas: economía, sociología, geografía, demografía, psicología, antropología, etnohistoria, etcétera. Sobre esa revolución en la teoría y en los métodos, que experimentaron en los últimos años ciencias más "prácticas" que la historia, se apoya el desafío lanzado a la tradición. Y así como el cambio sustancial, que todavía hoy no cesa de transformar a las ciencias humanas, vino de disciplinas no muy ortodoxas y con poca o ninguna tradición, así en historia los aires nuevos comenzaron a soplar desde posiciones de frontera, en el seno de especialidades mal definidas y decididamente sin prosapia. Un día, los historiadores inconformes y los vocados al experimento decidieron buscar en otras tierras el campo adecuado para realizar sus aspiraciones. En la aventura rebasaron los límites de su disciplina, penetraron en áreas antes vedadas y descubrieron que ahí se practicaban técnicas, ideas y experimentos mucho más audaces que los suyos. Superada esa barrera lo demás fue rápido y sencillo. De la apertura al diálogo y al experimento nació la necesidad de conocer esas prácticas y luego el deseo de adaptarlas a sus propias preocupaciones. El cambio no se hizo esperar. La comunicación entre historia, economía, sociología, demografía, antropología y otras ciencias, dio origen a las nuevas especialidades que desde hace más de treinta años revolucionan la vieja concepción de la historia: [2] historia cuantitativa —o *New Economic History*, como la llaman en Norteamérica—, demografía histórica, geografía humana, historia social, historia de las mentalidades, etcétera.

Revolución es la palabra justa para denominar ese cambio puesto que todo se transformó radicalmente. Del interés por los hechos singulares se pasó al estudio de los fenómenos colectivos, al examen de esos hechos económicos, sociales, demográficos y mentales que al repetirse diaria e indefinidamente a través de los tiempos, modelan la estructura profunda de una época. De una historia cuya finalidad era describir o "dejar hablar al documento", se dio el salto a una historia esencialmente explicativa, guiada por hipótesis y abierta a la imaginación. La afición por los hechos deslumbrantes, pero instantáneos, fue sustituida por el interés en los hechos de duración larga y media que condujo

---

[2] Véase los ensayos de Fernand Braudel reunidos en *Historia y ciencias sociales*. Alianza Editorial, Madrid, 1968. En ellos se traza el cambio operado en la historia por virtud del contacto con otras ciencias.

al descubrimiento de otros tiempos distintos a los de la cronología política. Del apego a las fuentes tradicionales se pasó a la búsqueda irrestricta y heterodoxa de nuevos testimonios que ampliaron los horizontes de la investigación. Y, en fin, por virtud de esos contactos y transformaciones, se pasó de una historia encerrada en sí misma y sin posibilidades de renovación interna a una historia dinámica, agresiva y abierta a todos los experimentos.

Tales son los aires que hoy transfiguran el fondo y la forma de la vieja historia. Pero lo importante es que si al principio sólo estimularon a quienes estaban dispuestos a aceptar el cambio, hoy inquietan y atraen a los historiadores más tradicionales. En muchos países la nueva historia ha dejado de ser una herejía. Sus aportaciones ya no se rechazan sin meditación ni se piensan exclusivas de las especialidades que las propiciaron. Poco a poco se integran a las preocupaciones de los demás historiadores y se establece un comercio activo entre viejas y nuevas concepciones. Una parte del ciclo se ha cumplido; su etapa siguiente es todavía impredecible; pero es seguro que el diálogo que hoy comienza entre las aportaciones de la vieja y la nueva historia lanzará a los historiadores a una nueva aventura, más osada y fructífera para el desarrollo de las ciencias del hombre.

Para nosotros, como lo señaló hace tiempo Alfonso Reyes, el problema es doble. Por un lado es obligatorio conocer lo que se produce en casa, y por otro es indispensable seguir de cerca lo que se hace en el exterior. Pero ocurre que en ocasiones la producción local nos absorbe de tal manera que por mucho tiempo nos desentendemos de la externa. Otras veces, movidos por el deseo de reparar esos olvidos y acortar distancias, trasladamos mecánicamente conceptos e ideas que en otras partes han probado sus bondades pero que no siempre se ajustan a nuestra realidad. En ambas situaciones tocamos los extremos. Hoy, por ejemplo, todo parece indicar que nos encontramos en el límite del primer caso. No sólo estamos bastante alejados de las corrientes que en el exterior transforman a la historia, sino que aun entre nosotros la comunicación es difícil o simplemente no existe. En una época en que abrirse al exterior es casi una cuestión de vida o muerte, seguimos empeñados en cultivar ese hermetismo que Octavio Paz destacó hace veinte años como una de nuestras tendencias más peligrosas.

En historia las pruebas de esta vocación al hermetismo son a tal punto abundantes que parecen increíbles. Los cultivadores de las diversas variantes de la Clío mexicana no sólo rechazan la posibilidad de establecer contactos entre sí. Cada quien procura andar tan separado de los demás como éstos de aquél, y algunos llegan al extremo de pontificar en sus cenáculos que no hay más ruta que la que ellos

322HISTORIOGRAFÍA DE LA VIDA ECONÓMICA

señalan. "Conocemos —dice Octavio Paz— el delirio, la canción, el aullido y el monólogo, pero no el diálogo."[3]

Una política que promoviera el diálogo entre nosotros y con el exterior bastaría para renovar nuestra historiografía y lanzarla hacia nuevas metas. Son hoy tan numerosas las aportaciones de cada una de nuestras especialidades que el solo esfuerzo de comparar entre sí sus resultados, de integrarlos en el todo de que forman parte, arrojaría una nueva visión de la historia mexicana. ¿Y qué decir de las perspectivas que abriría el intento de aplicar el instrumental teórico y metodológico de la "nueva historia" al material empírico acumulado por varias generaciones de historiadores? He ahí un primer paso que además de inyectarle sangre nueva a nuestra disciplina, ayudaría a corregir otra desviación suicida: la ausencia de comunicación entre ciencias vecinas. Recuerdo que en los manuales donde se explicaba qué era la historia, había un apartado donde se listaban las "ciencias auxiliares" de esta disciplina: geografía, sociología, economía, etcétera. Esos manuales eran obra de autores extranjeros. En México no existe esa concepción. Sería necesario una larga búsqueda para localizar un libro mexicano que integre de verdad los datos de la geografía a los problemas históricos. Y todavía es más desesperante no encontrar en las obras de los geógrafos las aportaciones de antropólogos, sociólogos o historiadores. ¿Y quién negará, en este país donde recorrer espacios equivale a transitar épocas históricas, que el enfoque combinado de historiadores y geógrafos no iluminaría muchos aspectos esenciales de nuestra historia pasada y presente?[4] Algo semejante puede decirse sobre la incomunicación entre historiadores, sociólogos y economistas. Sólo los antropólogos, y algunos especialistas que se ocupan de épocas que carecen de testimonios escritos, recurren con frecuencia a los métodos y conocimientos de otras ciencias.

Dialogar en familia, con los vecinos y el exterior, es sólo una manera de abrir las puertas a la renovación. Otra, también experimental y fecunda, es intentar un enfoque de nuestro pasado distinto del que hasta la fecha se ha practicado. Hace menos de tres años, en una reunión de historiadores europeos destinada a revisar lo hecho en historia social, decía Ernest Labrousse: "nous avons fait, jusqu'ici l'histoire des Mouvements et... nous n'avons pas fait assez l'histoire des Ré-

[3] *El laberinto de la soledad.* Fondo de Cultura Económica, México, 1959, p. 47.
[4] Uno de los muchos caminos posibles para unir con fruto las aportaciones de la historia y la geografía, lo ha señalado recientemente A. Moreno Toscano, *Geografía económica de México, siglo XVI.* El Colegio de México, México, 1968. Véase también su artículo "Toponimia y análisis histórico", *Historia Mexicana*, xix, 1969, pp. 1-10.

sistances".[5] Esas palabras tienen plena validez para el conjunto de la historiografía mexicana. Desde que hubo historia entre nosotros, el interés se concentró en los acontecimientos relampagueantes y de gran estruendo, generalmente de naturaleza política, que por su violencia e intensidad parecían ser los principales agentes del proceso histórico. Más tarde, y por contagio inevitable, los especialistas de la historia social, de las ideas y la cultura, dedicaron también su atención a los "momentos estelares". En suma, hasta aquí hemos hecho la historia de los cambios violentos, de las élites y de los triunfadores; rara vez la historia de los marginados, de los derrotados y de las masas; casi nunca la historia de los largos procesos que conforman la mentalidad de estos últimos grupos y explican sus aspiraciones, sus frustraciones.

La historia de México no es sólo la historia de "sus tres grandes movimientos triunfantes: Insurgencia, Reforma y Revolución". Es también, y en una proporción numérica mucho mayor, la historia de incontables movimientos fracasados, de resistencias seculares, de miles de pueblos y hombres marginados. ¿Qué es la historia de los indios y campesinos de México, si no una historia de resistencias al cambio y de explosiones frustradas? ¿Qué es la historia de la mayor parte de los pueblos y pequeñas ciudades del país, si no una historia cuyo ritmo marca un compás diferente y extraño al de "nuestros grandes movimientos", y donde todas las estructuras —económicas, sociales y mentales— ignoran o se oponen al cambio que estimulan desde fuera las élites?[6] Hablar de resistencias es una manera de referirse a las supervivencias, a esas voluntades que desafían el cambio porque están fincadas en estructuras cuya finalidad es coagular el tiempo, impedir la transformación que produciría su muerte. A una de esas supervivencias: la negativa de un grupo de comunidades campesinas a dejar de serlo, se refiere el hermoso libro de John Womak, Jr.[7] Sin embargo, sabemos poco o casi nada de las supervivencias religiosas, mentales, económicas, sociales y políticas que hoy todavía luchan por prolongarse. He ahí la otra, inmensa y oscura cara de nuestra historia que es preciso conocer para acercarnos a la verdadera imagen de este país contradictorio.

En historia de las ideas, una de las especialidades más innovadoras de los últimos años y menos aprovechadas, el maestro José Gaos había señalado un camino para estudiar el cambio y las constantes del pensamiento a través de lo que él llamaba *semántica cuantitativa*. Esto es, a través de la acumulación de las ideas que sobre un determinado

[5] *L'Histoire sociale. Sources et Méthodes.* Presses Universitaires de France, Paris, 1967, p. 5.
[6] Véase, en este sentido, el excelente libro de Luis González, *Pueblo en vilo. Microhistoria de San José de Gracia.* El Colegio de México, México, 1968.
[7] *Zapata y la revolución mexicana.* Siglo XXI, México, 1969.

aspecto se producen en un periodo, seguidas de su ordenación conceptual y cronológica, con el objeto de extraer de ahí un cuadro de las
ideas de una época que permitiera estudiar sus frecuencias, su continuidad, sus rompimientos y los grupos o individuos que las emitieron.
Este proyecto, como muchos otros que dio a conocer y comenzó a desarrollar con sus alumnos, era apenas la primera parte de lo que según
el maestro se podía hacer, *ahora*, en esta rama de la historia. Después
del periodo de las encuestas laboriosas, de la acumulación, ordenamiento y clasificación de las ideas, vendría una segunda etapa —que no vio
cumplida y en cuya falta se apoyan las principales críticas a este método—, el momento de conectar esas ideas con la realidad que las
genera, con los hechos políticos, económicos y sociales que las nutren
y explican.

Ésta y muchas otras ideas que sembró Gaos en México pueden ser
utilizadas provechosamente por los historiadores de la vida social, económica, del arte y de la cultura. Apoyados en esos catálogos y crono-
logías de ideas y acontecimientos grandes, pequeños, estables o fuga-
ces, podremos algún día fijar el movimiento, los ritmos y cadencias hasta
hoy desconocidos de nuestra historia social, económica y espiritual.
Por ese camino se podría obtener una historia del movimiento de esos
procesos apoyada en el estudio de su propio ritmo, no derivada de una
cronología ajena (la de la historia política, única disponible ahora),
sino inmanente a ellos. [8] Y conociendo individualmente los distintos
ritmos de un proceso y su tendencia general, podríamos entonces comparar ese movimiento con el que siguen los demás procesos, y así llegar
a registrar con exactitud esos momentos esenciales en los cuales los
procesos económicos, sociales, políticos y mentales confluyen o se des-
fasan. Esos desfases, esos diferentes ritmos de desarrollo que adoptan
los procesos que intervienen en la historia, ofrecen una nueva explicación de los cambios históricos; pueden ayudarnos a conocer las causas
profundas de esas grandes convulsiones que a menudo conmueven nuestra historia.

Apertura hacia nosotros y hacia el exterior, comercio activo con los
problemas e ideas de otras ciencias lejanas o próximas a la nuestra,
práctica de nuevos enfoques y métodos, todo ello nos puede llevar a
una nueva historia, a una historia que por lo pronto desearíamos
que fuera simplemente abierta y experimental. Abierta tanto a los
aires que vienen de la tradición, como a los nuevos que soplan por el
mundo. Y experimental, porque ésta ha sido siempre la tradición de la
ciencia, la única manera de renovarse sin cesar.

---

[8] El interés por conocer el ritmo (o los ritmos) de desarrollo de cada uno
de los múltiples procesos que intervienen en la historia, no tiene nada que ver
con el interés puramente calendárico de otros tipos de historia. Se trata de
un interés en los *movimientos*, no en las fechas.

Y seguramente cada una de las diversas variantes de Clío tiene algo que decir sobre este posible, deseable cambio. La historia económica, una especialidad reciente en nuestro medio, y, por tanto, abierta al cambio y a los experimentos, puede contribuir a esa renovación necesaria.

III. PERSPECTIVAS DE LA HISTORIA ECONÓMICA EN MÉXICO

La bibliografía que preparo sobre la historia económica de México (hasta la fecha he reunido un material considerable sobre los periodos prehispánico, colonial e independiente),[9] aunque todavía bastante incompleta, revela el enorme interés que en los últimos años han despertado estos temas. Lo comparten historiadores nacionales y extranjeros, pero puede decirse que las aportaciones de estos últimos, además de introducir novedades temáticas y metodológicas, mantienen un promedio de calidad más uniforme y son más numerosas en todas las épocas. Naturalmente, el predominio de la producción extranjera se debe a las aportaciones de los historiadores norteamericanos, aunque también son importantes los estudios de españoles, franceses, alemanes, sudamericanos e ingleses. Por último, el desequilibrio mayor se localiza en las preferencias que manifiestan los investigadores por determinadas épocas. El periodo colonial se lleva la parte del león, tanto en cantidad como en calidad. Le sigue la época prehispánica y en último lugar, queda el periodo independiente, pues en proporción a la gran riqueza de sus fuentes y las múltiples oportunidades que ofrece "para hacer un nombre en la historia", continúa siendo "un siglo olvidado".

No cabe hacer aquí el análisis detenido de esa inmensa producción. Pero sí es necesario, para los fines de esta ponencia, destacar algunas características generales de ella que tienen relación con el desarrollo y perspectivas de la historia económica en México.

Con las inevitables valiosas excepciones que confirman la regla, la mayoría de esos estudios exaltan al extremo las virtudes del trabajo monográfico. Elegido el tema, se va a los archivos a buscar exclusivamente lo que a él concierne, y si algo surge en la investigación que amenace con rebasar los límites previamente fijados, se le extirpa sin contemplaciones. Al menos ésa es la impresión que deja la lectura de esos estudios laboriosos donde no hay relación alguna con los temas ve-

[9] Actualmente preparo con la ayuda del Social Science Research Council una bibliografía del siglo XIX destinada a recoger fuentes estadísticas y documentos cuantitativos. Pienso reunir este material bibliográfico en un solo libro que sirva a todos los interesados en la historia económica de México. Por esa razón la bibliografía preliminar anexa a esta ponencia no se publicará en las *Memorias* del Congreso.

cinos y menos con los aspectos generales de la historia. Resultado: la mayoría de esas contribuciones requieren un esfuerzo posterior que las integre al todo de que son parte y permita entonces comprender su significado. Se confunde así la necesidad metodológica de aislar un fenómeno para estudiarlo mejor, con una manera de entender la historia, con la mala costumbre antes señalada de dividirla en estancos y parcelitas sin conexión entre sí. De esa práctica se derivan dos males que afectan tanto a la historia económica como a la historia sin adjetivos: al mismo tiempo que se anula la posibilidad de que el análisis económico enriquezca el análisis histórico, se frustra también el intento de crear contactos fecundos con los métodos y problemas de otras especialidades.

Nadie puede negar que esta tendencia al monografismo cerrado y erudito sirvió en un momento para frenar la "historia impresionista" que se venía haciendo con un mínimo de datos y un máximo de "imaginación". Pero hoy, sin duda para confirmar nuestra vocación a los extremos, estamos exactamente en el lado opuesto. Mientras se publican cientos de pequeños estudios valiosos o sin horizonte, carecemos de síntesis, de obras de imaginación que restituyan el todo e interpreten esa producción cada vez más ingobernable. Y para la historia económica, disciplina todavía sin arraigo en nuestro medio, esta situación no es nada favorable. ¿Cómo se puede pedir a los investigadores de otras áreas que fortalezcan sus interpretaciones con los datos de la realidad económica si no podemos ofrecerles ni siquiera un esquema de los principales procesos económicos que les sirva de apoyo? Teóricamente hasta el investigador más reacio a desprenderse de sus hábitos mentales podría aceptar que no se puede hacer historia social sin acudir a los hechos económicos que expliquen el origen de las diferencias y antagonismos sociales. Y lo mismo se podría decir acerca de la necesidad teórica de integrar el análisis económico al estudio de la historia política. Pero entre la teoría y la práctica, además del grueso colchón de tradiciones que dificulta el intercambio efectivo, hay un vacío: no existe ni una historia económica general, ni historias particulares sobre procesos capitales de la historia económica (geografía económica, historia demográfica, historia agraria, desarrollo industrial, comercio interior y exterior, política económica, clases sociales, poder económico e influencia política, etcétera). Y no veo ninguna posibilidad de que pueda establecerse un comercio activo entre historia económica y las demás especialidades mientras persistan estas grandes lagunas. Creo que todo proceso de intercambio opera sobre la base real de préstamos, enriquecimientos e influencias mutuas. Y mientras no exista esa base, *mientras la historia económica no se constituya como algo indispensable y necesario dentro de la práctica de las otras especialidades*, no habrá posibilidad de intercambio ni de transformación recíprocas.

En otras palabras, el asunto de integrar los métodos, las ideas, los problemas y resultados de la historia económica a la práctica corriente de nuestra historiografía, es en primer lugar un problema nuestro, como lo es también para los demás investigadores de especialidades nuevas que aspiran al mismo fin. Pero no se trabaja en favor de esa integración siguiendo los hábitos de la historiografía tradicional. No es por el camino de la monografía encerrada en sí misma como podremos hacer de la historia económica una disciplina viva, en estrecha comunión con los problemas de la historia. Y, por otro lado, hay problemas todavía más prácticos y serios que nos indican que debemos intentar otro camino: carecemos del tiempo, del material humano y de los recursos económicos para esperar a que por un proceso acumulativo que duraría largos años se llenen esas lagunas y comience entonces el proceso de integración.

Creo que todos los caminos para llegar a esa deseada integración quedarán abiertos si partimos de la idea de que la historia económica no es una parcela, ni un género ni un agregado de la historia, sino una parte consustancial del desarrollo histórico, en relación viva y permanente con los otros procesos que lo determinan. Los historiadores, aun los más especializados, no pueden dejar de pensar que su tarea comienza y acaba en ese punto central donde converge todo lo que es historia: el hombre. Un universo que no admite la especialización más que como un paso metodológico para acceder a una comprensión más amplia y profunda de él. Y en el caso que nos concierne, la historia económica, ésta ha probado en los países donde es vanguardia que puede penetrar profundamente en una de las partes de ese universo sin olvidar el todo. Creo que si esta idea se incorpora a nuestros estudios de historia económica, a la investigación más especializada y erudita o al intento de síntesis e interpretación más general, podremos llegar a esa integración portadora de cambio en un tiempo mínimo y aprovechando al máximo los recursos disponibles.

Las líneas que siguen pretenden mostrar, a través de ejemplos concretos, algunas de las muchas posibilidades que tiene la historia económica de llegar a esa meta utilizando los más variados caminos: desde la síntesis hasta el estudio monográfico.

A. *El análisis general: Las síntesis como interpretación de lo hecho y apertura de nuevos horizontes.*

La síntesis, el análisis general y todo esfuerzo con pretensiones totalizadoras son vistos a menudo como la última etapa de un camino previamente pavimentado por numerosas monografías. Tal vez esto sea cierto para quienes conciben la síntesis como mera ordenación de conocimientos dispersos. No lo es para quienes ven en ella la oportunidad de reflexionar sobre lo que es esencial en el desarrollo histórico. En esta última categoría se inscriben las síntesis creativas, aquellas que aparecen no al final de un proceso historiográfico, sino cuando las ideas tienen que señalar metas a la investigación. Recuerdo dos tipos ejemplares de esta clase de síntesis. Una es la obra de Marc Bloch: *Les caractères originaux de l'histoire rurale française*; la otra es el libro del historiador belga, Henri Pirenne: *Historia económica y social de la Edad Media*. Las dos fueron producto, más que de otra cosa, de la reflexión inteligente, puesto que en el caso de la obra de Bloch casi no había nada detrás, y en el de Pirenne quizá se había hecho demasiado. Ambas propusieron nuevos enfoques, plantearon otros problemas, señalaron nuevas perspectivas y finalmente fueron superadas. Ambas siguen siendo obras clásicas. De obras de esta especie requiere nuestra historiografía, tanto para otorgarle un sentido al conjunto de lo hecho, como para despejar el horizonte y mostrar otras perspectivas. En historia económica, campo virgen, el análisis general puede practicarse provechosamente en todas las escalas.

Síntesis de épocas. Entre los análisis de tipo general el más difícil quizá es el que intenta abrazar toda una época, el que penetra en todos los hechos para seleccionar y explicar sólo aquellos que fueron esenciales en el periodo. Dos épocas de nuestra historia, la prehispánica y la colonial, parecen dignas de un examen semejante. Las dos cuentan con suficientes estudios de carácter económico. Las dos han sido estudiadas con rigor en casi todos sus aspectos. Nadie ha intentado analizar su historia a través del cristal de lo económico.

Examinar la época prehispánica a través del maíz y la agricultura no sólo es apasionante, es fundamental. Es estudiar también el origen de la estructura familiar y social de esos pueblos; es un camino necesario para comprender tipos de poblamiento y de organización política; es la vía natural para penetrar profundamente en la cultura, la religión, los mitos y la visión del mundo del hombre prehispánico; en una palabra, el maíz está presente en todas las manifestaciones de esas culturas. [10]

Los libros sagrados de esos pueblos cuentan que el primer hombre fue hecho de maíz. Sus descendientes, todavía numerosos, no han podido romper ese hechizo original y, junto con el cultivo del cereal sagrado, han prolongado hasta estos días estructuras económicas, sociales y mentales de origen milenario. He ahí otra investigación, complementaria de la anterior, que aclararía mucho del pasado y del presente.

[10] Una bibliografía muy amplia sobre el maíz en esta época: Enrique Florescano y Alejandra Moreno Toscano, *Bibliografía del maíz en México*. Universidad Veracruzana, Jalapa, 1966.

¿Qué sobrevivió de la cultura indígena, mediante qué adaptaciones y cómo y por qué fue aceptado en la economía y la vida de los vencedores? Es la historia presentida pero no escrita de nuestras comunidades indígenas a través de pruebas de fuego sucesivas: Colonia, Independencia, Reforma, Porfiriato, Revolución... hasta los hijos de Sánchez. Un tema apasionante que ofrece la ventaja para el historiador de entrar en contacto con antropólogos, folkloristas, sociólogos y economistas, y desde luego con los restos vivos y muertos del mundo indígena.

La época colonial es una época más compleja: conviven en ella dos economías, y una de ellas está ligada a una metrópoli en crisis permanente que participa de la economía mundial. Puede decirse que casi todos los aspectos de la economía colonial, incluidas sus relaciones con el exterior, han sido tocados por la investigación reciente. Sin embargo, todavía no se llega a definir con claridad de qué economía se trata, ni cuáles son sus principales características. Comparando la economía de los centros de población blanca e indígena, algunos han hablado de "economía dual" y de "colonialismo interno". Otros, al examinar la minería y la industria textil, han dicho que se trata de capitalismo. Quien ha estudiado la agricultura señala que estamos ante una economía "eminentemente agrícola" y sugiere que los principales fenómenos económicos de la época tienen ese carácter. ¿Y qué decir acerca de aspectos menos estudiados pero tan conocidos como las diferentes economías que coexisten en una misma región, la pequeñez de los mercados, los problemas de transporte, la escasez de circulante o la tendencia a la inversión suntuaria de los ricos de la época? Todo ello habla en favor de un análisis que pondere esos elementos y les asigne su jerarquía e influencia en el desarrollo de la sociedad colonial.

Por otra parte, también esta época pide un análisis semejante al señalado para el periodo prehispánico: un enfoque montado entre dos épocas que distinga las esencias que el periodo colonial hereda al independiente. [11] Se verá entonces, como ya lo han mostrado algunos historiadores, que la división política que separa esas épocas es arbitraria, que muchas de las principales estructuras coloniales se prolongan sin modificación hasta muy avanzado el siglo xix. Y, sobre todo, un análisis de este tipo proporcionaría una base sólida para comenzar el estudio en profundidad de nuestro gran siglo olvidado. Pero para iluminar mejor este siglo, quizá convenga también ensayar otros métodos.

[11] Un modelo de este tipo de estudios lo ofrece el excelente libro de W. P. Glade, *The Latin American Economies. A Study of their Institutional Evolution*. American Book, New York, 1969; y el también excelente ensayo de Stanley y Barbara Stein, *The Colonial Heritage of Latin America. Essays on Economic Dependence in Perspective*, próximo a publicarse por Oxford University Press.

330HISTORIOGRAFÍA DE LA VIDA ECONÓMICA

Análisis general cuantitativo. El siglo xix, en efecto, no cuenta ni con suficientes estudios económicos ni con esa cantidad impresionante de valiosas aportaciones sobre la historia política, social, institucional o cultural que facilitan la tarea en otras épocas. Pero si es pobre en obras, es en cambio un siglo extraordinariamente rico en fuentes, sobre todo para la historia económica (estadísticas regionales, generales, sectoriales, diccionarios geográfico-económicos, memorias, censos, etcétera). Esta circunstancia, además de ofrecer la posibilidad de una interpretación nueva y bien fundada del periodo, agrega el atractivo de probar un método ya generalizado en los estudios de historia económica. Los historiadores lo llaman análisis cuantitativo. Su rasgo distintivo es el uso de datos seriados y su mecanismo es el siguiente. Primero: seleccionar algunas "variables" o sectores económicos significativos. Segundo: acumular la mayor cantidad posible de datos seriados y continuos sobre cada una de esas variables, de manera que éstos sirvan para construir series completas y dilatadas en el tiempo. Tercero: registrar las tendencias y movimientos de cada variable, establecer sus relaciones y determinar el sentido de la tendencia general. Cuarto: integrar el resultado de la investigación en el cuadro económico de la época y proceder a su interpretación. Un enfoque como éste se antoja útil, necesario y oportuno para el siglo xix. La selección y estudio de algunas "variables" representativas de su desarrollo demográfico, de la historia agraria, del desarrollo industrial, del comercio interior y exterior, de la hacienda pública y de la política económica, proporcionaría en corto tiempo un cuadro sólido de las principales tendencias económicas del periodo. [12] Un cuadro que propondría, además, problemas concretos para la investigación futura.

Pero tales empresas son generalmente colectivas y requieren de grandes inversiones. De manera que, más que de la voluntad de los historiadores, su realización depende de una "política institucional" que las estimule.

Análisis regional y local. Quien no tiene oportunidad de hacer la síntesis o el análisis general de toda una época, le queda como última perspectiva de conjunto intentar la historia económica regional o local. La importancia de este tipo de estudios para la historia general de

[12] En relación a este tipo de análisis véanse los modelos que ofrecen los economistas: Douglas C. North, *Growth and Welfare in the American Past. A New Economic History.* Prentice-Hall, New Jersey, 1966; J. Marczewski. *Introduction a l'histoire quantitative.* Droz, Ginebra, 1965; y los que proponen y aplican los historiadores: Pierre Vilar, *Crecimiento y desarrollo. Economía e historia.* Ariel, Barcelona, 1964; P. Goubert, *Beauvais et le Beauvaisis de 1600 a 1730.* SEVPEN, Paris, 1960; R. Baehrel, *Une croissance: La Basse-Provence Rurale (fin du XVIe siécle—1789).* SEVPEN, Paris, 1961; y P. Vilar, *La Catalogne Dans l'Espagne moderne. Recherches sur les fondements économiques des structures nationales.* SEVPEN, Paris, 1962.

México la señaló hace poco, de palabra y con obra, Luis González. [13] Y bastaría mencionar la variedad geográfica del país y el desarrollo desigual de sus regiones para admitir que estos estudios son también capitales para la historia económica. A pesar de ello no hay estudios históricos sobre el desarrollo económico del norte del país, ni sobre el centro, las zonas de tierra caliente o las regiones marginales. Aquí, como en otros casos, la magnitud de nuestra negligencia sólo es comparable a la importancia de lo que nos empeñamos en ignorar.

He ahí, pues, una meta más para la investigación futura: el estudio histórico del desarrollo regional. Un largo camino que se puede acortar si se establece diálogo con geógrafos, antropólogos, economistas, sociólogos e historiadores de la vida parroquial. [14]

Naturalmente que junto al estudio regional debe estimularse el estudio del desarrollo económico de pueblos y ciudades, pues así como el análisis regional corrige, apoya y vuelve profundo el análisis general, así también la historia del pueblo más pequeño enriquece y complementa el análisis regional. Metodológicamente el análisis de la unidad más pequeña debería preceder a los demás, pero eso está tan alejado de nuestras posibilidades que deben buscarse fórmulas mixtas que combinen la profundidad en el estudio con el conocimiento de espacios cada vez mayores. Pueblo, región, país, he ahí las metas de este triple enfoque. [15] El carácter alternativo o simultáneo que tienen todos estos enfoques, además de permitir intercambios siempre valiosos de métodos y experiencias, puede ayudar también a delinear una política de investigaciones, tan necesaria en un país donde los recursos humanos y materiales son escasos. Así, en algunos Estados puede pensarse en la posibilidad de que mientras una institución coordina el análisis económico regional interdisciplinario, otros investigadores estudien individualmente el desarrollo de pueblos y ciudades representativos de ciertas condiciones económicas de la región. Sólo a través de la jerarquización de nuestras necesidades y de la cooperación con otros investigadores podremos llegar a conocer, en un plazo corto, lo que por tanto tiempo hemos ignorado.

B. El análisis sectorial

Señalemos, por último, la conveniencia de estimular un tipo de aná-

[13] Véase en su libro ya citado, *Pueblo en vilo*, la introducción.
[14] A un antropólogo, Miguel Othón de Mendizábal, se debe el único estudio histórico sobre desarrollo económico regional que recuerdo: "Evolución del Noroeste de México", *Obras completas*. México, 1946, t. iii, pp. 7-86.
[15] Como modelo de análisis económico cuantitativo aplicado a regiones y pueblos, véanse las obras de P. Goubert, R. Baehrel y P. Vilar, citadas en la nota 12.

lisis económico que, además de venir en apoyo de los anteriores, combina las cualidades del análisis monográfico con las del análisis general: el análisis por sectores o ramas de la actividad económica. El objeto de este análisis es sólo una porción del todo económico —agricultura, desarrollo industrial, comercio, etcétera—; pero se trata de partes complejas cuya comprensión exige un análisis total de sus diversos elementos. Así, cuando el tema es demasiado vasto, es posible encerrarlo en límites geográficos o temporales y obtener entonces mayor profundidad. Otras veces, si hay ambición y recursos, puede intentarse una empresa más audaz, por ejemplo la historia agraria del periodo independiente, combinando el estudio de las estructuras (propiedad, cultivos, técnicas, trabajo, mercados, etcétera), con el análisis de los movimientos de la coyuntura económica (producción, precios, salarios, venta, etcétera). En ambos casos, sea que se limite a una época y lugar o que se extienda a varios espacios y tiempos, este análisis permite la aplicación de los métodos cuantitativos más recientes al lado de las técnicas tradicionales. Es decir, es un enfoque que como los anteriores puede adecuarse a las necesidades de cada investigador, y que por otro lado ofrece un sólido apoyo al análisis general. En los países donde más se practica se le concibe como un análisis en profundidad de una parte del hecho económico que enriquece la comprensión de hechos no económicos. Aquí, como en otros casos, el problema de pasar de lo económico a lo social y de ahí a otras realidades no es, nunca ha sido, un problema de método: depende de la concepción que cada investigador tiene del mundo y de su oficio.

Veamos, pues, muy rápidamente, algunos sectores de nuestra historia económica que podrían beneficiarse con este enfoque.

Geografía económica. Se ha dicho que la historia de México no se entiende sin el estudio de su geografía; que el destino de sus habitantes lo ha dictado una geografía complicada y hostil. Pero la geografía que por costumbre hemos estudiado no es la que se mueve con el hombre y le impone desafíos y servidumbres *históricas*: es una geografía detenida en el espacio, sin horizontes temporales. Y lo que necesitamos es justamente una geografía dinámica, una geografía que registre tanto los cambios naturales como los procesos que se inician cuando el hombre traba contacto con su medio natural.

Un ejemplo puede aclarar lo que quiero decir. Los geógrafos nos dicen que en este país hay tres grandes regiones naturales: 1. La región de las tierras secas extratropicales (el norte); 2. la región de las altas tierras tropicales (el altiplano) y, 3. la región de las tierras tropicales bajas y calientes. Sobre las tres hay valiosos estudios que explican su composición, desarrollo, flora, fauna, variaciones, características, etcétera. Todo, menos la historia de ese mundo en su relación con el hombre. Por su lado, los historiadores saben que de esas regiones sólo el altiplano ha sido centro de poblamiento estable desde hace miles de años; lugar de equilibrio entre el medio natural y las necesidades humanas, aunque en repetidas ocasiones ese equilibrio haya peligrado. En el norte no hubo esa adecuación y sólo cuando llegaron otros hombres con instrumentos y mentalidad diferente a la de los primitivos pobladores pudo romperse el límite natural que impedía penetrar la región. Por último, las tierras bajas y calientes, aunque pobladas intermitentemente desde la época prehispánica, son una conquista de nuestro tiempo, de la nueva tecnología y de un Estado con capacidad económica para hacer grandes inversiones en obras de infraestructura.

Es decir, en cada una de esas tres regiones ha habido una relación diferente entre el hombre y su ambiente, una historia cuyos avances, estancamientos y retrocesos no conocemos. Las huellas de esa relación entre el hombre y la naturaleza esperan al historiador que las reconstruya y exprese su dinámica: están en el paisaje mismo, en el nombre dado a la tierra y a los pueblos, en archivos y bibliotecas. [16] Su estudio requiere el contacto con otros especialistas y la experimentación de nuevos métodos y técnicas.

Historia demográfica. Por razones diversas —apego a las fuentes tradicionales, ignorancia de los métodos cuantitativos, etcétera— la demografía histórica que se practicaba en nuestro medio se había reducido a indagar el número total de habitantes que tuvo el país en diversas épocas, acudiendo en todos los casos a fuentes y cifras aisladas que no daban idea del movimiento de la población. Esta predilección por la imagen fotográfica cambió un poco cuando comenzaron a publicarse los estudios de la llamada "escuela de Berkeley". Se dieron a conocer entonces nuevas cifras sobre la población indígena, nuevas fuentes y métodos, nuevas explicaciones de las causas que provocaron la catástrofe que abatió al mundo indígena. Con todo, persistió una constante que había obsesionado a los viejos investigadores: el interés por determinar el número de pobladores que había inmediatamente antes y después de la llegada de los españoles. O sea que si exceptuamos unos pocos trabajos, la mayoría de las nuevas aportaciones siguen dominadas por la maldición del padre Las Casas: su problema es dilucidar si fue mayor o menor el derrumbe demográfico después de la Conquista. Esa obsesión explica la abundancia de estos trabajos en el siglo XVI y su pobreza exasperante en el resto de la Colonia y en todo el periodo independiente.

Sin embargo, desde hace poco se gesta una revolución que conviene

---

[16] Los estudios citados en la nota 4 contienen sugerencias temáticas y metodológicas de interés para la historia de la geografía económica en México.

precipitar: el estudio cuantitativo del movimiento y las estructuras demográficas basado en la explotación de los archivos o registros parroquiales. En Europa este análisis ha revolucionado los estudios demográficos porque a través del recuento y examen secular de bautismos, defunciones y casamientos ha sido posible reconstruir el movimiento y las principales tendencias demográficas de una época; y porque a través del llamado método de "reconstrucción de familias" se puede penetrar también en la estructura demográfica de las sociedades antiguas: fecundidad, mortalidad infantil y juvenil, crisis demográficas; pirámide de edades, proporción entre los sexos, población activa, etcétera. [17] Apoyado en estos datos y métodos el análisis demográfico se ha convertido en un instrumento esencial de la historia económica. Como resultado de otros factores —clima, epidemias, crisis agrícolas— o como factor de crecimiento o de parálisis económica, la "variable demográfica" es hoy imprescindible en todo estudio de historia económica, social o política.

Aplicar a la historia de México esos métodos y técnicas es sólo cuestión de tiempo, y mejor dicho, de apoyo institucional. Los archivos mejor conservados, los parroquiales, esperan a los investigadores. Algunos guardan libros de bautismos, defunciones y casamientos fechados desde 1550. La mayoría se prolonga hasta fines del siglo pasado, y en algunos pueblos apartados llegan hasta 1960. Esa magnitud obliga a pensar en la selección de pueblos representativos de ciertas regiones, para obtener pronto un "muestreo" de diversos desarrollos demográficos. [18]

Historia agraria. Quien recuerde algunos estudios clásicos sobre este tema, como el de Chevalier, por ejemplo, pensará que este sector es de los más conocidos de nuestra historia. Grave error: ignoramos quizá demasiado de él. ¡Y se trata del sector que por más tiempo ha señoreado la historia económica y social de este país!

País de grandes haciendas y de latifundistas, de indios sin tierra y peones endeudados, de tierra avara y cosechas "aventuradas a la voluntad del cielo"; país sacudido por interminables luchas agrarias. . . Y bien, todavía no hemos hecho la historia de esas haciendas dominadoras del campo y la ciudad: cerealeras, ganaderas, pulqueras, azucareras. Conocemos algunos de sus rasgos generales, no su historia interna: ¿Qué

---

[17] Sobre los métodos y aportaciones de este análisis véase el libro de P. Goubert, *Beauvais et le Beauvaisis*, ya citado; también D. V. Glass y D. E. C. Eversley, *Population in History*. Londres, 1965; M. Fleury y L. Henry, *Des registres paroissiaux à l'histoire de la population: manuel de dépouillement et d'exploitation de l'état civil ancien*. Paris, 1956; L. Henry, *Anciennes familles genevoises*. Paris, 1956.

[18] Se han hecho estudios, sin publicarse aún los resultados, en Acatzingo y Cholula (Puebla), sobre los registros de la época colonial.

producían y para qué mercados? ¿Qué técnicas y sistemas agrícolas aplicaban? ¿Cuál era su organización interna? ¿Cuáles eran sus ganancias y su destino? ¿Cuál fue su función social en la historia rural? ¿Qué cambios experimentó la hacienda desde su nacimiento en la época colonial hasta su muerte con la Reforma Agraria? ¿Qué importancia económica tuvo en el siglo xix? ¿Cuál fue su influencia en la vida social y política de ese periodo? Todo eso y más desconocemos de la hacienda. ¿Y qué se puede decir de la historia agraria de las comunidades indígenas, de las luchas y explosiones campesinas?

La historia de nuestro campo está todavía por hacerse. Cada nuevo estudio ofrece una sorpresa.

Industrias y artesanías. Una sola monografía, la de R. C. West sobre el real de minas de Parral, aunque excelente, no basta para formarse una idea de la principal industria de la época colonial. Tampoco es reconfortante señalar que las páginas que Humboldt dedicó a la minería hace más de siglo y medio se mantienen como la mejor visión de conjunto sobre el tema. Es, pues, imprescindible investigar los principales centros mineros (Zacatecas, Álamos, Chihuahua, Guanajuato, San Luis Potosí, Taxco, etcétera), para precisar las alzas y bajas de la producción minera y evaluar la importancia de esa actividad en el desarrollo económico y social de la Colonia. Por otro lado, las aportaciones recientes de D.A. Brading sobre la minería del siglo xviii muestran la conveniencia de combinar el estudio cuantitativo de la producción con el estudio de los hombres que desarrollaron esa actividad. Por ese camino la historia económica pasa a ser lo que siempre debe ser: historia social. Y hasta la fecha sabemos poco de los mineros, de los propietarios y de los trabajadores, de la vida de las minas y de su importancia social y política en el norte donde prosperaron.

En el siglo xix, mientras la mayoría de las minas se encontraban anegadas y destruidas, la minería atrajo los primeros capitales extranjeros y fue tema de graves reflexiones para hombres de Estado que vacilaban entre revigorizarla o impulsar otras actividades. Pero ni los capitales extranjeros ni el interés de algunos mexicanos pudieron reanimarla. Su postración produjo la ruina y el despoblamiento vertiginoso de ciudades antes prósperas, la desaparición de numerosos pueblos y un futuro oscuro para muchas regiones del país... Quizá por ser ésta una historia triste, sabemos tan poco de ella.

El estudio de las industrias y artesanías textiles ha tenido mejor suerte, pero hacen falta monografías que nos aproximen a su funcionamiento y vida interna, a la historia de su producción. Por otra parte, los grandes centros fabriles e industriales del siglo xix (Orizaba-Río Blanco, Puebla, Monterrey, Jalapa, etcétera), todavía esperan su historiador. Algunos, como Orizaba-Río Blanco, son representativos de las grandes transformaciones que sacuden ese siglo: su historia es la historia de los primeros centros fabriles, de la introducción de la tecnología más moderna, de la formación de un proletariado, de las primeras huelgas con reivindicaciones sociales y políticas ...

Comercio interior y exterior. El comercio interno ha sido un tema francamente menospreciado por los historiadores de la época colonial y apenas estudiado por los que se ocupan del siglo xix. Sin embargo, detrás del estudio de ese comercio, de las alcabalas, aduanas, ferias, caminos y transportes, está la clave para comprender una característica fundamental de la estructura de esas sociedades: la reducida extensión de sus mercados. Influyeron en la formación de esa estructura, todavía no sabemos exactamente cómo ni en qué proporción, los accidentes de la geografía, el autoconsumo y el casi nulo poder de compra de la gran masa indígena, la política proteccionista y elitista del imperio español, la situación colonial, el desarrollo de intereses monopólicos locales ... Todo ello limitó el desarrollo posterior del país: opuso un freno al crecimiento del periodo Porfirista y sigue siendo hoy uno de los grandes problemas nacionales. Los archivos de las oficinas que forjaron esas limitaciones (aduanas, peajes, alcabalas), contienen una impresionante documentación que puede manejarse cuantitativamente para fijar el volumen de la circulación comercial a escala citadina, provincial y nacional. Es un material virgen. [19]

En cambio, el comercio exterior ha sido un tema bastante frecuentado por los historiadores, especialmente por los extranjeros. Sin embargo, todavía hay que completar la larga serie construida por Huguette y Pierre Chaunu, sobre todo en la parte relativa al siglo xviii, para unirla a las series de minería y precios agrícolas y comprender mejor el crecimiento de fines de la Colonia. Por otro lado, todavía no se responde una pregunta fundamental tanto para la Colonia como para el siglo xix: ¿cuál fue la influencia real del sector externo en la economía del país? ¿Qué actividades y qué regiones fueron estimuladas o vieron limitarse su desarrollo como consecuencia de la demanda externa? ¿Cómo afectó al desarrollo general del país? ¿Qué estructuras internas determinaron que las relaciones con el exterior se establecieran de una manera y no de otra?

Hacienda pública y política económica. Una constante de los estudios de historia económica ha sido su interés en el desarrollo y los

[19] Para el tratamiento de este material y la posibilidad de aplicarle métodos cuantitativos véase Óscar Altimir, Ezequiel Gallo, Nicolás Sánchez Albornoz y Horacio Santamaría, "Las relaciones económicas interregionales. Metodología para su estudio en el Virreinato de Río de la Plata", *Moneda y Crédito*, 99, dic., Madrid, 1966, pp. 67-89.

problemas del sector privado. En cambio, se ha ignorado la organización económica y administrativa del Estado, y su participación como promotor o regulador del crecimiento económico. Un tema del que se habla mucho hoy día pero del que se desconoce su historia.

No fue sino hasta hace poco que un pequeño y excelente estudio de Andrés Lira vino a revelarnos la estructura de la Real Hacienda a fines del periodo colonial. En un apéndice el autor mostró también la posibilidad de cuantificar el ingreso y el gasto público, utilizando fuentes éditas. Los archivos españoles contienen el material suficiente para convertir esa posibilidad en realidad. ¿Y qué decir de lo que puede hacerse sobre el mismo tema en el siglo xix? Las fuentes de la época son tan abundantes que la investigación se puede hacer a escala estatal y nacional. Y quizá por este camino se aclaren, además de otras cosas, muchas de las interrogantes que rodean la disputa entre centralistas y federalistas. Queda, además, abierta la posibilidad de estudiar la intervención del Estado en la actividad económica a través de fuentes cualitativas: decretos, leyes, reales cédulas, códigos, etcétera. Lo cual llevaría, finalmente a comparar la legislación o las intenciones con la realidad.

Grupos económicos, clases sociales y participación política. Dejé para el final la consideración de esta trilogía no porque deba tratarse como un sector o una parcela más de la historia, sino porque creo que debe estar presente en todo estudio de historia económica. Nada impide transitar de los hechos económicos bien establecidos a los hombres que padecen y promueven la actividad económica; y si desde esta ventana observamos lo que impulsa y anima a esos hombres, sus esperanzas y sus ideas, sus intereses y sus pasiones, entonces estaremos haciendo historia a secas, historia del hombre entero. Esa aspiración, para muchos una utopía, puede satisfacerla el historiador que por preferencias metodológicas se especializa o parte de los hechos económicos.

Hay muchos estudios y materiales que apoyan ese enfoque que va de lo económico a lo socio-político. Sólo hace falta la concepción que guíe el proceso de integración. Las alzas y bajas de la actividad económica, sus crisis y contracciones, no son fenómenos que ocurren en el aire: afectan a empresarios, comerciantes, mineros, agricultores y compradores, a hombres concretos. ¿Por qué no observamos entonces las reacciones que cada uno de esos grupos adopta ante los acontecimientos? Como todos sabemos esas reacciones sobrepasan siempre la esfera de la actividad económica. Los hombres que forman grupos económicos poderosos son fáciles de conocer. Un historiador interesado, por ejemplo, en el crecimiento económico de fines del periodo colonial, podría integrar rápidamente una lista de los principales mineros, comerciantes y agricultores que se beneficiaron con el auge. Podría también hacer un cuadro de sus intereses económicos y ver en qué sectores de la actividad económica se reparten. Finalmente podría hacer un cuadro de sus relaciones familiares y sociales, y así poder establecer las relaciones entre intereses económicos, familiares y grupos sociales. Los acontecimientos políticos que se inician en 1808 y concluyen en 1821 le darían, por último, la oportunidad de estudiar la conducta y las decisiones políticas que esos grupos adoptan ante el proceso revolucionario. El resultado sería un estudio de historia social y política asentado en datos económicos.

Un estudio que combinara estos enfoques parece útil para el siglo xix. Seguramente podría dirimir muchas interrogantes sobre las luchas políticas y sociales entre conservadores y liberales.

En fin, el estudio económico, familiar, genealógico y social de los poderosos es siempre posible. Aparecen en todos lados y su relieve o su exhibicionismo los hacen presa fácil del historiador. Más difícil es precisar la situación económica, social o política de ese todo indiferenciado que llamamos pueblo, plebe, masa, campesinos, proletariado... Y, sin embargo, es indispensable que el historiador procure diferenciar hasta donde es posible los diversos contenidos y estructuras de un movimiento popular. Decir "rebeliones campesinas" sin precisar si se trata de indígenas desposeídos de sus tierras o de pequeños propietarios, es confundir, no hacer historia. Es ignorar que una determinada situación económica produce un tipo de reivindicaciones sociales y cierta praxis o conducta política. Parece a veces que son diferencias de matiz, pero son esenciales para comprender el sentido profundo de un movimiento popular. La revolución zapatista no se explica como movimiento campesino así a secas, sino como un movimiento de comunidades indígenas campesinas, según lo percibió Chevalier y lo demostró Womack. Aquí, como en muchos de los ejemplos anteriores, la relación entre historia económica y social se revela indispensable, necesaria.

THE ECONOMIC HISTORIOGRAPHY
OF TWENTIETH CENTURY MEXICO

CLARK W. REYNOLDS

Economic historiography in its contemporary form goes considerably beyond the recording of historical events. What is most appropriate to the discipline is the development of a framework of analysis whithin which a particular set of events may be ordered and employed to shed light on man's material behavior. Economic history according to Schumpeter- comprises one of the three fundamental building bloks of economic science, along with statistics and theory. He considered the interpretation of history to be the acid test of doctrine, each to be in continual interaction with the other, subject to the constraint of statistical verification. It is with this view in mind that the present paper is written. The fact that the Mexican economy since 1900 has passed through a series of internal and external shock waves that have more or less transformed the process of production, distribution, and final demand, along with most of the institutions upon which economic decisions are based, cannot be ignored in any attempt to comment upon the historiography of the period. One wonders whether conventional economic doctrine is competent to analyze so complex a set of political, social, economic, and even psychological relationships, all undergoing continual change.

What does the received body of doctrine on Mexican economic history of the present century provide in terms of the general themes of development economics? How does it serve to unify and hopefully to explain the events of the turmulous decades since 1910? A cursory glance at the bibliography appended to this paper indicates that there is no lack of material dealing with the period. Indeed almost every topic has received some treatment from *ixtle* to industrialization in monographs and essays touching every corner of the nation and every time period. Yet one may look in vain for general theories of twentieth century Mexican economic change or even for a complete analysis of the economic history of a single sector including the most basic units such as agriculture, industry, mining and services. In those cases where some organic unity does appear, more often than not it is purchased at the price of aprioristic periodization, theoretical determinism, or the judicious selection of data to support the writer's initial premises. Where these methods fail there has been the temptation to employ popular phrases in the place of logic in order to bestow an appearance of order on otherwise disjointed fact and opinion. Can this notable lack of analysis in the literature be attributable to the shortcomings of scholarship, the recent nature of the events, lack of adequate statistics and supporting evidence, or weaknesses in economic theory itself?

Such a question takes on even greater meaning when one surveys the body of received doctrine on economic growth and development under conditions of structural change. The models are generally of a beguiling simplicity, if not in their mathematics at least in their economic content. Moreover few if any are capable of incorporating noneconomic variables in an endogenous form rather than as stochastic "shocks" to the system. Despite the work of pioneers such as Kuznets, Seers, Ruggles, Goldsmith, Chenery and their students, all of whom are making progress in the identification of common structural characteristics among developing systems as well as the functional relationships between growth and structural change, the work is almost solely on economic variables an the results are yet inconclusive [1] The best models developed to date are confined to technological diffusion within single sectors (industry for Nelson; agriculture for David) or the interaction between two sectors, each of which has a high degree of symmetry, under extremely restrictive conditions (Jorgenson; Fei-Ranis; Johnston, etc.). In addition some scholars such as Mamalakis are busily engaged in the formation of development taxonomies, but these have yet to display the functional cohesion essential to models of growth, much less historical verisimilitude. [2]

It is therefore entirely appropriate to challenge the concept of contemporary historiography presented above as relevant to the analysis of developing countries. Can anything more be done than to catalogue events or to engage in partial analysis of single sectors or markets? This writer is convinced that although conventional economic analysis

---

[1] Simon Kuznets, *Economic Growth and Structure*, Norton, 1965.

———, *Modern Economic Growth: Rate, Structure, and Spread*, Yale, 1966. Hollis B. Chenery, "Patterns of Industrial Growth", *American Economic Review*, September, 1960, pp. 624-654.

——— and Lance Taylor, "Development Patterns: Among Countries and Over "Time", Center for International Affairs, Harvard, *Economic Development Report* Nº 102, June 1968 (draft), pp. 1-41.

Dudley Seers, "The Stages of Economic Development of a Primary Producer in the Middle of the Twentieth Century", *The Economic Bulletin of Ghana*, vol. xii, Nº 4, 1963. See also the monumental series of volumes, *Studies in Income and Wealth*, Conference on Research in Income and Wealth. National Bureau of Economic Research. Columbia University Press.

[2] Markos J. Mamalakis, "The Theory of Sectorial Clashes", paper presented at "Class-Sector" Conference, University of Wisconsin at Milwaukee, April 18-19, 1969. This paper and comments by the present writer and others will appear in a forthcoming issue of *Latin American Research Review*.

cannot completely determine the pattern of economic change in a developing system, it can be used to explain a significant portion of economic behavior, leaving a residual to be associated at a later stage with non-economic (or at least non-conventionally economic) factors. Moreover the application of theory to new historical situations will permit its modification and expansion, raising it to a higher order of generality. We may term this historical -*inductive approach* to the development of economic theory. In the Mexican case there is ample scope for the theorizing by induction, since all the best and worst features of both planning and the price system have been present at one time or another during the past half-century. The economy is a mixture of public and private enterprise, artisanry and machine manufacturing, collective and individual farming on both a subsistence and commercial bassi, and domestic and foreign enterprise. Moreover every conceivable type of shock has been experienced by the system from foreign occupation to the massive seasonal emigration of labor in one direction and tourists in the other, to internally and externally induced trade cycles with both surpluses and deficits, deflation and inflation, price stability, capital flight and capital repatriation, agrarian reform, over and undervaluation of the currency, and civil war. The country is an ideal proving ground for social scientific hypothesis-testers, among whom anthropologist, sociologists, and political scientists have figured prominently in recent years. But in the area of economic history caution has taken the better part of courage, perhaps to the relief of more traditional historians, and much of contemporary Mexican development remains an analytical question mark.

Let us examine the literature on the subject. Appendix B, "A Selective Bibliography of Mexican Economic History (Post 1900)", includes several hundred books, articles, and monographs as well as a substantial collection of basic source material on the period. Clearly scholars have been active in the field, and much raw material remains with which to analyze national, regional and/or sectorial relationships. Yet of the mountain of manuscripts which have appeared on the post 1900 economy, few are truly historical in scope, few employ more than the most elementary economic analysis, and still fewer attempt to relate their special topic to broader dimensions of economic and social change except in the most casual and intuitive manner. For example the term "Revolution" appears frequently in association with a host of topics from agriculture to manufacturing, yet with little specificity. If such facile slogans could provide a catalyst for history, this profession would be both richer and wiser. But, alas, terms such as this evoke more emotion than understanding and sell more books than arguments. What is needed is clarification of the postulational basis of such concepts as "Revolution", decomposing them into their institutional and behavioral roots, such that the social structural changes which they presently conceal rather than reveal may be brought to light. Once this is done, it then becomes possible to disaggregate the events which have taken place during the period of abrupt transition covered by the term and to relate these changes to their economic, social, and political determinants.

The same holds for periodizations of history, often taken from the misleading temporal specificity of political events. The abuse of periodization permits scholars to skip lightly over and even ignore important transitional mechanisms whereby one set of institutions and behavioral relations merges into another. It is of little help to those interested in investigating the mechanism of development for one to impose aprioristic time periods on the sequence of events. Instead one should attempt to uncover the synapses of change and, if necessary, induce periods from the data itself, with allowance for those relationships which do not change markedly as well as those which do. More light is often shed on the process of historical evolution by comparing sectors which continue as before with those which do not, than by forcing all observations into the same framework. Thus the continuity of production in the Mexican mining and petroleum industries through most of the period of armed conflict and political rivalry from 1910 to 1920 not only provides important evidence on the nature and intensity of the Revolution but also illustrates a general principal: that periods of major social and political transition tend to depend upon the maintenance of stable and substantional revenue flows, preferably from an export industry.

For Mexico it is beguiling to begin and end time periods with the dates of political administrations. The justification is that new brooms sweep clean and that the executive policies of a highly centralized political system are both the creatures of the current regime and of fundamental importance to the economic process. The dates 1910 and 1940 tend to be taken uncritically as watersheds not only of political but also economic change. Similarly the years 1934 and 1946 marking the beginning of the eras of Cárdenas and Alemán often appear as historical benchmarks. While this writer is as guilty as any of employing such shorthand methods for the classification of economic events, it should be note that the Mexican economy from 1909 to 1912 did not exhibit any notable variation in the pattern of development, nor did it from 1939 to 1941. Just as the rudder turns the vessel only by degrees, so the most basic intention to change policy will often anticipate the results by months and years. The "revealed preference" of planners is subject to a considerable lag. It is perhaps unfortunate, therefore, that most of the literature on modern Mexican economic history begins either with 1910 or 1940 while that of earlier periods tends to end with 1910. Little effort is made to describe or analyze the process by which one period of rapid economic growth such as the Porfiriato merges into a following period of social upheaval and economic disorder, or how a period of relative *laissez faire* such as the twenties might logically be followed by a decade of major institutional reform.

In addition to the aforementioned lack of theory and inattention to transitional detail, much of the literature of the period makes only minimum of use of available statistics and tends to accept the data which are presented with critical abandon. Highly questionable figures appear again and again, in a pyramiding of research, each additional level of which is built upon an initial foundation of statistical sand. The result is a product of scholarship having the same qualities of functionless endurance as the great pyramids themselves. Mexican economic statistics are no different from those of most developing countries. Though they rarely rise above repute and generally demand a considerable degree of cross checking for consistency, the figures can be profitably employed provided the scholar knows something of their sources and methods. Such information has not always been readily available to historians, since Mexican economic statistics have tended to be used as instruments of political prestige and power, rather than as the neutral sources of impartial information which they are supposed to be. Economists have been tempted to assume the role abandoned by court magicians and astrologers who, with their arcane paraphernalia and incantations, prophesied triumph or disaster. Thus economists have tended to keep their data in locked drawers to be drawn forth only at kingly command. Fortunately this situation is now beginning to change as *data power* is shifting to *analysis power* in the higher councils of state. Hopefully this will mark a trend toward a more thorough and critical application of statistics in subsequent writings on the period.

What we need, therefore, and what this paper calls for, is a fresh approach to the writing of contemporary Mexican economic history. Scholars must be prepared to forget whatever prejudices they have formed on the basis of insufficient evidence, in order to view the whole period in a new light. The existing literature must be called ruthlessly to separate the bits and pieces of hard analysis based on firm factual and analytical foundations from the rest. To these few building blocks it will be necessary to add great chunks of new research which require renewed attention to basic statistical detail, patient archival research in Mexico and abroad, interviewing where necessary to fill remaining gaps, and always subject to anaytical rigor. While this may seem an extreme objetive it is essential if the present state of mediocrity in the field is to end. Fortunately there is evidence that a generation of new scholars, well-trained in technical economics and econometric analysis, is already beginning to work on pre-19th century and post 1940 material. Hopefully this research will extend to the intervening years for which much raw data is now waiting to be analyzed.

In the process a whole new set of basic economic statistics will have to be generated, both at the national and regional level, a process which will require substantial institutional support. The Department of Economic Studies of the Bank of Mexico has already financed a considerable body of research on the pre-1940 economy, much of which is now beginning to appear in the form of aggregate indicators of economic activity (382) (388). These series need to be complemented with data on distributive shares, the composition of final demand, savings and investment. Foreign trade data similar to these generated by El Colegio de Mexico's research project on the Porfiriato, under the direction of Daniel Cosío Villegas, need to be extended to the period from 1910 to 1940. Moreover existing times series require considerable cross checking for accuracy both of level and trend, and especially those before 1950. The frequent revision of the national accounts by the Bank of Mexico, while praiseworthy, tends to wreak havoc with scholarship, and this writer has found his own efforts frustrated continually by the need to generate analysis capable of hitting a moving target. A glance at Appendix A ("A Brief History of National Account Estimation in Mexico") will suffice to illustrate the problems that can arise for quantitative historians dealing with Mexico. The estimates of national income and product for selected years vary from ten to fifty percent depending on the date of their derivation, the data then available, and the assumptions employed in their use. In adition the composition of output has changed notably from revision to revision of GDP, as has the rate of growth of such basic aggregates as agriculture, industry, services, and gross investment.

Despite these difficulties enough information now exists to make considerable progress in such broad areas of analysis as: a) the economic determinants of demographic change; b) proximate sources of productivity growth by sector and region; c) the effect of policy decisions on the pattern of resource allocation and growth; d) the effect of structural changes in output on income distribution, the formation of markets, and the pattern of final demand; e) trade and factor movements in relation to the internal structure of production and distribution; f) the regional pattern of economic growth as it has been influenced by public policy, migration, and innovations in transport. It is not that topics such as these have failed to receive attention until now, but rather that they have been placed low in the order of research priorities in favor of a largely descriptive treatment of individual sectors, institutions, and policy problems. While a postponement of attention to the broader issues of economic history may have been justified in the past by shortcomings in data and technique, these difficulties are being gradually overcome. It is hoped that the improved quality and accessibility of both statistics and technique will soon lead to a higher level of analytical research.

In addition to the pure economics of Mexican historiography, which as we have seen leaves much to be desired, there is a problem which we might term the *social scientific identification problem*. This problem has to do with the difficulty of analyzing economic relationships which are affected by the interaction of non-economic factors. The problem is especially complex when non-economic "inputs" are themselves at least partial functions of economic events in the past. In the broadest sense the history of developing countries involves a multidimensional interaction of social, political, economic, and even psychological variables. Thus to simulate, or "explain" the pattern of economic behavior using economic variables alone will tend to misspecify relationships and lead to erroneous conclusions. The more a social system is subject to structural change, the greater the likely error from one-dimensional economic analysis. This means that for countries such as Mexico which have experienced fundamental changes in their social structure in the course of economic development one cannot expect to explain the process of change with accuracy using a solely economic framework of analysis. Rather what is needed is an analytical model which is broad enough to accomodate non-economic factors in the transition process, yet narrow enough to permit the statement and testing of hypotheses. An example will help to illustrate this point.

The economic disturbances in Mexico in the late twenties and early thirties brought about import by the world depression, led to a shortage of liquidity, falling prices and wages, high unemployment, and general social unrest. This was compounded by the internal political and religious struggle, of which the Cristero Rebellion and the assassination of President-elect Obregón were but symptoms. It has been argued that deteriorating economic conditions brought about a growing lack of confidence in the *laissez faire* policies advocated by Calles and the hand-picked administrations from 1928-1934. Dissatisfaction with the state of the economy as it presently was run reawakened interest in more radical goals of the Revolution as expressed in the Constitution of 1917. This led to a groundswell of support for Cárdenas, a man backed by a coalition of progressive state governors, supported by General Calles, who had already proved his zeal for agrarian reform and labor organization as governor of Michoacán. The changing economic circumstances of the time, according to this view, laid the groundwork for political change.

Once in office Cárdenas invoked new policies, different in degree if not in kind, leading to wholesale reform of the land tenure system. This had been tried earlier by Portes Gil, but his term of office had been short-lived. The greater degree of economic policy space created by the depression was taken advantage of by Cárdenas from 1934 to 1938 and he acted boldly to alter the pattern of asset ownership. However he was limited as to the extent of actual income distribution which could be achieved, since income itself was depressed during the thirties through depression, pessimism regarding the treatment of private property, as well as general uncertainty about the future. Investment tended to dry up, along with tax revenues, and government expenditures were limited as the government attempted to avoid inflation and devaluation of the currency. In this case political action was both impelled and constrained by the level and growth of economic activity. At the same time the pattern of economic activity began to reflect the asset redistributive policies of Cárdenas. Thus the process of economic history of the period involved an interaction between economic and political events, not subject to any simple apriori model of material or political determinism.

To adequately interpret such political economic symbiosis calls for a modern Beard or Turner. Economic events should be characterized by the way in which they are interwoven into the fabric of social change as a simultaneously interacting recursive system. This is quite different from the tendency among Mexican writers dealing with the post-revolutionary period to impose aprioristic doctrines on events, sweeping all contravening evidence under the rug. It is time to break the chains of simple dialectical materialism and open the profession in Mexico to an objective analysis of the process of social interaction. This will lead to a true dialectic in which economic factors are seen to be both causes and effects of political, social, and attitudinal change. If the revolution can be ascribed in part to failures of the preceding economic production and distribution process, so it can be explained by the capacity of the same production process to provide material support for fundamental social and political change. Similarly changes in the economic process cannot be wholly attributed to prior economic events, but rather to the way in which society in response to these events, acted to change the nature of the economy and its direction of growth. Under the circumstances it is important to free the analysis of the period as much as possible form ex post doctrines of historical inevitability.

One way to overcome the natural tendency to regard observations as the inevitable consequence of their antecedents is to focus on the synapses of change mentioned earlier. It is useful to speculate on what might have happened had slight variations taken place at those transaction points. Such speculation, which would be idle without at least some simple analytical model, becomes possible once social theory is introduced into historiography. The "new economic history" is an example of the use of such models to predict what "might have been" under slightly different conditions, as a way of shedding light on what did in fact occur. This is more than the idle amusement of armchair brigadiers refighting Borodino with factors of production instead of troops and resource-allocation rules rather than military strategy. Counterfactual analysis can do much to clarify causal relationships in the historical process. By determining the limits of economic behavior under given conditions of factor endowments, supply and demand relationships, and public policy, subject to exogenous disturbances, it is possible to determine "residuals" in the pattern of change which cannot be accounted for by economic factors alone. For example, by estimating production functions for which assumptions are made about input-output relationships, one can discover the portion of observed changes in production which the analysis would not predict. An effort can then be made to account for this discrepancy in the analysis by respecifying the model, or by adding new factors which had preciously been ignored.

The entire growth process of an economy or sector is subject to this type of analysis. It is possible to estimate how change would have occured under conditions assumed to characterize the period under consideration. The extent to which actual events departed from the predictions of the model show up the strength of the initial assumptions, specification of equations, or degree of underdetermination of the model (more unknowns than equations). Among the missing elements it is quite possible that social and political factors will prove significant. The socially-conscious economic historian, by seeking to improve the explanatory power of the analysis, may be hoped to uncover important new dimensions of social interaction.

This method of using theory to shed light on the influence of non-traditional factors in economic change was experimented with by the writer in the case of Mexican agricultural development under circums- tances of radical land tenure change (94). Agricultural production functions were estimated independently for the five census zones of the country by decade from 1930 to 1960, and regional output was estimated back to 1900. The results showed significant differences in inputs, outputs, and productivity both by regional and decade. These disparities when associated with the differing regional and temporal pattern of tenure change, infrastructure investment, and rural population growth, do much to clarify the relationship between traditional and non-traditional factors in the development of this key sector of the economy. In addition the analysis lays the groundwork for subsequent research on the causes of change underlying the proximate sources of production and productivity growth measured here. Hopefully a literature will develop on rural technology, marketing, cropping, tenure conditions, incentives, migration, and institutional change, building on and modifying the results of these highly aggregative regional models.

A similar investigation at a higher level of aggregation was undertaken to uncover some of the possible consequences of social and political changes associated with the Revolution and subsequent Reform, during the years 1910 to 1940. [3] A simple model was employed to estimate the expansion of value added in seven principal production sectors for the period 1910 to 1940, under a range of assumptions about productivity and population growth in the absence of Revolution. The population growth assumptions were crucial, in that they supposed that those deaths during the decade 1910-20 attributable to the disturbances of the Revolution and its aftermath did not, in fact, occur. Non-agricultural output was projected on a commodity by commodity basis under various productivity assumptions, all of which were constrained from outperforming representative Latin American countries over the same period. Agricultural production for export was estimated on the same basis, while that for home consumption was related to the hypothetical rates of population growth assuming that actual per capita productivity trends would have held despite the considerably higher rate of population growth from 1910 to 1920.

The resulting estimates of gross domestic product (GDP) for the years 1925, 1930, and 1940 were subjected to consistency cheks in terms of domestic savings, foreign exchange, and labor and implicit productivity requirements necessary to achieve the projected levels of GDP by 1940. The two most optomistic projections indicated that the actual level of GDP in 1940 might have been achieved as early as 1925 had the losses of the Revolution not occured, and that GDP in 1940 might actually have been 36 to 61% above observed levels under alternative conditions. The two low projections, on the other hand, were considerably less favorable, the lowest placing GDP at only 12% above the observed level. All of these estimates were extremely sensitive to the assumed rate of population growth. Thus while projected GDP was shown to be as much as 61% above the actual 1940 levels, *per capita* product under the most optomistic alternative assumptions only reached 12% above observed levels of per capita GDP in that year. The range of per capita estimates was considerably narrowed, and the lowest figures were actually 2% *below* observed levels in 1940. What is evident from the results is that in the absence of Revolution Mexico might well have possessed a considerably larger population and corres-

[3] Reynolds, Clark W. *The Mexican Economy: Twentieth Century Structure and Growth* (94), Appendix B. See also, "Ideology and Economic Development in Mexico", Food Research Institute Discussion Paper N⁹ 69-1 (Revised). April, 1969.

pondingly greater absolute income, but even under the most optomistic assumptions it would not have enjoyed a much greater rate of growth in *per capita* income than did, in fact, occur during the thirty years after 1910.

This type of analysis is by no means intended to substitute for the hard factual research of traditional economic historiography. At best a complement to such investigation, it can nevertheless prove helpful in clarifying basic questions of interpretation such as alternative views institutional change. It enables one to uncover weaknesses in discriptive on the economic consequence of revolutionary political, social, and analysis, by forcing the scholar to determine an internally consistent set of relationships and to be explicit about the assumptions involved. Since any interpretation of history involves implicit if not explicit model-building, this approach simply allows the theorist to test out his hypotheses in terms of the best evidence available. Where evidence essential to the analysis is missing, it points to the direction in which statistical research should proceed. Where the model reveals the outcome to be extremely sensitive to certain relationships, one may then go to a more detailed institutional investigation of these relationships. For example in the case of the model above, the obvious next step is to investigate the limits between economic, social, political and demographic change for the period 1910-20 in order to isolate the underlying causes of massive loss of life during those years. To what extent were the causes associated with the Revolution, and to what extent were they randomly induced? Was the influenza epidemic of that period directly or indirectly attributable to the socio-economic disturbances of the time? If not, then the "opportunity cost" of the Revolution as measured above may be based upward by the assumption of population growth "as usual" in the absence of Revolution.

Similar work should be done on the market versus non-market influences on output and productivity over the period 1910 to 1940, including a clarification of what actually did occur in production, distribution, and final demand. For example in the case of agriculture the research mentioned above permitted the writer to engage in a major revision of the gross agricultural production index for the years 1910 to 1930. The figures turn out to be quite different from those in even the most recent Banco de México series (382), owing to the inclusion of a much wider sample of commodities in the index. The preponderance of traditional crops such as *maíz* and *frijol* in the earlier indexes bias them downward substantially (139) (262) (31) (382), since these commodities behaved far worse than cash crops during the period. The use of the new series on production, along with the regional disaggregation, permits a new interpretation of the consequences of armed conflict, population dislocation, agrarian reform, and world prices on the agricultural sector. For example production in the Northwestern region moved forward rapidly from 1910 to 1930, while that of the Center and South Pacific lagged far behind.

In addition to more quantitative exploration of aggregate and sectorial production, productivity, and distributional characteristics during the twentieth century, and particularly for the statistical and analytical "dark age" from 1910 to 1940, there is the need for critical investigation of key decision-making units and their historical evolution. Mexican economic activity has been profoundly influenced by the activities of such entities as the Banco de México, Nacional Financiera, Mexican Social Security Institute (IMSS), Banco de Comercio Exterior, CONASUPO, and private banking chains such as the Banco de Comercio. The major work and most conspicuous success to date in the area of institutional historiography has been on the development of financial intermediation. A descriptive literature on the history of banking and financial intermediation appears in the works of Bett (12), Shelton (119), Anderson (48), Goldsmith (49), Blair (119), and Aubey (3). This is supported by the somewhat more analytical studies of the relationship between growth and financial intermediation by Bennett (10), Campos Andapia (18) (333), Brothers and Solís (14), and Koehler (341). Piecing together this material, one begins to see a fairly clear picture of the broad lines of institutional change in the financial sector during the twentieth century. The decade from 1910 to 1920, during which repeated currency crises and bank failures severely upset the monetary system, is treated with the kind of critical insight that comes from close association with some of the institutions involved, by Kemmerer (60).

The inflationary years of the forties and early fifties are subjected to alternatively monetarist and structuralist approaches so ubiquitous to Latin American economics of the period in the works of Siegel (106), Navarrete (78) (354), Mueller (346), Brothers (155), and Solís (298). The transition from inflation to price stability between the mid-fifties and mid-sixties is skillfully handled by Brothers and Solís (14) and Koehler (341), with Koehler adding insights from a disequilibrium income-determination model (fixed interest rates, credit rationing, and restrictions on foreign investment) to the more conventional quantity-theoretical foundations of his predecessors. The twenties and thirties have yet to receive adequate attention by monetary historians. The earlier decade is of interest because of the association between liquidity shortages, falling prices and their possible impact on growth. The latter period combines expansion of liquidity in the form of paper pesos with a growing government deficit, both of which lead to moderate inflation. The affect of the silver agreements with the U. S. during the early thirties, their eventual expiration, and capital flight associated with the oil expropriation of 1938 deserve to be analyzed in more detail, especially in relation to income stability and growth.

Despite all of the institutional material on financial activities of the modern period, one looks in vain for a work comparable in depth and scope to the admirable historiography of Potash in his now-classic study of the nineteenth century Banco de Avío. What is lacking in these studies, from the viewpoint of the historian, is a fully fleshed contextual framework within which the institution finds its place. There is too little attention to the character and motivation of entrepreneurship involved, the alternatives facing the enterprise, its role in the broader cultural and political history of the time. One would hope that increased analytical sophistication would not drive out painstaking attention to institutional detail. Yet this seems to be happening in work on the twentieth century. Hopefully the theoretical and statistical rapacity of the modern economic historian can be combined with renewed enthusiasm for archival research. Until then the best that can be expected are well-sculpted systems of bone, nerves, and sinews, all of which distinguish anatomy from design and laboratory specimens from statuary.

More work is also needed on the history of policy-making than one now finds in the literature. The dimensions of policy space within which government decision makers operate are broadly defined and subject to considerable change over time. Historiography can be used to clarify these relationships and reveal their implications for economic activity. The transmission of information on market signals to decision makers, and the reverse flow of commands, are both subject to a greater or lesser degree of "noise" in the political system, if one may borrow from the terminology of communications theory. Socio-economic historians such as Vernon and Wionczek (118) (119) (126) (322) skillfully interpret the subtle interplay of social-psychological and economic factors underlying the pattern of public policy in Mexico. As such they set forth a pattern of research which might well be followed by other students of contemporary Latin American history.

Wionczek in his thoughtful analysis of the nationalization of electric power, and more recently that of the sulphur industry (126) comes to grips with problems which beset all developing countries forced to balance the requirements of foreign capital and technique against a mandate of national autonomy and maximum relative shares from domestic resources. While one might have hoped for more statistics and conventional economic analysis in his two important studies, including a fuller statement of sales, costs, profits, and returns to the domestic economy over time, as a basis for evaluating the purely economic content of the decisions both of industry and the government, it is perhaps fair to say that Wionczek offers the most carefully researched and conventionally historical scholarship of the modern period. Vernon on the other hand is at his best when dealing with the broad sweep of events and the atmosphere in which they take place (118). His insights, such as those concerning the role-playing of *políticos* versus *técnicos*, are often revealing, though he is content to paint history with a broad brush. One is left with a highly impressionistic set of interpretations of events, so much so that as hypotheses they are difficult if not impossible to test. There are few statistics employed in his analysis, and those which are (such as his now obsolete series on gross investment) lead to a quite erroneous view of the mechanism of income determination and stabilization in the postwar period. (See, for example, the detailed critique of the Vernon model by Koehler [341], as well as that of the writer [94]).

In calling for more detailed research on the individual subperiods of the modern era, one may point to the pathbreaking precedent of the Cosío Villegas series on the Porfiriato, and particularly the brilliant analyses of the development of industry, foreign trade, and the general economy prior to 1910 by Fernando Rosenzweig (280) (281) (282). This work provides not only an uncovering of hitherto buried factural evidence on the period, including structural evidence on the evolution from artisanry to machine manufacturing in such basic activities as textiles, but a sophisticated interpretation of the interaction between production and employment and its influence on the wage level and the rate of urbanization. [4] What Rosenzwieg did for the pre-Revolutionary period must now be done for the successive years, starting perhaps with the manufacturing sector. Mosk's classic o the subject (75), while still a vital source of institutional detail for the period of the forties, suffers from a reliance on production data which are now obsolete and tends to neglect the years before 1940 during which much capacity was installed which came into full production only after the beginning of World War II. For more recent years there is a growing literature on the process of import substitution and the use of commercial policy to promote industrialization, owing to the recent research fad in this area (see Izquierdo [119], Bueno [332], Bacha [144], Strassman [112] [208], King [339], Maneschi and Reynolds [343] and Reynolds [359]). However little of this material covers the prewar period, and most of it deals with the fifties and onward. (A longer study on industrialization by King has come to the attention of the

---

[4] In addition an analytical reworking of the census data on employment by sector for the period 1895 to 1950 has recently been prepared by Keesing (338), qualifying some of the earlier series in El Colegio de Mexico's sourcebook on the Porfiriato (396). This important study will shortly appear in the *Journal of Economic History*.

author but is still in draft form and was not available for examination
at the time of this writing.)

As to historiography of other sectors of the economy, agriculture
alone would deserve a paper in itself. Fully one quarter to one-third of
the references in the bibliography deal directly or indirectly with this
sector, yet, as has been mentioned above, the quantitative analysis of
agricultural development in Mexico remains fragmentary and relatively
unrelated to the general development process. Studies such as those
by Flores (44), and Moisés de la Peña (32), introduce important
issues of social and political development into the agrarian model. As
such they are written in the best tradition of post-Revolutionary Mexican historiography, but in such efforts there is a far greater need for
factual support and analysis than even a purely economic study would
require if the reader is to accept the conclusions on the basis of reason
rather than faith. Moreover the process of intersectoral flows of labor,
capital, and intermediate goods and services between the agricultural
and non-agricultural sectors has yet to be analyzed in detail, despite
the crucial nature of such flows to the development of agriculture itself.
Rural income distribution studies do not abound, though some material
is available in the works of Navarrete (79), Singer (367), Solís (368),
Sturmthal (302), Reynolds (94), and others. One of the critical issues
facing contemporary policy-makers is the eventual disposition of the
institution of the *ejido*. The history of this institution occupies a good
share of the literature on Mexican agriculture, from which we should
not omit the classical offerings of the Northamericans Simpson (109),
Seinor (102), and Whetten (123), as well as the important earlier
work on land tenure by McBride (68). Fernández y Fernández has
competently dealt with the dilemma of this curiously Mexican institution as it relates to the technological and sociological exigencies of
the modern era (43) (180) (181) (185) (186) (187) (188), while
Eckstein has employed econometric analysis to determine the productivity of a sample of agricultural units by size and tenure class (37).
This research sheds much light on the historical impact of agrarian
reform on production, since it combines the statistical analysis with
case studies. The first volume, which ends with the 1950 census data,
is brought up to date in a more recent study for CIDA (38) in which
agriculture is more explicitly related to the overall process of Mexican
development.

Considerable insight into broader issues of social change may often
be obtained by looking in detail at a given region or project. Project
analysis in Mexico has bee relatively popular in the thesis mills of
American universities, owing to the lure of the land and the romance
of its history and institutions. Two studies of river basin development
written under such circumstances deserve mention, those of Barkin

on the Tepalcatepec Region (328) and Kink (339) (to be published jointly in Spanish by Siglo XXI. To these should be added the work by Poleman on the Papaloapan Project (89). While these works represent useful applications of comparative cost analysis, they tend to be confined to the strictly economic dimensions of the subject and as such may not be said to qualify as economic history in the broadest sense. Indeed the impact of major expenditures on rural infraestructure in hitherto impoverished regions has an effect on the pattern of society, culture, and economic institutions far beyond those which are readily amenable to statistical measurement. What is called for if this impact is to be adequately interpreted, is *regional* rather than project historiography, in which the broad social characteristics of the region are examined in detail before, during, and after the advent of the project. While such an undertaking may require far more time and attention than a conventional Ph. D. dissertation in economic development, it is essential if we are to fully appraise the impact of a major exogenous economic shock on the economic life of the community.

Perhaps at this point it might be appropriate to note that the weaknesses of contemporary economic historiography, of which the work on Mexico is but a sympton, reflect the institutional contraints of the modern university system. In this system students are required to "do a thesis" in a circumscribed period of time, with limited resources. If the student is to research a foreign area, as is often the case for those who explore the curiosities of Mexican history, still more time is required in simply becoming acquainted with the lay of the land. It is not surprising, then, that the product of this type of scholarship is so frequently 40% hypothesis, 40% technique, and only 20% historical detail. What may be required if the products of scholarship are to be improved is a change in the conditions of research. Perhaps the period for writing of a Ph. D. dissertation in economic history should be extended to take into consideration the special requirements of the field. Perhaps more funds should be allocated to post-doctoral research in this area. Perhaps local institutions should support the kind of work on the post-1910 period that has been so impressively undertaken for the Porfiriato by El Colegio de México. Indeed there is no reason why Mexican students, with their rising degree of analytical sophistication, should not be incouraged to explore the neglected areas of contemporary economic history with the most powerful techniques at their disposal and with the requisite amount of time for careful attention to institutional detail.

A few other exemplary cases of historical research deserve mention. The work of Wilkie on oral history of the period promises to fill important gaps in the history of decision-making (124), while his comparison of the policy statements with actual expenditures of Post Revolutionary administrations throws considerable light on the revealed preferences of Mexican presidents (124). His indexes of social change represent a highly experimental and controversial application of quantitative indicators of welfare at the state, regional, and national level. While these indexes are arbitrary in their choice of indicators (relying on census reporting of social characteristics), weighting, and mixture of stocks and flows, they are indicative of the process of social change and offer something beyond the characteristic series on *per capita* income alone. Alas, they do not substitute for the kind of detailed welfare analysis which one might wish in attempting to interpret the social impact of economic change over the period. Here again one is happy to have at least a skeleton of information but will be more content once there is flesh upon the bones. What will perhaps prove to be Wilkie's most important work on contemporary Mexican history is yet to appear, that dealing with Cárdenas' governorship of Michoacán and later succession to the presidency. In this work the logical next step is taken, following the formulation of broad social-economic indicators, and that is to provide the institutional detail within which they take on meaning.

All too often it is to historians, rather than economists, that credit must be given for the broad-based research on which economic analysis must depend. In this respect Howard Cline's two volumes dealing with the pre and post-1950 periods respectively are invaluable sources of information on the panorama of change within which economic events play only a partial, if often crucial, role (24) (25). The bibliographical Appendix to the first volume is particularly helpful in bringing up to date (1953) the material in the Mexican section of *The Economic Literature of Latin America* (2 vols., 1935-36). Similarly Bernstein's massive volume on the history of Mexican mining provides much legal institutional and historical detail on the evolution of this sector which first led and then followed the general development process (11). One of his most provocative suggestions, worth testing in detail, is that U.S. ownership of the mining sector increased during the twenties. This is supported by Sherwell's data on the falling Mexican share of value added (105). Unfortunately the mining sector, despite its importance, has yet to be subjected to a thorough economic analysis. Except for some valuable estimates in the work of Navarrete on returns to Mexico from the extractive industries over time the wealth of statistics on mining remains largely unexplored. The petroleum sector has a relative large literature, especially in terms of the circumstances surrounding the expropriation in 1938, including a classic analysis of the history prepared at the time by Jesús Silva Herzog. The memoirs of U.S. Ambassador Josephus Daniels and Cronin's highly readable *Josephus Daniels, in Mexico* shed considerable light on the economic as well as political issues. A valuable collection of statistics and an insider's report on the industry from 1938 to 1960 appears in ex-PEMEX director Antonio Bermúdez' volume *The Mexican National Petroleum Industry* (Stanford, 1963). Nevertheless much remains to be done to analyze the economic causes and consequences of the petroleum seizure, a subject which could prove to be a scholarly bonanza.

Time and space do not permit attention to the fundamental contributions to scholarship of the national and international agencies whose concern has been to discover the economic structure on which economic and financial policy must depend. The annual surveys of the UN Economic Commission for Latin America, beginning with the essay on Mexico in the 1949 survey (430) are important sources of both data and interpretation of the economic growth process. Similarly the ECLA study of external disequilibrium, its causes and consequences, prepared in the mid-fifties by a group of extremely insightful political-economists including Víctor Urquidi, Juán Noyola, Celso Furtado, and Osvaldo Sunkel, all of whom were associated with the Mexico City office of ECLA at the time, proved highly prophetic in its projections of the balance of trade and constitutes one of the first attempts at model-building to simulate the process of Mexican economic development (431). The World Bank study of the structure of the Mexican economy from 1939 to 1950 and its implications for capital —absorptive capacity is another landmark, including some of the first estimates of the economic and functional distribution of income for that decade (55) (85). More recently the Banco de México has vastly improved the quality and availability of its economic statistics. Input-output tables have been prepared for 1950 and 1960. Time series on the level and distribution of income by activity and factor shares for the period 1950-1967 have just been released, on a provisional basis, and deserve careful attention (379). Earlier series used as a basis for policy making were prepared by the Banco de México and the Secretaría de Hacienda in a joint volume for the period 1939 to the mid-sixties (387). Economists Víctor Urquidi, Leopoldo Solís, Ernesto Fernández Hurtado, statistician Rubén Gleason, and numerous others have cooperated to bring about an outpouring of data which cannot help but revolutionize the interpretation of modern Mexican economic history. The profession owes a vote of thanks to the untiring efforts of these economic pioneers who have labored to bring order from chaos, both in terms of data and their interpretation.

In summary the ground has only been scratched in this field. There is need for considerably more attention to such basic issues as the economic impact of roads and railroads, technological innovations in construction and earth-moving as they have contributed to a unification of national markets, the regional pattern of internal trade and its relationship to natural and induced processes of sectorial expansion, the role of mining in the initial expansion of the modern period and the opportunity cost of policy-induced neglect of this sector in recent years, the economic impact of the bracero program and the unbalanced growth of the frontier economy along the U.S. border-its benefits and costs, the economic history of the cattle industry from the Porfiriato to the present —a virtually neglected sector, and that of the service sector which has absorbed most of the increase in the urban labor force since the Revolution, rather than industry. Foreign investment needs considerably more attention than it has yet received, the interesting interpretations of Ceceña (22), Wionczek (126), Brandenberg (153) (13), and others notwithstanding. Fertile ground still exists for work on the henequen industry and its impact on the export economy of Yucatán, the history of the sugar industry (including an investigation of its amazingly rapid recovery in the twenties), cotton, and textiles, all of which, by reflecting in a single sector the varying currents of economic, political, and social change, could provide vast amounts of new evidence for interpretation of the period. In short much remains to be done. The areas of analytical wilderness which remain are much wider than the present patches of plowed ground. Hopefully those who wish to clear the new land will be pioneers in social development analysis as defined above, rather than purely institutional or theoretical in focus. Disaggregation is likely to prove more helpful than aggregate analysis, in the future, provided that the broader set of social-economic relations are not forgotten in the process. Hopefully the methodology developed in connection with Mexican historiography will be applied elsewhere in those cases where the process of economic history involves broad interactions of regions, social classes, and production sectors subject to periods of profound political shocks. For one who feels that U.S. economic history leaves much to be desired in its dealings with times of major social-political-and institutional change, such as the Civil War, the Great Depression, both World Wars, and the postwar assimilation of racial and population explosions, Mexico may set a pattern of investigation. In all of this it should not be forgotten that economic historiography is the handmaiden of theory and policy. While events never exactly repeat themselves, their components often recombine in similar ways, allowing the insights drawn from earlier periods to be applied at great social saving.

COMMENTARY

STANLEY J. STEIN

INTRODUCTION: THE FLORESCANO BIBLIOGRAPHY

Enrique Florescano's contribution consists of two separate sections, bibliography and observations on the state of the discipline of history as it has been and is currently practiced in Mexico, and recommendations on how it ought to be practiced. Students of Mexican history are already in his debt for his insight, commitment and enthusiasm for the possibilities of the renovated and enlarged discipline of history and for 72 pages of bibliography. One need hardly add that he speaks with the authority of his recently published *Precios del maíz y crisis agrícolas en México* (1969).

His analytical bibliography lists major publications and articles on Mexico's economic and social history sweeping through more than four centuries from pre-conquest times to the end of the Porfiriato. Not only is the bibliography logically analytical and frequently annotated, it lists published materials on the new foci of the discipline, e.g., historical demography, economic history in particular agrarian history, price fluctuations, changing technology and agricultural crises. It is in no sense a criticism to note that bibliographical distribution among the three periods covered, preconquest, colonial and independence periods, is uneven. For Florescano has had to follow the distribution of historians' interests and consequently the colonial period occupies roughly sixty per cent of the total bibliography by pages. It should also be noted that the bibliography has no separate section devoted to the period of Insurgency, 1810-1821. This is a selective not a comprehensive bibliography, for published primary source are omitted; it is sparely but judiciously annotated. One suspects that Florescano will not be able to prevent its early publication in the Proceedings of this Reunion dispite his stated intention to withhold its publication until a later date.

OBSERVATIONS ON MEXICAN HISTORIOGRAPHY

Florescano has introduced the bibliography with a widely ranging review of the way in which the history of Mexico has been written and with suggestion for new themes and new methodology. By turn, he emphasizes the petrification of political history in Mexico, the isolation of practitioners of the discipline both from colleagues and from the potential advantages of other disciplines; he indicates the utility of economic history especially the quantitative over the purely descriptive; and he pinpoints the type of investigation potentially most fruitful at the macro— or national level, at the regional and local level, and by economic sectors; and he concludes with a plea for the integration of economic and socio-political factors to create a rounded history or in his eloquent phrase, "historia del hombre todo".

Although Florescano is impatient to see the new quantitative economic history incorporated into the research, reflections and writings of Mexican historians, he recognizes that one need not await decades of monographic accumulation for the appearance of works of synthesis. He recognizes too the danger that the narrowly focused monograph on one aspect of economic history may well leave the traditionally oriented political historians unimpressed. So he suggests that economic historians present their findings within a larger framework and that they, along with other types of historians, consider the heuristic synthesis, the synthesis based on insight derived from the monographic fragment, from the research probe in depth which has often opened up wider horizons. Above all, he offers no unilateral road to the understanding of an era via one variety of economic or any other history. There are, he indicates, many approaches to economic history.

A CRITIQUE

To fault so comprehensive and judicious an introduction to a substantial bibliography is not easy. Nor is there any reason to do so. What follows is not criticism but views that have been stimulated by his underlying emphasis and reliance upon the ambitious, comprehensive quantitative techniques of what may be termed the French school of "total" history.

Florescano's strongest criticism is directed against the persistent tradition of political history among Mexican historians despite the appearance elsewhere of new historical modes of thought and techniques of analysis, notably in Western Europe and the United States. His impatience is understandable; yet equally understandable is the fact that national historiographical trends reflect the predominant preoccupations of every epoch. No doubt the variety and utility of new analytical tools affect the mode of analysis; what precedes the choice of approach and technique, however, is primarily the desire to achieve explanations of the past more illuminating of the present than the accepted, that is, the traditional. But more baldly, pressures and interests determine the historians' interests and methodologies as historiographical trends of the twentieth century in the United States, France and Mexico indicate.

In the historiographical development of the United States interest in economic factors obviously antedates Charles Beard's *An Economic Interpretation of the Constitution of the United States* (1911). Beard was not the first in the United States to observe and document the relationship of economic interest to political structure, function and groups. What must be recalled is that the *Economic Interpretation* appeared precisely at that moment in US history when powerful monopolistic and oligopolistic business organizations had aroused the opposition of broad segments of the people of the US, when business organizations seemed to control effectively access to the political system and when the people of the US wondered whether the constitution was indeed a God-given instrument to permit the flowering of liberty for God's chosen people in the Promised Land. Not inappropriately, Beard and his Columbia University colleague, Robinson, were later to become the leading protagonists of integrated history rather than history as chronicle of past politics, what became the "new history" in the US.

In much the same light one may view the wide vogue of price and wage history in the post-World War I years of inflation terminated by the deflation of the Great Depression. Earl Hamilton, as Pierre Vilar has reminded us, was stimulated by profit inflation in the US between 1916-1919 and by the phenomenon of post-war inflation in Western Europe. These elements and —one may presume— the upsurge of socialism in once capitalist Russia led him to examine the origins of capitalism in Western Europe and to ascribe over-riding importance to price inflation and to profits developing from the lag of wages behind prices. To be sure, Hamilton was not the first historian to focus upon the sixteenth-century origins of capitalism or upon prices. Nor was he unique in the field at the time. His article on "American Treasure and the Rise of Capitalism, 1500-1700" appeared in 1929; the carefully elaborated monographs on Simiand (1932), Labrousse (1933) and Hamilton (1934) rapidly followed. Without streching the point unduly, these historians utilized a sectoral analysis to cast light upon capital formation in the long-term economic growth and development under capitalism.

The clearest example of methodology at the service of new foci of interest, and not the reverse, is offered by the French school of historiography. It may be facetious, but it is clearly beyond dispute that in this case quantity alone is not responsible for qualitative change. What characterizes the group which includes Braudel, Goubert, Baehrel, Meuvret, Leroy Ladurie and —in Iberian and Ibero-American studies— Chaunu and Vilar is their emphasis upon quantification in handling economic and social data and, in the second place, their attempt to view the past through many analytical prisms to achieve "total" history. They have been distinguished disciples of distinguished master —Lefebvre, Bloch, Febvre. More to our point, the historians who have focused upon French problems have structured their analyses around the problems of pre-industrial agrarian societies at the regional level in response to such nagging questions of their time as (1) the relationship between enduring agrarian structures and the timing and rate of French industrialization; (2) the factors responsible for long-term French demographic patterns, i.e., the role of the epidemic disease, subsistence and property size and ownership in demographic fluctuations; and (3) not to exhaust the catalogue, the role of market forces —supply, demand, prices— in agrarian production. In other words, this school, has furnished outstanding examples of aggregative regional studies, underscoring socio-economic factors, utilizing quantitative as well as descriptive data. Integrative at the regional level, these studies still await a new national synthesis of the character supplied almost forty years ago by Bloch. Admirable models of the historians' craft, the French studies have certain limitations in the Latin American context. First, their regionalist focus, and, second, the fact that with the exception of Lefebvre's *Les paysans du nord pendant la revolution* the French essays in "total" history simply omit the great watershed in French development, the Revolution.

Even de much studied French Revolution is a *terra incognita* from the viewpoint of long-term agrarian studies.

THE CASE OF MEXICO

It appears to be the burden of Florescano's argument that Mexico has lagged in the development of economic and social history and that where such studies have appeared since about 1940 the methodology employed indicates "los viejos hábitos, los métodos gastados, y la incapacidad creativa de la historia tradicional". By this he seems to mean that economic and social history is still descriptive rather than quantitative and that it lacks any new conceptual apparatus.

These phenomena are easily explained. In the first place, no one questions the high quality and volume of Mexican historiography of the nineteenth century from Bustamante and Alamán to Hernández y Dávalos, Paso y Troncoso and Genaro García. Their focus was properly that great single block of Mexican history and its inevitable sequel, the colony and the insurgency and its aftermath. That they emphasized politics and personalities reflects an age which saw in political structure and function the resolution of conflicts confined largely to the economic and social elite. On the other hand, at the end of the Porfiriato when the splendor of the age was already tarnished and dissent became more widespread and dangerous, there appeared the classic work of Molina Enríquez which economic and social historians may still consult with profit. The Mexican Revolution diverted and inevitably wasted energy and talent; it is only since the end of large-scale agrarian reform, the acceleration of industrial growth and the unbroken succession of governments that new cadres of historians have appeared. One might hypothesize that those talents which under other circumstances might have been channeled to economic and social history, have instead been absorbed by government and by the discipline of political science and especially economics. Clark Reynold's bibliography suggests that in Mexico the interest in economics has been sustained and substantial.

The end of the most recent, most profound and most popular of Mexico's historical cycles, the Revolution, offers historians an opportunity to employ a sophisticated and interdisciplinary methodology to illuminate Mexico's past. The opportunity, however, should not be limited to the Revolution; rather, we should examine all the great cycles of Mexico's past, conquest in the sixteenth century, rapid growth and change at the end of the eighteenth which culminated in anti-colonial warfare, then the Reforma and its sequel. It is not enough, for example, to formulate a balance sheet of the Revolution. Historians must sort out the unique and incidental from the perennial, the persistent, the enduring; in other words, now is the time to emphasize the structures, the *supervivencias*, the hard substrata of Mexico's history. This was the challenge before Lucas Alamán and later Molina Enríquez and each met it in his own way, through his own ideological prism. It is our challenge to examine an even longer time-span than theirs, to pinpoint the structures and to place them intelligibly within the context of the long-term or secular movements.

We must avoid the congenital tendency of historians to examine discrete elements and periods of the past, to confine our conclusions to the boundaries of one era. For example, we will continue to have an imperfect view of the society and economy that Spaniards erected in Mexico by the last quarter of the sixteenth century unless we review the pre-conquest cultures of Central Mexico, their society and economy and in particular the stresses and strains, the frictions and fissures that most certainly had developed in the fifteenth century when Central Mexico may have had a population upwards of 20 million. Put another way, historians must reflect upon the implications of the painstaking reconstruction of Mexico's historical demography by Simpson, Cook and Borah. In a similar vein, we have perhaps permitted the Insurgency to obscure our understanding of Mexico's great export cycle at the end of the eighteenth century and its relationship to demographic growth, increase in imports as well exports, and changes in land ownership, land use and output. To the economist of today, this pattern suggests a sort of archetype of enclave economy not so much in terms of linkages to the host or domestic economy as in the export of silver and the outflow of interest and profit. The Soviet historian, Alperovich, who has read his Humboldt carefully, has reminded us that Humboldt went to the core of Mexico's mining economy and its colonial function within Spanish imperialist structures when he wrote that "La Nueva España ... proporciona a la hacienda real dos veces más ingresos que la India británica con una población cinco veces mayor al erario". An equally careful reading of Pierre Vilar's *La Catalogne dans l'Espagne moderne* indicates the key role of the Mexican colony to what was perhaps Spain's most dynamic regional economy at the end of the eighteenth century, that is, Mexico's role as importer of Catalonian wines, brandies, textiles and paper, and as exporter of silver.

No doubt the Insurgency affected mining operations, particularly in the form of labor shortages and inadequate maintenance and pumping operations. Yet the production peak came perhaps a decade before the outbreak of revolution and there are reports of this period which affirm the apparently inexorable rise of cost levels reducing the profitability of most Mexican mines. A long-term examination of the mining sector, sweeping from the late eighteenth to the late nineteenth centuries may lead to the conclusion that there was in fact a mining crisis antedating 1810 and that the causes of collapse or contraction in the period 1820-1880 were less political and more technological.

The trajectory of the Mexican Revolution and the revindications demanded and sometimes achieved have lead historians often to view the movement as a revolution by peasants. No economic historian can deny that it was a peasant revolution; but it was this and something more. No doubt the grievances of Mexican peasants in 1910 go back in part to the land policies and practices of federal, state and local governments from 1857 onward. However, we cannot overlook that land concentration, rural unemployment and under-employment and just plain rural misery were clearly recognized and criticized at the end of the eighteenth century and thereafter in the nineteenth. Yet it seems to me that in our examination of the origins of the peasant contribution to the Revolution, we overlook the fact that the development of the Mexican hacienda in the late nineteenth century was closely linked to the revival of the Mexican mining economy after about 1880 in much the fashion that in the eighteenth century a developing mining sector had its direct linkages to the hacienda. When the economic historian views the Mexican economy under the Porfiriato he cannot help concluding that in terms of expansion of output, sources of investment flows, imports of technology and the creation of necessary infra-structure via railroads, the growth of the mining and petroleum sectors of the Mexican economy is another classic example of an export economy of an enclave type. Thus we may view the Mexican Revolution as the first of the twentieth-century upheavals in the neocolonial or Third World to uproot and export economy which, among other effects, exaggerated and exacerbated the secular agrarian problems of Mexico. At the risk of oversimplification, mining has been to Mexico at least until 1930 what sugar has been to Cuba in recent times.

One final example of the need to study long-term trends rather than discrete phenomena may be drawn from agrarian history and agrarian historiography since 1910. No one need be reminded of the vast literature of Article 27, the hesitant and often contradictory policies of the 1920's and in the 1930's massive land redistribution and the increase in the number of ejidos, in the overwhelming majority individually operated ejidos. A situation that appeared well on the way to solution by 1940 hardly seems so by the 1960's. Now the ejido program, we are informed, is in crisis and we are overwhelmed with statistics on rural poverty, rural unemployment and underemployment, rural illiteracy. To crown the calvary of agrarian reform, there are hard quantitative data to prove that in 1960 over 3.3 million rural Mexicans or 53% of the rural population were landless and that there were as many haciendas as in 1877. The quantitative and qualitative changes induced by the Mexican Revolution in the countryside cannot be denied. Yet the historian must be permitted his moment of cynicism when he dips into the literature on the contemporary rural scene of Mexico and encounters references to *grandes terratenientes*, *grandes propietarios*, *burguesía rural-comercial* and countless references to *campesinos sin tierras*. Since historians are tolerated by society for their possible moments of insight and not their cynicism, I suggest that a long-term perspective of Mexico's agrarian structures and agrarian fluctuations, a view sweeping back to the late sixteenth century, leads inescapably to the conclusion (or is it hypothesis?) that in 1969 Mexico's rural conditions are the product of more than four centuries of capitalistic development in agriculture, of the sometimes slow, sometimes rapid but always inexorable expansion of private enterprise into the Mexican countryside. In fact, this is what Clark Reynolds argues by suggesting that we look at the basic, unchanging economic and social patterns which persisted from the Porfiriato to the era of Cárdenas, at least. When he urges that we determine "the limits of economic behavior under certain conditions", I deduce that he proposes that we review the way in which structures and interests associated with them blocked significant economic change.

THE DIRECTION OF FUTURE STUDY

What the papers of Florescano and Reynolds share are a common insistence upon quantitative verification, periodization reflecting economic trends, and upon a conceptual framework. Both stress the need for methodological innovation; yet neither one is specific about defining a conceptual framework. Reynolds argues against what he calls "simple dialectical materialism" and for an examination of what he describes as a "multidimensional interaction of social, political, economic and even psychological variables". It is not clear, however, whether this conception deals with dialectics or interplay. What is encouraging is that an economist and a historian agree that we need a framework incorporating both economic and non-economic factors.

Such a framework must meet a number of criteria to have the widest applicability. First, it must grow inductively from the historical pattern of Mexico; and, second, it must permit relevant comparison with the growth patterns of other Latin American nations, of the so-called Third World and ultimately of Western Europe and the United States. In other words, only into a very broad framework can we fit logically and correctly small bits oldstone to form a large and coherent mosaic. That mosaic will never adequately be achieved by indiscriminate borrowing of reference framework and methodologies fashioned for different realities.

As at other times, so today social scientists find that the needs of their era shape the questions they ask of the past. The questions in turn grow out of distinctively different national historical patterns. In the United States, racism, poverty and imperialism have led to one syndrome of questions; another syndrome emerges in England where the promise of what was once the world's foremost industrial nation seems blighted. In Mexico, the shortcomings of the Revolution receive more attention than the gains perhaps because all revolutions fail in some degree. If I interpret accurately the uneasiness of historians looking at Latin America's past through the prism of western Europe's history, and of economists perplexed by Latin America's inability to close the gap between underdevelopment and development, that uneasiness may be located in the growing perception that Latin American conditions have been and still are different from those of Western Europe, that they may be characterized as typically colonial or neo-colonial. This explains the current vogue of the concept of dependence in Latin America's political, social and economic literature. For dependence seems to provide a general concept of backgroundness. I would refine that general concept slightly and propose that economic historians move toward an examination of the origins, patterns and stages of capitalism in dependent areas to arrive at a definition of colonial or peripheral capitalism.

To the weaknesses inseparable from capitalism developing in a colonial economy may be traced the failure of industrial capitalism to take deep root in Catalonia in the eighteenth century. Likewise, the inadequacy of data and indiscriminate application of a frame of reference developed for an area outside of Latin America may explain the confusing interpretation of the Mexican Insurgency. To Silvio Zavala the movement "esbozó . . . la revolución burguesa en un país señorial" and to M. S. Alperovich it created "condiciones muy favorables para el desarrollo de las relaciones económicas capitalistas y para la incorporación de México al sistema económico mundial" and was "en esencia una revolución burguesa anti-colonial" with "un carácter antifeudal". Later Alperovich argues that at independence, Mexico had solved "una de las tareas de la revolución burguesa", that the Plan de Iguala's guarantees blocked "una serie de transformaciones de carácter antifeudal" and that independence "no condujo a una transformación radical de la estructura económico-social de México". * Zavala and Alperovich are not the only historians to appear confused by the Mexican insurgency, by the wars of independence or by the Mexican Revolution. The confusion probably arises from the fact that in Mexico as in Latin America a variety of stages of capitalism have long co-existed symbiotically. Could it be otherwise in a continent conquered by Iberian entrepreneurs leaving a metropolitan economy already colonialized and who perpetuated in America relations of dependence?

* In Ricardo Levene, ed., *Historia de América* (Buenos Aires, 1940), vII, p. 10; M. S. Alperovich, *Historia de la independencia de México (1810-1824)*. (México, 1967), pp. 277, 279, 281.

COMENTARIO

JAN BAZANT

Enrique Florescano presenta muchas ideas interesantes. No estoy de acuerdo con él en lo siguiente: en las páginas 325-26, E. F. habla de "esos estudios laboriosos", de "estancos y parcelitas", del "monografismo cerrado y erudito"; en lugar de él, sugiere que se hagan síntesis, "obras de imaginación". Ya que no nombra ninguna obra en particular, los que hemos hecho una que otra monografía nos damos un poco por aludidos.

Creo que tiene razón en cuanto al periodo de 1867-1910, sobre el cual existen ya bastantes estudios parciales de los que se pudiera quizás intentar una síntesis. Pero creo que se equivoca si se refiere también a los años de 1821-67, sobre los cuales hay pocas monografías publicadas. Entre ellas quisiera yo mencionar el libro de Potash, Costeloe (que pertenece en parte a la historia social), y Turlington (en éste se basa en parte mi *Historia de la deuda exterior de México*); en la prensa del Colegio de México se encuentra el de R. Flores sobre la expulsión de los españoles, y en la de Cambridge University el mío sobre la desamortización de la riqueza clerical. Tengo la impresión de que como autores hemos procurado razonablemente situar nuestros cuadros dentro del marco histórico general. Lo dicho por E. F. se podría aplicar tal vez a la obra de Harris, *The Sánchez Navarros 1846-1853*. Pero no pretende ser una monografía sino sólo un ensayo —en 100 páginas no se puede hacer más. El estudio en sí es bueno y hacen falta otros trabajos sobre los mismos Sánchez Navarros aun cuando sin duda se requerirá "un esfuerzo posterior que los integre al todo de que son parte". Con los papeles de la Universidad de Texas se podría hacer también uno o más estudios útiles sobre la firma Manning & Mackintosh.

Del periodo de 1821-67 faltan monografías sobre precios (muchas veces intenté animar a E. F. para que lo hiciera), salarios, rentas... sobre agricultura y minería; es importante la historia regional y parroquial; de ésta habría que pasar a la minihistoria —historia de una casa o grupo de casas (una pequeña muestra la ofrezco en un artículo sobre 20 casas del Duque de Terranova, que se publica en el último número de *Historia Mexicana*); igualmente importante serían biografías de hombres de empresa como los hermanos Escandón y otros de esa época. Después llegará el momento de intentar una síntesis.

Por supuesto tal "obra de imaginación" se puede intentar antes, pero no olvidemos que, como alguien ha dicho, las ideas tienen una elevada mortalidad infantil. Un indicio de que aún no es tiempo de sintetizar el periodo de 1821-67, lo encuentro en el hecho de que los intentos hechos hasta ahora en este campo no pueden considerarse como bien logrados. Tomemos el que parece el mejor, *La estructura económica y social de México en la época de la Reforma* (1967) de F. López Cámara, quien en 240 páginas pretende abarcar *toda* (véase el índice) la economía y la sociedad de 1853-70. Es, pues, netamente, una síntesis. El autor está mal informado sobre varios puntos importantes: en la página 58 especula sobre el tamaño de las fábricas textiles en 1843 y como era de esperarse, llega a conclusiones erróneas. Si hubiera visto la *Memoria de la Dirección de Industria de 1844* y su lista detallada de todas las fábricas con el número de husos en cada una se habría ahorrado no sólo la especulación sino también el error. En la página 172 proporciona cifras incorrectas sobre el monto de la deuda exterior. Ignora que éste no creció entre 1837 y 1870 porque México logró mantenerlo en un nivel razonable. En la página 197 da una cuantía extravagante de los bienes clericales, basándose en los imaginativos pero poco exactos informes de los diplomáticos franceses quienes se proponían extraer del país mucho dinero por este concepto. Claro está, se podría argüir que con una información más sólida se podría hacer una síntesis mejor que la mencionada. De acuerdo. Pero aún así creo que la síntesis es un poco prematura en este momento en vista de las referidas lagunas en nuestro conocimiento.

Otra síntesis es *Historia social y económica de México 1521-1854* de A. Cue Cánovas. El autor subordina la economía a la política, como se ve en los títulos de los capítulos: Primer Imperio, República Federal, dictadura militar... la guerra con los Estados Unidos. Esto podría ser interesante si el autor mostrara el impacto de cada uno de estos eventos en la economía. Pero se contenta con intercalar en el relato político pasajes sobre el Banco de Avío, etcétera.

Esquema de la economía mexicana hasta antes de la Revolución de O. A. Hernández, en las 30 páginas sobre 1821-76, es francamente superficial.

Historia y pensamiento económico de México de D. López Rosado, obra planeada para 6 volúmenes, no es lo que llamaríamos una síntesis sino un bien documentado texto universitario.

Ignoro si al hacer una afirmación general sobre trabajos monográficos, Enrique pensó en su propia monografía, desde luego muy buena, sobre los precios del maíz o si la incluyó entre "las inevitables valiosas excepciones que confirman la regla". En su "estudio laborioso", F. omite el estudio de los precios de trigo, cebada, frijol, carne, queso, etcétera, los de inmuebles (alquileres), salarios y tasa de interés, aun cuando a dos de estos factores los menciona. Indiscutiblemente hay que preparar monografías sobre estos "temas vecinos" para obtener un cuadro más completo de la economía.

E. F. también "extirpó sin contemplaciones", por ejemplo, los grandes cambios en la tenencia de la tierra como la confiscación de los bienes jesuitas y la consolidación de los vales reales que, junto con otros acontecimientos o actos políticos o gubernamentales, deben de haber tenido un impacto en la agricultura. Él mismo se concentra correctamente en su "parcela" de maíz, porque en el trabajo monográfico, el que mucho abarca, poco aprieta.

P. S. La obra de M. López Gallo, *Economía y política en la historia de México*, trata muy poco de la economía en 1821-67. En el capítulo

"De 1800 a 1854" las referencias a la economía prácticamente terminan con la Independencia. Sobre el fomento de la industria por Alamán tiene un párrafo de 7 líneas.

El capítulo siguiente, "El movimiento liberal" (1855-75), es exclusivamente político excepto en sus páginas sobre la deuda exterior (tomado de Payno).

RELATORÍA

ALICIA ORIVE

La sesión se inició con la exposición de algunas de las principales ideas contenidas en las ponencias. El señor Víctor L. Urquidi presentó sus comentarios orales a la ponencia de Clark Reynolds. Consideró que algunas ideas contenidas en la ponencia no son del todo justas, especialmente cuando se señala que no hay teorías generales sobre las características del cambio económico en México y que no existe un análisis completo de un solo sector de la economía. Se recordaron algunos estudios de la CEPAL, dirigidos por Celso Furtado, en donde se intentó la utilización de un esquema teórico sobre el crecimiento de la economía mexicana y sobre las causas de sus desequilibrios originados por su crecimiento hacia el exterior. Igualmente se indicó que existen otros trabajos encabezados por Leopoldo Solís, en torno a un largo periodo de la economía mexicana, en donde se puede encontrar buena economía y, al mismo tiempo, buena historia. Los comentarios de Stanley Stein, aparecen reproducidos en esta sección.

En otra parte de la discusión general se adentró la urgencia de formular programas que sirvieran de guía para la investigación económica. Algunos recalcaron la importancia de analizar la influencia que sobre el crecimiento económico han tenido sectores tan importantes como de la tenencia de la tierra, la mano de obra y el de las comunicaciones.

El debate sobre los orígenes de la industrialización en México animó las discusiones. Algunos participantes señalaron la carencia de una política de industrialización antes de la crisis de 1929, y explicaron que el impulso y el estilo del crecimiento hacia adentro tuvo como antecedentes necesarios la política agraria de la Revolución Mexicana y los efectos derivados de la independencia de la economía mundial, puesto de manifiesto en la crisis de 1929. Otros consideraron que la industrialización fue un proceso continuo iniciado en los últimos años del siglo XIX, y que la movilidad de factores ocasionados por la Revolución dio un mayor impulso a la industrialización ya iniciada, pero no tan complejo ni tan generalizado como el de las últimas décadas.

Otro aspecto, igualmente interesante, fue el relacionado con la divulgación y utilización de los nuevos métodos y técnicas de investigación histórica, especialmente aquellos que rompen con la tradición de la historiografía política. Se señaló la urgencia de experimentar los nuevos métodos de la historia económica y social con el fin de fortalecer y apoyar las interpretaciones de la historia política. Se recalcó la evidente popularidad de la historia económica y las perspectivas que existen para los investigadores en este campo, principalmente abierto a la utilización de los métodos y las técnicas de otras ciencias. Se destacó la importancia de la utilización de las técnicas cuantitativas en la investigación de la historia de México, a pesar del reconocimiento de los problemas y las limitaciones en la obtención e interpretación de los datos.

VIII. HISTORIOGRAFÍA DE LA VIDA SOCIAL

Presidente: Gonzalo Aguirre Beltrán, director del Instituto Indigenista Interamericano.

Ponentes: Jean Meyer, profesor e investigador visitante de El Colegio de México; Frederick Turner, profesor asociado de ciencia política, Universidad de Connecticut.

Comentarista: Ramón Ruiz, profesor de historia, Smith College.

Participantes: Guillermo Bonfil, Sección de Antropología, UNAM; Woodrow Borah, profesor de historia, Universidad de California Berkeley; James Cockcroft, University of Wisconsin, Milwaukee; Barbro Dahlgren Jordán, subdirectora del Departamento de Investigaciones Históricas, INAH; Lucila Flamand, investigadora del Instituto de Investigaciones Bibliográficas, UNAM; Heather Fowler, investigadora asistente del Instituto de Estudios Latinoamericanos de la Universidad de Texas, Austin; Tarsicio García Díaz, director del Colegio de Historia, Universidad Iberoamericana, investigador de la Biblioteca Nacional de México; Alfonso García Ruiz, profesor en la Facultad de Ciencias Políticas y Sociales UNAM; Guadalupe Monroy, investigadora de El Banco de México; Pablo Marentes, director de la Dirección General de Información, UNAM; Luis F. Muro Arias, investigador de El Colegio de México; Margarita Nolasco, Departamento de Investigaciones Históricas, INAH; Alicia Olivera de Bonfil, Departamento de Investigaciones Históricas, INAH; Thomas G. Powell, editor asistente de *The Hispanic American Historical Review*; Evon Vogt, Universidad de Harvard; Arturo Warman Investigador y profesor del Instituto de Ciencias Sociales, Universidad Iberoamericana.

Participantes europeos: Michael Costeloe, Lector en el Departamento de Español y Portugués, Universidad de Bristol, Inglaterra; Magnus Mörner, Instituto de Estudios Iberoamericanos, Estocolmo.

Relator: Irene Vázquez Valle, estudiante del Centro de Estudios Históricos de el Colegio de México.

HISTORIA DE LA VIDA SOCIAL

JEAN A. MEYER

"La historia social es más bien un proyecto y una manera de ver que una ciencia sólidamente constituida", escribió Pierre Goubert en la página vii de su tesis; más recientemente ha dicho: "La historia social es una especie de convergencia, una especie de centro que, para mí, representa la historia simplemente." [1]

Precisemos que nuestra ambición es conocer la sociedad mexicana, sus clases, sus grupos y, en fin, la manera como esta sociedad se ha visto a sí misma. Si nos limitamos incluso a la época independiente, y si preferimos de todo este periodo el siglo xx, que nos es más familiar, debemos tener siempre presentes aquellas frases de Octavio Paz que son a la vez hilo de Ariadna y "garde-fou": "En nuestro territorio conviven no sólo distintas razas y lenguas, sino varios niveles históricos. Hay quienes viven antes de la historia; otros, como los otomíes, desplazados por sucesivas invasiones, al margen de ella. Y sin acudir a estos extremos, varias épocas se enfrentan, se ignoran o se entredevoran sobre una misma tierra o separadas apenas por unos kilómetros. Bajo un mismo cielo, con héroes, costumbres, calendarios y nociones morales diferentes, viven católicos de Pedro el Ermitaño y jacobinos de la Era Terciaria."

Queremos hacer la historia de la sociedad global, estudiar sus elementos constitutivos, individuales y de grupo, así como el encadenamiento de las relaciones que los animan. Pero no olvidamos que lo social está directamente ligado a lo económico, en cuanto que el hombre es productor/consumidor. Lo social penetra en los comportamientos de la vida cotidiana y en las ideologías. He ahí nuestro imperialismo: todo el dominio de la historia. ¿Por qué? Porque hasta la historia más tradicional contiene siempre algo de historia social, historia de los grupos sociales y de sus relaciones entre sí, historia del hombre en cuanto que está integrado a un grupo social. El grupo social, tomado desde un punto de vista antropológico, el más amplio y el más profundo, mantiene relaciones particulares con aquello que es económico y aquello que es mental. Hoy la nueva historia económica, la sociología en pleno auge y la antropología agresiva nos per-

[1] Pierre Goubert, *L'Histoire Sociale, sources et méthodes.* PUF, Paris, 1967, p. 97.

miten estudiar con mayor seguridad las relaciones entre lo económico, lo social, lo mental. Los hechos económicos influyen sobre las estructuras sociales, las ideas, las mentalidades; éstas a su vez los modifican y los transforman. La interacción dialéctica es la regla, y no podemos atrevernos a decir qué viene primero . . .

Lo que voy a decir ahora debe ser entendido como una interrogación y no como una afirmación. Como una invitación, no como una provocación. No se trata de llevar a cabo un balance de lo que se ha hecho —para eso están las bibliografías que son abundantes y están bien hechas, y un buen ejemplo es la de Susana Uribe, *Bibliografía histórica mexicana*—; sino más bien de diseñar un proyecto de investigaciones sobre algunos sectores poco explorados. Y si se quiere ver en ello una decisión de no conformismo, recuérdense las palabras de José Clemente Orozco: "en cuanto alguien diga SÍ, hay que contestar NO, debe hacerse todo a contra pelo y contra la corriente, y si algún insensato propone alguna solución que allane las dificultades, precisa aplastarlo, cueste lo que cueste, porque la civilización misma correría peligro". Sin ir tan lejos yo pretendería que lo propio de las ideas falsas, mientras señorean, es pasar por evidencias y no ser puestas en duda. En este sentido la regla de la evidencia propuesta por Descartes resulta inútil. La evidencia no es un criterio, sino más a menudo el lugar donde se esconden, bajo una luz aparente, los supuestos más dudosos. En fin, puesto que nosotros hacemos figura de cojos antes los ojos de nuestros colegas más "científicos", sepamos apoyarnos sobre el "bastón fecundo de la controversia herética".

Es un verdadero escándalo científico nuestra ignorancia acerca de la estructura social del México histórico. Muy pocos han intentado el examen de esa sociedad. No sabemos cuál fue su desarrollo sobre la tierra mexicana, sus verdaderas estructuras, sus necesidades, sus posibilidades. He ahí el gran tema. ¿Cuáles son los datos fundamentales del problema? El problema consistiría en principio en preguntarse ¿qué es una estructura social?

Mis maestros me han enseñado que en la base de todo se encuentra el hombre concreto. He ahí por donde debe comenzarse. La sociedad es un grupo de hombres. Debemos conocer la persona, la psicología, utilizar la demografía y tener un tinte etnológico para comprender los rasgos de este pueblo.

Cuando todos esos datos hayan revelado sus componentes, podrá abordarse el grupo. Si esos hombres están unidos por ciertas afinidades, estamos frente a una comunidad, tal como nos lo ha mostrado Luis González. [2] Si esos hombres se hallan encuadrados en algo más rígido, insertos en una cierta armadura, si mantienen entre sí ciertas rela-

---

[2] Luis González, *Pueblo en vilo: microhistoria de San José de Gracia*. El Colegio de México, México, 1968.

ciones institucionales, estamos entonces en presencia de una sociedad. La sociedad se caracteriza por la existencia de instituciones; instituciones que, si pasamos de la estructura a la dinámica, son ligas orgánicas en perpetuo movimiento, puesto que se trata de relaciones entre hombres, entre seres vivos, y de ninguna manera de relaciones algebraicas. La estructura social es una forma, concedido; pero una forma que no podría subsistir si no circulara en ella una vida, mucho más difícil de captar, para nosotros, que la forma misma.

Después de haber considerado las personas y las cosas, elementos de la estructura social, podemos pasar al estudio de las categorías dentro de las cuales evolucionan esos elementos: espacio y tiempo. El geógrafo, al estudiar los lazos entre el hombre y el medio, podrá hacer aparecer relaciones sutiles, correspondencias insospechadas. Y por otro lado, la profundidad temporal deberá mostrarnos esas desarmonías de la vida social tanto tiempo descuidadas por el sociólogo negligente, del espacio y del pasado; permitirá estudiar la psicología de las crisis, de las luchas, de las revoluciones. Esta medida temporal nos dará la dimensión que permita comprender una civilización. La categoría del tiempo encierra las tradiciones del grupo social, aquello que cree llevar unido a sus orígenes, sus costumbres, hábitos canonizados por el tiempo. Hay que tener en cuenta también su memoria colectiva, sus representaciones mentales. Pienso que nadie irá a auscultar un poblado de la Sierra Gorda sin evocar la imagen de la pacificación (no es casualidad que San Luis se llame "de la Paz"), o un poblado de Morelos sin evocar el zapatismo.

Aún más, falta construir la taxonomía de los tipos sociales. Existen tipos cerrados, de estructuras sociales replegadas sobre sí mismas y existen tipos abiertos, ligados al exterior. ¿Cómo explicar al Pueblito (Querétaro) actual, si no se sabe, gracias a José Miranda, que estuvo poblado de otomíes trasladados desde Jilotepec? ¿Cómo explicar el oeste y sudoeste de Michoacán y su historia de los últimos 150 años, tan diferentes por su personalidad y comportamiento de las demás regiones del Estado, si no se sabe que desde el siglo XVIII, por lo menos, esa región fue poblada por gente venida de los Altos de Jalisco? Hemos tocado aquí uno de los problemas más importantes, el de las mutaciones en el espacio y en el tiempo. De importancia semejante es el problema de los contactos que se establecen en una región con otras regiones: contactos de mercado, de feria, contactos por peregrinaciones, por la "leva", por la emigración definitiva o simplemente estacional... El problema de los contactos es capital, puesto que la entrada de elementos extraños en las estructuras sociales desquicia las costumbres, mientras que una comunidad aislada, replegada sobre sí misma, continúa viviendo su vida. ¿No es ésta una de las claves posibles del problema de la oposición entre baja planicie y altiplano, entre el "plan" y los "altos", "abajeños" y "alteños"?

He ahí nuestro método. Véamos ahora los sectores en que deberemos aplicarlo, los menos conocidos, los menos pensados. En algunos casos el tema ha sido tratado abundantemente, pero interpretado apenas. En otros casos la investigación no se ha comenzado siquiera.

Examinaré sucesivamente la historia rural y la historia obrera y capitalista, en cuanto que éstas atañen a estructuras sociales directamente ligadas a la historia económica. Después pasaré a la historia política vista desde nuestro ángulo: las motivaciones sociales de la conducta, fenómenos e instituciones políticas, las relaciones entre la sociedad y las ideologías, el nacionalismo, la violencia, etcétera. De la violencia a la historia militar no hay más que un paso. La "historia-batallas" se verá rehabilitada si nos interesamos en los ejércitos como grupos sociales y como estructuras; un enfoque semejante deberá rehabilitar la veta biográfica. Con la historia religiosa, la historia de las mentalidades y la de las ideas, nos encontramos frente a las superestructuras. Ya llegaremos a ellas. Las bibliografías correspondientes se encontrarán al final del texto.

I. LA HISTORIA RURAL

El siglo xix mexicano fue el gran siglo de disturbios rurales. La de 1911 fue la primera Revolución rural de América latina; la Reforma Agraria el gran acontecimiento del siglo xx mexicano; a pesar de haber concluido la fase militar de la Revolución, la violencia en fermento, esporádica, difusa, no ha cesado en el campo. Si estamos todos de acuerdo en la importancia de estos fenómenos y, por lo tanto, en la importancia del hecho campesino, debemos reconocer que nuestros conocimientos son bastante fragmentarios. La historia rural del siglo xix se encuentra en su infancia. Propiamente hablando no hay una obra que se consagre a este tema, lo cual parece una paradoja frente a la abundancia de literatura agraria, y las referencias abundantes a los precursores y a los movimientos que anuncian la Reforma Agraria. Pero la realidad es que las rebeliones indígenas del siglo xvii y del siglo xviii nos son más conocidas que los movimientos del xix. Los únicos trabajos que existen, y que no son muy recientes, salvo el que prepara Moisés González Navarro,[3] se refieren a la guerra de castas en Yucatán y a las guerras del yaqui. Es, pues, muy difícil hacerse una idea de la amplitud y del significado de un fenómeno cuya bibliografía es tan restringida. Todos estos movimientos esperan ser estudiados desde el punto de vista clásico antes de que podamos pasar a su análisis, a su clasificación, al

[3] Moisés González Navarro, trabajo en curso sobre la guerra de castas en Yucatán, problema racial y problema agrario.

estudio de su dinámica. Si los movimientos rurales son poco conocidos, los problemas agrarios se mantienen planteados en términos generales y a menudo superficiales, a tal punto que, aparte de las indicaciones precursoras de Luis Chávez Orozco y de los volúmenes de *Historia moderna de México*, carecemos de una verdadera historia económica y social del siglo XIX en la que podamos resituar los movimientos sociales.

Esto es menos cierto para el periodo revolucionario que cubre tradicionalmente los años de 1910 a 1940. Incluso si los historiadores deben sobrepasar obstáculos que no por ser de otro orden son menos considerables, la literatura es abundante aunque a menudo apologética, y siempre más política que social y económica. Se habla mucho de Zapata y de Villa, pero ¿en dónde están los zapatistas y los villistas? Nos interesamos en el carácter heroico de los héroes sin estudiar relamente sus movimientos dentro del contexto socioeconómico.

¿En qué medida las circunstancias, la coyuntura en el más amplio sentido del término, contribuyen a explicar las rebeliones? Podríamos preguntarnos si no son efectivamente el resultado de coyunturas más que de estructuras económicas o sociales. Pero también podemos preguntarnos si no son las estructuras las que imponen su destino a esta historia: el estado de la sociedad, los progresos del naciente Estado moderno, el desarrollo de una industria capitalista. ¿Quién ha tomado la iniciativa de las rebeliones, quién ha comenzado? He ahí el problema de la movilización, problema dinámico y bastante poco conocido.

En el estado actual de nuestros conocimientos, lo único que podemos decir es que se trata de problemas rurales de tipo clásico (antiguo) nacidos del combate desesperado que opone a los pequeños campesinos y a las comunidades contra el neolatifundismo del siglo XIX. Combate para proteger los derechos de las comunidades (pero ¿quién podría decirnos el grado de evolución de las comunidades en esta época, la fuerza de la psicología social, de las mentalidades, de las estructuras de las comunidades antiguas? La disgregación, la disolución de esas sociedades está seguramente en marcha, de una manera variable, según las regiones, según las alteraciones producidas por la economía de mercado. Nos gustaría saber qué es lo que sucedió entre 1810 y 1910). Combate para mantener un antiguo tipo de agricultura, combate de retaguardia, o mejor dicho, el fin de un largo combate que no se interrumpió con la Independencia, sino más bien lo contrario, puesto que la Independencia, criolla de 1821 significa la aceleración de la concentración de la propiedad territorial. Hay una continuidad entre el siglo XVIII y el XIX, la Independencia no es una línea de demarcación, el proceso estaba en marcha desde el momento en que puede hablarse de una racionalización de la agricultura.

El paso de la "hacienda" de tipo antiguo, paternalista, a la nueva exploración agrícola explica la permanencia de la crisis agraria y de

los disturbios. Pero si disponemos de una teoría general, ignoramos
casi todo de la realidad económica y social del campo. Si hay confrontación entre dos sistemas agrarios, siendo el primero un fin en sí mismo,
una sociedad, una civilización, y el segundo un modo de producción al
servicio de la moderna sociedad que se gestaba en las ciudades, y si creemos poder afirmarlo, nuestras teorías se quedan peligrosamente en las
nubes. ¿Cuáles son las estructuras económicas y sociales del campo?
¿En dónde predomina la "hacienda"? ¿Y cuál hacienda, la moderna o
la tradicional? Queda por hacer el estudio socioprofesional, y no únicamente el de la propiedad bajo todas sus formas, sino también el de la
explotación. Cuando este estudio se haya hecho, y sólo entonces, podrá
darse un sentido a la Reforma y más adelante al Porfiriato. Creemos
ver en la Reforma la alianza de la "pequeña burguesía" (las comillas
están ahí para señalar qué poco afortunado es el término) con los neo-
latifundistas y los caciques regionales contra el clero y los latifundistas
del antiguo sistema. Los bienes de las comunidades religiosas y civiles
destruidos por la Reforma (es cierto, pero ¿hasta qué punto? ¿qué comunidades lograron mantenerse? ¿cómo evolucionaron las demás? tantas preguntas aún sin respuestas) sirvieron para consolidar la posición
de los grandes propietarios y de la pequeña burguesía —pequeña burguesía de abogados liberales que no era más que el ala izquierda del neola-
tifudismo y para sellar la alianza que convirtió a los campesinos en obreros agrícolas. De la alianza de esos dos grupos sociales, poco o nada
conocidos, nació la "paz porfiriana"; de su divorcio en 1910, la Revolución. Es decir, que la historia política no podrá escribirse verdaderamente hasta el día en que dispongamos de esta historia económica y
social.

Por otro lado, al parecer, los campesinos no comenzaron el combate
en ninguna parte, quedaron a la defensiva. En 1910 la Revolución fue
preparada por opositores políticos al régimen, y sólo después de que
estalló el conflicto político se sublevaron los campesinos. Los revolucionarios mexicanos, cuyas ideas sobre la vida rural eran bastante suma-
rias en 1910, fueron conducidos por la fuerza de los acontecimientos
a tomar en cuenta las necesidades expresadas por el campo. La anarquía que siguió a la toma de Ciudad Juárez permitió a los campesinos
dar a conocer, bajo múltiples formas, su descontento. Los revolucionarios, lejos de haber tomado la iniciativa y expresado las necesidades
instintivas de la masa, se plegaron a las iniciativas y reclamaciones veni-
das del campo. Pero se tomaron su tiempo para ello, puesto que fue
necesario toda la obstinación de un Zapata para que en 1915 el carrancismo descubriera al fin el problema agrario.

La participación del campo en la Revolución no será conocida mientras no sepamos cuál era su situación en 1910. Se ha escrito mucho
sobre todo esto, pero se ha trabajado poco. Agreguemos a todo lo ante-

rior que no hay campesinado, sino medios rurales diversos, según la geografía que divide al país en grandes zonas agrarias. Todo ello explica la variedad considerable de las condiciones y de las mentalidades rurales. El movimiento campesino no logró casi nunca conquistar todo el territorio, sino que estuvo limitado a una o dos grandes regiones. ¿Porqué?

Cuando estallaron los acontecimientos de 1910 el campo no estaba listo para enfrentarse a una Revolución, y durante el primer momento de la Revolución, del 20 de noviembre a la llegada de Madero a México, no había ni siquiera 50 focos de agitación rural, exceptuando Morelos. Son llamaradas cortas que se apagan en seguida. Sólo más tarde, cuando las autoridades tradicionales desaparezcan, tratarán los campesinos de aprovecharse de la situación. En realidad Madero dispuso de una larga tregua que no supo utilizar, limitándose a tomar medidas simbólicas. El mundo rural, Zapata inclusive (pero no Genovevo de la O), pareció admitir que su situación podía esperar sin reclamar soluciones urgentes, así como el gobierno maderista no pensó en los campesinos ni tampoco la mayor parte de los hombres políticos. Nada de extraño entonces que Zapata en el sur y Orozco en el norte acaben por cansarse y reanuden el combate. Ese combate alimentado de odio de los campesinos (¿cuáles entre ellos?) debía conducir a una recuperación de la Revolución, como crisis permanente, chocará con los diferentes niveles de la sociedad: la edad media, los tiempos modernos, los mundos prehispánicos y la revolución industrial. ¡Qué campo tan hermoso para una historia social!

Después de la derrota de la División del Norte se asiste a una extensión de la anarquía, tan grande que las malas cosechas ligadas a condiciones atmosféricas serán suficientes para hacer de 1917 "el año del hambre". El campo se ve afectado profundamente por esa nueva agitación, mucho más violenta, puesto que el desorden se ha instalado y satisface a algunos. En consecuencia, el deseo de repliegue del campesino hacia los pueblos no hace más que acrecentarse. El pillaje asola al país entero, las destrucciones sin fin son la regla, y Zapata tiene que hacer lo imposible para evitar que sus hombres se conviertan en simples bandidos.

Todo ello explica la preocupación de los Constituyentes de 1917 sobre el problema agrario, problema que deberá reglamentarse antes que nada para calmar a esas masas y restablecer el orden necesario. El objetivo era ganarse a aquellos hombres rurales que según los oradores de la época eran tanto "los apoyos más seguros de la reacción" como los "mejores aliados de la Revolución". Obregón y Calles redactarán, más tarde, un balance poco estimulante de la agitación campesina en el que desempeñan un papel principal los viejos instintos de la envidia, el miedo al cambio, el individualismo, la venganza, el pillaje. Los campesinos se revelaron como el elemento más turbulento y más destructor.

¿Cómo reconstruir el Estado en plena anarquía rural? Tal era el problema de Obregón y de Calles. Ambos supieron resolverlo apaciguando a los campesinos, dividiéndolos, desarmándolos, volviéndolos al trabajo de la tierra que les concedía la Reforma Agraria y, después, apoyándose en los obreros para dar una base política a su poder. Pero ¿cómo fue distribuida esa tierra? ¿quiénes fueron los beneficiarios? He ahí un capítulo que queda por escribirse y que nos explicaría muchas cosas. Resumamos: no sabemos aún quién fue orozquista, villista, cedillista, zapatista; no sabemos quién fue revolucionario (y hay mil y una maneras de serlo), ni quién contrarrevolucionario. Para mostrar la complejidad del problema, y su interés, me permito referirme a los comentarios de Stresser Péan sobre esa huaxteca que conoce tan bien. En la huaxteca el indio no fue revolucionario. Pobre, sin armas, y a pie, no se abandona fácilmente una familia cuando se es sedentario y menos cuando ni siquiera se habla español. Revolucionario fue el mestizo, "vaquero", agresivo, móvil, que se aprovechó de la situación para apoderarse de las tierras de los indios.

"Los mestizos famélicos, pero enérgicos, descendidos de las regiones montañosas vecinas, aprovecharon los disturbios y las carencias gubernamentales para imponerse al indígena, las armas en la mano . . . Este último episodio de la conquista de México, viejo solamente de medio siglo, ha dejado un desagradable hedor de violencia y de antagonismo." [4] Y si relacionamos todo esto con una frase de Molina Enríquez ("el conflicto entre Madero y Orozco . . . no es más que el enfrentamiento violento entre los intereses de los criollos señores representados por Madero y los de los indios mestizos que Orozco representaba inconscientemente"), [5] veremos todo lo que se puede ganar al dar profundidad social a los movimientos campesinos de la Revolución.

El periodo cardenista, cuando de manera generalizada y masiva se lleva a cabo la Reforma Agraria, nos es más conocido, lo que no significa que todo esté claro. ¿Qué fue lo que condujo a Cárdenas a seguir esa política? ¿El factor determinante es su personalidad, la coyuntura económica mundial, la necesidad política o las presiones de los mismos campesinos? ¿Los campesinos son movilizados o se movilizan espontáneamente? ¿Quiénes son los agraristas y qué significa el antagonismo sangriento que los opone a menudo a los otros campesinos? En fin, ¿qué es el sinarquismo? ¿en dónde recluta a sus partidarios y por qué tiene seguidores, al menos por algún tiempo?

Es cierto que los campesinos fueron el motor de la Revolución, pero falta hacer el cuadro de esas rebeliones permanentes contra un lati-

[4] Guy Stresser Péan, "Les problèmes agraires de la Huaxteca", *Problèmes agraires des Ameriques Latines*. CNRS, Paris, 1967, p. 207.
[5] Andrés Molina Enríquez, *Historia de la Revolución agraria en México*, México, 1963. vol. v, p. 65.

fundismo persistente al que arrancarán poco a poco una Reforma Agraria. Existen, por un lado, esos disturbios continuos y sordos, una violencia cotidiana y poco espectacular, guerra de desgaste que continúa mucho más allá del fin de la Revolución armada, y por el otro, llamadas violentas.

Todo ese capítulo, lo que podríamos llamar ambiciosamente una problemática de la historia social del campo, está subyacente en las reflexiones que inspira el libro ejemplar de Luis González, *Pueblo en vilo. Microhistoria de San José de Gracia*, crónica de una comunidad largo tiempo replegada sobre sí misma y abierta brutalmente al mundo exterior por la Revolución. Luis González nos obliga a reflexionar sobre numerosos problemas y a replantear cuestiones que esperan una respuesta. [6]

[6] Bibliografía de trabajos recientes:

Almada, Francisco R., *La Revolución en el Estado de Chihuahua*. México, 1964 y 1965, 2 vols.

Beltrán, Enrique, "Fantasía y realidad de Pancho Villa", *Historia Mexicana*, XVI, 1, julio-sep. 1966. p. 71-84.

Berzunza Pinto, Ramón, *Guerra social en Yucatán*. México, 1965.

Chávez Orozco, Luis, "Servidumbre y peonaje", *Historia y Sociedad*, núm. 6, 1966, pp. 30-39.

Durán, Marco Antonio, *El agrarismo mexicano*. Siglo XXI, México, 1967.

Gamiz Olivas, Everardo, *La Revolución en el Estado de Durango*. México, 1963.

Gill, Mario, *Sinarquismo, origen y esencia*. México 1962.

Gómez, Marte R., *La Reforma Agraria en las filas villistas, años de 1913 a 1915 y 1920*. México, 1966.

González Navarro, Moisés, "Instituciones indígenas en el México Independiente", *Métodos y resultados de la política indigenista en México*. México, 1954, pp. 113-169.

González Navarro, Moisés, "Zapata y la Revolución Agraria mexicana", *Cahiers du monde Hispanique et Luso Brasilien (Caravelle)*, IX, 1967, pp. 5-31.

González Navarro, Moisés, *La Confederación Nacional Campesina. Un grupo de presión en la Reforma Agraria Mexicana*. México, 1968.

González Navarro, Moisés, "La guerra de castas en Yucatán y la venta de mayas a Cuba", *Historia Mexicana*, XVIII, 1968, pp. 11-34.

González Ramírez, Manuel, "La Revolución Social en México", *El problema agrario* (III). México, 1966.

González Roa, Fernando, *El aspecto agrario de la Revolución Mexicana*. México, 1919, vol. 3, pp. 2-120.

Horcasitas, Fernando, *De Porfirio Díaz a Zapata. Memoria nahuatl de Milpa Alta*. UNAM, México, 1968.

Jaramillo, Rubén y F. Manjarrez, *Autobiografía y asesinato*. México, 1967.

Ledit, Joseph, *El frente de los pobres*. México, 1957.

Mendieta y Núñez, Lucio, *El problema agrario de México*. México, 1966.

Mendieta y Núñez, Lucio, *Introducción al estudio del problema agrario*. México, 1966.

Meyer, Jean A., *Guadalajara et sa region: pour une étude de la personnalité du Jalisco*. CNRS, Paris, 1968, 25 pp.

Meyer, Jean A., "Movimientos campesinos y problemas agrarios, 1810-1968", reporte preparatorio para el Congreso de Historia Económica y Social de Moscú (1970), mimeografiado, 33 pp.

II. OBRERO, INDUSTRIA Y CAPITAL

La historia del movimiento obrero espera a sus historiadores; y aquí, más quizás que en otras zonas, los conocimientos económicos previos son indispensables para el conocimiento de lo social. El siglo xx ha visto agruparse a los hombres, reunirse bajo rasgos fundamentales de su situación y de su condición, capaces o no —el historiador no puede aún decirlo— de tomar conciencia de sus semejanzas, si no de su comunidad de clase. Tenemos necesidad de una buena historia económica del porfiriato y de la Revolución para conocer el clima, las bases de las distinciones sociales, las fuerzas respectivas de las diversas clases. Y ¿quién será el historiador audaz que sitúe en términos de clases a la sociedad mexicana en el curso de los tiempos? El movimiento obrero realiza sus selecciones, adopta sus tácticas en función de su propia organización, de su grado de evolución, de sus fuerzas, pero siempre dentro de los límites que le imponen las estructuras económicas y la coyuntura.

Burguesía de empresa, obreros de fábrica, nacen en México al mismo tiempo condenados a desarrollarse paralelamente. El crecimiento obrero responde al crecimiento económico, es fruto del éxito capitalista. Es necesario entonces conocer seriamente los medios de producción, su desarrollo y su control. En 1910 nos impresiona la debilidad numérica de los obreros, que son menos que los artesanos, nos impresiona también el hecho de que son los capitalistas europeos y norteameri-

Meyer, Jean A., "El ocaso de Manuel Lozada", *Historia Mexicana*, vol. xviii, núm. 4, abril, 1969.

Montejano y Aguiñaga, Rafael, *El Valle de Maíz*. México, 1967.

Navarrete, Heriberto, *El voto de Chema Gutiérrez relato de ambiente cristero*. México, 1964.

Peña, Moisés T. de la, *El pueblo y su tierra. Mito y realidad de la Reforma Agraria en México*. México, 1964.

Puente, Ramón, *Villa en pie*. México, 1966.

Sierra, Carlos J., "Zapata, señor de la tierra, capitán de los labriegos", *Boletín Bibliográfico de la Secretaría de Hacienda y Crédito Público*, 13: 361 (supl.), México, 1967.

Silva, Herzog, Jesús, *El agrarismo mexicano y la Reforma Agraria, exposición y crítica*. México, 1959.

Silva Herzog, Jesús, *La cuestión de la tierra* (4 vols.)

Sinarquista, Pedro, *Pedro Sinarquista, novela popular Histórica de la Unión Nacional Sinarquista*. México, 1959.

Stavenhagen, Rodolfo, "Social aspects of agrarian structure in México", *Social Reseach*, xxxii, 1966, pp. 463-485.

Torre Villar, Ernesto, "Algunos aspectos de las cofradías y la propiedad territorial en Michoacán". *Jahrbuch für Geschichte von Straat., Wirtschaft. Und Gesellschaft Lateinamerikas*, iv. Colonia 1967, pp. 410-439.

Vilanova, Antonio, *Muerte de Villa*. México, 1966.

canos quienes crearon la industria mexicana y en consecuencia también su proletariado obrero. Ese joven proletariado, poco numeroso, empleado por poderosas empresas extranjeras, ¿no experimenta acaso un sentimiento de debilidad que lo empuja a buscar protectores, a someterse al gobierno? La pequeña masa proletaria había nacido poco tiempo atrás, insegura de sí misma y poco consciente de sus problemas. Los verdaderos obreros llevaban tras de sí apenas diez años de fábrica. Su debilidad explica que hayan puesto sus esperanzas en el Estado. Su juventud explica que sus líderes sean extranjeros o que pertenezcan al viejo grupo obrero, semejante por su composición y estilo al de la Europa de 1848. Desde entonces el movimiento será fuertemente nacionalista y el odio al patrón se dirigirá más contra el extranjero que contra el capitalista. ¿No será acaso este nacionalismo la causa de la derrota final de la *International Workers of the World* y de los comunistas, dirigidos también por extranjeros, cuando después de 1921 se enfrentan también al nacionalismo de los obreros? Son estas otras tantas hipótesis, no afirmaciones, que hemos creído poder extraer de la literatura existente, de las memorias de los líderes y de la prensa de la época.

El obrero acaba de nacer apenas cuando, surgiendo de las ciudades que tienden a la creación de un mercado nacional y de los países industriales que procuran integrar a México a los mercados internacionales, se inicia el despegue del crecimiento económico. De 1910 asistimos al auge de la gran industria capitalista y a la declinación paralela del taller y del paternalismo social. La fábrica-industria toma el lugar de la fábrica-taller. El buen estado de las máquinas no impide un número elevado de accidentes debidos a la torpeza y a la ignorancia de los trabajadores, justificaciones ambas que servirán para mantener bajos los salarios. La mayor parte de las fábricas utilizan mano de obra mal remunerada, y peor remunerada aún después de 1905, cuando la situación obrera sufre la coyuntura económica internacional. Entre la sociedad rural y el mundo obrero se encuentra una multitud intermedia y mal conocida que trabaja de manera discontinua y abarca a artesanos rurales, mineros que a menudo son también campesinos y que forman la legión de los trabajadores temporales de la industria. Este sector inestable permite que se eviten concentraciones de desocupados en las ciudades durante los malos años que siguen al pánico de Wall Street de 1907 y la recaída de 1911.

¿Qué sucede durante la Revolución armada? ¿Qué sucede con la industria? ¿Qué resultados obtienen los esfuerzos de reconstrucción de Obregón y de Calles? ¿Cuál es el impacto de la crisis de 1929? ¿Cuáles son los frutos del plan de Calles, destinado a poner remedio a la crisis? ¿Cuál es el balance de la política económica cardenista? Preguntas todas difíciles de contestar en el futuro inmediato y cuya respuesta, sin embargo, es indispensable si queremos conocer al prole-

384 HISTORIOGRAFÍA DE LA VIDA SOCIAL

tariado mexicano y comprender la trayectoria política del movimiento obrero.

Y si pasamos de los medios de producción a los ingresos, puesto que en el edificio económico es donde toman cuerpo las diferentes clases sociales, nos enfrentamos al problema del estudio de los beneficios y de los salarios. Reparticiones, movimientos, correlaciones, rentas, provechos, utilidades, beneficios y salarios, hace mucho tiempo que Ricardo y Marx mostraron que su conocimiento es condición previa al análisis social. El *beneficio* escapa a la investigación por razones que sería inútil repetir, y el único salario que nos interesa, el salario real, el verdadero salario social que nace de la confrontación entre salario nominal y costo de la vida, no lo tenemos aún a nuestra disposición. De todas formas, aunque supiéramos la evolución del salario real desde 1880, no sabemos nada serio acerca de la extensión y de las fluctuaciones de la desocupación. Esta ignorancia, tanto como la de la desocupación y subempleo rural, es un pesado *handicap* en el conocimiento social de los siglos xix y xx. Insistir en el hecho de que las distinciones sociales reposan sobre criterios económicos no significa una reducción de lo social a lo económico. La historia social se hace con las relaciones entre elementos mensurables y elementos no mensurables, de ahí su dificultad. Si los grupos sociales tienen un alma, hay sentimientos sociales que son propios de los grandes grupos, de las clases, como por ejemplo el miedo de quienes poseen. ¿En dónde buscar los orígenes de esas ideas, de esos sentimientos, sino en las diferencias económicas entre las clases? ¿Quién se atrevería a negar que el conocimiento de esos fundamentos económicos (fortunas, ingresos, niveles de vida) es insuficiente para el conocimiento social completo? De ahí el interés del análisis social, que reagrupa los factores, los mecanismos aislados por el análisis económico previo, análisis económico que es condición de inteligibilidad, único medio para alcanzar una explicación si no queremos quedarnos condenados a la sola descripción. El análisis económico es de todas maneras indispensable si queremos evaluar las relaciones de fuerzas respectivas entre los grupos sociales. El poder económico es, para la clase que lo posee, el poder supremo. La historia social de los siglos xix y xx presenta esta profunda laguna. ¿Qué sabemos del poder económico de los liberales, de los conservadores, suponiendo que formen grupos sociales diferentes? ¿Qué sabemos del poder económico de los científicos? ¿Qué de los grandes hacendados, de la gran industria, de la banca? ¿Qué sabemos, de todo esto, en particular entre los años de 1880 a 1930 y de 1940 a 1968? 90 años de crecimiento capitalista y de poder efectivo de la gran burguesía que se nos escapan, aunque el avance sea más rápido (relativamente) en el conocimiento de las clases dirigidas que en el de la clase dirigente.[7]

[7] Bibliografía:

III. LAS MOTIVACIONES SOCIALES DE LA HISTORIA POLÍTICA

Que la verdadera historia política se encuentra estrechamente ligada a la historia social queda probado sin ambigüedades por el movimiento

Banco de Londres y México, *Cien años de banca en México*. México, 1964.

Bazant, Jan, "La desamortización de los bienes corporativos de 1856", *Historia Mexicana*, XVI: 2, pp. 193-212.

Brothers, D. y Solís Leopoldo, *Mexican Financial development*. Austin, 1966.

Calderón, Esteban, *Juicio sobre la guerra yaqui y génesis de la huelga de Cananea*. México, 1966.

Carmona, Pedro, "Reflexiones sobre el desarrollo y la formación de las clases sociales en México", *Cuadernos Americanos*, sept. 1967, pp. 89-119.

Carrera Stampa, Manuel, "Fuentes para el estudio de la estratificación social y las clases sociales en México", *Memorias de la Academia Mexicana de la Historia*, XXIV: 5. México, 1965, pp. 30-55.

Cerda Silva, Roberto de la, *El movimiento obrero en México*. México, UNAM, 1961.

Chapoy, Bonifaz, *El movimiento obrero y el sindicato en México*. México, 1961.

"Cincuentenario de los batallones rojos del ejército constitucionalista", *Memorias de la Academia Mexicana de la Historia*, XXIX: 1. México, 1965, pp. 92-106.

Documentos Históricos de la CTM 1936-1941. México, s. f.

Elizondo, J. M. y López Malo, Rafael, *La derrota de la clase obrera mexicana*. México, 1953.

Fuente, Julio de la, *Las clases sociales en México*. México 1960.

García, T., *Los mineros mexicanos* (2da. ed.) 1968.

Gill, Mario, "Veracruz, revolución y extremo", *Historia Mexicana*, VIII, 1953, pp. 618-636.

López Aparicio, Alfonso, *El movimiento obrero en México: antecedentes, desarrollo y tendencias* (2da. ed.), México, 1958.

López Cámara, Francisco, *La estratificación económica y social en México en la época de la Reforma*. Siglo XXI, México, 1967.

Medina Salazar, Lino, "Albores del movimiento obrero en México", *Historia y Sociedad*, IV. México, 1965, pp. 56-68.

Meyer, Jean A., "Les ouvriers dans la révolution: les bataillons rouges", *Anales, economies, societes, civilizations*, (próxima publicación), 35 pp.

Montes Rodríguez, Ezequiel, *La huelga de Río Blanco*. Río Blanco, 1965.

Neymet, Manuela de, "El movimiento obrero y la Revolución Mexicana", *Historia y Sociedad*, III. México, 1967, pp. 56-73.

Ochoa Campos, Moisés, *La Revolución Mexicana, sus causas económicas*. México, 1966.

Olivé Negrete, Julio y Barba de Piña Chan, Beatriz, "Estudio de las clases sociales en la ciudad de México, experiencias con un grupo obrero", *Anales del Instituto Nacional de Antropología e Historia*, XIV: 43. México 1961-62, pp. 219-281.

Revueltas, José, *Ensayo sobre un proletariado sin cabeza*. México, 1962.

Rodea, Marcelo, *Historia del movimiento obrero ferrocarrilero*. México, 1944.

Salazar, Rosendo, *La Casa del Obrero Mundial*. México, 1962.

Salazar, Rosendo, *Historia de la lucha proletaria en México 1930-1936*. México, 1956.

Tavera, Xavier, "Consecuencias económicas de la intervención", *Intervención francesa y el Imperio de Maximiliano, cien años después*. Asociación Mexicana de Historiadores. I. F. A. L., México, 1965, pp. 71-82.

obrero mexicano. Se ha podido pronunciar la palabra "oportunismo" para calificar la línea política del movimiento obrero. Vemos efectivamente que sus dirigentes abandonan muy pronto la intransigencia anarquista de los años 1910 a 1914 en favor de un "posibilismo" cotidiano. La clarividencia no les hace falta. Ven que el proletario, si existe (y es la historia social la que habrá de decirlo), no posee ninguna conciencia de clase (¿por qué?, hemos adelantado ya algunas hipótesis socioeconómicas) y no puede convertirse espontáneamente en revolucionario. Por esta razón abandonan el anarcosindicalismo y deciden que una pequeña minoría, formada por las élites sindicales, conducirá al movimiento obrero. De 1910 a 1918 el movimiento obrero pasa por una serie de fluctuaciones, fases de hostilidad hacia el Estado seguidas de fases de colaboración. Colaboración que se adopta definitivamente en 1918 durante el Congreso de Saltillo, organizado por las autoridades. ¿Por qué esta fascinación por el Estado? ¿Por qué esta estrecha dependencia, querida conscientemente y efectivamente buscada? ¿Habrá que ver en ella una herencia hispánica del Estado como fuente de ley y principio de autoridad, al servicio del bien común, al no poder ser el instrumento de dominación al servicio de una clase? O bien, ¿habrá que encontrar en ella el resultado de las estructuras sociales del proletariado? La colaboración, el socialismo de Estado, la influencia mutua entre ambos compañeros ¿no son en sí mismas una consecuencia de su posición social y política y por lo mismo de la situación del proletariado dentro de la sociedad? Los obreros no pueden nada por sí solos y lo saben perfectamente. Cuando Rosendo Salazar critica a Morones, precisa: "en menos de un año, Morones nacionalizó a la CROM, lo que ciertamente no le reprochamos, puesto que pensamos todavía hoy que en eso tenía razón... el trabajo ajusta sus demandas a las leyes del Estado, quien lo protege de los abusos patronales".[8]

Esta sumisión en tutela de la clase obrera se explicará bien el día que conozcamos la composición social del proletariado, sus fuerzas y sus debilidades. Explicar todo por el papel de los líderes obreros no es satisfactorio, aunque exista, en ello una parte de verdad. La Revolución constitucionalista pudo así, con éxito, incorporar la población urbana obrera a la burocracia gubernamental.

Esto que hemos tratado de adivinar para el mundo obrero, esta relación estrecha entre lo social y lo político, podría hacerse para muchos otros problemas: el del caciquismo como estructura política de base, el de la violencia como sistema permanente, el del nacimiento del nacionalismo, fenómeno reciente y estrechamente ligado a la historia económica, como lo prueba el caso del petróleo mexicano y de su nacionalización por Cárdenas. "El poder y la riqueza de las grandes compañías no tardó en herir el amor propio de las poblaciones nacionales

[8] Rosendo Salazar, *Líderes y sindicatos*. 1953, p. 14 y p. 82.

y más tarde vino a suscitar sus reivindicaciones y a servir de catalizador al país que así podía —según el dicho de Ranke— 'darse el sentimiento de su ser'. Bajo esa luz, justamente, conviene juzgar la nacionalización mexicana que se convirtió en el símbolo de la independencia económica del país." [9]

IV. LA HISTORIA MILITAR

La historia militar ha sufrido injustamente el descrédito de la tradicional "historia-batallas". Pero la historia militar es mucho más que eso. Por una parte es un aspecto del fenómeno social y político de la violencia, y por la otra, el campo de acción de esos grupos sociales que son los ejércitos, y que es necesario estudiar en sus dimensiones, organización, funcionamiento, jerarquía, espíritu, etcétera. Los ejércitos son solidarios del medio económico y social en que han nacido, y su análisis enseña mucho sobre ese medio. Las guerras del siglo xix, desde el bandolerismo de los plateados hasta las guerras de Reforma y del Imperio, las guerras del siglo xx, la Revolución (extraordinario elemento militar difuso) han sido insuficientemente estudiadas, y prácticamente no se conoce nada desde el punto de vista que nos interesa. Se hace necesario, además, examinar la guerra como un instrumento ambiguo, a la vez de preservación cultural y de integración nacional. En México, cada guerra es a la vez civil e intercultural; lo prueban la guerra de castas, las guerras yaquis, las guerras juchitecas, el zapatismo, la rebelión cristera.

En un artículo sobre Lozada [10] traté de mostrar todo lo que puede concluirse de la historia militar al analizar la batalla de la Mojonera, a las puertas de Guadalajara, el 28 de enero de 1873. Esta batalla muestra efectivamente cómo la derrota no se debió a un hombre,

[9] Bibliografía:

Casas Borja, Lidia, *Causas de la Revolución de la Acordada*. UNAM, México, 1965.

González Casanova, Pablo, *La democracia en México*. México 1967.

Jiménez Moreno, Wigberto, "Puebla como recuperación del orgullo nacional", *Intervención francesa y el Imperio de Maximiliano, cien años después*. México, 1965, pp. 51-5.

Langle R. Arturo, "Porfirio Díaz y la agitación popular", *Estudios de Historia Moderna y Contemporánea*, ii, 1967, pp. 157-66.

Pérez Maldonado, Carlos, "La pugna Juárez-Vidaurri", *Memorias de la Academia Mexicana de la Historia*, xxxix: 1, 1965.

Segovia, Rafael, "El nacionalismo mexicano: los programas políticos revolucionarios 1929-1964", *Foro Internacional*, viii, 1968, pp. 349-359.

Wionczek, Miguel, *El nacimiento mexicano y la inversión extranjera*. México, 1967.

[10] Jean Meyer, "El ocaso de Manuel Lozada", *Historia Mexicana*, xviii: 4, 1969.

Lozada, que ya había vencido ejércitos de línea superiores numéricamente, sino al propio carácter de sus tropas. Los acontecimientos militares revelan las debilidades estructurales del movimiento de Lozada.

A pesar de los numerosos trabajos publicados acerca del zapatismo, poco se ha dicho sobre el reclutamiento y las actividades de su ejército. Sin embargo, lo que podemos concluir al respecto es ya apasionante. La democracia extrema del movimiento zapatista realizaba un viejo ideal utópico de asociación libremente consentida de clanes rurales, y el ejército de Zapata era una liga armada de municipalidades. La democracia extrema trae en consecuencia la aversión a la disciplina. Cada jefe, cada soldado podía seguir su propio camino un día y otro. Yo creo que es muy reveladora la ausencia de un uniforme entre los zapatistas, y personalmente vería en ello una afirmación de civilismo igualitario. El individualismo que destila conduce al oportunismo militar y político, al bandidaje, al aventurerismo. Tanto la estrategia como la táctica revelan siempre una mentalidad que es, a su vez, proyección de un cuerpo social. Cuando se concierta la alianza con Villa, los zapatistas no muestran ningún ardor por batirse para conservar Puebla, posición estratégica esencial, cuyo control permite a Obregón lanzar su campaña victoriosa contra Villa, desdeñando al enemigo zapatista. ¿Es esto una manifestación concreta de lo que Azcárate llama el "parroquialismo" del movimiento? ¿Qué otra visión podrían tener campesinos que producían para comer y estaban condicionados por el aislamiento cultural que ese género de economía impone a la comunidad?

Sabemos poco acerca de los ejércitos, de las partidas zapatistas, fuera de generalidades; pero sabemos mucho menos de los ejércitos de Orozco y de Villa, de las tropas de Peláez, de la gente de Inés Chávez García o de los serranos de Meixueiro, casi nada sabemos acerca del ejército federal.

Para terminar digamos que cada región tiene una guerra muy propia. Estas son un producto local, como lo son el maíz y el frijol. [11]

[11] Bibliografía:

Almada, Francisco R., "La división de operaciones", *Humanitas*, 9, Universidad de Nuevo León, 1968, pp. 431-455.

Casasola, Gustavo, *Historia Gráfica de la Revolución Mexicana*. (4 vols.) 1960. (reed).

González Ramírez, Manuel, "La muerte del general Zapata y la práctica de las emboscadas",, *Estudios de Historia Moderna y Contemporánea*, II 1967, pp. 211-247.

Langle Ramírez, Arturo, "El significado de la toma de Zacatecas", *Estudios de Historia Moderna y Contemporánea*, 1, 1965, pp. 125-134.

Langle Ramírez, Arturo, *El ejército villista*.

Lozoya, Jorge A., "Un guión para el estudio de los ejércitos mexicanos del siglo XIX", *Historia Mexicana*, XVII, 1968, pp. 553-568.

V. BIOGRAFÍAS

La biografía, como la historia militar, es un pariente pobre entre las diversas ramas de la gran familia histórica; y sin embargo, ¡qué errónea- mente! ¡Qué daríamos por tener buenas biografías de los grandes perso- najes, desde Iturbide a Lombardo Toledano, pasando por Santa Ana, Miramón, Tomás Mejía, Juárez, Porfirio Díaz, Obregón, Calles, Cárde- nas, para no citar más que a algunos! El individuo histórico, lo mismo el típico, que el excepcional, es el reflejo de una colectividad, y su acti- vidad, la expresión definida de una necesidad general. De ahí que la personalidad y el grupo formen un todo indisoluble, y que el desti- no individual aparezca como el desarrollo de una personalidad y su respuesta a las presiones del medio circundante. La psicología social enseña que no puede aislarse una personalidad del grupo que la estre- cha, y la recíproca no es menos cierta, lo que nos obliga a llevar a cabo un zig-zag constante de lo colectivo a lo personal. Dos grandes capítu- los nos esperan, el de la vida de las grandes personalidades, en el que podamos analizar con precisión suficiente el comportamiento indivi- dual, y el de la vida de un individuo cualquiera, investigación mucho más ardua, sobre todo a medida que remontamos el pasado. Estos estudios biográficos darán mucho a la historia social, que no estará ya simplemente asociada, sino subordinada a la economía, y será mucho más rica y mucho más profunda.

La extraña personalidad de Santa Ana merece una revisión de un proceso y nos parecerá más comprensible ahora que hemos conocido a ciertos líderes carismáticos del Tercer Mundo. Más cercano a nosotros, Obregón espera todavía su biógrafo, y valdría la pena interesarse por él en cuanto que representa el oportunismo en su sentido de inteli- gencia política que, consciente del estado de la sociedad mexicana, escoge en consecuencia a sus aliados. Obregón supo meditar sobre la agitación campesina y concluir que para recuperar el desarrollo econó- mico era necesario apoyarse en los obreros para lograr una base política urbana que permitiera vigilar a la reacción en las ciudades y someter al campo, apaciguar a los campesinos dándoles la tierra. Obregón supo plegarse a las necesidades del momento sin perder de vista sus objetivos finales. Es a él a quien se deben los artículos favorables a los obreros en la Constitución de un país que carecía de obreros, y cuya aplicación

Lozoya, Jorge A., *El proceso de despolitización del ejército mexicano* (tesis). El Colegio de México, 1966.

Fernández de Velasco, Manuel, "El militarismo en la vida del mexicano hasta 1955", *Estudios de Historia Moderna y Contemporánea*, II, 1967, pp. 97-113.

Sánchez Lomego, Miguel, *Historia militar de la Revolución Constitucionalista.* (4 vols.) México, 1956-57.

Ramírez Flores, José, *El gobierno insurgente en Guadalajara.* Guadalajara, 1969.

hizo de los obreros de la CROM una verdadera aristocracia. Pero fue él quien, al mismo tiempo, después de los motines obreros de 1922-1923, aceleró la distribución de la tierra para obtener el apoyo del campesinado.

Todavía más interesante resultará la biografía de Calles, el hombre de las grandes decisiones, y que aún hoy, a más de 40 años de distancia, sigue determinando la suerte del país. De él sabemos casi nada; sigue siendo una Esfinge.

Nos hace falta también una biografía ejemplar de los jóvenes intelectuales que no tenían ni la edad ni la posibilidad de participar en la Revolución armada de 1910, a 1920, y que luego prestaron sus servicios a los gobiernos de la reconstrucción y de la institucionalización. El intelectual se volvió entonces el consejero de Obregón, de Morones (otro que merece su biografía), de Cárdenas, y se embarcó en una tarea inmensa, abarcadora de la política, de la vida económica, de la instrucción pública, etcétera. Nada más original que su situación, sobre todo si, como dice Octavio Paz, tuvieron que hacer del compromiso un estilo de vida y un arte para no perder sus posiciones materiales e ideológicas.

Hemos sido breves sobre este tema, pues una de las sesiones de la Tercera Reunión está dedicada a la historia biográfica, pero quise referirme a él para mostrar su profundidad social. [12]

[12] Bibliografía:

Bassols Batalla, Narciso, *El pensamiento político de Álvaro Obregón*. México, 1967.

Cosío Villegas, Daniel, "Sebastián Lerdo de Tejada, mártir de la República Restaurada", *Historia Mexicana*, XVII, 1968, pp. 169-199.

Cosío Villegas, Daniel, "Juárez", *Boletín Bibliográfico de la Secretaría de Hacienda*, p. 338-1967.

Fuentes Mares, José, *Y México se refugió en el desierto: Luis Terrazas, historia y destino*. México, 1954.

García Naranjo, *Memorias de García Naranjo*. (7 vols.). Monterrey, 1962(?).

Guzmán Esparza, Roberto (ed), *Memorias de don Adolfo de la Huerta según su propio dictado*. México, 1957.

Hernández Rodríguez, Rosaura, *Ignacio Comonfort, trayectoria política* (documentos). México, 1957.

Liceaga, Luis, *Félix Díaz*. México, 1958.

Mena, Mario, *Un clérigo anticlerical*. México, 1958.

Morales Jiménez, Alberto, *Hombres de la Revolución: 50 semblanzas biográficas*. México, 1960.

Rojas, Basilio, *Un gran rebelde, Manuel García Vigil*. México, 1966.

Semo Caley, Enrique, "El gobierno de Obregón, la deuda exterior y el desarrollo independiente de México", *Historia y Sociedad*, II, 1965, pp. 25-48.

Suárez G., Ignacio, *Carranza, forjador del México actual*. México, 1966.

Teja Zabre, Alfonso, *Vida de Morelos*. México, 1959.

VI. HISTORIA RELIGIOSA

Dentro del gigantesco drama de la historia, la religión comparte con la economía y la política el papel central. Pero ¿sabremos medir las fuerzas que presenciamos? Todos juzgan con seguridad sobre cuestiones religiosas que no han sido científicamente estudiadas, mientras que la sociedad católica "desempeña un papel tan importante que uno puede preguntarse cuál otro podría preferir un sociólogo que quisiera conocer todos los aspectos de la vida nacional" (Gabriel Le Bras). Toda religión encarna en una sociedad, y es indispensable establecer la relación entre la coyuntura social y las vicisitudes de la historia religiosa. Un programa como éste debería comenzar por la anatomía histórica de los fenómenos religiosos, de los catolicismos y protestantismos mexicanos y de todas las otras manifestaciones de religiosidad, como el espiritismo, por ejemplo. Aquí todavía sería posible avanzar rápida y eficazmente utilizando todos los artículos, todas las informaciones existentes, los archivos de la Iglesia y del Estado. Todo ese material podría reunirse e interpretarse de manera sistemática según el siguiente plan:

a) Los marcos humanos: clero y cofradías;

b) Actividad cultural y sacramental;

c) Religión doméstica y vecinal;

d) Generosidad temporal;

e) Moralidad familiar, económica y social;

f) Oposiciones a la Iglesia y al cristianismo (la historia de la masonería no se ha hecho a pesar del interés que ofrece);

g) El estudio de la crisis. Crisis en el interior de la Iglesia, ataques contra la Iglesia venidos del exterior.

Sería importante puntuar sobre un mapa los lugares en que se manifiesta el anticlericalismo y saber si éste es mestizo, urbano, rural, norteño, particular o de clase. De cualquier forma, no existe en este terreno ningún absoluto. Hay un anticlericalismo del pueblo cristiano que nada tiene que ver con el anticlericalismo de los enemigos del cristianismo. Si el anticlericalismo rural incluye a toda una serie de matices, por su naturaleza o por sus manifestaciones, el anticlericalismo urbano no parece ser menos difícil de definir. Por lo menos, mientras no conozcamos exactamente el reclutamiento sociológico de los conservadores y de los liberales. En el siglo XX, son las mismas clases medias las que forman la armazón del nuevo anticlericalismo y las que suministran los apoyos más ardientes a la ortodoxia católica. Todo ello queda por estudiarse, según las épocas, según las regiones, y habrá que multiplicar las monografías dentro del cuadro de las diócesis mismas y descender hasta las parroquias.

Sólo descendiendo a ese nivel podremos tener una idea de la fe, de la práctica, de las conductas del pueblo. Ese catolicismo débilmente intelectual (no tendremos de su fe dogmática más que testimonios indirectos: indiferencia a las herejías, al protestantismo...), pero lleno de confianza hacia el milagro, como lo muestran narraciones y leyendas, nos es bastante desconocido. Para medir el ardor patético y la gran fuerza de esos sentimientos tenemos que impulsar el estudio cuidadoso de los expedientes parroquiales y diocesanos.

Un corte histórico interesante, que resulta del libro ya citado de Luis González, podría ser el de los años 1850-1870. Antes la Iglesia se encuentra en plena crisis; después, el evangelio se predica, se practica nuevamente. El obispo Munguía representa la toma de conciencia de la crisis y el principio del despertar, en el umbral de dos épocas. Se trata, en efecto, de un despertar, más que de una reconquista. Por vez primera la instrucción religiosa se propaga con un método: todas las diócesis tendrán un seminario, y la ciencia nueva del clero se mantendrá por medio de conferencias eclesiásticas. Los obispos multiplican las visitas para controlar la administración y la conducta de los sacerdotes, tal como Munguía efectúa sondeos en las parroquias de varias diócesis. El recuento de las visitas pastorales sería indispensable para medir la amplitud de este fenómeno. Fenómeno que se limita a los marcos eclesiásticos, puesto que no se olvida la instrucción de los seglares: misiones, catecismo, predicación, escuelas... La piedad es estimulada por nuevas cofradías de devoción o de caridad y por peregrinaciones guiadas por un clero que comparte el amor de su pueblo a los seres sobrenaturales. Tales son los temas de otras tantas monografías que están por hacerse, y otros tantos capítulos que siguen vírgenes. La prueba del éxito de este despertar está en el aumento del número de las vocaciones, el crecimiento de esa plebe de sacerdotes pueblerinos que merecerían un largo estudio. Luis González nos presenta sólo algunos tipos. Esta religión clerical y popular hunde sus raíces muy hondo en el pasado, se remonta a los santos de las primeras épocas al siglo XVI *sembrado* por los grandes misioneros. La naturaleza de esta fe la percibimos más intuitiva que científicamente. Es una fe popular, y el papel del pueblo explica la ingenuidad de las creencias, el gusto por las manifestaciones masivas (de ahí los choques contra un Estado que prohíbe las manifestaciones exteriores del culto), la participación en la organización de la parroquia, de las cofradías. Dentro de esta tradición, casi exclusivamente sentimental e imaginativa, las ideas no tienen más que una parte débil. De ahí el desconcierto de los historiadores o, mejor dicho, su desinterés por el fenómeno. Por ese lado habremos de recibir mucho de los antropólogos, aunque no fuera más que para olvidar la noción de "fanatismo", noción anticientífica por excelencia. La imaginación que alcanza esencialmente a la muerte explica la fuerza del sentimiento experimentado hacia las personas divinas, santas o santificadas, y la predilección por la Virgen y los santos locales.

Por supuesto, esta historia deberá ser capaz de darnos cuenta de las personalidades religiosas y de la diversidad de catolicismos mexicanos. El México "católico" es un cliché, una ilusión verbal. Regiones de fervor colindan con zonas de tibieza o de irreligión. La región misma es una entidad demasiado grande. El Jalisco "fanático" o el Tabasco "indiferente" son en realidad centenares de municipios, cada uno con sus particularidades. La vida religiosa de esos millares de parroquias no ha tenido jamás historiadores, y es una lástima.

Para mostrar la complejidad del problema remitiré a una observación oral de Luis González sobre la gran diferencia entre los "alteños" y los "abajeños", y es que el poblado encaramado, aislado, guarda mejor sus tradiciones (y ése es el caso de San José de Gracia, Michoacán), mientras que en el poblado bien provisto de caminos, sobre la planicie, el hombre rural podrá dirigirse a la ciudad, al baile, al cine. Sería raro que al atardecer encontrara gusto en ir al templo a cantar las vísperas como lo hacía en San José, o como lo hace todavía en San Francisco de Asís. Además las ciudades también se dirigen al campo, envían sus hombres de negocios, sus paseantes, sus diputados, sus periódicos y sus modas. Esto explicaría la diferencia de naturaleza, o de nivel, entre la fe de los Altos de Jalisco y la de los Llanos.

Esta observación conduce al estudio de las relaciones con el mundo, puesto que la sociedad religiosa se halla inmersa en la sociedad global, en la que nada puede dejarnos indiferentes. Nos encontramos bajo el señorío de la interacción, sociedad profana y sociedad sagrada (pueblo de Dios y sociedad clerical) que se sostienen, se combaten y se influyen mutuamente. ¿Cuál es la acción de la sociedad religiosa sobre las familias, la economía, la política? La Iglesia refleja y refuerza, a menudo inconscientemente, las jerarquías y las oposiciones de la sociedad civil. Tiene como compañero al Estado, cuyas presiones le son en definitiva y casi siempre desfavorables, vengan de conservadores o de liberales, trátase de leyes hostiles o de privilegios, tal como lo muestra la historia de los siglos xix y xx.

Los factores de unidad están representados por el Estado, la Iglesia y la civilización (ciencia, pensamiento, modas, economía, técnicas), pero el juego entre esas fuerzas es difícil de determinar, puesto que todas esas potencias se sitúan bajo el signo de la complejidad. La Iglesia es un conjunto de fuerzas que a menudo se contrarrestan. Y otro tanto podemos decir del Estado. En cuanto a la civilización, nada contribuye mejor a la dispersión de las potencias que esa coexistencia, señalada por Octavio Paz, de épocas y costumbres.

La diferencia de comportamiento según los sexos, el pluralismo de las generaciones, las divergencias sociales que dividen a la sociedad en categorías socioprofesionales y arrastran una curiosa contradanza de las clases sobre el camino de la Iglesia, y en fin, las oposiciones regionales, todo ello viene a complicar nuestra labor y a multiplicar las contradicciones. Con elementos tan numerosos, las combinaciones que se ofrecen como posibilidades son casi infinitas. Y por si todo eso fuera poco, hay que tomar en cuenta las variaciones en el tiempo, hay que tomar en cuenta el hecho de que los cambios han sido rápidos y constantes, aun cuando las permanencias profundas no hayan sufrido sacudidas. Los cambios que afectan un sector social o geográfico se hacen sentir en otros sectores. La religión, como componente de la cultura mexicana, depende de la economía, de la política, y a su vez afecta a todas ellas. El catolicismo que encontramos en los diferentes niveles de las culturas mexicanas, cultura de una facción limitada por el espacio y en el tiempo, cultura de una clase, cultura regional, cultura nacional, tiene múltiples rostros y conoce múltiples cambios de ideas.

El estudio de las relaciones de esos grandes sectores de la historia necesita un material documental que está muy lejos de encontrarse reunido. Poseemos numerosas monografías sobre municipios o sobre pueblos. [13] Si los trabajos de los antropólogos se especializan en las comunidades indígenas, los eruditos locales de la historia "parroquial" han preparado ya otro camino. De todas maneras, estamos mejor informados acerca de los indios que de los mestizos (en el sentido cultural); conocemos mejor ciertos poblados mundialmente célebres como Tepoztlán, Chan Kom, o Zinacantán que las ciudades; y los dos últimos siglos nos son todavía menos conocidos que la época colonial.

Lo que sí tenemos es la posibilidad de estudiar las crisis, como indicadores del estado religioso de la sociedad. En efecto, podemos suponer que si antes de 1810 los mexicanos gozaban de disposiciones comunes, éstas no eran de ninguna manera unánimes y que, después de esa fecha, se produjeron crisis periódicas que manifiestan y amplían las oposiciones duraderas, puesto que sobreviven en los espíritus y en los grupos organizados. Un ejemplo de la complejidad del papel de esas crisis, que son a la vez causas y efectos y después causas de nuevas crisis, sería la expulsión de los jesuitas, expulsión que trajo, entre otras consecuencias, la primera huelga en México, la de los mineros de San Luis Potosí y de Real del Catorce, que no perdonaron ni al Estado ni a la Iglesia secular la expulsión de la orden que ellos conocían. De manera semejante, los huicholes de la Sierra de Nayarit, cuando les

[13] Véase la ponencia del grupo V, "Historias de tema regional y parroquial".

enviaron curas seglares, respondieron que querían a los frailes o no querían nada, y nada tuvieron hasta 1960.

La crisis, instante de gran brillo, decide por mucho tiempo la suerte de la práctica a causa de sus funciones o de sus ruinas, del impulso o de la negación. Fue así como la gran crisis provocada por el regalismo de los Borbones desembocó en la guerra de Independencia y explica la participación masiva del clero y ciertos aspectos de "Religión y Fueros". Es así como ese conflicto entre la Iglesia y el Estado, proseguido por ciertos liberales y ciertos conservadores, explica la decadencia de la primera mitad del siglo xix. Es así como la persecución religiosa de los años 1926-1938 explica el despertar de una fe más mística y ardiente que nunca.

Las primeras pasiones se desencadenan en torno a la riqueza de la Iglesia, desde los Borbones hasta Lerdo de Tejada. Se hace necesario perseguir de nuevo el crecimiento de la riqueza de la Iglesia para encontrar el crecimiento paralelo de la envidia y de la cólera que extirpan la devoción. La guerra, la gran crisis de la civilización, de 1810 a 1821, conmociona, disloca a la Iglesia y a la sociedad. Arrastra interrupciones, rupturas, exaltaciones también; los desastres del siglo xix, más tarde los de la Revolución, hicieron florecer mucho a las cofradías, mientras que disminuía la asistencia a la misa.

La persecución religiosa fue la gran prueba de la Iglesia. Convendría hacer la estadística y la sociología de los cismáticos de la Iglesia católica, apostólica, mexicana del patriarca Pérez. Incluso si fueron poco numerosos, o aunque el gobierno haya tirado de las cuerdas, el caso no carece de interés.

En agosto de 1926 se inicia la sublevación popular, en el momento en que los cultos se suspenden. ¿En qué medida el levantamiento se debe a la fidelidad religiosa? ¿Qué parte correspondió a cada localidad? Es éste el tema de mi tesis, pero aún es temprano para responder. En el curso de las crisis que la han afectado desde hace dos siglos, la Iglesia ha sufrido derrotas, y es necesario escribir el capítulo de los progresos de la irreligión, distinguiendo el anticlericalismo religioso del anticlericalismo dirigido contra la persona del sacerdote. La Iglesia se ha conservado en parte, ha resistido y ha reaccionado, como en el caso del despertar de finales del siglo pasado, o como en el caso de su actividad política y sindical de los años 1910-1925. La Revolución quebró los marcos del culto y del control, como la gran prueba de la práctica religiosa en el país (en ciertas regiones el bautismo fue prohibido). De ahí que todos los índices locales de supervivencia o ruina de los usos religiosos durante los disturbios sean más valiosos para nosotros que los enormes y pacíficos balances del porfiriato.

En fin, dos grandes problemas no han sido tratados aún: primero, ¿en qué medida el catolicismo resiente en México la marca del carácter nacional, en qué medida corrige las disposiciones ordinarias de los mexicanos? Y segundo, ¿cuáles son las relaciones entre religión y tensiones sociales? Cuestión ésta que podemos descomponer en dos interrogantes: ¿cuál es la actividad de los cuerpos religiosos frente a las tensiones sociales? (las política obrera y agraria de la iglesia, el sindicalismo cristiano, el partido católico nacional, todo esto entraría como ejemplo). ¿Es la religión un factor de conflictos? (toda la historia de México entra en esta pregunta).

Es justamente esta relación entre la Iglesia católica y las tendencias sociales la que permite aprehender el problema de los protestantismos mexicanos. Hasta hace poco se podía hablar de un fracaso relativo del protestantismo acompañado de éxitos locales bastante curiosos, como son los casos de las comunidades de la Sierra Gorda y de la huaxteca (entre Xilitla y Pisaflores) durante el siglo pasado. En un mundo que muestra tanta devoción a la Virgen y a los santos, a los seres sobrenaturales y a los difuntos, no es de extrañar que las predicaciones protestantes hayan encontrado poco éxito al atacar usos tan queridos. Y a pesar de todo hay un protestantismo mexicano, mal conocido ciertamente, pero apasionante. Sería fácil trazar su mapa, precisar su composición social y sus motivos, que siempre ven que el sentimiento vence a la argumentación teológica, como ocurre, por lo demás, también entre los católicos. Trabajo que se facilita por ser pequeño su número. Las causas de la resistencia o de la adhesión al protestantismo nos iluminarán acerca de la vitalidad del catolicismo. Distingamos un protestantismo del siglo XIX, mínimo, que logró un éxito bastante mediocre porque estaba apoyado por el Estado mexicano, por los Estados Unidos, porque se trataba de un protestantismo de Iglesia, y de Iglesia a Iglesia se prefirió entonces a la romana. Ello no excluye los interesantes éxitos rurales que responden justamente a situaciones de privación o de frustración. Y un protestantismo del siglo XX, pobre, de evangelización radical, baptista, adventista, pentecotista, protestantes de las asambleas de Dios que se dicen católicas y que mañana podrían serlo efectivamente, como esos protestantes de la Costa Grande de Petatlán, que retornaron al seno de la iglesia. Místico, inspirado, cercano a Dios, sin exigencias dogmáticas, ese protestantismo se asemeja a menudo a un catolicismo de los medios rurales, sin sacerdote, que esperan todavía a su misionero o su retorno. Se asemeja por lo demás a un catolicismo antisacerdotal, ya que el sacerdote desempeña un papel negativo en las tensiones sociales al estar en servicio de las potencias de opresión o al ser él mismo opresor (de ahí que sea esencial estudiar el clero, su formación, su actividad, su riqueza, su moral).

Es también el protestantismo de tierras recién pobladas donde la Iglesia no alcanza a los emigrados. Tierra caliente del oeste, del sur, del golfo, del norte, desde entonces más americanizado. He ahí una situación que puede cambiar, que está cambiando puesto que la Iglesia católica ha recogido el desafío y las dos confesiones luchan a toda prisa por cristianizar a individuos que nunca antes lo habían sido. Señalaré entre las numerosas familias espirituales protestantes, un curioso movimiento con fuertes tendencias milenaristas, el de los trinitarios o marianistas que no soportan que se les llame protestantes, y cuya fe se asienta en revelaciones privadas hechas al fundador y en el culto de la Virgen, del Sagrado Corazón, de San José y de la Trinidad. Movimiento sobrenatural y paracletista que afirma la salvación colectiva para sus fieles y la salvación terrestre para el Nuevo Mundo y para México, siendo México la Nueva Jerusalén en donde se fundirán todas las razas. La salvación es eminente y será total.

Nuestro mundo moderno, nuestra historia no será inteligible hasta que se haya definido claramente la parte de la religión en la vida de las masas. Ese programa de investigación incluye las representaciones, las prácticas, las organizaciones, los sistemas. Hay que estudiar las creencias, los dogmas, las reglas de derecho, las revelaciones, el culto, las artes, las formas, aquello que es a la vez la obra de hombres ilustrados, de grupos cerrados o de muchedumbres inmensas. ¿Por qué ha concedido hasta aquí tan poco interés a las religiones vivas y tanto a las religiones muertas? La obediencia a sus mandamientos ocupa, modela a millones de personas, puesto que la religión es un hecho social por excelencia, un tema de historia social pura, podría decirse. La sociología francesa ha llevado la demostración a su extremo diciendo que es lo social lo que crea lo sagrado. En todo caso, si las sociedades profanas no crean dioses, "ofrecen a toda religión una cuna y un alimento" (Le Bras). De la proposición inversa, que toda sociedad resiente la acción de las estructuras y de las fuerzas religiosas, no se ha comenzado, en lo que respecta a la historia de México, a sacar consecuencias. Es por ello que me he detenido a sugerir empresas científicas que deberían interesar a los hombres de acción, puesto que son ricas en enseñanza sobre el comportamiento de los hombres. [14]

[14] Bibliografía:

Alcalá Alvarado, Alfonso, *Una pugna diplomática ante la Santa Sede. El restablecimiento del episcopado en México, 1825, 1831.* México, 1967.
Barquín y Ruiz, Andrés, *José de Jesús Manríquez Zárate.* México, 1952.
Barquín y Ruiz, Andrés, *Monseñor J. M. González Valencia.* México, 1957.
Brambila, Cresenciano, *El Seminario de Colima,* 1966.
Brambila, Cresenciano, *El Obispado de Autlán.*
Brambila, Cresenciano, *El Obispado de Colima,* 1964.
Bravo Ugarte, José, *Cuestiones históricas guadalupanas.* México, 1966.
Bravo Ugarte, José, *Munguía, obispo y arzobispo de Michoacán (1810-1868) Su vida y su obra.* México, 1967.
Barba González, Silvano, *La rebelión de los cristeros.* México, 1967.
Camberos Vizcaíno, Vicente, *Francisco el Grande. Mons. Francisco Orozco y Jiménez, biografía.* (2 vols). 1966.

VII. HISTORIA DE LAS MENTALIDADES

No se trata aquí de una exposición de historia sociocultural, sino de proposiciones de investigación que nos permitirán rendir homenaje al doctor José Gaos, cuya reciente muerte fue (y perdonen el lugar común tremendo de la fórmula, pero ella corresponde a la realidad) una pérdida irreparable. La historia —nos solía decir— es inmensa, diversa, indefinida, a la vez científica, filosófica y estética. La historia social, de las ideas, de las creencias y de los sentimientos se encuentra en un cruce de caminos que señala la necesidad de encuentros interdiscipli-

Cassaretto, Mary A., *El Movimiento protestante en México 1940-1955*. Guadalajara, 1960.

Dávila Garibi, Ignacio, *Apuntes para la historia de la Iglesia en Guadalajara* (3 vols.), 1957-63 (sigue la publicación).

Escobedo Arana, Jesús Salvador, *Ideario y ambiente jurídico-político de Clemente de Jesús Munguía*. Guadalajara, 1953.

Garibay, Ángel Ma., *Presencia de la Iglesia en México*. México, 1966.

García Gutiérrez, Jesús, *La masonería en la historia y en las leyes de México*. México, 1957.

Hurtado, Arnulfo, *El cisma mexicano*. México, 1956.

López Austin, Alfredo, "Los temacpalitotique. Brujos, profanadores, ladrones y violadores", *Estudios de Cultura Náhuatl*, vi, 1966, pp. 97-117.

Estrada, Antonio, *Rescoldo*. México, 1961.

Meyer, Jean A., "Pour une sociologie des catholicisme mexicains", *Cahiers de Sociologie Economique*. Universidad de Rouen, Havre, 1965, pp. 82-103.

Peñaloza, Joaquín A., *Monseñor Miguel de la Mora, el obispo para todos*. 1963.

Navarrete, Heriberto, *Por Dios y la patria*. 1961.

Navarrete, Heriberto, *El voto de Chema Rodríguez*. 1964.

Navarrete, Heriberto, *Los cristeros eran así . . .* 1968.

Olivera, Mercedes, "Notas sobre las actividades religiosas en Tlaxiaco", *Anales de INHA*, 1962.

Oliveira Sedano, Alicia, *Aspectos del conflicto religioso 1926-9, sus antecedentes y sus consecuencias*. México, 1966.

Peñaloza, Joaquín Antonio, *La práctica religiosa en México siglo XVI. Asedios de sociología religiosa*. México. Jul., 1969, 282 pp.

Rius Facius, Antonio, *México cristero, Historia de ACJM*. México, 1960.

Ruiz Martínez, Jorge, *Apuntes históricos acerca de la venerada imagen de Nuestra Señora de los Dolores de Soriano*. México, 1967.

Rubio, Elena, *Aportación al estudio histórico de las relaciones entre la Iglesia católica y el Estado mexicano durante los gobiernos de Obregón y Calles*. UNAM, México, 1964.

Torre Villar, Ernesto de la "La Iglesia en México de la guerra de Independencia a la Reforma. Notas para un estudio", *Estudios de Historia Moderna y Contemporánea*, i, 1965.

Treviño, J. G., *Mons. Martínez, Arzobispo primado de México*. Madrid, 1959.

Vázquez Vázquez, Elena. *Distribución geográfica y organización de las órdenes religiosas de la Nueva España. siglo XVI*. UNAM, México, 1965.

Zambrano, Francisco, *Diccionario biobibliográfico de la Compañía de Jesús en México*, vol. vi, México, 1966.

nares. Es, a menudo, en las fronteras donde los pioneros realizan los descubrimientos más hermosos, y una frontera, por definición, se sitúa entre dos mundos. La fórmula "historia de las mentalidades" tiene el interés de no ser demasiado precisa, de mantener polivalente y factible la historia de las ideas: si los hombres están movidos por la razón no hay que olvidar que también lo están por sus intereses y sus pasiones. Paul Hazard, cuya lectura recomendaba el doctor Gaos, propuso una ley de los balances según la cual una cultura se afirma unas veces como dominantemente racionalista y otras como dominantemente sentimental, y limitaba inmediatamente su afirmación al precisar que los hombres de sentimientos y los hombres de razón coexisten en la misma sociedad y que la razón y la oscuridad se reparten el corazón del hombre mismo. Cuestión de dosis, cuestión de elementos dominantes que darán su color a una sociedad, a una época. Hay una historia visible, una historia solar, de superficie o más bien una serie de cimas, y una historia subterránea de la civilización, una historia según los latidos, marcada por el retorno de los reflujos. También lo irreductible, lo ilógico, es accesible a nuestra razón de historiadores. Daré sólo una prueba: el doctor Gaos propuso como tema de tesis, a una de sus alumnas de la última generación, el amor y sus representaciones a comienzos de la vida independiente de México.

No puede descubrirse ninguna ley, en el sentido físico del término, que presida los destinos de las mentalidades colectivas. Ninguna ley, sino la de las coexistencias. Michel Foucault desprecia la historia y su continuidad, se opone a toda doxografía y no admite las transmisiones de edad a edad. Ahora bien, no es evidente que todos los hombres de un mismo tiempo sean exactamente contemporáneos, ni siquiera que los pensamientos de un hombre pertenezcan al mismo universo mental. Podría demostrarse la sobrevivencia del universo borbónico o al contrario, del universo habsburgués entre los delegados mexicanos a las Cortes, y al mismo tiempo, la intrusión de un nuevo pensamiento que niega el universo anterior. Mora, por ejemplo, es el contemporáneo de los Borbones del siglo XVIII al mismo tiempo que de las Cortes. Sus parientes son a la vez dos españoles reformistas: reformismos de Jovellanos y liberalismo político y anticlericalismo regalojansenista.

No podemos fiarnos de las apariencias, pues una generación puede levantarse contra la herencia que le transmite la precedente al aceptarla como un hecho. Puede también, de hecho, tomar el curso inverso, o no. El problema de las continuidades, de las rupturas, es uno de los más espinosos. ¿Quién rompe verdaderamente con el pasado —y con cuál pasado—: los liberales o los conservadores? ¿La Revolución de 1910 se volvió hacia el futuro, o su inspiración es colonial? ¿El conflicto religioso de 1926, no continúa acaso el conflicto del siglo XVIII? ¿Zapata y sus hombres no sostienen el mismo combate, no tienen las mismas aspiraciones que las comunidades de la época colonial? Si no podemos aún responder a estas preguntas, ello prueba nuestro retraso en este terreno, y esos cambios de mentalidades, que en muchos casos condicionan las mutaciones estructurales, siguen siendo poco conocidos. En el extranjero se realizan trabajos y vemos aparecer nuevas definiciones de las clases sociales que ponen el acento en los caracteres psicológicos y culturales, el género de vida, la educación, las aspiraciones.

Por su parte la historia literaria, protegida de los peligros del esteticismo por la historia social, permite precisamente ese psicoanálisis histórico que tanta falta nos hace de un tema ausente, puesto que se evade en el pasado. Las preocupaciones sociales recientes de la historia literaria ayudan a definir al público, las relaciones entre la condición social del escritor y la creación literaria y, por fin, las razones del gusto de una sociedad. La historia literaria provee también testimonios para la historia social, y sería muy importante que comenzaran investigaciones sobre los hábitos de lectura de los grupos sociales y su evolución. Luis González da indicaciones de este tipo: "Había poca cultura literaria, no obstante los esfuerzos del padre Othón para que la gente leyera. Prestaba y recomendaba libros y él mismo ponía el ejemplo al terminar el rosario, cuando leía durante un cuarto de hora algunos párrafos de libros piadosos. El hábito de la lectura se inició antes en las mujeres que en los hombres. En las tertulias preponderantemente femeninas se leía el *Arco iris de la paz* (explicaciones de los misterios del rosario), el *Año cristiano* (colección de vidas de santos), la *Imitación de Cristo, Estaurófila* y la historia de *Genoveva de Bravante*." [15]

Este ejemplo prueba bien que no debemos limitarnos a las que llamamos las "grandes obras"; habrá que privilegiar obras mediocres, las novelas comunes que dan la representación que una sociedad se hace de sí misma y que por su éxito masivo y persistente revelan las estructuras profundas. En esta investigación no se habrán de olvidar los aspectos materiales de la producción y de la difusión. Al lado de la historia del libro, y algunas veces más importante que ella, sobre todo en el siglo XIX, la historia de los "folletos" puede revelar no solamente la invención, sino la difusión y esquematización de las ideas religiosas y políticas. Volviendo a Paul Hazard, nos falta el esfuerzo inmenso que se necesita para buscar el clima mental de una época en la correspondencia, en los diarios, las memorias. Es de una verdadera sociología histórica el inventario de las imágenes, de los esquemas, de los pensamientos, de las categorías mentales que varían de edad en edad, de grupo en grupo, de región en región.

Luis González nos invita a atacar la misma empresa en lo referente a la cultura popular, que, decididamente religiosa hasta hace poco, ganaría mucho al ser estudiada a la luz de la sociología religiosa evocada

[15] Luis González. *Pueblo en vilo*, p. 147.

antes. Sin hablar de la *Buena Prensa* del siglo xx, existieron en todo
tiempo editoriales especializadas en calendarios, folletos técnicos, innumerables obras de piedad, cancioneros, colecciones de cuentos, de diálo-
gos, recetas médicas y recetas de cocina. Veríamos entonces los dos
grandes niveles de la sociedad mexicana, por un lado los ilustrados, los
sabios, los filósofos y sus lectores, y por otro el pueblo que se preocupa
del viaje a la luna o de la llegada de las lluvias. Es a ese nivel a donde
apunta la intuición de Paz: la oposición entre los jacobinos y los pere-
grinos de Pedro el Ermitaño. García Icazbalceta pudo perfectamente
arruinar los fundamentos científicos de la Virgen de Guadalupe, pero
la consagración legendaria sobrevivió a esos relatos. Cuando conozcamos esos medios culturales, sus relaciones, o mejor, eso que a título
de hipótesis creemos que es la ausencia de comunicación, nos podremos
explicar cómo los jacobinos de 1926 pudieron lanzarse a la ligera en el
aventurismo antirreligioso.

Podrían inventarse medios de aproximación semejante para otras tantas formas de expresión: música, teatro, pintura, al relacionar las capas
sociales con el gusto de los públicos. Pastorelas, cánticos, alabados,
representaciones religiosas y procesiones para los "de abajo"; ópera,
teatro y pintura internacional para los de "arriba". Los gustos de los
segundos son bien conocidos, los de los primeros todavía se encuentran
en la oscuridad. El arte revolucionario, el muralismo en particular, sería
tratado aparte.

En fin inspirados y no inhibidos por el estructuralismo, sería necesario estudiar el lenguaje de los unos y de los otros, patrimonio social
y viviente. Luis González tocó el problema al hacer inventarios verbales, en desorden alfabético, que pudieron parecer a algunos como efectos de estilo, pero que son efectivamente poderosos reveladores: "Podría
imaginarse una psicología de los pueblos que reposara en el examen
de los sucesivos cambios semánticos atestiguados en las lenguas que se
hablan" (Vendryes). Podrían lanzarse encuestas limitadas a grupos escogidos, pero representativos de la élite y del pueblo para estudiar el vocabulario político, religioso, amoroso, y con esto no terminaríamos la lista.

Habría que comenzar, por ejemplo, por lo más sencillo, recoger de la
prensa política del siglo xix las nociones clave con sus frecuencias, trabajo previo para preparar una lista provisional, como hipótesis, de sus
nociones políticas. El doctor Gaos preparó a varias generaciones en ese
género de lectura. Estamos conscientes de los límites e inconvenientes
de la empresa, pero ésta no ha comenzado todavía y las ventajas son
tan grandes ...

En fin, las investigaciones acerca de la enseñanza no deben descui-
darse. En el Colegio de México se aceptó este año un tema de tesis
en ese sector. Cuando se sabe la importancia que dieron a la educación
el siglo xix y después de él la Revolución, se explica por qué ansiamos

conocer la historia de los profesores, de los alumnos, de los programas, de la pedagogía, pues si las instituciones escolares son el fruto de transformaciones socioeconómicas, contribuyen también a precipitarlas y revelan una sociología cultural. La enseñanza, como el lenguaje, está en retraso respecto de la cultura, y habrá que tomar en cuenta el grado de esa ruptura. Aquí el campo es todavía vasto: escuelas estatales, escuelas protestantes, colegios religiosos, seminarios, universidades, programas, reformas desde la escuela lancasteriana hasta la escuela socialista... No puede olvidarse que, por ejemplo, la enseñanza de la historia, después de su elaboración, revela ciertos aspectos de las mentalidades colectivas. No se trata evidentemente de la disciplina científica, sino de la leyenda sagrada al servicio de una ideología empeñada en "forjar patria".

Esos trabajos nos permitirán desenmascarar la ruptura que existe entre las ideologías y las realidades sociales y explicar así su importancia para reorganizar la realidad nacional. El fracaso final de los liberales, su mutuación porfirista, ¿no se explica acaso por la inadecuación entre la ideología y la realidad mexicana? Ideología burguesa sin burguesía que, sin las previsiones de Justo Sierra, debía engendrar esa burguesía indispensable para el desarrollo del país. Del positivismo nos ha dicho Leopoldo Zea, hace tiempo, que respondía a las necesidades del momento social, y al mismo tiempo, que su relación con el grupo social dirigente era muy diversa de la que existía en Europa. Es esto lo que Paz llama la "simulación porfirista", reveladora de una situación social peligrosa. Todas esas contradicciones aparentes entre ideología y sociedad exigen un nuevo examen, un nuevo acercamiento histórico a la cultura mexicana. [16]

[16] Bibliografía:

Las dos mesas redondas de la IIIª Reunión sobre "Problemas de Historia de las Ideas" y "El contenido Social de la Literatura y las Artes", nos permiten limitar al extremo las indicaciones bibliográficas en ambos sectores. Deberá consultarse la colección *El mexicano y lo mexicano*, 1969.

Bremauntz, Alberto, *Batalla ideológica en México*. México, 1962.

Cardiel Reyes, Raúl, *Del modernismo al liberalismo, la filosofía de Manuel María Gorrino*. México, 1967.

García Cantú, Gastón, *El pensamiento de la reacción mexicana. Historia documental 1810-1962*. México, 1965.

Gelskey Beier, Frank, *Las novelas cristeras de Jorge Gram*. UNAM, 1957.

Gelskey Beier, Frank, *La literatura cristera después de Jorge Gram*. UNAM, 1958.

Gelskey Beier, Frank, *Historia e ideología de la filosofía cristera*. Universidad de Salamanca, 1961.

González Casanova, Pablo, *La democracia en México*. México, 1965.

Ibargüengoitia, Antonio, *Filosofía mexicana en sus hombres, en sus textos*. México, 1967.

López Cámara, Francisco, *La génesis de la conciencia liberal en México*. 1954.

VIII. PERMANENCIA DE LOS PROBLEMAS E HISTORIA DE LAS RESISTENCIAS

Lo que resalta de lo poco que sabemos es, finalmente, la estabilidad de las estructuras, mal conocidas y tan permanentes como los proble-

Melma Sztein, Anita, *El pensamiento sociológico del positivismo mexicano.* UNAM.

Reyes Heroles, Jesús, *El liberalismo mexicano* (3 vols.) 1961.

Moreno, Daniel, *Manuel Crescencio Rejón, pensamiento político.* 1968.

Tavera Alfaro, Xavier, *Tres votos y un debate del congreso constituyente 1856-7.* Xalapa, 1958.

Valadés, José, *El pensamiento político de Benito Juárez.* 1956.

Valadés, José, *Don Melchor Ocampo, reformador de México.* 1954.

Villoro, Luis, *La revolución de independencia. Ensayo de interpretación histórica,* 1953. (reed. 1958).

Yáñez, Agustín, *Don Justo Sierra, su vida, sus ideas, su obra.* 1962.

Zuno, José G., *Nuestro liberalismo,* Guadalajara, 1956.

Historia de la educación

Almada, Francisco R., "La Reforma educativa a partir de 1812", *Historia Mexicana.* 1968, pp. 103-125.

Alvear Acevedo, Carlos, *La educación y la ley, la legislación en materia educativa en el México independiente.* México, 1963.

Bravo Ugarte, José, *La educación en México.* México, 1966.

Bravo Ugarte, José, "Datos sobre la fundación de los seminarios diocesanos de México y sus confiscaciones", *Memorias Academia Mexicana de la Historia,* xi: 2, 1952, pp. 150-157.

Cantón, Wilberto, *Justo Sierra.* México, 1967.

Gallegos, José Ignacio, *Apuntes para la Historia del Instituto Juárez de Durango.* Durango, 1950.

Gallo Martínez, Víctor, "La educación preescolar y primaria", *México 50 años de revolución, la cultura.* 1962.

García Ruiz, Ramón, "Historia de la educación en Jalisco", *Historia Mexicana,* vi: 4, 1957, pp. 548-71.

González de Cossío, Francisco, "Disertación queretana", *Historia Mexicana,* vi: 4, 1957.

González Navarro, Moisés, "La instrucción pública" en Cosío Villegas, Daniel, *Historia moderna de México, El Porfiriato, La vida social.* 1957.

Hernández Espinosa, Francisco, *Historia de la educación en Colima.* 1950.

López Carrasco, *Historia de la educación en el Estado de Oaxaca.* 1950.

Manzano, Teodomiro, *Historia de la educación primaria en el Estado de Hidalgo.* 1950.

Mayo, Sebastián, *La educación socialista en México, el asalto a la Universidad Nacional.* 1954.

Mendirichaga Cueva, Tomás, "La Universidad socialista de Nuevo León", *Humanistas",* 9, 1968, pp. 361-88.

Romero Flores, Jesús, *Historia de la educación en Michoacán.* 1950.

Vázquez de Knauth, Josefina, "La República Restaurada y la educación: un intento de victoria definitiva", *Historia Mexicana,* 1968, pp. 200-211.

Deberán consultarse también los volúmenes de La Vida Social de la *Historia Moderna de México* y el tomo iv de *50 años de Revolución Mexicana.*

mas. Si la historia de los movimientos no se ha hecho, no tenemos tampoco historia de las resistencias que nos han descubierto los sociólogos cuidadosos de suprimir todos los obstáculos al "social change". Es esta historia de profundidad de las mentalidades la que nos permi-

Historia literaria

Abreu Gómez, E., *Martín Luis Guzmán*. México, 1968.

Cardoza y Aragón, Luis, *Círculos concéntricos*. Xalapa, 1967.

Castellanos, Luis, A., "La novela de la revolución mexicana", *Cuadernos Hispanoamericanos*, 62. Madrid, 1965.

Estrada, Ricardo, "Los indicios de Pedro Páramo", *Universidad de San Carlos*, I. Guatemala, 1965.

González Peña, Carlos, *Historia de la literatura mexicana desde los orígenes hasta nuestros días* 9ª ed., 1967.

Maza, Francisco de la, "Un libro romántico", *Anales del Instituto de Investigaciones Estéticas*, 36, 1967.

Monterde, Francisco, "La Intervención, tema en el teatro mexicano", *Intervención francesa y el Imperio de Maximiliano*, 1965, pp. 150-159.

Ochoa Campos, Moisés, *La oratoria en México. Antología desde la independencia a la época actual*. México, 1968.

Valenzuela Rodarte, Alberto, *Historia de la literatura en México e Hispanoamérica*. México, 1967.

Historia del arte

Arteaga, Beatriz (ed.), "Documentos para la historia del arte en México en el siglo XIX", *Anales del Instituto de Investigaciones Estéticas*", XXXVI, 1967.

Fernández, Justino, *El arte del siglo XIX en México*. México, 1967.

Baqueiro Foster, Gerónimo, "Apuntes para la historia de la música en México", *Boletín Bibliográfico de la Secretaría de Hacienda*, XVI, 1967.

Guillén. Fedro, "El mural y el libro en la Revolución", *Política*, 23 agosto, 1962.

Pupo Walker, Enrique, "Los de abajo y la pintura de Orozco. Un caso de correspondencia estética", *Cuadernos Americanos*, sept.-oct., 1967, pp. 237-254.

Reyes, Valerio Constantino, "Las pinturas en el papel de amate de Ixmiquilpan", *Boletín del INAH*, 27, 1967.

Reyes de la Maza, Luis, *El teatro en México durante el porfirismo, 1900-1910*. México, 1968.

Tibol, Raquel, *Historia general del arte mexicano, época moderna y contemporánea*. México, 1965.

Tibol, Raquel, *Siqueiros, introductor de realidades*. UNAM, México, 1961.

Toscano, Salvador, *Juan Cordero y la pintura mexicana en el siglo XIX*. 1946.

Siqueiros, David, *El Muralismo en México*. 1950.

Arte y pueblo

Baqueiro Foster, Gerónimo; "La revolución y sus cantos", *Revista del conservatorio*, oct. 1964. "La charrería", *Artes de México*, XIV: 99, 1967.

Flores Guerrero, Raúl, "El barroco popular de Texcoco", *Anales del Instituto de Investigaciones Estéticas*, 24, 1956.

García Maroto, Gabriel, *Arquitectura popular*. 1954.

Montenegro, Roberto, *Retablos de México*. 1950.

Mendoza, Vicente T., *Nuevas aportaciones a la investigación folklórica de México*. México, 1958.

tirá alcanzar las resistencias (juicios, sentimientos, actitudes) variables según los grupos y según los problemas. Al lado de estas resistencias de lo mental, se encuentra el problema del freno de la estructura social. Las condiciones del tradicionalismo, del conservadurismo real, aun cuando las apariencias engañen, aquello que Véliz llama el "hábito hispánico" ha sido demasiado descuidado. En el presente se interesan por ello los sociólogos, y aun cuando las dificultades que encuentran resultan de su insuficiente formación histórica, yo no podría reprochárselos. Por el contrario, ellos tendrían derecho de reprochar a los historiadores su falta de interés por esos problemas que no pueden comprenderse con profundidad de un pasado, algunas veces demasiado cercano, otras ya muy lejano. Hasta ahora nos hemos interesado en las revoluciones, porque aparentemente han triunfado, aun cuando nada prueba que el conservadurismo haya sido vencido con los conservadores, puesto que Lucas Alamán mismo se complace en denunciar el conservadurismo social de los liberales, cuando en su *Historia de México* los conmina a escoger entre Hidalgo, seguido por hordas populares, e Iturbide, el padre de la Independencia criolla. De labios afuera cantan las alabanzas de Hidalgo, pero Zavala, Mora, Gómez Farías, ¿acaso no votaron por el Imperio? La ruptura política entre los liberales y conservadores no se logra antes de la Reforma, y las décadas que siguen muestran que el conservadurismo social criollo continúa a todo lo largo del siglo. En fin de cuentas el liberalismo había quizás contribuido a minar las conductas tradicionales, pero muy tardíamente, y quizás nada efectivamente. Conservadores y liberales, ¿no son en realidad más complementarios, que antagonistas? Ésa es al menos la impresión que tenemos en el plano de las ideas. ¿Cuál es la realidad social?

Cuando tengamos respuestas o principios de respuestas a todos esos problemas, podremos escribir esas historias sociales que nos hacen falta, de la Independencia, de la Reforma, del Imperio, del Porfiriato y de la Revolución. Para limitarnos sólo a la Revolución, señalemos algunos problemas: ¿Por qué la fuerza campesina fue puesta finalmente a disposición de otros grupos? (Grupos mal conocidos también, como los demás, pues ¿quiénes son los reyistas, lo felicistas, etcétera?) La Revolución triunfante que volvió a lanzar a México por las vías del progreso y de la modernización ¿acaso no hizo imposible la utopía que soñaban los zapatistas? La Revolución rompió el antiguo sistema agrario, pero permitió que surgieran nuevas formas de explotación. Cuando el esfuerzo de los hombres rurales no coincidió ya con el de las clases dirigentes, su papel se hizo nulo, o fueron barridos. ¿Podemos proponer esto

Zuno, J. G., *Las artes populares en Jalisco*. Guadalajara, 1957.
Habrá siempre que recurrir a la *Historia Moderna de México* para la época 1867-1910. Para evitar repeticiones no hemos incluido los títulos de esta obra en las bibliografías parciales.

como hipótesis de trabajo? ¿Podrá decirse que una "burguesía" en formación tomó el poder mientras que la dominación de los notables rurales se mantenía casi intacta en el campo, y que para asegurar la hegemonía tuvo una inteligencia política tan grande como la de los liberales del siglo pasado? Era bien difícil apoyarse sobre un campesino cuyos proyectos eran divergentes y hasta opuestos entre sí, como lo prueban la muerte de Orozco, de Zapata, de Villa. Era necesario, pues, apoyarse en las ciudades y en el proletariado urbano y fomentar la unión de las nuevas clases dirigentes con los obreros, lo que significaba una política de progresismo social y de desarrollo económico. ¿No es acaso ésa la significación simbólica de los Batallones Rojos, del pacto entre los obreros y el constitucionalismo?

¿Sobre qué fuerzas sociales se apoyaba Calles para ser capaz de resistir a tantos enemigos e iniciar la edificación del México contemporáneo? ¿Qué representa el cardenismo? No podemos más que presentar esquemas que serán verificados, desechados o modificados el día en que conozcamos la realidad de cada uno de esos periodos.

Notas Técnicas

A. El historiador puede sacar un enorme provecho de los trabajos de sus colegas en disciplinas vecinas. Encontrará al sociólogo y al antropólogo, que son historiadores sociales en potencia y que nos ofrecen hermosas monografías descriptivas, más sociográficas que sociológicas. Remitimos a los títulos de publicaciones de la UNAM, Museo y Escuela de Antropología, *Revista de Sociología Mexicana* y *América Indígena*.

B. Para la historia contemporánea, historia en archivos hoy encerrados y mañana tal vez destruidos, historia que habrá que preparar para nuestros sucesores, todos los medios son buenos y toda información preciosa. El historiador tendrá interés en transformarse en encuestador, entrevistador: ya que "pocos compatriotas nuestros, así se cuenten entre los más destacados por su papel político, militar o social, escriben sus memorias... Tampoco abundan en México los diarios, los epistolarios, o los archivos privados, ni nada, en fin, capaz de contrarrestar, al menos en parte, las consecuencias negativas que para el sentimiento global de los mexicanos tiene nuestra repugnancia a ponernos por escrito. Callamos, junto con el relato de nuestra vida, la propia interpretación o valoración de los hechos, en que nos tocó estar". Martín Luis Guzmán: "Las memorias de Luis Aguirre Benavides", *Revista de la Universidad*, xxi, núm. 1, sept., 1966, p. 5.

HISTORICAL SOCIOLOGY
AND MEXICAN SOCIAL HISTORY

FREDERICK C. TURNER

Divergent lines of scholarship in sociology and history have emphasized respectively theory and description. Many historians have presented the facts of a social situation without drawing out their more theoretical implications, while sociologists have spun off general and middle-level theories with little but impressionistic grounding in facts and specific circumstances. [1] What is needed is a more integrative approach which allows historians and sociologists to make joint, mutually corrective contributions to our understanding of both particular historical situations and the general processes of social change.

Students of Mexico are in an especially advantageous position to make such contributions. Until recently, they neglected the approaches of historical sociology, and the best known work in this field dealt with other cases. In a large volume of writings in historical sociology collected during the early 1960's, there appear numerous selections on Europe, the United States, Asia, and Africa, but none dealing with Mexico or even with Latin America. [2] The national pride of many Mexican scholars has naturally focused their attention on the autochthonous rather than the broadly comparative aspects of Mexican history and society, [3] and the inherent interest of Mexican phenomena has often led foreign scholars as well to concentrate on the specifics of

[1] These tendencies appear in the writing on most countries and most topics. In Mexico, for example, the volumes in the *Historia moderna de México* series typify the descriptive approach. With their objetivity, careful scholarship, and overwhelming comprehensiveness, these volumes are indeed impressive, and it is no criticism of them per se to indicate that they neither raise nor test social theories in relation to social history. Embodying the contrasting tendency for many sociological theories to be unrelieved by historical data are such books as Alfredo Niceforo, *Líneas fundamentales de una sociología general* (México, 1958); and Francisco Ayala, *Ensayos de sociología política* (México, 1951).

[2] Werner J. Cahnman and Alvir Boskoff, eds., *Sociology and History: Theory and Research* (New York. 1964).

[3] An outstanding exception to this tendency has been Lucio Mendieta y Núñez. Material from Mexican history repeatedly modifies the conceptualizations in his *Teoría de la revolución* (México, 1959). He has also produced volumes which are more descriptively oriented, such as *El problema agrario de México* (9th ed., México, 1966); and volumes which are more generally theoretical, such as *Teoría de los agrupamientos sociales* (2nd. ed., México, 1963), and *Sociología de la burocracia* (México, 1961).

those phenomena rather than on the processes behind them. Since source material for historical sociology is widely available in Mexico, however, it is only natural that Mexicanists should more recently have begun to apply its approaches. Although historians have demonstrated the effectiveness of quantitative data in historical interpretation, contemporary community studies in Mexico show no uniform or consistent tendency correspondingly to weigh the historical dimensions of the issues which they raise. After evaluating the general relevance of historical sociology to Mexican experience and the development of quantitative and community studies, it should prove useful to consider an area where historical sociology is particularly significant: the study of social class.

I. THE USES OF HISTORICAL SOCIOLOGY

As applied in Mexico or anywhere else, the approaches of historical sociology encompass significant advantages and severe limitations. Concepts drawn from sociology can alert historians to look for new relationships and influences, while historical materials offer sociologists a series of potential testing grounds for general propositions and hypotheses. Attempts to realize these dual advantages are likely to fall flat, however, if researchers hunt only for universal laws, if they answer the seductive calls of policy-oriented research, or if they apply quantitative techniques to areas better studied through other methods. Once such limitations are clearly in mind, the comparative framework and specific approaches of historical sociology are especially useful in the study of problems in social change, institutional adaptation, class relationships, and historical causation.

Concern for comparison and empiricism is the essence of historical sociology. Implicit and sometimes unrecognized theorizing lies behind all historical generalizations, and making this theorizing explicit would often leave it more open for constructive criticism and revision. Such criticism advances understanding and strengthens interdependent efforts, even if it occasionally wounds individual pride. When researchers or their critics test the explanatory significance of sociological concepts in historical situations, their prime motivation may be to evaluate the concepts or to understand the situations. In either case, recurrent interplay occurs between fact and theory, and, at times, the same piece of research may realize both objectives.

This approach implies that social history should not be a mass of untested generalizations, but rather a composite picture built from detailed and, where possible, empirical and theoretically-oriented case studies. Folke Dovring claims that a lack of need for detail makes synthesis easier in the writing of social history than in political history or biography, [4] but this should not in fact be the case. Effective synthesis is as difficult from mass data as from personal data, because so many facets of the social situation demand detailed scrutiny and understanding. Since this is so, historians shoull, in addition to documenting individual episodes in social history, become increasingly concerned with testing new concepts in relation to that history and with verifying generalizations about it.

This emphasis on comparison does not force historical sociology into a search for universally valid propositions. The need is for empirical theory, not in the sense of the broad "social theory" of the classical sociologists [5] or the vast generalizations of Spengler or Toynbee, but in the sense of empirically testable propositions derived from these and other sources. A theoretical orientation refers here only to what Phillips Cutright describes as the situation where "one has a hypothesis to test using a set of predicting variables that are 'given' by the theoretical scheme". [6] Such "theoretical" study of Mexico would not lead us to the formulation of universal laws, to what Samuel Beer rightly rejects as the "misleading dogma of universality", [7] but it might lead to better understanding of both general social processes and specific historical situations. The point of historical sociology is not to uncover new facts of an historical period, but rather to work out the more general relationships among aggregations of facts and to verify social hypotheses against them. In working to refine specific propositions or theories, the historical sociologist may unearth facts as well as relationships which have been forgotten or neglected, but this is a side effect rather than his primary purpose.

Such an approach assumes compatibility rather than conflict between humanism and social science. As H. Stuart Hughes emphasizes, history should be a combination of both art and science, [8] and so indeed should sociology. Historians do not uniformly use the "scientific meth-

---

[4] Folke Dovring, History As a Social Science: An Essay on the Nature and Purpose of Historical Studies (The Hague, 1960), 81-82.

[5] See Chapter 1, "On Sociology As a Humanistic Discipline", in Hans L. Zetterber. On Theory and Verification in Sociology (3rd. ed., New York, 1965).

[6] Phillips Cutright, "National Political Development: Measurement and Analysis", in Charles F. Cnudde and Deane E. Neubauer, eds., Empirical Democratic Theory (Chicago, 1969), 195.

[7] Samuel H. Beer, "Causal Explanation and Imaginative Re-enactment", History and Theory, iii (1964).

[8] H. Stuart Hughes, "The Historian and the Social Scientist", American Historical Review, lxvi (October 1960). For a contrasting plea in behalf of the primacy of art in Mexican history, see Arturo Arnáiz y Freg, "Mexican Historical Writing", in A. Curtis Wilgus, ed., The Caribbean: Mexico Today (Gainesville, 1964), 221-222.

od" as Boyd C. Shafer assumes that they do,[9] but at least many historians recognize the limited benefits of doing so. Sociologists do not all appreciate the relevance of historical cases, but enough sociologists have returned to the use of historical materials to show their present utility.[10] The question is not whether a particular discipline lies among the humanities of the social sciences, not whether individual investigators should be humanists or behavioralists, but whether any investigator should, where applicable, combine the humanist's desire sympathetically to understand humanity with the social scientist's concern with the ways of doing so. Polemics which disregard the essential duality of this relationship misinterpret the real meaning of the fact-value controversy and do a disservice to whichever narrow discipline they try to uphold.

For those interested in pursuing the dual advantages of historical sociology, Mexico provides special research opportunities through the isolation of its commuities and the amount of past documentation concerning them. In a major study in historical sociology, Kai Erikson chose to analyze social deviance among the Puritans of the Massachusetts Bay colony for these very reasons: the relative isolation of the colony and the extensive documentation on it.[11] Mexican social history offers these same benefits. The isolation which geography once imposed upon Mexican commuities permits study with fewer extraneous variables entering in, while the more recent overcoming of geographic barriers encourages examination of the changes in the communities which outside influences bring.

Of equal importance, the literature on Mexican history and society is also ample and extensive, enabling us, as Merle Kling has pointed out, to go more easily beyond the stage of data collection to the active formulation and testing of hypotheses and generalizations.[12]

[9] Boyd C. Shafer, "History, Not Art, Note Science, But History: Meanings and Uses of History", *Pacific Historical Review*, xxix (May 1960), 160.

[10] During the 1960's, sociologists interested in questions of development and cultural change have increasingly turned to historical cases in order to expand the range of situations in which they can study aspects of the development process. For a discusion of this trend in historical sociology, see Seymour Martin Lipset, "History and Sociology: Some Methodological Considerations", in Seymour Martin Lipset and Richard Hofstadter, eds., *Sociology and History: Methods* (New York, 1968), especially 20-23, 50-53. On the use of sociological models in development studies, see Chapter 4, "Explanatory Models and Development", in J. A. Ponsioen, *National Development: A Sociological Contribution* (The Hague, 1968). A list of additional works on the interrelatinoship of history and sociology appears in Appendix D., "Social and Behavioral Sciences and History", in Robert Jones Shafer, ed., *A Guide to Historical Method* (Homewood, Ill., 1969).

[11] Kai T. Erikson, *Wayward Puritans: A Study in the Sociology of Deviance* (New York, 1966), vi-vii.

[12] Merle Kling, "Area Studies and Comparative Politics", *American Behavioral Scientist*, viii (September, 1964), 10.

For realistic interpretation of both past and present, it is necessary to devise what Roberto Agramonte calls "the most complete analysis of the events of our region, collected from the most varied and reliable sources, using the most trustworthy scientific methods of observation". [13] Despite gaps in aspects of the historical record, historical as against contemporary studies enjoy the major advantage that historians can check and reinterpret the results of the process under inspection. [14] Research on the social history of any country can then relate it to processes in other contexts and periods, so working toward the goal of treating time as an analytical whole. [15]

If the extensiveness of Mexican historical documentation facilitates social interpretation, so does Mexico's sociological tradition. In spite of pleas that Latin American sociology should become more ideological and more preoccupied with politics and policies, [16] Mexican sociologists have built up and maintained a long tradition of objective research. [17] They have recognized that objectivity in no way prevents asking the socially relevant questions of development, and that the rejection of ideological stereotypes is necessary for effectively answering such questions. The general climate of opinion in a society unavoidably influences scholarly interpretations of history and society, [18] but it has proved possible for Mexican historians and sociologists both to reflect the moral and intellectual concerns of their period and to attempt to reach more objective understanding of social processes and history.

Historical sociology also has the advantage of treating an area which Mexican scholars find to be important, since many of its natural contributions are to concepts of social development. As only one indication of Mexican interest in this area, a recent survey of 166 Mexican social scientists and government officials indicated their feeling that social research should relate especially to the problems of social justice, development, and human welfare. [19] To understand better the impe-

[13] Roberto Agramonte, "La moderna civilización latinoamericana y su itinerario histórico-social", *Revista Mexicana de Sociología*, xxv (mayo-agosto 1963), 440.

[14] For a discusion of this advantage, see Ben Halpern, "History, Sociology, and Contemporary Area Studies", *American Journal of Sociology*, LXIII (July 1957), 3-4.

[15] Robert F. Berkhofer, Jr., A *Behavioral Approach to Historical Analysis* (New York, 1969), 292.

[16] Jorge Graciarena, "Sociología e ideología: Algunos problemas en la orientación de la formación de sociólogos en América Latina", *Revista Mexicana de Sociología*, xxx (octubre-diciembre, 1968), 805-815.

[17] A description of the development and present status of sociology in Mexico appears in Lucio Mendieta y Núñez, "La sociología en México", *Revista Mexicana de Sociología*, xxvii (mayo-agosto, 1965).

[18] See Robert Allen Skotheim, ed., *The Historian and the Climate of Opinion* (Reading, Mass., 1969), especially Part Four, 167-213.

[19] Leticia Ruiz de Chávez and Gitta Alonso, "Los problemas sociales que deben

diments to greater equality and prosperity, new studies in historical sociology would complement present research. They would not eliminate the necessity for other lines of related research, but they could enlarge the perspective in which contemporary issues and theories are now viewed.

A tantalizing danger, however, is that such studies become too narrow in their orientation to present policies or their justification of them. If Ortega y Gasset is even partially correct in saying that human reflection is the source of future history, that man "has no nature other than what he has himself done", [20] then this mutability of men requires a more precise knowledge of past social processes for their future amelioration. But such knowledge arises from impartial research; it can not grow in an atmosphere of policy justification.

Although research needs in the field of social history do not revolve around the issue of "relevance" as policy-makers would define it, interpretations of those needs nevertheless influence present attitudes and policies. Whether or not scholars, polemicists, or popularizers are fully aware of the influence of their views, their explanations help to shape the perceptions of their audience. Myths of the past influence views of the present, and for scholars to write only for the scholarly community is to abandon the field of popular social history to mythologizers and polemicists. Although Mexican policy-makers seldom come to historians or sociologists with specific requests to enlighten or to justify their policies, historical interpretations affect the underlying assumptions and individual reactions of the decision-making elite as well as of the mass of citizens. The question is not whether historical research will have a social impact, therefore, but rather what the extent and direction of that impact will be. Besides maintaining balance and perspective in their writings, scholars can positively affect views and policies by uncovering the real nature of those social processes and relationships which, either directly or indirectly, alter present situations. To the extent that more scientifically oriented lines of research do influence the policies of governmental and private organizations, it becomes especially important that Latin Americans discover these implications themselves rather than leaving them to foreign interpretation and action. [21]

A contrasting danger of historical sociology is to forget that much

ser estudiados en México", *Revista Mexicana de Sociología*, xxx (abril-junio, 1968), 418-420.

[20] José Ortega y Gasset, *History As a System and Other Essays Toward a Philosophy of History*, Helene Weyl, trans. (New York, 1961), 217.

[21] A sympathetic discusion of new methods in the social sciences, which also points to the danger of their one-sided utilization from outside Latin America, is Florestán Fernández, "Las ciencias sociales en Latinoamérica", *Revista Mexicana de Sociología*, xxviii (abril-junio, 1966).

social history does not profit from attempts to test broad generalizations, to establish comparative frameworks, or to restrict analysis to detailed empirical verification of one aspect of a situation. In the case of Mexico, Manuel González Ramírez provides the sort of thoughtful, perceptive synthesis which touches upon social history in a particular period. [22] Ramón Ruiz traces changes in rural education through a descriptive and critical approach which greater concern for models or quantification could not improve. [23] Their books, and others like then, stand on their own merit as interpretations and documentations of general or specific aspects of social change, and in doing so they incidentally provide generalizations and some of the data upon which more self-consciously empirical studies can draw.

Limitations in the contemporary methodology of other academic disciplines point to the need for more catholic, eclectic, and pragmatic approaches in all fields. A danger of the new emphasis upon quantification in political science, for example, is that political scientists will look simply or predominantly at variables which can be measured in quantitative terms, neglecting variables of equal or greater importance which are not subject to such measurement. This may easily lead to what Oran R. Young calls "the fallacy of puristic induction: the collection of empirical materials *as an end in itself* and without sufficient theoretical analysis to determine appropriate criteria of selection". [24] But, just as political science needs approaches which are normative and historical as well as quantitative and theoretical, so historians should shake loose from the frequent assumption that a book or article is automatically best when it tries to be "definitive" in the sense of looking at a small incident or social group in greater detail than other works have done before. With regard to sociology, Karl Popper was wrong in assuming that what he praised as the "technological approach to sociology" would, in contrast to historicism, naturally lead to the researching of theoretically significant questions. [25] Sociology, like social history or political science, must self-consciously

[22] Manuel González Ramírez, *La revolución social de México. I. Las ideas-la violencia* (México, 1960). For a list of studies in Mexican social history, see the extensive, annotated bibliography of Enrique Florescano and Alejandra Moreno Toscano, "Historia económica y social", *Historia Mexicana*, xv (octubre, 1965-marzo, 1966).

[23] Ramón Eduardo Ruiz, *Mexico: The Chalenge of Poverty and Illiteracy* (San Marino, Calif., 1963).

[24] Oran R. Young, "Professor Russett: Industrious Tailor to a Naked Emperor", *World Politics*, xxi (April, 1969), 489-490. Young's italics. Related discussions of the assets and liabilities of new, quantitative approaches to international relations appear in Klaus Knorr and James N. Rosenau, eds., *Contending Approaches to International Politics* (Princeton, 1969).

[25] Karl R. Popper, *The Poverty of Historicism* (New York, 1960), 59.

strive to be qualitative as well as quantitative, developing qualitative impressions and hypotheses from research situations along with measures for those impressions. Historians, political scientists, and sociologists all enjoy the option of developing meaningful generalizations and theories, even if some members of each group have refused to exercise the option.

More specifically, one line of research for members of various disciplines could trace the situational similarities between Mexico, other countries, and the theories developed in each context. The emphasis here is upon delineating variables and testing them in historical frameworks which have both similarities and differences in terms of the variables in question. [26] The situations would not be chosen on the usual criteria of chronological periodization or geographical propinquity. Researches could, for example, analyze the Mexican Revolution of 1910 in terms of the theories of revolution which Crane Brinton and others have worked out from the historical experiences of other countries. [27] Many discussions of Mexico mention work done in other contexts, but they have yet fully to analyze Mexican experience in terms of detailed and explicit theories. Alternatively, students who have worked out propositions on consensus-building or other processes in terms of Mexican data [28] may test them through consideration of other historical situations. Since general theories contain many facets, and since the contexts with which to compare Mexican experience are so numerous, the possibilities for more comparative research remain extensive.

Interviews and questionnaire techniques have potential relevance in this type of research, although here, as elsewhere, their utility remains limited. As sources for historical investigation, surveys are defective in that they measure opinions at the time that they are taken rather than at the time that decisions were made, and respondents are infamous for masking their prejudices and real feelings in order to say what they believe that they *ought* to think or feel.

[26] In one sense, most historical quantification refers to more precise formulation of variables and to hypothetical verifiable statements of the relationships among them. As William O. Aydelotte argues, "The great step forward is to take the objective or unequivocal definition as the norma, as describing the entity that will be subjected to analysis, and to demote the subjective or vague concept to a subordinte position". Aydelotte, "Quantification in History", *American Historical Review*, LXXI (April, 1966), 814.

[27] Crane Brinton, *The Anatomy of Revolution* (New York, 1956). In "Theories of Revolution", *World Politics*, XVIII (January, 1966), Lawrence Stone usefully criticizes this and other general theories of revolution.

[28] One attempt to develop a theory of nationalism and consensus-building through the use of Mexican data is Frederick C. Turner, *The Dynamic of Mexican Nationalism* (Chapel Hill, 1968). Editorial Grijalbo is publishing a Spanish translation of this study under the title of *Dinámica del nacionalismo mexicano*.

Skillful survey techniques can reduce such difficulties, however, and, once their limitations are recognized, interviews and polls offer significant information. Researchers who interview the participants in events which are now long past sometimes uncover little helpful material, either because the participants have forgotten the important details, or because the details remain too sensitive to be revealed. As opposed to students of political or diplomatic history, however, social historians do not regularly have to reconstruct a particular chain of events in which specific individuals were involved. Instead, since they deal more broadly with the issues of social change and adaptation, the perspectives of persons from differing classes, occupations, and regions take on special significance. In an approach to historical adaptation which has gained little usage so far, researchers can survey the same individuals or gruops at distant points in time, estimating the reasons for changes in perspective along with developments in the society at large. Historically-oriented survey research in Mexico could provide a more substantial basis for generalizations about such contrasting issues as student activism, the role of women, or the interpretations which different groups now give to the events and figures of Mexico's past.

An alternative line of research could concentrate on combinations of social indicators. A North American geographer has recently suggested that we should define a region, like a social class, through classification of many indicators. [29] For the historian interested in comparisons of social processes, attitudes, and customs, the regional unit analyzed should not be arbitrarily delimited as a state or a corner of the country. We often think of Mexico in terms of states, geographic differences, Indian groups, or the folk-urban continuum, but the work of Howard Cline and James W. Wilkie shows that more meaningful units of comparison may result from combining a series of social indicators and seeing what "regions" naturally emerge. [30] Building upon previous works in Mexican regional history, future analyses can more precisely select the variables which set regions apart and more systematically explore the differences among them. Regional studies of social movements, together with sequential comparisons of such variables as occupation, income, attitude, age structure, and public expenditures, can —within regions as well as among them— indicate various dimensions of how regions change over time.

[29] Kevin R. Cox, "On the Utility and Definition of Regions in Comparative Political Sociology", *Comparative Political Studies*, ii (April, 1969), 69-71.
[30] See Chapter 5, "Regionalism and Sectionalism", in Howard F. Cline, *Mexico: Revolution to Evolution, 1940-9160* (New York, 1963); and James W. Wilkie, *The Mexican Revolution: Federal Expenditure and Social Change Since 1910* (Berkeley, 1967), 232-245.

Still another line of research can analyze more effectively the inter-relationships between the changing needs and attitudes of the Mexican people and the formal institutions set up to deal with those needs. In a recent doctoral dissertation, Martin Greenberg considered the social and political issues of water resources in Mexico, evaluating the operations of the Secretaría de Recursos Hidráulicos (SRH), the ministry which has dealt with these issues. [31] By interviewing person-nel both inside and outside the SRH, he was able to go well beyond the written sources in documenting the ways in which a Mexican ministry and the Mexican political system have reacted to the perceived priorities of irrigation, popular welfare, and political necessity. The work is one of the first in-depth case studies which take up the social responsiveness of a public agency in a transitional society, and compa-nion studies in Mexico could contrast the programs of other public agencies dealing with such revolutionary goals as education, land re-form, health, and social welfare. The topic is really much broader than the connection between social goals and public agencies, however. A great virtue of the SRH study is that it actively tests prior hypothe-ses and assumptions concerning bureaucratic responses, and researchers should similarly test other assumptions about the wider series of proces-ses which shape new attitudes, social relationships, and institutions. In this sense, the approach of the SRH study resembles that of several recent, quantitatively-oriented descriptions of Mexican history and society.

II. QUANTITATIVE APPROACHES TO MEXICAN HISTORY

Individual historians and sociologists have already developed quan-titative data of major importance for the Mexican case, and the past research strategies of James Wilkie and Joseph Kahl enjoy particularly wide applicability and significance. Although their work illustrates how much can be revealed in comparisons of governmental expenditures or attitudes toward modernism, however, other lines of quantitative research remain largely unexplored. While some lines of inquiry, such as electoral analysis, hold little promise for Mexico, others, such as content analysis, hold a great deal.

One of the most successful attempts at quantification and empiri-cism in Mexican history is Wilkie's The Mexican Revolution, a book which won the Bolton Prize of the American Historical Association in 1968. Wilkie analyzes the goals and achievements of Mexican re-

[31] Martin Harry Greenberg, "Bureaucracy in Transition: A Mexican Case Study" (unpublished Ph. D. dissertation, University of Connecticut, 1969).

gimes from 1910 to 1963 by contrasting the social, economic, and administrative expenditures in projected and actual budgets of the Mexican government, and by constructing a Poverty Index based on seven census items which measure social change. Budgetary statistics provide yearly checks on the plans and decisions of each Mexican president, while the Poverty Index measures social achievements in each census period. Far from being dry or tring Wilkie's skillful uses of statistical data make the reader continually want to skip from one section of the book to another in order to find out how particular interpretations of Mexican history relate to the data under consideration. The book exemplifies the intellectual excitement of the best empirical research.

Wilkie's findings alternatively support or contrast the findings and assumptions of earlier scholarly studies. He concludes that budgetary expenditures indicate four periods in recent Mexican history: political revolution from 1910 to 1930, social revolution from 1930 to 1940, economic revolution from 1940 to 1950, and balanced revolution from 1959 to 1963. [32] His data confirm the essential conservatism of Francisco Madero, show that Lázaro Cárdenas worked to invigorate and institutionalize the Revolution in budgetary as well as land and labor policies, and demonstrate a drastic reduction in spending for social as opposed to economic reform under Miguel Alemán. [33] Surprisingly, however Wilkie indicates that the period of economic revolution after 1940 brought about more rapid social modernization than had the period of social revolution during the 1930's. [34] Wilkie's approach allows him quantitatively to define "social modernization" as a decrease in his Poverty Index, and this Index comes far closer to measuring social change than do the aggregate economic statistics from which so many descriptions of social change derive. Although Wilkie literally fails in his misnamed attempt "to quantify political ideology", [35] his breakdowns of governmental expenditures do indicate presidential priorities, and his Poverty Index does contrast the results of the revolutionary ideology for different periods and regions.

On the matter of constant and relative expenditures, Wilkie's interpretation requires qualification. He recognizes that sharp absolute increases in the size of government budgets allow new types of expenditure without reductions in the old, yet he concludes that "the real test of ideology of each president is in how he has allocated federal

[32] See Chapter 2, "A Résumé of Comparative Presidential Budgetary Policies", in Wilkie, *The Mexican Revolution.*
[33] *Ibid.,* 43-49, 74-79, 85.
[34] *Ibid.,* 265.
[35] *Ibid.,* xix. In a more precise sense, attitude surveys are the more usual vehicle to measure "ideology".

expenditure in percentage terms". [36] His book concentrates on the rise of the "active state", where the Mexican government actively promotes social and economic development while meeting the administrative expenses of the public debt, the military, and other government agencies. On a fundamental level, the study measures government capabilities as much as ideology, however; with more financial resources, the government has been more able as well as more willing to finance development.

Wilkie's view of military expenditure provides a case in point. The monetarily constant but proportionally declining expenditures on the military since the 1930's do reflect the decrease in the military's political influence, [37] but the essentially stable nature of these expenditures also reflects the relatively unchanging nature of Mexico's defense needs and the resulting possibility for new revenues to be spent in the social and economic areas. Other administrative expenditures have risen since the 1920's, but not as rapidly as increased revenues have allowed other expenditures to rise. Here and elsewhere, "ideology" is only one of the variables. The relationship of increasing revenues to constant and relative costs has as much explanatory significance as does the "ideology" variable on which Wilkie concentrates.

On specific as well as fundamental issues, *The Mexican Revolution* remains open to debate. The claim that there has not been "a free election" in Mexico since the time of Madero requires clarification, [38] as the accuracy of the statement depends upon which aspects of electoral freedom one considers. Wilkie's detailed interviews with Mexican leaders provide some important new material, although, as in his tacit assumption that Lázaro Cárdenas' way of looking at politics was the same in 1962 as it had been between 1934 and 1940, [39] Wilkie's interpretations of the interview material may be questioned. One might also question Wilkie's assertion that during the depression of the 1930's "the poverty of the masses could no longer be ignored". [40] Even if expenditures did rise sharply after this period, earlier revolutionaries had not "ignored" poverty but had established the ideological superstructure which effectively demanded the major struggle against poverty both in the 1930's and after wards. If students of Mexican history can debate these and other issues, a real value of the Wilkie

[36] *Ibid.*, 35.

[37] *Ibid.*, 105-106. See also, Edwin Lieuwen, *Mexican Militarism: The Political Rise and Fall of the Revolutionary Army, 1910-1940* (Albuquerque, 1968); and Frederick C. Turner "México: Las causas de la limitación militar" *Aportes*, núm. 6 (octubre 1967).

[38] Wilkie, *The Mexican Revolution*, 95, 179-182.

[39] *Ibid.*, 72-73.

[40] *Ibid.*, 66.

volume is that it provides both empirical evidence for such debates and a framework of analysis for similar studies in other developing countries. Through the contrasting quantifications of survey research, Joseph Khal compares values and modernization in Mexico and Brazil. Kahl is primarily interested in understanding "modernism", the attitudes and values which naturally cluster together to form a modernist outlook, and the social characteristics which lead particular groups to accept the modernist viewpoint. The answers to Kahl's questionnaires provide information of even broader interest to sociologists and social historians, however. He found, for instance, that Mexican workers widely recognize the importance of education for occupational mobility, that workers in Mexico City were more conservative than those in the states, and that Mexicans appeared more traditional than Brazilians in family matters but more modern than Brazilians in attitudes toward work. [41] These findings provide useful information and suggest other questions and possible relationships.

Although Kahl's survey does not have an historical dimension per se, there are several ways in which such research could develop one. Investigators could ask for respondents' views of historical events, persons, and processes, thereby acquiring deeper understanding of the meaning which national history has for different groups. In Mexico, it would be helpful to see through attitude surveys how various age, occupational, or regional groups now view elements of the Independence period, the Porfirio Díaz era, or the activities of Lázaro Cárdenas. As such retrospective interpretations of national history are compiled in Mexico and elsewhere, they themselves become historical data and the contrasts between them over time may point to distinctions among the respondents of different periods.

Although abstract, mathematical formulations now have far less relevance to Mexican history, simpler forms of quantitative representation are most revealing. Mathematical interpretations of the French and Russian Revolutions remain so general as to have very little applicability to Mexico at this time. [42] Although, if they again elaboration and a more solid grounding in actual historical processes, they may come to relate to the Revolution of 1910. In contrast, much can be

[41] Joseph A. Kahl, *The Measurement of Modernism: A Study of Values in Brazil and Mexico* (Austin, 1968), 60, 112, 146.

[42] See N. Rashevsky, *Looking at History through Mathematics* (Cambridge, Mass., 1968), Chapters 9, 10. On p. ix Rashevsky admits that his first mathematical treatments are "apallingly crude" and remain "oversimplified and in many respects unrealistic". More general critiques of historical quantification include Chapter 14, "Quantification and Uniqueness in History", in Walter T. K. Nugent, *Creative History: An Introduction to Historical Study* (Philadelphia, 1967); and Chapter 12, "The Evidence for Generic Statements —Myths, Impressions, and Quantification", in G. Kitson Clark, *The Critical Historian* (New York, 1967).

gained when social historians simply attempt to uncover and summarize whatever quantitative data shed light upon the topics which they research. The feasibility of such attempts appears clearly in the exemplary work of Moisés González Navarro, as he presents ratios and comprehensive tables on investments, deaths, and migration in the 1910 Revolution to help gauge the level and nature of xenophobia in it. [43] By adding such data to other types of information taken from others sources, González Navarro is able to go well beyond previous interpretations in his balanced understanding of the subject.

Electoral analysis holds comparatively little promise for historical sociology in Mexico, even though it has proved most worthwhile in other contexts. Lee Benson is quite right in asserting that action is the best test of opinion, but his view that voting behavior is the best single measure for past public opinion requires qualification for Mexico and other countries whose history of voting behavior differs so markedly from that of the United States. [44] The work of Benson and his followers derives chiefly from the study of United States history, [45] and his views have the greatest relevance there and in a limited number of other countries with similar regularity of elections and differentiation in voting behavior. The Mexican case is not open to the same analysis, however, because of the dubious impact of Mexican votes on public programs, the resulting ambiguity of voting decisions, and the gross inaccuracies in published electoral results.

Despite limitations in electoral data, researchers can go much further than they have gone so far in drawing social implications from other statistical sources. The work of Raúl Benítez Zenteno typically provides excellent information, graphs, and tables on such topics as Mexican mortality and migrations, but it largely neglects the social implications of these statistics. [46] On the other hand, a case study of *bracero* mi-

---

[43] Moisés González Navarro, "Xenofobia y xenofilia en la Revolución Mexicana", *Historia Mexicana*, xviii (abril-junio, 1969). For a discusion of xenophobia in terms of 1960 Mexican census data, see Óscar Uribe Villegas, "Diagrama estadístico-social de México", *Revista Mexicana de Sociología*, xxvi (septiembre-diciembre 1964), 913.

[44] Lee Benson, "An Approach to the Scientific Study of Past Public Opinion", *Public Opinion Quarterly*, xxxi (Winter, 1967-1968), especially 551-567. See also, Lee Benson, *The Concept of Jacksonian Democracy: New York As a Test Case* (Princeton, 1961).

[45] See, for instance, Ronald P. Formisano, "Analyzing American Voting, 1830-1860: Methods", *Historical Methods Newsletter*, ii (March, 1969).

[46] Raúl Benítez Zenteno, *Análisis demográfico de México* (México, 1961). The later research of Benítez Zenteno has taken social variables more consistently into account. In "Cambios demográficos y la población en México", *Revista Mexicana de Sociología*, xxx (julio-septiembre, 1968), he specifically criticizes "demographic fatalism" and treats such topics as the relationship of education and fertility.

gration from Chihuahua indicates that *braceros* who returned from labor in the United States evidenced increased selfconfidence, decreased dependence upon local politicians and patrons, and a more friendly attitude toward the United States than was shown by members of the Mexican middle class who had not traveled there. [47] These alternative approaches of demographic description and case-study interpretation should be integrated and interrelated, so that their overall meaning becomes more clear. [48]

Building on past formulations, the study of periodic violence in Mexico can advance considerably. David L. Raby's numerical evaluation of the recorded cases of violence against Mexican rural teachers during the 1930's has indicated that, contrary to popular impressions, the major part of the violence against the teachers resulted, not from their antireligious stance, but from their roles in social innovation and rural politics. [49] Other groups and periods deserve similar attention. Given the applicability of Harry Eckstein's hypotheses to sporadic violence as well as to prolonged civil wars, it would be useful to test his hypotheses and his summary paradigm against Mexican data. [50] The repeated transitions from periods of civil war to intermittent violence and rebellions in Mexican history make Mexican experience especially inviting for such study.

Although we lack Mexican prototypes on which to build in the formal methodology of content analysis, its counting and comparisons of key words, symbols, or ideas could open a variety of topics for quantitative research The work of Richard Merritt on the meanings of community in colonial America during the mid-1700's illustrates the potential for studies in other countries where the attitudes of past generations at first seem unresearchable in quantitative terms. [51] Content analysis for Mexican social history can operate in the wide context of periodicals covering the colonial period as well as the nineteenth and twentieth centuries. [52] It could provide more information on social interpretations

[47] Richard H. Hancock, *The Role of the Bracero in the Economic and Cultural Dynamics of Mexico: A Case Study of Chihuahua* (Stanford, 1959), 122, 124.

[48] Frederick C. Turner, "Nacionalismo e internacionalismo, sus relaciones con la demografía", *Foro Internacional*, v (octubre-diciembre, 1964), is a general attempt to draw out some of the social implications of demographic analysis in terms of loyalty to different types of communities.

[49] David L. Raby, "Los maestros rurales y los conflictos sociales en México (1931-1940)", *Historia Mexicana*, xviii (octubre-diciembre, 1968), especially 213-215.

[50] Harry Eckstein, "On the Etiology of Internal Wars", *History and Theory*, iv (1965).

[51] Richard L. Merritt, *Symbols of American Community, 1735-1775* (New Haven, 1966).

[52] Helpful summaries of these periodical sources are Stanley R. Ross, "El historiador y el periodismo mexicano", *Historia Mexicana*, xiv (enero-marzo 1965);

of national heroes,[53] or test to what extent particular lines of propaganda have indeed tried to make propaganda play what Luis Castaño describes as its positive role of providing popular cooperation for public goals.[54] Content analysis may be applied to Mexican *corridos*, novels, or documents, while analysis of statements by leaders of the Independence struggle, Reforma, or 1910 Revolution could examine to what extent their statements were increasingly consistent with the "democratic", antiaristocratics tenets which Robert R. Palmer draws out of eighteenth-century revolutionary experience.[55] In the case of specific towns or communities, content analysis could even help to deepen the background for contemporary community studies whose authors sometimes imply that written records in the communities have little relevance to their members' present attitudes and behavior.

III. COMMUNITY STUDIES

To build up any consistent body of social science theory, research projects must be cumulative. When researchers study similar issues in slightly altered situations, they can more easily find which variables account for the observed differences. This does *not* mean that United States scholars should carry down ethnocentric theories to be tested in Latin America, because the fundamentally different historical experience of Mexico and the other Latin American countries frequently nullifies notions derived from the experience of the United States. The framework of questions for social investigation must relate to the context under study rather than to an alien or artificial context. What cumulative research does means is that scholars should apply parallel research strategies and frameworks to situations which differ in their temporal or contextual dimensions. Studies of towns and communities provide an apt focus for such research, because, as Woodrow Borah

and Stanley R. Ross, comp., *Fuentes de la historia contemporánea de México. Periódicos y revistas* (México, 1965).

[53] It could, for example, test and refine the various myths which Enrique Beltrán shows to have grown up around the figure of Pancho Villa. See Beltrán, "Fantasía y realidad de Pancho Villa", *Historia Mexicana*, XVI (julio-septiembre, 1966). Beltrán already treats the myths in categorical fashion, and it would be revealing to go on to see which myths found particular support in different periods and types of literature.

[54] Luis Castaño, "La propaganda, catalizador democrático de los proyectos planificadores", in *Temas de sociología política mexicana* (México, 1961), 61-80.

[55] Robert R. Palmer, "Generalizations about Revolution: A Case Study", in Louis Gottschalk, ed., *Generalization in the Writing of History: A Report of the Committee on Historical Analysis of the Social Science Research Council* (Chicago, 1963), 69-70.

pointed out in the early 1950's the town has been the dominant organizing unit in Mexican social life. [56]

Community studies have a long tradition, with the work of Robert
and Helen Lynd, W. Lloyd Warner, and Robert Dahl in the United
States, or that of Manuel Gamio, Robert Redfield, and Oscar Lewis
in Mexico. Such studies are especially effective when they incorporate
historical data, when they elicit contemporary evaluations of the past
history of the community or the society and/or test such evaluations
against other sources of evidence. Communities, like societies, are not
static entities, and neglect of their transformations is likely to produce
interpretations of questionable validity. One of the values of an historical dimension for community studies is that it can indicate which
social processes and values are *comparatively* static, gradual, or rapid
in their transformation. The significance of the historical dimension
makes it worthwhile to investigate the ways in which particular studies
have used or neglected it.

In controversial case studies of Tzintzuntzan, Michoacán, George
M. Foster sets out a model explaining peasant attitudes and behavior
in Mexico and other societies. The model postulates that Tzintzuntzeños perceive everything which is "good" in their enviroment to be
in limited and finite supply, so that whenever persons acquire more of
what is good they must do so at someone else's expense. This perception sharply restricts cooperative efforts and eliminates effective participation in groups, so maintaining the status quo of the peasant society.
The marginality of the peasant's life reflects in his often accurate
perceptions of its nature; innovation becomes difficult when peasants
suspiciously reject joint efforts and assume that wealth, manliness, and
even friendship and love remain unexpandable except at the expense
of another. [57] The peasant's fundamental assumption of "Limited
Good" seems to explain his consistently individualistic behavior, in
which Foster finds Tzintzuntzeños rejecting institutional ties and
maintaining personal, contractual relationships with individual collea-

[56] Woodrow Borah, "Race and Class in Mexico", *Pacific Historical Review*, XXIII
(November 1954), 334. Borah drew the observations in this paper from his year
of travel and study in Mexico during 1951-1952, and first read the paper at a
meeting of the Pacific Coats Branch of the American Historical Association in
December, 1952.

[57] Foster's most complete exposition of this model appears in *Tzintzuntzan:
Mexican Peasants in a Changing World* (Boston, 1967). Foster began study of
Tzintzuntzan between 1944 and 1946, on the basis of which he published *Empire's
Children: The people of Tzintzuntzan* (México, 1948). He returned to Tzintzun-
tzan in 1958 and, since then, has repeatedly revisited the town and published articles
concerning it.

gues and with those saints who they hope will intervene with God for them. [58]

Anthropologists have attacked Foster's model for being tautological, [59] for the degree to which it hopes to generalize about peasant behavior, [60] as well as for its inadequate criteria of applicability, its original assumption of a closed system, and its undue faith in the malleability of adult cognitive orientations. [61] The tautology criticism appears unnecessarily casuistical when one keeps in mind the mutually supportive relationship of Foster's data and his explanation, while the degree of generalization and the criteria of applicability can be worked out in more detail as scholars approach other communities with Foster's model in mind. Foster's book expands on his earlier articles by showing more outside influences on what he first described as the closed system of Tzintzuntzan. The criticism of cognitive malleability cogently questions the prescriptive, policy-oriented conclusions to which Foster comes, but even it fails to deal with another fundamental problem of Foster analysis: its fundamentally ahistorical character.

The ahistorical nature of Foster's approach appears most clearly in his neglect of the Revolution of 1910, a part of Mexico's historical experience which most observers agree had a profound effect on the views and behavior of Mexican citizens. In his chapter on "The Historical Roots", Foster skips directly from a single paragraph on the *porfiriato* to a mission which Lázaro Cárdenas sent to Tzintzuntzan in 1930. [62] In trying to establish a model of general explanatory power for peasant communities, Foster writes that "in Tzintzuntzan real behavior probably more nearly coincided with this ideal type fifty years ago [c. 1917] than it does now". [63] Were peasant attitudes actually the same or even closer to the assumptions of Foster's model during the violent years of the Mexican Revolution, however? Do

[58] George M. Foster, "The Dyadic Contract in Tzintzuntzan, II: Patron-Client Relationship", *American Anthropologist*, LXV (December, 1963).

[59] David Kaplan and Benson Saler, "Foster's 'Image of Limited Good': An Example of Anthropological Explanation", *American Anthropologist*, LXVIII (February, 1966). For a more sympathetic view of Foster's findings, see the review of *Tzintzuntzan* by Irwin T. Sanders in the *American Journal of Sociology*, LXXIV (September, 1968).

[60] John G. Kennedy, " 'Peasant Society and the Image of Limited Good': A Critique", *American Anthropologist*, LXVIII (October 1966).

[61] Steven Piker, " 'The Image of Limited Good': Comments on an Exercise in Description and Interpretation", *American Anthropologist*, LXVIII (October, 1966).

[62] Foster, *Tzintzuntzan*, 26. Although Fosters' earlier book on Tzintzuntzan provides excellent, detailed description of the community in the 1940's it too largely neglects historical material and especially the Revolution. See *Empire's Children*, 6-22, 188-189.

[63] Foster, *Tzintzuntzan*, 123.

periods of massive violence really fail to affect peasant values and behavior? Should distinctions be made for the peasants of Morelos, Yucatán, and Michoacán, and, if so, what kinds of distinctions should they be? Foster never proposes even tentative answers to these questions, because he never seems to feel that they are worth asking.

In contrast to Foster, May N. Díaz actively uses historical detail, not to test general propositions but to show the vast distance between historical reality and contemporary myth in a Mexican community. As one aspect of a larger project on cultural change which Foster supervised, she studied the effects of industrialization in Guadalajara upon the small outlying town of Tonalá. Although finding very little historical material which dealt with Tonalá after the period of Spanish conquest, Mrs. Díaz shows how far myths of the conquest have strayed from the harsh realities of the actual situation. Legends claim that the Spaniards defeated the Indians of Tonalá because Saint James came riding across the sky on his white horse at the climax of the battle between them. The Tonaltecans renamed their town in honor of Saint James, and until recently they annually re-enacted his symbolic domination of the Indians. Tonaltecans have forgotten the ugliness which a contemporary soldier attributed to the Indian queen of the region, and they have accepted a mythology where town pageants show her as a young and beautiful person whose acceptance of Christianity became copied and admired. [64] Mrs. Díaz' prototypical contrasts of historical reality with contemporary mythology, which require both detailed consultation of historical sources and personal observation of pageants and propaganda, provide an important means of gauging the social meaning of history itself.

In the study of communities, therefore, we require expanded concepts of models and comparisons. Foster's view of a "model" or "principle" as "an inferential construct or an analytic abstraction derived from observed behavior" [65] is not really as temporally circumscribed as it appears, since historians can reconstruct social principles through careful analysis of past observations in a manner which relates them directly to the present observations of social scientists. Just as Edith Boorstein Couturier's intensive study of a progressive hacienda points up the limited malleability of the hacienda as an institution in the decade before the 1910 Revolution, [66] so analysis of Mexican towns

[64] May N. Díaz, Tonalá: Conservatism, Responsibility, and Authority in a Mexican Town (Berkeley, 1966), 19-25.

[65] George M. Foster, "Peasant Society and the Image of Limited Good", American Anthropologist, LXVII (April, 1965), 294. Foster goes on at some length here to discuss such model construction.

[66] Edith Boorstein Couturier, "Modernización y tradición en una hacienda (San Juan Hueyapan, 1902-1911)", Historia Mexicana, XVIII (julio-septiembre

can probe their relationship to social innovation during crucial periods in the past. Historical sociology similarly indicates the importance of detailed comparisons between coeval communities, as when Charles Tilly studied the process of counter-revolution by systematically contrasting the various characteristics of those communities in the Vendee which actively supported the French Revolution or the counterrevolution of 1793. [67] In addition to looking at issues of social innovation, urbanization, or violent confrontation in Mexican society, community studies, like the other approaches of historical sociology, should also come to focus on the crucial area of social classes.

IV. THE STUDY OF SOCIAL CLASS

As Sylvia Thrupp indicated more than a decade ago, social stratification is an especially promising area for joint research by historians and sociologists. [68] This continues to be true, not only because of the overlap between historical and sociological materials and interests in this area, but also because of the inadequacies of nonempirical research and the key role which class variables are assumed to play in social processes and confrontations. When Kahl discovered social status to be a more consistent predictor of modernist attitudes in Mexico than geographic location or any other variable, [69] his work underscored the importance of past as well as present class analysis. Althoug recent studies illustrate ways in which to approach past Mexican stratification, the real work, from an empirical standpoint, remains to be done.

An absence of adequate class studies now seriously hampers social science theorizing in Latin America, especially when models from outside the region are superimposed without recognition of the contrasts in Latin American experience. As Sugiyama Iutaka points out in his evaluation of the literature on Latin American stratification, this literature tends to be polemically contentious and abstractly theoretical rather than empirical. [70] Milton I. Vanger, after testing the 1911 election of José Batlle y Ordóñez against present notions of middle class-lower class coalitions, rightly concludes that our general class hypotheses do not satisfactorily explain the tendencies of Latin American politics. Although Vanger cogently argues that his findings

1968). See also Charles H. Harris, III, *The Sánchez Navarros: A Socio-economic Study of a Coahuilan Latifundio, 1846-1853* (Chicago, 1964).

[67] Charles Tilly, *The Vendée* (Cambridge, Mass., 1964).

[68] Sylvia Thrupp, "History and Sociology: New Opportunities for Co-operation", *American Journal of Sociology*, LXIII (July 1957), 13.

[69] Kahl, *The Measurement of Modernism*, 21, 134.

[70] Sugiyama Iutaka, "Social Stratification Research in Latin America", *Latin American Research Review*, I (Fall 1965), 8.

demonstrate the need for studies of such variables as leadership and the role of political mythology, [71] his argument also emphasizes the need to generate sounder class studies from which fresh hypotheses can be developed and tested. As Eric Wolf said in a 1959 waring which has too often gone unheeded, the realities of class structure and relationships in Mexico and Middle America differ radically from the European prototypes to which they are regularly compared. [72]

In the case of Mexico, empirical class studies are necessary partly to form the basis for broader interpretations of Mexican history. Charles C. Cumberland has recently been criticized for failing to deal with social classes in his comprehensive treatment of Mexico, [73] but the lack of detailed monographic studies of Mexican classes prevents Cumberland and other synthesizers from giving classes the full coverage which their significance seems to warrant. Researchers may turn to Nathan Whetten's classic study of the Mexican middle class, [74] to John Johnson's interpretation of the "middle sector", [75] or to the estimates of class change which Howard Cline painstakingly derived from the data of José Iturriaga and other sources. [76] With the exception of broadly descriptive material on the *porfiriato*, [77] however, researchers can not draw upon monographic interpretations of class structure during different periods of Mexican history. In the absence of such works perhaps Cumberland is to be admired rather than blamed for his refusal to drag out class clichés or to reprint the estimates of others.

Detailed verification should have a special place in the development of these sources, because only through careful analysis of the social origins of different groups can historians test the guesswork generalizations which polemicists make about classes and their conflicts. The circumstantial work of Crane Brinton and Donald Greer on the social origins of the Jacobins and the victims of the Terror in the French

[71] Milton I. Vanger, "Politics and Class in Twentieth-Century Latin America", *Hispanic American Historical Review*, XLIX (February 1969).

[72] Eric R. Wolf, *Sons of the Shaking Earth* (Chicago, 1959), 241-243.

[73] Charles A. Hale, review of Charles C. Cumberland, *Mexico: The Struggle for Modernity* in the *Hispanic American Historical Review*, XLIX (May 1969), 342.

[74] Nathan L. Whetten, "The Rise of a Middle Class in Mexico", in Theo R. Crevenna, ed., *La clase media en México y Cuba: Cuatro colaboraciones*, vol. 2 of *Materiales para el estudio de la clase media en América Latina* (Washington, D.C., 1950).

[75] Chapter 7, "Mexico: Reorientation of a Revolution", in John J. Johnson, *Political Change in Latin America: The Emergence of the Middle Sectors* (Stanford, 1958).

[76] See Chapter 11, "Society in Transition", in Cline, *Mexico*, especially Table 30 on p. 124.

[77] Luis González y González, Emma Cosío Villegas, and Guadalupe Monroy, *La República restaurada: La vida social*, vol. 3 in *Historia moderna de México* (México, 1956), 329-450.

Revolution, for example, has disproved simplistic theories of class conflict and shown that large groups of both Jacobins and Terror victims
came from different social classes. [78] Students of Mexican class behavior can now enhance the approach of Briton and Greer by coding
data and working out the relationships among masses of data with the
aid of a computer. For more precise study of social status and inter-
generational mobility, Jacques Dupaquier has suggested putting into
machine-readable form specific information on individuals' antecedents,
descendants, sector of activity, occupation, social status, legal status,
income, wealth, family situation, age, geographic origin, and other
variables. [79] Correlations made from such data would allow comparisons
of the smaller socio-professional groups which make up social classes,
and the plan is as applicable to the social history of Mexico as it is to
that of France.

In a period of Mexican history for which no such detailed data are
available, the careful work of Alfonso Caso has already provided important class analysis of the Aztecs at the time of the Spanish conquest.
Just as polemical writers on the French Revolution assumed a simplistic dichotomy of nobles and plebians, so writers on Aztec organization
assumed the same dichotomy or believed that Aztec organization followed Iroquois or Roman lines. Caso shows, however, that the function
of individuals was not the sole determinant of their social class, so
that military and priestly classes did not in fact exist. In addition to the
land-owning nobility and the plebians who worked clan lands, Aztec
organization encompassed a middle class, freemen who rented land,
serfs who were bound to the land but maintained rights on it when
its ownership changed, and slaves who had no rights concerning land
and whom a noble could arbitrarily assign to other tasks. [80] If painstaking survey of original sources can provide so much fresh insight into

[78] Clarence Crane Brinton, *The Jacobins: An Essay in the New History* (New
York, 1930); and Donald Greer, *The Incidence of the Terror during the French
Revolution: A Statistical Interpretation* (Cambridge, Mass., 1935).

[79] Jacques Dupaquier, "Problèmes de la codification socio-professionelle", in
Ernest Labrousse, and others, *L'Histoire sociale: Sources et Méthodes* (Paris, 1967),
especially 163-167. S. W. F. Holloway has further suggested the need to draw up
and relate more precise indices of social class and class conflict, and the interrelationship of these measures of occupational groupings and wealth distributions with
violence, strikes, or class literature stands as a challenging if difficult task for
students of Mexico. See Holloway, "History and Sociology: What History Is and
What It Ought to Be", in W. H. Burston and D. Thompson, eds., *Studies in the
Nature and Teaching of History* (London, 1967), 20-21.

[80] Alfonso Caso, "Land Tenure among the Ancient Mexicans", *American Anthropologist*, LXV (August 1963), 865, 871. See also, Charles Gibson, *The Aztecs
under Spanish Rule: A History of the Indians of the Valley of Mexico, 1519-1810*
(Stanford, 1964), 153-165.

Aztec social organization, then examination of the later and better documented periods of Mexican social history should provide even more. Situational limitations impose some restraints even on the best documented periods, of course. Mexico has had an official peerage only in certain periods of her history, so that Mexican historians remain more limited than British historians in the degree to wich they can replace ambiguous terms like "aristocracy" or "oligarchy" with precise studies of peers and their sons. [81] Alternatively, many Mexican towns are so small and so homogeneous as to preclude class differentiations and internal political conflicts. In Tzintzuntzan, Foster found that "social classes are absent, and there are no families or individuals of disproportionate power and influence". [82] A clear parallel exists here between the highly personalized and essentially apolitical pattern of relationships is small towns in Mexico and the United States. As in Tzintzuntzan, a recent survey shows the politics of a small Connecticut town to be similarly nonideological, focused upon personalities rather than issues, and devoid of arguments on the role of government in effecting social change. [83] Even if studies of social class among some Mexican groups or communities, become difficult or irrelevant, howwever, it remains of prime importance to understand the nature and roles of Mexican classes in the social context of larger communities.

One direction which inspection of these roles may take appears in the research of Andrew Whiteford. Although Whiteford bases his conclusions on contemporary observation and wide reading in secondary sources rather than upon more quantitative evaluations of historical data, he presents persuasive interpretations of historical as well as contemporary class structures. The telling nature of his findings results partly from the restricted and comparative framework within which he operates, and partly from the years of research which he spent in the two communities whose classes he examined: Popayán, Colombia, and Querétaro, Mexico. Whiteford discovered considerably more historic continuity in the upper class of Popayán, which reflects what he delineates as the fundamentally different experience of civil strife in Mexico and Colombia. In Querétaro, he analyzes the presence of a self-conscious but generally unrecognized remnant of the pre-revolutionary upper class, and the transfer of real power from the

[81] In "The Oligarchy Muddle", World Politics, xx (April 1968), James L. Payne presents an extended discussion of other difficulties of elite analysis in Latin America.

[82] George M. Foster, "The Dyadic Contract: A Model for the Social Structure of a Mexican Peasant Village", American Anthropologist, LXIII (December 1961), 1176.

[83] Everett Carll Ladd, Jr., Ideology in America: Change and Response in a City, a Suburb, and a Small Town (Ithaca, 1969). In particular, see Chapter 6, "Putnam: The Ideological Life of an American Small Town", and Ladd's concluding remarks on Putnam on pp. 346-347.

porfirian elite, to revolutionary generals and politicians, to the present industrial leaders and entrepreneurs. [84] Particularly in conjunction with more quantitative approaches to the study of past classes, Whiteford's approach points the way to fruitful and revealing comparisons with other cities and regions.

In complementary fashion, another line of research can quantitatively summarize characteristics of the Mexican elite, much as William P. Tucker has done for its changing demographic characteristics on the basis of material published in biographic repertories at five-or six-year intervals between 1935 and 1961. [85] Tucker's work confirms some prior impressions, such as the preponderance of training at the National University for members of the Mexican elite or the shift after 1935 from Europe to the United States as its favored location for foreign study. Comparisons of biographic data on the Mexican and United States elites seem to indicate that journalism, law, and art are the most common occupations for the Mexican elite, while teaching, business, and law are most common for that of the United States.

Social research of this kind remains potentially ambiguous, however, as it often reveals far more about the particular repertories consulted than about the elites which they supposedly describe. The formal and informal criteria for individual inclusion in a repertory tend to vary considerably over time and among countries, and they may favor groups or occupations out of all proportion to their actual influence or their size in comparison to more objectively defined social or economic groupings. It at first seems suggestive for Tucker to point out that Mexican repertories contain a far higher proportion of government personnel than do those of the United States, or that United States repertories show a steadily increasing proportion of nonmilitary government personnel since the 1930's. Such findings hardly indicate that government officials enjoy more popular respect in Mexico, however, or that United States officials have steadily gained in respect rather than merely in numbers. The figures indicate more about repertory selection criteria and overall group size than they do about social norms in either country. Similarly, the fact that only 2 per cent of the persons in a Mexican repertory in 1961 were women, as compared to 6 per cent or more women in United States repertories for the earlier years of 1934, 1942, and 1948, does not prove that women professionals have gained more general status and prestige in the United States than in Mexico. Such quantitative evaluations deserve consideration, but they can not be interpreted at face value.

[84] Andrew Hunter Whiteford, *Two Cities of Latin America: A Comparative Description of Social Classes* (Garden City, N.Y., 1964), especially 15-16, 224-226, 248.

[85] William P. Tuckner, "Las élites mexicanas", *Aportes*, núm. 13. (julio, 1969).

Still another line of research can test contemporary findings on stratification against the historical experience of towns and groups. In a major program of ongoing research, members of the Harvard Chiapas Project have found considerable social stratification in the community of Zinacantan. Communal behavior works to maintain this stratification, as in the case of the religious cargo system where a person's wealth affects his ability to progress as a cargoholder and so partially determines his social standing. Display of wealth in the cargo system insures commitment to common values and also tends to maintain the community by using up excess wealth in ways which do not permit social change and development. [86] One way to approach the modernization process in such communities is to trace, as the members of the Harvard project plan to do, the future changes in Zinacantan. An alternative method, which relies upon historical rather than anthropological research, could trace past changes in a village which had once been essentially closed in the pattern of Zinacantan but has now been forced to become more completely integrated into Mexican national life. In both approaches to modernization, shifts in patterns of stratification take on particular significance.

Many other general findings similarly invite historical exploration. Despite the impressive literature on the *porfiriato*, we have yet to develop comparative studies which test Stanley Stein's idea that the Revolution of 1910 came to Mexico and not to other Latin American countries because Mexico had a relatively "open" society with high mobility. [87] Work in the 1940's suggested that Mexican women upheld class differences more than did men, [88] yet research on Mexican women has not tried to probe this apparent variation. How, in individual communities, has class structure been related to miscegenation and what Gonzalo Aguirre Beltrán calls a resulting "desire for unity, an ideal of nationhood as the harmony and union of segregated groups"? [89]

[86] Frank Cancian, *Economics and Prestige in a Maya Community: The Religious Cargo System in Zinacantan* (Stanford, 1965), Chapters 10-13. Kimball and Romaine Romney have likewise stressed the high cost of religious fiestas, their prevention of capital accumulation, and their effect of setting the Indian community off from other Mexicans. For the fiesta of a patron saint in a barrio where men regularly earned about 3 pesos a day, the Romneys found costs to amount to 1500 pesos for the mayordomo, 250 pesos for each of his helpers, and 3 pesos for each guest. They did not find, however, that this participation in the fiestas conferred special prestige or status on the persons involved. See Kimball Romney and Romaine Romney, *The Mixtecans of Juxtlahuaca, Mexico* (New York, 1966), 57-63.

[87] Stanley J. Stein, "Latin American Historiagraphy: Status and Research Opportunities", in Charles Wagley, ed., *Social Science Research on Latin America* (New York, 1964), 94, 96.

[88] Norman Daymond Humphrey, "Social Stratification in a Mexican Town", *Southwestern Jorunal of Anthropology*, v (Summer 1949), 143.

[89] Gonzalo Aguirre Beltrán, "Indigenismo y mestizaje: Una polaridad bio-cultu-

What historical verification is there for that part of Rodolfo Stavenhagen's model of Mexican organizations which hypothesizes that such
groups operate more in the interests of the personal advancement of
their leaders than on the basis of articulated demands from group
members? [90]

Historical testing may also lead to the generation of new hypotheses.
Looking once again at earlier interpretations may contradict or redefine
their conclusions, just as a fresh appraisal of Robert Redfield's data
has seriously challenged his concept of classless homogeneity in Chan
Kom. [91] The relationships of Indian and ladino communities offer other
opportunities for new hypotheses on social structure, caste, and class
interaction. [92] Survey research has indicated that education and socio-
economic status have considerably more influence upon dogmatism
and authoritarianism than do religious beliefs in contemporary Mexico, [93] and that family ties in cities have more influence in encouraging
Mexicans to accept factory employment than does the pressure of low
incomes in the countryside, [94] but did similar relationships hold true
in an earlier period when religious values were stronger and cities were
smaller? To what degree would historical research confirm the contemporary finding that *compadrazgo* performs alternate functions among
different social classes, and, when it cuts across class lines, tends to
reinforce the class structure by maintaining client relationships? [95]

In an overall sense, if it is correct to assert that students of social
history should thus develop wider concern for the theoretical significance and empirical orientation of their studies, then this is at the

ral", *Cahiers d'Histoire Mondiale*, vi (1960), 160. In " El mestizaje mexicano en el
periodo nacional", *Revista Mexicana de Sociología*, xxx (enero-marzo, 1968), Moisés
González Navarro presents a statistical summary and careful evaluation of the
process of miscegenation in Mexico.

[90] Rodolfo Stavenhagen, "Un modelo para el estudio de las organizaciones
políticas en México", *Revista Mexicana de Sociología*, xxix (abril-junio, 1967),
334.

[91] Victor Goldkind, "Social Stratification in the Peasant Community: Redfield's
Chan Kom Reinterpreted", *American Anthropologist*, lxvii (August 1965); and
Victor Goldkind, "Class Conflict and Cacique in Chan Kom", *Southwestern
Journal of Anthropology*, xx (Winter 1966).

[92] See the challenging conclusions in Chapter 8, "Estructura de casta y clase",
in Gonzalo Aguirre Beltran, *Regiones de refugio: El desarrollo de la comunidad
y el proceso dominical en mestizo América* (México, 1967).

[93] Glaucio Ary Dillon Soares and José Luis Reyna, "Status socio-económico,
religiosidad y dogmatismo en México", *Revista Mexicana de Sociología*, xxviii (octubre-diciembre, 1966).

[94] Frank W. Young and Ruth C. Young, "Individual Commitment to Industrialization in Rural Mexico", *American Journal of Sociology*, lxxi (January 1966).

[95] Gwendoline van den Berghe and Pierre L. van den Berghe, "Compadrazgo
and Class in Southeastern Mexico", *American Anthropologist*, lxviii (October
1966).

very most only one of the fruitful paths open to historical scholarship. Lewis Hanke has argued persuasively that, in order to engage the commitment of students who will make better scholars and citizens in the years ahead, we must produce more effective teaching materials as well as more effective scholarly monographs. [96] The contrasts and inherent excitement of Mexico's violent and constructive history make it a prime subject for engaging analysis. Scholarly approaches to this subject which stress empirical testing of significant propositions complement rather than contradict the concern for better teaching materials, and neither of these orientations supersedes the need for descriptive treatments or traditional case studies. Greater emphasis upon theory and empiricism could deepen and extend, therefore, but not fundamentally reorient, the academic trend of Mexican historiography.

[96] Lewis Hanke, "Studying Latin America: The Views of an 'Old Christians' ", *Journal of Inter-American Studies*, ix (January 1967).

COMMENTARIES

RAMÓN EDUARDO RUIZ

I

The study of Mexican history represents a paradox. Few peoples in Spanish America have been scrutinized with the care lavished on Mexicans, yet the history of Mexico, particularly since independence, reveals gaps not only in chronology but in the carefully and analytical examination of social phenomena at almost every stage. A mere handful of historians has taken the time to study the campesino, the class structure, or urbanization on the eve of the Revolution, the most singular event of the last century.

In their papers, both Frederick C. Turner and Jean A. Meyer stress this obvious absence of research, and its implications for a knowledge of what really transpired in Mexican history. To fill the gaps and to expand the horizons of knowledge, Turner writes about the necessity to study Mexican history by comparing it with others, that is by the comparative method. In defense of his plea, he argues, and rightly so, that the end is not the "misleading dogma of universality"—a quote he has taken from Samuel Beer— but that the comparative approach "might lead to better understanding of both social processes and specific historical situations". In addition, he advocates, among a variety of approaches, the use of "historical sociology" which, in reality, is a principal theme of his paper: the need of both historian and sociologist to employ each others disciplines.

Turner stresses the reliance on historical sociology because he believes that the study of Mexican society lends itself to that method. He emphasizes the relative isolation of the country and the extensive documentation available for its study as important reasons for his view. As he points out, geography isolated the Mexican community over a long period of time, and thus only a number of "extraneous variables" influenced it, while the transformations that have modified geographical limitations in recent years permit the scholar to analyze the factors that encourage change.

Turner's suggestions are both sound and provocative. Mexican history, indeed, has been both studied intensively and neglected. Much is known about the course of historical development in Mexico, but few attempts at theoretical analysis are available. When Turner argues that much can be learned about the nature of the Mexican Revolution of 1910 if Crane Brinton's theories are applied to it, he stands on solid grounds. Not only will the comparative method shed new light, but Brinton's suppositions, gleamed from his study of the French, American, English, and Russian revolutions, aid the scholar to understand the character of the Porfirista regime, as well as the basic nature of nineteenth century Mexico.

Brinton's labors represent one source. Much more lies close at hand to the historian who seeks fresh insights and perspectives into the Mexican Revolution. On the subject of man's protests against tyrannical regimes a wealth of information awaits the imaginative student. One has merely to turn to "Brinton's bibliography, in a book published approximately thirty years ago, to learn how much had been done on the subject then. Today studies of the revolutionary process literally pour from the presses. Among the new works that help the scholar to focus a new on the upheaval of 1910 is Chalmers Johnson's *Revolutionary Change* which adds a new dimension to earlier contributions. Even the polemical tract authored by Regis Debray, *Revolution in Revolution*, may steer the scholar towards a better comprehension of the events of 1910-1917.

Since the Revolution, in the standard mythology that passes for the true version, stands as an agrarian uprising in which land-hungry peasants played a leading role, why not employ for purposes of comparison and analysis the challenging thesis advanced by Barrington Moore in his justly controversial *Social Origins of Dictatorship and Democracy?* No book that discusses peasant involvement in political protests can ignore Moore's sections dealing with the question of why peasants rebel. His interpretation may compel the scholar to rethink —and perhaps to deemphasize?— the significance of the peasant's participation in the Mexican upheaval of 1910, a view, that in my opinion, cries for recognition. George Foster, an anthropologist whose interpretations are questioned by Turner, may well be correct in his assumption that the Revolution had little impact on the peasants (campesinos?) of Tzintzuntzan.

All of this can be accomplished —to move historical studies of Mexico to a higher theoretical plane— because, as Turner believes, enough of the groundwork has been done to provide for profitable use of theory. That, in turn, should point the way to new directions in research and to the collections of empirical data that will either support theory or indicate fresh theoretical possibilities. The collection of data, the activity that leads to the preparation of the narrow monograph, goes hand in glove with the attempt at generalization based on the use of theory. The two complement each other; at this stage of Mexican research, one need not wait for the other.

Comparing the Mexican Revolution with other movements offers additional advantages. It helps to define more precisely the nebulous term "revolution", which scholars of Mexico interpret loosely. Succinctly, what makes up the revolutionary process? In their study of Mexico since 1910, scholars, particularly Northamericans, often prostitute the term. To accept what may well represent the majority version, itself a reflection of the political conservatism of historical scholarship in the United States since the end of World War II (interpretations now under heavy attack from the revisionists), is to believe that Mexico has enjoyed a revolution for nearly sixty years. That is historically impossible! No revolutionary process, if revolution means drastic and violent socio-economic change, can endure for long. Societies simply will not suffer unstable conditions for more than brief periods; too quickly the people yearn for a return to peace, stability, and order, conditions that are the antithesis of revolution. If the

Mexican Revolution survives, it is unique to the experience of mankind
on this earth while the Mexican is a rare breed of animal found only in
that region lying between the Río Bravo in the north and Guatemala
to the south. And that, as any study of the species man in Mexico amply
demonstrates, is untrue.

The confusion stems from the misleading interpretation applied to the
term revolution. Proponents of the "continuing revolution" thesis, that
credo of PRI politicians since the days of Ávila Camacho, confuse evolutionary middle-class change, which may or not be reform, with revolution.
If attention were paid to France in the years after its justly famous revolution, or to Russia in its post-revolutionary era, perhaps the question of
whether or not the Mexican Revolution survives 1917 (or 1940?) might
not exist. Because, if Mexico suffered a revolution in the true sense of that
term —violent and drastic socio-economic upheaval— that condition ended
long before the 1920's disappeared into the past. That President Cárdenas
carried on an extensive program of social change does not necessarily
demonstrate that he either continued or revived the movement launched
by Madero and brought to fruition in the Constitution of 1917. Why not
speak of a Cardenista revolution, separate and distinct from the earlier
upheaval, which had long ago collapsed if land distribution statistics provide
and index to change in Mexico? Cardenistas spoke for a new generation
that, with some exceptions, had only indirectly or in secondary roles participated in the crusade that began in 1910. Certainly, the Mexico of
1935 bore little resemblance to the nation of Zapata and Villa or even
Obregón.

Of course, none of this denies the necessity to keep firmly in mind the
"uniqueness" of the Mexican experience. Turner rightly reminds us of
the validity of Eric Wolfe's admonition that the "realities of class structure
and relationships in Mexico ... differ radically from the European prototypes ..." Still, granted the need to recall that Mexico is Mexico, comparisons with foreign models can stimulate the historian to formulate not
only fresh views of Mexican history but distinct approaches to its study.
If care is taken to bear in mind obvious differences, no harm can come
from the use of outside experience to measure and evaluate Mexican
development.

II

Perhaps, if the student of Mexico had employed the comparative method
more frequently, Jean A. Meyer might have had answers to many of the
questions he asks. Further, he might have questioned some of the assumptions he takes for granted. After all, was the nineteenth century in Mexico
the age of rural conflict? Is the Mexican Revolution of 1910 the "first
rural revolution in Latin America?" Why not ask if that upheaval was
indeed a "rural revolution?"

Yet these questions are asked, not merely because the study of rural
Mexico in the past century is in its "infancy", but because most of the
popular assumptions (stereotypes) of Mexican history seldom confront

serious challenges. What passes for Mexican social history in the age of Mora, Juárez, and Díaz lies mired in a cycle without end. The absence of careful monographic investigations leaves intact old views that may not stand the light of scrutiny, while the lack of new theories applicable to the era discourage revisionist scholarship.

Much of this, as Meyer recognizes, applies to the Mexican Revolution. We know something about the heroes of the strife —what historian cannot describe Zapata?— although almost nothing of their followers. Villa represents a classic case illustrating the inconsistency of research. On Villa, books and articles galore lie in libraries; but who investigates the character of his followers? Who were the men of the *División del Norte?* Peasants? Where these peasants —or campesinos?— identical to the men who farmed the hacienda lands of the central and southern zones? Might not Villa's army, as a few scholars have suggested, speak for the small-town proletariat of the north, a group that because of its *ambiente* and resulting goals and beliefs, differs radically from the followers of a Zapata or a Buelna —a point raised by Meyer when he speaks of the importance of background to the understanding of individuals and groups?

Of the questions formulated by Meyer, that of greatest implications centers on the causes of rebellion, both in the nineteenth century as well as of the Revolution. Who, he asks, was responsible for the protest? Who took the initiative in forming an active opposition? Applied to the Revolution, the question invites further examination of the premise that peasant unrest underlies rural protest. Did the peasants revolt every where in 1910, or only in certain geographical zones? Morelos, for example? If only in Morelos and other isolated spots, why? Or did peasant uprisings, if indeed any existed, correspond to the challenge of individual leadership? Or to economic changess that had transformed the peasant into an agricultural wage laborer? These questions, says Meyer, have not been answered and, often, not even asked.

Unfortunately, in terms of the Revolution of 1910, these vital questions cannot be answered until more information is available. To cite Meyers again, studies of the haciendas of nineteenth-century Mexico are needed, studies that would analyze by regions the institutions, especially in order to see whether the hacienda is one or many types, and whether or not it suffered transformations in the years between independence and 1910. Did the introduction of capitalism and trade ties with industrial Europe and the United States alter the pattern of the colonial haciendas, and with that transformation the role of the peasants on them? If changes took place, which of them encouraged the peasant activity that led to the Revolution? Until we know more about these aspects of socio-economic history, Meyer correctly insists, much political phenomena cannot be understood or brought to light. For example, why did peasant unrest fail either to spread throughout the Mexico of 1910 or to capture the Revolution —if peasant unrest truly characterized Porfirista Mexico? Why did a so-called agrarian revolution not produce meaningful agrarian reform until 1935, and then under circumstances that cast doubt on the survival of the movement launched in 1910?

Might not the campesino, as Meyer suggests, represent as much the "reaction" to (as in the Huaxteca?) as the "best allies" of the revolutionaires? That the Revolution never advanced much beyond the "bourgeois" stage may be traced to the fact that it was basically impossible to politicize illiterate rural masses, except in places such as Morelos where the introduction of railroads and a modern sugar system tied to export markets wrought profound changes?

Clearly, the theories advanced above, the questions posed, represent only a variety of possible explanations for the historical phenomena of the time. All are tentative. To affirm them categorically as true cannot be done because the spadework remains unfinished. Yet the total picture of Mexican development, in a social as well as a political sense, awaits the bold pioneer who will both "dig" out the facts as well as interpret the large currents. In that task he can expect that history by comparison and by theoretical analysis will open new and exciting avenues of thought.

RELATORÍA

IRENE VÁZQUEZ VALLE

El debate se inició con algunas consideraciones en torno a las ventajas y desventajas de realizar la investigación de la historia social basada en enfoques interdisciplinarios. Se destacaron los peligros de este enfoque, especialmente el peligro de que la historia, como disciplina, fuera considerada como un agregado de la sociología. Varios participantes expresaron críticas hacia los historiadores que quieren hacer las veces de sociólogos y los sociólogos metidos en el campo del historiador.

Los participantes estuvieron de acuerdo en la urgencia de establecer un marco teórico que guiara las investigaciones, así como la de ponerse de acuerdo sobre la definición de conceptos y términos que manejan, con diferentes significados historiadores y sociólogos; entre los que mencionan el de "clase social".

En relación con la teoría se señaló que deberían tenerse en cuenta los problemas sociales contemporáneos porque sirven de pauta de los temas que debe investigarse en el pasado. Algunos participantes expresaron que no les sorprendía tanto que todavía se utilizaran métodos derivados del neopositivismo, sino más bien ese constante volver a la búsqueda de los datos por los datos mismos.

La ponencia del profesor Jean Meyer fue leída en su ausencia. En relación a algunas preguntas formuladas en la ponencia un grupo de participantes consideró que eran muy interesantes pero que no entendían su formulación cuando se indicaban las fuentes donde se podrían encontrar las respuestas; o formularse las preguntas cuando el autor indicaba que la respuesta se encontraba en la utilización de métodos cuantitativos. Igualmente se advirtió que ya existen estudios sobre varios de los temas propuestos por el profesor Meyer.

Otro grupo de participantes destacó el hecho de que la ponencia es una invitación a la investigación y que la formación de preguntas no es de suyo una deficiencia ya que tocaría a los investigadores dilucidarlas. Por otra parte se consideró que lo importante no es que ya existan estudios sobre algunos de los temas propuestos por el autor, sino que era preciso reestudiarlos y darles un nuevo contenido dentro de un contexto social más preciso a la luz de nuevos métodos de análisis.

IX. HISTORIOGRAFÍA DE LA VIDA POLÍTICA

PONENCIAS

"El liberalismo triunfante y el surgimiento de la historia nacional." María de la Luz Parcero

"Political Historiography of the Porfirian Period of Mexican History." Laurens B. Perry

"Mexican Political Historiography, 1959-1969." John Womack, Jr.

COMENTARIOS

Rafael Segovia
Albert Michaels
Nettie Lee Benson

RELATORÍA

Jorge Jufresa

6 de noviembre de 1969

Presidentes: José C. Valadés, investigador de historia de México; Rafael Segovia, profesor e investigador del Centro de Estudios Internacionales de El Colegio de México.

Ponentes: Ma. de la Luz Parcero, investigadora del Departamento de Investigaciones Históricas, INAH; Laurens Perry, investigador de la Universidad de las Américas; John Womack Jr. instructor, Universidad de Harvard.

Comentaristas: Rafael Segovia, profesor e investigador de El Colegio de México; Albert Michaels, profesor asistente, State University of New York, Buffalo; Nettie Lee Benson, directora de la Biblioteca del Instituto de Estudios Latinoamericanos, University of Texas, Austin.

Participantes: Arturo Arnáiz y Freg, Academia Mexicana de la Historia; Lyle Brown, profesor asistente de ciencias políticas, Baylor University; James Cockcroft, profesor asistente de historia, Universidad de Wisconsin, Milwaukee; Eugenia Meyer, investigadora del Departamento de Investigaciones Históricas, INAH; Martín Quirarte, subdirector del Archivo Histórico de la Secretaría de Relaciones Exteriores; Andrea Sánchez Quintanar, investigadora de la Universidad Iberoamericana; Robert Scott, profesor de ciencia política, Universidad de Illinois; Charles Hale, profesor asistente de historia, Amherat College; Paul Vanderwood, profesor asistente San Diego State College.

Participantes europeos: M. S. Alperovich, Instituto de Historia Latinoamericana, Moscú; Friedrich Katz, Universidad de Humboldt, Alemania.

Relator: Jorge Jufresa, estudiante del Centro de Estudios Históricos de El Colegio de México.

EL LIBERALISMO TRIUNFANTE
Y EL SURGIMIENTO DE LA HISTORIA NACIONAL

MARÍA DE LA LUZ PARCERO

I

Raras veces las actividades históricas en México han sido estrictamente académicas. Desde que nuestro país surgió como Estado moderno su historia ha sido, en primera instancia, la búsqueda permanente de su libertad, libertad concebida como un medio de progreso económico, social y político. La historiografía mexicana no es sino la manifestación más concreta de los procedimientos que, en opinión de los patriotas más ilustres o de los hombres más interesados en el bien común, pueden aplicarse a la consecución de esa meta.

En la crisis que afectó al mundo entre los siglos XVIII y XIX, y que sigue inexorablemente afectando a muchos pueblos, entre ellos el nuestro, la historiografía no podía ser una actividad erudita: tenía que estar, y está, vinculada a los problemas inherentes a su desarrollo. Era, en aquel periodo, arma de lucha, parte siempre de un programa orientado a encaminar el rumbo de la sociedad mexicana; era apoyo de actos bélicos y de los programas legislativos y educativos de las fuerzas en pugna. Para quienes la escribían la historia era asimismo acto de conciencia, experiencia que enseñaba; instrumento político, lección franca y bien intencionada que dejaban los miembros de los grupos contendientes.

El estado de agitación en que se debatía el país, poco después de lograr su Independencia, hizo que la labor histórica aun de escritores tan destacados como Alamán o Zavala y Bustamante y Mora, resultara circunstancial y poco esclarecedora aun para los hombres de la segunda mitad del siglo XIX.

Hacia 1865 Manuel Larrainzar, para quien la historia, "base de la experiencia", "maestro de la vida", debía ser también un espectáculo del acontecer humano destinado a servir de lección moral, científica y política; y a cuyo estudio debían dedicarse los hombres más penetrantes y los más reconocidos por su saber o su interés social, revisando en el seno de la Sociedad Mexicana de Geografía y Estadística toda la producción histórica del país, encontraba obras parciales sobre todos los periodos, pero no una historia general. Esta clase de trabajos, decía, son obra del tiempo y de muchas circunstancias; están en relación con el adelanto de los pueblos. En todas las obras que se han elaborado falta unidad de pensamiento y, por consiguiente, uniformidad en el plan y en la ejecución. Hay lagunas y vacíos en las épocas de que tratan; todos los trabajos son estimables, pero es preciso reunir lo más memorable, lo más útil e instructivo, refundir y formar en un solo cuerpo, bajo un plan más extenso y mejor combinado, todas las historias particulares purgándolas de los errores que pudiesen contener. Un trabajo así será de difícil ejecución, reconoce, pero la conveniencia pública, la marcha de la civilización, el lustre de la nación y los adelantos que ha hecho así lo exigen. [1]

Tendrían que pasar varios años para que esa aspiración, generalizada ya entre los escritores mexicanos como exigencia de una nueva época, se viera alcanzada.

II

Al franquear el siglo XIX se inicia en el país un largo proceso de revolución en el que se enfrentan dos órdenes y pelean uno con exclusión de otro: el colonial y el democrático; las tendencias y los grupos se alían según los intereses que se juegan al pretender cambiar o perfeccionar la estructura social y la organización política heredadas de la dominación española. En medio de la versatilidad de los partidos y de las discrepancias ideológicas, los historiadores de aquella etapa exteriorizan en sus diversos matices los ideales del partido del orden, tradicionalista, católico y monarquizante, y las aspiraciones del partido del progreso, racionalista, liberal y republicano, conceptos que suponen un modo especial de entender el ser y la historia del pueblo mexicano.

El problema básico que se presentaba a la historiografía, explica el doctor O'Gorman, era explicar el aparente fracaso de la guerra de Independencia. El país, lejos de haber entrado a la senda risueña de la paz y del progreso, yacía en el abismo de la discordia y de la guerra civil. Liberales y conservadores se inculpaban mutuamente del desastre, y desembocaban, al tratar de comprender el pasado mexicano, en una contradicción irreductible. [2]

La disputa por el poder fue larga y cruenta; en ella se jugaban los dos partidos su propia existencia y el rumbo que tomaría la nación recién emancipada. Al mediar el siglo, Otero, Payno, Altamirano, Ignacio Ramírez, Ocampo, Arriaga y muchos otros escritores exhibían la continuidad de la lucha entre los dos sistemas y mostraban soluciones

[1] Larrainzar, Manuel, *Algunas ideas sobre la historia y maneras de escribir la de México, especialmente la contemporánea desde la declaración de Independencia en 1821 hasta nuestros días.* Imprenta de Cumplido. México, 1865.
[2] O'Gorman, Edmundo, "Tres etapas en la historiografía mexicana". *Anuario de Historia.* Facultad de Filosofía y Letras, UNAM. T. II, 1962.

cada vez más variadas y ricas a las exigencias vitales de su tiempo. No obstante, por la inestabilidad continua anunciadora de los cambios notables que sufría socialmente la nación, era imposible vislumbrar con claridad los sucesos de un presente fluctuante, y al encontrar en el pasado indígena o en el colonial la raíz y el origen de cualquiera de los sectores en oposición, tampoco llegaron a entenderlo en su integridad y ni menos podía servir de inspiración o de orgullo a los partidarios de uno u otro bando.

Sólo después de la gran década de la Reforma y la Intervención (1857-1867), al observarse plenamente la toma de conciencia de la propia nacionalidad por parte de los grupos que reclamaron desde 1810 el goce de su soberanía, pudo hacerse una revisión y un balance de todo lo acontecido; sólo entonces se volvió con amor al pasado para esclarecer el significado del presente y para definir los contornos movedizos de ese pueblo que llegaba al ejercicio del poder.

Fue ese el momento en el que pudo originarse la historia nacional. Colaboraron en esa gran empresa Alfredo Chavero, Vicente Riva Palacio, Julio Zárate, Juan de Dios Arias, Enrique de Olavarría y Ferrari y José María Vigil al publicar *México a través de los siglos*,[3] obra cumbre del siglo xix por su significado histórico; apareció entre 1887 y 1889 después de una larga gestación, en la que tal vez Larrainzar y Altamirano tuvieron no poca parte.[4]

Otros autores, con intereses sectarios los más, habían intentado una revisión de la historia de México en sus diversas etapas. Ninguna, sin embargo, animada por los intereses conciliadores del círculo de *El Renacimiento*, había emprendido el estudio sistemático de toda la historia del país desde los orígenes prehispánicos hasta la consolidación de la República. Fueron los liberales, como miembros de una clase ya dueña del poder, los que se dieron a la tarea de integrar una historia general filosófica y razonada "conforme a los adelantos del arte y a las reglas de la escuela moderna" tal como la quería Larrainzar: una historia interesante e instructiva de lo que la nación había sido en cada época, en que los acontecimientos presentados en su orden natural se explicaban en todas sus relaciones y combinaciones, en que se señalaba

[3] *México a través de los siglos*. Historia general y completa del desenvolvimiento social, político, religioso, militar, artístico, científico y literario de México, desde la antigüedad más remota hasta la época actual. Ballesca-Espasa. México-Barcelona, 1887-1889.

[4] Nos inclinamos a creer que la base de que partieron los autores de *México a través de los siglos* es el trabajo de Larrainzar antes mencionado por la completa identidad de los objetivos que proponen, por las fuentes que se consideran importantes y por el esbozo de la historia de México que aquel historiador presentara a la Sociedad Mexicana de Geografía y Estadística de la que Altamirano —conocedor sin duda de este proyecto— impulsor y amigo de Riva Palacio y sus colaboradores, fue luego miembro y vicepresidente.

con la debida distinción y claridad la parte que las leyes, las costumbres o las circunstancias habían tenido en los adelantos que se habían logrado o en su abatimiento y decadencia y, en que se resaltaba la instrucción que se desprendía de esos hechos y en que se procuraba que cada cosa apareciera con el color que le era propio, con fidelidad, exactitud y la firmeza que inspiraban el culto a la verdad y a la justicia.

Esta obra heredera de las inquietudes históricas de Alamán, Bustamante, Orozco y Berra, Fernando Ramírez, Larrainzar y Altamirano, anuncia una concepción nueva de la historia mexicana en que el pasado indígena y español se presentan como base del desarrollo de todos los órdenes de nuestra cultura. Su aspiración básica era definir el ser de la nación mexicana y sus adelantos alcanzados en el camino del progreso.

Allí, en ese pasado, una obra hecha con el afán más erudito y científico de su tiempo, bajo el signo de Vico, Taine, Comte, Spencer y los historiadores alemanes, encontraba también la tesis por la que el presente de México y su destino se esclarecían, por la que sus luchas terribles e ininterrumpidas se justificaban y por las que se abría al pueblo un cauce a seguir. Con esa obra se entregaba al país una posibilidad de comprenderse como ente histórico y una lección moral, científica y política, aún no superada. [5]

III

Los intelectuales que fraguaron ese puntal de nuestra historiografía eran hombres hondamente arraigados a los intereses de su tiempo. Habían participado en las luchas políticas del país y se encontraban familiarizados con los asuntos del gobierno, pues habían desempeñado diversos cargos que les permitieron estar en contacto con los intereses públicos. Eran liberales cultos saturados de ideales positivistas y de empeños románticos. Chavero, celebrado como dramaturgo en su tiempo, por su erudición era amigo y discípulo de García Icazbalceta y Orozco y Berra, y era también un romántico apasionado de la nacionalidad, fuerza espiritual que a partir de la Independencia afectara todos los órdenes de nuestra cultura en que participaron los liberales; a Riva Palacio, alma de la ejecución de la obra, político de múltiples actividades, se le conocía por su fecunda vena novelística; a Zárate se le consideraba un diestro investigador de la historia; Vigil era periodista y un

[5] De lo que se ha caminado en el terreno de la interpretación histórica, desde que apareció esta obra monumental, habla atinadamente el doctor Edmundo O'Gorman en su ensayo "La Revolución Mexicana y la historiografía". *Seis ensayos históricos de tema mexicano.* Universidad Veracruzana, Xalapa, 1960.

bibliófilo destacado; Juan de Dios Arias, poeta y periodista como Olavarría y sus compañeros de trabajo, pertenecía al círculo de Altamirano que se empeñaba en forjar una literatura orientada a la afirmación de los valores nacionales.

Bajo el influjo de las tesis positivistas de Comte, divulgadas en el país desde 1857 por Gabino Barreda, y de las tesis románticas de la nacionalidad popularizadas ya entre los liberales al mediar el siglo, *México a través de los siglos* intentó explicar cómo se formó esa nacionalidad que se exaltaba en la tribuna y en las letras. Sus autores se consideraban parte de una corriente nueva que tendía a reformar el trabajo histórico mediante una cuidadosa selección y un análisis lógico de los testimonios; a su juicio, el periodo científico en que se encontraba ya la humanidad había dado un giro diferente al estudio tradicional de la historia y por lo mismo ya no les interesaba tanto la narración de los hechos y de los movimientos políticos como reflexionar filosóficamente "sobre las evoluciones sociales y sobre la marcha y el progreso del espíritu humano; sobre el influjo de la ley de la herencia en el pasado y en el porvenir de la nación; sobre la geografía política del mundo y sobre la relación que el territorio habitado y el medio tienen con los caracteres nacionales". Creían que la historia detallada y minuciosa iba separándose de la historia sin personajes y que esta última, aunque sostenida por aquélla, era la que debía prestar positiva utilidad en lo porvenir. Investigaron, pero trataron de que su historia estuviera fincada en la sociología para que pudiera ser realmente útil.

Quisieron presentar los hechos en su "verdadera luz", alejados de cualquier propósito sectario, imparcialmente, sin apasionamientos ni falsos criterios políticos, seguros como estaban de que la época en que emprendían su extraordinaria labor, era propicia, técnica y espiritualmente, para reconstruir la histroia mexicana, impulsados sólo por su acendrado amor a la patria y con el deseo de servir de guía a la juventud, "esperanza de la nación". Su historia aspiró a presentar no una infinidad de detalles sino los grandes hechos en su conjunto, mostrándolos como fruto de las exigencias y necesidades de una época y no del egoísmo humano; un cuadro así, creían, "debía encerrar útiles y fecundas lecciones al mostrar el camino recorrido por el pueblo mexicano desde sus orígenes hasta su época y los senderos por los que la nación debía caminar de una manera reflexiva para corresponder al destino de su siglo".

Novedosa era la técnica y todavía más lo era el enfoque; el postularse el ser nacional como producto del mestizaje físico y espiritual de las razas indígena y española, al antítesis liberal-conservadora se liquidaba ante un nuevo criterio histórico que respondía en su más hondo significado al deseo de unificar los intereses de los grupos en pugna, después de la Reforma y la Intervención.

IV

El pueblo que advino a la vida moderna, pensaban, no era la nación que había sido conquistada y tampoco conquistadora, era un pueblo cuya "embriogenia y morfología" debía estudiarse durante los tres siglos de la dominación española en los cuales se había formado la individualidad social y política que sintiéndose viril y robusta proclamó su independencia en 1810. Resultante de un proceso que incluía el pasado indígena y el pasado español, era un pueblo cuya historia comenzaba precisamente en el momento en que se encontraron las dos razas a las que debió su nacimiento. La historia precortesiana se presentó así como el primer gran capítulo de la historia nacional.[6]

Al esbozar el cuadro de la cultura prehispánica, Chavero quiso presentar los adelantos de la sociedad indígena en su propia luz, desechando todo lo que podía ser fruto de la imaginación o del engaño, separando las fábulas de lo que realmente aconteció. Con este afán erudito se volcó en el estudio de las fuentes; no pretendía hacer alardes de erudición y por ello omitió notas aclaratorias, pero reconocía que su labor es fruto de la investigación de sus antecesores, de quienes da amplia cuenta en la revisión de las fuentes que le sirvieron de base para componer su libro. Códices indígenas, crónicas españolas, así como historiadores y lingüistas, le proporcionaron datos que le permitieron ahondar en ese pasado y plantear hipótesis superadas ya, y hasta algunas veces confirmadas por la arqueología como testimonio de su estudio concienzudo y sistemático del mundo prehispánico.[7]

Para él las manifestaciones culturales de los antiguos superaron en mucho a las del viejo mundo; sin embargo la historia precortesiana no sólo le parecía digna y valiosa como aportación genuina para conocer una fase del desarrollo de la humanidad; era importante sobre todo, porque constituía parte de la historia mexicana moderna, en cuanto raíz de una de las dos razas que habían dado origen al pueblo mexicano, y en tanto que ese pasado remoto, se recuperaba como base de la nacionalidad y de la historia de una nueva generación deseosa de sacrificar sus tendencias políticas en aras de la comprensión del ser nacional a la luz de la gran ley de la evolución del espíritu humano.

La empresa conquistadora le parecía una hazaña grandiosa dotada de un doble significado. Había sido destructora pero también creadora. Chavero se duele de la destrucción de lo indígena bajo el impacto de

[6] Chavero, Alfredo, Historia antigua. T. I. Primera Época.
[7] Para quienes el sentido de la historia se reduce a la verificación de los datos, el mérito de toda la obra se juzga en la medida que resiste la crítica apoyada en conocimientos actuales. El trabajo de Chavero, por ejemplo, no sólo se juzga cursi sino "poco serio e inútil" porque sus datos han sido desechados o porque no menciona prolijamente las páginas de sus fuentes.

la Conquista. Por eso siente que ellos, con sus esfuerzos, reconstruyen un pasado que es título de orgullo para los mexicanos. La superioridad de civilización, piensa, dio el triunfo a los españoles y la religión les aseguró el dominio de los indios y sus posesiones. No obstante, siendo la Conquista obra de la fatalidad, terminó con el señorío de Moctezuma sobre multitud de pueblos heterogéneos que al convertirse en aliados de Cortés sacudieron el yugo de aquel déspota y decidieron el triunfo para España, país a cuya sombra surgiría el pueblo mexicano. Lejos ya del antihispanismo o del indigenismo de la primera mitad del siglo, eligió a Cortés y a Bernal como fuentes más dignas de crédito para el estudio de esta etapa. Atacó los aspectos deprimentes de la obra conquistadora, pero juzgó la obra misionera de un gran valor y por encima de todo, el empeño que tuvieron los religiosos en proteger a los indios y en preservar las notas sobresalientes de su cultura le parece meritorio.

En el siglo XVI se formó el embrión de un pueblo que debía ser con el tiempo una República independiente, asienta Riva Palacio. Laboriosa y difícil evolución tenía que consumar aquel informe agrupamiento de familias, de pueblos y de razas unidos repentinamente por un cataclismo social y político para constituir un pueblo que ni era el conquistado ni el conquistador, pero que de ambos heredaba virtudes y vicios, glorias y tradiciones, características y temperamento para unirse en una sola bandera, constituyendo un solo pueblo, reinos y repúblicas que no sólo eran independientes sino enemigas. Las leyes y las costumbres proclamaban la división de razas y de castas, pero los intereses y las familias se fueron identificando y confundiendo hasta formar "el alma nacional". [8]

La Conquista fue generadora de la nueva nacionalidad y *El virreinato* era la historia del desarrollo y desenvolvimiento del pueblo mexicano. Riva Palacio nos explica ampliamente las líneas de ese desarrollo.

Neutralizadas sus tendencias políticas por sus intereses románticos y su filosofía positivista, pudo ver con simpatía a España y a sus reyes. A Isabel, impulsora de la empresa del Almirante, la encuentra noble y poética y aun cuando la Conquista fue al fin una manera de esclavizar a los indios, las protestas de la reina en favor de sus nuevos vasallos hacen que a los ojos del autor liberal, la dinastía austriaca se salve. Sus leyes, aglutinadas por la *Recopilación* de Carlos II, le parecen verdaderas avanzadas de liberalismo y hasta las equipara con las del siglo XIX. Si se cometieron crímenes y se abusó de las leyes, indica, en nada se empaña el reflejo de la gloria y gratitud a que es acreedora aquella mujer "modelo de reinas, de esposas y de madres". Estableciendo el paralelo sobre los reinados de la Casa de Austria y la de Borbón, cree, apartándose de los cánones históricos de los ilustrados, que muy a pesar

---

[8] Riva Palacio, Vicente, *El virreinato*. T. II. Segunda época.

de que se considere mejor el ejercicio del poder por los Borbón, después de un balance analítico, puede afirmarse que los Austria tuvieron un mayor número de dificultades que vencer si bien aquellos lograron desenvolverse con mayor facilidad por haber encontrado españolizada ya la Colonia.

La historia de la dominación española aparece en su esquema como una etapa sin brillo que prepara otra. En esa especie de Edad Media de la historia mexicana lo único realmente notable fue, para él, la formación del pueblo mexicano.

Fue la Colonia un periodo tranquilo de crecimiento interrumpido apenas por tumultos locales y sin consecuencias o por invasiones piráticas en las costas que no tenían más resultado que el saqueo o la destrucción de algún puerto, afirma. La vida se deslizaba sin ruido y sin brillo. Vanamente, agrega, se buscarán en esos tres siglos, los grandes acontecimientos que perpetua resonancia dejan en el mundo; inútilmente querrán encontrarse allí esas luchas apasionadas de los partidos políticos o religiosos, esa efervescencia de los ánimos tan fecunda en rasgos deslumbrantes que caracteriza en las épocas críticas de los pueblos a las grandes convulsiones de la madurez y virilidad. El saqueo de un puerto, las noticias de la corte que una o dos veces al año llegaban con las flotas, las funciones religiosas, los actos literarios de la Universidad y algunas veces las ejecuciones de justicia o actos de fe eran los acontecimientos que turbaban la monotonía de aquella existencia.

La historia del virreinato, señala, es un capítulo de la historia de España, porque fueron los españoles los que siempre ocuparon la atención de los cronistas que poco se preocuparon del nacimiento y desarrollo del pueblo que llegó a formar una nacionalidad independiente. Pero ese pasado, ajeno en Riva Palacio, se vuelve parte entrañable de la historia de México con la existencia de los hijos de los conquistadores y los conquistados, semilla mestiza que había de formar el núcleo de la nueva raza que en trescientos años había de crecer y extenderse por toda la Nueva España sobreponiéndose a las razas que la originaron. El agrupamiento, la analogía en sus costumbres y tendencias los hizo reconocerse como sociedad, dice; el deseo de gobernarse por sí mismos y el odio a la dominación los impulsó a proclamarse nación independiente y a conquistar a base de combates y de sangre su autonomía.

La tendencia natural de los habitantes a la libertad, la predisposición orgánica de los individuos, el ejemplo de otras naciones y el influjo progresista del siglo xix inspiró y alentó a la nación mexicana a convertirse en pueblo estableciendo la democracia y consignando los derechos del hombre como base de sus instituciones políticas, concluye.

Julio Zárate imprimió también el sello liberal, romántico y positivista al enfoque novedoso y certero con el que analiza la guerra de Independencia. [9] Los intereses patrióticos en que se abriga le obligaban a escribir con sinceridad, buena fe y firme intención de rendir culto a la verdad y a la justicia.

A la luz de sus tesis evolucionistas la guerra de Independencia se muestra como una cadena de luchas necesarias para el desarrollo de la sociedad, pues estaba convencido de que la patria se había ya encaminado en la marcha del progreso. Esa lucha parece a su sensibilidad romántica, un hecho grandioso y digno de la mayor exaltación, aun cuando cree que su historia puede escribirse ya sin odio y sin lisonjas.

La guerra dividió a la sociedad que formaba la Nueva España —dice— y todos los elementos de esa sociedad hubieron de modificarse. El estudio de esas modificaciones es lo que persigue al investigar, ayudado por todos los historiadores del siglo xix y sobre todo por Alamán y Bustamante; los rasgos fundamentales de esa etapa que decidieron al pueblo a proclamar su Independencia y romper sus lazos con España.

Afirma Zárate que en los tres siglos de dominación se produce el trabajo lento de identificación entre los diversos grupos que componían socialmente a la Colonia y del cual resultara el "alma nacional". No obstante que las costumbres eran fiel reflejo de la separación de razas que favorecieron los reyes, el pueblo que se formó a la sombra de la dominación, a la hora de proclamar su Independencia, se vio respaldado por los indios y rompieron juntos la aparente armonía que había existido por tres centurias.

Los acontecimientos que se produjeron en Europa después de la Revolución Francesa, así como el ejemplo de la Independencia norteamericana, favorecieron el estallido de la revolución y alteraron la tranquila marcha de una sociedad poco acostumbrada a sacudidas revolucionarias.

A mediados de 1808 llegaron las noticias del motín de Aranjuez y de la abdicación de Carlos IV, de la entrada de Fernando VII, de la prisión de la familia real en Bayona, del patriótico levantamiento del pueblo de Madrid y de la erección de juntas provinciales.

Se percibió de inmediato la separación entre la autoridad constituida, defendida por los dominadores y el alto clero, y los representantes del pueblo apoyados en las masas que serían acaudilladas por simples sacerdotes y oficiales.

Hidalgo concentró las aspiraciones justísimas de la nación iniciando una lucha terrible en que la insurgencia se levantaba como un mar encrespado. Morelos fue el gran capitán de la guerra, campeón de la Independencia y enemigo formidable del régimen español. La envidia que inspiró su gloria hizo prosélitos hasta en sus propios compañeros de lucha, se le inutilizó y su muerte fue el triunfo de cien victorias para el enemigo.

[9] Zárate, Julio, *La Independencia*. T. iii, Tercera Época.

Otro gran momento de la guerra fue Mina. Al final de la guerra Vicente Guerrero ofrece el ejemplo del patriotismo más ardiente e inquebrantable por la lucha heroica con que mantiene el fuego de la Independencia cuando parecía haberse extinguido. No obstante tocó a Iturbide —instrumento de las clases privilegiadas para sustraerse al régimen liberal que se instituyó entre 1820 y 1821 en España— ser el unificador de todos los intereses y el consumador de la independencia.

En esa etapa el estruendo de la guerra ahogó las otras manifestaciones de la vida social, explica Zárate. La lucha, con todos sus desastres, es por espacio de once años, la condición en que vive un pueblo que parecía destinado a dormir indefinidamente. La guerra marca un periodo importantísimo en la vida histórica de la nación mexicana. Decídese allí si ha de ser libre o ha de continuar sujeta; pero al fragor de los combates se efectúa un rápido cambio en los espíritus. Antes que las armas, ya la opinión, y el sentir público han obtenido un triunfo completo. La Independencia, más que aspiración, era la única manera posible de ser del pueblo mexicano.

Sobre las ruinas de la antigua dominación, declara, surge un nuevo pueblo que trae, aparte de la entereza para conservar su autonomía, el valor ingénito de sus antecesores y las ideas, hábitos, educación y tendencias que habían heredado del pueblo que les dio civilización a cambio de su Independencia.

Cayó la dominación española cuando había cumplido su destino y México entra, a partir de la guerra de Independencia, en la vida tempestuosa de los pueblos jóvenes y libres. Comienza a marchar por el sendero glorioso y difícil de las naciones independientes, afirma convencido Julio Zárate, y agrega: trae a su nueva existencia los errores y defectos que le han legado sus dominadores, pero ha heredado también sus altas virtudes y ellas le bastarán para mantener su Independencia y cumplir las leyes inmutables del progreso.

Tenaces y naturales debían ser las resistencias al empuje de los soplos renovadores que ofrecían seductores horizontes de libertad y de progreso, afirma Juan de Dios Arias al entrar al estudio del México independiente. [10]

El medio actúa sobre el hombre y los pueblos no pueden liberarse de la influencia del medio; al emprenderse el cambio, al verificarse el choque de intereses, el país tuvo que pasar por las características revolucionarias que presentaban todos los pueblos desde el siglo XVIII.

La revolución cuandió no por convencimiento sino por sentimiento. Era un contagio moral determinado más por la imaginación que por los razonamientos. Todos los elementos que componían al pueblo mexicano había entrado en actividad. Al sentimiento de emancipación política, lo acompañaban exigencias de carácter social que envolvían refor-

[10] Olavarría y Ferrari, Enrique, *México independiente 1821-1855.* T. IV.

mas profundas. La colisión entre los intereses nacionales y los de las clases privilegiadas era fatalmente necesaria al consumarse la Independencia, con el giro que le dio Iturbide para sustraer a México de las reformas efectuadas entonces en España. El país entró a un estado de disolución cuyo signo positivo era, a pesar de la miseria pública, del desorden social, de la inestabilidad política, preparar una etapa favorable al desenvolvimiento, sin trabas del pueblo mexicano.

El principal obstáculo con el que debía enfrentarse la nación era el poder eclesiástico, cimentado en las creencias religiosas y ligado con el profundo respeto a las autoridades constituidas. El clero, poderoso y rico, monopolizador de las tierras y del crédito, a la par que acumulaba riquezas y fuerza política, perdía las virtudes que en los tiempos de la Conquista le ganaron respetabilidad y prestigio. El recuerdo de las virtudes de los primeros religiosos, sólo servía para establecer un ingrato paralelo con los frailes del presente sumidos en la ignorancia y entregados a la ociosidad y el lujo.

Otro obstáculo casi insuperable lo representaban los intereses del ejército unido por un fuerte espíritu de corporación igual que el clero. Llevado por sus ambiciones atizaba la guerra y se convertía en árbitro de las contiendas políticas. El espíritu partidarista hacía aun a los mejores caudillos víctimas del encono político, habiendo sido esa la suerte del general Guerrero.

El vértigo de la discordia se traducía en desorden crónico, se habían perdido todas las nociones de honor y religiosidad; la estabilidad de los gobiernos dependía de voraces agiotistas y especuladores. De todas estas fuerzas se nutrió el partido conservador que estaba formado por cristianos timoratos y monarquistas convencidos defensores nada más de su situación privilegiada.

Este periodo, que corre desde la consumación de la Independencia hasta la Revolución de Ayutla, era expresión de la lucha necesaria que se había desatado entre los intereses democráticos de la nación y los de la oligarquía de las clases privilegiadas; y lección de liberalismo que presentaba los horrores de los regímenes oprimidos y la confirmación de las tesis propagadas por Gabino Barreda al mostrar que la marcha hacia el progreso era inevitable.

José María Vigil, romántico y positivista, presenta el movimiento de Reforma y la Intervención, como consecuencias de antecedentes que sitúa en los orígenes de México. [11] A través de la Colonia analiza el desarrollo del conflicto que se plantea entre los poderes civil y eclesiástico en los momentos de surgir la Colonia, conflicto que le parece el hilo conductor sobre el que se desarrolla el drama de nuestra historia. La Reforma era para él un problema social y político que resultaba imprescindible liquidar ya en su tiempo.

[11] Vigil, José María, *La Reforma*. T. v.

Al consumarse la Conquista, no obstante que los reyes procuraron mantener a la Iglesia bajo su dependencia, se estableció una dualidad entre los poderes espiritual y temporal sobre el cual se erigió el edificio religioso y político, señala Vigil. Así, desde un principio, se dieron choques violentos entre las autoridades civiles y el clero que dieron origen a disposiciones tendientes a moderar un celo respetable en su base, pero que podía degenerar en elemento de anarquía.

Las circunstancias especiales de una sociedad embrionaria en que luchaban razas y civilizaciones tan diversas; la distancia a que se hallaba el país recién conquistado del agente político que daba vida a un nuevo ser; los intereses y pasión de corporación que movía a los evangelizadores, produjeron una lucha en el seno de los mismos y fue así como se vieron surgir enconadas luchas entre el clero secular y regular, entre los frailes y los obispos y dentro de las propias órdenes religiosas que se disputaban la dominación de los indígenas. Los conflictos, surgidos de este afán de dominio, favorecieron la relajación del elemento eclesiástico, los conventos se multiplicaron fuera de las necesidades civiles, las riquezas que acumularan adquirieron proporciones extraordinarias y esto, unido a la influencia que ejercía una clase revestida de carácter sagrado y con la superioridad de cultura intelectual, inspiró en los pueblos un respeto y una veneración sin límites que trascendía a todos los actos de la vida pública y privada, en el individuo, la familia y la sociedad.

Los más ilustrados estadistas españoles habían comprendido, desde mucho tiempo atrás, la necesidad de poner un límite al poder absoluto de la Iglesia, iniciando saludables reformas que se dejaron sentir en toda su fuerza desde que entró a reinar la dinastía de Borbón.

El poder absoluto de los reyes, asentado en el respeto tradicional de los pueblos, podía luchar ventajosamente con su rival, que se inclinaba sumiso ante la disminución del poder inquisitorial, la supresión de las órdenes religiosas, la supresión de bienes de manos muertas y otras reformas que sin grandes obstáculos se establecían progresivamente en el Imperio.

La invasión de Napoleón a España determinó una crisis en Nueva España que venía gestándose hacía mucho tiempo.

El clero bajo, seguido por las masas populares, enarboló la bandera de insurrección, que no sólo luchaba por la separación de la metrópoli, sino también por la extirpación de los abusos inveterados de que adolecía todo el cuerpo de la monarquía española, sintetizando de esta manera el deseo de sustituir el régimen absoluto por el orden constitucional.

Se opusieron el alto clero y las clases privilegiadas, núcleo del partido conservador que odiaba especialmente al espíritu innovador, abusando los eclesiásticos de una manera escandalosa de las armas que la religión y el fanatismo habían puesto en sus manos.

En medio de la guerra, y correspondiendo a sentimientos análogos, España daba un golpe de muerte al régimen absoluto al proclamar la Constitución de 1812. Los forcejeos entre Fernando VII y los revolucionarios se decidieron en 1820 con la supresión definitiva del Santo Oficio y la libertad de imprenta otorgada por el nuevo régimen. El clero de Nueva España, viéndose amenazado en su poder y sus riquezas por el nuevo orden de cosas, confeccionó el Plan de Iguala y proclamó la Independencia como un medio eficaz de conjurar la tempestad paralizando así el movimiento reformista que en la propia España se efectuaba desde muchos años atrás.

La Constitución de 1824 dio existencia oficial en México al clero, que estableció relaciones necesarias con el Estado.

Se entabló una lucha entre ambos poderes que arrojó al país en el abismo de la anarquía que por muchos años agitó a la República.

La mudanza de las instituciones, el cambio de regímenes, los movimientos de reacción entre 1821 y 1855 no cortaron, sin embargo, la marcha ascendente del espíritu reformista lenta o rápida, pero siempre segura.

En medio de aquel torbellino de revoluciones, que alejaba toda esperanza de paz, se fue simplificando el problema: llegóse a comprender, por las lecciones de la experiencia, que existía una suma de intereses radicalmente hostiles a los de la nación, vinculados en un cuerpo poderoso por los medios materiales de que disponía y por la influencia incontrastable que ejercía en las conciencias. Se había visto que las condescendencias sólo habían servido para exagerar las pretensiones clericales, que a la primera oportunidad se levantaron contra un gobierno cuya timidez no había conseguido más que su desprecio, coadyuvando a la creación de una dictadura tiránica que trató de ahogar las tendencias del pueblo a la libertad en todas sus fecundas aplicaciones. Desde ese momento la violencia de la reacción tenía que producir una acción enérgica, el moderantismo era sólo una doctrina inaplicable, el pensamiento de la revolución quedó perfectamente definido, tales eran las convicciones de quienes sostuvieron la Revolución de Ayutla.

No había lugar a términos medios indica Vigil. Los dos partidos ventilaban en la lucha su propia existencia, y en oposición a los intereses nacionales el partido que se jugaba el todo por el todo apelaría a todos los recursos sin excluir el del auxilio extranjero. La sociedad mexicana, bajo el impacto de la Reforma preparada por tantos años y tantos hombres, se sacudió en sus cimientos.

La Intervención fue un hecho de trascendencia internacional que obedecía a los designios de Napoleón para extender su poder a América, bajo el pretexto de proteger a la raza latina del avance sajón. Los miembros de la reacción, en contra de toda evidencia, ignorando el espíritu de la época, olvidando las lecciones de su propia historia, se imaginaron que el monarca francés y el archiduque austriaco les servirían de instrumentos para asegurar sus intereses. Los conservadores fueron cogidos por sus propias redes.

Los proyectos de Napoleón no sólo lastimaron a México; hirieron a todo el continente. La cuestión de México se tornó continental. Las simpatías estaban con el gobierno republicano. El pueblo no hizo otra cosa que defender sus derechos y su soberanía. Juárez fue el único hombre capaz de efectuar tamaña empresa.

Maximiliano no satisfizo los anhelos conservadores. Víctima de un engaño y de sus propios compromisos e intereses, desconocía enteramente la índole de la sociedad en medio de la cual se encontraba y todos sus actos políticos, aun los más bien intencionados resultaron desaciertos.

Su sacrificio fue necesario para consolidar la Independencia del país y fue también una fuente de calumnias para México, que mostró al mundo su inquebrantable decisión de mantener sus derechos y su capacidad para conjurar los grandes obstáculos que se oponían a su progreso.

Con el triunfo liberal los intereses del país se unían y se liquidaban las causas de su abatimiento. [12] Después de terminar heroicamente con todos los escollos que habían entorpecido su entrada a la ruta franca de la paz, el orden y el progreso a que aspirara desde el momento de surgir como Estado independiente, México, en opinión de nuestros autores se adentraba en ella con paso firme y seguro.

¿Cabía el porfirismo en esta imagen optimista? La exaltación demagógica de Juárez y de la Constitución de 1857 en el régimen porfirista así lo indican. Es más, el discípulo más notable de Altamirano, Justo Sierra, no sólo reafirmó los puntos de vista de los autores de *México a través de los siglos*, sino que mostró al gobierno de Díaz como centro de acción del orden y el progreso que estos habían anunciado en su obra. [13]

Al derrumbarse la dictadura en 1910, cayó también por tierra esa visión fantástica de nuestra historia, que vista a distancia se nos muestra como expresión y justificación de las aspiraciones y luchas de una clase, que al llegar al poder se sustentaría ideológica y políticamente en el estatismo positivista que garantizaba la permanencia de su triunfo.

[12] O'Gorman en su trabajo "Precedentes y sentido de la Revolución de Ayutla", *Seis ensayos históricos de tema mexicano*. Universidad Veracruzana, Xalapa, 1960, instruye sobre el proceso ideológico de liquidación de la contradicción liberal-conservadora que hizo posible la dictadura. En otros aspectos, no han surgido trabajos tan esclarecedores de este proceso de síntesis.
[13] *Evolución política del pueblo mexicano*. UNAM, 1948.

Con la Revolución de 1910, observa O'Gorman, la definición del
ser mexicano alcanzada por el liberalismo entró en crisis.

Sin embargo pocos autores se han percatado de esa crisis que impone
una nueva perspectiva. Los más siguen la huella trazada por los crea-
dores de *México a través de los siglos*, pero de sus plumas no ha salido,
no digamos una obra comparable en significación a lo que esta obra
fue en su tiempo como ha indicado ya el Dr. O'Gorman: ni siquiera una que supere su contenido general.

POLITICAL HISTORIOGRAPHY
OF THE PORFIRIAN PERIOD
OF MEXICAN HISTORY

LAURENS B. PERRY

This essay will embrace three subjects, corresponding to three sections. The first is almost entirely inspired by the exceptionally important works written and edited by Daniel Cosío Villegas, who has provided me with many pleasurable hours of reading. The second section is a partial listing of unused documentary sources in the city of Mexico useful for the writing of political history in the age of Porfirio Díaz. The third section is a consideration of studies which seem to me to be necessary for better understanding that important period.

I

Political historiography of the Porfirian regime, as we all know, has been characterized by factional studies. If this is true of all Mexican history, the problem has been compounded by additional factors in the case of the *Porfiriato*. First, the epic revolution transformed the Porfirian period into the *Ancien Regime* of Mexican history, attended by all the passions and political propaganda which abound in the wake of true revolution, to the disadvantage of objective analysis. Secondly, Porfirio Díaz and the men who surrounded him are suspended between two sets of patriot-heroes, those of the "Second Independence" and those of the "National Revolution", denegrating the *Porfiriato* and making it less attractive for study. Thirdly, there is some reluctance to enter porfirian historical studies because of the social pressure to support the Revolution. Other factors, such as the wholesale destruction of documents during the revolution, have retarded porfirian studies. This poverty of twentieth century studies has afforded little opportunity to experiment with periodization in nineteenth century political history.

During the last two decades we have been told that Mexico's "Modern History" began in 1867 with the collapse of the Maximilian monarchy and ended in 1911 with the collapse of the porfirian dictatorship. This periodization, although useful for attracting historians to the least studied period of Mexican history since 1810, has as many disadvantages as advantages. The school of historians headed by Daniel Cosío Villegas, who promote this view, then proceed to do violence to periodization by dividing it into the "Restored Republic" and the "Porfiriato". At least they find 1876 so significant a watershed that not only the volumes on political history were proposed to divide there, but so too are the volumes on social and economic history. The major political work covering the first decade of the period was written by Dr. Cosío Villegas himself. [1] The theme of the work is that the principal leaders of the Reform and of the Republican resistance to the French Intervention tried to establish a viable progressive democracy in Mexico, and that the prime obstacle upon which success was shattered was the bastard ambitions of a group of unprincipled militarists, led by Porfirio Díaz. This group sapped the energies of the feeble government, forced the diversion of resources by constant rebellion and terminated the experiment in liberal government by insurrection in 1876. Whether or not the interpretation is valid and it is useful for some purposes —the periodization logically should commence in 1854 and terminate in 1876. Logical with the interpretation, the twenty-two year period was the rise, challenge and fall of the liberal democratic dream. The dramatic tragedy is only opening onto the third act in 1867.

The *Porfiriato* then comprises another period, one that might best be studied as a unit from 1876 to 1914, to the overthrow of the regime of Victoriano Huerta, or even to 1938, the liquidation of the last of the oligarchic forces which characterize *porfirismo*.

Of course, other historians will immediately take issue, insisting that many of the principal *porfiristas* were within the liberal tradition of Juárez and Lerdo, and that the liberal period ended in 1884 or 1888 or even 1900. The frequently held view that Díaz was good for Mexico until about 1900 (he solved, in this view, the perennial problem of militarism, balanced the budget, developed the infrastructure and brought international respect to Mexico) is enhanced by this periodization and shortens the *Ancien Regime* to the first decade of the twentieth century. Revolutionary history then begins about 1900 (Old Regime) or 1908 (open and significant opposition).

José Bravo Ugarte uses a periodization similar to that of Cosío with different results, more caustic and cynical, by stressing other characteristics of the period. [2] He designates the period from 1867 to 1943 as one of constitutional dictatorship —"constitutional" because of the recognition of a supreme law, but "dictatorship" because the law was

[1] Daniel Cosío Villegas, *Historia moderna de México. La república restaurada. La vida política*. México, Editorial Hermes, 1955.

[2] José Bravo Ugarte, *Historia de México*, vol. III (3rd edition, revised). México, Editorial Jus, 1962, pp. 345-346.

not observed in practice. He, too, divides this period into two phases, "personal dictatorship" from 1867 to 1914, and "revolutionary dictatorship" from 1917 to 1943. It is the first phase that is almost coterminous with the periodization of Cosío Villegas. In Ugarte's interpretation Juárez, Lerdo and Díaz were all dictators; the difference was that the regimes of the former two were disorderly and unprogressive and the latter one was orderly and progressive. This is also a useful interpretation, and is internally logical.

Other periodizations of nineteenth century political history immediately come to mind to all of us. The point here is that just as different interpretations of the facts beg different periodization, so too, different periodizations beg different interpretations. I personally have the uneasy feeling that the void in scholarly studies of Mexican history between the dates of 1867 and 1911 was to some important degree a factor for the periodization chosen by the school of historians who gathered around Daniel Cosío Villegas. As great as is the debt which we owe to Cosío Villegas, other historians will best serve the knowledge of history by a continued examination of the periodization they decide to adopt. If in the future 1867 and 1911 are generally accepted as standard divides, the credit will go to the Cosío school for its untiring efforts to convince us, and we shall have abandoned other viable interpretations by default.

Anyone coming to the study of the political history of the porfirian regime understands that he will deal with the works of Daniel Cosío Villegas, although the most important work for the political history of the period will not be written: *Historia moderna de México. El porfiriato. La vida política interior.* * Cosío announced two reasons for his decision to substitute *La vida política exterior* for the former. [3] One seems to me good, the other bad. The inaccessibility of documentation is valid and tragic. We can only hope the situation is temporary and remediable. However, the second reason, that "... about the internal political life of the *Porfiriato* much has been written, ..." [4] is true only

---

* About a month before the Oaxtepec Conference where this paper was presented, but after it was submitted to the organizational committee, don Daniel Cosío Villegas informed me that he had not abandoned the project of the internal political history of the Porfirian period. Therefore, some of the judgments and implications of this *ponencia* are premature. The author offered apologies at the conference and wishes to repeat them here, hoping that his assumptions have caused no inconveniences to anyone.

[3] Daniel Cosío Villegas, *Historia moderna de México. El porfiriato. La vida política exterior.* Primera Parte. México, Editorial Hermes, 1960, pp. XIV-XVI.

[4] *Ibid.*, p. XIV.

of quantity rather than quality. Cosío Villegas himself has said the same. [5] The decision is regretable, however necessary.

A second misfortune resulting from Cosío's abandonment of his original plan is the loss of a final statement by Cosío Villegas concerning Porfirio Díaz as a man, politician and statesman. This is of interest because of the suspicion that a mellowing evolution is discernible in the attitude of Cosío Villegas toward Díaz. This supposed evolution has been discerned for some time and might be accounted for in a number of ways. Has it been the influence of further study? The thought here is that Díaz has slowly advanced in the approbation of Cosío as the latter has come to appreciate the former. If this were true, in no way would it reflect disparingly upon the historian in question.

The implication, however, is that Cosío began his works with a decided prejudice against Díaz. Silvio Zavala noted that Juárez came off better than Díaz in one of Cosío's early works "in part for historic reasons, in part for reasons personal to the author". [6] A second Mexican historian refered in 1956 to Cosío's "notorious *antiporfirismo*", but a third was happy to note that Cosío was escaping his early prejudice. [7] Interestingly, in 1949 Cosío applauded Valadés for escaping the same prejudice in the latter's work on porfirian history. [8] However, it is not possible that Cosío Villegas has found more to approve in Díaz' later career than in his rebel career?

To rephrase: is it not possible for a moderate man who believes that Juárez and Lerdo were trying to reconstruct Mexican political life for the solution of national problems in the image of the liberal program —to despair of Díaz, whose goals and methods ran contrary to the program of the former men? One might disagree that such was the program of Juárez and Lerdo, or even that Cosío has successfully described porfirian goals and methods. Nevertheless, could not the "evolution" seen in Cosío Villegas, and which he sees in Valadés, better be applied to Díaz? Could those historians have been disgusted with

[5] Daniel Cosío Villegas, "El Porfiriato: Su Historiografía o Arte Histórico", *Extremos de América*. México, Tezontle, 1949, pp. 115-147. This excellent essay, followed by 276 titles, is an appraisal of the printed works on the political history of the Porfirian regime and is the best bibliography of the period.
[6] Silvio Zavala, "Cosío Villegas, historiador", *Historia Mexicana*, vol. III, núm. 12 (April-June, 1954), p. 608.
[7] The "second Mexican historian" was José Fuentes Mares, "Sobre la Historia Moderna de México", *Historia Mexicana*, vol. V, núm. 19 (January-March, 1956), p. 464. The author cannot relocate the criticism of the third historian mentioned, and believes it appeared in the Mexican press in the mid-1950's and that it was written by José Bravo Ugarte. If this is inexact, apologies are extended.
[8] Daniel Cosío Villegas, "El Porfirismo: Su historiografía", *Extremos de América*, México, Tezontle, 1949, p. 141. Cosío was remarking about *El Porfirismo* by José C. Valadés. México, vol. I, José Porrúa e Hijos, 1941, vol. II, Editorial Patria, 1947.

Díaz the rebel and later have approved of Díaz the statesman? If so, is the evolution in the historian? Or is it not in Díaz!

Arguing for this proposition is evidence that Cosío early in his career recognized an evolution in Díaz. In 1953 Cosío asked, "How can it be explained that Porfirio, who until 1876 was a simple soldier, a *militarote*, ... was able to transform himself... into a *gobernante extraordinario* (?)"[9] The question is perhaps not the best one. The historian should perhaps have chosen to note and explain why a large and important group of people between 1867 and 1876 thought of Díaz as a *militarote* and then why a large and important group of people years later considered him a *gobernante extraordinario*. Cosío might have asked these questions: How large and important was the group which thought such-and-such a way? Who were those people? Were they the same people in the two periods? How did those beliefs manifest themselves in action? How important were those beliefs in the determination of developments? Who thought differently and what was their source of strength? These and other questions might better have been asked. Nevertheless, the fact that Cosío Villegas was asking when Díaz changed, and what were the influences upon him which caused that change, is indicative that from the beginning of Cosío's career as an historian he recognized an evolution in the person of Díaz.

There is yet another explanation for evolution in porfirian historians. The consideration here is that over the past two decades the Mexican intellectual climate of which Dr. Cosío is a part has perceptively chifted. The shift itself is away from the emotional necessity of justifying the Revolution by denegrating the *Porfiriato*. Certainly the factor of time is important. One has less commitment to the justification of the Revolution if not involved personally; every year fewer Mexican were. A prerequisite for objectivity is the subordination of emotional involvement, which is facilitated by the absence of the need for justification.

A further refinement of the argument for a shift in the intellectual climate of contemporary Mexico might be based upon the belief that the Revolutionary development parallels the development of *porfirismo*. A policy of political concentration and the bringing of all political ambition into a common fold by the rewarding of loyalty and effort through controlled promotion of careers; an early period of international difficulty with problems of recognition, pivoting on foreign debts and privileged foreigners with claims and concessions; a Mexican diplomatic victory in the face of greater foreign power, followed by a period of international good will and cooperation, investment and increasing trade; political problems solved, particularly that of succession, with a change of emphasis to economic development, characterized by low priority

[9] Daniel Cosío Villegas, "Porfirio contra Juárez", *Excelsior*, 14 October 1953.

for widespread distribution; overwhelming financial difficulties followed by budgetary and monetary stability and international credit; a relaxation of tensions between church and state following an earlier period of considerable hostility; recognition of indigenous problems but with hopes placed on a final absorption into the national culture without bold attempts to protect the former; all of this describes both the *Porfiriato* and the Revolutionary period. Should not the present historian note these parallels and reevaluate the *Porfiriato*?

If the early twentieth century historians who were apologetic to *porfirismo* were frank *porfiristas* —men like Salvador Quevedo y Zubieta, Pablo Martínez del Río, Alberto María Carreño, Justo Sierra, Emilio Rabasa— not the same can be said of others. Genaro Fernández MacGregor, José Bravo Ugarte, José C. Valadés, Jorge Fernando Iturribarría, Ángel Taracena —these are more moderate historians, neither claiming for the *Porfiriato* an Augustinian age, nor feeling the need to demonstrate hatred for it. They all weigh and measure —each in his own way; they all find much that is decent and progressive in the pre-revolutionary period. These men are Cosío's contemporaries; he must have respect for some of them; they undoubtably influenced one another. They are part of a new intellectual climate which is neither reactionary nor radically revolutionary. This is the shifting intellectual climate to which an evolution in Cosío Villegas might be accredited.

As for me, however, I think the way to view Cosío Villegas is not primarily as an increasingly more knowledgable historian, nor as an increasingly objective twentieth century revolutionary, but rather as a nineteenth century Juárez liberal. Certainly Cosío was part of the idealistic generation of the Revolution. [10] Nevertheless, the Revolution has many traditions, one of which was the early belief that the ideals of the Reform were alive and about to be effected. The very questions Cosío formulates, "... whether political institutions were consolidated during the Porfiriato"; "Is it possible to respect a law that is not enforced?"; "Can a law which is not enforced remain in force?"; "Can a law which is not enforced someday recover its ascendancy?"; [11] these are the type of question asked by the men at the constituent assembly of 1856-1857, not by the men of the *Partido Revolucionario Institucional*. The age of Porfirio Díaz, like the age of the PRI, is the direct heir of the best and the worst of Mexican history. The values of the

---

[10] Of Cosío's extensive writing, the most autobiographical piece known to me, in which he recalls his revolutionary ardor "to do something for Mexico", is his introductory essay in *Ensayos y Notas*, México, Editorial Hermes, 1966.

[11] Daniel Cosío Villegas, "El porfiriato, era de consolidación", *Historia Mexicana*, vol. XIII, núm. 49 (July-September), p. 85.

Juárez liberals, in whose image Cosío Villegas studies and judges the politics of *porfirismo,* are admirable but limited criteria.

More important than has been the supposed evolution in Cosío Villegas was the real evolution of Juárez Liberalism. The ideals of the Reformers of 1854-1857 suffered two great attacks, the Three Years War and the French Intervention. The composition of Juárez Liberalism was chemically altered by those conflagrations and emerged in 1867 a different compound with tendencies toward different characteristics. Díaz merely carried those tendencies to their final reality: the concentration of power in a single individual, extolling the forms of the constitution of 1857, while controlling substance by dominating the personnel of government. I expect that had Cosío Villegas written the promised detailed story of that political consolidation, he would have acknowledged Díaz as a successful politician, but would nevertheless have judged the system harshly. Not only did it fail to answer the social and economic needs of Mexico, but it violated everything held holy by the Reformers of 1857, which by 1867 was being abandoned by most of the remaining Reformers.

From the beginning of the project which has produced the *Historia moderna de México* critics have discussed the methodology and the sources. There was fear that the team could never synthesize the material researched as well as the individual historian, or that the synthesizing historian would inevitably misuse the *fichas* gathered by the researchers. The fears have been largely unfounded; the project is enormously successful. Error has doubtlessly crept in; a note on a card is used by the synthesizer in a way which he might not have used it had he the whole document before him. A mistake is passed along which the master would have caught. So Díaz is accused of blackmail on page 869 of *La república restaurada. Vida política,* based on a letter Carreño attributed to Díaz. A reading of the whole letter rather than the part quoted by Cosío shows that Díaz was the recipient of the letter, Servando Canales the sender. [12] There are other mistakes, but perhaps fewer than the individual historian makes, and few have I caught in relation to the number of notes I have checked.

My objections are two. First, I regret the system of notations. Cosío felt it necessary to compromise between the full academic notation and the needs of the general reader. [13] My own view is that the

[12] Porfirio Díaz to Servando Canales (sic), 23 March 1876; *Archivo del General Porfirio Díaz, Memorias y Documentos,* Alberto María Carreño, ed., vol. XII, 106-107. Díaz, not Servando, had recently moved his forces and was in a position to march quickly on Matamoros.

[13] Daniel Cosío Villegas, *Historia moderna de México. La república restaurada. La vida política.* México, Hermes, 1953, p. 39.

standard footnote is already a compromise between, on the one hand, repeating whole passages and arguing questions with previous authors directly in the text, and on the other hand, omitting all notation. The collective citation is unusable. The system used in *La Noria*, the time-honored footnote, is far better. [14]

Secondly, the argument for relying so heavily on newspapers in *Vida política* is in my opinion mistaken. Don Daniel argues that newspaper reporting was more reliable during the Restored Republic because "there have never been governors of Mexico more determinedly respect-ful of press liberty than Juárez and Sebastián Lerdo de Tejada". [15] However, the salient feature of the Mexican press during the Restored Republic was not its liberty, but its irresponsible factionalism. That is, although the press was free, that freedom was utilized to beguile the reading public to interpret news in the interest of the politics of each newspaper's owner. Not even reported fact is above suspicion, for the editor's sense of responsibility was not above blantent lie. The saving grace in the work cited is Dr. Cosío's critical use of the press —as a reflection of factionalism rather than as a source of information. The alternative to general confidence in Dr. Cosío's competance and integrity in the use of newspapers is shattering in the extreme, but relative faith may be restored by a comparison of Cosío's section IV, on the insur-rection of Tuxtepec, to the book on the same subject by Ciro B. Ce-ballos. [16] One observes with great relief that archival sources predominate over newspapers in the two fine volumes on foreign affairs. [17] If abandonment of the political history of the *Porfiriato* saved us from an account based largely on newspapers, we can probably sigh with relief.

II. SOME UNUSED MATERIALS USEFUL FOR PORFIRIAN POLITICAL HISTORY IN ARCHIVES OF MEXICO CITY

The following description is the result of a preliminary search which is by no means complete. The hope was to have much more information

[14] Daniel Cosío Villegas, *Porfirio Díaz en la Revuelta de la Noria*, México, Edi-torial Hermes, 1953.

[15] Daniel Cosío Villegas, *Historia moderna de México. La república restaurada. La vida política*. México, Editorial Hermes, 1953, p. 37.

[16] Ciro B. Ceballos, *Aurora y Ocaso, la historia de la revolución de Tuxtepec*, México (publisher not mentioned), 1912. Ceballos despaired so deeply of the press that he frequently printed versions from two capital papers of the same military action, versions which reason can hardly convince one to believe refer to the same events.

[17] Daniel Cosío Villegas, *El porfiriato. La vida política exterior*. Primera Parte. Segunda Parte. México, Editorial Hermes, 1960 and 1963.

available before submitting this paper. However, some archives are in such disorder that even extensive searching has not enabled a report to be made, while conditions of access to others proscribes making a report. As it is, no claim is made that these materials exhaust the possibilities. Indeed, the contrary is true: there is an enormous amount of materials available in Mexico City. Some of it is without organization even in major archives, some well organized and readily available, and some in private collection with limited access. More materials are in private hands awaiting the collector. Hopefully all these materials will soon be collected in adequate depositories, organized, catalogued, made available to historians and described in a single bibliographical guide.

The *Archivo General de la Nación* is the single most important source of materials on the *Porfiriato*. Not yet used thoroughly for porfirian political history, it is rich in both printed primary sources and documents. The former include innumerable political pamphlets, annual reports (*Memorias*) of the various ministries, presidential informes, the congressional debates, proceedings and records of the state governments, budgets, projects, and copies of many kinds of materials from government and private presses. The single most important *ramo* of documents I have surveyed at present is the *Ramo de Gobernación*. The *Ramo de Gobernación* is grouped in 2,041 *legajos*, of which 1,196 are from the porfirian years. A full seventy-eight percent of these pertain to the *Cuerpos Rurales*. Materials in other *legajos* include militia reports, decrees of the national, state and local governments, police reports, budgets, salary schedules, employee registers, government circulars, muster reports of military units, inventories, receipts, records of expenses of various departments, inter-office correspondence, developmental proposals and estimates, lottery reports, election results, correspondence to state officials, sanitation reports, Monte de Piedad records, contracts, etc. A forty-two page typewritten calendar is available in the library of the AGN noting the *legajo* number, the year of the materials and the general subject. Other *ramos* exist which this compiler has not yet consulted.

The Library in the National Museum of Anthropology and History (*Biblioteca Nacional de Antropología e Historia*) is divided into three sections, the collection of books, the microfilm section and the documentary archive, all under the direction of Sr. Antonio Pompa y Pompa. The latter two sections are of interest here. The microfilm section (*Fondo de Microfotografía*, formerly the *Centro de Documentación* housed at Chapultepec Castle) is composed of some 20 to 25 "series", each dedicated to a different topic or region of the republic. Some series are anthropological materials, other historic. Of the historic materials the majority are official and parroquial records from the provinces, and the majority of those are from the colonial period. Collections of provincial newspapers and a few private collections of correspondence and manuscripts complete the microfilmed materials. In the selection of materials to be microfilmed little emphasis was placed on the years after 1876, probably on the assumption that priority had to be given to older materials in the attempt to preserve them from decay. Almost all of the rolls are briefly described in eleven typed calendars arranged by roll number within each series. These *catálogos* total between one and two thousand typed pages. From those pages I have extracted the following register of materials of use for the political history of the *Porfiriato*, which is doubtlessly the least representative period in this collection.

Serie Acolman

> *Rollo* 1497. *Archivo del exconvento de Acolman. Defunciones.* 1881-1913.

Serie Archivo Judicial de Puebla

> *Rollo* 11. *Lista de las causas criminales. Tribunal Supremo de Justicia, juzgado de sentencia.* 1836-1894. *Causas criminales. Relación. Cuadro Sinóptico. Juzgado de sentencia.* Teziutlán. 1893-1894.

> *Rollo* 30. *Inventario en el avalúo de la hacienda de Tres Jahueyes.* 1888.

> *Rollo* 37. A few documents of *Tierras y Aguas.*

> *Rollo* 56. *Impresos oficiales de Puebla.* Including: *Decretos que el gobernador da a conocer a los ciudadanos.* 1881-1882, 1889. *Ley y reglamento del impuesto del timbre sobre bebidas alcohólicas.* 1895. *Memoria que el departamento ejecutivo presenta al XVIII congreso.* 1903.

Serie Archivo de Matías Romero

> *Rollos* 1-72. This is the microfilm of the famous collection housed at the *Banco de México* and forms for porfirian history the most important part of the microfilms of the *Biblioteca Nacional.* The materials include letters, newspaper clips, copies of public documents and even books. Dates range from 1837 to 1900.

Serie Chiapas

Rollo 77. *Archivo Histórico Chiapaneco. Palacio de la Cultura.* Tuxtla Gutiérrez. *Ramo Civil* 1875-1890.

Rollo 78 & 79. Documents from the *Archivo de la Alcaldía de Chiapas.* 1881-1899.

Rollos 82-84. *Ibid. Decretos.* 1877-1898.

Rollo 85. *Memorias del Sargento José María Montesinos.* Ms. 1866-1878.

Rollos 87, 88, 91. Various newspaper collections from Chiapas.

Rollo 96 & 97. San Cristóbal de las Casas. Chiapas. *Libro de Actas de la Cofradía del Santísimo Rosario.* Comitán. 1885. *Defunciones.* 1862-1900.

Rollo 98. *Archivo Parroquial.* Comitán. Chiapas. *Libro de Gobierno de la Parroquia.* 1873-1889.

Rollo 107. Tenejapa, Chiapas. *Archivo Parroquial. Circulares.* 1876-1889.

Serie Guadalajara

Rollo 97. *Colección particular de D. Ricardo Delgado. "Escritos relativos a la persona del Gral. D. Porfirio Díaz".* Ms. Letter from Hilario Frías y Soto to Diputado Francisco Bulnes. 1903.

Rollo 103. *Colección de Acuerdos sobre Bienes de Indígenas y Fundos Legales.* T. IV. 1879.

Rollo 104. *Ibid.* T. VI. 1882. *Noticia Geográfica Estadística del Partido de Sánchez Román. Estado de Zacatecas al Cd. T. de la Cadena.* 1881. A few copies of *Juan Panadero,* a political weekly of Guadalajara. 1871. *"Noticia Geográfica, Estadística y Administrativa del Partido de Juchipila formada por Juan I. Matute".* 1885. Correspondence of Francisco del Paso y Troncoso.

Rollo 115 & 116. *Libro de patentes.* 1853-1925.

Rollo 117. *Apuntes para la Historia del Pueblo de Etzatlán.* Jalisco. By Apolinar Pérez Alonso.

Serie Guatemala, 3ª Serie

Taken from *Secretaría de la Defensa Nacional de México. Archivo Histórico, Estado de Chiapas.*

Rollo 3. Military and political documents of Chiapas, some pertaining to boundary problems with Guatemala. 1856-1885.

Serie Hidalgo

Rollos 7-9. Mostly newspapers from the state of Hidalgo. Some official documents in roll 7.

Serie León

Rollos 43-49. Mostly newspapers from the state of Nuevo León.

Rollos 54-57. Official documents of the state and other reports and manuscripts.

Serie Miscelánea

Rollo 16. *El Lapso más Tormentoso de la Dictadura porfirista.* By Jesús González Monroy. *El porfirismo y la oposición Cananca.* Typescript. Oct. 30, 1965, pp. 538.

Rollo 25. Correspondence of Rufino José Cuervo to Joaquín García Icazbalceta. 1885-1889.

Rollo 27. *Colección de Cuadros Sinópticos de los Pueblos, Haciendas y Ranchos del Estado Libre y Soberano de Oaxaca.* 1883.

Rollo 79. About 600 letters to Pbro. Fortino Hipólito Vera. 1870-1896.

Serie Monterrey

Rollo 1. *Inventarios de la documentación del Archivo Municipal de Monterrey.* 1860-1907.

Rollos 28-38. Newspapers of the day from Monterrey and other northern cities.

Rollos 42 & 43. *Índice del Archivo General del Edo. de Nuevo León.*

1866-1898. 1879-1923. Also: *Archivo del Gral. Francisco Naranjo*, from the *Fondo Alberto Naranjo* in the *Biblioteca Universitaria Alfonso Reyes.* Monterrey. Nuevo León. Letters from 1900-1907.

Rollos 44 & 45. *Ibid.* 1904.

Rollos 46-49. Newspapers.

Rollos 50-54. *Correspondencia del Lic. Genaro Garza García, Gobernador de Nuevo León.* 436 letters. 1865-1878.

Rollos 56-72. *Archivo Jerónimo Treviño*, from the *Biblioteca Universitaria Alfonso Reyes.* Letters from 1865-1872.

Serie Morelia

Rollo 3. Contains some official documents from Michoacán.

Rollos 13 & 14, 16-19. Michoacán newspapers.

Serie Relación de Conflicto Religioso

Rollo 1. *El Catolicismo social en México.* 1903-1911.

Serie San Juan Teotihuacán

Rollos 10-12, 16, 17, 22, 23. Baptisms. Marriages. Burials. 1857-1911.

Serie San Luis Potosí

Rollo 46. *La Unión Democrática*, official newspaper of the state. 1877. *Acta levantada por la guarnición de San Luis Potosí uniéndose al plan de regeneración política reclamada en Guadalajara.* 1876.

Rollo 53. *Archivo Municipal del Río Verde.* 1882. *Libro de Actas. Proyecto original del ferrocarril de Río Verde.* 1882. *Actas del Cabildo Río Verde.* 1876-1890. *Archivo del Juzgado de la primera instancia.*

Rollos 55 & 56. *El Estandarte.* Newspaper of San Luis Potosí. 1885-1893.

Serie Sonora

Rollo 1. *Leyes, Decretos y Reglamentos del Estado de Sonora.* 1884-1899.

Rollos 6-9, 11 & 12. *Documentos para la historia de Sonora, compilados por don Fernando Pesqueira.* 1869-1944.

Rollo 13. *La Estrella de Occidente.* Sonora newspaper.

Rollo 14. Materials concerning the Yaqui War.

Rollos 19 & 20. Materials concerning the Apache campaigns.

Rollo 25. Documents for the history of Sonora. 1857-1882.

Serie Yucatán

Rollo 33. *Archivo de Cabildo de la Ciudad de Mérida. Actas de la Junta patriótica de Mérida.* 1874-1877. *Acuerdos.* 1877-1879.

Rollos 34 & 35. *Copiadores de oficios del Ayuntamiento.* 1879-1882 & 1887. *Acuerdos.* 1880-1887 & 1891.

The second part of the *Biblioteca Nacional de Antropología e Historia* in the *Museo Nacional* of interest to porfirian domestic political history is the documentary archive. Here too, the emphasis lies in colonial history. Only a scattering of materials are of use to the historian of *porfirismo*. From the several collections catalogued in a crossindex card catalogue —including the *Colección Francisco Paso y Troncoso* and the *Colección García de Orozco*— only fifteen items useful to porfirian history emerged from 2,000 cards checked. Another collection merits more attention, the *Correspondencia del Archivo del Ejército de Oriente.* Numbered consecutively, it is composed of two parts, the *Archivo del General Porfirio Díaz,* and the *Archivo del Licenciado Justo Benítez.* The former is composed of 6,739 documents —letters to Porfirio Díaz, with a few *borradores* of outgoing letters, *oficios* and reports. The Justo Benítez collection (2,624 items, numbered 6719-9343) is essentially incoming letters during that period when Lic. Benítez was working for Porfirio Díaz and promoting his career. Both collections are more important for Reform and Intervention history than for the history of either the Restored Republic or the *Porfiriato.* Indeed, only some ten percent of those nearly 10,000 documents are useful for the *Porfiriato, per se,* and probably more than ninety percent of those pertain to the years 1876 and 1877. Nevertheless, the historian interested in the founding of the *Porfiriato* cannot afford to overlook this collection, particularly in view of the important political role played by Lic. Justo Benítez, comparable only to the latter role of Manuel Romero Rubio. A calendar exists for both the Díaz papers and the Benítez papers, giving the document number, the identification of the document (*carta, oficio, minuta, borrador, decreto,* etc.) the author of the document, the recipient and the date. Resumes are included only for manuscripts and odd materials other than the correspondence. Because the order of the documents is chronological only within each *legajo, paquete, sobre* and *carpeta,* and the calendars are included within each group, use of the collection requires opening each of the hundredood packages. The collections may with time expand to include these.

The Documentary Archive of the University of the Americas (also *Archivo Documental de la Universidad de las Americas*) is a newly founded archive having as its purpose the preservation and cataloguing of documents and other research materials for the history of Mexico. Its major holding, and only holding at present for the political history of the *Porfiriato,* is the *Colección General Porfirio Díaz,* the private papers of Porfirio Díaz principally from 1876 to 1915. This is the collection which Dr. Alberto María Carreño began to publish in a selected and annotated form to 1880. (*Archivo del General Porfirio Díaz, memorias y documentos.* México: Editorial Elede, S. A. 30 vols., 1947-1961). On permanent loan to the University of the Americas from the Díaz family, the collection covers 109 meters of shelf space and contains 663,843 items of the following types: letters, almost entirely addressed to Porfirio Díaz, 500,699; telegrams, both incoming and outgoing, 161,275; *copiadores,* bound outgoing correspondence from Porfirio Díaz, 9,000 letters; pamphlets, newspapers, maps, reports, manuscripts and other bound materials, 858; and codes, principally used for telegraphic communications, 228. The entire collection is arranged chronologically, numbered, housed in 1,451 titled archive boxes, in seventy-two *legajos.* The collection is microfilmed —nearly one million frames— on 374 rolls of 16 mm film. The collection is of primary use for three kinds of studies, political history, Díaz family history, and economic history. Two archival tools have been developed for its use, first a 58 page published guide,[18] which identifies the materials in each *legajo* and roll of microfilm by date and number, and which contains an alphabetical table of persons who used the codes; and a 60 page calendar of *legajo* 42 *Folletos y periódicos, de la Colección General Porfirio Díaz* for internal work in the archive. The major tool

[18] Laurens B. Perry, *Inventario y Guía de la Colección General Porfirio Díaz,* México, University of the Americas Press, 1969, 58 pp.

will be the name-place-subject catalogue, which is presently underway, after which the collection will be opened for historical investigation. It should perhaps be noted that there are approximately 10,000 documents covering the period which Carreño published —documents which he did not have— and an unknown number of items in the *Museo de Historia* on the *Plaza Carlos Pacheco* —documents which Carreño excluded from publication after appraising them. We may presume that most of those latter documents were so unimportant that no one will care to look at them, but some of them may be coded letters and telegrams for which codes exist in the *Colección General Porfirio Díaz*.

The *Archivo Histórico del Ex-Ayuntamiento de México*, located on the Zócalo, has a useful and well organized collection of materials. A fifty-two page typewritten guide describes the materials in two sections. The first section is for documents found on the ground floor, which are primarily *Actas de Cabildo* bound in 2,700 volumes in chronological order from 1524 to 1928. The seventy volumes numbered from 208 to 277 refer to the years 1876 to 1911, as well as the fourteen volumes, volumes 316 through 329, entitled *Actas de Cabildo — Originales de Sesiones Secretas*, and nineteen volumes, numbers 393-411, covering the period 1879-1899, *Actas de Cabildo, Índices*. Also on the ground floor are the following: #422, *Índice Alfabético-Cronológico*, 1878; # 514-626, *Actas de Cabildo Borradores*, 1876-1911; # 677-750, *Actas de Cabildo Libros Impresos*, 1879-1903; # 775-841, *Diario Oficial*, 1900-May, 1911; # 1052-1271, *Sub-Dirección de Ramos Municipales - Pólizas y Comprobantes de Ingresos - Egresos*, 1905-1912; #1272-1596, *Dirección General de Obras Públicas*, 1866-1923; and # 1597-2003, and 4660-4662, *Obras Públicas del Distrito Federal*, 1903-1914. The second section of the archive is arranged by subject in alphabetical order in 4,721 bound volumes found on the first, second and third floors of the *Ayuntamiento* building. The guide in the reading room will suffice to indicate to the investigator what subjects are to be found in this magnificent collection. Although this material will be more useful for social and economic history that for purely political history, the political implications of much of the materials will be recognized. The following partial listing will indicate the types of materials available for the *Porfiriato*: # 862-869, elections, 1820-1921; # 2272-2275, innundations, 1714-1903; # 2725-2728, *judiciales*, 1871-1919; # 2730-2737, *jurados criminales*, 1869-1880; # 3649, *incendios*, 1774-1886; # 3676 and 3678-3682, *salubridad-epidemias*, 1879-1915 and 1832-1892; # 4019, *teléfonos*, 1883-1905; # 4020, *telégrafos*, 1857-1916; # 4577-4579, *dirección de aguas*, 1898-1902; # 4586-4589, *actas impresas del cabildo*, 1879, 1880, 1894, 1903; # 4592, *censos*, 1838-1909. Other volumes of documents pertain to vaccination, drainage, beautification, public instruction, slaughterhouses, theaters, parks, markets, etc.

Tantalizing in its potential is the new private archive of Condumex, S. A., under the able directorship of Sr. Juan Luis Mutiozabal V. de L. Called the *Centro de Estudios de Historia de México*, the collection contains both a 20,000 volume library on the history of Mexico, and a documentary archive of some quarter million documents. At present the archive contains materials for the colonial period, the national period to 1867 and the twentieth century after 1911. For the porfirian years the archive has only two research tools, a complete set of *Diario Oficial* and a complete collection of the newspaper *Hijo del Ahuizote*. Thus this archive does not at present hold private or official correspondence from the porfirian period. It is mentioned here to bring to the historian's attention the existence of an active and extremely well organized archive, which may in the future expand its holdings to rectify its lecunae, to mention the newspaper collection, and parhaps to save the porfirian historian valuable investigation time and effort.

III. SUGGESTIONS FOR FUTURE INVESTIGATION

At regular intervals there appears the judgement that a more systematic approach be made to the study of Mexican history, replacing the hit and miss results of current practice.[19] This inevitably means a preference for social, economic and intellectual history over political-military history. I dissent. Even while recognizing the short-term value of the results, I feel that historical investigation must remain the choice of individual scholars. The systematic approach implies a degree of compulsion with a simultaneous loss of intellectual satisfaction, which would be disastrous over the long run. I can do no better than quote the emminant Latin Americanist, France V. Scholes:

> I hope that this Congress recognizes and will assert the right of the individual historian to pursue his labors in his own way and according to his own lights; the right freely to choose his own subject for investigation; the right not to be placed under pressure, direct or indirect, by any agency, private or governmental (including universities); the right to channel his investigations along lines for which funds may be available, without sacrificing research projects of his own preference or choice.[20]

[19] See, for example, the remarks attributed to C. Harvey Gardiner in Robert A. Naylor, "Research Opportunities: Mexico and Central America", *Americas*, 18 (March, 1962), p. 557.
[20] France V. Scholes, "Freedom for the Historian", *The New World Looks at its History: Proceedings of the Second International Congress of Historians of the United States and Mexico*, eds. Archibald R. Lewis and Thomas F. McGann

There are numerous biographical studies yet to be done. One merely need reflect upon the lack of biographical studies of such persons as Protasio Tagle, Justo Benítez, Carlos Pacheco, Luis Mier y Terán, the Baranda brothers, the Díez Gutiérrez brothers, Servando Canales, Felipe Berriozábal, Pablo Macedo, Ignacio Vallarta, to lament the efforts in this genre of historical investigation. Although biographical work has been done on some figures, for example Teodoro Dehesa, Luis Terrazas, Bernardo Reyes, Gerónimo Treviño, Ignacio Mariscal, Manuel Romero Rubio, José Ives Limantour, Ramón Corral, Enrique Creel, and Manuel González, there is still much more to do with these individuals. More has been done with intellectual figures like Ignacio Altamirano, Justo Sierra, Francisco Bulnes, Francisco Paso y Troncoso and Manuel Orozco y Berra than with purely political and military figures. Indeed, it may be said that there is to date no study of a single figure from the political history of the porfirian period, which is adequate by modern historical standards.

Not even Porfirio Díaz himself, whose biographies have formed a life of their own, has received a definitive study. The two best biographies are recent and should be given more attention than has yet been done, those by Jorge Fernando Iturribarría and Ángel Taracena. [21] Also an attractive study, from the point of view of philosophic positivism as applied biography, is the work of Agustín Aragón. [22] These works will be the point of departure for future Díaz biographies, disregarding all others prior to them, with the exception of two or theer still useful works, to be used with care. [23]

A useful study yet to be done of an analytical rather than narrative nature is the study of backgrounds of the many governors, generals, senators, ministers, ambassadors, and deputies of the period. A tabu-

(Austin, University of Texas Press, 1963), pp. 173-183. Reprinted in Lewis Hanke, ed., *History of Latin American Civilization; Sources and Interpretations,* vol. II, Irvine: University of California, 1967, pp. 492-495.

[21] Jorge Fernando Iturribarría, *Porfirio Díaz ante la historia,* México (publisher not mentioned), 1967, and Ángel Taracena, *Porfirio Díaz,* México, Editorial Jus, from the series "Figuras y episodios de la historia de México", núm. 88, 1960. The three volumes by José C. Valadés, cited above, are not exactly biographical, but rank with the very best literature on the period.

[22] Agustín Aragón, *Porfirio Díaz,* 2 vols., México, Editora Intercontinental, 1962.

[23] Francisco Bulnes *El Verdadero Díaz y la Revolución,* México, Eusebio Gómez de la Puente, Editor, 1920 is an *a la Tocqueville* analysis of *porfirismo* as *Ancién Regime.* Rafael de Zayas Enríquez (*Porfirio Díaz,* New York, D. Appleton and Company, 1908) is useful as a contemporary appraisal of political problems in the late *Porfiriato.* If a third standard may be named, the biography by Nemesio García Naranjo (*Porfirio Díaz,* San Antonio, Casa Editorial Lozano, 1930) is still influential and to be consulted, at least partially, because of the author's active opposition to the Madero government.

lation of the political and economic background of some two hundred
of those figures would tell us a great deal about vested interests, of
the "policy of conciliation" and of social mobility in the *Porfiriato*.
The figures might be classified in one correlation as "Maximilian Conservatives", "Juarista Liberals", "Lerdo Liberals", "Iglesistas", "Tuxte-
pecanos", "Gonzalistas", and "New Porfiristas", In what proportions
were they in inner circles of government in 1876? 1880? 1888? 1900?
Did a significant number of them become *hacendados* during the
period? Did they gain advantages by government concessions in banking, industry and commerce? To what extent were they related by
blood ties, marriage and *compadrazgo*? A competent prosopographical
study of this nature carrying over from the Reform Period to the
Porfiriato, relating the early *Porfiriato* to the late *Porfiriato*, and ultimately tying in the late *Porfiriato* to the Revolutionary Period, would
teach us a great deal about oligarchy, political dictatorship, and even
about revolution.

Election studies, particularly on the local level, need to be written.
The object should not only be to determine the degree of corruption
and fraud, but also to understand local issues and local factions, how
those issues and factional struggles were used for the benefit of the
regime, and whether systematically or sporadically. Who voted, who
were the opposition candidates, what were their connections with the
ruling oligarchy and what did they do thereafter; these questions need
answers and will have bearing on special interests and political stability When returns of this kind of study are in, useful comparative
studies can be made with other countries and with other periods of
Mexican history, such as twentieth century Mexican revolutionary
history.

Documents recently published in the Mexican press by Ángel Taracena concerning incidents of land distribution in the *Porfiriato*, attempts
by Díaz to curb the rapacity of *hacendados* and examples of reprimand-
ing cruelty to *hacienda* peons and communal Indians must be examined at length. [24] It is important to learn if the porfirian regime in the
last years was losing *hacendado* support, as did the Spanish regime and
the Maximilian regime in their last days.

An area of investigation urgently needing study is the process of
government, its structure, its administration, its internal movement,
the relationships between branches of government and between departments, the working of pressure groups, the formation of public
opinion, and all the other concerns of the political scientist. That
procedural practice did not reflect the constitution will make the study

[24] See, for example, Ángel Taracena, "Otra Carta de don Porfirio en defensa
del campesino mexicano", *Sol de México*, 8 February 1969.

difficult. However, much material is already available in memoir literature, contemporary and later criticisms, and in proposals for reform. Thus the historian of governmental procedure need not start from scratch, but the material must be collected, organized, analyzed and supported with archival study. Perhaps the most certain beliefs we hold are only true for one phase of a continual evolutionary process. Perhaps we will be suprised by the similarities between porfirian governmental practices and those of former and more recent times.

A vital study for our understanding of the *Porfiriato*, one done by the legal historian, is the sifting and analyzing of court cases. The bald statement that the judiciary was used to reward the supporters of the regime and was completely dominated by the president of the nation must be authenticated or modified by careful investigations. The ramifications of such a study will only be known once the project is underway, but may be great indeed.

These are some of the areas which occur to me. Every historian will be able to think of others, perhaps parallel to studies done for other times and places. Frequently these investigations are of even greater value in comparative studies. Again I suggest that the most interesting comparative studies might be between porfirian and Revolutionary Mexico, but comparative studies with other contemporaneous societies would do a great deal to place the *Porfiriato* in perspective.

MEXICAN POLITICAL HISTORIOGRAPHY, 1959-1969

The building and uses of power still fascinate historians of Mexico. Despite the calls for attention to economic, social, and intellectual history, political history remains our favorite enterprise. We go on telling time here by how a government goes.

My purpose is to discuss the work on Mexican political history since the meeting in Austin in 1958. I do not intend to deliver a bibliographical essay, there already being several such essays with passages on politics. [1] (We need more essays, focussed on specific questions. But those that we now have are good guides.) Nor will I comment on popular history, vulgarization in the French sense, because I think that by now our work is professional, that in intent and in practice professional history is different from popular history, and that our primary obligation in a meeting of professionals is the evaluation of how we have done. Nor will I confine my discussion to the work of younger historians. This would have an interesting point: presumably their work is least familiar in the field and yet of most potential effect there, since they may reshape the lay of the intellectual land during the next generation; we would like to see now what their ideas on political history are. The difficulty is in deciding which historians are young. Most of us juniors and seniors have behaved as if we were still in the 1920's as if we had never heard that we should study several languages, linguistics, sociology, law, statistics, geography, theology, economics, philosophy, ecclesiology, demography, or political science, as if we could not imagine revisions. What I will try in this discussion is simply to determine the character of the professional political history of the last decade, to clarify its main accomplishments and its main problems.

The literature is now considerable. As a body it has grown much larger than it was 10 years ago, when we had little to recommend to scholars in other fields who wanted to read in ours, and even less to recommend to scholars in other sections of our own field, in the

---

[1] See the articles by Stanley R. Ross and Luis González y González in the *Handbook of Latin American Studies*, Nos. 23, 24, 25, 26, 28, and 30. See also Martín Quirarte, "Historia Política: Siglo xix", *Historia Mexicana*, xv, 2-3 (October 1965-March 1966), 408-424; and Stanley R. Ross, "Historia Política: La Revolución", *Historia Mexicana*, xv, 2-3 (October 1965-March 1966), 425-433, and "Introduction" and "Additional Readings" in *Is the Mexican Revolution Dead?* (New York, 1966), 3-34, 247-255.

economic or social history of Mexico, who wanted to read about the politics of their periods. By various criteria 60 to 100 books on Mexican political history appeared in the last decade in Mexico, the United States, Great Britain, and France, not to mention eight or 10 documentary collections, 60 to 80 articles in professional journals, and probably 40 or 50 doctoral dissertations. If this is small compared to the work on American or European political history, it is nevertheless a great growth in our field.

The reasons for the surge in the production of political history are, I think, clear. Several major political anniversaries occurred in Mexico in the 1960's —the fiftieth anniversaries of the Maderista, the Zapatista, and the Constitutionalist revolutions, the Sovereign Revolutionary Convention, and the Constitutional Convention, and the hundredth anniversary of the French Intervention— each creating a market for books in the events celebrated, each giving Mexican authors a chance to publish, and Mexican publishers a chance to sell. Also the United States government took a special interest in Mexico during the last decade, in part because of the general American worry over the effects of the Cuban revolution in Latin America, but in particular because of the official desire to show that serious revolutions (Mexico's being the prime example) could take place "democratically", as the official phrase went, without help from the Russians, it meant. This was good advertising, though bad history, and in the allotment of new American resources for the study of Latin America it enabled us Americans interested in the historical disposition of power in Mexico to seize a good share of the money, jobs, and time for research. (I must insist on our independence from Camelot that our work has been free of official dictation, that our insights and mistakes have been our own, that as historians we have not cared to prove the "preferability" of the Mexican Revolution but only the truth about it as we see it, and that as historians we have hardly propagated the myth of American benevolence here.) But most important for the increased production was the professional work already established in the field during the previous decade, the work that we could depend on, the work out of which our work could grow. [2] Without this basis, without its professional sobriety and integrity, we could not have produced much of value. The Mexican volumes for the anniversaries would have been only merchandise, and the American volumes on the Revolution would have been only propaganda for the Alliance for Progress. Because the field was already

---

[2] For the previously established work, see Carlos Bosch García, *Guía de instituciones que cultivan la historia de América* (México, 1959), and Robert A. Potash, "Historiography of Mexico since 1821", *Hispanic American Historical Review*, XL, 3 (August 1960), 383-424.

respectable 10 years ago, we have been able to produce the respectable growth of the last decade.

As a body the recent writing on Mexican political history is traditional in style, which is in part a new development. I do not mean that it has all come out of the same school, or that it has all gone along the same lines of interpretation, for it has been a literature of diversity, not to say disparity. Nor do I mean that its arguments have not been original, or that its conclusions have not been novel, for in fact it has also been a literature of discovery. But I do mean that as a body it fits the traditional canon of political history. Let me note two of its traditional features. One is the assumption, which is new, that the political history of Mexico is a comprehensible question — comprehensible because, the assumption now is, life in Mexico in no period has been just chaos, irrational and absurd, but has always been a series of patterns, usually obscure but sometimes definite, anyway accessible to our understanding; and a question because life in Mexico, the assumption is, has not been a mere automatic evolution but rather a struggle that has taken surprising turns that require our investigation. (The reason for the new development is still in the dark, but I would guess that it results from the new sense of maturity in contemporary Mexico.) On the assumption that our work is on a comprehensible question we have sorted ourselves out from the popular historians, who alone go on treating periods of the past as chaos.

The other traditional feature of our recent writing that I would note is the assumption, a classical one, which we inherited and have carried on, that politics in Mexico (and elsewhere) is a formal activity —that the study of politics is the study of government, or of institutions and individuals that have directly to do with government. With rare exceptions we have studied power here when it has taken territorial shape and partaken of sovereignty, and rather ignored it in its other, vaguer moments, in families, for instance, or in business, or the Church, which we leave for the anthropologists to study.

Broken down into categories of coverage, the literature is very irregular. During the last decade there were no professional attempts at a grand synthesis of the politics of the whole national epoch, which I take as a sign of wisdom in our profession, a recognition that no one, however ambitious, is yet capable of dominating all the new and old monographs. There were scattered books on specific matters running through the whole epoch, like Turner's on nationalism or García Cantú's on conservatism, but they did not impose a new organization on our section of the field. There were also a few general boks, like Bravo Ugarte's or Cumberland's but they did not reorganize our section either.

As for the differing coverage of different political periods within the national epoch, the period getting most coverage was still the Great

Revolution of 1910-20 —especially the years from 1910 to 1915. There was only one professional attempt at a synthesis of the Revolution, that of Valadés, a massive and admirable enterprise but (I think) nevertheless dubious. It was actually more a multi-volume monograph then a synthesis; when synthetic organization did take hold, it was too stiff, and the data got loose again. Valadés's rambling through the Revolution evoked the Revolutionary experience, as his earlier command of the Porfiriato evoked the Porfirian experience. But no more in history than in other arts do the aesthetics of imitation convey conviction.

The normal approach to the revolution was still explicitly monographic —the study of specific phases or movements or men, more or less to the neglect of other issues. As in a blunt fashion this was the approach of the popular historians of the Instituto Nacional de Estudios Históricos, so in a sophisticated fashion it was the approach of professional historians —Mexicans like Amaya C. writing on the Revolutionary Convention or Valadés writing on Madero, and Americans like Blaisdell writing on the Magonistas in Baja California, Clendenen on Villa and the United States, Michael Meyer on Orozco, Quirk on the Revolutionary Convention and on the American Intervention in Veracruz, Sherman and Greenleaf on Huerta, and me on the Zapatistas; in the same sophisticated fashion it was also the approach of Calvert to the Anglo-American involvement in the Revolution, and Katz in his chapters on the German involvement.

This approach, I think, is still the best for us. For though we now have many monographs on the Revolution, we need several more before we can make a good case about it. What, for instance, did the industrial working class do from 1910 to 1920, both the organized and the unorganized workers? Reference to the Casa del Obrero Mundial and the Red Battalions is not enough. We need to know if workers themselves ever tried to seize a factory or a mine and manage it as their own, if their strikes were often political, if the workers of one industry were more political than those of another, and if so why, for economic or ideological or other reasons —all this and much more we need to know, in order to say whether industrial workers made a difference in the disposition of power during the Revolution, or even tried to make a difference. And what about monographs on Carranza's government preconstitutional and constitutional, or the Constitutional Convention, or the Revolutionary governments in certain states like Oaxaca or Sonora or Tamaulipas? The suggestion of these and other new topics for research can plunge us into manic depression —so much to do, too much to do. Even the episode most studied so far, the Sovereign Revolutionary Convention, needs more analysis. The first national assembly of revolutionary characters, stacked with licenciados but still in its composition the most popular of all the national revolutionary conventions, rowdy and confused, much more deeply soaked in popular hopes and fears than the Constitutional Convention, it was the closest that plain Mexicans came to deciding how they wanted Mexico to be. With the documents that Barrera Flores has collected, we can now get a sense of what they thought their revolution was and what they tried to make it. But the analysis is still there to do.

Saying which of the other periods received most coverage during the last decade is difficult, depending on whether we call a pamphlet a volume. The French Intervention and the Mexican Resistance certainly had much treatment, again wisely (I think) in monographs. But the treatment was not as extensive or as good as it should have been. The publications from the Historical Section of the Mexican Society of Geography and Statistics are, I think, almost all disappointments. More helpful are the collection of essays on the Intervention published by the Instituto Francés de América Latina, the book by Dabbs on the French Army in Mexico, the volumes of French documents that Lilia Díaz collected, the works on Juárez and Zaragoza, and the sets of documents that de la Torre Villar is now having published. But we still need monographs on how the Resistance operated locally, not only in military but also in political terms, how Juárez even in El Paso del Norte and even in a political crisis could retain authority over loyal Republicans throughout the country, how the Republican army redeveloped after its initial collapse, and so on. Most of all we still need a study of the most interesting episode during the Intervention, which is the Mexican Collaboration. No doubt this is a sore spot in Mexican history, which explains why we hesitate to touch it, but the fact is that many honorable Mexicans collaborated with the French and served the Emperor Maximilian —probably in severe tension but nevertheless respectful of a foreign solution to their country's misery. About this episode we still have only the foggiest notions. But we cannot understand Mexican political history before 1863 or after 1867 unless we understand the politics of the years in between. There is one recent piece of exciting writing on the Intervention, a seminal essay that may generate a comprehension of the Resistance and the Collaboration, the essay by Chevalier on the sociology of Liberalism and Conservatism. If Chevalier's earlier piece on Zapatismo put agrarian movements in a context explaining Mexico's social history in the 19th century, then this piece on Liberals and Conservatives may put the Intervention in a context explaining Mexico's political history in the 19th century.

The period since around 1920 also had much coverage, in syntheses and in monographs. Most of the work was that of political scientists, economists, and sociologists, not that of political historians. Most of the interest was in how systems, institutions, and agencies function, not in how they developed. In this work there was a tacit admission that the explanation of a function requires a brief relation of its development, but the purpose was still to satisfy the curiosity of political scientists, economists, and sociologists, not the curiosity of political historians. The work of these specialists in other fields remains important to us, however; some of them showed better historical imagination than we historians did. It honors us to discuss their work together with our own.

The syntheses were impressive. The arguments of Brandenburg, Cline, González Casanova, Padgett, and Scott, with their different emphases on lobbies, mobility, presidentialism, elites, marginality, are now a regular school for political historians. We have here nothing comparable to the arguments on American or European politics. But we do at last have a serious debate going on, informed as never before and in intelligent control as never before. Therefore we may expect more precise and more persuasive syntheses and more pertinent monographs.

The monographs, without anniversaries to concentrate them, varied widely in focus and in quality. They ranged from González Navarro's thorough and thoughtful study of agrarian organizations and Wionczek's fine study of economic nationalism down to Millon's indefensible hagiography of Lombardo Toledano, from Bazant's careful chapters on the foreign debt and Lorenzo Meyer's excellent book on the struggle over oil down to Dulles's credulous chronicle. Most of the monographs were sound productions but not strong enough to change the shape of the field —Ashby's book on Cárdenas and the CTM, Brothers's and Solís's on official financing, Cancian's on Indian villagers, Cronon's on Ambassador Daniels, Lieuwen's on militarism, Moore's on official financial institutions, Olivera Sedano's on the Cristeros, Orive Alba's on irrigation, Ruiz's on education, Schmitt's on the Communist movement, and Shafer's on planning, to mention a few stout examples, and Ezcurdia's book on the PRI, Kling's on Monterrey lobbies, and Morton's on female suffrage, to mention a few thin examples. In this middling range I think the most interesting effort was Wilkie's, on federal budgets and expenditures. The book had a tremendous impact; it is important for the study of Mexican political history. That the analysis had faults —the easy reliance on official statistics (without research, difficult but not impossible, into the economic conditions during the period), the mechanical identification of ideology with spending (without taking politics into account), the brief glance at inflation (without making allowances for its different effects on different items of budgeting and spending), the practical supposition of Mexico's fiscal autonomy (without locating the country in shifting international currents) —this does not lessen the book's importance. Simply to note that it will move us into serious research on Mexico's central government is to indicate the strength of its contribution to our field.

The monographs we still need on this period are numerous. Topics obviously waiting for treatment for 20 years remain virgin. At least we can wonder where the histories are of the Labor party, the Vasconcelista movement, the PNR-PRM-PRI, and the several federal elections, and where the biographies are of all the ranking politicians. The plea that entry into private archives of the period is difficult, often out of the question, does not convince me. I wonder then why we have not consulted archives we could have entered, or even public records like those that political historians of other countries have put to good use.

Attracting less coverage during the last decade was the Porfiriato, and that again in monographs. For this period the professional work was mainly in three volumes on Mexico's international politics, the two magnificent productions of Cosío Villegas on Porfirian foreign relations with Central America and with the United States, and the rich study by Katz on the German relations with Mexico. Here we have major refinements in our knowledge. But the recent treatments of Porfirian domestic politics were few and more puzzling than enlightening. Bernstein, despite his promise, hardly helped us to understand the politics behind Porfirian mining legislation. Cockcroft, although he provided much interesting information about the opposition centered in San Luis Potosí, hardly explained why the dictator tolerated its appearance or how young sycophants of his could have joined it. Gutiérrez Santos, absorbed in the defeats of the Porfirian army, hardly outlined its construction. Lemus, who reanimated the animated Bulnes, hardly deciphered his odd political career. Niemeyer, concentrating on Bernardo Reyes as the public man, hardly revealed to us the *presidenciable*.

Again we need many more monographs —especially on institutions, both formal (Congress, the jefatura política, the Law School, the Judiciary, the rural police, the army, the press, the rural school, the state governorship and legislature, the Ministries), and informal (the científico clique, the Porfirista circles, the Jockey Club, the groups in opposition, the foreign colonies), to mention only a few examples. These studies I think we need more than biographies, which are liable in this period, I think, to distort our image of how the structure of power developed. Now that Díaz's archive is open, it is incumbent upon us to do justice to the man and the age we have named for him.

Even skimpier was the recent coverage of what I would call the period of the Bourbon Republic, from 1821 to 1854. But the coverage, in a synthesis and in a few monographs, was high in quality. (Why this is so, and whether we should devise a motto —the less the better —I cannot say. But I would guess that we should not flaunt a poverty of aspiration.) The synthesis was Hale's work on Mora and the age

he called the Age of Liberalism. It is, I think, another important book
for the study of Mexican political history, nicely organizing its period.
Though ist main argument on Liberalism was not original, Tena Ramírez having already advanced a similar thesis, and though the implication
was wrong that Mora cast as much weight in political action as in
political thought, the book did give an analysis of Liberalism that
explained its appeal and its frustrations —not only in Mora's time but
in the times after him. If disagreements will inevitably persist about
the period, at least we now have terms in which to debate them.
Another attempt at synthesis, that of Reyes Heroles, did not (I think)
succeed, falling between mere exposition of Liberal positions and mere
assertion of Liberal cogency. The monographs have been among the
best in the field —Costeloe's neat study of the Church as a financial
agency, Potash's superb book on the Banco de Avío, and Reyes Heroles's sharp essays on Mora, Otero, and Zavala. Again our cry is for more
monographs —on the masonic clubs, the cathedral chapters, the semi-
naries, the officer corps, the institutos, the familial connections among
Liberals and Conservatives and between Liberals and Conservatives, the
politics of strategic states, and so on. Our hope is only that the high
standards now established for this period do not collapse in the new
research and writing.

On the Reforma and the Restored Republic, after the flurry of anniversary volumes in the 1950's the coverage during the last decade
was scanty. The publication of documents (like the Comonfort papers)
is a valuable service we all appreciate, but it is only the commencement
of our task. With all the primary and secondary materials that have
been available for the study of these periods, we should have several
new syntheses and monographs to discuss. But we have only a few,
like Fuentes Mares's, "welcome additions", as we say in reviews, but
no great shakes in the field. Most embarrassing is that we do not even
know what the political continuity was between the Reforma and the
Restored Republic. The legend is that the first climaxed in the second,
but without the monographs we still cannot say *en cristiano* what the
climax amounted to in terms of power.

Almost all our recent work has painfully conspicuous shortcomings.
It has suffered from our traditional assumption from the classics that
politics is governance. This formalism is snobbery, and it has impaired
our professional vision. We know that manifold relations of power have
existed in Mexico besides those between the government and the
governed, that formal politics is only one kind of politics, and that
politics is only one kind of social action, yet generally we have persisted
in researching and writing as if we could understand formal power
without understanding social power. Few among us resemble the model
described in the preface to a recent book on 19th-century European
politics, the scholar who proceeds "not as a political scientist with a

penchant for history but as a social historian interested in perceiving
how change in governamental and political institutions affects and
expresses social change". [3] Because we have remained traditionalists
in defining Mexican politics, we have missed seeing it as a theme in
Mexican social history. Our work has also suffered from our acceptance
of the established periods, 1821 to 1854, 1854 to 1876 to 1910, and so
on (not to raise questions about how long the Revolution lasted). This
rigidity has cramped us badly. We know that the history of power
does not start and stop like tenure in office, yet generally we have
hesitated to listen again to the past's political rhythms. Because we
have heard the same old beat, we have danced the same old steps. The
worst shortcoming that our work has suffered, I think, has been our
astonishing failure to try a comparative method. We know that for
two generations historians working on European countries have taken
for granted that they should make comparisons, yet generally we have
gone on as if we could rightly interpret Mexican political history
without keeping in mind that Mexico is in Latin America. The result
is that we have often misconstrued local or national developments of
power in only local or national terms, ignorant of the fact that they
were local or national versions of continental developments requiring
interpretation in continental terms. Because we have studied only
Mexico, we have learned less about Mexico.

All this production during the last decade is nevertheless a substantial
accomplishment. Given the inherent difficulties of the field, the still
relatively few men regularly researching and writing on political history,
and the still relatively scarce resources to subsidize them, we have
consolidated the professional temper of our work and dutifully extended
its application through layer upon layer of rhetoric to all the recognized
periods of power in the Republic's history. Our shortcomings, I think,
are not very worrisome. Once we are aware of them, we can correct
them. And in time, I imagine, we and the historians wetrain may move
—not in legions, because no one would support so sizable an army of
scholars here, but at least as the point-men for squads— to study power
in Mexico in its social dimensions, to define new periods for telling
time in the country's political history, and to place the country in the
continental context where it belongs. Then we could conceive of
questions we cannot dream of now. At the moment we can only record
the limited but fairly solid and promising advances that we have made.

Imbedded in this accomplishment are problems much more dangerous for us than simple shortcomings in conception and method. They
are philosophical problems of history, which, unless we understand
them, will impede our work and sap our confidence that we can do

[3] Eugene N. and Pauline R. Anderson, *Political Institutions and Social Change
in Continental Europe in the Ninettenth Century* (Berkeley, 1967), VII.

better. Mexican political historiography as a whole is now in a state of analysis like that of medieval European historiography two generations ago, when Marc Bloch wrote that " 'analysis' can only be transformed into 'synthesis' if it has had the latter in view from the beginning and has been deliberately designed to serve that purpose". [4] Unless we understand the philosophical problems of designing historical analysis for historical synthesis and of turning analysis into synthesis, we will soon find ourselves in the most frustrating debates.

The problems express themselves in certain contradictory mistakes that we often make. One is to treat episodes happening at one moment in Mexico's past as no more than preparation for other episodes happening at a later moment in the country's past, as if we meant that the first episodes had happened so that the second could happen. This is the mistake of "precursorism", the Latin American counterpart of the notion now current in the United States that all history is the history of modernization, both mistakes being variants of what I learned from my teachers to call "the Whig interpretation of history". I am not arguing generally that history is not in the great chain of being, "the seamless web", as we are fond of saying when we cannot explain how a change happened. Nor am I arguing in particular that some men did not try and fail at ventures that other men later tried and succeeded at. Granting that time is coherent and that men do carry on heritages, I am arguing that the past has a right to our professional respect —that as professionals we are under the obligation of seeing how men made history as they really and bravely made it, without knowing beforehand how it would turn out.

Let me cite a couple examples, to show that "precursorism" infects our explanations of not just one period but the whole epoch. (I will not cite the most blatant example, the official argument that Mexican governments represent the Revolution of 1910, as if Madero had revolted to the cry —"On November 20, 1910, let us become the precursors of the PRI!" Take our ideas on Liberals and Conservatives in the 19th century, from the 1820's through the 1860's. Without professionally argued evidence we still write as if the gomezfaristas of 1833 were embryonic puros of 1856, who were themselves homuncular juaristas of 1865, and as if Lucas Alamán were the natural father of Juan Nepomuceno Almonte. We should at least wonder whether the developments within the parties amounted only to crystalizations of already established patterns, and whether the conflict between the parties was the same in the 1860's as in the 1850's, or in the 1830's. This is not necessarily to imply that partisan traditions were weak, or that new generations developed new disputes. But maybe the terms of Mexican

[4] Marc Bloch, *Land and Work in Medieval Europe, Selected Papers* (New York, 1969), 72.

political development did change profoundly from 1821 to 1867. Actually we do not know.

Take for another example our ideas on the opposition to Díaz from around 1900 to around 1910, in paricular Cockcroft's recent book on the Liberal clubs. Here is the word itself —the growing opposition among young intellectuals in the 1890's and early 1900's was the action of "precursors", whose cause the Maderistas took as their own, which cause the Zapatistas and the Constitutionalists took as their own, so that is finally flowered in the Constitution of 1917. I doubt that this conveys much sense of what really happened. I am not denying the courage of those who spoke out against dictatorship and even organized clubs to act on their feelings, nor am I denying their claim on us to remember them in respect. I am also not denying that in the Liberal clubs many young men learned to think programmatically about free politics, social welfare, and national pride, nor am I denying that individuals who were Liberals in 1901 or 1906 werer later Maderistas and Constitutionalists. What I do deny is that the connection of the facts is easy, that it is like a flow of water from one spring through one channel to the sea. We cannot imagine Ricardo Flores Magón and his cohorts saying, "Let's oppose Don Porfirio so that we can get new articles 3, 27, and 123 in a new constitution in 1917". We cannot even imagine them saying, "Let's oppose Don Porfirio so that what will happen from 1910 to 1920 will happen". But this is what treating the Liberals as "precursors" boils down to. To treat the past as a series of precursory events is to lose the sense of the past as it was for the people who lived it —a series of difficult presents, one difficult present after another.

Another mistake we often make, contradictory to "precursorism" but born of the same philosophical problems, is to treat one period as radically different from periods before and after it, as if the codes of living and understanding were entirely different from one period to the next. This is the mistake of "age-ism". Certainly "times do change" in México, as elsewhere. Certainly there have been stages and periods in Mexican political history, and logically therefore differences between them. And certainly the political alterations from one period to the next have been great. But it is not certain that the essential patterns of one age are thoroughly different from those of another age, that time cracks when one age ends and another age begins.

Let me again cite a couple examples, again to show the variety of the mistake. Take the 1920's. They were the first years of the new revolutionary age, the new nationalist state, the new political organization of the masses. But were not the men then politically active in the new republic all products matured in the Porfiriato? Consciously or unconsciously did they not revive many old habits of political thought and action, bred into them during the Porfiriato? In this perspective, despite official declarations of socialism, is the official encouragement of capitalism so bizarre? I am not arguing that Mexico in 1926 had not changed from 1906, but only that the change was a matter of elaboration as well as a matter of revolution, that the nature of the change was not simple but complicated and subtle.

Take the Porfiriato for a more familiar example. Supposedly in 1876 a radical change occurred in Mexico, separating the Age of the Republicans from the Age of Don Porfirio and bringing in the científico theory and practice of politics. Certainly the Mexico of 1892 was quite different from the Mexico of 1872, not least in the prevailing political attitudes and procedures, in particular because of the científicos' rise into national authority. But did Mexico not become what is was in 1892 with the full participation of many old republicans, who made the country into a place where the científicos could rise into authority? If the change was radical, how do we explain Carlos Pacheco, heroic republican soldier, rich porfirista minister, patron of science in agriculture and industry —all before the científico entry into national authority? Was not the Republic a premonition of the Porfiriato?

These contradictory mistakes of "precursorism" and "age-ism" derive from another mistake we often make —which is to mistake the explanations of social science for the explanations of historiography. Both social scientists and historians study processes, a modern concern with movement distinct from the ancient concern with great deeds. But the process the social scientist studies is operational, whereas the process the historian studies is after all chronological. Linguistically the work of explaining an operation is distinct from the work of explaining a chronology. The essence of social scientific explanations is timelessness, its essential categories being regularity and universality. Its paradigm is a law. The essence of historical explanation is time, its essential categories being endurance and change. Its paradigm is a narrative. As we have to our credit learned the tricks of social science, we have to our confusion tried to treat history as social science in time —as social science factored through time. This is a gross mistake, to confuse categories, to confound explanatory laws and explanatory narratives. Tire is the condition of history, not a factor in it, which is an image leaking into history from mathematics and eroding our sense of what we professionally should be doing. The mistakes in our language reveal the problems of our field. Time in itself does not, as we often write, make a political difficulty easier or harder. Time only tells —who did make the difficulty easier or harder.

It is beyond me here to go into the dialectics of induction and deduction, the dispute between methodological individualists and methodological socialists, or the contention between the idealist proponents of "understanding" and the materialist proponents of "explanation"; on this I will only recommend a recent book by Arthur C. Danto analyzing the philosophy of history. [5] But let me cite one example of how the mistake of confusing social science with historiography has affected our work. The example is an essay that I think is exciting and seminal but loaded with a problem, Chevalier's essay on Liberalism and Conservatism. What we as political historians want is an essay in political history —the definition of the historical subject, a discovery of its origin, an account of its development, and a conclusion about it at a moment manifestly crucial to it, with maybe an epilogue suggesting its subsequent fate. What we have instead from Chevalier, as he subtitles it, is "An Essay in Political Sociology and Geography". In fine French style it broaches the political history for a illuminating sketch of the social origins of both parties, their geographical distribution around the country, and the local clans into which they organized for action. But it does not continue into political history, to trace the parties' developments, to explain their chronologies. What we as historians miss is the narrative —of how the escoceses became the centralists, the mochos, the greens, and the monarchists, if they did, and how the yorkinos became the federalists, the puros, the reds, and the republicans, if they did. This precisely it is the historian's obligation to produce. But this precisely it ruptures the social scientist to produce. The instinct to tell a story to explain what happened is, I think, the mark of the profession we now belong to —the legitimate ground of its vitality after two and a half millenia, the inexhaustible source of its insights. The search for factors to balance an equation is a response to another calling. Until we clarify the claims on us, we will hardly get out of the debate whether time is continuous or discontinuous and into the stories where time is our element.

These mistakes all derive, I think, from a problem of meaning in Mexican political historiography that still afflicts us. It is not that we merely disagree about what it means to say, for instance, that Lucas Alamán was conservative, nor that we merely disagree about what it means to say, for another instance, that Cárdenas was an agent of reform. It is also not that we grandly disagree on whether the meaning of all Mexican political history is a meaning we cheer or deplore. For light on these problems of meaning, which I cannot now give, I can only recommend close reading of the essays in Gardiner's book on theories of history. [6] Our problem of meaning is rather immediate, in that generally we have not yet recognized what we want to mean in our section of the field. If the paradigm of a historical explanation is a narrative, a story meaningful not only because it hangs together, from the beginning through the middle to the end, but also because it has a role in a big story, a transcending creation, then our problem is that

[5] Arthur C. Danto, *Analytical Philosophy of History*. Cambridge, 1968.
[6] Patrick Gardiner, ed., *Theories of History*. Glencoe, 1959.

we often do not know what the stories are that we want professionally to tell.

We have an excuse for why we do not know what we want to mean, for why we do not know what stories we want to tell. It is that we feel we do not know for sure what the big stories are that our stories would fit into. This is because the biggest story for us, the story of the Great Revolution of 1910-20, is not only a story of the result of the politics of the last century, which is political history, our professional concern, but also a story of the origin of the politics of the present century, and by implication a judgment of the present government, which is political criticism, not our professional concern. The classic exercise of scholarship is to make a hypothesis to explain why the big story turned out as it did, then tentatively fill in the data, then mark the incredible leaps in the explanation, then re-make the hypothesis. But in Mexican political historiography the exercise is still suspect, because the very declaration that the big story has or has not turned out for us to make hypotheses about rings not like scholarship but like politics. In Mexico the present still seeps back into the past, and the past up into the present, like blood through a bandage. Let me cite a final example. I would argue now that after all the popular strain and sacrifice the meaning of the Great Revolution is that it issued in the regime prevailing since the 1940's, which itself issued in the government that massacred the citizens in Tlatelolco Plaza in October 1968. My position, I would admit, has political implications. Suppose a colleague argued instead that the meaning of the Great Revolution is that it issued in a workers' resort in Oaxtepec. His position, I would insist, is implicitly political too. But suppose that another colleague argued instead that the meaning of the Great Revolution is still at issue because the Revolution itself is still at issue, that neither the griefs of Tlatelolco nor the delights of Oaxtepec are warrant for drawing conclusions, that the meaning of the Revolution will come clear only when the Revolution triumphs. His position, I would insist, is no less political. The history of power that we try to make sense of depends inevitably on a criticism of power that we try to steer away from.

But there is a resolution of this problem of meaning, and of the derivative mistakes and confusion. It lies not in logic or in time, but, I think, in a new trust in the profession we have made. It is to argue our cases about the past regardless of their political import in the present, on the faith that our profession can stand our contentions and prejudices and even blend them into moments of the truth. Now that we are professionals, we can count on each other to do responsible work in professional terms without worrying about its import in other terms. We can count on each other to take our explanations, our big stories and our little stories, with regard only to their quality, without suspicion of their politics —as citizens of a democracy take each other's opinion "for what it's worth" without suspicion of treason. We can count on each other to write history, not briefs of indictment or defense. Trusting in our profession, we may improve our practice.

COMENTARIO

RAFAEL SEGOVIA

De las ponencias presentadas parece derivar un cierto acuerdo sobre el tema de la historia política. El poder, su formación, distribución, ejercicio, etcétera, es el campo de estudio de esta historia adjetivada.

Salta de inmediato una primera objeción: ¿hay posibilidad de historiar un campo previamente acotado del pasado o, por el contrario, éste forma un todo tan estrechamente interrelacionado que toda división sólo conduce a oscurecerlo? Aceptemos la posibilidad de aislar un fenómeno —el poder— para mejor observarlo, analizarlo, y explicarlo. En esto nos encontraríamos con la incapacidad de marcar el límite inferior, el dintel donde se origina el poder. Segunda objeción que, de hecho, invalida la primera "concesión" —la posibilidad de estudiar el poder como un fenómeno analíticamente aislado. Extender el estudio hacia unas raíces lleva indefectiblemente a salirse del campo de la historia política para entrar de lleno en otros: historia social, económica, cultural, etcétera, con lo que volveríamos a toparnos con la unicidad de todo fenómeno histórico. Problema bizantino, si se quiere, pero sólo soluble si se acepta previamente una filosofía de la historia capaz de jerarquizar los hechos estudiados y de explicar los cambios originados en un sector de estudio de la historia —económica, pongamos por caso—, u otro —la política, pongamos también por caso. Lo que sí no se encuentra en ninguna parte es la filosofía de la historia —o ideología, no importa la palabra— subyacente o manifiesta en los historiadores: éstos siguen obstinados en ver una garantía de seguridad en los fenómenos estudiados, como si la garantía jerárquica se desprendiera de ellos sin más esfuerzo ni trabajo que observarlos.

Otras filosofías de la historia o ideologías repercuten directamente en la metodología: quien vea en la historia "mi interpretación Whig" acudirá a la transposición de los métodos de la ciencia política —y sobre todo de la sociología política— al pasado. Al escribir su *The structure of politics at the accession of George III*, S. Lewis no hacía sino implantar —con su genio inefable, hasta hoy no igualado los métodos de A. Siegfried y Charles a un tema histórico. Admitamos que este tipo de corriente —el estudio de la modernización de las sociedades— es hoy absolutamente dominante o casi y, por ello, no es extraño que los sociólogos lo encuentren en México.

COMMENTARY

ALBERT MICHAELS

Although the terms, political history or political historiography, feature in the title of this session and both papers, I am relatively disturbed that neither author has bothered to clearly define his own meaning of political history. Professor Perry avoids the problem completely; Professor Womack often refers to "power", "study of government", and "historical disposition of power in Mexico", without clearly trying to show *where political history might end and economic and social history might begin*. Although both authors might believe an attempt to define these terms either impossible or counterproductive in relation to space and time, the lack of clear definition limited the overall coherence of both these papers.

My own approach would have been to confront the problem by dividing Mexican political history into two blocs, the Marxist or materialist, and the traditional. The historian following the materialist approach seeks to establish the relationship between political history and the social and economic interests of its participants. He would argue the impossibility of understanding the political activities of a power oriented group without a thorough understanding of their economic interests. (Professor Womack shows perception of the importance of this interrelationship in his brilliant study of the Morelos aristocracy on the eve of the Revolution and in his brief allusion to the importance of the connections between formal power and social power.) The traditionalist on the other hand usually sees the political process occurring in a more pluralistic context often independent of social and economic motivations; thus the leaders or the parties act more from a desire for power or for purely personal reasons rather than to gain, or protect, vested economic or social interests. This latter approach has often led historians of Mexico to view the De la Huerta rebellion, the Escobar rebellion, or the Calles-Cárdenas split purely in terms of the political ambitions of the individual participants without trying to relate their activities to contemporary social and economic developments. This methodology limits the validity of some of the important North American and Mexican work on the Mexican Revolution; such as the general Studies by Parkes, Valadés, Taracena, and Tucker and the political monographs by Meyer, Blaisdell, Ashby, Dulles, and numerous Mexican historians.

Although most historians of Mexico might desire to establish a closer identification of economic and social power with the political they face staggering problems in doing so. In Mexico where most important politicians describe themselves as "Revolutionaries" the records of financial holdings of public figures are not open to public scrutiny. This leaves us with the problem of trying to use the meagerest of evidence to explain the economic motivation and class bias of political leaders. Such superficial evidence as a villa in the Lomas de Chapultepec or a ranch in Michoacán do not prove corruption or even great wealth. Furthermore, many Mexican leaders have certainly acquired their wealth legitimately after leaving office; there would be no justice in citing possessions often obtained after political power was lost. Yet recently both Womack and Cockroft have shown the results of imaginatively applying available economic information to political developments.

Professor Womack has pointed out the vast number of articles, books, dissertations, and documentary collections on Mexican political history which have appeared in the last decade, yet he chooses only to discuss a handful, mainly the better known books and one article. Obviously, he could not have read all of these but I would have been interested to have seen more of an attempt to bring some of the better articles and dissertations into his general discussion. Most important, I came to realize my own ignorance of the volume of this work and was struck by the urgent professional need for a working bibliography of Mexican history, including purely economic, social and foreign policy studies as well as history.

Both Perry and Womack call for a reexamination of the current periodization used in Mexican history and try to suggest refinements. Both also discuss the need for more studies comparing Mexican developments to those in other societies. However, neither paper convinces me that we presently have the depth of quality monographs that might allow us to attempt such refinements or comparisons. A case in point is the period after 1920 of which we know so little. Professor Perry suggests that "the oligarchic forces which characterized Porfirismo lasted until 1939". Given our knowledge of recent Mexican history such a suggestion seems premature. We have much to do before such suggestions can be proved or seriously discussed. Most of our reperiodizations or comparisons would have to be based on general works which, despite their high quality, still rest upon a bedrock of insufficient monographic material.

Perhaps the setting of priorities for future research is the most urgent task confronting us. Whatever our approach to history, whatever our goals in studying Mexico, we should try to define the most urgent tasks to be completed in the next decade. Perhaps we might stop studying Woodrow Wilson's foreign policy and the oil controversy and get down to studying Mexico's perplexing internal problems and institutional growth. Such priorities coming out of a meeting such as ours might help to avoid the duplication and wasted effort that has characterized some of our work. Professor Perry has capably suggested some possibilities for the Porfirian period. Professor Womack has concentrated on the 1910-1920 period in which he has done most of his work. Rather than duplicate or even discuss these suggestions, I will try to point out some important gaps in our knowledge of Mexican history concentrating on the 1920 to 1940 period; the decades most neglected by those currently interested in Mexican political history.

One task of immediate importance would be a close examination of the many evidences of social protest, armed or otherwise, which occurred far more often after 1867 than we once realized; such a study might begin with the movement around Manuel Lozada in Nayarit and include the Yaqui revolt in Sonora, the Caste Wars in Yucatán, various agrarian revolts, the Liberal party, social catholicism, and Maderismo. With such a study we could then better judge Professor Chevalier's contention that the Zapata uprising in Morelos "was an explosion in a critical zone of the deep social disorder whose more noteworthy manifestations had been banditry... and above all the most uninterrupted succession of peasant and indigenous insurrections based essentially on agrarian issues". If Chevalier's thesis depicting the Porfiriato as a time of dynamic tension proves correct, we will no longer see the 1876-1910 period as a necessary respite connecting two violent anarchical eras. Perhaps we might then look elsewhere than Madero and the events of 1910 for the Revolution's starting point. Already Cockcroft, Wilkie and Womack have clearly shown Madero as a social conservative concerned mainly with political reform. Could not the real Revolution have begin with Lozada in the 1860's or Zapata in 1912?

The political historians with an interest in computers can have a vital role to play in making the Revolution more comprehensible to us. The important post-Revolutionary positions, national, regional, and local, can be isolated and those officials who held them can be listed. A team of researchers could then compile short biographies of at least some of those men as to birthplace, background, and career during and following the Revolution. The biographical information could be fed into a computed and the results would surely help to correlate the relationship between changes in the executive with individual political mobility, the regional basis of important power groups and the importance or lack of importance of the age differential in various governments. Perhaps this study would show us who really has ruled twentieth century Mexico. Professor Wilkie has tested the ideology of the Revolutionary governments by examining the federal budgets, but nobody has tested changes in personnel. I expect that the results might show us that Mexican politics particularly between 1920 and 1933 were more than a game of musical chairs.

Womack's excellent historical analysis of recent works of the period between 1910 and 1920 needs little elaboration. Yet there are some important possibilities which he has not mentioned. A study of the movement around Pancho Villa similar to Womack's study of Zapata would be extremely instructive. Particularly valuable would be a survey of Chihuahua on the eve of the Revolution with a special emphasis on the expansion of the vast estates of the Terrazas family. Another important contribution might be a study of Carrancismo between 1914 and 1920; at the present we know little about the "First Chief", his ideas, his relationship with his followers, and the true configurations of the power groupings which he apparently cleverly manipulated. Finally, one might cover Múgica and Blanco's attempt to carry out agrarian reform in Tamaulipas; Múgica's experience there might have colored his future career and the advice he later gave to Lázaro Cárdenas. Many other important political problems (in the Revolution's first decade) have not been studied but the gaps in the next twenty years really define the depths of our lack of knowledge of revolutionary Mexico.

At present we lack even one good political monograph on the 1920-1940 period. The best work, Lyle Brown's study of Lázaro Cárdenas and his manipulation of power, still remains unpublished. Both authors bemoan the lack of political biographies of prominent Mexican leaders. Although such studies appear non-existent, what seems more urgent is not to write biographies but to identify if possible the political movements of the 1920's and decide how, if at all, they differed from one another. Once these movements have been clearly defined, they must then be studied as to social composition, objectives, and reasons for success or failure. Surveys such as these will help us to better explain the differences, if there are any, between the movements represented by Carranza, Obregón, Calles, De la Huerta, Escobar, Vasconcelos and Cárdenas. We must also decide whether the struggle for power between 1921 and 1933 was purely political and personal as Dulles implies or whether the often bloody disputes of these years signified a deep ideological or social split in the so-called Revolutionary family. Such a deduction might clarify the enigmatic role played by Plutarco Elías Calles who I believe showed a greater ideological consistency throughout his long career than many of his critics have yet suggested.

The role of the church in the 1920's and 1930's also remains largely unresolved. After an intensive study of the many polemics of these years one can not easily decide whether the bishops and their lay supporters really believed that the government threatened the church's existence or whether they hoped to use the constitution's anti-clerical laws as a pretext for a conflict which would cause a North American intervention and a counterrevolution. Another possibility often suggested is that Calles and Obregón frequently used the danger of church opposition to the government as an excuse for curtailing social reform. An examination of church leadership during these years might help us to more fully understand the relationship between social background and clerical resistance to the Revolution; it might also suggest that an important turnover in clerical leadership helped account for the church-state detente arranged under the government of Lázaro Cárdenas. The Cristero rebellion has been the subject of several monographs but we still know little of the socio-economic background of the Cristeros themselves. We could in addition formulate a study comparing Cristero leadership and ideology with that of the Sinarquistas to better understand the variety of Catholic opposition to the Revolution.

Álvaro Obregón's death in 1928 ushered in one of the most confusing periods in Mexico's political history. The only coverage of these years is in a few memoirs and the narrations by Taracena, Valadés and Dulles. These inform us about day by day events but shed little light on the realities of power. They do not help us to understand the extent of Plutarco Elías Calles' rule over Mexico or anything about his relationship with CROM, Portes Gil, Ortiz Rubio and Rodríguez. More important, no historian economic, or otherwise, has fully evaluated the full effect of the World Depression upon Mexico. Without such analysis how can we entirely understand the economic factors limiting political and social action and the desire for change wich clearly influenced the rise of Cárdenas to the presidency. Finally, what can be concluded from Cárdenas' nomination in 1933? Does this nomination show us that Calles power has been overestimated or that he made a wrong calculation in thinking that Cárdenas would be a malleable puppet?

Cárdenas' political period is somewhat more completely covered in several dissertations and it will be shortly covered by a book of essays by Brown, Wilkie, and Michaels. However, today we have little easily obtainable information of the political struggle of the 1934-1940 era. Books by Millon and Ashby cover labor-government relations but both lack profound analysis. Lieuwen's chapter on civil-military relations adds little to the earlier work of Virginia Prewett. We still do not understand the economic and social implications of the Calles-Cárdenas split, the reason for the quixotic Cedillo rebellion, the forces around Almazán and Ávila Camacho, and the 1931 Shift of the Revolution to the right. We know Cárdenas expropriated much of Mexico's land, but we have little idea of who owned the land and how they obtained it during earlier administrations. With so much unanswered in what is probably the Revolution's pivotal period how can we even begin to speak of historical synthesis?

Local political history, above all, has been the most sadly neglected. What little that does exist has been the result of local historians trying to glorify their home towns or states and in the mostly superficial volumes stemming from the Instituto Nacional de Estudios Históricos de la Revolución. Although we lack the resources, human and financial, to study every state or region throughout the Revolution, we can research particular problems in order to better comprehend certain important problems already touched on in this discussion. Michoacán, from 1921 to 1933 is the scene of events and personalities whose influence spread far beyond the states borders. Pascual Ortiz Rubio, Francisco Múgica, Lázaro Cárdenas, Benigno Serratos, Gildardo Magaña all interact within the state. Múgica's struggle with Ortiz Rubio explains much about the eclipse of the former and the latter's rise to the presidency; it also helps us understand the methods by which Álvaro Obregón so successfully ruled Mexico. In 1926 Lázaro Cárdenas as governor of Michoacán began a series of reforms that in many ways anticipated the national changes he initiated in mid 1930. He also acted as a lodestone for many young radicals seeking refuge from the government's increasing conservatism after 1929. Calles later replaced Cárdenas with the more conservative Serratos raising important questions about both Cárdenas-Calles relations prior to 1933 and Cárdenas' eventual rise to the presidency.

Another example of a state which served as a stage for events and personalities that far transcended its overall political importance is Yucatán. Both Salvador Alvarado and Felipe Carillo Puerto carried out important reforms supposedly benefiting the states' impoverished Maya Indians; yet the latter had to wait for the visit of Cárdenas to Yucatán in 1937 before they actually received their lands. A study of this area would enlighten us to the interesting careers of both Carillo Puerto and Alvarado but more significant it would show how a small group of wealthy landowners worked to successfully thwart social justice despite articulate local radical leadership.

A study of Tabasco under Tomás Garrido Canabal also might deepen our understanding of Mexico's revolutionary process. The controversial caudillo apparently neglected or abused agrarian reform while he terrorized the Catholics. He entered the government under Cárdenas but appeared to remain loyal to Calles thus losing his baliwick in 1935. A history of his rule would divulge the relationship between agrarian reform and anti-clericalism as well as the diversity of those around Calles. Garrido's relationship with Archbishop Pascual Díaz also raises questions about the Cristero rebellion and the churchman who negotiated the truce.

Finally, a study of San Luis Potosí after the revolutino would be of the utmost importance: First we could use Professor Cockcroft's study to compare the states social and economic structure before and after the Revolution. Second, we then could understand the rise and fall of Saturnino Cedillo whose history has meaning for Caudillismo and its role in the Revolution, agrarianism, Cárdenas' rise to the Presidency, and the church-state conflict. Third, by tracing developments in the state we would need to examine the roles played by Aurelio Manrique and Graciano Sánchez in their attempt to promulgate agrarian reform and political democracy in their home state. These suggestions of the inherent possibilities in the state and regional history are hardly exhaustive. Any of these studies could for example be related to Dr. Wilkie's poverty index to help us explain the lag in the economic development of certain states. It is certain however that if we are ever to understand power, both formal and social, in Mexico, we must know more about what was going on outside Mexico City.

I agree with Professor Womack that we historians of Mexico have made great progress in the past ten years. An impressive number of monographs has appeared along with articles, document collections, and dissertations. Yet too much still remains to be done. Perhaps it is now time for our better scholars to stop compiling overviews of the modern period and concentrate on less impressive but more needed in-depth studies of specific situations. Perhaps we must also stop allowing graduate students to persist in studying United States —Mexican relations and direct them towards Mexico's neglected internal history. Finally, many of us must stop narrating the struggle for power in México as solely a personalistic rivalry between ambitious politicians and begin to investigate the social, economic, and ideological factors which underly these rivalries. Yet here too we must avoid the temptation of attributing all political action to selfish economic motives. After all, man's actions are usually complex and traditional narrative must not be replaced by Marxist polemic.

COMMENTARY

NETTIE LEE BENSON

The papers by Dr. John Womack and Dr. Laurens Perry offer us various suggestions for continued investigation as well as additional information on archival sources which need study and analysis.

Dr. Perry seems to attribute the current periodization of Mexican history of the middle nineteenth and early twentieth centuries to those historians gathered around Cosío Villegas. But, in fact, this form of periodization was used long before Cosío Villegas entered the field, and debate over periodization will continue as long as historians write. Periodization will always depend largely on the knowledge and interest of each individual historian. It is more a useful tool for a beginning or ending of a study than a limit that can be finally established. Many historians would periodize the rural police as of the period of the Porfiriato, but a careful study by Paul J. Vanderwood shows that this institution did not begin with Porfirio Díaz or close with his departure from the scene. Doubtless a careful study of the *jefe político* would reveal a similar story. To place the period of the Mexican independence struggle between 1808 and 1821 is just as unsatisfactory. Periodization will always depend on varied factors since political history is a continuous matter and does not begin and end on set dates.

Te most surprising statement in Dr. Perry's paper is that Cosío Villegas stated that he did not intend to write the political history of 1876-1910. Nowhere have I been able to find that Cosío Villegas ever thought of not writing the political history of the Porfiriato. In fact, he has been writing this very history for the past several years, has already completed some 2200 pages of it and hopes to send the completed work to the press before the end of this year. What Cosío Villegas really said was that he would not complete the political history until after the work on the economic, social and diplomatic history of the Porfiriato was available. Thus he would be able to write far more intelligently the political history of those years.

Based on the false assumption that Cosío Villegas did not intend to write this political history, Dr. Perry attempts to explaint the decision on the basis of a change in attitude of Cosío toward Díaz *. Cosío Villegas, like any true historian, is the first to admit that as he has learned more and more of the period, his concept of Díaz has changed and developed and never has he considered that this change reflects in any way upon him as a historian.

The second part of Dr. Perry's paper dealing with materials for Porfirian political history in archives of México City is useful to those not already aware of this material. It might be indicated here that Cosío Villegas has been aware of this material as well as of other archival material that needs careful study and analysis. He would like to see the Archivo de Limantour, which still exist and is in the hands of the Iturbes and the musician Limantour, the Archivo de Manuel González presently in the hands of the sons of Dr. Fernando González Montesinos and the Papeles de Rosendo Pineda once possessed by Aurelio Manrique and now in the hands of José Valadés made available for study in order that an even more complete appraisal of the Porfiriato can be made. The Archivo de Iglesias in the Archivo General de la Nación needs to be made more readily available through a guide to it. Also before the final story is written, the papers and archives of other men —both Díaz's supporters and opponents— need to be located and made available.

Dr. Womack's analysis of Mexican political historiography for the period 1959-1969 is a useful evaluation of the accomplishments of historians in those years. His suggestions for future investigation are also valuable. Especially welcome is his comment that "life in Mexico in no period has been just chaos", for the frequently held assumption that life between 1821 and 1857 was chaos has tended to drive historians away from a study of those years or has caused them to rely almost exclusively for their study or analysis on the limited printed materials produced largely by participants in the events of that time. Because of this mistaken assumption we still lack sound monographic studies based on the wealth of archival material available for the writing of a good history of those years. In the same way that the composition and work of the revolutionary congresses of the twentieth century require more study, the many congresses and conventions of the early nineteenth century —their composition, operation, failures and successes— must be studied along with the activities of the other institutions and events of that time —epidemics, natural calamities and economic and social developments. To date little basic monographic material is available.

RELATORÍA

JORGE JUFRESA

La sesión se inició con la evaluación de la producción historiográfica profesional publicada durante la década de los 60. Se reconoció el valor del trabajo de otros historiadores realizado antes del periodo revisado, como base para el incremento en el volumen y refinamiento en la calidad de la nueva producción. Sin embargo se estuvo de acuerdo en que una comprensión cabal de la historia política mexicana dependía del estudio de algunas lagunas todavía notables. Los participantes advirtieron que, por su relevancia, las épocas de la Intervención Francesa y la Revolución de 1910, así como el estudio de sus héroes, atrajo casi todo el interés de los investigadores, quedando el Porfiriato y el periodo posrevolucionario escasamente atendidos. Por otra parte algunos consideraron que se advierte una presión para sostener los estudios sobre la Revolución, lo cual dificulta el estudio de periodos aparentemente olvidados. A pesar de esto se manifestó una preferencia sobre la monografía más que en la síntesis, porque, se dijo, "aún no estamos en posibilidad de manejar todo el material".

En relación con la periodización de la historia mexicana se estableció que, si bien algunas divisiones de la historia sirven para ciertos propósitos historiográficos y didácticos, en cambio violentan muchas veces la realidad. Por esta razón varios participantes consideraron que debería examinarse la continuidad y discontinuidad en los periodos con más cautela.

El debate sobre la consulta de nuevos depósitos documentales provocó interesantes intervenciones. Se llamó la atención sobre la falta de exploración extensiva e intensiva por desconocimiento o negligencia de algunas fuentes y acervos. Se criticó, en particular, la actitud de la excesiva custodia del archivo del general Porfirio Díaz por limitar el acceso a muy pocos investigadores.

X. PROBLEMAS COMUNES EN LA INVESTIGACIÓN HISTÓRICA EN MÉXICO Y LOS ESTADOS UNIDOS

PONENCIAS

"Problems of a Northamerican Scholar Working in Mexican History." Marvin D. Bernstein

"Archivos, bibliotecas e historiadores." Romeo Flores Caballero

COMENTARIOS

Woodrow Borah
Howard F. Cline
J. Ignacio Rubio Mañé

RELATORÍA

Victoria Lerner

5 de noviembre de 1969

Presidente: Roberto Burr, profesor e investigador de la Universidad de California, Los Ángeles, en ausencia de la doctora Nettie Lee Benson, directora de la Colección Latinoamericana; Biblioteca de la Universidad de Texas.

Ponentes: Romeo Flores Caballero, profesor e investigador de El Colegio de México; Marvin D. Bernstein, profesor asociado de ciencias sociales, Universidad del Estado de Nueva York, Fredonia.

Comentaristas: Ernesto de la Torre, director de la Biblioteca Nacional de México; J.Ignacio Rubio Mañé, director del Archivo General de la Nación; Howard F. Cline, The Hispanic Foundation, Biblioteca del Congreso, Washington; Woodrow Borah, profesor de historia, Universidad de California, Berkeley.

Participantes: Carlos Bosch García, profesor de historia, Facultad de Filosofía y Letras UNAM; Robert Burr, Universidad de California, Los Ángeles; William S. Coker, Universidad de West Florida; Josefina V. de Knauth, profesora e investigadora de El Colegio de México; Eugenia Meyer, investigadora del Departamento de Investigaciones Históricas. INAH; Juan Luis Mutiozábal, director del Centro de Estudios de Historia de México de Condumex, S. A.; David Trask, Universidad del Estado de Nueva York, Stony Brook; Berta Ulloa, investigadora de El Colegio de México; Paul Vanderwood, profesor asistente, San Diego State College; John Womack, instructor, Universidad de Harvard.

Relator: Victoria Lerner, estudiante del Centro de Estudios Históricos de El Colegio de México.

PROBLEMS OF A NORTHAMERICAN SCHOLAR
WORKING IN MEXICAN HISTORY

MARVIN D. BERNSTEIN

For many years a saying has been current in Mexico: "Poor Mexico: so far from God and so close to the United States." While I would not venture to pass judgement on Mexico's proximity to the Almighty, its nearness to the United States certainly has affected northamerican historians. Only a decade ago the late George Boehrer complained that the professional Brazilianists in the United States could hold their national convention in a telephone booth; it has been a long time since the same could be said of Mexicanists. A recent survey indicated that about half of the United States scholars working in the field of Latin American history consider the study of some aspect of Mexican history as their specialty. In fact, when the number of professional and amateur northamerican historians interested in Mexico was small enough to meet in a telephone booth, that useful structure had not yet been invented. As a result of the northamerican's long-term interest in Mexican affairs, there are impressive resources and facilities —material and human— available in the United States for the study of Mexico. As for the future, one scholar at the University of Buffalo has broached the idea, and even organized a conference to explore the possibility of having a consortium formed by the major research libraries of the United States to microfilm in their entireity every public archive in Latin America. The cost of the project staggered the assembled librarians more than it did the scholar who had received numerous foundation grants.

When first asked to comment on the problems encountered by those engaged in historical research on Mexican topics, I was highly tempted to begin with the problems which haunted me in my formative years: How do you order scrambeld eggs in a Mexican restaurant and not end up with an omelette? And where do you stay on a short-term basis with a bed whose mattress will be kind to soft gringo bones at a rent which will be kind to a graduate student's wallet? For the man working on the United States side of the border, southern cooking —Florida or Texas style— or the more imaginative California salads can pose as great a threat to his well-being as the "Aztec Revenge". Like Karl Marx's boils —to which are attributed many of the more acerbic passages in *Das Kapital*— damnable living conditions can be a major problem for the historian. But enough of everyday matters; let us turn our attention to more professional problems which the historian faces in undertaking research in Mexican history.

In the matter of northeamerican scholars, the graduate school experience is, in the majority of cases, the key to a man's life. In fact, I would venture a guess that the three to five or more years of concentrated research, study, and writing necessary for the typical Ph. D. dissertation and its conversion into a publishable book would constitute a major fraction of many men's scholarly lives. There is, of course, the college or university professor carryin on research as part of his adopted or compulsive life's work and pattern; and there is the teacher plugging away under the spur of publish-or-perish or its variant, publish-and-prosper. But it is the Ph. D. candidates who constitute half, if not more, of those men actively working on a Mexican history topic in the United State or in Mexico itself. Heaven knows, each summer Mexico is covered with a swarm of would-be Bancrofts and Boltons armed with the names of their dissertation directors as their entree to the sacred precincts.

On the positive side, and helping to alleviate so many problems that researchers have had in the past, we are finding that the preparation of predoctoral researchers in the United States has improved tremendously in the last two decades. Young men interested in Mexican history now speak as well as read Spanish fluently in addition to a working konwledge of Portuguese or even Nahuatl. They are prepared in some of the other social sciences as well as history; they read Mexican novels and are interested in politics and art and the culture in general of both modern and prehistoric Mexico. They are better prepared in historical methodology and critical methods, and they do not start their work with H. H. Bancroft and Lucas Alamán as basic sources. In fact, historiographical surveys and analyses by Potash, Ross and Meyer introduce him to the field of historical writing in Mexico. The day of the *alles*, the universal Latin Americanist, equally at home in colonial Argentina or 19th century Santo Domingo is over, and well-trained Mexicanists have taken over.

But the profession has neglected some facets of these young scholars' professional preparation for we have not helped these eager and often extremely bright young men find themselves as scholarly personalities nor have we introduced them to some of the mysteries and idiosyncracies of the organization of their chosen field of study. Their topics, while interesting, are shot-gun like scatterings of interests. Some reflect their director's biases and interests —and many of them have tied their futures to this omniscient man for reasons that are far from rational. For many other graduate students, sheer happenstance determines whether he writs a dissertation on Punta Arenas or Nogales.

Indeed, the choice of a topic is no small matter for in many cases the topic itself can ease the way in finding financing, building a bibliography, securing research materials, and gaining entree to the necessary archives and private collections of materials. For some men, in major research centers, virtually any topic can gain financial support and secure materials. However, men in smaller institutions and younger Ph. Ds. would do well in selcting a topic with great care and foret-hought.

Lodged in my memory is the anecdote of the young man who met Lion Feuchwanger, the German novelist, and said that he too would like to be a novelist, but he could not think up any plots. The older man assured him that detail should not stop him from pursuing his ambition since is had not deterred so many others. At times I am moved to think that perhaps the object of writing history is to fill blank pages, and the object of historical research is to find *any* unex-plored corner and bring some light to bear upon it. (The lantern, however, should be filled with oil purchased with foundation money.) In short, it is impossible to pontificate on intellectual freedom and arrive at the conclusion that given a policy of laissez faire in the choice of topics a sort of invisible hand will guide us to the greatest benefit for all mankind and the best of all possible worlds. In the end, not only will researchers be more highly motivated and better trained thereby in their profession, but that in time the whole of history will be illumined.

The older professors guiding large numbers of graduate students in Latin American history did not follow consistent patterns: some had plans, of sorts, for their students' topics while others appeared to give their students a freer hand. Herbert Eugene Bolton wrote and inspired a series of works on Spain and Mexico in the American Southwest which systematized this fascinating period in New World history and spawned a school wihch, aided and abetted by ancestor-seekers, is fecund even in the third generation. Charles Wilson Hackett directed several dozen of his students into the field of biography resulting in over a score of studies of Mexican leaders of the early nineteenth century. On the other hand, while the late Professor Frank Tannen-baum, one of the leading Mexicanists of his time, trained and inspired many excellent Latin Americanists, his students ranged almost helter-skelter over the entire specturm of the region's history from urban growth in Brazil to the ill-fated Francisco Madero, to use a grab-sample. Professor Clarence Haring similarly guided students whose work ranged from Las Casas to Yucatan textile mills and from the origins of Argentine federalism and Argentine foreign relations to the Mexican Revolution. Under this system of freedom of choice men have unearthed numerous neglected facets of Mexican history to con-tribute to the never completed mosaic.

Certainly the history of every nation is an unfinished mosaic in that certain important events have not been thoroughly researched, or new sources force a re-writing of established expositions, or new viewpoints are borrowed from the other social sciences, or some bright, hard-working historian stops following the leader and asks new questions of the material which yields new interpretations.

An attack on the unorganized state of research in Latin American topics is now in progress. The disorganization can be documented. Howard F. Cline in his anthology *Latin American History: Essays on its Study and Teaching, 1898-1965* has conveniently gathered —with footnotes to yet other such studies— discussions of the random scattering of a goodly portion of northamerican research. Several of the papers reprinted here decry the past pattern of topics chosen and fields neglected and indicate the topics which in the opinion of the leaders of the profession in the United States should be researched.

It ought to be recognized that fashions change in the study of history; certain topics such as Mexican militarism and certain historical periods become more popular, for example the Mexican Revolution and Agrarian Reform because of its "Golden Anniversay" and the outbreak of social unrest in many other countries, or newer types of investigations which are capturing the imagination of historians such as computerized quantitative research and economic time-series. Apparently cross-fertilization with social sciences is the latest order of the day with projects being mounted to study history and regional development, economics and political interpretation, history and the miltary, history and government finance, history and political leadership (holigarchical, military and radical), and history and the black problem. Historians of the pre-columbian, colonial and modern periods have eagerly embraced the social sciences, and only those of the first century of independent national Mexico have still remained more orthodox, although the Díaz period is now yielding to multidisciplinary attacks.

To help the investigator through the maze of conflicting attractions, several studies have appeared to aid the puzzled historian. The list of guides to "research opportunities" in the history of the individual Latin American nations is now quite formidable, and Dr. Cline is to be thanked for collecting so many of them in previously his mentioned book, *Latin American History*. The Joint Committee of Latin American Studies of the Social Science Research Council and the American Council of Learned Societies has published two volumes, *Social Science Research on Latin America* (1964) and *Social Science Research in Latin America* (1967) which are filled with suggestions. The introductory essays in the annual *Hanbook of Latin American Studies* and the excellent seminal articles in the *Latin American Research Review* are replete with leads. In addition, the running inventory of research in the LARR and the United States State Department's *External Research* apprises the scholar of the work in progress. And, I might add, the informal channels of communication maintained by historians during annual meetings of various historical and professional associations in the United States not only spread the word of what is in progress, but permit the historian to try out his ideas on his peers for their reaction.

The Latin American Studies Association Consortium has moved into a consideration of research guidelines. It proposes to rationalize research and coordinate fellowships in order to avoid overlapping and to cover previously neglected areas. To me, it appears that the field of Latin American studies is moving toward over-organization which, through its influence over many sources of research funds, would stress and steer researchers into areas favored by an in-group. Over-bureaucratization can be counter-productive. There may well be too much lost if the impulsive young scholar is dissuaded from pursuing his hunch and works in a recommended field instead. In any event, the reading and convention attending necessary to keep up with the analyses of new trends may take so much time that the scholar will hardly be able to research in his chosen field!

With a topic in mind and, possibly, a project outline in hand, the scholar is now ready for the venture of seeking money. Having pointed out that in the United States research topics and financial support are offen two sides to the same coin, perhaps we can note a few of the effects of this relationship. Off times the desire for money or subsidized travel may precede the project itself, for Americans are as prone to collect research grants in their earlier years as they are to collect honorific titles and visiting professorships in their later ones. Like the mountain climber contemplating a lofty peak, the grant-seeker wants some of that money because it is there to be had. Or his wife wants a change of scenery. Some projects are literally dreamed up, and then financing is sought for the dream. An anthropoligist once told me that his wife had fallen in love with a spot in Mexico during their honeymoon, so he wrote up a plan for a study to contrast the way of life of two villages near that city. His university financed a year's residence and study in Mexico and, two years later, another six month's residence to fill in the gaps in his research. Historians also play at that game. A young man who wrote his doctoral dissertation on the Spanish epoch of one of the southern states of the United States decided that summer research trips there would be miserably uncomfortable and inconvenient for his family. So he worked up a project concerning problems and methods of Spanish colonial adminstration which justified several trips to South American interspersed with visits to Simancas. Perhaps I am speaking from pique: my wife constantly accuses me of lacking initiative and imagination in being stuck in modern Mexican economic history with virtually no prospect of visiting Spain or the Argentine Alps.

For the younger scholar, most graduate schools either have funds to subsidize their students for their initial venture into foreign archives —at some universities acceptance into doctoral candidacy implies an obligation to provided money for the budding scholar— or use their influence to secure a grant for him from a foundation or a government source. The Fulbright grant is the most common among United States government grants, giving the young man the privilege of living abroad in a harried fashion. Among private foundations, a grant from the Doherty Foundation is almost sort of a fraternity pin among Latin American specialists. Most important is the Joint Committee on Latin American Studies of the American Council of Learned Societies and the Social Science Research Council which presents a large number of grants for historical and social science studies. The Joint Committee has been described as the great funnel to the profession for money from various sources to be disbursed to applicants at several levels of age and scholarship. Additional help is often available from the American Philosophical Society in the form of small grants to meet out-of-the-pocket expenses such as Xeroxing and short trips in connection with a project.

Once established at a university teaching post, the young savant finds a number of possibilities offered by his school such as summer fellowships, research aid money, provisions for semester leaves, and, after a suitable length of time, sabbatical leave. However, with the greater opportunities for obtaining funds from other sources for foreign area studies that longing for a year off at half pay every seventh year is not as great as it used to be. In fact, modern pressures are such that in area studies six years away from his region or nation of specialization can be ruinous as well as hobbling a man in the publish-or-perish race. Still, historians find that funds for history projects are scarcer than for other social science disciplines. Many historians have to be resigned to teaching one summer to finance the next summer's research in order to underwrite their research abroad. In the case of United States government sponsored research, the historian, unless he has an adaptable specialty in fields such as social or economic history, finds little money available. In any event, officially sponsored research has not recovered from the Project Camelot fiasco. And today federal budgetary stringencies have forced numerous cutbacks. An estimate in March 1969 placed the amount of money appropriated for government sponsored research in the social studies at $ 13.5 million of which $ 3.5 million was for research overseas. By 1970 that amount will be reduced to less than $ 1 million for all areas including Latin America. The Department of Defense, which has subsidized most of the social and behavioral science research abroad and has consequently been the butt of most of the criticism from Congress as to its objective, wishes to shift the burden to the Department of State which, surprisingly, has sponsored little social and behavioral science research outside that done by its own staff.

Although U. S. government research sponsors some very fine work, like smallpox it leaves marks. A very fine study of the mining industry of Chile by a geographer sponsored by the Geography Branch of the Office of Naval Research through the National Academy of Sciences and the National Research Council omitted any mention of labor unions, United States capital, and the policies of the Chilean government. In any event, the historian qua historian has little place in the scheme of government-sponsored research. In addition, he is assigned topics for research which are not of his choosing —although at times they have been used to support doctoral dissertations.

Given the reality for many scholars of a long-term visit to Mexico only once every three to five years or more infrequently, the availability in the United States of research materials is of critical importance. Topics which offer substantial amounts of source material in American libraries, depositories and collections, and large numbers of background and secondary sources —particularly topics in which the United States government was a participant— are especially appealing.

The professional status of the researcher is an important factor in securing materials for his use. Graduate students working on their doctorates cannot influence the collection at a large university, while college teachers at smaller institutions find that their funds to acquire materials as well as funds for photocopies quite limited. On the other hand, a well-established man at a larger and wealthier university not only has a strong voice in directing library acquisitions, but the costs of photoduplication are regarded as merely nuisances —in fact, graduate students can be used to wear out their eyesight perusing microfilm— and time off and financing for trips to other libraries in the Unites States and to Mexico are more easily secured.

A substantial boost for the scholar in moderate-sized institutions is the planned purchasing by the Stechert-Hefner book company under the Latin American Cooperative Acquisitions Program of the outstanding current publications throughout Latin America. The plan has made it possible for libraries with even modest budgets to begin the accumulation of a respectable Latin American collection, and it has relieved major libraries of the routine of ordering directly volumes which can be obtained from Stechert and concentrate their energies upon pursuing more specialized and esoteric items needed for advanced research.

Northamerican scholars can do a large portion of their work on their home campuses without interruption in their teaching duties through the use of bibliographic and reproduction facilities coupled with a lending system. I, for one, am not too happy with this trend of events. I am reminded of a friend of mine, an American colonial historian, who had written on British policy toward the North American colonies after perusing literally miles of microfilm in several United States libraries and the Manuscript Room of the Library of Congress before a rather short trip to London. He told me of a fellow historian who spent two years in England doing research on a facet of 17th century Virginia history. Only when this fellow returned to the United States did he discover that virtually all of his material had been microfilmed as part of the Library of Congress program to copy documents pertaining to United States history in foreign archives. The moral of the story, said my friend, was that he ought to have done his homework. I, myself, thought that the man studying Virginia's history had two years in England instead of a case of eyestrain and heat rash from two years in Washington!

While it is true that the research resources for the study of the history of foreign nations to be found in the United States are considerable, in the case of Mexican history, research abroad is still a necessity for any major work. For the scholar of slender means, the proximity of Mexico is truly providential.

As Dr. Manuel Carrera Stampa has written, Mexico is a country of archives and can be proud of its enormous quantity of documental wealth from archaeological sites and colonial architecture to vast collections of paper —despite the attempts of revolutionaries and erstwhile defenders of the established government to burn them. At times, however, the destruction can be exaggerated and the historian in Mexico should be part-time detective and part-time scout. Of great help in understanding the labyrinth of depositories is Dr. Carrera Stampa's *Archivalia Mexicana*, particularly when supplenmented by Lino Gomez Canedo's *Los archivos de la historia de América* and the Columbus Momorial Library's *Guía de las bibliotecas de la América Latina*.

When working with older Mexican archives and more recent administrative files, it is almost impossible to plan without extensive letter-writing and personal enquiry to determine where items may be located, and, equally important, what is and what is not open to the public. For a northamerican planning on a relatively costly hegira, the inconvenience of enquiry is a necessity in order to avoid even greater inconveniences.

The young researcher who shows up in Mexico without a more experienced hand at his side needs a single source to indicate the location of printed sources, journals, and serials and major secondary works such as the *National Union Catalogue* and an inclusive archive checklist. The Luis Gonzalez *Fuentes de la historia contemporánea de México* with notations on the locations of its bibliographic items is particularly commendable in offering the novice an introduction to major depositories of contemporary materials. Many documentary collections, particularly in modern and contemporary history, are in private hands, and introductions and tact are essential in obtaining permission to use them. But when the sources can be consulted, the result may be excellent, such as Ross's *Madero* which is based entirely upon primary sources. For the present it would appear that full biographies of Limantour and Carranza will not be possible because of the unavailability of many private papers. The guidance of the staff of *El Colegio de México* is as indispensable as it is warm, and the aid offered by a Robert Cuba Jones is comforting. It is to be hoped that the newly founded *Centro de Estudios de Historia de México* will be equally useful. In short, working in the archives of Mexico depends a great deal on personal contact and the passing on of leads to information by word of mouth.

Two difficulties which pose particular problems for researchers working in Mexican history are statistics and interviews. Mexican statistics can be the despair of anyone who attempts to use them. We are indeed to be thankful to *El Colegio de México* for undertaking the publication of systematically arranged economic and social statistics of the porfiriato and hope that longer time-series will be elaborated. Meanwhile, the statistics themselves are plagued with inaccuracies ranging from the level of a typesetter's error in the copper production figures for 1915 which caused metric tons of copper to be recorded as kilograms, to the absolutely botched census figures for 1921 which reported Mexico's population at from 400,000 to 500,000 people fewer than there were, throwing off all economic analyses of per capital figures based on that total. Foreign trade figures are often result of a Kafka-like drama. In order to justify the actual tax receipts, officials manipulated the merchandise figures which in any event were not corrected for contraband trade. These numbers were then submitted to clerks who, in turn, used them as production figures for certain products —such as minerals— whose domestic consumption was generally low. Hence, nobody really knows how much was produced because the figures would be embarrassing to tax collectors and customs inspectors. Even today United States official agencies adjust the Mexican official figures on the basis of consular and trade association reports before preparing their analyses. The United Nations, however, must take everything at face value.

Gaining accurate information through interviews can also be a frustrating experience. The popularity of contemporary history in the United States is reflected by students of Mexican history choosing topics set in the post-1917 period, which opens a new source of information: the personal interview and oral history. As one who failed rather dismally in gaining reliable information from corporation executives about their companies' history and policies, I can but wish Dr. James Wilkie and those with whom he is working Godspeed. My experience was to receive from businessmen —American, British, and Mexican— a combination of evasive answers, curt replies, half-truths, misleading prevarications, and public relations oficialese designed to answer without explaining. But then, they were talking of money, not merely public acts. By a combination of patience, persistence, and meticulous background research, Dr. Wilkie has been able to record the thoughts, the observations, and the justifications or rationalizations of a growing number of men in Mexican public life. While the technique of oral history has been extensively criticized, it is also true that some light can be cast on many obscure incidents and vagrant thoughts and interpretations. While tempered with time and hindsight, these remarks still compare favorably with that old historical standby —the diary. And while a diary may be an unorganized catch-all, the interview technique can focus its interest more intelligently. It is to be hoped that as the tapes and printed collections of these materials grow, they will become the basis of a new tool for the historian's hand.

It would seem that being a northamerican scholar in the field of Mexican history is not one of the hardest rows to hoe in academe. Excellent training in the graduate divisions of several universities, in languages, history, and the auxiliary social sciences is available to students who show aptitude, while travel and residence in Mexico for a student is not an unbearable cost. His training completed, the young acolyte can venture forth to his job with a strong background set off by residence abroad and possibly by this time a dissertation holding the seeds of several articles or a book. Except for the case of those men who end up in quite small and out-of-the-way institutions, they can continue their scholarly pursuits between the resources available to one residing in the United States through inter-library loans, microforms, and library purchases, and periodic visits to Mexico for more highly specialized materials. It can be a full and rewarding life with enough adventure and accomplishment to delight a researcher's soul.

A NOTE ON FINDING AIDS

The researcher in the United States has several finding aids with which to start his research, ranging from C. K. Jones' somewhat dated *Bibliography of Latin American Bibliographies* updated by Arthur E. Gropp's *Bibliography of Latin American Bibliographies* (1968) and the American Historical Association's *Guide to Historical Literature* to R. A. Humphrey's practical *Latin American History:*

A *Guide to the Literature in English* and the recently issued volume
by David and Roger Trask and Michael C. Meyer, *A Bibliography of
United States-Latin American Relations* whose title belittles its rich
contents. Furthermore, even smaller libraries in the United States
carry copies of the products of Mexican bibliographers such as the
three volume bibliography on contemporary Mexican history by Luis
González supplemented by Ross's tome, and the Colegio de México's
excellent *Veinticinco años de investigación en México* (1966),
which covers all periods and all topics. Reprint editions of the
great Mexican bibliographics of the past such as Beristáin's are
paralleled by the reappearance of Joseph Sabin's indispensable
work on early New World history. The indispensable annual
Handbook of Latin American Studies, whose quality has risen so
markedly in the past two decades, is obligingly kept in print by
the University of Florida Press back to 1935, while the Pan- American
Unions' *Revista Interamericana de Bibliografía* and the Public Affairs
Information Service *Bulletin* contribute numerous items as do the
various *Indexes* and *Guides* of the H. W. Wilson Company. And
the most valuable *Dissertation Abstractes* should not be forgotten
for many surprises and gems. Furthermore, there are the bibliographies
of S. A. Baytich and Martin Sable and the specialized bibliographies in
economic history by Professor Tom Jones and by the Harvard Bureau
for Economic Research in Latin America. With the reprint house
publication of the Columbus Memorial Library of the Pan-American
Union's *Index to Latin American Periodical Literature*, items are
found going back to 1929. The United States Government has also
been most active in this field with the Library of Congress' *Guide
to the Official Publications of the Other American Republic* —now
reprinted— Annita Ker's lamentably scarce *Mexican Government
Publications* and Carpenter's *Government Publications in late 18th
Century Mexico*. Dr. John Harrison's *Guides* to Mexican and Latin
American material in the United States National Archives has opened
leads to many nuggets of material particularly in the Department
of State sections. This material is already photocopied or can be
copied to order. All of these guides are available in even smaller
libraries to any researcher in Mexican history.

Since a storehouse is valueless without a guide to indicate where
the material is to be found, union lists and inventories of many
collections have been made and can be consulted or obtained without
too much trouble. These listings serve the dual function of helping
to locate historical materials and of being bibliographic aids as well.
The Library of Congress *National Union Catalogue* —soon to be
published in its entireity in book form— is the prime source for
locating catalogued materials in print or typescript in the major
libraries of the United States. To complement the *Union List of*

Serials in Libraries of the United States and Canada with its numerous supplements, the University of Texas Press has issued the *Union List of Latin American Newspapers in United States Libraries* prepared under the auspices of the Conference on Latin American History. Equally important is the project begun in 1965 by the University of Florida and shortly to appear in print to list holdings in the United States and Canada for as many serial documents as can be identified for individual Latin American countries including publications of government agencies, national museums, libraries, universities and autonomous entities.

An invaluable service has been rendered researchers by the appearance of numerous card catalogues of specialized collections printed in book form, beginning with the reproduction of the entire Library of Congress collection in 1942. In time it has been followed by publication in book form of the catalogues of the major libraries in the United States with Latin American holdings: Texas, Bancroft, New York Public, the Hispanic Society, and the Columbus Memorial Library of the Pan American Union. The publication of the *Latin America and Latin American Periodicals* shelflist by the Weidner Library of Harvard University has facilitated calling upon the resources of that library by scholars throughout the United States.

Manuscripts can be traced through publications such as Philip Hamer's *Guide to Archives and Manuscripts in the United States* and the *National Union Catalogue of Manuscript Collections*. The now primitive microfilm has spawned a host of versatile microforms which make possible the widespread, if not exactly cheap, distribution of what were relatively inaccessible research materials of all sorts. Since this technological revolution has struck information dissemination, Richard W. Hale Jr.'s *Guide to Photocopied Historical Materials in the United States and Canada* supplemented by the commercial ventures, *Guide to Microforms in Print* and *Subject Guide to Microforms in Print*, now lead to a wealth of materials. A companion listing, *Guide to Reprints* covers books, journals, and other materials now back in print by virtue of reproduction processes such as photo-offset. University Microfilms of Ann Arbor, Michigan not only has a long list of materials on microfilm in its storehouse, but it is willing, for a rather nominal charge, to microfilm (subject to copyright laws) any book or manuscript submitted to it or which it can borrow and by use of the Xerox Copyflo machine reproduce the material in book form.

Since these listings can be virtually endless, let me conclude them by reference to specific guides to some of the major library and archival holdings of Mexican historical material in the United States. An overview is given by Ronald Hilton's general *Handbook of Hispanic Source Materials and Research Organizations in the United*

States. Examples of particularized listings would be Lotta M. Spell's *Research Materials for the Study of Latin America at the University of Texas* and the several other guides written by Castañeda and Dabbs, and the University of California's publication, *Mexico: Works in the Bancroft Library* which adds to their venerable *Spain and Spanish America in the Libraries of the University of California.* An interesting example of a guide to the materials in a smaller manuscript and archival collection is Clery L. Stout's *A Catalogue of Hispanic Documents in the Thomas Gilcrease Institution* (Tulsa, Oklahoma).

ARCHIVOS, BIBLIOTECAS E HISTORIADORES

ROMEO FLORES CABALLERO

Mucho se ha hecho por mejorar las condiciones de los centros de investigación histórica existentes en el país, desde que el doctor Herbert E. Bolton publicara su *Guide to the Materials for the History of the United States in the Principal Archives of Mexico.* Sin embargo, a pesar del tiempo transcurrido, algunas críticas y observaciones, presentadas por el doctor Bolton en 1913, son de una vigencia evidente para los investigadores de la historia de México en 1969.

El propósito de este trabajo es estudiar y analizar algunos de los problemas a los que se enfrenta el investigador de la historia de México, mediante la descripción de la situación general de los centros de investigación histórica existentes en el país. El estudio está basado en la literatura existente sobre el tema, entrevistas realizadas entre historiadores mexicanos y extranjeros, y en experiencias del autor.

Para comprender la situación en que se encuentran los archivos, bibliotecas y, en general, los centros de investigación del país, es necesario ubicarlos dentro del estado de desarrollo general de la República. Vivimos en un país subdesarrollado y, como tal, las inversiones del sector público se destinan a resolver los problemas económicos y sociales más apremiantes de la nación. El gobierno federal, y los gobiernos estatales y municipales, no tienen una política bien definida de inversiones. Éstas, con frecuencia, obedecen a razones políticas, o son condicionadas por los grupos de presión existentes en el país. Sin embargo, a pesar de esto, se ha mantenido un ritmo constante y acelerado de crecimiento económico. Es de lamentarse, sin embargo, que el avance de los centros de investigación, especialmente los de la investigación histórica, no hayan mejorado al mismo ritmo que los otros sectores.

Los gobiernos en todos los niveles, por lo general, están interesados en invertir en obras notorias al público y de lucimiento. Consideran, erróneamente, que las inversiones en centros de investigación no son vistosas. La inversión en educación, una de las más apremiantes, está enfocada principalmente a resolver el problema de la educación mínima que requiere la industrialización del país y, a pesar de que es una de las inversiones más altas del sector público, no lo es tanto la que, dentro de este sector, se dedica al fomento, mejoras y actualización de los servicios que prestan los archivos y bibliotecas.

Los problemas de la investigación histórica están muy relacionados con esta situación. Están relacionados en cuanto que es indudable que el progreso de la investigación histórica ha crecido a un ritmo mucho más acelerado que el ritmo de los servicios de los archivos y bibliotecas de los cuales se nutre.

En esto último tiene mucho que ver la carencia de especialistas. Éstos están sujetos a la falta de incentivos que, a su vez, son determinados por la subestimación en que se tiene a los archivistas y bibliotecarios del país, cuando debiera considerárseles indispensables en la planeación educativa. Es evidente que este problema no es exclusivo de México, existe también en Estados Unidos, sólo que hay una diferencia de grado.

Quizá algunas estimaciones nos ayuden a comprender mejor este problema. En México hay únicamente 24 bibliotecarios profesionales titulados; de ellos, 14 se graduaron en universidades extranjeras. Existen en el país solamente dos escuelas de biblioteconomía y archivonomía: el Colegio de Biblioteconomía de la Universidad Autónoma de México, fundado en 1956; y la Escuela Nacional de Bibliotecarios y Archivistas dependiente de la Secretaría de Educación Pública, cuyos orígenes se remontan hasta 1916. De la primera se han graduado seis estudiantes aunque hay 25 pasantes; de la segunda, hasta la fecha, han terminado tres y quedan 21 pasantes. [1]

El círculo vicioso de la falta de incentivos económicos y psicológicos ha ocasionado que la archivonomía y la biblioteconomía se hayan quedado en la infancia en que la encontró el doctor Herbert E. Bolton en 1913. [2] No es de extrañar, por lo tanto, que desde que se fundó el Archivo General de la Nación en 1823, y en general desde que se fundaron los archivos del país, las personas que los han dirigido no hayan sido especialistas sino destacados historiadores, profesores distinguidos o bibliófilos notables. Estas distinguidas personalidades, como es de suponer, no se dedican en exclusivo a sus archivos y bibliotecas, y se ven en la necesidad de combinar sus labores con el fin de aumentar sus ingresos. Los jóvenes, en general, no aspiran a dirigir centros de investigación, o están excluidos de antemano, por carecer, tanto de "madurez" como de "obra", o por falta del "criterio" necesario para dirigirlos.

El problema de los centros de investigación histórica no es de organización o de administración, sino de recursos. Todos los directores de los archivos del país, como se ha dicho, son personas distinguidas, con méritos y conocimientos suficientes para ocupar los puestos

[1] AMBAC, *Estado actual de los servicios bibliotecarios en la República Mexicana: evolución y necesidades* (informe mecanoescrito), pp. 1-4.

[2] Herbert E. Bolton, *Guide to Materials for the History of the United States in the Principal Archives of Mexico*. Carnegie Institution, Washington, D. C., 1913, p. VI.

directivos. Sin embargo, a pesar de sus empeños, no logran actualizar sus acervos. La organización, administración, catalogación, clasificación y los demás servicios, no son obra de un solo hombre, sino del conjunto de especialistas, investigadores y empleados que dependen de él y del presupuesto que se les asigne. Es difícil exigir eficiencia a un técnico que percibe el salario mínimo, o a un investigador que recibe $ 1,200.00 pesos mensuales de pago por sus servicios profesionales.

En tales circunstancias no debería extrañarnos que los centros de investigación estén olvidados, fuera del alcance de los estudiantes y del público en general. Y mientras éste y el gobierno no logren descubrir su carácter indispensable y sigan creyendo que son repositorios de libros viejos y de material inservible, jamás formarán parte de los planes de inversión del gobierno.

ARCHIVOS

En cierto sentido los archivos del país, el General de la Nación, los de las secretarías, los estatales, los 2,264 municipales, los 2,200 parroquiales y los privados, tienen características muy similares y, por consiguiente, presentan problemas comunes al investigador: están localizados en edificios inapropiados y mal ubicados; se han formado con los fondos existentes de las secretarías de las principales autoridades, de las dependencias gubernamentales y eclesiásticas, y su importancia está en relación con la jerarquía respectiva al puesto; están incompletos, desorganizados y descuidados; carecen de catálogos, índices y guías, o están deficientemente clasificados y catalogados y, a pesar de su importancia, son desconocidos; carecen de presupuesto adecuado y ofrecen servicios deficientes. El personal es improvisado y está mal remunerado, aunque es solícito y servicial al grado de suplir muchas veces por su conocimiento del archivo, la información contenida en guías existentes.

En la actualidad los administradores de los archivos del país se han preocupado por elaborar guías, catálogos e índices. A pesar del empeño dedicado a estas labores básicas es de suponerse que, por la escasez de recursos, la tarea no progresará mucho. Los problemas de catalogación y de clasificación del material son los más graves. El Archivo General de la Nación, por ejemplo, tiene aproximadamente 35,000 legajos o volúmenes a vistas del público, de ellos la mitad está organizada de acuerdo con la clasificación establecida en la Colonia y heredada del siglo XIX. Si tomamos en cuenta, por ejemplo, que se cataloga un promedio de un volumen por mes; que en el Ramo de Tierras faltan por conocerse 1,500 volúmenes aproximadamente, y que solamente una persona se encarga de su clasificación, ésta, su catalogación final se realizaría en 1,500 meses, es decir, en aproximadamente, 30 años; así que el material se conocerá alrededor del año 2000.

Hemos advertido que son 35,000 volúmenes los que se pueden ver, o a los que, por lo menos, tiene acceso el investigador. Bolton anotaba desde 1913, [3] que existía una cantidad semejante amontonada en una bodega, cuyo contenido se desconocía completamente. El actual director del Archivo declaraba, hace 20 años, en el Primer Congreso de Historiadores Mexicanos y Norteamericanos, que había "masas enormes sin ningún plan y menos orden cronológico que tienen el pecado original y la escasa destreza de los que trabajan en la organización de estas secciones". [4]

Es de suponerse que el Archivo General de la Nación continuará aumentando su material, puesto que a sus fondos deberán llegar los expedientes concluidos de las diferentes Secretarías del Gobierno. En tales circunstancias es posible, que a pesar de la buena disposición de sus administradores e investigadores, se agrave aún más el problema de la accesibilidad y difusión del material.

Los archivos de las Secretarías de Hacienda, de Relaciones, de Gobernación, especialmente los archivos privados de los presidentes de 1910 a 1940, y el de la Secretaría de la Defensa Nacional aunque tenga secciones vedadas a cualquier investigador, son los más accesibles de los archivos de las dependencias federales. Están bien cuidados y responden a las necesidades de las Secretarías.

Los archivos estatales son, por lo general, los más descuidados y desorganizados del país. En ellos se manifiesta más claramente las pérdidas del material ocasionado por abandono, incuria, desórdenes políticos, efectos de roedores, descuido, humedad, polilla, pérdidas por ventas para material de coheterías y envolturas para tiendas de abarrotes, o pérdidas por fuego, como el caso del Tribunal Superior de Justicia de Oaxaca. [5] Otros desaparecieron en el traslado de un sitio a otro durante crisis políticas, o simplemente por la ignorancia de algunos gobernantes, como el caso de un gobernador de Michoacán, "tan inepto como irresponsable", que ordenó la venta del reducido material del archivo a una fábrica de cartón. [6]

Entre los archivos municipales que se destacan por su organización y cuidado están los de México, Puebla, Monterrey, Guadalajara, Morelia y Oaxaca. Estos archivos han tenido entre sus directores a

[3] Ibid., p. 1.

[4] J. Ignacio Rubio Mañé, "La Historia de las Provincias Internas en el Archivo General de la Nación", Memoria del primer congreso de historiadores de México y los Estados Unidos... Ed. Cultura, México, 1950, p. 64.

[5] Jorge Fernando Iturribarría, "Oaxaca: la historia y sus instrumentos", Historia Mexicana, vol. ii, núm. 3, enero-marzo, 1953, pp. 459-476.

[6] Joaquín Fernández de Córdoba, "Michoacán: la historia y sus instrumentos", Historia Mexicana, vol. ii, núm. 1, julio-septiembre 1952, p. 536.

distinguidos profesores con vocación, carácter y capacidad necesaria para realizar las tareas que requieren la clasificación y catalogación del material y su divulgación, a través de la elaboración de índices y guías. Algunos de estos archivos han permanecido casi intactos por haber estado fuera del alcance de los conflictos políticos y militares; otros, como el caso de Puebla, "uno de los mejores y más completos" de la República, mantienen su integridad porque, además del diligente cuidado de sus conocedores, "está situado en un rincón del segundo piso del Palacio Municipal", y por lo tanto alejado del público e ignorado, como dice el doctor Borah, de los invasores extranjeros y de los disturbios políticos.[7] Los archivos municipales, en general, son los que más han sufrido de saqueos tanto de extranjeros como nacionales.

Según el profesor Manuel Carrera Stampa existen alrededor de 2,200 archivos parroquiales en el país.[8] Estos archivos, a pesar de su importancia para la genealogía, la etnología, la historia económica y la historia demográfica, son los menos conocidos de los investigadores. La mayoría de ellos están incompletos y mal clasificados y catalogados. El más importante es el de la Catedral de México. Sin embargo ninguna de sus colecciones está completa. Casi todos perdieron parte de sus acervos durante la segunda mitad del siglo XIX como consecuencia de la Reforma. En el caso del archivo de la Catedral no existen documentos anteriores a 1870, pero el investigador los puede encontrar en el Archivo General de la Nación. Además una gran parte de los documentos localizados en la Catedral está bajo llave y es sólo accesible para unos cuantos investigadores.[9]

La investigación de los archivos personales se encuentra obstaculizada por el excesivo celo de los que guardan los documentos de algún ilustre antepasado. A pesar de ello es posible ganarse la confianza de los dueños e investigar en ellos. Una de las limitaciones de estos archivos, o al menos la más obvia, es que están formados principalmente de la corresponencia recibida, y no es frecuente encontrar las respuestas a ésta. Aunque no es general esta limitación se explica por la carencia de métodos de reproducción en el siglo XIX. El archivo de don Matías Romero y el de Benito Juárez deberán considerarse como excepciones a la regla.[10]

Los esfuerzos por mejorar los servicios de los archivos, como se

---

[7] Woodrow Borah, "El Archivo Municipal y la Historia de Puebla", *Boletín del Archivo General de la Nación*, vol. XIII, núms. 2-3, 1942, pp. 207-239, 423-464.

[8] Manuel Carrera Stampa, *Archivalía Mexicana*. UNAM, México, 1952 p, 121.

[9] Michael C. Costeloe, "Guide to the Chapter Archives of the Archbishopric of Mexico", *Hispanic American Historical Review*, vol. XLV, núm. 1, February, 1965, p. 63.

[10] Guadalupe Monroy Huitrón, *Archivo histórico de Matías Romero: catálogo descriptivo, correspondencia recibida*. Banco de México, S. A., México, 1965 I, VIII, XX.

ha dicho, están enmarcados dentro del subdesarrollo general del país. Sin embargo, poco a poco, se ha logrado que los documentos sean accesibles a los investigadores mediante la elaboración de índices, guías y catálogos, tarea en la que han colaborado organismos nacionales e internacionales.

Junto a la formación de índices estos organismos han facilitado el manejo de los archivos regionales mediante métodos modernos de reproducción. El primero fue el Centro de Documentación, planeado en 1949, y en el que participaron la Comisión de Historia del Instituto Panamericano de Geografía e Historia, el Instituto de Historia de la UNAM, la Secretaría de Relaciones Exteriores, el Archivo General de la Nación, el Fondo de Cultura Económica, la Fundación Rockefeller, la Biblioteca del Congreso de los Estados Unidos, la Bibioteca Franklin y la Institución Carnegie. El centro funcionó de 1950 a 1963, su tarea consistió en fotocopiar los archivos regionales, en particular, los archivos del centro y sur del país, especialmente su material de los siglos XVI y XVII por haberse perdido del Archivo General de la Nación como consecuencia del incendio que sufriera en 1692. También se fotocopió material del siglo XIX. Dentro de los planes se lograron sacar 655 rollos de micropelícula de los materiales de los archivos de Puebla, Oaxaca, Guadalajara, Michoacán, Tlaxcala y Guanajuato, que cubren más del 60% del total de los documentos fotocopiados y los archivos de los municipios de Durango, Zacatecas, Monterrey y Parral.

El manejo de los documentos mediante este procedimiento facilitó la tarea de catalogación y clasificación. El material se organizó no sólo por orden cronológico, sino también por temas. La fotocopia de los documentos no fue exhaustiva pero se reprodujeron las piezas más importantes. El contenido de los 655 rollos se ha dado a conocer en los Anales del Instituto Nacional de Antropología e Historia, y en las Memorias de la Academia Mexicana de la Historia. [11]

Después de los resultados alentadores del Centro de Documentación, la Academia Mexicana de Genealogía y Heráldica, en asociación con la Sociedad Genealógica de Utah, promovieron la microfilmación del material de todos los archivos civiles, eclesiásticos y privados de la República. El propósito de esta empresa ha sido el de salvaguardar el material de estos archivos y ponerlos a disposición de los investigadores. Hasta el momento se han invertido alrededor de 30 millones de pesos. Del Archivo General de la Nación se mocrofilmaron alrededor de 2,000 volúmenes. Existen 64,000 rollos de micropelícula que contiene más de 80 millones de páginas. Hasta el momento

[11] Berta Ulloa, "Centro de Documentación del Museo Nacional de Historia del Castillo de Chapultepec", *Historia Mexicana*, vol. IV, núm. 2, octubre-diciembre, 1954, pp. 275-280.

se han clasificado 46,000 rollos y los índices se encuentran en Salt Lake City. [12]

Por su parte el Instituto Tecnológico de Estudios Superiores de Monterrey, gracias al interés de sus historiadores y a la cooperación de fundaciones nacionales y extranjeras, ha auspiciado la fotocopia de los archivos municipales del noreste del país.

Estos grandes proyectos constituyen un gran paso hacia el conocimiento, consulta y divulgación del material de nuestra historia regional y han contribuido a facilitar la tarea de los historiadores.

BIBLIOTECAS

En 1965 el país contaba con 463 bibliotecas, cuyo acervo superaba a los 1,000 volúmenes. De ellas 206 se encontraban en el Distrito Federal y 257 en los Estados. La cantidad de volúmenes existentes en estas bibliotecas asciende a casi 4.7 millones de libros, de los cuales 2.9 millones se localizaban en las bibliotecas de Distrito Federal y 1.7 en el resto de la República; de éstos, 1.2 millones, aproximadamente, estaban en los Estados de Jalisco, Nuevo León, Puebla, Michoacán, Veracruz, Guanajuato y Coahuila, con un acervo superior a 100,000 volúmenes en cada caso; 500,000 volúmenes aproximadamente se encontraban distribuidos en las bibliotecas del resto de los Estados.

De los acervos bibliotecarios localizados en el Distrito Federal, 1.2 de los 2.9 millones de volúmenes del total, correspondían a las bibliotecas de la Universidad Nacional Autónoma de México; 220,000 volúmenes aproximadamente pertenecían a bibliotecas de Secretarías, organismos descentralizados y a instituciones culturales y científicas, y 650,000, aproximadamente, a bibliotecas de la Secretaría de Educación. [13]

El número de bibliotecas y el acervo bibliográfico son muy deficientes si se comparan con los países altamente desarrollados. La Unión Soviética registra en 1953, 380,000 bibliotecas con un acervo de 1,000 millones de volúmenes. [14] En Estados Unidos sólo las bibliotecas universitarias tenían 200 millones de libros aproximadamente, [15] sin incluir el acervo de las bibliotecas públicas que suman una cantidad equivalente a la de las bibliotecas de la Unión Soviética. De acuerdo

[12] Entrevista con el Lic. G. Romo Celis de la Academia Mexicana de Genealogía y Heráldica, Gante núm. 7, 4º piso.

[13] AMBAC, *Estado actual de los servicios bibliotecarios. Op. cit.*

[14] "La organización de las bibliotecas en la Unión Soviética", *Boletín de la UNESCO para las Bibliotecas*, vol. VIII, núms. 5-6, mayo-junio, 1954, pp. 97-100.

[15] Pedro Zámora y Pablo Velázquez, "Planeamiento Nacional de Servicios Bibliotecarios en México", *Pan American Union, Columbus Memorial Library...* v. 2 por países. Chile y México, 1966. (Estudios bibliotecarios, núm. 8.)

con un estudio elaborado por Pedro Zamora y Pablo Velázquez hay, en América Latina, ciudades como Río de Janeiro, Buenos Aires y Santiago de Chile, que tienen más libros que todas las bibliotecas de México juntas.

Las bibliotecas de la República no se adaptan a las necesidades que demandan los intelectuales y los investigadores del país. La calidad de la investigación está, en gran medida, relacionada directamente con las facilidades que se ofrecen a los investigadores. Los resultados de la recopilación de material bibliográfico, una de las primeras etapas de la investigación, no dependen únicamente de quienes lo emprenden, sino de las fuentes de donde se nutren. [16]

En cierto sentido las bibliotecas tienen los mismos defectos que los archivos: edificios improvisados, escasez de personal técnico, bajos salarios, reducido acervo bibliográfico, métodos y sistemas de catalogación deficientes, ausencia de departamentos de adquisiciones y carecen de servicios de reproducción de documentos.

A pesar de la tradición cultural del país son pocas las bibliotecas que sirven para la investigación histórica. Entre ellas la Bibioteca Nacional, la mejor de país, la Biblioteca del Banco de México, la Biblioteca "Lerdo de Tejada" de la Secretaría de Hacienda y Crédito Público, la Biblioteca del Instituto Nacional de Antropología e Historia que, junto con la del Instituto Tecnológico de Estudios Superiores de Monterrey y la Biblioteca de la Ciudad Universitaria, tienen las mejores y más modernas instalaciones y servicios del país; la Biblioteca de la Universidad Iberoamericana, la Biblioteca Alfonso Reyes de la Universidad de Nuevo León, Biblioteca de México, Biblioteca de la Universidad de Veracruz, Biblioteca del Congreso de la Unión, Biblioteca de la Universidad de San Luis y la Biblioteca del Colegio de México, la única totalmente catalogada y clasificada. En estas bibliotecas el historiador encuentra la más amplia libertad para la investigación y cuenta con la mejor disposición de sus directores.

Quizá el problema más grave al que se enfrentan, especialmente las bibliotecas oficiales, es la falta de buenas y suficientes obras secundarias, y la carencia de estudios recientes sobre temas históricos. Situación que se explica porque se nutren de donativos particulares y carecen de un presupuesto adecuado para adquisiciones.

Mención especial merece la Biblioteca Palafoxiana de Puebla, que constituye uno de los esfuerzos culturales más notables del 'siglo xvii. Esta biblioteca se conserva intacta con sus 25,000 volúmenes en su propio local. [17]

[16] Daniel Cosío Villegas, *Nueva historiografía política de México moderno.* Colegio Nacional, México, 1965, p. 12.
[17] Ernesto de la Torre Villar, "Nuevas aportaciones de la Biblioteca Palafoxiana", *Boletín de la Biblioteca Nacional,* vol. xi, núm. 1 (2a. época), enero, marzo, 1966, p. 35; Juan B. Iguíniz, *Disquisiciones bibliográficas, autores, libros, bibliotecas, artes gráficas.* El Colegio de México, México, 1943, p. 237.

Los mejores centros para la investigación histórica son, además del Archivo General de la Nación y la Biblioteca Nacional, las bibliotecas privadas. En cada Estado de la República existen cinco bibliotecas con acervos de obras raras básicas para el historiador. Muchas de ellas se han nutrido de bibliotecas oficiales a través de varios métodos, entre los que destacan adquisiciones mediante la compra de libros antiguos en las librerías de viejo. Hay muchas, sin embargo, que todavía tienen los sellos de las instituciones de donde proceden.

La subsistencia de bibliotecas privadas y la insistencia de formarlas en la actualidad, resulta anacrónica; especialmente cuando el avance académico e institucional hacen imposible mantenerlas al corriente con el progreso académico e intelectual en cualquiera especialidad. La biblioteca personal, de acuerdo con Carl M. White, es la forma más primitiva de desarrollo bibliotecario de un país. [18]

En la actualidad algunas empresas privadas, interesadas en promoción de investigación histórica, han iniciado la formación de archivos y bibliotecas con base en la compra de colecciones privadas. El esfuerzo más notable lo ha hecho Condumex que, a través de su Departamento de Relaciones Públicas, ha creado un centro de estudios históricos muy importante para la historia de México del siglo xix. Aunque hasta ahora muy pocos historiadores han tenido acceso a este centro de investigación, pronto estará en condiciones de abrirse al público. El acervo ha estado en proceso de catalogación, clasificación y reproducción, con el fin de facilitar el manejo de los documentos.

Es posible que otras empresas imiten el ejemplo de Condumex, aunque sería recomendable que, dada la situación de las bibliotecas del país, destinen sus fondos al enriquecimiento de las bibliotecas de algunas instituciones ya establecidas como el Instituto de Antropología e Historia, la Biblioteca Nacional y el Colegio de México. Lo mismo podrían hacer los poseedores de bibliotecas privadas. De esa manera contribuirían genuinamente al progreso de la investigación de la historia de México y evitarían su salida del país.

HISTORIADORES

Entre la variedad de investigadores de las ciencias sociales, los historiadores son los que más utilizan los archivos y bibliotecas; lo mismo sucede en Estados Unidos. [19] Por esta razón los historiadores son los investigadores que mejor comprenden los problemas que

---

[18] Carl M. White, *Library and Information Services in Mexico. A Study of Present Conditions & Needs.* Unpublished Manuscripts.

[19] Walter Rundell Jr., "Relations between Historical Researchers and Custodians of Source Materials", *College & Research Libraries,* vol. 29, núm. 6, November, 1968, p. 467.

implica la búsqueda de documentos y, por lo mismo, han sido los mejores aliados de los administradores de los centros de investigación histórica y los que más han colaborado con ellos en facilitar las labores de investigación de sus colegas.

El Centro de Estudios Históricos de El Colegio de México ha auspiciado y publicado en su revista *Historia Mexicana* una serie de artículos de historiadores mexicanos y extranjeros, con la finalidad de orientar a los investigadores acerca de la situación de los centros de investigación en los Estados de la República. Un esfuerzo igualmente importante han realizado la Biblioteca Nacional, el Archivo General de la Nación, el Instituto Nacional de Antropología e Historia; algunas universidades e institutos de enseñanza superior como las Universidades de Veracruz, Nuevo León, Puebla, Guadalajara; el Instituto Tecnológico de Estudios Superiores de Monterrey, y asociaciones como la Asociación Mexicana de Bibliotecarios. Los resultados de estos esfuerzos se pueden consultar en los anales, boletines y revistas de estas instituciones.

Todos estos estudios han contribuido a facilitar la tarea del historiador. Sin embargo, a pesar de estos esfuerzos, es muy frecuente escuchar críticas exageradas sobre los servicios que prestan los archivos y bibliotecas y, en particular, sobre la falta de guías, catálogos e índices. A este respecto es necesario decir que, si bien es cierto que adolecen de graves defectos, también los hay, y muy serios, entre algunos historiadores. Muchos piensan que los archivos existen sólo para ellos y creen que con sólo visitarlos están haciendo un favor, no sólo a los archivos, sino a la nación. La verdad es que los investigadores deberían estar agradecidos por tener el privilegio de poderlos consultar. En muchas ocasiones la actitud del historiador, y su comportamiento en los archivos, es la causa de que se eliminen las posibilidades de realizar una buena investigación antes de emprenderla.

La personalidad del historiador, por difícil que sea definirla, juega un papel muy importante en el proceso de la investigación; especialmente en un país como México en el que las relaciones personales son determinantes y adquieren una importancia preponderante para conseguir el acceso a los documentos. Esto no significa, por supuesto, que se intente cambiar la personalidad de los historiadores. Sin embargo es necesario advertirlos de la existencia del fenómeno y hacerles ver que de su actitud depende en buena medida el éxito de la investigación.

Muchos historiadores, especialmente los jóvenes, desconocen los problemas particulares de los archivos y bibliotecas y llegan a consultarlos sin tener una idea previa de sus características y sin conocer la técnica del manejo de los materiales que solicitan. Otros, especialmente norteamericanos, sujetos al sistema de "Publish or Perish", se desconsuelan al no encontrar guías, catálogos e índices. Con frecuencia sólo visitan los archivos mejor organizados, seleccionan unos cuantos documentos y se consideran listos para vaciar los resultados. Esto, por supuesto, no es investigar. Desde este punto de vista los problemas de la investigación no son de los archivos sino del investigador.

La investigación histórica implica el examen detallado de documento por documento y quien no esté dispuesto a aceptarlo debería cambiar de profesión. Los resultados de una buena investigación histórica no descansan en la responsabilidad de los archivistas, bibliotecarios y administradores, ni en las guías e índices de los archivos y bibliotecas, como muchos lo suponen, sino en los historiadores mismos. Por esta razón es necesario advertir a quienes exageran la importancia de los índices y guías, que éstos nunca serán lo suficientemente detallados para satisfacer la curiosidad de un verdadero investigador.

CONCLUSIONES

a) A pesar del material que en libros y documentos se ha perdido, o ha pasado a bibliotecas privadas, o salido del país, es indudable la existencia de una gran riqueza bibliográfica y documental que permite la investigación histórica en México;

b) El problema principal, en relación con las bibliotecas y los archivos, es la falta de suficiente personal capacitado para organizar y completar las colecciones;

c) En tal virtud una de las mejores inversiones que pueden hacerse para resolver el problema es, por una parte, fortalecer las escuelas de archivistas y bibliotecarios ya existentes y, por la otra, multiplicar las facilidades para la preparación de bibliotecarios y archivistas a niveles más altos que los que pueden ofrecer las escuelas nacionales;

d) En segundo lugar habría que pensar en un financiamiento adecuado para mantener salarios estimulantes para profesionales de primera, enriquecer las colecciones y mejorar los servicios que únicamente pueden ofrecerse con locales, mobiliario y equipo adecuados;

e) Aunque es muy encomiable el interés de algunas empresas del sector privado por adquirir colecciones importantes para los estudios históricos, sería conveniente proponerles que elaboraran convenios con bibliotecas y archivos preexistentes, y bien organizados, que pudieran ofrecer un servicio eficiente a todos los investigadores;

f) El creciente interés y la indudable importancia de la conservación y difusión de los documentos de todos los archivos del país, mediante el uso de métodos modernos de reproducción, hace pensar en la conveniencia de que se establezca un organismo coordinador de las actividades y proyectos de microfilmación que se realizan en el país por el Instituto Nacional de Antropología e Historia, el Instituto Tecnológico de Estudios Superiores de Monterrey y la Academia Mexicana de Genealogía y Heráldica;

g) Finalmente, en vista de que el historiador es el que mejor conoce los problemas de los centros de investigación histórica, es de esperar que continúe colaborando con los bibliotecarios, archivistas y administradores en la clasificación y catalogación de los materiales de los archivos y bibliotecas del país.

COMMENTARY

WOODROW BORAH

We have before us two papers which might be called reflections on the human condition in its special effects upon the sub-sub-variety called historian. The papers are highly disparate, yet they mesh in a rather odd way. That by Dr. Romeo Flores Caballero deals with the problems of historical research in a country that for historians is still under-developed in the organization of its archives, in the endowment of public libraries, and in the training and numbers of its personnel. Under-development means lack of facilities, inadequate provision for scholars, and steady wastage as students and scholars re-do work already done because they do not have access to bibliographies and libraries. Dr. Flores Caballero mentions advances that have been made in provision and training of scholars, and points to a remedy, namely, better marshalling of resources and, even more, persuading private enterprises to make more efficient use of their benefactions by improving existing public facilities rather than creating numbers of private ones. All that Dr. Flores Caballero has to say is true although I am led to reflect that Mexico, despite a continuing and profligate destruction of its records that can perhaps best be compared with our own gutting of the resources of an entire continent, still remains the possessor of vast archival wealth.

The paper by Dr. Marvin Bernstein shows the reverse picture, the generally rich endowment and ample provision of an affluent society, even though despite affluence there are some minor complaints such as the need for students and scholars on field trips to live in something less than the comfort that they are used to at home. Yet —and an odd aspect— the ability to assemble materials in the form of books, manuscripts, and photocopies of all kinds has led to a peculiar dispersal and disorder, for without adequates indexes to what is available and where, especially for photocopies, students and scholars are unable to make adequate use of, let alone master, the materials they need. If one adds to this statement what Dr. Bernstein does not mention, the increasing pressure upon facilities in the United States, one is left with a picture of increasing disorder as wealth multiplies, and so in the United States as in Mexico, scholars are forced in the end to build private libraries and so we return to "la forma más primitiva de desarrollo bibliotecario de un país." Dr. Bernstein points at some lenght to the creation of guides and indexes that are helping to solve some of the disorder, and all that he has to say is true, but again I am led to reflect that neither in the United States nor in Mexico has there been written a general guide to the sources for the history of Mexico comparable to the extraordinarily useful manual of Raúl Porras Barrenechea, *Fuentes históricas peruanas.* Both Dr. Flores Caballero and Dr. Bernstein in their suggestions for remedies approach the idea of central direction and central ordering although Dr. Bernstein, on a perhaps closer look at the remedy, enters a hasty caveat. I should add in justice to both papers that, in addition to the elements I have indicated, they cover many other aspects of difficulties in research and training.

I both agree and disagree with the two papers. The problems and difficulties they point to are very real and very much with us in the two countries. Nevertheless, from an experience as student and perhaps scholar that reaches back to the middle 1930's, I do think that there has been considerable change for the better. When I first visited Mexico in 1938, I remember the far more meager endowment of facilities for scholars and the far greater sacrifice that dedication to historical research then meant. Dr. Flores Caballero's paper itself mentions, for example, the contributions of El Colegio de México, and the various entities of the Instituto Nacional de Antropología e Historia, including the Centro de Documentación and its notable labor of preserving local records by a beneficent seizure on microfilm. One may point to the remarkable growth of the Universidad Nacional Autónoma de México, the creation of the Instituto de Investigaciones Históricas, and the rise of state universities. There is far more historical research and I have the impression that much of it is of the quality that only a small proportion of work done earlier attained. In the United States, I can recall the range and quality of instruction and published research of the 1930's and compare it with somewhat more thoughtful offerings, oral and written, today. Charles Gibson's careful summary of work done in Latin American history since 1904, especially in the United States, in his *Spain in America*, is a heartening testimony, for his summary shows substantial advance in range of question and examination of older questions. Perhaps most encouraging is the fact that the overwhelming bulk of the contribution has been by relatively small accretion. The extent of support for students and scholars in the United States, even for us troglodytes in history, has become far more generous and at times munificent. It may have reached the point of bringing us to a standard of living that hampers study and reflection, or even worse leads us to shy away from thoughts that might imperil the flow of funds.

Let me come now to those problems that are common to the condition of historian in general, rather than to people in the United States and México who study Mexican history. Much in the two papers really relates to these latter but much is really a complaint on the human condition. I refer especially to statements on problems of training, of selecting topics, and of carrying out certain kinds of work such as inquiries that may use statistics. Here I think one must distinguish among the uses of history and the kinds of history, and here there is a marked difference between the United States and Mexico, for in the United States higher productivity and automation create a need to absorb into suitable activities, population that would otherwise be redundant. Among such activities, the pursuit of history is a decorous and favorite choice. México with its lesser degree of industrialization has yet to reach this need. As to the kinds and uses of history, one must distinguish among a number each of which imposes its own requirements. Much of what is complained of in the two papers is apprentice work, the necessary training exercises that teach students the nature of materials and the techniques of inquiry. To ask that these exercises advance collective knowledge is to set a high goal indeed that can be reached only occasionally. A great deal more of historical writing represents what I shoul call the renewal of national myth and of items of popular entertainment. It is generally true that much of such writing is best called artful repetition, but it is equally true that such affirmation in a perhaps slightly updated idiom seems to be a matter of national demand as to myth and of popular need in the materials of public entertainment. There is in the latter a demand for something that can be called new even if it is not and for the kind of updating that will substitute for the biographies of saints those of revolutionary heroes in accordance with changes in taste.

There is indeed a category of new work, that is research that genuinely moves to something different, but such research depends either upon the uncovering of new materials, the development of a new point of view, or the use of new techniques of treatment. These do not spring to the hands of multitudes.

This category of new work, because it does mean moving beyond established lines, has in it the normal human problems of arriving at adequate formulation of concepts, methods, and questions —the age— old human difficulties as we try to encompass within our own understanding a vastly complex and puzzling universe. Furthermore, we are led to demand of the relatively limited materials of past years the answers to questions we now formulate on the basis of conceptions of new kinds of gathering. The vessel frequently cannot take the pressure, and yet oddly enough, handled with some care, can take a good deal more than most scholars think.

At this point I should perhaps give a word of encouragement in that the problems in statistics that Dr. Bernstein points to need upset us less than one might think. The undercount in the Mexican census of 1921 added an error of less than 10 percent, and can easily be handled by known techniques of adjustment from earlier and later counts. The other censuses in turn, by the way, contain margins of error as do all censuses. As for data on imports and exports, the problems in Mexican statistics are no worse than those in the statistics of most countries, and hardly worse than those in data on movement of specie. The truth is that all data, statistics included, have their problems, and we work with greater or lesser margins of error. The important thing is to be aware that we do and not to commit the idiocies of one man who translated the depth of a harbor from meters into feet and inches to the fourth decimal place and so reached a statement that became inaccurate every time a few grains of sand moved on the bottom. In the end, in most research, we do not see all of the material or we never get down to writing, and what material we do see is pervaded with various kinds of error and bias. Our defence is to resort to sampling techniques of various kinds. Sampling techniques is frequently applied to quantitative data; it can be applied to materials of a qualitative nature, especially if the points of view and interests can be sorted out. That means that our search in archives is not to see all but to get adequate samples. Beyond that most masses of documents tend to repeat themselves.

A major problem not put forth in either paper is the need to make available to students and scholars more time for reflection and to decrease the amount of writing they do. What we need is more concise and meaningful writing, that is the elimination in historical writing, except for the tasteful reassertion of myth and popular tale, of writing which has little to say. Today most people write books to convey a few additional points or a suggestion for another interpretation when a few pages would handle the matter fully and well. What are published as articles could better be handled by the learned note of a few paragraphs. That kind of change would require far greater emphasis on quality and disapproval of quantity unless the number of printed pages clearly justified their existence. With the time for reflection thus made available, we in the United States could profit more fully from our studies in Mexico, which have the inestimable benefit of immersing us in another culture and so of enriching our personalities and our existence. For Mexico, with its different conditions, the benefits might come more slowly. They will show up more rapidly as historical inquiry in Mexico expands beyond national history to other countries, a phenomenon that is now well under way.

COMMENTARY

HOWARD F. CLINE

The two papers by Professors Flores Caballero and Bernstein, plus the comments by Professor Borah, collectively pose baffling problems for one like me who has been assigned to make further formal comments. In each instance we have a fascinating and informative individual contribution that merits serious consideration. At the same time they seem unrelated to one another or to some general topic. Originally the planners of this Third Meeting had hoped that this session would address itself to some *common* problems faced by students of Mexican history, whether in Mexico, the United States, or Europe, with discussions revolving about some of the professional and intellectual problems inherent in such historiography. Generally speaking, however, our three documents here have in common only the delineation of disparate socio-economic problems that require administrative and political decisions and solution beyond the power of our small and unorganized band of professional historians here to make, or even influence to any real degree.

Perhaps we can take as axiomatic that at the present, and in the forseeable future, the historiography of Mexico will continue to operate within the economics of poverty, not of affluence. Improvements will come incrementally, not by quantum jumps. This approach applies even more specifically to developments in the indispensable auxiliaries, libraries, archives, research centers. As Dr. Flores Caballero cogently and correctly points out, growing demands on public funds in Mexico consistently outstrip available fiscal resources. Support for intellectual enterprises in general, and for historiography and its infrastructures in particular, traditionally have occupied and probably will retain a low national priority. As all of us agree, there has been improvement in these matters in Mexico over three decades, quantitative and qualitative, seen in expanded facilities and in more and better historical studies. I would hope and expect such advances to continue, but at their present evolutionary, not a revolutionary pace. Compared to conditions in some other Latin American countries, Ecuador, Bolivia, Venezuela, for instance, conditions for carrying on historical studies in Mexico are very favorable indeed.

Dr. Flores Caballero also mentioned that many of the same obstacles to historical research seen in Mexico are also found in the United States. I would like to extend slightly his carefully worded statement on this matter. Both my colleagues from the United States have mentioned our purported affluence, but I should like to stress here that the historians as a group have shared in it to a very limited degree. Even that relatively "Golden Age" of the past decade or so is drawing abruptly to a close. Dr. Bernstein has correctly indicated that the United States Government has been a relatively negligible factor in the support of any historical studies, let alone those dedicated especially to Mexico. The National Science Foundation, a major official national element in aiding scientific research, has never supported historical studies, the only exception being history of science. The defense establishment, which has made research money available to selected social sciences for what is essentially applied research, has had and manifests no interest in professional historiography except of its own past. The National Endowment for the Humanities, although headed by an historian, has a very small annual budget, and in its brief existence has been able to do little for the study of foreign cultures, inundated as it has been with applications for funds to carry on investigations of our own national history.

Much of the burden in the United States of supporting research abroad, or investigations concerning foreign cultures, thus has traditionally been borne by the private sector, notably the major foundations. Especially significant was the entrance of the Ford Foundation into this arena. Its several Latin American programs got under way about 1960, but for all intents and purposes they have now been closed out. From previous expenditures that hovered around $ 21 million a year, the figure for all Latin American undertakings has dropped to around $ 4 million, and this reduced sum is restricted to programs on recent and contemporary problems, carried on by its own personnel. But even in the recent heydey of its aid, the Ford Foundation normally eschewed (with minor exceptions) direct support to working historians. It did in 1964 provide the Conference on Latin American History, our professional association, with a small grant of $ 125,000 which permitted it to undertake preparation of things like the Charles Griffin *Guide to the Historical Literature of Latin America* and other generally useful tools. But Ford Foundation renewal funds were not forthcoming last year to publish them. In this connection it might be worth noting, in line with Borah's implied and useful suggestion that needed for improvement of Mexican historical studies is a manual like Porras Barrenechea *Fuentes Históricas Peruanas,* that the Griffin *Guide* which attempts to provide such coverage for the historical literature of Latin America as a whole, required about $ 100,000, including costs of publication, and that such sums are now no longer available from United States sources. In short the so-called affluence was never very great, and it was short-lived.

Rather than being depressed at the thought that we may now again be driven back on the small individual resources we can muster among ourselves, I tend to be calm, and even perhaps relieved. Rather than indulging in some of the gamesmanship and grantsmanship to which Professor Bernstein alludes, both students and their mentors may well be forced to think more clearly about the main business of historical scholarship: to find significant problems and to bring personal ingenuity and dogged persistence to bear in solving them. In this new intellectual Darwinism that has already begun, the fittest will survive. We shall fortunately reduce the number of marginal figures who invade México and perform disgracefully in archives and libraries in the manner Professor Flores Caballero describes so restrainedly in the closing paragraphs of his paper. I might add that they often act much the same in U.S. repositories, where they are equally arrogant and demanding.

In short, we are more and more directly facing an enforced academic birth control situation. Our planned families of young scholars may well be the better for facing some of the austerities that many of us took for granted in the far-off days when young people actually paid to go to graduate school. Their seniors, too, may be forced to sharpen their own pencils.

Thus I foresee that some if not most of the redundant population whom Professor Borah views as becoming academic historians of Mexico merely because it is a decorous activity is likely to emigrate to greener scholarly pastures, and God-speed. The hardy band that survives in Mexico, the United States, and elsewhere will find many useful things to do, often capable of accomplishment without much more investment than personal dedication, and a willingness to help one another. I have been struck by the fact that the Brazilianists, who mushroomed in number far beyond the telephone-boothful mentioned by Professor Bernstein, created within an academic generation a remarkable group of young scholars. Among other things these graduate students and recent Ph.D. degree recipients cooperated to produce a field guide to Brazil which covers many of the practical aspects of pursuing historical work there, such as how to cash a check, as well as invaluable notes on archives and other scholarly resources, based on their own recent personal experience. Such a compilation for Mexico, brought together by our young people, in cooperation with their Mexican peers, might well improve the efficient use of valuable scholarly time by all.

At least two problems mentioned by my North American colleagues are likely to diminish, if my estimate has any validity. Dr. Borah notes that the financial support available to historians in the United States in the past few years "has reached the point of bringing us to a standard of living that hampers study and reflection, or even worse, leads us to shy away from thought that might imperil the flow of funds". We are past that era already. Apparently it will take a little time to see if the quality of writing improves now that lack of munificence will automatically provide enforced leisure and time for reflection. But I think that the time for study and reflection is not something we see as a problem, but rather something that we now should welcome and must me prepared to live with.

Dr. Bernstein in passing mentions a problem, also touched on peripherally by Professors Flores Caballero and Borah, that concerns us all, and to which there are no ready answer. It concerns the increasing amount of research materials becoming available and a wastage of scarce human resources by duplicated research, in the face of dwindling financial support, seemingly calling for some mechanisms providing central direction and central ordering of scarce human resources. I am not quite sure of Professor Bernstein's position on these matters, nor how to interpret his statement that "it is impossible to pontificate on intellectual freedom and arrive at the conclusion that given a policy of laissez-faire in the choice of topics, a sort of invisible hand will guide us to the greatest benefit for all mankind and the best of all possible worlds". I do not know if he believes in such invisible hand, or if he does, whether he favors laissez-faire or some planning. In discussing the proposed plans of the Latin American Studies Association for some rationalization of these matters, he says it appears to him "that the field of Latin American studies is moving toward over-organization which, through its influence over many sources of funds, would stress and steer researchers into areas favored by an in-group. Over-bureaucratization can be counter-productive". This requires comment.

In the first place, I think the kind and degree of coordinating activity proposed by the Association is rather different from those implied in this statement. So far as I know, there is absolutely no intention of imposing some monstrous Politbureau plan worked out by a secret elite to direct scholarly lives. This attempt would not only be unwise, but wholly impossible within the academic community as now constituted. This is a bogus issue. The Association's role is to aid, not control research. For it as for us here the problem obviously becomes one of devising or suggesting the means to overcome as a group certain common problems that seemingly are beyond the abilities of an individual scholar to solve.

It is, of course, to these latter problems that this Session was presumably dedicated. Some of the assumptions on which discussion can fruitfully be based include the proposition that history and its writing is a house of many mansions, and historiography thrives within a pluralistic intellectual universe where no single orthodoxy (except a sincere search for historical truth) dominates. Infinite are the combinations of materials, techniques, and frames of reference which may be legitimately employed to write history. No one general program could hope to provide each researcher with all the source materials he needs, or even information on where to find them. However, as Dr. Borah correctly notes, no one ever sees everything he needs. We all do the best we can with what we have, but there are general improvements that reasonably can be discussed.

One is greater accessibility to materials, both in the United States and in Mexico. This poses less problem to the colonialist than to the specialist in the national period, where it grows more acute in almost geometric proportion by years from the turn of the twentieth century, and is often insuperable for recent times. This unavailibility of sources applies not only to the personal papers of important or even lesser individuals mentioned by our speakers, but is particularly serious for records in public but bureaucratic hands. One group of such records of special interest and concern relates to various joint enterprises undertaken by the United States and Mexican government; neither side can or will release them to scholarly eyes without permission from the other partner, normally nearly impossible to obtain. In both countries access to diplomatic papers seems much more difficult and complicated than any real or assumed threat to national security justifies, but I am at a loss to suggest any viable solution to the problem.

In mentioning the problem of sources for recent and contemporary history, I should like to enter a caveat against the unbridled and often witless use of oral history techniques mentioned by Dr. Bernstein. I do not refer to the carefully controlled approach by Dr. Wilkie and some others. I do deplore the growing notion that a North American graduate student barely fluent in English, let alone Spanish, can be turned loose on busy Mexican nationals with a tape-recorder and the conviction that it somehow replaces dreary archival research and that they have an obligation to be interviewed.

Obviously a catalog of gaps and barriers to particular research can be augmented infinitely by each researcher. However, despite them I should like to echo the muted notes of optimism sounded by three scholars whose remarks I have reviewed. Even in the face of inadequate financing, scattered and intractable source materials, and the other drawbacks, a very respectable body of Mexican history is being written by capable historians in many lands. Its quantity and quality need no extended apology.

COMENTARIOS

J. IGNACIO RUBIO MAÑÉ

I

Interesante es la exposición de cómo se desarrollan en Estados Unidos de América las investigaciones históricas relativas a la América Latina y muy especialmente a México. Pondera ese progresivo interés de los estudiosos norteamericanos, afirmando que muy cerca de la mitad considera algún aspecto de la historia de México como su especialidad. Ilustra ese gran interés con la referencia de un plan que se presentó en la Universidad de Buffalo para fotocopiar todos los archivos de la América Latina.

Señala cómo ha mejorado el nivel de preparación de los jóvenes que en los Estados Unidos de América se interesan en la historia de México: hablan la lengua española con mayor fluidez, procuran aumentar sus conocimientos en otras ciencias sociales, amplían su atención en el arte, en los problemas económicos y políticos, y en la cultura general tanto del México moderno como del prehistórico. Afirma también que se ha elevado el nivel de la metodología histórica y su sentido crítico. Sin embargo confiesa que en esa preparación profesional se ha descuidado el conocimiento de los misterios del alma mexicana y la idiosincracia de la organización del campo que se ha escogido para estudio.

Indica que la preocupación de maestros y alumnos en Estados Unidos de América es acertar en la selección de temas adecuados para conducir un estudio o una investigación en el campo de la historia de la América Latina. Que ya se van agotando las tradiciones que dejaron Bolton, Hackett, Haring y Tannenbaum. Sin embargo confiesa que todavía es inagotable el mosaico que presentan ciertos sucesos importantes, que no han sido debidamente investigados, o que necesitan revisarse exposiciones ya establecidas a causa de nuevas fuentes descubiertas, o por nuevos puntos de vista que se reflejan de otras ciencias sociales.

Puntualiza que el panorama presenta algunos aspectos de desorganización de tantos temas latinoamericanos, que requieren mayor atención, aunque ahora ya se progresa en ese análisis. Recomienda conocer ese examen en la antología que Howard F. Cline ha publicado con el título de *Latin American History: Essays on its Study and Teaching, 1898-1965.*

Considera que en la selección de temas se sigue mucho lo que está de moda: el militarismo mexicano, la Revolución Mexicana y la Reforma Agraria. Que de otras ciencias sociales puede hallarse repertorio de asuntos que despierten interés, como interpretaciones económicas y políticas, finanzas gubernamentales, desarrollo regional, caudillajes, oligarquías, gobiernos encabezados por militares y radicales.

Encarece el asombroso progreso que se ha alcanzado en los Estados Unidos de América en proporcionar guías de investigación en la historia de los países latinoamericanos. Recomienda para conocer esto la obra del doctor Cline, *Latin American History*. Menciona publicaciones recientes que informan de esos progresos. Aduce, asimismo, el gran despliegue de información de los trabajos que se preparan, que se escucha en las reuniones de historiadores. Cita las funciones del Latin American Studies Association Consortium, que labora en coordinar investigaciones y becas. Refiere los esfuerzos, las aventuras y las experiencias para financiar investigaciones. Puntualiza que si se comparan los fondos destinados a esas inversiones en otras disciplinas de las ciencias sociales con los que se aportan para las averiguaciones históricas, la desproporción es evidente porque éstos son escasos. Que muchas veces tienen los maestros que combinar su tiempo consagrado a la enseñanza para que los recursos adquiridos con estos esfuerzos les sirvan para investigaciones en archivos y bibliotecas. Proporciona algunas noticias sobre las inversiones destinadas a proteger esas investigaciones históricas.

Indica el asombroso crecimiento de los materiales y de las técnicas de la investigación histórica en los últimos veinte años, con la publicación de bibliografías, guías, manuales, índices, listas, catálogos, boletines y revistas que informan dónde pueden hallarse las fuentes históricas en los Estados Unidos de América. Cita como ejemplo el caso de un historiador interesado en la vida colonial de Virginia. Pasó dos años en los archivos británicos y a su retorno supo que toda la documentación que había ido a consultar en Londres se hallaba ya fotocopiada en la Biblioteca del Congreso, en Washington.

Señala cómo es grande la cantidad de archivos mexicanos que todavía están sin explorarse debidamente y la riqueza documental que en ellos se custodia. Advierte que no se debe confiar mucho en ciertas estadísticas publicadas en México, porque no se ajustan a realidades investigadas a conciencia. Observa también los riesgos que corren en confiarse en cuestionarios, como asimismo en informes que se consiguen con entrevistas o por noticias orales.

Ante toda esta exposición del autor tengo cuatro puntos que comentar:

1. Si es evidente el asombroso desarrollo técnico de bibliografías, guías, catálogos, índices, etcétera, resalta también que hay desproporción en la producción de obras de alto nivel de investigación histórica que haya aprovechado tanto material acumulado. ¿No sería más conveniente desviar algo tantos esfuerzos técnicos hacia la rendición de frutos de asimilación de tantos elementos?

2. Es asimismo admirable el crecido interés de los estudiosos en los Estados Unidos de América que tienen enfocada su atención hacia la historia de la América Latina y especialmente de México; pero esto se hace con el unilateral punto de vista de ellos. ¿No sería conveniente que surgiera también el interés por considerar los puntos de vista de los latinoamericanos, especialmente de los mexicanos? Así se acallaría la crítica acerba de los enemigos de los Estados Unidos de América, que maliciosamente suponen que ese movimiento de estudios es una de las características del imperialismo yanqui.

3. Si los archivos mexicanos carecen de guías que ilustren su contenido,

convendría que esto se hiciera con mayor interés general y no exclusivo de un país. Es evidente que la guía de Bolton ha sido muy útil y es la única que se ha hecho hasta hoy, pero fue hecha exclusivamente para servir a los historiadores de los Estados Unidos de América y no para otros países. Es más amplio el interés de las guías que el doctor Harrison ha hecho de los Archivos Nacionales en Washington, en donde todos los países latinoamericanos tienen algo que estudiar.

4. Procurar una mejor selección de las becas que se conceden a estudiosos mexicanos, cuidando otorgarlas a los que han demostrado vocación y austeridad, además de obra hecha. Que no se utilicen para intereses personales, fomentar turismo intelectual y menos para abrir oportunidades a la emigración de nuestros valores.

II

Examina el autor el estado de la investigación histórica en México, señalando como mayor impedimento para su desarrollo la poca atención que el sector público tiene para esta clase de trabajos intelectuales. Explica con evidente realismo por qué sucede esto, afirmando que a la resolución de problemas económicos y sociales muy apremiantes se destinan las inversiones de dicho sector público. Que es cierto que hay un ritmo constante y acelerado de crecimiento económico en México; pero que el avance de los centros de investigación no tienen ese mismo progreso.

Advierte, con el mismo tono de realismo, que a pesar de que las inversiones del sector público, en educación son las más altas de su presupuesto en general, su mayor atención está enfocada hacia el problema de la educación mínima, uno de los más apremiantes de este país. Que, a pesar de esa fuerte inversión, no hay la debida atención a los servicios que debían prestar los archivos y las bibliotecas a la cultura nacional.

Si en esto que el autor expone hay realidad, creo que hay tanta o mayor en otros aspectos que intento ahora comentar. Si analizamos la actividad intelectual en México, podemos distinguir que hay pobreza de investigación histórica. Se prefiere la exposición ideológica o la interpretación de los hechos. Y es que la tarea del investigador de la historia en México requiere una vocación heroica de renunciación a cierto porvenir económico, la vocación propia de los religiosos benedictinos que deban hacer votos de permanente austeridad. Si a esto agregamos que a los jóvenes mexicanos no se les encauza por el camino de una verdadera vocación, que tienen apremios económicos y se les mal conduce, tenemos entonces un lamentable panorama de frustraciones.

La enseñanza de la historia en México no promueve la investigación histórica. En muchas cátedras universitarias se tiene muy triste idea de lo que es la búsqueda en los archivos, considerándola como un trabajo de curiosidad, una industria de eruditos, una fábrica de fechas y de nombres en las montañas de miles de documentos. Se prefiere fomentar la agilidad ideológica, de la filosofía, revisar teorías novedosas y presentar interpretaciones deslumbrantes con matices de originalidad. La mayoría de las tesis son reflejos de esas deficiencias de investigación documental.

Si el poder público no invierte mucho en archivos es porque en gran parte es mínima la atención de los intelectuales mexicanos a la utilidad de esos repositorios para sus trabajos. Si los archivos mexicanos se confunden con las bodegas comerciales es porque no hay la debida demanda de sus funciones. Si no se elevan los sueldos de los archivistas es porque no hay la correspondiente capacidad de preparación estudiosa de ellos, ni la vocación, ni la disciplina. Si no hay archivistas competentes es por la carencia de una preparación de alto nivel que incumbe a los maestros. Creo que en todo esto hay eslabones de la mala organización de los estudios.

El verdadero investigador de la historia en México tiene que formarse por sí solo y aislarse del ambiente de ideas peregrinas. Si es cierto que hay muy lamentables deficiencias en los servicios de los archivos y que el sector público no les ha prestado toda la atención debida, iguales o tal vez mayores son las deficiencias en la preparación académica de un verdadero investigador. Si muy pocos mexicanos utilizamos los archivos para preparar trabajos históricos, no es extraño que el poder público no los atienda. Tengo un ejemplo que ilustra esta situación. Hace poco más o menos dieciséis años fue nombrado director del Archivo General de la Nación todo un señor profesor de filosofía que enseñaba en la Universidad Nacional Autónoma de México. En el momento que recibió dicho nombramiento surgió entonces para él la cuestión de averiguar dónde se hallaba esa institución, pues ignoraba su existencia. Otro fue el de un estudiante universitario que lo envió su maestro al Archivo General de la Nación para buscar el documento original en que constara la frase que se atribuye a Álvaro Obregón, cuando dicen que dijo que no había general mexicano que aguantara un cañonazo de cincuenta mil pesos. Otro que quiso ver documentos del siglo XVI y reclamó que los quería escritos en español y no en árabe, como los que estaba viendo. Si éste es el triste nivel de la investigación histórica en México, ¿cómo puede exigirse mejor organización de los archivos?

Es muy cierto que hay un pequeño grupo de verdaderos investigadores que luchan en este México de los grandes contrastes, en que no falta confusión de valores y ambiciones desorbitadas. Ilustraré con ejemplos algunos casos. Un investigador que se dolía de haberse quemado las pestañas con fatigosas búsquedas en los archivos, durante diez años, y no tener recursos para comprar un coche último modelo. Otro que pretendía una beca doble para pasar en Europa o en Estados Unidos de América una soñada luna de miel con su prometida. No hay conciencia de que estas actividades de investigaciones históricas no darán nunca para ser un magnate con grandes posibilidades económicas.

México carece de especialistas en archivos históricos, es cierto; pero antes de conceder las remuneraciones y los alicientes debemos prepararlos adecuadamente y encauzar sus vocaciones. Cuando ya existan, exigir entonces la base económica de esos valores intelectuales.

Es cierto, también, que las tareas de la catalogación y clasificación del Archivo General de la Nación no progresan mucho. Esto se debe a la carencia de material humano debidamente preparado y disciplinado, más que a razones presupuestales.

Observo que hay alguna confusión en lo que el autor menciona del

Archivo de la Catedral de México, que debe en realidad llamarse del Arzobispado de México. Dentro de ese archivo está el del Cabildo de la Catedral, donde se custodian las actas. También hay cedularios, de los cuales
algunos publicó don Alberto María Carreño, pero no todos. Mucha de esta
documentación permanece guardada como secreta y el público no tiene
acceso a ella. Los archivos de carácter económico están en la sección de
Hacedería, dentro del Archivo del Arzobispado, y de éstos son los que
no hay anteriores a 1870. Algunos de esos expedientes, no todos, están en el
Archivo General de la Nación, en la sección llamada Papeles de Bienes
Nacionales.

Se queja el autor del trabajo que comento, respecto a que el Archivo
General de la Nación y otros no han estado bajo la dirección de especialistas en la investigación histórica y que los titulares no se dedican totalmente a esa dirección por necesidades económicas de combinar esas labores
para lograr algún aumento a sus ingresos. Reconoce que han sido destacados
historiadores, profesores distinguidos y bibliófilos notables. Sin propósitos
de egolatría, el actual director del Archivo General de la Nación prefiere
declinar los honores de contarse entre los así elogiados y afirma que desde
las 8 de la mañana hasta las 14.30 horas está en su despacho para
atender los servicios de la investigación histórica.

Como recomendaciones encarezco los puntos siguientes:

1. Que se concedan becas a archivistas profesionales mexicanos para
conocer las técnicas de los archivos nacionales de los Estados Unidos.

2. Que se concedan becas en escuelas especialiazdas de Estados Unidos
a estudiantes postgraduados, que hayan demostrado toda una vocación para
la especialidad de archivos.

3. Promover conferencias de archivistas profesionales de Estados Unidos
en centros de investigación histórica en México.

RELATORÍA

VICTORIA LERNER

El debate general se inició con una discusión relacionada con lo que debió incluirse en las ponencias según el título de la sesión. Algunos participantes consideraron que los ponentes expusieron y analizaron los problemas prácticos a los que se enfrentan los investigadores de la historia, pero que descuidaron otros de los aspectos que se consideró debía ser el contenido de los escritos; es decir, el tratamiento de áreas de estudios comunes, tales como los problemas derivados de la vecindad o fronterizos, que interesen a investigadores de ambas nacionalidades. Se hizo hincapié en que debía revalorarse lo que se ha hecho en relación con estos problemas y de intentar una historiografía doble de mexicanos y norteamericanos.

Los ponentes defendieron el contenido y enfoque de sus escritos, considerando que en toda la III Reunión se estaban tratando problemas comunes de investigación y que ellos habían escogido un aspecto de ellos. Reconocieron que sólo habían tocado una parte del complicado tema general y que el estudio que se les pedía necesitaba de mayor tiempo y espacio.

Se acordó por unanimidad en la necesidad de establecer una mayor comunicación entre los historiadores de ambos países, de procurar un mayor intercambio de información y de materiales y de revalorar, en conjunto, los temas comunes que se desprenden del hecho de que una parte de nuestra historia y nuestros problemas nos son comunes. Se concluyó que éste debería ser el contenido de las ponencias dedicadas a esta sesión en la próxima Reunión de Historiadores Mexicanos y Norteamericanos.

XI. HISTORIOGRAFÍA
DE LAS RELACIONES INTERNACIONALES

Presidente: Roque González Salazar, director del Centro de Estudios Internacionales de El Colegio de México.

Ponentes: Sheldon Liss, profesor asistente de Estudios Latinoamericanos, Indiana State College; Berta Ulloa, profesora e investigadora del Centro de Estudios Históricos de El Colegio de México.

Comentaristas: M. S. Alperovich, Instituto de Historia Latino Americana, Moscú; Carlos Bosch García, profesor de historia, Facultad de Filosofía y Letras, UNAM y director de C.I.L.A.; Lyle C. Brown, University of Texas, Austin; Horst Drechsler, Centro de Estudios Latinoamericanos, Universidad de Rostock, República Federal Alemana.

Participantes: Robert Burr, Universidad de California, Los Angeles; Howard F. Cline, The Hispanic Foundation, Biblioteca del Congreso de Washington; Daniel Cosío Villegas, El Colegio Nacional; Mario Ojeda, profesor del Centro de Estudios Internacionales de El Colegio de México; César Sepúlveda, profesor e investigador de las Relaciones Internacionales de México; David Trask, Universidad del Estado de Nueva York, Stony Brook; Lyle Brown, profesor asistente de ciencia política, Baylor University.

Participantes europeos: M. S. Alperovich, Instituto de Historia Latino Americana, Moscú; Horst Drechsler, Centro de Estudios Latinoamericanos, Universidad de Rostock, República Federal Alemana; Peter Calvert, lector de historia política, Universidad de Southampton, Inglaterra; Gordon Connel-Smith, Universidad de Hull, Inglaterra.

Relator: Miguel Marín, Secretaría de Relaciones Exteriores.

RELACIONES INTERNACIONALES DE MÉXICO: ¿DÓNDE ESTÁN LOS YANQUIS?

In the recently published historical literature of Mexico, international relations have generally been eclipsed by the vital debates on the Revolution. The history of ideas, with economic, political and social themes, has taken precedence over international politics. Few historians have viewed the Mexican Revolution as an international experience and new attempts to do so might prove pointless. Despite recent United States emphasis on training diplomatic historians, university programs devoted to Latin America, easier access to archival collections, and new research libraries, individuals who have utilized these resources have concentrated on Mexican-United States relations to the exclusion of Mexico's dealings with the rest of the world.

Within the past decade many traditional political scientist have been replaced by data quantifiers or sociologically oriented technicians. This has been particularly so in the United States where as a consequence diplomacy and the study of international politics has been hindered. Historians are increasingly alone in the quest to chronicle and interpret past interplay between nations.

This work focuses on the literature, published within the last decade, concerning Mexico's twentieth century internacional relations, exclusive of the realm of Mexican-United States diplomacy. The paucity of materials in the field permits the handling of a broad range of topics that fall within our general scope. By no means is this work comprehensive. Nor is it confined exclusively to the work of young scholars, as originally suggested by those who established the framework for the paper. The imposition of such restrictions would preclude its writing. No picayune attempts will be made to differentiate between diplomatic history, foreign policy, or international relations. The works under discussion will primarily be those of a specialized nature which deal with all the aforementioned topics. The major emphasis will be upon scholarly monographs, although a few articles which have appeared in English will be examined. [1] The writer has at times been compelled to analyze Mexican international relations, but for the most part indicates existing gaps and areas for potential development, and raises questions for future scholarship to answer.

---

[1] To do likewise for Spanish language articles would be impossible within the confines of this paper.

In addition to works on Mexican-United States relations, this paper will also exclude the many excellent legal treatises, particularly on international law, which have been published recently in Mexico, as well as literature on foreign economic relations and development. The last decade has also produced an abundance of journal articles and monographs dealing with France in Mexico, adding information to major secondary works on diplomacy prior to the intervention, [2] the French in Mexico, [3] and the aftermath, [4] none of which fall within the purview of this paper. Also omitted is the early Diaz era and a few significant volumes dealing with relations with Guatemala, [5] Central America, France, Great Britain, Spain and the Vatican [6] during that period.

FOREIGN POLICY

Virtually no literature, either monographic or in article form, by a citizen of the United States has appeared on the making and conduct of Mexican foreign policy. Frank Brandenburg's "Foreign Policy And International Affairs", which appeared as a chapter in his *The Making*

[2] See, Carl H. Bock, *Prelude to Tragedy. The Negotiation and Breakdown of the Tripartite Convention of London, October 31, 1861.* Philadelphia Univ. of Penna. Press, 1966. Jose Fuentes Mares, *Juarez y la intervención.* Mexico, Editorial Jus, 1962.

[3] See, Jack A. Dabbs, *The French Army in Mexico, 1861-1867.* The Hague, Mouton & Co., 1963. Arturo Arnáiz y Freg & Claude Bataillon (eds), *La intervención francesa y el imperio de Maximiliano. Cien años después, 1862-1962.* México, Asociación Mexicana de Historiadores e Instituto Francés de América Latina, 1965. Lilia Díaz (trans. & ed.), *Versión francesa de México. Informes diplomáticos,* vol. II, 1858-1862, vol. III, 1862-1864, vol. IV, 1864-1867. México, El Colegio de México, 1964-1967.

[4] See, Lucía De Robina (ed.), *Reconciliación de México y Francia, 1870-1880.* México: Publicaciones de la Secretaría de Relaciones Exteriores, 1963.

[5] See, Ministerio de Educación Pública de Guatemala, *Memoria sobre la cuestión de límites entre Guatemala y México. Presentada al Señor Ministro de Relaciones Exteriores por el Jefe de la Comisión Guatemalteca, 1900, & Límites entre Guatemala y México.* I: *La cuestión de límites entre México y Guatemala, 1875.* II: *Cuestiones entre Guatemala y México, 1895.* Guatemala, Centro Editorial, 1964. Daniel Cosío Villegas, *El Porfiriato. La vida política exterior.* Parte 1, vol. v. of *Historia moderna de México.* México, Editorial Hermes, 1960.

[6] See, Daniel Cosío Villegas, *El Porfiriato. La vida política exterior.* Parte 2. (Vol. VI. of *Historia moderna de México*) México, Editorial Hermes, 1963. José Bravo Ugarte, *Historia de México,* t. III, *Relaciones internacionales territorio, sociedad y cultura.* México, Editorial Jus, 1959. Javier Malagón Bárcelo, Enriqueta López Lira & José María Miquel I. Vergés, *Relaciones diplomáticas hispano-mexicanas, 1839-1898. Serie I, Despachos Generales, IV, (1846-1848).* México, El Colegio de México, 1968.

Of Modern Mexico, [7] merits attention. More than half of this unusual treatment is devoted to foreign policy and its formulation, with stress on economic factors. Brandenburg contends that the basic guiding principles of Mexican policy often prove paradoxical. He cites collective security, juridical equality of nations, national sovereignty, national self-determination, non-intervention, pacific settlement of international disputes, protection of basic human rights, regionalism, and universalism as the cardinal principles which often, because of delicate inter-relationships, cause conflicts. [8] For example, how does Mexico maintain diplomatic relations with Cuba and not offend the Organization of American States or its respective members Brandenburg poses many such questions and presents insights into a multitude of unexplored facets of Mexican foreign policy.

Mexican foreign policy has been unique in that the nation has generally had no ideological, political, or territorial interests beyond her own borders. Her primary quests have been peace and independence, and she has tried to avoid international entanglements. However, the nationalistic nature of the 1917 Constitution, which guides Mexican foreign policy, has caused problems with other nations. Article twenty-seven of that document contains the basic international goals of the Revolution, those being agrarian reform, and the recovery of natural resources from foreign ownership. In "Revolution And Foreign Policy: Mexico's Experience", Jorge Castañeda emphasizes that, prior to the Revolution, expropriation was traditionally valid in international law only in the maintenance of public order. [9] Castañeda points out that Mexican style expropriation, with compensations not being paid immediately, but rather when best suited to the economic stability of the expropriator, has established a hemispheric trend [10] which has touched off numerous international quarrels. He mentions basic principles of equality of rights between nationals and aliens, non-responsibility of a state for damages suffered during civil strife, and the concept of non-recognition of territorial conquest, which have been violated during the Revolution as Mexico has assumed abligations for acts committed by Revolutionary forces, and has expressed a moral commitment to compensate. [11]

In "The Foreign Policy of Mexico", [12] Francisco Cuevas Cancino presents an excellent historical analysis of his nation's international

[7] Frank R. Brandenburg, *The Making of Modern Mexico.* Englewood Cliffs, Prentice Hall, Inc., 1964.

[8] *Ibid.,* p. 320.

[9] Jorge Castañeda, "Revolution And Foreign Policy: Mexico's Experience", *Political Science Quarterly,* vol. 78 (Sept., 1963), 391-417.

[10] *Ibid.,* p. 398.

[11] *Ibid.,* p. 394.

[12] Francisco Cuevas Cancino, "The Foreign Policy of Mexico", *Foreign Policies In A World Of Change.* New York, Harper & Row, 1963.

behavior. He indicates the adaptation of an individualistic foreign policy to the nation's historical configurations, an area that needs further elucidation. From his cursory treatment of the subject one sees that an interpretative history of the changes in the course of Mexican foreign policy throughout the phases of the Revolution is feasible. A work that deemphasizes the narrative approach in favor of analysis is in order. Cancino states Mexico depends on a spiritual interpretation of history, and displays a contempt for the materialistic shaping of diplomacy. [13] Exposure to Cancino's work leaves many questions unanswered or half explained. Why has Mexico's foreign policy always been cautious and even defensive within Latin America? Why has Mexico not been more active in post-World War II international affairs? After all, is not Mexico confronted with the problems of diplomatic recognition, or even the threat of war? The preliminary works by Brandenburg, Cancino and Castañeda constitute a challenge to further scholarship in the foreign policy domain.

INTERVENTION

A basic component of Mexico's foreign policy has been an overwhelming desire to preserve her independence. This, coupled with numerous tragic experiences with foreign powers, has made her sensitive to intervention of any type. Mexican literature consistently mentions the Argentine legalist Carlos Calvo who stated in 1863 that sovereignty is inviolable and precludes resident aliens from requesting their own governments to intervene on their behalf. Mexico has followed the precepts of Luis Maria Drago, of Argentina, who reiterated Calvo's ideas in 1902 by asserting that public debts cannot be cause for armed intervention or occupation of territory of an American state. The doctrine of non-intervention eminates from Mexico's basic belief in the state's right to guide its own destiny. It even extends to the right of recognition as exemplified by the well known derogation of the Mexican policies of Woodrow Wilson as moral imperialism.

Both at Montevideo in 1933 and Buenos Aires in 1936, Mexico strove vociferously for hemispheric acceptance of non-intervention, and the belief that states determine their own forms of internal government and protect human rights themselves. Mexico rejected the doctrines of Uruguayan Foreign Minister Rodriguez Larreta who, in 1945, proposed collective action by hemispheric republics to safeguard endangered human rights. Paradoxically, in 1960 at the San Jose Conference, Mexico opposed all types of intervention and simultaneously supported the idea that the inter-American system was incompatible

[13] *Ibid*, p. 652.

with totalitarianism. Is the belief that international Communism is inimical to OAS principles reconcilable with a strict non-intervention policy? How does one explain Mexico's position in light of her often professed belief that defense against foreign ideology is a matter of domestic rather than international jurisdiction? Numerous similar conundrums currently exist, involving intervention, which have yet to be investigated and analyzed by non-Mexican historians.

The Mexican point of view has been presented sagaciously by Isidro Fabela in *Intervención*, [14] which deals with the legalistic aspects of non-intervention. His book probes Mexico's position at various Pan American Conferences and strongly reenforces the policy of absolute non-intervention. This piece of scholarship is justifiably anti-United States, and opens many avenues of historical scrutiny. For example, one might elaborate upon the theme that the Revolutionary commitment to non-intervention has precluded Mexico from becoming a hemispheric leader in the sense of exercising hegemony over lesser Latin American nations. Is it not feasible to examine more fully the concept of leadership by abstention and genuine national sovereignty?

Numerous inconsistencies remain to be explained. Can Mexico pursue an independent international position and successfully defend the values of Western Civilization? If one is truly independent do values need to be defended? How can Mexico subscribe to the belief in non-intervention and the rights of nations to form their own destiny and yet have aided the Spanish Republican government against Franco? Why does Mexico at times refute the idea of coexistence within the context of self-determination among peoples? Is the concept of non-intervention reconcilable with the defense of democracy, or is the defense of democracy, beyond national boundaries, of itself non-democratic? The answers to these and other questions have not as yet been explored by historians and experts in international relations.

INTERNATIONAL ORGANIZATIONS

International law has been the cornerstone of Mexican foreign policy because the Spanish concept of a community of states which follow similar juridical principles has endured from colonial times. Throughout the twentieth century Mexico has subscribed to the ideas of international cooperation. Yet the literature discussing the subject is sparse.

When the League of Nations was founded in 1919, Mexico was one of four countries, excluding the Central Powers, which was not invited to join. When Mexico finally joined the League in 1931 she repudiated

[14] Isidro Fabela, *Intervención*. México, Escuela Nacional de Ciencias Políticas y Sociales, UNAM, México, 1959.

the Monroe Doctrine, subsequently favored China in the Manchuria matter, opposed Italy in the case of Ethiopia, protested against the Anschluss and the German occupation of the Sudetenland, and supported the Republic of Spain. All of these policies, along with others pertaining to Mexico's participation in the League of Nations and the Permanent Court of International Justice, need contemporary critical investigation and appraisal.

In the United Nations, Mexico has constantly supported the rights of all governments, regardless of size. Certainly within the confines of this body room exists for ample investigation. As of now Jorge Castañeda's *México y el orden internacional*, [15] which was subsequently published as *Mexico and the United Nations*, [16] remains the lone recent volume on the subject. This work, which evolved from the labors of a study group at *El Colegio de México*, presents a chauvinistic view of Mexican foreign relations and policies towards other nations. At this juncture a revised and less partisan edition is in order, one which stresses Mexico's action in the UN *per se*, rather than general policies with the member states. It should include Mexico's reaction to an organization where some members are more equal than others, as well as answers to the following questions. How has Mexico, as a nation with a lengthy colonial past, enunciated her displeasure towards twentieth century colonialism? How does she define colonialism in the ideological context? What has she done to diminish the power of the Security Council, aside from proposing that it be increased in size? In light of her non-interventionist principles how has Mexico reacted to the collective security measures which have necessitated military action on the part of the UN? Why has Mexico generally refused to recognize her potential leadership position among Latin American nations? Is it attributable to her strict adherence to the precepts of national sovereignty? If Mexican sensitivity to imperialism has impeded her leadership capabilities in international organizations, why has she taken the lead in advocating Latin America as a denuclearized zone?

Are professors in the United States disinterested in such matters? Only John Faust and Charles Stansifer in "Mexican Foreign Policy in the United Nations: the Advocacy of Moderation in an Era of Revolution", [17] have explored the situation. They alone, in rudimentary fashion, have chronicled some of the Mexican votes in the UN. They point out that Mexico has generally supported the Russian concept

[15] Jorge Castañeda, *México y el orden internacional*. México, El Colegio de México, 1956.

[16] Jorge Castañeda, *Mexico and the United Nations*. New York, Manhattan Publishing Co., 1958.

[17] John R. Faust & Charles L. Stansifer, "Mexican Foreign Policy in the United Nations: the Advocacy of Moderation in an Era of Revolution", *Southwestern Social Science Quarterly*, vol. 44 (Sept., 1963), 121-129.

of universal membership for all ideologies, and yet has condemned Soviet intervention in Hungary. Paradoxically, Mexico has supported the admission of Albania, Bulgaria, Hungary and Rumania, while simultaneously refusing to seat China. Additional scholarship on many of these points will undoubtedly produce valuable insights into Latin American policy in general, as well as enhance comprehension of Mexican policy.

Since the Chapultepec Conference of 1945, Mexico has pursued a more Pan Americanistic attitude than the United States in both the UN and the OAS. A need exists for thorough studies of Mexico's policies in the Inter-American system. An abundance of research materials, many of which are a matter of public record, have gone unscathed. For example, in the realm of collective security alone, sufficient data exists to form the nucleus of a multivolume series.

THE WESTERN HEMISPHERE

Because of her prominent position in Spain's colonial empire, after independence it was believed that Mexico would exercise hegemony over Latin American affairs. But only during the tenure of Alamán, Gorostiza, Ramos Arizpe, Azcárate and Herrera did México manage her foreign policy on the assumption that she was a great power. [18] Subsequently Mexico fell prey to increased instability and her pretensions towards Latin American leadership diminished. During the twentieth century the nation has not resorted to "bloc" influences for fear that to do so might be intervention. Mexico's profound belief in sovereignty has weakened her in terms of hemispheric power. Despite the lack of an assertive regional policy, the Mexican Revolution has enabled the nation to lead primarily by setting an example for international morality.

How far this moral example has extended in the foreign policy sphere has never been studied. One wonders, to what extent the Latin American nations have endeavored to emulate Mexico's Revolutionary foreign policy. By remaining true to the precepts of peace, not maintaining a large standing army, and keeping military expenditures to a minimum, Mexico has not shared common objectives with many of the nations of the region. Nevertheless, Mexico has been in agreement with most hemispheric states with regard to the need for international economic cooperation. Even in this area of accord, little literature exists, outside of publications produced under the auspices of the UN, the OAS, the Inter-American Development Bank and their respective affiliates.

[18] Cancino, *op. cit.*, p. 643.

The major works dealing with Mexico in hemispheric affairs dwell primarily on relations with the United States. If anything, the proximity of Mexico to the United States and preoccupation with mutual diplomacy should have awakened academic interest as to the other Latin American reactions to Mexican foreign policy. Why have there been no extensive studies on the attitudes of Argentina, Brazil, Chile, the Caribbean, or Central American countries towards Mexico? Have not Bolivia, Cuba, and Guatemala been interested in the foreign policy of the Mexican Revolution? Is it unrealistic to expect commentaries from other Latin American nations on Mexican international relations, when so few works exist on their own foreign policies?

One recently published piece of Mexican literature was Alonso Aguilar's *El Panamericanismo de la Doctrina Monroe a la Doctrina Johnson.* [19] This indictment of Pan Americanism emphasizes an inept OAS controlled by the United States. He touches upon the portents of the Tricontinental Conference of Havana and the possibility of Latin American orientation away from the United States, and links with África and Asia. In espousing Latin American withdrawl from the OAS, Aguilar reiterates the anti-*Komunismo* theories of the Guatemalan scholar-statesman, Juan José Arévalo. [20] Although it is a general work, not primarily designed for scholarly consumption, the book reflects one Mexican viewpoint and might serve as a model for a more specific study of Mexico's hemispheric relations.

If one were confined to works like that of Alonso Aguilar, he might soon come to believe that the United States has a monopoly on hemispheric imperialism and that Mexico has remained unsoiled. However an examination of border relations with Guatemala would reveal that Mexico too has at times been hypocritical. The story of Mexico's annexation of Chiapas and Soconuzco should be analyzed, as should her involvement with Great Britain concerning the proposed transfer of British Honduras to Guatemala. These long-standing problems ought to be studied in depth in orden to add to our growing fund of knowledge about Mexican diplomacy.

Recently there has been an upsurge of Mexican interest in Cuba and *vice versa*. The events of the Cuban revolution of Fidel Castro cannot yet be considered with proper historical perspective. Twenty years hence scholars will want to analyze the early moral support given Castro by the *cardenistas*. Analogies will be drawn between the Mexican and Cuban revolutions, and the current deluge of polemics will be sifted through carefully for historical relevance. Works like

[19] Alonso Aguilar, *El Panamericanismo de la Doctrina Monroe a la Doctrina Johnson*. México, Cuadernos Americanos, 1965.
[20] Juan José Arévalo, *Anti-Komunismo en América Latina*. Buenos Aires, Editorial Palestra, 1959.

Isidro Fabela's *El caso de Cuba*, [21] will be given more credence. Perhaps by the 1980's a comparative study of Castro's endeavors to export Cuba's revolution and Mexico's lack of messianism will prove rewarding. However, a more immediate need os to address the basic question of why Mexico has not consciously exported her Revolution.

Daniel Cosío Villegas' *Cuestiones internacionales de México, una bibliografía*, [22] provides an excellent backlog of materials on hemispheric affairs, many with emphasis on Mexico. Eeach subdivision of this work could be expanded into an historical volume or even a bibliography of its own. Literally dozens of areas within hemispheric re'ations remain untouched. New works dealing with Mexican diplomacy with virtually every Latin American nation remain to be written, and ancient scholarship needs revision in light of new data. At this point, would it be audacious to suggest that Mexico's relations with Canada provide virgin territory for the scholar?

THE EARLY REVOLUTION

After the unimaginative foreign policy of the Díaz years one would hope to find that the Revolution rekindled a literary interest in Mexican international relations. The preponderance of scholarship dealing with the early years of the Revolutions is based upon the México-United States theme. Young scholars from north of the Río Grande remain content to explore the intricacies of their own nations' involvement with the various Revolutionary governments. However, in the past decade Europeans have expanded their horizons, and some heretofore neglected archival collections have been used to produce cogent works which examine Mexican foreign policy from different perspectives.

From behind the Iron Curtain came Friedrich Katz's *Deutschland, Díaz un die mexikanische Revolution. Die deutsche Politik im Mexiko 1870-1920*, [23] a Marxist oriented diplomatic history of German-Mexican relations. Based primarily on German Mission reports from Mexico, this interesting work details European imperialist rivalries and increases the knowledge about the World War I era and the German struggle to enlist the aid of Mexico in the battle against the United States.

[21] Isidro Fabela, *El caso de Cuba*. México, Cuadernos Americanos, 1960.

[22] Daniel Cosío Villegas, *Cuestiones internacionales de México, una bibliografía*. México, Secretaría de Relaciones Exteriores, 1966.

[23] Friedrich Katz, *Deutschland, Diaz un die mexikanische Revolution. Die deutsche Politik im Mexiko 1870-1920*. Berlin, VEB Deutsche Verlag de Wissenschaften. Schriftenreihe des Institutes für allgemeine Geschichte und der Humboldt-Universitat, 1964.

From this volume one discovers a vast store of untapped materials on Mexico in the German Central Archives. A similar treatment of the inter-war years and the World War II period should now be prepared.

Two articles from the United States have recently appeared to supplement the Katz volumen. Warren Schiff's "German Military Penetration into Mexico During the Late Díaz Period", [24] illustrates the influence of the German military ower that of France in Mexico prior to World War I. It points out Germany's faidure to institutionalize her gains, thus enabling United States' influence to remain dominant. This article begins to penetrate the German Foreign Ministry Archives for materials relevant to Mexico. "The Mexican-German Conspiracy of 1915", [25] by Michael Meyer also accentuates German interest in Mexico from the Díaz era. Meyer's piece, which deals with the abortive Mexican-German Cabal of 1915, breaks new ground concerning numerous facets of German-Mexican relations which should be explored. Too little has been written about Mexico's World War I policy, especially with reference to Germany. Even Bárbara Tuchman's *The Zimmerman Telegram*, [26] which deals with a well-know aspect of World War I diplomacy, is primarily based upon sources available in the United States. More pervasive research into German archives should be conducted and the results published.

In conjunction with the Katz volumen *Meksikanskaia revoliutsiia 1910-1917, gg. i. politika SShA*, [27] by the Russians Alperovich and Rudenko, should be read. Another example of Marxian historical analysis, this Soviet view of the Revolution places particular emphasis on United States diplomacy towards Mexico. It also makes one wonder if the Russians have fallen into the pattern of viewing Mexico only in the light of the United States. Or is it the ideological conflict between Communism and capitalism which compels this trend?

Helping the United States save face, the late Alfred Tischendorf authored *Great Britain and Mexico in the Era of Porfirio Díaz*. [28] Tischendorf began to penetrate into Anglo-Mexican diplomacy, a task which was taken up by British political scientist Peter Calvert in *The Mexican Revolution, 1910-1914: The Diplomacy of Anglo Ame-*

[24] Warren Schiff, "German Military Penetration into Mexico During the Late Díaz Period", *Hispanic American Historical Review*, vol. 39 (Nov., 1959), 568-579.

[25] Michael C. Meyer, "The Mexican-German Conspiracy of 1915", *The Americas*, vol. 23 (July, 1966), 76-89.

[26] Barbara W. Tuchman, *The Zimmerman Telegram*. New York, Dell Publishing Co., 1958.

[27] M. Al'Perovich & B. Rudenko, *Meksikanskaia revoliutsiia, 1910-1917 gg. il politika SSha*. Moscow, 1958.

[28] Alfred Tischendorf, *Great Britain and Mexico in the Era of Porfirio Díaz*. Durham, Duke Univ. Press, 1961.

rican Conflict.[29] Although the latter work deals with the diplomacy of the United States, it is cited here for its explorations of British diplomacy during the early years of the Revolution. A clear picture unfolds of British finances being used to counteract American diplomatic and political pressures in Mexico, and British dollar diplomacy is contrasted with the Yankee version. The writer concludes that Great Britain did not emulate the United States by persuing moralistic foreign policy in Mexico. He leaves the impression of British order versus United States chaos in foreign policy. As a study in contrasting styles of diplomacy, Calvert's work is an ideal model for future histories.

Upon turning attention to Mexican titles, one is initially attracted to *Historia diplomática de la Revolución mexicana, 1912-1917,*[30] by Isidro Fabela the ex-Constitutionalist Foreign Minister. Unfortunately the title is somewhat misleading, as both volumes deal essentially with diplomacy between Mexico and the United States. However, Volume II does contain a section dealing with Mexico's neutrality during World War I. Another work by the same person, *Documentos históricos de la Revolución,*[31] contains numerous useful selections pertaining to the early Revolution as excerpted from the Foreign Relations Archives in Mexico City. An additional deceptive title *La política internacional de la Revolución,*[32] by Aarón Sáenz, turns out to deal primarily with United States-Mexican relations during the Obregón years. However, it makes one aware that a similar treatment for relations with the rest of the world is lacking.

THE LATER REVOLUTION

In a statement to the press on September 30, 1930, Mexican Foreign Minister Genaro Estrada issued *La doctrina mexicana* which stipulated that automatic recognition of a government should be accorded, but that when so granted by México it does not imply judgment. From the issuance of this maxim it became an integral part of Mexican Revolutionary foreign policy and a topic of conversation in diplomatic circles throughout the hemisphere. In June of 1964 the Estrada Doctrina was refined by the Mexican government when it stated that the nation would henceforth maintain and with-

[29] Peter Calvert, *The Mexican Revolution, 1910-1914: The Diplomacy of Anglo-American Conflict.* London, Cambridge Univ. Press, 1968.
[30] Isidro Fabela, *Historia diplomática de la Revolución Mexicana, 1912-1917.* México, Fondo de Cultura Económica, vol. i, 1958, vol. ii, 1959.
[31] Isidro Fabela, *Documentos históricos de la Revolución.* México, Fondo de Cultura Económica, 1964.
[32] Aarón Sáenz, *La política internacional de la Revolución.* México, Fondo de Cultura Económica, 1961.

RELACIONES INTERNACIONALES

draw diplomatic agents when it considered it advisable, without judging the right of any nation to accept, preserve, or change its government or authorities. In other words, Mexico would no longer "recognize" governments, but rather just establish diplomatic relations. In light of Mexico's Revolutionary experience, the fact that this doctrine has endured for over three decades and its more recent ramifications, up-to-date monographic literature about it is conspicuous by its absence.

The foreign policy and international relations of the Cárdenas years is of Revolutionary salience. Although the *cardenistas* have not been a political group in the conventional sense, they have had a profound affect upon the course of Mexican history. The Russian author Shul'govskii in his work [33] dealing with the anti-imperialism of the Cárdenas Administration, touches upon the liberation of the Mexican people during the 1930's His analysis of Mexico's emerging socialism provides diverse insights into the nations' role in foreign affairs as the Revolution matured. There remains a need to develop the international aspects of *cardenismo*. For example, considerable Mexican diplomacy ensued following the oil expropriations of 1938. In *México y Estados Unidos en el conflicto petrolero*, [34] Lorenzo Meyer hints at the complexities of Anglo-Mexican diplomacy over the petroleum crisis, but the major focus of his study is United States-Mexican relations. Nevertheless, Mayer's well documented work clears the path for future investigations.

Economists have often attributed the success of the industrial phase of the Mexican Revolution to World War II. Although it is exceedingly difficult to disassociate Mexican foreign policy from relations with the United States with whom she was inextricably bound during the conflict, little monographic literature has been written strictly on Mexico's role in the war. The academic world is currently inundated with literature concerning the diplomacy of the Allied-Axis struggle. Archival collections encompassign the early war years are now accessible, sets of valuable documents have been cataloged and even published. Materials pertaining to the international policies of the later Revolution are beginning to be made available in Mexico by the *Secretaría de Relaciones Exteriores*, [35] as well as

[33] A. Shul'govskii, *Meksika na krutom povorote svoe i istorii: osvoboditel 'naia i antiimperialisticheskaia bor'ba meksidanskogo maroda v 30-e gody i problema vybora puti sotsial' nogo razvitiia*. Moscow, Izdatel'stvo Prosveschenie, 1967.

[34] Lorenzo Meyer, *México y Estados Unidos en el conflicto petrolero, 1917-1942*. México, El Colegio de México, 1968.

[35] For example, see, México: Secretaría de Relaciones Exteriores. *Labor internacional de la Revolución Constitucionalista de México: libro rojo*. México, Ediciones de la Comisión Nacional para la Celebración del Sesquicentenario de la Proclamación de la Independencia Nacional y del Cincuentenario de la Revolución Mexicana, 1960.

abroad, and hopefully an energetic group of embryonic scholars will seize upon them.

INTERNATIONAL IDEOLOGY

With the advent of the Cold War the production of literature pertaining to international ideology, particularly of the leftist variety, increased in Mexico. While leftism in Mexico attracted considerable attention in Mexican academic circles, in the United States it was generally ignored in print. Perhaps this is attributable to the mentality which pervaded the United States during the McCarthy scare which may have subconsciously frightened academicians in subsequent years.

In *La batalla ideológica en México*,[36] Alberto Bremauntz delves into the history of ideas and ilulstrates the importance of Marxism-Leninism to Mexico's development. He derogates the United States, the Roman Catholic Church and capitalism as inimical to the Revolution which he visions being completed only through socialism. Like Juan José Arévalo, he inveighs against anti-*Komunismo* which he claims is detrimental to development. His brief examination of the international aspects of the ideological struggle in Mexico proves enlightening. Like Aguilar and Arévalo he is highly critical of the Latin American military regimes which are sustained by their constant quest to eradicate Communism and buttressed in their endeavors by the State Department.

From the United States and the pen of Karl Schmitt came *Communism in Mexico: A Study in Political Frustration*,[37] which distinguishes between the multifarious Marxist groups in Mexico. Although primarily oriented to internal politics, a chapter on international Communism does discourse on recent relations. This chapter could be expanded into a book, beginning with the early struggles to ignite the fires of international Marxist ideology in Mexico and terminating with the impact of Castroism upon the nation. Schmitt's work is a welcome addition to the literature in the field, but obviously much remains to be done in this highly controversial area. Perhaps a "New Left" historian, if such a person exists among Mexicanists in the United States, might author a work on Communism in Mexico. Also, a history of Communism's affect upon Mexican foreign policy by an American would be thought provoking.

Prior to the emergence of Castro, the Soviet Embassy in Mexico City served as a focal point for dissemination of Communist materials

[36] Alberto Bremauntz, *La batalla ideológica en México*. México, Ediciones Jurídico Sociales, 1962.
[37] Karl M. Schmitt, *Communism in Mexico: A Study in Political Frustration*. Austin, Univ. of Texas Press, 1965.

for Central America, and the Russians have long expressed an interest
in the Mexican Revolution. Rodrigo García Treviño, a former socialist
leader of the *Confederación de Trabajadores de México*, in *La ingerencia rusa en México*, [38] has written an introductory history of the
Mexican Communist Party from its inception under Russia's Michael
Borodin, Japan's Sen Katayama, and India's N. M. Roy. He deals
effectively with the Communism of the 1930's and the impact of
the Comintern upon Mexico. The writer even examines the diplomacy
of international Communism's alignment with England and the
United States against Nazism.

Despite disunity among Marxists in Mexico, for many years the
late Vicente Lombardo Toledano was a major link to international
Communism. For purposes of meeting the minimum electoral requirements Lombardo's *Partido Popular Socialista* supplanted the Communist Party. His Marxist-Leninist writings were prolific and said
by many to have an affect upon the course of the Mexican Revolution.
The writings are analyzed by Gerardo Unzueta in *Lombardo Toledano
y el marxismo leninismo.* [39] In his own volume *¿Moscú o Pekín? La
vía mexicana hacia el socialismo,* [40] the leader of the PPS dealt with
world problems as he made a doctrinaire analysis of the future of
Mexican socialism. Even a scholar in the United States has endeavored
to capture the message Lombardo struggled so long to convey. In
Mexican Marxist: Vicente Lombardo Toledano, [41] published prior to
the labor chief's death, Robert Millon offered a biography of the
leader of the international Communist movement in Mexico. Signi-
ficantly, the author deals with the attitudes of Lombardo with respect
to international affairs.

In explaining why Mexico's Communist Party has made no headway,
journalist José Revueltas, in *Un proletariado sin cabeza,* [42] offers a
disillusioned version of Communism in Mexico. Although he has
not lost his faith in the Communist doctrines, he proposes that the
Mexican Communist Party as early as 1929 failed to organize itself
as the conscience of the proletariat, a role that was assumed by the
Official Party. Also of interest to the student of Mexican Communism
is a work by the artist David Alfaro Siqueiros, *Mi respuesta. La*

[38] Rodrigo García Treviño, *La ingerencia rusa en México.* México, Editorial
América, 1959.
[39] Gerardo Unzueta, *Lombardo Toledano y el marxismo-leninismo.* México,
Fondo de Cultura Popular, 1966.
[40] Vicente Lombardo Toledano, *¿Moscú o Pekín? La vía mexicana hacia el
socialismo.* México, Partido Popular Socialista, 1963.
[41] Robert Millon, *Mexican Marxist: Vicente Lombardo Toledano.* Chapel Hill,
Univ. of North Carolina Press, 1966.
[42] José Revueltas, *Un proletariado sin cabeza.* México, Ediciones de la Liga
Leninista Espartaco, 1962.

historia de una insidia. ¿Quiénes son los traidores a la patria? [43] This collection of documents supplementes the work of Revueltas. The writer criticizes the PRI for its failure to follow a true revolutionary path, and insists that the Communist Party is still capable of rectifying the situation.

Many north of the Río Grande have long believed that the Mexican left will never succeed as long as it espouses foreign ideology which is inimical to a basic tenet of the Revolution. Nevertheless the writings of Jesús Silva Herzog about a world dominated by the Soviet Union and the United States, have been well received in Mexico and Latin America. In *El mexicano y su morada y otros ensayos,* [44] he deals specifically with these themes. Similarly in *American Extremes,* [45] an updated version of *Extremos de América,* [46] the old master Daniel Cosío Villegas confronts the attractions of Communism for those suffering from economic inequality. Cosío differs from Silva Herzog, in that he asserts Communism sounds the death knell to national independence and personal freedom. In a more contemporary vein he treats the impact of Communism upon the world from Russia and Korea to Cuba and the Castro rebellion.

The study of international Communism has considerable appeal in Mexico, where many attribute the success of the Revolution to the borrowing of ideology without adherence to international conspiracies. The appeals of Communism have been apparent to United States historians of Mexican international relations, but lack of productivity in the area indicates disinterest in writing about what has been highly unpopular in their country.

Mexican international relations viewed in terms of the class struggle is an area open to scholarly objectivity, for a great deal of the work in the field has been biased. Notgithstanding the writings on international ideology, a strong anti-foreign sentiment in Mexico is discernable. Xenophobia is still ripe in the Mexican literature on international themes and this pertains to Russia as well as the United States. Marxism seems to be gathering acceptance, while anti-Stalinism remains in evidence. Opponents of the Marxian interpretation of history, such as Antonio Caso, are on the decline. In the final analysis, the study of Marxism in Mexico is still underdeveloped when compared to that of liberalism.

One's readings on Mexican international ideology might culminate

---

[43] David Alfaro Siqueiros, *Mi respuesta. La historia de una insidia. ¿Quiénes son los traidores a la patria?* México, Ediciones de Arte Público, 1960.

[44] Jesús Silva Herzog, *El mexicano y su morada y otros ensayos.* México, Ediciones Cuadernos Americanos, 1960.

[45] Daniel Cosío Villegas, *American Extremes.* Austin, Univ. of Texas Press, 1964.

[46] Daniel Cosío Villegas, *Extremos de América.* México, Tezontle, 1949.

with *Los signos de nuestro tiempo. Extrema izquierda y democracia integral*, [47] which includes brief papers analyzing the fair left and investigating the possibility of a third position in foreign policy. An historical work contrasting Mexican foreign policy with that of De Gaulle, Nasser, or Perón, might enhance the feasibility of this argument.

Because of the nature of the Mexican Revolution, World War II, and the impact of numerous Spanish Republican exiles upon Mexico's intelligentsia, literature concerning right wing ideology has been meager both quantitatively and qualitatively. During the past decade there has been more academic concern with Communism, and fascism, except for the Spanish variety, has been almost dormant in the literary sense. However, with the majority of the peoples of Latin America living under the aegis of militarism, at this time of writing, the scarcity of works involving Mexico's diplomacy with right wing governments is regrettable from the standpoint of utilizing history as a means of furthering comprehension of the present.

NEW DIRECTIONS

The above paragraphs have by no means uncovered all of the voids existing in the recent literature on Mexican international relations. In skimming through some of the areas in which monographs relevant to Mexico's twentieth century international policy have been produced during the past decade, the writer has no doubt been guilty of countless omissions. He has probably offended some of his Mexican *compañeros* by neglecting to mention their works of which he was unfamiliar. The difficulties of preparing this type of paper were many and varied. The shortcomings in collections of over 6.000,000 volumes in Northeastern Ohio, including the Cleveland Public Library's extensive Latin American section, make it evident that more viable and rapid means of exchanging information concerning Mexican scholarly publications have to be devised. To broaden the understanding of Mexico and capture the fancy of potential Mexicanists the immediate need for more translations of basic scholarly works from Spanish to English, and *vice versa*, must be filled.

In addition to the numerous literary deficiencies noted throughout the previous pages, many others exist. For instance, Mexican relations with nations of the Soviet Bloc have not been examined. Not only are there opportunities for scholars to penetrate the history of relations between Mexico and Russia, but diplomacy with Czechoslovakia and Poland, with whom ties have been established the longest,

[47] Víctor Manzanilla Schaffer, *Los signos de nuestro tiempo. Extrema izquierda y democracia integral.* México, Editorial Libros de México, 1961.

should be studied. Mexican relations with France, Great Britain, and Spain during the twentieth century have not been covered in detail. Despite the existence of *México y el Vaticano*, [48] by the Jesuit Luis Medina Ascensio, considerable remains to be done in the field of Mexican—Church diplomacy. Non-Catholic insights into the subject might prove illuminating.

Works are needed which deal with the historical, rather than the legal side of Mexico's treaty commitments. In the realm of legal history a gap exists in literature on Mexico's territorial claims. For example, what have been the international consequences of Mexico's claims to waters extending nine miles beyond her coast as opposed to the generally accepted practice of claiming only three miles jurisdiction? Numerous alien vessels, which have intruded in Mexico's territorial waters, have been seized over the years, and a comprehensive examination of these events has yet to appear in print. Mexico has long been interested in international arbitration and the history of her relations in this field would make interesting reading. Occasionally a work appears like *México y el arbitraje internacional. El Fondo Piadoso de las Californias. La Isla de la Pasión. El Chamizal*, [49] by Antonio Gómez Robledo, which enhances the understanding of Mexican relations. His work corroborates the idea that Mexico's primary diplomatic objective has been the conservation of her territory, a topic alone deserving of an historical tome.

After perusing the volumes on Mexican international relations dealing with the twentieth century and published within the past ten years, the lack of diplomats' published memoirs, biographies, and autobiographies is also apparent. The most important figures in the formulation of Mexican foreign policy, Presidents and Foreign Ministers, have often been men of letters, and their papers should be compiled and published in a useful format.

Mexican historians might also consider using features found in scholarly books published in other countries. Lately, Mexican literature has been appearing with more footnotes, but far too many volumes still lack bibliographies and indices.Paradoxically, the bibliography, which is an integral part of scholarship, has recently emerged as a separate entity. No finer example can be found than *Revolución mexicana, 1910-1920*, [50] a prodigous guide to the contents of multi-volumes in the section on the Mexican Revolution of the Archives

[48] Luis Medina Ascensio, *México y el Vaticano*, vol. i: *La Santa Sede y la Emancipación Mexicana*. México, Editorial Jus, 1965.

[49] Antonio Gómez Robledo, *México y el arbitraje internacional.. El Fondo Piadoso de las Californias. La Isla de la Pasión. El Chamizal*. México, Editorial Porrúa, 1965.

[50] Berta Ulloa Ortiz, *Revolución Mexicana, 1910-1920*. México, Secretaría de Relaciones Exteriores, 1963.

564   RELACIONES INTERNACIONALES

of the Secretary of Foreign Relations, compiled by Berta Ulloa
Ortiz. The format of this well indexed monumental work could
be duplicated for material from other nations including the United
States. Above all, let its contents now direct historians of Mexican
international relations into new and more perspicacious endeavors.

In conjunction with *Revolución mexicana,* the external politics
section of *Fuentes de la historia contemporánea de México,* [51] edited
by Stanley Ross and associates, provides a solid foundation for those
interested in pursuing the literature of Mexico's international relations
up to 1940. Similar proyects must be completed to catalog the
existing literature published in the 1940-1960 era.

FINAL OBSERVATIONS

Over the past ten years the volume of historical studies concerning
Mexico has grown rapidly. As Mexico has gained in international
stature, the overall quality of her native historians has improved.
Greater emphasis has been placed on international relations in
Mexico, as reflected by the increased number of degrees granted
in the field. Under the institutional leadership of *El Colegio de
México,* which has engaged experienced scholars on worthwhile pro-
pects, young academicians of the future have been trained. Names
like Daniel Cosío Villegas and Isidro Fabela are known throughout
the hemisphere for their contributions on Mexican international
relations, and younger scholars are beginning to be noticed. However,
the name of a sing'e historian from north of the Río Grande,
who has distinguished himself in this field, outside of the area of
Mexican-United States relations, fails to come to mind. The few
United States scholars who have ventured into this area have generally
been unimaginative and their work has yielded little in the way
of new interpretations.

The Mexicans too have not been faultless. From the standpoint of
proportionate number of works they have produced in the field, more
interpretative histories should be forthcoming. These could easily
eminate from the published document collections and bibliographies
which have tended to dominate the international relations field in
Mexico over the past decade. That is not to say that bibliographical
and documentary work must be curtailed, but only to suggest that it
is time to divert attention to the more analytical aspects of diplomatic
history. For example, could not existentialist philosophy be applied to
international relations? Might not the historian inquire into the essence

[51] Stanley R. Ross, *et al., Fuentes de la historia contemporánea de México.
Periódicos y revistas,* vol. i. México, El Colegio de México, 1965.

of diplomatic reality? Is it not feasible that from this approach there might evolve a true interpretation of Revolutionary foreign policy? Even if such an effort proved futile from the standpoint of literary production, it could be a worthwhile mental exercise.

In an atempt to gain perspective, a cursory survey of the literature reviewed in the *Hispanic American Historical Review* for the years 1959 to 1968 was conducted and divulged some interesting statistics. [52] During that period thirty-six volumes on Mexican-United States relations were reviewed, with twenty-two originating in the United States and thirteen in Mexico. [53] In contrast, twenty-eight published volumes were reviewed in other areas of Mexican international relations. Of these only five came from the United States, and twenty from Mexico. [54] In light of the fact that in the overall production of historical monographs Mexicanists in the United States have generally kept pace with those in Mexico, obviously the field of Mexican international relations has, for the most part, been overlooked by United States historians. Only Great Britain, among the European countries, has recently made major advances in Mexican studies. Consequently, literature on Anglo-Mexican diplomacy is beginning to emerge.

In general, scholars in the United States have not involved themselves in the controversies evolving out of recent Mexican diplomacy with nations other than their own. Perhaps they have been unaware of the existence of numerous research possibilities. Maybe they have been too cognizant of the hazards of writing diplomatic history involving living individuals and institutions that are vulnerable to criticism. Nevertheless, historians of international relations must be courageous and engage in research and writing about the recent past.

Radical views of Mexican diplomacy and foreign policy have been verbalized in the United States, but have yet to appear in print. To increase the core of knowledge, the depth and scope of scholarship must be expanded. This can be accomplished by new and innovative interpretations of international diplomacy. It might now be opportune to ascertain whether or not orthodoxy in this historical pursuit is healthy, or conducive to intellectual sterility.

In the realm of thought the United States can invade Mexico without trepidation, as cerebrative imperialism is non-existent. Academicians in the United States must delve more deeply into the field of Mexican international relations and atone for past derelictions, so that no longer can it be justifiably asked: *¿Dónde están los yanquis?*

[52] Bear in mind that the *HAHR* generally reviews all works published in the United States, but not in Mexico.

[53] Twenty-three volumes were produced in English, twelve in Spanish, and one in Russian.

[54] Four volumes were published in English, twenty-two in Spanish, and one each in German and Russian.

LA HISTORIOGRAFÍA DE LAS RELACIONES DIPLOMATICAS DE MÉXICO ENTRE 1940 Y 1969

BERTA ULLOA

Intentamos presentar un panorama general de lo que se ha escrito por mexicanos sobre el tema de las relaciones internacionales de nuestro país con otros países, desde su emancipación política de España hasta 1940. Ante todo conviene señalar que entre las dependencias oficiales e instituciones que han patrocinado la publicación de obras históricas o de co!ecciones de documentos, antecedidos de estudios, sobre las relaciones diplomáticas de nuestro país en el periodo señalado, destacan la Secretaría de Relaciones Exteriores, la Universidad Nacional Autónoma y El Colegio de México. La primera reanudó en 1943 la publicación del *Archivo Histórico Diplomático Mexicano* con el subtítulo de Segunda Serie * usando para ella el método monográfico; además en 1961 inició una variante, la de preparar y editar *Guías* de sus grandes fondos documentales, que incluyó en 1966 una excelente *Bibliografía* sobre cuestiones internacionales de México. En cuanto a la Universidad Nacional Autónoma, en sus facultades de Derecho y de Filosofía y Letras, así como en su Escuela de Ciencias Políticas y Sociales, ha preparado profesionistas que en sus tesis para exámenes de grado, sus cátedras y obras escritas posteriormente, se han ocupado de las relaciones internacionales de México. Finalmente, al fundarse El Colegio de México en 1940, en sus centros de Ciencias Sociales (1940), de Historia (1943) y de Estudios Internacionales (1961), ha formado profesionistas en el campo, patrocinado obras, difundido estudios sobre la materia en sus revistas *Historia Mexicana* y *Foro Internacional*, publicado colecciones documentales procedentes de archivos españoles y franceses, y adquirido copias en micropelícula de documentos depositados en Estados Unidos, Francia y la embajada de España en México y, entre 1959 y 1961, se echó a cuestas el trabajo de ordenar algunos ramos presidenciales de este siglo en el Archivo General de la Nación y de elaborar guías para otros ramos de los Archivos Históricos de las Secretarías de la Defensa Nacional y de Relaciones Exteriores. También ha publicado bibliografías, hemerografías y otras obras sobre relaciones internacionales de México, tanto de sus investigadores como de funcionarios de la citada Secretaría de Relaciones

---

* La primera serie abarcó 40 volúmenes, publicados entre 1923 y 1940. Ésta, a su vez, fue precedida por 3 volúmenes de la *Diplomacia Mexicana* que aparecieron de 1910 a 1913.

Exteriores. Sin olvidar que, en combinación con otras instituciones nacionales y extranjeras, ha facilitado los estudios de sus egresados e investigadores más allá de nuestras fronteras. En todas las actividades que ha emprendido El Colegio de México, sobresale la excelente obra de don Daniel Cosío Villegas.

A las instituciones citadas hay que agregar otras que, teniendo un campo diferente de actividades u otros temas de estudio, han colaborado en el de la historia diplomática, como son la Comisión de Investigaciones Históricas de la Revolución Mexicana, fundada por Isidro Fabela y especializada en la publicación de documentos de su archivo y de los de las Secretarías de Relaciones y de otros que conservan en su poder algunos particulares; el Instituto Nacional de Estudios Históricos de la Revolución Mexicana, dirigido por Salvador Azuela, y el Patronato de la Historia de Sonora dirigido por Manuel González Ramírez, que iniciaron sus actividades a partir de 1950 y han publicado un número considerable de obras. La Sociedad Mexicana de Geografía y Estadística que, entre 1962 y 1963, publicó veintiocho volúmenes del Congreso Nacional de Historia para el Estudio de la Guerra de Intervención; las Secretarías de Hacienda y Crédito Público y la del Patrimonio Nacional, así como el Senado de la República que conmemoran con diversas publicaciones en 1962 y 1967, victorias mexicanas contra la Intervención Francesa y la restauración de la República. Por otra parte, la Cámara de Diputados editó en 1965 y 1966 los informes presidenciales y las constituciones mexicanas, y la Secretaría de la Presidencia algunos volúmenes sobre El Chamizal, a raíz de su devolución a México en 1962 por el presidente John F. Kennedy. En menor escala contribuyeron con publicaciones sobre cuestiones internacionales la Secretaría de Educación Pública y la Academia Nacional de Historia y Geografía.

En el siglo y cuarto de las relaciones internacionales que estamos viendo en estas páginas, ciertos acontecimientos propiciaron el estudio y la producción de obras: la expropiación de las compañías petroleras en 1938, el centenario de la invasión norteamericana en 1947, el sesquicentenario de la Independencia y cincuentenario de la Revolución Mexicana en 1960; los centenarios de la batalla del 5 de mayo y de la restauración de la República en 1962 y 1967, respectivamente, y la devolución de El Chamizal, iniciada a partir de 1962. En consecuencia éstos han sido los temas de estudio más socorridos y están en relación con Estados Unidos, Gran Bretaña, Francia, España y las repúblicas de Centro y Sudamérica, en obras escritas sobre todo por licenciados en derecho, ya que de los autores que hemos estudiado más de veinte tienen dicha profesión y más de la mitad de ellos, además, son diplomáticos e internacionalistas, uno presidente de la República, cinco secretarios y un subsecretario de Relaciones Exteriores, dos secretarios de Hacienda y otro de Instrucción Pública. Anotamos también a cinco economistas, tres médicos y otros tantos ingenieros, sacerdotes y filósofos. Entre maestros y doctores en historia egresados de la Universidad Nacional Autónoma contamos quince y seis graduados en El Colegio de México. Asimismo en la Escuela de Ciencias Políticas y Sociales de la Universidad, cerca de cuarenta egresados han escrito sus tesis de grado sobre problemas internacionales. Otra veintena de autores la componen literatos, profesores y aficionados a la historia, seis militares y un número similar de periodistas. La mayor parte de las obras producidas por estos autores han sido históricas y jurídicas y, recientemente, la investigación ha ido cobrando auge en el campo político propiamente, así como en el económico, el social, el cultural, etcétera. *

En el análisis hemos incluido obras que no son totalmente de historia diplomática, pero que tratan este aspecto en alguno o algunos de sus capítulos; además abarcamos las publicaciones de colecciones documentales, sobre determinados periodos de las relaciones internacionales y las provenientes o tocantes a los principales personajes que intervinieron en ellas o por el valor que en sí mismas representan y porque la mayoría va entecedida de estudios valiosos sobre los temas correspondientes; a otras más las incluimos porque aun cuando tratan asuntos internos de México, éstos estuvieron muy vinculados a los de índole exterior. Finalmente también tomamos en cuenta biografías, bibliografías, hemerografías y guías de archivos, que consideramos necesarias para el estudio de las relaciones internacionales de México.

De los ciento veinticinco autores que entre 1940 y 1969 produjeron ciento treinta y un obras de acuerdo con los temas en que se dividió la bibliografía anexa a este análisis, destacan los rasgos siguientes: en las historias generales de la sección general, tanto para el aspecto internacional como para el nacional, contamos ocho volúmenes de una obra de valor excepcional, la *Historia moderna de México* que abarca los aspectos políticos, económicos y sociales de 1867 a 1911, y en los dos volúmenes especialmente dedicados a *La vida política exterior*, trata las relaciones con Guatemala en especial y con Centro América en general, así como las indirectas y directas con Estados Unidos, y las cuestiones internacionales con España, Francia e Inglaterra, apoyados en fuentes primarias y secundarias de primera calidad, tanto mexicanas como extranjeras. Otros dos libros de Cosío Villegas, *Extremos de América, ensayos y notas,* tratan certera y agudamente los problemas más recientes de este hemisferio. Esquivel Obregón y Bravo Ugarte, en sus obras respectivas, dedican un volumen completo a las relaciones internacionales de México con España,

* Daniel Cosío Villegas, *Cuestiones internacionales de México. Una bibliografía.* Secretaría de Relaciones Exteriores, México, 1966. xvii, 588 pp. (Archivo Histórico Diplomático Mexicano. Guías para la Historia Diplomática de México, 4), p. xii.

Gran Bretaña, Francia, la Santa Sede, Estados Unidos, Centro y Sur América; ambas obras, en conjunto, abarcan de 1821 a 1917; se basan en fuentes secundarias nacionales y extranjeras y su criterio es político jurídico. En el tema del panamericanismo, incluyendo al hispanoamericanismo y al interamericanismo, sobresalen los estudios de Cuevas Cancino sobre Bolívar, Franklin D. Roosevelt etcétera, en los que el autor utilizó fuentes nacionales y extranjeras, tanto primarias como secundarias; los estudios de González Navarro sobre Alamán son igualmente valiosos. Las relaciones diplomáticas con Estados Unidos tienen una historia formal con Luis Zorrilla y otra polémica con Carreño, la primera basada en fuentes primarias de México y ambas en secundarias nacionales y extranjeras; además hay un número considerable de obras de tipo político jurídico sobre tratados de límites y distribución de aguas, El Chamizal, el Istmo de Tehuantepec y la "mala vecindad" con Estados Unidos, casi todos apoyados en fuentes secundarias del país y extranjeras, escritos con tendencia nacionalista. Enfoque, tendencia y fuentes que también se usan al tratar la cuestión de Belice; las relaciones diplomáticas han sido vistas en relación con El Salvador y Guatemala y las comerciales con Centro América en general. De nuevo una obra indispensable para nuestras relaciones con Guatemala en especial y con Centro América en general, es la de Cosío Villegas: *Historia moderna de México. La vida política exterior.* Parte primera. Para finalizar la sección general está el apartado titulado "Varios" que incluye diversos temas del pasado, tratados durante periodos largos, como México y el arbitraje internacional, la deuda exterior y la historia militar de México. Sobre el primer asunto destaca la excelente obra de Gómez Robledo y, sobre el segundo, la de Jan Bazant, hecha en colaboración con Gloria Peralta, Guadalupe Nava y Enrique Semo; en ambas obras se utilizaron fuentes secundarias nacionales y extranjeras. Por último toda la sección general cuenta con valiosas colecciones documentales: las constituciones de América; un proyecto de unidad panamericana y la conferencia celebrada en México en 1895 y 1896; relatos de viajes a Texas, y cuestiones internacionales de México con Belice y Brasil; compilaciones de artículos de diversos autores tocantes a El Chamizal, el pensamiento económico, social y político de México, y una guía de documentos sobre las relaciones franco-mexicanas. De las reediciones, destaca la de Justo Sierra.

La iniciación de la vida independiente cuenta con relatos sobre la situación en los Estados del Norte y con estudios bien documentados en fuentes primarias y secundarias, nacionales y extranjeras, sobre las relaciones diplomáticas con Estados Unidos, Francia, Gran Bretaña: Medina Ascencio y Miquel i Vergés; así como con otros estudios sobre Manuel Crescencio Rejón, Lorenzo de Zavala y Joel M. Poinsett. Esta división tiene también colecciones de documentos de Agustín de Iturbide, Rejón, Zavala y Poinsett; sobre California y las relaciones diplomáticas con el Vaticano, las hispano-mexicanas, las franco-mexicanas y las mexicano-norteamericanas.

En la era de Santa Anna hay un marcado resentimiento con Estados Unidos y con el propio Santa Anna, por la intervención armada que sufrió nuestro país, el tratado de Guadalupe-Hidalgo, la venta de La Mesilla, etcétera. Sobresalen los estudios de Fuentes Mares y Álvaro Acevedo sobre Santa Anna y la intervención, así como de otros autores sobre Juan N. Pereda, Gastón de Raouset-Boulbon, Bustamante y Sierra O'Reilly, además de documentos o colecciones de los ya citados, así como de Alamán, Juan N. Almonte, Maximiliano, Mariano Otero, Roa Bárcena, José Bernardo Couto y Polk.

En la Reforma y la Intervención encontramos nuevamente un acrecentamiento del nacionalismo y del resentimiento, ahora con respecto a Napoleón III y aún más mezclado a las corrientes políticas, en obras polémicas sobre los tratados Mon-Almonte y McLane-Ocampo, así como sobre la actitud de Juárez; pero también hay estudios documentados sobre ellos, así como de Maximiliano, Francisco de Paula Arraingoiz, Zarco, Vallarta, José Ma. Iglesias, Jesús Terán y el General Prim, sustentados en fuentes primarias y secundarias, nacionales y extranjeras, debidos a Fuentes Mares, Quirarte, González Navarro y Miquel i Vergés, así como una interpretación de posibles antecedentes de la Intervención, hecha por Margarita Martínez Leal. Visiones muy partidaristas o francamente polémicas son las obras producidas por Bulnes, Cue Cánovas, Blanco Moheno, Sánchez Navarro, Salmerón, Villaseñor y Villaseñor, y Junco; en esta sección hay además varias historias militares; abundan las colecciones documentales sobre Maximiliano, Jesús Terán y el General Prim, las de fuentes francesas, traducidas y editadas por Lilia Díaz, Ernesto de la Torre y Manuel Tello; el *Diario personal de Matías Romero*, editado por Emma Cosío Villegas; las compilaciones de artículos de prensa que fueron redactados por contemporáneos de la Intervención, así como de otros artículos hechos recientemente para conmemorar las victorias mexicanas contra los franceses y que fueron editados por Arnáiz y Freg y Catalina Sierra.

No cabe duda de que el periodo mejor estudiado es la de la restauración de la República y el Porfiriato, por contar con la *Historia moderna de México*, de la cual fue director don Daniel Cosío Villegas y, además, autor de tres volúmenes: *República restaurada. Vida política* (1955), *El Porfiriato. Política exterior*, Parte primera (1960) y Parte segunda (1963) y de las "llamadas particulares" que anteceden los volúmenes, así como de la revisión y unificación de *El Porfiriato. Vida económica*, 2 vols. (1965), encomendados a Nicolau d'Olwer. Francisco Calderón, Guadalupe Nava, Fernando Rosenzweig, Luis Cossío, Gloria Peralta y Enrique Coello. De los otros dos volúmenes de la

República restaurada, el de la V*ida económica,* correspondió a Francisco Calderón (1955) y el de la V*ida social* a Luis González, Emma Cosío Villegas y Guadalupe Monroy (1956); y *El Porfiriato. Vida social* a Moisés González Navarro (1957). La culminación de esta magna obra la esperamos con verdadera ansiedad en el volumen o volúmenes que escribe don Daniel sobre la vida política interna del Porfiriato. El periodo citado cuenta además con los estudios de Fuentes Mares sobre Juárez, de Moisés González Navarro sobre Vallarta, de Espinoza de los Reyes, relaciones económicas con Estados Unidos, de Valadés sobre el "Porfirismo". Además de varias tesis presentadas en la Escuela de Ciencias Políticas y Sociales que, en general, son contrarias al imperialismo yanqui y están basadas en fuentes secundarias nacionales y extranjeras. También se cuenta con las memorias de Limantour, Tomás Mejía y Salado Álvarez, y con la compilación de artículos de varios autores que editó la Secretaría de Hacienda en 1967 para conmemorar el centenario de la restauración de la República. Por otra parte se publicaron colecciones de documentos: el archivo de Porfirio Díaz y el de Benito Juárez, editados por Carreño y Tamayo, respectivamente; la entrevista Díaz-Creelman; la huelga de Cananea; discursos políticos de Juárez y una colección de artículos sobre su natalicio; la promoción de las relaciones comerciales entre México y Estados Unidos, según Matías Romero; así como el catálogo de su archivo histórico, elaborado por Guadalupe Monroy; la reconciliación de México y Francia, editada por Lucía Robina, y las reclamaciones Weil y la Abra por César Sepúlveda. Además se reeditó el libro de Sierra sobre Juárez.

Aunque para el periodo de Revolución Mexicana 1910-1940 aumenta considerablemente el número de publicaciones, * adolece de la falta de una obra o de un conjunto de ellas que tengan un valor similar al de la *Historia moderna.* Tanto en el ramo general como en los temas específicos de la Revolución hay obras de tipo político, social, económico, cultural, ensayos, historias, crónicas, "hechos reales", ideológicas, gráficas, de caricaturas, biográficas, memorias, de divulgación, polémicas y formales, basadas en toda clase de fuentes, desde las primarias y secundarias, nacionales y extranjeras, hasta las experiencias vividas y los relatos de otras personas; obras en las que en general se nota una marcada tendencia nacionalista, antiyanqui y de polémica partidarista, sobre todo entre carrancistas y obregonistas. Hay dos obras sobre historia diplomática de la Revolución escritas por Fabela y por Aarón Sáenz; dos más, que son propiamente de política interna y de divulgación, de Silva Herzog y de Valadés; y un valioso estudio

* Ascienden a 164 mientras que para los otros periodos tenemos: 89 en la era de Santa Anna, 65 en Reforma e Intervención, y 31 en República restaurada y Porfiriato.

de César Sepúlveda sobre las relaciones diplomáticas entre México y Estados Unidos en el siglo xx. En las obras que van en la sección de temas específicos los asuntos que tratan son definidos y por lo general en relación con Estados Unidos, por ejemplo: los hermanos Flores Magón y el problema de Baja California; el resentimiento por la actitud del embajador Henry Lane Wilson, especialmente en la Décena Trágica, así como por la ocupación armada de Veracruz; el ataque de Villa a Columbus y la expedición punitiva; contra el imperialismo yanqui y la política de Woodrow Wilson; los conflictos petrolero y religioso, etcétera. Entre los buenos estudios que hay destacan el de Gómez Robledo sobre los Tratados de Bucareli y el de Lorenzo Meyer acerca del conflicto petrolero con Estados Unidos, apoyado en fuentes nacionales y extranjeras, tanto primarias como secundarias. Recientemente circuló entre un número reducido de personas un estudio monográfico de la autora de esta ponencia sobre la Revolución Mexicana y los Estados Unidos, basado en historia diplomática entre 1910 y 1914, basado en fuentes primarias y secundarias, mexicanas y del extranjero. La era de la buena vecindad cuenta con el magnífico estudio de Cuevas Cancino y con otros de Fabela y de Silva Herzog, los de éste, sobre todo, relativos a la expropiación petrolera. Finalmente en la sección de varios incluimos algunas memorias y biografías; estudios sobre braceros, tratados internacionales, el reconocimiento de gobierno, una antología, etcétera. Así como el ensayo de Cosío Villegas sobre las revoluciones mexicana y cubana. El periodo de Revolución Mexicana cuenta con varias colecciones documentales: la de Fabela sobre Flores Magón, Madero y Carranza; de reproducciones fotográficas y de caricaturas políticas; las relaciones internacionales de México a través de los mensajes presidenciales; la guía del ramo Revolución Mexicana del Archivo de la Secretaría de Relaciones Exteriores; una compilación de artículos en *México, 50 años de revolución*, además de algunas reediciones.

Por último, mencionaremos otra de las obras de don Daniel Cosío Villegas en El Colegio de México, la fundación en 1957, y la dirección posterior, del Seminario de Historia Contemporánea de México, como resultado del cual ya fueron publicadas las investigaciones bibliográficas que estuvieron a cargo de Luis González, Guadalupe Monroy, Susana Uribe y Luis Muro; así como de Stanley R. Ross con la colaboración de Alicia Bazán, María de Jesús Cubas, Lilia Díaz, Lucila Flamand y Fernando Zertuche, correspondiente a libros y folletos, periódicos y revistas; la de Berta Ulloa sobre el Archivo Histórico de la Secretaría de Relaciones Exteriores y la de Luis Muro sobre el Archivo Histórico de la Secretaría de la Defensa Nacional, no ha sido publicada, pero sus ficheros se pueden consultar en El Colegio de México. El Seminario de Historia Contemporánea de México tuvo una segunda etapa, la de investigación histórica, a la cual pertenecen los trabajos casi concluidos de Moisés González Navarro sobre la vida social de 1910 y 1965 y de Berta Ulloa sobre las relaciones entre México y Estados Unidos entre 1910 y 1914.

Finalmente hacemos notar que la inmensa mayoría de las obras revisadas fue publicada en la ciudad de México, con excepción de catorce que vieron la luz en el interior de la República: cuatro en Guadalajara, tres en Mérida, dos en Monterrey y una, respectivamente, en Chetumal, Chihuahua, Jalapa, Campeche y Saltillo. Por otra parte han habido obras o traducciones de ellas publicadas en el extranjero: dos en Buenos Aires, dos en Madrid, una en Austin, una en Lincoln y otra más en Caracas.

Una última aclaración: en las fichas y en el cuadro, anexos a estas páginas, contra lo que es usual, se sumaron las páginas de los prólogos e introducciones con las de los textos, y en general las de los varios volúmenes de una misma obra. Además, para este trabajo, utilizamos el libro de David Trask, Michael C. Meyer y Roger Trask: A bibliography United States-Latin American Relations since 1810. A selected list of eleven thousand published references, Compiled and edited by... Lincoln, University of Nebraska Press, 1968. 441, pp. Libro que no citamos en la sección de bibliografía por ser un trabajo hecho exclusivamente por norteamericanos.

BIBLIOGRAFÍA

I. SECCIÓN GENERAL

a) Historias generales

Bravo Ugarte, José: Historia de México. T. III, vol. II. Relaciones internacionales, territorio, sociedad y cultura. México, Editorial Jus, 1959. 564 pp.

Cámara de Diputados. XLVI Legislatura del Congreso de la Unión: Derechos del pueblo mexicano. México a través de sus Constituciones, México, Cámara de Diputados, 1967. 8 vols. 7237 pp.

Cámara de Diputados. XLVI Legislatura del Congreso de la Unión: Los presidentes de México ante la Nación, Informes, manifiestos y documentos de 1821 a 1966. Recopilación bajo la dirección de Luis González. México, Cámara de Diputados, 1966. 5 vols. 5022 pp.

Cosío Villegas, Daniel: Ensayos y notas. México, Editorial Hermes, 1966. 2 vols. 828 pp.

Cosío Villegas, Daniel: Extremos de América. México, Tezontle, 1949. 331 pp.

Publicaciones en inglés por The University of Texas Press, 1964. 227 pp. (The Texas Pan-American Series).

Cosío Villegas, Daniel: *Historia Moderna de México*. México, Hermes, 1955-1965. 8 vols. 7652 pp.

Esquivel Obregón, Toribio: *Apuntes para la historia del derecho en México*. Tomo IV, *Relaciones Internacionales 1821-1860*. México, Robredo, 1948. 836 pp.

García Granados, Ricardo: *Historia de México, desde la restauración de la república en 1867, hasta la caída de Huerta*. México, Jus, 1956. 2 vols. [800] pp.

Junco, Alfonso: *Un siglo de México, de Hidalgo a Carranza*. México, Jus (5ª ed.), 1963. 244 pp.

Romero Flores, Jesús: *Estudios históricos*. México, Ediciones B. Costa-Amic, 1969. 3 vols. [1200] pp.

Sierra, Justo: *Evolución política del pueblo mexicano*. México, UNAM (4ª ed.), 1957. 426 pp.

b) Panamericanismo

Aguilar, Alonso: *El panamericanismo: de la Doctrina Monroe a la Doctrina Johnson*. México, Cuadernos Americanos, 1965. 186 pp.

Alba, Pedro de: *Breve reseña histórica del movimiento panamericanista*. [México], Antigua Imprenta de E. Munguía, 1940. 62 pp. (Instituto Panamericano de Geografía e Histoira, 49).

Alba, Pedro de: *De Bolívar a Roosevelt. Democracia y unidad de América*. México, Cultura, 1949. 290 pp.

Arroyo Rivera, Alberto: *La no-intervención en el derecho internacional americano*. México, s.p.i., 1952. 116 pp.

Ávila Vizcarra, Gloria: *La solidaridad de América y sus proyecciones hacia el futuro; una interpretación del interamericanismo*. México, s.p.i., 1956. 89 pp.

Barquín y Ruiz, Andrés: *Agustín de Iturbide campeón del hispanoamericanismo*. México, Editorial Jus, 1968. 203 pp. (México Heroico, 77).

Borrego, Salvador: *América peligra*. México, Impresos Aldo (2ª ed.), 1965. 647 pp.

Cortés Medina, Hernán: *Iberoamericanismo y panamericanismo. Hacia una verdadera comprensión americana*. México, s.p.i., 1953. 76 pp.

Cuevas Cancino, Francisco: *Bolívar. El ideal panamericano del libertador*. México, Fondo de Cultura Económica, 1951. 330 pp. (Colección Tierra Firme, 50).

Cuevas Cancino, Francisco: *Del Congreso de Panamá a la Conferencia de Caracas, 1826-1954. El genio de Bolívar a través de la historia de las relaciones interamericanas*. Caracas, Editorial Ragón, 1955. 2 vols. 642 pp.

Cuevas Cancino, Francisco. *El Pacto de familia. Historia de un episodio de la diplomacia Mexicana en pro de la anfictonía.* México, Publicaciones de la Secretaría de Relaciones Exteriores, 1962. 357 pp. (Archivo Histórico Diplomático Mexicano, Segunda Serie, 14).

Estrada, Genaro: *La doctrina de Monroe y el fracaso de una conferencia Panamericana en México.* México, Secretaría de Relaciones Exteriores, 1959. 136 pp. (Archivo Histórico Diplomático Mexicano, Segunda Serie, 11).

Fabela, Isidro: *La doctrina Drago.* México, Secretaría de Educación Pública, 1946. 84 pp.

Fabela, Isidro: *Las doctrinas Monroe y Drago.* México, UNAM, Escuela Nacional de Ciencias Políticas y Sociales, 1957. 266 pp.

García Robles, Alfonso: *El panamericanismo y la política del Buen Vecino.* México, Comité Mexicano para el Estudio Científico de las Relaciones Internacionales, 1940. 84 pp.

García Zapata, Lamberto: *El panamericanismo base del derecho internacional público americano.* México, s.p.i., 1940. 102 pp.

Gómez Robledo, Antonio: *Epopeya del monroísmo.* México, Jus, 1940. 126 pp.

Gómez Robledo, Antonio: *Idea y experiencia de América.* México, Fondo de Cultura Económica, 1958. 250 pp.

Gómez Robledo, Antonio: *La seguridad colectiva del Continente Americano.* México, UNAM, 1960. 229 pp.

González Navarro, Moisés: *El pensamiento político de Lucas Alamán.* México, El Colegio de México, [1952]. 178 pp.

Martínez, Ricardo A.: *De Bolívar a Dulles: el panamericanismo, doctrina y práctica imperialista.* México, América Nueva, 1959. 229 pp.

Moreno Méndez, Adalberto: *Las instituciones y las doctrinas americanas, garantía de la independencia de los estados.* México, s.p.i., 1954. 112 pp.

Padilla, Ezequiel: *El hombre libre de América.* México, Nuevo Mundo, 1943. 288 pp.

Pasquel, Leonardo: *Las constituciones de América. Textos íntegros vigentes.* México, s.p.i., 1943. 2 vols. [800] pp.

Pereira, Carlos: *El mito de Monroe.* Buenos Aires, El Búho, 1959. 236 pp.

Pereira, Carlos: *El fetiche constitucional americano. De Washington al segundo Roosevelt.* Madrid, Aguilar, 1942. 299 pp.

Pérez Cabral, Pedro Andrés: *Raíces de la política yanqui en América: un estudio de preimperialismo.* México, 1964. 284 pp.

Zea, Leopoldo: *América en la historia.* México, Fondo de Cultura Económica, 1961. 280 pp.

c) Relaciones con Estados Unidos

Berdeja Galeana, Sergio: *El tratado de aguas internacionales celebrado entre México y Estados Unidos el 3 de febrero de 1944 y la convención del 21 de mayo de 1906.* México, Autor, 1944. 63 pp.

Carreño, Alberto M.: *La diplomacia extraordinaria entre México y Estados Unidos, 1789-1947.* México, Jus (2ª ed.), 1961. 2 vols. 591 pp.

Carvajal Rodríguez, Carlos: *La solución al caso de "El Chamizal".* México, UNAM, Escuela de Ciencias Políticas y Sociales, 1964. 48 pp.

Castañeda Alatorre, Fernando: *El tratado de 1906 celebrado entre México y los Estados Unidos de Norteamérica sobre la distribución de las aguas del Río Bravo, en el Valle de Juárez, Chih. Su historia y crítica. Y estudio sobre el derecho de México para utilizar las aguas del Río Bravo en el propio Valle Juárez, Chih., México.* México, UNAM, Facultad de Derecho y Ciencias Sociales, 1944. 63 pp.

Comisión de Límites: Viaje a Texas en el año de 1828. México, Vargas Rea, 1948. 77 pp.

El Chamizal, monumento a la justicia internacional. México, Secretaría de Hacienda y Crédito Público, 1964. 125 pp.

Escoto y Ochoa, Humberto: *Integración y desintegración de nuestra frontera norte.* México, Stylo, 1949. 213 pp.

Fernández Mac Gregor, Genaro: *El istmo de Tehuantepec y los Estados Unidos.* México, [Editorial Elede], 1954. 238 pp.

Gill, Mario: *Nuestros buenos vecinos.* Prólogo de Narciso Bassols. México, Editorial Azteca (4ª ed. ampliada), 1959. 331 pp. Otra edición en: México, Paralelo, 1957. 275 pp.

Jury Germany, Sonia Helena: *Un siglo de negociación diplomática de los límites entre México y los Estados Unidos (1819-1900).* México, UNAM, Escuela de Ciencias Políticas y Sociales, 1965. 204 pp.

Macías, Pablo C.: *El Chamizal, territorio de México en poder de los Estados Unidos.* México, Magisterio, 1961. 69 pp.

Mendoza, S.: *El Chamizal: un drama jurídico e histórico.* México, 1963. [70] pp.

México recibe "El Chamizal". Introducción de Antonio Luna Arroyo. México, La Justicia [1963], 284 pp. (Documentos para la historia de un gobierno, 136).

Posada Noriega, Juan: *México y Estados Unidos.* México, León Sánchez, 1941. 84 pp.

Roel, Santiago: *Malinchismo Nacional.* Monterrey, Autor, 1954. 170 pp.

Sodi Álvarez, Enrique: *Istmo de Tehuantepec.* México [Talleres Gráficos de la Nación], 1967. 204 pp.

Tratado de aguas internacionales celebrado entre México y los Estados Unidos el 3 de febrero de 1944. Antecedentes, consideraciones y resoluciones del problema de las aguas internacionales. México, Secretaría de Relaciones Exteriores, 1947. 142 pp.

Vargas Silva, J. A.: *El caso del Chamizal: sus peculiaridades jurídicas.* México, 1963. [70] pp.

Victoria del derecho y la moral en la histórica recuperación del Chamizal. Introducción de Antonio Luna Arroyo. México, Editorial "La Justicia", 1963. 279 pp. (Documentos para la Historia de un Gobierno, 109).

Vivó, Jorge A.: *Informe de la comisión nombrada para dictaminar sobre el problema del trazo de la línea internacional entre México y Estados Unidos.* México, Sociedad Mexicana de Geografía y Estadística, 1950. 449 pp.

Zorilla, Luis G.: *Historia de las relaciones entre México y los Estados Unidos de América, 1800-1958.* México, Editorial Porrúa, S. A., 1965. 2 vols. 1218 pp.

d) La cuestión de Belice y Relaciones con Centro América

Alcalá Quintero, Francisco: *El comercio de México con Centroamérica.* México, Publicaciones Especializadas, 1965. 101 pp.

Castellanos, Francisco Xavier: *La intendencia de Yucatán y Belice.* México, Autor, 1962. 62 pp.

Castillo Mayorga, F.: *Relaciones entre México y la República de El Salvador; examen histórico diplomático.* México, s.p.i., 1960. 78 pp.

Cosío Villegas, Daniel: *Historia Moderna de México. El Porfiriato. Vida Política Exterior. Primera Parte.* México, Hermes, 1960. 845 pp.

Cravioto, Adrián: *La paz de América. Guatemala y Belice.* México, Cultura, 1943. 56 pp.

Fabela, Isidro: *Belice, defensa de los derechos de México.* México, Editorial Mundo Libre, 1944. 423 pp.

Gallegos, Aníbal: *El Belice Mexicano.* México, Autor, 1951. 110 pp.

González Blanco, Pedro: *El problema de Belice y sus alivios.* México, Galatea, 1950. 129 pp.

González Ramírez, Baltasar: *Tratado Spencer-Mariscal. La cuestión de Belice.* México, UNAM, aula de Ciencias Políticas y Sociales, 1962. 150 pp.

López Jiménez, Ramón: *Belice tierra inédita.* México, Mundo Actual, 1943. 232 pp.

Martínez Alomía, Santiago: *Belice.* Campeche, Autor, 1945. 374 pp.

Martínez Palafox, Luis: *La cuestión de Belice.* México, Polis, 1945. 135 pp.

Peniche, Manuel: *Historia de las relaciones de España y México con Inglaterra sobre el establecimiento de Belice.* Mérida, Tipografía Yucateca (3ª ed.), 1940. 83 pp.

Publicada la primera vez con el *Boletín de la Sociedad Mexicana de Geografía y Estadística en 1869.* La segunda en la *Revista de Historia de América.* núm. 10, 1940.

Pérez Trejo, Gustavo A.: *Documentos sobre Belice o Balice.* México, Secretaría de Hacienda, 1958. 209 pp.

Rebolledo, Miguel: *Quintana Roo y Belice.* México, Stylo, 1949. 106 pp.

Romo García, Eloy: *Los derechos de México sobre Belice.* México, s.p.i., 1942. 88 pp.

Sandoval Sandoval, Héctor: *Relaciones diplomáticas México-Guatemala.* México, UNAM, Escuela Nacional de Ciencias Políticas y Sociales, 1965. [70] pp.

e) Varios

Bazant, Jan: *Historia de la deuda exterior de México (1823-1946).* México, El Colegio de México, 1968. 277 pp. (Centro de Estudios Históricos, Nueva Serie, 3).

Cota y Soto, Guillermo: *Historia militar de México. Ensayo. Recopilación de datos de la historia militar de México desde la guerra de Independencia en 1808 hasta la participación de México en la II Guerra Mundial, inclusive.* México, Talleres Gráficos de la Nación, 1947. 335 pp.

Chavarri, Juan N.: *El heróico Colegio Militar en la historia de México.* México, Libro Mex, 1960. 346 pp.

Gómez Robledo, Antonio: *México y el arbitraje internacional. El fondo piadoso de las Californias. La Isla de la Pasión. El Chamizal.* México, Editorial Porrúa, 1965. 424 pp.

González de Mendoza, José María y Américo J. Lacombe: *Relaciones diplomáticas entre México y Brasil, 1822-1923.* T. I (1822-1867). Preliminar de Manuel Tello. México, Secretaría de Relaciones Exteriores, 1964. 539 pp. (Archivo Histórico Diplomático Mexicano, Segunda Serie, 18).

Edición bilingüe: español, portugués.

Gutiérrez Santos, Daniel: *Historia militar de México, 1876-1914.* México, Ediciones Ateneo, 1961. 3 vols. 1210 pp.

Silva Herzog, Jesús: *El pensamiento económico de México.* México, Fondo de Cultura Económica, [1947]. 199 pp.

Silva Herzog, Jesús: *El pensamiento económico, social y político de México, 1810-1964.* México, Instituto de Investigaciones Económicas, 1967. 748 pp.

Siqueiros Prieto, José L.: *Las reclamaciones internacionales por intereses extranjeros en sociedades mexicanas.* México, Imprenta Universitaria, 1947. 143 pp.

Torrea, Juan Manuel: *Funcionarios de la Secretaría de Relaciones desde el año de 1821 a 1940.* México, Talleres Gráficos de la Nación, 1940. 205 pp.

Torrea, Juan Manuel: *Tampico (apuntes para su historia): su fundación, su vida militar.* Época contemporánea por Ignacio Fuentes. [México, Nuestra Patria], 1942. 448 pp.

Weckmann, Luis: *Las relaciones franco-mexicanas (1823-1867).* Prefacio de Daniel Cosío Villegas. México, Secretaría de Relaciones Exteriores, 1961-1962. 2 vols. 1,111 (Archivo Histórico Diplomático Mexicano, Guías para la Historia Diplomática de México, 1 y 2).

II. INICIACIÓN DE LA VIDA INDEPENDIENTE

Alessio Robles, Vito: *Coahuila y Texas.* México, Cultura, 1938, 1945-1946. 3 vols. [1200] pp.

Alessio Robles, Vito: *La correspondencia de Agustín de Iturbide después de la proclamación del Plan de Iguala.* México, Talleres Antográficos, 1945. 2 vols. 544 pp. (Archivo Histórico Militar Mexicano, 1 [2]).

Bosch García, Carlos: *Historia de las relaciones entre México y los Estados Unidos, 1819-1848.* México, UNAM, Escuela de Ciencias Políticas y Sociales, 1961. 297 pp.

Bosch García, Carlos: *Material para la historia diplomática de México (México y los Estados Unidos, 1820-1848).* México, UNAM, Escuela de Ciencias Políticas y Sociales, 1957. 654 pp.

Bosch García, Carlos: *Problemas diplomáticos del México Independiente.* México, El Colegio de México, 1947. 334 pp.

Carreño, Alberto M.: *Los españoles en el México Independiente.* México, Sociedad de Beneficencia Española, 1942. 478 pp.

Castilleros S., Andrés: *Papeles de las Californias: apuntes que hace el comisionado de las Californias al Exmo. Sr. General don Anastasio Bustamante.* México, 4 de octubre de 1837. México, Vargas Rea, 1944. 37 pp.

Comisión de Relaciones Exteriores: naciones bárbaras de las indias angloamericanas. Dictamen presentado a la Soberana Junta Gubernativa del Imperio Mexicano, por . . . en 29 de diciembre de 1821, primero de la Independencia (Dictámenes 1 y 2). México, Vargas Rea, 1944. 56 pp.

Cuevas, Mariano: *El Libertador: Documentos selectos de D. Agustín de Iturbide.* México, Patria, 1947. 480 pp.

Echánove Trujillo, Carlos A.: *Correspondencia inédita de Manuel Crescencio Rejón relativa a su misión diplomática a la América del Sur, a sus car-*

gos de ministro de Relaciones Exteriores y de Gobernación, de senador...
Recopilación, semblanza biográfica, notas y comentarios por... México, Secretaría de Relaciones Exteriores, 1948, 117 pp. (Archivo Histórico Diplomático Mexicano, Segunda Serie, 5).

Echánove Trujillo, Carlos A.: *La vida pasional e inquieta de don Crescencio Rejón*. México, El Colegio de México, 1941. 479 pp.

Flores D., Jorge: *Lorenzo de Zavala y su misión diplomática en Francia (1834-1835)*. Prólogo y compilación por... México, Secretaría de Relaciones Exteriores, 1951. 277 pp. (Archivo Histórico Diplomático Mexicano, Segunda Serie, 8).

Fuentes Mares, José: *Poinsett. Historia de una gran intriga*. México, Jus (4ª ed.) 1964. 258 pp. (Colección México Heroico).

Otra edición, Jus, 1951. 343 pp.

García Monraz, Manuel: *La diplomacia mexicana en la guerra de Independencia*. México, ?, 1955. 92 pp.

Malagón Barceló, Javier, Enriqueta López Lira y José María Miquel i Vergés: *Relaciones diplomáticas hispano-mexicanas (1839-1898). Documentos procedentes del Archivo de la Embajada de España en México. Serie I, Despachos Generales* [1839-1848]. México, El Colegio de México, 1949, 1952, 1966, 1968. 4 vols. 1489 pp.

Los prólogos de los vols. II y III por Nicolau D'Olwer.

Medina Ascencio, Luis: *La Santa Sede y la emancipación mexicana*. Guadalajara, Imprenta Gráfica, 1946. 243 pp.

Miquel i Vergés, José María: *La diplomacia española en México, 1822-1823*. México, El Colegio de México, 1956. 195 pp.

Moreno, Daniel: *Manuel Crescencio Rejón, pensamiento político*. Prólogo, selección y notas por... México, UNAM, 1968. 237 pp.

Ramírez Cabañas, Joaquín: *Las relaciones diplomáticas entre México y el Vaticano*. Editor... México, Secretaría de Relaciones Exteriores, 1958. 332 pp.

Rejón, Manuel Crescencio: *Discursos parlamentarios (1822-1847)*. México, Secretaría de Educación Pública, 1943. 279 pp.

Torre Villar, Ernesto de la: *Correspondencia diplomática franco-mexicana, 1805-1839*. Editor... México, El Colegio de México, 1957. 424 pp. 1 vol.

III. LA ERA DE SANTA ANA

A cien años de la epopeya. México, A. F. del Castillo, 1947. 63 pp.

Alamán, Lucas: *Iniciativa de Ley proponiendo al gobierno las medidas que se deberán tomar para la seguridad del estado de Texas y conservar la inte-*

gridad del territorio mexicano de cuyo proyecto emanó la ley de 6 de abril de 1836. México, ? , 1946. [50] pp.

Alcaraz, Ramón (et. al.): *Apuntes para la historia de la guerra entre México y los Estados Unidos.* México, Editora Nacional (2a. ed.) 1952. 401 pp. Edición facsimilar de la de 1848.

Almonte, Juan N.: *Correspondencia entre los señores J. N. Almonte Arrangoiz, cónsul en Nueva Orleans y los señores Pedro Fernández del Castillo y Joaquín Velázquez de León sobre Texas y los Estados Unidos. 1841-1843.* México, Vargas Rea, 1949. 57 pp.

Alvear Acevedo, Carlos: *La guerra del 47*, México, Jus, 1957. 70 pp. (Figuras y Episodios de la Historia de México, 41).

Apuntes históricos sobre los acontecimientos notables de la guerra entre México y los Estados Unidos. México, Vargas Rea, 1945. 77 pp.

Berrueto, Ramón: *En defensa de un verdadero México.* Saltillo, s.p.i., 1957. 84 pp.

Breve reseña histórica de los principales acontecimientos ocurridos con motivo de la rebelión de la colonia de Tejas y guerra con los Estados Unidos de Norteamérica. México, ? ; 1941. [100] pp.

Bustamante, Carlos María de: *El nuevo Bernal Díaz del Castillo. O sea historia de la invasión de los angloamericanos en México.* Introducción de Salvador Noriega, México, Secretaría de Educación Pública, 1949. 369 pp. (Testimonios mexicanos, Historiadores, 2).

Cabrera, Luis: *Diario del presidente Polk (1845-1849).* Editor... México, Robredo, 1948. 2 vols. 1267 pp.

Castillo Nájera, Francisco: *Invasión norteamericana, efectivos, y estado de los ejércitos beligerantes.* [México, Empresa Editorial "Beatriz de Silva"], 1947. 49 pp.

Castillo Nájera, Francisco: *El Tratado de Guadalupe; ponencia al Congreso Mexicano de Historia VIII reunión (Durango, Sep. 17-26 de 1947).* México Talleres Gráficos de la Nación, 1943. 102 pp.

Documentos para la historia de la guerra de Tejas. México, Nacional, 1952. 136 pp.

Fernández Mac Gregor, Genaro: *En la era de la mala vecindad.* México, Ediciones Botas, 1960. 434 pp.

Flores D., Jorge: *Juan Nepomuceno de Pereda y su misión secreta en Europa. 1846-1848.* México, Secretaría de Relaciones Exteriores, 1964. 476 pp. (Archivo Histórico Diplomático Mexicano, Segunda Serie, 19).

Fuentes Díaz, Vicente: *La intervención norteamericana en México (1817).* México, Nuevo Mundo, 1947. 303 pp.

Fuentes Mares, José: *Santa Anna. Aurora y ocaso de un comediante.* México, Jus (2a. ed.) 1958. 334 pp. (Figuras y episodios de la Historia de México, 73).

Primera edición en 1956.

Izquierdo, José J.: *Con la primera brigada de caballería del ejército del norte en 1847.* México, s.p.i., 1945. 84 pp.

Lemoine Villicaña, Ernesto: *Crónica de la ocupación de México por el ejército de los Estados Unidos.* México, UNAM, 1950. 103 pp.

Livermore, Abiel A.: *Revisión de la guerra entre México y los Estados Unidos.* México, Talleres Gráficos de la Nación, 1948. 350 pp.

Luelmo, Julio: *Los antiesclavistas norteamericanos. La cuestión de Texas y la guerra con México.* México, Secretaría de Educación Pública, 1947. 92 pp. (Biblioteca Enciclopédica Popular, 181).

Méndez, Carlos R.: *La célebre misión del doctor don Justo Sierra O'Reilly a los Estados Unidos de Norteamérica en 1847 y 1848.* Mérida, Compañía Tipográfica Yucateca, 1945. 303 pp.

Mestre Ghigliazza, Manuel: *Invasión norteamericana en Tabasco (1846-1847).* Documentos, selección de... México, UNAM, Instituto de Investigaciones Históricas, 1948. 369 pp. (Serie de Historia Moderna y Contemporánea de México, 1).

Murguía Rosete, J. A.: *El tratado de Guadalupe y el problema de las islas Catalinas, archipiélago de Santa Bárbara.* México, s.p.i., 1957. 117 pp.

Otero, Mariano: *Exposición que hace el ciudadano... diputado de Jalisco, al congreso nacional, al supremo gobierno del estado, sobre la guerra que sostiene la República contra los Estados Unidos del Norte. Toluca, 1847.* México, Vargas Rea, 1944. 65 pp.

Peña, J. E. de la: *La rebelión de Texas: manuscrito inédito de 1836 por un oficial de Santa Anna.* México, ?, 1955, [60] pp.

Ramírez Cabañas, Joaquín: *Gastón de Raousset, conquistador de Sonora.* México, Xochitl, 1941. 192 pp.

Rivera Cambas, Manuel: *Antonio López de Santa Anna.* México, ?, 1959. pp.

Roa Bárcena, José María: *Recuerdos de la invasión norteamericana (1846-1848).* Prólogo y edición de Antonio Castro Leal. México, Porrúa (3a. Ed.), 1947. 3 vols. 1191 pp. (Colección de Escritores Mexicanos, 46-48).

La primera edición en 1883.

Rojas Garcidueñas, José: *Don José Bernardo Couto; jurista, diplomático y escritor. Con un apéndice que contiene cuatro obras de Couto: la exposición de motivos del Tratado de 1848 con los Estados Unidos y biografías de*

Andrés Cavo, Francisco Javier Echeverría, Pedro José Márquez y José Ma. Luis Mora. [México, Universidad Veracruzana, 1964]. 127 pp. (Cuadernos de la Facultad de Filosofía y Letras y Ciencias, 24).

Sánchez Garza, J.: La rebelión de Texas, manuscrito inédito de 1836. Editor ... México, Sánchez, 1955. 321 pp.

Sánchez Lamego, Miguel A.: El Colegio Militar y la Defensa de Chapultepec en septiembre de 1847. México, s.p.i., 1947. 73 pp.

Sierra O'Reilly, Justo: Segundo Libro del Diario de mi viaje a los Estados Unidos. (La pretendida cesión de la península de Yucatán a un gobierno extranjero). Prólogo y notas de Marte R. Gómez. México. Porrúa, 1953. 159 pp.

Sobarzo, Horacio: Crónica de la aventura de Raousset de Boulbon en Sonora. México, Porrúa, 1954. 222 pp.

Torrea, Juan Manuel: A cien años de la Epopeya. Rendido homenaje a los héroes. Colaboración a la VIII Reunión del Congreso de Historia. [México, Beatriz de Silva], 1947. 65 pp.

Trueba, Alfonso: California, tierra perdida. México, Jus, 1958. 2 vols. 400 pp.

Valadés, José C.: Breve historia de la guerra con los Estados Unidos. México, Patria, 1947. 236 pp.

Valadés, José C.: Santa Anna y la Guerra de Texas. México, Patria (2a. ed.), 1951. 379 pp.

Reedición de la publicada en 1936 por Imprenta Mundial.

IV. REFORMA E INTERVENCIÓN

Aguirre, Manuel J.: La intervención francesa y el imperio de México. México, B. Costa-Amic Editor (2a. ed.), 1969. 149 pp.

Arnáiz y Freg, Arturo y Claude Bataillon: La intervención francesa y el imperio de Maximiliano cien años después. 1862-1962. Edición preparada por ... México, asociación Mexicana de Historiadores, Instituto Francés de la América Latina, 1965. 217 pp.

Arrangóiz, Francisco de Paula: México desde 1808 hasta 1867. Prólogo de Martín Quirarte, México, Editorial Porrúa, S. A. (2a. ed.), 1968. 1009 pp.

Bernal, Sofía Verea de: Cartas de José Manuel Hidalgo y Esnaurízar. Ministro en París del emperador Maximiliano. Recopilación y notas de ... México Editorial Porrúa, S. A., 1960. [200] pp.

Bernal, Sofía Verea de: Un hombre de mundo escribe sus impresiones (José Manuel Hidalgo). México, Editorial Porrúa, S. A., 1960. 35 pp. (Biblioteca Porrúa, 16).

Blanco Moheno, Roberto: Juárez. Ante Dios y ante los hombres. México, Libro Mex, 1959. 288 pp.

Bulnes, Francisco: *El verdadero Juárez y la verdad sobre la intervención y el imperio.* México, Editora Nacional, 1951. 973 pp.

Reedición de la publicada en 1904 por la Librería de la vda. de Ch. Bouret.

Bulnes, Francisco: *Las grandes mentiras de nuestra historia. La nación y el ejército en las guerras extranjeras.* México, Editora Nacional, 1951. 921 pp. (Biblioteca de Historia Mexicana).

Reedición de la publicada en 1904 por la librería de la vda. de Ch. Bouret.

Carranco Cardoso, L.: *Acciones militares en Guerrero. Primer Congreso Nacional de Historia para el Estudio de la guerra de Intervención.* México, ? , 1963. 93 pp.

Castañeda Batres, Óscar: *Francisco Zarco.* México, Club de Periodistas Mexicanos, 1961. 437 pp. (Biblioteca del Periodista).

Castañeda Batres, Óscar: *Francisco Zarco ante la intervención francesa y el imperio (1863-1864).* Compilación y prólogo de... México, Secretaría de Relaciones Exteriores, 1958. 216 pp. (Archivo Histórico Diplomático Mexicano, Segunda Serie, 10).

Castañeda Batres, Óscar: *La Convención de Londres (31 de octubre de 1861).* México, Sociedad Mexicana de Geografía y Estadística, 1962. 80 pp. (Colección del Congreso Nacional de Historia para el Estudio de la Guerra de Intervención, 1).

Causa de Fernando Maximiliano de Hapsburgo y sus generales Miguel Miramón y Tomás Mejía. Guadalajara, Jal., I. J. A. H., 1967. 410 pp. (Instituto Jaliciense de Antropología e Historia, Serie de Historia, 10).

Cosío Villegas, Emma: *Diario personal de Matías Romero (1855-1865).* Edición, prólogo y notas de... México, El Colegio de México, 1960. 676 pp.

Cué Cánovas, Agustín: *El Tratado McLane-Ocampo. Juárez, los Estados Unidos y Europa.* Prólogo de Vicente Sánchez. México, América Nueva, 1956. 304 pp. (Colección de Autores Contemporáneos, 7).

Cué Cánovas, Agustín: *El Tratado Mon-Almonte, Miramón, el partido conservador y la intervención europea.* México, Los Insurgentes, 1960. 97 pp.

Chávez Orozco Luis: *Maximiliano y la restitución de la esclavitud en México. 1865-1866.* Investigación y prólogo de... México, Secretaría de Relaciones Exteriores, 1961. 168 pp. (Archivo Histórico Diplomático Mexicano, Segunda Serie, 13).

Díaz, Lilia: *Versión francesa de México. Informes Diplomáticos. Documentos del Ministerio de Negocios Extranjeros de Francia, rubro 1853-1867.* Traducción e introducciones por... Prefacio de Luis González. México, El Colegio de México, 1963-1965, 1967. 4 vols. 2021 pp.

Frías y Soto, Hilarión: *Juárez glorificado y la intervención y el imperio, ante la verdad histórica: refutando con documentos la obra del señor Francisco Bulnes intitulada El verdadero Juárez.* México, ? , 1957, 450 pp.

Reedición de la publicada en 1905 por la Imprenta Central.

Fuentes Díaz, Vicente: *La intervención europea en México, 1861-1862.* México, Ediciones del Autor, 1962. 236 pp.

Fuentes Mares, José: *Juárez y el imperio.* México, Jus, 1963. 252 pp. (Colección México Heroico, 25).

Fuentes Mares, José: *Juárez y la intervención.* México, Jus 1962. 244 pp. (Colección México Heroico, 8).

Fuentes Mares, José: *Juárez y los Estados Unidos.* México, Jus (4a. ed.) 1964. 243 pp.

Fuentes Mares, José: *Proceso de Fernando Maximiliano de Hapsburgo y Tomás Mejía.* Prólogo de... México, Jus, 1966. 283 pp. (Colección México Heroico, 57).

Fuentes Mares, José: Y *México se Refugió en el desierto: Luis Terrazas: Historia y destino.* Prólogo de Nemesio García Naranjo. México, Jus, 1954. 323 pp.

García Gutiérrez, Jesús: *La Iglesia mexicana en el segundo imperio.* México, Editorial Campeador, 1955. 111 pp. (Figuras y Episodios de la Historia de México, 28).

González Navarro, Moisés: *Vallarta en la Reforma,* Prólogo, selección y notas de... México, UNAM, 1956. 265 pp. (Biblioteca del Estudiante Universitario, 76).

González Navarro, Moisés: *Vallarta y su ambiente político jurídico.* México, Junta Mexicana de Investigaciones Históricas, 1949. 165 pp.

González Ramírez, Manuel: *Los Tratados McLane-Ocampo. Ignominia y realidad.* Chetumal, Revista América, 1944. 80 pp.

Grajales, Gloria: *México y la Gran Bretaña durante la intervención (1861-1862).* México, Secretaría de Relaciones Exteriores, 1962. [300] pp.

Hernández Tapia, Germán: *Ensayo de una bibliografía de la intervención europea en México en el siglo xix (1861-1867).* México, Sociedad Mexicana de Geografía y Estadística, 1962. 143 pp. (Colección del Congreso Nacional de Historia para el Estudio de la guerra de Intervención, 13).

Hidalgo, José Manuel: *Proyectos de monarquía en México.* México, Jus, 1962. 240 pp. (Colección México Heroico, 3).

Ibarra de Anda, Fortino: *Carlota, la emperatriz que gobernó México.* México, Xóchitl, 1944. 192 pp.

Iglesias, José María: *Revistas Históricas sobre la intervención francesa.* Prólogo de Martín Quirarte. México, Editorial Porrúa, 1965. [500 pp]. (Sepan cuantos).

Junco, Alfonso: *Juárez intervencionista.* México Jus, 1961. 192 pp. (Figuras y Episodios de la Historia de México, 101).

León Toral, José: *Historia Militar: La intervención francesa en México.* México, ? , 1962. [100] pp.

List Arzubide, Germán: *La batalla del 5 de mayo.* México, Margen, 1962. 93 pp.

Loredo y Aparicio, José: *El general Prim en México.* México, El Libro Perfecto, 1947. 188 pp.

Malo, José Ramón: *Diario de los sucesos notables (1832-1864).* Arreglados y anotados por Mario Cuevas. México, Patria, 1948. 2 vols. 792 pp.

Martínez Leal, Margarita: *Posibles antecedentes de la intervención francesa de 1862 a través de las obras de viajeros franceses.* México, Autora, 1963. 256 pp.

Minvielle Porte Petit, Jorge y Rafael Tafolla Pérez: *Antecedentes de la intervención. El Imperio y la República.* México, Sociedad Mexicana de Geografía y Estadística, 1963 191 pp. (Colección del Congreso Nacional de Historia para el Estudio de la Guerra de Intervención, 23).

Miquel i Vergés, José María: *El general Prim en España y en México.* México, Hermes, 1949. 459 pp.

Monroy, Guadalupe: *Archivo Histórico de Matías Romero. Catálogo descriptivo. Correspondencia recibida I. 1837-1872.* Edición y prólogo de... México, Banco de México, 1965. 764 pp.

Moreno, Daniel: *Los intereses económicos en la intervención francesa.* México, Sociedad Mexicana de Geografía y Estadística, 1962. 43 pp. (Colección del Congreso Nacional de Historia para el Estudio de la Guerra de Intervención, 5).

Murillo Revelles, José Antonio: *Jesús Terán, embajador universal de la República juarista en Europa.* México, Sociedad Mexicana de Geografía y Estadística, 1963. 191 pp. (Colección del Congreso Nacional de Historia para el Estudio de la Guerra de Intervención, 25).

Pani, Arturo: *Jesús Terán, Ensayo biográfico.* México, A. Mijares, 1949. 146 pp.

Rangel Gaspar, Eliseo: *La intervención francesa en México. Consideraciones sobre la soberanía nacional y la no intervención.* México, Sociedad Mexicana de Geografía y Estadística, 1963. 72 pp. (Colección del Congreso Nacional de Historia para el Estudio de la Guerra de Intervención, 21).

Rivera Cambas, Manuel: *Historia de la intervención y del imperio de Maximiliano.* Prólogo de Leonardo Pasquel. México, Academia Literaria, 1961. 100 pp. (Colección Reforma e Imperio, 5).

Reedición.

Saldívar, Gabriel: *La misión confidencial de don Jesús Terán en Europa, 1863-1866.* Prólogo de... México, Secretaría de Relaciones Exteriores, 1943. 107 pp. (Archivo Histórico Diplomático Mexicano, 1).

Sánchez Navarro y Peón, Carlos: *Miramón y el caudillo conservador*. México, Jus, 1945. 414 pp.

La 2a. edición en 1949 por Editorial Patria, 296 pp.

Rubio Mañé, Ignacio: "El General Prim y el ministro de Hacienda don José González Echevarría. La crisis ministerial en México, 1961". México. *Boletín del Archivo General de la Nación*, Segunda Serie, III, IV, V, 1962-1964.

Salmerón, Celerino: *Las grandes traiciones de Juárez a través de sus tratados con Inglaterra, Francia, España y Estados Unidos*. México, Jus, (3ª edición aumentada), 1966. 199 pp.

Las ediciones anteriores son de 1960 y 1962.

Sierra, Catalina: *A cien años del 5 de mayo de 1862*. Dirección de ... Supervisión Agustín Yáñez. México, Secretaría de Hacienda y Crédito Público, 1962. 527 pp.

Sierra, Carlos J.: *La prensa liberal frente a la intervención y el imperio*. México, Secretaría de Hacienda, 1962. 205 pp.

Sierra, Carlos J.: *Periodismo mexicano ante la intervención francesa; hemerografía, 1861-1863*. México, Sociedad Mexicana de Geografía y Estadística, Sección de Historia, 1962. 173 pp. (Colección del Congreso Nacional de Historia para el Estudio de la Guerra de Intervención, 6).

Solana Gutiérrez, Mateo: *Maximiliano de Hapsburgo*. México, Polis, 1940. 175 pp.

Tello, Manuel: *Voces favorables a México en el cuerpo legislativo de Francia (1862-1867)*. Recopilación, prólogo, notas y traducción por ... México, Edición del Senado de la República, 1967. 2 vols. 1040 pp.

Terrazas Valdés, Alberto: *Chihuahua en la intervención francesa*. Chihuahua, ?, 1963. 143 pp.

Toro, Oliverio: *La quimera, el trono y el suplicio; ataujía histórica de la intervención francesa, del imperio de Maximiliano y de la segunda guerra de la independencia nacional*. México, Continente, 1949. 369 pp.

Torre Villar, Ernesto de la: *Las fuentes francesas para la historia de México y la Guerra de Intervención*. México, Sociedad Mexicana de Geografía y Estadística, 1962. 124 pp. (Colección del Congreso Nacional de Historia para el Estudio de la Guerra de Intervención, 10).

Velázquez, María del Carmen: *Documentos para la historia de México en colecciones austriacas*. México, Secretaría de Hacienda y Crédito Público, 1963. 252 pp.

Villaseñor y Villaseñor, Alejandro: *Antón Lizardo. El Tratado Mc Lane-Ocampo. El brindis del desierto*. Prólogo de Carlos Alvear Acevedo. México, Jus, 1962. 355 pp. (Colección México Heroico, 4).

Reedición de la publicada por Victoriano Agüeros en 1897, con el título de *Estudios Históricos I.*

Villaseñor y Villaseñor, Alejandro: *El 14 de marzo de 1858. El Tratado Wyke-Zamacona. El golpe de Paso del Norte. Juárez y la Baja California.* Prólogo de Carlos Alvear Acevedo. México, Jus, 1962. 331 pp. (Colección México Heroico, 5).

Reedición de la publicada por Victoriano Agüeros en 1909, con el título de *Estudios Históricos II.*

Zamarripa M., Florencio: *Anecdotario de la insurgencia.* México, Editorial Futuro, 1960. 196 pp.

Zendejas, Adelina: *La mujer en la intervención francesa.* México, ?, 1962. 108 pp.

V. REPÚBLICA RESTAURADA Y PORFIRIATO

A cien años del triunfo de la República. México, Secretaría de Hacienda y Crédito Público, 1967. 509 pp.

Avilés, René: *Benito Juárez el hombre ejemplar.* Idea y notas de... México, Sociedad de Amigos del Libro Mexicano, 1956. 76 pp.

Carreño, Alberto María: *Archivo del general Porfirio Díaz. Memorias y documentos.* Obra publicada en colaboración con el Instituto de Historia de la UNAM. México, Editorial "Elede", S. A., 1947-1961 (Colección de Obras Históricas Mexicanas, 2-3).

Cosío Villegas, Daniel: *Estados Unidos contra Porfirio Díaz.* México, Hermes, 1956. 344 pp.

Publicada en inglés por University of Nebraska Press, 1964. 259 pp.

Cosío Villegas, Daniel: *Historia Moderna de México.* México, Hermes, 1955-1965. 8 vols. 7652 pp.

Entrevista Díaz-Creelman. Prólogo por José María Luján. Traducción de Mario Julio del Campo. México, UNAM, 1963. 50 pp. (Cuadernos del Instituto de Historia. Serie Documental, 2).

Espinosa de los Reyes, Jorge: *Relaciones económicas entre México y Estados Unidos, 1870-1910.* México, Nacional Financiera, 1951. 189 pp.

Flores, Jorge D.: *La labor diplomática de don Ignacio Luis Vallarta como secretario de Relaciones Exteriores.* Estudio preliminar de... México, Secretaría de Relaciones Exteriores, 1961. 334 pp. (Archivo Histórico Diplomático Mexicano, Segunda Serie, 12).

Fuentes Mares, José: *Juárez y la República.* México, Jus, 1965. 198 pp. (Edición México Histórico, 45).

González Navarro, Moisés: *La colonización en México, 1877-1910.* México, Secretaría de Hacienda. Estampillas y Valores, 1960. 160 pp.

González Ramírez, Manuel: *La huelga de Cananea*. Editor... México, ?, ? pp.

Henestrosa, Andrés: *Colección de discursos de Juárez*. Editados por... México, ?, ? pp.

Henestrosa, Andrés: *Flor y látigo, ideario político de Benito Juárez*. Selección y prólogo de... México, Ediciones del Boletín Bibliográfico de la Secretaría de Hacienda y Crédito Público, 1964. 81 pp.

Lara Pardo, Luis: *De Porfirio Díaz a Francisco I. Madero*. México, ?, ? pp.

Limantour, José Yves: *Apuntes sobre mi vida pública (1829-1911)*. México, Editorial Porrúa, S. A., 1965. 337 pp.

Memorias de Don Francisco Mejía, secretario de Hacienda de los presidentes Juárez y Lerdo. México, Ediciones del Boletín Bibliográfico de la Secretaría de Hacienda y Crédito Público, 1958. 192 pp.

Palacios Galera, Lucía: *México vuelve a la comunidad internacional después de la intervención*. México, autor, 1956. [70] pp.

Río González, Manuel del: *Juárez; su vida y su obra*. Jalapa, Dirección General de Educación Popular, [1966]. 251 pp.

Robina, Lucía: *Reconciliación de México y Francia (1870-1880)*. Selección y prólogo de... México, Secretaría de Relaciones Exteriores, 1963. 257 pp. (Archivo Histórico Diplomático Mexicano, Segunda Serie, 16).

Romero, Matías: *La promoción de las relaciones comerciales entre México y Estados Unidos*. México, Banco de Comercio Exterior, 1961. 333 pp.

Roux López, Francis Bodhi J.: *El surgimiento del imperialismo económico y los Estados Unidos. La penetración económica en México (1896-1910)*. México, UNAM, Escuela de Ciencias Políticas y Sociales, 1963. 135 pp.

Salado Álvarez, Victoriano: *Memorias. I Tiempo Viejo. II Tiempo Nuevo*. México, Ediapsa, 1946. 342 pp.

Sepúlveda, César: *Dos reclamaciones internacionales fraudulentas contra México. Los casos de Weil y La Abra, 1868-1902*. México, Secretaría de Relaciones Exteriores, 1965. 273 pp. (Archivo Histórico Diplomático Mexicano, Segunda Serie, 17).

Sierra, Carlos J.: *Juárez en la inmortalidad del 21 de marzo*. Estudio por... Prólogo de Manuel J. Sierra. México, Secretaría de Hacienda y Crédito Público, Dirección General de Prensa, Memoria, Bibliotecas y Publicaciones, 1965. 162 pp.

Sierra, Justo: *Juárez, su obra y su tiempo*. Edición anotada por Arturo Arnáiz y Freg. Prólogo de Agustín Yáñez. México, Editora Nacional (3ª edición), 1965. 500 pp.

Tamayo, Jorge L.: *Benito Juárez. Documentos, discursos y correspondencia*.

Selección y notas de... Prólogo de Adolfo López Mateos. México, Secretaría del Patrimonio Nacional, 1964-1967. 10 vls. 6943 pp.

Taracena, Ángel: *Porfirio Díaz*. México, Jus, 1960. 211 pp. (Figuras y Episodios de la Historia de México, 88).

Torrea, Juan Manuel: *El general de división Ramón Corona. Excelsitud como ciudadano, como militar, como gobernante y como diplomático.* [Guadalajara, 1944. i.e. 1945. 150 pp.]

Valadés, José C.: *El pensamiento político de Benito Juárez.* México, ?, 1957. [200 pp.]

Valadés, José C.: *El porfirismo: historia de un régimen.* México, Antigua Librería Robredo de J. Porrúa e hijos y Editorial Patria, 1941 y 1948. 2 vols. [850 pp.]

Zamarripa, Florencio M.: *Apuntes para mis hijos; datos autobiográficos del Benemérito de las Américas, tomados de su archivo privado.* Prólogo y compilación de... México, Editorial Futuro, (4ª ed.), [1963]. 207 pp.

VI. REVOLUCIÓN, 1910-1940

a) Panoramas generales

Alessio Robles, Miguel: *Historia política de la Revolución.* México, ? (3ª ed.), 1946. [100 pp.]

Amaya, Juan Gualberto: *Síntesis social de la Revolución Mexicana y doctrinas universales.* México, s.p.i., 1947. 271 pp.

Beteta, Ramón: *Pensamiento y dinámica de la Revolución Mexicana.* México, Editorial México Nuevo, 1950. 579 pp.

Otra edición en 1951.

Blancas, Benito R.: *Ensayo histórico sobre la Revolución Mexicana.* México, autor, 1963. 176 pp.

Blanco Moheno, Roberto: *Crónica de la Revolución Mexicana.* México, Libro-Mex Editores, 1957, 1959, 1961. 3 vols. 1162 pp.

La Editorial Diana, S. A., ha publicado dos ediciones posteriores, una en 1967 y otra en 1968. (Colección Moderna).

Bremauntz, Alberto: *La batalla ideológica en México.* México, Ediciones Jurídico-Sociales, 1962. 304 pp.

Calzadíaz Barrera, Alberto: *Hechos reales de la Revolución.* México, Editores Mexicanos Unidos, (3ª ed.), 1965. 3 vols. 805 pp.

La segunda edición por Patria, 1961.

Casasola, Gustavo: *Historia Gráfica de la Revolución Mexicana, 1900-1960.* México, Editorial F. Trillas, S. A., 1960. 3 vols. 2207 pp.

Reedición.

Castillo Torre, José: *Palabras de paz y de guerra.* México, Botas, 1942. 338 pp.

Ceniceros, José Ángel: *Actitud internacional de México.* México, Botas, 1941. 69 pp.

Crónica ilustrada de la Revolución Mexicana. Director responsable Rubén Guerrero Caballero. Director de la obra Vicente Casarrubias. Asesor Diego Arenas Guzmán. México, Publex, S. A., 1966-1968. 6 vols. 78 núms. 1500 pp.

Encina, Dionisio: *¡Fuera el imperialismo y sus agentes!* México, Popular, 1940. 168 pp.

Fabela, Isidro: *Defensa de los derechos de México.* México, Mundo Libre, 1944. 423 pp.

Fabela, Isidro: *Historia diplomática de la Revolución Mexicana.* México, Fondo de Cultura Económica, 1958. 2 vols. 828 pp. (Vida y Pensamiento de México).

Fabela, Isidro: *Por un mundo libre.* México, Secretaría de Educación Pública, 1943. 148 pp.

Fabela, Isidro y Josefina E. de Fabela: *Documentos históricos de la Revolución Mexicana.* Editados por... México, Fondo de Cultura Económica y Jus. (Fuentes y Documentos de la Historia de México), 1960-1966. 10 vols. 4782 pp.

Fernández Mac Gregor, Genaro: *El río de mi sangre.* México, Fondo de Cultura Económica, 1969. 544 pp.

Ferrer de Mendiolea, Gabriel: *Historia de la Revolución Mexicana.* México, "El Nacional", 1956. 198 pp.

García Rivas, Heriberto: *Breve historia de la Revolución Mexicana.* México, Editorial Diana, 1964. 246 pp.

Gastélum, Bernardo J.: *La Revolución Mexicana. Interpretación de un espíritu.* México, Editorial Porrúa, S. A., 1966. 576 pp.

González Blanco, P.: *Una experiencia política: Las memorias del licenciado Portes Gil.* México, ?, 1945. [70] pp.

González Ramírez, Manuel: *Fuentes para la historia de la Revolución Mexicana. II La caricatura política.* México, Fondo de Cultura Económica, 1954. 500 pp.

González Ramírez, Manuel: *La revolución social de México.* México, Fondo de Cultura Económica, 1960, 1965-1966. 3 vols. 1717 pp.

Hermosillo Azpeitia, María de L.: *Política intervencionista americana.* México, autor, 1963. 173 pp.

Las relaciones internacionales de México, 1935-1956 (a través de los mensajes presidenciales). Prólogo de Luis Padilla Nervo, secretario de Relaciones Exteriores. México, Secretaría de Relaciones Exteriores, 1957. 130 pp. (Archivo Histórico Diplomático Mexicano, Segunda Serie, 9).

Continuación de *Un Siglo de Relaciones Internacionales de México* de Genaro Estrada, que concluye en 1934.

Mancisidor, José: *Historia de la Revolución Mexicana.* México, El Gusano de Luz, 1958. 293 pp.

Mejía Zúñiga, Raúl: *La revolución constitucionalista.* México, Secretaría de Educación Pública, Instituto Federal de Capacitación del Magisterio, 1964. 164 pp. (Técnica y Ciencia, 33).

México. Cincuenta años de Revolución. Prólogo de Adolfo López Mateos. México, Fondo de Cultura Económica, 1960-1961. 4 vols. 2342 pp.

Morales Jiménez, Alberto: *Historia de la Revolución Mexicana.* México, Partido Revolucionario Institucional, 1951. 307 pp.

Moreno, Daniel: *Los hombres de la Revolución; 40 estudios biográficos.* México, Libro-Mex Editores, 1960. 366 pp.

Muñoz, Ignacio: *La verdad sobre los gringos. ¡Defendámonos!* México, Ediciones Populares (4ª ed.), ¿1962? 240 pp.

Muñoz, Ignacio: *Verdad y mito de la Revolución Mexicana (relatada por un protagonista).* México, Ediciones Populares, 1960-1964. [1600] pp.

Parra, Manuel Germán: *La industrialización de México.* México, Imprenta Universitaria, 1954. 203 pp.

Portes Gil, Emilio: *Autobiografía de la Revolución Mexicana; un tratado de interpretación histórica.* Con ensayo crítico sobre la vida del autor por Antonio Luna Arroyo. México, Instituto Mexicano de Cultura, 1964. 881 pp.

Sepúlveda, César: *Las relaciones diplomáticas entre México y los Estados Unidos en el siglo XX.* Monterrey, s.p.i., 1953. 64 pp.

Silva Herzog, Jesús: *Breve historia de la Revolución Mexicana.* México, Fondo de Cultura Económica, 1960. 2 vols. 614 pp.

Silva Herzog, Jesús: *Trayectoria ideológica de la Revolución Mexicana. Del Manifiesto del Partido Liberal de 1906 a la Constitución de 1917.* México, Cuadernos Americanos, 1963. 135 pp.

Taracena, Alfonso: *La Revolución desvirtuada.* México, Costa-Amic, 1966-1967. 2 vols. 686 pp.

Continuación de *La verdadera Revolución Mexicana*, que publicó Jus hasta 1965.

Taracena, Alfonso: *La verdadera Revolución Mexicana.* México, Jus, 1960·

1965. 19 vols. 4370 pp. (Figuras y Episodios de la Historia de México y México Heroico).

Ulloa, Berta: *Revolución Mexicana, 1910-1920.* México, Secretaría de Relaciones Exteriores, 1963. 538 pp. (Archivo Histórico Diplomático Mexicano. Guías para la Historia Diplomática de México, 3).

Valadés, José C.: *Historia General de la Revolución Mexicana.* México, M. Quesada Brandi, 1963-1967. 10 vols. 4000 pp. (Obras Selectas sobre Historia de México).

Vera Estañol, Jorge: *La Revolución Mexicana: orígenes y resultados.* México, Editorial Porrúa (2ª ed.), 1957. 3 vols. 2409 pp.

b) Temas específicos

Aguirre, Enrique y F. Harris: *La no intervención y la quiebra de la soberanía nacional.* México, Tipografía Camionera, 1946. 183 pp.

Aguirre, Manuel Jesús: *Cananea: Las garras del imperialismo en las entrañas de México.* México, Libro-Mex, 1958. 398 pp.

Almada, Francisco: *La revolución en el Estado de Chihuahua.* México, Talleres Gráficos de la Nación, 1964-1965. 2 vols. 773 pp. (Biblioteca del Instituto Nacional de Estudios de la Revolución Mexicana, 35).

Álvarez Sepúlveda, Enriqueta: *Las relaciones de México y los Estados Unidos durante el periodo en que fue presidente, el general Calles, 1924-1926. Antecedentes y proyecciones.* México, ?, 1966. 412 pp.

Alvear Acevedo, Carlos: *Lázaro Cárdenas: El hombre y el mito.* México, Jus, 1961. 363 pp. (Figuras y Episodios de la Historia de México, 94).

Amaya C., Luis Fernando: *La soberana convención revolucionaria, 1914-1916.* México, Editorial F. Trillas, S. A., 1966. 468 pp.

Amaya, Juan Gualberto: *Los gobiernos de Obregón, Calles y regímenes "Peleles" derivados del callismo: tercera época, 1920-1935.* México, ?, 1947. 464 pp.

Amaya, Juan Gualberto: *Madero y los auténticos revolucionarios de 1910, hasta la Decena Trágica y fin del general Pascual Orozco: Primera etapa, 1900-1913.* México, ?, 1964. [400] pp.

Amaya, Juan Gualberto: *Venustiano Carranza, caudillo constitucionalista: Segunda etapa, febrero de 1913 a mayo de 1920.* México, ?, 1947. [400] pp.

Anguiano Equihua, Victoriano: *Lázaro Cárdenas: su feudo y la política nacional.* México, Ed. Eréndira, 1951. 361 pp.

Arenas Guzmán, Diego: *Historia de la Cámara de Diputados de la XXVI Legislatura Federal. La Revolución tiene la palabra. Acta del "Diario de los Debates" de la Cámara de Diputados, 14 de septiembre de 1912 al 19 de febrero de 1913.* Selección y guías por ... México, Talleres Gráficos de la

Nación, 1961, 1963. 4 vols. 2141 pp. (Biblioteca del Instituto Nacional de Estudios de la Revolución Mexicana, s/n).

Barragán Rodríguez, Juan B.: *Historia del Ejército y de la Revolución Constitucionalista.* México, Talleres de la Editorial Stylo, 1946. 2 vols. 1953 pp.

Barrera, Carlos: *Obregón: estampas de un caudillo.* Prólogo de Aarón Sáenz. México, s.p.i., 1957. 253 pp.

Barrera Fuentes, Florencio: *Historia de la Revolución Mexicana: la etapa precursora.* México, Talleres Gráficos de la Nación, 1955. 339 pp. (Biblioteca del Instituto Nacional de Estudios Históricos de la Revolución Mexicana, 1).

Bojórquez, Juan de Dios: *Hombres y aspectos de México en la tercera etapa de la Revolución.* México, Talleres Gráficos de la Nación, 1963. 243 pp. (Biblioteca del Instituto Nacional de Estudios Históricos de la Revolución Mexicana, 30).

Bonilla Jr., Manuel: *El régimen Maderista.* Prólogo de Joaquín Fernández de Córdoba. México, Editorial Arana, 1962. 351 pp. (Biblioteca de Historia Mexicana).

Reedición de la publicada en 1922.

Bravo Covarrubias, Hipólito: *La reforma agraria y los Tratados de Bucareli.* México, autor, 1961. 101 pp.

Bulnes, Francisco: *Toda la verdad acerca de la Revolución Mexicana. La responsabilidad criminal del presidente Wilson en el desastre mexicano.* México, Los Insurgentes, (2ª ed.), 1960. 354 pp. (Colección Reforma-Revolución, 4).

Calzadíaz Barrera, Alberto: *Villa contra todo y . . . en pos de la venganza sobre Columbus, N. M.* México, Editorial Libros de México, 1960. 177 pp.

Carrión, Ana María Rosa: *La intervención americana en Veracruz.* México, autora, 1964. [200] pp.

Cervantes M., Federico: *Francisco Villa y la Revolución.* México, Ediciones Alonso, 1960. 828 pp.

Cué Canovas, Agustín: *Ricardo Flores Magón, la Baja California y los Estados Unidos.* México, Libro-Mex Editores, 1957. 121 pp.

Diario de los Debates del Congreso Constituyente, 1916-1917. México, Ediciones de la Comisión Nacional para la celebración del sesquicentenario de la Proclamación de la Independencia Nacional, 1960. 2 vols. [800] pp.

Esquivel Obregón, Toribio: *La propaganda protestante en México a la luz del derecho internacional y del más alto interés de la nación.* México, s.p.i., 1946. 67 pp.

Fabela, Isidro: *El canal de Panamá y el ferrocarril de Tehuantepec.* México, s.p.i., ?, 51 pp.

Fabela, Isidro: *Intervención*. México, UNAM, Escuela de Ciencias Políticas y Sociales, 1959. 376 pp.

Franco, Luis G.: *Glosa del periodo de Gobierno del C. General e Ingeniero Pascual Ortiz Rubio, 1930-1932. Relaciones Exteriores de una actuación histórica*. Libro núm. 10. México, Meximex, 1947. 217 pp.

Gómez Robledo, Antonio: *The Bucareli Agreements and international law*. Traducción de Salomón de la Selva. México, The National University of Mexico Press, 1940. 229 pp.

Publicada en español por Polis en 1938.

González Fernández, A. R.: *La servidumbre de tránsito sobre el istmo de Tehuantepec en favor de los Estados Unidos y su abrogación definitiva*. México, s.p.i., 1958. 74 pp.

González Monroy, Jesús: *Ricardo Flores Magón y su actitud en la Baja California*. Prólogo de José Vasconcelos, México, Editorial Academia Literaria, 1962. 180 pp. (Testimonios Documentales de México, 1).

Guzmán, Martín Luis: *Febrero de 1913*. México, Empresas Editoriales, S. A., 1963. 133 pp.

Guzmán Esparza, Roberto: *Memorias de don Adolfo de la Huerta según su propio dictado*. Transcripción y comentarios de... México, Ediciones Guzmán, 1957. 335 pp.

Hidalgo, Ernesto: *La protección de mexicanos en los Estados Unidos*. México, Secretaría de Relaciones Exteriores, 1940. 72 pp.

Huerta, Victoriano: *Memorias de...* México, "Vértice", 1957. 137 pp.

La cuestión internacional mexicano-americana, durante el gobierno del Gral. don Álvaro Obregón. Prólogo de Alberto J. Pani. México, Editorial Cultura, (3ª ed.), 1949. 300 pp.

Reedición corregida y aumentada de las de 1924 y 1926.

Labor internacional de la Revolución Constitucionalista de México; Libro Rojo. México, Secretaría de Relaciones Exteriores, 1960. 445 pp. (Ediciones de la Comisión Nacional para al celebración del Sesquicentenario de la proclamación de la Independencia Nacional y del cincuentenario de la Revolución Mexicana).

Reedición de la que publicó la Secretaría de Relaciones en 1918.

Lara Pardo, Luis: *Matches de dictores. Wilson contra Huerta, Carranza contra Wilson*. México, Márquez, 1942. 303 pp.

Lascurráin y Osio, Ángel: *La segunda intervención americana*. México, Jus, 1957. 120 pp. (Figuras y Episodios de la Historia de México, 42).

List Arzubide, Germán: *El México de 1910: El Maderismo*. México, ?, 1963. [100] pp.

López Gutiérrez, Ma. Eugenia: *Procedimientos diplomáticos del régimen obregonista; antecedentes y proyecciones*. México, s.p.i., 1959. 268 pp.

Luquín, Eduardo: *La política internacional de la Revolución Constitucionalista*. México, Talleres Gráficos de la Nación, 1957. 281 pp. (Biblioteca del Instituto Nacional de Estudios Históricos de la Revolución Mexicana, 10).

Luquín, Eduardo: *México en el extranjero. Ensayo*. México, Ed. Costa-Amic, 1961. 91 pp.

Luquín Romo, Eduardo: *El pensamiento de Luis Cabrera*. México, Talleres Gráficos de la Nación, 1960. 252 pp. (Biblioteca del Instituto Nacional de Estudios Históricos de la Revolución Mexicana, 17).

Mancisidor Ortiz, Anselmo: *Veracruz recuperado*. México [Talleres Gráficos de la Nación], 1968. 178 pp.

Manero, Antonio: *La reforma bancaria en la revolución constitucionalista*. México, Talleres Gráficos de la Nación, 1958. 512 pp. (Biblioteca del Instituto Nacional de Estudios Históricos de la Revolución, 14).

Manero Sánchez, Adolfo y José Paniagua Arredondo: *Los Tratados de Bucareli ¡Traición sobre México! Un capítulo del "Libro Negro" de las relaciones entre México y los Estados Unidos durante la Revolución*. México, ? , 1958. 2 vols. 800 pp.

Martínez, Pablo L.: *El magonismo en Baja California, documentos*. México, Editorial Baja California, 1958. 63 pp.

Melo de Remes, Ma. Luisa: *¡Alerta Baja California!* México, Jus, 1964. 173 pp.

Melo de Remes, Ma. Luisa: *Veracruz Mártir. La infamia de Woodrow Wilson (1914)*. México, ? , 1966. 191 pp.

Mena Brito, Bernardino: *Hasta dónde llegaron los contrarrevolucionarios combatiendo a Carranza y a la Constitución de 1917 (villistas, zapatistas, pelaecistas, felixistas, mexueristas y obregonistas)*. México, Ediciones Botas, 1960. 50 pp.

Mena P. Mario: *Álvaro Obregón. Historia militar y política, 1912-1929*. México, Jus, 1960. 157 pp. (Figuras y episodios de la Historia de México, 90).

Menéndez, Gabriel A.: *Doheny el cruel; episodios de la sangrienta lucha por el petróleo mexicano*. México, Bolsa Mexicana del Libro, 1958. 309 pp.

Meyer, Lorenzo: *México y Estados Unidos en el conflicto petrolero, 1917-1942*. México, El Colegio de México, 1968. 273 pp.

Moctezuma, Aquiles P.: *El conflicto religioso de 1926: sus orígenes, su desarrollo, su solución*. México, Jus, (2ª ed.), 1960. 868 pp. (Figuras y Episodios de la Historia de México, 80).

Moreno, Daniel: *Francisco I. Madero. José Ma. Pino Suárez. El crimen de la embajada.* México, Libro-Mex, 1960. 57 pp. (Colección de Figuras Mexicanas, 3).

Muñoz Cota, José: *Ricardo Flores Magón. Un sol clavado en la sombra.* México, Editores Mexicanos Unidos, S. A., 1963. 125 pp.

Origel Sandoval, Cristina: *La Decena Trágica.* México, autora, 1963. [100] pp.

Palomares, Justino N.: *La invasión Yanqui en 1914.* Prólogo de Juan Sánchez Azcona, México, ? , 1940. 280 pp.

Pani, Alberto J.: *Apuntes autobiográficos.* México, ? , 1951. 2 vols. [800] pp.

Pani, Alberto J.: *Las conferencias de Bucareli.* México, Jus, 1953. 228 pp.

Pasquel, Leonardo: *Manuel y José Azueta. Padre e hijo. Héroes de la gesta de 1914.* México, Editorial Citlaltépetl, 1967. 229 pp. (Colección Suma Veracruzana. Serie Biográfica).

Portes Gil, Emilio: *Quince años de política mexicana.* Prólogo de Alfonso Teja Zabre. México, Ediciones Botas, (3ª ed.), 1954. 566 pp.

Prida, Ramón: *La culpa de Lane Wilson, embajador de los Estados Unidos, en la tragedia mexicana de 1913.* México, Ediciones Botas, 1962. 214 pp.

Puente, Ramón: *Villa en pie.* México, Editorial Castalia, (2ª ed.), 1966. 181 pp.

Ramírez Plancarte, Francisco: *La Ciudad de México durante la Revolución Constitucionalista.* México, Ediciones Botas, (2ª ed.), 1941. 598 pp.

La primera edición en 1940.

Rius Facius, Antonio: *La juventud católica y la Revolución Mexicana, 1910-1925.* México, Jus, 1963. 324 pp.

Rius Facius, Antonio: *Méjico cristero. Historia de la A.C.J.M., 1925-1931.* México, Editorial Patria, 1960. 510 pp.

Roa González, Luis: *La doctrina Estrada.* México, autor, 1952. 125 pp.

Sáenz, Aarón: *La política internacional de la Revolución. Estudios y Documentos.* Prólogo de Manuel González Ramírez. México, Fondo de Cultura Económica, 1961. 551 pp. (Vida y Pensamiento de México).

Sánchez Azcona, Juan: *Apuntes para la historia de la Revolución Mexicana.* México [Talleres Gráficos de la Nación], 1961. 391 pp. (Biblioteca del Instituto Nacional de Estudios Históricos de la Revolución Mexicana, 25).

Sánchez Azcona, Juan: *La etapa maderista de la Revolución.* México, [Talleres Gráficos de la Nación], 1960. 91 pp. (Biblioteca del Instituto Nacional de Estudios Históricos de la Revolución Mexicana, 22).

Santana Bravo, J.: *El problema del reconocimiento del gobierno de D. Venustiano Carranza.* México, autor, 1963. 88 pp.

Suárez G., Ignacio: *Carranza, forjador del México actual: su vida-su muerte.* México, B. Costa-Amic Editor, 1965. 221 pp.

Taracena, Alfonso: *Madero, el héroe cívico.* México, ? , 1946 [200] pp.

Taracena, Alfonso: *Madero, víctima del imperialismo yanqui.* México, Clásica Selecta-Editora Librera, 1960. 270 pp.

Taracena, Alfonso: *Venustiano Carranza.* México, Jus, 1963. 319 pp. (Colección México Heroico, 22).

Torrea, Juan Manuel: *La Decena Trágica. Apuntes para la historia del Ejército Mexicano. La asonada militar de 1913.* México, ? , 1960. [100] pp.

Trujillo, Rafael: *Adolfo de la Huerta y los Tratados de Bucareli.* México, Porrúa, 1957. 233 pp. (Biblioteca Mexicana, 19).

Ulloa, Berta: "La Revolución Mexicana y los Estados Unidos. (Historia diplomática 1910-1914)". México, El Colegio de México, 1969. 600 pp. mimeógrafo.

Urquizo, Francisco: *Carranza: el hombre, el político, el caudillo, el patriota.* México, [Ed. Muñoz], (6ª ed.), 1957. 111 pp.

Urquizo, Francisco: *La Ciudadela quedó atrás: escenas vividas de la Decena Trágica.* México, B. Costa-Amic Editor, 1965. 170 pp.

Urquizo, Francisco: *Páginas de la Revolución.* México, Instituto Nacional de Estudios Históricos de la Revolución Mexicana, 1956. 274 pp. (Biblioteca del Instituto Nacional de Estudios Históricos de la Revolución Mexicana, 3).

Valadés, José C.: *Imaginación y realidad de Francisco I. Madero.* México, Antigua Librería de Robredo, 1960. 2 vols. 571 pp.

Wallerstein Derechin, Eugenia: "Tierra y hombre del México revolucionario, 1913-1914. (Visión histórica de Edith O'Shaughnessy)". México, UNAM, Facultad de Filosofía y Letras, 1962. 354 pp. en mimeógrafo.

c) La era de la Buena Vecindad

Arellano Belloc, Francisco: *La exclusividad del estado en el manejo de sus recursos petroleros.* México, Concamal, 1958, 145 pp.

Botella Asensi, J.: *La expropiación en el derecho mexicano. El caso del petróleo.* México, Moderna, 1941. 222 pp.

Calvillo P., Horacio: *¿Está obligado México a someter a arbitraje las expropiaciones agrarias y petroleras?* México, ? , 1942. 250 pp.

Castillo Nájera, Francisco: *El petróleo en la industria moderna: las campañas petroleras y los Gobiernos de México.* México, Cámara Nacional de la Industria de Transformación, 1949. [70] pp.

Cuéllar, Alfredo B.: *Expropiación y crisis en México.* México, UNAM, 1940. 629 pp.

Cuevas Cancino, Francisco: *Roosevelt y la Buena Vecindad.* México, Fondo de Cultura Económica, 1954. 551 pp.

Enríquez, Ernesto: *Problemas internacionales: reclamaciones y petróleo.* México, Botas, 1942. 166 pp.

Fabela, Isidro: *Buena y mala vecindad.* Prólogo de Vicente Sáenz. México, América Nueva, 1958. 330 pp. (Colección de Autores Contemporáneos, 10).

Fabela, Isidro: "La política internacional del presidente Cárdenas". México, *Problemas agrícolas e Industriales,* 7: 4 (oct-dic 1955), pp. 3-117.

Fabela, Isidro: *Mentalidad . . . La Sociedad de Naciones y el Continente Americano entre la guerra 1939-1940.* México, Biblioteca de Estudios Internacionales, 1940. 325 pp.

González Ramírez, Manuel: *El petróleo Mexicano; la expropiación petrolera ante el derecho internacional.* México, América, 1941. 333 pp.

Hay, Eduardo: *Discursos pronunciados en su carácter de Secretario de Relaciones Exteriores, 1936-1940.* México, Talleres Gráficos de la Nación, 1940. 97 pp.

Lavín, José Domingo: *Petróleo: pasado, presente y futuro de una industria mexicana.* México, EDIAPSA, 1950. 401 pp.

Márquez Padilla, Tarsicio: *Consideraciones sobre la interpretación mexicana de la política del Buen Vecino.* México, s.p.i., 1944. 120 pp.

Silva Herzog, Jesús: *Historia de la expropiación de las empresas petroleras.* México, Instituto Mexicano de Investigaciones Económicas, 1964. 221 pp.

Silva Herzog, Jesús: *Historia de la expropiación petrolera.* México, Cuadernos Americanos, 1963. 171 pp.

Silva Herzog, Jesús: *Inquietud sin tregua. Ensayos y artículos escogidos, 1937-1965.* México, Cuadernos Americanos, 1965. 367 pp.

Silva Herzog, Jesús: *México y su petróleo.* Buenos Aires, 1959, 74 pp.

Silva Herzog, Jesús: *Nueve estudios mexicanos.* México, Imprenta Universitaria, 1953. 315 pp. (Colección Cultura Mexicana, 8).

Silva Herzog, Jesús: *Petróleo Mexicano. Historia de un problema.* México, Fondo de Cultura Económica, 1941. 305 pp.

Tribunales extranjeros reconocen el indiscutible derecho con que México expropió los intereses extranjeros. México, Secretaría de Relaciones Exteriores, 1940. 94 pp.

d) Varios

Alba, Pedro de: *Siete artículos sobre el problema de los braceros.* México, s.p.i., 1954. 56 pp.

Álvarez del Castillo, Juan Manuel. *Memorias.* Guadalajara, 1960, 635 pp.

Cosío Villegas, Daniel: *Change in Latin America, The mexican and cuban revolution.* Lincoln, University of Nebraska, 1961. 54 pp.

Enríquez, Ernesto: *Evolución del derecho internacional mexicano en los últimos treinta años (1912-1942).* México, Jus, 1943. 58 pp.

Frías Loyola, G.: *Constitución y tratados diplomáticos; su relación y posibles conflictos.* México, UNAM, 1952. 62 pp.

García Treviño, Rodrigo: *La ingerencia rusa en México (y Sudamérica).* Pruebas y testimonios. México, Editorial América, 1959. 233 pp.

Manero, Antonio: *México y la solidaridad Americana.* Madrid, s.f. 245 pp.

Olea Morca, José R.: *El reconocimiento de gobiernos.* México, s.p.i., 1948. 111 pp.

Orden Mexicana del Aguila Azteca. Ley y reglamento. México, Secretaría de Relaciones Exteriores, (2ª ed.), 1941. 61 pp.

Palacios y Bermúdez de Castro, Roberto: *El artículo 33 Constitucional.* México, Antigua Librería Robredo, 1949. 119 pp.

Reyes Lemoine, Marina Beatriz: *La diplomacia contemporánea, notas para su estudio.* México, UNAM, Facultad de Derecho, 1967. 237 pp.

Rojas Garcidueñas, José: *Genaro Fernández Mac Gregor, escritor e internacionalista; discurso de ingreso a la Academia Mexicana leído el 22 de junio de 1962, por...* México, UNAM, 1962. 72 pp.

Ruiz Olvera, Estela: *La mujer mexicana y la diplomacia.* México, UNAM, Escuela de Ciencias Políticas y Sociales, 1963. [100] pp.

Segura García, Baldomero: *Antología del pensamiento universal de Isidro Fabela.* Prefacio y selección de... México, UNAM, 1959. 2 vols. 1502 pp.

Sepúlveda, César: *La responsabilidad internacional del estado y la validez de la cláusula Calvo.* México, ? , 1944. 83 pp.

Taracena, Alfonso: *Cartas políticas de José Vasconcelos (Primera Serie, 1924-1936).* Preámbulo y notas de... México, Clásica-Selecta. Editora Librera, 1959. 312 pp.

Tratados y convenciones vigentes entre los Estados Unidos Mexicanos y otros países. México, Secretaría de Relaciones Exteriores, 1930-1965. 9 vols. [3600] pp.

VII. BIBLIOGRAFÍAS

Anuario Bibliográfico Mexicano de 1940. Catálogo de Catálogos e índice de periódicos 1941-1942. México, Secretaría de Relaciones Exteriores, 1942. 316 pp.

Bibliografía Histórica Mexicana. I y II. Compiladora Susana Uribe de Fernández de Córdoba. México, El Colegio de México. 1967-1968.

Buenrostro, Felipe: "Documentos diplomáticos relativos a la política exterior de México". *Historia del Primer y Segundo Congresos Constitucionales de la República Mexicana. IX.*

Cosío Villegas, Daniel: *Cuestiones internacionales de México. Una Bibliografía.* México, Secretaría de Relaciones Exteriores, 1966. 588 pp. (Archivo Histórico Diplomático Mexicano. Guías para la Historia Diplomática de México, 4).

Cosío Villegas, Daniel: *La historiografía política del México Moderno.* México, El Colegio Nacional, 1953. 91 pp.

González, Luis, Guadalupe Monroy, Susana Uribe y Luis Muro. *Fuentes para la Historia Contemporánea de México. Libros y Folletos.* México, El Colegio de México, 1961-62. 3 vols. i, lxxxi, 527. 688. 651 pp.

Guía del Archivo Histórico Diplomático de la Secretaría de Hacienda. Siglos XVI-XIX. México, Secretaría de Hacienda y Crédito Público, 1940.

Hernández Tapia, Germán: *Ensayo de una bibliografía de la intervención europea en México en el siglo* XIX. México, Sociedad Mexicana de Geografía e Historia, 1962. 143 p.

Muro, Luis F.: "Guía del Archivo Histórico de la Secretaría de la Defensa Nacional". Inédita. Depositada en el Colegio de México desde 1962. Cerca de 10000 fichas.

Ross, Stanley R.: *Fuentes para la Historia Contemporánea de México. Periódicos y revistas.* México, El Colegio de México, 1965, 1967. 2 vols. 2001 pp.

Ulloa, Berta: "Historia diplomática". *Historia Mexicana No. 60. (Veinticinco años de investigación histórica en México. II).* México, El Colegio de México, 1966. pp. 497-530.

Porrúa, Manuel (ed.): *Catálogo le libros de ocasión. México y Estados Unidos. Relaciones internacionales y controversias sobre límites.* México, Stylo, 1948. 48 pp.

Ramos, Roberto: *Bibliografía de la Revolución Mexicana.* México, Secretaría de Relaciones Exteriores, 1931-1940. 3 vols.

Segunda edición en 1959.

Saldívar, Gabriel: *Bibliografía de la Secretaría de Relaciones Exteriores.* México, Secretaría de Relaciones Exteriores, 1943. 96 pp.

COMENTARIO

HORST DRECHSLER

Me permito hacer unas observaciones acerca de la ponencia del profesor Liss. Si se comparan las dos ponencias sobre relaciones internacionales lo primero que se nota es que no hay unanimidad sobre lo que hay que analizar. El profesor Liss analiza las relaciones internacionales de México en el siglo xx, mientras que la profesora Ulloa lo hace desde la emancipación hasta 1940. El profesor Liss se concentra en la producción científica de la última década, mientras que la ponencia de la profesora Ulloa abarca casi 30 años. Es decir, que no hay unanimidad sobre el punto de partida.

Me ha gustado mucho el hecho de que la ponencia del profesor Liss abarque el periodo actual. Pero hay una contradicción en ella: dice que es pobre la producción científica sobre las relaciones internacionales de México y yo comparto esta opinión. Pero concentrándose, en primer lugar, en monografías cita solamente los artículos sobre nuestra materia que fueron publicados en inglés. Si no existe bastante literatura sobre un tema es ilógico excluir los artículos en otras lenguas, sobre todo en español. A mi parecer faltan, por ejemplo, los artículos sobre "La política exterior de México", publicados en un número especial de la revista *Foro Internacional* con motivo del 25 aniversario de El Colegio de México. Faltan otros artículos, por ejemplo el de Roque González Salazar sobre "La política exterior de México", publicado en un libro germano-occidental *Mittlere Mächte in der Weltpolitik* (Opladen, 1969) y otro artículo de Modesto Seara Vázquez sobre el mismo tema publicado en la revista *Ciencias Políticas y Sociales*. Me ha gustado además que el profesor Liss haya mencionado unos libros sobre su tema que fueron publicados en alemán y en ruso. Pero, analizando el libro de mi amigo y colega Katz, no era necesario añadir que este libro haya venido "from behind the iron curtain". Es una vuelta al idioma de la guerra fría. Y, como ustedes ven, el hecho de que tres historiadores de la República Democrática Alemana participen en su Reunión, muestra, a mi parecer, que la llamada cortina de hierro está haciéndose más y más transparente. Quiero añadir que los dos libros publicados en ruso, mencionados por el profesor Liss, existen también en lengua española.

Después de haber hablado sobre la situación bibliográfica, permítanme unas palabras sobre los problemas. El profesor Liss ha enumerado muchos problemas y plantea muchas preguntas desde un punto de vista a veces subjetivo. Por ejemplo, no puedo comprender que Liss trate de convencer —cinco veces en su ponencia— a México de adoptar un papel de "hemispheric leader over lesser Latin American nations". ¿Para qué? México no puede intervenir en América del Sur ingiriéndose en las rivalidades entre el Brasil y la Argentina sobre la hegemonía. Otra cosa es que México juegue un papel importante en América Central, especialmente en el campo de la economía. Su ponencia tiene una gran deficiencia que consiste en el hecho de no mencionar problemas económicos. No se puede hablar sobre relaciones internacionales sin tomar en cuenta los factores económicos. Por eso en toda la ponencia no existe la integración económica de América Latina que es, a mi parecer, un problema que influye mucho sobre las relaciones internacionales de cada país latinoamericano en la última década. En este contexto es necesario analizar la posición de México frente a la integración económica de América Latina. México pertenecía a los tres grandes países de América Latina que eran los verdaderos protagonistas y beneficiarios de la ALALC. Pero las cosas cambiaron cuando hace tres años los norteamericanos descubrieron su interés en un Mercado Común Latinoamericano e impusieron a la Conferencia Cumbre de Presidentes Americanos de Punta del Este en abril de 1967 su concepción de integración económica de América Latina. Desde este momento disminuyó constantemente el interés de México por la integración económica de América Latina y en 1969 el conocido documento "Consenso Latinoamericano de Viña del Mar" ya no mencionó este tema.

Otra cuestión que falta completamente en la ponencia del profesor Liss es el hecho de que no menciona la fuerte oposición de México al envío de una llamada Fuerza Interamericana de Paz a la República Dominicana en 1965 y después contra el establecimiento de tal fuerza militar interamericana.

Creo que en general se puede decir que México prefiere la Organización de las Naciones Unidas a la OEA que, hace algún tiempo, Carrillo Flores la ha calificado como una institución "cuya característica principal es la peculiar y abrumadora falta de equilibrio entre las fuerzas que la componen".

En conclusión, quisiera repetir que la ponencia del profesor Liss es, a pesar de mis objeciones, rica en sugerencias y por eso es un buen punto de partida para una discusión sobre relaciones internacionales de México. No es culpa suya que haya en ella más preguntas que respuestas.

CARLOS BOSCH GARCÍA

La lectura cuidadosa del trabajo de Sheldon B. Liss desconcierta. Quizá ésta sea la forma mejor de describirlo. Treinta y tres páginas de texto y más de cinco de notas que desconciertan porque no atina uno a percibir el verdadero objetivo del autor. Si todo responde a la preocupación de por qué no han escrito los autores estadunidenses sobre este tema en los últimos diez años, quizá el propio trabajo del autor pueda revelar el porqué. Se limita a presentar dudas sobre la política externa de México sin resolverlas. Si no nos hacemos a la idea de que debemos entrar en los temas a fondo, ¿cómo hemos de resolver los problemas que presentan?

Creemos, además, que limitarse a la bibliografía publicada en los últimos diez años es un error. Hablar de la pobreza de materiales aparecidos en esa época es intrascendente, porque el periodo es demasiado corto. Que apareciera una gran cantidad de bibliografía en ese tema sería casualidad.

El tema nunca fue de los más populares para los historiadores y, quienes lo hemos trabajado, sabemos por qué. Es molesto de trabajarse porque siempre se tropieza con las posturas políticas de los países y de los propios intelectuales. Molesto en cuanto a que se debe apoyar en archivos gubernamentales pertenecientes a Secretarías de gobierno que sirven a la Secretaría y no al investigador. Pero, además, molesto porque en él se discuten todos los motivos de fricción entre las naciones en un periodo en que se deseen ignorar todos los problemas incómodos.

Pero hay otros puntos de importancia; entre ellos los que, a los historiadores mexicanos, nos interesa analizar, con preferencia la postura de los Estados Unidos y los principios de su política que chocan con nuestro país y con los demás de América Latina. Es precisamente en este campo donde deseamos y nos esforzamos por encontrar una interpretación que nos sirva también para entender nuestra propia historia. En este punto estoy de acuerdo con el autor, debemos ir en busca de la interpretación o, por lo menos, de la interpretación mexicana de la política exterior de los Estados Unidos, porque es fundamental para nosotros. Pero no ignoramos, y seguro que el profesor Liss tampoco lo ignora, que lograr una interpretación en nuestra especialidad es quizá más difícil que en otras de la misma historia. Es, además, un proceso lento que parte del estudio de archivo —la bibliografía hay que manejarla con cuidado— y luego el conocimiento se eleva poco a poco hasta lograrse la interpretación. Quienquiera que intente esta tarea se dará cuenta de que significa un trabajo de muchos años y que no se pueden salvar conductos si se desea un producto bien acabado, por lo menos, para uno mismo.

El trabajo que nos concierne parece responder a la inquietud juvenil de nuestra época, por su interés sobre lo inmediato, por la limitación sobre la bibliografía de un lapso de tiempo muy corto y por la falta de satisfacción que obtiene de la respuesta de autores, elegidos por haber publicado sus trabajos dentro de la década escogida. Algunos de ellos quizá no hayan publicado su mejor libro en ese periodo, sino en épocas anteriores. Ellos son: Daniel Cosío Villegas, Isidro Fabela, Lucía de Robina, Jorge Castañeda, Francisco Cuevas Cancino, Aarón Sáenz, Lorenzo Meyer, Alberto Bremauntz, Rodrigo García Treviño, Vicente Lombardo Toledano, José Revueltas, David Álvaro Siqueiros, Jesús Silva Herzog, Víctor Manzanilla Schaffer, Luis Medina Ascencio, Antonio Gómez Robledo, Berta Ulloa. Todos ellos de diferentes objetivos e intereses al publicar sus libros y representantes también de estudios muy variados en el estudio de las relaciones entre los dos países, pues van desde el puro interés bibliográfico hasta el político, pasando por infinidad de intermedios.

Nos enfrentamos, pues, a un proceso de trabajo lento, en el que ya han trabajado varias generaciones y apenas empezamos a despejar algunas de las incógnitas más conspicuas. La experiencia muestra, de manera clara, cómo es imposible encontrar respuestas en una bibliografía limitada a los últimos diez años, tal como lo trata de hacer el autor.

Sus inquietudes, en cuanto a la pasividad de México en la política exterior de la postguerra, en cuanto al problema de la no intervención, o de la actitud jurídica, posiblemente se disiparían si recurriera a enlazar la bibliografía y los temas de preocupación con la bibliografía y los periodos históricos precedentes. De hecho debería remontarse sin prisa, ni ansias, hasta el principio del siglo XIX. ¡Cuán bizantinas resultarían muchas de las preguntas que plantea!

Todos admiramos el trabajo dinámico y quisiéramos absorber el contenido de los archivos en un momento para poder llegar a estadios superiores del estudio. Nos preguntamos también si la razón de ser de las dudas y de los temas, que se señalan para futuro estudio, no resultan de la falta de paciencia para investigarlos a fondo. Algunas de las preguntas que hace están resueltas, otras no. Puede ser que con el transcurso del tiempo el autor logre el equilibrio y la calma que le hará ver cómo los historiadores de los Estados Unidos, en la última década, han tenido temas de preocupación que han disminuido de manera aparente el interés por los temas cercanos, como lo son los de América Latina para ellos y, sustituirlos, abocándose a los temas de Oriente o África que responden a inquietudes de su propia nación y que, por ello, han sido subsidiados ampliamente.

Quienes manejan bibliografía pueden notar el aumento considerable de la producción norteamericana en esos campos y su disminución en el campo latinoamericano que ha llegado casi a desaparecer de las publicaciones.

II

El trabajo de la señorita Berta Ulloa está dividido en dos partes, a saber: la primera, un comentario general hecho en 13 páginas y la segunda, que consta de una bibliografía de alrededor de 40 páginas, si se cuentan los cuadros estadísticos que ha logrado montar.

El trabajo de conjunto significa un esfuerzo cuidadoso para mostrar lo que se ha producido en la materia que nos contrae. Reúne y clasifica las

fichas bibliográficas de las publicaciones aparecidas y las organiza en apartados idóneos.
Su clasificación comprende:

I. Sección general:
   a) historias generales;
   b) panamericanismo;
   c) relaciones con Estados Unidos;
   d) la cuestión de Belice y relaciones con Centroamérica;
   e) varios.

II. Iniciación de la vida independiente.

III. La era de Santa Anna.

IV. Reforma e Intervención.

V. República, restauración y Porfiriato.

VI. Revolución 1910-40:
   a) panoramas generales;
   b) temas específicos;
   c) la era de la buena vecindad;
   d) varios.

VII. Bibliografías.

VIII. Cuadro resumen.

El cómputo final no puede considerarse malo, pues se trata de 82 obras, sin contar las reediciones que entran en la sección general; 24 dedicadas a la iniciación de la Independencia; 35 a la era de Santa Anna; 59 a la Reforma e Intervención; 51 a la República restaurada; 178 a la Revolución cubriendo el periodo de 1910 a 1940. Significa un total de 429 títulos que han aparecido sobre las relaciones exteriores de México durante el lapso de veinte y nueve años. La estadística que presenta Berta Ulloa hace notar, además, cómo a partir de 1959 la producción se acelera y ello quiere decir que el interés por el tema va en aumento de manera considerable; pues si en el primer periodo, que va desde 1940 a 1958, se publicaron 193 obras en el segundo aparecen 266 lo que significa, en un lapso de sólo once años, casi un tercio de aumento.

Desde este punto de vista debemos sentirnos satisfechos, pues los esfuerzos llevados a cabo en el campo de las relaciones internacionales están rindiendo frutos y el tema en sí llama la atención de los estudiosos, a pesar de todos los pesares, que son muchos. Tampoco desanima observar los nombres de las personas que se han dedicado a este estudio, pues, al revisar las fichas con cuidado, notamos cómo se encuentran los nombres de personas ilustres de nuestro mundo intelectual, y político, entre los autores.

Creemos que el historiador mexicano de temas internacionales empieza a contar con una tradición y su estudio se debe al hecho real de que la vida internacional adquiere cada día más importancia en el país. Sin embargo el tema todavía no ha sido totalmente incorporado a la historia general de la nación y se sigue entendiendo como un aspecto paralelo de la historia. El paso, que significa la incorporación de nuestros temas a la historia general necesita, todavía de muchos esfuerzos. La bibliografía de Berta Ulloa nos lo muestra así, pero debemos satisfacernos al pensar que hemos logrado abrir un campo nuevo de estudio, que es importante y que contribuye al conocimiento de nuestra historia, al situarla en una tercera dimensión por relacionarla con la de otros países.

Ahora bien, el análisis que de su propia bibliografía hace Berta Ulloa no alcanza su propio significado, pues aunque menciona cómo 13 instituciones se han interesado por la publicación de las obras que nos conciernen, sólo tres parecen ser las patrocinadoras importantes de los libros y creemos que su misión va mucho más allá, ellas son: la Secretaría de Relaciones Exteriores, la Universidad y El Colegio de México. En esas tres instituciones el objetivo ha sido mucho más importante y la señorita Ulloa debe hacerlo resaltar con mucha claridad pues en ello se diferencian de las demás. La función de la Secretaría fue de publicar y difundir el conocimiento del tema y así lo intenta a través del Archivo Histórico Diplomático, desgraciadamente falló en su distribución como la mayoría de las publicaciones oficiales, que no siempre llegan a las manos de quienes en ellas se interesan. A la vez la Secretaría se convierte en la fuente primordial de documentación, porque posee el archivo donde los investigadores deberían encontrar todas las facilidades y libertad de trabajo.

En cuanto a la Universidad creemos que su función es, como dice la autora, la de preparar profesionales y ciertamente ha producido un buen grupo de egresados, que han mostrado solidez y dedicación por el tema, como sucede en sus tesis profesionales que, tanto por la temática como por el trabajo que acumulan, pueden considerarse de alto significado.

El Colegio de México ha sido la institución que pudo aprovechar a muchos de esos profesionales al utilizarlos en sus aulas, donde se prepararon funcionarios para la Secretaría, o dedicándolos a la investigación facilitando becas en el propio Colegio o ayudándolos a obtenerlas en el extranjero para viajar y a ampliar sus conocimientos. En esta forma sus egresados vieron su campo de investigación ampliado, pues tuvieron ocasión de consultar y utilizar materiales que se encuentran en archivos lejanos.

Las demás instituciones que menciona Berta Ulloa no se han preocupado, en la mayoría de los casos, por el estudio de nuestros temas. Se han limitado a patrocinar algunos de los libros y nada más. Es posible que esto explique la existencia de una lista de autores bizarros, no profesionales, que por afición producen manuscritos cuya salida es institucional por razones muy diversas. Esa lista de autores parece mostrar también que otro aspecto importante de esta especialidad es la falta de profesionalidad, pues trata de autores cuyo quehacer no es la historia, sino que va desde las tareas del curato hasta las guerreras y recordamos la frase famosa de "cuando tengo tiempo no tengo pan y cuando tengo pan no tengo tiempo", que explica y describe el verdadero fondo del asunto.

La autora pasa, después, a analizar el contenido de sus propios apartados bibliográficos y es una lástima que no se haya detenido en ellos con calma y precisión, pues sólo así nos hubiera presentado una historiografía, como dice el título, de mucha importancia para todos nosotros. ¿Qué tendencias hay en esos libros? ¿Cómo interpretan los problemas? ¿En qué forma los presentan? ¿Qué problemas tocan? Éstas y muchas otras preguntas son preocupaciones que, si bien se intenta descubrir en las páginas que analizamos, no se han logrado resolver. En este último tramo es donde la ponencia amerita todavía un esfuerzo supremo, pues apenas esboza sin lograr profundizar sus propios conceptos.

COMMENTARY

LYLE C. BROWN

Within the limits which he has set for himself, Professor Liss has done an excellent job of identifying the writings of Mexican and United States historians in the area of Mexico's international relations since the beginning of this century. After excluding from his survey those works which deal mainly with United States-Mexican diplomacy, international law, and foreign economic relations and development, he observes that *los yanquis* have failed to make significant contributions to the body of historical literature concerning Mexico's recent relations with other nations. At the same time, however, he has made imaginative suggestions regarding important targets for research that should be attacked by diplomatic historians on both sides of the Río Bravo.

We can agree, I am sure, that there is a need to learn more of Mexico's twentieth century relations with Great Britain, France, Germany, Cuba, Guatemala, the Soviet Union, and many other countries. Certainly, those *yanquis* with special interests in United States-Mexican relations can come to understand their subject better as they extend investigation to all matters embraced by Mexico's foreign policy. Nevertheless, we are reminded that diplomatic history is a relatively new field; even the popular subject of United States-Mexican relations began to receive needed attention only in the World War II period. No doubt it was logical that citizens of the United States should first study the history of their own country's relations with the neighbor to the south before attempting to become authorities on Mexico's dealings with other nations. After all, vision is first developed by identifying big objects near at hand before straining the eye to identify things of lesser magnitude which are more distant. Our border problems, an expandig volume of trade, the growing tourist traffic, and the importance of United States-Mexican financial ties —all of these seem to have justified a preoccupation with United States-Mexican diplomacy.

At this time, are *los yanquis* prepared to undertake the investigation of Mexico's relation with other countries? An examination of abstracts of doctoral dissertations recently completed at universities in the United States reveals that among thirteen studies dealing with Mexico's international relations, only one writer has concerned himself with Mexico's total involvement in world affairs;[1] the others have confined their attention to matters involving Mexico and the United States. Hopefully, some of these young scholars will respond to Professor Liss's challenge and will focus future research efforts on Mexican relations with other countries in this hemisphere or with the nations of Europe, Africa, and Asia.

[1] David Anthony White, "Mexico in World Affairs, 1928-1968" (Ph.D. dissertation, University of California at Los Angeles, 1968).

Although not the work of a *yanqui*, mention must be made of a book which deals in part with Mexican foreign policy and which has been published in the United States this year. It is *Latin American International Politics* edited by Professor Carlos A. Astiz, an Argentine citizen who received B. A., M. A., and Ph. D. degrees at Pennsylvania State University and who is a member of the faculty of the State University of New York at Albany. As an introduction to Section II of his book, which includes four previously published articles on Mexican foreign policy, the *gaucho* scholar has written a brief essay which suggests that he will have more to offer us on this subject in the future. [2]

Professor Liss has pointed out that in this past decade there has been a conspicuous lack of published biographical and autobiographical literature concerning Mexican diplomats. Miguel A. Marín's article on the life and work of Isidro Fabela (1882-1964) indicates the great need for a biography of this statesman and man of letters, who played an important role in Mexico's international affairs for half a century. [3] Fabela has been described by Jesús Silva Herzog as "el internacionalista con preocupaciones literarias" [4] and "uno de los mejores mexicanos de su tiempo". [5] Another example of biographical writing, which suggests the need for more extensive scholarly treatment of the lives of persons who have formulated and administered Mexican foreign policy since 1900, is a recently published article dealing with the diplomatic activities of Victoriano Salado Álvarez (1867-1931), who served during the later years of the Díaz era and under De la Barra, Madero, and Huerta. [6] Emilio Portes Gil's second

---

[2] Carlos A. Astiz (ed.), *Latin American International Politics: Ambitions, Capabilities and the National Interest of Mexico, Brazil and Argentina*. Notre Dame, Ind., University of Notre Dame Press, 1969, pp. 81-88. Two of the articles included in this collection have been noted by Liss: John R. Faust and Charles L. Stansifer, "Mexican Foreign Policy in the United Nations", pp. 100-110 (originally published in *Southwestern Social Science Quarterly*, XLIV [September, 1963], 121-129); and Jorge Castañeda, "Revolution and Foreign Policy: Mexico's Experience", pp. 137-165 (reprinted from *Political Science Quarterly*, LXXVIII [September, 1963], 391-417). The latter is essentially a translation of the author's "México y el exterior" in *La política*, vol. III of *México: cincuenta años de la Revolución* (4 vols.) México, D. F., Fondo de Cultura Económica, 1961-1962, pp. 267-289. Also included are two articles by Mexican writers which are printed in English for the first time: Luis Padilla Nervo, "The Presence of Mexico at the United Nations: The Cuban Case", pp. 89-99 (originally published as "Presencia de México en las Naciones Unidas. El Caso de Cuba", *Cuadernos americanos*, XX [May-June, 1961], 72-83) and Javier Rondero, "Mexico at Punta del Este", pp. 111-136 (originally published as "México en Punta del Este", *Ciencias Políticas y Sociales*, VIII [January-March, 1962], 49-72).

[3] Miguel A. Marín, "Isidro Fabela", *Foro Internacional*, V, October-December, 1964, pp. 151-182. Also see Comité de Amigos de Isidro Fabela, *Homenaje a Isidro Fabela* (2 vols.). México, D. F., Universidad Nacional Autónoma de México, 1959.

[4] Jesús Silva Herzog, *El pensamiento económico, social y político de México, 1810-1964*. México, D. F., Instituto Mexicano de Investigaciones Económicas, 1967, p. 616 and pp. 635-651.

[5] *Ibid.*, p. 651.

[6] José Rojas Garcidueñas, "Don Victoriano Salado Álvarez como diplomático", *Historia Mexicana*, XVII, April-June, 1968, pp. 569-586.

autobiographical work appeared only five years ago, [7] but the former President (1929-1930) and Secretary of Foreign Relations (1934-1935) gives us very little information about Mexico's international affairs during his years in office, except for an account of the breaking of diplomatic relations with the Soviet Union in January, 1930. [8] On the other hand, publication of the memoirs of Juan Manuel Álvarez del Castillo has provided us with a detailed account of a diplomatic career that extended from 1923 to 1955 and involved service in Europe and the Western Hemisphere. [9] Also, within recent weeks the atoubiography of Genaro Fernández MacGregor (1883-1959), a distinguished writer and international affairs specialist, has been published. [10]

The paucity of autobiographical literature indicates the importance of the oral history technique which has been employed by James W. Wilkie and Edna Monzón de Wilkie. To date they have conducted interviews with twenty-eight prominent Mexicans, thus accumulating 158 hours of tape recordings which have produced an archive of 3,500 pages of typescript. [11] Recently the recorded interviews with Ramón Beteta, Marte R. Gómez, Manuel Gómez Morín, Vicente Lombardo Toledano, Miguel Palomar y Vizcarra, Emilio Portes Gil, and Jesús Silva Herzog have been published in a well-indexed volume entitled *México visto en el siglo XX.* [12] Although the interviews are focused mainly on Mexican political history, this book offers much interesting testimony concerning Mexico's twentieth century international relations. Some of the Mexicans interviewed by the Wilkies have written autobiographical works, while others have not but still may find time to do so; nevertheless, the typescript of a tape-recorded interview constitutes a unique personal document. For those people who have neither the time nor the inclination for autobiographical

---

[7] Emilio Portes Gil, *Autobiografía de la Revolución Mexicana: un tratado de interpretación histórica,* México, D. F., Instituto Mexicano de Cultura, 1964. The third edition of his *Quince años de la política mexicana.* México, D. F., Botas, 1954; had appeared a decade earlier.

[8] Portes Gil, *Autobiografía de la Revolución Mexicana,* pp. 607-610.

[9] Juan Manuel Álvarez del Castillo, *Memorias.* Guadalajara, Talleres del Instituto Tecnológico de la Universidad de Guadalajara, 1960.

[10] Genaro Fernández MacGregor, *El río de mi sangre.* México, D. F., Fondo de Cultura Económica, 1969. Also see Genaro Fernández MacGregor, "Las relaciones exteriores de México y el derecho internacional" in Arturo Arnáiz y Freg *et. al., México y la cultura.* México, D. F., Secretaría de Educación Pública, 1961, pp. 961-1005.

[11] The twenty-eight persons interviewed are Salvador Abascal, Aurelio R. Acevedo, Juan Andreu Almazán, Silvano Barba González, Clementina Batalla Bassols, Ramón Beteta, Juan de Dios Bojórquez, Alfonso Caso, Luis Chávez Orozco, Daniel Cosío Villegas, Carlos Fuentes, Francisco Javier Gaxiola, Jr., Marte R. Gómez, Manuel Gómez Morín, Martín Luis Guzmán, Luis L. León, Germán List Arzubide, Vicente Lombardo Toledano, Aurelio Manrique, José Muñoz Cota, Melchor Ortega, Ezequiel Padilla, Miguel Palomar y Vizcarra, Emilio Portes Gil, Manuel J. Sierra, Jesús Silva Herzog, David Alfaro Siqueiros, and Jacinto B. Treviño.

[12] James W. Wilkie and Edna Monzón de Wilkie, *México visto en el siglo XX: entrevistas de historia oral.* México, D. F., Instituto Mexicano de Investigaciones Económicas, 1969.

writing, such tape-recorded interviews represent the only possibility for
first-person accounts by men who have influenced the course of public
affairs and who have made history. These records provide important
supplements to the printed documents, official records, manuscript materials,
statistical data, and other sources commonly used by historians. [13] Thus, if
better Mexican diplomatic history is to be written, many of us must undertake a portion of the task of tape-recording interviews with diplomats and
other government officials who may never write the memoirs that we
need. [14]

[13] For examples of effective utilization of oral history materials in the writing
of Mexico's political history, see quotations from Ramón Beteta in James W.
Wilkie, *The Mexican Revolution: Federal Expenditure and Social Change Since
1910*. Berkeley and Los Angeles, University of California Press, 1967, pp. 8-9,
90-91; also see quotations from Daniel Cosío Villegas and Manuel Gómez Morín
in James W. Wilkie and Albert L. Michaels (eds.), *Revolution in Mexico: Years of
Upheaval, 1910-1940*. New York, Knopf, 1969, pp. 4-7 and pp. 257-261, respectively.

[14] For description of the Wilkies's oral history methodology and explanation
of concepts on which their program is based, see their *México visto en el siglo XX*,
pp. 3-18. Also see James W. Wilkie, "Postulates of the Oral History Center for
Latin America", *The Journal of Library History*, ii, January, 1967, 45-55; and
James W. Wilkie, "Oral History of 'Biographical Elitelore' in Latin America",
unpublished paper presented at the Social Science Research Council Conference
on Folklore and Social Science, New York City, November 10, 1967.

COMENTARIO

M. S. ALPEROVICH

El profesor Liss justamente señala que la mayoría de los trabajos históricos acerca de las relaciones internacionales de México tratan principalmente de las relaciones entre México y los Estados Unidos, al mismo tiempo que las relaciones de México con otros países se estudian en mucha menor medida. Sin embargo, es de lamentar que el informante no mencionó siquiera algunos de los trabajos publicados en los últimos años que tratan esta cuestión. Quiero, en parte, recordar aquellas publicaciones mexicanas como: Manuel Ramírez Reyes, *La posición de México ante la OEA* (México, 1965); Alberto Bremauntz, *México y la revolución socialista cubana* (Morelia, 1966); Manuel Tello, "Algunos aspectos de la participación de México en la sociedad de las naciones" (*Foro Internacional*, 1965-1966). [1]

Quisiera también hacer hincapié en el libro del investigador norteamericano Frederick C. Turner *The Dynamic of Mexican Nationalism* (Chapel Hill, 1968). [2] El autor de este interesante trabajo, al analizar el nacionalismo mexicano desde principios del siglo pasado y, principalmente, bajo la influencia de la Revolución de 1910, subraya el importante rol de la xenofobia en este proceso.

Muy valiosa visión de la política de la Alemania hitleriana con relación a México en los años 1938-1941 contiene el artículo de Friedrich Katz "Einige Crundzüge der Politik des deutschen Imperialismus in Lateinamerika 1898 bis 1941" [3] en el volumen *Der Deutsche Faschismus in Lateinamerika, 1933-1943* [4] (editado en 1966 por la Universidad de Humboldt en Berlín).

En Moscú acaba de aparecer una recopilación del historiador soviético Alexander Sizonenko *En el país del águila azteca*. Está dedicado a la vida y funciones de los primeros embajadores soviéticos en México (hasta el final de la Segunda Guerra Mundial).

Una observación más. Quisiera manifestarme en contra de la afirmación del respetable profesor Liss, relacionada con las aparentes contradicciones entre los principios básicos de la política exterior de México y su realización práctica. En lo que a mí se refiere, no entiendo ¿por qué la doctrina de no intervención en los asuntos internos de otros Estados y la autodeterminación de los pueblos parece contradecir la ayuda que, en su tiempo, México brindó a la España republicana? ¿por qué los miembros de la Organización de Estados Americanos no pueden mantener relaciones diplomáticas y comerciales con Cuba?, etcétera. Y, por último, no es comprensible por qué el problema de la influencia del marxismo y las ideas comunistas

---

[1] Nota del traductor: En español en el original.
[2] Nota del traductor: En inglés en el original.
[3] Nota del traductor: En alemán en el original.
[4] Nota del traductor: En alemán en el original.

en México que se debe, más que nada, a meros factores internos, se examina en conexión con el problema de las relaciones extranjeras. Por supuesto la teoría del marxismo constituye una doctrina internacional. Puede asimilarse o no, pero, desde mi punto de vista, no hay base para analizarla como ideología "extranjera" para México así como para cualquier otro país.

RELATORÍA

MIGUEL MARÍN BOSCH

La discusión se inició con un análisis de las ponencias presentadas. Se destacó el hecho de que una fuera una bibliografía y la otra un ensayo bibliográfico; en consecuencia, se puntualizaron los defectos naturales de ambos tipos de trabajos.

Los participantes consideraron que las limitaciones de los estudios de historia diplomática a las relaciones entre México y Estados Unidos se explicaba, en gran parte, porque el campo es relativamente nuevo. Por esta razón se hizo una exhortación para que se investigaran las relaciones de México con otros países tales como Alemania, Gran Bretaña, Francia, y la Unión Soviética. Igualmente se invitó a los historiadores para que estudiaran las relaciones de México con el resto de los países de América Latina, así como su posición frente a la integración económica de la región. Se destacó el hecho de que los investigadores mexicanos tuvieran una oportunidad única y exclusiva para realizar estudios sobre las relaciones con Cuba.

Aludiendo a los trabajos teóricos que sobre la diplomacia se han escrito en Europa, algunos participantes propusieron que los historiadores de las relaciones internacionales de México colaboraran en un esfuerzo multinacional con el fin de estudiar las bases teóricas de las relaciones, especialmente consideradas, en función de la proximidad con Estados Unidos. Entre los temas posibles de estudio se mencionaron la situación geográfica del país, la explotación de los recursos naturales, los presupuestos militares, la ideología nacional y el papel desempeñado en los foros internacionales.

Los debates sobre la carencia de estudios de historia diplomática, así como las dificultades para consultar los archivos que nutren estudios de esta naturaleza, ocupó buena parte de la discusión. Sin embargo, se concluyó que los problemas de consulta de acervos documentales no era exclusiva de México sino de todos los países, citándose entre ellos a los más avanzados.

XII. MESA REDONDA: A) "NUEVOS MÉTODOS Y TÉCNICAS DE INVESTIGACIÓN HISTÓRICA"

PONENCIAS

"Mr. Historian meet Mr. Demographer." Harley L. Browning

"New Directions and Methods in Historical Investigations." Peter Boyd Bowman

"La antropología y la investigación histórica: el estudio del indio." Pedro Carrasco

"New Approaches in Contemporary Mexican Historical Research." James W. Wilkie

MR. HISTORIAN, MEET MR. DEMOGRAPHER

HARLEY L. BROWNING

My comments on "New Directions in Historical Research" will not be in my professional role as sociologist, though it would be tempting to pose some of the unexplored problems of social classes and social mobility as they were affected by the Mexican Revolution, or the applicability of the Barrington Moore Jr. thesis, as elaborated in his book, *Social Origins of Dictatorship and Democracy: Lord and Peasant in the Making of the Modern World*, to the Mexican or the Latin American experience, the world area which he almost completely neglects. Instead, I want try to point out ways in which historians, at least those concerned with economic and social history, can benefit from a better understanding of the demographic perspective and particularly demographic theoretical models.

As a sociologist who works continually with demographic data, sometimes within the historical context of trend analysis, I am often puzzled by the historian's general orientation to demographic factors as they might help in accounting for social change. With but few exceptions, most historians make little or no effort to introduce population variables and population change as an integral part of their interpretation of social change. It is for me striking how rarely population change, including population redistribution in the form of internal migration and urbanization, is seen as a dynamic force whose causes and consequences are worthy of analysis in their own right. I make this charge of historians generally, not limiting it to those concerned with Latin America, and I would recommend to you a recent article by David Landes who takes European and American historians to task on this point in a recent issue of *Daedalus* devoted entirely to historical demography. [1] This volume, I might point out, provides a good recent overview of the vitality and creativity of historical demography as practiced in Europe, particularly among the English and the French. [2]

If you will permit me a sweeping generalization, my impression is that historians tend either to ignore demographic data, either through sheer ignorance of available data or in the belief that the

---

[1] Landes, David, "The Treatment of Population in History Textbooks", *Daedalus*, 1968, 97:2: 363-384.

[2] See also the impressive collection edited by D. V. Glass and D. E. C. Eversley, *Population in History: Essays in Historical Demography*. Chicago, Aldine Publishing Company, 1965.

data are unimportant or unreliable or both, or they introduce population data but in a completely uncritical and mechanical fashion. The same historian who is unsparing of himself in spending many days and weeks to track down and verify some fact that may be only tangentially related to his argument, will at the same time accept without hesitation or question population figures that even upon visual inspection appear suspect. Can it be that historians have such complete confidence in the accuracy of anything issued under the aegis of a governmental agency, as for example a census bureau? I doubt it. I think the main reason for the uncritical acceptance of population figures and the often weak and unsatisfactory analyses of these data is due mainly to the fact that historians simply are unfamiliar with demographic procedures and therefore are ill-equipped to evaluate and effectively utilize demographic data. It is highly unlikely that most historians have been exposed to any sort of formal training in demography and they seldom give the reader any evidence of familiarity with the demographic literature.

Let me illustrate these general comments by reference to the case of Mexico. This is a case where the need for the incorporation of demographic factors in the interpretation of Mexican history needs little defense. Surely the interpretation of the entire colonial period can never be made secure until the controversy surrounding the population of pre-conquest Mexico and of New Spain is in one way or another resolved. I have followed for some years the efforts of the "Berkeley Group" (Borah, Cook and Simpson) as reported in *Ibero-Americana* to attack earlier conceptions of population trends during this period. Without pretending to the specialist's knowledge, I find myself in sympathy and general agreement with their effort to radically revise the demographic history of Mexico. Their patient, skillful and dedicated search for archival material bearing on the question I find most impressive. But I am not impressed by their neglect, at least if one is to rely upon citations in their publications, of demographic methodology that could help them better to evaluate and interpret their data.

Since I have criticized an American group, let me not exempt the Mexicans. Just before leaving for this conference there came into my hands a book-length manuscript by Moisés González Navarro entitled, *Historia Demográfica del México Contemporáneo*, and covering the period 1910 to 1964. I had time only to skim the chapter headings and to glance at the bibliography. I have no doubt that this volume will be an important addition to the literature, but again I am struck by the lack of any reference to technical demography sources in the bibliography. Certainly the impact of the Mexican Revolution upon the population of Mexico, particularly between the years of 1910 and 1921, still remains to be written. The demographic cost of the Revolution both at the national as well as state and regional levels, has been inadequately specified. I say this because we cannot accept at face value the figures of the 1910 census, but most particuarly that of the 1921 census. No one doubts that the 1921 census left much to be desired in terms of accuracy —considering the circumstances in which it was undertaken, it is indeed remarkable that any census whatever was carried out— but as yet the problem has not been attacked with the full armory of demographic techniques. Hopefully, someone within the demographic section of *El Colegio de México* sooner or later will address himself to this particular problems.

I know that the reaction of some historians to my remarks will be to the effect that it is unreasonable of me to ask of the historian that he also become a formal demographer, trained and well practiced in advanced statistical and mathematical analysis. I will grant that some corners of demographic theory and methodology are highly technical and that they can be quite intimidating to those without training in advanced mathematics, at least I must report that I am myself intimidated by much of this work. But I am prepared to argue that social and demographic historians will find it of lasting benefit to make rather modest investment in time —a matter of several months at the most— to acquaint themselves with the fundamentals of demographic and methodological perspectives and their logic of analysis. This I believe can be made accessible to the historians with only a minimum of training in statistics or mathematics.

Within the last decade or so there have been a number of significant developments within the fields of demography that warrant the attention of historians. First of all, the fund of reliable census and vital statistics data has enormously increased since World War II, partly as a consequence of the encouragement of international agencies such as the United Nations as well as the conduct of censuses in many countries of the world previously lacking such information. While it is true that these data are for quite recent time periods and therefore not ostensibly of concern to most historians, as I shall try to point out later, this accumulation has made more clear the probably range of demographic behavior. Along with the mounting data, there has been a concomitant concern with the development and elaboration of techniques protesting the accuracy of these demographic data. While some of this material is quite technical and forbidding in nature, there are a number of more elementary discussions that are available to the historian. For example, the book by Barclay, *Techniques of Demographic Analysis*. [3] and a number of

[3] Barclay, George W., *Techniques of Population Analysis*. New York, John Wiley & Sons, Inc., 1958.

the inexpensive manuals issued by the United Nations [4] are clear and effective expositions of data evaluation techniques.

The second feature worthy of not is linked to the accumulation of data. The computer has been recently enlisted in the processing of this vast amount of data in a systematic fashion and this has greatly encouraged and facilitated the development of useful comparative and historical surveys. A recent example is the book by Keyfitz and Flieger, *World Population: An Analysis of Vital Data.* [5] In the words of Philip M. Hauser, "...this volume opens new vistas of opportunity for comparative demographic study. It permits, among other things, more careful examination of population dynamics —the interplay of fertility and mortality over time as it affects population growth and changes in the age structure. It affords a basis for evaluating the accuracy of vital statistics in census data, and the power of diverse techniques of population estimation".

The second point leads into the third significant development in demography which has been a florescence in theory and formal model construction. Deriving mainly from the earlier work of Lotka, stable population theory has developed some of the most powerful and useful models outside of the physical sciences. The fundamental assumption of demographers, whether it be in evaluation of the accuracy of some set of data or in the preparation and use of model life tables in stable populations, is that human demographic behavior within "closed" populations (that is, those not greatly affected by migration) is not unrestricted in its range. If we can have some degree of confidence that the components of population change, fertility and mortality, vary within known and predictable limits, then our chances of correctly "placing" a particular population, even on the basis of fragmentary data, will be greatly enhanced. The analogy of the paleontologist who is able to create a complete skeletal structure from a few surviving bones is perhaps appropriate.

It is precisely this orientation that has guided the authors of a manual recently prepared for a United Nations demographic series and appropriately entitled, *Methods of Estimating Basic Demographic Measures From Incomplete Data.* [6] Coale and Demeny have also published a much more elaborate set of reference tables entitled,

[4] *Manual I: Methods of Estimating Total Population for Current Dates*, ST/SOA/Series A/10. Also *Manual II: Methods of Appraisal of Quality of Basic Data for Population Estimates*, ST/SOA/Series A/23. Also *Manual III: Methods for Population Projections by Sex and Age*, ST/SOA/Series A/25.

[5] Keyfitz, Nathan and Wilhelm Flieger, *World Population: An Analysis of Vital Data*. Chicago, University of Chicago Press, 1968.

[6] United Nations, *Manual IV: Methods of Estimating Basic Demographic Measures from Incomplete Data*, ST/SOA/Series A/42.

Regional Model Life Tables and Stable Populations. [7] I would recommend the United Nations publication both because an edition is in preparation in Spanish and also because it is inexpensive. In the words of the authors, "there was therefore an apparent need for a manual that would make it possible for a demographer-statistician with only a moderate level of training, perhaps working in isolation in a provincial capital of a less developed country, to derive the maximum of reliable information from data in a census or demographic survey". It is not possible here to take up the range of topics and problems that the authors review.

Let me, however, try to indicate the utility for a historian of the two appendix tables that really represent the heart of their work. First is a series of model life tables by sex which encompasses a range of demographic behavior for all except very exceptional cases. The range of life expectancy for the female varies from a low of 20.00 years at birth to a high of 75.00 and that of males is 18.03 to 71.10. Let us assume that the historian is interested in some given period of colonial Mexico and that he has reason to believe that male life expectancy was quite low but not at the very lowest level. Choosing "level 5" he has a model life table indicating expectancy at birth of 27.67 years. Having selected this table, what can the historian then derive from it? It will provide him with life expectancy for age one and by five-year intervals from five through eighty. He also will have the mortality rates for these particular ages, including the number surviving to these ages from an original hypothetical number or "radix" of 100,000 at birth. For the life table in question, for example, the figure of 100,000 will be reduced to 70,454 by age one. By age 15 little more than one half (53,393) will still be alive. Indeed, the extremely high mortality in the first years accounts for the apparent anomaly that life expectancy at age five (42.05 years) is considerably greater than that at birth. Incidentally, this point relates to the naive error sometimes made by those who, upon seeing an extremely low life expectancy such as 27.67, assume that few people live beyond that age. By use of this model life table, however, one can readily see that once a male reaches age five he then has a one in two chance of surviving to age 50. Mortality takes a terrible toll at all levels, but it is particularly damaging in the first years of life.

If, after selecting a model life table, it can also be assumed that there has been relatively constant fertility and mortality rates for some decades prior to the date in question, then one can turn to the set of model stable populations given in the second appendix

[7] Coale, Ansley J. and Paul Demeny, *Regional Model Life Tables and Stable Populations*. Princeton, N. J., Princeton University Press, 1966.

table. This will also require us to select an annual rate of increase.
For the purposes of argument, let us assume that there is reason to
believe that it is positive but low (.005 or 1-½ percent per annum).
(The stable population tables contain an annual rate of increase range
of-.010 to .050.) What can this table add to that of the model life
table? It can tell us the age distribution of the population (in
categories of under one, one to four, and then by five-year intervals
from five to seventy-nine and then eighty and over). It can further
provide us with birth and death rates, which in this case respectively
are 41 and 36 per thousand. It gives us the average age of this
male population, 25.9 years, and the gross reproduction rate.

I have deliberately simplified this exposition. The United Nations
manual is filled with cautionary statements and technical suggestions
for the adjustment of faulty data. I think it useful for historians to
take the trouble to acquaint themselves with this part of the
manual and not to limit themselves to the two appendix tables.
Doubtless the text may appear forbidding at first glance, but it
really requires very little mathematical sophistication. I will say that
Coale and Demeny impose more rigorous requirements upon their
data than it is likely that a historian working for example with colonial
population data would demand. In the end, he may be forced
to make some guesstimate of the population "parameters" needed to
select the proper model life table and the stationary population tables.
I believe that the gains to be derived from such a practice will far
outweigh the risks involved. At the very least, these model tables
will force the historian to think through some of the implications
of his data and his assumptions and this cannot help but strengthen
his own argument.

I hope that the plea that I have just made will not fall upon
barren soil. Had I been addressing a meeting of demographers, I
would have attempted to persuade them that they need much greater
familiarity with historical data and historical methodology. We talk
a good deal in the social sciences about the need for interdisciplinary
investigation. I am convinced that the interplay between the historian
and the demographer is one of the most fruitful possible combinations and their respective skills will greatly strengthen and enrich the
subject of their common concern; namely, social change.

NEW DIRECTIONS AND METHODS
IN HISTORICAL INVESTIGATIONS

PETER BOYD-BOWMAN

Though I have had a life-long interest in history I am by profession a linguist rather than a historian, and all my ventures into the historian's field have been in search of solutions to primarily linguistic problems, such as the origins of dialect differentiations in American Spanish today.

These differences are attributable to a number of highly complex factors, among which I will mention only the regional (i.e. dialectal) origins of the early Spanish settlers of the New World, the rapidly changing features of Spanish as spoken during the last decade of the xvth century and much of the xvith, the interaction of Spanish and native tongues in certain parts of the New World, the varying degrees of contact with metropolitan Spain enjoyed by different colonies throughout the colonial period, and the linguistic contributions of immigrants from a number of European countries in the xixth and xxth centuries.

In some coastal or tropical areas the phonological influence of certain African languages may yet prove to have been significant, though this significance has not yet been adecuately demonstrated.

The oft-noted phonetic division between two broad types of American Spanish, *highland* Spanish (marked by strongly articulated consonants and weakly articulated vowels) and *lowland* Spanish (where the reverse is the case), and the curious resemblance of the latter to the Spanish of Andalusia, gave rise to Max Leopold Wagner's ingenious but until recently unsupported climatological theory which held that emigrants to the New World tended to settle in areas whose climate most closely resembled that of their own native region in Spain.

It was to shed light on such disputed problems that I began, while still an instructor at Harvard in 1950, to analyze the regional origins of as many xvith century emigrants to the New World as I could uncover in the copious records of the period, taking into account such factors as parentage, exact year of departure, destination in America, occupation, social and marital status, and any additional important data that could be recorded without undue difficulty.

The information that I was able to assemble from xvith Century passenger lists and other sources proved to be so unexpectedly plentiful that my files now bulge with biographical information —including in every case the place of origin— on over 45,000 individuals who had emigrated to American by 1580 alone.

This biographical data, together with statistical studies, demographic charts, maps and copious indices to facilitate use (surnames, place names, occupations, social status, and even expeditions in the New World), is the substance of a chronologically organized series, now in its fourth volume, entitled the *Índice geobiográfico de 40,000 pobladores españoles de América en el siglo* xvi. (The actual figure now exceeds 46,000 and may top 60,000 when I add volume v to complete the xvith century.)

Volume i features data on 5,481 emigrants during the Antillean period (1493-1519), volume ii data on another 13,626 who emigrated between 1520 and 1539, volume iii (complete but still awaiting its turn to be published) provides biographical data on 9,044 who emigrated between 1540 and 1559, while volume iv, which I have just finished within the last few days, offers data on 17,580 more who emigrated between 1560 and 1579. Each volume also contains a relatively small number of additional emigrants on whom information came to light too late to be included in the statistical analyses.

One of the principal facts to emerge from this demographic reference work is the leading and often overwhelming role played throughout the formative period of colonial society by the Andalusians and, not suprisingly, by the province and city of Seville. In a series of articles, both in Spanish and English, I have stressed the important part played by the Andalusian women in xvith Century America and the statistical evidence that both shipping and commerce were largely in the hands of merchants and sailors born or domiciled in Andalusia.

Evidence is piling up to support both the theory of an Andalusianized base for several of the American-Spanish dialects and incidentally Wagner's climatological theory also, for it is wellknown that New World ports were often more closely linked to each other by sea than they were with their own mountainous hinterlands, and it is precisely the maritime regions, whose pronunciation most strikingly resembles that of Andalusia, where my statistics are beginning to show that Andalusians settled in greater proportions than anywhere else.

Before leaving this subject I would like to remark that it is my overall impression, based upon the many tens of thousands of individual settlers examined, that the proportion of hidalgos and literate persons among those who emigrated to the New World was roughly the same, or perhaps even slightly higher, than among those who remained behind.

The LASCODOCS Project

In the process of sifting through vast quantities of colonial records in search of biographical data for the *Índice geobiográfico de pobladores,* I had been much impressed by the unsuspected material waiting to be mined as well. These prosaic, non-literary documents, drawn from every region of Spanish America throughout the colonial period, might well hold the key to the early beginnings of dialect differentiations which are so evident today, for interspersed with archaic legal formulae can be found many indications of the colloquial language of earlier periods, recorded not only in the verbatim testimony of witnesses in law-suits, hearings, and trials, but also in private letters, contracts, minutes, confidential reports, commercial records, and countless other colonial documents. Most of these have the further unique advantage, from the linguist's point of view, of furnishing explicit information as to both authorship and place and date of origin.

With the aid of two grants from the ACLS totalling $ 4,000, another grant from the Graduate School of SUNY at Buffalo in the amount of $ 2,680, and 50 hours of IBM 7,044 computer time generously donated by our own computer center, I and a team of graduate assistants have in the past two years extracted, categorized, and key-punched well over 75,000 lexical, syntactical, and morphological items from xvith Century Mexico and the Caribbean area alone, each labeled as to source, reference, date and place of composition, and pertinent linguistic category. Enough of the contextual environment is furnished in each case to establish rather precisely both function and meaning. All computer output is arranged in two different formats: one (key words in alphabetial order) represents the first stage of what will eventually become the first, sorelyneeded *Dictionary of American Spanish on Historical Principles.* The other (linguistic categories) will form the basis for a large number of well-documented monographs such as the disputed chronology of distinctive sound changes, early nautical and mining terms, the use of diminutives and forms of address, word-formation, semantic changes, the penetration of Indian words into the daily speech of the colonists and the manner in which these words spread to other regions of America, and the emergence of regional peculiarities of every sort. Because of the way in which the data is being organized, numerous linguistic processes will be discernible for the first time and the erstwhile meanings of obscure or forgotten words brought into relief.

Only the last of nine computer runs in still needed to complete Phase I of the main proyect, which is the preparation of a *Vocabu-*

lario hispanoamericano del siglo XVI, but already the main proyect has generated a host of ancillary ones. In addition to a paper entitled "El español hablado en México en el siglo XVI", scheduled to be published in the *Actas del III Congreso de la Asociación Internacional de Hispanistas,* no less than two doctoral dissertations have been started to study some of the data already assembled. One of them proposes to examine the phonology of XVIth Century Spanish colonial documents, the other the penetration of American Indian terms into the colonists' daily vocabulary. But since time is short and this is a meeting of historians rather than of linguists, I will not dwell here on our linguistic findings, interesting though they are, but will go on to enumerate other studies of a more definitely historical kind that LASCODOCS helped inspire. Curiously enough it was the relative dearth of unmodernized, paleographically reliable sources for LASCODOCS that rekindled in me an interest in paleography that had been dormant since 1956 and 1957 when I spent several months working with XVIth Century passenger registries in the Archivo de Indias in Seville. Thanks to a collection of early documents from Nueva Granada owned by our library and some of the 60,000 rolls of archival documents already microfilmed by the Academia Mexicana de Genealogía y Heráldica, I and some of my Spanish research assistants have over the past two years transcribed with great accuracy the substantive portions of over 2,000 XVIth Century documents, the majority of them executed in Puebla between 1540 and 1556.

The notarial archive of the Mexican city of Puebla de los Ángeles, virtually complete from 1540 on, is a veritable treasure-house of information about social and economic life in the early colony. Many of its earliest documents are, however, in deplorable physical condition, unindexed and chronologically unorganized, which makes them extremely difficult and time-consuming to consult. In order to remedy this condition and make the archive more accessible to scholars both in Mexico and elsewhere, I have indexed and extracted from microfilm the substance of over 1,600 documents executed betwen 1540 and 1555. These will probably appear in a two-volume collection published by the Editorial Jus in Mexico City and entitled *Índice y extractos del Archivo de Protocolos de Puebla (1540-1556)* The documents make fascinating reading. There are wills, dowries, contracts, law-suits, partnerships, promissory notes, rentals, powers of attorney, as well as bills of sale itemizing every imaginable kind of property from real estate to livestock to produce to general merchandise.

Though serious financial problems are delaying publication of the collection itself, the linguistic data from it has already been fed into the computer for use by LASCODOCS, one especially interesting list of merchandise has been published in translation (*Buffalo Studies,* vol. iv, Aug. 1968, pp. 45-56) and another, featuring *inter alia* a library of theological books shipped from Spain to the Dominican monastery in Puebla, has been submitted to the *Latin American Research Review*. In addition, the collection was my source for an article appearing in this October's issue of *The Americas* entitled "Negro Slaves in Early Colonial Mexico: Based on Unpublished Manuscript Documents from Puebla de los Ángeles (1540-1556)", in which I was able among other things to record the African tribal origins of 124 Negro slaves who were bought and sold in Puebla in the mid-sixteenth century.

My little historico-linguistic Latin-American colonial research center at Buffalo now occupies a converted classroom equipped with a seminar table, two large microfilm readers (one of them a 3-M reader-printer), three electric typewriters with international keyboards, a small but well-stocked library of historical and linguistic reference works, and a part-time staff of sixteen graduates and undergraduates, most of them native speakers. I teach a credit course for graduates, entitled "Paleografía hispanoamericana", which is equipping a growing number of students at Buffalo to do research in the colonial field.

Our most current grant-supported project is a reconstruction of Puebla's *vecinos* and their families as of the year 1554, based on copious information contained in the notarial archive material already extracted and indexed. With the valuable help of three graduate research assistantes I am now tabulating the contents of all the documents up to and including the year 1554 with a view to determining the personal history of each *vecino* residing in Puebla in that year —his age, parentage, place of birth, relatives and frieds, his occupation and other sources of income, his business investments and associates, his real estate, live-stock, merchandise, slaves, and the cost and location of his home. We also propose to examine the social, political and economic structure of Puebla in 1554, and do a demographic (i.e. statistical) analysis of various occupations, social groupings, and types of family.

My assistants and I have prepared and stencilled sets of biographical data sheets onto which information on each *vecino* is being systematically and chronologically entered for later evaluation.

It should be apparent from the foregoing report that in the course of my own basic research in Spanish American linguistics I have crossed the boundaries of various other disciplines. As a humanist my only excuse is that, in this age of ever-increasing specialization, the generalist's interdisciplinary training and broad cultural perspective may on occasion have something worthwhile to contribute.

LA ANTROPOLOGÍA
Y LA INVESTIGACIÓN HISTÓRICA:
EL ESTUDIO DEL INDIO

PEDRO CARRASCO

Del hombre de Tepexpan a los hijos de Sánchez los antropólogos se han ocupado en una multitud de aspectos de la sociedad y cultura de los grupos humanos que han vivido en México a través de su historia. Son muchos los intereses de los antropólogos y no todos responden a un mismo concepto de esta ciencia. La antropología como los demás estudios sociales incluye planteamientos teóricos distintos y a veces antagónicos que producen contribuciones inconexas. Los linderos de la antropología frente a otras disciplinas son vagos; hay muchos intereses comunes a varias de ellas y los antropólogos cada vez adquieren más, unos como adiciones permanentes, otros tal vez como modas pasajeras.

Se ha discutido si la antropología es una "ciencia" dedicada a la formulación de generalizaciones o leyes acerca de la sociedad y la cultura humanas, o bien si es una rama de la historia y como tal describe secuencias de acontecimientos únicos. No creo necesario discutir aquí tema tan trillado. Doy por sentado que los "científicos" que asisten a esta conferencia se interesan en los hechos individuales de la historia de México aunque sea únicamente para usarlos en la búsqueda de leyes generales. También supongo que los "historiadores", por más enfrascados que estén en los hechos individuales y únicos de la historia mexicana, no negarán el uso de generalizaciones sobre procesos culturales y sociales.

Parte del interés "científico" de la antropología es el uso del método comparativo y se ha dicho que el uso de este método es característico de la antropología. Cierto que es mayor la importancia de los estudios comparados en la antropología que en la historia, pero los estudios de historia comparada muestran un interés semejante en estudios comparativos dentro de la historia.

El concepto cultura también se da a veces como fundamento de los estudios antropológicos, pero hay antropólogos que lo han negado y aunque la "cultura" del antropólogo sea un concepto más amplio que el del historiador no se puede negar que los historiadores también estudian la cultura.

Se dice, otras veces, al describir los estudios antropológicos de sociedades contemporáneas tratadas generalmente por sociólogos e historiadores, que lo distintivo del estudio antropológico es la investigación detallada de localidades pequeñas, grupos familiares o minorías étnicas —microestudios como alguien los ha llamado. Sí es verdad, pero no podemos decir que el estudio detallado de lo pequeño sea nuevo o exclusivo de los estudios antropológicos; también se encuentra en la historia local y en la biografía, enfoques bien tradicionales en la historia. Frente a la generalidad de los estudios históricos los antropólogos recomendarían mayor énfasis en estudios comparados, en el estudio de instituciones más que de individuos y en estudios intensivos de comunidades, pero al hacer esto expresamos nuestra preferencia por algunas de las cosas que los historiadores ya hacen y nuestras preferencias son semejantes a las que sugerirían otras disciplinas como la sociología.

Aunque para algunos de mis colegas sea una idea anticuada y rechazada, creo que la definición teórica de la antropología, que resulta más adecuada para describir los estudios realizados en México por los antropólogos, es la del estudio de sociedades primitivas. Con este punto de partida el antropólogo se ha dedicado principalmente al estudio del indio. Tratando el periodo prehispánico mediante las técnicas de la arqueología; en el caso de los indios modernos con el estudio etnográfico de campo. Estos dos temas rara vez han sido tocados por el historiador. En el caso de las culturas prehispánicas más antiguas por la falta de documentos escritos; en el caso de los indios actuales por tratarse de sociedades vivas del presente. Los grupos indígenas del tiempo inmediatamente anterior a la conquista y de la época colonial han sido estudiados tanto por historiadores como por antropólogos, predominando los estudios antropológicos para el periodo prehispánico a base de fuentes escritas de tipo histórico o etnográfico. Los estudios del indio colonial a base de la rica documentación de archivos han sido realizados principalmente por historiadores.

Los trabajos etnográficos de comunidades modernas comenzaron con el estudio de pueblos indios. Al darse cuenta que éstos no son pueblos "primitivos" sino en su mayoría campesinos, el antropólogo ha extendido su interés a las comunidades campesinas en general y aun a las clases bajas de la sociedad moderna. En esta nueva orientación de la antropología, general en todo el mundo, los estudios hechos en Mesoamérica se cuentan entre los que iniciaron esta ampliación del interés antropológico.

Al tratar de la contribución de la antropología a los estudios de historia de México dejo de lado los temas de prehistoria, provincia exclusiva de la antropología. No trato tampoco la contribución que la antropología aporta al ofrecer al historiador conceptos generales, como su insistencia en el método comparativo y el refinamiento en estudios del parentesco, o palabrejas y conceptos nuevos como "patrones" culturales, sociedad "folk", cultura de la pobreza, etcétera. Me limito a los estudios acerca del indio.

El estudio de las culturas prehispánicas difiere en mucho del de las culturas indígenas actuales, aunque ambos hayan sido cultivados por antropólogos. Por una parte, las características de las culturas mismas —el contraste entre las antiguas civilizaciones aborígenes y las pequeñas comunidades rurales de hoy— forman la base para esas diferencias. Pero a ello se une la visión fragmentaria de las culturas antiguas determinada por lo limitado de la información que se encuentra en las fuentes escritas y, sobre todo, en el material arqueológico, en contraste con la posibilidad de estudiar todos los temas imaginables al tratar de las comunidades vivas como lo hace el etnógrafo de campo. A todo esto se añaden, además, las diferencias de orientación que han caracterizado a los estudios de uno u otro tipo: la prevalencia de las distintas escuelas de "antropología social" en los estudios del indio moderno contrasta con los estudios de arqueología y etnohistoria donde ha dominado el enfoque puramente descriptivo o "histórico", y los intereses teóricos más usados han sido los derivados de la tesis de Morgan y Bandelier acerca de la sociedad prehispánica o las interpretaciones ecológicas, ambos distintos a los intereses dominantes en la antropología social.

De este modo los estudios de las distintas épocas en el desarrollo de las culturas indígenas de México han sido hechos por grupos de investigadores diferentes que han concentrado su atención en los materiales que sus fuentes hacen más fácilmente accesibles, recalcando las peculiaridades típicas de los distintos periodos y elaborando las diferencias de orientación o las modas que ha desarrollado cada disciplina. Exagerando podemos decir que los arqueólogos estudian cerámica, pirámides, inscripciones y calendarios, con alguna especulación acerca de los sistemas agrícolas practicados y el tipo de organización política que pudiera haber sido determinado por ellos. Para el etnohistoriador hay abundante material sobre fiestas religiosas, sacrificios humanos, leyendas migratorias y dinastías y se ha especulado sobre ciertos problemas planteados por la interpretación de Morgan y Bandelier; por ejemplo la existencia de propiedad privada o si el calpulli era un clan. En los estudios del indio colonial encontramos otros temas dominantes como el tributo, los servicios personales, las congregaciones, la cristianización y la demografía. En los estudios de etnografía moderna el tratamiento suele ser más completo pero también se han favorecido ciertos temas como mercados, compadrazgo, mayordomías o relaciones interétnicas y se ha especulado acerca de la naturaleza "folk" o campesina de las comunidades indígenas.

En la medida en que los intereses especiales estudiados en cada etapa histórica responden a las características de ese periodo encontramos una buena definición de las trasformaciones que han sufrido las culturas indígenas a través de la historia; pero en la medida en que los distintos especialistas han favorecido lo que les era más fácil estudiar o más de moda en su especialidad encontramos contrastes creados por los mismos investigadores que dificultan los estudios comparativos de distintos periodos históricos.

El hecho de que los antropólogos hayan estudiado las etapas prehispánicas y moderna ha llevado a algunos de ellos a hacer comparaciones directamente entre estos dos periodos sin tomar en cuenta los materiales coloniales, o a lo sumo han buscado datos en trabajos de historiadores y frecuentemente no los han encontrado. Son pocos los antropólogos que han buscado en documentos coloniales datos para discutir los problemas planteados por el estudio de las culturas prehispánicas o modernas. La visión que se puede obtener de esta manera sobre la evolución de las comunidades indígenas sirve para definir contrastes entre los dos puntos extremos de la línea evolutiva, pero no nos dice cómo se efectuó el proceso de cambio.

Por otra parte los historiadores que han tratado el indio de la época colonial o del siglo XIX, raramente toman en cuenta los estudios etnográficos del presente, los cuales plantean problemas de importancia para la investigación histórica, porque definen situaciones cuyos comienzos y antecedentes se deben investigar en la Colonia y porque nos dan una guía para la interpretación del documento escrito, especialmente de disposiciones legales e informes administrativos a menudo apartados de la realidad social.

A continuación enumero algunos de los temas en que creo necesaria mayor compenetración de los estudios históricos del indio colonial y del siglo XIX con los productos de la etnografía moderna. Me limito a las regiones de antecedentes indígenas mesoamericanos.

En estudios de tecnología sabemos bastante acerca de la introducción de nuevas plantas de cultivo, animales y técnicas en los comienzos de la Colonia. Poco se ha hecho, sin embargo, para reconstruir la importancia cuantitativa y la distribución geográfica de las distintas técnicas en el curso de la historia colonial. Sabemos quién sembró el primer trigo y cuándo y dónde se construyeron las primeras carreteras, por por ejemplo; pero los indios todavía consumen poco trigo y hay regiones donde las carreteras nunca tuvieron importancia ni la tendrán debido a la introducción de nuevas formas de transporte. En éstos como en muchos otros elementos de la técnica tenemos una idea general acerca de su distribución en la actualidad. Sería importante tener información comparable a través de la historia. Hay un buen estudio de este tipo en el trabajo de West sobre Michoacán y estudios semejantes se deberían hacer para todo el país.

En el estudio de la economía indígena hay notables diferencias en la importancia dada a distintos temas en los trabajos etnográficos en comparación con los de la época colonial que sólo en parte se deben a las diferencias entre las economías de estos dos periodos. Los estudios de la Colonia dan la importancia debida al papel del indio como aportador de tributo y de trabajo. Que estos temas apenas aparezcan en estudios etnográficos se entiende por haberse realizado la mayor parte de éstos en comunidades de pequeños productores y por el cambio efectuado en el sistema tributario del país. Pero cómo se realizó este cambio y qué parte tocó al indio es tema que todavía requiere cantidad de estudios que serán indispensables para comprender la trasformación del indio colonial en el moderno.

El sistema de tenencia de la tierra ha sido objeto de estudios, sobre todos los periodos de la historia de México, pero falta todavía mucho antes de poder integrar los materiales sobre los grupos indígenas. Los estudios sobre los periodos colonial e independiente nos dicen poco acerca del régimen de la tierra dentro de las comunidades campesinas, tema que hay que tratar a base de estudios monográficos de comunidades determinadas o a lo menos de regiones, debido a la gran diversidad regional. Del mismo modo la aplicación de las Leyes de Reforma, las revueltas agrarias durante la Revolución, la introducción del ejido, son temas que hay que estudiar monográficamente en distintas regiones y que sólo así se pueden relacionar satisfactoriamente con los estudios etnográficos.

Los mercados regionales más o menos han recibido la atención de todos los estudios etnográficos. Faltan estudios comparables acerca del comercio indígena en las épocas colonial e independiente.

La estratificación social es tema que se presta a estudios comparados de importancia entre los materiales etnográficos e históricos. La estratificación étnica de la Colonia, reglamentada por la ley, era un rasgo fundamental en la organización social de la época. La situación moderna sin sanciones legales y con una población indígena de mucha menor cuantía presenta en muchas regiones características muy distintas pero en otras todavía subsiste una estratificación étnica semejante a la colonial. El tema de relaciones interétnicas en la actualidad ha sido bastante bien tratado. Sin embargo es mucho lo que todavía hay que hacer con el material histórico. La documentación del siglo xviii no ha sido bien estudiada desde este punto de vista y el siglo xix, un periodo clave para la trasformación del sistema étnico de estratificación social en el centro y sur del país, todavía no ha producido ningún estudio de importancia sobre este tema.

Dentro del sistema de estratificación social en cuanto a los indios se refiere fue importante la nobleza indígena y hay varios buenos estudios sobre ella en el siglo xvi. Faltan sin embargo estudios detallados acerca de la nobleza indígena en el siglo xviii y su extinción o transformación a principios del xix.

La organización política de las comunidades indígenas es un tema tratado en detalle tanto por etnógrafos como por historiadores. La documentación acerca de los cabildos de las repúblicas de indios es abundante y los etnógrafos han encontrado que la organización política local con todas sus conexiones económicas y ceremoniales es la institución que da más cohesión a la comunidad indígena. Las organizaciones colonial y moderna presentan toda una serie de semejanzas y contrastes que no han sido estudiados en detalle. Faltan estudios monográficos de comunidades para las cuales tengamos información detallada de todas las principales etapas históricas y faltan en general estudios sobre el siglo XIX. Aun para los periodos coloniales mejor estudiados faltan datos acerca de algunos de los rasgos que la etnografía moderna ha puesto de relieve, bien sea por falta de documentos o porque los investigadores no han escudriñado las fuentes desde el punto de vista de los problemas planteados por la etnografía moderna. Por ejemplo los etnógrafos han notado que parte de la unión de los organismos políticos y religiosos locales es la existencia de una jerarquía que combina en un escalafón único puestos civiles y religiosos. Los orígenes coloniales de este sistema no se han documentado en detalle. Faltan especialmente estudios de las cofradías coloniales que se puedan comparar directamente con las organizaciones modernas. Baste un ejemplo para mostrar la falta de relación que todavía existe entre los estudios etnográficos y los históricos. Cualquier etnografía de los tarascos hará notar que el "hospital" que hoy existe en casi todos los pueblos tarascos es un descendiente de los hospitales establecidos por Quiroga. Los historiadores que han tratado este tema se han concentrado en la personalidad y las teorías del obispo. Todavía no hay un estudio que nos diga cómo fueron los hospitales que de hecho funcionaron en el siglo XVI y qué forma tomaron en el curso del periodo colonial.

Para el estudio de la religión indígena en los periodos colonial e independiente el historiador suele estar mejor preparado que el antropólogo en el conocimiento de los usos e instituciones de la Iglesia católica. Mucho cabe todavía esperar en la investigación de modalidades locales del culto católico desarrolladas en los distintos obispados o por distintas órdenes religiosas, así como en el estudio de cofradías ya mencionado. La distinción que hay que hacer a menudo entre el cuadro presentado por los documentos oficiales y la realidad social es de máxima importancia en el caso de la religión debido a la ocultación de prácticas religiosas no aprobadas por la Iglesia y que sólo salen a luz con motivo de las investigaciones que seguían al descubrimiento de idolatrías. El análisis de estos documentos sobre idolatrías y supersticiones es uno de los temas que más se presta a comparaciones con las religiones prehispánicas y modernas y en que más puede aportar el antropólogo. Es de esperar que aparezcan más documentos de este tipo, aunque todavía queda bastante por hacer en la interpretación de fuentes ya publicadas desde hace tiempo. La actitud del clero que administraba a los indios hacia las supersticiones de éstos es otro tema que se debe estudiar en detalle a través del tiempo y que nos da parte importante de la situación social que permitió la sobrevivencia de prácticas paganas. Los informes de Cortés y Larraz sobre Guatemala tienen buenos datos sobre

la indiferencia o falta de conocimientos de los párrocos y debe haber
materiales semejantes para México.

El parentesco es un campo trabajado especialmente por la antropología. Queda mucho por hacer en el análisis de documentos coloniales
poco usados para estos estudios como padrones y registros parroquiales.
Otros documentos como pleitos sobre tierras también pueden aportar
datos, especialmente en lo referente a la herencia. Dado el interés de
los antropólogos en estos temas es de esperar que sean ellos los que
más se dediquen a estos asuntos si bien los historiadores están probablemente más familiarizados con las normas de derecho civil y canónico
que deben haber afectado el desarrollo de las instituciones indígenas.

En resumen: El estudio de las culturas indígenas de México a través
de los distintos periodos de su historia ha ocupado en el pasado la atención de historiadores y antropólogos y es de pensar que continue esta
cooperación. Para lograr una mejor integración de los estudios de ambas
disciplinas conviene que los especializados en una de ellas obtengan el
mejor conocimiento posible de los estudios realizados en la otra y
prosigan en su propio campo de estudios los problemas planteados por
los otros. Concretamente y desde el punto de vista de la antropología
sugiero que los estudios etnográficos de los indios actuales plantean
una serie de problemas cuyos orígenes y desarrollo los historiadores,
debido a su mayor familiaridad con las fuentes documentales, pueden
estudiar mejor que los antropólogos. Como parte de estos estudios
sugiero especialmente el estudio monográfico de regiones o comunidades determinadas con énfasis en la historia social local perfilada según
el patrón de las monografías etnográficas. Muy especialmente para
ligar los periodos más cultivados hasta ahora, es decir el siglo XVI, por
una parte, y la etnografía moderna por otra, conviene desarrollar la
investigación del indio a fines de la Colonia y durante el siglo XIX.

NEW APPROACHES IN CONTEMPORARY
MEXICAN HISTORICAL RESEARCH

Possible new approaches in twentieth- century Mexican history not only include utilizing new methods such as oral history, but developing interpretations of historical statistics. Since my thoughts on oral history have been presented in a recent book, *México visto en el siglo XX; Entrevistas de historia oral*. [1] I will confine myself here to the latter topic. This essay will present some *debatable* hypotheses in order to suggest examples of little examined political, economic, and social data which might fruitfully be investigated in historical research.

I

A major source of data which often has been overlooked in Mexico is election statistics. Perhaps because the honesty of some elections has been questioned, generally scholars have not examined, for example, patterns in presidential voting by state; apparently researchers assume that altered results will not help them to determine regional interests and influences upon policy or other questions concerning the nature of constituencies which have intrigued political analysts in other countries. In order to suggest a way of using presidential voting statistics, however, for the sake of argument let us hypothesize that, though time-series election data have been manipulated, they may reveal strength of regional opposition to the official party. In this regard, we may view the number of votes conceded to opposition presidential candidates as being related to the government's desire to make the election appear to be valid yet take into account varying amounts of dissent. [2]

Table 1 shows the percentage of vote won by the official candidate for the presidency in 10 presidential elections since 1917; low percen-

---

[1] James W. Wilkie y Edna Monzón de Wilkie, *México visto en el siglo XX; Entrevistas de historia oral: Ramón Beteta, Marte R. Gómez, Manuel Gómez Morín, Vicente Lombardo Toledano, Miguel Palomar y Vizcarra, Emilio Portes Gil, Jesús Silva Herzog*. México, D. F., Instituto Mexicano de Investigaciones Económicas, 1969.

[2] The hypothesis that the results of Mexican presidential elections have been manipulated ignores possibilities that the Mexican populace generally has supported official candidates by massive majorities, especially with economic development in the last 30 years.

tages (boxed) portrary the extent of major dissent. In Mexico, low percentages won by the official party include all figures below 80 per cent, a figure that would be considered a land-slide victory in the United States. Marte R. Gomez, Minister of Agriculture under President Manuel Avila Camacho, has noted that in 1940 Avila Camacho won the national vote but lost the Distrito Federal.[3] Table 1 reveals, however, that official election results gave Ávila Camacho 72 per cent of the votes! If a generalization might be drawn from this case, amounts less than about 70 per cent could be considered a loss to the government.

It is interesting to note that in 323 cases given in Table 1, only 57 or 17.6 per cent are presented in boxes (if the cut off point for boxes were reduced to amounts under 70 per cent, only 27 cases or 8.4 per cent would be included). Incredibly, the official tally of votes shows that only in 2 cases (Baja California and Sinaloa in 1924) was the official candidate not supported by a majority of voters. Among Mexico's 32 federal entities, Baja California and the Distrito Federal are exceeded only by Chihuahua for number of cases with percentage scores less than 80 per cent.

A glance at Table 1 raises a number of questions. Did national discontent with the "economic revolution" of the period 1940-1960 force the government to admit in 1946 and 1952 to the greatest amount of election dissent since 1924? (The year 1924 witnessed an outright rebellion against the government's candidate.) Given widespread social disorders after the election of 1958, did a renewed lack of voting opposition in that year represent a return to "authoritarianism"[4] reminiscent of the very controversial election of 1940? What were the circumstances that would permit the government to announce in 1917 and 1934 that the lowest percentage won by the official party did not go below 80 per cent in any entity? Was the result in 1964 chosen at 89 per cent in order to take advantage of relative political peace yet fix an amount for advertising purposes? (Certainly the validity of 89 per cent might be more credible than 90 per cent.) Or did the introduction of opposition "diputados de partido" in the Chamber of Deputies obviate the need for concessions in presidential voting results?

In suggesting that Mexican presidential statistics might serve as a rough gauge of official party power, it is important to note that we could develop many alternative hypotheses, including one that would give presidents of the period of economic revolution credit for attempting to develop a more democratic count of the vote. Such hypotheses could be tested against aspects of oficial party strength in state and

[3] Wilkie y Wilkie, *México visto en el siglo XX*, p. 120.
[4] Philip B. Taylor, "The Mexican Elections of 1958: Affirmation of Authoritarianism?", *Western Political Science Quarterly* 13 (1960), pp. 722-744.

TABLE 1

PRESIDENTIAL ELECTION VICTORY PERCENTAGES WON BY THE OFFICIAL PARTY OF THE REVOLUTION, 1917-1964 [a]

	1917	1920	1924	1929	1934	1940	1946	1952	1958	1964
Total	97.1	95.8	84.1	93.6	98.2	93.9	77.9	74.3	90.6	89.0
Aguascalientes	98.9	98.0	77.7	94.0	96.0	93.9	70.4	67.9	93.2	91.2
Baja Calif.	95.3	96.4	44.7	91.6	97.2	93.9	63.6	61.7	60.7	78.6
Baja Calif. Terr.	b	b	b	b	b	100.0	b	91.7	82.3	93.4	96.8
Campeche	98.8	99.9	100.0	94.2	100.0	98.1	75.1	87.1	87.7	95.9
Coahuila	98.8	99.5	72.2	80.4	93.5	95.1	81.4	80.7	94.9	93.4
Colima	98.7	74.4	94.0	96.0	94.8	95.3	66.8	80.1	89.7	87.3
Chiapas	100.0	98.3	99.9	99.6	100.0	98.1	87.3	90.5	98.0	98.9
Chihuahua	98.2	99.7	68.9	78.9	99.8	92.6	75.7	63.9	64.6	78.7
Distrito Federal	96.6	96.0	94.9	97.0	97.3	72.0	57.0	51.4	79.9	74.9
Durango	88.5	97.8	69.8	84.1	99.7	96.8	65.4	65.0	84.8	90.0
Guanajuato	92.0	96.0	66.4	91.6	98.1	95.9	64.0	64.1	89.5	79.6
Guerrero	100.0	99.9	83.2	99.5	100.0	95.4	85.0	82.5	98.2	97.0
Hidalgo	98.4	99.7	87.1	96.0	100.0	99.5	90.4	88.7	98.1	98.4
Jalisco	99.7	73.2	87.4 .	93.9	99.1	98.7	78.8	64.7	89.0	87.0
Mexico	96.0	98.5	86.3	100.0	99.7	94.9	84.1	81.1	98.9	91.7
Michoacan	93.9	97.4	79.4	92.1	99.8	92.9	67.3	55.4	87.2	86.0
Morelos	b	91.7	93.6	87.1	99.8	98.1	57.3	68.5	95.8	94.2
Nayarit	98.3	87.4	59.0	100.0	100.0	97.0	85.3	76.0	98.7	91.6
Nuevo Leon	99.9	96.8	96.7	95.5	84.5	89.3	70.4	80.8	90.3	84.3
Oaxaca	99.5	96.9	98.8	99.7	100.0	99.4	90.2	79.8	95.6	96.9
Puebla	97.6	93.7	90.6	98.0	99.3	98.8	81.9	80.9	95.2	93.7
Queretaro	95.0	96.5	90.8	95.4	99.5	98.7	84.3	82.0	89.5	91.3
Quintana Roo	99.4	100.0	98.5	91.5	b	95.7	91.4	95.3	79.9	96.6
San Luis Potosi	98.5	99.3	93.0	99.7	100.0	98.2	80.2	88.9	94.3	91.6
Sinaloa	98.2	99.9	34.7	75.9	97.7	89.5	89.9	73.9	98.1	92.1
Sonora	97.9	96.2	84.5	68.9	100.0	92.4	81.5	81.1	97.3	98.4
Tabasco	99.7	100.0	100.0	93.1	100.0	99.8	95.6	79.3	98.9	99.3
Tamaulipas	95.5	100.0	90.3	94.9	97.1	88.1	72.4	69.5	94.8	96.5
Tlaxcala	98.4	99.6	81.4	97.9	99.6	95.7	81.1	81.2	98.4	98.4
Veracruz	98.8	98.3	88.1	89.3	94.9	94.8	90.5	91.5	97.6	96.8
Yucatan	99.7	100.0	99.8	100.0	99.4	88.1	75.9	81.5	77.4	85.8
Zacatecas	97.9	90.7	54.6	93.8	93.8	94.3	67.6	71.8	91.7	79.5

[a] Excludes election of 1928 when Alvaro Obregón was unopposed.
[b] No data given in source.
Source: México, Cámara de Diputados, *Diario de los Debates*, April 26, 1917; Oct. 26, 1920; Sept. 27, 1924; Nov. 28, 1929; Sept. 12, 1934, 1940, 1946, 1952; Sept. 10, 1958; *Dictamen* published in *El Día*, Sept. 9, 1964.

municipal elections as well as related to the number of members in governmental affiliated labor unions or beneficiaries of land reform by state. In this manner we could revise and refine our concepts of the Mexican electoral process.

II

An example of economic data which has been involved in controversy for a number of years includes expenditure of Central Government income. Many observers have felt that Central Government capital investment has been overly concentrated in the Distrito Federal. One possible implicit corollary of this argument is that the population in the country is being taxed to support the growth of a great metropolis in the Distrito Federal which thus attracts ever greater concentration of capital and population. Because little "hard data" has been available to support such contentions, [5] it is important to consider several factors.

By comparing data on actual origin of income taxes to projected capital expenditures and population by entity given in Table 2, we may hypothesize that the Distrito Federal has received less than an equitable share of capital in relation to its contribution of income taxes and population to national totals. If the 1960's, when data are available, are indicative of earlier years, the Distrito Federal has provided tax revenue to support development in the rest of Mexico by a margin which leaves relatively little funds to meet its own great needs generated by growth which is most productive.

Though projected outlay may have little to do with actual investment, [6] Table 2 suggests that in 1961, 1964, and 1967 only Mexico's North Zone had anywhere near a balance of federal investment in relation to population and collection of revenue. In contrast, the South, which contributed the least in revenue was projected to receive investment exactly in proportion to its share of population in 1960, 11.9 per cent. If this pattern has historical validity (a supposition which needs investigation), heavy capital investment in the North during earlier years probably was in excess of collections; thus we might assume that if such a policy were applied to the South, in the long run that poor area might show increased economic development and tax collections. The present data, however, do not tell us how much invesment might be required for the South (even assuming that the areas have the same requirements for development) because we have no idea about the level of investment to collections in the North prior to 1961.

None of this discussion answers the question as to where capital investment might better be spent in order to encourage economic production. If development of a national market for goods is dependent upon social affluence in the entire country, then the Government must

[5] *Cf.* Ifigenia M. de Navarrete, *Política fiscal de México.* México, D. F., Universidad Nacional Autónoma de México, 1964, p. 38.

[6] See James W. Wilkie, *The Mexican Revolution: Federal Expenditure and Social Change Since 1910* (2nd ed., revised). Berkeley, University of California Press, 1970, Part i.

TABLE 2

SHARE OF CENTRAL GOVERNMENT INCOME TAX REVENUE BY
FEDERAL ENTITY COMPARED TO POPULATION AND PROJECTED
CENTRAL GOVERNMENT CAPITAL INVESTMENT,
SELECTED YEARS, 1959-1967

(In Percentages)

Collections by Entity	Population (1960)	Investment (1959-1963)	Income Tax Revenue [a]		
			1961	1964	1967 [b]
Revenue (millions of pesos)			4,036	7,254	10,168
Total Per Cent	100.0	100.0	100.0	100.0	100.0
North	15.8	16.5	18.5	16.8	15.0
Baja California	1.5	2.3	2.4	2.2	1.6
Chihuahua	3.5	5.8	3.1	2.3	1.6
Coahuila	2.6	1.7	3.3	2.7	1.8
Nuevo León	3.1	1.8	6.4	6.4	6.9
Sonora	2.2	2.7	1.9	1.9	1.9
Tamaulipas	2.9	2.2	1.4	1.3	1.2
West	14.1	15.6	4.7	4.5	4.3
Aguascalientes	.7	.4	.1	.2	.3
Baja Calif. Terr.	.2	.5	.1	.1	.1
Colima	.5	1.0	.1	.1	.1
Durango	2.2	2.1	.3	.3	.3
Jalisco	7.0	2.8	2.8	2.7	2.7
Nayarit	1.1	.7	.2	.1	.1
Sinaloa	2.4	8.1	1.1	1.0	.7
West Central	16.8	8.1	5.9	7.4	9.2
Guanajuato	5.0	1.6	.7	.9	.9
México	5.4	3.5	4.4	5.4	7.5
Michoacán	5.3	2.4	.4	.7	.4
Morelos	1.1	.6	.4	.4	.4
East Central	15.8	7.6	2.7	2.7	3.2
Hidalgo	2.8	1.2	.5	.3	.5
Puebla	5.7	1.0	1.1	1.2	1.2
Querétaro	1.0	.6	.3	.5	.7
San Luis Potosí	3.0	2.9	.6	.5	.6
Tlaxcala	1.0	.5	.1	.1	.1
Zacatecas	2.3	1.4	.1	.1	.1
South	11.9	11.9	.8	.9	.8
Chiapas	3.5	4.6	.3	.3	.2
Guerrero	3.4	2.6	.3	.4	.4
Oaxaca	5.0	4.7	.2	.2	.2
Gulf	11.6	9.3	2.3	3.1	2.4
Campeche	.5	1.2	.1	.1	.1

Collections by Entity	Population (1960)	Investment (1959-1963)	Income Tax Revenue [a] 1961	1964	1967 [b]
Quintana Roo	.1	.7	c	c	c
Tabasco	1.4	2.2	.2	.2	.2
Veracruz	7.8	3.7	1.5	1.9	1.8
Yucatán	1.8	1.5	.5	.9	.3
Distrito Federal [a]	14.0	31.0	65.1	64.6	65.1

[a] Excludes payments made directly to the Federal Treasury; payments not determined by entity are not taken into account here.

[b] Excludes collections of previous years.

[c] Less than .05 per cent.

Source: Tax revenue is from México, Secretaría de Hacienda y Crédito Público, *Cuenta Pública*, (Dark-colored Edition), 1961, 1964, 1967. Regions, population and investment are presented according to methodology given in James W. Wilkie, *The Mexican Revolution: Federal. Expenditure and Social Change Since 1910* (2nd ed.; Berkeley: University of California Press, 1970), Table 10-1.

traverse a difficult path which will encourage balanced growth. What share of scarce resources can be devoted to a poverty-stricken South Zone (which because of its isolation and lack of transport infrastructure does not enjoy the North's border advantages of market and tourism)? Also, given scarce resources, one could argue that the Mexican policy of offering tax incentives to industry initiated outside of the Distrito Federal has been the wisest policy, except that some intellectuals now claim that funds must be massively diverted from Mexico City to the countryside. Thus, the real "dilemma of Mexico's economic development" may not stem from the fact that the Central Government has been eased into a "political strait jacket", as Raymond Vernon would have us believe, but that it must conduct a "balanced revolution" which will encorage social justice along with economic growth. Though Vernon views presidential actions of the early 1960's as evidence of weak and vascilating policy, I have portrayed the same actions as indicating a strong shift in policy from economic to balanced revolution which would attempt to meet some of the problems posed by uneven economic and social development. [7]

Has recent Mexican governmental policy slowed the growth of the Distrito Federal? Has Mexico City's share in industry, commerce and

[7] See Raymond Vernon, *The Dilemma of Mexico's Development: The Roles of the Private and Public Sectors*. Cambridge, Harvard University Press, 1963, Chapter 7, especially p. 188. Shift from economic to balanced Revolution is analyzed in Wilkie, *The Mexican Revolution*, Part i.

services, and motor transportation and gasoline consumption decreased? As I have shown elsewhere, these total shares did not increase between censuses in 1960 and 1965. Slight decreases in 1965 reversed a trend of increasing importance of the Distrito Federal in Mexico's economic life. Given the overwhelming economic importance of Mexico City, perhaps we might ask ourselves the following question: Why has the population of the capital grown so slowly? By 1965 the Distrito Federal only had an estimated 15 to 16 per cent of the population and persons economically employed compared to over one half of commercial and service activity, over one third of industrial activity, and over one quarter of all motor vehicles and gasoline consumption.[8]

In addition to the above figures which suggest that Mexico City's importance might soon reach a plateau, Table 2 shows that in 1961, 1964, and 1967 the capital's share of tax revenues remained about 65 per cent. Thus, if we are to understand the regional development process, we must suggest a number of factors for which study might be undertaken. We not only need to investigate the historial relation of regional tax collection and investment but to examine the relation of migration patterns to regional share in GNP and economically active population.

III

An example of socio-economic data which has been overlooked for historical analysis involves the interpretation of statistics on unemployment. Table 3 gives total figures on male unemployment for the 1930's and for 1940, 1950, and 1960 when data are available. Most observers think that these figures are too low to be meaningfully compared to time series for a more developed country like the U. S. The following oral history interview with Jesús Silva Herzog, however, reveals one possible approach to these statistics:

JW [James Wilkie]: ¿Hubo mucha desocupación en México [durante la crisis mundial de los años de 1930]? . . .
JSH [Jesús Silva Herzog]: Aquí en México, como en otros países subdesarrollados, hay siempre desocupación oculta. Pero aquí sucede algo que no sucede en los países altamente desarrollados; lo que sucedió entonces y que se puede repetir en distintos momentos es que el hermano que tiene trabajo acoge al otro hermano; que hay una familia, el padre, la madre, tres hijos. Si un hermano no tiene trabajo, le dicen: "Vente acá; aquí repartiremos los frijolitos." Y llega el hermano, muchas veces

---

[8] James W. Wilkie, "La Ciudad de México como Imán de la Población Económicamente Activa, 1930-1965", *Historia y Sociedad en el Mundo de Habla Española; Homenaje a José Miranda.* México, D. F., El Colegio de México, 1970.

con la esposa y dos hijos. Y se avienen a vivir en un pequeño cuarto o en dos pequeñas habitaciones. De suerte que no hubo manifestaciones de desocupados ni el gobierno de México tuvo que acudir durante la crisis en auxilio de los desocupados. Eso es muy interesante apuntar.

. . .

JW: Bueno. Hablando de la estadística de desocupación: se comenzaron a reunir las estadísticas de desocupación al venir la Depresión en México y subió el número —el porcentaje de la población de trabajadores— del dos por ciento, más o menos, al cinco o al seis por ciento de la población. Pero no dicen las estadísticas qué son los desocupados, quiénes son los que tenían trabajo, y ya no lo tienen. ¿Perdieron su trabajo por culpa de la Depresión? No se dice nada de estas estadísticas ocultas de que usted habla. Y las estadísticas de hoy tampoco . . . ¿El gobierno no puede tratar de averiguar cuánto es el porcentaje?

JSH: Es sumamente difícil. Son casos verdaderamente interesantes éstos de la desocupación oculta. Miren ustedes, a medida que el nivel económico en este país es más bajo, hay una mayor solidaridad entre los componentes de las personas de ese bajo nivel económico y se ayudan unos a otros. Por ejemplo, nosotros tenemos aquí una criada que tiene bastantes años con nosotros. Tiene una casita y seguido sabemos que tiene recogido a un señor o a una mujer en su casa, que "porque están más pobres que ella" . . . Sería necesario hacer una encuesta de muestreo en varias regiones del país para poder tener una idea de este fenómeno. [9]

A second possible approach to statistics in Table 3 might involve a hypothesis that in a less developed country high unemployment rates occur only with increasing affluence or serious depression. Alternatively, low rates occur because unemployment benefits are not available, and persons must find a way to make a living even if it involves selling lottery tickets in the streets or becoming a professional beggar. Thus a rate of 1 to 2 per cent male unemployment in 1930, 1950, and 1960 would offer a rough gauge of low Mexican social affluence. Increase of this rate to between 3.1 and 6.5 per cent in the Mexico of the period 1931-1940 would indicate a lingering aftermath of depression in the early 1930's rather than affluence. The nomination of Lázaro Cárdenas to the presidency in 1933 and the nature of his government between 1934 and 1940 can be related to this social and economic problem.

Variation of the above hypothesis might be developed to relate unemployment in Mexico to the U. S., a ratio showing the difference in the level of social affluence in the two countries. Examination of the 13 years under consideration in Table 3 reveals that except for 2 years (when the depression was at its worst in Mexico during 1931-

---

[9] Wilkie y Wilkie, *México visto en el siglo XX*, pp. 677-678.

1932), the U. S. had 4 to 5 times as much unemployment as Mexico. (If circumstances have not changed, and if the ratio has any meaning for the first nine months in 1969 when data are not available for Mexico, the official rate of unemployment in Mexico might currently be less than 1 per cent). [10]

TABLE 3

UNEMPLOYMENT, AVAILABLE YEARS, 1930-1960 [a]

| | Mexico | | | U.S. | |
Year	Men [b] Unemployed [c] (1)	Economically Active Pop. [b] (2)	Per Cent Unemployed [d]	Total [e] Per Cent Unemployed [f] (3)	Ratio U.S./Mexico
1930 [g]	89,690	5.165,803	1.7	8.7	5.1
1931 [h]	287,462	5.188,245	5.5	15.9	2.9
1932 [h]	339,378	5.238,124	6.5	23.6	3.6
1933 [h]	275,774	5.307,090	5.2	24.9	4.8
1934 [h]	234,538	5.386,192	4.4	21.7	4.9
1935 [h]	191,371	5.428,121	3.5	20.1	5.7
1936 [h]	186,904	5.482,307	3.4	16.9	5.0
1937 [h]	180,128	5.573,809	3.2	14.3	4.5
1938 [h]	209,332	5.649,142	3.7	19.0	5.1
1939 [h]	198,593	5.787,109	3.4	17.2	5.1
1940 [h]	184,247	5.858,116	3.1	14.6	4.7
1950 [g]	91,095	8.345,240	1.1	5.0	4.5
1960 [g]	160,147	11.253,297	1.4	5.6	4.0

[a] No data available for 1941-1949 and 1951-1959.

[b] Over age 12.

[c] Including men unemployed for more than 1 month in 1930 and 1940 and for 12 weeks or less as well as over 13 weeks in 1950 and 1960.

[d] Women unemployed (not included) in 1960 constituted .2 per cent of the economically active population.

[e] Men and women over age 14.

[f] Including persons not at work during the survey week.

[g] Census.

[h] Monthly average.

Source: Columns 1 and 2: México, Dirección General de Estadística, Anuario Estadístico, 1938, p. 158 and 1940, p. 431; Resumen del Censo, 1940, p. 17; 1950, p. 58; and 1960, pp. 1, 3, 363. Column 3: Statistical History of the United States from Colonial Times to the Present (Stamford, Conn.: Fairfield Publishers, [1965]), pp. 73, 100A.

[10] The average unemployment rate in the U. S. for the first 9 months of 1969 was 3.5 per cent; see Newsweek, October 20, 1969, p. 89.

Assuming that unemployment is related to affluence, theoretically in 1930, 1940, 1950, and 1960 when data are available, [11] the Distrito Federal should have had greater unemployment than the national average. In fact, most cases did exceed the national average; figures for the D. F. were 3.6 in 1930; 1.5 in 1940 (incomplete); 1.7 in 1950; and 2.0 per cent in 1960. [12]

Unemployment also is related to a political factor. Until a political decision is made in Mexico to provide unemployment benefits, it may be argued that some persons can not afford to be unemployed regardless of the level of affluence in the society. Furthermore, given the view presented by Jesús Silva Herzog, we may suspect that the decision to expand unemployment benefits will intrude upon Mexico's tradition of extended family solidarity, a tradition that in the U. S. did not withstand the impact of urbanization and industrialization.

IV

There are a great number of historical time series which have not been investigated for purposes of historical research. Almost every central government agency and decentralized institution have generated statistics. Several guides to this material have been prepared by the Dirección General de Estadística, one of the most useful being the *Inventario de Estadísticas Nacionales*, 1966. [13] This work gives information on the nature and coverage of data, frequency of tabulation, initiation of series, and where published or unpublished figures may be obtained.

Though the Mexican population census is one of the best in Latin America, with regard to coverage and consistency of time series it could be greatly expanded to provide data on political attitudes as well as social modernization. In order to suggest possible improvements in national population censuses (and local surveys) in Latin America, a Social Census Conference recently met at the University of California in Los Angeles to consider a questionnaire developed from the point of view of historians who generally have not made their views known concening data needed for analysis. [14]

[11]Data on economically unemployed population for the D. F., are not available for the period 1931-1939.

[12] Calculated from sources in Table 3 and *Anuario Estadístico*, 1938, p. 52. Data on unemployment for 1940 are contradictory; the monthly average during the year was higher than figures given on the date of the census, except for the D. F. where the monthly average was incomplete or not measured during the period 1931-1940. I have used the monthly average as more representative of the entire year for national totals of unemployed but have used census data for the D. F.

[13] See also *Catálogo General de las Estadísticas Nacionales* and its separate *Índice* (1960).

[14] See James W. Wilkie, John C. Super, Edna M. Wilkie (eds.), "A Social Census Questionnaire for Latin America", draft, January 1970.

In spite of limitations, existing census data could serve as a guide to researchers in several disciplines who are interested in such fields as local and regional investigation. Some years ago, for example, Howard F. Cline showed that if statistics on location of communities which have been studied (and on size of their populations) were taken into account, scholars might advantageously investigate a greater variety of villages in Mexico. [15] We might add here that social and economic characteristics from the population and agricultural censuses could be used for developing parameters by which individual communities could be selected and introduced in a national setting. Yet one of the most innovative community studies published in recent years, economist Michael Belshaw's valuable work on Huecorio, Michoacan, excludes the use of census data which would allow us to understand the *municipio* context of village life in a country which in 1960 had 2,377 *municipios*. Indeed, Belshaw not only implicitly assumes that Huecorio is representative of Mexican village life, but explicitly suggests that it has an "uncanny resemblance to an underdeveloped country in miniature". This latter assertion is made without supporting data and despite his findings that one third of the adult males of the community had been to the U. S. to works as braceros! [16]

Examination of consistency and meaning in census materials themselves provide opportunity for scholars. An example of the kind of work which should be encouraged is found in Robert G. Greer's M. A. thesis at the University of Texas. Writing on "The Demographic Impact of the Mexican Revolution, 1910-1921", Greer concluded in 1966 that the period of violence of the teens held Mexico's population at a virtual standstill for 10 years in which the country could have been expected to increase by about 2 million persons. His calculations and review of the literature lead him to the interesting view that only about 75,000 to 100,000 persons were killed in military action in contrast to previous estimates reaching as high as 1.200,000 deaths. [17]

In the political and administrative appointments of the "permanent revolution" since 1910 we have an example of information from which data can be generated to test hypotheses about outcomes of the Revolution. Has the Revolution opened opportunity for advancement through a dynamic bureaucracy?

During the past several years I have encouraged several individual scholars to examine the role of bureaucracy in Mexico in order to trace patterns in the way the government fills its positions. Though some observers maintain that the Mexican political system is "open" com-

[15] Howard F. Cline, "Mexican Community Studies..." *Hispanic American Historical Review* 32 (1952), pp. 212-242.
[16] Michael Belshaw, A *Village Economy: Land and People of Huecorio.* New York, Columbia University Press, 1967, pp. XI-XIV, 123.
[17] Pp. 9 and 21.

pared to the closed Porfirian system, others feel that this year's middle-
aged senator will be next year's director of a descentralized agency, and
a future cabinet minister before he returns to the Senate. Such generalizations might be tested by establishing a pool of important positions
for which appointees could be listed in a year-by-year scheme cross-
related to individual career biographies. In this manner we could develop statistics in order to pinpoint periods of bureaucratic expansion as
well as investigate the "openness" of an expanding system. Such an
analysis might begin by considering a bureaucratic pool of 1048 offices
given in the *Directorio del Poder Ejecutivo Federal, 1961* (including
ministerial and departmental offices, embassies, consulates, etc.), and
316 organizations given in the *Directorio General de Organismos Descentralizados, Empresas de Participación Estatal, Establecimientos Públicos, Comisiones, Juntas e Institutos Dependientes del Gobierno Federal* (1964). [18] A work contributing to the feasibility of this analysis
is the extremely useful *Manual de Organización del Gobierno Federal,
1969-1970* which deals with the public sector in general. [19]

CONCLUSION

Historical statistics provide threads by which many aspects of contemporary Mexican history can be reexamined. One advantage which
we enjoy in working with data in our own age is that frequently we
are able to question persons who have compiled materials in order to
clarify meaning and formulation of time series. Nevertheless, few
aspects of Mexican history have been investigated in light of patterns
in time series; whole fields of political, social, and economic history are
open to this type of research. In offering some debatable hypotheses
about time-series data which many have found particularly questionable,
I have tried to suggest that statistics might be useful for interpreting
history in new ways. Examples are given here to indicate approaches
which need research, and several series are presented here for the first
time in order to make figures available to scholars.

---

[18] Both directories are published by the Secretaría del Patrimonio Nacional.
[19] Prepared by the Secretaría de la Presidencia, Comisión de Adminstración
Pública.

XIII. MESA REDONDA: B) "PROBLEMAS DE LA HISTORIA DE LAS IDEAS"

ANTONIO CASO: A REJECTION OF THE IDEA OF PROGRESS

JUAN GÓMEZ QUIÑONES

"El progreso (*pro* hacia adelante *gressus* marcha) no puede afirmarse como ley de la humanidad."

CASO

STATEMENT OF PURPOSE

The purpose of this paper [1] is to ascertain and analyze the *Idea of Progress* as found in the writings of Don Antonio Caso, [2] a Mexican philosopher and educator of the twentieth century. To this end Caso's concept of progress shall first be established and then related to his larger views on history and society, and his observations on the Mexican scene both past and present. [3] At the close of the paper

---

[1] Perhaps in a discussion which has as its point of departure the idea of progress, this paper is a negative statement. But in view of the fact that our larger area of study is Latin America, an examination of Antonio Caso is well worth the effort, and in his own right as a representative of a tradition.

[2] Antonio Caso y Andrade was born on December 19, 1883 and died on March 6, 1946. He rarely left his native Mexico City. He received his degree in law. His most influential teacher was Justo Sierra. Caso repaid the debt to his mentor in the beautiful essay "Justo Sierra, el amante".

He was appointed professor of philosophy in 1910 and held this post, along with other appointments, until his death. He often suffered from shifting political winds. The cause and the nature of these political embarrassments are obscure; they are referred to obliquely here and there.

Caso held various administrative posts: head of the National Preparatory School, Secretary and Rector of the National University, and Director of the University's Faculty of Philosophy and Letters. During his life he received many honors, both at home and abroad. For a brief period he was appointed roving ambassador to Perú, Chile, Argentina, Uruguay and Brazil.

Shortly before his death he was working on a series of lectures entitled, "The Problem of the Philosophy of History". He would no doubt, at least in passing, have addressed himself to the question of progress. But in my opinion it is doubtful that he would have presented a radically different viewpoint. For further information on his life see Luis Garrido, *Antonio Caso una vida profunda* (México 1961) and the essay by the Spanish philosopher José Gaos "Las mocedades de Caso", in Roberto Gómez Robledo, et. al. *Homenaje a Antonio Caso* (México, 1947) hereafter cited as *Homenaje*.

[3] Antonio Caso has received the attention of a number of writers and his ideas have been examined to some extent. However, his rejection of progress has not been related to his other views. Hopefully this paper does. In the writing of this paper I am most heavily indebted to: Juan Manuel Terán, "Caso y la filosofía de la historia"; José Gaos, "Las mocedades de Caso" in Gómez Robledo, *Homenaje*; and Patrick Romanell, "The Christian Dualism of Antonio Caso", in Romanell

a series of critical summaries and conclusions shall be presented and an attempt shall be made to relate Antonio Caso to the larger intellectual spectrum.

In the course of the analysis, scant attention shall be paid to biographical data (see footnote two) and to the writings of the man which are exclusively aesthetic and critical in nature. In addition, a general familiarity with modern Mexican history shall be assumed. If by chance the argument compels attention to any of these factors, the matter shall be dealt with in a footnote.

INTRODUCTION

The idea of progress holds that man in community, and man alone, is capable of infinite perfectability; and that continual amelioration occurs and that it is discernible and obtainable through the rational faculties of man. Optimism is the touchstone of this doctrine. [4] Some, however, demur from this Penglossian perspective.

The idea of progress has within its premises two contradictory elements: the absolute and the relative. If their conflict is not resolved, the value of the abstraction as a conceptual frame of reference is negated. Both elements are due to the expression of progress as a continuum. On the one hand, an absolute is posited toward which the continuum is in motion; but on the other hand, the goal is relative to the notion made. Achilles never overtakes the hare. Thus the idea of progress is reduced to the most vain of philosophical conceits: a syllogism which denies its own premises. Pervading this concept is a nebulous teleological air which is at once distasteful and untenable to an age of quantun physics in which the only certainties are those of the abstruse mathematics of probability.

A REJECTION OF PROGRESS

The teleological aspect of the idea of progress leads Antonio Caso to reject the entire concept as a philosophical tool. He was aware of the significance of the concept of man's intellectual evolution and was acquainted with its historical trajectory. [5] To him, it was

The Making of the Mexican Mind (Lincoln, Nebraska, 1952). The two monographs dealing with the subjet's life and thought, Luis Garrido, Antonio Caso una vida profunda (México, 1961) and Rosa Krause de Koltenink, La filosofía de Antonio Caso, though enlightening do little more than provide background and sketch his ideas.

[4] The best treatment available on the concept of progress is J. B. Bury, The Idea of Progress. New York, 1955.

[5] Antonio Caso, El concepto de la historia universal y la filosofía de los valores. México, 1933 — hereafter cited as El concepto, p. 15.

handmaiden to the philosophy of history which held that there was design and purpose in the historical continuum and which made of the abstraction "humanity" a concrete entity. The works *El concepto de la historia universal* and *La existencia como caridad* contain his most extensive considerations on the subject. In them he categorically denies the possibility of attaining the perfection of man, because in his opinion it implies an acceptance of a collective improvement which is verifiable through the course of history. This he disdained as a modern myth. It was his opinion that progress can only be considered within the premises of extreme rationalistic philosophies such as positivism. Socially he characterized it, somewhat disdainfully, as:

> es la ilusión de la burguesía,
> militante y triunfante. [6]

Caso pointed out that belief in progress had resulted from confusion between the technological and moral spheres, a confusion which could be dated as far back as the first Bacon. On examining three fields of man's endeavors, the technological, the philosophical and the moral, Caso could find evidence of progress only in the first. [7] Neither philosophy, nor art, nor morality could demonstrate comparable advancement. After two thousand years, it is difficult to make an empirical evaluation between Democritus and Hegel. In the field of art, relativism reigns supreme for genius makes all works equal. Similarly, in the moral sphere, he found variety but not progress. Caso labeled as anthropormorphic vanity, all efforts to discover perfectability. On viewing history, the *pensador* agreed with Schopenhauer, and echoed the poet:

> . . . a tale
> Told by an idiot, full of sound and fury,
> Signifying nothing.

As can be seen from the foregoing, the eminent philosopher found himself in the worst of possible philosophical quandaries. In working his way clear of this intellectual morass, Caso established premises for a more vital relationship between man and universe, and in so doing, issued a call for a more positive dialogue among Mexican thinkers. To a certain extent, he gave impetus to the Mexican cultural renaissance which continues to this day.

His doubts on the validity of the idea of progress are not the

---

[6] *Ibid.*, p. 38.
[7] Caso, *La existencia como economía, como desinterés y como caridad*. México, 1943 — hereafter cited as *La existencia*, pp. 150-152.

whole, only a part of his larger philosophical opinions. Intimations of these doubts are found in the premises of his personal philosophy and in his discourse on history and society; and they cast a shadow on his reflection on México.

A PHILOSOPHIC SYNTHESIS

Accepting philosophy as that discipline which endeavors to establish the relationship between man and the universe, i. e., nature, arriving thereby at a veredict on life, philosophers may be separated into two broad camps: those who preach *attachment to life* and those who counsel *detachment from life.* In the latter group belongs Antonio Caso: He styled his philosophy *Cosmovisión cristiana.* [8] He first wrought his synthesis in an attempt to exhibit the development of Christian Ideas and sentiments through the centuries. [9] The cornerstone of his philosophy is that the universal law in operation is death; nature is in a constant process toward death. * In view of this, Caso concludes that man in his existence must somehow transcend the universal law; he must overcome time and nature. [10] The methodology the Mexican selected was "intuitionism", [11] his general ethical outlook is an agnostic Christian [12] skepticism.

Before life and the world environment, Caso distinguished two attitudes which he generalized as the "Christian" and the "Utilitarian". The latter was life as economy, the governing principle being *life: the most for the least effort.* [13] In contrast to it, arose the Christian attitude which views life as charity. The categorical imperative as formalized by Caso in this case is, *life: the least for the most effort.* [14] In sum, his synthesis holds that existence could only achieve meaning through *caridad,* the virtue of self-denial. In this effort, man is alone.

Along with the antithesis between the utilitarian and the moral, there are those between the aesthetic and the logical and between

[8] *Ibid.,* p. 13.

[9] It is significant to note that those who are distinguished in this outline are nay-sayers to life, Christian pessimists such as John the Baptist, St. Paul, St. Augustine, St. Francis of Assis, Kierkegaard, Tolstoi, etc.

* the energy of the universe is constantly diminishing.

[10] Caso, *La existencia,* pp. 25-32.

[11] Intuition is a direct apprehension of truth which is not the result of reasoning or sense perception; an immediate, non symbolic, non discussive penetration into the nature of the object.

[12] Caso's religious beliefs are difficult to define. He was not an orthodox Catholic. He considered himself an agnostic Christian. He called himself "Christian" because he believed that Christ exemplified the most ethical of lives. In ethics we should strive to imitate him.

[13] Caso, *La existencia,* p. 44.

[14] *Ibid.,* p. 154.

the metaphysical and the historical. He believed that the task of philosophy is to synthesize these contrasts through the employment of intuition. He never did; hence, the inconsistencies in his work. Caso, in effect, presupposes a dualism: Culture and Nature. However, he apparently did not recognize this. His thought moves on two planes one is the universal, the realm of the spirit in which man is alone; the other is the plane of the biological, the social and the concrete. He rarely bridges the gap.

The American philosopher, Patrick Romanell, has distinguished three stages in Caso's intellectual development: 1) the anti-intellectualist; 2) the pragmatist, and 3) the dualist. [15] Our reading has led us to believe that this is too fine and arbitrary a distinction and comes from a consideration of works individually. Considering his avowed intuitionism and mysticism, he could never be considered a pragmatist: the dualism was always present in his thought and, from the time of his rejection of positivism, he remained and anti-intellectualist. From the beginning, Caso chose a philosophical path and stuck to it.

In sum, Caso's general philosophy is a call to individual realization; in essence it is a rejection of the world. His view of history and society, as well as his observations on México, were deeply affected by this.

A VIEW OF HISTORY AND SOCIETY

History, to Caso, is an effort at reconstruction of the particular; a study of particular acts related in time. [16] As such, it is not a science, but a very special form of knowledge. In itself, as a process, it has neither sense nor value; it acquires these only through the individual —man provides contingency for the events isolated in time. If it were to have independent validity, one would have to accept the abstractions, "humanity" and "progress' as concrete; they are, however, merely ontological notions, illusions. In Caso's view, the term "philosophy of history" is a contradiction, since philosophy is a universal synthesis and history has reference only to things and beings unique and individual whose relation is contingent: Again, it is an individualistic view:

> Toda esta marcha de la historia, toda esta sucesión de sociedades, Estados, naciones, religiones, filosofías, técnicas, artes, litias y ciencias por todos elaborada cobra sentido, únicamente en la integración de individuos humanos superiores. Por esto se ve que la humanidad no va reali-

---

[15] Patrick Romanell, *The Making of the Mexican Mind*, p. 71.
[16] Caso, *El concepto*, pp. 136-137.

656 HISTORIA DE LAS IDEAS

zando ningún plan o propósito trascendente. Su fin es inmanente: realizar hombres cabales. [17]

Caso relegates society, like history, to a subordinate role in the process of man's individual development. He acknowledges that man is a social being, but he is also a spiritual being, and the spiritual takes precedence. Society is not an end in itself; neither it nor culture, of which it partakes, are justifiable except as they serve man. Caso conceives societal values as norms existing between the human and the divine; they are real and objective and serve to normalize relationships between men by counseling mutual respect.

In view of his larger philosophy, it is not surprising that Caso could regard the State as a necessary evil. He visualized the state as the formalization of social intercourse amongst men. In its purpose there was no equivocation:

> El Estado es la fuerza coactiva
> que debe garantizar a cada quien,
> la posibilidad de desarrollar su
> propia personalidad. [18]

All forms of government are bad, or at least imperfect; government is a sad necessity of communal life. The ideal of sovereign individual liberty is very far off. For Caso, civil and political liberties are only means to the achievement of personal development. To this end the state must preserve liberty of conscience, private property and political freedom. He believed that the best government would be one of enlightened despotism, but even this would be the lesser of many evils. [19]

Of the many political alternatives, Caso acknowledges Democracy as the most viable, given the realities of the twentieth century. [20] Democracy is the vehicle for individual self-identification with the governing process, an irritating necessity in Caso's opinion. Technological change and the resulting social upheaval have wrought havoc on former traditions and ideals. In surveying this century's society Caso saw only one ideal, only one tradition: the masses. This made democracy imperative. However, Caso observed that the very nature of mass culture will prohibit its perfection. He posed the internal conflict of democracy as this: Modern social and psychological temperament demand it, yet the reality of poverty and ignorance make it difficult to fully develop. Nevertheless he counseled that it must

[17] *Ibid.*, pp. 119-120.
[18] Caso, *La persona humana y el Estado totalitario*. México, 1941, p. 201.
[19] Caso, *Discursos heterogéneos*. México, 1925, p. 29.
[20] Caso, *México* (apuntamientos de cultura patria). México, 1943 — hereafter cited as *México*, p. 7.

be accepted and be given loyalty, for in the face of reality it is at once a necessity and an ideal.

In the concept of progress, man has a positive relation with society; man improves as society improves. There is a mutual beneficial intercourse. History is testimony of this in the past, and sheds light on future development. Reason is the key for the interpretation of history and the tool for the establishment of the proper relations between man and society. Life is seen in positive terms. Caso establishes his philosophic premise on a negative view of life and in his quest for meaning in the individual existences he rejects society and history. The *Pensador* has convinced himself that man can create good only within himself and in this effort he cannot depend on reason.

OBSERVATION ON MÉXICO

Turning to México, the mild, individual, Christian skepticism of Antonio Caso served him no less well in letter, but perhaps not in spirit. If there are contradictions in his views on society and history, they occur when he deals with problems of his native land. Barely would he admit to even the possibility of material and political improvement in the Mexican situation, and yet, reading between the lines, one almost senses, on his part, a desire to believe in positive cultural and moral progress. But in the end he remains faithful to his avowed skeptical individualism. He concludes that national problems will never be solved in his final analysis they are "Un arcano problema de amor". [21]

On consideration of his own country Antonio Caso at times displayed acute perceptivity; on other occasions his personal intellectual proclivities led him to rather unreal considerations. Perhaps this is because he could never bridge the gap between the ideal and the concrete. A biographical incident in his life may illustrate the point: In the 1910 elections, he was in the forefront of the Re-elecionista * ranks, editor of a party organ and leader of the younger generation. At the opening session of the party convention he made an elegant speech in behalf of electoral and constitutional liberties; he could not understand the wild applause of the galleries ** and the stony silence of his fellow delegates. [22]

[21] *Ibid.*, p. 21.
* The sham party advocating the re-election of Porfirio Diaz. In later years he repudiated his adherence to the regime.
** Madero was already developing his campaign.
[22] José Gaos, "Mocedades de Antonio Caso", in Gómez Robledo, *Homenaje*, p. 38.

His general pessimism did not preclude his making perceptive remarks. Caso believed that two factors operated to the detriment of the national scene: one was the propensity of the Mexican mentality to a *Bovarismo nacional,* [23] and the other was the sad fate of societies such as México to live at *destiempo.* More often than not such societies are out-of-step with the ideological march of the more advanced societies, often necessitating violent remedial action in order to keep abreast. He believes that both *Bovarismo* and *destiempo* are rooted in the Conquest, which initiated the assimilation of two radically opposed societies. [24] The synthesis of these two groups, in his opinion, is still far off; and not until it is accomplished will México be able to embark upon a more orderly evolutionary development. Above all, cultural unity must be achieved so that the country can face the future with one countenance. As yet México has not realized, has not discovered, its true identity. To Caso, Mexican history, politics, and society gave ample evidence of this lack of self-awareness. Mexicans suffer from a myopic vision that has frequently led them to place their faith in a lie, an involvement often resulting in death and sacrifice. His contribution to the national dialogue lies in the fact that he counseled generations of Mexican students to, above all, root their thought in the national reality; that they must actively seek to form and direct the intellectual currents of their time —but as Mexicans. He did not ask that they accept his own ideas, but only that they take into account the national needs in forming their own philosophies.

Caso maintains that México has experienced three ideologies: [25] *Catolicismo, Jacobinismo, y Positivismo,* and is now in the midst of a fourth, *Revolucionarismo.* The nation never fully assimilated the first three; what it will do with the fourth the future will decide. Catholic humanitarian ideals never entirely took hold in Indian Mexico. Caso considers the nineteenth century Jacobin liberals as Don Quixotes after the chimera of liberty. They distinguished themselves in the twin malaise of *Bovarismo* and *destiempo.* To them, the word was reality. The Indian past, the colonial experience, the very society around them was dismissed, and the Constitution of 1857 came into being. The skeptic Caso is amazed at groups of men seriously proposing to legislate the perfect government. To Caso, the imperial interlude was no less of a Quixotic venture. Positivism was as absurd as Jacobinistic idealism and lacked the saving nobility of the latter. Under the banner of *organic progress* and *social stability,* it served the interests of an extremely mediocre

[23] Caso, *Discursos a la nación mexicana.* México, 1922, p. 80. After Flaubert's character Madame Bovary who lived in a make believe world.

[24] Caso, *México,* p. 24.

[25] Caso, *Discursos a la nación mexicana,* p. 53.

bourgeoisie. Positivism in his eyes was a disruption of the normal intellectual evolution. [26]

Demonstrably, Jacobinism and positivism had failed. In the Mexico of Caso's day, it is the ideology of the Revolution which demands allegiance. The Revolution is a justifiable moral reaction, its task is no less than the construction of the foundation of the future. Caso warned, however, that to be viable a creed must be rooted in the imperatives of the national realities and must partake of the ideal and the concrete: "Alas y plomo". [27] These two must be cautiously mixed.

In one essay, Caso outlines a number of factors that must be taken into account in the formalization of a political structure. [28] These are: the army, capital, labor, the Catholic church, and the United States. Recognizing the general nationalistic milieu, Caso admits, the last two must be considered, but not formally recognized. In effect, Caso is suggesting the vague outlines of the then nascent PRI. As far as current ideologies he felt that perhaps Socialism had relevance and justice. Any ideology, the philosopher pointed out, must pay special heed to two areas: education and industry. There must be an industrial and educational patriotism. For México, he stated, the day of the warrior and the apostle are over; it is now that of the industrialist.

Caso points out that through the centuries México has sought the ideal of liberty; the various revolts have had it as a goal. In a skeptical way he suggests that perhaps the lie will, in time, become a truth, but he very much doubts it. Yet, nonetheless, the ideal must be sought. In order to accelerate the process, Caso states that three spheres must be satisfied: the economic, the judicial and the intellectual; in other words, the nation must endeavor to obtain wealth, justice, and enlightenment. [29] These he believes are found already in most of the western democracies. Díaz began the obtainment of the first, but his error was in ignoring the other three. Madero deserves praise for calling attention to the disequilibrium, if for nothing else, in Caso's eyes. Mexico must develop the three spheres; if not, it will continue as before. Caso advised his students that México is imperfect, but this does not make of it a freak among nations; it is one among many. Considering the liabilities under which it labors, this is understandable. He told his listeners that if they wished to improve Mexico to begin with themselves.

[26] *Ibid.*, p. 70.
[27] Caso, *México*, p. 30.
[28] *Ibid.*, pp. 23-30.
[29] *Ibid.*, p. 14.

SUMMARY AND CONCLUSIONS

Philosophically, Caso's thesis is, in many instances, analogous to *Idealistic Pessimism* and *Religious Perfectionism*. The former, as exemplified in Schopenhauer, maintains that nature and man are manifestations of will, and therefore, existence is a never-ceasing struggle, meaningless in itself. Salvation temporarily may be obtained through denial of the will-to-live and aesthetic contemplation of ideas. Caso combines this with the more transcendent metaphysical way of Christian self-denial, as exhibited in Aquinas. This perfectionism defines purpose as supernatural and subordinates the natural; it gives as a guide to the moral life, the cardinal virtues and the three theological virtues: faith, hope and charity.

Caso offered a moral ideal. Since the universe is a process toward death, in his brief life man must transcend the universe or he lives meaninglessly. Throught a life of charity and self-denial, the individual provides himself with purpose. For Caso, sense is good action. Eeach man alone must be his own saint.

Caso's philosophy is a moral reaction in face of world circunstance. Reflecting of the World War and its aftermath, he concluded the age to be one of decline, with moral magnanimity absent and with vague and sterile ideals. The two contending ideologies, Capitalism and Communism were only shades apart; their base was the same, avarice and selfishness. [30] These same vices were no less evident in his own country. The first edition of *La existencia como caridad* which propounded his basic thesis, came out in 1915 when the savagery of the Revolution was at its height, as the country was beign devastated in the three-cornered war between Villa, Zapata and Carranza. Mexico was a part of his pessimism.

This writer cannot accept the efforts of Zea [31] to make the philosopher into a nationalist spokesman. This comes from considering exclusively his essays on national affairs and often taking statements out of context. Caso was aware of his country's travails but would never consider himself merely a nationalist spokesman. The leading intellectual of a country undergoing radical transformation was not vitally concerned or involved. [32]

Caso, upon occasion, could make perceptive generalizations on the Mexican phenomena. But they were just that, generalizations. His

[30] Caso, *Discursos heterogéneos*, p. 45.

[31] For his argument see Leopoldo Zea "Antonio Caso y la mexicanidad" in Gómez Robledo, *Homenaje*, pp. 95-108.

[32] For a very caustic view of Caso with special reference to his intellectual pretensions and ivory tower attitude, see Antenógenes Pérez y Soto, *La simulación filosófica y educativa del Lic. Antonio Caso*. México, 1919.

comments were always on the abstract plane; never did they deal with concrete means, problems or solutions. He considered himself an academic philosopher and so acted: "Sereno meditador intelectual". His contribution to the national dialogue is, nonetheless, not insignificant. He is one of the initiators of the search for national identity; he urged concern for: "México y lo mexicano...", though he himself did not practice what he preached. He taught several generations of Mexican intellectuals that regardless of what avenue they took in their quest their base should be their own native environment. A list of his more distinguished students is nearly a who's who of Mexican intellectual and political life. He was more than a professor to many of these; for the more serious and outstanding, he cultivated a life-long friendship.

As an intellectual, he was well-acquainted with the concept of progress, its origins, development and significance. But he could not accept it as valid, his rejection was consistent with his philosophy and his views on history and society. Though one senses, is his writings with reference to México, that at times, he wished that his conviction would be otherwise. There is no doubt of his perceptivity concerning the historical and contemporary travails of his country, and that he earnestly sought to provide insight and solutions to the national problems; but his personal inclinations and philosophical orientation precluded the suggestion of viable alternatives. In a world of hard and ugly facts, mystics have little to suggest.

Antonio Caso chose a different route. In action, he does not cut the figure of the romantic and heroic Martí; in style he does not breathe the fire of the satanic iconoclasm of González Prada. Instead of the masses, he chose the individual; instead of the material, the spiritual. Life to Antonio Caso was:

"un arcano problema de amor".

BIBLIOGRAPHY

A. Primary Sources

Caso, Antonio, *El acto ideatorio y la filosofía de Husserl*. México, Stylo, 1945.
———, *El concepto de la historia universal y la filosofía de los valores*. México, Ediciones Botas, 1933.
———, *Discursos a la nación mexicana*. México, Porrúa Hnos., 1922.
———, *Discursos heterogéneos*. México, Herrero Hnos., 1925.
———, *Doctrinas e ideas*. México, Ediciones Botas, 1924.
———, *Ensayos críticos y polémicos*. México, Cultura, 1922.
———, *La existencia como economía, como desinterés y como caridad*. México, Secretaría de Educación Pública, 1943.

———, *La filosofía de la cultura y el materialismo histórico.* México, Ediciones Alba, 1936.

———, *Historia y antología del pensamiento filosófico.* México, Secretaría de Educación Pública, 1926.

———, *México* (apuntamientos de cultura patria). México, Imp. Universitaria, 1943.

———, *Nuevos discursos a la nación mexicana.* México, Robredo, 1934.

———, *El peligro del hombre.* México, Stylo, 1942.

———, *La persona humana y el Estado totalitario.* México, Universidad Nacional Autónoma de México, 1941.

———, *El problema de México y la ideología nacional.* México, Libro-Mex., 1955.

———, *Los problemas filosóficos.* México, Porrúa Hnos., 1915.

———, *Sociología.* 4th Edition. México, Stylo, 1945.

B. Secondary Sources

ALBA, Víctor, *Las ideas sociales contemporáneas en México.* México, Fondo de Cultura Económica, 1960.

BECKER, Carl, "Progress", *Encyclopedia of the Social Sciences*, XI, pp. 495-499. New York, The Macmillan Company, 1937.

BURY, J. B., *The Idea of Progress.* New York, Dover Publications, 1955.

CRAWFORD, Rex, W., *A Century of Latin American Thought.* Cambridge, Massachusetts, Harvard University Press, 1963.

DAVIS, Harold Eugene, *Latin American Social Thought: The History of its Development since Independence, with Selected Readings.* Washington, D.C., The University Press of Washington, D.C., 1963.

GARCÍA MÁYNEZ, Eduardo, *Caso.* México, Secretaría de Educación Pública, 1943.

GARRIDO, Luis, *Antonio Caso: Una vida profunda.* México, Universidad Nacional Autónoma de México, 1961.

GÓMEZ ROBLEDO, Antonio, *Homenaje a Antonio Caso.* México, Stylo, 1947.

KRAUZE DE KOLTENINK, Rosa, *La filosofía de Antonio Caso.* México, Universidad Nacional Autónoma de México, 1961.

PAZ, Octavio, *The Labyrinth of Solitude: Life and Thought in Mexico.* Tr. Lysander Kemp. New York, Grove Press, Evergreen, 1961.

PÉREZ Y SOTO, Antenógenes, *La simulación filosófica y educativa del Lic. Antonio Caso.* México, Imprenta de J. I. Muñoz, 1919.

RAMOS, Samuel, *La historia de la filosofía en México.* México, Universidad Nacional Autónoma de México, 1943.

ROMANELL, Patrick, *The Making of the Mexican Mind.* Lincoln, Nebraska, University of Nebraska Press, 1952.

SÁNCHEZ, Pedro Troncoso and Salazar, Joaquín, *Homenaje a Antonio Caso.* Ciudad Trujillo, Universidad de Santo Domingo, 1946.

ZEA, Leopoldo, *The Latin American Mind.* Tr. James H. Abbot & Lowell Dunham. Norman, Oklahoma, University Press, 1963.

THE ENLIGHTENMENT
AND THE IDEA OF AMERICA

MAX SAVELLE

PREFATORY REMARK

My interest in exploring the thoughts of the men of the Enlightenment about America was aroused, over a period of many years, by my reading of the documents pertinent to the international history of Angloamerica in the colonial period. For as I studied the more or less petty bickerings between European nations over boundaries, islands, lands, trade, or the freedom of the seas, and the treaties with regard to America that issued from them, I was led into an interest in the larger assumptions and ideas that lay behind those activities in the minds of the European statesmen.

One was led most obviously and directly from diplomacy to the study of international law and its principles relative to America in the writings of the great legal theorists from Pufendorf to Vattel and beyond. From the study of international law one moved into the schemes for international peace —of Willian penn, of the Abbe St. Pierre, the great Kant himself, and the part America played in the thought and in the hopes of those idealists. And from ideas in international law one moved, perforce, into the writings of the more general political theorists, Locke, Montesquieu, Rousseau, Franklin, Condorcet. But one did not stop there; one must study the ideas of the economists, the geographers, the anthropologists, the historians, the theorists of religion, especially of Christian missions, the litterateurs, and the philosophers.

Obviously, any project to isolate, to master, and to analyze the thinking with regard to America of all or most of the important men of the Enlightenment would be a project beside which the "moon walk" would be hardly more than a mathematical *paseo*.

I take as my definition of the Enlightenment Peter Gay's definition of it as "a family of philosophers", but, also, "a cultural climate —a world in which the philosophers acted, from which they noisily rebelled and quietly drew many of their ideas, and on which they attempted to impose their program", a world which flowered, roughly, in the century between the birth of Montesquieu (1689) and the death of Holback (1789). [1] (For the purposes of this report I think

---

[1] Peter Gay, *The Enlightenment: An Interpretation. The Rise of Modern Paganism*. New York, Alfred Knopf, 1699, pp. x-xi, 17.

of the Enlightenment as including the work of Condorcet, Humboldt, and the early Goethe.)

Many men, of course, have studied the Enlightenment as an European phenomenon. Others such as Gilbert Chinard, [2] Silvio Zavala, [3] Benjamín Bissell [4] and others, have done magisterial work in certain limited areas of European thought with regard to America. Many more special studies such as theirsare needed. But no one known to me has studied the problem as a whole. No one, as far as I know, had addressed himself to the whole mind of the Enlightenment with regard to the new world of America, or, more specifically for the purposes of this conference, what the men of the Enlightenment thought about Angloamerica and México.

Thus, if there is anything new about the outline presented here, that newness lies in the fact that it proposes to study European thought with regard to America in its entire perspective. That perspective is characterized by two aspects: 1) It is international. It is not limited to any one of the European countries interested in the new world but it considers them all: France, Spain, Germany, Holland, England, Portugal and, in some areas of thought, Italy. Indeed, any study of the Enlightenment as an international phenomenon must include many Americans as well as Europeans. This plan, therefore, is interested in all the Europeans and Americans who expressed noteworthy thoughts about America, and it seeks to discover, by comparing and collating them with each other, whether the "mind" of the Enlightenment with regard to America was, in fact, an international mind.

2) In the second place, this proposed program is intended to study all the areas of thought to which the men of the Enlightenment devoted themselves. Thus, it is interested in the place of America in scientific thought, in geography, in anthropology, in history, in political theory, in economics, in religion, in literature, in philosophy, and in the rising mood of nationalism. Again, by studying all these areas of thought in a total perspective, it is hoped to arrive at some viable conclusion to the existence —or non-existence— of common general ideas that ran through the areas of thought.

By about the middle of the eighteenth century, the vast phenomenon called the Expansion of Europe, already three centuries old, had called into being, among European thinkers and observers of the human drama a great corpus of thought relative to that phenomenon. This thought was an integral part of the thinking of the

[2] Gilbert Chinard, *L'Amérique et Le rêve exotique dans la littérature française au XVIIᵉ et XVIIIᵉ siècle.* Paris, E. Dioz, 1934.

[3] Silvio Zavala, *América en el espíritu francés del siglo XVIII.* México, Colegio Nacional, 1949.

[4] Benjamin Bissel, *The American Indian in English Literature of the Eighteenth Century.* Hamden, Conn., Archon Books, 1968.

Enlightenment; and the thinking of the *philosophes* with regard to the "new world" in general and about the new world of America in particular involved every division of the intellectual life of the eighteenth century.

He who would seek to understand this eighteenth-century "rationalization" of the Expansion of Europe must therefore be prepared to read widely and deeply into the writings of the eighteenth-century savants in all the western nations and in all the fields of thought and to examine the questions the *philosophes* asked themselves with regard to the new world, and their answers. Such questions, for example, as:

> What was, for them, the nature and the historical, cultural and spiritual significance of the expansion of Europe?
> What was the nature of colonies —economic, political, sociological, imperial and national?
> What was the meaning and the significance of the new Euro-American civilization —or civilizations— for the nature and destiny of man?
> What role did America play in the development and the flowering of that mystical quality so dear to the minds of the *philosophes*, the "human spirit?"

If there was one basic assumption of all, or nearly all the *philosophes*, it was their faith in science, or, rather, in "nature" as they thought it to berevealed by science. Thus, one of the most intense interests of the men of the Enlightenment in America was in the picture of natural science revealed there —the botanists, such as Peter Kalm and Georges-Luis Leclerc de Buffon, the physicists, such as Benjamin Franklin, the anthropologists, such as Cornelius de Pauw, and, above all, the geographers. Map-making flourished; and men such as G. Delisle, J. B. B. D'Anville, and Doctor John Mitchell, achived high levels of scientific accuracy in their maps of America. Descriptive and theoretical geographers like Alexander von Humboldt and Karl Ritter, especially the former, [5] whose highly significant works on the geography of America constitute a magnificant culmination to a century of Enlightenment geography relative to the new continent. Above all, the great philosopher, Immanuel Kant, although he wrote little or nothing about America, placed geography in the great corpus of organized knowledge (science), linking geography, which is a study of phenomena that exist beside each other in peace, with history, which is the study of phenomena that follow each other in time. Geography is a sort of summary of nature —a philosophy of man's place in nature: mathematical, moral, political, commercial, and theological.

[5] See, for example, Alexander von Humboldt, *Voyage de Humboldt et Bonpland...* 23 vols. Paris, F. Schoell, 1805-34.

But the study of the geography of America was not merely an examination of physical features of the continent, nor even as Kant would have organized it, a "summary of nature", in mathematical, moral, political, commercial and theological divisions. It was more than that: it was a study of the earth and of man which contributed to one's perspective, and to an understanding of humanity and its problems.

The *philosophes* were also interested in, and curious about, the races of men, particularly those in America. Voltaire devoted many pages in his *Histoire des Moeurs* to the American Indians and to the Negroes of Africa and America. He finds these races different from, and inferior to, the white Europeans; his racism is reflected in the writings of many another anthropologist, such as Cornelius de Pauw and M. Engel, of the *Encyclopédie*. Indeed, this "scientific" racism may be said to have been typical of the men of the Enlightenment; it was shared by David Hume, Benjamin Franklin, and many others. For them, the differences between races and the superiority of the whites were obvious, clearly demonstrated by the scientific, comparative study of the other races. [6]

Many of the *philosophes* were deeply interested in the history of America; many of them found in that history the confirmation of their own Enlightenment predispositions, but they also saw in it the narrative of one of the most significant events in the history of humanity. We are not accustomed to think of Voltaire, for example, as an historian of America, yet much of his writing, especially his *Histoire des Moeurs*, is devoted to commentary upon the rise of the Euroamerican civilizations on this continent. With regard to the expansion of Europe, led by the Portuguese, he says that "C'est ici le plus grand evenment sans doute de notre globe, dont une moitié avait toujours été ignorée de l'autre. C'est une espèce de création nouvelle". [7]

The deep historical significance of this great phenomenon, however, lay not in the quantity of the gold and silver brought back to Europe, nor yet in the new products of America that changed the way of life of the Europeans, but the expansion of man's knowledge of the world and of himself. It lies in the greatness of this phenomenon as an expansion of the human spirit:

> L'objet [de notre Histoire des moeurs y incluse l'histoire de l'Amérique] était l'histoire de l'esprit humain, non pas de faits presque toujours défigurez, mais de voir par quels degrés on est parvenu de la rusticité barbare de ces temps [de Charlemagne] à la politesse des notre ...
> C'est donc l'histoire de l'opinion qu'il fallut ecrire; et par là ce chaos

[6] See, for example, Cornelius de Pauw, *Recherches Philosophiques sur les Américains*. Paris, 1768-1770.
[7] Voltaire, *Histoire des Moeurs...*, *Oeuvres*, Moland, ed., XII, 376.

d'événements, de factions, de révolutions, et de crimes, devenait digne
d'être présenté aux regards des sages...

On voit dans l'histoire ainsi concise les erreurs et les préjugés se suc-
céder tour a tour, et chasser la vérité et là raison ... [Mais] Enfin les
hommes s'éclairent un peu par ce tableau de leurs malheurs et de leurs
sottises. Les sociétés parvenirent avec le temps a rectifier leurs idées; les
hommes apprennent a penser. [8]

In writing thus, Voltaire spoke for his time. There were many *philosophes*, as Peter Gay says, and they differed widely from each other
in the details and in the individualism of their thinking. But nearly
all of them shared this devotion to the grand idea of the progress of
the human spirit, despite, as Voltaire says, the stupidity, the savagery, the bigotry, the cruelty, the crimes and all the other animalistic ins-
tincts of men.

Other historians must be considered. The most important of all,
perhaps, was the Abbé Raynal, whose monumental *Histoire philosophique et politique des Établissements et du Commerce des Européens
dans les deux Indes*, [9] for all its vagaries, was a genuine effort to interpret the expansion of Europe in terms of the welfare of humanity;
as such, it is a highly significant example of the mind of the Enlightenment with regard to the "new world", including America.

David Hume's History of England [10] has much to say about the
English colonies in America and the "noble principles" upon which
they were founded. William Robertson's *History of America* [11] followed Raynal and Voltaire in his acceptance and elaboration of *La
Leyenda Negra*. Juan Bautista Muñoz was commissioned by Carlos III
to write a new history of the New World, but only the first volume
of his projected work ever appeared, in 1793. [12]

One of the major concerns of the political theorists of the Enlightenment was the political nature of colonies and their relationship
with the mother countries. For the Europeans, the most common
assumption was that colonies had been established, in the first place,

---

[8] François-Marie Arouet de Voltaire, *Remarques pour servir de supplement a
l'Essai sur les moeurs et l'esprit des nations et sur les principaux faits de l'histoire,
depuis Charlemagne jusq'a la mort de Louis XIII, Oeuvres*, Moland, ed., xxiv,
pp. 547-548.

[9] There were many editions of Raynal's *Histoire philosophique*, which was first
published in 1770. The edition used here is the one published in Geneva, in five
volumes, "Chez Jean-Leonard Pellet", in 1780.

[10] David Hume, *The History of England from the Invasion of Julius Caesar to
the Revolution in 1688*, 10 vols. London, J. Wallis, 1803.

[11] William Robertson, *History of America*, 2 vols. London, William Strahan,
1777.

[12] Juan Bautista Muñoz, *Historia del Nuevo Mundo*. Madrid, Vda. de Ibarra,
1793.

as a sort of distant factory for the promotion of the commerce of
the mother countries. Thus Montesquieu wrote, in *L'Espirit des Lois*:

> Les Espagnols regardèrent d'abord les terres découvertes comme des
> objêts de conquête; des peuples, plus rafinés qu'eux trouvèrent qu'elles
> étaient des objêts de commerce, & c'est là-dessus qu'ils dirigèrent leurs
> vues. Plusieurs peuples se sont conduits avec tant de sagesse, qu'ils ont
> donné l'empire a des compagnies de negocians, qui, gouvernant ces états
> eloignés uniquement pour le négoce, ont fait, une grande puissance
> accessoire, sans embarrasser l'état principal.
> Les colonies qu'on y a formées sont sous un genre de dépendance
> dont ou ne trouve que peu d'exemples dans les colonies anciennes, soit
> que celles d'aujourd'hui relèvent de l'état même, ou de quelque com-
> pagnie commerçante établie dans cet état.
> L'objêt de ces colonies est de faire le commerce à de meilleures
> conditions qu'on ne le fait avec les peuples voisins, avec lesquels tous les
> avantages sont reciproques. On a établi que la metropole seule pourrait
> négocier dans la colonie; & cela avec grand raison, parce que le but de
> l'établissement a été l'extension du commerce, no la fondation d'une
> ville ou d'un nouvel empire. [13]

Naturally, it follows from this concept of economic dependence that
colonial government should be similarly politically dependent upon
the imperial government of the metropolis.

But a new political concept of the colonial societies was gestating
in America —most clearly in Angloamerica. Thus Richard Bland, of
Virginia. basing his ideas, in typical Enlightenment fashion, upon the
notions of natural law and natural rights, explained the nature of
the colonies as that of new societies, each enjoying sovereignty within
its own boundaries:

> Men in a state of Nature absolutely free and independent of one
> another as to sovereign Jurisdiction, but when they enter into a Society,
> and by their own Consent become Members of it, they must submit
> to the laws of the Society according to which they agree to be govern-
> ed; ... But though they must submit to the Laws, so long as they
> remain members of the Society, yet they retain so much of their natural
> Freedom as to have a Right to retire from the Society, to renounce the
> Benefits of it, to enter into another Society, and to settle in another
> Country; ... This natural Right remains with every Man, and he cannot
> justly be deprived of it by any civil Authority ... Now when Men
> exercise this Right, and withdraw themselves from their Country, they
> recover their natural Freedom and Independence: The Jurisdiction and
> Sovereignty of the State they have quitted ceases; and if they unite,

---

[13] Charles Louis de Secondat, Baron de Brede et de Montesquieu, *De l'Esprit
des Lois, Oeuvres complets de Montesquieu*, André Masson, ed. 3 vols., Paris,
Éditions Nagel, 1950, I, pp. 518-519.

and by common Consent take Possession of a new Country, and form themselves into a political Society, they become a Sovereign State, independent of the State from which they separated. [14]

And Benjamin Franklin applied this theory to the structure of the British Empire, describing it as sort of confederation of sovereign societies bound together by their loyalty to a common monarch and by the functional necessity for some central administration of the affairs of the whole confederation. In this he echoed the thought of Adam Smith that:

> The colony assemblies... cannot be supposed the proper judges of what is necessary for the defense and support of the whole empire... The assembley of a province, like the vestry of a parish, may judge very properly concerning the affairs of its own particular district; but can have no proper means of judging concerning those of the whole empire. It cannot even judge properly concerning the proportion which its own province bears to the whole empire; ... What is necessary for the defense and support of the whole empire, and in what proportion each part ought to contribute, can be judged of only by that assembly which inspects and superintends the affairs of the whole empire [i.e., Parliament]. [15]

But Bland's and Franklin's new concept of colonial empires as federations of sovereign states involved, also, a new concept of sovereignty, that is, a concept of sovereignty as divided between imperial sovereignty, inherent in the monarch, and colonial sovereignty, inherent in the colonial legislature. This new concept ran counter to the notion of the indivisible nature of sovereignty as expounded by Rousseau and as adhered to in the practice of the statesmen who administered the affairs of the British Empire. One is inclined to see in these ideological phenomena the appearance of a new school —an American school— of thought as to the nature of colonial empires, although it is to be recognized that a few men, such as Richard Price and Anne-Robert-Jacques Turgot, came very close to seeing the growth and the resolution of the political structures of empires in quite similar terms.

Many other political thinkers, such as Edmund Burke, the Earl of Halifax, Josiah Tucker, and Lord Mansfield, in England, and Turgot and Moreau de St. Méry in France addressed themselves to the constitutional theory and intra-imperial institutions of the colonies, or involving them. There is a sharp contrast between the "integral im-

---

[14] Richard Bland, *An Inquiry into the Rights of the Colonies* (1776). Richmond, edited by Earl Swem, 1922, pp. 9-10, 14.

[15] *An Inquiry into The Nature and Causes of the Wealth of Nations.* Edited by Edwin Cannan, 2 vols. London, Methuen: University Paperbacks, 1961, ii, p. 134.

perialism" of Mansfield, for example, and the "separatism" of Tucker and Turgot.

Thought relative to intra-imperial relations could not avoid consideration of theory relative to inter-imperial relations, that is to say, international law and diplomacy. What part did America or the overseas colonies play in the thinking of Pufendorf or of Vattel? Inevitably, they were forced to consider such questions as those involved in the establishment of national title to unoccupied lands overseas; what rights did the Indians have over the land they occupied? What rights did the trading nations have upon the sea that separated America from Europe? What rights, if any, had the European inhabitants of a colony ceded by one imperial state to another? How were boundaries to be determined? What rights did one empire have with regard to visit to, or trade with, the colonies of another?

Vattel, as the great moralistic philosopher of international law, placed his heaviest emphasis upon *"la loi naturelle"* and the moral duty of kings and of states to observe that law. [16] But other theorists saw the necessity for international organization to implement international morality. What part was envisaged for America in the schemes of William Penn, the Abbé de St. Pierre, and Immnauel Kant for international peace?

The economic philosophers of the Enlightenment had their own problems with regard to America. As already noted, such philosophers as Montesquieu though of the colonies as sort of commercial "factory" which existed for the economic benefit of the mother country. On the basis of this assumption, they justified the system of national-imperial monopoly of the colonial economies. As François Véron Duverger de Forbonnais put it, in the *Encyclopédie*:

> Toutes celles de ce continent [l'Amérique] ont eu le commerce & la culture tout-a-la-fois pour objêt de leur etablissement, ou s'y sont tournées: dès-lors il était nécessaire de conquérir les terres, & d'en chasser les anciens habitants, pour y transporter de nouveaux.
>
> Ces *colonies* n'étant établies que pour l'utilite de la metropole, il s'ensuite:
>
> 1º Qu'elles doivent être sous sa dépendence immédiate et par conséquent sous sa protection.
>
> 2º Que le commerce doit en être exclusif aux fondateurs...
>
> Ainsi le profit du commerce & de la culture de nos *colonies* est précisément, 1º le plus grand prodution que leur consommation occasione au

16 Emmerich de Vattel, *Le droit des gens; ou, Principes de la loi naturelle appliqués à la conduite ou aus affaires des nations et des souverains*, 3 vols. Washington, Carnegie Institution, 1916.

proprietaire de nos terres, les frais de culture deduits; 2º ce que reçoivent nos artistes et nos matelots qui travaillent pour elles, & à leur occasion; 3º tout ce qu'elles suppléent de nos besoins; 4º tout le superflu qu'elles nous donnent à exporter . . .

[Il y en résultent plusieurs conséquences:]

La première est que les *colonies* ne seroient plus utiles, si elles pouvoient se passer de la métropole: ainsi c'est une loi prise dans la nature de la chose, que l'on doit restraindre les arts & la culture dans une *colonie*, à tels & tels objects, suivant les convenances du pay de la domination.

La second conséquence est que si la *colonie* entretient un commerce avec les étrangers, ou que si l'on y consomme les merchandises étrangères, le montant de ce commerce & de ces merchandises est un vol fait a la métropole; vol trop commun, mais punissable par les lois, & par lequel la force réele & relative d'un état est diminuée de tout ce que gagnent les étrangers. [17]

By the third quarter of the eighteenth century a number of men had arisen to challenge this assumption and the mercantilist system that had been built upon it. The greatest of these challengers, of course, was the Scottish Adam Smith, whose *Wealth of Nations*, published in 1776, the year of Angloamerican independence, riddled the economic thinking upon which the mercantilist system was built. As for colonies:

The colonists carry out with them a knowledge of agriculture and of other useful arts, superior to what can grow up of its own accord in the course of many centuries among savage and barbarous nations. They carry out with them too the habit of subordination, some notion of the regular government which takes place in their own country, of the system of laws which supports it, and of a regular administration of justice; and they naturally establish something of the same kind in the new settlement . . . Every colonist gets more land then he can possibly cultivate. He has no rent, and scarce any taxes to pay. No landlord shares with him in its produce, and the share of the sovereign is commonly but a trifle. He has every motive to render as great as possible a produce, which is thus to be almost entirely his own . . . Plenty of good land, and liberty to manage their own affairs their own way, seem to be the two great causes of the prosperity of all new colonies. [18]

It is to be noted that Smith attributes the relatively great prosperity of the British colonies to the fact that they enjoy freer political institutions than other colonies. Others, such as the Reverend Josiah Tu-

[17] *L'Encyclopédie*, article "Colonie", III, p. 650.
[18] Adam Smith, *op. cit.*, II, p. 83.

cker and David Hume, went even further and, while minimizing the economic profitableness of the colonies to the mother country, proposed that the colonies be given their independence entirely. It is to be noted, also, that in all of the major Euroamerican empires American-born colonials were appearing to challenge, in the name of natural economic laws and natural economic rights, the old mercantilistic system of laws and regulations under which the economies of the colonies were controlled by the metropoli.

Most of the religions of Euroamerica had their centers in Europe. Only the Indian and the African religions had no European connections.

In general, the Christian leaders in Europe assumed that America, in addition to being, in a religious sense, an extension of Europe, was also a rich field for missionary enterprise for the extension of the faith among the Indians and Negroes. George Berkeley, for example, the Anglican Bishop of Cloyne, in Ireland, expressed what seems to have been the generally accepted English attitude when he wrote that:

> Although there are several excellent persons of the Church of England, whose good intentions and endeavours have not been wanting to propagate the Gospel in foreign parts ... it is nevertheless acknowledged that there is at this day but little sense of religion, and a most notorious corruption of manners, in the English colonies settled on the Continent of America, and the Islands. It is also acknowledged that the gospel hath hitherto made but a very inconsiderable progress among the neighboring Americans [Indians], who still continue in much the same ignorance and barbarism in which we found them about a hundred years ago. [19]

Meanwhile, the Jesuits, for example, among the Catholics devoted a major part of their activity in America, from Canada to Paraguay, to the work of converting the Indians to Catholicism and protecting the Indians from the European Christians. [20] The rationalization of this great religious expansive movement constitutes a vast field for investigation.

But European Christianity, itself, was passing through a sort of revo-

[19] George Berkeley, "A Proposal for the better supplying of churches in our foreign Plantations and for converting the savage Americans to Christianity by a College to be erected in the Summer Islands, otherwise called the Isles of Bermudas", *The Works of George Berkeley, D.D.; Formerly Bishop of Cloyne, Including his Posthumous Works*, edited by Alexander Campbell Frazer, 4 vols. Oxford, The Clarendon Press, 1901, IV, pp. 341-364, IV, p. 346.

[20] For example, one needs only to mention the vast collection of the *Jesuit Relations*, — not only those from North America (*The Jesuit Relations and allied Documents*... Edited by Reuben Gold Thwaites... 73 vols. Cleveland, O.: Burrows Brothers, 1896-1901), but those from other parts of the hemisphere, published and unpublished as well.

lution as one of the effects of the rationalism of the Enlightenment. From the English rationalists through the naturalism of the Deists to the atheism of such *philosophes* as Dennis Diderot and the Baron d'Holbach, the old theology and the old religious institutions were coming under fire. The activities of the Christians in America, whether Catholic or Calvinist, were attacked with vitriolic criticisms by such historical writers as Voltaire, Robertson, Raynal and a host of others; The *Encyclopédie* was thoroughly saturated with criticism, explicit or implied, of the religious Establishment.

In America, too, religious thinking tended to become "American", as against that of the European establishments, and their "American", localized versions of Christianity tended to align themselves with the other ideological forces, economic, political, and psychological, that were working with increasing clarity, during the middle decades of the century, toward the moods that eventuated in indepedence.

In the literature of the European Enlightenment, America looms large. For America provided literary themes derived from heroic deeds and the conflicts of civilizations, as in Voltaire's *Alzire, ou les Américains,* and from nationalistic fervour, such as in James Thomson's *Britannia and Liberty.* At the same time, the American experience provided nationalistic themes for the nascent literature of the Angloamericans themselves. Thus, Voltaire uses his novellette, l'Ingénu, as a vehicle for his moral conviction that men reared in a state of nature, as among the Hurons, were more sincere, honest, direct —in short, more "natural"— than men reared in the corrupt, selfish, conspiratorial, hypocritical society of Europe. In his *Alzire, ou les Américains,* Álvarez say (of Alzire), on the theme of the conflict of the two cultures, Spanish and Indian:

> Son coeur aux Castillans va donner tous les coeurs;
> L'Amérique à genoux adoptera nos moeurs;
> La foi doit y jeter ses racines profondes;
> Votre hymen est le noeud qui joindra les deux mondes;
> Ces feroces humains, qui détestent nos lois,
> Voyant entre vos bras la fille de leurs vois,
> Vont, d'un esprit moins fier et d'un coeur plus facile,
> Sous votre joug heureux baisser un front docile;
> Et je verrai, mon fils, grâce a ces doux liens,
> Tous les coeurs désormais espagnols et chretiens. [21]

And Alzire says of herself:

> Je fus instruite, Émire, en ce grossier climat,
> A suivre la vertu sans en chercher l'éclat.

[21] Voltaire, *Alzire, ou les Américains,* (*Oeuvres,* Moland, ed.), III, pp. 367-438, III, p. 390.

L'honneur est dans mon coeur, et c'est lui qui m'ordonne
De saüver un héros que le ciel abandonne. [22]

James Thomson, in his panegyric on British freedom, *Liberty*, glo-
rifies what he feels to be British cultural supremacy and the expansion
of British freedom overseas:

> Despairing Gaul her boiling youth restrains,
> Dissolv'd her dream of universal away:
> The winds and seas are Britain's wide domain:
> And not a sail, but by permission, spreads.
> Lo! swarming southward on rejoicing suns,
> Gay colonies extend; the calm retreat
> Of undeserv'd distress, the better home
> Of those whom bigots chase from foreign lands,
> Not built on rapine, servitude, and woe,
> And in their turn some petty tyrants prey;
> But, bound by social freedom, firm they rise;
> Such as, of late, an Oglethorpe has form'd,
> And, crowding round, the charm'd Savannah sees.

The literature of the Enlightenment is abundantly rich in thought
about America. Is there a general concept, or "idea" of America revealed in that literature? [23]

Among the Angloamericans, the early stirrings of an Angloamerican
nationalism is to be heard in the "Poem on the Rising Glory of America" by Philip Freneau and H.H. Brachenridge:

> This is they praise America, thy pow'r,
> Thou best of climes by science visited,
> By freedom blest and richly stor'd with all
> The luxuries of life. Hail happy land,
> The seat of empire, the abode of kings . . . [24]

Aagain, as in other areas of thought, it may conceivably be discovered that the "mind" of the Enlightenment of the eighteenth century
was really two minds, an European mind and an American mind, an
European "idea" of America and an American "idea" of America conceived by the Americans themselves.

Eighteenth century philosophy, as such, concerned itself little, directly, with America. In the writings of Immanuel Kant, perhaps the
greatest of the eighteenth-century formal philosophers, the student

[22] Voltaire, *Alzire, ou les Américains*, (*Oeuvres*, Moland, ed.), III, p. 432.
[23] Watter Wàdepuhl, *Goethe's Interest in the New World*. Jena, Frommann, 1934.
[24] Philip Freneau and H. H. Brackenridge, *Poem on the Rising Glory of America*. Philadalphia, 1772, p. 28.

finds extremely little, if anything, that is of direct reference to the new world.

And yet, in the general philosophical outlook of the men of the Enlightenment, America looms large. John Locke, for example, was of high importance among philosophers for his sensationalism that seemed to justify the philosophers in much that they thought, relative to America or to anything else; but his great place in the Enlightenment philosophy, or "idea", of America derived not so much from what he said about America as for the vast influence he exercised upon the gestating mind of America itself.

David Hume, as a philospher, wrote little that directly involved America; but in his *History of England* he gives much attention, as has been noted, to the development of the Angloamerican colonies and the "noble principles" upon which they were founded. And as the tension between the colonies and England developed, Hume became an ardent, often vitrolic, partisan of the Americans, to the point of actually advocating their independence.

And George Berkeley, the great immaterialist, could see in America, as did Voltaire, a stage for the further progress of the human spirit:

> The Muse, disgusted at an age and clime
> Barren of every glorious theme,
> In distant lands now waits a better time,
> Producing subjects worthy fame:
>
> There shall be sung another golden age,
> The rise of empire and of arts
> The good and great inspiring epic rage,
> The wisest heads and noblest hearts.
>
> Not such as Europe breeds in her decay;
> Such as she bred when fresh and young,
> When heavenly flame did animate her clay,
> By future poets shall be sung.
>
> Westward the course of empire takes its way,
> The four first Acts already past,
> A fifth shall close the Drama with the Day;
> Time's noblest offspring is the last. [25]

The fragments of Enlightenment thought that have been pieced together here are offered only as examples of the thinking that the *philosophes* were doing, both in Europe and in America. They are presented only as opening dors, as it were, into the mind of the

[25] George Berkeley, "Verses on the Prospects of Planting Arts and Learning in America", *The Works of George Berkeley*, edited by A. C. Frazer (4 vols.) Oxford, The Clarendon Press, 1901, IV, pp. 365-366.

Enlightenment with regard to America. The pattern here is, of course, but the merest sketch, a sort of *esquisse*, of the problem, if even that. It has been presented in this way for the sake of suggesting an *überlick* of the eighteenth-century "mind" with regard to America, in perspective both of time and of place and of the Enlightenment "mind" in general.

Is it possible to make any generalization as to the Enlightenment "mind" with regard to America? Were there any ascertainable "common denominators" that ran through most of the thinking of most of the *philosophes*, or were they but "a family" of thinkers, an host of individual men who did their own thinking individually, each having little in common with the others?

It does appear that there were certain concepts and assumptions that were shared by most of the intellectual leaders of the century, no matter which the fields in which they worked. To suggest only a few, one might refer, first, to the faith of most of them in science: not only the factual and mathematical knowledge of the universe and of man that derived from science but, also, the enthusiastic faith that men could know and understand more, and that, knowing and understanding, they could influence or control the material universe and its laws for the physical, moral, and spiritual betterment of the human condition. This was their belief in progress, their faith that man *could* improve his condition, if he would, by the use of his mind.

In the second place, it seems to be clear that, for most of the *philosophes*, the great *leit-motif* in their thinking was the "human spirit". This was the essence of their metaphysic. Most of them, from the geographers to the political scientists to the nationalists to the philosophers, held this ideal before them. The bulk of the *philosophes'* writing constituted a great morality, even a religion. It was a sort of metaphisic derived from the notion of "nature" and of "nature's God". functioning in a system of "natural Law" through an ethic based upon scientific knowledge and interpreted by human reason.

So far as the idea of America was a part of this metaphysic this new world was unlerstood to be at once the scene of terrible aberrations from the moral principles of natural law among men and a stage upon which might enacted, at last, the victorious drama of liberty, of human rights, and of human felicity. In America, itself, there seems to have appeared a new idea of America, expressing a new concept of what America was and what its destiny, in terms of the "human spirit", might be.

Most of the quotations cited here are expressions of ideas that are generalizations derived from the observation of actual experience. They are, in a sense, rationalization of experience. It might be thought to be possible to write the history of these ideas, therefore, only in a context of an history of experience, or events. Yet, how much of demonstrable connection is there between events and Voltaire's *"esprit humain"* or Vattel's *"amour universel du genre humain?"* Our historian of ideas is confronted, again, with a sort of modern version of the age-old realist-nominalist dilemma: the ideas are real, certainly, but is their reality an existence in events only, or do they exist only in the minds of many different men a sort of existence that is independent of events, an existence which gives these ideas a life of their own, and, therefore, a history of their own?

Ahí está el problema. It is a problem in generalization. It is an invitation to the labors of many minds.

NATURALEZA DE LA IDEA Y DE SU HISTORIA

ABELARDO VILLEGAS

1. Una reflexión sobre la idea y su historia requiere, cuando menos, tres puntos a tratar, en relación a la idea misma:

   a) La naturaleza del objeto a la que ella se refiere;

   b) La naturaleza de ella misma y del método que la produce;

   c) Y las vinculaciones sociales e históricas y características personales de quien la concibe.

2. Como se sabe el sentido o significado de una idea radica en el señalamiento del objeto a que se refiere. Este objeto u objetos pueden ser de diferente índole: la idea puede referirse a ella misma o a otra idea. Un ejemplo del primer caso es obvio; uno del segundo lo tenemos cuando la idea se refiere a un triángulo o a un punto o a cualquiera otra entidad matemática o abstracta, tales como el absoluto, la nada, etcétera. Puede también referirse a relaciones entre ideas o entre ideas y cosas. Y, por último, también a algo que no es ella misma y que designaremos con el nombre de cosas, hechos o fenómenos.

La validez o verdad de una idea depende de la vinculación que hay entre ella y su objeto. Pero esta vinculación de verdad no es un problema exclusivamente metódico o teórico, sino que depende también de la naturaleza del objeto.

Hay objetos, como las cosas naturales, que son reiterativos, que se repiten como cosas o como desarrollos y procesos. Con ello queremos decir que la naturaleza tiene toda ella un carácter reiterativo o cíclico, aunque no absolutamente. Gracias a este carácter las ideas del conocimiento natural, si logran describir bien esos procesos, pueden alcanzar un alto grado de validez objetiva y de generalidad.

Este grado de validez y generalidad aumenta si las ideas se refieren a ideas generales o a relaciones entre ellas, como en el caso de la matemática y de la lógica a las cuales llamaremos, echando mano de una terminología muy conocida, ciencias *eidéticas*. Los fenómenos y cosas naturales son de una enorme variedad y constantemente descubren nuevos aspectos y zonas que rectifican el conocimiento de la naturaleza. Esta variedad y reiterabilidad natural permiten al mismo tiempo el progreso y acumulación de los conocimientos naturales. En tanto que el conocimiento eidético, aunque muy exacto, es bastante limitado.

Los fenómenos humanos se desarrollan en el marco de la naturaleza. Y no sólo eso, sino que, por así decirlo, la substancia de que están constituidos es natural. Podríamos decir que lo específicamente humano del hombre es su comportamiento. La estructura de su comportamiento, de su actividad, es la fuente del mundo humano que es, desde luego, diferente al del mundo de los otros seres vivos.

Entre otras características este comportamiento posee la de no ser reiterativo como los procesos de la naturaleza. Aquí cabe aclarar que ningún individuo humano natural, determinado o limitado en el espacio y en el tiempo, se repite; la espacialidad y la temporalidad es justo lo que determina la individualidad y singularidad de cosas y hombres. Lo que se repite en la naturaleza son los procesos y esta repetición, como dijimos, por su regularidad permite la generalización de las ciencias de la naturaleza.

Los procesos humanos pueden repetirse, pero no lo hacen necesaria y regularmente. Y este aspecto de irrepetibilidad es lo que da lugar a la ciencia histórica, como un conocimiento más bien de lo particular que de lo general. Sin embargo, no quiero decir que en la ciencia histórica sea imposible la generalización. Tomemos este enunciado: "las revoluciones triunfantes se dividen". Tal enunciado se refiere a lo que suele ocurrir en forma general, pero no pretende alcanzar el grado de exactitud que puede tener una ley natural.

La irrepetibilidad condiciona el que la ciencia histórica no tenga ante sí el fenómeno mismo que estudia, sino sólo su huella, su vestigio. Por eso el método histórico debe consistir principalmente en inferir los acontecimientos a partir de su huella. Por eso mismo la ciencia histórica no sólo es poco generalística, sino que el grado de exactitud de sus verdades es bastante menor que el que poseen las ciencias naturales y las ciencias eidéticas, que pueden "traer a la vista", prácticamente en forma voluntaria, los fenómenos que desean estudiar.

Pero si tal es el carácter de la historia, es a todas luces incorrecto tratar de extender su inexactitud al resto de los conocimientos, como quiere hacerlo alguna tendencia filosófica.

Uno de los objetivos centrales de la ciencia histórica consistiría precisamente en el registro del cambio o de la reiteración del comportamiento humano. En rigor éste es *su* objeto de estudio. Lo cual no tiene que llevarnos necesariamente a la conclusión de que lo humano es el cambio. Lo humano, valga nuevamente la paradoja, es todo el mundo humano, y el cambio supone factores cuya permanencia lo hacen posible. Mencionemos de pasada algunos de estos factores permanentes: uno de ellos es la naturaleza misma, otro es el comportamiento psíquico y otro más es la sociedad.

No se trata aquí de enumerar o jerarquizar esos factores, sólo en forma provisional sostenemos que la diferente estructuración de ellos es el cambio humano mismo.

Ahora bien, la ausencia de repeticiones regulares en la actividad humana, ya lo señalamos, determina el bajo grado de exactitud de la ciencia histórica; y aquí cabe otra aclaración, pues varios de los pensadores que han trabajado la historia de las ideas en América con frecuencia han partido del supuesto de que este grado de inexactitud se debe al sujeto que piensa y a sus determinaciones históricas. Esta suposición tropieza con el hecho de que estando todos los pensadores sometidos a las variantes históricas, los grados de exactiutd de los distintos conocimientos varían, desde la física y la matemática hasta la historia. Ello sólo puede explicarse a partir de los distintos tipos de objetos y no de las puras características de los sujetos.

3. Pasemos ahora a la idea como objeto de estudio y en especial como objeto de la historia.

Tenemos que pasar por alto aquí una posible disquisición sobre su substancia. Ya se la conciba como esencialmente diferente de la substancia natural, como un fenómeno natural más o como una simple palabra, vamos a tratar de determinar algunas peculiaridades de ella que no tienen relación con esta cuestión.

Las ideas tienen distinto grado de extensión o generalidad, y en virtud de esto y de sus peculiaridades comprensivas, unas se pueden derivar de otras, en los dos sentidos de la generalidad ideas particulares de generales o viceversa. Con ello queremos afirmar que es propio de la idea el poder ser estructurada en sistemas, en tanto que esta característica no se presenta en los fenómenos naturales. Y, así, cuando hacemos la historia de tal o cual región del conocimiento en vez de encontrarnos con ideas aisladas nos enfrentamos con paquetes de ideas o sistemas de ideas.

En los sistemas de ideas pueden distinguirse con facilidad algunas que son prácticamente determinantes de todas las demás y a las cuales bien podemos denominar *principios*. El carácter de estos principios varía según las diferentes regiones del conocimiento.

Vamos a incursionar un poco en esta dirección. Dijimos antes que el significado de una idea es la relación que tiene con un objeto. Ahora bien, a las ideas les ocurre un poco lo que a los fenómenos de la naturaleza, que sin ser cíclicas pueden ser traídas voluntariamente a la mirada empírica, cosa que, por ejemplo, no ocurre con un hecho histórico; no podemos traer a la mirada empírica los episodios de la Revolución Francesa, por ejemplo. Pero entonces tenemos casos como los siguientes: podemos traer a examen, tantas veces como queramos, el pensamiento de Sarmiento, sin embargo ocurre que los objetos a que se refiere ese pensamiento ya no están a la vista y sólo quedan vestigios de ellos. Uno de esos vestigios es el propio pensamiento de Sarmiento. La tiranía de Rosas ya no está a la vista y por eso es difícil determinar la veracidad de las ideas que Sarmiento emitió sobre ella, aunque éstas las podamos examinar todas las veces que queramos.

Así, los principios que rigieron la filosofía política liberal en América Latina tienen un carácter semejante al del ejemplo que acabamos de mencionar.

Pero también hay historias de otros tipos de ideas, el problema puede surgir de otro modo; una historia de las ideas científicas podrá determinar mejor la validez de los principios del pensamiento científico que como lo puede hacer una historia con los principios del pensamiento político.

En nuestra América se han cultivado bastante estos tipos de historia de las ideas, pero también cabe la posibilidad de hacer una historia del pensamiento en la vida cotidiana. Puede hacerse una historia del positivismo en México como capítulo de la historia de la filosofía en este país, y también se puede averiguar si la gente de la calle, de las ciudades y los campos, tenía ideas semejantes a la élite científica, o si las tenía derivadas de aquéllas u otras completamente diferentes.[1] Se pueden hacer ambos tipos de historia a la vez, pero es necesario reconocer que se trata de dos géneros diferentes, que requieren distinta metodología sin que se renuncie a encontrar sistemas, principios y validez del pensamiento popular o cotidiano. La distancia que va de éste al otro es la misma que hay entre el conocimiento popular y el científico.

4. Con esto ya estamos enunciando algunos problemas del método de la historia de las ideas. Ella puede tratarlos en forma aislada, pero una historia omnicomprensiva tiene que tratarlos todos y otros más a los que nos referiremos adelante.

De hecho la historia no puede soslayar el carácter sistemático de las ideas. Por ejemplo, si hacemos una historia del liberalismo en México, o en Argentina o en cualquier otra parte, nos encontraremos con ideas políticas liberales, ideas económicas liberales, o ideas pedagógicas liberales, con conceptos artísticos liberales, etcétera, todos estos géneros distintos de ideas son tributarios de principios comunes, y su historia no puede evadir tal carácter sistemático sin perder capacidad explicativa.

También tiene que referirse a la validez o verdad de una idea; su cumplimiento en los hechos puede determinarse por la historia de esos mismos hechos o por otra ciencia contemporánea, según de la idea de que se trate. La validez o verdad del sistema de Ptolomeo es determinada por la física y la astronomía contemporáneas. Pero sólo la histo-

---

[1] Cf. William D. Raat, "Leopoldo Zea y el Positivismo: una Revolución", en *Latinoamérica*. Anuario del Centro de Estudios Latinoamericanos, UNAM, núm. 2. México, 1969.

ria fáctica nos puede dar elementos para ponderar la afirmación de
Lorenzo de Zavala referente a la negatividad del régimen colonial para
constituir la nación mexicana.

Empero, en la historia de las ideas no sólo se trata de determinar
la validez de la idea sino también su *eficacia*, su poder de persuasión,
su capacidad para engendrar hechos. Algunos historicistas confunden
la validez con la eficacia, pero en rigor se trata de dos cosas distintas.
Una idea puede tener eficacia independientemente de su validez, e
incluso hay ideas que sólo tienen eficacia sin que presenten el problema de validez. Un ejemplo ilustre de esto último es la idea antifictió-
nica de Bolívar. La historia de las ideas pondría en claro sus antecedentes ideológicos, tendría que hacer un análisis minucioso de la misma
y un examen de sus consecuencias posteriores, pero para determinar
su grado de eficacia tendría que acudir a la historia fáctica para que
mostrara sus antecedentes en los hechos y para explicar por qué no se
puso en práctica y por qué, a pesar de eso, siguió teniendo poder de
convicción. Pero no tiene caso averiguar si es verdadera o falsa.

También dentro de este terreno de la eficacia se puede investigar
hasta qué punto las ideas de una élite científica o política penetran
en lo más de la población y determinan sus creencias y formas de
acción, o viceversa, etcétera.

Sin embargo el problema central de la historia de las ideas, que implica a los anteriores, es explicar el cambio de las mismas, pues, como
dijimos, el objeto de estudio de la historia es el cambio, la temporalidad. A este respecto una posición que tratara de explicar el cambio
de las ideas como consecuencia de los cambios históricos o sociales de
las sociedades que la sustentan, estaría apelando a un mecanisismo no
confirmado en la experiencia y además trasladaría el problema a otra
zona, la fáctica, de cuya explicación no se siente responsable. Las
nociones de sistematicidad, validez y eficacia de las ideas tienen mucho
que ver en la explicación del cambio.

Sin embargo consideramos, con la dialéctica, que para explicar el
cambio de las ideas, lo mismo que cualquiera otro, la noción de contradicción es indispensable. Sólo que este término debe entenderse en un
sentido lato. En rigor lógico sólo dos proposiciones que tengan el mismo
predicado y el mismo sujeto, pero que una afirme y la otra niegue y
una sea universal y otra particular, pueden ser llamadas contradictorias
(como: todos los A son B y algunos A no son B).

Ésta es la definición de contradicción de la lógica formal tradicional,
pero de la filosofía dialéctica se desprende otra definición que implica
pugna o lucha o antagonismo o incompatibilidad entre diferentes términos. Tal contradicción, en consecuencia, puede darse entre concepto,
entre proposiciones, o bien entre una proposición y su cumplimiento
en los hechos, o, en el nivel de la eficacia, entre una idea y la acción
que engendra, o, en el nivel fáctico, entre dos hechos, etcétera.

También quizá habría que desterrar la idea de que la contradicción es sólo entre dos términos. Tal bipolaridad no es necesaria, los términos contradictorios pueden ser múltiples formando un todo estructural contradictorio.[2] La agudeza de las contradicciones, en el caso de las ideas, que es el que ahora nos ocupa, determinaría la celeridad de los cambios, aunque esto no puede afirmarse de manera absoluta. Asimismo, podría explicar la calidad de los mismos.

Vamos a unos ejemplos: Leopoldo Zea en sus estudios sobre el positivismo en México y Latinoamérica encontró que las ideas comtianas sufrían una transformación al adoptarse en esta parte del mundo como consecuencia del gran impulso que había adquirido el liberalismo. Desde un punto de vista ideológico el positivismo de Comte, era una ideología de la restauración antiliberal, pero aquí apareció en distintas etapas al servicio de revoluciones liberales. O sea que el impacto y contradicción del liberalismo con la teoría positivista determinó la transformación de ésta y luego su posterior abandono y substitución por el evolucionismo. Es éste un caso de contradicción entre los fenómenos políticos y la teoría política.

Pero puede darse otro en que la contradicción sea en el puro nivel de las ideas, en que la contradicción entre dos concepciones del mundo origina una tercera; como el de la Ilustración hispano-mexicana que trató de conciliar la concepción católica del mundo con la idea de progreso y obtuvo como resultado un eclecticismo, de honda repercusión en los hechos históricos posteriores.

Pero hay otros aspectos de la misma cuestión, el ritmo de los cambios históricos es diferente aun en el seno de un solo país y de una misma época. Por ejemplo, es fácil notar en algunos países de la América Latina que en ciertos niveles presentan un agudo antagonismo como, por ejemplo, el que hay entre una minoría muy enriquecida y la pobreza de la mayoría, pero que este antagonismo va acompañado de un estancamiento de esta situación. Y ocurre que, mientras las estructuras económicas y sociales permanecen estáticas, hay en esos mismos países una extraordinaria movilidad política e intelectual. Es un fenómeno común en la América Latina que las élites intelectuales con frecuencia vayan mucho más aprisa que las élites políticas y económicas. Lo cual produce una serie de fenómenos que han sido ya estudiados por los historiadores de las ideas.

Esta diferencia de ritmos en el cambio en distintos niveles de un solo país o de una sola región no puede ser explicada por el puro método de encontrar contradicciones bipolares, sino que, como ya dijimos, la multiplicidad de términos contradictorios forma estructuras de contra-

[2] Cf. Louis Althusser, *La Revolución Teórica de Marx*. Siglo XXI Editores, México, 1967. Y también del mismo autor junto con Étienne Balibar: *Para leer el capital*. Siglo XXI Editores, México, 1969.

dicciones, de tal manera que es un problema para el historiador establecer las relaciones entre estas diferentes estructuras. Siguiendo una sugerencia de José Gaos los historiadores de las ideas podrían proponerse la formulación de categorías propias de esa historia, es decir, criterios generales por medio de los cuales se organizan y conectan los datos que proporciona la investigación. Pero es evidente que las categorías de la historia del pensamiento no son las mismas que las categorías de la historia fáctica porque sus estructuras son diferentes y que el estudio de las relaciones entre ellas es un problema todavía en pie para la ciencia histórica.

5. Pasemos por último a examinar la situación del sujeto de las ideas, es decir, del que las concibe y sus vinculaciones con la sociedad o con la circunstancia histórica en la cual se encuentra inserto. Como ya lo anotamos, tenemos que rechazar la idea de que las ideas son sólo explicables a partir de las características del sujeto que las concibe, creemos que todo lo anterior habrá mostrado que las ideas se van determinando por el objeto a que se refieren, por el método que las trata y por el sujeto que las concibe. Pero es evidente que, a pesar de ello, la idea no es un objeto opaco que tiene que ser explicado absolutamnte desde afuera, extrínsecamente; la idea, el proceso del pensamiento todo, es un proceso mediante el cual nos abrimos al mundo para conocerlo, metafóricamente podríamos decir que es nuestra ventana al mundo y no cosas opacas cuya explicación parte de la sociología, de la economía, o de la historia fáctica. La idea revierte sobre sus factores determinantes e informa acerca de ellos procurando formular su verdad o su razón acerca de ellos, adquiriendo incluso efectividad sobre ellos.

Por esa razón tenemos que rechazar la opinión de que el mundo de las ideas forme parte de una superestructura, determinada por una estructura más radical o anterior, que sea un simple epifenómeno de los fenómenos económicos. O, para decirlo más concisamente, que sea el resultado del manejo de los instrumentos de producción y de las relaciones de producción. La experiencia en el cultivo de la ciencia histórica nos muestra que esto no ocurre así. Rechazando la división entre estructuras y superestructuras Claude Lévy-Strauss ha mostrado en sus estudios sobre la cultura de los hombres primitivos que la llamada superestructura es tan determinante como la estructura misma, así por ejemplo, en algunos tipos de sociedades las relaciones familiares, y la posición que en virtud de ellas tienen sus integrantes, determina sus formas de trabajo y producción, [3] esto es, que las relaciones de producción se dan en el marco de las relaciones sociales, y sin estas últimas no serían posibles las primeras. No sería difícil aplicar este razonamiento ya no a las sociedades primitivas, sino a los países latinoame-

[3] Cf. C. Lévi-Strauss, *El pensamiento salvaje*. Fondo de Cultura Económica, México, 1962.

ricanos en donde, según las investigaciones de la CEPAL, la economía sigue siendo familiar aun en nuestras grandes ciudades aparentemente modernas. [4]

Y lo que se dice de las relaciones sociales puede decirse también del mundo de las ideas. La historia latinoamericana del siglo xix está llena de ejemplos de la influencia ideológica en las actividades económicas y sociales. A esta influencia le llamamos antes la eficacia de las ideas. Menciono sólo un ejemplo al respecto, muchos de nuestros historiadores han hecho hincapié en el utopismo de nuestros ideólogos, y han mostrado cómo ese utopismo ha operado sobre los acontecimientos obteniendo resultados generalmente diferentes de los que se proponía. En la segunda mitad del siglo xix encontramos casos como el de Alberdi que propuso la apertura irrestricta de América Latina ante el capital moderno con el fin de que nuestra América se modernizara y se industrializara. Esta ideología tuvo eficacia aunque los resultados no fueron los que la misma preveía.

Entonces, si rechazamos el economicismo, por la misma razón tenemos que hacerlo con el sociologismo, que trata de buscar la determinación de las ideas en la pura estructura de las relaciones sociales. Es cierto que todos los individuos están determinados por la estructura de la sociedad en que viven, pero no sólo por ella, ya mencionamos aquí las determinantes naturales, y tenemos que mencionar otras más como las determinantes culturales y las propiamente individuales. Lo que piensa un individuo también es determinado por lo que pensaron otros, aparte de las condiciones sociales o económicas en que éste se encuentra. Si a todas estas determinantes les llamamos *sociedad*, entonces el problema es sólo de nombre. Pero lo que es necesario aclarar también es que, como lo ha advertido muy bien el filósofo checo Karel Kosik, [5] los individuos, si bien determinados por su circunstancia no lo son absolutamente en tanto que ellos mismos también son determinantes, esto es en tanto que ellos forman parte de la circunstancia determinante. De este modo es lícito tratar de precisar las determinantes sociales e históricas de la obra y el pensamiento de Simón Bolívar, pero también lo es el precisar las determinantes que él mismo creó; y este mismo proceso puede efectuarse no sólo con los individuos históricos sino incluso con fenómenos más amplios que los individuales, tales como las consecuencias y efectos de una revolución.

Esta misma objeción puede hacérsele a cierto tipo de historicismo que apela a la circunstancia para explicar las ideas. Estas corrientes agravan todavía el problema porque suelen no precisar los perfiles de la circunstancia, o no definirlas simplemente. En todo caso, cuando se

---

[4] Cepal, *El desarrollo social de América Latina en la postguerra*. Solar Hachette, Buenos Aires, 1963.

[5] Karel Kosik, *Dialéctica de lo concreto*. Editorial Grijalbo, México, 1967.

trata de señalar alguna determinante de un cuerpo de ideas, es necesario precisarla con rigor. Si consideramos que tal o cual conjunto de ideas tiene una vinculación con tal o cual fenómeno social, se requiere precisar el fenómeno que la produce y el tipo de vinculación que hay entre ambos. Sólo así podremos averiguar en concreto si una idea tiene una causa social, económica, natural o individual, o todas a la vez. Tales son las sugerencias que, en forma sintética, tenemos que hacerle al trabajo del historiador de las ideas.

IDEAS AND HISTORY IN MEXICO: AN ESSAY ON METHODOLOGY

WILLIAM D. RAAT

In approaching the study of the relationship of ideas to history the inquiring student can easily be lost in a jungle of ambiguity not always of his own making. Well armed with Bernheim's canons as derived from the *Lehrbuch*, our adventurer eagerly seeks his prey. But unfortunately the path is difficult to follow having been obscured by an overgrowth of confused and confusing terminology. And if this welter of "World Spirits", "Ideal Forms", "Unit-Ideas", and "Mexican Minds" does not send our trained scholar back into the refuge of empirical and institutional studies; and again, if our man does take the time to observe his fellow hunters, he will notice that the object of his quest tends to blur and transform before his very eyes with no two hunters seeking the same end.

The problem, not always noticed by the participants in the chase, is primarily that of a methodological dilemma. Simply stated, this dilemma derives from a distinction between an internal and an external approach to ideas in historical study. Internal analysis usually studies ideas apart from questions of social origin. External analysis, on the other hand, traces the relationship of ideas, not to each other, but to events. The dilemma is one of resolving the often different conclusions which are obtained from two distinctive methods. The approaches, based upon different philosophical and methodological assumptions, produce if not conflicting at least very dissimilar results.

This distinction between internal and external analysis, while not often noted by Mexican writers, is easily distinguishable in the vocabulary of many North Americans. Arthur Lovejoy, R. W. B. Lewis, and Roy H. Pearce, who are all committed to an internal approach to ideas, speak of their task as that of the "history of ideas". In contradistinction to these scholars, historians like James Harvey Robinson, Crane Brinton, and Franklin L. Baumer refer to their own external analyses as that of "intellectual history". [1] And even if the terminology of the researcher does not indicate this difference, as it does not with

---

[1] Rush Welter surveys a list of writers who make the distinction between internal and external history of ideas in his "The History of Ideas in America: An essay in Redefinition", *The Journal of American History*, LI (March 1965), pp. 599-614.

John Higham for example, at least most North American historians of ideas are aware of the distinction. [2] In either case, most of these writers would not consider their activities as being synonymous with that known as the philosophy of history. [3]

The foregoing has been stated as part of the following major contention of this essay. These differences between the history of ideas, intellectual history, and the philosophy of history are not only important as problems in semantics. Rather, these differing activities reflect moods, intellectual attitudes, and philosophical traditions which distinguish North American from Mexican historiography of ideas. Thus before future trends for research into the relationship of ideas to history can be suggested, it will be necessary to understand the present status and nature of our inquiry and its current methodological problems. For this reason I have chosen to examine these approaches and their expressions in Mexican and non-Mexican writing in some detail.

Although there have been some attempts to resolve the dilemma of internal history of ideas versus external intellectual history, and to further prevent one discipline from splitting into two, [4] a synthesis of both is a difficult task since at bottom each approach is based upon divergent philosophical views. The internal approach to ideas assumes that the human mind has a creative vitality which is not dependent upon external circumstances; that is, ideas have a life of their own which transcend ordinary experience. Thus ideas create and/or reflect

---

[2] John Higham uses the term "intellectual history" in a general sense but does refer to the "...internal or the external view of intellectual history". See his essay "Intellectual History and Its Neighbors", *Journal of the History of Ideas*, xv (June 1954), pp. 339-347. Similarly, the Latin Americanist Harold Eugene Davis uses the term "the history of ideas" in an inclusive way to mean history of ideas, thought, and philosophy. Yet Davis does distinguish those writers who view ideas as autonomous from those, like Víctor Alba or Jesús Silva Herzog, who see ideas as expressions of cultural conditions and social situations. Refer to Davis' essay, "The History of Ideas in Latin America", *Latin American Research Review*, iii (Fall 1968), pp. 23-44.

[3] Some thinkers like Maurice Mandelbaum go further to distinguish the history of ideas and intellectual history from the history of philosophy. For Mandelbaum the formal thinking of the philosopher only represents one particular strand within the intellectual history of any period and he further suggests that philosophy has its own internal history in which specific ideas, or unit-ideas in Lovejoy's sense, are only one part. All of this is quite unlike the synthetic and speculative activity of the philosopher of history. See Mandelbaum, "The History of Ideas, Intellectual History, and the History of Philosophy", *The Historiography of the History of Philosophy* ("*History and Theory*: Studies in the Philosophy of History", Beiheft 5; The Hague, 1965), pp. 33-66.

[4] Both Rush Welter and John Greene argue, although in different ways, for an inclusive approach which would synthesize internal and external analysis. See both Welter, "The History of Ideas in América", pp. 599-614 and Greene, "Objectives and Methods in Intellectual History", *The Mississippi Valley Historical Review*, xliv (June 1957), pp. 58-74.

a separate world of values and aesthetics. This "idealist" view is quite different from the "functionalism" of the historian of external intellectual history. To the latter, mind is not characterized so much by vitality as by utility and ideas are important to the extent that they act as agents for adaptation and survival in the concrete realm of a socio-biological world.[5] In effect, it would appear that the two approaches reflect the differences between the philosophical traditions of Germanic Idealism on the one hand, and British Empiricism, Utilitarianism, and "positivism"[6] on the other.

While both internal and external analysis when pursued in isolation from one another lead to difficulties, the former lends itself to a special criticism. If ideas have no reference to the material conditions of human experience, then they become intangibles not subject to the ordinary canons of historical evidence. Historical inquiry can become a subjective process which is no longer distinguishable from philosophy, literature, arts, and letters. To say this is to only assert that which is not surprising, i.e., history, especially intellectual history, is a branch of the humanities.

Now it is certainly true that a philosopher like Arthur Lovejoy has contributed greatly to our understanding of the underlying unities of thought, and that a literary critic like Henry Nash Smith has aided in our knowledge of the role of myth and symbols in history.[7] Yet philosophy is only one aspect of human thought, and a formal one at that, and when intellectual history becomes a tool of literary criticism the tendency is one of illustrating aesthetic judgments rather than that of understanding human thought in an historical context. In addition, if the subjective and imaginative artist is given full rein his art becomes that of polemics.

Another difficulty with the internal approach lies with its intellectualistic bias. A philosophical and/or literary analysis often narrows the quest to that of the biography of an idea with the materials of history being restricted to autobiographies of literary giants or important philosophers and thinkers. When ideas are endowed with a special potency intellectual history is narrowed to become the history of intellectuals. Hegelians will be tempted to write an elitist history in which the "great man" or Hero will be the center of focus as the best or

[5] John Higham, "Intellectual History and Its Neighbors", p. 341.

[6] Although the term "positivism" has misleading connotations it is here used to refer not to any systematic philosophy in particular but to scientific thinking in general. In philosophy the term is used to distinguish scientific inquiries from idealist traditions. The positivist historian would argue for the validity of historical generalizations and the inductive nature of causal explanations. See William H. Dray, *Philosophy of History*. Englewood Cliffs, New Jersey, 1964, pp. 1-58.

[7] See Arthur O. Lovejoy, *The Great Chain of Being: A Study of the History of an Idea*. Boston, 1936 and Henry Nash Smith, *Virgin Land: The American West as Symbol and Myth*. New York, 1950.

most adequate expression of the (World) Spirit of the Age. What started as a humble pursuit to understand historical thought becomes a speculative activity in which a higher reality is asserted which is not subject to any objective analysis of the role of ideas in history. History now becomes metahistory and the historian of ideas has become a grand theorist and a philosopher of history. [8]

Now it should be understood that philosophy of history is a credible and valiant activity. [9] But that is not the point. My concern is one of encouraging the historian to distinguish between the history of ideas and the idea of history. And, it should be noted, that distinction is not one of history writ small in contrast to universal history.

The task of universal history is one of discovering or interpreting general trends, directions, and patterns in world history. To this extent the activity of a A. J. Toynbee, for example, only differs in scope from that which the ordinary historian does. It is only when Toynbee, or Hegel, or any other grand theorist for that matter, attempts to answer larger questions that he leaps from history to philosophy (and maybe even theology). Thus when Toynbee asserts a mechanism like "challenge-and-response", or when Hegel speaks of the "dialectic", they are postulating not hypotheses to be verified but models which are intended to show how historical change *in general* takes place. The transcendence from ordinary history becomes even more obvious when these thinkers speculate about the meaning of human history. Toynbee thus concludes his A *Study of History* by suggesting that human history is purposive in that the history of civilizations, in spite of the cyclical growth patterns of organic birth and death, has been moving in a progressively linear direction towards transcendence from materiality to spirituality. This claim, while possibly true, is certainly beyond the capacities of historical demonstration. [10]

Having said all this it is time to determine what historians and scholars have said about the role of ideas in Mexico's history and to

[8] P. P. Wiener, in describing six types of history of ideas, mentions four which appear to be quite similar and would fit my description of the relationship of the history of ideas to the philosophy of history. These four are the biographical, the philological, the metaphysical and theological, and subsumption of ideas under patterns (e.g. Hegel's dialectic). See Wiener, "Some Problems and Methods in the History of Ideas", *Journal of the History of Ideas*, xxii (Oct.-Dec. 1961), pp. 538-546.

[9] By "philosophy of history" I mean what many philosophers call "speculative philosophy of history" in contrast to "critical philosophy of history". This is primarily a metaphysical, not a epistemological, actitvity in that the task is one of answering the question of what is ultimate historical reality instead of how does the historian know reality. For a more detailed treatment of this topic refer to W. H. Walsh, *Philosophy of History*. New York, 1960, pp. 13-28.

[10] See Dray, *Philosophy of History*, pp. 60-97. For a critique of Toynbee in particular see Charles Frankel, *The Case for Modern Man*. Boston, 1959, pp. 164-195.

establish, where possible, the methodological and philosophical concerns of these writers. To do this I have chosen to treat primarily the
traditions as they exist in Mexican, not non-Mexican circles.

Intellectual history writing in Mexico has been, with few exceptions,
a mid-twentieth century development. Late nineteenth century writers
contributed more to the world of polemics and apologetics than they
did to history proper. A few writers, of course, like Justo Sierra or
Agustín Aragón do not fit this description. [11] In the early twentieth
century the development of the history of ideas was delayed by the
chaos of revolution and the urgencies of reform. Only Samuel Ramos,
writing in the 1930's, was an important exception to this generalization. [12] Since 1940, however, at least two generations of Mexican
historians have been extremely prolific in writing and publishing works
in the area of the history of ideas. Primarily this has been due to
individuals like José Gaos, Edmundo O'Gorman, Leopoldo Zea and
other members of the Faculty of Philosophy and Letters of the University of Mexico. [13]

Many authors, Mexican and non-Mexican, have examined the intellectual antecedents of both contemporary Mexican historiography in
general, and of the history of ideas in particular. Although these antecedents are varied in number, a similar quality of mood and attitude is
shared by all of them. In effect the current situation is this: Many of
Mexico's historians, and especially those who have been trained in the
Gaos-Zea school of the history of ideas, are still waging a continuing
spiritual revolt against positivism.

This "revolt", at least in philosophical terms, has been one of
moving away from the external to the internal, from the objective
to the subjective, from the universal to the particular, from scientific
history to history as romantic art or philosophy. Rejecting scientism,
an historian like José Gaos speaks in humanistic terms about history
while Leopoldo Zea argues for the interdependence of history and
philosophy. And, of course, O'Gorman in typical cavalier fashion
dismisses scientific history and historians with informative epithets
like "blind", "brutal", and "foolish". [14]

[11] The contemporary historian especially owes a debt to Aragón for his outline
of Comtean Positivism in Díaz's Mexico. See his study entitled *Essai sur l'histoire
du positivisme au Mexique*. Mexico and Paris, 1898.

[12] Ramos, *El perfil del hombre y la cultura en México*. México, 1934. See also
his later work *Historia de la filosofía en México*. México, 1943.

[13] Luis Villoro, "Historia de las ideas", *Historia Mexicana*, xv (October 1965-
March 1966), p. 163.

[14] See both José Gaos, "O'Gorman y la idea del descubrimiento de América",
Historia Mexicana, i (January-March 1952), p. 488 and Leopoldo Zea, *El positivismo en México*. México, 1943, p. 25. O'Gorman's comments about scientific
history were quoted from *Crisis y porvenir de la ciencia histórica* by Merrill Rippy
in his article "Theory of History: Twelve Mexicans", *The Americas*, xvii (January
1961), p. 227.

As has been indicated, the ideological sources of Mexico's contemporary historical thinking are many. They include, among others, Hegel's dialectic, Dilthey's neo-Kantian views, Croce's presentism, Bergson's vitalism, Mannheim's relativism, the humanism of Ramos, Ortega's perspectivism, and Heidegger's existentialism. All have influenced the recent attempt by Mexican writers to construct a national ethos and discover true Mexicanism through an awareness of "lo mexicano". [15]

The philosophical tradition which Mexico's historians of ideas have inherited is primarily that of Germanic Idealism. It started with Hegel and Kant, found expression in the writings of Wilhelm Dilthey, and has emerged in more recent times with the theoretical works of the historian Friedrich Meinecke. Of this general idealist tradition, the philosophy of history is only one concern. Influenced by Dilthey, idealist philosophers of history have developed their own thinking along separate lines in several countries outside Germany. Some of these spokesmen would include Benedetto Croce in Italy, José Ortega y Gasset in Spain, R. G. Collingwood in England, and of course, Leopoldo Zea in Mexico. If one word could possibly define this idealist type of philosophy of history it would be "historicism".

The importance of idealism and historicism for the history of ideas in Mexico has been recognized by the Mexican practitioners in the field. Thus Leopoldo Zea can readily assert in a recent article that "Romanticism in the nineteenth century and historicism of our times have offered the adequate methods for reverting to the past in order to delineate a basic, unique spirit". [16] The next issue to logically explore is this: since historicism is the source of the Mexican historian's methodology in the history of ideas, what are the philosophical assumptions of historicism and how do they affect the methodology?

The basic thesis of historicism seems to be that the subject matter of history is human life in all of its multiplicity. These "facts" of history are peculiar ones involving concrete, unrepeatable events and personalities. Because the subject matter of history is unique, any intellectual pursuit which only describes the common properties of historical entities will be inadequate since it will not lead to understanding of specific differences, i.e., the very "stuff" of history. Thus the rational and abstract systems of the philosopher, as well as the empirical explanations of the scientist, are to be rejected. In this respect history is more akin to literature than science in that the primary aim of a

[15] Some of these influences are noted in John L. Phelan's survey of Mexican writers entitled "México y lo mexicano", *Hispanic American Historical Review*, XXXVI (August 1956), pp. 309-318. See also Martin S. Stabb, *In Quest of Identity*. Chapel Hill, 1967, pp. 182-217.

[16] Leopoldo Zea, "Philosophy and Thought in Latin America". *Latin American Research Review*, III (Spring 1968), p. 12.

historical narrative is to reconstruct events in terms of their individuality, not to formulate general laws. [17]

If then, history cannot be approached through a rational or empirical system, what method will suffice? It is here that the historicist affirms the principle of empathy. The "facts" of the past are only grasped in the mind of the present. The historian must recreate the past by feeling himself in the past. What the historian calls historical evidence is nothing other than the physical remains of past memory, and historical knowledge is not gained through direct experience but rather in the historian's thinking about past thought. This is why Collingwood speaks of "re-enacting past thinking in the thought of the present" or why Croce argues that "every true history is contemporary history". [18] In the final analysis historicism merges with Idealism by asserting that reality is spiritual with the ultimate constituents of the historical world consisting in human motives, purposes, and thoughts, rather than in social or institutional factors.

Now it is obvious that any study of ideas in history which is derived from and based upon the assumptions of historicism will be what I have referred to as internal history of ideas rather than external intellectual history. In addition, it would appear that there are very few individual Mexican historians who are working in the field of intellectual history proper. The genre of history of ideas has been appropriated primarily by philosophers. A few references to Mexican historical literarure should suffice to demonstrate this statement.

Illustrative of this is a volume which has been recently translated into English by A. Robert Capronigri of the University of Notre Dame and which first appeared in 1963 under the title of *Estudios de historia de la filosofía en México*. Papers presented by historians and philosophers at the Thirteenth International Congress of Philosophy in Mexico City form the content of this volume. Now the historian who reaches for this book in hopes of finding an "objective" intellectual history will be disappointed. For example, with Rafael Moreno's essay on New Spain the reader is not presented with the historical impact of the Enlightenment or Jesuitic Humanism upon eighteenth-century Mexican thought, but rather with an internal study of the writings of Sor Juana Inés de la Cruz and Don Carlos de Sigüenza y Góngora. Edmundo O'Gorman's study on American begins as a biograpy of the idea of the "New World" and ends as a religious testimony to the truthfulness of the gospel of the universalization of Western culture. And Leopoldo Zea, while entertaining the problem of the relationship of positivist ideology to the middle class, fails to demonstrate that relation-

[17] For both a definition and a critique of historicism refer to Hans Meyerhoff's anthology, *The Philosophy of History in Our Time*. New York 1959.

[18] See both Collingwood, *The Idea of History*. New York, 1956, pp. 282-314 and Meyerhoff, pp. 43-57.

ship. The "nativist" point of view of the writers leaves the reader feeling that the book is not really a history of philosophy, but rather a collective philosophy of history. [19]

Mention has been made about the tendency of internal history to become a narrow biography about the ideas of important individuals. Harold Davis, in writing about the literature of the history of ideas in Latin America, has noted that "Much of it treats the ideas of individuals; [which], while useful in filling out the picture ... lacks any general concept, either of national intellectual history or of that of Latin America as a whole ". [20] This is also the case when Mexican literature is surveyed. Of the one hundred and fifty works cited by Luis Villoro in a recent bibliographical essay on the history of ideas, [21] nearly forty per cent could be classified as biographies of men and/or ideas. Another forty per cent could be considered either history of philosophy or philosophy of history. The conclusion is evident. Very few Mexican writers employ an external analysis and produce histories which could properly be called intellectual.

In this context the writings of Leopoldo Zea should be briefly considered since the limitations of the internal approach to the history of ideas are well exemplified in Zea's classical two volumes on Positivism in nineteenth century México. [22] Like Villoro and O'Gorman, Zea's histories are goal-oriented since true history in the historicist sense must be contemporary history. Politically this end is one of developing a unitary society upon the foundations of a conscious Mexicanism. In philosophy the concern is that of deriving from New World conditions a universal and ethical system of thought. Unwilling to detach history from present or future concerns, viewing his role as that of a philosopher-savior who will direct Mexico's destinies toward a genuine historical consciousness in the Hegelian sense, Zea's subjective histories invite honest criticism. [23]

Two examples should suffice at this point to show how Zea's subjectivity and philosophical propensities lead him into historical

[19] The translated version is called *Major Trends in Mexican Philosophy*. Notre Dame and London, 1966. See also my review of this volume in *The Western Humanities Review*, xxi (Spring 1967), pp. 173-175.

[20] Davis, "The History of Ideas in Latin America", p. 27.

[21] Villoro, "Historia de las ideas", pp. 167-195.

[22] Zea, *El positivismo en México*. México, 1943 and *Apogeo y decadencia del positivismo en México*. México, 1944. For a more inclusive list of Zea's works along with a critique of his methodology see my article "Leopoldo Zea and Mexican Positivism: A Reappraisal", *Hispanic American Historical Review*, xlviii (February 1968), pp. 1-18.

[23] To paraphrase Villoro: Mexico's history is purposive. Ideas and philosophies like historicism, existentialism, and humanism are manifestations of a single purpose, more or less conscious, in the development of Mexico's history. The role of the historian of ideas is that of making this purpose conscious. See Villoro, "Historia de las ideas", p. 163.

distortions. Zea argues, like Hegel, that México, and America for that matter, has not had a true history since México and Mexicans have not negated the past *dielctically* through assimilation but have only rejected the past *logically*. In Zea's words, "As long as such negation or such assimiliation is not carried out, American will continue being a continent without history, a dependency of European history". [24]

Unfortunately, as Charles Hale has observed, Zea's concept of nineteenth century Mexican thought as an effort at mental emancipation is both inadequate and misleading. It is an interpretation based for the most part upon the rhetoric of liberal thinkers and as such it ignores conflicting evidence found in the personal correspondence and parliamentary debates of the era. For example, it can now be demonstrated that José María Luis Mora, one of Zea's mental emancipators, did not reject his Spanish heritage at all. On the contrary, Mora often sought intellectual inspiration from the reformers of late eighteenth and early nineteenth century Spain. [25]

The concept of mental emancipation is also misleading in the context of the Porfiriato. My own research indicates that Comtean Positivism, one form of logical rejection and imitation for Zea, was not as widespread or as important for Mexico's late mineteenth century history as Zea would have us believe. Again Zea's argument or brief for Positivism was based mostly upon the rhetoric of liberals, clerics, and intelectuals. These sources weare highly polemical and tended to exaggerate the actual diffusion of Positivism in México. [26]

The tendency for intellectual history to become the history of intellectuals has been noted before in this paper. Like many writers, Zea's history of ideas was in reality a history of the ideas of a few academics and intellectuals. Mexico's intellectual history was the history of a few elites which did not even include a large section of the reading public. Philosophical assumptions and logical propositions were emphasized while emotional attitudes and evocative symbols were ignored. The thinking of a very few individuals on the staff of *La Libertad* or the científicos within the ranks of government became, for Zea, representative of the age. The somewhat confused and inarticulate war against Positivism by the Reyistas, the army, the workers, and the Church was ignored in Zea's account. [27]

[24] Zea, *The Latin-American Mind*. Norman, 1963, p. 4.

[25] Charles A. Hale, "Colonial Values and Contemporary Latin America: The History of Ideas" (Unpublished essay first delivered to the Conference on Latin American History at the American Historical Association meeting in Toronto, December 1967), pp. 13-15. See also Hale, *Mexican Liberalism in the Age of Mora, 1821-1853*. New Haven and London, 1968.

[26] William D. Raat, "Positivism in Díaz Mexico" (Unpublished dissertation, University of Utah, 1967).

[27] *Ibid.*, pp. 226-254.

The intent is not to belittle Zea's works. Rather, and this distinction is primarily for the benefit of my North American audience, it is that since Zea's studies are based upon the idea of the historicity of philosophy it is not always easy to determine whether he is writing history of philosophy. For Zea, the importance of his volumes on Positivism is found in their relationship to a larger context and concern, that of the philosophy of the history of the New World. Zea's synthesis has been described in some detail elsewhere.[28] Here it should suffice to point out the key elements of pattern, mechanism, and purpose in his philosophy of history.

For Zea, Mexico's history from the conquest to the Revolution of 1910 was "unauthentic" in that México was indiscriminately imitating European culture writ large. This trend was first changed with the Revolution which ushered in the beginnings of a conscious Mexicanization of thought and society. The mechanism behind this process of history has been a kind of Ortegian dialectic in which "Utopian views" were in constant conflict. Thus in the colonial period the native and retrogressive Oriental population collided with the progressive forces of Spain resulting in an "immoral union". The logical dialectic of the nineteenth century was one of romantics, liberals, and positivists in opposition to the scholasticism and conservatism of an earlier era. In spite of the dialectics a genuine triad or synthesis did not result and the Mexican remained a European colonist.

Only in 1910 did the Mexican first begin to have a genuine history and assimilate his past. The universal was assimilated and applied to the Mexican circumstances. Now the Mexican as an American can universalize from his particular Mexican situation to develop a New World philosophy which can be shared with all humanity. American philosophy will save Occidental culture from the spiritual crisis of our times and turn the tide of dehumanization.

This, then, is Zea's grand scheme and hope for the future. It has been argued that philosophy of history is poor philosophy and bad history. All I can claim is that in the final analysis Zea's speculation about history is beyond the realm of ordinary historical analysis. It is metahistory, not intellectual history.

It is a bit inexplicable that North American historians, with some obvious exceptions like Irving Leonard's *Baroque Times in Old México* or Charles Hale's *Mexican Liberalism in the Age of Mora*, have not been as prolific as their Mexican counterparts, and have often based their own research and writing upon the assumptions of their Mexican colleagues. Several scholars have written on Latin American positivism in Zea's terms. Two examples would be Karl

[28] See both Patrick Romanell, *Making of the Mexican Mind*. Notre Dame, 1967, pp. 166-176 and Harold Davis, "The History of Ideas in Latin America", pp. 32-36.

M. Schmitt's essay entitled "The Mexican Positivists and the Church State Question" and Patrick Romanell's description of positivism in his book, *Making of the Mexican Mind*.[29] This is even more surprising when one remembers that the historicist tradition has never been strong in the universities of the United States.

The subjective view of historical knowledge has never been as popular in the United States as it has in Latin America. A belief in the objective nature of historical reality has been the primary theory of several generations of United States' historians since the turn of the last century. The neo-Kantian thought of Dilthey is still missing from most discussions on historical methodology with that man's major works not being available in English as late as 1960. Only in the 1930's did relativism become attractive with Carl Becker's literary histories and Charles Beard's flirtations with Croce. Yet, even then most historians would have agreed with Arthur Lovejoy and other traditionalists that historical understanding requires transcending the biases of the present. This continuity of objectivity is noted by John Higham in an introduction to a study of history-writing in the United States when he says: "No one, including the 'literary' historians, rejected the ideal of objectivity in the ordinary sense of unbiased truth; no one gave up the effort to attain it; and no one thought it wholly unapproachable".[30] Even if the quest itself were subjective, relative, partial, and limited, the object of the quest remained real and external. The task of the historian was not to bring certainty, but to approximate objectivity.

In the special area of history of ideas, where the historian often argued for the autonomy of thought, the objective theory of historical knowledge was not only not rejected, but, in fact, openly defended. Arthur Lovejoy, a pioneer in developing internal analysis and in writing the history of an idea (or as he preferred, unit-ideas), argued against the neo-idealism of Croce and the relativism of Mannheim. The idealist doctrine of the "internality of all relations" was for him, a pluralist, incompatible with the correspondence theory of truth. To confuse a present idea with the past events to which it refers violated the basic canons of temporalism. And the relativism or relationalism of the sociologists was absurd, since even Karl Mannheim did not really believe "that the proposition that George Washington was a great landed proprietor is true for a Virginia Episcopalian but false for a Chicago Baptist".[31] This objective tradition

---

[29] Schmitt, *Church and State*, VIII (Spring 1966), 200-213 and Romanell, pp. 42-66.

[30] John Higham, et. al., *History: the Development of Historical Studies in the United States*. Englewood Cliffs, New Jersey, 1965, p. 90.

[31] See Maurice Mandelbaum, "Arthur O. Lovejoy and the Theory of Historiography", *Journal of the History of Ideas*, IX (October 1948), pp. 412-423. The

has enabled the historian of ideas in the United States to avoid the
pitfalls of subjectivity which often accompany the internal approach.

Having made this brief survey the present need becomes obvious.
There has been very little intellectual history written on México
either by Mexicans or non-Mexicans. The available studies in the
history of Mexican philosophy, art, and literature should be complemented with new studies that will seek to demonstrate the external
relationship between ideas and society. In fact, the need is even
greater than this. The historian of the near future should be
encouraged to combine the skills and techniques of the philosopher
with the understanding and methods of the empirical historian, in
other words, a synthesis of internal and external history of ideas. And
fortunately the models are available, one being the work of Elie
Halevy.

Why does Halevy epitomize the ideal of the intellectual historian?
Because he attempted with success to balance the results of internal
analysis with external analysis. In his definitive work on the development of Benthamite utilitarianism in England entitled *The Growth
of Philosophic Radicalism,* Halevy began as a philosopher in analyzing
the basic tenets of utilitarianism. By so doing he was able to
demonstrate how a dichotomy in the system led to inconsistent activity
on the part of many utilitarians. Yet even though he made clear
the analytical structure of the doctrine, he never detached ideas from
their historical context. Not only did he assert an influence for
utilitarianism, but he ended his study by outlining the channels
through which utilitarianism permeated English society. These means
of intellectual diffusion included the universities, adult education
centers, the press, Parliament, and Bentham's own correspondence.
Needless to say the entire study was based upon extensive primary
and secondary documentation with Halevy being the first of scholars
to ever read and digest the Bentham manuscripts. [32]

This kind of task and achievement still awaits the historian of
Mexican ideas and culture. The idealist tradition of historicism has
been an important corrective to some of the naive assumptions of
scientific history. Historical explanation it not analogous to that
of the sciences. Concepts of causation do involve value considerations.
The task is both subjective and limited. This the idealists have taught
us in their revolt against positivism. Now it is time to seek a new
historical understanding which will strive for the impossible by seeking
the past while using the resources of the present, and which will

quote was taken from Lovejoy's essay, "Reflections on the History of Ideas",
Journal of the History of Ideas, i (January 1940), p. 18.

[32] Élie Halévy, *The Growth of Philosophic Radicalism.* Boston, 1960. See also
the review article by Charles C. Gillespie, "The Work of Élie Halévy: A Critical
Appreciation", *The Journal of Modern History,* xxii (September 1950), pp. 232-249.

be responsive to our own age while remaining faithful to the integrity of an age gone by. Perhaps it will be the disinterested quest which will finally enable México and humanity to know itself.

COMENTARIO

ANDRÉS LIRA GONZÁLEZ

En la mesa redonda sobre historia de las ideas, que tuvo lugar el día 6 de noviembre, se presentaron cuatro ponencias. De éstas sólo tres llegaron con anticipación a mis manos, de tal suerte que fueron las únicas que pude apreciar con detenimiento para elaborar este comentario. Ellas son: la ponencia del doctor Max Savelle, "The Enlightenment and the Idea of America"; la del profesor Abelardo Villegas, "Naturaleza de la idea y su historia" y la del doctor William D. Raat, "Ideas and History in Mexico: An Essay on Methodology".

Los tres trabajos tienen un carácter muy diverso, pero es posible que su apreciación nos indique puntos de coincidencia en cuanto a la problemática que plantean, a fin de poder extraer un contenido común en cierto aspecto: cuál es el problema para historiar las ideas, si se toma en cuenta el medio social en que se dan. ¿Será posible historiarlas independientemente de los hechos contemporáneos a ellas? ¿De ser posible, se deberá hacer siempre?

La ponencia del doctor Savelle es la que presenta mayores rasgos de particularidad, pues constituye el desarrollo de un tema concreto dentro de la historia de las ideas: la Ilustración y la idea de América. Pero el tema en sí es embrión de reflexiones generales: dentro del hecho histórico que es asunto del tema —la idea de América en los "filósofos de la Ilustración"— caben un sinnúmero de cuestiones parciales, que bien vistas, son problemas que se plantean al pensamiento "universalista e internacional" del xviii. Problemas que Savelle ha presentado siguiendo autores europeos y americanos que se ocuparon del Nuevo Mundo con distintos puntos de vista (histórico, político, económico, cultural y religioso).

En el último punto concluyente, Savelle enuncia una cuestión que será el tema central de las otras ponencias. Ante la variedad de ideas que ha mostrado en su monografía, se pregunta si éstas cobran realidad de los hechos y del mundo de la facticidad que las rodea; o, si bien es posible que las ideas tengan una existencia y realidad independiente de los hechos, de tal suerte que exijan una historia aparte de la que se hace para explicar éstos.

A esta cuestión responde en forma directa la ponencia del profesor Villegas. Se trata de una reflexión de filosofía crítica en torno a lo que considera es y debe ser la labor en la historia de las ideas.

Villegas, por principio de cuentas, sostiene que las ideas, en cuanto objetos a estudiarse, presentan características propias, de tal suerte que comprensión como entes históricos puede hacerse y requiere de una manera propia, diversa en cierto modo de la que se emplea para elaborar la historia de los hechos, estrictamente hablando.

Pero Villegas en ningún momento hechaza la posibilidad de acercar o de referir la historia de las ideas a las de los hechos sociales, económicos, políticos, etcétera; sólo que advierte, con acierto, los peligros que implica el tratar de establecer una relación simplista, en la cual las ideas resulten reflejos o meros efectos de los hechos, como lo han querido entender algunas concepciones estrechas. También se ocupa del problema de la efectividad de las ideas; es decir, de la influencia de éstas como conformadora de la realidad misma; de su influencia sobre un número menor o mayor de personas. Pero para Villegas estos problemas son ya algo diferente a la historia de las ideas mismas. En todo caso el autor señala la posibilidad y la necesidad de ver las ideas para historiarlas; por una parte, como ideas en sentido estricto, y, por otra, como ideas en relación con los hechos o acontecimientos que las rodean dentro del medio histórico en que se producen y cobran realidad.

El trabajo del doctor Raat constituye una crítica, como el de Villegas, pero, a diferencia de éste, la ponencia se ciñe a las cuestiones que implica el método empleado hasta ahora por los historiadores que se han ocupado de la historia de las ideas en México. Raat no hace, como Villegas, una crítica filosófica, más bien, una crítica científica, en la que ha tenido el cuidado de tomar en cuenta lo que se ha hecho en historia de las ideas. No por ello deja de atender a los elementos filosóficos que aparecen en nuestra historiografía de las ideas; su visión de este aspecto es cuidadosa.

Raat comienza estableciendo una diferencia entre "historia o análisis interno de las ideas" (en el que por lo general, dice, "se estudian las ideas fuera del problema de su origen social"), e "historia externa o análisis externo de las ideas", en la que el propósito principal es precisamente establecer la relación entre las ideas y el medio social en el que se originan. A este tipo de historia la llama el autor, siguiendo la tradición norteamericana, "historia intelectual" (intellectual history), y es, por lo que se desprende de su ponencia, la que le interesa más.

Para Raat, la mayoría de los trabajos sobre historia de las ideas en México constituyen historia o análisis interno; la historia externa o intelectual se encuentra escasamente, y sólo a partir de los 1940's.

Después de un breve inventario y comentario en torno al desarrollo de la historia de las ideas en México, el autor inicia una apreciación de los elementos filosóficos que cree han determinado semejante historiografía mexicana. Considera que han predominado el historicismo, el relativismo histórico y el existencialismo. También advierte un desvío en el objetivo principal de la historia; más que historia de las ideas, dice, se ha tratado de construir una filosofía basándola en las ideas historiadas; para Raat, los problemas que han presidido nuestra historia de las ideas han sido más bien cuestiones filosóficas (por temas elegidos y finalidades en las obras) que afán de contemplar una facticidad. Se ha buscado "lo mexicano" como algo indispensable para expresarse filosóficamente.

El blanco de la crítica de Raat es la obra de Leopoldo Zea, filósofo historiador, a quien había ya criticado con éxito en un célebre artículo. [1]

[1] "Leopoldo Zea and Mexican Positivism: A Reappraisal", *Hispanic American Historical Review*, XLVIII, febrero, 1968, pp. 1-18 (premiado como el mejor artículo de esa revista). Traducción española de Josefina Vázquez de Knauth en *Latino-*

Raat ha tomado esta obra como representativa de la historiografía mexicana de las ideas, en cuanto que en ella se pone muy claro lo que implica la "limitación del análisis interno". No descartamos la validez de la crítica a la obra de Zea, y aceptamos que como crítica es útil; pero es necesario advertir que la crítica que hace Raat implica ya un punto de vista: el de su preferencia por el análisis o historia externa de las ideas, cosa que Zea nunca se propuso realizar en su obra. La crítica parece referirse más a lo que no hizo Zea, que a lo que ha hecho efectivamente. No obstante, decíamos, vemos en la crítica algo positivo: la exigencia de una nueva historia de las ideas que está por hacerse en México.

La crítica se revela como positiva en cuanto descubre en la obra de Zea un "filosofismo", —si se nos permite el término—; por una parte se destaca muy claramente el afán de encontrar una filosofía en la historia de las ideas en México (idea por demás consciente en la época en que escribió Zea *El positivismo en México,* y claramente expresada por su maestro, José Gaos en obras compuestas *En torno a la filosofía mexicana).* [2] También es positiva la crítica en cuanto revela la limitación de material empleado por Zea, el esquema vigente en su interpretación de la historia, y la poca referencia a la situación social en que surge el positivismo. Pero estos hechos señalados son en realidad limitaciones propias de la índole de la obra; jamás se pretendió desbordarlos. Ahora bien, es útil que se nos indiquen a quienes pretendemos hacer historia de las ideas para aceptarlos o rechazarlos en nuestro trabajo.

Todo lo anotado es algo que se había venido señalando sobre la obra de Zea, tomada como expresión más representativa de la historia de las ideas en México. Pero lo que a nosotros se nos ocurre es que si la obra de Zea es, con merecimiento, la más conocida hasta ahora, no es la única, y quizá no sea para estos momentos la que más represente la labor historiográfica de las ideas que se realiza actualmente en México.

Creemos que el filosofismo en los temas y objetivos de la historiografía de las ideas va siendo desplazado, al menos en buena parte, en favor de temas que no se ocupan de ideas filosóficas, y también por personas que no se empeñan en encontrar o de aplicar esquemas o visiones filosóficas. Téngase presente que aquellos que escribieron poco tiempo después que Zea no siempre han elegido ideas filosóficas para historiarlas.

Raat ha hecho un esfuerzo por encontrar ejemplos en el desarrollo de la historia de las ideas, siguiendo su clasificación de historia interna y externa; y es entendible y justificable que ignorara lo que actualmente se viene preparando por generaciones recientes: por una parte, un acercamiento a ideas la vida diaria como objeto de la historia, y también un desvío hacia el estudio sociológico de las ideas (análisis externo, en la terminología de Raat); que tardará en completarse, según nos parece, hasta que no se tengan suficientes estudios de historia social en México. En otras palabras, esos inicios que Raat ve en los 1940's para la historia intelectual, parecen afirmarse como tendencia.

América. Anuario de Estudios Latinoamericanos de la Facultad de Filosofía y Letras, UNAM, núm. 2, pp. 171-189.

[2] México, Porrúa y Obregón, 1951-1952 (números 7 y 11 de la colección "México y lo Mexicano").

Cabe mencionar que ese acercamiento a la historia de las ideas diversa de las filosóficas, y no sólo a ellas, sino que también a hechos de la vida mental y psicológica en general, fue estimulada por el propio José Gaos, maestro de Zea, y de otras generaciones de historiadores de las ideas, al ponerse en contacto con estudiantes de historia, pues los historiadores que había formado hasta antes de la última época de su seminario de tesis (interrumpida por su muerte este año) eran estudiantes egresados de la Facultad de Filosofía, con formación de filósofos. Esto explica sin duda la preferencia por los temas de filosofía en las tesis anteriores a las que se prepararon en los últimos años y las que se preparaban cuando murió; tesis que por los temas y por la manera de enfocarse difieren de las anteriores. (Ejemplos de ellas son la de Victoria Lerner, "La idea de Estados Unidos en los viajeros mexicanos", tema que toca ya problemas de actitudes; también la de Françoise Carner, "La idea del amor en la literatura del siglo xix", o la de Jorge Jufresa, "La moralidad en la primera mitad del siglo xix".) [3] En términos generales podemos decir que las tres ponencias coinciden en un problema general:

La posibilidad (y la necesidad para Raat) de referir la historia de las ideas a la historia de los hechos; siempre y cuando se tome en cuenta que esta referencia es un modo especial de ver las ideas, y que implica la necesidad de construir una historia social, que, por otra parte, debe recibir impulso de la historia de las ideas, pues ésta alumbrará sobre muchos aspectos de lo social.

[3] A los trabajos de José Gaos y a su labor en relación con los estudiantes de historia de los años 1966-69 nos hemos referido en particular en "José Gaos y los historiadores", *Revista de la Universidad de México*, v. xxiv, número 9, México, mayo de 1970, pp. 28-32.

XVI. MESA REDONDA: C) "EL CONTENIDO SOCIAL DE LA LITERATURA DE LAS ARTES"

SOCIAL CONTENT IN THE MEXICAN PLASTIC ARTS OF THE COLONIAL PERIOD

This paper will give a definition of "Social Content in the Arts" and demonstrate how social content can be determined by investigators. In the examples discussed and analyzed we shall concentrate on painting but also refer to the arts of sculpture and architecture. Dealing only with the major plastic arts, we shall omit any discussion of literature, music, the dance, and the minor plastic arts such as ceramic, metal working, textiles, costume, and furniture, among others. We shall also omit consideration of the corroborating evidence conveyed by archival and other documents.

The social content of the arts comes from the wishes and demands of the patron, the training (*i.e.*, the level of skill) of the artist, and the social role the work of art plays. They all reflect the taste of their times and thus the social ambiente in which the work of art was produced. Social content is conveyed to the beholder explicitly and directly through direct communication in what we can call the iconographic component of the work of art, and implicitly and indirectly through the style of the work of art.

Social content in the plastic arts so defined derives from the wishes and demands of the patron, the skills and training of the artist and reflects the socio-economic level of the patron, the technical level of the artist's training, and the level of taste of the public for whom it is made.

What can be deduced about Colonial Mexican society through a study of its major plastic arts thus can come from the explicit, overt, and direct statement and also the covert, implicit, or indirect information we derive from study of such aspects of the work as style, materials used, size, and even financial resources of the patron.

Social content can be determined directly in the several arts by the statements of meaning conveyed directly to the beholders. In domestic architecture, for instance, this can be conveyed through the use of towers and coats of arms to indicate the titles of nobility of the owners. In religious architecture there is a hierarchy paralleling the clerical hierarchy. The Cathedral of México is the prime cathedral church, seat of the archbishop; the other cathedrals follow, just as the other Colonial schools fell in order of social importatnce below the university. The parish church is by definition lower in the architectural as well as the religious hierarchy. Mission churches in remote parts

708 LA LITERATURA Y LAS ARTES

of the country are of simpler and more modest construction and decoration than the great pilgrimage churches. The monastic establishments of wealthy and powerful orders, such as the Jesuits, are larger than those of the smaller orders; parish churches in the great colonial centers are ordinarily larger and more luxurious than those of small country pueblos. Conventional establishments, especially for nuns had their own social stratification —those for Indians, for Mestizos, and for Spaniards, for the rich with a dower fee of 4,000 pesos or the poor, for the ordinary citizen and for the nobility. The very name of the order can conjur up for the student the status of its inhabitants and thus the social position of the community as surely as the coat of arms emblazoned over the doors of city palaces or the battlements and fortified towars of remote estates in the northern cattle country indicate the title of the owner of a noble palace or social status of the hacienda owner. These insignia of rank state the owner to belong to the high social strata closest to the viceregal court; usually they belonged either to the agricultural aristocracy or the mining magnates of the Colony.

Painting in the Baroque period, however, gives us even more clear-cut indications of social content. Secular painting, through most of the colonial period was by and large limited to portraiture and here, through coats of arms and the descriptive text of the labels on the painting, the life, deeds, and social position of the sitter are spelled out in almost painful detail. His position in the secular, religious or military hierarch defined, dates of birth and death or the time when the portrait was painted are usually included. The setting for the sitter in the portrait merely reinforced this social message. Splendor and richness of costume give indication of profession, trade or occupation through attributes such as clerical garb, regular or secular costume indicating a nun's order, the sword of the nobleman, the books of the attorney, the studio of the writer, and the hacienda setting; all are elements of the explicit social content of Colonial portraiture.

Paintings were made of the various physical types resulting from the inter-marriages of whites, Indians, and Negroes and the various permutations, each with its own name. Again, such paintings explicitly point out the racial mixtures through the use of written descriptions with the commonly used name for the result of each mixture and additionally show typical costumes and occupations of these members of the lower socio-economic classes.

The student of Mexican culture and history, having examined the work of art under consideration in terms of its overt statement, may find answers complete enought to enable him to place the work in its social milieu and thus have no further need of analysis. However, it is quite possible that the direct statement will not give the required information, that the primary message is not clear enough. In that case he must turn to other methods of dealing with the work of art to decipher the social content. These can deal with the patron (although patronage is either stated directly or is a much clouded and difficult matter to decipher solely from the work of art), the social role of the work in itself, or finally, the social role and status of the artist.

The social role of the work of art in itself can be resolved into two major categories: public and private. By these we mean that the work is displayed in a public context such as a religious painting or sculpture in a church or a public building, a cabildo, for instance, or it can appear in a more private context —a portrait from a private collection, the residence of a private person even though a member of the Colonial nobility. There is another way of dividing the material, however, since the division between public and private may be with some justice considered somewhat artificial. Perhaps another distinction might be more useful for our purposes: the distinction between works of art produced in the metropolitan ambiente and those made in the provincial ambiente. The provincial ambiente, in this context, refers to provincial centers, cities and villages, and the artists working in them, but also by extension those working in the capital itself if they are remote from the *avant-garde* tendencies of metropolitan art or removed from the rigorous and specific training demanded of artists working in the highest echelons of courtly art.

The sixteenth century gives us the clearest examples in painting and sculpture of the indirect expression of social content in the plastic arts. The very existence of a large monumental conventual establishment points to its social role the seat of the first missionary groups, the seat of the educational effort aimed at bringing the Indians into the orbit of Europeanized society in the varying degrees the Church and State had decided this should be done. The College of the Holy Cross at Tlatelolco, a liberal arts college established for Indians, played a somewhat specialized role in Colonial life; however, it was below the University in prestige. Equally specialized, the University played a distinct role at the highest levels in terms of education, in terms of students, in terms of relation to the viceregal court and Colonial society, especially in its social aspect. Other Colonial educational institutions fell in ranks below the University in their importance in society.

Architectural decoration, as in the flat two-dimensional sixteenth century facade et Tepoztlan, indicates the greater remove of its sculptor from European antecedents than the fine plasticity closer to European sources of the example of the facade at Acolman.

Paintings show similar differences, afford similar clues, and give similar knowledge about the artists, the patrons, and the public they were destined for. The early Colonial manuscript paintings with their survival of Pre-Colombian artistic modes are aimed either at native viewers and readers or at Spaniards, most probably either government officials or clerical intellectuals interested in understanding the Indian culture, then on the wane.

Fresco decorations of sixteenth century convento walls, on the other hand, were destined for almost as restricted an audience, the inhabitants of the convento only and their permitted guests, and exhibit closer ties with Europe because of the heavy degree of reliance on illustrations in printed books for inspiration. One does not know for sure who the painters were, but they were clearly closer to European counterparts or at least the European sources than the manuscript painters.

At the same time, in the second half of the sixteenth century, European-born and trained painters began arriving in the New World, bringing with them the art of painting as practiced in Europe. European forms are clearly seen in their style —figural proportions, figures set in landscape with assurance, the use of sophisticated antitheses of light and shade, and the European materials— stretched canvases (lienzos) and oil paint, none used in the acculturated world of the native-born artists to any significant degree that we know of.

The painters arrived from Europe were organized into a guild following European practices and were employed by the highest ranking persons and public institutions in Colonial society. A painting on a stretched canvas is, by its very nature, speaking to us from an assured position in the top strata of this society. The convento fresco, more private than lienzo altarpeices in the same church, is in a somewhat middle position. It is in a European ambiente, but so far as we know, not executed by artists trained in Europe but rather made by skilled copyists from European prints for the more restricted contemplation of cloistered clergy. The Indian manuscript painting was made in a world of anonymous masters working either for themselves or for Spanish clients who certainly did not consider them on the same level as a Simon Pereyns or a Francisco de Zumaya.

In addition to documentation from historical archives and signatures, traditional methods for making attributions, we can also tell the social position of the artist by his style, by something as discernible as closeness to or remoteness from European modes of painting. This is, in truth, a way of arriving at some aspects of the social content of Colonial painting.

Indirect evidence of the social status of owner and architect and the role played by secular buildings in the Baroque period is the magnitude of the palace: the large size of the plan of the whole and its complexity, the large number, and very indicative of status, the specialization of rooms — a family chapel, for instance, or specialized patios for the masters or for service. Sculptural elaboration of the facade, even its very size (height and width fronting the street) and materials (stone in México, stucco and ceramic tile in Puebla) are in contrast to the more humble buildings of adobe. Interestingly enough, the architects of Baroque palaces could sign their work with an inscription, permitted to do so no doubt by a noble patron proud of having his palace designed by a distinguished architect. Lower down in the social hierarchy, such signatures are extremely rare if not non-existent.

The style of the painter in the Baroque period gives important data on the sitter and his ambiente. A portrait by Cabrera was sought after in the highest social circles of the Viceroyalty. In the small country pueblos or even in relatively large country towns painters of much less training, sometimes called folk-artists, were also busy making portraits. The "Mayor of Pátzcuaro" is an example of such a portrait. Somewhat ungainly, unable to place his figure convincingly in space, and not giving us a convincingly three-dimensional human form not complex patterns of light and shade, the artist was clearly a provincial painter, and the style of his painting tells us this. Other suggestions also come from the painting which one would hope could be investigated through documentation. Why, for instance, did these provincial sitters of patrons not employ the services of more expert, sophisticated, and metropolitan painters? Was it because they could not convince the courtly painter of the capital to come to the provincial city or the patron himself could not go to México City for sittings? Was it because the scale of prices in the capital was too high for such provincial officials? Another possibility is that the provincial patron preferred the style of the princial artist. All these are questions posed, in effect, by the style of the painting aside from the explicit statements in the painting, and to answer them we must turn to the documentary materials of the archive.

Religious painting can also convey social content in a very significant way. Great paintings of such subjects as the "Triumph of the Eucharist" or the "Triumph of the Church", bespeak patronage of a sophisticated type knowledgeable of the highest reaches of the theology of the Church, steeped in the complexities of its iconography.

Popular saints, on the other hand, can also give us parallel insights. Guadalupe, the Mexican Saint, par excellence, born on the standard of the revolutionaries of the War for Independence, was opposed to the Virgen de los Remedios portrayed on the banners of the royal government forces. A study of the various paintings of Guadalupe could show the student the whole range of social position of patron and artist and propinquity to and remoteness from the main streams of official and popular art.

Some of the most unsophisticated and direct examples of Guadalupe paintings link us to the world of the primitive artist, the untrained painters who even now are making the retablos and ex-votos of Mexican churches. Usually unsophisticated as artists, working in the main for themselves, or at times others, they demonstrate a remoteness from the high styles of the capital today just es they did in the eighteenth and nineteenth centuries. As in the great Baroque portraits, labels are usually used to indicate the stimulus calling forth the picture. A miraculous intervention to save the life of improve the health of the donor whose portrait is usually shown, an equestrian accident in a swollen river, a train wreck, or a miraculous cure for internal infirmities are typical subjects recorded and dated on the labels.

How the donor figure is painted is a far cry from the Baroque portrait in size, in artistic skill and even material: small opposed to large, sheet metal opposed to lienzo, primitive versus sophisticated. One might remark there, as an aside, that the retablo or ex-voto paintings and the provincial paintings are very often as interesting in some ways as the metropolitan state portraits. The "Mayor of Pátzcuaro", for instance, for all of the evidence of the primitive painter, is a powerful and direct statement in which inconsequential details have been suppressed to give a concentrated image of the man. The art of the primitive painter is often extremely linear, lacking soft trasitions from light to shadow, and more closely adheres to the two-dimensional plane of the painted surface.

Among the metropolitan painters, on the other hand, we find skill in depicting the three-dimensional form convincingly in the three-dimensional space; their sophisticated and intricate compositions often use patterns of light and shade as integral parts of the design as well as devices for showing depth. The work of Cabrera is a good example of the subsidiary social content to be found in the oeuvre of such painters. His paintings in the Church of Sta. Prisca and Sebastian in Taxco demonstrate in their facility his cosmopolitan training and associations. Their presence in what was one of the most ambitions and complete patterns of architecture, sculpture, painting and minor arts (silver work, embroideries, even furniture) of the Baroque period is a clear demonstration that Borda, the patron of the church, who spared no pains in collecting artists to work for him, must have considered Cabrera the supreme painter of the time. His position is thus verified in Colonial society by the importance of his sitters for portraits and for the imporntance of his religious paintings with their architectural associations. In this he follows Villalpando and Correa in their suite of paintings in the Sacristy of the Metropolitan Cathedral. The most esteemed artists received the most important and thus from the artist's point of view, the most coveted commissions Colonial society had to offer.

The variety of style to be found in the paintings of Cabrera is possibly a reflection of the nature of his work from a social point of view. We know that the prodigious amount of work attributed to him could hardly have been painted by one man, and we also that he had a shop with assistants to help him with his large commissions and suites of paintings. The social status of Cabrera thus was more than respectable from the point of view of the commissions he received and from the size of the "operation" he headed.

The Baroque painters supported and even proclaimed the power, wealth and oppulence of the Baroque Church in Mexico. Baroque sculptors too were called upon to proclaim the Church. One of the most obvious examples is the seminary-monastery church of Tepotzotlan where sculpture ranging from the retablos of the midseventeenth century to the facade of the church are complemented by the Loreto Chapel, the Domestic Chapel and the works of art embellishing them. An interesting contrast with the wealth of works of art from the metropolitan sphere of Colonial life at Tepotzotlan is the parallel wealth of richness in the Rosary Chapel of Santo Domingo, Puebla. Set in the richness of polychromed-stucco sculpture, both proclaim the heights of Colonial stucco workers. The Puebla Rosary Chapel is in its opulence a proclamation of the aims of the Colonial masters. At the same time, it seems to have been the inspiration for artisans, if not artists, operating on a different level of society in the decoration of the chapel of Santa María Tonantzintla. Here the richness of Puebla is transmuted by the folk-artist into something even more overwhelming. The Indian nature of the pueblo of Tonantzintla is apparent in a study of the polychromed-stucco work with the naïveté of forms and coloring and the overall richly plastic drenching of surfaces.

Isolated examples of sculpture, such as the Santos or Bultos of New Mexico with their almost hieratic dignity derived from frontality and even a rigid stiffness reminiscent of archaic Greece or the Egyptian royal icon, show remoteness from the sopristicated and metropolitan work its polychromy over gold or the use of ivory for faces and hands, with its swirls of drapery echoing European masters and again proclaiming the pride, wealth, power and dominance of the Church in the arts.

We can call attention, in closing, to a certain continuation into the nineteenth century of older modes of thought and behavior. Academic paintings and sculpture demonstrate continued dependence upon contemporary European styles such as Classicism or Romanticism but side by side with this an adumbration of the twentieth century in that Mexican subject matter such as the "Torture of Cuauhtemoc" or the "Invention of Pulque" are the subjects. European styles become more and more merely the vehicle, and the latent indigenism of the subject matter has as its fruit the nationalism of the mural masters of the

714

es of this century a national subject matter and a national
style.

Velasco stands out as one of the great nineteenth century landscape
painters, and yet, in his panoramic views of the Valley of Mexico with
its prosperous agriculture or railroad trains crossing trestles in wild
gorges, he paints as social content the *Orden y Progreso* of the late
nineteenth century.

Boari's post office in Mexico City is one example out of many where
we can point out social content in architecture to parallel that in
painting and sculpture. The Venetian Gothic exterior, clearly an importation, is an example of the eclecticism dominating Europe and
North America at the time; however, the construction of such buildings
with their massive use of materials and mechanical devices imported
from abroad show clearly the dependence upon things foreign in more
fundamental aspects than just the style with which the building is
draped. Perhaps the importation of modern technology in the beginning
of this century and the end of the last is, in a way, the continuation of
a certain colonialism but at the same time a necessary preparation for
the flowering of a distinctly Mexican modern architecture in our own
time.

The work of art, a worthy object of study in itself, should be used
as a primary document for the general historian both for the direct
message it carries and for the indirect information one can deduce
from it. It should be used, as should all other documents, with the
critical analysis and the acumen of the historian.

SOCIAL CONTENT OF LITERATURE AND THE ARTS

JOHN S. BRUSHWOOD

It is possible that a discussion of this subject might find itself turning unproductively on the word "content". The term "social content" suggests that a work of art (I include literature) may contain an element that can be identified as "social" and studied apart from the work as a whole. Indeed, in some cases it may be possible to do so, but such a separation is not generally characteristic of creative work. A discussion of the subject will state more truth with greater clarity if it considers the function of the work of art within the whole society. The consideration of "social content" suggests the static characteristics of a document, which art is not. A description of "function", on the other hand, suggests dynamism which is the very essence of creativity.

From this point on, I will refer only to literature because I will be on surer ground and because I can avoid the complication of referring to the difference between literature and the other arts. We must recognize of course that literature is distinguished by the use of words. Words, in our culture, are inevitably associated with ideas, ideas with reason, and reason with reality. This whole series of associations is an enormous fabrication supported by wishful thinking rather than by truth. But so long as we insist on keeping faith with this fiction, literature will often be expected to do something its creators do not usually intend —simply because it uses words.

In order to appreciate the relationship of literature and society, we must work with two reciprocating views. Society includes literature just as it includes all other things that men do. And literature generally reveals its kinship with the total circumstances. At the same time, literature includes society because it often deals with social attitudes, aspirations, even events. The crucial fact is that the literary work is not a doctrine or a document but an experience like watching a sunset, falling in love, driving a car, robbing a bank, making soup, climbing a mountain. The essence of the experience is the act of climbing, not the fact of the accomplishment.

Since novels and plays tell stories, they are more vulnerable than poetry to misuse as documents. Poetry is misused as philosophy. The relationship of novels and plays to daily living suggests that they may be valuable as sociology or as history. And indeed they may be so, but preferably if the sociologist or historian understands the literary function. It would be absurd to use *Romeo and Juliet* as a source of information about marriage customs in Verona. But many works that are

not protected by the status of being masterpieces are often expected
to produce information of this kind.

We must be clear that society as seen in literature does not lend
itself to quantitative studies. We may find a very limited semi-docu-
mentary value if we identify the action of a novel with experience past.
But such use is a serious distortion of the work, because literature
is experience present. Reading a literary work is a unique experience.
It is made so by the fact that it is a creation.

I do not mean that literature does not contribute to our knowledge
of society. Quite to the contrary, it offers a kind of information that
is essential to understanding and which cannot be gotten anywhere else.
Here we run into a problem created by the arbitrary limits we place
on the ways of knowing. We tend to admit only what can be authenticated by critical examination and reference to past experience. Much
more can be learned by surrendering to the function of art.

As an example, we may consider a novel now about a year old, *Los
juegos verdaderos*, by Fernando de los Rios, a Peruvian. I choose this
work because it is neither Mexican or Northamerican, it is too recent
to have acquired any particular status in literature, it has received
generally favorable reviews with some reservations, and it has an obvious
base in a recognized social problem.

The book brings into focus three sets of circumstances: 1) a guerrillero in a prison in the Peruvian jungle, 2) a young man about to leave
Peru ostensibly to study in Mexico but really to go to Cuba for guerrilla
training, and 3) a young boy among his childhood friends. The novelist
allows us to assume that the protagonist is the same in all three circumstances. But he does not tell us that is the case. Our attitude,
therefore, is different from our attitude toward a hero-protagonist whose
character is logically developed throughout a novel. We do not feel we
are dealing with a single person. Still the communication of emotion
in each of the three circumstances is so intimate that we feel more
involved than we would with an abstraction or a mass protagonist.
What we have then is a kind of intimate generalization of a guerrillero.

What do we learn about society? Certainly not how many guerri-
lleros there are in Peru, nor anything about the probability of their
success. We do experience the revolutionary impulse as we never could
on the basis of document or statistics. I am not able to communicate
it here. I cannot *say* the impulse; I can only talk about it. The knowledge *is* the experience. And the experience, in turn, has two facets.
One is the reader's vicarious reaction to the three circumstances; the
other is his awareness of the novelist's creative act in making the circumstances. This second awareness is what makes the novel different
from a newspaper account. It is also what makes the work a unique
experience —a creation cannot be created more than once.

Most of us have been indoctrinated in fiction and theatre that is based on observed reality. We forget that this basis has served authors for a relatively short time. Novels of chivalry, pastoral novels, even sentimental novels came from the imagination rather than from observation. Even the picaresque novel takes a restricted and somewhat stylized view of society. Only Realism and Naturalism attempted a reproduction of social actuality. They have been misused more than purely imaginative works because it is easier to read possible documentary value into their apparent verisimilitude. But if awareness of creation-in-progress is lost, even in a Realist novel the work is only partially understood. What is even more important to an understanding of the relationship of literature and society is the fact that novels based on observed reality have been disappearing for quite a while, and purely imaginative fiction has been gradually taking its place. This change may very well be corollary to a change in the social structure. The possibility is much too complicated to be dealt with at this point. But we should understand clearly that these novels are not reconstructions of social reality in the usual sense. They bear little or no resemblance to that restricted view supported by the association of word to idea to reason to reality. Indeed, these novels may be utterly unreal from this limited viewpoint, but they are no less experience. They are experience just as poetry is, without reproduction of the social scene.

Because of the factor of experience, literature is essential to the process of education. Education is concentrated experience or it is nothing. This description applies even to highly specialized, technical education. It is even more applicable to what we call "liberal education" —that is, the development of the individual's capacity for exercising all his human functions. Ideally, the concentration of experience through education should give every generation an advantage over the preceding.

Although we have approached this ideal, it has never been achieved, for a variety of reasons. One of these reasons is that we tend to understand experience as past rather than as present. When we speak of "experience", we really mean "experienced". Our appreciation of experience allows it to be passive. It becomes a tool or a criterion which we use but which has lost its own vitality.

The use of the literary experience in this way does increase to some extent the reader's capacity to exercise his human capabilities. To say it in a more commonplace way, he gains some knowledge of what life is like. But the potential of literature is very limited unless a work is treated as actual experience. Experience that is not observed from a distant point, but acknowledged in the act itself. This experience is not simply identification with the characters or theme of a literary work. It is this identification plus an awareness of the author's creative act, a sense of witnessing a coming-into-being. (The most important job of literary criticsm is to reveal and analyze the various aspects of a work in such a way that the reader may realize more fully both the identification and the creative movement.) The reader himself becomes a third factor in the experience.

This sense of becoming, of the process of creation, is the major social content of literature. One of the paradoxes of our attempts to understand our circumstance is that we insist on using static means of appreciating dynamic reality. Society is always dynamic, though the intensity of movement varies. Dynamic reality is always present in literature.

We must also recognize the possibility that what visual observation calls "society" may not be reality at all. To put it another way, the whole structure may be antagonistic to what is authentically human. Recent novels, in their movement away from reproduction of visible realities, create worlds that seem more real than reality, fictions that seem truer than truth. These apparent paradoxes can be understood only if readers enter the creative process.

If many should do so, it is possible —just barely— that the creative imagination of men might come into the mainstream of life and produce an exercise of the human capability which, up to now, has existed only in the wildest dreams of a few. It is lamentably probable that the creative imagination will continue to be relegated to a peripheral importance, from which position it goads us, frustrates us, keeps us alive but never authentic. In terms of what literature may do, I fear that the reecent novels I have referred to may reach only a very small audience, while the great majority watch television, which is considered more down-to-earth. In other words, these novels may join poetry in relative oblivion.

Let me say clearly that I do not wish to plead the case of a few novels. I use them only as a symbol. The point is that we have a chance to discover reality. This reality is the awareness of creation, of dynamic life that Jorge Guillen's reader experiences when the poet says

Soy, más, estoy. Respiro.	I am; I am here and now.
Lo profundo es el aire.	I breathe the deepest air.
La realidad me inventa,	Reality invents me.
Soy su leyenda. ¡Salve!	I am its legend. Hail! *

* The verse is from *Cantico* and is cited here from *Affirmation: A Bilingual Anthology, 1919-1966*, with translations by Julian Palley (Norman, University of Oklahoma Press, 1968), pp. 30-31.

SOBRE EL ARTE "MESTIZO" HISPANO-AMERICANO

LEOPOLDO CASTEDO

INTRODUCCIÓN

Mucho se ha escrito, y mucho ha de escribirse aún, acerca del encuentro (o desencuentro) de Hispanoamérica con su propia esencia. La literatura de introspección es abundante. Estas notas tienen por objeto añadir una contribución más, convencidos de que entre los muchos caminos recorridos, y entre los que han de recorrerse forzosamente en esta necesaria búsqueda, el ya abierto por la historia del arte es el más representativo, como oportunamente ha señalado en reiteradas formas y ocasiones Justino Fernández.

La ocasión es propicia. La motivación de esta Mesa Redonda, también. Séanos por ello permitido proponerles a ustedes un tema que, no por muy discutido, ha superado ya los límites de una contumaz controversia: el de la existencia real o imaginada de un arte colonial americano, expresado en sus aportaciones no europeas. En efecto, al referirnos a ciertas formas artísticas de expresión de la sociedad colonial hispanoamericana, ¿debemos tratarlas como derivadas de un arte "provincial" o "folklórico", o bien "mestizo", o "tequitqui", o puramente imitativo? ¿Son originales en algún grado? ¿Son dignas o indignas de figurar honorablemente en la historia general del arte?

Es muy probable que nunca se llegue a total acuerdo en este litigio, litigio que en los círculos especialistas se mantiene desde hace medio siglo. Mas parece oportuno reactualizarlo puntualizando los argumentos con el correspondiente análisis de las fuentes documentales y bibliográficas.

I

En el terreno de la historiografía iberoamericana los planteamientos se iniciaron en 1914 en Argentina [1] y culminaron en la encuesta solicitada por el profesor Graziano Gasparini en Venezuela [2] en 1964 y en los artículos publicados a continuación, especialmente

---

[1] El arquitecto Martín S. Noel realizó un viaje de estudio a Perú y Bolivia en 1913. En septiembre de 1914 propuso en una conferencia en el Museo Nacional de Bellas Artes de Buenos Aires la definición de una arquitectura "hispanoamericana" diferenciada de la europea.

[2] Encuesta sobre la significación de la arquitectura barroca hispanoamericana. *BCIHE*, I, enero Caracas, 1964, pp. 9-42. Respondieron a la encuesta: arquitectos: Carlos Arbeláez Camacho, Mario J. Buschiazzo, José García Bryce, Teresa Gisbert

en el *Boletín del Centro de Investigaciones Históricas y Estéticas* de la
Facultad de Arquitectura y Urbanismo de la Universidad Central
de Venezuela. En cuanto a la historiografía norteamericana, los dos
trabajos que abren y (al parecer en cuanto al último) cierran la
controversia se deben a Alfred Neumeyer [3] en 1948 y a George
Kubler [4] en 1961, sin menoscabo de otras publicaciones que comen-
taremos más adelante, a partir de la obra de Sylvester Baxter [5] en 1901.

La tarea emprendida por el profesor Gasparini es digna de elogio.
Muchos factores de confusión han sido en parte aclarados. Otros,
en cambio, son ahora más oscuros que nunca. Como la controversia
ha adquirido a veces tonos agrios, pareciera correrse el riesgo de
abrir nuevas trincheras erizadas de bayonetas entre los diversos bandos:
acusaciones de nacionalismo o racismo, de limitaciones profesionales,
de "hacer literatura", de confusiones en la terminología, de intromisión en terrenos no genuinamente histórico-artísticos, entre otras.

Tratemos de enumerar algunos factores de confusión.

Al repasar minuciosamente las citas en apoyo de autoridades, se
advierten las omisiones de autores que, por su visión histórica, su capacidad de análisis o su conocimiento documental y artístico han escrito
capítulos sapientísimos al respecto. Baste citar los casos flagrantes de
Mariano Picón Salas [6] en su *Barroco de Indias*, una sola vez citado
de pasada, por Mesa-Gisbert [7] y el aún más grave de José Moreno
Villa, [8] también citado una sola vez por Kubler [9] si bien con mayor
interés. Lo anterior no quiere decir que los autores en cuestión
eviten a los "no especialistas". En un artículo incendiario [10] Gasparini
cita a Salazar Bondi [11] precisamente en una de las partes más agrias
de su apasionante ensayo, *Lima la horrible*. [12]

Emilio Harth-terré, Carlos Maldonado, José de Mesa, Ricardo de Robina y Germán
Téllez; profesores: Diego Angulo Iñíguez, George Kubler y Sidney D. Markman.

[3] Alfred Neumeyer, "The Indian Contribution to Architectural Decoration in
Spanish Colonial America", *Art Bulletin*, June, 1948.

[4] George Kubler, "On the Colonial Extinction of the Motifs of Pre-Columbian
Art. Essay 2", *Essays in Pre-Columbian Art and Archaeology*: Cambridge, Mass
1961, pp. 14-34.

[5] Sylvester Baxter, *Spanish-Colonial Architecture in Mexico* (with Photographic
Plates by Henry Greenwood Peabody and Plans by Betram Grosvenor Goodhue),
s/h, 1901.

[6] Mariano Picón-Salas, *De la conquista a la independencia*. México-Buenos Aires,
1944.

[7] José de Mesa y Teresa Gisbert, "Renacimiento y manierismo en la arquitectura
'mestiza'", BCIHE, 3, junio, Caracas, 1965, pp. 9-44 (nota 40, p. 35).

[8] José Moreno Villa, *La escultura colonial mexicana*. México, 1942. *Lo mexicano*.
México 1948.

[9] George Kubler, "On the Extinction...", pp. 16-17.

[10] Graziano Gasparini, "Opiniones sobre pintura colonial", BCIHE, 8, noviembre.
Caracas, 1967, pp. 133-142 (nota 11, p. 142).

[11] Sebastián Salazar Bondi, *Lima la horrible*. México 1964.

[12] p. 85 de la edición peruana. Publilibros. Lima 1964.

La mayor parte de los juicios de valor se ha centrado en la arquitectura. [13] En cuanto a la pintura y a la escultura, pese a los bene-
méritos esfuerzos de Martín Soria, [14] Enrique Marco Dorta [15] el
matrimonio Mesa-Gisbert, [16] Francisco de la Maza, [17] Héctor Schenone, [18] Elizabeth Wilder Weismann, [19] Gabriel Giraldo Jaramillo, [20]
Alfredo Boulton, [21] entre otros, pareciera existir consenso acerca de
su calidad imitativa. Los juicios oscilan desde el académico principio
de Martín Soria, [22] hasta las conclusiones ambivalentes de Mesa-
Gisbert [23] (relacionados sólo con la altoperuana). En cuanto a México

[13] A la citada encuesta (vid. nota 2) que, por su mismo índole, atañía sólo a la
arquitectura, respondieron 9 arquitectos y sólo 3 profesores-historiadores no arquitectos.

[14] Martín Soria, vid. Kubler-Soria nota 22: "Colonial Painting in Latin America", AIA, pp. 47-3; Fall 1959, pp. 32-39. Una nota sobre pintura colonial y
estampas europeas: AIAAIE/A, 5, 1952, pp. 43-49. La pintura del siglo xvi en Sud
América. B. A. 1958; "La pintura en el Cuzco y el Alto Perú, 1550-1700: rectificaciones y fuentes", AIAAIE/A, 12, 1959, pp. 24-34.

[15] Enrique Marco Dorta: En Diego Angulo, Enrique Marco Dorta y Mario
Buschiazzo, Historia del arte hispanoamericano. 3 vols., Barcelona, 1954-1956, t. ii.,
cap. ix. "La escultura en Colombia, Venezuela, Ecuador, Perú y Bolivia." t.
ii, cap. xii. "La pintura en Colombia, Ecuador, Perú y Bolivia."

[16] Vid. nota 23.

[17] Francisco de la Maza, Los retablos dorados de la Nueva España. México.
1950. "La decoración simbólica de la Capilla del Rosario de Puebla", AIIE/M
6:23, 1955."Las estampas de Alconedo", AIIE/M 6:23, 1955, pp. 69-74. "Arte
colonial en Chiapas", Ateneo, 6, mayo, Chiapas 1956, pp. 59-122. "Un carpintero
poblano. Documentos", AIIE/M, 31, 1962, p. 143). "Una pintura de la 'Ilustración' mexicana", AIIE/M, 32, 1963, pp. 37-51.

[18] Héctor H. Schenone, Pinturas de Las Mónicas de Potosí, Bolivia, 1952.
"Acerca de una pintura de Manzoni", AIAAIE/A, 6, 1953, p. 103-104. "Tallistas
portugueses en el Río de la Plata", AIAAIE/A, 8, 1955, pp. 40-56. "Escultura
funeraria en el Perú", AIAAIE/A, 13, 1960, pp. 35-40. "Esculturas españolas en
el Perú, siglo xvi", AIAAIE/A, 14, 1961, pp. 58-72.

[19] Elizabeth W. Weismann, Mexico in Sculpture: 1521-1821. Cambridge, Mass.
1950.

[20] Gabriel Giraldo Jaramillo, Bibliografía selecta del arte en Colombia. Bogotá,
1955. El Museo del Seminario Conciliar de Bogotá. Bogotá, 1954. Notas y documentos sobre el arte en Colombia. Bogotá, 1954. Pinacotecas bogotanas: "El Museo
Colonial". Bolívar, Bogotá 29, 1954, pp. 729-738. "El grabado en Colombia". Bogotá.
1959. Pinacotecas bogotanas: "La galería del Colegio Mayor de N. Sra. del Rosario".
Bolívar, Bogotá, 38, mayo 1955, pp. 635-668. "Humboldt y el descubrimiento
estético de América", Cp/F, 20:18, marzo-abril 1959, pp. 10-19.

[21] Alfredo Boulton, Historia de la pintura en Venezuela. t. i, época colonial.
Caracas, 1964.

[22] Martín Soria, En George Kubler and Martín Soria: Art and Architecture in
Spain and Portugal and their American Dominions. 1500-1800: "... Colonial
painting usually lacks originality and slavishly follows prints from Antwerp and
Roma..." p. 303. Sin embargo en "Una nota sobre pintura colonial y estampas
europeas" (AIAAIE/A, 5, 1952, pp. 43-49) acepta la distinción en el arte colonial
entre europeo, mestizo e indio (p. 48).

[23] José de Mesa y Teresa Gisbert, Historia de la pintura cuzqueña. Buenos Aires,
1962: "(los) maestros (del) siglo xvii siguieron las tendencias europeas......Quis-

los valores se sintetizan en una brillante frase de Francisco de la Maza, [24] sin menoscabo de los esfuerzos del propio De la Maza, de Xavier Moyssen, [25] de Abelardo Carrillo, [26] sobre los enigmáticos frescos de Ixmiquilpan y de tantos otros ilustres investigadores del Instituto de Arte Americano de la UNAM. [27] Mención especial y elogiosa merece el trabajo exhaustivo de Alfredo Boulton en Venezuela, [28] así como los estudios sobre la sobrevivencia del arte precolombino en los manuscritos coloniales, especialmente de Robertson [29] y Tudela de la Orden. [30]

Por lo que atañe a la escultura, salvo los escasos trabajos especializados, incluyendo el clásico de Elizabeth Wilder Weismann, [31] el de Berlín [32] y las partes correspondientes de Wethey, [33] Kelemen, [34] Soria, [35] Toussaint, [36] Angulo y Marco Dorta, se incluye con frecuencia en los panoramas generales o en las formas integradas de la arquitectura.

pe Tito... es el directo responsable de(l) cambio... (hacia) la pintura cuzqueña popular del s. XVIII... En su trabajo.. se señalan sus raíces hispanoindígenas", (p. 12). "El pintor Diego Quispe Tito", *AIAAIE/A*, 8, 1955, pp. 115-122. "La pintura boliviana en el siglo XVII", E. A, 11, 52-1956, pp. 19-42 "Nuevas obras y nuevos maestros en la pintura del Alto Perú", *AIAAIE/A*, 10, 1957, pp. 9-46 *Holguín y la pintura altoperuana del Virreinato*. La Paz, 1956. *Fray Francisco de Salamanca, pintor orureño del siglo XVIII*. Khana —36— 1962. *Gaspar Berrío*. La Paz, 1962.

[24] Francisco de la Maza, *El pintor Cristóbal de Villalpando*. México, 1964. "Toda creación es rebeldía y toda escuela es obediencia. Y nosotros, en la Colonia, fuimos obedientes. Creamos muy poco y mucho copiamos. Pero, eso sí, tuvimos buenos, maestros." p. 1.

[25] Cf. especialmente su magnífico trabajo (rectificaciones a Toussaint, Kubler y Angulo, entre otros) sobre el caso de transculturación en "Tecamachalco y el pintor indígena Juan Gerson", AIIE/M, 33, 1964, pp. 23-39.

[26] Abelardo Carrillo y Gariel, *Ixmiquilpan*. México, 1961 Cf. asimismo: *Imaginería popular novoespañola*. México, 1950.

[27] Cf. Justino Fernández, *Bibliografías de los investigadores*. Instituto de Investigaciones Estéticas, México, 1961. (Colosal muestrario del trabajo de los investigadores mexicanos. Romero de Terreros figura con 466 títulos y el propio Fernández con 341 hasta 1960 ...)

[28] Vid. nota 21.

[29] Donald Robertson, *Mexican manuscript painting of the early colonial period: The Metropolitan schools*, New Haven, Conn. Yale University Press, 1959.

[30] José Tudela de la Orden, "Las primeras figuras de indios pintadas por españoles", *Homenaje a Rafael García Granados*. México, 1960, pp. 319-329.

[31] Vid. nota 19.

[32] Heinrich Berlin, *Historia de la imaginería colonial en Guatemala*. Guatemala, 1952.

[33] Harold Edwin Wethey, *Colonial Architecture and Sculpture in Peru*. Cambridge, Mass.

[34] Paul Kelemen, *Baroque and Rococo in Latin America*. New York, 1951.

[35] Vid. nota 22

[36] Manuel Toussaint, *Arte colonial en México*. México, 1949. Cf. además "Huellas de Diego Siloee en México", AIIE/M, 6:21, 1953, pp. 11-18.

II

Otro factor de confusión lo determina la manía de los encasillamientos. Nadie podría poner en tela de juicio la importancia que
para la historia en general y para la historia del arte en particular
tienen las clasificaciones y las "teorías". Erwin W. Palm puntualiza
de manera elocuente y con un acopio sistemático de referencias la
evolución y reflejo en la historiografía del arte colonial, de las teorías,
casi todas alemanas, que han pretendido sistematizar la interpretación
de los fenómenos histórico-artísticos. [37] Desde Riegl hasta Landolt,
los historiadores del arte de ambas Américas se han abanderizado en la
teoría a la sazón prevalente. Ángel Guido [38] tratando de embutir
su teoría indoamericana en las categorías, bastante rígidas por cierto, de
Wölfflin y de Worringer, Dvorak y Pinder [39] pareciera que, merced
a la energía y a la consecuencia de Gasparini, está por inaugurarse la
era Hanspeter Landolt. [40] El caso del manierismo es tal vez el más
ilustrativo. Kubler emplea el término desde su primera obra básica
de 1948; [41] Mesa-Gisbert [42] y Santiago Sebastián [43] abundan en su
aplicación. En la larga lista de los "resistentes", actitud que Palm
censura sin ambages, [44] figuran casi todos los historiadores mexicanos
y desde luego, Mario Buschiazzo.

No es éste el lugar para analizar más a fondo el atractivo tema.
Mas baste plantear las incógnitas que crearía la interpretación "manierista" del trabajo de Francisco Guerrero y Torres en la elevación
de la Capilla del Pocito, a pesar de su modelo "serliano", o la
proyección de Vignola en el barroco americano.

No menos limitadoras son las confusiones derivadas de la discre-
pancia en la terminología. Con todos los respetos, que son muchísimos,
por la obra ejemplar del maestro Toussaint, pareciera que el término
"ultra-barroco" (aunque él no lo inventara, lo hizo popular) encerrara
un contrasentido flagrante, si consideramos que el concepto barroco, en

[37] Erwin W. Palm, "Perspectivas de una historia de la arquitectura colonial
hispanoamericana", BCIHE, 9, abril, Caracas, 1968, pp. 21-37.
[38] Ángel Guido, La filosofía del arte en la actualidad. Cap. ii de "Redescubrimiento de América en el Arte". Buenos Aires, 1944.
[39] "La arquitectura hispanoamericana a través de Wolfflin". Ibid.
[40] Véase más adelante el análisis del concepto del espacio en la arquitectura
colonial.
[41] George Kubler, Mexican Architecture of the Sixteenth Century. New Haven,
1948.
[42] José de Mesa y Teresa Gisbert, "Renacimiento y manierismo en la arquitectura mestiza", BCIHE, 3, Caracas, 1965, pp. 9-44.
[43] Santiago Sebastián, "La decoración llamada plateresca en el mundo hispánico",
BCIHE, 6, Caracas, 1966, pp. 42-51. "La influencia de los modelos ornamentales
de Serlio en Hispanoamérica", BCIHE, 7, Caracas, 1967, pp. 30-73.
[44] Erwin W. Palm, "Perspectivas..." (vid. nota 37), p. 29.

sí, es ya el "non plus ultra". Más grave es el caso del "churrigueresco", asunto dilucidado definitivamente por Kubler. [45] Puestos a hacer teorías, por qué no establecer la del atractivo onomatopéyico que para los españoles tiene la salomónica forma del popular "churro", y su identificación con las torceduras del último de los Churriguera.

III

Hemos señalado ya que los empeños por la determinación de un arte provincial, "folklórico", de segunda mano o "mestizo" y original se han centrado en los análisis de las obras arquitectónicas. Diversas posiciones se disputan el favor del lector estudioso.

Acerca de la posición "indigenista" ya hemos hecho varias alusiones al principio de este trabajo. [46] Conviene, en materia de atribuciones, rectificar la información dada por el matrimonio Mesa-Gisbert acerca de la paternidad del adjetivo "mestizo" para singularizar el fenómeno, que la ilustre pareja atribuye a Wethey. [47] Mucho antes que Wethey la usaron el propio Guido en 1936, Noel (aunque no en los mismos términos pero sí el mismo sentido) desde 1914 [48] y, desde luego, y con más alcance, Buschiazzo en 1944. [49] La posición "indigenista" *à outrance* ha producido obras deliciosas, como la de Cali. [50]

Al margen de la crítica formal y académica, cuesta creer —con Guido— que los indios rebeldes aprovechaban el pesado sueño de los frailes coloniales para esculpir "cantuctas" y "alkumaris" de contrabando en las fachadas de los templos católicos. [51] Pero ningún estudioso del arte americano puede dejar de reconocer los muchos méritos en la obra de Martín S. Noel [52] que abrió el paso en América

[45] *vid.* nota 14.

[46] *vid.* notas 1, 3 y 38.

[47] Mesa-Gisbert, Renacimiento... p. 9, nota 4: La denominación de "arquitectura mestiza" se debe a Wethey en... 1949 y... 1960

[48] *vid.* nota 1.

[49] Mario J. Buschiazzo, *Estudios de arquitectura colonial hispanoamericana.* Buenos Aires, 1944.

[50] François Cali, *L'Art des Conquistadors. Photos de Claude Arthaud et François Hèert-Stevens.* Paris, 1960. En contraste con la magnificencia de las fotografías, el texto de este "Coffee-table book" es una cadena de asociaciones marginales que poco tienen que ver con el título y las fotos. Tal vez sea mejor así. Por ejemplo: Santiago Pomata está influenciado por la Estela Raimondi y, por supuesto, el famoso indio Kondori es el autor de la fachada de San Lorenzo de Potosí (p. 283 y 198).

[51] Cf. además de la *op. cit.* la proposición de Guido en ([Catálogo de la] Exposición de Arte Religioso Retrospectivo, octubre 1950. Rosario, 1950) para definir el arte colonial como barroco hispano, barroco criollo y barroco mestizo. *La arquitectura mestiza en las riberas del Titikaca.* Buenos Aires, 1956.

[52] Martín S. Noel, *Contribución a la historia de la arquitectura hispanoamericana.* Buenos Aires, 1921. (Proposición de clasificar las artes americanas en "hispano-aztecas" e "hispano-inkaicas".) *Fundamentos para una estética nacional.* Buenos

del Sur a las interpretaciones más ecuánimes de sus colegas y continuadores, desde los tiempos ya remotos de su conferencia en el Museo de Bellas Artes de Buenos Aires en 1914, al final de la cual, y luego de mostrar diapositivas de los monumentos religiosos del Collao, propuso definirlos como propios de su "arquitectura Ibero-Andina".

Fogoso adalid de la posición "espacial" es el profesor Graziano Gasparini. [53] Para Gasparini los "valores esenciales de la arquitectura" sólo atañen al espacio. Todo lo demás (función, ornamento, supeditación al ambiente, razón económica y sociológica de ser, integración con las artes no espaciales, etcétera) pareciera no tener vigencia. Además el enjuiciamiento "estético" de un arte, que no debe ser mistificado con la pintura y la escultura, le lleva a concluir que "es imposible admitir la existencia de una arquitectura barroca hispano-americana, por cuanto no pertenecen a América los conceptos espaciales que originaron su expresión". Por cierto no hubo Borrominis americanos, aunque sí borrominismo en América. Para Gasparini el "carácter americano reside entonces en la reinterpretación y reelaboración de conceptos arquitectónicos importados (sic) y eso impide considerar este fenómeno como la aparición de un arte 'americano' surgido de un impulso creador autóctono". [54] Con la misma argumentación "antinacionalística" podría sin duda argüirse que el barroco español y el portugués son también formas provinciales y derivadas. El único barroco auténtico parece ser el italiano y, como consecuencia, el alemán. Es curiosa la identificación de Gasparini con Hanspeter Landolt. Según el distinguido analista de la arquitectura barroca: "La arquitectura no es, única y simplemente, 'arte espacial'; tiene por sobre todo dos aspectos diferentes: en el primero, e incluso el principal, se manifiesta como cuerpo arquitectónico de naturaleza plástica, sin contar el espacio y sólo en segundo plano es un arte moldeador de vacíos espaciales." [55] La teoría de la negación de creatividad americana en materia de espacio se contrapone con varios

Aires, 1926. *Teoría histórica de la arquitectura virreinal.* Buenos Aires, 1932. *El arte en la América española.* Buenos Aires, 1942. (En esta obra emplea ya el término "indomestizo".) *La arquitectura mestiza de las riberas del Titikaca.* Buenos Aires, 1952. *En la Arequipa indohispánica.* Buenos Aires, 1957.

[53] Graciano Gasparini, "Análisis crítico de las definiciones de 'arquitectura popular' y 'arquitectura mestiza'," *BCIHE* 3, junio, Caracas, 1965, pp. 51-66. "Significación de la arquitectura barroca en Hispanoamérica", *BCIHE,* 3, junio, Caracas, 1965, pp. 45-50. "Las influencias indígenas en la arquitectura barroca colonial de Hispanoamérica", *BCIHE,* 4, enero, 1966, pp. 75-80.

[54] Gasparini, "Las influencias . . ." p. 77.

[55] Hanspeter Landolt, "El espacio en la arquitectura barroca". Traducción del alemán por los arquitectos Joaquín Rodríguez Saumell y Patricio H. Randle. *AIAAIE/A,* 9, 1956, pp. 53-69.

trabajos publicados antes y después de los artículos del distinguido
profesor de la Universidad de Venezuela. Los que más se relacionan
con el tema son los dedicados al estudio formal y "espacial" de
posas, capillas abiertas y atrios en el plateresco mexicano y en menor
proporción en América del Sur. Algunos autores, como Arbeláez
Camacho [56] y McAndrew, [57] consideran tales formas como inventos
americanos, sea de los frailes en el XVI o bien supervivencias de
conceptos precolombinos. Otros, por el contrario, como Mesa-Gisbert [58]
y Erwin Palm [59] las consideran readaptaciones de viejas formas europeas
olvidadas. El autor de este trabajo opina lo mismo. [60] Mas creemos
que lo que da valor "americano" a tales desarrollos espaciales es
su carácter de arquetipo repetido, su capacidad para convertirse en
una verdadera constante de la arquitectura colonial americana, a
diferencia de los esporádicos y aislados ejemplos que de sus antecedentes encontramos en Europa. Otra forma de adaptación o modificación espacial se produce en la arquitectura rural, como lo han
demostrado los trabajos de Heinrich [61] y Romero de Terreros. [62]
También debieran considerarse en este capítulo los análisis estructurales y, sobre todo, de las técnicas de construcción en la arquitectura
de las misiones, especialmente en Mojos y Chiquitos, tema trabajado
por Busaniche [63] y por Buschiazzo. [64]

Además de las posiciones interpretativas criticadas cabría comentar
la que, con cierto eclecticismo, nos atreveríamos a llamar "académica".
Esta posición está representada por distinguidos profesores norteame-

[56] Carlos Arbeláez Camacho, "Nueva visión de la arquitectura colonial", BCIHE,
2, Caracas, 1965, pp. 27-46.

[57] John McAndrew, The Open-air Churches of Sixteenth-Century Mexico. Cambridge, Mass. 1965. Sostienen también la tesis Obregón Santacilia y, en cierto
modo, Tounsaint y Angulo.

[58] José de Mesa y Teresa Gisbert, Iglesias con atrio y posas en Bolivia. La
Paz, 1961. "La capilla abierta de Copacabana", AIAAIE/A, 15, 1962, pp. 103-108.
"La iglesia de Caquiaviri", Khana, 4, 7-8, marzo, 1955, pp. 27-35.

[59] Erwin W. Palm, "Las capillas abiertas americanas y sus antecedentes en el
occidente cristiano", AIAAIE/A, 1953, pp. 47-64.

[60] Leopoldo Castedo, "El plateresco americano". Finis Terrae, 20, 4º trimestre,
Santiago de Chile, 1958, pp. 53-58. A History of Latin American Art and Architecture. New York, 1969, p. 320.

[61] Heinrich Berlin, "Una iglesia rural mexicana", SGHG/A, 29: 1-4, enero-dic.,
1956, pp. 46-54.

[62] Manuel Romero de Terreros, Antiguas haciendas de México, 1956.

[63] Hernán Busaniche, La arquitectura en las misiones jesuíticas guaraníes. Santa
Fe, 1955.

[64] Mario J. Buschiazzo, "La arquitectura de las misiones de Mojos y Chiquitos", AIAAIE/A, 5, 1952, pp. 34-49. "La arquitectura de las misiones de Mojos
y Chiquitos", Sudamérika, 4: 3, Nov., Dez., 1953, 14 pp. "La arquitectura en
madera de las misiones del Paraguay, Chiquitos, Mojos y Maynas", en International
Congress of the History of Art 1963. pp. 173-190.

ricanos, especialmente Kubler,[65] Markman,[66] Baird,[67] además del español Angulo[68] y del alemán Palm.[69] Si hubiéramos incluido al Brasil en este análisis deberíamos añadir el nombre no menos distinguido de Germain Bazin.[70] Esta "escuela", si así podemos denominarla, prefiere opinar lo menos posible, ceñirse a los hechos. Y los hechos, en la historia de la arquitectura, son las plantas, las fachadas, la identificación de los autores, la determinación de los monumentos de acuerdo con determinados criterios estilísticos. Obra meritísima, absolutamente necesaria. Tal vez por sus mismas características rehuye la intromisión de la historia en la historia del arte, conflicto que trató con devoción Kelemen[71] y planteó erradamente Cali.[72] La selección del grupo mencionado de ninguna manera significa la eliminación de él de otros historiadores que, además de la erudición teórica y del dominio de la información documental, tratan (y no pocas veces consiguen) darle ese doble contenido, a nuestro juicio necesario. En general la posición "académica" considera el arte colonial como

[65] George Kubler, además de las numerosas obras ya citadas: "Indianismo y mestizaje como tradiciones americanas medievales y clásicas", BCIHE, 4, enero, Caracas, 1966, pp. 51-61. "El problema de los aportes europeos no ibéricos en la arquitectura colonial latinoamericana", BCIHE, 9, abril, Caracas, 1968, pp. 104-116. "Latin American Art and the Baroque Period in Europe (studies in Western Art)" Actas del vigésimo Congreso Internacional de Historia del Arte. Princeton III, 1963, pp. 145-146.

[66] Sidney D. Markman, Colonial Architecture of Antigua Guatemala. Philadelphia, 1964. "The Plaza Mayor of Guatemala City",JSAH, vol. xxv, núm. 3, pp. 181-196. "Santa Cruz, Antigua, Guatemala, and the Spanish Colonial Architecture of Central America", JSAH, vol. xv, núm. 1, pp. 12-19. "Las Capuchinas: an Eighteenth Century Convent in Antigua, Guatemala", JSAH, vol. xx, núm. 1, pp. 27-33. "La mano de obra indígena (no española) en el desarrollo de la arquitectura colonial de Guatemala", BCIHE, 3, junio, Caracas, 1965, pp. 88-97.

[67] Joseph A. Baird Jr., The Churches of Mexico 1530-1810. Berkeley, 1962. "The Ornamental Niche-Pilaster in the Hispanic World", JSAH, vol. xv, núm. 1, pp. 5-11.

[68] Diego Angulo Iñíguez (en colaboración con Mario J. Buschiazzo y Enrique Marco Dorta), Historia del arte hispanoamericano. 3 v., Barcelona, 1945-1956, Planos de monumentos arquitectónicos de América y Filipinas existentes en el Archivo de Indias. 7 vols., Sevilla, 1933-39. "Andrés y Francisco de Ocampo y las esculturas de la catedral de Comayagua, Honduras", AAF, 2: 4, 1952, pp. 113-120. "La capilla de indios de Teposcolula y la catedral de Siena", AAF, 25: 98, abril-junio, 1952, pp. 170-172. "Planos y documentos de América. Catedral, Santiago de Cuba, 1731-1784", Arquitectura, 21: 238, mayo, Habana, 1953, pp. 211-218. "Eighteenth-Century Church Fronts in Mexico City", JSAH, vol. 5, 1946-47, pp. 27-32.

[69] Erwin Walter Palm, Los monumentos arquitectónicos de la Española. 2 vols., Santo Domingo, 1955. "El arte del nuevo Mundo después de la conquista española", BCIHE, 4, enero, Caracas, 1966, pp. 37-50. "Plateresque and Renaissance Monuments of the Island of Hispaniola", JSAH, vol. 5, pp. 1-14. "Introducción arte colonial", Cuadernos Americanos, año 16, 92: 2, marzo-abril, 1957.

[70] Germain Bazin, L'Architecture Religieuse Baroque au Brésil. Paris-São Paulo, pp. 956-58. Aleijadinho et la sculpture baroque du Brésil. Paris, 1963.

[71] Vid. nota 34.

[72] Vid. nota 50.

derivado del español, rechaza de plano el supuesto "mestizaje", altoperuano e incluso el "criollismo" mexicano. Más que arte americano, se trata de arte en América.

IV

Entre los lectores de habla inglesa y los especialistas de otras latitudes era forzada obra de referencia la de Kelemen [73] hasta la publicación del tomo correspondiente a la *Pelican History of Art* de Kubler y Soria. [74] Como ya se ha indicado, Kelemen trató de vincular un caudal nutrido de noticias al transfondo histórico-social. Kelemen afirma un "arte americano". En el prólogo señala: "The farther I traveled, the more I became aware that the artistic production ... under Spanish administration —which resulted in a conglomeration of transplanted styles— is surpassed by more original manifestations on this continent. For the Indian and mestizo craftsmen and artists had yet to pour their imagination, their tremendous artistic talent, and their ancestral skills into the service of the new religion." Y añade: "Until recently the art of colonial Latin America either has been treated in a most perfunctory manner, merely as an appendix to that of the Iberian Peninsula, or ignored. As a rule, the more a building, statue, or canvas resembled a European prototype, the greater reverence it was accorded." [75] El pretérito empleado por Kelemen puede bien trocarse por un presente que tal vez dure. Kelemen apoya decididamente la nomenclatura de Wethey acerca de un "mestizo style". [76]

Kubler, en cambio y como hemos visto, apostrofa del término "mestizo". [77] En su obra básica, señala, refiriéndose a Arequipa, Cajamarca y Puno: "This style os often called 'mestizo'. The term is abusive to nearly everyone in the Andean region, to the mestizo people, whom it singles out, as well as to the creoles, Spaniards, Indians, and Negroes, whose many contributions it excludes. Hence it is preferable to discuss the style in question as 'provincial highland' architecture..." Al margen de la obsesión por negar la fusión de valores estéticos que cristaliza en una nueva forma (similar actitud se manifiesta al negar la presencia de una "arquitectura de retorno" en la Cartuja de Granada), [78] la obra de Kubler es definitivamente la más sólida y perdurable escrita en lengua no española.

[73] *Vid.* nota 34.
[74] *Vid.* nota 22.
[75] *Op. cit.*, p. VIII.
[76] *Op. cit.*, p. 167.
[77] *Op. cit.*, pp. 91-92 (*vid.* nota 4).
[78] George Kubler, "Arquitectura de los siglos XVII y XVIII", *Ars Hispaniae, Historia universal del arte hispánico.* Vol. XIV. Madrid, 1957. También *vid.* nota 4.

La obra de Wethey,[79] no obstante su antigüedad, sigue siendo también de consulta obligada. Durante dos años el distinguido profesor de Michigan realizó investigaciones de primera mano, ampliadas después en Bolivia.[80] Wethey es, si no autor, al menos difusor de la nomenclatura "arquitectura mestiza" en el Alto Perú.

Erwin Palm, profesor de la Universidad de Heidelberg, ha consagrado sus mejores esfuerzos al estudio del arte antillano del siglo XVI. En su obra básica[81] Palm acepta la denominación de "barroco americano", pero limita su "voluntad artística" (Riegl y después Worringer) a una actitud inconsciente, de reacción más que de acción volitiva, tesis que, según el mismo Palm, podría ser rectificada con la acumulación de nuevos documentos que demuestren lo contrario. En su reciente análisis crítico de la historiografía del arte americano[82] rectifica, en parte, su antigua opinión.

Markman[83] representa a nuestro juicio un modelo de investigación documental, de análisis formal y de profundidad de conocimientos históricos. Para dilucidar (al menos en la reducida área de su campo de acción) el supuesto y discutido "mestizaje", Markman ha realizado una profunda labor en los archivos guatemaltecos para determinar el número y el color de los artesanos que trabajaron en Antigua. Sus conclusiones lo alínean, con la mayor parte de los estudiosos norteamericanos, en la línea de un "arte en América".

El profesor Baird[84] niega cualquiera aportación no europea al desarrollo de la arquitectura mexicana a partir de 1570 u 80. Sigue literalmente la posición de Kubler. A la fachada de Tepalcingo, por ejemplo, la adjetiva de "folk oriented" y "unusual"[85] y de Santa María Tonantzintla dice: "there is a pronounced folk character here, which has inevitably attracted the indigenists and elicited enthusiastic comparisons of this decor with 'Indian' 'native' traditions. As suggested elsewhere in the text and catalogue of this book, there is comparatively little real 'Indian' influence in Mexican viceregal art after 1570 or 1580. There is, however, a marked folk fantasy to much of colonial art, persisting down to the twentieth century".[86]

---

[79] Vid. nota 47.

[80] Harold E. Wethey, "Hispanic Colonial Architecture in Bolivia", *Beaux Arts*, 39, 1952, pp. 47-60; 40, 1952, pp. 193-208. *Arquitectura virreinal en Bolivia*. Recopilación y traducción de José de Mesa y Teresa Gisbert. La Paz, 1960-1961. "La Merced en Cuzco, Perú", *JSAH*, vol. 5, 1946-47, pp. 35-38.

[81] Erwin W. Palm, *Los monumentos arquitectónicos de la Española*. 2 vol. Ciudad Trujillo, 1955.

[82] Vid. nota 37.

[83] Vid. nota 66.

[84] Joseph A. Baird Jr., *The Churches of Mexico 1530-1810*. Photographs by Hugo Rudinger. Berkeley, 1962. "Mexican architecture and the baroque", *International Congress of the History of Art*, 1963, p. 191-202.

[85] *Op. cit.*, p. 114.

[86] *Op. cit.*, p. 122.

Cabría preguntar al profesor Baird quiénes son los autores de tal "folk fantasy". Para Baird, también, no hay arte americano, sino arte en América. Aparte interpretaciones, su acopio documental es excelente, así como las aclaraciones sobre algunas dudas en cuanto a atribución de obras.

Muchas más notas podrían añadirse a la crítica de la abundante literatura histórico-artística norteamericana. La necesidad de apretar este texto, excesivo, nos fuerza a omitirlas.

V

El análisis crítico de la historiografía de la arquitectura sobre temas americanos ha sido recientemente realizado en forma panorámica, como hemos visto, por Palm [87] y el particular mexicano por Pedro Rojas. [88] No obstante, y dada la índole de esta Mesa Redonda, creemos oportuno hacer algunas acotaciones a las referencias críticas de Rojas. Primero, porque el historiador mexicano, por razones de elemental discreción y buen gusto, no opina acerca de sí mismo. Segundo, porque es nuestro intento apoyar (o disentir) tales puntos de vista críticos desde el que pretende justificar el título de este trabajo.

Los historiadores españoles mantienen con ejemplar constancia la imagen de un arte hispanoamericano en cuanto provincia de un gran arte hispano. Tiene razón Kubler al proponer una revisión sistemática de los orígenes directos no españoles del arte colonial. [89] Sin embargo, puestos a establecer una competencia sistemática en los orígenes de las ideas arquitectónicas (en otros términos, a determinar quién fue el creador de la idea), resultaría que la arquitectura española no es española. Ni la románica, ni la gótica, ni la isabelina, ni la mozárabe (¿típico caso de arquitectura "mestiza"?) ni la plateresca ni menos la barroca. Tal vez sólo se salven (y apenas) el arte trentino, Gaudf y Torroja.

Kubler censura un "imperialismo" español en su visión del arte colonial americano. Salvo las alusiones a supuestas supervivencias mayas o aztecas y la atribución a ideas precolombinas de las capillas abiertas (Angulo) o el elaborado y fructífero trabajo sobre la decoración "planiforme" del Alto Perú (Marco Dorta), para los autores españoles de la obra más contundente publicada en castellano, se trata de un arte "en" América, de un arte español, en este caso. La posición del tercer coautor, Mario J. Buschiazzo, merece párrafo aparte, y muy especial.

[87] *Vid.* nota 37.
[88] Pedro Rojas, "Historiografía del siglo XX sobre la arquitectura de la Nueva España", *BCIHE*, 9, abril, Caracas, 1968, pp. 74-103.
[89] George Kubler, "El problema de los aportes europeos no ibéricos en la arquitectura colonial latinoamericana", *BCIHE*, 9, abril, Caracas, 1968, pp. 104-116.

La obra en cuestión es, por cierto, la historia del arte hispano-americano. [90] Angulo escribió los capítulos sobre México, Centroamérica y las Antillas; Buschiazzo los de Brasil, Paraguay, Misiones de Mojos y Chiquitos, Argentina y Chile; Marco Dorta el resto. El primer tomo de los tres publicados (se anuncia desde hace tiempo un cuarto para los siglos XIX y XX y los índices) apareció hace ya 24 años. La obra es, sin embargo, y lo será probablemente durante mucho tiempo, fundamental acopio de referencias y de materiales diversos.

Angulo ha continuado, desde Sevilla y Madrid, su trabajo meticuloso de esclarecimiento documental. Marco Dorta sigue viajando por América del Sur y mantiene su producción de monografías. [91]

Formado en tan rigurosa escuela, mas animado por el noble empeño de "modernizar" técnicas y puntos de vista estilísticos, otro español, Santiago Sebastián, realiza en Colombia una labor sistemática de permanente redescubrimiento. [92] Circunscrito a los límites geográficos de su campo de estudio, Sebastián no se ha interesado todavía por extenderlos y aquilatar, por esta vía, sus posibilidades de ampliar paralelos y comparar modalidades contemporáneas. Su posición gravita entre un arte "en" y un arte "de" en su visión americana. Lo importante es que la ve desde dentro y su acto volitivo de radicación en el propio escenario le permite identificarse más con el objeto tratado.

Similar en cuanto al honesto rigor pero diferente en cuanto a las inquietudes por ampliar el horizonte de sus trabajos es el caso del matrimonio Mesa-Gisbert. Dueños de una disciplina en el sistema de vieja cepa europea, Teresa Gisbert y José de Mesa jamás aventuran una teoría sin antes haberla comprobado documentalmente. [93] Ambos

[90] Vid. nota 68.

[91] Enrique Marco Dorta, "Iglesia del siglo XVIII en Bolivia", AAF, 2:4, 1952, pp. 237-256. El barroco en la arquitectura de la villa Imperial de Potosí. Potosí, 1955. "Andean Baroque Decoration", JSAH, 5, 1946-47, pp. 33-34. La arquitectura barroca en el Perú. Madrid, 1957.

[92] Santiago Sebastián: Álbum de arte colonial de Tunja. Tunja, 1963. "Hacia una valoración de la arquitectura colonial colombiana", ACHSC, 1-2, Bogotá, 1963, pp. 219-238. En este trabajo el autor destaca el "mestizaje" en la escultura integrada en la arquitectura y describe la flora nativa en la decoración. "Notas sobre la arquitectura manierista en Quito", BCIHE, 1, enero, Caracas, pp. 113-120. "Relación de los monumentos de Mompox con el arte venezolano", BCIHE, 10, nov., Caracas, 1968, 73-92.

[93] Vid. notas 7, 23, 42, 47, 58. Además: José Mesa y Teresa Gisbert, "Noticias para la historia del arte en La Paz", AEA, 10, 1953, pp. 171-208. "El estilo mestizo en la arquitectura virreinal boliviana", Khana, 4: 7-8, marzo 1955, pp. 9-26. "Un arquitecto potosino del siglo XVIII: Bernardo de Rojas", Khana, 4: 2: 19-20, oct., 1956, pp. 195-199. San Francisco de La Paz. La Paz, 1962. "La arquitectura 'mestiza' en el Collao. La obra de Diego Choque y Malco Maita", AIAAIE/A, 15, 1962, pp. 53-65. Contribuciones al estudio de la arquitectura andina. La Paz, 1966. "Determinantes del llamado estilo mestizo. Breves consideraciones sobre el término". BCIHE, 10, nov., Caracas, 1968, pp. 93-119.

pertenecen al grupo de los que creen en las peculiaridades originales de un arte americano. Sus aportaciones, por ejemplo, a la reinterpretación de conceptos espaciales en Bolivia son convincentes y originales.

Entre los consagrados a la valoración "desde dentro", el ilustre arquitecto peruano Emilio Harth-terré ocupa también lugar de honor. Sus ideas están resumidas en la respuesta a la mencionada encuesta de Gasparini. "Por fuerza el vocablo 'mestizo' se acomoda con un temple del barroco americano; creemos que el calificativo es más lato que lo que hasta ahora se entiende por él; despojado de toda la singularidad étnica que se le puede atribuir, pensando sólo en obra de gentes de sangre mediatizada, puede y debe ser empleado." [94] Harth-terré ha dedicado toda una vida al estudio del arte peruano colonial. [95]

Mario J. Buschiazzo, en suma, representa la síntesis entre erudición e interpretación. Su capacidad de análisis y su visión panorámica del fenómeno continental, hacen de él, especialmente en su sintética *Historia de la arquitectura colonial*, un adalid de la posición americanista. [96]

Durante el desarrollo de estas notas hemos procurado ceñirnos al comentario de las obras que de manera directa atañen al planteamiento inicial. Unas son panorámicas, abarcan todo el territorio hispanoamericano. Otras se limitan a lo nacional incluso considerando las notorias diferencias que existen entre la "geografía política" (respetada rigurosamente por Angulo) y la "geografía artística" que hace, v.gr., a Tunja más afín con Quito que con Cartagena y a Puno más cerca de La Paz que de Lima.

VI

El análisis crítico de la historiografía de la arquitectura, como hemos visto, ha sido realizado en forma cabal por Palm. [97] El particular mexicano, por Pedro Rojas. [98] No obstante, y dada la índole de esta Mesa

[94] Vid. nota 2.

[95] (Sólo señalamos algunas obras en la vasta bibliografía del arquitecto e historiador peruano) Emilio Harth-Terre, *Artífices en el virreinato del Perú*. Lima, 1945. "El indígena peruano en las bellas artes virreinales", *UNCRU*, 49: 118. 1. sem. 1960, pp. 46-95. Y Alberto Márquez Abanto, "El artesano negro en la arquitectura virreinal limeña", *RPEANR*, 25: 2 jul.-dic., 1961, pp. 360-430. "Arequipa. Genio y donaire de un estilo peruano", *BCIHE*, 1, enero, Caracas, 1964, pp. 51-63.

[96] Mario J. Buschiazzo, *Historia de la arquitectura colonial en Iberoamérica*. Buenos Aires, 1961. "Exotic influences in American Colonial Art", *JSAH*, 5, 1946-47, 21-23. Vid. notas 49, 64 y 68.

[97] Vid. nota 37.

[98] Pedro Rojas, "Historiografía mexicana del siglo xx sobre la arquitectura de la Nueva España", *BCIHE*, 9, abril, Caracas, 1968, pp. 74-103.

Redonda, creemos oportuno hacer algunas acotaciones a las referencias críticas de Rojas. Primero, porque el historiador mexicano, por razones de discreción y buen gusto, no opina acerca de sí mismo. Segundo, porque su análisis persigue otros propósitos.

Singulares coyunturas históricas, culturales y aun políticas generaron las condiciones para el desarrollo espectacular de la historiografía artística nacional en México: la disciplina del positivismo, con todas sus taras, la reacción contra el afrancesamiento del porfiriato, la autoafirmación artística concomitante con la Revolución agraria, la cristalización de toda una tecnología moderna en la investigación histórica (Alfonso Reyes, Silvio Zavala, Cosío Villegas, Edmundo O'Gorman, Gaos y Zea, El Colegio, el Fondo).

Tan heterogéneos y ciertamente constructivos elementos transformaron el movimiento inicial narcisista que en hora oportuna llevara el Dr. Atl a lo sublime con mucho de descomedido. El deslumbramiento por la forma artística del pasado nacional originó, como era lógico, una literatura ditirámbica. Duró poco. Y de todo ello surgió, explícito o implícito, un programa que, con las alternativas del caso, se cumple y se mantiene.

En sus líneas generales este programa consiste en el agotamiento de la investigación monográfica, en la cautela para emitir opiniones, en una mesura muy mexicana. Tal vez estas virtudes se hayan convertido, al juicio de algunos, en limitaciones. Más adelante veremos cómo Justino Fernández, desde su ejemplar Instituto (hace aún muy poco tiempo que ha dejado de dirigirlo) trató de equilibrar investigación e interpretación. Según Rojas [99] el programa trata también de... "establecer las filiaciones para diferenciar dentro de la funcionalidad de las obras de arte lo que es variante, invariante y original". Hay además una confusa obsesión esteticista. Tratemos de ejemplarizar el proceso.

Todo parte, al parecer, de Revilla. [100] Confesamos que nuestras opiniones al respecto son de segunda mano. No hemos manejado esta obra primigenia (se publicó en 1893, hace ya 76 años) simplemente porque la de Toussaint hizo innecesaria su consulta. Pero las opiniones de los historiadores mexicanos acerca de ella son abundantes y creemos que valederas, especialmente las de Fernández y Rojas.

Según Fernández el valor principal de Revilla estriba en la vigencia de sus interpretaciones acerca de un arte que, superando los modelos peninsulares (o modificándolos), adquirió expresiones propias. [101] A pesar de su preocupación en la búsqueda de lo mexicano parece que la escala de valores, atribuyendo méritos decrecientes a las tres cate-

[99] "Historiografía . . ." p. 79.

[100] Manuel C. Revilla, *El arte de México en la época antigua y durante el gobierno virreinal*. México, 1893. (2ª ed., 1923.)

[101] Justino Fernández, *El Retablo de los Reyes. Estética del arte de la Nueva España*. México, 1959, p. 129.

gorías de un arte español, criollo e indígena, sirvió de pauta para el
reducido número de historiadores partidarios de clasificar el arte mexicano como provincial. Tal es el caso de Francisco Díez Barroso [102] que
lo juzga como "una rama del maravilloso arte español". [103] Conviene
incluir en este grupo, salvando las grandes distancias en el tiempo y
en la intención, a Víctor Manuel Villegas [104] que trató de destruir, en
un voluminoso libro, el "mito del estípite". También desde ángulos muy
distintos y dispares, cuadra considerar aquí a Francisco de la Maza, no
por ser "provincialista", que no lo es, sino tal vez por no ser nada más
(y nada menos) que un rigurosísimo intérprete de la realidad artística
colonial sin condescender con encasillamientos rígidos y mutables. Digamos de paso que Francisco de la Maza posee otros atributos. Entre ellos
(se lo han dicho muchas veces) el de ser un excelente escritor. A la
mayor parte de los historiadores del arte, en el mejor de los casos, se
nos consulta, a él se le lee. [105]

Inicia el empeño por establecer diferencias espirituales y formales
entre el barroco de México y el de España (nadie se preocupa a la
sazón de Europa) Manuel Romero de Terreros. La obra de Romero
es enorme. En la bibliografía de Justino Fernández [106] figura con 466
títulos. José Juan Tablada [107] entra de lleno en el capítulo de los diti-
rámbicos, y el "caso Atl" es, [108] al mismo respecto, conmovedor en
cuanto a sus interpretaciones, espléndido en cuanto a la documentación
gráfica. Para el Dr. Atl el "ultrabarroco" (sic) es exclusivamente mexicano. El arquitecto Obregón Santacilia, [109] usa sin ambajes el término
"mestizo". También para él las posas y las capillas abiertas son producto
del arrastre precolombino. MacGregor [110] habla de un "plateresco indígena". Su trabajo sobre la arquitectura y la decoración del siglo XVI
tiene, entre otros, el interés por aportar abundantes testimonios gráficos.

Constreñidos por las limitaciones de tiempo y espacio, que un trabajo
de esta índole determinan, no pueden incluirse en la ya larga lista todos
los investigadores del Instituto. [111] Debemos mencionar, sin embargo, la
obra del profesor Xavier Moyssen, especialmente por tratarse del único
historiador mexicano que, hasta ahora, ha manifestado interés creciente

[101] Francisco Díez Barroso, El arte en Nueva España. México, 1921.
[102] Cita de Justino Fernández en El Retablo... (vid. nota 101), p. 152.
[104] Víctor Manuel Villegas, El gran signo formal del barroco. Ensayo histórico
del apoyo estípite. México, 1956.
[105] Vid. notas 17 y 24.
[106] Vid. nota 27.
[107] José Juan Tablada, Historia del arte en México. México, 1927.
[108] Atl, Dr. (Gerardo Murillo), Manuel Toussaint, José R. Benítez, Iglesias
de México. México, 1924-1927.
[109] Carlos Obregón Santacilia, México como eje de las antiguas arquitecturas de
América. México, 1947.
[110] Luis Mac Gregor, El Plateresco en México. México, 1954.
[111] Vid. nota 27 y núm. 30 en adelante de AIIE/M.

por el arte colonial de América del Sur. [112] En sus trabajos Moyssen suscribe sin reservas la realidad de un carácter indocristiano.

Párrafo especial merece Constantino Reyes Valerio. [113] Bien es cierto que Tepalcingo (y sus proyecciones) había sido "descubierto" por Toussaint. [114] El mérito de Reyes Valerio estriba en su planteamiento valorativo de todo un estilo, proyectado en los límites de los Estados de Morelos y Puebla. Sus análisis lineales e iconográficos son de extraordinario valor. El "estilo Tepalcingo" plantea la reinterpretación de la iconografía tradicional cristiana europea, con evidentes resabios medievales, en un medio nuevo y "mestizo". Esperamos que Reyes Valerio se decida a elaborar un trabajo mayor, que podría dar la clave a muchas incógnitas vigentes.

La figura culminante de la historiografía colonial del arte mexicano es, sin lugar a dudas, la benemérita de Manuel Toussaint. Es lamentable que su muerte haya privado a la historiografía del arte hispanoamericano de su proyección analítica continental, una sola vez por él llevada a cabo en su trabajo sobre el mudéjar en América. [115] La sólida cultura de Toussaint, su capacidad de observación, trascienden en su identificación entre formas artísticas y formas de vida. Su obra es un monumento en la historia colonial de México. Hasta donde es posible establecer los principios de una técnica basada en la obra de un autor, creemos que éstos podrían resumirse de esta manera: ante todo "vivir" y amar la obra de arte, entendiéndose por vivirla el identificarse con el medio en el cual la obra fue concebida y realizada; escarmenar hasta el fondo los datos disponibles y lograr los que faltan; situar el juicio crítico de la obra en el tiempo histórico, es decir, saber qué opinaban de ella los que la veían o usaban; resumir todas estas experiencias en el papel, tratando de sofrenar (en buena hora muchas veces Toussaint no lo conseguía) el entusiasmo. Los libros de Toussaint son académicos. Nuestra preferencia se inclina, sobre todo, por sus iglesias de Puebla, [116] aunque tal vez el trabajo que hemos leído más veces (sonriendo no pocas de ellas ante su enternecedora pasión) es su "Apología. . ." [117]

La función de Justino Fernández podría resumirse como la de autor, catalizador y animador de este florecimiento de la historiografía artística mexicana. Con erudición ejemplar, Fernández acumula en su Retablo [118]

[112] Xavier Moyssén, "La catedral de Puno", AIIE, 31, 1962, pp. 43-55. "Las cruces de Toluca", AIIE, 27, 1958, pp. 33-46.

[113] Constantino Reyes Valerio, Tepalcingo. México, 1960. Trilogía Barroca. México, 1960.

[114] Manuel Toussaint, "Una joya de arte desconocida: el Santuario de Tepalcingo", AIAAIE/A, 6, 1953, pp. 39-44.

[115] Manuel Toussaint, Arte mudéjar en América. México, 1946.

[116] Manuel Toussaint, La catedral y las iglesias de Puebla. México, 1954.

[117] Manuel Toussaint, "Apología del arte barroco en América", AIAAIE/A, 9, 1956, pp. 13-20.

[118] Vid., nota 101.

todas las opiniones que los contemporáneos manifestaron acerca del
arte colonial, a las que suma sus propios juicios críticos sobre la obra
historiográfica posterior. Es un arsenal de encontradas valoraciones que
representa una forma diferenciada de llegar a la valoración sintética.
Justino Fernández, tanto en su abundante obra monográfica como en
sus libros de síntesis, sostiene la vigencia de un gusto "mestizo". Ya
se ha indicado que su obra de investigador corre paralela a la del organizador directriz. También hemos mencionado la vigencia de un programa que se cumple. La papeleta, el plano, el diagrama y el análisis
de la forma, el encuentro del dato, o la rectificación gracias a la búsqueda de nuevas fuentes, son tareas necesarias, imprescindibles, pero no
únicas. Justino Fernández se ha pedido a sí mismo y ha pedido a los
investigadores e historiadores mexicanos, simplemente opinar. En cuanto
a la motivación de este trabajo, ese opinar sobre el hecho y el objeto
documentados consiste en la aclaración del dilema propuesto al principio.

Creemos que Pedro Rojas lo ha resuelto. [119] Y para no hacer más
largo este largo pergeño de notas, resumamos con el índice de su obra
lo que pareciera ser la clave del asunto: "Primera parte: Las artes en el
ámbito de los indios; Segunda parte: Las artes en el ámbito de los
españoles."

[119] Pedro Rojas, *Historia General del Arte Mexicano. Época Colonial.* México,
1963.

NOVELA DE LA REVOLUCIÓN: CRITERIOS CONTEMPORÁNEOS

JOSEPH SOMMERS

Es ya hora de que se vuelva a examinar la llamada "novela de la Revolución", la cual se encuentra en peligro de caer en un olvido casi completo, o, en el mejor de los casos, en un destierro injusto al salón de clases y al manual de historia literaria.

El mismo paso de los años, que ha venido perfilando con contornos más nítidos los acontecimientos y el significado de la Revolución Mexicana, hace posible ahora que a través de la distancia temporal veamos desde nuevas perspectivas el proceso de la novela mexicana. La definición operante en el presente trabajo tiene como base la temática: denominamos "novelas de la Revolución" las obras cuya última significación humana depende de los conflictos y los problemas engendrados por la lucha revolucionaria en México con el fin de cambiar las instituciones nacionales —lucha que estalla en noviembre de 1910 y cuya trayectoria termina en 1940. Para nosotros, pues, la Revolución Mexicana constituye un fenómeno de treinta años.

Desde nuestra perspectiva no sirven ya las viejas categorizaciones de este género que abundaban en los 1940 y 1950: "memorias más que novelas; ya el relato episódico que sigue la figura central de un caudillo, o bien la narración cuyo protagonista es el pueblo; perspectiva autobiográfica, etcétera. Tampoco nos parece adecuada la afirmación del profesor Manuel Pedro González, escrita en 1950: "el tema de la Revolución parece haberse agotado sin agotarse. Quiero decir que el asunto ha dejado de tener virtualidad inspiradora para los novelistas..." [1]

El hecho es que para los novelistas modernos de México, de los últimos veinte años, la Revolución, en una u otra de sus etapas, ha sido el trasfondo y ha tenido una presencia activa en algunas de sus obras importantes. Aquí me refiero a Agustín Yáñez, a Juan Rulfo en varios de sus mejores cuentos, a Elena Garro, a Fernando Benítez, a Rosario Castellanos y a Carlos Fuentes. Este fenómeno de las últimas dos décadas hace posible ampliar el enfoque tradicional. Nos proponemos en el trabajo presente trazar, en términos sintéticos, cómo es interpretada y entendida la Revolución Mexicana en seis de las novelas más significativas que se escribieron en México entre 1915 y 1962.

[1] *Trayectoria de la novela en México.* México, Botas, 1951, p. 92.

Esta manera de formular el problema lleva implícitas tres premisas: 1) Que la novela como género está íntimamente vinculada con la experiencia nacional. De ahí que se espere que las conclusiones tengan interés historiográfico; 2) Que cuanto más se aferra la novela a las exigencias del género, es decir, a las normas formales de la novela, tanto más expresiva resulta ser. Es decir, damos por supuesto, que las novelas de más alcance literario son las que desarrollan una visión más profunda de la experiencia mexicana; 3) Que un método válido de resumir el proceso histórico de la novela es el de seleccionar novelas claves, ejemplares, en vez de esforzarse por abarcar toda la producción novelesca, reduciéndose así a generalizaciones diluidas aplicables a todas las obras, pero útiles sólo en cuanto el denominador común es útil.

Las obras que estudiaremos a continuación son: *Los de abajo*, [2] de Mariano Azuela; *La sombra del caudillo*, [3] de Martín Luis Guzmán; *El resplandor*, [4] de Mauricio Magdaleno; *Al filo del agua*, [5] de Agustín Yáñez; *Oficio de tinieblas*, [6] de Rosario Castellanos y, *La muerte de Artemio Cruz*, [7] de Carlos Fuentes.

Casi sin excepción son las mismas novelas que hemos analizado en un libro reciente: *After the Storm: Landmarks of the Modern Mexican Novel*. [8] Aquí el propósito no es repetir conceptos ya expresados, sino dirigirnos a problemas de historiografía literaria e intelectual.

Escrita en 1915 *Los de abajo* no sólo sienta la base de la novelística de la Revolución, sino que es la obra de ficción narrativa más importante que se da a luz en México hasta el advenimiento de la novela moderna tres décadas más tarde. En términos literarios alcanza un alto nivel de adecuación entre técnica y temática.

El adjetivo "episódico" aplicado a esta obra puede confundir. En realidad un análisis cuidadoso revela una arquitectura literaria bastante nítida, basada en múltiples interrelaciones —las más de las veces paralelos o contrastes— entre paisajes, personajes, segmentos narrados. Por ejemplo, la estructura circular encierra en sí misma un tema central: el retorno eterno al punto de partida. La muerte trágica de Demetrio Macías en el mismo cañón desde el cual él y sus hombres se lanzaron a la bola comunica un significado irónico. A pesar de luchas revolucionarias y del heroísmo personal el destino del hombre consiste en cerrar el círculo que niega significancia a su vida. Otra técnica de Azuela es la

[2] Para este trabajo nos hemos referido a la edición de la Colección Popular, México, Fondo de Cultura Económica, 1960. Las citas que se hagan serán a esta edición y aparecerán en el texto.

[3] Para este trabajo nos hemos referido a la última edición: México, Cía. General de Ediciones, 1968. Las citas que se hagan serán a esta edición y aparecerán en el texto.

[4] México, Botas, 1937.

[5] México, Porrúa, 1947.

[6] México, Joaquín Mortiz, 1962.

[7] México, Fondo de Cultura Económica, 1962.

[8] Albuquerque, University of New Mexico Press, 1968.

de extender, por medio de una serie de acciones simbólicas y metáforas sugestivas, el significado de la trama. De ahí que se establezca por debajo de la superficie una segunda trama. En primer plano está la historia personal de Macías. Relacionada con ella, y siguiendo la misma trayectoria trágica, está la Revolución Mexicana.

El hábil manejo de una serie de subtramas contribuye al sentido de estructuración cuidadosa. Éstas desempeñan la función interna de interrelacionar las tres secciones de la novela y el papel temático de reforzar la visión irónica que constituye la médula de la obra. Otra técnica de que se sirve Azuela es la de plantear un tema desde el punto de vista de un personaje y posteriormente elaborarlo dentro de la acción misma. En la escena final de la primera parte Solís, el intelectual desilusionado, condena la inmoralidad de los revolucionarios mexicanos, "La psicología de nuestra raza, condensada en dos palabras: ¡robar, matar!" (p. 72). Unas páginas, y unos días después, sentados los revolucionarios en un restaurante, surge en la conversación el tema de "yo maté" y cada cual narra un homicidio, generalmente gratuito, del cual ha sido responsable. Hacia el final de la segunda parte, en la escena XIV, estando el grupo de Demetrio en un tren rumbo a Aguascalientes, la conversación gira alrededor de los robos que han cometido los partidarios de Macías. En esta ocasión se elabora el tema de "yo robé". El autor logra establecer relaciones entre distintas escenas de su obra, relaciones que realzan en forma irónica la temática de la desilusión.

Se podrían seguir precisando otros aspectos de la forma de esta novela, tales como el empleo del lenguaje, la compresión, y el ritmo. Estos elementos contribuyen a una serie de conceptos paradógicos de donde emana la cosmovisión de Mariano Azuela. Entre las ironías principales figuran éstas: 1) La conducta y el parecer físico del hombre son presentados a través de imágenes normalmente aplicables a bestias; 2) Los de abajo, al posesionarse de los haberes y los bienes de la gente rica, que a su vez se había enriquecido injustamente, se comportan de una manera igualmente cruel e inmoral; 3) La educación y las ideas no sirven ningún propósito positivo en el huracán de la Revolución; 4) Sólo ante la inminencia de la muerte encuentra el hombre una relación armoniosa con la naturaleza, la cual "se viste de nupcias" y se vuelve fuerza purificadora.

La visión del mundo que se puede abstraer de la novela de Azuela encierra una valorización trágica del mexicano y de su Revolución. Al mexicano lo vemos como prisionero de sus pasiones, como miembro de una raza de alguna manera irredenta, que ha perdido la gracia. Hasta un Demetrio Macías, dotado de honestidad y decencia campesinas, cae en la inmoralidad. Otro aspecto de la visión de Azuela se deriva del enfoque colectivo de la obra. No hay personajes bien desarrollados, que reflexionen, que tengan vida interior, cuya formación particular prerrevolucionaria conozcamos. Al contrario, *Los de abajo* es

novela de masas, y este enfoque le da un cariz naturalista, destacando
la impotencia del individuo frente a la presión de los acontecimientos
y de la historia.

Por otra parte, Azuela simplifica enormemente la historia. En una
novela que se concentra en las presiones sociales hace falta que se nos
comunique un análisis de la dinámica de estas presiones. Aquí me refiero
a lo que para E. M. Forster se llama "causalidad". A pesar de su talento
literario en extender el significado de las acciones, Azuela, cautivado
por el drama del presente, deja de establecer una relación entre pasado
y presente. Como consecuencia, parece interpretar la Revolución como
fenómeno altamente espontáneo y superficial.

Relacionado con la ausencia de análisis es el marcado tono anti-
intelectual de la novela. Para Azuela las ideas no tienen cabida en el
transcurso de la Revolución. En ningún momento se notan rastros del
fermento ideológico que tradicionalmente ha sido la contribución de la
clase media educada a las situaciones revolucionarias. Al contrario las tres
figuras de posible categoría intelectual en la novela son un oportunista
corrompido, Cervantes, un idealista amargado y cínico, Solís, y un poeta
loco, Valderrama.

Por otra parte, si *Los de abajo* comunica una visión de la Revolución
como fracaso y del mexicano como prisionero de sus circunstancias, esta
visión está comunicada en términos mexicanos. Es decir, a partir de
Azuela la novela empieza el proceso de mexicanización, con personajes
de habla popular, cuya experiencia más vital es la experiencia nacional.

Si *Los de abajo*, protagonizada por las masas campesinas, trata la
etapa violenta de la Revolución, en un ambiente rural del norte del
país, *La sombra del caudillo*, de Martín Luis Guzmán, escrita en 1929,
se sitúa en un mundo y un periodo distintos. Refleja la lucha política
de los 1920, y se concentra en los de arriba —el pequeño grupo de
políticos en la capital nacional que se disputan el poder. Otro contraste notable entre esta obra y la de Azuela es la preocupación estilística en Guzmán, cuyo lenguaje, con toques de elegancia impresionista,
refleja la herencia del modernismo mexicano.

No obstante estos contrastes, en sus aspectos claves las dos novelas
se prestan más a la comparación. Técnicamente, la de Guzmán sigue
una secuencia cronológica, demuestra una circularidad anecdótica semejante a la de *Los de abajo*, y se aferra a la Revolución como base de la
trama novelesca. Conceptualmente las dos obras trazan en sus personajes centrales una trayectoria gradual de corrupción y frustración que
termina en la muerte violenta y trágica, muerte que niega que haya
habido progreso hacia las metas de la Revolución. Tal como Azuela,
Guzmán amplía el significado de su narración infundiendo en las relaciones personales y los acontecimientos políticos ironías profundas. El
tema central —la corrupción y la tragedia que acompañan inevitablemente la lucha por el poder— es reforzado por la inversión irónica entre

el principio y el fin de la obra. En la última escena, el *Cadillac* de Aguirre, símbolo en el primer capítulo de su autoridad, se ha vuelto propiedad del asesino del joven general enérgico.

Tal como su predecesor en la novela, Guzmán no desarrolla personajes complicados. Más bien vemos desde el exterior a un protagonista interesante, y seguimos el proceso de su destrucción por las circunstancias sociopolíticas. Asimismo, hay una carencia absoluta de antecedentes históricos y personales que nos ayudarían a entender la formación del personaje y la causalidad de la crisis política que constituye el eje de la novela. El enfoque, pues, se limita al presente.

La visión del hombre resulta ser la de un ente inadecuado. La barbarie del palenque de la política mexicana vence las aspiraciones de cualquier individuo que tenga nociones de un código moral, siquiera parcial y limitado. Como dice Olivier, uno de los expertos: "La política de México, política de pistola, sólo conjuga un verbo: madrugar" (p. 208).

En el mundo imaginario que Martín Luis Guzmán construyó a base del México que vio e interpretó, los valores intelectuales desempeñan un papel mínimo. Los pocos campesinos e indios que aparecen están vistos como simples, dóciles, incapaces de entender las maniobras de sus jefes. La clase media, que hubiera podido proporcionar dirigentes y un sentido de valores para la Revolución en estos años, se presenta como un grupo que se mantiene aparte.

Los personajes de Guzmán, generales y políticos en su gran mayoría, casi nunca discuten de ideas. En la única ocasión en que figuran conceptos intelectuales —un discurso de Axkaná a los campesinos— los conceptos resultan ser precisamente el aspecto menos significativo de su oratoria:

> En su discurso no vivían los conceptos: vivían las palabras como entidades individuales, estéticas, reveladoras de lo esencial por la sola virtud de su acción inmediata sobre el alma (p. 101).

En *Los de abajo* vimos a las masas en movimiento sin que hubiera líderes capaces que supieran interpretar sus anhelos revolucionarios. *La sombra del caudillo* en cierta forma es la otra cara de la moneda: el mundo de los caudillos, con toda la sutileza de las rivalidades personales y las maniobras maquiavélicas, presentado como un mundo hermético, en el cual las aspiraciones populares no pesan en las decisiones políticas. Se podría decir que las dos novelas se complementan en su tratamiento temático, y que comparten el enfoque de crítica moral, basada en una interpretación de la experiencia inmediata de la Revolución Mexicana.

El resplandor, de Mauricio Magdaleno, novela indigenista, producto de la década de los 1930, representa un paso adelante en el desarrollo de la novela de la Revolución. Implícita en esta obra está la premisa de que hay que tomar en cuenta el pasado para apreciar el significado del presente.

Escrita en 1937, y situada históricamente en la época de Calles, la novela encierra una nota fuerte de protesta social, presentando el sufrimiento del indio como repetición sin fin de un sistema básico de explotación, sea a manos del conquistador español o de sus herederos criollos.

Una vez más la circularidad de la trama subraya una nota final de angustia. En la primera sección de *El resplandor* un gobernador de Estado, seudobenevolente, visita el pueblo otomí de San Andrés de la Cal y escoge a un niño, Saturnino Herrera, para llevarlo a la capital donde se educará. Al final de la novela, después de que el joven ha crecido, ha entrado en el mundo mestizo, ha engañado a su pueblo, llegando a ser gobernador él mismo, después de que la rebelión desesperada de San Andrés ha sido reprimida cruelmente, retorna Saturnino Herrera a su pueblo para repetir el mismo rito: escoge a un niño para llevarlo a educarse a la capital. El círculo de angustia y de explotación se cierra, para que la historia se repita. Esta continuidad de la condición sufrida del indio implica que la Revolución sirve sólo para darle una forma nueva a la vieja serie negativa de relaciones humanas. La novela sufre de verbosidad, fragmentos ensayísticos y un tono a veces retórico, debido al empeño del autor en imponer al lector su propia actitud de simpatía por el indio. Sin embargo se pueden notar ciertos avances técnicos y literarios, además de la conciencia histórica. Se introducen varias secuencias oníricas para comunicar cómo la magia forma parte de la realidad india. Es más, se nota un intento de manejar la técnica del fluir de la conciencia. Desgraciadamente se trata de ejemplos aislados más que de técnicas empleadas coherentemente e incorporadas dentro de la textura de la novela.

A Mauricio Magdaleno, igual que a sus predecesores, le importaba más el drama de los acontecimientos y las circunstancias sociales que los personajes individuales. Tal como queda simplificada su interpretación de la historia en categorías blanquinegras, así están presentados *a grosso modo* los caracteres, fácilmente divisibles en dos grupos. Los otomíes aparecen simpáticos, estoicos, sufridos. Los mestizos, casi sin excepción, son codiciosos, hipócritas, explotadores. Pasado y presente, pues, vienen a constituir un solo tejido monótono, sin complejidades ni variaciones. El hecho trascendental de la subordinación económica determina de una manera unilateral los valores fundamentales en el mundo de *El resplandor*.

Por simplista que sea el análisis de las relaciones humanas, la visión del mundo de Magdaleno es más avanzada que la de Azuela y Guzmán. Refleja el indigenismo de los 1930, y por implicación sugiere la necesidad de la Reforma Agraria y la eliminación del soborno político.

Por otra parte, mientras que la novela lanza una protesta en contra del despojo de los indios por los herederos de la tradición hispanocatólica, el retrato de los indígenas que nos ofrece demuestra una base conceptual de filiación paternalista. Tal como nos los presenta Magdaleno, en sus creencias y sus acciones, los otomíes de San Andrés son prisioneros de una cultura basada en supersticiones que los mantienen en un estado de ignorancia inocente, surtiendo como defensa solamente el resguardo del estoicismo y la resignación fatalista ante el sufrimiento preordinado. Parecen comportarse de una manera infantil, y su cultura está descrita desde una perspectiva no india. La voz narrativa, más o menos la del autor, cataloga creencias totémicas, una religión empapada de paganismo y una disposición a la medicina popular, todo en un tono que sugiere la inutilidad de estas prácticas en una sociedad occidental. Pocos son los ejemplos de sensibilidad narrativa hacia el papel de tales creencias dentro de la cosmovisión indígena.

El tono antintelectual de las novelas anteriores se repite en *El resplandor.* Para Saturnino las ideas sirven meramente como *slogans,* vehículos de engaño. Para el vate Pedroza, su teniente político pseudointelectual, constituyen el embellecimiento del poder político. Pero vista en un contexto histórico, la novela sirvió un propósito más positivo. El énfasis de Magdaleno en desarrollar una perspectiva histórica; su esfuerzo por establecer la noción de causalidad, por unilateralmente económica que fuera; la nota de protesta que circuló en el México cardenista sobre el abuso de los indios en la década anterior; estos elementos representaban un reto para los intelectuales mexicanos de 1930-1940, década del auge del nacionalismo, cuando se buscaban definiciones nuevas de la nacionalidad mexicana. En la categoría de historia literaria *El resplandor* es la novela indigenista más seria y más elaborada de los primeros treinta años de la Revolución. Extiende el alcance temático de la novela de la Revolución, y anticipa, en sus innovaciones técnicas, la llegada de la novela moderna.

Vistas en su totalidad, como novelas escritas a través del proceso histórico de la Revolución, estas obras permiten que se establezcan algunas conclusiones para la historiografía literaria:

1. Se valen, como materia prima, de personajes, lenguaje, y paisaje mexicanos;

2. Afirman la validez de la experiencia nacional como base de una novela auténticamente mexicana. En este sentido, representan un avance nacionalista, y en este sentido tiene razón Castro Leal al referirse a una "novela de afirmación nacionalista". [9]

[9] Antonio Castro Leal, ed., *La Novela de la Revolución Mexicana.* México, Aguilar, 1960, I, xxix.

3. Se desarrollan como novelas de estructura circular, dependiendo de la acción dramática como núcleo de la trama, acción que resulta ser superior al personaje individual; desarrollan una visión unidimensional de la Revolución, básicamente moralizante; carecen de perspectiva histórica o intelectual, encerrando una valoración crítica negativa y una actitud sumamente pesimista;

4. Llegan a constituir todo un género. Con este ciclo la novela mexicana deja de ser un producto cultural derivativo. Las obras provocan polémicas públicas, los autores reciben reconocimiento, ganan premios, su obra se lee, se sienten "dueños de su propia casa".

Se ha afirmado o, por lo menos implicado, que la novela de la Revolución fue revolucionaria y que, conscientemente, pretendió avanzar la causa revolucionaria. Por ejemplo, dice Frederick Turner en su libro recién publicado: "*Los de abajo* presents the need for love of country by portraying men without patrotism ... It is precisely by showing the lack of unifying ideals that Azuela emphasizes the need for them." [10] Sin embargo se puede hacer constar que sí promovió la conciencia de la experiencia nacional, pero al limitarse al drama de los acontecimientos inmediatos, mostró una actitud de derrota y desilusión.

Otro concepto historiográfico relacionado con estas obras es el del nacionalismo cultural —una tendencia menospreciada en estos días tanto en México como en los EE.UU. Las novelas discutidas hasta aquí demuestran que, dentro de un contexto bien definido, esta tendencia puede producir valores positivos. En efecto, en México durante las décadas que van de 1915 a 1947, Azuela y sus seguidores establecen una tradición novelesca nacional. Sientan las bases de la novela auténticamente mexicana.

En lo que se refiere a las relaciones y posibles paralelos entre literatura y arte, en el proceso de su desarrollo, caben algunas observaciones. Cierto es, como señala Stanley Ross, que hubo un "fenómeno al que sólo puede llamarse renacimiento cultural, que acompañó y fue parte esencial de la Revolución Mexicana —influyendo en el arte, la música, la literatura y la filosofía". [11] Hecha esta observación vale la pena precisar unas diferencias entre la novela y la pintura mural, diferencias de tradición, de espíritu y de función:

1. El arte fue nacionalista en sus temas y revolucionario en su espíritu. La novela es semejante en el primer aspecto pero no en el segundo;

2. El arte, al rechazar un papel derivativo, pudo recurrir, para una nueva vitalidad, no solamente a una tradición popular, sino asimismo

[10] *The Dynamic of Mexican Nationalism.* Chapel Hill, University of North Carolina Press, 1968, p. 262.

[11] "Imágenes de la Revolución Mexicana", *Latino América.* UNAM, Centro de Estudios Latinoamericanos, 1, México, 1968, p. 46.

a tradiciones del arte indígena. La novela pudo nutrirse de la cultura popular, pero no de una narrativa indígena comparable al arte plástico de las culturas prehispánicas;

3. El arte mural de Rivera, Orozco, Siqueiros y Tamayo, a grandes rasgos, sí se preocupa por interpretar la historia mexicana, estableciendo interpretaciones causales, que relacionan pasado y presente. La novela es mucho más limitada;

4. El arte mural llega a influir en el proceso ideológico de la Revolución misma, desempeñando un papel activo. La novela, por más que se discuta en polémicas literarias, no logra tener semejante papel;

5. El arte mural de 1920-40 influye en la novela, pero la influencia de la narrativa apenas se siente en la pintura de los grandes.

II

Las tres novelas posteriores, escritas durante la postrrevolución, forman parte de la novela moderna en México. En técnica y visión del mexicano, son obras de orientación universal.

Agustín Yáñez, Rosario Castellanos y Carlos Fuentes se esfuerzan por incorporar los nuevos conocimientos y descubrimientos intelectuales del mundo occidental, en filosofía, psicología, y antropología. Para comunicar estas nuevas perspectivas en términos literarios se valen de nuevos procedimientos artísticos. En Yáñez observamos el monólogo interior. Castellanos desarrolla un tratamiento dualista del tiempo, por medio del proceso mitificador. Fuentes fragmenta la secuencia temporal y los planos narrativos. Por medio de estas técnicas los autores quieren, en vez de aislar al mexicano y su mexicanidad, iluminar la experiencia mexicana, viéndola a la luz de la experiencia del hombre moderno. En este sentido, estas tres novelas representan una reacción en contra de las anteriores, superando la etapa nacionalista.

Asimismo trascienden la postura moralizante, unidimensional, de sus antecesores. Sin prescindir del contexto social, la novela moderna penetra en la complejidad del hombre a través de personajes "redondos" (para emplear la clásica formulación de E. M. Forster) —personajes individualizados, con problemática personal más profunda, más contradictoria, y por eso más difícil de enjuiciar. Para llegar a entender y valorizar a figuras como el padre Dionisio, la india tzotzil Catalina, o Artemio Cruz, ya no sirven las categorías fáciles del bien y del mal. Las novelas ya no se cierran en estructuras circulares. Ahora se relativiza la visión implícita del hombre, porque para los nuevos novelistas, el dilema del hombre encierra de una manera u otra ciertas ambigüedades básicas.

En su interpretación novelística de la Revolución, Yáñez, Castellanos y Fuentes examinan las estructuras sociales en conflicto, estableciendo un sentido causal, un entendimiento de los orígenes de la lucha y las fuerzas en pugna. En gran parte, estos autores, especialmente Rosario Castellanos y Carlos Fuentes, comunican una visión dolorosa, en términos humanos, de la desviación o la traición de las normas revolucionarias. Pero no encuentran la culpa en un hombre corrompido, a quien inherentemente le falta la capacidad de cambiar, sino que nos hacen ver por qué era inevitable la Revolución, y cuál fue su dinámica subyacente.

Yáñez, conocedor de los principios freudianos, explora las tensiones individuales y colectivas puestas de relieve por el sistema porfiriano en un pueblo remoto de Jalisco que vive "al filo del agua", ante la inminencia de la Revolución. Entre las varias instituciones que determinan la vida rural, la narrativa se concentra en la iglesia y las múltiples represiones que ésta impone en las vidas privadas y las prácticas sociales. El lenguaje mismo de Yáñez —elaborado, ornamental, cargado de ritmos y giros arcaicos— comunica el sabor de estancamiento en este pueblo de mujeres enlutadas, pueblo que parece revivir formas medievales y barrocas. Pero la superficie arcaica de la rutina diaria, regida por el calendario religioso, oculta presiones irreprimibles en distintos individuos tanto como en el pueblo entero, presiones que fatalmente buscan salida en el estallido de 1910.

Acierto notable de esta novela es el desarrollo amplio y multifacético del personaje, don Dionisio, sacerdote del pueblo. Recto, austero, fiel en todo momento a las premisas ortodoxas de su oficio eclesiástico —así lo vemos en su conducta, su habla, sus relaciones con sus feligreses, en su reacción a las crisis que en el pueblo se manifiestan con un ritmo cada vez más acelerado. Pero como complemento de su figura externa, su vida interior, asequible por medio de la técnica de Yáñez, lo humaniza. Su mente es un campo de batalla, en el cual compiten fuerzas opuestas. Por sus sueños y sus monólogos interiores vemos crecer sus dudas, vemos minada la confianza en la ortodoxia a medida que, una tras otra, sus ovejas protegidas, dejan el rebaño. En un esfuerzo cada vez mayor por mantenerse fiel y por purificarse, se flagela, y logra imponer su voluntad consciente sobre sus vacilaciones subconscientes. Yáñez presenta como auténtica la religiosidad de don Dionisio, a la vez que saca a luz las fallas psicológicas de sus premisas. El cura resulta ser una figura verdaderamente trágica, quien organiza todo su ser en un intento sincero e inútil de detener el proceso de la historia y la naturaleza humana.

La acción de *Al filo del agua*, casi contemporánea con *Los de abajo*, está presentada desde una perspectiva doble, la subjetiva de los personajes y la más objetiva del narrador. Vemos en el hombre la capacidad y la necesidad de luchar por un equilibrio entre aspiraciones personales y fuero interior, por una parte, y su vida social, sexual, y artística, por otra.

Castellanos, enfocando el choque de dos culturas, demuestra el impacto traumático que produce en individuos de cada grupo —indio y ladino— el dominio socioeconómico, apoyado por el racismo. En *Oficio de tinieblas* la perspectiva crítica, más profunda que la de Mauricio Magdaleno, se logra presentando la cultura indígena de acuerdo con sus propias normas. La protagonista india se nos ofrece con sus propias sensibilidades, su vida interior, su modo particular de entender la realidad. La autora ha aprovechado un acontecimiento histórico del siglo XIX, una rebelión indígena inspirada en el culto de ídolos prehispánicos. Al situar la novela en la era cardenista y al ampliar los datos históricos de acuerdo con las necesidades internas de su obra literaria, les infunde una referencia y un significado modernos. Al final de la novela, aplastada su rebelión, los indios tzotziles recurren al proceso tradicional que siempre ha sido su modo de enfrentarse a su historia trágica: la asimilan transformando realidad histórica en leyenda mítica. Sin idealización, y por medio de personajes válidos, Rosario Castellanos afirma el valor y la dignidad del indio, por su tenaz insistencia en sobrevivir. La situación paralela de angustia, en que se encuentra la mayoría de los personajes ladinos, está vista implícitamente como el precio humano que ha tenido que pagar la cultura dominante para imponer su hegemonía racista.

En *La muerte de Artemio Cruz* Carlos Fuentes traza la vida de un hombre que surge de la obscuridad a participar en la lucha armada revolucionaria. Después, por medio de la traición sistemática y consciente de los ideales de la Revolución, alcanza un puesto de poder político y económico en el mundo del México postrrevolucionario. La novela, con vistas retrospectivas al siglo diecinueve, implica una interpretación de tipo marxista del desarrollo histórico de México en los últimos cien años. Vemos cómo los terratenientes de la época porfiriana, aprovechando la Ley Lerdo y el juarismo, alcanzan el poder, para ser reemplazados en el siglo veinte por una nueva minoría poderosa —los arribistas exrevolucionarios que han sabido encauzar la fuerza dinámica de la Revolución hacia el neocapitalismo.

Pero Fuentes va más allá de la historia, concentrándose en la trayectoria y la problemática de su personaje central. El marco es la inminencia de la muerte. En la luz penetrante de esta inminencia la personalidad del Artemio Cruz moribundo se refracta, a medida que éste agoniza, siente desmoronarse su cuerpo, revive sus decisiones personales, y contempla el significado último de su vida. Técnicamente, Fuentes, para construir la visión multidimensional de la vida y el tiempo de Artemio Cruz, alterna entre tres planos narrativos. En primer lugar, la acción se nos presenta en forma de monólogo interior, en primera persona, aproximando el fluir de la conciencia del Cruz agonizante; el protagonista se dirige directamente al lector, comunicando su conciencia moribunda. Sus sensaciones agudizadas de dolor y del funcionamiento defectuoso del sistema fisiológico encuentran correspondencias en sus pensamientos negativos sobre el sacerdote y los familiares que lo rodean. La codicia y la hipocresía que observa en ellos acentúa su malestar, y en un nivel más profundo, su sentido de culpa.

A continuación hay pasajes narrados en la voz de un "otro" misterioso, probablemente el *alter ego* de Cruz, quien se dirige a él de "tú", y emplea el tiempo futuro, aunque se refiere a sucesos del pasado. El lector se vuelve casi un testigo, escuchando, como si estuviera al lado de Cruz, oyendo con él esa voz. El empleo del futuro sitúa a Cruz en el pasado, como si los acontecimientos no hubieran sucedido todavía. Como consecuencia, se enfocan las opciones disponibles en distintos momentos de crisis, y las elecciones —los actos— de Cruz para salir de sus apuros. Indirectamente se acentúa la nota de examen moral.

Los segmentos narrados en tercera persona, más tradicionales, son los más largos. En ellos una voz omnisciente, externa, reconstruye fragmentos del pasado de Artemio Cruz, en secuencia acronológica. Ordenando estos fragmentos el lector va forjándose gradualmente una visión total de la vida del protagonista, visión que no se completa hasta el capítulo final. Esta secuencia temporal, aparentemente caótica, está organizada de una manera que da relieve a las decisiones claves que definen la trayectoria personal de Artemio Cruz.

Con esta técnica, se produce un énfasis existencial. Se dan por supuestas la lucha de clases y la traición de la Revolución, y se examinan dentro de estas fatalidades históricas las posibilidades de que dispone un individuo que se empeña en lograr sus aspiraciones y satisfacer sus necesidades personales. Por encima de la dimensión histórica, y basándose en ella, quedan planteadas una serie de problemas de índole moral y filosófica: la vida vista como suma de las decisiones del individuo, la vida definida por la muerte, la responsabilidad moral del individuo por sus actos. Artemio Cruz, revolucionario transformado en capitalista, resulta ser una figura para quien Fuentes demuestra un desprecio profundo, pero a quien desarrolla comprensiva y sensiblemente, hasta con compasión.

Decir que determinadas obras se caracterizan por su universalidad no proporciona en realidad índice alguno de su sistema de valores, el cual puede asociarse con una u otra de la posibilidades, que se extienden desde el abstraccionismo hasta el *engagement*. Esta última tendencia es la que han preferido los escritores modernos al analizar desde una perspectiva crítica las causas de la Revolución, las formas en que fue frenada, y, en el caso de Castellanos y Fuentes, distorsionada. Sus obras, aprovechando los recursos técnicos de la novela moderna occidental de Joyce, Faulkner y Woolf, postulan una causalidad más compleja en significado filosófico, y más profunda en extensión temporal. Marcan una ruptura, en forma y fondo, con la novela anterior. Los intérpretes modernos de la Revolución no continúan la tradición establecida, sino que rechazan los modelos nacionalistas e intentan trascenderlos en una suerte de proceso dialéctico para llegar a un nuevo orden ontológico. Al poner en tela de juicio en sus obras la Revolución y sus frutos, están más en consonancia con la juventud intelectual universitaria que con los partidarios oficiales que sostienen la versión de una Revolución que mantiene desde 1910 su marcha infatigable al futuro.

Vista la novela de la Revolución a través de casi medio siglo, 1915-1962, se nota que llega a su apogeo al pasar de la primera etapa a la segunda; de la visión inmediata a la reflexiva; del empeño nacionalista al universal; de una técnica decimonónica a la conciencia artística moderna; de una actitud cerrada arraigada en criterios moralistas a una mentalidad abierta, consciente de la complejidad del hombre; de una crítica profunda dirigida hacia las instituciones de México antes, durante, y después de la Revolución.

COMENTARIO

JORGE ALBERTO MANRIQUE

1. Que las artes revelan su medio social y el *tempo* histórico de una sociedad parece una verdad incontestable. Desde, por lo menos, los tiempos de Taine ha quedado tal cosa esclarecida. De entonces a acá la crítica enfocada en esa dirección no ha hecho sino afinar los medios para esclarecer y deslindar el contenido social de las artes, evitando (verbigracia en A. Hauser) las simplificaciones que parecían más obvias.

La utilidad de esa crítica es indudable; se establece una recíproca corriente interpretativa: la historia (a secas) ayuda a una "explicación" de las obras de arte y, en correspondencia, la historia del arte proporciona apoyos a la comprensión del fenómeno histórico y social en su totalidad. Así, hace algunos aspectos más evidentes que lo que resultaría en otra forma de investigación, detecta quizá matices que de otro modo permanecerían desapercibidos. La historia del arte se muestra, entonces, como un valioso auxiliar de la historia y de la historia social: tal vez en esta reunión —que es de historiadores y no de historiadores del arte— destacar esa su función resultaría suficiente.

2. Pensando en términos de historia del arte y de crítica de arte, sin embargo, se imponen otras reflexiones.

No coincido con la idea de Croce —que, matizada, persiste de alguna manera en estudiosos actuales— según la cual la belleza y perfección son unas solas, únicas, que se arropan en diversos vestidos formales según las épocas en que han sido creadas.

Para quien piensa así la labor del crítico es detectar el ropaje circunstancial y temporal para, una vez conocido, desecharlo y permitir de ese modo el brillo de lo eterno, bello, perfecto; y puede acontecerle que al desechar lo circunstancial se quede sin nada en las manos: habrá topado con una obra pseudoartística.

Creo firmemente que el conocimiento de las implicaciones sociales y temporales es necesario para la comprensión de la obra de arte, no nada más como un arbitrio a la manera crociana, sino porque es parte esencial de su belleza, que entiendo justamente circunstancial y temporal.

Pero si bien considero el estudio de ese contenido social como indispensable, nunca puedo considerarlo suficiente para la comprensión de la obra. Alguna vez dijo Malraux que "la obra se debe tanto a su medio como a las obras que le antecedieron", y en esto estoy con él: porque si es cierto que en una obra podemos reconocer a la sociedad que la creó, el conocimiento de esa sociedad no basta para decirnos por qué esa obra tiene esas formas que vemos, oímos, leemos, *ésas precisamente* y no otras. Es decir, podemos encontrar la correspondencia entre la sociedad criolla novohispana del siglo XVIII y el barroco estípite que ella creó, o la que hay entre el gótico flamígero y la sociedad del "otoño de la edad media",

pero para comprender las formas del barroco estípite y del flamígero necesitamos, además, acudir a una "historia interna" de las formas artísticas.
Porque la obra se debe tanto a su momento como a su propia historia, y
sólo considerando ambas cosas nos es dable sentar las bases del juego de
categorías propias a un estilo o a una modalidad: y sin haber establecido
en nuestra conciencia tal esquema de categorías y convenciones no veo
que sea posible acercarse a una obra con probabilidades de éxito al com-
prenderla y juzgarla.

3. Un problema al margen, tal vez excesivo y fuera de lugar para esta
reunión, pero que quizá valga la pena siquiera citar, es el de la apurada
situación en que se encuentra quien abandona el esencialismo. Aceptando
un relativismo o un historicismo aplicado a las obras de arte, es necesario
hacerse ciertas preguntas: ¿*Todas* las obras que se dicen o se presentan
como artísticas lo son realmente? Si no lo son ¿cómo podemos distinguir
una obra artística de otra que no lo es? o, por lo menos, ¿cómo distinguir una buena obra de otra menos buena? ¿Cómo decir que Velázquez
es superior a otros pintores de su tiempo? ¿Cómo decir que es "el más
grande" o "uno de los más grandes" de la historia? Y suma y sigue.

4. El objeto de estos párrafos es el de incitar a una discusión, que
seguramente no nos dará soluciones puesto que nunca en discusiones de
este tipo puede llegarse a ellas, pero quizá sí pueda llevarnos, a cada uno,
a ver las cosas más claras a partir de planteamientos que no eran los
nuestros iniciales. Así, pues, y pensando en la mutua ayuda que historia
e historia del arte pueden darse, propongo invertir los términos de la proposición que da título a esta mesa redonda: no nos preguntemos por "el
contenido social de la literatura y las artes", sino hagámoslo más bien
por "el contenido literario y artístico de la sociedad". Porque si bien es
cierto que una sociedad responde a las condiciones materiales que la sustentan, tampoco creo que se deba sólo a eso. Toda sociedad es un proyecto
de vida (siempre frustrado, porque a ella se superpondrá otra sociedad
diferente; o siempre logrado, si se quiere, puesto que toda sociedad se debe,
y no puede no deberse, a la anterior); y como tal proyecto responde
también a una vida imaginada. Podemos decir que la realidad copia a la
imaginación. De alguna manera una sociedad se inventa a sí misma,
y lo hace respecto a unos ideales, unas fobias, unos deseos, unos temores:
éstos son los que en forma excelente se manifiestan en la filosofía, en la
literatura, en las artes. ¿Por qué no nos empeñamos en descifrar de qué
manera una sociedad consigue adecuarse a su arte?

ÍNDICE

En la Imprenta Universitaria, bajo la
dirección de Jorge Gurría Lacroix, se
terminó la impresión de *Investigaciones contemporáneas sobre Historia de
México*, el día 8 de septiembre de 1971.
La composición se paró en tipos Electra
11:12, 10:11, 9:10, 8:10 y 8:9. Se
tiraron 1,500 ejemplares